Intellectual Property in Business Organizations

Cases and Materials

Richard S. Gruner

Professor of Law
Whittier Law School

Shubha Ghosh

Professor of Law
Southern Methodist University
Dedman School of Law

Jay P. Kesan

Professor of Law
University of Illinois College of Law

LexisNexis™

Matthew Bender®

Library of Congress Cataloging-in-Publication Data

Gruner, Richard S., 1953-
   Intellectual property in business organizations : cases and materials / Richard S.
Gruner, Shubha Ghosh, Jay P. Kesan.
      p. cm.
   Includes index.
   ISBN 0-8205-6150-9 (hardbound)
   1. Intellectual property — United States — Cases. 2. Business enterprises — Law
and legislation — United States — Cases. I. Ghosh, Shubha. II. Kesan, Jay P.
III. Title.
KF2980.G78 2006
346.7304'8 — dc22

                                                          2006012386

Editorial Offices
744 Broad Street, Newark, NJ 07102 (973) 820-2000
201 Mission St., San Francisco, CA 94105-1831 (415) 908-3200
701 East Water Street, Charlottesville, VA 22902-7587 (434) 972-7600
www.lexis.com

                                                      (Pub. 3205)

DEDICATION

For Marie — R.S.G.

For Soma — S.G.

For my parents, maternal grandmother and maternal uncles — J.P.K.

PREFACE

Intellectual property is a pervasive concern in modern society. Individuals regularly utilize diverse items from computer software to pharmaceutical drugs that are the products of innovation and subject to intellectual property protection. Businesses have developed new operating models based on extensive use of intellectual property and transfers of the embodiments of such property to their customers. Law schools and business schools are expanding their course offerings concerning intellectual property and its business implications. Academic journals in many disciplines publish articles on the impact of intellectual property and related laws in those fields. The popular press is filled with news stories on intellectual property laws, efforts to reform those laws, and lawsuits over infringing software, hardware, books, and movies.

Despite all this attention, the concept of intellectual property is far from well understood. Many people, including leading scholars, question whether intellectual property is really property. Others struggle to reconcile intellectual property law's right to exclude with the restrictions on exclusionary conduct in antitrust law. Another focus of attention is on how intellectual property laws further and/or hinder progress in particular industries, such as the biotechnology, software, and the entertainment industries, both in the United States and world-wide.

Into these debates, we introduce the following casebook, "Intellectual Property in Business Organizations." Our perspective is unique and central to the modern role of intellectual property. We propose that intellectual property should be studied and understood in its business context. This approach helps to resolve many of the current policy questions and substantive uncertainties surrounding intellectual property laws. Like other business assets, such as securities, intellectual property has characteristics of more traditional forms of property. Furthermore, when viewed in business contexts, intellectual property's role in markets and industries can be more systematically appreciated and analyzed. Given its importance in modern society as a whole, there is a surprisingly limited amount of scholarship focused on intellectual property as a business asset and its role in business organizations. A few scholars have addressed intellectual property in these contexts, and their work is cited in many places in our book. We hope that this casebook will stimulate further study of how businesses use intellectual property and how intellectual property law shapes markets and the structure of business activities.

The focus of our casebook reflects our professional and academic interests as attorneys and law professors. We have brought our own combined expertise in economics, engineering, and law, developed through our experience in law firms and in industry, to bear in assembling cases, statutes, regulations, and articles written by practitioners and professors in the fields of business organizations, commercial law, taxation, and intellectual property. The materials are designed to present a wide-ranging picture of the different roles that intellectual property plays in various stages of business activity, ranging from business formation and initial ownership structuring processes, to bankruptcies, mergers, and acquisitions, to public stock offerings and other advanced business transactions. Students using these materials will gain a rich exposure to the place of intellectual property in the contemporary business world, an exposure that will inform their subsequent activities in legal practice or business contexts and their understanding of intellectual property policy.

The topics of business organizations and intellectual property can each be intimidating to students. Putting the two together may be doubly intimidating. We hope that by bringing intellectual property and business organizations together, we can illuminate both fields and make each more understandable for students. In law school settings, we feel these materials will be useful as a basis for a survey course introducing students to the fields of intellectual property and business transactions. If used in more depth, this casebook can also serve as the basis for a capstone course for students who may have taken other intellectual property and business courses and are seeking a practical and applied course that focuses on important aspects of the relationship between intellectual property and various business organizations with differing scope, size and focus. In order to facilitate usage of this casebook without requiring any prior knowledge of intellectual property law, we have included an Appendix that provides a brisk introduction to different intellectual property regimes for the uninitiated. In choosing and organizing the materials, we have been sensitive to the multiple needs of different types of students and law school and business school professors. We have also sought to assemble materials that demonstrate how intellectual property interests figure in contemporary business and legal environments. By using this text to provide students with illustrations of the business significance of intellectual property, we also hope that professors in both law schools and business schools will make use of these materials in other courses on intellectual property, business transactions, and technology management.

Because of the salience of intellectual property, it is important that we recognize and study how to conduct business transactions involving intellectual property. While other intellectual property materials have largely focused on litigation involving intellectual property, our book provides a unique and comprehensive overview of transactional lawyering and management decision-making regarding intellectual property. Whether you approach these materials as an instructor or as a student, we hope that we are able to give you a deeper appreciation of the richness of intellectual property and its importance in shaping modern technology, industry, and business organizations.

The writing of this casebook was a truly collaborative enterprise. We each learned a great deal about the fundamental character of intellectual property issues from the authors of the materials used in our text as well as from reviewing the work of our co-authors. We also benefited from the generosity and expertise of the many colleagues, students, and staff members who contributed to the completion of this text at various stages. We particularly wish to thank Professor John R. Allison, Professor Ronald J. Mann, and Professor Peter Yu, who provided insightful comments on early chapters and the original proposal that was the seed for this casebook.

Richard Gruner benefited from repeated instances of research support from the Whittier Law School and especially appreciates the support of Dean Neil Cogan for the research activities leading to the completion of this text. He is deeply grateful for the dedicated, detailed, and unflagging assistance with manuscript changes provided by Karl Friedrich and Henrietta Johnson. He is also indebted to Christian Lopez, Whittier Law School Class of 2005, and Gloria D. Sefton, Whittier Law School Class of 2008, for their extensive efforts in identifying potentially useful sources and in reviewing drafts of chapters.

Shubha Ghosh benefited from the students and staff of two wonderful institutions as well as from support from two deans: Dean John Attanasio of Southern Methodist University Dedman School of Law and Dean Nils Olsen of The University at Buffalo, SUNY, Law School. He would like to thank Michelle Oswald of Southern Methodist University Dedman School of Law and Sandy Conti of The University at Buffalo, SUNY, Law School for tremendous secretarial support. He would also like to thank several student research assistants and readers: Ruth Freeburg, University at Buffalo, SUNY, Law School Class of 2005; Harven DeShield, University at Buffalo, SUNY, Law School Class of 2007; Christine Petersen, Southern Methodist University Dedman School of Law Class of 2005; and James Taber, Southern Methodist University Dedman School of Law Class of 2008. Each of these students took an extraordinary amount of time and effort to proofread and comment on drafts of individual chapters.

Jay Kesan would like to thank his colleagues and Dean Tom Mengler and Dean Heidi Hurd for their support and commitment to the highest academic standards at the University of Illinois College of Law. He is also grateful to Patty Pisut, University of Illinois College of Law Class of 2006 for her dedicated and responsive assistance with various tasks during the course of completing this book. He would also like to thank Kevin Brown, University of Illinois College of Law Class of 2004, for his assistance during the early stages of this effort.

Richard S. Gruner, Los Angeles, California
Shubha Ghosh, Dallas, Texas & Buffalo, New York
Jay P. Kesan, Champaign, Illinois
October 2005

TABLE OF CONTENTS

Page

INTRODUCTION   1

CHAPTER 1   CREATING AND PROTECTING THE BUSINESS MODEL   7

    Problem   7

    Focus of the Chapter   7

    Readings   8

  A. Capturing Value Through Intellectual Property   8

      Jon E. Hokanson & Sa'id Vakili, Intellectual
Property Issues for the Technology Startup
Company Los Angeles Lawyer, February 2000,
at p. 21   8

      Victoria A. Cundiff, How a Startup Company
Can Put Its Intellectual Property at Risk,
Practicing Law Institute, Patents, Copyright,
Trademarks and Literary Property Course
Handbook Series No. G0-00CW (September, 2000)   12

      Motor City Bagels, LLC. v. American Bagel Co.   20

      Notes & Questions   24

  B. Valuing Intellectual Property   25

      Ted Hagelin, Valuation of Intellectual Property
Assets: An Overview, 52 Syracuse Law Review
1133 (2002)   25

      Robert Goldscheider, The Negotiation of Royalties
and Other Sources of Income from Licensing
36 IDEA 1 (1995)   30

      Hughes Tool Co. v. Dresser Industries Inc.   40

      Notes & Questions   43

  C. Avoiding Forfeitures of Intellectual Property Interests   44

      Pfaff v. Wells Electronics, Inc.   45

      Notes & Questions   49

  D. Establishing and Policing Intellectual Property Licenses   50

Dennis Braswell, Setting Business Objectives and
Negotiating Valuable Licenses, Practising Law
Institute Patents, Copyrights, Trademarks, and
Literary Property Course Handbook Series
No. G0-01GM March–May, 2004   50

Notes & Questions   57

E. Tax and Accounting Issues Raised by Intellectual Property   57

Joseph Bankman & Ronald J. Gilson, Why Start-ups?
51 Stanford Law Review 289 (1999)   57

Syms Corp. v. Commissioner of Revenue   60

Edward J. Jennings, The Taxation and Reporting of
Distributions Derived from Licensing Intellectual
Property 15 Taxation of Exempts 207
(Mar/Apr 2004)   64

Notes & Questions   70

F. Intellectual Property in Special Contexts   72

1. Universities   72

Madey v. Duke University   72

Fenn v. Yale University   76

2. Federally Funded Research   84

University of Rochester v. G.D. Searle, Inc.   84

*Public Citizen Health Research Group v. National
Institutes of Health*   85

Trinity Industries, Inc. v. Road Systems, Inc.   85

3. Federal Government   88

Embrex, Inc. v. Service Engineering Corp.   88

4. State Government   90

*University of Colorado Foundation, Inc. v.
American Cyanamid Co.*   90

*Xechem Intern., Inc. v. Univ. of Tex. M.D.
Anderson Cancer Center*   92

Notes & Questions   96

G. Patenting Methods of Doing Business   97

Brian M. Buroker, Business Method Patents:
They are Not Just for Dotcom Companies
Anymore, 16(9) J. Proprietary Rights 1 (2004)   97

Robert P. Merges, As Many as Six Impossible
Patents Before Breakfast: Property Rights for
Business Concepts and Patent System Reform
14 Berkeley Tech. L. J. 577 (1999). 102

Notes & Questions. 106

**CHAPTER 2   ORGANIZING AND FINANCING AN
INTELLECTUAL PROPERTY BASED
STARTUP COMPANY**   107

Problem 107

Focus of the Chapter 108

Readings 109

A.   Commercializing Intellectual Property: Selecting a Business
Entity and Obtaining Initial Financing   109

Richard A. Mann, et al. Starting From Scratch:
A Lawyer's Guide to Representing a Start-up
Company, 56 Ark. L. Rev. 773 (2004) 109

Kristopher D. Brown & Graham D. S. Anderson,
Financing and Strategic Alliances for the New
Media Company, Practising Law Institute,
Representing the New Media Company
1999 545 PLI/Pat 709 113

Notes & Questions. 122

B.   Venture Capital Financing 123

Manuel A. Utset, Reciprocal Fairness, Strategic
Behavior & Venture Survival: A Theory of Venture
Capital-Financed Firms, 2002 Wis. L. Rev. 45 123

Ronald J. Mann, Do Patents Facilitate Financing in
the Software Industry? 83 Tex. L. Rev. 961 (2005) 130

Michael H. Brodowski, Ph.D., Kirkpatrick & Lockhart
Nicholson Graham, Boston, MA, Making Intellectual
Property Portfolios Attractive to Venture Capitalists
http://www.buildingipvalue.com/05_NA/159_162.htm
(last visited on May 20, 2005) 139

Beverly A. Berneman, J.D., LL.M., Benjamin,
Berneman, and Brom, LLC, Venture Capital Financing
for the Development of Intellectual Property Assets:
A Marriage of Convenience, Practising Law Institute,
Handling Intellectual Property Issues in Business
Transactions 2005 824 PLI/Pat 223 (2005) 141

Notes & Questions. 145

C.   Financing Through Loans Secured by Interests in Intellectual
     Property 145

         In re Peregrine Entertainment, Ltd................... 146

         Notes & Questions..................................... 153

D.   Tax Considerations in Allocating Intellectual Property
     Ownership and Licensing Among Business Entities 158

         Deborah Diehl, Whiteford, Taylor & Preston L.L.P.,
         Is the IP Holding Company Dead? Maryland Bar
         Journal (January/February 2004) 158

         Notes & Questions..................................... 163

E.   Fiduciary Duties of Corporate Officers Regarding Intellectual
     Property Development and Management 163

         Farwell v. Pyle-National Electric Headlight Co. 164

         Vendo Company v. Stoner 167

         Henderson v. Axiam, Incorporated.................... 175

         Rexford Rand Corp. v. Ancel 184

         Notes & Questions..................................... 189

**CHAPTER 3   MISSTATEMENTS IN STOCK SALES
              REGARDING INTELLECTUAL PROPERTY
              INTERESTS** 191

         Problem 191

         Focus of the Chapter 193

         Readings 195

A.   Standards Governing Securities Fraud 195

         Robert A. Prentice & John H. Langmore, Beware of
         Vaporware: Product Hype and the Securities Fraud
         Liability of High-Tech Companies, 8 Harv.
         J.L. & Tech. 1 (1994) 195

B.   Examples of Fraudulent Representations Regarding
     Intellectual Property 216

         Pommer v. Medtest Corporation...................... 216

         Notes & Questions.................................... 220

         Alna Capital Associates v. Wagner 220

         Notes & Questions.................................... 228

         Gompper v. VISX, Inc............................... 229

         Notes & Questions.................................... 231

         Nathenson v. Zonagen, Inc. 233

Zirn v. VLI Corporation 239

Notes & Questions 250

CHAPTER 4 TRADE SECRETS 253

    Problem 253

    Focus of the Chapter 254

    Readings 254

A. Introduction — What is a Trade Secret? 254

    Notes & Questions 255

B. Civil Protection of Trade Secrets 257

    1. Uniform Trade Secrets Act 258

      a. Introduction 258

      b. Application of the UTSA 258

      Learning Curve Toys, Incorporated v.
      Playwood Toys, Incorporated 258

      Mangren Research and Development Corporation v.
      National Chemical Company, Incorporated 266

      Notes & Questions 273

      c. Elements of Trade Secrets 273

        i. Information 273

      DeGiorgio v. Megabyte International, Inc. 273

        ii. Value Through Secrecy 274

      Buffets, Inc. v. Klinke 274

      Notes & Questions 277

        iii. Reasonable Efforts of Protection 279

      Notes & Questions 280

    2. Non-UTSA Jurisdictions 280

      E.I. DuPont DeNemours & Company, Inc. v.
      Christopher 281

      Notes & Questions 284

      a. The Honest Discoverer 286

      b. The Innocent Wrongful User 287

C. Criminal Protection for Trade Secrets 288

    1. Federal Protection 288

      a. Economic Espionage Act of 1996 288

Notes & Questions 289

    b. Actual Theft of Trade Secrets 290

        United States v. Lange 290

    c. Conspiracy to Steal Trade Secrets 293

        United States v. Martin 293

        Notes & Questions 299

  2. State Protection 299

      People v. Pribich 300

      Notes & Questions 304

CHAPTER 5 **EMPLOYMENT ISSUES** 307

      Problem 307

      Focus of the Chapter 308

      Readings 309

A. Ownership of Intellectual Property 309

  1. Statutory Default Rules 309

    a. Patents 309

      i. Shop Right 310

      Max C. McElmurry and White River Tech., Inc. v.
      Arkansas Power & Light Co., Entergy Corp. and
      Middle South Utilities 310

      ii. Hired to Invent 314

      Standard Parts Co. v. Peck 314

      Notes & Questions 316

    b. Trade Secrets 317

      i. Introduction 317

      Wexler v. Greenberg 318

      Notes & Questions 321

      ii. Implied Duties of Employees 323

      Harry R. Defler Corporation v. Kleeman 323

      Notes & Questions 327

    c. Copyrights 327

      Community for Creative Non-Violence v.
      James Earl Reid 328

  2. Private Adjustments Through Employment Contract
    Terms 333

a. Introduction 333

b. Invention Assignments 334

Freedom Wireless, Inc. v. Boston Communications Group, Inc. 335

Notes & Questions 338

B. Transfers of Intellectual Property Upon Changes in Employment 339

  1. Enforceability of Restrictions on Subsequent Employment for Parties Holding Trade Secrets 339

    a. Nonuse and Nondisclosure Agreements 339

    Union Pacific Railroad Company v. Brent Mower 339

    Notes & Questions 344

    b. Covenant Not to Compete 345

      i. Generally 345

    Nike, Inc. v. Eugene McCarthy. 345

    Notes & Questions 351

      ii. Hold-Over/Trailer Clauses 352

    Ingersoll-Rand Co. v. Armand Ciavatta 352

    Notes & Questions 361

      iii. Nonsolicitation Agreements 362

    Palmer & Cay of Georgia, Inc. v. Lockton Companies, Inc. 363

  2. Inevitable Disclosures of Trade Secrets as a Basis for Preemptive Employment Limitations 365

    a. Generally 365

    Pepsico, Inc. v. William E. Redmond, Jr., and the Quaker Oats Company. 365

    Notes & Questions 374

    b. Hazards of Applying the "Inevitable Disclosure" Doctrine 375

    William LeJeune v. Coin Acceptors, Inc. 375

  3. Risks to New Employers From Hiring Experienced High Tech Employees 383

    a. Misappropriation: Wrongful Use or Disclosure 383

      i. Acts Giving Rise to Third Party Liability 383

    Colgate-Palmolive Co. v. Carter Products 384

    Notes & Questions 388

b. Intentional Interference with Contractual or
Fiduciary Relationship 391

i. Generally 391

Reeves v. Hanlon 391

Storage Technology Corp. v. Cisco Systems, Inc. 397

Notes & Questions 401

CHAPTER 6 LICENSING IN BUSINESS ORGANIZATIONS 403

Problem 403

Focus of the Chapter 404

Readings 405

A. Patent Licensing 405

1. The Right to Sue for Infringement 405

Abbott Laboratories v. Diamedix Corporation 405

Notes & Questions 409

2. Challenges to Patent Validity 410

a. Res Judicata 410

*Blonder-Tongue Laboratories, Inc. v. University of
Illinois Foundation* 410

Notes & Questions 416

b. Estoppel 416

Lear, Inc. v. Adkins 416

Notes & Questions 422

3. Duration of Obligation to Pay Royalties 425

a. Post Patent Expiration Royalties 425

Brulotte v. Thys Co. 425

b. License Royalties on Unpatented, Publicly-disclosed
Products 427

Aronson v. Quick Point Pencil Co. 427

Notes & Questions 432

4. Implied Transfers 433

a. Patent Exhaustion and the First Sale Doctrine 433

Jazz Photo Corp. v. International Trade Commission ... 433

Notes & Questions 440

b. Compulsory Licenses 443

5. Cross-Licensing 444

a. Why Enter Into a Cross-Licensing Agreement? 444

Texas Instruments v. Hyundai Electronics Industries ... 444

Notes & Questions 449

b. Antitrust Considerations and Patent Misuse: the *Texas Instrument* Saga Continues 452

Texas Instruments v. Hyundai Electronics Industries ... 452

6. Patent Pools 459

Matsushita Electrical Industrial Co., Ltd. v. Cinram International, Inc. 459

U.S. Philips Corporation v. International Trade Commission 465

Notes & Questions............................ 476

7. Patent Packages 477

Well Surveys, Inc. v. Perfo-Log, Inc. 477

Notes & Questions 480

8. University Licensing 480

B. Trade Secret Licensing 481

1. Introduction 481

Notes & Questions............................ 482

2. Duration of Trade Secret Royalties 483

Warner-Lambert Pharmaceutical Company v. John J. Reynolds, Inc. 483

Notes & Questions............................ 488

C. Trademark Licensing 489

1. Requirement of Good Will: Prohibition Against "Bare" or "Naked" License 489

International Cosmetics Exchange, Inc. v. Gapardis Health & Beauty, Inc. 489

Notes & Questions............................ 492

2. Control Over the Mark 493

Dawn Donut Company v. Hart's Food Stores, Inc. 493

Notes & Questions 498

3. Antitrust Concerns: Tying 500

Principe v. McDonald's Corporation 500

Notes & Questions 503

D. Copyright Licensing 504

    1. Introduction 504

        Nancey Silvers v. Sony Pictures Entertainment, Inc...... 504

        Notes & Questions 509

    2. Scope of the Use: Unforeseen Uses 511

        Boosey & Hawkes Music Publishers, Ltd. v. The Walt Disney Company 511

    3. Performance Rights Organizations: ASCAP & BMI 515

E. Licensing Multiple Types of Intellectual Property: Hybrid Licensing 516

    1. Patent and Trade Secret Licensing 516

    2. Patent and Trademark Licensing 516

CHAPTER 7   INTELLECTUAL PROPERTY ASSETS AND THE TERMINATION OF A BUSINESS 519

    Problem 519

    Focus of the Chapter 519

    Readings 520

A. Termination Through Bankruptcy 520

    1. The Bankruptcy Estate 522

        Patrick A. Casey, P.A. v. Joel S. Hochman, M.D. 522

        Penick Pharmaceutical, Inc. and Unofficial Committee of Equity Holders of Penick Pharmaceutical, Inc. v. McManigle 525

        Simplified Information Systems, Inc. v. Cannon 529

        C Tek Software, Inc. v. New York State Business Venture Partnership 530

        Notes & Questions 536

    2. The Automatic Stay and Intellectual Property Litigation 538

        Checkers Drive-in Restaurants, Inc. v. Commissioner of Patents and Trademarks 538

        In re: The Singer Company 544

        Notes & Questions................................ 548

    3. The Intellectual Property License in Bankruptcy 549

        a. Statutory Background 549

Notes & Questions. 551

　　b.　Licensor as Debtor 554

　　　In re: CellNet Data Systems, Inc.. 554

　　　*Lubrizol Enterprises, Inc. v. Richmond
　　　Metal Finishers, Inc.* 562

　　　Notes & Questions 566

　　c.　Licensee as Debtor 568

　　　Institute Pasteur v. Cambridge Biotech Corporation 568

　　　In re Catapult Entertainment, Inc.. 572

　　　Notes & Questions. 578

B.　Termination Outside of Bankruptcy 579

　　　Hapgood v. Hewitt. 579

　　　Pav-Savr Corp. v. Vasso Corp.. 584

　　　Southwest Whey Inc. v. Nutrition 101, Inc. 591

　　　Ronald S. Laurie, Intellectual Property Allocation
　　　Strategies in Joint Ventures, Inflexion Point Strategy,
　　　LLC, Practising Law Institute, Patents, Copyrights,
　　　Trademarks, and Literary Property Course
　　　Handbook Series, PLI. No. 5923 (March 2005) 598

　　　Notes & Questions. 605

**CHAPTER 8　INTELLECTUAL PROPERTY ISSUES IN
　　　　　　　MERGERS AND ACQUISITIONS** 607

　　Problem 607

　　Focus of the Chapter 607

　　Readings 609

A.　Some Basic Terminology 609

B.　Ownership Issues 613

　　　David H. Kennedy, Intellectual Property Issues Arising
　　　Out of Acquisitions, Practicing Law Institute, Patents,
　　　Copyrights, Trademarks, and Literary Property Course
　　　Handbook Series PLI. No. 6056 (March-May 2005) 613

　　　PPG Industries, Inc. v. Guardian Industries Corp. 625

　　　*Verson Corporation v. Verson International
　　　Group, PLC* 633

　　　Motorola, Inc. v. Amkor Technology, Inc.. 639

　　　Notes & Questions. 644

C. Liability Issues 645

      Ed Peters Jewelry Co., Inc. v. C & J Jewelry Co., Inc. 645

      TXO Production Co. & Marathon Oil Co. v. M.D.
      Mark, Inc. 650

      Notes & Questions 653

D. Transfer Issues 654

      BioLife Solutions, Inc. v. Endocare, Inc. 654

      Notes & Questions 661

E. Impacts of Ineffective Transfers and Inadequate Diligence 662

      Paragon Trade Brands, Inc. v. Weyerhaeuser
      Company 662

      Notes & Questions 674

CHAPTER 9 INTELLECTUAL PROPERTY DUE DILIGENCE
PRECEDING PUBLIC SALES OF STOCK 677

      Problem 677

      Focus of the Chapter 680

      Readings 682

A. Features of Due Diligence Reviews of Intellectual Property 682

      Diane J. Kasselman, Intellectual Property Due
      Diligence in Business Transactions, Practising Law
      Institute, Patents, Copyrights, Trademarks, and
      Literary Property Course Handbook Series
      No. G0-011U (October, 2002) 682

      Mary J. Hildebrand & Jacqueline Klosek, Intellectual
      Property Due Diligence: A Critical Prerequisite to
      Capital Investment, http://library.findlaw.com/2003/
      Dec/1/133278. html (last visited on May 15, 2005) 698

B. Legal Tests for Reasonable Due Diligence Reviews 700

      Feit v. Leasco Data Processing Equipment
      Corporation 700

      Notes & Questions 710

C. Maintaining and Waiving Privilege Protections in Due
Diligence Reviews 714

    1. The Scope of Privilege Protections 715

      Knogo Corporation v. United States 715

      Notes & Questions 720

2. Maintaining Privilege Protections in Due
Diligence Reviews 721

Eric K. Steffe, W. Blake Coblentz & Jessica Parezo,
The Common-Interest Doctrine and Intellectual
Property Due Diligence, 24 Biotechnology L. Rep. 1
(Feb. 2005) 721

Notes & Questions 728

**CHAPTER 10 DISCLOSURES OF INTELLECTUAL PROPERTY
INTERESTS AND RISKS CONCERNING
PUBLICLY TRADED COMPANIES** 729

Problem 729

Focus of the Chapter 731

Readings 733

A. Introduction: Goals and Required Contents of a Prospectus 733

1. Drafting a Prospectus for a Public Offering 733

a. Goals in Drafting a Prospectus 734

b. Typical Contents of a Prospectus 734

c. Disclosures in Prospectuses Regarding Intellectual
Property 736

2. Regulatory Standards 739

SEC Standards for Prospectus Contents, Regulation S-K
(Excerpts), United States Securities and Exchange
Commission 17 C.F.R PART 229 739

3. Examples of Intellectual Property Disclosures 742

S.E.C. Form S-1, Santarus, Inc (Excerpts), Filed:
March 31, 2004 742

B. Misstatements in Prospectuses Regarding Intellectual
Property Interests or Their Business Implications 750

In re Stac Electronics Securities Litigation 750

*Sherleigh Associates, LLC v. Windmere-Durable
Holdings, Inc.* 755

In re SeaChange International, Inc. 766

*In re Alliance Pharmaceutical Corp. Securities
Litigation* 772

Burstein v. Applied Extrusion Technologies, Inc 778

Notes & Questions.............................. 785

CHAPTER 11   ADVANCED TECHNIQUES FOR MAXIMIZING INTELLECTUAL PROPERTY VALUE IN MATURE COMPANIES 787

  Problem 787

  Focus of the Chapter 788

  Readings 790

A. Allocating Business Resources to Innovation 790

  1. Multi-Divisional Corporations as Internal Capital Markets 790

    George G. Triantis, Organizations as Internal Capital Markets: The Legal Boundaries of Firms, Collateral, and Trusts in Commercial and Charitable Enterprises, 117 Harv. L. Rev. 1102, 1105, 1109-15 (2004) 791

    Dan L. Burk, Intellectual Property and the Firm, 71 U. Chi. L. Rev. 3 (2004) 796

  3. Allocations of Research Activities Among Firms and Distributed Communities: The Open Source Experience . . . 808

    David McGowan, Legal Implications of Open-Source Software, 2001 U. Ill. L. Rev. 241, 242-45, 285-87 (2001) 808

    Notes & Questions 812

B. Intellectual Property Securitization 812

    Hewson Chen, Don't Sell Out, Sell Bonds: The Pullman Group's Securitization of the Music Industry, 2 Vand. J. Ent. L. & Prac. 161 (2000) 813

    Notes & Questions 816

C. Intellectual Property Enforcement Insurance 817

    JumpSport, Inc. v. Jumpking, Inc. 818

D. Corporations as Long-term Intellectual Property Users: Anticipating New Modes of Use and Distribution 828

    New York Times Company, Inc. v. Tasini 829

    Amy Terry Sheehan, Tasini Aftermath: The Consequences of the Freelancers' Victory, 14 DePaul-LCA J. Art & Ent. L. 231 (2004) 835

    Notes & Questions 837

E. Valuable Dispositions of Intellectual Property 838

  1. Auctions 838

    In re: Commerce One Inc. 839

    Commerce One Operations, Inc. 841

Notes & Questions.................................. 843

   2. Donations to Charitable Organizations 844

General Explanation of Tax Legislation Enacted
in the 108th Congress (2005), Joint Committee
on Taxation 845

Charitable Contributions; Patents, Internal Revenue
Service Revenue Ruling 2003-28 (Feb. 26, 2003)....... 849

Notes & Questions.................................. 852

   3. Releasing Intellectual Property to Enhance Open Source
Product Development 854

Steve Seidenberg, Big Blue Discovers New Way to
Leverage Patents: Open-Source Revolution
Keeps IBM in the Black, Corporate Legal Times,
p. 24 (April 2005)................................... 854

Notes & Questions.................................. 857

**CHAPTER 12 ADVANCED TECHNIQUES FOR MINIMIZING
RISKS OF INTELLECTUAL PROPERTY
INFRINGEMENT IN MATURE COMPANIES** 861

Problem 861

Focus of the Chapter 862

Readings 863

A. Responding to Partially Understood Intellectual Property
Threats: The Example of Risks Associated with Open Source
Products 863

Lori E. Lesser, Simpson Thacher & Bartlett, LLP,
A Hard Look at the Tough Issues in Open Source
Licenses, Practising Law Institute, Open Source
Software 2005: Critical Issues in Today's Corporate
Environment (2005)................................. 864

Notes & Questions.................................. 871

B. Infringement Insurance 872

Steven E. Tiller & Briggs Bedigian, Intellectual
Property and Technological Insurance Coverage,
Maryland Bar Journal, Nov./Dec. 2001, p. 35 872

Mez Industries, Inc. v. Pacific National Insurance
Company 877

Notes & Questions.................................. 890

Zurich Insurance Co. v. Killer Music, Inc 890

Notes & Questions.................................. 894

State Farm Fire and Casualty Insurance Company v. White 895

Notes & Questions 897

American Century Services Corp. v. American International Specialty Lines Insurance Co. 897

Notes & Questions 903

C. Liability of Corporate Officers and Directors for Infringement of Intellectual Property Interests 904

Steven E. Bochner & Susan P. Krause, Intellectual Property Management and Board Liability, Practising Law Institute, Advanced Securities Law Institute 1065 PLI/Corp 453 (1998) 904

Notes & Questions 907

CHAPTER 13   THE ANTITRUST PERILS OF A DOMINANT INTELLECTUAL PROPERTY POSITION 909

Problem 909

Focus of the Chapter 910

Readings 911

A. Statutory Overview 911

Sherman Act 911

Clayton Act 911

Federal Trade Commission Act 912

National Cooperative Research Act 912

Antitrust Guidelines for the Licensing of Intellectual Property, Issued by the U.S. Department of Justice and the Federal Trade Commission, April 6, 1995 914

Notes & Questions 923

B. The Antitrust-Intellectual Property Interface 927

R. Hewitt Pate, Competition and Intellectual Property in the U.S.: Licensing Freedom and the Limits of Antitrust, Assistant Attorney General, Antitrust Division, U.S. Department of Justice, 2005 EU Competition Workshop, Florence, Italy, June 3, 2005 927

Notes & Questions 934

C. Improper Conduct 936

1. Restricting Competitors   936

    United States v. Microsoft   936

    Notes & Questions   948

2. Tying Arrangement   950

    United States v. Microsoft   950

    Notes & Questions   958

D. Cooperative Ventures   959

    In the Matter of Dell Computer Corporation Consent
    Order, etc., In Regard to Alleged Violation of Sec. 5
    of the Federal Trade Commission Act, Docket
    No. C-3658, Decision, May 20, 1996   959

    Notes & Questions   970

E. International Perspective From the European Union   971

    European Union Competition Commission Decision of
    March 24, 2004, relating to a proceeding under Article 82
    of the EC Treaty, Case COMP/C-3/37.792 Microsoft   971

    Notes & Questions   983

**CHAPTER 14   MANAGING THE INTELLECTUAL PROPERTY
PORTFOLIO**   987

    Problem   987

    Focus of the Chapter   987

    Readings   988

A. Identifying the Patent Portfolio   988

    R. Polk Wagner & Gideon Parchomovsky, Patent
    Portfolios, 154 U. Penn. L. Rev. 1 (2005)   988

    Notes & Questions   991

B. The Challenges of Joint Ventures   993

    Kurt M. Saunders, The Role of Intellectual Property
    Rights in Negotiating and Planning a Research Joint
    Venture, 7 Marq. Intell. Prop. L. Rev. 75 (2003)   993

    David J. Teece, Profiting from Technological
    Innovation: Implications for Integration, Collaboration,
    Licensing and Public Policy, Practising Law Institute,
    Patents, Copyrights, Trademarks, and Literary
    Property Course No. G0-007N (October 7-8, 1999)   996

    Notes & Questions   1000

C. Patent Protection for Research Tools and
Experimental Use 1001

    Merck KGaA v. Integra Lifesciences I, Ltd. 1001

    Merck KGaA v. Integra Lifesciences I, Ltd. 1007

    Merck KGaA v. Integra Lifesciences I, Ltd. 1016

    Notes & Questions 1024

**APPENDIX INTRODUCTION TO INTELLECTUAL
PROPERTY FOR THE NON-SPECIALIST** 1027

TABLE OF CASES TC-1

TABLE OF STATUTES TS-1

INDEX I-1

INTRODUCTION

This casebook focuses on the legal problems of businesses that develop and utilize intellectual property as the businesses are founded, financed, expanded, transferred to others, or terminated. The legal issues presented in this text are important to law students in both substantive and practical terms. These issues are substantively important because they turn on fundamental policy questions of intellectual property and business organization law that have yet to be fully resolved and that will have a bearing on a broad range of important intellectual property and business organization controversies. At the same time, the intellectual property issues in business organizations are practically important because they correspond to areas of highly active legal practice where law students will need special training and have ample opportunities to apply it.

The text addresses the distinctive roles played by intellectual property at three stages of business development: the startup phase (where intellectual property often plays key roles in business formation and venture capital financing), the mid-life phase (where intellectual property is often an important factor in going public or selling a business through a merger into a larger concern), and the mature company phase (where successful firms must deal with problems such as preventing abuses of dominant intellectual property positions and remaining competitive in complex high tech markets despite being innovators in only small components of those markets).

The text is designed for law students in advanced classes concerning intellectual property, business organizations, and the law of science and technology as well as intellectual property survey courses. It will also be suitable for business school students in classes with a substantial focus on legal problems of developing businesses. A strong background in intellectual property law is not assumed. Rather, background material on important intellectual property standards is provided in an appendix to the text. In addition, detailed notes on particular intellectual property laws and legal issues raised in the materials are included with the readings.

The readings in the text revolve around the problems faced by a hypothetical company, the Digital Ignition Systems Corporation ("Digital Ignition"). The concerns that face this company as it develops serve as the background or "backstory" for problems raised in the text regarding specific intellectual property issues. Individual chapters in the book focus on particular types of intellectual property problems encountered at different stages of this company's history. Additional factual accounts elaborating on some of the incidents mentioned in the following overview of Digital Ignition's history are presented in each chapter to highlight particular contexts and intellectual property problems faced by businesses as they develop.

The Saga of Digital Ignition:
Intellectual Property and Business Growth
in a "Start Up" Company

Digital Ignition Systems Corporation (Digital Ignition) was established in Salem, Oregon, in 1980. The company was founded by Y.L. See to develop and manufacture computer-based ignition systems for automotive engines. These ignition systems monitor the conditions inside an automotive engine, analyze those conditions through a specialized computer system and associated software, initiate the injection of fuel into the cylinders of the engine, and precisely control the timing of the ignition of fuel in each cylinder in relation to the position of the cylinder components and the fuel and oxygen content of the cylinder. By using these systems, automobile owners gain significant engine power and fuel conservation benefits over engines with prior ignition systems.

Dr. See received a doctorate in computer science in 1970 from the Nevada Institute of Technology, a prestigious university. From 1970-1975, he worked as a designer of engine parts for the International Motors Corporation, a multinational corporation engaged in the design, manufacturing, and marketing of diverse types of automobiles and automotive equipment. Dr. See worked as part of a design group that specialized in the design of electronic ignition systems for automobile engines.

Frustrated by the unwillingness of engineers at International Motors to pursue improved ignition system designs based on new types of computer analyses of engine operating conditions, Dr. See left International Motors in 1975 to form a consulting business aimed at helping designers of race car engines improve the designs and performance of their ignition systems. While engaged in this consulting business, he discovered a series of computer processing methods, which, when applied to electronic ignition designs, produced substantially better engine performance and gas mileage results than prior ignition system designs. In 1980, Dr. See obtained several United States patents covering aspects of his new ignition system designs. Separate patents were obtained for: (1) the computer software implementing his new ignition system control method, (2) an ignition system device incorporating the software and an associated computer and designed to operate in accordance with the method, and (3) the method of information processing in the ignition system itself.

After having obtained these patents, Dr. See formed Digital Ignition to commercialize his designs. His company initially had five financial backers. All of these backers were co-owners of the company along with Dr. See. The five backers included Thomas Carlise, a Salem investment counselor; two former college professors who were also planning to serve as salaried product designers for Digital Ignition; a local dentist; and a member of Dr. See's family.

Digital Ignition's engineers worked for a year to produce a commercially viable ignition system based on Dr. See's designs. Their efforts focused on producing a modified version of an International Motors brand ignition system, altered to incorporate Dr. See's patented software and to operate in accordance with his patented method. Dr. See and fellow executives at Digital Ignition developed a business plan calling for the manufacturing of ignition system units based on this new design and the marketing of these units to builders of race cars and other high performance vehicles sold to select consumers at premium prices. Following a review of this business plan, Future Ventures, LLP, a venture capital partnership in Palo Alto, California, agreed to invest $10 million in Digital Ignition in exchange for a substantial percentage of stock ownership in the company.

Digital Ignition proceeded to manufacture and sell ignition systems in accordance with its initial business plan for three years. Its ignition systems received a considerable amount of favorable publicity when several race car drivers and owners cited the systems as a significant factor in their racing success.

Given the favorable public attention their ignition systems were receiving and having gained substantial experience in the operation and manufacturing of these systems, Digital Ignition's engineers developed a version of the company's ignition equipment that was suitable for retrofitting on standard model cars sold by International Motors and other manufacturers. Installation of the new Digital Ignition system as a substitute for a car's original ignition system was easily accomplished by a car owner or mechanic and significantly improved a car's performance and gas mileage. Demand for these "plug compatible" substitutes for original equipment ignition systems was brisk, and Digital Ignition's revenues and profits grew rapidly. However, Digital Ignition found that its manufacturing and marketing capabilities were not sufficient to keep up with the new levels of consumer demand for its products.

Digital Ignition's executives considered two options to respond to this identified but unmet demand for its products: (1) a merger with a larger concern having sufficient manufacturing and financial resources to expand the company's production and marketing efforts and (2) a public offering of Digital Ignition stock that would raise sufficient funds for the company to expand its production and marketing.

Company managers approached International Motors and several other large automobile parts manufacturers concerning a possible merger. The objective of these discussions with the larger companies was to obtain a "buy out" price in a merger that would compensate Digital Ignition's founders and initial investors for their efforts in bringing the company to its present stage of business success and positive public reputation. A merger partner acquiring Digital Ignition would effectively acquire several key assets allowing the partner to expand on the business opportunity identified and partially developed by Digital Ignition. Key assets that would come under the control of the merger partner included Digital Ignition's patents, its product production and marketing facilities, and its customer lists and other marketing and production know how and trade secrets. Of these, the company's primary assets to be transferred in the merger were its patents giving it practical control over the market for ignition systems based on Dr. See's designs for approximately ten more years.

International Motors initially expressed interest in such a merger and Digital Ignition's lawyers drafted a proposed merger agreement. However, merger discussions between the companies ultimately fell through because International Motors refused to pay what Digital Ignitions executives felt was a sufficiently high cash price. Executives for International Motors felt that Digital Ignition did not provide sufficient proof of the probable validity and scope of the company's patents to justify a higher price.

Digital Ignition's executives then shifted their primary attention to a possible public offering of the company's stock. Lawyers for the company spent a considerable amount of time resolving two issues related to this public offering: (1) how should the scope and value of the company's intellectual property interests be evaluated and described in pre-offering discussions with investment bankers and in further public disclosures required by securities laws and (2) what types of risks of patent invalidity or other sources of weakness in the companyís intellectual property interests would need to be disclosed in connection with its public offering? The company ultimately filed a registration statement with the SEC and completed its public offering in 1990, raising a total of $40 million in the process. However, sales of the company's products were poor during the two years following the public offering. The price of the company's stock dropped by 50%, motivating several shareholders to file federal and state securities law suits against the company and several of its senior officers. The plaintiffs claimed that the company's disclosures at the time of the public offering overstated management's understanding of the commercial advantages provided by Digital Ignition's intellectual property interests and omitted mention of known risks regarding Digital Ignition's business plans. These suits were ultimately settled through modest payments to the shareholder plaintiffs.

Eventually, Digital Ignition's sales of plug-compatible ignition systems substituting for original equipment systems were highly successful and the company and its ignition systems gained a positive reputation among a widespread portion of the public. Company executives sought to capitalize on Digital Ignition's favorable public reputation in four ways: (1) developing new products and gaining further patents to extend the duration of its control over key technologies in the area of ignition systems, (2) licensing its patented technology to other companies, (3) offering new products under the trademark "Digital Ignition," and (4) attempting to market further unpatented products in conjunction with its popular patented components.

In new product development, Digital Ignition sought to produce patentable ignition system improvements and advanced products that would maintain its technological dominance over this narrow area of the automotive products market and allow the company to continue to maintain its image as a product innovator in the eyes of consumers. The company sought to produce advanced products in the ignition equipment field that were unavailable from other sources by both developing and patenting improvements in its own initial products and by obtaining exclusive licenses to produce and sell products incorporating certain patented advances discovered by several other small, innovative companies.

At the same time as it acquired further intellectual property rights from other concerns, Digital Ignition also attempted to maximize the value of its own patents and other trade secret rights by licensing other parties to make and sell products based on Digital Ignition's patented designs and transferring related trade secret know how to these licensees. International Motors, by now regretting that it had not acquired rights to Digital Ignition's products through the previously proposed merger, sought to obtain an exclusive license to include products based on Digital Ignition's designs in newly manufactured International Motors vehicles. As part of the resulting license agreement, Digital Ignition agreed not to license any other car manufacturer to include products based on Digital Ignition's designs in newly manufactured vehicles. However, Digital Ignition retained the right to continue to manufacture and sell ignition systems based on its patented designs for use as plug-compatible replacement parts substituting for original equipment ignition systems in diverse types of cars.

International Motors enjoyed a significant increase in auto sales following the addition to its cars of ignition systems based on Digital Ignition's designs. The success of the company coupled with the apparent inability of other new car manufacturers to offer automobiles with similar ignition systems caused several of the other manufacturers to complain to the Federal Trade Commission (FTC) regarding Digital Ignition's licensing practices. The FTC initiated an investigation of Digital Ignition to determine if its licensing practices constituted an unfair trade practice in violation of federal laws.

A further problem arose when Digital Ignition developed and patented an improved ignition system five years after its original license agreement with International Motors. The improved design incorporated and extended Digital Ignition's original patented design. Digital Ignition contended that its licensing agreement with International Motors did not require it to license the new patent to International Motors. However, since the licensing agreement provided that the right to produce and sell ignition systems conforming to the original patented design could not be transferred to any new car manufacturer other than International Motors, Digital Ignition was practically precluded from licensing its new patent to any other company because it could not validly authorize any other company to produce the ignition system features covered by the original patent that were also incorporated in the new design. Negotiations between Digital Ignition and International Motors regarding a license to the new patent broke off after the parties failed to reach agreement on royalty terms.

Impressed by the positive image of Digital Ignition among automobile owners, the company sought to capitalize on the use of the "Digital Ignition" trademark. It sought to manufacture and market its own line of automobile repair products under this trademark, to license other manufacturers to market automotive products under this trademark, and to license further manufacturers to market tee shirts, hats, and other clothing items bearing this trademark.

Digital Ignition also sought to use its success in marketing its initial patented products to expand its sales of related, non-patented products. It developed and sold a new version of its patented ignition system that could only be bought in conjunction with cables that were included in the product packaging. Previous Digital Ignition products had not been packaged with such cables, but the company asserted in its product marketing literature that the new design of its product was particularly sensitive to the use of the proper cables and that, to ensure consumer satisfaction, the new design was being sold only in conjunction with the bundled cables. Both consumers and independent cable sellers raised complaints about this new marketing practice of Digital Ignition, asserting that it improperly precluded free competition for sales of the relevant cables.

This brief overview identifies the many important roles that intellectual property and related legal problems can play in a company like Digital Ignition. The readings in this text address some, but not all, of these key developments in the founding and growth of Digital Ignition. In addition, further legal problems that the company encountered in developing and marketing its intellectual property are examined in particular chapters. Collectively, these problems represent critically important challenges faced by many companies in our modern economy and correspondingly significant opportunities for attorneys to aid businesses as problem solvers regarding intellectual property assets and infringement threats.

CHAPTER 1

CREATING AND PROTECTING THE BUSINESS MODEL

PROBLEM

You are working as an associate in a law firm and are given a case file for Dr. See, a computer scientist who plans to form a new company named Digital Ignition. The case file indicates that Dr. See has received several patents to cover his software based ignition system that provides better engine performance and gas mileage. The file also indicates that Dr. See will be meeting with several potential investors in a few weeks and is in the process of putting together a business plan to present to the investors. You are asked to review the plan in order to identify potential intellectual property issues raised by the business plan that Dr. See would like addressed before his meeting.

FOCUS OF THE CHAPTER

The following reading materials provide a useful checklist of what to consider in advising Dr. See about his plan and his meeting. Specific topics to keep in mind include recognizing the value of intellectual property, putting a dollar estimate on this value, identifying pitfalls to protecting intellectual property and structuring licensing, and becoming aware of tax issues. Additional readings in this chapter focus your attention on contemporary problems that confront many start-ups, such as issues involving university-industry collaboration, federal funding, and negotiating with federal and state governments. As you work through the readings, think about the ways in which you would advise start-up companies on how to identify and manage their intellectual property resources. The materials are divided into subsections addressing the following seven issues:

    a. Identifying what can be protected as intellectual property;

    b. Valuing intellectual property assets once identified;

    c. Avoiding forfeiture of intellectual property rights through failures to register and public uses;

    d. Licensing intellectual property assets;

    e. Identifying tax issues raised by intellectual property licenses;

    f. Identifying special issues raised by intellectual property in the context of universities and state and federal governments;

    g. Protecting business plans themselves as intellectual property through business method patents.

As you work through these readings, think about how these seven issues might arise and intersect in the course of starting up a new business.

READINGS

A. CAPTURING VALUE THROUGH INTELLECTUAL PROPERTY

Jon E. Hokanson & Sa'id Vakili, Intellectual Property Issues for the Technology Startup Company
Los Angeles Lawyer, February 2000, at p. 21*

. . .

When starting up a technology company, there are so many details to consider that intellectual property questions are often overlooked. The consequences of this oversight can be considerable: greatly increased expenditures or, even worse, unrecoverable loss of valuable rights that could have been secured by taking simple, relatively inexpensive actions at an earlier date. It is therefore important for a startup, at an early stage, to identify the key issues and milestones in the life of its intellectual property and recognize the measures that should be taken to protect its valuable intellectual property rights in a cost-effective manner.

In technology companies, intellectual property issues tend to cluster around three basic areas: utility patents, trademarks used in interstate commerce, and copyrights. While each of these areas is governed by its own statutes and rules, in real life the challenge of securing these rights often cuts across two or even all three of the categories.

A technology company often begins its life with the single objective of exploiting an invention. Even for startups with a broader business plan, a critical first step is to identify any subject matter that may qualify for patent protection. . . .

Once the protectable subject matter has been identified and a decision to seek patent protection has been made, it is often best to file a provisional patent application. The costs of preparing and filing the application are relatively low and depend on the degree of complexity of the invention and the extent to which the inventors are able to provide a full written description of exactly how to make and use the invention.

A provisional patent application is generally considered to be the most cost-effective means of securing the earliest priority right to the invention, which is important for several reasons. First and most important, an early provisional application minimizes the amount of "prior art" that may be used to prevent a patent from being issued. Put another way, the longer that a company waits to file a provisional patent application, the greater will be the

---

developments in the field that will affect the consideration of the patent application.

In addition, an early priority right can become critical when filing for a patent in foreign countries, because most countries other than the United States are governed by the first-to-file rule. Under this principle, if two or more applications are filed for the same invention, the patent is awarded to the application having the earliest priority right. In contrast, U.S. patent law is governed by the first-to-invent rule, under which the patent is awarded to the party that can demonstrate that it was the first to invent the patentable subject matter, even if that party's patent application has a later file date than that of a competing party. Even in the United States, an early priority date is important when more than one applicant applies for the same patentable invention. In this situation, the patent application with the earliest priority date is accorded important procedural rights that place its inventor in a much stronger position to be declared the first to invent and thus eventually to earn the U.S. patent.

It is usually best to file a provisional patent application as soon as the inventor knows how to make and use the invention. At the very least, the patent application should be filed prior to any offer for sale, public disclosure, public use, or sale of the invention. Failure to file a patent application prior to any of these events may reduce the available patent rights in certain countries and even prevent a valid patent from issuing.

This dire result is a consequence of a patent rule known as absolute novelty, which is operative in many countries. In order to obtain patent protection in absolute-novelty countries, a patent application must be on file prior to any disqualifying public disclosure, public use, or sale of the invention. The nuances and specific definitions of these rights-losing-events vary from country to country, and a patent attorney should be consulted regarding potential loss of rights in any specific country and under any particular set of circumstances. A failure to file an application on a timely basis prior to making the invention public will prevent the company from obtaining valid patent rights in most countries outside the United States.

Relatively few countries — but including the United States, Canada, and Mexico — provide a one-year grace period within which the potential commercial success of the invention may be tested prior to making an investment in patent protection. In these countries, an offer for sale, public disclosure, public use and/or sale of the invention typically triggers the one-year period. If by the end of that year an application for a patent has not been filed, the rights to obtain a valid patent are lost. . . .

The second critical component of a patent rights strategy is to provide a full and complete written description of how to make and use the invention for which the patent is sought. Startups (and mature companies rushing to bring a product to market) too often leave the patenting process to the last minute or consider it only as an afterthought. Then, faced with a deadline under which valuable patent rights will be lost if an application is not filed, a barely adequate, or in some cases an inadequate description of the invention is prepared and filed.

The consequence of having a legally adequate but less than complete written description of the invention is that the maximum scope of patent protection available from the application will not truly match the scope of the invention, and will thus be less than could have been obtained. For example, a legally adequate application might omit a certain claim, which would then give competitors a head start in developing a competing product.

In the worst case, a less-than-complete application might not even be legally adequate. For example, it might omit some critical feature of the invention or a discussion of the "best mode" of practicing the invention at that time. If the U.S. Patent and Trademark Office discovers such inadequacy during its consideration of the application, it may refuse to grant a patent. Even if the Patent Office does not discover the inadequacies and issues a patent, the patent is not secure. If the patent later becomes the subject of litigation, it is likely that the inadequacies will then be exposed, the likely result of which is that a federal court will invalidate the patent.

The additional cost of providing a full and enabling disclosure, compared to an inadequate or barely adequate disclosure, would typically be in the hundreds of dollars or, at most, a few thousand dollars. On the other hand, if the patent application is rejected, the cost of challenging a patent examiner's decision at the Patent Office Board of Appeals, or eventually on appeal to the U. S. Court of Appeals for the Federal Circuit, would be measured at several thousand to potentially tens of thousands of dollars. If the patent is ultimately invalidated in litigation because of a failure to provide an enabling disclosure of the invention and/or to detail the best mode of carrying out the invention, the cost would run at least many tens of thousands to hundreds of thousands of dollars, considering the cost of obtaining the patent, paying the maintenance fees, and defending the validity of the patent in litigation. In some cases, the cost of losing the patent on an invention could be measured in the millions of dollars.

Trademark Rights

Acquisition of federal trademark rights is invariably less risky and less costly if an organized, intelligent approach is made at or near the beginning of the lifetime of a new product, rather than waiting until the product's launch date or even beyond. Once a decision is made to market an invention, the company should begin to select candidates for marks that will be used to identify the product or service in interstate commerce. At this stage, two considerations are paramount:

1. Whether the company can adopt and use the mark in interstate commerce free from the legitimate assertion of rights by another.

2. Whether the company can obtain a federal trademark registration (and in some instances corresponding foreign trademark registrations) for the mark.

As an initial step, a relatively inexpensive computer database search should be made from records available at the U.S. Patent and Trademark Office. The objective of this search is to eliminate bad candidates and thereby save costs that might otherwise be spent on the clearance of marks that are not likely to win approval. Once this initial clearance search is complete, it is wise to conduct a full search beyond the Trademark Office database and include the databases of all state registries, common law databases, and Internet domain names. In situations in which the product is destined for global distribution, it is also worthwhile to commission searches in foreign countries. . . .

Copyright

Copyright registration is a relatively inexpensive form of legal protection available to a technology startup company. On the other hand, the financial consequences of not obtaining appropriate copyright protections are typically not as high as the costs that accompany the failure to obtain patent and trademark protection. Companies often use copyright as a complementary form of protection for promotional materials, manuals, and, most importantly, computer software.

Copyrightable subject matter is referred to as a "work of authorship," and registration may be obtained once the work of authorship has been reduced to a tangible medium, such as a printed page, computer file, and the like. The cost of registration at the U.S. Copyright Office varies, but typically runs only several hundred dollars, including the government filing fee and the associated costs of preparing and filing the application.

Two major benefits accrue from the early filing of an application for registration of copyright if an infringement is discovered and spawns litigation. In a lawsuit brought on a registered copyright, the copyright owner has the ability to obtain 1) statutory damages, without the need to comply with costly discovery requests or offer evidence to prove the damage amounts, and 2) an award of attorney's fees and costs. On the other hand, failure to register the copyright in a timely manner may result, as a practical matter, in not being able to enforce the copyright against infringements.

For technology companies, an important element in copyright registration is to ensure that the documentation reflects the company's ownership of the copyrights, rather than the individual who created those works. This is especially true when the employment relationship between the company and the individual who created the work is unclear. Except for "work made for hire," ownership of the copyright as a matter of law belongs, in the first instance, to the human beings who authored the work rather than to the company who may have paid those humans for creating it. Whereas the cost of obtaining documentation that clearly identifies the company's ownership of the work is typically trivial if completed in conjunction with or prior to the authoring of the work, these costs can become devastatingly high if the work becomes valuable and the company cannot establish through proper documentation that it owns the copyright to the work. As always, if a dispute can only be resolved through litigation, the costs to obtain or prove ownership may reach into the hundreds of thousands of dollars, with typical presumptions working in favor of the human author as opposed to the company. This increases the risk that the company ultimately will not be determined to be the owner of the copyright.

Intellectual property issues often arise in the life of a startup company in the context of company patents, trademarks, and copyrights. Employees and consultants who participate in product development can claim an ownership or co-ownership right to the company's intellectual property unless a written agreement clearly provides that the ownership of the intellectual property right is held by the company.

An employee's claim of right to a company's intellectual property can be devastating in situations in which a company product or trade name becomes a valuable asset. Typically, employee claims of ownership can be prevented by an employee agreement assigning all intellectual property rights to the employer. Because such agreements involve the surrender of prospective employee rights, they need to be drafted in compliance with applicable state labor laws. When dealing with consultants or other independent contractors, the company should have a written agreement providing that the company retains ownership of all intellectual property.

Victoria A. Cundiff, How a Startup Company Can Put Its Intellectual Property at Risk,
Practicing Law Institute, Patents, Copyright, Trademarks and Literary Property Course Handbook Series No. G0-00CW (September, 2000)*

While there may be as many ways to jeopardize intellectual property rights as there are new startup companies, here are some of the most common mistakes, and some solutions.

1. Start up the new company while working for the old.

Starting a successful new company requires good ideas, intense commitment, and the willingness to take risk. Many entrepreneurs try to put off the risk-taking by staying in a salaried job for as long as possible. This approach can lead to a lawsuit — and even to the loss of intellectual property developed for the new company.

While the law is clear that one can prepare to start a new business and can even prepare to compete while working for one employer, the law is equally clear that actually starting a new job or competing while employed is a breach of fiduciary duty. The employee has a duty of undivided loyalty to his or her employer.

What this means, in practical terms, is that an employee who is supposed to be developing software for a current employer should not be developing software for a new company, even at home and even after hours. Otherwise, the soon-to-be former employer may have a viable claim that it owns the software, particularly if the software relates in any way to work the employee was supposed to be doing while on salary or was created using property of the former employer. *See, e.g., Health Care Affiliated Services, Inc. v. Lippany*, 701 F. Supp. 1142 (W.D. Pa. 1988). Even if that claim ultimately fails, time and money spent litigating the issue with the prior employer can quickly drain startup capital.

Further, while working for one company, the employee should not be soliciting its employees or customers to move to a new company. *See, e.g., Duane Jones v. Burke*, 306 N.Y. 172, 117 N.E.2d 237 (1954). The employee needs to quit first and, unless contractually prohibited from doing so, recruit later. The employee should not be soliciting new customers on behalf of the new company, either, since the claim could readily be made that by so doing, the employee was diverting a business opportunity that should have been shared with the employer.

Finally, the employee should not permit work to get the new company up and running to interfere with his or her work for the employer. Doing so may lead to a claim that the employee must repay the salary received during the period of overlap. *See, e.g., Maritime Fish Products, Inc. v. World-Wide Fish Products, Inc.*, 100 A.D.2d 81, 474 N.Y.S.2d 281 (1st Dep't.), *app. dism'd*, 63 N.Y.2d 675 (1984).

2. Wait to search and register trademarks or domain names until just before a public announcement or product release.

Many entrepreneurs conceive of clever, memorable names they plan to use once their business gets started. That name dominates their thinking, their presentations to investors and potential employees, and their graphics and product design. When they finally get around to conducting a trademark search, however, they may discover that someone else has already registered, or is using, the very name they had counted on for similar goods or services. While that earlier registration may be the result of misappropriation — the registrant learned the entrepreneur's intended trademark and pirated it for its own use — more often the problem is simply that someone else independently thought of, and protected, the same name first.

To prevent the attendant loss of momentum, the entrepreneur should conduct a trademark search as soon as he or she comes up with an appealing name. The greater the commitment to the name, the more comprehensive that search should be. An initial screening of Federally registered trademarks, which can be done free on-line by checking www.uspto.gov, may knock out some proposed marks early on or raise some red flags by showing that others have registered or claim rights in the same or a similar name or logo.

This limited search cannot, however, "clear" a proposed name or logo. In trademark law, one gains rights by using the mark, whether or not one seeks a Federal registration. Thus, someone else may have acquired rights in the proposed mark by using it without filing for a Federal registration. A good example is one of the designs for the Coca Cola bottle, which was only registered as a trademark many years after it was first used. *See also BIEC Int'l, Inc. v. Global Steel Services, Ltd.*, 791 F. Supp. 489, 533 (E.D. Pa. 1992).

If the entrepreneur starts using a mark someone else had been using, the "prior user" may be able to put a stop to the new use in the territories where the prior user had used it first. Such "common law" rights enabled the University of Nebraska to stall NBC's proposed national launch of its new stylized "N" logo several years ago, for example. Exacting common law searches conducted by trademark search organizations are necessary to detect such use of proposed marks in commerce by third parties. These searches check telephone directories, trade journals, domain name registrations, state filings, and other resources. Experienced counsel can help interpret those reports so that the fledgling company can more accurately assess whether third parties indeed have a superior claim to a chosen mark.

How can the Company protect the mark it selects? Obtaining a Federal registration can certainly help. Many entrepreneurs believe that they cannot register their own proposed mark until they can prove that they are actually using it. Since 1989, however, the Trademark Office has allowed parties to "reserve" trademarks they hope to use shortly but are not yet using in interstate commerce. By filing an "intent-to-use" application, they can get the trademark approval process underway and, if successful, obtain a Federal registration once they begin using the mark which will be effective as of the date of the intent-to-use application. 15 U.S.C. § 1051(b) (1998). In most instances, an entrepreneur will want to consider this approach, since a Federal registration can generally give the applicant nationwide rights against later, or "junior," users of the mark even if the applicant has not actually used the mark nationwide. . . .

But obtaining a Federal registration is not the only way, or the final step to protect a trademark. Recall that trademark rights come from use. Once the entrepreneur settles on a name, the Company should begin using it in commerce just as soon as it makes business sense to do so. Failing to use the mark can result in forfeiture of rights. "Token" use, such as in shipments to out-of-state friends, however, does not generally establish rights. Lucent Information Management ("LIM") recently learned this in its unsuccessful effort to claim superior rights over Lucent Technologies, Inc., which filed an intent-to-use application and aggressively promoted the mark after LIM, had made only a single sale. *Lucent Information Management, Inc. v. Lucent Technologies, Inc.*, 186 F.3d 311 (3d Cir. 1999). Using the mark in a concerted and consistent fashion will both build consumer recognition and help establish legal rights.

3. Ignore trademarks and concentrate solely on domain names.

Many entrepreneurs seek domain name registration the moment they think of a name. If they succeed, they believe they have protected "their trademark" and that others will not be allowed to use similar marks, on-line or elsewhere. This belief confuses domain name rights with trademark rights. The two are related, but are not identical.

Registering a domain name, such as "goodidea.com," simply gives the registrant the right to use that precise name as an Internet address. Obtaining a domain name, however, does not even prevent others from registering similar domain names, such as "good-idea.com". Nor does it stand as a certification that third parties are not already using the name. Apart from seeking some representations from the applicant, the domain name registrar does not make an independent determination of the applicant's right to use a particular name. This means that the party that registers a name as a domain name will not necessarily prevail in an infringement lawsuit if another party has used the name first.

Many readers are familiar with this principle in the context of "cyber pirates" who register domain names incorporating well-known trademarks intending to sell them back to the trademark owner. The pirate who first registers "cocacola.com" will not thereby gain rights superior to those enjoyed by the Coca Cola Company. *See, e.g., Panavision Int'l, L.P. v. Toeppen*, 141 F.3d 1316, 1327 (9th Cir. 1998). But the distinction between domain name rights and trademark rights can also affect the innocent domain name owner who has simply never checked to see if others are using the same or similar name as a trademark. . . .

The lesson? By all means obtain a domain name. But do some research into whether others are using similar names. If so, investigate further. If not, don't simply let the domain name lie dormant and unused. "Trademark protection" does not stop with domain name registration. It begins with careful selection, and is maintained by proper use.

Finally, be aware that registering a name with the Secretary of State, while often a prerequisite to doing business in that state, does not establish trademark rights, either. Only use, and, if appropriate, federal trademark registration, can.

4. Just assume that the Company owns what it pays others to create.

Once they are up and running, many startup companies understandably rely on consultants, part time employees, or "jacks-of-all-trades" who do everything from marketing to raising capital to writing software. Each of these approaches at the very least complicates the question of whether the Company owns the intellectual property it has paid others to create.

Contrary to popular belief, simply paying someone who winds up creating intellectual property does not make the work created a "work-for-hire" belonging to the Company. Nor does the fact that an employee created intellectual property necessarily make that property an asset of the company if it was created outside the scope of the employee's duties or without using company property. Under many circumstances, failing to obtain properly worded written assignment or work-for-hire acknowledgments will leave the Company with only non-exclusive rights in the intellectual property. The parties who created the property will also be able to exploit and license it — with no obligation to pay any proceeds to the Company. Moreover, by the time the lack of assignment agreements becomes apparent, many of the contributors to the intellectual property may have scattered or be unavailable, making it difficult if not impossible to cure the problem.

The conscientious entrepreneur would do well, therefore, to work with counsel to develop and use appropriate assignment agreements and keep careful track of who has contributed to each item of intellectual property developed for the Company. . . .

A related mistake is failing to keep copies of intellectual property created for the Company. If the Company has overwritten the software it wishes to protect, for example, or has failed to keep clear records of how and when its invention was developed, it may not be able to seek a copyright registration or apply for a patent. Moreover, the intellectual property owner who claims that a third party has infringed an early version of its software but does not have a copy of that version to introduce into evidence may face dismissal of the case. Even well-established companies have suffered these consequences of sloppy early record keeping. *See Computer Associates International v. American Fundware, Inc.*, 831 F. Supp. 1516, 1520 (D. Colo. 1993).

The solution? Archive and retain in Company files all material variations of the intellectual property created for the Company. Careful recordkeeping will also make it easier to sell or license intellectual property later on.

5. To generate excitement, freely disclose the Company's plans and intellectual property without a confidentiality agreement.

Entrepreneurs typically need to present their ideas to many people before they can get up and running or take the business to the next level. Bankers, "angels," venture capitalists, strategic alliance partners, and key customers, among others, may all need to investigate the entrepreneur's ideas before they can commit to back them.

But the more people who learn the plan, the more people who can divert it to their own use.

While under certain circumstances courts may be willing to impose a duty of confidentiality on potential investors and others with whom the entrepreneur has shared his or her ideas, counting on these "implied" protections is foolish. Before presenting confidential intellectual property or business plans, or even proposed trademarks, the entrepreneur should get a written commitment that the information will not be used or disclosed except for purposes the entrepreneur specifies, and that all documents, including notes, discussing the disclosures will be returned or destroyed once the specified use ends. (Filing an intent-to-use application should give further protection for the proposed trademark.) Failure to obtain such an agreement in writing has sparked costly litigation between kozmo.com and urbanfetch.com, among others.

Many entrepreneurs fear that insisting that potential financial partners enter into confidentiality agreements will scare them away. It is true that many venture capitalists are so inundated with business plans to which they give only cursory attention that as a matter of policy they will not assume duties of confidentiality with respect to initial submissions from those seeking investment capital.

Once past the initial submission, however, some venture capitalists increasingly view a request for a confidentiality agreement as an indication that the entrepreneur is taking proper measures to protect his or her ideas and, by extension, the value of what the investors are being asked to invest in. Thus requesting a confidentiality agreement before revealing confidential details makes good business sense as well as legal sense. Indeed, at least one venture capital firm has commenced litigation to enforce its own confidentiality rights against its former employees. . . .

The party receiving the disclosure may want to negotiate some limitations on the duties of confidentiality. Many may well be appropriate, such as mechanisms for determining whether the receiving party has already seen or separately developed similar intellectual property, or acknowledgments that the party receiving the disclosures is making no advance commitment to finance the project. But while the entrepreneur may be willing to be flexible as to certain details, he or she must be adamant about limiting and protecting the disclosures he or she does make. This is not an area to compromise. Otherwise, someone else may turn those ideas into the next successful IPO. . . .

The Company needs to be just as careful to insist that its own employees, consultants, and suppliers keep Company secrets under wraps. Some startup companies start out well, carefully developing assignment agreements, confidentiality procedures and policies, non-compete/non-solicitation agreements, and other safeguards. But as time goes on, they get sloppy. They stop legending documentation as confidential. They freely display their breakthroughs to suppliers and potential customers. They "assume" consultants have signed non-disclosure and assignment agreements and "imagine" employees have signed appropriate covenants. They "expect" departing employees to understand their continuing obligations, but stop conducting exit interviews to remind them. Then they are surprised when their expectations are dashed.

Finally, take care not to post secrets on the Company web page. It is amazing how many startup companies post customer lists, employee rosters, joint venture plans and technical papers for all the world — including all the competition — to see.

Establishing proper internal protective measures can help — but only if the Company follows them. Otherwise, their major function is to serve as powerful evidence that the Company did not follow what it knew were reasonable measures to protect its own property. As one court has emphasized, "One who claims that he has a trade secret must exercise eternal vigilance." *Baystate Technologies, Inc. v. Bentley Systems, Inc.*, 946 F. Supp. 1079 (D. Mass. 1996). Investors and intellectual property owners alike should recognize, however, that even well-crafted protective measures are not infallible. Thus entrepreneurs should not overreach in describing the likely efficacy of their confidentiality procedures and agreements. *Cf. Steinberg v. PRT Group, Inc.*, 88 F. Supp.2d 294 (S.D.N.Y. 2000) (dismissing claim that prospectus misrepresented the nature and importance of its non-compete agreements, concluding that the "subdued description of the non-compete agreements" reflected no more than "general optimism" and holding that company had no obligation to disclose that such agreements are sometimes ignored).

6. Assume the founders and other key employees will stay with the Company forever.

Many startup companies are started by a few friends who spend 120 hour weeks establishing the Company, creating the intellectual property at its heart, and developing its customer base. When these efforts succeed, the Company is often sold to third parties or taken public. What happens to the founders then?

Often they stay on as key employees or full-time consultants. But frequently they leave to pursue new undertakings. The far-sighted company will consider entering early on into agreements that provide for a smooth transition, limit immediate head-to-head competition, and prohibit use of the Company's intellectual property and use and disclosure of its trade secrets. Without such protections in place, a startup company will be far less attractive to investors, including the public. Few announcements scuttle a public offering so quickly as those reporting that the founders are starting NewCo 2000 to market version 2.0 of the Company's intellectual property.

Anticipating key departures is important even if a sale or IPO seems far away. Particularly in the early stages of a company, the loss of a single employee or key consultant to a competitor can endanger the Company. Stock option agreements may entice employees to stay, but what if they do decide to leave? The legal protections available to an employer depend on state law. The contractual safeguards that work for a New York company, for example, may not be enforceable in California. But companies need to work with counsel before departures to plan how to prevent the loss of a key contributor from transferring Company secrets, technology, and business to a competitor.

7. Ignore invasions of Company rights by third parties.

The last thing a company in the process of establishing its business usually wants to do is become embroiled in a lawsuit. Thus, when startup companies detect evidence that others may be adopting similar names or slogans or may be copying the technology, some corporate founders simply shrug and say there's nothing they can afford to do about it. An almost equally common reaction is to threaten to sue the offender for punitive damages and injunctive relief — and then either fail to sue, or sue and devote far too much money and corporate time to the effort.

Deciding what to do about an apparent infringement of the Company's intellectual property rights is a delicate balancing exercise. Every infringement does not warrant a lawsuit. Generally speaking, the courts do not require an intellectual property owner to sue everyone who encroaches upon its rights. But if the owner of a trademark does not protest now when others use substantially similar marks to promote their similar products, it may have to justify its inaction later when it does sue someone else for using marks similar to those ignored in the past.

Or, if a trademark owner has known of an apparent infringement for years but did nothing to challenge it, it may be found to have forfeited its rights against that specific infringer. The trademark owner may become, as one court has said, "the hapless victim of his own lethargy." This problem is by no means limited to startups. The famous French fashion house, Hermés, for example, was recently found to have forfeited its rights to sue a New York firm for handbag copies Hermés had been aware of — but remained silent about — for nearly twenty years. The Court held that even "a single warning letter would have been sufficient to lessen this severe delay." *Hermés Int'l v. Lederer de Paris Fifth Avenue, Inc.*, 50 F. Supp.2d 212 (S.D.N.Y. 1999).

Thus, even if the Company is not prepared to file a lawsuit, it may still make sense to send protest letters making clear that the Company objects to the infringing activity. The Company should also document internally the reasons it decides not to file suit in particular cases, such as the very limited geographic scope of the infringement, the limited overlap in products, etc. The reasoning that seems logical now may be forgotten, and difficult to explain, in the future. The Company should maintain records of any agreed compromises, as well. Such records can be used in the future to explain how an infringement that does lead to a lawsuit differs from events in the past.

Protest letters should be carefully reviewed with counsel to prevent them from being used by the alleged infringer as the basis for starting a lawsuit in an unfriendly jurisdiction to declare the parties' rights.

One type of misappropriation the intellectual property owner will almost always want to challenge at the outset is use or disclosure of trade secrets. Unlike other forms of intellectual property, a trade secret, once freely disclosed, is as a practical matter, lost forever. *FMC v. Taiwan Tainan Giant Indus. Co.*, 730 F.2d 61, 63 (2d Cir. 1984). Others who learn it without knowledge that it has been misappropriated will generally be free to use it without limitation. While the party disclosing it may well be liable for damages, that fact may be of little comfort, especially if that party has few assets. Thus, at a minimum, a protest letter to the potential discloser and to those likely to receive the disclosure is almost always in order, although it must be carefully drafted and circulation properly controlled to prevent claims of libel. Injunctive relief to "keep the cat in the bag" may also be warranted.

Trade secret owners who believe their valuable secrets have been stolen may also want to consider presenting their claims to the U.S. Attorneys' office for potential prosecution under the Economic Espionage Act, a Federal criminal statute. 18 U.S.C. §§ 1831–1839 (1996). While such actions are not routinely brought and do not lead to financial recovery by the trade secret owner, they may save the secret and punish the thief at minimal cost to the trade secret owner.

8. Ignore protest letters from third parties.

Finally, the entrepreneur needs to be careful not to infringe on the intellectual property rights of others. Following the tips outlined in this article should reduce the risk. Requiring employees and consultants to certify that they are not incorporating the property of others into work they create for the Company and are not using the confidential information of others should also help. But if protest letters come, the startup company, in particular, must pay attention.

Some protest letters are clearly unwarranted or overreaching. Some are sent by third parties who can be easily shown to have inferior, or no, rights to the name or writings or technology. If so, say so — in writing. Many intellectual property lawsuits are filed simply because an initial protest letter was never answered. Ex parte restraining orders are sometimes entered for the same reason. The plaintiff is able to persuade the court that nothing short of a court order will make the accused infringer pay attention and explain the conduct at issue.

Sometimes a protest letter does seem to have substantial merit. Better to try to address it informally than to bog down in litigation. In the case of a trademark dispute, perhaps a license can be worked out permitting use of the name in a specific geographic area or for particular types of goods. Or perhaps the trademark owner could assist the innocent infringer in developing a new mark, or allow some time to phase in the new mark. In the case of a copyright dispute, perhaps certain segments of the computer code could be rewritten in a new version. In the case of potential use or disclosure of a trade secret by a former employee, perhaps the employee could be assigned to new duties which would not put the information at risk.

Not every dispute can be readily resolved, of course. But confronting the risks early on, rather than simply ignoring them, may help prevent a lawsuit or, at the least, a major damages award. By contrast, companies that have simply ignored others' successful claims to intellectual property may find themselves having to pay multimillion dollar damages awards, or even stop selling their products altogether.

Intellectual property can be among a company's most valuable assets, but only if the company works hard to protect it, and to ensure that it does not belong to others. An ongoing partnership with intellectual property counsel can protect the Company when it starts out — and once it becomes a market leader.

MOTOR CITY BAGELS, LLC. v. AMERICAN BAGEL CO.
United States District Court for the District of Maryland
50 F. Supp. 2d 460 (1999)

Beginning in the fall of 1993, Plaintiff, Joseph Anthony, began researching franchise opportunities as a possible entrepreneurial venture. At that time, Mr. Anthony had an M.B.A. in finance and accounting from the Tuck School of Business Administration at Dartmouth College and had extensive experience in commercial real estate investment and management. By the spring of 1994, Mr. Anthony intensified his evaluation of potential franchise opportunities, focusing particularly on the bagel industry. While researching various bagel franchisors, Mr. Anthony initiated discussions with Chesapeake Bagel Bakery through its sales representative Steve Vierra. After some preliminary discussions on the telephone, Mr. Anthony traveled to McLean, Virginia during the spring of 1994 to meet with Mr. Vierra and to tour a handful of Chesapeake stores in the Washington, D.C. area.

Early in the summer of 1994, Plaintiff, Randall Flinn, teamed with Mr. Anthony in assessing the feasibility of operating a bagel franchise. Mr. Flinn, a friend of Mr. Anthony's from college, had an M.B.A. from the J.C. Kellogg Graduate School of Management and was working as a Senior Product Manager for Teradyne, an Illinois telecommunications concern. By late July 1994, Mr. Anthony and Mr. Flinn received an American Bagel Uniform Franchise Offering Circular, dated August 23, 1993 ("1993 UFOC"), which disclosed information about the Chesapeake Bagel Bakery franchise system, including estimates of initial investment costs experienced by franchisees.

The 1993 UFOC provided an estimate for initial investment costs for Chesapeake Bagel Bakeries, "based on the latest available data," ranging from $240,400 to $304,500. 1993 UFOC at 8. Mr. Anthony and Mr. Flinn used the cost figures provided in the 1993 UFOC as a central assumption in an extensive, written business plan analyzing the viability of owning and operating Chesapeake Bagel Bakery franchises. The plaintiffs used the midpoint in the range provided in the disclosure document, $275,000, to determine the amount of capital required to open an individual store.

Although the plaintiffs used the cost figures from the August 23, 1993 UFOC in drawing up their business plan, American Bagel had actually updated its disclosure information through a revised UFOC, filed in Mr. Anthony's home state of Indiana on April 21, 1994 ("1994 UFOC"). This revised UFOC contained a higher range of estimated initial investment costs than was included in the 1993 UFOC. The 1994 UFOC stated that, "based on the latest available data," start-up costs for individual Chesapeake Bagel Bakery stores ranged between $288,300 and $376,000.

In November 1994, American Bagel mailed Mr. Anthony a second UFOC. The defendants contend that they sent the 1994 UFOC with the revised estimates of initial investment costs. The plaintiffs, however, vehemently deny this assertion, claiming that they received a UFOC with the same cost estimates that they had received in July. In any event, Plaintiffs, Mr. Anthony, Mr. Flinn, and Motor City Bagels, L.L.C., signed an Area Franchise Development Agreement ("AFDA") on December 3, 1994 pursuant to which they received the exclusive right, subject to certain terms and conditions, to develop Chesapeake Bagel Bakeries in Oakland County, Macomb County, and the city of Grosse Pointe, Michigan. Under the agreement, the plaintiffs had to pay $25,000 at the time of signing, $10,000 prior to December 31, 1994, and an additional $50,000 within forty-five days. That same day, the plaintiffs also entered into two franchise agreements, obligating the plaintiffs to pay license fees of $22,500 and $20,000 by December 31, 1994.

On June 15, 1995, the plaintiffs signed another AFDA pursuant to which they were granted, under certain terms and conditions, the exclusive right to develop Chesapeake Bagel Bakeries in Washtenaw, Livingston, Clinton, Eaton, and Ingham Counties, Michigan, another franchise agreement, and a promissory note for $10,000 payable to American Bagel. Under the AFDA, the plaintiffs paid to American Bagel $60,000 in franchise fees and the franchise agreement required the plaintiffs to pay an additional $17,500 in license fees.

Allegedly unbeknownst to the plaintiffs, American Bagel had again updated its UFOC between the signing of the first wave of agreements on December 3, 1994, and the second wave on June 15, 1995. On January 25, 1995, the Federal Trade Commission approved the revised offering circular submitted by American Bagel ("1995 UFOC"). In this updated disclosure form, American Bagel had again increased the estimated initial costs that prospective franchisees could expect to spend to a range of $328,800 to $431,000.

Pursuant to the two franchise agreements signed on December 3, 1994, the plaintiffs opened a Chesapeake Bagel Bakery on December 27, 1995 in Northville, Michigan, and a second one in Troy, Michigan on March 6, 1996. According to the plaintiffs, their start-up costs greatly exceeded the amounts represented by the defendants in the 1993 UFOC. Mr. Anthony estimated that in the Northville store, the plaintiffs spent $425,000 on tenant improvements and equipment, and that franchise fees and expenses associated with training, advertising, and deposits pushed the total cost of the store over $500,000. Similarly, the plaintiffs assert that it cost approximately $400,000 to construct and equip the Troy store, even before accounting for franchise fees, advertising, training, and other sundry start-up expenses.

After Northville and Troy, the plaintiffs failed to open up any additional Chesapeake Bagel Bakery restaurants as required by the Consolidated, Amended and Restated Area Development Agreement, signed by the plaintiffs on August 10, 1996. Mr. Flinn testified at his deposition that the plaintiffs refused to open more stores because they had "been fraudulently induced into signing the contracts and the agreement with [American Bagel] to open these stores through the representation of construction costs that were dramatically lower than the actual costs." The plaintiffs had exhausted their capital in starting up the Northville and Troy restaurants, and the debt burden resulting from the unexpectedly high construction costs was "putting a real strain on the profitability of the stores." Mr. Flinn explained that "at $400,000 to open a store, it's not a viable business. So, yes, we said if it's going to cost us $400,000 to open stores, we are not going to be able to open any additional stores." In addition to not constructing additional stores, the plaintiffs, in November 1996, likewise decided to stop paying various monthly franchise fees to American Bagel and its successor, Defendant, AFC Enterprises, Inc. ("AFC"), arising from the ongoing operations at their Northville and Troy stores.

As a result of this failed business relationship, the plaintiffs filed an eight-count suit against the defendants alleging violations of Indiana franchise law, fraud, negligent misrepresentation, violations of Maryland franchise law, breach of contract, unjust enrichment, and misappropriation of trade secrets. In addition, the plaintiffs seek declaratory judgment against AFC, arguing that the contracts at issue in this case are void ab initio and thus unenforceable. Additional facts will be discussed, as needed, within the framework of the legal issues presented in the individual claims. . . .

. . . .

IX. Misappropriation of Trade Secrets

The plaintiffs have asserted that the defendants' distribution of the business plan, in violation of [its] promise [of confidentiality] to the plaintiffs, constitutes a misappropriation of trade secrets in violation of the Maryland Uniform Trade Secrets Act ("MUTSA"). Md. Com. Law II Code Ann. §§ 11-1201 to 11-1209. At the outset, the Court is unclear as to the basis for applying Maryland law when the alleged misappropriation of the plan actually occurred in Virginia. However, the same analysis would apply under either Virginia or Maryland law as both states have adopted trade secret statutes which closely track the Uniform Trade Secrets Act. In addition, the Maryland legislature has dictated that the MUTSA "be applied and construed to effectuate its general purpose to make uniform the law with respect to" trade secrets among the states that have enacted the Uniform Trade Secrets Act. Md. Com. Law II Code Ann. § 11–1208.

The MUTSA defines "trade secret" as follows:

[I]nformation, including a formula, pattern, compilation, program, device, method, technique, or process, that:

> (1) Derives independent economic value, actual or potential, from not being generally known to, and not being readily ascertainable by proper means by, other persons who can obtain economic value from its disclosure or use; and
> (2) Is the subject of efforts that are reasonable under the circumstances to maintain its secrecy.

Stated succinctly, "to be protected under Maryland law, information must be secret, and its value must derive from the secrecy. In addition, the owner of the information must use reasonable efforts to safeguard the confidentiality of the information."

As an initial matter, the Court must determine whether the business plan constitutes a "secret" as required under the MUTSA. The Court of Special Appeals of Maryland has noted that a manufacturer's marketing plan did not constitute a protectable trade secret under Maryland law, in part, because it was based on information "readily available from the marketplace." The court specifically observed that the defendants could have obtained the same information in the plaintiff's marketing plan "simply by talking with prospective customers." While the business plan at issue in the case at bar does contain some public information and facts ascertainable from the marketplace, it likewise includes personal insights and analysis brought to bear through diligent research and by marshaling a large volume of information. [A]n attempt to independently duplicate the plaintiffs' efforts in the instant case would be an onerous task.

The United States District Court for the Eastern District of Pennsylvania has recognized that "[t]he fact that individual forms in marketing material or in plaintiff's proposal book were compilations of public information does not itself preclude a finding that the combination of the included elements affords a competitive advantage and is not itself in the public domain." The court continued:

> The combination of information in the proposal book reflected market research preformed [sic] by plaintiff and decisions to include and exclude certain elements from a larger pool of data. It is this, rather than the data contained in the individual forms generally known in the self insurance business, which may arguably contain a significant degree of novelty, however, slight, to be excluded from general knowledge, and may qualify the proposal book as a trade secret.

. . . Thus, applying the rationale set forth in these decisions, the Court concludes that the plaintiffs' extensive compilation of information and analysis in their business plan qualifies as a trade secret.

Likewise, the Court finds that the business plan derived value from its secrecy. . . . However, the MUTSA provides that damages caused by misappropriation . . . "may be measured by imposition of liability for a reasonable royalty for a misappropriator's unauthorized disclosure or use of a trade secret." Under this provision, the plaintiffs in the case at bar could argue that they are entitled to monetary damages in the form of royalties as a result of the defendants' unauthorized distribution of their business plan to prospective franchisees. Based on these potential royalty payments, the business plan "[d]erives independent economic value . . . from not being generally known to, and not being readily ascertainable by proper means by" the defendants and prospective Chesapeake franchisees.

The final prong that the plaintiffs must prove in bringing their misappropriation claim is that they took reasonable measures to ensure the secrecy of their business plan. The Fourth Circuit has noted that "[s]ecrecy is a question of fact" to be determined by the circumstances presented in each case. In the case at bar, the plaintiffs drafted an extensive confidentiality agreement that they had "most potential investors sign" when they received a copy of the business plan. The problem for the plaintiffs is that they only produced five executed copies of the confidentiality agreement when they distributed the business plan to over fifteen individuals. When questioned as to whether he recalled ever receiving any confidentiality agreements from other individuals who were given the business plan, Mr. Anthony responded, "I mean I don't remember. I think I probably got — had more of them but maybe not. This might be it." Mr. Anthony's equivocating response to this question reveals that the plaintiffs did not act diligently to protect the secrecy of their business plan. The Supreme Court has observed that the disclosure of a trade secret "to others who are under no obligation to protect the confidentiality of the information" extinguishes the property right in the disclosure. Under this reasoning, the plaintiffs' failure to exact agreements from potential investors to maintain the secrecy of the business plan is inconsistent with recognition of the document as a trade secret under the MUTSA.

In addition, the Court does not find the boilerplate language on the cover of the business plan stating that "[t]his memorandum is for the exclusive use of the persons to whom it is given and is not to reproduced or redistributed" precludes the denial of trade secret status. This sentence appears at the end of a general disclaimer, cautioning investors as to the risks involved in making an investment in the business described in the plan. The language is not highlighted or isolated so as to put one on immediate notice that the plan constitutes a trade secret that the authors of the plan are actively seeking to protect.

Taking the facts as a whole, the Court concludes that the plaintiffs simply did not act reasonably in seeking to ensure the secrecy of their plan. Because the plaintiffs have failed to adduce sufficient proof of this essential element of their misappropriation claim to ward off summary judgment under Anderson and Celotex, and the defendants' motions for summary judgment on this count will be granted.

NOTES & QUESTIONS

1. The readings in this section illustrate some of the intellectual property issues that confront a new business. The Cundiff reading is applicable to both high technology and low technology enterprises. The Hokanson & Vakili reading focuses specifically on technology based businesses, such as in the software and biotechnology sectors. Do the issues confronting high technology and low technology business start-ups differ? If so, how?

2. What could the plaintiffs have done differently in the *Motor City Bagel* case to protect their business plan as a trade secret? Are there tort or contract theories they could have pursued to protect their interests? What would be the likely results?

3. We will discuss forfeiture of intellectual property interests in greater detail below in section C. Notice how entrepreneurs have to be careful about their actions early on to make sure valuable intellectual property is not lost in the future. If you are a business person, at what stage should you consult an attorney? When you first come up with the idea? When you first decide to share the idea with someone else? If you are an attorney, knowledgeable in the fine details of intellectual property law, what should you be aware about from a business perspective?

4. What advice would you give Dr. See about sharing his business plan with potential investors in light of *Motor City Bagels?* In light of the Cundiff and Hokanson & Vakili readings?

B. VALUING INTELLECTUAL PROPERTY

Ted Hagelin, Valuation of Intellectual Property Assets: An Overview
52 Syracuse Law Review 1133 (2002)*

Introduction

The value of intangible assets relative to the value of physical and financial assets has continuously increased since the early 1980s. In 2000, the market-to-book value for the S&P 500 companies showed that approximately 83.3% of the companies' market values stemmed from intangible assets. For many companies, the ratio of intangible assets to physical and financial assets is considerably higher. The importance of intangible assets has created an urgent need to value these assets in many contexts including intellectual property management, acquisitions, sales, joint ventures, and licensing.

This article will briefly review the three basic valuation methods, then discuss the valuation methods developed for intellectual property and finally present a new valuation method — Competitive Advantage Valuation.®

I.   Valuation Methods

There are three basic methods of valuation: the cost method, the market method, and the income method. The cost method of valuation measures the value of an asset by the cost to replace the asset with an identical or equivalent asset. The assumption underlying the cost method of valuation is that the cost to purchase or develop a new asset is commensurate with the economic value that the asset can provide during its life. The market method values an asset based upon comparable transactions between unrelated parties. The income

---

method values an asset based upon the present value of the net economic benefit (net future income stream) expected to be received over the life of the asset.

II.   Valuation Methods Developed for Intellectual Property

There are seven commonly used valuation methods developed for use with intellectual property: the 25 Percent Rule, Industry Standards, Ranking, Surrogate Measures, Disaggregation Methods, the Monte Carlo Method, and Option Methods. The 25 percent rule is the most simple, flexible, and often referenced valuation method. Although there are many variations on the 25 percent rule, the most often given definition is that the licensor should receive 25 percent of the licensee's gross profit from the licensed technology. This statement of the 25 percent rule makes clear that its purpose is not the valuation of a technology per se, but rather the apportionment of a technology's value between the licensor and licensee. Discussions of the 25 percent rule generally provide that the percentage split between the licensor and licensee should be adjusted upwards or downwards to take into account the parties' respective investment and risk in the licensed technology.

Valuation of intellectual property by industry standards is another widely used valuation method. The industry standards method, also referred to as the market or comparable technology method, attempts to value an intellectual property asset by reference to royalty rates in similar past transactions. Information on royalty rates is available from a number of different sources such as articles on royalty rates and licensing terms, specific publications, price lists, contracts filed with the Securities and Exchange Commission and court decisions in infringement cases. The industry standards method of valuation is subject to a number of limitations because intellectual property is inherently dissimilar, intellectual property exchanges are motivated by unique strategic considerations, and published royalty rates are often based on broad industry classifications and provided in terms of wide percentage ranges, which might provide little guidance on an appropriate royalty rate for a specific intellectual property asset being valued.

The ranking method of valuation compares the intellectual property asset to be valued to comparable intellectual property assets on a subjective or objective scale. The ranking method is often used in conjunction with the industry standards method to determine a more precise royalty rate within an industry royalty rate range. There are five components to a ranking method: (i) scoring criteria; (ii) scoring system; (iii) scoring scale; (iv) weighting factors; and (v) decision table. These five components are used to calculate a composite score for an asset. That score is then compared to the average score for a comparable intellectual property asset to determine the relative value. The major disadvantages of the ranking method of valuation are the identification of comparable (benchmark) intellectual property asset transactions, the subjectivity of the criteria, and the translation of the composite score into a royalty rate or dollar adjustment. Furthermore, comparability is as much of a challenge in the ranking method as it is in the other methods for the same reasons.

Surrogate measures have been developed to value patents. Surrogate measures do not value patents by reference to profits, industry standards or rankings, but by reference to the patents themselves. The three most common types of surrogate measures are the number of patents issued to a company, payment of patent maintenance fees, and prior art citations. These measures have been shown to correlate, on average, with a firm's market value, suggesting that investors use these measures explicitly or implicitly in making investment decisions. The utility of surrogate measures, however, is limited because they can be inherently misleading, they can be manipulated, and they can only be used to value patent portfolios rather than individual patents.

There are two basic types of disaggregation methods — value disaggregation and income disaggregation. Value disaggregation seeks to apportion some fraction of total value to intellectual property assets by setting the value of intangible assets equal to the value of a firm (or a subdivision of a firm) minus the firm's monetary assets (cash, securities, receivables, inventories, prepayments, etc.) and tangible assets (land, buildings, equipment, furniture, vehicles, etc.) to determine the value of the intangible assets. This form of disaggregation is useful to provide perspective on the importance of intangible assets to a firm, but cannot be used to value different types of intangible assets or to value individual, or related groups of, intangible assets.

Income disaggregation seeks to apportion some fraction of total earnings of a firm, based upon various factors, to intellectual property assets. Two forms of income disaggregation are the "Technology Factor" method developed for the Dow Chemical Company and the Knowledge Capital Scorecard.

The Monte Carlo method of valuing intellectual property assets is primarily used as a refinement of the income method discussed earlier. Whereas the income method assigns a single value to the variables used in calculating the net present value (NPV) of an asset, the Monte Carlo method assigns a range of values to the variables and the probability of each value. Using the range of values and probabilities, the frequency of specific NPVs are calculated and plotted to provide an indication of the most likely NPV. The benefits of the Monte Carlo method are that it can calculate minimum and maximum NPVs, can associate intermediate NPVs with the probability of their realization, and can determine how different variables affect the uncertainty of the NPV calculation. The challenge in implementing the Monte Carlo method is obtaining the necessary information.

Option methods of valuing intellectual property assets are based on a widely used method for valuing stock options, known throughout the financial industry as the Black-Scholes formula. Under the Black-Scholes formula, the essence of a stock option's value lies in the right to wait and see what happens to a stock's price and to exercise or not exercise the option accordingly. The adaptation of stock option valuation to intellectual property valuation is based on the same "wait and see" value. Option valuation of intellectual property views an investment in intellectual property as an option to develop the intellectual property further, or to abandon the intellectual property, depending upon future technical and market information. The advantages of option valuation are that it avoids exaggerating the risk of investing in intellectual property assets and provides an objective, repeatable means for calculating intellectual property value. The disadvantages of option valuation are its complex mathematics and its requirement of extensive information databases.

III.   Competitive Advantage Valuation®

Competitive Advantage Valuation® (CAV) is a new method to value intellectual property assets. The CAV method was developed over a number of years through a series of research projects undertaken in the Technology Transfer Research Center at Syracuse University on behalf of a variety of client organizations. These research projects assessed the commercial potential of many different types of early-stage technologies by analyzing the engineering, marketing, licensing and intellectual property advantages and disadvantages associated with these technologies. When presented with the final research findings, the question most often asked by client organizations was, "So, what's the invention worth?" CAV was developed to answer this question in a simple and direct way.

In comparison to other valuation methods, the CAV method combines a number of unique features. Most importantly, the CAV method is specific. It can be used to value individual intellectual property assets and to determine differences in value within a group of intellectual property assets. The more specific a valuation method is, the more useful it is in managing intellectual property assets. The other unique features of the CAV method are:

> The CAV method is understandable to the broad cross-section of professionals practicing in the fields of licensing and intellectual property management. The easier a valuation method is to understand, the lower the transaction costs of negotiation and the quicker the parties can know whether an agreement can be reached.

> The CAV method is repeatable and not dependent upon the subjective choices of individuals or groups. The more repeatable a valuation method is, the easier it is for parties to focus their attention on the variables and value inputs on which they agree or disagree.

> The CAV method is affordable in terms of the time and cost of obtaining necessary information and performing the valuation analysis. The more affordable a valuation method is, the more broadly it will be adopted and the more likely it will be standardized.

> The CAV method is flexible and can be used to value any type of intellectual property as well as licenses, prospective research and development investments, and pre-market products. The more flexible a valuation method is, the more it can be shared across business divisions and used as a common benchmark.

> Finally, the CAV method is scalable. A simple CAV analysis can be performed using built-in default formulas to calculate values and more advanced CAV analyses can be performed using statistical software tools to calculate values. The more scalable a valuation method is, the greater the user's ability to choose the trade-off between the time and cost of the valuation, and the desired degree of accuracy of the result.

The major premise of the CAV method is that intellectual property assets have no inherent value; the value of intellectual property assets resides entirely in the value of the tangible assets which incorporate them. The minor premise of the CAV method is that the value of a given intellectual property asset can best be measured by the competitive advantage which that asset contributes to a product, process, or service. For the purpose of explanation, I will discuss the CAV method with respect to an existing product.

The CAV method is a novel combination of the income and disaggregation approaches to valuation. In its most general form, the CAV method consists of six basic steps:

(1) The intellectual property asset to be valued (IPA) is associated with a product and the product's net present value is calculated.

(2) The product's net present value is apportioned among tangible assets, intangible advantages and intellectual property assets. (There are three groups of intellectual property assets: technical [utility patents, functional software copyrights and technical trade secrets]; reputational [trademarks, service marks and brand names]; and operational [business method patents and proprietary business processes].

(3) The product is associated with competition parameters which can be used to compare the product to substitute products and competition parameter weights are calculated. (There are three groups of competition parameters: technical [price and performance], reputational [recognition and impression], and operational [cost and efficiency]. Weights are calculated for each parameter group and for individual parameters within each group.)

(4) The IPA is associated with an individual competition parameter and the IPA's competitive advantage relative to substitute intellectual property assets is calculated. (Substitute intellectual property assets are assets which are incorporated in substitute products and associated with the same competition parameter as the IPA.)

(5) The IPA is associated with complementary intellectual property assets and the IPA's competitive advantage relative to complementary intellectual property assets is calculated. (Complementary intellectual property assets are assets which are incorporated in the same product and associated with the same parameter group as the IPA.)

(6) The value of the IPA is calculated by apportioning a share of the product's intellectual property asset value to the IPA based upon the IPA's competitive advantage contribution relative to substitute and complementary intellectual property assets.

If the IPA is associated with multiple products, the IPA's relative competitive advantage contribution to each product is calculated and these contributions are summed to calculate the total value of the IPA. If the IPA is associated with multiple parameters, the IPA's relative competitive advantage contribution for each parameter is calculated and these contributions are summed to calculate the total value of the IPA.

Conclusion

The valuation of intellectual property assets is a trillion dollar problem in today's economy. The success of companies, and indeed the welfare of society, increasingly depends on intellectual property; and intellectual property assets cannot be effectively managed or efficiently transferred without adequate means to value them. Fortunately, a number of new methods to value intellectual property have been developed in recent years. Although each of these methods has certain limitations, together they have provided intellectual property managers a very useful new set of decision-making tools.

As with the valuation of tangible assets, no single method for valuing intellectual property assets will be definitive. Also, as with the valuation of tangible assets, the methods for valuing intellectual property assets will be subject to continuing research and refinement. The development of valuation methodologies has no terminal completion point, but is an ongoing, evolutionary process. The CAV method is proposed as part of this evolutionary process. The CAV method is not a definitive valuation method and further research will be required to refine the method. However, the unique features of the CAV method make it a useful addition to the existing methods. Hopefully, the CAV method will contribute in a small way to increase company values and investor returns.

Robert Goldscheider, The Negotiation of Royalties and Other Sources of Income from Licensing
36 IDEA 1 (1995)*

I. INTRODUCTION

Technology transfer agreements involving long-term relationships should be creative in both organization and structure. In fact, long-term profitability is often achieved by subtle and indirect forms of consideration. Accordingly, skilled practitioners of licensing should not be slaves to a "plain vanilla" approach. Rather, by combining resources from several aspects of various intra-party business dealings, practitioners can frequently generate greater income for both parties to a negotiation.

Without the prospect of substantial benefits, there is no point in making a deal. Thus, when valuing a prospective transfer of technology, one should first quantify the total possible profit. This valuation should include the effect of combining the rights and resources which each party is expected to contribute. Only after making this determination may parties logically negotiate their portion of the profit. If the preliminary apportionment is realistic and equitable, the parties may achieve the ultimate goal of licensing professionals: the "win-win" relationship.

The above approach may seem strange to newcomers to the licensing field who are only familiar with licenses based on royalty rates, which are often a simple percentage of the licensee's net sales of the licensed product. Indeed, the thought of basing a license upon a profitability analysis is distasteful to many in the licensing field. But royalty rates are merely expressions, or mechanical forms of calculation, employed by parties when making decisions or assumptions based upon profitability. Thus, many people make decisions based on profitability without even realizing it.

Parties to potential licensing transactions should remember that a technology transfer may have broad, corporate implications. Transactions susceptible to these implications may include: licensing in technology to complement existing core technologies; licensing out technology to a larger company to fund further research; or, for a small proprietor, generating capital funds for growth by selling a minority equity interest to the licensee. Later, the licensee might also consider acquiring the proprietor.

License creations are often important transactions in their own right. However, they may also be integrated into multi-faceted arrangements to meet both the short and long-term objectives of the parties. Furthermore, licenses are not the only way to realize returns on investments made during discovery, creation, and development of the subject technology; many alternatives exist. This article exposes and discusses many profit-generating alternative methods for achieving a mutually-satisfactory bottom line. . . .

III. CONCEPT OF INHERENT VALUE

When attempting to license an invention, a proprietor will sometimes justify a high royalty rate by noting that it has expended enormous time, effort, and money to create and develop the subject technology. To counter this argument, astute licensees should characterize those expenditures as the proprietor's "sunk-costs." As such, they are irrelevant to the licensee, who is only interested in the technology's future profitability.

Fortunately for the licensor, there is a way to trump this "sunk-costs" theory. Consider, for example, a pharmaceutical company which, with very little out-of-pocket expense, discovers a new application or use for an existing drug. Assume further, that the licensor has existing, fully-depreciated production facilities to satisfy the large and urgent need for this new use. In such a case, the proprietor might alternatively choose to exploit the opportunity directly. This extra option provides the proprietor with enough leverage to demand a high royalty rate; thus, the proprietor can afford not to make a deal.

The element of risk is also important in determining which party should realize the lion's share of the return from a licensing relationship. The licensor typically bears the principal risk, since that party usually makes the initial investment required to introduce the subject technology. When the subject of the license is a process, however, licensees may have to make investments as well. Often, their existing production facilities must be reorganized, and sometimes, completely new facilities are needed in order to exploit the license. In situations where no such licensee capital outlays are needed, a high royalty rate would be justified. A high rate will serve to compensate the proprietor for the risks associated with its initial investment.

IV.   RELATIVE CONTRIBUTIONS OF PARTIES

After reaching a consensus about the overall profit potential, the parties should establish a profit-sharing ratio. This apportionment of future profit rarely occurs on a conscious level, but it is nevertheless important.

It is here that the so-called "25 percent rule" can be put to useful effect. The rule compares the licensee's expected pre-tax profitability rate from the combined resources of the parties to the expected profitability of a similarly-situated, model license. It cannot be overemphasized that this technique merely provides a starting point from which the parties can often gain a better perspective on their relative contributions. Although helpful, the "25 percent rule" is not universally applicable. If it were, there would be no point in applying it in the first place.

Apparently, the "25 percent rule" was utilized by practitioners even prior to 1971. The late Worth Wade, citing Albert S. Davis, Jr., listed three basic patent licensing considerations: "(1) scope of patents, (2) validity of the patents, and (3) profitability of the patents' use. If the patents protect the licensee from competition and appear to be valid, the royalty should represent about 25% of the anticipated profit for the use of the patents."

Accordingly, if the existing factors correspond closely to the model, the parties should seriously consider adopting a 25 percent to 75 percent profit split between the licensor and licensee. But where the circumstances differ from those in the ideal model, the ratio should be adjusted accordingly. . .

Elements that increase the strength of a prospective licensor's assets include the following:

(1)   the existence of relevant, assumable, and enforceable patents;

(2)   the existence of trade secrets and know-how that are related to the subject technology;

(3)   the existence of ancillary trade secrets and know-how, including marketing insights and contacts;

(4)   one or more established product trademarks, house marks, or logos that could promptly contribute goodwill and credibility to the licensee;

(5)   software programs, advertising support and other expressions of creative work, whether or not protected by copyright;

(6)   an active, well-financed and historically-productive R&D facility that could reinforce the licensed technology on a regular basis;

(7)   a pattern of successful licenses between the licensor and similar or current licensees;

(8)   a reputation for diligence in pursuing infringers of its rights; and

(9)   a reputation for protecting its licensees from independent actions initiated by third parties.

Licensee risk assumption is probably the most contested factor in the entire profit-apportionment equation. Prospective licensees who assume unusual risks should expect to adjust their portion of the profit up from the standard 75 percent. For instance, licensees may need to make substantial investments in new plants and staffing. They may also face serious competition in the relevant market. From the licensee's perspective, other risk-related factors exist and may include:

(1) the possession of a pre-existing manufacturing plant and the capacity to produce the licensed product or process;

(2) the possession of a skilled marketing force that can effectively reach the licensed technology's intended market; and

(3) the availability of critical raw materials, local government approvals, or financial grants that can have an impact on both short and long-term success.

To the extent that the licensee and licensor have overlapping resources, the licensor's leverage is reduced. However, the contemplated technology transfer may enable the licensee to make better use of under-employed resources. When this is the case, the licensee's overall risk is reduced, and the licensor's leverage is increased.

The 25 percent rule is not actually a rule, in the formal sense. It is merely a rough guideline that should be refined to fit a given situation. While licensing professionals sometimes follow other royalty setting approaches, careful presentation of licensing terms based on the 25 percent rule is usually well-received. Because it was originally conceived in the real world, this rule has a ring of common sense and is becoming widely accepted.

In a recent negotiation, the parties reached a consensus on several projections: the costs of production, including raw materials to the licensee; the selling prices obtainable; the levels of sales; and the expected market share. This data, along with predicted inflation rates and expected market demand, made it possible for the potential licensor to construct a ten year spreadsheet.

During the following negotiating session, the potential licensee offered to pay a 5 percent royalty rate on the mutually agreed royalty base. The licensor then presented its spreadsheet. The spreadsheet illustrated that the licensee could expect a weighted pre-tax profitability of more than 40 percent over the next ten years. Based on the value of the intellectual property offered, the proprietor requested a minimum of 25 percent of this revenue, which was actually a 12 percent royalty rate. The spreadsheet's numbers were indisputable and the 12 percent royalty was adopted. Additionally, since the "bottom line" achieved in the negotiation was supported by credible figures, the contracting parties' boards of directors accepted it as well.

V. SETTING RATES

Quite often, parties will agree that the division of profits will be manifested in practice as a percentage royalty of the licensor's net invoiced sales. This mechanism is frequently chosen for two basic reasons:

(1)   licensees operating at "arm's length" with their licensors often prefer to release raw sales figures over actual profit margins; and

(2)   this approach compensates for inflation.

Although commonly used, a "percentage of sales" approach actually disfavors licensees. This is because it regularly generates royalties to the licensor, regardless of the actual future profit performance of the licensee. Consider the following situation:

(1) suppose, at the outset, a licensee is able to sell the licensed products at $100 and has total material labor and overhead costs of $70. This yields a pre-tax net profit of $30. Accepting the 25 percent rule, the licensor is entitled to 25 percent of the pre-tax net profit. Therefore, the parties should agree to a 7.5% royalty rate, because: 25% of pre-tax profit = (.25 × (100–70)) = 7.5%; and

(2) if conditions change, and costs increase from $70 to $94, without a corresponding increase in licensee prices above $100, the pre-tax net profit would be only $6. If the parties previously agreed to a royalty of 7.5% of the licensee's net invoiced sales, the licensor would be entitled to the same royalty rate, but the licensee would actually be incurring a loss. (100-94 = 6% pre-tax net profit; a 7.5% royalty would mean a 1.5% loss to the licensee).

This "heads I win, tails you lose" aspect of royalty calculations based on a percentage of sales can provide licensees with an argument to fix the royalty rate lower than the 25 percent guideline. An increased likelihood of substantial market fluctuations may also aid the licensee in arguing for a lower rate when applying the 25 percent rule.

VI.   ROYALTIES AS A PARTICIPATION IN SUCCESS

Licensors who have confidence in the future performance of their licensees may maintain a high royalty rate by offering to share in the fortunes of the licensee, good or bad. This approach is often useful in licenses for processes designed to improve efficiency or lower costs. For example, a confident licensor might set royalties at 25 percent of the savings the licensee realizes from the improved process. The danger here is that the licensor must forgo royalties if the licensed technology fails to achieve its predictions.

Indeed, by assuming this added element of risk, the licensor might even attempt to negotiate a bonus for exceptional performance attributable to the licensed process. This bonus is a logical request, because even marginal increases in efficiency often produce increases in profit.

When the above "cost savings" approach is used, the parties must agree upon exactly how the "cost savings" will be calculated. This type of planning reduces the likelihood of disputes related to royalty amounts later on, and therefore, helps maintain long-term business relationships.

Even where product licensing is concerned, licensors sometimes offer to share the licensee's risk by accepting royalties calculated as a given percentage of profit. If royalties are based upon an objectively-determined profit calculation formula that allows for verification, this method is an effective way to license products.

VII. OTHER FORMS AND APPROACHES TO LICENSING REMUNERATION

Although running royalties account for most of the remuneration received by licensors, additional approaches exist. These include the following:

A. Lump-Sum Payments

A would-be licensor (now called the proprietor) can simply sell its technology for a so-called "lump-sum payment." This approach is useful for technology that licensors no longer need. It is often used when a given technology falls outside the proprietor's business or when, as is common after a policy shift, the proprietor abandons activities relating to the subject technology. Care should be exercised before choosing this method because it may elicit capital gains tax treatment if the technology's cost basis can be established.

After quantifying the payment, the proprietor's minimum acceptable amount should, at least, account for the disposal costs and any risk arising from the purchaser's possession of the technology. The proprietor may also justify a higher selling price by pointing out the benefits the sale will bring to the purchaser.

The upper boundary of lump-sum payments is the purchaser's cost to duplicate or "invent around" the technology. If the technology is patented, the remaining patent life should be considered. Similarly, a body of know-how or trade secrets can also be transferred, with the cost and time needed for duplication accounting for its purchase price.

The same 25 percent rule which is useful in setting periodic royalties may also be used to set lump-sum payment prices. To apply the rule to lump-sum payments requires the following steps:

(1)   perform a 25 percent rule analysis and arrive at a royalty rate;

(2)   project the economic life of the technology in question;

(3)   project a royalty base for the technology, taking into account the significance of such technology to the product, process, or service being transferred; and

(4)   multiply the rate by the base and perform a discounted cash flow analysis on the product of such multiplication, using the interest rate for borrowing available to the technology purchaser.

Of course the sum reached by the foregoing method is subject to final adjustments. Often these adjustments reflect the parties' need to complete the transfer.

B. Periodic Lump-Sum Payments

Sometimes it is onerous for parties to calculate royalties on the use of a particular invention because it is a component of a complicated piece of equipment or system. In these cases, an annual lump sum may be a more practical approach.

For instance, suppose an auto manufacturer licenses technology that improves its current technology. Assume further that the invention is incorporated into each of the millions of vehicles produced by such licensee each year. If an annual lump sum of $1 million were fixed as a "paid-up royalty" for that year, it would represent a very narrow slice of the profit generated by the total sales of the vehicles concerned. Nevertheless, the actual payment may well be reasonable to the parties concerned. Because the auto market's and the licensee's gigantic proportions are not attributable to the licensor or its invention, a more "normal," heavily discounted royalty rate is appropriate.

An alternate approach involves charging a fixed royalty per item sold or used by a licensee. This method is favored because it affords easy royalty calculation. Whatever method is used, it is advisable to key the lump-sum royalty to a recognized economic indicator. This link will facilitate later increases in the payments, consistent with inflation or other economic events.

C.   Initial Payments

The availability of initial payments is very important in the negotiation of licenses. It is also important during the calculation of the parties' relative profit entitlement. Initial payments are popular because they provide front-end cash to a licensor, which can immediately be applied to recover the costs associated with developing the licensed technology. Additionally, because the costs must be recouped before a licensee can begin to realize profit, these payments are strong evidence of licensee commitment. The licensee's maximum payment should correspond to the reasonable amount of working capital earmarked by the licensee for the license.

D.   Prepaid Royalties

Sometimes a licensor is financially weaker than the licensee, but is required to further develop the licensed technology. The licensee may provide these needed funds. The amount paid in excess of the reasonable initial payment can sometimes be applied against future running royalties, depending on how they are calculated.

In a current negotiation, this device is being cleverly employed by a start-up licensor who has patented a significant invention, for which there are several powerful licensees. The licensor requires significant working capital to grow its business and to further develop its technology. However, the entrepreneurs who founded the business do not currently wish to dilute their equity holdings by bringing in equity funding. So each licensee is required to pay, in lieu of an initial fee, a pre-paid royalty of $250,000 in U.S. currency. This sum is then recovered by the licensee at the rate of one-half of the running royalties as they accrue.

In other words, if a licensee sells $5,000,000 of the licensed products at a 10% royalty rate, then $500,000 in royalties would accrue. The licensee would pay $250,000 in running royalties to the licensor and would credit the remaining $250,000 to the prepaid royalty previously advanced to the licensor. This device provides the licensor with funding, while helping the licensor maintain its ownership position.

E. Minimum Royalties

Minimum royalties are another device which can ensure commitment and adequate licensee performance. The word "adequate" is used advisedly because the level set is usually less than excellent performance. Instead, it reflects results which are at the low end of the licensor's acceptable range. It has been said that "minimum royalties are the handmaiden of exclusive licenses." This is because the minimum amounts must be paid in order to assure the continued exclusivity of the licensees.

Minimum royalties can also be employed when non-exclusive licenses are involved. They can improve a licensor's cash flow, especially in times of high interest rates, by requiring each licensee to pay the greater of the minimum or the accrued royalties at the end of each calendar quarter, with the possibility of a final adjustment at the end of each reporting year. Minimum royalties may also be used to eliminate licensees who cannot perform adequately by providing a mechanism to "weed out" the unsuccessful licensees.

The licensor has three recourses to enforce the minimum royalty, which vary in severity. In ascending order of impact, they are as follows:

(1)   if the activity level of a licensee is insufficient to generate enough accrued royalties to exceed the minimum level, a licensee may merely pay the difference;

(2)   on the same facts, even if a licensee pays cash to cover its shortfall, a licensor has the discretionary right to reduce the rights of the licensee (e.g., by retracting exclusivity, by reducing the scope of the products licensed, or by narrowing the territory covered by the license); and

(3)   on the same facts, a licensor has the discretionary right to cancel a license.

The agreement may provide that remedies (2) or (3) would only be available to a licensor if a licensee had failed to accrue sufficient royalties to meet or exceed the minimum level in more than a set number of years or consecutive reporting periods.

Minimum royalty levels usually increase from zero, during the initial year of a license, up to a maximum level during later years. For instance, a license which starts on February 1, 1995, might provide the following royalty payments:

Until 12/31/95	10,000 U.S. Dollars
From 1/1/96 to 12/31/96	25,000
From 1/1/97 to 12/31/97	50,000
From 1/1/98 to 12/31/98	75,000
Every calendar year thereafter	100,000

In some instances, parties can also provide that minimum royalty requirements will decrease over time to reflect the maturity of the licensed technology. Providing for inflation by tying minimum royalty figures to some recognized index (e.g., the Producer's Price Index of the U.S. Department of Labor) is a useful device that is frequently employed.

F. Sale of Key Ingredients, Components, or Special Items by Licensor to Licensee

A licensee may purchase a key component from a licensor at a price sufficient to eliminate the licensor's need to exact royalties in any form. Provided the purchased item is truly proprietary to the licensor, these arrangements need not run afoul of tying prohibitions under the antitrust laws.

Frequently, it is cheaper for a licensee to purchase certain components from a licensor who is prepared to make the components and can take advantage of long production runs. By exploiting their production ability, some licensors may offer a price and royalty combination that makes the subject technology cheaper than if the licensee produced it. Licensors who do this can sell the component at a price that includes incremental profit; they can also charge running royalties.

Sales also occur when licensed products are available in a range of sizes or models, with some being much more in demand in a licensee's territory than others. In these cases, it may be more economical for a licensee to purchase the less popular sizes or models from a licensor. Royalty payments may or may not attach to resales by the licensee of those items, depending on the circumstances, including the relative bargaining strengths of the parties.

G. Barter and Payments in Kind

Barter and payments in kind are common when licensing to third world countries and to the People's Republic of China because these countries have insufficient hard currency available to fund their licensing interests. A barter system frequently utilizes specialized intermediaries who arrange the trade of goods offered as payment by the licensees.

Alternatively, licensees may offer to sell goods made under the license back to the licensor, at attractive prices. This system works when the licensor makes a resale profit that is sufficient to compensate the licensor for granting the license. However, arrangements of this sort are not frequently of interest to licensors because there are often ample supplies of the subject goods available.

H. Receipt of Equity

Skeptics of the licensing process claim that these transactions educate future competitors. To reduce this risk, licensors should require interested potential licensees to form a new corporate entity for the purpose of executing the substance of a proposed license. As total or partial consideration for a license grant, the licensor should receive a mutually agreed percentage of the voting stock of the new corporate licensee, usually with the right to veto decisions that are considered important to the continued viability of the venture.

There are many possible variations on this theme, including provisions for royalty payments to the licensor or potential dividends from the licensor's holdings in the licensee corporation. Also, the licensor might sell or increase its holdings, in accordance with some express formula.

I. Sublicensing

By granting licensees the right to appoint one or more sublicensee, a proprietor can increase its earning potential. To do so, the licensor should require that sublicensors remit a pre-agreed percentage of the income from sublicensees, e.g., from 5 to 95 percent, depending upon the role of the licensee. Another approach is to require the licensee to remit to the licensor the same sum per licensed product that the licensee pays on its direct sales, with the understanding that the sublicensees will pay a somewhat higher royalty; the difference being retained by the principal licensee.

VIII. SUPPLEMENTAL FORMS OF REMUNERATION TO LICENSORS

By performing special, additional services for its licensees, technology proprietors can often increase the profitability of licenses. Proprietors often provide consulting or trouble-shooting services. Profits from these services can come from annual retainers or per diem charges. To encourage licensees to utilize these licensor-operated services, a certain (usually modest) amount of the service may be offered free of charge, with fees only attaching to the excess.

Licensors can also increase their profitability by retaining marketing rights to products produced by licensees outside the licensed territory. This clearing house function can enable licensors to earn commissions on sales from a licensee, who is a very efficient producer, to other licensees, who may be less efficient or not manufacturing a full line. Moreover, such an arrangement may allow a licensor to better protect and serve its home market. For example, if the licensor has a highly proficient Japanese licensee, the licensor may be able to make some high quality and cost-effective purchases from its Japanese licensee, while also protecting its home market from competition by the same Japanese licensee.

IX. FAIRNESS DOCTRINE

One overall consideration applicable to licensors' management of licensees is the "fairness doctrine." Its basic concept is that although an unaffiliated licensee is an independent party, a licensee is somehow part of the licensor's family. There exists an underlying, and often unspoken, critical bond between a licensor and a licensee; they are collaborating on a business venture in which, in effect, they are sharing profits.

The sharing may be spelled out in black and white terms, e.g., five percent of net sales. Yet, in key ways, a licensing agreement is more involved for both sides than is a straight arm's length sale. First, the relationship is long term. Second, it usually involves an exchange of know-how, personnel, and management techniques; it is not merely a sale of goods. If one side is too demanding, the other may simply find the venture unprofitable and either abrogate the agreement or treat it in such a haphazard manner that both sides lose potential profits.

Perhaps more of the responsibility for maintaining a fair relationship rests with the licensor than with the licensee, if only because the licensor has more to give. Ultimately, both must share in making the relationship work. However, if the licensor demands too much, the deal will not be mutually profitable and will fail. By comparison, it is less likely that a licensee who is realizing an unforeseen windfall will voluntarily offer a corresponding increase in its royalty rates. Such an initiative would not be counterproductive, however, because it could inspire the licensor to be more active in supplying improvements and other services back to the licensee.

X. STANDARD INDUSTRY LICENSING RATES

Negotiators or so-called "licensing experts" often suggest that standard, industry-specific royalty rates exist and that it is very difficult to depart from them. Indeed, there have been efforts to publish standard rates as guidelines to practitioners. However, since the author feels that royalties are essentially an expression of underlying contemplated profitability, he disapproves of royalty rate standardization.

For example, third-party licenses are rare in the agricultural chemical industry. Instead, they are kept within the immediate corporate "family," and are usually handled by close affiliates. Only less important technology is licensed. Therefore, if negotiated royalties were to be tabulated and averaged in the agricultural chemical business, the results would be unrealistically low.

It is believed that the same considerations hold true for many other industries, particularly those in which multi-national companies are active. If industry trends indicate low royalties, they could merely be a reflection of the general level of profitability in that industry. To limit innovation in that industry to an artificially low royalty standard would be inappropriate. The licensing process should not be subject to the pressures of Gresham's law.

HUGHES TOOL CO. v. DRESSER INDUSTRIES, INC.
United States Court of Appeals for the Federal Circuit
816 F. 2d 1549 (1987)

RICH, Circuit Judge.

[The following is a summary of the district court opinion on damages excerpted from the Federal Circuit opinion:]

Although Hughes Tool sought damages based on its lost profits with respect to the TCI journal bearing bits Dresser sold to customers within the United States, the court concluded that Hughes Tool "failed to demonstrate with 'reasonable probability' an approximation of the profits it would have made on the infringing Dresser sales." The court then set out to determine, "under the 'willing buyer — willing seller' rule, what a reasonable royalty" would have been.

In assessing the evidence on the damages issue, the district court found that customer demand for the patented rock bits was strong and that no acceptable non-infringing alternative existed. However, the court also found that Hughes

Tool failed to demonstrate the manufacturing and marketing ability to meet the demand for at least part of the period of Dresser's infringement.

Turning specifically to the commercial situation as it existed in 1973, the district court noted that Hughes Tool was experiencing a rising demand for its patented journal bearing bits and that Hughes Tool believed that those bits were more profitable than its sales of certain other tools. Although Hughes Tool had a company policy of not licensing its patented inventions to major competitors, the court did note evidence of forty-five prior licenses and offers of licenses under other patents owned by Hughes Tool at royalty rates of six percent or less. The court did not give much weight to those prior royalty rates, however, because those licenses were for widely diverse products. Similarly, the court acknowledged the existence of one license at four percent to a non-competitor, Gault, and specifically held that it would not consider a fifteen percent license agreement made in 1983 in settlement of litigation with Hughes Tool's competitor, Rock Bit Industries. The court ultimately concluded that Hughes Tool showed no desire to license direct competitors under the '928 patent.

The court also found that Dresser was concerned about a potential loss of fifty to sixty percent of its rock bit market to Hughes Tool; that when Dresser considered beginning to manufacture the patented journal bearing bits itself in 1973, it projected total profits of 60% on sales of the new bits; and that its total profits on all sales the year before had been 7.2%. The district court also noted that Hughes Tool asserted profits of 49-54% on sales of the patented journal bearing insert bits.

The district court found, however, that Hughes Tool did not realize that the demand for rock bits other than sealed journal bearing bits would drop as sharply as it did. In addition, Hughes Tool was aware that its competitors were working diligently to produce competitive rock bits. Finally, the district court found that the '928 patent did not give the new rock bits their essential market value, but rather that the patented O-ring seal was only one of numerous parts that contributed to the overall value of the rock bit.

Although Hughes Tool's expert at trial asserted that 52.8% was a reasonable royalty for both the patents in suit, that assertion was based on the assumption that the patented combination with the O-ring seal was responsible for most of the value of the bit. The district court disagreed, stating that the '928 patent contributed only part of the total value of the bit, and concluded that 25% of the gross sales price would have been a reasonable royalty had the parties negotiated for a license in 1973. . . .

On May 31, 1985, Dresser appealed the district court's judgment with respect to the validity of the '928 patent and the amount of damages, as well as the district court's denial of its post-trial motions. Hughes Tool filed its cross-appeal on June 13, 1985, seeking review of the district court's failure to award increased damages as well as its failure to award prejudgment interest for the period the '928 patent had temporarily been under the cloud of a district court holding of invalidity.

[The following is the Federal Circuit's opinion on the reasonable royalty rate:]

The district court's award of damages to Hughes calculated as a royalty of 25% of the dollar amount of Dresser's total sales of certain infringing bits is based on a finding of fact with respect to Dresser's projected profits which Dresser asserts is clearly erroneous. The basic predicate for the district court's 25% royalty determination is that Dresser projected "total profits of 60% as a percent of sales." That 60% "profit" figure was then contrasted with Dresser's 1972 actual profits of 7.2% for all of its sales. The 60% profit projection is referenced repeatedly in the court's analysis and is clearly critical to its damage award:

> ". . . the projection of 60% profit in the present case, admitted by Dresser"

> "Hughes's 49% and 54% royalty requests would be 81.6% and 90% of Dresser's projected 60% profits in this case."

> "15% profit" in other Hughes litigation is "considerably lower profit than those projected in the present case."

> "the parties in 1973 projecting 49% [Hughes] to 60% [Dresser] profits."

> "Dresser projected 60% profits on the sale of bits with the '928 seal."

> "Hughes suggests it realized profits of 49% and 54% on its '928 bits sold in the United States and abroad."

> "This figure [25% of sales price] would still have allowed Dresser to realize a large profit on its sales of the bits."

> "Of these various considerations [relevant to setting a reasonable royalty] the expected profit from making and selling the patented invention is the primary consideration."

Before this court Hughes Tool argues: "The magnitude of this 'large profit' of 60% less the royalty award of 25%, left Dresser a 35% profit from sales — as contrasted with its usual profit of 7.2% of sales on all of its products." Hughes's simple arithmetic, however, is a gross distortion of reality.

The evidence of Dresser's projected profitability does not show, as the trial court found and Hughes asserts here, that, in 1973, Dresser was projecting 60% profit on the proposed new product line. Rather, Dresser's projection was a 60% return on the additional investment required to make the bits. Thus, the 60% projection of such return cannot be compared meaningfully with the 7.2% actual profits of 1972.

The evidence . . . on which the district court relied for its finding is set forth below in pertinent part:

> During the year 1973, defendant, Dresser Industries, anticipated that its incremental future sales of Insert Rock Bits with Journal Bearings would provide defendant with profits, on an earnings before tax basis, of not less than 60% of dollar sales of such Rock Bits.

> During the year 1973, for the purposes of capital appropriations only, personnel of Defendant at one time forecast that its incremental future sales ascribable to that particular appropriation request of insert Rock Bits with Journal Bearings would provide Defendant with

profits, on an earnings before tax basis, of not less than 60% of dollar sales of such Rock Bits.

During its fiscal years 1972 through 1981, defendant, Dresser Industries, was making profits, on a before tax basis, as a percentage of net dollar sales of all of its products and services as set forth below:

YEAR	PROFIT AS % OF NET DOLLAR SALES	NET DOLLAR SALES (Millions)
1972	7.2	906.2
1973	7.1	1,025.2
1974	8.2	1,398.0
1975	11.2	2,011.6
1976	12.2	2,232.2
1977	13.2	2,538.8
1978	12.4	3,054.0
1979	11.8	3,457.4
1980	11.2	4,016.3
1981	11.5	4,614.5

. . .

The testimony of Dresser's controller, Mr. Munnerlyn, and Hughes Tool's Chief Accounting Officer, Mr. Willis, is consistent with the above evidence that the expected profit on incremental sales would yield a 60% return on incremental investment. There is no evidence to the contrary.

Thus, this case closely parallels Georgia-Pacific Corp. v. U.S. Plywood-Champion Papers, Inc. The question in Georgia Pacific was the reasonableness of a royalty of $50 per thousand square feet of certain plywood sales. There, the district court (as did the district court here) accepted that a reasonable royalty must be fixed so as to leave the infringer a reasonable profit. To calculate the royalty, the Georgia Pacific trial court erroneously used a figure of $159.41, which represented Georgia Pacific's average "realization" on plywood sales [possibly margin], rather than a figure of $50.00, which represented Georgia Pacific's expected profit on such sales. Thus, the award of a $50.00 royalty, which would leave no profit, was set aside on appeal as excessive.

The royalty of 25% set in this case, being based on a clearly erroneous finding of projected profits of 60% as a percent of sales, is ipso facto arbitrary and must be set aside.

NOTES & QUESTIONS

1. Why did the Federal Circuit reject the special magistrate's decision to use a 60 per cent figure for projected profits in determining damages? Does the Federal Circuit offer an alternative approach? If so, what effect would this approach have on damages?

2. How does a decision like *Hughes Tool* affect negotiations for start-up companies over the licensing of intellectual property? Do you think the decision would lead potential licensors and licensees to adopt more specific terms, such as liquidated damage clauses, to specify a reasonably royalty in terms of breach?

3. The reading by Professor Hagelin identifies three ways to value intellectual property: the cost method, the market method, and the income method. Professor Hagelin discusses these methods as a way to determine royalty rates for licenses. Do these methods have any applicability to the calculation of damages? If so, which one is the most appropriate? How does Professor Hagelin's proposed CAV method compare to these other three in determining damages?

4. Professor Goldscheider discusses the "25 % rule" for establishing base royalty rates. What is this rule and how does he propose it be applied? What result if the rule is applied to the facts of *Hughes Tool*?

5. Suppose a potential investor in Dr. See's company asks for a valuation of the patents that Dr. See has obtained and any trade secrets he may have. How would you proceed to address the investor's valuation question?

C. AVOIDING FORFEITURES OF INTELLECTUAL PROPERTY INTERESTS

Patent act conditions for patentability; novelty and loss of right to patent

35 USC § 102 (2001)

A person shall be entitled to a patent unless —

(a) the invention was known or used by others in this country, or patented or described in a printed publication in this or a foreign country, before the invention thereof by the applicant for patent, or

(b) the invention was patented or described in a printed publication in this or a foreign country or in public use or on sale in this country, more than one year prior to the date of the application for patent in the United States . . .

Copyright act registration and infringement actions

17 USC § 411 (2002)

(a) . . . no action for infringement of the copyright in any United States work shall be instituted until registration of the copyright claim has been made in accordance with this title. In any case, however, where the deposit, application, and fee required for registration have been delivered to the Copyright Office in proper form and registration has been refused, the applicant is entitled to institute an action for infringement if notice thereof, with a copy of the complaint, is served on the Register of Copyrights. The Register may, at his or her option, become a party to the action with respect to the issue of registrability of the copyright claim by entering an appearance within sixty days after such service, but the Register's failure to become a party shall not deprive the court of jurisdiction to determine that issue.

PFAFF v. WELLS ELECTRONICS, INC.
525 U.S. 55

Justice STEVENS delivered the opinion of the Court.

Section 102(b) of the Patent Act of 1952 provides that no person is entitled to patent an "invention" that has been "on sale" more than one year before filing a patent application. We granted certiorari to determine whether the commercial marketing of a newly invented product may mark the beginning of the 1-year period even though the invention has not yet been reduced to practice.

I

On April 19, 1982, petitioner, Wayne Pfaff, filed an application for a patent on a computer chip socket. Therefore, April 19, 1981, constitutes the critical date for purposes of the on-sale bar of 35 U.S.C. § 102(b); if the 1-year period began to run before that date, Pfaff lost his right to patent his invention.

Pfaff commenced work on the socket in November 1980, when representatives of Texas Instruments asked him to develop a new device for mounting and removing semiconductor chip carriers. In response to this request, he prepared detailed engineering drawings that described the design, the dimensions, and the materials to be used in making the socket. Pfaff sent those drawings to a manufacturer in February or March 1981.

Prior to March 17, 1981, Pfaff showed a sketch of his concept to representatives of Texas Instruments. On April 8, 1981, they provided Pfaff with a written confirmation of a previously placed oral purchase order for 30,100 of his new sockets for a total price of $91,155. In accord with his normal practice, Pfaff did not make and test a prototype of the new device before offering to sell it in commercial quantities.

The manufacturer took several months to develop the customized tooling necessary to produce the device, and Pfaff did not fill the order until July 1981. The evidence therefore indicates that Pfaff first reduced his invention to practice in the summer of 1981. The socket achieved substantial commercial success before Patent No. 4,491,377 ('377 patent) issued to Pfaff on January 1, 1985.

After the patent issued, petitioner brought an infringement action against respondent, Wells Electronics, Inc., the manufacturer of a competing socket. Wells prevailed on the basis of a finding of no infringement. When respondent began to market a modified device, petitioner brought this suit, alleging that the modifications infringed six of the claims in the '377 patent.

After a full evidentiary hearing before a Special Master, the District Court held that two of those claims (1 and 6) were invalid because they had been anticipated in the prior art. . . . Adopting the Special Master's findings, the District Court rejected respondent's § 102(b) defense because Pfaff had filed the application for the '377 patent less than a year after reducing the invention to practice.

The Court of Appeals reversed, finding all six claims invalid. 124 F.3d 1429 (C.A.Fed. 1997). Four of the claims (1, 6, 7, and 10) described the socket that Pfaff had sold to Texas Instruments prior to April 8, 1981. Because that device had been offered for sale on a commercial basis more than one year before the patent application was filed on April 19, 1982, the court concluded that those claims were invalid under § 102(b). That conclusion rested on the court's view that as long as the invention was "substantially complete at the time of sale," the 1-year period began to run, even though the invention had not yet been reduced to practice. *Id*. at 1434. The other two claims (11 and 19) described a feature that had not been included in Pfaff's initial design, but the Court of Appeals concluded as a matter of law that the additional feature was not itself patentable because it was an obvious addition to the prior art. Given the court's § 102(b) holding, the prior art included Pfaff's first four claims.

Because other courts have held or assumed that an invention cannot be "on sale" within the meaning of § 102(b) unless and until it has been reduced to practice, *see, e.g., Timely Products Corp. v. Arron*, 523 F.2d 288, 299–302 (C.A.2 1975); *Dart Industries, Inc. v. E.I. du Pont De Nemours & Co.*, 489 F.2d 1359, 1365, n. 11 (C.A.7 1973), cert. *denied*, 417 U.S. 933, 94 S.Ct. 2645, 41 L.Ed.2d 236 (1974), and because the text of § 102(b) makes no reference to "substantial completion" of an invention, we granted certiorari. 523 U.S. 1003, 118 S.Ct. 1183, 140 L.Ed.2d 315 (1998).

II

The primary meaning of the word "invention" in the Patent Act unquestionably refers to the inventor's conception rather than to a physical embodiment of that idea. The statute does not contain any express requirement that an invention must be reduced to practice before it can be patented. Neither the statutory definition of the term in § 100 nor the basic conditions for obtaining a patent set forth in § 101 make any mention of "reduction to practice." The statute's only specific reference to that term is found in § 102(g), which sets forth the standard for resolving priority contests between two competing claimants to a patent. That subsection provides:

> "In determining priority of invention there shall be considered not only the respective dates of conception and reduction to practice of the invention, but also the reasonable diligence of one who was first to conceive and last to reduce to practice, from a time prior to conception by the other."

Thus, assuming diligence on the part of the applicant, it is normally the first inventor to conceive, rather than the first to reduce to practice, who establishes the right to the patent.

It is well settled that an invention may be patented before it is reduced to practice. In 1888, this Court upheld a patent issued to Alexander Graham Bell even though he had filed his application before constructing a working telephone. . . . When we apply the reasoning of *The Telephone Cases*[, 126

U.S. 1 (1888),] to the facts of the case before us today, it is evident that Pfaff could have obtained a patent on his novel socket when he accepted the purchase order from Texas Instruments for 30,100 units. At that time he provided the manufacturer with a description and drawings that had "sufficient clearness and precision to enable those skilled in the matter" to produce the device. *Id.*, at 536. The parties agree that the sockets manufactured to fill that order embody Pfaff's conception as set forth in claims 1, 6, 7, and 10 of the '377 patent. We can find no basis in the text of § 102(b) or in the facts of this case for concluding that Pfaff's invention was not "on sale" within the meaning of the statute until after it had been reduced to practice.

III

Pfaff nevertheless argues that longstanding precedent, buttressed by the strong interest in providing inventors with a clear standard identifying the onset of the 1-year period, justifies a special interpretation of the word "invention" as used in § 102(b). We are persuaded that this nontextual argument should be rejected.

[Section] 102 of the Patent Act serves as a limiting provision, both excluding ideas that are in the public domain from patent protection and confining the duration of the monopoly to the statutory term.

We originally held that an inventor loses his right to a patent if he puts his invention into public use before filing a patent application. "His voluntary act or acquiescence in the public sale and use is an abandonment of his right." *Pennock v. Dialogue,* 2 Pet. 1, 24, 7 L.Ed. 327 (1829) (Story, J.). A similar reluctance to allow an inventor to remove existing knowledge from public use undergirds the on-sale bar.

Nevertheless, an inventor who seeks to perfect his discovery may conduct extensive testing without losing his right to obtain a patent for his invention — even if such testing occurs in the public eye. The law has long recognized the distinction between inventions put to experimental use and products sold commercially. In 1878, we explained why patentability may turn on an inventor's use of his product.

> "It is sometimes said that an inventor acquires an undue advantage over the public by delaying to take out a patent, inasmuch as he thereby preserves the monopoly to himself for a longer period than is allowed by the policy of the law; but this cannot be said with justice when the delay is occasioned by a bona fide effort to bring his invention to perfection, or to ascertain whether it will answer the purpose intended. His monopoly only continues for the allotted period, in any event; and it is in the interest of the public, as well as himself, that the invention should be perfect and properly tested, before a patent is granted for it. Any attempt to use it for a profit, and not by way of experiment, for a longer period than two years before the application, would deprive the inventor of his right to a patent." *Elizabeth v. American Nicholson Pavement Co.,* 97 U.S. 126, 137, 24 L.Ed. 1000 (1877).

The patent laws therefore seek both to protect the public's right to retain knowledge already in the public domain and the inventor's right to control whether and when he may patent his invention. The Patent Act of 1836, 5 Stat. 117, was the first statute that expressly included an on-sale bar to the issuance of a patent. Like the earlier holding in *Pennock*, that provision precluded patentability if the invention had been placed on sale at any time before the patent application was filed. In 1839, Congress ameliorated that requirement by enacting a 2-year grace period in which the inventor could file an application. 5 Stat. 353. . . .

Petitioner correctly argues that these provisions identify an interest in providing inventors with a definite standard for determining when a patent application must be filed. A rule that makes the timeliness of an application depend on the date when an invention is "substantially complete" seriously undermines the interest in certainty. Moreover, such a rule finds no support in the text of the statute. Thus, petitioner's argument calls into question the standard applied by the Court of Appeals, but it does not persuade us that it is necessary to engraft a reduction to practice element into the meaning of the term "invention" as used in § 102(b).

The word "invention" must refer to a concept that is complete, rather than merely one that is "substantially complete." It is true that reduction to practice ordinarily provides the best evidence that an invention is complete. But just because reduction to practice is sufficient evidence of completion, it does not follow that proof of reduction to practice is necessary in every case. Indeed, both the facts of *The Telephone Cases* and the facts of this case demonstrate that one can prove that an invention is complete and ready for patenting before it has actually been reduced to practice.

We conclude, therefore, that the on-sale bar applies when two conditions are satisfied before the critical date. First, the product must be the subject of a commercial offer for sale. An inventor can both understand and control the timing of the first commercial marketing of his invention. The experimental use doctrine, for example, has not generated concerns about indefiniteness, and we perceive no reason why unmanageable uncertainty should attend a rule that measures the application of the on-sale bar of § 102(b) against the date when an invention that is ready for patenting is first marketed commercially. In this case the acceptance of the purchase order prior to April 8, 1981, makes it clear that such an offer had been made, and there is no question that the sale was commercial rather than experimental in character.

Second, the invention must be ready for patenting. That condition may be satisfied in at least two ways: by proof of reduction to practice before the critical date; or by proof that prior to the critical date the inventor had prepared drawings or other descriptions of the invention that were sufficiently specific to enable a person skilled in the art to practice the invention. In this case the second condition of the on-sale bar is satisfied because the drawings Pfaff sent to the manufacturer before the critical date fully disclosed the invention. . . . When Pfaff accepted the purchase order for his new sockets prior to April 8, 1981, his invention was ready for patenting. The fact that the manufacturer was able to produce the socket using his detailed drawings and specifications demonstrates this fact. Furthermore, those sockets contained all the elements of the invention claimed in the '377 patent. Therefore, Pfaff's '377 patent is invalid because the invention had been on sale for more than one year in this country before he filed his patent application. Accordingly, the judgment of the Court of Appeals is affirmed.

NOTES & QUESTIONS

1. This section revisits some of the issues discussed at the beginning of the chapter, particularly those issues relating to identifying ideas and innovations potentially protected by intellectual property law. Rethink the question raised previously of the best time to first discuss a business plan with an attorney. Would Pfaff have benefited from working with counsel earlier in the invention and dissemination process? When would intervention have been helpful?

2. How would you advise Dr. See in light of the Supreme Court's decision in *Pfaff?* Notice that Dr. See already has obtained several patents. The problem that may arise as Dr. See speaks with potential investors is that of follow-on inventions. Dr. See must be careful that he does not "give away" potentially patentable inventions as he speaks with the public. How would you advise Dr. See to avoid this problem?

3. Software inventions can be protected by both patent law and copyright law. Patent law protects software as a process when it produces a concrete, tangible, and useful result, but does not protect the written code. Instead, copyright protects the written code, and derivatives, as a literary work, but does not protect any methods or processes. Are patent and copyright complementary? Suppose one of the investors wants to inspect Dr. See's code. How would you advise Dr. See on satisfying this request? Keep in mind that in addition to patent and copyright, trade secret law also protects software.

4. Suppose Dr. See suspects that a former colleague is infringing the copyright in his software. Dr. See has not registered the copyright. Can he bring suit? There is a circuit split on how this situation is handled. The Second Circuit, for instance, will dismiss the complaint if the copyright has not been registered. *See Well-Made Toy Mfg. Corp. v. Goffa Intern Corp.*, 354 F.3d 112 (2nd Cir. 2003); *Morris v. Business Concepts Inc.*, 283 F.3d 502 (2nd Cir. 2002). Other circuits permit the complaint to be amended once registration has been obtained. *See Syntek Semiconductor Co. Ltd. v. Microchip Technology Inc.*, 285 F.3d 857 (9th Cir. 2002); *Bouchat v. Baltimore Ravens, Inc.*, 228 F.3d 489 (4th Cir. 2000); *Raquel v. Education Management Corp.*, 196 F.3d 171 (3rd Cir. 1999). Notice that under the Copyright Act, the copyright owner loses the right to obtain statutory damages and attorney's fees and costs if she fails to register either before the work is published or within three months of publication.

5. How about intellectual property protection in other countries? Although our primary focus is on the issues confronting intellectual property related businesses in the United States, it is worth noting that most countries other than the United States adopt an absolute priority rule, meaning that the ability to

patent is forfeited for any disclosure of the invention prior to the date of application. On the other hand, other countries are less formalistic and more flexible when it comes to registration of copyright.

D. ESTABLISHING AND POLICING INTELLECTUAL PROPERTY LICENSES

Dennis Braswell, Setting Business Objectives and Negotiating Valuable Licenses,
Practising Law Institute Patents, Copyrights, Trademarks, and Literary Property
Course Handbook Series
No. G0-01GM March–May, 2004*

In negotiating any deal, it is imperative that everyone on the negotiating team understands the objectives. Unless they are known, it is very difficult to evaluate whether a deal is good, and you will have conflicting opinions as to whether to do the deal. This is very important in intellectual property licensing, where the value is often not well established, in contrast to most goods or services deals. With clear objectives, a potential deal can be fairly evaluated and entered into (or not) with confidence. Moreover, as part of this process of setting objectives, you must set firm walk-away conditions, and know what you will do if negotiations are unsuccessful.

Far too often there is no communication among a negotiating "team," resulting in frustration for the other side. If the frustrated side is the licensor, it may sue, or grant another a license. Granting another such a license may destroy the potential first licensee's competitive advantage. If the frustrated side is the licensee, it may move on to other technologies, leaving the licensor in the dust. In most cases, focused negotiations result in fair and fast licenses; unfocused babble results in lawsuits.

There are many reasons for licensing, and, not surprisingly, they all boil down to economic gain. However, the specific reasons dictate your negotiating decisions, and they should be well articulated before you begin. For example, if one has determined to widely license a technology on a non-exclusive basis, it may be desirable to sign the first licensee up at a cut rate, to get the ball rolling. I'll now summarize the most common reasons for licensing, and the basic questions that should be answered before embarking on a licensing program.

I.A. WHY ARE YOU LICENSING?

To make or save money. For the licensor, the license agreement should make at least as much as could be made if it goes into the business for itself, or if it sued. For the licensee, the license must provide a way to make at least as much money as the license payments, or to save at least that much. To accomplish these goals, one must understand the real value of the technology, and the costs involved if litigation is required. And, as will be discussed later,

---

central to this question of how much money will be made is whether the licensee is, or licensees are, able to exploit the technology to its fullest. Of course, one can implement high minimum royalties, but often a better approach is to limit the licenses by non-exclusivity, fields of use, territories, or (if practical) time.

To avoid litigation or to survive. Other than plaintiff's attorneys, few people relish litigation. Obviously, a lawsuit is usually only attractive where damages (or an injunction) are bigger than the costs of litigation. So, if you are staring down a litigator's gun barrel, use all the right resources to make that balance look unattractive. You must evaluate the IP and make your case against big damages, including invalidity attacks. I'll never forget my civil procedure teacher's simple rule: Demur, Deny, Defend, Attack. So, analyze whether you have, or could secure rights to, IP that could be asserted against the aggressor. However, the price of all technology is not the cost of litigation (and plaintiffs know that too). So, explore ways to minimize cash outlays, like cross licensing, supply relationships, and joint developments, as these alternatives may provide the rationale to do a deal.

To enter a particular market. If a licensor is not now in a particular market (whether it be a new geographic market, a new product, or a new industry), the entry costs may be too great to allow exploitation of intellectual property in that market. If another has the expertise to exploit that market better or faster than a licensor can, it makes sense to share the profits through a license. This expertise may be in the form of manufacturing, marketing, customer lists, distribution, knowledge of foreign language or culture, or regulatory expertise, among many others.

For example, a manufacturer of beverage dispensers, with expertise in pumping liquids, may have technology that applies to dosing of pharmaceuticals. It may be the wisest course to license the technology to a company with the marketing and distribution infrastructure that can efficiently exploit the market. Another example is the licensing of movie characters to the toy industry. Another example is in the biotech field, where small biotech companies may license larger drug companies to manufacture and market new products.

To incorporate your technology with another more readily purchased product. The classis example here is software bundled with a PC.

To accelerate growth of an industry. In some industries, like semiconductors in the 1980s, it's wise to recognize that some competitors are developing technology just as well and fast as each other. Rather than risking lawsuits or being out maneuvered, a cross-license allows the players to focus on overall growth and development of the industry. This is particularly appropriate where common technology is used across a wide range of products (like semiconductor processing technology), and no one company can (should?) exploit each product segment (microprocessors, memory chips, DSPs).

To gain access to another's innovations. As in the last example, licenses allow sharing of IP without the need for joint development or joint venture arrangements. Very often this objective is met in a cross license or IP grant-back clause. This can also be important where there are many licensees, and there is a desire to create a "technology pool" for all to share in.

To maintain quality and goodwill. In trademark licenses where technology is important to the product, it is imperative that the appropriate license is in place.

To obtain or maintain control of a market. With IP in a standard, like an operating system or industry wide protocol, licensing may allow one to maintain control of a market and provide more certainty that future R&D will find a home.

To keep competitors from leapfrogging. A competitor may be less inclined to develop a better mousetrap if offered a reasonable license.

I.B.   WHAT ARE YOU LICENSING?

As basic as this concept sounds, it is often overlooked. Just what is being licensed is a very important question, with profound consequences. If the definition is too narrow, a licensee may find itself paying twice for what it should have paid for only once. If it is too wide, the licensor may lose income, or be burdened with onerous technology transfer obligations.

Define the IP. If a patent license is what is being considered, define which patents are involved, and address all continuations, continuations-in-part, reissues, reexaminations, and divisionals. If the license is for know-how or trade secrets, define what they are. Also, address later developed or acquired IP. When later developed or acquired IP is involved, time limits are critical.

Fields of use or embodiment restrictions. Both sides should be careful in defining these kinds of restrictions. Too narrow and the licensee may get less than it is bargaining for. Too wide, and the licensor may be losing out due to unexploited applications.

Define the trigger for the royalty obligation. Make sure it is clear what triggers the royalty. This is usually a sale, but it could be manufacturing. Also, where trade secrets are involved, you should define which products the royalty is based on (those that are made on process x, or those that include feature y).

Define the base to which the royalty applies. Make sure that you don't leave open the question of how much of a sale is subject to a royalty (for example, if there are significant installation charges associated with a licensed product, does a royalty rate apply to revenue from the installation?).

Know the weaknesses of the licensed IP. Both sides should know the strengths and weaknesses of the IP. Without knowing this going in to the negotiation, you may find your bargaining position weakened. Knowing the information ahead of time helps you develop answers to strengthen your position.

Consider what you are willing to do after signing the deal. Define the licensor's obligations to transfer technology (such as documentation, training (on or off site), on-going communications, etc.). You don't want to pay for something you don't really receive. These transfer obligations can be onerous, and unless specifically spelled out, the licensee may expect much more than the licensor plans to provide.

On the licensee's side, it should be very clear what the expectations are for exploiting the technology. You don't want the case of the 100 mile per gallon carburetor put on the shelf. Of course, there are ways to cover those risks, such as minimum royalties, but you should also consider dividing the market into segments or territories, or licensing only particular embodiments. If the licensee wants more than the licensee is comfortable giving, options to add to the license may be included if certain conditions, such as having a serious business plan and success in other segments, are met.

Draft with clarity. License agreements are often long term arrangements, and the original players move on. Don't ever believe that ambiguity is good (for example, in defining fields of use, sublicensing rights, gross revenues, scope of trade secrets).

Value over time. Include mechanisms for fairly valuing the IP over time. In patent licenses, the patent life is often a good measure. When there are multiple patents, you may want to consider lowering the rate when the main patent expires. With trade secrets, you must consider whether a product includes the IP, and at what point is the original trade secret not truly valuable any more. As the licensee, you don't want to be in the position of having to prove that the secret is now well known, because (1) that may be hard to prove, and (2) what if you caused it?

I.C.   WHERE ARE YOU LICENSING?

It is important to consider the geographic scope of the license. Unless a licensee is able to exploit a technology in all the world, you should consider territorial restrictions on the license. Otherwise, the unexploited territory is unproductive. Thus, for example, you should understand the distribution channels that may dictate certain natural territories. In trade secret cases, territorial restrictions are sometimes difficult, as one licensee may resist allowing another to share in the secret (for if they divulge anywhere, the first licensee may lose his advantage).

Another issue to consider is whether the country in question has a reliable justice system for enforcing the agreement. If not, perhaps control of the licensee is important (e.g., through a joint venture, equity investment, or tying the license to other business or equipment). As an aside, even in countries that do not have reliable justice systems, obtaining patents can be important. In particular, if you will license a reputable multinational, it will be willing to pay royalties in the questionable countries because the patent is there (as a matter of company policy to respect others' intellectual property).

I.D.   WHO ARE YOU LICENSING (TO OR FROM)?

"Thus it is said that one who knows the enemy and knows himself will not be endangered in a hundred engagements. One who does not know the enemy but knows himself will sometimes be victorious, sometimes meet with defeat. One who knows neither the enemy nor himself will invariably be defeated in every engagement." — Sun-Tzu, The Art of War (Planning Offensives).

Knowing your adversary (or "partner") is extremely important, as Sun-Tzu knew thousands of years ago. I'm not about to discuss the psychology of negotiations, but, it is sufficient to say that it is a very important part of IP licensing. What I do want to touch on are two main themes: (1) the importance of knowing the history, plans, and capabilities of the other party; and (2) knowing how many potential licensees there are.

Require exploitation. As I have mentioned already, as a licensor, you must have some assurance that the licensee will really exploit the technology. If you use a minimum royalty, don't just stick your finger in the air and say, how about $100,000? You need to set it at a level that is consistent with proper exploitation. So, I suggest that it grow over time, to reflect roll-out realities. Of course, this is most often used in exclusive arrangements, but it can be used in non-exclusive ones as well, since the very grant of a non-exclusive precludes obtaining from another the greater income that may be derived from an exclusive license.

Also, you must know what the licensee's real strengths are. Don't license a party to do something it really can't (or won't). So, consider field of use type restrictions.

Know whether you are creating a competitor. If the other party is already a competitor, then you must understand, before granting a license, not just the value of the royalty stream, but the value of having the technology exclusively to yourself. If not a competitor, might the license make it one? If so, consider fields of use or territory restrictions.

Know the licensee's IP (and your own). Before getting too aggressive, you'd better be sure your "licensee" is not a sleeping giant with an IP armory. I know of at least two companies that tried to poke Texas Instruments in the eye and ended up wishing they had never taken their hand out of their pocket. And, if you are a potential licensee, consider whether you have IP to bring into the mix to lower, eliminate, or generate royalties.

Know the ethical reputation of the other party. Will the licensee keep the secrets secret? Will royalties be accurately reported? Will the licensee in any way reflect badly on the licensor? All these questions will bear on the strength of audit and enforcement clauses.

Know the number of players in the market. Is it a one-player, two-player, oligopolistic, or many player market? You must consider whether an exclusive license is more valuable than a non-exclusive. Of course, this depends on the nature of the technology (are there alternatives), and on the nature of the competitors. But, in a market with a small number of players, an exclusive license to a particular technology could be devastating to those left out, and the value may therefore be very great. In contrast, if offered to all on a non-exclusive basis, the value may be less (but not to one not taking a license).

In a market with many players, it is advisable to make it easy to license, for any one objector could overturn the apple cart by pressing for invalidity. As a corollary, licensees in such markets should fight like crazy for low royalties.

II.   LICENSING STRATEGIES (AVOIDING LITIGATION)

First off, you may not want to avoid litigation. If you can prove lost profits, damages may be very, very large. And, even in reasonable royalty cases, courts have often found 20% or higher royalty rates to be acceptable. Also, from the licensee's viewpoint, there are too many invalidity decisions out there to rule out the possibility of a complete (albeit expensive) victory if you fight in court.

In general, however, negotiated solutions are superior to litigation. Even though licensing may be calmer than litigation, the parties are not excused from doing a very thorough job of analysis. The better prepared you are to show your case, the more likely you are to avoid litigation. If you are a licensee, do your homework on invalidity. And, whoever you are, do not be arrogant. Do not dismiss another's claims without really counting the costs. There are a number of jury verdicts in patent infringement and trade secret cases that exceed 50 million dollars, and many invalidity decisions.

Of course, to avoid litigation, the deal has to look to both sides to be better than the uncertainties of litigation. So, you should be able to show what you would show to a jury — make sure the other side understands the strength of your position.

II.A.   WHAT IS THE VALUE?

Perhaps the paramount licensing issue is value. To get the result you think fair, you must be able to create a compelling case for your valuation of the technology. One way to do this is to come up with different methods of valuing the technology (such as (1) what's it worth to have it, (2) what's the cost of not having it, and (3) what are the risks of litigation). In the best scenario, these valuations converge, but you can always just average them. With such an approach, it is difficult to argue against the numbers.

Know the market. You must understand the real costs and profits of the industry. Use annual reports, former industry players, or whatever you can to obtain credible numbers. I've seen people with good technology get bounced out because they wanted $10 or $20 million up front for something that just wouldn't deliver the profit to support such numbers.

Understand practical design arounds or alternatives. You can drive a potential licensee away by asking for too much. You must understand the ability of an industry to use an alternative technology.

Understand manufacturing and distribution. Savings or costs associated with a new technology should be well understood.

Understand consumer receptivity. What are the additional sales or profit margins that will be delivered? Will there be any convoyed sales?

Know the effect of exclusivity. You should quantify the value of exclusivity, both where the potential licensee gets it, and where its competitor does. Also, you should understand the value of exclusivity versus non-exclusivity.

Know the cost of litigation. That's about $3 million plus possible damages to the defendant.

Balance risk. One way to balance risk is with more or less in up-front money for less or more royalties later. Also, arguments for invalidity must be factored in.

II.B.   WHAT IS THE RIGHT SPLIT OF THAT VALUE?

Few licensees will take a license that gives all the value to the licensor. So, there must be a split, a sharing of the profit. Of course, every case is different, but licensors can easily argue that a fair split is 50%/50%. However, licensees often argue that they are taking all the risk, so they should get 99% of the value.

In the reasonable royalty cases, where courts award the outcome out of a hypothetical negotiation, courts have many times granted reasonable royalties of over 20% of gross sales. You should read the case law to see whether there are cases in your technology area that could be instructive and persuasive in a negotiation.

Also, you should know traditional industry royalty rates, but don't be bound to them. Each technology is different, and some are just more valuable than others. Another source for royalty rate data is university web sites. Many schools (such as Stanford) have technology licensing offices, and they sometimes provide the royalty rates they are offering. . . .

III.   CROSS LICENSES

Cross licenses allow companies to share in technology, and usually involve access to future developments. Before entering into such a license, it is important to understand why you are doing it. You do not want to trade away a future gem for present light affliction.

- Is it to avoid specific litigation? How weighty is it?

- Is it to get an industry off the ground, and is there room for two players? For how long will the license last?

- Is it for peace of mind (general access to technology)? Are you really anxious?

- Is it as a grant back in a licensee? For what areas? Don't be too generous.

- Is it for patents only, or is it for other know how or trade secrets? If for the others, are the technology transfer provisions clear?

Cross licenses are often between competitors. So, consider field of use or territorial restrictions, to protect your own strengths (e.g., one company might license its semiconductor processing technology for use in digital signal processors, but not in microprocessors for PCs). However, consult you competition counsel to ensure no agreements in restraint of trade are created by such restrictions.

Most of the points made earlier apply to cross licenses. But, a couple are worth stressing. Because these agreements often address future technology, make sure they are time bound. Also, consider mechanisms for payment that reflect the reality of the balance of technology. It may be that one company creates more valuable IP than the other (indeed, one may significantly reduce its R&D), and that should be reflected in the agreement.

IV.   ROYALTY STACKING

How can one avoid paying multiple royalties on one product? If there are many licensors, it's tough, but try to find someone with the right to sublicense others. As to one licensor, simply put in a clause that says you pay only once, no matter how many claims or patents cover the product. But, for this to work, you must be sure to make very broad the definition of what is licensed - including later developed or licensed technology. You don't want to find out that you licensed x only, but also need y.

NOTES & QUESTIONS

1. The licensing of technology, both protected and unprotected by intellectual property law, raises a host of questions that we will discuss at various points in this book, including income taxation (the topic of the next subsection), trade secret law, and antitrust law. The last two will be discussed extensively in separate chapters below.

2. Suppose Dr. See tells you that he has learned that one of the potential investors has developed software that allows his software system to run more efficiently. The same investor has also created hardware that permits diagnostic testing and repair of Dr. See's software. What would you advise on the best ways to obtain the most value from this set of inventions? How would you implement your advice in the negotiation and transaction process?

3. Review the materials on valuation of intellectual property discussed above. What special issues of valuation does licensing raise? How are the methods of valuation discussed above applicable to the licensing situation?

E.   TAX AND ACCOUNTING ISSUES RAISED BY INTELLECTUAL PROPERTY

Joseph Bankman & Ronald J. Gilson, Why Start-ups?
51 Stanford Law Review 289 (1999)*

Assume that we have a risk-neutral, established employer and a group of risk-averse engineers. Each of the engineers is competent at pursuing the employer's ongoing business — normal science — and each has a positive probability of developing an innovation that would give rise to a new business. Neither the engineers nor the employer can identify ex ante which of the engineers actually will develop the innovation. The obvious risk-sharing

---

arrangement is for the employer to hire all the engineers, pay each the mean expected value of the group, and receive in return the engineers' contribution to the employer's ongoing business and all discoveries made by any of them.

Of course, once the uncertainty is eliminated — when the passage of time reveals which engineers have won the innovation lottery — the engineers' attraction to ex ante risk sharing gives way to an incentive for ex post opportunism. The winning engineer wants to keep the discovery for herself. Thus, the risk-sharing arrangement must have some characteristics that protect it from the corrosive effect of learning which engineer wins. And it should be apparent that, whatever the arrangement, it is not perfect. There must be a problem in prospectively transferring ownership of the engineers' discoveries to the employer. If the property rights could be fully specified and transferred ex ante, we would not observe start-ups. Thus, the puzzle is premised on a contracting failure.

However, contracting failure alone is insufficient to account for the existence of start-ups. Even if the employee retains some property right in her discovery, commercializing the idea requires starting a business. In return for some portion of the future earnings from the innovation, other parties still must put up the factors of production the employee lacks: (1) capital; and (2) managerial, manufacturing, and marketing expertise. A conventional solution to this problem is venture capital financing. A venture capital fund contributes capital to the start-up as well as noncapital contributions such as management consulting, monitoring, and reputation, in return for an ownership stake in the start-up. But suppose we recharacterize the venture capital process as an auction. The engineer leaving her position with the employer is selling off a portion of her innovation to the highest bidder. When all else is equal, the employer has advantages — tax, information, and scope — that should result in it consistently winning the auction.

A.   The Employer's Tax Advantage

Under current law, the tax treatment of corporate investment depends on the tax history of the organization making that investment. An investment made by a company with sources of past or present income is subject to a symmetrical tax regime: The expenses of the investment are deductible and produce tax savings, while the gains from investment are subject to tax. An investment carried out by a start-up, in contrast, is subject to an asymmetrical tax regime: Gains are fully taxed, but losses may be deducted only against future income. As discussed in more detail below, this difference in tax regime operates in the circumstance of interest here to provide a substantial subsidy for an employer's efforts to develop an employee's innovation internally.

Under Internal Revenue Code (I.R.C.) § 172, a start-up may deduct expenses only against income — expenses in excess of current income (a net operating loss) may generally be carried forward for fifteen years and deducted against future income. In contrast, a company with sources of past or present income from other activities — we will call it an "established company" — may deduct expenses of the start-up activity that exceed start-up activity income as they are incurred: The expenses of the start-up activity are set off against the income from other activities. The significance of the divergent tax treatment of innovation expenses incurred by established companies on the one hand, and start-ups on the other, depends on the timing for tax purposes of expenses and income. For a number of reasons, the consequences of this divergent tax treatment are likely to be particularly important for start-ups.

First, a significant number of start-up companies never earn profits. For these companies, the limitation on deductibility amounts to a permanent loss of the tax benefit. For more successful start-ups that ultimately do earn profits, the combination of staged financing, often involving new investors at each round, and the exercise of employee stock options, likely will result in an identifiable group of five percent shareholders increasing their ownership interests by at least fifty percentage points within a three-year period. This triggers a change of ownership under I.R.C. § 382 which, in turn, sharply restricts the value of the net operating loss. Even companies that reach profitability within the carry forward period and escape the change of ownership limitation still require many years before generating sufficient taxable incomes to take full advantage of early losses. Thus, the tax benefit of the eventual deduction is limited by the loss of value inherent in deferral.

For new ventures carried out by established companies the tax picture is quite different. Such companies face no special limitations on otherwise deductible expenses, and the availability of tax credits and deductions for research and development ensures that most expenses of internally developing an innovation can be immediately offset against income from other activities. Expressed in terms of net present value, the effect of the tax differential is quite stark. Consider, for example, an investment that costs $100 in year one and has the following probability distribution of returns: a 40 percent chance of returning nothing; a 40 percent chance of returning $100 in year ten; and a 10 percent chance of returning $700 in years six through twelve. At a discount rate of 15 percent (quite conservative in light of the 40 to 60 percent rate said to be applied by venture capitalists), the investment has a net present value of approximately $141.

Now assume that the combined state and federal tax rate is 40 percent; that an established company is able to deduct the investment ratably over three years; and that the company is able to gross up the investment by the present value of the tax savings. The investment now shows an after-tax present value of approximately $135. The relatively small reduction in present value as a result of the 40 percent tax reflects that the value of deducting the venture's losses in the first few years offsets most of the future tax on the later occurring venture income. In contrast, a start-up loses the entire deduction on the investments that never generate profit, and loses most of the present value of the deduction for break-even and successful investments. As a result, the after-tax net present value of the investment to the start-up is only $95 — $5 less than its cost, and $40 less than the value of the same investment to an established company.

Our analysis thus far has focused only on the corporate tax. A more complete analysis would also include the tax paid by shareholders of start-ups on the proceeds from the sale of their stock. In general, taking the shareholder-level tax into account would lessen the start-up's disadvantage. For unsuccessful start-ups, the inability to deduct expenses would exacerbate losses on the corporate level and lead to greater losses on the shareholder level; for successful start-ups, the deferral of deduction at the corporate level would reduce gains at the shareholder level. In either event, the result would be a reduction in shareholder-level tax. Tax savings at the shareholder level, however, would be of second-order magnitude. At best, given a 40 percent combined state and federal tax rate, shareholders would recoup only 40 percent of the tax disadvantage experienced by the corporate start-up. In all cases, this partial recoupment of the tax disadvantage would require disposal of the underlying stock. For unsuccessful investments, such recoupment would be hampered by I.R.C. limitations on deduction of capital losses. . . .

SYMS CORP. v. COMMISSIONER OF REVENUE
Supreme Judicial Court of Massachusetts
765 N.E.2d 758 (2002)

1. Background. Syms is a New Jersey corporation engaged in "off-price" retailing, which is the retail sale of brand name clothing at prices lower than those in department stores. It was founded in 1959 by Sy Syms. It operates two stores in the Commonwealth and therefore is subject to Massachusetts corporate excise tax.

During the years in question, Sy Syms was the chairman of the board of directors and the dominant shareholder, owning fifty-six per cent of the stock and controlling the votes for another twenty-four per cent held in trust for family members. His daughter, Marcy Syms, was the president of the company.

Syms used several marks in its business, including the "Syms" name, a "multiple 'S' logo" that it placed on its own brands of clothing, and the slogan, "An Educated Consumer is Our Best Customer." Prior to December, 1986, Syms owned these marks.

The idea of a trademark holding subsidiary was first brought to the attention of Syms in early 1986 by Irv Yacht, a consultant with a company called Coventry Financial Corporation. Yacht broached this idea in a letter to Syms's chief financial officer, Richard Diamond, in which he promised that he "had a method of saving state taxes." Immediately after their first meeting in the spring of 1986, Yacht and Diamond signed an agreement, which recited that Coventry "has developed a program . . . for reducing [Syms's] income taxes by reorganizing the business activities of [Syms] in certain areas." Yacht's proposal was for Syms to form a Delaware subsidiary, transfer the marks to that subsidiary, and then execute a license agreement under which Syms would continue to use the marks as it had before the transfer (Coventry plan).

Under the license agreement, Syms would pay a large royalty to the subsidiary, thereby generating a deduction for Syms on its State excise taxes. The subsidiary, however, would not pay any State tax on the royalty income because, under Delaware law, corporations that hold intangible assets are exempt from income tax. Syms was to pay Coventry twenty-five per cent of the tax savings realized in the first year, with a declining percentage for the next four years.

In considering whether to engage in the Coventry plan, Syms recognized the risk of a tax audit. In a memorandum to Sy Syms, Diamond wrote, "There have been cases when corporations attempted to do this and did not do it properly and thus had problems in various states. It is everyone[']s feeling that New York is the most sophisticated state in terms of tax audits and most other states will not even realize the impact of the transactions." As a precaution, Syms held part of Coventry's compensation in escrow in case the hoped-for tax savings were disallowed in an audit.

Syms also consulted its trademark attorneys about risks attendant to the transfer of the marks under trademark law, and was advised that the transfer would be valid as a matter of trademark law because "Syms Corp. will own and control the subsidiary. Whether or not the subsidiary is an active entity, its assets (consisting of the trademarks) belong to the parent company. Syms Corp. will, in fact, continue to stand behind the goods and services identified by these marks."

Syms decided to proceed with the Coventry plan and SYL was incorporated in Delaware on December 4, 1986, as Syms's wholly owned trademark holding company. Its board of directors and officers were Sy Syms, Marcy Syms, Richard Diamond, and Edward Jones, a partner in a Delaware accounting firm. SYL and Syms executed a license agreement on December 18, 1986. SYL, acting as the owner of the marks, granted to Syms the right to use the marks nationally for a royalty equal to four per cent of Syms's annual net sales. The marks were transferred from Syms to SYL the next day, December 19, 1986.

For the calendar year 1986, Syms paid SYL a royalty for the marks that constituted four per cent of its annual net sales from October 1, 1986, until the end of December. The 1986 royalty was approximately $2.8 million. In subsequent years, the royalty amount increased from nearly $10 million in 1987 to $12.7 million in 1991. In each of these years SYL received one annual royalty payment from Syms, which it held in Delaware for a few weeks before paying it back to Syms, with interest (minus expenses) as a tax-free dividend. SYL's only income came from Syms's annual royalty payments, and its expenses amounted to approximately one-tenth of one per cent of its income.

SYL's corporate "office" consisted of an address rented from Jones's Delaware accounting firm, for an annual fee of $1,200. The accounting firm provided this same service to "a couple of hundred" other corporations that used Delaware subsidiary corporations to hold their intangible assets. Jones was not only a partner of the accounting firm, he was SYL's only employee, serving in a part-time capacity for which he was paid $1,200 per year.

The business operations of Syms did not change after the transfer and license-back of the marks. All of the work necessary to maintain and protect the marks continued to be done by the same New York City trademark law firm that had previously performed those services, and Syms (not SYL) continued to pay all the expenses attendant thereto. All efforts to maintain the good will and thus to preserve the value of the marks were undertaken by Syms, and all advertising using the marks was controlled and paid for by Syms or by a wholly owned Syms subsidiary formed solely to do advertising. The choice of which products would be sold under the marks, as well as the quality control of those products, remained the responsibility of the same persons who had done that work before the transfer — Sy Syms himself, and the Syms staff of buyers.

2. Sham transaction. Syms does not contest the validity of the "sham transaction doctrine" and the commissioner's authority under that doctrine to disregard, for taxing purposes, transactions that have no economic substance or business purpose other than tax avoidance. It is a doctrine long established in State and Federal tax jurisprudence dating back to the seminal case of *Gregory v. Helvering*, 293 U.S. 465, 55 S.Ct. 266, 79 L.Ed. 596 (1935). It works to prevent taxpayers from claiming the tax benefits of transactions that, although within the language of the tax code, are not the type of transactions the law intended to favor with the benefit. "Usually, transactions that are invalidated by the doctrine are those motivated by nothing other than the taxpayer's desire to secure the attached tax benefit," and are structured to completely avoid economic risk.

Syms contends that the doctrine does not apply in this case because it had business purposes, other than tax avoidance, for incorporating SYL and then transferring to it and licensing back the marks which it previously owned. It complains that the board ignored the "uncontroverted" evidence of these other business purposes, and based its decision on the record in another case litigated shortly after this one, and on an across-the-board policy of the "disallowance of deductions for all related trademark protection companies."

The question whether or not a transaction is a sham for purposes of the application of the doctrine is, of necessity, primarily a factual one, on which the taxpayer bears the burden of proof in the abatement process. . . .

The board found that the transfer and license back transaction had no practical economic effect on Syms other than the creation of tax benefits, and that tax avoidance was the clear motivating factor and its only business purpose. The board rejected the other business purposes claimed by Syms during the hearing, finding them to be "illusory, not supported by the evidence, or contrary to the weight of the evidence."

[Syms proffered, and the board rejected, almost a dozen nontax business purposes to support its claim that the transfer and license-back was not intended solely to avoid taxation. For example: Syms's assertion that the transfer would protect the marks from claims of Syms's creditors was rejected by the board, because creditors could reach assets of Syms's wholly owned subsidiary; Syms's claim that the transfer would protect the marks from a hostile takeover was rejected, because Syms could only have achieved that goal by transferring the marks to an independent third party, and with eighty per cent of the stock controlled by the company founder, such a takeover was hypothetical at best; Syms's claim that the transfer would result in better management of the marks was rejected because Syms retained the same responsibilities for managing and maintaining the marks after the transfer; and Syms's assertion that the formation of the subsidiary would enhance Syms's ability to borrow funds was rejected because creditors would have viewed the two entities as intermingled and would not have offered any different financing arrangements, Syms's founder strenuously opposed borrowing money, and the subsidiary never borrowed any money.]

While there may be many important business purposes attendant to the transfer and licensing back of intangible assets within corporate families, to be viable for the purposes claimed by Syms, they must be more than theoretical musings, concocted to provide faint cover for the creation of a tax deduction.

3. Ordinary and necessary expense. General Laws c. 63, § 1 ("[n]et income"), provides that corporations may take business deductions allowable under the Internal Revenue Code (Code). Under the Code, only "ordinary and necessary" business expense deductions are allowable. I.R.C. § 162. Deductions are not permitted if the expense was "created solely for the purpose of effectuating a camouflaged assignment of income.". . . . As an alternative ground for the disallowance of Syms's deduction for royalty expense, the board concurred with the commissioner's position that the royalty payments were not an "ordinary and necessary" business expense.

The board found that the value of the marks had been created entirely by Syms, and even after their transfer and the payment of the royalties, Syms continued to pay the expenses associated with owning them, including the legal expenses incurred in maintaining them. It concluded that, in such circumstances, Syms's royalty payments to SYL for the use of the marks was unnecessary. In effect, Syms was paying twice for their use. The board further reasoned that it was irrelevant that the measure of royalty payments might have been equivalent to what would have been paid in an arm's-length transaction where, as here, the payments were not for services provided by SYL but rather part of a contrived mechanism by which affiliated entities shifted income, tax free, between themselves in a circular transaction for the benefit of Syms.

Syms counters that, having validly transferred the trademarks to SYL in consideration for receipt of SYL stock, it was required to pay royalty fees, and, therefore, they were a necessary business expense. It also argues that there is no requirement that owners add value to assets before allowing their use by another entity, and that the sole test whether the royalty payments are deductible is whether they were made at "arm's length."

These arguments closely mirror those made on the question whether the transfer and license back of the marks constituted a "sham" transaction. The central issue for the court to decide is whether the board's finding that there was no business reason for Syms to incur the expense of millions of dollars in royalties other than to create tax deductions is supported by the record. As we have already concluded, it is. The royalty expense to Syms "resulted not as an ordinary, necessary incident in the conduct of the taxpayer's business, but instead was created solely for the purpose of effectuating a camouflaged assignment of income. It was properly disallowed.

6. Penalties. The board acted within its discretion in refusing to abate penalties levied on Syms. General Laws c. 62C, § 33(f), provides for an abatement of penalties "[i]f it is shown that any failure to file a return or to pay a tax in a timely manner is due to reasonable cause and not due to willful

neglect." . . . Here, the board found that the plan was not drafted or reviewed by a competent tax professional on behalf of Syms. An internal company memorandum submitted by Syms indicated that the plan had been "looked at" by "Mann Judd Landau," who believed that it was "within the state tax laws," but that "[t]hey can not give an opinion as to what might occur during a tax audit." On this record, the board was within its discretion to conclude that the taxpayer had not relied on the advice of a competent tax professional, had understood the risks inherent in the tax plan, and, therefore, its failure timely to pay the corporate excise deficiencies resulting from the disallowance of its royalty payment deductions was not due to reasonable cause.

Decision of the Appellate Tax Board affirmed.

Edward J. Jennings, The Taxation and Reporting of Distributions Derived from Licensing Intellectual Property
15 Taxation of Exempts 207 (Mar/Apr 2004)*

. . .

Patents and know-how.

The courts have analyzed the taxation of patents invented by employees by whether there is a transfer of the property and, if so, whether the payments made to the employee attach or relate to that property. The reasoning is that without property to transfer, or with transferred property but no consideration attributed to it, the distributions constitute compensation for services rendered. The analysis for independent contractors with respect to patent and secret know-how property is merely whether those distributions were made in relation to the transfer of the property.

Hired-to-invent. When interpreting the regulations on patents, the courts have applied a "hired-to-invent" principle to determine whether an employee transferred property. Reg. 1.1235–2(a) expressly provides "that payments received by an employee for services rendered as an employee to transfer to the employer the rights to any invention by such employee are not attributable to a transfer to which section 1235 applies." If the employee was hired-to-invent a specific product as part of the employment agreement, the payments are classified as compensation because the consideration is "for his labor, not for the product" whereby, the "invention" is the "property of his employer." As a point of distinction, the courts recognize that the initial ownership of property rights vests with the employees, permitting employees to transfer property. Thus, assignment agreements standing alone are not sufficient to divest the employees of ownership. These agreements are commonplace between employees and employers within the technology community under which, as a condition of employment, any and all inventions made by the employee become the sole property of the employer.

The court cases provide guidance as to the use of the term "hired-to-invent" based on a detailed review of the facts and circumstances of each arrangement. In *Blum* (11 TC 101 (1948)), the employer hired the taxpayer for the specific purpose of making adaptations to a particular chain saw that the company intended to sell. While performing his responsibilities, the taxpayer made certain inventions regarding the chain saw and, based on the employment agreement, these inventions became the property of the company. In reading the terms of the contract, the court held that the taxpayer entered into a "contract to invent" and that the employer owned the property outright. Thus, without the transfer of property, the payments made to the taxpayer were compensation for services rendered.

The court in *McClain* (40 TC 841 (1963)), however, held that the inventor was not hired-to-invent. McClain, who had entered in an "assignment of inventions agreement" as a condition of employment, invented two patents while working at Lockheed where he was assigned as a layout draftsman to design window installations for the cockpit section of the fuselage of the Model 44 aircraft. He conceived and invented a new and different windshield construction to be used on the aircraft, a polymerized vinyl butyral for use between the windshield glass. It was anticipated by Lockheed that McClain would use the existing state of the arts materials and techniques to perform his duties. The court found that the employee was clearly not hired-to-invent and that the patented property did transfer.

The court in *Chilton* (40 TC 552 (1963)) gives a more likely scenario in the sense that the employee was hired to render 'engineering work relating to the improvements of existing types of aircraft engines' as well as to "apply his experience and his inventive ability to problems." He entered into an assignment arrangement whereby the employer owned the rights to any inventions until after 90 days from the date of completion of the development tests. Thereupon, if the employer did not pursue developing the technology, the employee was free to apply for a patent on this invention for himself. Based on a close examination of the facts, the court held that the employee was clearly not hired-to-invent.

Bona fide transfers. If it is determined that the employee was not hired-to-invent, the courts examine the facts and circumstances of the agreement, relying on certain factors to indicate a bona fide transfer of property rights. These factors include a legally binding agreement to make a fixed payment amount that continues regardless of termination or changes in policy and after employment or death. Also, the payments should be dependent on the use of the invention. The rationale is that the payment stream is beyond the discretion and control of the employer to attribute compensation. The courts use these same factors for distributions made to independent contractors. . . .

The IRS recently released TAM 200249002, which agrees with the analysis put forth by the courts. The facts pertain to a university setting in which a professor at a state university who performs multiple tasks of teaching, conducting research, and various administrative tasks, with research efforts varying anywhere between 50% to 100% in any given academic term, agreed to transfer rights of future inventions in his employment contract. It is university policy to assess the value of the property transferred and, if the school chooses to commercialize the invention, it will pay royalties to the researcher based on the use of the property. Should the institution elect not to exercise the property rights, however, the invention is returned to the employee to do with as he or she sees fit. This TAM concludes that the property transferred constitutes a royalty that was entitled to capital gain treatment.

This same analysis is used with respect to know-how property. Wall Products, Inc, a closely held corporation that manufactured and sold "Plastorene" and "Morene" products, made payments to principal stockholders in exchange for the use of a secret formula. The IRS argued that payments to the researchers were compensation for services rendered under the premise that non-secret know-how is not considered property and, therefore, any related payments constitute compensation. However, the court held that there was a bona fide transfer of property in the form of secret know-how. The court did not address the hired-to-invent principle since the corporation did not hire the employees to perform the research and the research was conducted outside the scope of employment.

The challenge for research institutions is to define "secret" know-how and apply it to the facts and circumstances of each transfer. The value of secret know-how is not the information transferred but the fact that the information is kept confidential. Thus, it is the wall of concealment built around the information that the licensee/buyer is willing to pay for that determines whether the know-how constitutes intellectual property. Historically, the IRS applies a higher standard than the courts when defining the term "secret."

The IRS limits transferable property to information that is secret formulas or secret processes. Rev. Proc. 69-19 provides that only the owners and confidential employees know of the information and that safeguards are taken to prevent unauthorized disclosure. The information must be more than merely rights to tangible evidence, such as blueprints, drawings or other physical material. Further, technical information that relates to the property must not be furnished on a continuing basis. Non-secret know-how may qualify for capital gains treatment only when in the form of services and those services are ancillary to the technology transferred. The IRS has defined ancillary services as promoting the transferred property or by assisting or performing under a guarantee the start-up of the property.

In *Wall* (11 TC 51 (1948)), the court defined the concrete curing process as secret know-how even though the process was readily disclosed by performing a 'reverse engineering' procedure. The court in *DuPont* (389 F.2d 904 (Ct. Cl. 1961)) held that secret information includes customer lists, customer credit lists and news, suggesting secrecy attaches to a series or set of known materials. In another case, the taxpayer found that the transfer of manuals that were available to competitors did not prevent permitting capital gains treatment. Accordingly, an institution or researcher relying on these court cases should consider the tax risks that may arise with respect to the positions taken by the IRS. Legal definitions aside, the authorities clearly demonstrate that in determining the transfer of know-how property, the facts of each case dictate the outcome. Consequently, research institutions may avoid reporting the taxation of distributions as compensation by modifying policy and procedure statements, and assignment agreements. For example, institutions may require that the distributions paid from commercialized technology preclude revenues related to hired-to-invent agreements. Furthermore, hired-to-invent arrangements should be contracted for separately and distinctly from other licensed properties.

A large majority of licenses entered into by the higher education community includes non-secret know-how as services that are ancillary to the technology transferred. However, to the extent that non-secret know-how is more than ancillary or unrelated to the transfer, institutions need to make allocations necessary to report such payments as compensation. Similar to the hired-to-invent arrangements, it is recommended that research institutions enter into separate contracts when licensing such non-secret know-how services.

Moreover, such policies and agreements should be revised to include those factors that ensure a bona fide transfer of technology. Payments should evidence a legally binding agreement to pay a fixed amount that should continue regardless of changes to or termination in policy and after employment or death. Further, the payments should be in relation to the use of the property.

Copyrights.

The courts apply the same analysis to the transfer of copyrights that is applied to patents and know-how, but replace the hired-to-invent principle with a 'work-made-for-hire' principle. Similar to patents and secret know-how properties, ownership of copyrights initially vests in the author. However, a provision in the federal copyright law provides that ownership of the property initially vests in the employer when the employee created the work within his or her scope of employment as work-made-for-hire unless the parties expressly contract otherwise. This principle extends to independent contractors as well. The consequence is that the researcher cannot transfer property he or she does not own and, thus, any distributions made constitute compensation.

The courts' interpretation of the work-made-for-hire provision is similar to and parallels the hired-to-invent provision. The court in *Boulez* (83 TC 584 (1984)) held that a world-renown musical conductor who was hired exclusively by the employer for the purpose of making phonograph records created copyright property that the employer owned. In *Hill* (47 TC 613 (1967)), the court held that the payments made to an employee who was hired to produce programs as directed by the employer resulted in compensation. A case on copyright infringement (*Scherr v. Universal Match Corp.*, 417 F.2d 497 (2nd Cir. 1969)) found that the property rights belonged to the Army regarding a statue created by soldiers who were relieved from regular military duties to work on the statue as part of a formal government-commissioned project.

Research institutions should make the same adjustments to distribution policies and contracts for work-made-for-hire cases as with the invent-to-hire arrangements. Also, these documents should include the necessary factors to indicate a bona fide transfer of property rights.

Income recognized as royalties or as sales of capital assets

Once it has been determined that a bona fide transfer of property took place, the question becomes whether the researcher is entitled to capital gains treatment on the distributions he or she receives. The courts use the same analysis under both the patent and capital asset provisions to determine capital gains treatment (1) whether the property transferred is a recognized patent or a capital asset, (2) if so, whether the transfer constitutes a sale rather than a license arrangement and, (3) if so, whether the holding period for long-term assets is met. When these provisions are met, the income derived is entitled to the capital gains tax rate. However, when these requirements are not met, the payments are classified either as royalty income or income derived from the sales of short-term capital assets, both of which are subject to ordinary income tax rates.

Patent provision.

Congress introduced this provision in 1954 to provide lower tax rates to individuals — in particular, professional inventors who typically are denied capital gains treatment under the capital asset provision.

A capital asset. Regulations under Section 1235 define patents using the terms provided under the provisions of title 35 of the United States Code, or as any foreign patents that grant rights similar to those of U.S. patents. It is not necessary that the patent or patent application for the invention be in existence for this provision to apply. Also, a patent includes future improvements and undivided interests or fractional interests in the property as a whole.

This provision, however, excludes sales of patentable property that are made to related persons, either directly or indirectly. Reg. 1.1235-2(f) defines "related person" as a member of the family, including a spouse, ancestors, and lineal descendants. Brothers and sisters, however, are excluded. "Related person" also includes corporations, partnerships, and certain trusts in which the holder maintains an ownership interest of 25% or more. The rationale is to prevent an effective transfer when a sale of patents is within the same economic family.

Consequently, researchers should be made aware when licensing property independently that transfers to limited liability companies, corporations, or partnerships in which the researcher maintains a 25% interest or more may deny him or her capital gains treatment. In the alternative, if institutions make patent transfers to such entities on behalf of their researchers, they should maintain documentation to indicate that the transactions were at arm's length and not directed or controlled by the researcher in any way.

A sale or exchange. Section 1235 defines a "sale or exchange" as the transfer of all substantial rights to a patent, including undivided interests, by a holder. The terms may call for payment over a period generally coterminous with the use of the patent or contingent on the patent's productivity, use, or disposition. "Holder" is defined to include individuals whose efforts created the patent or those individuals, but for the creator's employer and related parties, who acquired an interest in the payment prior to actual reduction to practice of the property. The rationale is that a transfer of all substantial rights is deemed a sale since the researcher has given away all the bundle of rights, keeping nothing of substance.

Reg 1.1235 provides examples of transfers that meet, may meet, and do not meet the "all substantial rights" standard. The holder can qualify for capital gains when retaining the following rights:

1. Legal title for the purpose of securing performance or payment with exclusive licenses or reservation in the nature of a condition subsequent.

2. Rights that are not inconsistent with the passage of ownership, such as a security interest or a vendor's lien.

The holder may meet the "all substantial rights" requirement when he or she retains the following:

1. The right to prohibit sublicensing or subassignment by the transferee.

2. The right to use or sell the property.

Conversely, retention of other rights defeats the applicability of this provision. Examples include:

1. Limiting the rights geographically within the country of issuance.

2. Limiting by agreement the duration to a period less than the remaining life of the patent.

3. Terminating the transfer at will.

4. Granting less than all claims or inventions in the patent that exist and have value at the time of the grant.

5. Granting fields of use that are less than all the rights covered by the patent that exist and have value at the time of the grant.

The court in *Taylor* (TCM 1970–325) gives guidance as to the application of the term "all substantial rights." William Taylor, who patented in the U.S. a "square" manhole (advertised as the "safe" and "silent" answer to sewage repair), entered into three agreements to transfer the patent rights. In the first agreement, the right to "manufacture" was exclusively transferred to a manufacturer to make products in Ontario. However, the remaining fundamental rights to "use" and "sell" were not clearly transferred as exclusive rights. In the second agreement, the inventor transferred non-exclusive rights to "make, use and sell" the invention throughout Canada's maritime provinces, keeping the rights to transfer the patent to other parties. Both agreements limited the transferees' rights to assign any rights and prevented them from suing in their own name for infringement cases.

In the third agreement, the inventor, in general terms, transferred expressly the exclusive rights to "make and sell" the invention and by implication "use" the property in the United Kingdom. Taylor limited the duration of the agreement to one year with an option by the transferee to renew the contract for the term of the patent. The arrangement also allowed the transferee the right to institute or join Taylor in any infringement proceedings at his request. Further, Taylor retained the right to veto assignments to other parties.

The court held that the first two agreements constituted licenses but found the third agreement transferred "all substantial rights," effecting a sale. In the first two agreements, the failure to transfer exclusively two of those essential rights to a patent, "use and sell," combined with limitations on assignments and infringements, resulted in the inventor retaining substantial rights significant to defeat the transfer as a sale. In the third agreement, however, the transfer, taken as a whole, represented the appropriate "bundle of rights." The agreement transferred all essential rights to the patent and did not impair the duration of the arrangement when allowing the transferee under the option to either terminate or continue the arrangement. The agreement permitted the transferee to sue in its own name for infringement cases and the retention of the rights to veto assignments, by itself, was not enough to prevent a sale.

The determination of whether the conditions of the assignment agreement meet the "all substantial rights" standard is based on the facts and circumstances of each transfer, including providing documentation that gives the values of the rights at the time of the transfer. For example, property transferred by an inventor who retained a substantial right, the right to terminate the exclusivity of the agreement, qualified for capital gains treatment since the right had no significant, practical or commercial value when the contract was entered into and the clause was not exercised. Also, this standard is not affected by licenses previously granted to the federal government for government purposes. The court in *First National Trust and Savings Bank of San Diego* (200 F. Supp. 274 (D.C. Cal. 1961)) held that the exclusive license to a local business constituted a sale regardless of the fact that the patent had a pre-existing non-exclusive license to the U.S. government to manufacture and sell devices.

Holding period. Section 1235 defines the holding requirement as a long-term period per se. The effective transfer of "all substantial rights" by definition deems the holding period to be met when it provides "a transfer . . . of all substantial rights . . . by any holder shall be considered a sale or exchange of a capital asset held for more than 1 year."

Alternatively, when the patent fails to meet the requirements under this provision, it may qualify for capital gains treatment under the capital asset provision. For example, a transfer to a related party will cause the transfer to fall outside this provision. Reg. 1.1235-1(b) provides that when this provision does not apply, the "tax consequences of such transactions shall be determined under other provisions of the internal revenue laws." The IRS confirmed this position when it applied the 'all substantial rights' standard to those patents that seek capital gains treatment under the capital asset provision in default of this provision.

NOTES & QUESTIONS

1. The tax treatment of intellectual property is a difficult and technical subject, covered in a class of its own. Our purpose here is to make you aware of some of the issues and alert you to the need to have clients consult relevant tax counsel for problems that you may identify as a business attorney. For an excellent source on the taxation of intellectual property, see JEFFREY MAINE & XUAN THAO-NGUYEN, INTELLECTUAL PROPERTY TAXATION (BNA 2003).

2. The reading by Professors Bankman and Gilson raise a startling question: why do entrepreneurs form start-ups as opposed to having all innovation occur within existing companies? What is the tax argument against start-ups? Despite the tax impediments that the professors identify, what

are the countervailing benefits of start-ups? A very important tax question that is beyond the scope of this book, but nonetheless worth recognizing, is the relevance of taxation for the choice of business form. Remember that a corporation is a separate entity and is taxed at a different rate and in a different manner from partnerships. One importance difference in manner is that corporation income is paid by the business entity while partnership income passes through to the partners and is taxed at the partner level at the partnership rate. There are also significant differences in deductions and in the treatment of property and service contributions between corporations and partnerships.

3. The *Syms* case illustrates the tax treatment of an intellectual property holding company. Why would someone transfer ownership of intellectual property, or any property for that matter, to a separate entity and then license or lease the property back? Do you see the tax advantages of such an arrangement? Why did the Internal Revenue Service disallow the arrangement as a "sham transaction?" Does the analysis presented in the case make clear what a "sham transaction" is?

4. Delaware has been an attractive jurisdiction for forming subsidiaries to hold intellectual property assets because Delaware law does not tax corporate revenues derived from intellectual property. However, several states have enacted Add-Back legislations that allow state taxation of intellectual property revenues earned by these Delaware subsidiaries. Corporate challenges to these statutes have been mixed with a pro-taxpayer ruling in Massachusetts, and an anti-taxpayer ruling in New York. *See Sherwin-Williams Co. v. Commissioner of Revenue*, 778 N.E.2d 504 (2002); *Sherwin-Williams Co. v. Tax Appeals Tribunal Of The Department Of Taxation and Finance Of The State Of New York*, 12 A.D.3d 112 (N.Y. Sup. Ct. App. Div. 2004). In the New York case, the following testimony was key to the ruling against the taxpayer:

> Shapiro [expert witness for the State] testified that the subsidiaries were unable to add value to the trademarks and that, objectively viewed, the transaction lacked economic substance because there was no reasonable expectation of benefits exceeding costs. He explained that the value of a trademark is principally tied to it being recognized and reflecting the quality and service associated with products bearing that trademark. Thus, according to Shapiro, trademarks cannot be managed "independently of the core branded products and the knowledge that comes from managing those products." He further set forth the reasons for his conclusions that the subsidiaries failed to provide any meaningful quality control, that the arrangement did not protect against a hostile takeover and that creating the subsidiaries did not advance the goal of limiting liability.

12 A.D.3d at 114. What lessons can be learned from the New York case? The Massachusetts court concluded that "[b]ecause the record in this case establishes that the reorganization and subsequent transfer and licensing transactions were genuine, creating viable businesses engaged in substantive economic activities apart from the creation of tax benefits for Sherwin-Williams, they cannot be disregarded by the commissioner as a sham regardless of their tax-motivated

purpose." 778 N.E.2d at 519. How do you think the Massachusetts court distinguished *Syms*?

5. The *Syms* case deals with trademarks. Would the analysis have been different if patents, copyrights or trade secrets were at issue? How would you have set up the holding company and licensing arrangements differently in light of the result in *Syms*? In thinking about this question, focus on any relevant differences among the various types of intellectual property.

6. The Jennings reading addresses the treatment of income from intellectual property licenses. The key question is when such income will be treated as returns to a capital investment and when it will be treated as ordinary income. Pay particular attention to the tax treatment (1) of inventions and works made in an employment context and (2) of transfer of intellectual property interests.

7. In the case of intellectual property transfers, the "all substantial rights" test will determine whether such transfers will constitute a sale or a license. Review carefully the discussion of the test. Suppose Dr. See decides to enter into a cross-licensing arrangement with one of the potential investors who has developed hardware that permits efficient diagnostic testing and debugging of Dr. See's software. Under this arrangement, Dr. See will give the investor rights to copy and adapt the software in exchange for exclusive use of the hardware for diagnostic purposes. In light of the "all substantial rights" test, how would you structure the cross-license so that Dr. See obtains favorable tax treatment?

F. INTELLECTUAL PROPERTY IN SPECIAL CONTEXTS

1. Universities

MADEY v. DUKE UNIVERSITY
United States Court of Appeals for the Federal Circuit
307 F. 3d 1351 (2002)

In the mid-1980s Madey was a tenured research professor at Stanford University. At Stanford, he had an innovative laser research program, which was highly regarded in the scientific community. An opportunity arose for Madey to consider leaving Stanford and take a tenured position at Duke. Duke recruited Madey, and in 1988 he left Stanford for a position in Duke's physics department. In 1989 Madey moved his free electron laser ("FEL") research lab from Stanford to Duke. The FEL lab contained substantial equipment, requiring Duke to build an addition to its physics building to house the lab. In addition, during his time at Stanford, Madey had obtained sole ownership of two patents practiced by some of the equipment in the FEL lab.

At Duke, Madey served for almost a decade as director of the FEL lab. During that time the lab continued to achieve success in both research funding and scientific breakthroughs. However, a dispute arose between Madey and Duke. Duke contends that, despite his scientific prowess, Madey ineffectively managed the lab. Madey contends that Duke sought to use the lab's equipment for research areas outside the allocated scope of certain government funding, and that when he objected, Duke sought to remove him as lab director. Duke eventually did remove Madey as director of the lab in 1997. The removal is not at issue in this appeal; however, it is the genesis of this unique patent infringement case. As a result of the removal, Madey resigned from Duke in 1998. Duke, however, continued to operate some of the equipment in the lab. Madey then sued Duke for patent infringement of his two patents, and brought a variety of other claims.

A. The Patents and Infringing Equipment

One of Madey's patents, U.S. Patent No. 4,641,103 ("the '103 patent"), covers a "Microwave Electron Gun" used in connection with free electron lasers. The other patent, U.S. Patent No. 5,130,994 ("the '994 patent"), is titled "Free-Electron Laser Oscillator For Simultaneous Narrow Spectral Resolution And Fast Time Resolution Spectroscopy." The details of these two patents are not material to the issues on appeal. Their use in the lab, however, as embodied in certain equipment, is central to this appeal.

The equipment at the Duke FEL lab that practices the subject matter disclosed and claimed in the patents is set forth in the list below, which first lists the equipment and then the patent(s) it embodies.

- An infrared FEL called the "Mark III FEL," embodying the '994 patent and the '103 patent (by incorporating the microwave electron gun in the infrared FEL).

- A "Storage Ring FEL," embodying the same patents as the Mark III FEL because it incorporates a Mark III FEL.

- A "Microwave Gun Test Stand," embodying the '103 patent (by incorporating the microwave electron gun).

The three alleged infringing devices are the Mark III FEL, the Storage Ring FEL, and the Microwave Gun Test Stand. Although it is not clear from the record, perhaps because Duke defended by asserting experimental use and government license defenses, Duke seems to concede that the alleged infringing devices and methods read on the claims of the patents. Although the three devices were housed in Duke's physics facilities, the Microwave Gun Test Stand was not Duke's asset, but rather belonged to North Carolina Central University ("NCCU").

B. Duke's Relationship with NCCU

Madey and Duke built the Microwave Gun Test Stand as a subcontractor to NCCU after the government awarded NCCU a contract to study microwave guns (the "AFOSR Contract"). Professor Jones of NCCU was the principal investigator under this government project. The Microwave Gun Test Stand was built and housed in the Duke FEL lab. The AFOSR Contract listed the Microwave Gun Test Stand as NCCU's asset.

. . .

D. The District Court's Summary Judgment Opinion

The Patent Motion and the Experimental Use Defense

The district court acknowledged a common law "exception" for patent infringement liability for uses that, in the district court's words, are "solely for research, academic or experimental purposes." The district court recognized the debate over the scope of the experimental use defense, but cited this court's opinion in *Embrex, Inc. v. Service Engineering Corp.*, 216 F.3d 1343 (Fed.Cir.2000) to hold that the defense was viable for experimental, non-profit purposes.

After having recognized the experimental use defense, the district court then fashioned the defense for application to Madey in the passage set forth below.

> Given this standard [for experimental use], for [Madey] to overcome his burden of establishing actionable infringement in this case, he must establish that [Duke] has not used the equipment at issue "solely for an experimental or other non-profit purpose." More specifically, [Madey] must sufficiently establish that [Duke's] use of the patent had "definite, cognizable, and not insubstantial commercial purposes."

Summary Judgment Opinion at 10.

. . .

Before the district court, Madey argued that Duke's research in its FEL lab was commercial in character. . . . Based on language in Duke's patent policy, Madey argues that Duke is in the business of "obtaining grants and developing possible commercial applications for the fruits of its 'academic research.'"

The district court rejected Madey's argument, relying on another statement in the preamble of the Duke patent policy which stated that Duke was "dedicated to teaching, research, and the expansion of knowledge . . . [and] does not undertake research or development work principally for the purpose of developing patents and commercial applications." The district court reasoned that these statements from the patent policy refute any contention that Duke is "in the business" of developing technology for commercial applications. According to the district court, Madey's "evidence" was mere speculation, and thus Madey did not meet his burden of proof to create a genuine issue of material fact. . . .

The District Court's Overly Broad Conception of Experimental Use

Madey argues, and we agree, that the district court had an overly broad conception of the very narrow and strictly limited experimental use defense. The district court stated that the experimental use defense inoculated uses that "were solely for research, academic, or experimental purposes," and that the defense covered use that "is made for experimental, non-profit purposes only." Both formulations are too broad and stand in sharp contrast to our admonitions in *Embrex* and *Roche* [*Products, Inc. v. Bolar Pharm. Co.*, 733 F.2d 858 (Fed.Cir. 1985)], that the experimental use defense is very narrow and strictly limited. In *Embrex*, we followed the teachings of *Roche* and *Pitcairn* [v. United States, 547 F.2d 1106 (Ct.Cl. 1976),] to hold that the defense was very narrow and limited to actions performed "for amusement, to satisfy idle curiosity, or for strictly philosophical inquiry." Further, use does not qualify for the experimental use defense when it is undertaken in the "guise of scientific inquiry" but has "definite, cognizable, and not insubstantial commercial purposes." The concurring opinion in Embrex expresses a similar view: use is disqualified from the defense if it has the "slightest commercial implication." Moreover, use in keeping with the legitimate business of the alleged infringer does not qualify for the experimental use defense. . . .

Cases evaluating the experimental use defense are few, and those involving non-profit, educational alleged infringers are even fewer. In [*Ruth v. Stearns-Roger Mfg. Co.*, 13 F.Supp. 697, 713 (D.Colo. 1935)], the court concluded that a manufacturer of equipment covered by patents was not liable for contributory infringement because the end-user purchaser was the Colorado School of Mines, which used the equipment in furtherance of its educational purpose. Thus, the combination of apparent lack of commerciality, with the non-profit status of an educational institution, prompted the court in *Ruth*, without any detailed analysis of the character, nature and effect of the use, to hold that the experimental use defense applied. This is not consistent with the binding precedent of our case law postulated by *Embrex*, *Roche* and *Pitcairn*.

Our precedent clearly does not immunize use that is in any way commercial in nature. Similarly, our precedent does not immunize any conduct that is in keeping with the alleged infringer's legitimate business, regardless of commercial implications. For example, major research universities, such as Duke, often sanction and fund research projects with arguably no commercial application whatsoever. However, these projects unmistakably further the institution's legitimate business objectives, including educating and enlightening students and faculty participating in these projects. These projects also serve, for example, to increase the status of the institution and lure lucrative research grants, students and faculty.

In short, regardless of whether a particular institution or entity is engaged in an endeavor for commercial gain, so long as the act is in furtherance of the alleged infringer's legitimate business and is not solely for amusement, to satisfy idle curiosity, or for strictly philosophical inquiry, the act does not qualify for the very narrow and strictly limited experimental use defense. Moreover, the profit or non-profit status of the user is not determinative.

In the present case, the district court attached too great a weight to the non-profit, educational status of Duke, effectively suppressing the fact that Duke's acts appear to be in accordance with any reasonable interpretation of Duke's legitimate business objectives. On remand, the district court will have to significantly narrow and limit its conception of the experimental use defense. The correct focus should not be on the non-profit status of Duke but on the legitimate business Duke is involved in and whether or not the use was solely for amusement, to satisfy idle curiosity, or for strictly philosophical inquiry.

FENN v. YALE UNIVERSITY
United States District Court for the District of Connecticut
283 F. Supp. 2d 615 (2003)

I. Findings of Fact

A. Introduction

John B. Fenn ("Dr. Fenn") is a leading scientific expert in the field of mass spectrometry, which determines the masses of atoms and molecules. Mass spectrometry has important uses in the development of medicines and the mapping of genes. In 1967, Dr. Fenn joined the faculty of Yale University ("Yale") as a tenured full professor. In 1987, as required by Yale's then-mandatory retirement policy, Dr. Fenn retired from his position as a full professor, but continued his work at Yale for another seven years as a "Professor Emeritus" and "Senior Research Scientist." In 1994, Dr. Fenn left Yale and became a research professor at Virginia Commonwealth University.

This case concerns a dispute between Yale and Dr. Fenn over an invention in the field of mass spectrometry which he developed while at Yale. In the following findings of fact, the Court will first address the various Yale policies that concern the inventions of its faculty members such as Dr. Fenn, then the particular policy that applied to him for this invention, then the particular invention here.

B. Yale's Patent Policy

From before Dr. Fenn joined its faculty, Yale's administrative policies have provided that patentable inventions resulting from a faculty member's research conducted at Yale belong to Yale and not the faculty member unless Yale expressly releases its interest in such inventions. These policies have also provided, though, that licensing royalties resulting from such inventions would be shared by Yale and the faculty member/inventor. After Dr. Fenn came to Yale in 1967, Yale made changes to its patent policy in 1975, 1984, 1988, and 1989, but these changes dealt primarily with the division of net licensing royalties between Yale and the inventor. The policy that inventions belong to Yale and not the inventor remained unchanged throughout Dr. Fenn's employment at Yale.

In 1967, when Dr. Fenn began his employment at Yale, the Faculty Handbook, dated July 1, 1966, contained provisions about Yale's patent policy with regard to inventions by its faculty members (the "1966 policy"). Pursuant to that policy, a faculty member was required to report to the university any invention resulting from "research conducted under University auspices or with the use of facilities under its control" and Yale owned the invention. The patent policy further stated that Yale did not typically keep title to patents resulting from those inventions; Yale arranged with the "Research Corporation" to carry out the patenting and commercializing of the inventions and to retain title to the subject patents. The policy also indicated that an inventor's share of any net royalty income from such inventions was "usually"

15%. The policy further stated that the University could abandon its interest in an invention and that in such circumstances, "the inventor is free to handle or dispose of his invention as he wishes." Dr. Fenn does not dispute that this patent policy applied to him.

On July 1, 1970, Yale prepared and distributed an updated Faculty Handbook with a section setting forth a patent policy identical to the 1966 policy. Subsequently, Dr. Fenn wrote a letter to Yale's Provost expressing his opinion that the inventor's share of royalty income provided by that patent policy was inadequate.

In 1974, the Yale Provost appointed a committee of faculty and administrators, including Dr. Fenn, to review the patent policy. The committee's work resulted in the 1975 patent policy, which increased the faculty member/inventor's share of net licensing royalties from 15% to 50%. The policy reiterated that all discoveries and inventions which result from "teaching, research, and other intellectual activity performed under University auspices" must be reported to Yale and provided that:

> [t]he [Yale] Treasurer shall refer inventions to Research Corporation or make other arrangements for evaluation of them in accordance with this policy. . . . In addition, the inventor may propose, even though the invention is one in the patenting or licensing of which the University wishes to participate, that the patenting of the invention or the licensing of the patent shall be arranged by the inventor at the inventor's expense, and if his proposal is accepted by the University, he shall proceed in accordance with an agreement to be made between the inventor and the University providing for such patenting or licensing by the inventor. Finally, if the University decides that although patenting or licensing of an invention is not contrary to University policy or the University does not wish to participate in the patenting or licensing, the University shall release to the inventor the University's interest in the invention, and the inventor shall be free to dispose of the invention as he wishes.

The 1975 patent policy also provided that it was "subject to revocation or amendment by the [Yale] corporation at any time." Dr. Fenn concedes that he was contractually bound by this 1975 patent policy.

In the early 1980s, a committee headed by Yale Professor Clement L. Markert ("the Markert Committee") was convened and charged with the task of reviewing the 1975 patent policy, faculty research sponsored by private entities, and commercial activities of faculty members. The Committee also recognized a need to re-examine the patent policy in light of the Bayh-Dole Act's changes in federal law and a shift in responsibilities from the Research Corporation to the Yale Office of Cooperative Research. Dr. Fenn served on the Markert Committee.

The Markert Committee produced a "Report of the Committee on Cooperative Research, Patents, and Licensing" ("the Markert Report"), setting forth specific recommendations, including changes to Yale's 1975 patent policy. The report's recommendations were embodied in a revised draft of the Faculty Handbook and a revised draft patent policy. Among other things, the

Markert Report recommended reducing the share of licensing royalties for faculty members set forth in its 1975 patent policy. In particular, the Markert Report provided that inventors should receive 30% of net royalty income up to $200,000 and 20% of net royalty income in excess of $200,000.

Professor Markert presented Yale's then-president, A. Bartlett Giamatti ("President Giamatti"), with a draft of the Markert Report by letter dated November 18, 1983. In that letter, Professor Markert indicated that the report "represents a consensus of diverse views held by members of the committee." In a reply letter dated November 28, 1983, President Giamatti thanked Professor Markert for the Committee's work and informed him that the Markert Report would be circulated to the faculty for their comments. President Giamatti wrote that "[a]s I receive comments, I will share them with you and the members of the committee. Sometime early in the next semester, having taken into account the advice of the faculty, I will take, with the Provost, the report to the [Yale] Corporation. My intention is to ask the Corporation to approve as university policy those relevant portions of the report." Subsequently, President Giamatti circulated the Markert Committee Report to faculty and research scientists. Dr. Fenn received a copy of the Markert Report.

On February 29, 1984, Dr. Fenn wrote to President Giamatti concerning the Committee's Report. Dr. Fenn wrote: "In the covering letter that accompanied the draft copy of the Report of the Committee on Cooperative Research, Patents and Licensing (CCRPL), Chairman Markert indicated that the views set forth comprised a consensus of the committee membership. Lest you harbor the illusion that this consensus was unanimous I write to record one member's dissent with respect to some of those views." Dr. Fenn's letter set forth his objections to the Markert Report, particularly taking exception to the Committee's recommendation to reduce the inventor's share of royalty income through licensing.

On March 10, 1984, the Yale Corporation "[v]oted, to accept in principle 'the Report of the Committee on Cooperative Research, Patent, and Licenses [the Markert Report].'" On March 23, 1984, President Giamatti responded to Dr. Fenn's February 29, 1984 letter in which he had objected to the Markert Report. In his letter, President Giamatti specifically told Dr. Fenn that "[t]he final draft has been approved by the Corporation in principle. The Report was modified in a few places, specifically with regard to copyright issues, in response to faculty comment." The draft patent policy dated March 6, 1984 became Yale's patent policy on March 10, 1984 through the approval of the Markert Report. As mentioned, that policy provided inventors with 30% of net royalty income achieved through licensing up to $200,000 and 20% of net royalty income in excess of $200,000. The policy also required that inventions be "reported promptly" to Yale and that Yale may release its interest to the inventor should it decide it does not wish and has no legal obligation to participate in the patenting or licensing of the invention. The 1984 policy, like the 1975 patent policy, specifically provided that it was "subject to revocation or amendment by the [Yale] corporation at any time."

In 1986, Yale prepared a revised edition of its Faculty Handbook which contained a section titled "Policy on Patents, Copyrights, and Licensing." The section indicated that a "full statement of the University policies on patent, copyrights, and licensing is available from the Office of the Provost, the Office of Cooperative Research, or the Office of Grant and Contract Administration." The section indicated that licensing royalties would be divided "in accord with the University patent policy," and reiterated that the patent policy required faculty to disclose "[a]ny potentially patentable invention or any potentially licensable computer program" to the Committee on Cooperative Research, Patent, and Licenses through the Office of the Director of Cooperative Research.

In June 1988, the Yale Corporation adopted a patent policy developed by the Committee on Cooperative Research, Patent, and Licenses and published the text of that policy in the October 10-17, 1988 Yale Weekly Bulletin and Calendar. The policy, consistent with the prior policies, stated that "all inventions . . . shall be reported promptly in writing to the provost through the director of the Office of Cooperative Research" and that "[i]f the University decides that it does not wish and has no legal obligation to participate in the patenting or licensing of an invention, the University may release to the inventor the University's interest in the invention, and the inventor shall then be free to dispose of the invention as he or she wishes." The 1988 policy continued the royalty sharing provisions set forth by the 1984 policy, providing 30% of net royalty income up to $200,000 to the inventor and 20% of net royalty income in excess of $200,000 to the inventor. The policy provided that it was effective as to "all inventions/discoveries made on or after June, 1988." It also provided that it was "subject to revocation or amendment by the [Yale] Corporation."

In October 1989, Yale published another patent policy which it indicated applied retroactively to "all inventions/discoveries made on or after June 1988." Like the policy set forth in the October 1988 bulletin, this policy stated that "all inventions . . . shall be reported promptly in writing to the Provost through the Director of the Office of Cooperative Research" and that "[i]f the University decides that it does not wish and has no legal obligation to participate in the patenting or licensing of an invention, the University may release to the inventor the University's interest in the invention, and the inventor shall then be free to dispose of the invention as he or she wishes." The 1989 policy changed the royalty sharing as follows: for the first $100,000, 50% to the inventor; for amounts between $100,000 and $200,000, 40% to the inventor; and for amounts exceeding $200,000, 30% to the inventor. Like all the policies since 1975, it provided that it was "subject to revocation or amendment by the [Yale] Corporation."

C. The Invention and Licensing of the '538 Patent

Prior to June 1988, Dr. Fenn, together with Matthias Mann and Chin-Kai Meng, Yale graduate students working with Dr. Fenn at Yale, invented a method for determining the molecular weight of particles through the use of multiply charged ions, which relates to the field of mass spectrometry. The research that led to that invention was conducted under Yale's auspices, on the Yale campus, and was funded by grants from the National Institutes of Health ("NIH") awarded to Yale.

Dr. Fenn first publicly disclosed this invention in San Francisco at the Annual Conference of the American Society for Mass Spectrometry ("ASMS") in June 1988. The paper he presented to the ASMS met the ASMS's novelty requirements because it demonstrated for the first time that the electrospray ionization process could produce ions from large molecules.

Fenn and others recognized the importance of the invention in medical diagnosis and treatment at the 1988 conference because it solved a "long-standing scientific problem" and was believed to "revolutionize the way that one could analyze peptides and proteins." Dr. Mann, Dr. Fenn's co-inventor, believed in 1988 that the invention was "revolutionary" and a "scientific breakthrough."

Dr. Fenn did not disclose the invention to Yale's Office of Cooperative Research ("OCR") in 1988. It was not until April 6, 1989 that Dr. Fenn submitted a completed invention disclosure form to the OCR regarding the invention. However, at least by the end of 1988, Dr. Fenn knew of the great importance of the invention and its commercial value. In his invention disclosure — which only generally and briefly summarized the invention — Dr. Fenn indicated that any patent application would have to be filed by June 1, 1989 — within one year of the patent's public disclosure at the San Francisco conference. He also noted that co-inventor Mann would be out of the country until May 15, 1989.

After the Yale OCR received Dr. Fenn's invention disclosure, Dr. Robert Bickerton ("Dr. Bickerton"), the head of the OCR, telephoned Dr. Fenn to find out more about the invention. Dr. Bickerton specifically inquired as to the potential commercial value of the invention. Dr. Fenn stated to Dr. Bickerton that he did not believe the invention had the potential for much commercial value because any patent issued on it would be a "use" patent as opposed to an "apparatus" patent and, as such, it would difficult to protect against its infringement. Dr. Fenn did not disclose that Pfizer Corporation, colleagues at the Yale Medical School and others had previously expressed a strong interest in the commercial viability of the invention. Dr. Fenn also did not disclose his own view, and the view of others, that the invention was in fact "revolutionary" or "important" and that it would likely have substantial commercial value.

Dr. Bickerton asked Dr. Fenn if Analytica of Branford, Inc. ("Analytica"), a company founded in 1987 to pursue electrospray technology by Dr. Fenn and Craig Whitehouse, one of Dr. Fenn's former graduate students, would be willing to pay for a patent application in return for Yale's commitment to license the invention to Analytica. As mentioned, Analytica was founded for the purpose of exploiting Dr. Fenn's two previous mass spectrometry inventions, which were owned by Yale, and Dr. Fenn was a 49% shareholder of Analytica. Though Dr. Fenn had already discussed the '538 invention with Mr. Whitehouse, also a 49% shareholder-owner of Analytica, he stated to Dr. Bickerton that he did not know if Analytica would be interested. Contrary to Dr. Fenn's representation to Dr. Bickerton, Dr. Fenn knew that Analytica was very much interested in the invention and its potential for commercial success.

On May 5, 1989, Dr. Bickerton called Dr. Fenn to discuss the invention again. When Dr. Bickerton noted that any patent application would have to be filed within a month, Dr. Fenn replied that he would be "up to his ears" preparing for several upcoming scientific conferences and that, beginning on May 20, 1989, he would be absent from the Yale campus for several weeks in Miami and Europe attending those conferences. Dr. Fenn stated that he was not scheduled to return from Europe until the end of June 1989, after the statutory deadline for filing a patent application had passed. Dr. Fenn did not tell Dr. Bickerton that co-inventor Meng was on the Yale campus during that same period of time and would be available to assist Yale with a patent application.

Dr. Fenn knew at that time that it would be difficult for Yale to prepare a patent application without his assistance in the limited time remaining. He also understood that he would have to assist Yale in preparing a patent application because information far beyond the inventors' disclosure document he gave the OCR would be needed for a proper patent application.

Yale did not file a patent application before the statutory deadline of June 1, 1989. In making this decision, Yale relied on Dr. Fenn's representations about the importance of the invention. Recognizing that Dr. Fenn was an expert in the technology, Yale accepted Dr. Fenn's statement that the invention and any resulting patent would have little commercial value. Dr. Fenn's representation that the invention was of limited value was very significant to the OCR staff and signaled that it should not expend its resources on a patent application.

In his own name and without Yale's knowledge, however, Dr. Fenn filed a patent application for the invention on May 19, 1989, which was financed by Analytica. In an October 19, 1989 letter to Provost Turner regarding the invention, Dr. Fenn continued to conceal from Yale that he had filed the patent application. Dr. Fenn testified that he did so in order to "let[ ] the scheme play out so the incompetence of [the OCR] would emerge." Dr. Fenn stated at trial:

> I ha[d] made a number of complaints to Yale, the fact that I thought that [OCR] was incompetent. And here was a case which I had filed a patent application, it had nothing further, and I thought we'll let it go because if it culminates in a patent this will be first rate evidence that I've been trying to convince Yale of for a long time that these guys over there weren't doing their job. . . . And I knew that if I, from Bickerton's previous behavior, confirmed by subsequent behavior, that if I had told him that I had filed a patent application at that time he would have immediately said, well, that belongs to Yale. And there would have been a confrontation. And if no patent issued, the confrontation would have been pointless but, moreover, if the patent didn't issue, then he'd be off the hook in a sense because he could say, well, I knew it wasn't going to result in a patent. So I was essentially making my case.

Dr. Fenn stated that he "was trying to show up how [the OCR] handled its business which in my view was incompetent."

Also in the fall of 1989, Dr. Henry Lowendorf of the Yale OCR, not knowing of Dr. Fenn's pending patent application, wrote to the NIH that "Yale is reporting an invention which was disclosed to NIH on 17 May 1989 to be unpatentable. . . . The invention is not patentable because enabling information on this invention was published in an abstract, enclosed, at a conference in June of 1988 and Yale did not file a patent application between the time the invention was disclosed to this Office, 6 April 1989, and the one year anniversary of disclosure." Dr. Fenn received a copy of Dr. Lowendorf's letter to NIH. Dr. Fenn knew that this letter was untrue, but he did nothing to correct Dr. Lowendorf's unintentional misrepresentation to the NIH that no patent application had been filed.

Without telling Yale, Dr. Fenn licensed the invention to Analytica on July 31, 1991. On July 14, 1992, United States Patent No. 5,130,538 ("the '538 patent") issued to Dr. Fenn for the "Method of Producing Multiply Charged Ions and for Determining Molecular Weights of Molecules By Use of the Multiply Charged Ions of Molecules." Dr. Fenn also failed to let Yale known of the issuance of the patent.

Yale first learned about the '538 patent when Aldo Test, an attorney for the Finnigan Corporation, wrote to Dr. Bickerton on January 20, 1993 inquiring about the possibility of licensing the '538 patent. Mr. Test explained in his letter that he had tracked the patent to Yale through its NIH grant number. Mr. Test also indicated that the patent had issued to Dr. Fenn, that Analytica claimed control over the licensing of the patent through its assignment from Dr. Fenn, and that Analytica had refused to sub-license the invention to Finnigan. Dr. Fenn received a copy of Mr. Test's letter.

Upon receiving Mr. Test's letter, Dr. Bickerton spoke with Dr. Fenn and forwarded to him a form asking him to assign the patent to Yale pursuant to the patent policy. The form was attached to a letter dated March 2, 1993, in which Dr. Bickerton wrote:

> As we discussed last month, the University recently became aware that you had filed a patent application, and obtained one or more patents, on an invention disclosed by you to my office in 1989. The invention was made by you and your students in the course of research at Yale funded by NIH . . . We have looked into the matter and concluded that Yale's patent policy requires that the invention and the patents be assigned to the University. Enclosed is a standard assignment agreement for your signature.

Yale's Committee on Cooperative Research, Patents and Licensing had determined that Yale was the rightful owner of the invention and '553 patent, and that Dr. Fenn should assign the patent to Yale. Dr. Fenn, nevertheless, refused to assign the patent to Yale.

Concerned with its ability to pursue infringers of the '538 patent because of the question whether its assignment from Dr. Fenn was valid, Analytica then asked Dr. Fenn to also assign the patent to Yale so that Yale could then license the patent to Analytica. Although Dr. Fenn "thought Analytica had a legitimate concern," he refused to assign the patent to Yale. Analytica then asked Yale for a license to any rights Yale possessed. In a meeting with

Dr. Bickerton, Mr. Whitehouse "emphasized the critical nature of the invention to his company and indicated that it was imperative that they have a license." In September 1993, Yale entered into a licensing agreement with Analytica granting Analytica a "worldwide exclusive license in and to any and all interest Yale has or may have in the licensed patents [i.e. '538 patent]."

Since January 30, 1997, Analytica has been paying into escrow amounts calculated pursuant to the royalty provisions of the Fenn-Analytica agreement to which Dr. Fenn would otherwise be entitled. Before Analytica began to deposit the royalties into the escrow accounts, it had paid out $302,435.16 in royalties to Dr. Fenn and his designees in accordance with the Fenn-Analytica license agreement. At the time of trial, the escrowed amounts through the third quarter of 2000 totaled $2,108,820.90. Analytica has been depositing in escrow only amounts calculated pursuant to the terms of the Fenn-Analytica agreement and has not also deposited additional amounts calculated pursuant to the Yale-Analytica agreement. Amounts calculated pursuant to the Yale-Analytica agreement total $1,717,975.92 of the $2,108,820.90 in escrow through the third quarter of 2000. Beginning in the first quarter of 1995, Analytica ceased making royalty payments to Yale. Up until that time, Analytica had paid Yale $43,011.30 pursuant to the Yale-Analytica license agreement. At the time of trial, the earned, but unpaid, royalties due Yale under the Yale-Analytica license amounted to $1,760,987.22.

[Based on these facts, Fenn alleged conversion, theft, tortious interference with business relationship, and violation of the Connecticut Unfair Trade Practices Act against Yale University. The University counterclaimed for breach of contract and fiduciary duty, fraud, negligent misrepresentation, conversion, theft, unjust enrichment, and unfair trade practice violations and sought an accounting of profits from Fenn on the '538 patent. The district court made the following determinations:]

Dr. Fenn's contributions to the science of mass spectrometry, including the invention that led to the '538 patent, are significant and beneficial to many. As evidenced by his receipt of the 2002 Nobel Prize for Chemistry, the invention that led to the '538 patent is one of far-reaching import and magnitude. Indeed, the Nobel Foundation stated that the invention has "revolutionized the development of new pharmaceuticals" and that "[p]romising applications are also being reported in other areas, for example foodstuff control and early diagnosis of breast cancer and prostate cancer." The Nobel Foundation, Press Release: The Nobel Prize in Chemistry 2002, at http:// www.nobel.se/chemistry/laureates/2002/press.html.

However, Dr. Fenn failed to promptly disclose the '538 invention to Yale, misrepresented its importance and commercial viability, and actively discouraged Yale from preparing and filing a patent application by the statutory deadline. At the same time, Dr. Fenn secretly prepared a patent application in his own name and licensed the '538 invention to Analytica without notifying Yale and the NIH. Those actions not only violated Dr. Fenn's obligations to Yale, but also violated Connecticut state law. Moreover, his actions were intentional and without justification.

Accordingly, the Court finds for the defendant and counter-plaintiff, Yale University, as indicated above. However, in order to fashion a judgment consistent with this memorandum of decision, the Court directs the parties to file supplemental papers.

Specifically, the Court hereby orders the parties to file proposed findings of fact with factual support and proposed orders concerning the relief requested by Yale. The parties shall address: (1) Yale's request for an accounting/assignment of the patent; (2) the amount of damages under the 1989 patent policy and how they should be awarded; and (3) whether punitive damages should be awarded and their amount, including proof as to reasonable attorney's fees. Those proposed findings and orders are due within thirty days of the date of this order. Both parties are also ordered to file memoranda regarding Yale's theft and conversion claims within thirty days.

2.   Federally Funded Research

UNIVERSITY OF ROCHESTER v. G.D. SEARLE, INC.
United States Court of Appeals for the Federal Circuit
358 F.3d 916 (2004)

[The University of Rochester owned a patent for a method of treating inflammation without undesirable side effects. In the infringement suit brought against G.D. Searle, the federal district court in the Western District of New York invalidated the patent. The Federal Circuit addressed the Bayh-Dole Act issues raised on appeal as follows:]

Rochester argues that "[t]he appealed decision vitiates universities' ability to bring pioneering innovations to the public," and that:

> Congress has determined that licensing of academia's inventions to industry is the best way to bring groundbreaking inventions to the public. See 35 U.S.C. § 200. By vesting in universities the patent rights to their federally funded research, the Bayh-Dole Act of 1980 encouraged "private industry to utilize government funded inventions through the commitment of the risk capital necessary to develop such inventions to the point of commercial application." H.R.Rep. No. 96-1307, pt. 1, at 3 (1980).

Further, amici the University of California and the University of Texas assert that "[t]his Court's decision will have a significant impact on the continuing viability of technology transfer programs at universities and on the equitable allocation of intellectual property rights between universities and the private sector."

That argument is unsound. The Bayh-Dole Act was intended to enable universities to profit from their federally-funded research. It was not intended to relax the statutory requirements for patentability. As pointed out by amicus Eli Lilly, "no connection exists between the Bayh-Dole Act and the legal standards that courts employ to assess patentability. Furthermore, none of the eight policy objectives of the Bayh-Dole Act encourages or condones less stringent application of the patent laws to universities than to other entities. See 35 U.S.C. § 200."

PUBLIC CITIZEN HEALTH RESEARCH GROUP v. NATIONAL INSTITUTES OF HEALTH
United States District Court for the District of Columbia
209 F. Supp. 2d. 37 (2002)

[A public interest group requested releases of patent royalty information from the National Institute of Health under the Freedom of Information Act. In rejecting the request, the Institute argued that compliance would interfere with the goals of the Bayh-Dole Act. The district court addressed the argument as follows:]

In this case, under the Bayh-Dole Act, Congress has directed federal agencies to use the patent system to promote inventions arising from federally supported research. 35 U.S.C. § 200 (2001) ("It is the policy and objective of the Congress to use the patent system to promote the utilization of inventions arising from federally supported research or development; to encourage maximum participation of small business firms in federally supported research and development efforts; to promote collaboration between commercial concerns and nonprofit organizations, including universities."). Thus, under the Bayh-Dole Act, the function of commercializing invention is left up to the private sector. Additionally, under the FTTA, Defendant is encouraged to work with private organizations to assign rights to a collaboration without going through the licensing regulation required by the Bayh-Dole Act.

The Court finds that if the royalty information were disclosed, the effectiveness of Defendant's licensing program would be impaired. Plaintiff first argues, without any support, that as there is no competitive harm in releasing this information, licensees will not stop working with the agency in order to collaborate on certain technologies. Additionally, Plaintiff contends that because Defendant offers a "treasure trove" of new technologies, there will always be potential licensees ready to partner with the agency. Plaintiff's arguments are wholly unsubstantiated and without merit.

TRINITY INDUSTRIES, INC. v. ROAD SYSTEMS, INC.
United States District Court for the Eastern District of Texas
235 F. Supp. 2d 536 (2002)

[Trinity Industries, Inc. had worked with Texas A&M University ["TAMU"] to develop a patent for a method of treating highway guardrail ends. In the infringement suit brought against Road Systems, Inc., the defendant alleged that the patent was invalid because of fraud on the patent office. The district court addressed the defense as follows:]

Defendants claim, and Plaintiffs admit, that TAMU did not disclose to the PTO that the federal government helped fund the research that led to the development of the '928 patent. . . . Therefore, the court must decide three issues: (1) whether TAMU was required to disclose the federal government's funding of the research leading to the '928 patent; (2) whether such funding and possible governmental rights were material to patentability; and (3) whether Defendants have presented sufficient evidence of TAMU's intent to deceive the PTO in order to prevail on the affirmative defense of inequitable conduct at the summary judgment stage.

The United States government has an interest in a patent developed under a "funding agreement". 35 U.S.C. § 202(c)(4) (also known as the "Bayh-Dole Act"). Defendants claim that the '928 patent was the product of a "funding agreement" and thus the federal government automatically had rights to the patent. Furthermore, Defendants claim TAMU had a statutory and contractual duty to disclose to the PTO the government's funding and consequential rights in the '928 patent. Plaintiffs contend that although federal funds were used to develop the '928 patent, there was no "funding agreement" to which TAMU was a party. Therefore, Plaintiffs argue that the federal government has no rights to the '928 patent and there was no duty to disclose the source of the funding. And, even if there were a duty to disclose, Plaintiffs' contend that the failure to do so is not inequitable conduct.

Within the specification of an application for a patent developed under a "funding agreement", there must be a statement specifying that the "invention was made with Government support and that the government has certain rights in the invention." 35 U.S.C. § 202(c)(6). In order to determine if there was a duty to disclose in the instant case, the court must first determine if federal funding went into the development of the '928 patent pursuant to a "funding agreement" as used in the Bayh-Dole Act:

> The term "funding agreement" means any contract, grant, or cooperative agreement entered into between any Federal Agency, other than the Tennessee Valley Authority, and any contractor for the performance of experimental, developmental, or research work funded in whole or in part by the federal government. Such term includes any assignment, substitution of parties, or subcontract of any type entered into for the performance of experimental, developmental, or research work under a funding agreement as herein defined. 35 U.S.C. § 201(b).

Under the Act, a "contractor" is "any person, small business firm, or non-profit organization that is a party to a funding agreement." 35 U.S.C. § 201(c) (emphasis added). The Act grants the funding federal agency a "nonexclusive, nontransferable, irrevocable, paid-up license to practice or have practiced for or on behalf of the United States any subject invention throughout the world." 35 U.S.C. § 202(c)(4) (emphasis added). A "subject invention" is "any invention of the contractor conceived or first actually reduced to practice in the performance of work under a funding agreement." 35 U.S.C. § 201(e). Thus, if TAMU, a non-profit organization, received funds from the Federal Highway Administration ("FHwA"), a federal agency, through the terms of a subcontract with the Texas Department of Transportation ("TxDOT"), in order to develop the '928 patent, a subject invention, the federal government automatically had an irrevocable license to the '928 patent, and TAMU had a statutory duty to disclose the existence of those rights during the patent application process.

FHwA, a federal agency within the United States Department of Transportation, provided money to the Texas State Department of Highways and Public Transportation in 1985 and 1986. The agreements under which the federal money was given by the federal agency to TxDOT are "funding agreements". *See* 35 U.S.C. § 201(b). TxDOT, in turn, used that federal money to fund research projects at the Texas Transportation Institute ("TTI") to develop guardrail end treatment technology. Between September 1, 1985 and August 31, 1987, TxDOT provided TTI with $216,608.92 for the guardrail end treatment project. The funding of the specific guardrail end treatment project described in the 1985 Study Proposal Agreement was made pursuant to the more general research agreement embodied in the 1985 Cooperative Research Agreement between TxDOT and TAMU.

Thus, funding was given by the federal government through its agency, FHwA, to TxDOT in order to conduct research. TxDOT forwarded a part of those funds to TAMU in order to develop new guardrail end treatment technology. The '928 patent resulted from the research. The 1985 Study Proposal Agreement and the 1985 Cooperative Research Agreement are "subcontracts" as used in 35 U.S.C. § 201(b). Therefore, a "nonexclusive, nontransferable, irrevocable, paid-up license" arose pursuant to the Bayh-Dole Act. See 35 U.S.C. § 202(c)(4). Furthermore, a contractual right to an interest in the patent arose from the 1985 Cooperative Agreement. The language of paragraph IV.(a) mirrors the language of the statute.

Because TAMU can accurately be labeled a "contractor" due to its status as a party to a "funding agreement", Section 202(c)(6) and the Manual of Patent Examining Procedures Section 310 issued by the PTO required the disclosure of the federal government's rights during the prosecution of the '928 patent. See 35 U.S.C. § 202(c)(6); Manual of Patent Examining Procedure § 310.

Plaintiffs did not disclose, as required, the government funding or the United States' rights in the '928 patent during the prosecution process. Defendants assert that this nondisclosure is "concealment" that amounts to sufficient inequitable conduct to preclude the Plaintiffs' ability to enforce the '928 patent against alleged infringement.

Parties before the PTO are charged with a duty to disclose information material to patentability:

> [I]nformation is material to patentability when it is not cumulative to information already of record or being made of record in the application, and (1) It establishes, by itself or in combination with other information, a prima facie case of unpatentability of a claim; or (2) It refutes, or is inconsistent with, a position the applicant takes in: (i) Opposing an argument of unpatentability relied on by the Office, or (ii) Asserting an argument of patentability. 37 C.F.R. § 1.56(b).

Information is "material" when there is a "substantial likelihood that a reasonable examiner would have considered the information important in deciding whether to allow the application to issue as a patent." To be material, the information must be the type that a reasonable examiner would consider in allowing the patent.

Although Defendants concede that most findings of inequitable conduct have involved the omission of prior art, they have failed to link the nondisclosure in the instant case to patentability. Even if TAMU had a duty to disclose the information, and it breached that duty by failing to disclose, Defendants have presented nothing more to show how the omission has affected the patent examiner's decision to accept or reject TAMU's patent application. Defendants have offered no evidence, other than the mere breach of a duty, to establish that Plaintiffs failed to disclose material information. Defendants have shown that Plaintiffs failed to disclose information, but the court finds the information to be less than material. Defendants have not even suggested that the information regarding funding and the government's subsequent rights would possibly cause an examiner to deny the patent. Had the information been disclosed, it would not have been considered by the examiner, because the funding information does not have a logical relationship to the decision on whether or not to issue the '928 patent.

Similarly, Defendants offer no proof to support their conclusory statement that Plaintiffs intentionally deceived the PTO. While Defendants do not need to present direct evidence of intent, they do need to present sufficient evidence to allow an inference of wrongful intent from the surrounding circumstances. [*Baxter Int'l, Inc. v. McGaw, Inc.*, 149 F.3d 1321, 1329 (Fed.Cir.1998)]. There must be clear and convincing evidence that the Plaintiffs made a deliberate decision to withhold a known material reference. Due to the court's conclusion that the information in question was not material, it is impossible for the Defendants to clear the high burden required on this issue at the summary judgment stage.

Defendants have not presented sufficient evidence of materiality and intent to deceive the PTO to warrant summary judgment in their favor on the affirmative defense of unenforceability due to inequitable conduct.

3. Federal Government

EMBREX, INC. v. SERVICE ENGINEERING CORP.
United States Court of Appeals for the Federal Circuit
216 F.3d 1343 (2000)

Embrex is the exclusive licensee of the '630 patent from the United States Government under the Bayh-Dole Act. A scientist at the U.S. Department of Agriculture developed the patented technology. The '630 patent claims methods for inoculating birds against disease by injecting vaccines into a specified region of the egg before hatching. In its commercial application, the claimed invention immunizes chickens in ovo, i.e., while they are still in the egg. Thus, the claimed method reduces the risk that chickens will succumb to infections that often infect an entire flock. This method represents an advance over the prior art method, which inoculated several days after hatching, leaving the chicks unprotected. . . .

Upon obtaining its license to the '630 patent, Embrex began designing machines to perform the claimed method in large scale industrial chicken farms. After learning of Embrex's products, Service Engineering Corporation ["SEC"] attempted to interest Embrex in using its device for automatically transferring eggs from egg-supporting flats to hatching trays about three quarters of the way through the incubation period. SEC also expressed to Embrex its interest in manufacturing Embrex's in ovo injection machines. Embrex rebuffed SEC's advances. SEC then contacted two other companies about collaborating to design around the '630 patent. Embrex sued SEC and its collaborators for infringement of the '630 patent. That litigation resulted in a settlement agreement, and a dismissal of the infringement suit.

Despite this history, SEC continued its attempts to build an in ovo injection machine. SEC developed a prototype device, and engaged the services of two scientists to investigate the possibility of injecting chicken embryos outside the region covered by the '630 patent claims. Dr. Vergil Davis suggested that the embryos could be inoculated by injecting vaccine into the chorioallantoic sac (CAS), a part of the egg not mentioned in the '630 claims. Mr. Bounds and Dr. Davis experimented to determine whether they could target the CAS by injecting India ink into several eggs. To address the difficulty of injecting into the CAS, Mr. Bounds devised a test stand to reliably inject into predetermined depths beneath the shell of the egg.

SEC also retained Dr. Rosenberger, a professor at the University of Delaware. SEC gave Dr. Rosenberger the test stand, with which he performed several tests to determine the practicability of injection into the CAS. These tests injected India ink into some eggs and vaccine into others. The India ink tests sought to target the CAS, whereas the vaccine tests sought to evaluate the effectiveness of the inoculations. According to the trial record, the Rosenberger tests showed that the injected embryos received little immunity, and that most injections penetrated beyond the CAS and into the amnion/yolk sac — areas covered by the '630 patent.

While preparing its prototype and performing tests, SEC began soliciting orders for its in ovo injection device. Specifically, Embrex alleges that SEC offered to sell its machines to Hudson Foods in the U.S. and Courvoir Dufo in Canada, effectively depriving Embrex of the sales.

Upon learning of SEC's testing and its attempts to market the nascent in ovo injection device, Embrex again sued SEC. Embrex's suit alleged willful infringement of the '630 patent. . . . The district court . . . granted Embrex's summary judgment motion on SEC's defense that Embrex did not have standing to sue for infringement of the '630 patent because its license from the U.S. government violated the Bayh-Dole Act. . . .

SEC appeals the district court's grant of Embrex's motion to dismiss SEC's defense, which challenged the government's grant of the exclusive license to Embrex, which in turn gave Embrex standing to sue for infringement. . . . The district court determined that the standing defense was precluded by res judicata, in view of the consent judgment in prior litigation between the parties. That consent judgment incorporated by reference the parties' settlement agreement. That agreement stated, "Embrex has standing as exclusive licensee under the '630 patent." . . . [A]ssuming that the district court erred in granting Embrex's motion to dismiss, this court concludes that the same issues have been fully litigated in another case. Before the district court's entry of judgment in this case, SEC filed suit in the United States District Court for the District of Maryland, challenging the government's grant of the exclusive license under the '630 patent to Embrex. In [*Service Eng'g Corp. v. United States*, No. CCB-97-833 (D.Md. Mar. 30, 1999)], SEC challenged the original grant of the exclusive license to Embrex as well as the subsequent amendments thereto. In a well reasoned thirty-page opinion, the Maryland district court addressed and disposed of each of SEC's assertions, ruling against SEC on every issue. Because SEC has had a full and fair opportunity to litigate the standing issue at least once, this court will not disturb the judgment of the North Carolina district court dismissing the standing defense.

4. State Government

UNIVERSITY OF COLORADO FOUNDATION, INC. v. AMERICAN CYANAMID CO.

United States Court of Appeals for the Federal Circuit
196 F.3d 1366 (1999)

Materna 1.60 (Materna) is a prenatal multivitamin/mineral supplement produced and sold by Lederle Laboratories, a division of Cyanamid. In 1981, Cyanamid began selling a reformulation of Materna. The reformulated product improved iron absorption over the previous version of the product. Cyanamid filed a patent application claiming the reformulation. The application named Dr. Leon Ellenbogen, a Cyanamid chemist, as the inventor. The '634 patent issued from this application in 1984.

[Doctors at The University of Colorado] first learned of the '634 patent in 1993. The University and the Doctors then brought suit in federal district court against Cyanamid and Dr. Ellenbogen. That lawsuit alleged (1) that the Doctors (who were medical researchers at the University of Colorado Health Sciences Center) invented the reformulation of Materna covered by the '634 patent claims and communicated the invention to Dr. Ellenbogen, (2) that Dr. Ellenbogen intentionally omitted the Doctors as co-inventors in the patent application, and (3) that Cyanamid intentionally hid the patent from the Doctors.

In response, Cyanamid asserted that Dr. Ellenbogen hired the Doctors to perform research that convinced Cyanamid to reformulate Materna. According to Cyanamid, the Doctors transmitted the results of their research to Cyanamid with the intention that Cyanamid would reformulate Materna and thereby profit. Cyanamid further asserted that Dr. Ellenbogen was the true inventor. Consequently, Cyanamid argued that it had no duty to notify the Doctors of the patent and denied any liability to the University. The district court granted summary judgment to Cyanamid on the § 256 claim refusing to substitute the Doctors as the named inventors on the '634 patent. The district court also granted summary judgment to Cyanamid, denying the University's claims of patent infringement and ownership of equitable title to the '634 patent. The district court also granted summary judgment to the University on copyright infringement. Specifically, the district court found that four bar graphs and a table in the Doctors' published article were copyrightable subject matter and copied by Cyanamid into the patent application.

Following a bench trial, the district court found that the Doctors invented the Materna reformulation and that Dr. Ellenbogen was not an inventor of that composition. To determine inventorship, the district court applied state common law, rather than federal patent law. . . .

[The Federal Circuit reversed the district court on its finding of inventorship and addressed the issue as follows:]

Field preemption describes exclusive regulation of a legal subject by federal law. To preempt a field, federal law must evince "a scheme of federal regulation so pervasive" that no room remains for a state to supplement. Alternatively, federal law preempts a field by addressing a "federal interest . . . so dominant that the federal system will be assumed to preclude enforcement of state laws on the same subject."

A primary purpose of patent law is to reward invention. The law of inventorship, which has heretofore developed solely under federal law, supports this purpose by identifying the actual inventors of an invention eligible for patent protection. With its advent in Article 1 of the Constitution, patent law has developed under federal law to achieve the objective of national uniformity.

An independent inventorship standard under state law would likely have different requirements and give rise to different remedies than federal patent law. A different state inventorship standard might grant property rights to an individual who would not qualify as an inventor under federal patent law, or might grant greater relief to inventors than is afforded by federal patent law. Either situation might frustrate the dual federal objectives of rewarding inventors and supplying uniform national patent law standards.

The federal Patent Act leaves no room for states to supplement the national standard for inventorship. Title 35 contains explicit and detailed standards for inventorship. *See, e.g.,* 35 U.S.C. §§ 101-03, 116-20, 254-56, 261-62 (1994). Moreover, federal law has provided this court with jurisdiction to enforce these comprehensive provisions to provide a uniform national standard for inventorship. *See In re Snap-On Tools Corp.,* 720 F.2d 654, 655, 220 U.S.P.Q. 8, 9 (Fed.Cir.1983). Therefore, the field of federal patent law preempts any state law that purports to define rights based on inventorship. Consequently, this court vacates the district court's conclusion that the Doctors were the inventors of reformulated Materna and that Dr. Ellenbogen was not the inventor. Upon remand, the court must apply federal patent law principles to determine whether the Doctors and/or Dr. Ellenbogen were inventors of the technology of the '634 patent.

[The Federal Circuit addressed the copyright issue as follows:]

The district court found that Cyanamid copied Figures 1-4 and Table 1 of the Doctors' journal article into the patent application. Because these depictions of data in the Figures and Table were protectable expressions under the copyright statute, the district court determined that Cyanamid infringed the Doctors' copyright in the article. However, the district court concluded that the University did not prove any damages from the copyright infringement.

The University argues that its proof of Cyanamid's gross revenues from sales of reformulated Materna shifted the burden of proof to Cyanamid under 17 U.S.C. § 504(b) (1994) to prove deductible expenses and to prove those elements of its profits that were attributable to factors other than copyright infringement. The University's argument presumes that the sales of reformulated Materna were due to Cyanamid's copyright infringement. The University had the burden to show this connection. See 4 Melville B. Nimmer and David Nimmer, Nimmer on Copyright § 14.03[A] (1999) (noting that plaintiff's claims for indirect profits rarely succeed). The district court found that the University did not meet this burden. This court detects no clear error in this finding. This court therefore affirms the district court's decision.

XECHEM INTERN., INC. v. UNIV. OF TEX. M.D. ANDERSON CANCER CENTER
United States Court of Appeals for the Federal Circuit
382 F.3d 1324 (2004)

PAULINE NEWMAN, Circuit Judge

Xechem International, Inc., a biopharmaceutical company, brought suit against the University of Texas M.D. Anderson Cancer Center and the Board of Regents of the University of Texas System (collectively "the University") in the United States District Court, raising several federal and state counts arising from a collaborative project between Xechem and the University. In response to the complaint the University asserted its Eleventh Amendment and state immunity from suit, and the United States District Court for the Southern District of Texas granted the University's motion to dismiss on the pleadings. . . . The only issue on appeal is whether the University is subject to suit in federal court to obtain correction of the inventorship of United States Patents No. 5,877,205 and 6,107,333, the patents flowing from the project.

We affirm the dismissal, for Supreme Court precedent controls the arguments raised by Xechem with respect to waiver or abrogation of the University's Eleventh Amendment immunity.

BACKGROUND

The basic facts are generally undisputed: Xechem and the University in 1995 entered into a Sponsored Laboratory Study Agreement, with financial and technical support by Xechem, for the purpose of developing a pharmaceutical formulation that would enhance the solubility and thereby the effectiveness of the cancer drug paclitaxel. The persons principally involved in the project were Dr. Ramesh C. Pandey, president and CEO of Xechem; Dr. Luben K. Yankov, a scientist employed by Xechem; and Dr. Borje S. Andersson and Dr. Elias Anaissie, scientists employed by the University.

The complaint states that a successful formulation was developed, and that Xechem prepared a patent application naming Dr. Pandey of Xechem and Dr. Andersson of the University as joint inventors, and in early 1996 sent the draft application to the University. The University objected to the designation of inventorship, and on June 28, 1996 the University filed a patent application in the United States Patent and Trademark Office, naming Dr. Andersson as sole inventor. . . .

On August 18, 1997 Xechem and the University entered into a Patent and Technology License Agreement whereby Xechem received the exclusive worldwide license to manufacture and market these paclitaxel formulations, and

Xechem agreed to pay certain continuing sums and a royalty. Xechem also agreed to pay the costs of obtaining the patents in the United States and foreign countries. The University's patent application issued as the '205 patent on March 2, 1999, and a divisional application, also naming Dr. Andersson as sole inventor, issued as the '333 patent on August 22, 2000. Both patents were assigned by Dr. Andersson to the University.

On February 15, 2000 Xechem was notified that the University considered the License Agreement to have terminated automatically no later then December 31, 1998, due to Xechem's alleged insolvency, and that any use of this technology by Xechem was deemed to be patent infringement. Xechem then filed suit in federal court, presenting several counts sounding in tort and contract and also seeking correction of inventorship and a declaration of non-infringement. Xechem stated that Dr. Pandey made a mistake when he acquiesced in the naming of Dr. Andersson as sole inventor, and asked the court to determine the correct inventorship. Apparently upon the University's claim of sovereign immunity from state as well as federal action, the state law tort and contract counts were withdrawn by Xechem. This appeal relates only to the dismissal, on Eleventh Amendment grounds, of the inventorship correction claim.

DISCUSSION

The University of Texas is deemed to be an arm of the State of Texas, and Xechem does not dispute that the University is properly accorded Eleventh Amendment immunity.

The Supreme Court has addressed Eleventh Amendment immunity as it pertains to violation of federal patent and trademark laws. In *Florida Prepaid Postsecondary Education Expense Board v. College Savings Bank,* 527 U.S. 627, 119 S.Ct. 2199, 144 L.Ed.2d 575 (1999) and *College Savings Bank v. Florida Prepaid Postsecondary Education Expense Board,* 527 U.S. 666, 119 S.Ct. 2219, 144 L.Ed.2d 605 (1999), the Court invalidated the legislative abrogation of state immunity from suit under these laws. In *Florida Prepaid*, the Court ruled that the Eleventh Amendment was violated by the Patent and Plant Variety Protection Remedy Clarification Act of 1992). . . . The Court held that Eleventh Amendment immunity may be abrogated "only where the State provides no remedy, or only inadequate remedies, to injured patent owners for its infringement of their patent could a deprivation of property without due process result," thereby invoking the Fourteenth Amendment. The Court also referred to lack of a "pattern of patent infringement by the States," in suggesting that legislative remedy had not been shown to be necessary. . . .

Xechem argues that the University waived its Eleventh Amendment immunity when it entered into this collaborative research agreement, and further waived its immunity by contracting with Xechem in the License Agreement for purposes of commercial gain. Xechem argues that by entering into these contractual and commercial arrangements the University waived objection to federal court jurisdiction to secure constitutionally protected property rights, and for issues that can be decided only in federal court under preemptive federal statutes. . . .

In [*Parden v. Terminal Railway of the Alabama State Docks Department*, 377 U.S. 184, 84 S.Ct. 1207, 12 L.Ed.2d 233 (1964)] the Court had relied on the Commerce Clause to hold that when a state voluntarily enters into federally regulated activity — in *Parden*, operating a railroad — the state is deemed to have consented to federal jurisdiction arising from that activity, in that case an action under the Federal Employers' Liability Act. In overruling *Parden*'s constructive waiver, the Court stressed in College Savings that a state's waiver of Eleventh Amendment rights cannot be imposed or implied based on a state's entry into commerce, but must be founded on a "clear declaration" by the state of its intent to submit to federal jurisdiction. Such a declaration was not made by the University in entering into its various relationships and contracts with Xechem. . . .

Xechem also argues that the University constructively consented to federal jurisdiction by causing its employee Dr. Andersson to apply for United States patents. Xechem argues that the University made a clear and voluntary waiver of immunity when it entered the Patent and Trademark Office and sought its legal benefits, and that the University cannot both obtain patents and "hide behind the Constitution." . . .

Xechem also argues that a state's invocation of the authority of the PTO to grant patents is analogous to the state's invocation of federal authority to enforce its patent rights at state initiative, the latter clearly serving to waive Eleventh Amendment immunity. Such analogy does not withstand scrutiny, for waiver must be clear, explicit, and voluntary, and cannot be imposed on a state that has not voluntarily entered federal jurisdiction. Thus the argument must be rejected that a state's entry into the patent system is a constructive waiver of immunity for actions in federal court against the state under the patent law. . . .

Xechem also argues that the grant of a patent is a "gift or gratuity" by the government, whereby acceptance of the grant is a constructive waiver of immunity. The Court confirmed in *Petty* and again in *Dole* that Congress can condition receipt of federal funds on a commensurate waiver of state immunity. However, in College Savings the Court explained that such conditions on federal disbursements are "simply not analogous to *Parden-style* conditions attached to a State's decision to engage in otherwise lawful commercial activity." . . .

Patent activity is commercial activity, not governmental beneficence. The holdings of [*Seminole Tribe of Florida v. Florida*, 517 U.S. 44, 116 S.Ct. 1114, 134 L.Ed.2d 252 (1996)], and the overruling of *Parden*, have foreclosed the broad ruling that by obtaining patents the state constructively waived its Eleventh Amendment immunity as to any federal proceeding involving those patents. . . .

AFFIRMED.

NEWMAN, Circuit Judge, additional views.

I write separately to state my concern lest the caveats and safeguards recognized by the Supreme Court in its rulings in *Florida Prepaid* and *College Savings* become submerged in generalizations of absolute state immunity. The Court observed in *Florida Prepaid* that if no state court remedy were available for patent infringement, such failure of recourse could raise the due process concerns of the Fourteenth Amendment. Although Xechem is here seeking judicial, not legislative, relief, its due process claims on the ground that there is no alternative remedy have not been fully explored.

In *Florida Prepaid*, the Court, discussing abrogation of Eleventh Amendment immunity, stated that "only where the State provides no remedy, or only inadequate remedies, to injured patent owners for its infringement of their patent could a deprivation of property without due process result." . . . Throughout the evolution of Eleventh Amendment jurisprudence the Court has stressed the rigor of the restraint imposed by the Fourteenth Amendment on the federal government as well as on the states. Thus the Court found in *Florida Prepaid* that patent infringement by states did not appear to be a sufficiently prevalent national problem to warrant § 5 abrogation. And in College Savings the Court held that unfair competition by a state based on false advertising did not raise a Fourteenth Amendment property issue; the Court observed that general business interests are not property rights, and held that while trademarks are constitutionally protected property, false advertising has no relation to the right to exclude and does not raise a constitutional issue. The Court recognized, however, that "the assets of a business . . . unquestionably are property, and any state taking of these assets is unquestionably a 'deprivation' under the Fourteenth Amendment."

Xechem has asserted that in this case inventorship controls ownership and the right to practice the patented invention — fundamentals of patent property. Xechem's claim on its face raises issues of property and due process. The Court explained in *Florida Prepaid* that "[i]n procedural due process claims, the deprivation by state action of a constitutionally protected interest . . . is not in itself unconstitutional; what is unconstitutional is the deprivation of such an interest without due process of law." However, the Court in *Florida Prepaid* required a showing — more than an allegation — of the unavailability of adequate remedy in state court. Although Xechem argues that only federal courts can order a change of inventorship, precedent has not dealt with whether state courts are precluded from resolving issues of ownership of patent property when ownership is based on inventorship.

In *Florida Prepaid* the Court noted that patent infringement by the state might be remedied in state court on the traditional state law grounds of taking of property or conversion, observing that a factor in the due process provision of the Fourteenth Amendment is whether any remedy is otherwise available. However, precedent establishes no ready rule as to when the nature of the wrong and remedy warrant recourse to the Fourteenth Amendment. On the record before us, and the premises of Rule 12(b)(6), the question of alternative remedy was not explored. We are told that various state law counts were withdrawn from the complaint in the district court; however, the potential presence of other issues does not avoid this dismissal on the pleadings. These questions are not resolved by today's decision. . . .

The circumstances of this case illustrate that when a state is charged with contravention of federal law in a way that directly affects private property, and if no remedy is indeed available within the state's tribunals — whether by the state's invocation of immunity or by federal preemption of the cause of action — there can arise an affront to the fundamentals of due process. Respect for the principles of federalism does not automatically immunize the state from due process considerations. The Court in *Florida Prepaid* kept this door ajar. I write to the same purpose, for there is an increasing urgency, as the states enter the private competitive arena governed by the laws of intellectual property, to establish fair relationships and just recourse.

NOTES & QUESTIONS

1. The materials in this subsection illustrate the legal issues raised by university-industry-government collaborations. Many of these issues are raised throughout the Digital Ignition narrative and arise specifically in the context of the hypothetical meeting between Dr. See and the potential investors. In synthesizing these readings think of the concerns that a potential investor in Digital Ignition may have.

2. First, why might an investor be concerned about any agreements between Dr. See and a university that he has spoken to or collaborated with? Does the Federal Circuit's decision in *Madey* alleviate any of these concerns? Do you think the narrow view of experimental use adopted by the Federal Circuit helps or hurt private industry? Do you think the Federal Circuit's decision reduces or increases incentives for university-industry collaboration? Does the court's decision in *Fenn* aid or hinder university-industry collaboration? How would you address the concerns of potential investors in inventions that arose from university-industry collaboration in light of *Madey* and *Fenn*?

3. The Bayh-Dole Act provided a major impetus for university-industry collaboration as the three excerpted cases illustrate. What issues do you think a potential investor will have in light of Bayh-Dole? What specific obligations does the Bayh-Dole Act impose on patent applicants?

4. Both federal and state governments are key players in the process of acquiring and licensing intellectual property. As the *Embrex* case illustrates, the federal government can own patents and the Bayh-Dole Act governs how these patents can be licensed to private individuals. *The University of Colorado* and *The University of Texas* cases illustrate the role of state governments, particularly state universities as players. Do you think better contracting and internal policies would have avoided the dispute in *The University of Colorado* case? If so, how would you draft these policies? Would these policies run the risk of being pre-empted by federal law?

5. State sovereign immunity from suits for intellectual property infringement clearly affects the balance between private industry and state governments in the innovation process. Discuss the arguments for and against waiver in *The University of Texas* case. As a legal matter, which side has the better argument? Which side is more persuasive as a matter of social or business policy? How does sovereign immunity affect the discussion of university-industry collaborations as illustrated by *Madey* and *Fenn*? Notice that private universities do not have the immunity. Does this absence of immunity for private universities alter in any way the dynamics of university-industry collaboration discussed in note (2) above?

G.   PATENTING METHODS OF DOING BUSINESS

Brian M. Buroker, Business Method Patents: They are Not Just for Dotcom Companies Anymore
16(9) J. Proprietary Rights 1 (2004)*

General Motors, TV Guide, Nintendo, Pharmacia, and Johnson & Johnson. These companies share common traits, some of which may be surprising. Each was a successful company well before the dotcom boom. Each was awarded at least one so-called business-method patent from the US Patent and Trademark Office (PTO) in the past three years.

Some readers will be surprised to learn that such venerable companies are pursuing patents in an area that many still consider controversial. . . . [F]ew companies have adapted their intellectual property strategy to include patents on the very business methods that differentiate those companies from their competitors. While many reasons contribute to companies' failure to file for business-method patents, the most common explanation is the misperception that business-method patents are only for companies whose name ends with "dotcom."

Bringing Business-Method Patents into the Business World's Consciousness

The origin of this misconception can be traced to the lawsuit Amazon.com filed against BarnesandNoble.com. That lawsuit received widespread press coverage in the mainstream and business communities, raising awareness of business-method patents in the business community. As a result, in 1999, Amazon.com's so-called one-click patent became the center of the debate over the propriety of patents for business methods. Just one year earlier, in early 1998, the US Court of Appeals for the Federal Circuit cleared the way for Amazon's suit with its *State Street Bank v. Signature Financial Services* ruling. Specifically, the *State Street* decision held that business methods, just as many other types of methods, were patentable. Amazon.com's patent infringement action against its online book-selling competitor BarnesandNobel.com was the first highly publicized, post-State Street lawsuit involving a so-called business-method patent. Other business-method patents receiving scrutiny included those issued to Priceline.com and Coolsavings.com.

As in the past when the concept of patenting software and genes was "new," the thought of allowing patents business methods sparked a vigorous debate. Meanwhile, the number of patents on business methods filed with the PTO skyrocketed. Congress weighed in with several proposed legislative initiatives. The PTO held open forums and eventually implemented additional levels of review for business-method patents. Intellectual property bar organizations voiced their opinions.

---

* Reprinted/Adapted with the permission of Aspen Law & Business, from Brian M. Buroker, "Business Method Patents: They Are Not Just for Dotcom Companies Anymore," 16(9) J. Proprietary Rights 1 Copyright 2004.

Now, more than four years later, the PTO issues another group of business-method patents each Tuesday. Congressional initiatives on business-method patents have stalled. The public PTO hearings are over. The press on business-method patents has quieted. Business-method patents are here to stay for the foreseeable future. Nevertheless, despite the availability of business-method patents to all industries, the public still associates business-method patents with dotcom companies. Practitioners still frequently hear, "I thought patents on business methods are just for Internet companies." That misperception has lead many companies to forego patent protection on some of their most valuable intellectual property — their new business methods.

Hesitation to File Business-Method Patents Could Cost Dearly

While some Fortune 500 companies such as General Motors, Baxter International, Pharmacia, and Becton Dickinson seized the opportunity and began filing business-method patent applications with the PTO, a stay-the-course mentality pervades at many others. To this day, many companies develop new methods of doing business at tremendous expense to their bottom line, yet fail to seek patent protection to protect that investment. While it is hard to imagine that any publicly traded company would ever develop a new product without seeking expansive patent protection, those same companies spend millions developing and honing their business methods only to have their competitors copy and adopt those business methods for a fraction of the cost.

If success of a US business in the future economy will depend on the strength of its intellectual capital, as many economists opine, then the companies that build up their valuable intellectual capital, including protection of their innovative business methods, stand a greater chance of success in the future. Those companies that refuse to change may wonder how they allowed their competitors to copy their innovative business methods without any recourse. Worse, they may be foreclosed from a potentially profitable business because a competitor patented its business methods. When that happens in this era of corporate scrutiny, shareholders will wonder who was responsible for failing to protect a valuable corporate asset and why their company did not have valuable business-method patents as leverage to keep them in that line of business. Failure to protect valuable business methods may eventually be considered tantamount to a failure to protect corporate assets.

Although the business method patent era is only beginning to play out, historically, those companies that have been slow to pursue patents in areas that were considered "controversial" have paid in the long run. Just as many companies today may be heard saying that "no one in our business files business method patents," back in the 1980s, Microsoft could be heard saying that software patents would never play a factor in their business either.

At that time, another vigorous debate raged over whether computer software should be patentable. Despite many US Supreme Court and other appellate court decisions approving patents on software, the software industry generally scoffed at patent protection for software, including the largest software company of all — Microsoft.

Although Microsoft filed a few token patent applications in the 1980s, a huge jury award changed its view on software patents forever. In 1994, a federal court jury returned a verdict for more than $132 million, largely due to Microsoft's infringement of a software patent owned by a small software company called Stac Electronics. Unlike many of the bigger players in the software industry, Stac had read the Federal Circuit's decisions and pursued patent protection for its valuable data compression software. That huge verdict and potential injunction against a key component to Microsoft's platform product, its Windows operating system, resulted in a settlement between Stac and Microsoft. More importantly, however, it resulted in Microsoft's changing its entire corporate philosophy. Whereas prior to 1990 Microsoft has received a mere eight patents, since then it has earned almost 2,500.

Businesses that choose to take the sit-back-and-wait approach to business-method patents may find themselves in Microsoft's shoes. Maybe their competitors will do the same, and they will not be faced with a multimillion dollar lawsuit and a potentially devastating injunction. The question is whether such businesses are willing to take that risk.

Perhaps Ford Motor Company's recent published patent application provides some insight into how Ford responded to GM's business-method patent. On January 2, 2003, a Ford patent application for a "[m]ethod for implementing a best practice idea" was published. Similarly, in response to Johnson & Johnson's business-method patent in the blood assessment area, a Baxter patent application entitled "System and method for tracking a blood collection kit in a blood collection facility" was published on January 2, 2003.

Although pending patent applications are maintained in secrecy, at least until 18 months after filing, the PTO's statistics indicate that many others have decided to join the business-method patent battle, and filings have skyrocketed. If motor companies, pharmaceutical companies, and magazine publishers are among those filing business-method patents, any business that takes a chance that its competitors have not already begun filing business-method patents is risking its future. A company's own business-method patent portfolio may be just the advantage that it needs to prevent a competitor from knocking on its door seeking an injunction.

Implementing a Business-Method Patent Program

Although the task may seem daunting, implementing a business-method patent program can be done with a few modifications to existing programs. The key change, however, has to be a change in corporate attitude toward business-method patents, from the company's top executives and throughout the organization. Experience with corporate intellectual property programs indicates that companies whose executives value and emphasize intellectual property development have a strong intellectual property portfolio. Employees take their cues from their management. If a supervisor does not value and recognize an employee's submission of invention disclosures, then employees consequently do not submit invention disclosures. Potential intellectual assets are thus wasted. Everyone from the top executives to the lower level managers must understand the importance of recognizing innovative business methods and bringing that information to the attention of the intellectual property program decision makers.

. . .

Common Factors Used in Assessing a Potentially Patentable Business Method

Some of the factors used to determine whether to file a patent application on a new business method require knowledge of the competition and where the company's future lies.

For example, one factor useful in assessing a business method for potential patenting is whether that new business method can be detected by competitors. If a competitor will readily detect the business method as soon as it is implemented, filing for patent protection is the only way to protect the idea. Otherwise, the company's entire investment in developing the business method could be lost because a competitor would be able to copy the business method without incurring the same amount of start-up costs. Disclosure and reporting laws now require many business practices to be disclosed to investors. For example, recent Internal Revenue Service regulations requiring disclosure of tax-shelter transactions on income tax returns have led some tax advisors to file for patent protection on their new tax savings plans. Disclosure obligations, reverse-engineering, and accessibility to the public of a business method all weigh in favor of patent protection.

If, on the other hand, the business method is internal to the business and virtually impossible for a competitor to detect, then the company may forgo patent protection and rely instead on trade secret protection. In general, trade secret law can protect an idea for far greater time than the current 20-year term for US patents and does not require the expenditure of filing for patent protection. On the downside, trade secret law does not prevent a company from independent development of the same idea. Misappropriation of trade secrets may be difficult to determine and even more difficult to prove in court, leading to the following factor.

A second factor often considered is whether it is likely that a competitor could independently develop the business method. If so, then patent protection could provide leverage against that competitor. If a new business method can be internally protected by trade secret laws and competitors are unlikely to be able to independently develop the idea, then the cost of pursuing patent protection on that business method may not be warranted. Each of these last two factors then leads to the next.

A third factor for consideration is the likely useful lifecycle of the business method on the company or competitor's ongoing operations. If the business method is likely to have long-term application, either for the company or its competitors, then that weighs heavily in favor of patent protection. The time between filing for patent rights and obtaining enforceable rights in the business method patent area will take at least a year, and generally much longer. If a business method is not likely to be in use two years from the time a patent application filing would be made, then filing for patent protection would likely be a waste of resources. If the new business method is going to be in use, in some form, two years in the future, patent protection for the new business method may be worth pursuing.

Fourth, the patent filing strategies of competitors related to business methods should be considered. Obviously, there are advantages of being ahead of competitors in filing for business method patents. Nevertheless, if competitors are unlikely to file business-method patents of their own, a company may view business-method inventions with slightly more scrutiny. In contrast, if a company knows that its competitors will file for business-method patents, a more aggressive approach would be warranted.

A fifth factor to consider is the value in being able to exclude competition from the business method in the future. Some new business methods do not necessarily contribute to the bottom line; therefore, it may have little or no impact on the originator if a competitor adopted the new business method. Moreover, if competitors are not litigious or confrontational, the likelihood of ever needing a business-method patent as bargaining leverage goes down significantly. As a result, the nature of competition in any particular line of business must be considered in determining whether to file on new business methods.

Sixth, as a corollary to the first factors, the detectability of infringement by competitors is important. Just as a competitor may not be able to detect a business method from the originating company, it may be equally difficult to determine whether a competitor is infringing on a business-method patent. As a result, the company could have a difficult time assessing whether its rights were being violated. A business-method patent covering difficult-to-detect methods would thus have less value because the company would never know whether it could be enforced. For example, if the business method relates to a method of internally auditing performance of its workers, the patent owner would have a difficult time determining whether a competitor was performing this method. Determining infringement may even require breaching the competitor's confidentiality obligations with its employees. If so, the company would have a difficult time enforcing the patent without being faced with a trade secret misappropriation lawsuit for using the competitor's confidential information to determine that infringement occurred. . . .

Make Invention Disclosure Procedures Available

Another process to implement a business method IP program involves educating key business personnel on company invention disclosure procedures. If the company offers online invention disclosure systems, key business personnel need to be trained and provided access to these systems. Just as engineers are expected to consider invention disclosure procedures as part of any research and development act, all new business initiatives should be considered for patenting. If technical employees are evaluated based on invention submissions at the company, so should business employees. In other words, business personnel should be incentivized to submit their business methods as part of their daily activities. A patent consideration protocol should become part of the standard procedures with any new business initiative before implementation.

. . .

Robert P. Merges, As Many as Six Impossible Patents Before Breakfast: Property Rights for Business Concepts and Patent System Reform
14 Berkeley Tech. L. J. 577 (1999)*

[S]oftware, once thought too purely mathematical, and now business "methods" or concepts, once thought too abstract, have become perfectly acceptable subject matter for patents. For better or for worse, whole new landscapes have been opened to the possibility of patents.

To get right to the heart of the issues surrounding patents for business concepts, log on to <http://www.walkerdigital.com/html/information.html>. This is the website of Walker Digital, Inc., the company that recently "spun off" its Priceline.com subsidiary, a separate company that uses the Internet to match buyers with sellers. Here is what you will read:

> We [Walker Digital, Inc.] conceive, research, and prepare our patented business systems in-house. Our team of specialists prepares cases that solve real-life problems for a wide variety of industries such as retail, telecommunications, credit cards, casinos and more. So far, we've filed over 250 U.S. and international patent applications to create a portfolio that we believe is unlike anything anywhere else in the world.

Until very recently, Walker Digital would not have existed. The patent system did not embrace the abstract patents on business concepts that are the company's key assets. There would be no cornerstone patents on internet price-matching, personified by Walker Digital's "Priceline.com" subsidiary. Without patents, in fact, it is difficult to see how a firm could survive as an independent "idea factory" for Internet commerce.

Walker Digital is therefore a perfect test case. It can tell us whether formerly "impossible" patents on business concepts are a good idea. If there were some way to determine whether this firm had initiated business concepts that no one else would have, or had hurried them into practice faster, we could ask: is the game worth the candle? Alas, no such knowledge has been revealed to us. The instruments we have at hand are simply too imprecise, at least for the time being. We may see an explosion of activity. Or we may hear horror stories about good, solid businesses abandoned in the face of predatory patent extortionists. It is simply too soon to tell.

But there are some positive steps we can take to limit any negative effects from business method patents. The most important is to make sure that the business concept patents that do issue are good, solid patents. It may be too late to argue to a court that business concept patents are universally bad. And it may be too early to ask Congress to rein them in. But it is neither too late nor too early to argue forcefully that bad business concept patents are bad. In fact, the time is just right: minimizing the number of worthless business concept patents makes a great deal of sense just now. Only by improving the overall quality of these patents can we begin to determine whether or not they

---

make any sense. Once we disentangle the bad from the good, we can see whether the good ones are worth the trouble. If, in the process, this entails improving the overall quality of issued patents, all the better. If it tweaks us into fixing some deep-seated flaws in the way the Patent and Trademark Office ("PTO") examines patents, the advent of business method patents may even turn out to serve a useful purpose.

. . .

[L]et us first consider how we came to patent this subject matter in the first place. Although the older cases do not articulate their reasoning very clearly, they seem to center around one idea: that the patent system was meant to protect technology — actual machines, devices, and new chemical compositions — rather than pure concepts. Because business methods are not tied to particular machinery or devices, they are clearly not patentable under this view.

This antipathy to patenting mere abstractions actually grew out of older cases which questioned the patentability of processes per se. How, it was asked, could a list of steps not tied to particular machinery or devices be patentable? In time, the opposition to process patents died away, partly because they came to be understood as physical transformations rather than mere abstractions. It also did not hurt that they were perceived as crucial to the growing chemical industry of the early twentieth century. Yet, the prohibition on patents for business methods lived on.

With the acceptance of patents for software, courts could no longer persuasively rely on the distinction between concepts and machines. Even so, for a brief time the rule against business method patents survived. Those who defended this rule justified it on other grounds. Most powerfully, it was argued that such patents were simply not necessary. After all, there seemed to be no shortage of new accounting methods, financial instruments, or financial services techniques throughout the history of the American economy, when business methods were not patentable. Even into the mid-1980s, when business method patents were just beginning to appear, the U.S. was considered the world leader in this service industry. Thus, according to this view, the proper question is: why fix it if it ain't broke?

The conventional answer is dictated by the logic of patent principles and current practices. It holds that there is no sound reason not to protect business methods. The history, logic, and accepted practices of our method of granting patents essentially compels us to allow patents on business concepts, because there is no principled basis on which to distinguish this "industry" from the myriad other industries that routinely obtain patents. Further, we should all have faith that this wave of patenting will unleash an Edisonian tidal wave of inventiveness — that, if we thought entrepreneurs rapidly introduced new ideas such as overnight package delivery and 1-800-Flowers without patents, then Watch Out!, because we haven't seen anything yet in this field!

Certainly Walker Digital sees it this way. Again, their web page:

> We're not believers in traditional commercial inventing, where old methods are shoehorned into new technologies. Rather than think outside the box, we seek to reinvent the box. We create practical new ways

to do things based on the inherent benefits of new technologies. We then take our core ideas, protect them with patents and establish licensing partnerships with major industry players who bring our ideas to market. These ideas are our intellectual property, our product.

Our team includes entrepreneurs, inventors, technologists, patent attorneys, industry analysts and even a world-renowned cryptographer. It also includes folks who, in previous lives, were some of the country's top CEOs and marketing executives. It's a group of highly intelligent, inventive, business-savvy people, with plenty of room for even more bright people, like you.

We earn profits from our intellectual property through a variety of business strategies ranging from direct licensing agreements — selling an idea to another company — to spinning off new businesses in which we retain an equity stake. Our first business spin-off was a home run — Priceline.com, our patented buyer-driven commerce system.

Priceline.com is the only system, on or off the Internet, where buyers can name their own price for specified goods and services. Like all of our spin-offs, its success has become our success.

Not surprisingly, the patent covering the Priceline.com service is in dispute. A rival inventor — a patent lawyer, in fact — had filed a patent application with somewhat analogous claims earlier. An interference is now afoot. And so commences the inevitable shakeout period when rival patentees jockey for position. This much, at least, is not new. For example, the Bell System had 600 patent infringement suits pending in the late nineteenth century, and the past fifteen years have seen a steady stream of foundational litigation in the biotechnology industry.

What is new is this: the shakeout has begun without answers to some important threshold questions. Chief among these is whether Walker Digital and other firms like it are doing anything that would not be done in the absence of patents. Put another way, in an ideal world, society would have addressed whether or not the types of business concept patents sought by these firms contributed any value in excess of what they cost society. If the answer was no, we would deny patents to them; if yes, patents would be allowed.

Defense to Infringement Based on Earlier Inventor ("First Inventor Defense")

35 U.S.C. § 273 (2002)

(a) Definitions. — For purposes of this section —

(1) the terms "commercially used" and "commercial use" mean use of a method in the United States, so long as such use is in connection with an internal commercial use or an actual arm's-length sale or other arm's-length commercial transfer of a useful end result, whether or not the subject matter at issue is accessible to or otherwise known to the public, except that the subject matter for which commercial marketing or use is subject to a premarketing regulatory review period during which the safety or

efficacy of the subject matter is established, including any period specified in section 156(g), shall be deemed "commercially used" and in "commercial use" during such regulatory review period;

(2) in the case of activities performed by a nonprofit research laboratory, or nonprofit entity such as a university, research center, or hospital, a use for which the public is the intended beneficiary shall be considered to be a use described in paragraph (1), except that the use —

(A) may be asserted as a defense under this section only for continued use by and in the laboratory or nonprofit entity; and

(B) may not be asserted as a defense with respect to any subsequent commercialization or use outside such laboratory or nonprofit entity;

(3) the term "method" means a method of doing or conducting business; and

(4) the "effective filing date" of a patent is the earlier of the actual filing date of the application for the patent or the filing date of any earlier United States, foreign, or international application to which the subject matter at issue is entitled under section 119, 120, or 365 of this title.

(b) Defense to Infringement. —

(1) In general. — It shall be a defense to an action for infringement under section 271 of this title with respect to any subject matter that would otherwise infringe one or more claims for a method in the patent being asserted against a person, if such person had, acting in good faith, actually reduced the subject matter to practice at least 1 year before the effective filing date of such patent, and commercially used the subject matter before the effective filing date of such patent.

(2) Exhaustion of right. — The sale or other disposition of a useful end product produced by a patented method, by a person entitled to assert a defense under this section with respect to that useful end result shall exhaust the patent owner's rights under the patent to the extent such rights would have been exhausted had such sale or other disposition been made by the patent owner.

(3) Limitations and qualifications of defense. — The defense to infringement under this section is subject to the following:

(A) Patent. — A person may not assert the defense under this section unless the invention for which the defense is asserted is for a method.

(B) Derivation. — A person may not assert the defense under this section if the subject matter on which the defense is based was derived from the patentee or persons in privity with the patentee.

(C) Not a general license. — The defense asserted by a person under this section is not a general license under all claims of the patent at issue, but extends only to the specific subject matter claimed in the patent with respect to which the person can assert a defense under this chapter, except that the defense shall also extend to variations in the quantity or volume of use of the claimed subject matter, and to improvements in the claimed subject matter that do not infringe additional specifically claimed subject matter of the patent.

(4) Burden of proof. — A person asserting the defense under this section shall have the burden of establishing the defense by clear and convincing evidence.

(5) Abandonment of use. — A person who has abandoned commercial use of subject matter may not rely on activities performed before the date of such abandonment in establishing a defense under this section with respect to actions taken after the date of such abandonment.

(6) Personal defense. — The defense under this section may be asserted only by the person who performed the acts necessary to establish the defense and, except for any transfer to the patent owner, the right to assert the defense shall not be licensed or assigned or transferred to another person except as an ancillary and subordinate part of a good faith assignment or transfer for other reasons of the entire enterprise or line of business to which the defense relates.

(7) Limitation on sites. — A defense under this section, when acquired as part of a good faith assignment or transfer of an entire enterprise or line of business to which the defense relates, may only be asserted for uses at sites where the subject matter that would otherwise infringe one or more of the claims is in use before the later of the effective filing date of the patent or the date of the assignment or transfer of such enterprise or line of business.

(8) Unsuccessful assertion of defense. — If the defense under this section is pleaded by a person who is found to infringe the patent and who subsequently fails to demonstrate a reasonable basis for asserting the defense, the court shall find the case exceptional for the purpose of awarding attorney fees under section 285 of this title.

(9) Invalidity. — A patent shall not be deemed to be invalid under section 102 or 103 of this title solely because a defense is raised or established under this section.

NOTES & QUESTIONS

1. The readings by Buroker and Merges offer contrasting perspectives on the desirability of business method patents. Which author do you think has the better side of the argument from a policy perspective? As a business lawyer, how would you advise clients about pursuing a strategy of patenting business methods? Do the benefits outweigh the costs of such a strategy? Is there a downside from a business perspective to the strong pursuit of patents?

2. Review the *Motor City Bagels* case, excerpted at the very beginning of the chapter. What strategies did the parties pursue to protect their business plan? Were patents viable for the business methods at issue in that case? What would you think of as possible alternatives to business method patents? How do the different ways to protect business patents and plans that you come up with compare?

CHAPTER 2

ORGANIZING AND FINANCING AN INTELLECTUAL PROPERTY BASED STARTUP COMPANY

PROBLEM

After several years as a successful consultant regarding race car ignition systems and after having obtained several patents regarding new ignition system designs, Dr. See has decided to form a new business (to be called "Digital Ignition Systems Corporation" or "Digital Ignition") in order develop and market products incorporating his patented designs. Dr. See plans to hold a significant ownership share in the new concern reflecting his contribution of key technologies and his ongoing role in the leadership of the new business. Dr. See has identified five additional individuals who are interested in being initial co-owners of the new business. Some of these co-owners plan to be actively involved in the management and operation of Digital Ignition, while others expect only to be investors. The anticipated roles and financial contributions of the six initial co-owners of Digital Ignition are as follows:

Dr. See will:

- transfer ownership of his patents to Digital Ignition
- invest $100,000
- serve as chief executive officer

Thomas Carlise (an investment counselor) will:

- invest $100,000
- serve as chief financial officer

Mary Sanchez (a college professor of engineering) will:

- serve as chief product engineer
- make no investment

Tom Johnson (another, less experienced college professor of engineering) will:

- serve as Sanchez's assistant
- also make no investment

Hameed Bukhari (a local dentist and friend of Dr. See's) will:

- contribute $500,000 (in a combination of loans and direct invest-ments of funds, with the fraction of each to be determined)

- play no active management role in the business

Sally Loo (a successful clothing store operator and Dr. See's cousin) will:

- invest $500,000

- play no active management role in the business

Dr. See has come to your law firm for help in setting up Digital Ignition. He is seeking advice on what type of legal entity to pick for this business, how the fractional ownership interests in the business might best be allocated given the anticipated activities and contributions of the six initial co-owners, conflicts of interest and fiduciary obligations that may arise among the co-owners once the business is established, and means to generate additional financing for Digital Ignition using loans and, eventually, venture capital financing.

Please provide Dr. See with advice on these questions, with particular atten-tion to how Digital Ignition's present and anticipated intellectual property interests may influence the answers.

FOCUS OF THE CHAPTER

This chapter considers business formation and financing issues that are peculiar to start-up companies with significant intellectual property assets. Section A describes some of the types of business entities that can be useful vehicles for developing and commercializing new intellectual property, with emphasis on features of those business entities that aid business executives in making effective use of intellectual property interests and that prepare the entities for additional investment and growth. Section A also describes some of the common sources for initial financing of start-up companies seeking to commercialize intellectual property assets. Section B examines the expecta-tions of venture capitalists in financing start-up companies. This section also addresses the impact of venture capitalists' expectations in shaping start-up business enterprises, the initial ownership structures of such enterprises, and the business goals of these enterprises as they look ahead to possible venture capital financing. Section C addresses the use of security interests in intellec-tual property as means either to promote lending to developing companies or to enhance the attractiveness of those companies as they seek venture capital. Section D discusses how tax considerations may affect the allocation of intel-lectual property ownership and licensing among business enterprises. Section E explores how corporate law duties applicable to corporate directors, officers, and shareholders may constrain how these individuals utilize or dispose of the intellectual property assets of a business.

READINGS

A.   COMMERCIALIZING INTELLECTUAL PROPERTY: SELECTING A BUSINESS ENTITY AND OBTAINING INITIAL FINANCING

Richard A. Mann, et al. Starting From Scratch: A Lawyer's Guide to Representing a Start-up Company
56 Ark. L. Rev. 773 (2004)*

. . .

Along with protecting intellectual property, establishing a business entity in order to conduct the business is high priority. Business entities considered by entrepreneurs include: (1) sole proprietorships, (2) partnerships and limited partnerships, (3) corporations, and (4) limited liability companies. Each of these entities has advantages as well as disadvantages.

. . .

B.   Sole Proprietorships

The simplest form of business association is the sole proprietorship. A sole proprietorship is an unincorporated business consisting of one person who owns and completely controls the business and is personally liable for all the obligations of the business. The costs in establishing and running a sole proprietorship are minimal; it is formed without any formality. The profits from the business are taxed to the individual owner and filed on the individual's tax returns. The business is freely transferable by sale, gift or will. Finally, the sole proprietorship may have a relatively short life span because the death of the sole proprietor dissolves the sole proprietorship. Typically, the sole proprietorship is used for small family businesses.

C.   Partnerships

Broadly speaking, partnerships are either general partnerships or limited partnerships. A general partnership (usually referred to simply as a partnership) is an unincorporated business entity that is formed when two or more persons join together to co-own a business for profit. No formal agreement is necessary to create a general partnership. Thus, if two or more people conduct a business, under normal circumstances a general partnership will result by default. Each partner is personally liable for an unlimited amount of the

---

obligations of the general partnership. The cost to create and run a general partnership depends on the complexity of the ownership arrangement.

A general partnership is not a separate taxable entity. Consequently, the taxation of a general partnership is comparable to a sole proprietorship as the profits and losses "pass-through" to the general partners. Income allocated to the partners is subject to the self-employment tax. The partnership must file an informational return with the Internal Revenue Service (IRS). A general partnership is very flexible in that the management responsibilities can be divided among the partners in virtually any way the partners agree. In the absence of a specific agreement, each partner has an equal right to control of the partnership. Partners may assign their financial interest in the partnership, but the assignee may become a member of the partnership only if all of the members consent. Lastly, under the original UPA, the death, bankruptcy, or withdrawal of a partner dissolves the general partnership. Under the Revised UPA, these dissociations of a partner result in dissolution only in limited circumstances; in many instances, they will result merely in a buyout of the withdrawing partner's interest rather than a termination of the partnership.

In contrast to the informal creation of a general partnership, a limited partnership must be established by filing a certificate of limited partnership with the appropriate state office. The limited partnership is a creation of state statute, and the members of the limited partnership must strictly comply with the state laws. A limited partnership must have at least one general partner and one limited partner. General partners have unlimited personal liability for the partnership's obligations, whereas limited partners have limited liability. The costs of creating and managing a limited partnership will typically be more expensive than a general partnership. Each general partner has an equal right to control of the partnership; limited partners have no right to participate in control. Partners may assign their financial interest in the partnership, but the assignee may become a limited partner only if all of the members consent. Unless otherwise agreed, a limited partnership must dissolve if a general partner dies, goes bankrupt, or withdraws. The limited partnership will survive the death, bankruptcy, or withdrawal of a limited partner. A limited partnership is not a separate taxable entity, so income of the partnership is deemed to be distributed to the partners, similar to a general partnership. Limited partnerships are frequently used to raise capital and to bring together passive investors with managerial talent.

D.   Corporations

A corporation has a separate legal existence apart from its owners. A corporation is created by filing articles of incorporation with the appropriate state office. Because each state has adopted its own corporate statutes, the rules governing the creation, internal affairs, and dissolution vary from state to state. A board of directors elected by the shareholders manages the corporation but the board normally delegates to certain officers the oversight of day-to-day activities. Owners are not liable for the actions of the corporation. However, under certain circumstances, state courts will strip away the corporation's protective shield and expose the owners to liability. State courts will "pierce the corporate veil" in extreme cases where shareholders do not follow corporate formalities or intentionally undercapitalize a corporation. The costs of creating and running a corporation may be significant depending upon the complexity of the corporation's organizational documents. A corporation is a more formal entity that requires many administrative tasks such as regular board meetings, shareholder votes, and other corporate governance formalities. The taxation considerations for corporations are also considerable. One tax disadvantage to becoming a corporation is that corporate profits are subject to double taxation: a corporation is taxed as a separate entity, and shareholders are taxed on corporate earnings that are distributed to them. Some corporations, however, are eligible to elect to be taxed as Subchapter S corporations, resulting in flow-through taxation of the shareholders. There are substantial advantages, however, to selecting the corporate form of business. Corporate structures permit the creation of sophisticated financial structures in which variable ownership classes are entitled to different rights and preferences. Also, absent shareholder agreements restricting transfers, an ownership interest is freely transferable. Finally, the corporation's existence can be perpetual.

E.   Limited Liability Companies

A limited liability company (LLC) is a relatively new form of business that combines the "pass-through" tax advantages of partnerships while providing limited liability to all its owners. As the name suggests, the owners of a limited liability company are not personally liable for the LLC's obligations. Also, all members of a member-managed LLC may participate in the management of the business. LLC statutes permit LLCs to be managed by one or more managers who may, but need not, be a member. In a member managed LLC, the members have actual and apparent authority to bind the LLC. In a manager-managed LLC, the managers have this authority; while the members have no actual or apparent authority to bind the manager-managed LLC. The ownership interests are transferable and assignable with the consent of the other owners. Depending on the state in which the LLC is organized, the LLC will dissolve on the death, bankruptcy or withdrawal of a member, unless the remaining members take action to prevent the dissolution.

F.   Choice of Business Entity Analysis

In [*The UCLA Tax Conference: The Structure of Silicon Valley Start-Ups,* 41 UCLA L. REV. 1737 (1994),] a 1994 article examining the choice of entity by high-tech start-ups, Professor Joseph Bankman argued that, because of tax advantages, using an entity with pass-through taxation is a better choice than using a corporation. Given that the start-up costs of a high-tech company are tax deductible, his premise was that a partnership structure would allow the inevitable losses in the early stages of the start-up to pass through to each individual partner. These losses could be used to offset income from other sources and reduce the partner's tax liability. On the other hand, if the new entity is a corporation, only the corporation can deduct the losses. As Bankman points out, "[t]he newly-formed company, however, has no material source of present or past income against which to deduct the expense." Yet, Bankman found that most start-ups incorporate and thereby forego many of the tax advantages that partnerships receive. While the theory regarding the value of losses is interesting, as a practical matter, these losses have little if any value to the traditional venture fund supported by institutional investors.

By mid-1996 every state had enacted an LLC statute. LLCs became popular because they combined the best attribute of partnerships, pass-through taxation, with the best attribute of corporations, limited liability. Therefore, some commentators have argued that the LLC is the best initial choice for entrepreneurs. On the other hand, one of the advantages of incorporating is separating equity ownership from control, an attribute not always present with an LLC. LLCs are specifically designed to be more flexible than corporations and can be organized as manager-managed entities. However, venture capitalists appear to be cool to this approach: "Conventional wisdom holds that venture capital firms generally do not invest in limited liability companies."

Not surprisingly, the choice of entity for high-tech start-ups often is driven by their subsequent need for additional money from venture funding. Venture capitalists invest in companies that statistically are likely never to go public. As private company investors, the venture capitalist seeks as much certainty as possible in an investment. In this respect corporations have the advantage because they have many years of case law providing much greater predictability relating to shareholder rights and director duties. Furthermore, even those arguing that the LLC should be the entity of choice, acknowledge that if the start-up ever goes public, the market will require it to incur the costs of restructuring as a corporation. Nevertheless, they contend that the transaction costs associated with a restructuring are less than the tax benefits derived from starting out as an LLC.

In explaining the higher incidence of incorporation over partnership formation, despite the theoretical tax advantages of not incorporating, Bankman suspected that entrepreneurs simply did not value tax savings as a priority. Some entrepreneurs were not even aware of the tax consequences of incorporating. Since Bankman's study, LLCs have become more widely accepted as a viable start-up entity choice. Nevertheless, corporations remain the preferred vehicle for high tech start-ups. The following is an explanation for the persistence of incorporation despite the tax advantages of an LLC:

> To the extent participants in this market continue to choose the corporate form over theoretically available LLC structures, it may be because innovation may not promise sufficient advantages over the customary structure . . . . [V]enture capital firms structure investment relationships through legal forms that create significant rights in firm governance. If these rights are valuable, sophisticated investors are not likely to experiment with organizational innovations that carry uncertain consequences.

[Deborah A. DeMott, *Agency and the Unincorporated Firm: Reflections on Design on the Same Plane of Interest,* 54 WASH. & LEE L. REV. 595, 609, 611 (1997).] In addition to corporate governance issues, most venture capital firms have restrictions in their fund documents that prohibit investing in flow-through entities due to certain adverse income tax consequences to their limited partners. Further, the flow through of losses to pension plans and other tax-exempt entities is in most cases meaningless, so there may be no tax advantage ever under any circumstances. In addition, the body of case law available to interpret stockholder rights, and director duties is well established for corporations but virtually barren for partnerships and LLCs. Finally, venture investors look for methods to enhance cash flow after a start-up reaches profitability. If net operating losses have flowed through to investors, the losses are no longer available to the enterprise. For corporations, the incurred losses are available to shelter future taxable income and support future tax-free growth of the enterprise.

An entrepreneur should weigh the advantages and disadvantages of each business entity, taking into account whether the nature of the entity matches the type of investor that is being targeted. For example, a venture that can be financed by a few high net worth investors may be a candidate for operating as an LLC, but a biotechnology company requiring institutional investors would not typically be a candidate.

. . .

Kristopher D. Brown & Graham D. S. Anderson, Financing and Strategic Alliances for the New Media Company
Practising Law Institute,
Representing the New Media Company 1999
545 PLI/Pat 709*

[The following reading describes typical financing options for new media companies — companies that are frequently concerned with sales of intellectual property via the Internet and other new media — as well as for other start-up companies with products based on intellectual property.]

I. INTRODUCTION TO FINANCING NEW MEDIA COMPANIES

Every new company eventually requires capital beyond the means of its founders in order to finance its operations. This inevitability creates significant obstacles for the company to overcome including (i) identifying a source of capital, (ii) minimizing the cost of any secured capital, (iii) negotiating a deal to the satisfaction of both parties, and (iv) maintaining a stable flow of capital going forward.

While each obstacle can be overcome through careful planning and diligence efforts by both the company, its lawyers and other advisers, the structure of any new financing will ultimately depend on (i) the amount of capital needed, (ii) the company's operating history (to the extent there is any), (iii) the company's current financial condition, and (iv) the risks associated with the company's business.

Founders of new media companies will generally face the same obstacles as any other start-up. However, because new media companies have, by definition, a limited operating history and are considered fairly risky ventures, simple financing arrangements are few and far between. Therefore, the planning process involved in anticipation of securing third-party financing is all the more important.

A.   Formulating a Plan and Assessing Costs

Accepting complexity as a certainty, the founders of a new media company must diligently consider their need for capital and what they would be willing to part with in order to secure this capital. Entrepreneurs too often wait until negotiations have reached a standstill before considering these issues. The result is often that the cost of capital is much higher than what otherwise should have been necessary. It is the responsibility of lawyers to raise these issues early on.

The company must have an acute understanding of its needs going forward to insure that it avoids unnecessary costs. Putting together a detailed and highly specific budget will help to adequately assess the needs going forward. Once the capital requirements are in place, the founders will then be in a position to consider the possible cost of such capital. All third party investors will demand certain concessions in order to mitigate the risk associated with their investment. Such concessions may include (i) control of the company or a percent thereof, (ii) in the case of debt financings, possibly a security interest in the company's assets, (iii) a right to veto certain material corporate transactions, and/or (iv) under certain special circumstances, a right to exit or even take control of the company in the event certain operating goals are not met within a specified time frame. A lawyer should be prepared to advise the company on the pros and cons of each of these terms when working with a company on a financing transaction.

A new media company has much better negotiating leverage with potential investors if it begins its capital raising efforts early on. If a company waits too long to begin trying to identify financing sources, its ongoing costs combined with diminishing financial reserves will put pressure on the company's management to cut any deal they can make with an investor. Accordingly, the average early stage new media company should begin preparing for capital raising activities typically six to twelve months before they anticipate needing the funds. Of course, this is not always possible at the stage where a new media company is first being formed, and lawyers should advise clients seeking to build a new media business that they may be required to finance the operation out of their own pockets for a long period.

For both securities law purposes and to ensure that young companies with limited personnel and other resources are not focusing solely on raising capital to the detriment of building their business, companies also should not be continuously entering into small financing transactions. Instead of raising money on an ad hoc and continuous basis, a company's fund raising activities should be carefully coordinated, with the company first attempting to line up or commit financing sources and then working with its lawyer to finalize the deal with an individual or group of investors. A lawyer should let the company know that this approach is also cheaper for them in terms of his or her time.

Furthermore, the conditions of the new media market amplify the need for a company to adequately consider its position with respect to a financing, i.e., there are now many potential investments and, ultimately, only a finite amount of potential investors. Companies are therefore not only forced to compete with one another in the marketplace, but also for the attention of investors. This situation can increase the cost of capital for new media companies even more than the typical start-up venture.

. . .

B.   Identifying Sources of Capital

Armed with knowledge of both their basic needs and potential concessions, the new media company's founders will be in a good position to know what type of third-party investor to pursue. The traditional sources of capital, i.e., private placements and/or bank lending, are reserved for more established and tested companies and are offered to start-up ventures on an extremely limited basis, and often only with the support (e.g., through a guaranty) by an institutional venture capital firm or strategic partner that is already committed to the company. Nevertheless, there are a number of other options for start-up ventures, and specifically new media companies, to explore.

The major sources of capital for these organizations are detailed below. Generally, they are (i) seed capital for companies looking for small amounts of cash to finance the initial stages of a venture, (ii) venture capital for companies in need of larger amounts of financing for a longer term and willing to give up certain corporate powers, and (iii) strategic alliances for companies looking for an established business partner to mold and shepherd the company into a successful enterprise going forward.

. . .

II.   TRADITIONAL METHODS OF SECURING CAPITAL

A.   Bank and Asset Based Lending

Banks are a major source of both short-term and long-term funds. Through borrowing, an entrepreneur is able to acquire the funds she needs to operate her business without giving up control or a piece of any future growth. The principal downside to borrowing is that, in addition to charging interest, banks often require their borrowers to adhere to very strict operating standards to keep the loan in good standing. The pressures of operating in such an environment could outweigh the benefits.

Furthermore, for the start-up company and specifically for the new media company, there are a number of barriers to access to commercial bank loans which must be overcome before a loan will be actually approved. When making a decision as to whether to extend a loan to a small company, banks pay strict attention to the financial history and projections and the management of the business. The bank will also consider the past relationship it has had with the company and its principals. Unfortunately, since these companies rarely have more than a business plan and budget, qualifying for bank lending is often not possible for a start-up company.

An additional difficulty associated with borrowing money is that banks will often not lend funds without collateral or a recognized institutional investor to secure or guarantee the loan. In fact, banks commonly will require collateral valued at more than two times that of the principal of the loan. Most start-up companies are not able to provide such security. Furthermore, as new media companies typically are not "asset-intensive" businesses, it is difficult to qualify even for the most mature new media company.

The most common solution to the aforementioned difficulties is for the founders of the new media company to take a personal interest in the venture, i.e., a home equity loan (assuming the entrepreneur owns a home) or personal guarantee. The price of such a commitment is of course that should the company fail, the bank will seek to collect as much of its loan as possible and the entrepreneur could lose her home and/or other personal property.

1.   National Banking Act

Although many new media companies fail to qualify as borrowers under the stringent criteria of commercial banks, most qualify for direct loans and/or awards from Small Business Investment Companies (SBICs). The structure of SBICs is discussed below, but it is worth mentioning that the National Banking Act, which sets the guidelines for the operation of national banking associations, allows banks to invest 5% of their capital in one or more of these entities. As a result, many national banks, which otherwise are restricted from making equity investments, have formed SBICs to make investments in small businesses. Access to this capital is not as difficult as to actual loans from the bank itself, but as discussed later below, it presents certain other issues for the entrepreneur to consider.

2.   Venture Lending

Increasingly, more established new media companies are seeking and obtaining bank debt, either in the form of revolving or term loans to finance certain aspects of their business and operations. Equity is typically used to fund a new media company's highest risk expenses, such as start-up, product development and market entry expenses. A loan or debt, on the other hand, is typically used to fund assets which generate cash, such as products, equipment and facilities, as well as certain lower risk expenses, such as working capital, research and development and administration. Accordingly, as discussed earlier, most early stage new media companies, that are focusing on creating and starting the business, are not appropriate candidates for debt and so do not have access to traditional lenders.

Venture lending, where traditional lending is combined with the grant by a company to the lender of warrants (i.e., rights to buy a proportionate amount of common stock at a specified price) or some other form of equity, is being used more and more to adjust the risk premiums for a lender. New media companies that can obtain venture lending are able to minimize overall equity dilution and diversify sources of capital. In most cases, however, it remains the case that only those new media companies that have already raised some money and are affiliated with institutional venture capital firms can obtain venture loans. Typically, this is because the venture lender will want the new media company to have at least some assets (such as equipment or accounts receivable) that can serve as collateral to secure the loan obligation. Guaranties may also be sought from the venture capital firms affiliated with the company as a condition to any loan.

A lawyer advising a new media company that is seeking to obtain a loan should be familiar with the general legal provisions found in loan documents. Among other terms, the representations, warranties and covenants in such loan documents will need to be carefully analyzed to ensure that they are tailored to the company's business and do not restrict in any material way the company from operating in the normal course. After the loan documents have been entered into, the lawyer should also stay in touch with the client to advise about the importance of not violating certain restrictive and other ongoing covenants contained in such documents. For example, failure in some instances to stay in compliance could cause the company to become in default, triggering the lender's right to seize the company's assets.

3.   Venture Leasing

Early stage new media companies will typically lease most of the equipment used in their business (e.g., copiers, telephones, computer systems). Leasing equipment instead of purchasing it outright allows the new media company to limit overall expenditures, helping to ensure that it develops its business in accordance with its budget. Accordingly, for lawyers advising new media companies, it is essential to have at least some basic understanding of equipment or operating leasing issues and the contractual provisions of leases.

Lessors typically present standard form operating leases to start-up new media companies, on a "take-or-leave-it" basis, since a young new media company has very little leverage with which to negotiate and is typically not considered a good credit risk. The lawyer must analyze the lease form presented to the new media company with reference to the company's specific objectives, and with the goal that a demand be made to the lessor to at least modify the standard form to address the company's unique business objectives. It is also critical that the operating lease not be structured in such a way that the new media company will be in violation simply by operating its business in the ordinary course. Most importantly, the lawyer should help the new media company to negotiate the representations, warranties and covenants in the operating lease as they relate to the default provisions.

For most new media companies, it is very difficult to obtain any form of leasing until the company has received at least one or more rounds of venture financing, and has developed a strong relationship with an institutional venture capital firm. In some cases, the lessor may even require that the venture capital firm give it a guaranty as a condition to entering into the operating lease with the new media company. Earlier stage companies (even ones without venture capital firm involvement) may, however, be able to receive such leasing arrangements if they have between $0.5 million to $5 million of non-custom, fungible assets that can be used as collateral, such as personal computer hardware and off-the-shelf software. High end servers and other specialized items, even if owned outright by a new media company, may be too specialized to serve as such collateral.

Increasingly, so-called "venture leasing firms" are seeking warrants or other forms of equity from new media companies in exchange for providing the company with an operating lease. A warrant can serve as "sweetener" to enhance the marketability of the lease. In exchange for the warrant, new media companies will sometimes negotiate to remove all covenants and other restrictive terms from the operating lease. As the number of venture leasing firms has increased in recent years, many such firms appear to be more willing to negotiate such provisions, particularly as they seek to attract the long-term business of good new media customers.

B.   Private Placements

Private placements, another traditional source of financing, consist of the offer and sale of equity or debt securities in an offering exempt from both federal and state securities laws. The prime purpose of such an offering is to quickly raise capital without having to contend with the heavy disclosure requirements associated with a public offering.

In order to qualify for any securities law exemption, private placements are normally restricted to wealthy individuals and institutional investors known as accredited investors. The advantage of such an offering is that the company is able to control its cost of capital by setting the terms of the sale and merely selling to those parties willing to buy. In addition, the company is able to avoid the burdensome disclosure requirements required in public offerings. Unfortunately for emerging new media companies, these investors are often not willing to make such an investment in young companies competing within high-risk industries.

As a result of the above, executing a private placement is normally not a viable option for a new media company to pursue. At the early stage of development, a new media company . . . will likely find it difficult to even retain a placement agent to market the securities. Such a company will likely have to raise its initial financing from some of the other sources discussed below.

III.   SEED CAPITAL (PRIMARILY EQUITY)

Given the difficulties of raising capital by traditional means, an immediate issue for any new company to face is how it will finance its operations. Although the proposed business plan is still in its formative stage, the entrepreneur must consider this issue. To do so intelligently, the entrepreneur must understand two things: (i) any potential investor will likely evaluate the entrepreneur as much as (and in many cases more than) the business plan she proposes; and (ii) any eventual negotiated deal will likely include the sale of a significant portion of the company.

Investors willing to provide a start-up company with its initial funds, or seed capital, generally trust their ability to evaluate people more than their ability to evaluate an untested business plan. Therefore who the entrepreneur is and how she comes across will play an enormous role in whether any seed capital will ultimately be secured. In addition, the investor will almost certainly demand a significant amount of ownership of the company, usually in the form of common stock. As a common stockholder, the investor can maintain significant control over the affairs of the company and also share in any achieved growth.

Given these truths, the difficult question becomes where to actually find the money. Three sources of seed capital are detailed below.

A.   Entrepreneur's Personal Resources

The primary source of third party financing for early stage new media companies is the entrepreneur's "friends and family." Considering that access to seed capital is heavily dependent on the entrepreneur herself, it makes sense that the chief source of capital will be from those with whom she is personally familiar. However, certain potential problems with this form of financing should be considered.

First and foremost, is that the potential pool of funds for most entrepreneurs is limited; i.e., not everyone is related to or friendly with a millionaire. Therefore, a new company will often find that as soon as it secures these funds, it requires more. Second, the costs of any failed enterprise are multiplied when one considers the guilt and emotional pain associated with losing the capital of a loved one. As most start-up companies, including new media companies, are extremely risky investments, there is a strong chance that any invested capital will be lost. As a result, the possibility exists that friends could turn into enemies.

B.   Government Sources

A potential way to avoid the pitfalls of "friends and family" money is for a new company to secure its seed capital from the government. Both Federal and various state government agencies fund organizations which help finance small businesses in a variety of ways, including (i) the issuance of a direct financial award (more typical among state organizations), (ii) the extension of a low-rate loan and/or (iii) the guaranty of a commercial bank loan. The federal government's Small Business Administration (the "SBA") is probably the most popular of these organizations.

Most new media companies in search of seed capital will qualify as small businesses by the SBA definition since both their employee base and annual sales are typically small. The most common form of SBA funding is through the guaranty of a commercial loan. In order for the SBA to guaranty a commercial loan, the company must grant a security interest in its assets and, in certain cases, the entrepreneur must also sign a personal guaranty for both the SBA and the lending bank. As a result, the same difficulties previously discussed as relating to bank loans will again be encountered. In addition, these loans are initially offered only in small amounts. However, the potential for additional loans, in higher principal amounts, increases as the company pays off its debt and establishes a favorable credit rating.

As discussed earlier, the SBA also licenses private capital funding organizations known as SBICs. With their own capital and with funds provided by the federal government at favorable rates, SBICs provide capital to small independent businesses, including new media companies. Special SBICs are even formed specifically to provide financing to entrepreneurs who have been denied access to capital because of their race or socio-economic class. The form of financing provided by SBICs is typically debt, but some forms of equity investments are also possible.

. . .

C.   Wealthy Individuals and Other Private Sources (Angels)

Increasingly, new media entrepreneurs are seeking to raise capital in the private sector. A fast-growing source of such money comes from "angel" investors, who in 1998 reportedly provided over $10 billion in seed capital to start-up companies. Angels are typically wealthy individuals, usually former entrepreneurs, who look to grow their fortunes by investing in new start-up ventures. It is estimated that there are approximately 300,000 such people in the United States today. Angels will normally provide capital in the range of few hundred thousand dollars, but sometimes as high as 2 million dollars. In return they will demand various forms of equity including common stock and options for additional shares. As discussed, however, tapping into angel capital is perhaps one of the most burdensome obstacles facing entrepreneurs today.

1.   Significant Barriers to Financing

Angel investing is a relatively recent phenomenon that has surfaced to fill a void in the private equity market, notably seed financing for start-up companies. Ten years ago, venture capital organizations filled this void, but insofar as these organizations have significantly larger pools of capital to invest, they no longer make as many small start-up investments. Unfortunately, it is precisely the noninstitutional nature of angel investing that creates the obstacles that entrepreneurs in search of capital must overcome.

First, the angel market is highly fragmented. Angels do not operate as investment companies; they operate as sole proprietorships. The angel usually invests her own capital in one or two investments at a time. Second, most angels restrict their investments to industries they are familiar with or have competed in. Consequently (and unfortunately for new media companies), the more innovative the product or industry, the less chance there will be of finding an angel willing to invest. Third, angels usually like to keep a close personal watch on their investments and as such, they will typically not invest in a company that operates too far away from their home. Again, this poses a difficulty for new media companies which often are located in lessor populated and inexpensive locales.

. . .

4.   Typical Angel Transactions

The most common form of angel financing is equity. Normally, because the founders are usually the only other stockholders, the angel is satisfied to receive common stock in return for his investment. The rights enjoyed by the angel and how great a percentage of the company the angel receives will vary depending on the size of the investment and the maturity of the company.

As mentioned, the typical angel invests his own capital in usually one or two companies. As a result, the angel will feel a personal stake in the company. The entrepreneur should thus expect that the angel will play a significant role in the management of the company. Angels, whether or not in control of the company, will still negotiate a great many rights to assure their ability to closely monitor the day to day operations of their investment. Examples include the right (i) to specifically appoint certain board members, (ii) to approve of certain management appointments and/or (iii) to control a variety of common management functions, including check writing, salary structure and the formulation of the business plan.

5.   Cost/Benefit of Angel Capital

The above discussion alludes to some of the many advantages and disadvantages of securing angel financing. The prime advantage of angel capital is that the angel, as a former entrepreneur, is likely to be more understanding of the wants and needs of the company's founders. In addition, as angels are experienced business people, they typically offer a company more than financial assistance; their business sense and personal network of contacts are often great sources of knowledge and capital for the growing company. Finally, because angels are usually investing their own capital they offer more flexibility than do some other more institutional investors. Angel investors are not bound by time windows or performance goals; their capital is truly invested for the long term.

There are certain disadvantages. As discussed, angels are normally more "hands-on" than other private investors. Despite the fact that securing such a partner may not have been what the entrepreneur bargained for, it may be exactly what she gets. In addition, because the angel has negotiated a substantial amount of control over the enterprise, the entrepreneur may experience problems if her vision for the future of the company differs from that of the angel. Finally, as most angel investments are not more than a few hundred thousand dollars, angel capital will only get the company so far. Therefore, although they are willing to keep their money invested for a long time, the company will still have to look for more substantial investors going forward.

NOTES & QUESTIONS

1. Assuming that venture capital financing is not presently an option, what forms of business entity will best serve a company like Digital Ignition in the short-term as it develops new products and defines its manufacturing and marketing techniques for those products? To what extent are the business entity selection issues confronting Digital Ignition typical of those facing start-ups generally? How does the company's plan to rely on intellectual property protections in commercializing products in a new technology area affect the choice of a desirable business form and ownership structure for Digital Ignition's future activities?

2. What considerations should govern the percentages of ownership interests allocated to each of the six initial owners of Digital Ignition? If Digital Ignition is operated as a corporation, what percentage of the corporation's stock should each of the six parties receive? What role should loans from one or more of the initial owners play in funding Digital Ignition's startup activities? How might preferred stock — which typically gives the holder a right to corporate dividend payments ahead of any payments made to general or "common" stock holders — be used in combination with common stock to adjust the ownership interests of the six co-owners to their investment risk preferences? For example, what would be the implications for the company and for Hameed Bukhari if he were to invest his $500,000 in exchange for preferred or common stock versus loaning Digital Ignition a similar amount? If, as is usually the case, holders of preferred stock do not vote on matters that are controlled by a majority vote of the holders of common stock (such as the election of corporate directors or the approval of a merger), how might this affect investors' preferences regarding their receipt of preferred versus common stock?

3. Corporate stock options giving the holders the right to purchase stock from a corporation for a specified price can be means to create useful incentives for corporate owners who are also managers or employees of a firm. For example, if a company's stock has a present value of about $10, stock options that are exercisable — that is, can be used to force a sale of stock to the option holder — at $15 per share will encourage the option holders to manage corporate affairs to drive the value of the company's stock above $15 per share. If the company's stock becomes worth, for example, $17 per share, each option to buy at $15 per share has an immediate value of $2 (the difference between the exercise price and the value of the stock at the time of exercise).

Stock options may also be used to ensure that key managers and employees "stick with" a corporate enterprise for a substantial period. This can be accomplished by specifying that stock options received by the key individuals only vest — that is, become exercisable — after the recipient has completed a specified period of service to the company involved.

How might stock options granted to some or all of the six initial owners of Digital Ignition help the company to realize its goals and ensure that these individuals pursue desirable actions on behalf of Digital Ignition?

B.   VENTURE CAPITAL FINANCING

Manuel A. Utset, Reciprocal Fairness, Strategic Behavior & Venture Survival: A Theory of Venture Capital-Financed Firms
2002 Wis. L. Rev. 45*

Introduction

Venture capitalists serve as a major source of capital for young, risky firms with high growth prospects, primarily high-technology firms such as those in the computer, biotechnology, or telecommunications business. They identify, nurture, package, and eventually sell these start-up firms, either through an initial public offering or a private sale to a third party.

. . .

[I]t is useful to isolate three factors that will affect the actions taken by parties in any long-term venture, such as that between a venture capitalist and an entrepreneur: (1) the extent to which each party has mistaken beliefs about the nature of the transaction; (2) the ability of each party to freely maneuver during the venture, i.e., to take actions that negatively affect the other party; and (3) the ability of each party to exit the venture. The venture capital literature has primarily focused on how venture capitalists structure transactions paying close heed to these three factors. For example, venture capitalists know that they may have mistaken beliefs regarding the viability of the innovation or the abilities of the entrepreneur. Moreover, venture capitalists recognize that an entrepreneur's knowledge and skills — her human capital — will be critical to the venture until the innovation is finished, but will not be as valuable during the marketing and production stages. At those latter stages, the venture will be best run by an individual with well-developed managerial skills.

As a result, venture capitalists structure transactions so as to retain control. Among other things, control gives venture capitalists the ability to freely maneuver during the venture, including the ability to dismiss entrepreneurs when their services are no longer deemed valuable — e.g., entrepreneurs whose managerial skills are sub-par compared to those of professional managers. In addition to retaining control, venture capitalists adopt mechanisms to reduce their costs of exiting the venture and mechanisms that make it very costly for entrepreneurs to exit. Entrepreneurial exit is penalized whether the exit is voluntary or at the hands of the venture capitalist. For example, a fired entrepreneur will lose access to her innovation, will be subject to restrictions on competing employment, and under certain instances will even lose all or part of her equity in the venture

The existing venture capital literature has analyzed the effects of mistaken beliefs, maneuverability during the venture, and the ability to exit from the point of view of venture capitalists. This Article takes the opposite tack, analyzing the effects of these three factors from the point of view of entrepreneurs. This allows us to bring to the foreground the following three facts that generally hold when an entrepreneur transacts with a venture capitalist: (1) at the time of contracting, the entrepreneur will tend to have substantial mistaken beliefs, a fact that she will recognize as she interacts with the venture capitalist and as onerous provisions in venture capital contracts are triggered; (2) the entrepreneur has the ability to freely maneuver during the venture, given that her human capital is critical to the success of the venture; and (3) there is a high penalty attached to entrepreneurial exit, whether the exit is voluntary or involuntary.

. . .

I.   The Agency Theory of Venture Capital Contracts

Investments in innovation-intensive start-ups are particularly risky, given uncertainties surrounding the innovation process, and potential opportunistic behavior and managerial incompetence on the part of the entrepreneur. Venture capitalists and entrepreneurs enter into a set of highly standardized contracts aimed at reducing the contractual risks faced by venture capitalists. I will use the phrase venture capital contracts to refer to this set of highly standardized written contracts.

Over the years, scholars studying the venture capital process have made a variety of theoretical claims about venture capital contracts using an agency theory approach. Whenever one individual acts on behalf of another, a potential agency problem arises: the agent (the person acting) will undoubtedly have interests incongruous with those of her principal. One would expect that a bona fide, self-interested agent, such as an entrepreneur, would take self-serving actions at the expense of her principal, the venture capitalist. Agency theory provides important insights into the costs of such self-serving actions.

As monitoring costs — that is, informational costs — increase, an agent will be less constrained, allowing her greater freedom to take actions detrimental to the principal. Financing innovation-intensive firms involves numerous informational problems, making the theoretical agency literature a natural starting point. With few exceptions, this literature, following the agency paradigm, has focused on the screening and monitoring difficulties faced by venture capitalists. In keeping with the agency paradigm, the venture capitalist's informational disadvantage vis-à-vis the entrepreneur and the potential for entrepreneurial opportunism are given a central role. Accordingly, this literature focuses on the role of venture capital contracts in reducing venture capitalists' risks arising from informational asymmetries and entrepreneurial opportunism.

A.   Contractual Risks Faced by Venture Capitalists

1.   Informational Risks

It is fair to assume that at the time of contracting, an entrepreneur has superior information vis-à-vis the venture capitalist regarding the innovation and whether she is a hard worker with the required managerial skills to run the venture. Therefore, before investing in a start-up, a venture capitalist will acquire information about the innovation, such as how feasible and marketable it is, as well as information about the entrepreneur — whether she is the real thing or just a crank, honest or a thief, hard-working or taken to leisure.

During the life of the venture, informational asymmetries continue to be a source of risk to the venture capitalist. A venture capitalist is not involved in the day-to-day managing of the venture and will not have first-hand knowledge of how much time and effort the entrepreneur is dedicating to the venture. This is typical of the delegation implicit in any agency relationship. However, the informational problems in high-tech start-ups are exacerbated by the fact that managerial decision-making requires more than general managerial skills; it also requires an ability to understand, verify, and apply technical information necessary for the managerial decision-making process. The entrepreneur, in managing the venture, will not only have greater access to information related to the ongoing development of the innovation, but will also have a better ability to judge and use that information since she will generally have superior technical knowledge.

2.   Risks Related to the Intangible Nature of the Assets in High-Tech Start-Ups

The principal assets of high-tech start-ups, such as the entrepreneur's know-how (her human capital) and intellectual property (e.g., patents and trade secrets), are highly intangible in nature. Firms whose principal assets are intangible are riskier to finance than those with tangible assets, such as manufacturing equipment, since investors can always recuperate some of their investment by selling those tangible assets. Intangible assets like intellectual property are harder to value and sell to third parties.

Reliance on the entrepreneur's human capital exposes a venture capitalist to a "hold-up" risk: after the venture capitalist makes its investment, the entrepreneur can threaten to quit the venture (taking her human capital) unless the venture capitalist agrees to "renegotiate" the bargain to give the entrepreneur a larger portion of the venture's surplus. For example, assume that a venture capitalist invests one million dollars with an entrepreneur to finance the development and marketing of a new drug. This investment is, to some degree, irreversible since it is venture-specific; the venture capitalist will receive less than one million dollars if the entrepreneur quits without developing the drug. Since the value of the venture capitalist's investment depends, in large part, on the entrepreneur remaining in the venture, the entrepreneur has some ability to act opportunistically

Of course, the venture capitalist will be able to anticipate this behavior and will require some assurances that the entrepreneur will not threaten to quit the venture. However, the venture capitalist's inability to force an entrepreneur to perform against her will means that some other governance mechanisms are needed, such as non-compete agreements or other penalties for exiting the firm inappropriately.

3. Contractual Risks Associated with the Uncertainty Surrounding the Innovation Process

There is a large degree of uncertainty surrounding the financing of high-tech start-ups. This uncertainty is due to a number of factors, including unknowns surrounding the technical viability and market potential of the innovation, the potential for new competitors, as well as the inherent uncertainties surrounding any new venture. Moreover, contracting for innovations and enforcing those contracts is made more difficult by the inherent novelty of innovations, which in some instances may require the development of new ways of perceiving, processing, transferring, and referring to information.

4. Contractual Risks Due to the General Illiquidity of Venture Capital Investments

The relative illiquidity of the venture capitalist's investment produces another contractual risk. As in most close corporations, the venture capitalist's ability to exit by selling its shares is limited. This illiquidity is due to the absence, prior to an initial public offering, of a public market in which the venture capitalist can sell its shares. From the venture capitalist's perspective, the illiquidity problem is exacerbated by the fact that when a venture capitalist attempts to sell its shares it may inadvertently signal to potential buyers that there are undisclosed problems with the venture. This is because a venture capitalist is in a better position to know about the prospect of the venture. Therefore a potential buyer faces the same informational asymmetry problems discussed above in connection with a venture capitalist's initial investment in the venture.

B.   Institutions Adopted to Deal with Contractual Risks

In this Section, I describe the principal contractual mechanisms used by venture capitalists to address the four contractual risks described in the prior Section. The agency literature on venture capital contracts describes venture capital contracts as a reaction to these contractual risks. There are two textbook reactions to contractual risks: discounting for the risk and adopting governance structures.

In view of these risks, standard venture capital contracts encompass four principal goals. The first goal is to provide venture capitalists with very high rates of return — usually a ten-fold return of capital over a five-year period. The second goal is to give control of the start-up firm to the venture capitalist. By retaining control over the venture, venture capitalists can change the "rules of the game" and interpret ambiguous rules instead of requiring the intervention of third parties, such as courts or arbitrators. The third goal is to provide a set of high-powered incentive mechanisms aimed at increasing entrepreneurial effort and reducing opportunistic behavior. The final goal is to provide exit mechanisms for venture capitalists.

1. Giving Control over the Start-Up to the Venture Capitalist

The contractual sources of venture capitalist control are (1) the preferred stock purchase agreement, (2) the terms of the preferred stock, (3) the stockholders' agreement, and (4) employment agreements. By controlling the venture, a venture capitalist can keep a "tight leash" on entrepreneurs, thereby reducing their ability to act opportunistically. Control allows greater access to information needed to monitor entrepreneurs and provides venture capitalists with various mechanisms to discipline errant entrepreneurs, including the ability to fire or demote a managing entrepreneur with little difficulty (other than meeting the provisions of the employment agreement).

A venture capitalist's control over a start-up's board of directors is a critical source of its governance powers. Venture capitalists in most instances negotiate to get outright control of the board. Although the board does not usually run the day-to-day affairs of a company, it is vested with the ultimate power and responsibility of managing the corporation. It selects the officers who will actually manage the corporation (including, in our case, the entrepreneur), sets their salaries, and replaces them when necessary.

Additionally, the stock purchase agreement and stockholders' agreement will contain affirmative and negative covenants, whereby the entrepreneur agrees to take certain actions or to forego taking certain actions, respectively. For example, an entrepreneur may agree to certain affirmative covenants, such as giving the venture capitalist financial statements as well as other types of information. Moreover, an entrepreneur will typically be prohibited from amending the certificate of incorporation, changing the nature of the business, entering into self-dealing transactions, making unauthorized dividend payments, entering into a merger agreement, and selling all or substantially all of its assets.

2. Incentive-Based Mechanisms

Venture capital contracts adopt a variety of incentive mechanisms aimed at better aligning the interests of the entrepreneur with those of the venture capitalist. A principal goal of these incentive mechanisms is to provide an impetus to entrepreneurs to exert the right amount of effort and to dissuade them from acting opportunistically. Under venture capital contracts, the entrepreneur will contribute to the venture her capital, intellectual property, labor, and expertise needed to develop, manufacture, and market the innovation. In return, the entrepreneur retains some of the venture's equity with the expectation that it will provide her with a high rate of return if the venture were to be successful. The higher the intensity of the incentive mechanisms deployed, the greater will be the amount of the venture's risk that is transferred from the venture capitalist to the entrepreneur.

a. Compensation Schemes as High-Powered Incentives

Venture capitalists use compensation schemes to provide entrepreneurs with an incentive to exert the right amount of effort. If a venture capitalist could adequately observe and quantify the effort level of the entrepreneur (and it knew the optimal effort level to be taken), it could then base the entrepreneur's compensation on the amount of effort exerted. However, a venture capitalist cannot fully observe entrepreneurial effort. As a result, an entrepreneur's compensation must be tied to an observable metric, such as the venture's performance, that can act as a proxy for entrepreneurial effort. Stock options can play such a role and, thus, comprise a large part of the compensation package.

Generally, entrepreneurs are paid a salary that is below market with the expectation that the bulk of their compensation will come from appreciation of their base equity holdings and be supplemented by stock options awarded during the venture. The stock options will vest over a period of years, heavily weighed towards the back end. If an entrepreneur leaves the company or is fired (for cause) before the shares have vested, she loses her right to exercise the options.

b. Staged Financing

Unlike banks, which will often disburse borrowed funds in a single transaction, venture capitalists disburse funds over time, in succeeding stages. By staging investments and not pre-committing to financing future stages, venture capitalists, in essence, create a series of call options. At the time each stage arrives, the venture capitalist will decide — given the current valuation — whether to continue investing in the project or to dissolve the company and salvage what it can. In a sense, staged financing gives venture capitalists an "option to abandon."

According to the venture capital literature, the principal function of staged financing is to reduce the amount of a venture capitalist's investment that is put in jeopardy by an entrepreneur's threat to quit the venture. Staged financing also helps reduce a venture capitalist's informational hazard by allowing it to acquire information about the entrepreneur and the innovation before putting too much of its capital at risk.

Several academic observers of the industry have argued that staged financing is the most effective control mechanism available to a venture capitalist. A venture capitalist can discipline an entrepreneur by threatening not to fund any more stages of the project. The ability to credibly threaten to liquidate the firm at the time of negotiating over a stage gives the venture capitalist bargaining leverage. To increase their leverage, venture capitalists often delay their funding until close to the date when the venture's working capital is completely exhausted — what is referred to in the industry as the "burn date." A venture capitalist's leverage is further strengthened by contract provisions giving it a monopoly over future financing. Moreover, even if a venture capitalist allows an entrepreneur to seek additional outside funding, the very refusal by a venture capitalist to provide that additional funding will send negative signals to other potential financiers, making it harder for the entrepreneur to convince third parties to invest in the venture.

c. Power Exerted over the Entrepreneur's Equity Stake

The employment agreement usually provides that if the entrepreneur leaves the venture, she has to, at the option of the venture capitalist, sell back at book value (rather than current market value) any stock she owns. Upon exiting the venture, an entrepreneur will also lose any stock that had been allocated to her — through options, for example — but that had not yet vested. Additionally, the stockholders' agreement will restrict the ability of the entrepreneur to sell her shares.

Venture capitalists make their capital contribution through convertible preferred stock. Like all convertible securities, the preferred stock will have provisions to protect against dilution, in case of stock splits, or issuances of common stock at a lower price than the conversion price. Anti-dilution provisions adjust the conversion price to the price of new shares offered or rights issued. A type of anti-dilution provision often used by venture capitalists is the ratchet-down anti-dilution provision. Such a provision mandates that if even one share is sold at a lower price, the conversion price of all the venture capitalist's preferred stock is adjusted. Once triggered, anti-dilution provisions can wipe out all or most of an entrepreneur's equity stake. Anti-dilution provisions can be used opportunistically, particularly given that the venture capitalist controls the infusion of new capital and the board of directors (which sets the issuance price).

d. Providing Disincentives for Entrepreneur Exit from the Venture

A venture capitalist can increase the entrepreneur's cost of exit by having her sign a non-disclosure agreement. This agreement, which is standard in these transactions, prohibits an entrepreneur from disclosing trade secrets to third parties and requires her to disclose and transfer to the venture any invention or other innovation developed while she was still with the venture. An entrepreneur may also be required to sign an agreement promising not to compete directly with the venture. Although non-compete agreements may be hard to enforce in court, a well-drafted non-disclosure agreement can achieve many of the same results. The entrepreneur's value to other employers (or even as a single proprietor) is significantly reduced by these agreements given the threat of lengthy and expensive litigation. For example, a new employer can be sued for stealing trade secrets, for interfering with an agency relation under agency law, or for tortious interference with a contract.

3. Venture Capitalist Control over Exit Mechanisms

Venture capital contracts give venture capitalists the ability to liquidate the venture or to sell it through a private sale or initial public offering. Venture capital contracts achieve this through three principal mechanisms: (1) a registration rights agreement, which usually requires that the venture file a registration statement with the Securities and Exchange Commission in order to effectuate an initial public offering; (2) the venture capitalist's voting control over the company's equity and control over the board of directors; and (3) redemption rights — that is, a "put" that forces the venture to buy back the venture capitalist's preferred stock (of course, this is of little use if there are no assets to pay for the redemption). Control over these exit strategies will help alleviate the venture capitalist's liquidity hazard.

. . .

Ronald J. Mann, Do Patents Facilitate Financing in the Software Industry?
83 Tex. L. Rev. 961 (2005)*

. . .

To understand the effect of patents on software development, I focus on small firms, which typically are venture backed. . . . First, I discuss the goals of the venture capital investors, which relate to the likelihood that a [firm with a portfolio of patents] can differentiate itself from its competitors in a reliable way. Second, I analyze the ability of patents to provide that reliable differentiation. Although the discussion evinces pessimism about patents as a mechanism for appropriating the value of innovations in the software industry, it also emphasizes a shift in the efficacy of patents as firms pass through the early stages of growth. To that end, I discuss a number of reasons why patents are not likely to allow such appropriation in the earliest stages of a software firm, before it has revenues or begins shipping a product. Then, I show how once the firm moves beyond infancy — to a stage with revenues or a product — patents can have a variety of beneficial effects. That section provides a framework for relating the evidence drawn from my interviews to the existing analytical literature, teasing out of that pattern a set of direct and indirect positive effects that patents can have in various circumstances.

A. Venture Capitalists and Sustainable Differentiation

The development of software is expensive and time consuming. Thus, it is not common for a successful product to be developed by an individual developer working in his spare time. Rather, most commercial software products are the result of years of effort. That effort, in turn, inevitably requires the expenditure of considerable monetary resources. Of course, young firms can — and normally are expected to — go a considerable way toward developing their concept without using the funds of third parties. At some point, however, the individuals within young firms will exhaust their own resources and the readily available resources of friends and family members.

In most cases, the firm then will turn to institutional investment. One of the most prominent and common sources of that investment is a venture capitalist. Venture capital firms are intermediaries that raise funds from institutional investors (corporate pension plans and the like) and invest those funds in startup companies in technology areas. There is a vast literature on the structure of the venture capital industry, including detailed studies of many aspects of the contract structures that firms use in dealing with their investors and with the portfolio companies in which the firms invest. For the purposes of this project, however, the structure of the venture capitalist is relatively unimportant. What is important is to understand as precisely as possible [are the] characteristics of a portfolio that lead venture capitalists to invest. Although there is little quantitative empirical work on that question, the most obvious role that [intellectual property (IP)] protection might play in that process is that the monopoly that IP protection grants on the exploitation of a covered technology could cause investment to flow into the firm that has created the technology. The monopoly supports such a flow of investment — at least in theory — by creating market power that allows the firm to earn supranormal profits by exploiting the technology in question.

The first point to understand about startup companies is that the uniqueness of a firm's product is not likely to be one of the primary issues a potential venture capital investor will analyze in deciding whether to invest in the firm. The investor is likely to examine a large number of plans and invest in only a small number of them — perhaps 6 out of every 1,000. In deciding whether to invest, the investor is likely to start by focusing on issues that validate the firm's competency to execute its concept successfully. For example, investors will be interested in such things as experience in the relevant market and the skills of the management team. One remarked: "Every company of mine that has failed has been [due to] mismanagement of executives, not technical failure." Similarly, even before investors consider whether a firm can protect a market leader position, they will want to know whether the product is one that customers need so desperately that the firm could earn significant revenues from sales of the product.

Still, for firms that have a credible product idea and the expertise to implement it, venture capitalists plainly accept the idea that their goal is to identify firms that will have sufficient market power to earn extraordinary profits. IP protection is important only indirectly, as a tool that might provide that market power. The key is "sustainable differentiation": something special about the particular firm that will enable it to do something that its competitors will not be able to do for the immediate future. The interviews reflect more picturesque terminology — referring to "secret sauce" or "magic dust." But it is clear that the key to a desirable investment opportunity is in the expectation of market power, and all other attributes of the company are indirect predictors of that ultimate goal.

For example, investors commonly referred to lead time or first-mover advantages. The premise is that a portfolio company that truly is the first to provide a sophisticated and functional response to an important problem can expect to earn a supranormal return for years to come. Interestingly enough, that expectation rested on the perception that a firm can maintain a lead on its rivals as long as it keeps improving its technology as quickly as its competitors. I rarely if ever heard investors (as opposed to developers) voice an expectation that portfolio firms obtain and keep a strong market position through "lock-in" or "bandwagon" effects.

That is not to say that IP protection is unimportant. It is clear, however, that different investors have different views about it. Some feel that intellectual property always is important and claim that they never invest without strong patentable technology. Even those investors, however, go on to say that they are not as interested in the IP protection as they are in technology that is sufficiently cutting edge to warrant protection. Others, however, particularly those that emphasize early-stage companies, say IP protection is unimportant for software investments. Still others take a middle position, holding that IP protection matters some, but not all, of the time. Most of those who addressed the subject recognized differing perspectives on the point and argued that those with the other perspectives are misguided. The most likely explanation is that investors are simply implementing different investment models based on their particular expertise.

B.   Patents and Sustainable Differentiation

If understanding what venture capitalists want answers the first question, the second question is whether they believe that patents can provide it. This subpart looks quite closely at the various stages of relatively small private firms and suggests that investors and developers discern a balance of interests that shifts as firms grow from the earliest stage, where patents are not often helpful, through intermediate stages to the terminal stage of venture-backed firms (just before an acquisition or IPO), where patents are almost universally viewed as useful.

1. The Basic Problem: Patents and Appropriability. — A basic problem for software firms at all stages is the sense that even with a patent it often is difficult for a firm to "appropriate" the value of its invention. Specifically, my interview subjects agreed that competitors usually could, without infringing a patent, implement most of the aspects of a patented software product. One reason for that problem is the multifarious nature of software innovation, which permits many solutions to any particular problem. Another contributing factor is the poor match between patents and products in the industry: it is difficult to patent an entire product in the software industry because any particular product is likely to include dozens if not hundreds of separate technological ideas. Thus, it may take a number of novel ideas — and patents — to build a defensible barrier around a product. Another problem is that technology tends to develop so rapidly that by the time a patent is issued — and the formal right to exclusivity commences — the technology may be obsolete. Litigation at that point will involve efforts by the patent owner to challenge technology of a subsequent generation to which application of the patent may be less clear. Yet another problem emphasized in my interviews is the problem of detectability — the difficulty of being sure that a competing product infringes a patent.

The problem of appropriating the value of software through patents is not universal. As I discuss below, some patentees manage to obtain patents of sufficient breadth to cover all possible solutions to an important problem. More broadly, some knowledgeable observers attribute the difficulty of appropriation not to the nature of software technology, but to the infancy of the industry. Because the industry is developing so rapidly, some argue, the nature of technology and even of technological developments is so poorly understood that firms do not recognize the value they could appropriate from patents if they pursued them in an informed way. From this perspective, the relatively limited appropriability provided by software patents should be compared not to the relatively high appropriability of hardware patents, but to the even more limited appropriability that software patents provided a decade ago. Those observers expect that in a matter of decades software technology will be as effectively subject to patent protection as the related hardware technology is at this time.

For now, despite those qualifications, the relevant point is that for most firms, most of the time, there is little prospect that the patents they obtain will provide market power that they can use to exclude competitors. That point is underscored by the relative infrequency with which venture-backed software startups obtain patents. For comparative purposes, consider that only about twenty percent of venture-backed software companies have a patent within five years of their first financing (with each of those firms holding, on average, about two patents), while more than half of biotech startups have patents by that time (with each of those firms averaging about seven patents). Thus, even the tenuous exclusivity such patents could provide is usually not a factor for early-stage software startups because so few of them in fact have patents.

The point is further underscored by the statistical relation between the success of venture-backed software startups and their patenting practices. The general theme of the preceding pages is that there are many factors that play into the ability of a startup firm to obtain funding and success and that intellectual property has a low place on the list of factors, if it appears on that list at all. The data I have collected with Tom Sager supports that view — indicating that patenting practices have at best a minuscule ability to predict the success of a venture-backed software startup.

2. Patents and Prerevenue Startups. — In addition to the problem that patents often are not an optimal mechanism for appropriating the value of software innovation, a number of considerations make it particularly difficult for early-stage companies to employ patents effectively. The key points here are the limited efficacy of litigation for those firms, the constraints on resources that make it infeasible to focus on patenting, and the limited value to prerevenue firms of excluding competitors.

a. The Perils of Small-Firm Litigation. — On the first point, even if an early-stage company had a patent, it is unlikely that it would have resources available to enforce the patent through litigation against a competitor. That is particularly true when the competitor is a large firm. One problem is the disparity in litigation resources. One investor emphasized the concern that a large defendant would "rain lawyers on your head and tie you up in court for the next ten years." A somewhat different concern is the likelihood that the large firm might have a patent that the small firm infringes. If so, the lawsuit might simply alert the large firm to the presence of the small firm.

A related concern is that firm culture is degraded when a firm must rely on licensing revenues instead of developing its own product. Interestingly enough, that sentiment was expressed even at firms that rely heavily on licensing revenues. Those firms encouraged efforts to maintain a product-centered culture that emphasizes production of the firm's own products. One executive explained that a cultural risk arises when a company pursues patent litigation and licensing, explaining that such a strategy unfavorably affects the company's needs. "You don't need sales people; you need attorneys. You don't need solutions architects; you need accountants. So you wind up losing the very people who are, who were, and who continue to be constructive . . . and innovative and help you build things and would give us a continuing competitive advantage."

Indeed, the one interviewee whose firm had a major licensing program related that the entire program was entrusted to third-party professionals so that it would not interfere with the focus of the onsite software engineers.

b. Diversion of Focus. — Similarly, many investors and developers emphasized that attention to patents can be damaging to a startup because it has the potential to divert limited time and resources from what is likely to be a highly time-pressured effort to develop a product and convince customers and investors of its worth before the firm runs out of capital resources. One investor explained: "[We] typically find that the companies that focus on just patents don't have the right view of what is important, and they really are therefore not successful in business. And they're usually not around to prosecute their patents." Developers understand the point well. As one said: "Every dollar we spend on [patenting] is a dollar we can't spend on a software engineer." Another, with a patent-leaning background from his days at IBM, commented: "Patentability is something we will pursue, but let's get the product out first."

Thus, a young company is presented with a challenging task. If the nature of the firm's innovation is such that IP is ever likely to be important, it must spend sufficient resources on the protection and development of intellectual property from the earliest days of the company — as an investment in the possibility that the firm might grow to the point at which IP is useful. The firm that fails to protect its IP at the earliest stage is like a desperate ship at sea that empties its drinking water in the hope of evading a faster pursuer: it might survive for the time being, but it may have sown the seeds of its inevitable failure if it survives to a later stage. On the other hand, it must not spend so much that the company fails before it is able to recoup its investment.

Firms have developed a number of strategies for dealing with that problem. Some involve using half measures to protect the IP, such as filing provisional applications or omitting standard practices related to documentation of the work of engineers. Those practices do not directly abandon the IP, but they may make it more costly and difficult to protect it in the future. The bottom line is that even for companies that have begun to earn substantial revenues it often does not seem appropriate to devote the resources necessary to ensure that all of the firm's innovations are patented. Others — it must be said that executives with prior experience at large IP-sensitive firms like IBM or Bell Labs populate this category — seem to relish the discipline of making sure that the IP is pinned down no matter how difficult it may seem to find the time and resources to do so. The difficulty of this strategic choice, coupled with the difficulty in accurately predicting the future prospects for their products and their IP, is a problem about which startup software executives worry constantly.

Investors, of course, are aware of this problem. Their approach typically does not extend to forcing (or even urging) their portfolio companies to seek patent protection. However, they do go to considerable lengths to evaluate the IP that potential portfolio companies have. In a typical process, the venture capitalist (VC) knows most of the reputable patent attorneys in the local community. If one of those attorneys has filed a patent for a potential portfolio company, the VC discusses the patent with that lawyer. If an attorney with whom the VC did not have a preexisting relationship filed the patent application, the VC has the patent studied by an attorney in whom he has confidence. In the context of the interviews, it was clear that the intent of this examination is not purely technical — whether this is a patent likely to be granted — but also a broader exercise to understand what type of market power the patent might (or might not) provide. Indeed, the current practice-oriented literature characterizes examination of market power as central to careful due diligence practices. The practice at first seems to be in tension with the thesis of this section — that patents have little value for the earliest-stage startups. In fact, however, it leads into the point of the next section: the firms that survive their earliest days may reap substantial value from patents.

c. The Limited Benefits of Exclusion. — One final element of the patenting calculus for small firms may seem obvious, but is so important to the overall framework as to warrant brief notice. Because those firms do not yet have a product, they have no opportunity for revenues. Thus, the benefits they reap from excluding competitors are minimal at best. Only if they survive to a later stage — in which they can hope to profit from their own exploitation of that product — will they be able to reap any substantial value from the exclusion of competitors.

3. The Increasing Value of Patents for Later-Stage Startups. — When firms mature to the point of having revenues, the systematic difficulties that plague the efforts of prerevenue startups to obtain and exploit patents dissipate. That does not mean, however, that patents suddenly become a philosopher's stone that will turn their creative endeavors into IPOs. Rather, the underlying problem of appropriability continues to plague most efforts to use patents directly to exclude competitors. Still, my interviews suggest a series of benefits that patents might provide for later-stage software startups. This section describes those benefits by reference to the bodies of existing literature that have offered them as theoretical possibilities.

a. Direct Effects: Protecting a Space for Innovation. — The most important point concerns the direct ability of a software patent to carve out for the firm a space in which it can innovate without competition. I explain above that my interview subjects often complain about how difficult it is to use patents to exclude competitors. Although there is some truth in this complaint, it is an overgeneralization, at least once a firm reaches the stage at which it has designed a product that it can market to customers.

First, it is clear that some firms in the industry obtain a substantial amount of revenues by licensing the use of their patents to competitors that need to use the patented technology in their own products. Indeed, even in my limited sample, three small Austin companies — Applied Science Fiction, Bluecurrent, and Forgent — have obtained substantial revenues from patent licenses. I do not believe that industry wide statistics quantify the size of that market, but it plainly is substantial. Those transactions — and others like them — demonstrate that some software patents are sufficiently robust to allow their holders to appropriate substantial value from the underlying inventions. Licensing transactions are noteworthy given the difficulties small firms face in enforcing patents against large firms. [T]he small firm with a revenue producing product must be quite confident in the value of its technology before it wisely can cross swords with a company like IBM.

More generally, it seems clear that the received wisdom that patents are not useful to appropriate software-related inventions is overstated. Two separate points are important. The first is the distinction between the relative rarity of observed offensive patent use — for out-licensing or litigation — and the use of patents to exclude competitors. The relative rarity of offensive use of patents does not prove that the patents are insufficiently robust to exclude competitors. As discussed in the previous section, there are many reasons why a firm might want to wait until late in its development to advertise the nature of its technology and its proprietary claims to that technology.

A firm can refrain from offensive use of its patents and still derive important value from the patents as an exclusion device. Contrary to the perception that patents tilt the playing field in favor of large incumbent firms to the disadvantage of small firms, patents in this context afford a unique opportunity to the small startup. The patent system grants the small firm an automatic stay of competitive activity that remains in force long enough for the firm to attempt to develop its technology. For large firms, the marginal increase in appropriability that comes from patents may have little benefit: IBM could compete quite successfully against smaller firms even if it did not have patents protecting its product from copycat competitors. For the smaller firm, however, the ability of the implicit threat of patent litigation to prevent incumbents like IBM and Microsoft from taking its technology can be the difference between life and death. As one executive put it: "What's protected me from other people ripping [off our product] has been the specter of patent infringement."

It is instructive to think of the offensive uses of software patents reported in the press. Among the most famous incidents are the successful attempts by small firms — Stac in the mid-1990s and Eolas in 2003 — to force alterations in Microsoft products that arguably infringed patents held by those firms, and the similar attempt by InterTrust to assert rights to digital rights management technology that was important to several Microsoft products. The profits from suing other small firms seem to be so much smaller that it is easy to see why that kind of "horizontal" litigation is apparently less common. I note that the story depicted in the press is consistent with empirical work suggesting that patents held by small firms are more likely to be litigated than patents held by large firms. This also finds strong support in Bronwyn Hall's recent work suggesting that patent rights in complex product industries are more valuable for younger firms than they are for older incumbent firms.

Second, the ability of a patent to appropriate the value of an innovation is often said to vary along several dimensions. One of the most common is the nature of the particular innovation. Thus, it is often thought futile to rely on a patent if the innovation lies in a method of writing software code. At the other end of the continuum, patents that protect an ultimate functionality that the software provides or an algorithm necessary to provide that functionality are more likely to be important in excluding potential competitors. Interestingly, that distinction seems to undermine the conventional wisdom dividing patents along another dimension, in which "process" patents tend to be less valuable than "product" patents. In the software industry, a patent on the product tends to have relatively little value because of the ease of designing a distinct product. A patent on the process that the product implements is much more likely to be valuable, if only because it often is possible for the claimed process to be defined broadly enough to include all practicable methods of competition.

A sectoral variation in patenting appears to be related to those dimensions of analysis. As the empirical data presented in a related paper I authored with Tom Sager demonstrates, there is a strong variation in the rate of patenting by venture-backed firms in different sectors of the software industry. For example, the average number of patents in the dataset was about 0.6 patents per firm. Several sectors, however, had markedly higher rates, including graphics and digital imaging, expert systems and natural language, multimedia, and security. At the same time, some relatively important sectors had unusually low rates of patenting, including email and internet software, applications software, and financial software. That variation is interesting because it can be discerned in a quantitative way even though patents are thought to be less valuable for software than they are for hardware, and even though patents are much less common in the software industry than in some other industries.

This is not a topic on which my interviews produced constructive results. I focused several of my interviews on firms known to me to have commercially valuable patents. Notwithstanding the discussion and empirical evidence above, executives of those firms that expressed a view as to why their patents were valuable generally believed it had nothing to do with the nature of the innovation. Rather, they attributed it to the firm's ability to obtain a patent that staked out a sufficiently large field to cover all plausible variations on the relevant technology. Still, it seems likely that variation is related at least in part to the nature of innovation in different sectors, with higher rates of patenting associated with types of innovation more susceptible to appropriation by patent. However strongly my interview subjects rejected such a distinction, the data powerfully suggest that further inquiry is warranted. For now, my intuition is that the patterns of patenting rates most likely relate to the distinction between product firms (for which patents would be more useful) and service firms (for which patents would be less useful).

Taken together, those two points portray a world in which small firms struggle to innovate, facing the pervasive concern that a competitor might appropriate any useful invention at any time. Given the difficulties those firms face in sustaining differentiation, the possibility that patents can provide shelter for some firms is important. The extent of shelter may be difficult to predict because it depends primarily on the breadth of market protection a patent has by the time it is issued. Furthermore, the frequency of shelter is open to doubt; it plainly was not relevant to most of the firms that I interviewed. The interviews that I discuss above, however, do suggest that shelter is real in the place where its effect would be most important — in the minds of firms doing the innovation. It certainly would be valuable to know more about the frequency with which small firms obtain patents of sufficient strength to use in this way. However, even without quantitative information, it is difficult to believe that this is not a major part of what makes patents and their breadth an item of interest to investors.

b. Indirect Effects. — The most intriguing information from my interviews relates to patent benefits that do not involve direct exploitation of the patents. Those benefits fall into two classes: facilitation of a litigation-free zone through a pattern of cross-licensing; and a set of what I call "information" effects — beneficial effects that patents have on information related to the firm's technology.

(1) Facilitating a Licensing Equilibrium. — As suggested above, many in the industry completely deny any substantial use of patents to exclude competitors. Rather, the most prominent explanation for patents in the interviews was that patents are useful as "barter" in cross-licensing agreements that the firm enters if it reaches a sufficiently mature stage to be a significant player in the industry.

. . .

(2) Information Effects. — The last set of effects relates to information generated through a firm's participation in the patent system. Moving along the course of a firm's development, these effects fall into three classes: (A) the ability of patents to facilitate the firm's efforts to codify tacit knowledge, (B) the firm's subsequent ability to signal the discipline and technical expertise that allowed it to codify that knowledge, and (C) the use of the patent as a signal of the underlying technology.

. . .

4. Patents and Large Firms. — Although the bulk of my interviewing base is small venture-backed startups, the interviews and publicly available information do provide enough information to give a good idea of the role that patents play in large firms. Because much of the information is plain from the discussion above, I discuss that topic briefly solely to complete the picture.

First . . . large firms gain relatively little through litigation or the exclusion of competitors from patented spaces because large firms often can compete successfully with small firms without excluding the competitor. The saying that "nobody ever got fired for buying IBM [or Microsoft]" is not baseless, and in a contest between IBM and a small startup, both with equivalent products, IBM (or Microsoft) often will prevail. In contests among large firms, litigation is rare because of cross-licensing of portfolios.

Second, patents provide considerable benefits to large firms by enabling them to participate in cross-licensing agreements that give them the freedom of action to design and deploy products as they wish, without regard to the IP portfolios of competitors. It may be, as I argue above, that large firms that use their portfolios solely for that purpose would be better off without the costs of developing and maintaining those portfolios, but in the existing milieu, each firm has a strong incentive to collect patents for that purpose.

Third, many — though certainly not all — large firms obtain substantial revenues from directly exploiting their patent portfolios. IBM, for example, earns literally billions of dollars each year exploiting its patent portfolio; a significant share of the revenue comes from its software patents. Thus, although different firms have different strategies, the potential for large firms to earn substantial revenues from direct exploitation of patents does exist. Information about the amount of those revenues would be valuable in assessing the net effect of patents, but that data is not readily available.

Michael H. Brodowski, Ph.D.,
Kirkpatrick & Lockhart Nicholson Graham, Boston, MA,
Making Intellectual Property Portfolios
Attractive to Venture Capitalists
http://www.buildingipvalue.com/05_NA/159_162.htm
(last visited on May 20, 2005)*

Intellectual property (IP) rights, especially patents, often are a cornerstone for building a company. Not only do IP rights provide an avenue for entry into a marketplace, they facilitate raising the capital required for the company's development and growth. Venture capitalists frequently look for early-stage companies or raw ideas that have commercial potential, provided that adequate IP rights have been or can be secured to protect the underlying business. Because IP rights can play a substantial role in the success of the business, an attractive IP portfolio can increase the likelihood of investment.

Accordingly, from its infancy, a company seeking funding should consider strategically creating an IP estate. Following good IP practices from the outset can ease the preparation and organization involved in marketing the business to investors and subsequent due diligence inquiries, which have become increasingly more thorough. Therefore, important considerations to keep in mind while building a business include developing a portfolio of IP rights protecting the business, which may include licenses and other agreements; establishing the ownership of those rights; and avoiding infringing upon the IP rights of third parties.

Portfolio Development

Investors occasionally are impressed with the total number of properties in an IP portfolio. However, savvy investors are more interested in whether there is a strategic relationship between the IP and the business. Consequently, a company needs to devise an IP portfolio development strategy that integrates its business plan with its IP. Although the underlying technology may be very sophisticated, it is insufficient to understand and promote merely the science. Rather, it is also important to understand the use of the technology in a business context so as to maximize the value of the IP rights. For example, a patent that fully describes the technology, including its commercial applications, instead of reading like a scientific journal article, communicates its potential value to would-be investors as well as supports protection of the significant commercial embodiments.

Although typically focused on patents, an IP portfolio should include other rights depending on the particular business and industry. Copyright protection can be valuable for internet, software and information technology-based businesses. For certain industries and technologies, trade secrets and proprietary information can form the basis of or supplement an IP portfolio. Trademark or service mark protection can be important for a consumer products or services company. While each type of IP can be independently effective, combinations of IP can provide layers of protection. For example, computer software may be protected with both patents and copyrights.

Among the various IP rights available to a business, patents tend to provide the most common and important rights for start-up and early-stage companies, especially in the life sciences area. Unlike computer-related businesses, biotechnology and small molecule therapeutics companies often require many years to bring a product to the marketplace and achieve profitability. Thus, the initial value of such companies often lies in their patent portfolios.

Because resources usually are limited, a company initially should focus its patenting efforts on its core technologies. The claims of a patent determine the breadth of protection. Accordingly, the claims should be of the appropriate scope commensurate with the underlying idea. For a pioneering invention in a new technological field, the claims should be written to encompass the idea as generically as possible with the least amount of description. Consequently, competitors should confront a broad barrier to enter the field. If the idea is an improvement of an old technology, the claims will need to be more focused to avoid being indistinguishable from the pre-existing technology. In either case, narrower claims directed to specific embodiments can result in quicker issue of a patent, which may be desirable in rapidly developing technological fields.

Regardless of the scope of the claims, it is paramount to craft them to include the company's important commercial applications. Although a patent application may be well written and include applications of the technology, if the claims are not carefully drafted to coordinate with the business plan, the resulting patent is less valuable. That is, the claims of a patent application should be drafted not only to be patentable, but also to cover aspects of the technology that are commercially significant. For example, a patent application regarding a new diagnostic assay typically would include claims to the test method itself. However, if the diagnostic assay will be embodied in a test kit sold to consumers, then claims directed to the test kit also should be pursued.

. . .

An important component of a company's strategic patent plan is determining in which countries to obtain patent protection. The costs of multiple filings tend to mount quite rapidly so the goal should be to formulate a global strategy that will adequately protect the company's proprietary technology within a sound budgetary framework. Companies should consider filing patent applications in countries in which they make and/or expect to make substantial sales of their patented products or services. Companies could also look at those markets in which their competitors are most likely to manufacture infringing products. In this way, the company may be able to stop an infringing product at its source rather than pursue the infringer in each geographic market.

Companies that rely on internally developed processes and research tools, such as drug candidate screening methods, may find it more beneficial to protect their technology as trade secrets, as patents relating to methods of making products or of conducting research often are difficult to enforce. Patent protection, however, is typically the more prudent way to proceed as it prevents a company from being blocked from practicing its own technology if a third party independently develops and successfully patents the same idea. However, protection as a trade secret potentially permits the company to practice the technology into perpetuity without the time limit of a patent term. If a company does maintain trade secrets, it should have a formal policy in place to ensure that the trade secrets remain as such and are protected under law. An adequate policy should at least include appropriate confidentiality and non-compete agreements for key personnel, limit disclosure of important information and documents to a need-to-know basis and maintain physical security of the company's facilities, including its computers.

Beverly A. Berneman, J.D., LL.M.,
Benjamin, Berneman, and Brom, LLC,
Venture Capital Financing for the Development of Intellectual Property Assets: A Marriage of Convenience
Practising Law Institute,
Handling Intellectual Property Issues in
Business Transactions 2005
824 PLI/Pat 223 (2005)*

I.   INTRODUCTION

For the entrepreneur, [a period encompassing] the development of a new idea can be a heady time. The entrepreneur has a great idea that has marketing potential. But, the entrepreneur needs funding in order to develop the idea. Thus, the excitement of developing an idea can be tempered by the inability to find development financing. When that idea involves different types of patents, copyrights, trademarks and trade secrets, finding financing to develop the idea can be grueling and frustrating.

The financing world offers a wide variety of financing opportunities. The entrepreneur must find the right fit for idea development. Financing schemes range from finding "angels" to obtaining conventional asset based loans.

Within the range of possible financing schemes falls venture capital. Venture capital groups provide financing to riskier and unproven enterprises. Venture capital serves the start up firm in development. In exchange for the needed capital to fund the enterprise, the venture capital investor usually demands stock or subscriptions to acquire stock. Venture capital financing offers many advantages to the entrepreneur such as the availability of funds for assets in development.

Unfortunately, since the recent dot.com debacle, venture capital financing groups have a healthy skepticism when the enterprise has primarily intellectual property assets.

For both entrepreneur and the venture capital group, the pre-relationship due diligence period can be critical. If both parties pay attention to the pre-relationship due diligence, the ultimate relationship will benefit both parties. The entrepreneur and the venture capital group must first find each other and they must engage in an elaborate mating ritual to confirm that they have a future together. Thus, the entrepreneur's future enterprise and the venture capital group can look upon their pre-relationship investigation as a form of courtship and marriage.

As will be discussed below, the phases of meeting, courting, and wedded bliss can provide the entrepreneur's enterprise with financing and the venture group with a successful investment.

II.   THE HOMEWORK PHASE

The entrepreneur must strive to make the current status of the enterprise and its future potential attractive to the venture capital group. Before the entrepreneur even begins to search for the perfect venture capital mate, the entrepreneur has to have a good idea of at least three things:

1.   What business plan will the enterprise operate under?

2.   What assets will the enterprise need to operate?

3.   What management organization will help the enterprise accomplish its goals?

The formulation of the business plan and the assets needed to operate often go hand in hand. The entrepreneur should have a clear idea of what the goals of the enterprise will be and how those goals will be accomplished. Once the goals are identified, the role of intellectual property assets can be assessed.

The entrepreneur should identify his assets by conducting his own due diligence that consists of the following:

1.   Asset audit where the entrepreneur identifies each of the types of intellectual property assets that will be owned or developed by the enterprise;

2.   Value investigation of the intellectual property assets, including researching market impact, the risk of third party development and the risk of infringement; and

3.   The asset audit and value identification can and should be as extensive and detailed as the venture capital group's suggested due diligence that will be discussed further below.

The entrepreneur should also take steps to build a strong organization before approaching a venture capital firm. Building a strong reference list will add credibility to the enterprise. Many startup businesses are long on innovation but short on skilled management. The enterprise can address this problem in two primary ways. First, the enterprise should build an active advisory board. This will demonstrate to the venture capital group that the entrepreneur has a strong basis for innovation as well as management. Second the entrepreneur should identify its key personnel and document their relationship to the enterprise through employment agreements and shareholder agreements (where appropriate).

III.   THE MATCHMAKING PHASE

While most venture capital groups prefer to invest in an enterprise that has some operating history, a select few will invest in the entirely new venture. Venture capital groups usually concentrate in a specific area such as pharmaceuticals, electronics or biotechnology. Some firms also focus their efforts in certain geographical areas.

Each side must do a lot of "dating" before finding the right match. Venture capital groups receive thousands of business plans each year. They cull out those proposed enterprises that have very little chance of success. On the other side, an entrepreneur will pitch to dozens of venture capital groups before finding a venture capital firm that will fund the enterprise. When the venture capital group has a basic knowledge of the enterprise's industry, the match between venture capital and the enterprise has a better chance for success.

This 'match making' phase involves effort on both sides to find the right fit both in terms of industries and amount of capital needed to fund the enterprise's success. Once the right "match" is found, the parties then enter into phase.

IV.   THE COURTING PHASE

During the courting phase, the parties need to learn more about each other to insure that a formal relationship between them will be a comfortable fit. The parties should focus on the exchange of reliable information. The venture capital group will look to the entrepreneur to provide as much information as possible. The more reliable the information from the entrepreneur, the more comfortable the venture capital group will feel during the courting phase. The courting phase is made up of four stages of due diligence.

[These stages of due diligence entail the following types of information gathering steps and analyses:

1. Identifying intellectual property assets that are integral to the function of the enterprise, verifying the ownership of those assets, and ensuring that these assets are free from encumbrances;

2. Reviewing the features and background of the individual intellectual property interests identified in phase 1 to determine the scope of rights associated with these interests and possible grounds for unenforceability of those rights;

3. Verifying key information relied upon in prior phases of due diligence reviews through such investigative techniques as obtaining and evaluating documents used to register interests, searching databases to verify rights, and interviewing key business and technology staff members; and

4. Interpreting the relationship between the confirmed intellectual property interests of the company under scrutiny and the probability of success of the

company, taking into account such factors as how those interests are used in the enterprise, how the interests relate to the company's present and projected products, and the expertise and experience of the company's management regarding means to commercialize products based on the type of intellectual property assets held by the company.]

V. THE PRENUPTIAL PHASE

Once due diligence has been completed and the parties determine that they can go forward with the relationship, they enter the prenuptial phase. During this phase, the parties define the structure of their relationship. In a successful venture capital relationship, both parties understand the rules. Thus, the written agreement between the venture capital group and the enterprise should:

1. Define each and every assumption and expectation;

2. Clearly set forth any expectations regarding the progress of research and development and marketing of the enterprises products or services;

3. [Specify the] stages at which funds will be disbursed over time; and

4. Provide disincentives for key personnel to leave the enterprise putting the entire venture at risk.

Once the parties have a written document to describe their relationship, the enterprise can begin using the financing.

VI. THE WEDDING PHASE

Once the venture capital group and the enterprise have reached an agreement, the marriage can be a happy one. However, as with any marriage, both parties must continue to work together in order to keep the relationship functioning. Ongoing disclosures on both sides aid in the progress of the relationship. Both sides should also be aware of and plan for a few situations that may derail the happy relationship.

"Founder's disease" occurs when the entrepreneur, who is good at innovation but not so good at day to day management, becomes discouraged and leaves the enterprise. The parties should have incentives in place to keep the founding entrepreneur in a position where he or she can do the most good.

The possibility of a change in circumstances, such as a change in laws or a shift in projected market conditions may eviscerate the success of the enterprise. If so, the parties should have an exit strategy for the liquidation of the venture.

VII. CONCLUSION

Venture capital financing can be the perfect way to finance the development of an enterprise's intellectual property assets. However, no matter how perfect it is, the experience will not be a successful one unless both the venture capital group and the entrepreneur carefully navigate the road to their ultimate relationship.

As discussed above, the proper due diligence and information exchange can make for a happy marriage between the entrepreneur and the venture capital group.

NOTES & QUESTIONS

1. What features of Digital Ignition's initial plans for developing its business and related technologies may make the firm unattractive as a candidate for venture capital financing? What aspects of the company's ownership structure may impede further investment by venture capitalists? What weaknesses in the company's present intellectual property interests may concern venture capitalists? What types of intellectual property will Digital Ignition be counting on using that may be freely used by its competitors, leaving the company with little competitive advantage?

2. How can Digital Ignition improve its likelihood of obtaining venture capital financing? What types of legal strategies and steps will be helpful in this regard? How will changes in the company's ownership structure that are likely to attract venture capitalists affect Digital Ignition's initial investors? What types of steps can the company take to clarify the strength and value of its present intellectual property interests? What additional intellectual property interests (or programs to systematically obtain such interests) might be attractive to venture capitalists?

C. FINANCING THROUGH LOANS SECURED BY INTERESTS IN INTELLECTUAL PROPERTY

Intellectual property interests can secure loan repayments and thereby further the financing of business activities at various stages of company growth. A security interest in intellectual property allows the holder to claim ownership of the intellectual property upon the occurrence of a specified event such as the failure of a borrower to make required loan payments. Early in the development of a company, security interests in intellectual property may be granted to key lenders in exchange for substantial infusions of operating funds. In later stages of business development, mature companies with valuable intellectual property assets such as film libraries or complex software may obtain loans secured by these assets to accelerate the companies' access to the value of these properties. Through these loans, a company can gain immediate access to the loan proceeds, while spreading and balancing the timing of loan repayments against the pattern of licensing royalties or sale proceeds obtained as slowly realized returns on the assets.

As with security interests generally, a security interest in intellectual property is typically established through two sets of steps: initial actions to attach a security interest to a particular intellectual property asset and additional actions to perfect the security interest. Absent successful completion of both these types of steps, a purported security interest in intellectual property may not be enforceable against parties who succeed to ownership of the intellectual property without knowledge of the security interest. This means that a party relying on an improperly created security interest in intellectual property to reduce the risks associated with repayment of a loan may have her security interest cut off by an assignee of the intellectual property involved. A party relying on an improperly created security interest in intellectual property may also have that interest cut off in the course of a bankruptcy proceeding involving a borrower as the intellectual property interests of the borrower are sold off in order to satisfy claims against the bankrupt. *See generally* H. Jason Gold & Christopher M. Mills, *Intellectual Property and Bankruptcy: Protecting Your Investment*, Metro. Corp. Couns., March 2004, at 7.

Unfortunately, the actions needed to establish properly perfected and enforceable security interests in some types of intellectual property remain in doubt. The main source of uncertainty in this area stems from the interplay of federal and state standards governing the creation and perfection of security interests in intellectual property. In general, the creation of security interests in intellectual property is a function of state laws modeled after the provisions of Article 9 of the Uniform Commercial Code (UCC). These provisions treat intellectual property interests as intangible assets and describe how a party may create and perfect enforceable security interests in such assets.

However, many important intellectual property interests — such as patents, copyrights, and federally registered trademarks — are products of federal law. The provisions of federal statutes specifying the proper means for recording these federally-defined interests may preempt and trump state law provisions regarding the proper means to create and perfect security interests. Courts have reached mixed results in analyzing whether federal statutory standards for recording intellectual property interests arising under federal laws were intended by Congress to preempt state standards governing the recording and perfection of security interests.

The court's opinion in *In re Peregrine Entertainment, Ltd.* below describes the UCC's standards for the perfection of security interests in intellectual property and the possible preemption of those standards under federal copyright laws. The impacts of federal standards on the perfection of interests in patents, trademarks, and trade secrets are discussed in the notes following the *Peregrine* case.

IN RE PEREGRINE ENTERTAINMENT, LTD.
United States District Court for the Central District of California
116 B.R. 194 (1990)

KOZINSKI, Circuit Judge[1]

This appeal from a decision of the bankruptcy court raises an issue never before confronted by a federal court in a published opinion: Is a security interest in a copyright perfected by an appropriate filing with the United States

---

[1] [FN*] Sitting by designation pursuant to 28 U.S.C. § 291(b) (1982).

Copyright Office or by a UCC-1 financing statement filed with the relevant secretary of state?

I

National Peregrine, Inc. (NPI) is a Chapter 11 debtor in possession whose principal assets are a library of copyrights, distribution rights and licenses to approximately 145 films, and accounts receivable arising from the licensing of these films to various programmers. NPI claims to have an outright assignment of some of the copyrights; as for the others, NPI claims it has an exclusive license to distribute in a certain territory, or for a certain period of time.[2]

In June 1985, Capitol Federal Savings and Loan Association of Denver (Cap Fed) extended to American National Enterprises, Inc., NPI's predecessor by merger, a six million dollar line of credit secured by what is now NPI's film library. Both the security agreement and the UCC-1 financing statements[3] filed by Cap Fed describe the collateral as "[a]ll inventory consisting of films and all accounts, contract rights, chattel paper, general intangibles, instruments, equipment, and documents related to such inventory, now owned or hereafter acquired by the Debtor."[4] Although Cap Fed filed its UCC-1 financing statements in

---

[2] [FN1] . . . For purposes of presenting the legal issues raised by this appeal, it is sufficient if at least one of the films in NPI's library is the subject of a valid copyright. Cap Fed has stipulated that there is at least one such film, the unforgettable "Renegade Ninjas," starring Hiroki Matsukota, Kennosuke Yorozuya and Teruhiko Aoi, in what many consider to be their career performances.

[3] [FN2] All references are to the California version of the Uniform Commercial Code.

[4] [FN3] The UCC-1 [financing statement filed to perfect the security interest] described the collateral as follows:

> All inventory consisting of films and all accounts, contract rights, chattel paper, *general intangibles,* instruments, equipment, and documents related to such inventory, now owned or hereafter acquired by the Debtor, including, but not limited to:
>
> > (i) all accounts, contract rights, chattel paper, instruments, equipment, *general intangibles* and other obligations of any kind whether now owned or hereafter acquired arising out of or in connection with the sale or lease of the films, and all rights whether now or hereafter existing in and to all security agreements, leases, invoices, claims, instruments, notes, drafts, acceptances, and other contracts and documents securing or otherwise relating to any such accounts, contract rights, chattel paper, instruments, *general intangibles* or obligations and other documents or computer tapes or disks related to any of the above; and
> >
> > (ii) all proceeds of any and all of the foregoing property, including cash and noncash proceeds, and, to the extent not otherwise included, all payments under insurance (whether or not the Secured Party is the loss payee thereof), or any indemnity, warranty or guaranty, payable by reason of loss or damage to or otherwise with respect to any of the foregoing property.

See Memorandum of Decision re Motion for Partial Summary Adjudication (Nov. 14, 1989) at 4 (emphasis added). The security agreement described the collateral in nearly identical language. *See id.* at 3.

UCC § 9106 defines "general intangibles" as "any personal property (including things in action) other than goods, accounts, chattel paper, documents, instruments, and money." The official commentary to section 9106, adopted by numerous states (including California), specifically identifies "copyrights, trademarks and patents" as included in the definition of general intangibles. *See United States v. Anderson,* 895 F.2d 641, 647 (9th Cir.1990) (Kozinski, J., dissenting)

California, Colorado and Utah,[5] it did not record its security interest in the United States Copyright Office.

NPI filed a voluntary petition for bankruptcy on January 30, 1989. On April 6, 1989, NPI filed an amended complaint against Cap Fed, contending that the bank's security interest in the copyrights to the films in NPI's library and in the accounts receivable generated by their distribution were unperfected because Cap Fed failed to record its security interest with the Copyright Office. NPI claimed that, as a debtor in possession, it had a judicial lien on all assets in the bankruptcy estate, including the copyrights and receivables. Armed with this lien, it sought to avoid, recover and preserve Cap Fed's supposedly unperfected security interest for the benefit of the estate.

The parties filed cross-motions for partial summary judgment on the question of whether Cap Fed had a valid security interest in the NPI film library. The bankruptcy court held for Cap Fed. *See* Memorandum of Decision re Motion for Partial Summary Adjudication (Nov. 14, 1989) [hereinafter "Memorandum of Decision"] and Order re Summary Adjudication of Issues (Dec. 18, 1989). NPI appeals.

II

A. *Where to File*

The Copyright Act provides that "[a]ny transfer of copyright ownership or other document pertaining to a copyright" may be recorded in the United States Copyright Office. 17 U.S.C. § 205(a); *see* Copyright Office Circular 12: Recordation of Transfers and Other Documents (reprinted in 1 Copyright L.Rep. (CCH) ¶ 15,015) [hereinafter "Circular 12"]. A "transfer" under the Act includes any "mortgage" or "hypothecation of a copyright," whether "in whole or in part" and "by any means of conveyance or by operation of law." 17 U.S.C. §§ 101, 201(d)(1); *see* 3 *Nimmer on Copyright* § 10.05[A], at 10-43 to 10-45 (1989). The terms "mortgage" and "hypothecation" include a pledge of property as security or collateral for a debt. *See Black's Law Dictionary* 669 (5th ed. 1979). In addition, the Copyright Office has defined a "document pertaining to a copyright" as one that

> has a direct or indirect relationship to the existence, scope, duration, or identification of a copyright, or to the ownership, division, allocation, licensing, transfer, or exercise of rights under a copyright. That relationship may be past, present, future, or potential.

(although legislative history generally is a poor source of guidance for statutory interpretation, official commentaries are persuasive).

[5] [FN4] Under UCC § 9103(3)(b), "[t]he law . . . of the jurisdiction in which the debtor is located governs the perfection and the effect of perfection or nonperfection of the security interest" in a general intangible. "A debtor shall be deemed located at the debtor's place of business . . . [or] at the debtor's chief executive office if [it] has more than one place of business. . . ." U.S.C.§ 9103(3)(d). Because NPI is a Utah corporation that conducts much of its business in California, Cap Fed apparently deemed filing in both states prudent. Presumably, Cap Fed filed in Colorado because its own headquarters are located in Denver.

37 C.F.R. § 201.4(a)(2); *see also* Compendium of Copyright Office Practices II ¶¶ 1602-1603 (identifying which documents the Copyright Office will accept for filing).

It is clear from the preceding that an agreement granting a creditor a security interest in a copyright may be recorded in the Copyright Office. Likewise, because a copyright entitles the holder to receive all income derived from the display of the creative work, *see* 17 U.S.C. § 106, an agreement creating a security interest in the receivables generated by a copyright may also be recorded in the Copyright Office. Thus, Cap Fed's security interest *could* have been recorded in the Copyright Office; the parties seem to agree on this much. The question is, does the UCC provide a parallel method of perfecting a security interest in a copyright? One can answer this question by reference to either federal or state law; both inquiries lead to the same conclusion.

1. Even in the absence of express language, federal regulation will preempt state law if it is so pervasive as to indicate that "Congress left no room for supplementary state regulation," or if "the federal interest is so dominant that the federal system will be assumed to preclude enforcement of state laws on the same subject." *Hillsborough County v. Automated Medical Laboratories, Inc.,* 471 U.S. 707, 713, 105 S.Ct. 2371, 2375, 85 L.Ed.2d 714 (1985) (internal quotations omitted).[6] Here, the comprehensive scope of the federal Copyright Act's recording provisions, along with the unique federal interests they implicate, support the view that federal law preempts state methods of perfecting security interests in copyrights and related accounts receivable.

The federal copyright laws ensure "predictability and certainty of copyright ownership," "promote national uniformity" and "avoid the practical difficulties of determining and enforcing an author's rights under the differing laws and in the separate courts of the various States." As discussed above, section 205(a) of the Copyright Act establishes a uniform method for recording security interests in copyrights. A secured creditor need only file in the Copyright Office in order to give "all persons constructive notice of the facts stated in the recorded document." 17 U.S.C. § 205(c).[7] Likewise, an interested third party

---

[6] [FN6] The Copyright Act does expressly preempt state law in respect to the exclusive rights possessed by holders of copyrights under federal law. *See* 17 U.S.C. § 301(a). In *Del Madera Properties v. Rhodes & Gardner, Inc.,* 820 F.2d 973 (9th Cir.1987), the Ninth Circuit adopted the "extra element" test, holding that in order to survive a federal preemption challenge under section 301, a state law must involve rights that are qualitatively different from the exclusive rights established by section 106 of the Copyright Act. *Id.* at 977. The exclusive rights listed in section 106 include the rights to reproduce the copyrighted work, to distribute the work, to prepare derivative works and to display or perform the work. *See* 17 U.S.C. § 106.

Section 301 is inapplicable because here we are concerned not with the creation of the exclusive rights under section 106, but rather their transfer through the creation of a security interest. The transfer of a copyright interest is fundamentally different from the creation of exclusive rights to a work itself, and is governed by separate provisions in the Copyright Act. *See* 17 U.S.C. §§ 101, 201(d), 205. Therefore, under the rationale of *Del Madera Properties,* the preemptive language of section 301 has no bearing on the issues presented in this case.

[7] [FN7] For a recordation under section 205 to be effective as against third parties, the copyrighted work must also have been registered pursuant to 17 U.S.C. §§ 408, 409, 410. *See* 17 U.S.C. § 205(c)(2). Of course, registration is also a prerequisite to judicial enforcement of a copyright,

need only search the indices maintained by the Copyright Office to determine whether a particular copyright is encumbered.

A recording system works by virtue of the fact that interested parties have a specific place to look in order to discover with certainty whether a particular interest has been transferred or encumbered. To the extent there are competing recordation schemes, this lessens the utility of each; when records are scattered in several filing units, potential creditors must conduct several searches before they can be sure that the property is not encumbered. It is for that reason that parallel recordation schemes for the same types of property are scarce as hens' teeth; the court is aware of no others, and the parties have cited none. No useful purposes would be served — indeed, much confusion would result — if creditors were permitted to perfect security interests by filing with either the Copyright Office or state offices.

If state methods of perfection were valid, a third party (such as a potential purchaser of the copyright) who wanted to learn of any encumbrances thereon would have to check not merely the indices of the U.S. Copyright Office, but also the indices of any relevant secretary of state. Because copyrights are incorporeal — they have no fixed situs — a number of state authorities could be relevant. Thus, interested third parties could never be entirely sure that all relevant jurisdictions have been searched. This possibility, together with the expense and delay of conducting searches in a variety of jurisdictions, could hinder the purchase and sale of copyrights, frustrating Congress's policy that copyrights be readily transferable in commerce.

This is the reasoning adopted by the Ninth Circuit in *Danning v. Pacific Propeller*. *Danning* held that 49 U.S.C.App. § 1403(a), the Federal Aviation Act's provision for recording conveyances and the creation of liens and security interests in civil aircraft, preempts state filing provisions. According to *Danning*,

> [t]he predominant purpose of the statute was to provide one central place for the filing of [liens on aircraft] and thus eliminate the need, given the highly mobile nature of aircraft and their appurtenances, for the examination of State and County records.

620 F.2d at 735-36. Copyrights, even more than aircraft, lack a clear situs; tangible, movable goods such as airplanes must always exist at some physical location; they may have a home base from which they operate or where they receive regular maintenance. The same cannot be said of intangibles. As noted above, this lack of an identifiable situs militates against individual state filings and in favor of a single, national registration scheme.

Moreover . . . the Copyright Act establishes its own scheme for determining priority between conflicting transferees, one that differs in certain respects from that of Article Nine. Under Article Nine, priority between holders of conflicting security interests in intangibles is generally determined by who perfected his

---

except for actions for infringement of copyrights in foreign works covered by the Berne Convention. 17 U.S.C. § 411; *International Trade Management, Inc. v. United States*, 553 F.Supp. 402, 402-03, 1 Cl.Ct. 39 (1982).

interest first. UCC § 9312(5). By contrast, section 205(d) of the Copyright Act provides:

> As between two conflicting transfers, the one executed first prevails if it is recorded, in the manner required to give constructive notice under subsection (c), *within one month after its execution in the United States or within two months after its execution outside the United States,* or at any time before recordation in such manner of the later transfer. . . .

17 U.S.C. § 205(d) (emphasis added). Thus, unlike Article Nine, the Copyright Act permits the effect of recording with the Copyright Office to relate back as far as two months.

Because the Copyright Act and Article Nine create different priority schemes, there will be occasions when different results will be reached depending on which scheme was employed. The availability of filing under the UCC would thus undermine the priority scheme established by Congress with respect to copyrights. This type of direct interference with the operation of federal law weighs heavily in favor of preemption.

The bankruptcy court below nevertheless concluded that security interests in copyrights could be perfected by filing either with the copyright office or with the secretary of state under the UCC, making a tongue-in-cheek analogy to the use of a belt and suspenders to hold up a pair of pants. According to the bankruptcy court, because either device is equally useful, one should be free to choose which one to wear. With all due respect, this court finds the analogy inapt. There is no legitimate reason why pants should be held up in only one particular manner: Individuals and public modesty are equally served by either device, or even by a safety pin or a piece of rope; all that really matters is that the job gets done. Registration schemes are different in that the *way* notice is given is precisely what matters. To the extent interested parties are confused as to which system is being employed, this increases the level of uncertainty and multiplies the risk of error, exposing creditors to the possibility that they might get caught with their pants down.

A recordation scheme best serves its purpose where interested parties can obtain notice of all encumbrances by referring to a single, precisely defined recordation system. The availability of parallel state recordation systems that could put parties on constructive notice as to encumbrances on copyrights would surely interfere with the effectiveness of the federal recordation scheme. Given the virtual absence of dual recordation schemes in our legal system, Congress cannot be presumed to have contemplated such a result. The court therefore concludes that any state recordation system pertaining to interests in copyrights would be preempted by the Copyright Act.

2. State law leads to the same conclusion. Article Nine of the Uniform Commercial Code establishes a comprehensive scheme for the regulation of security interests in personal property and fixtures. By superseding a multitude of pre-Code security devices, it provides "a simple and unified structure within which the immense variety of present-day secured financing transactions can go forward with less cost and greater certainty." UCC § 9101, Official Comment. However, Article Nine is not all encompassing; under the "step

back" provision of UCC § 9104, Article Nine does not apply "[t]o a security interest subject to any statute of the United States to the extent that such statute governs the rights of parties to and third parties affected by transactions in particular types of property."

For most items of personal property, Article Nine provides that security interests must be perfected by filing with the office of the secretary of state in which the debtor is located. *See* UCC §§ 9302(1), 9401(1)(c). Such filing, however, is not "necessary or effective to perfect a security interest in property subject to . . . [a] statute or treaty of the United States which provides for a national or international registration . . . or which specifies a place of filing different from that specified in [Article Nine] for filing of the security interest." UCC § 9302(3)(a). When a national system for recording security interests exists, the Code treats compliance with that system as "equivalent to the filing of a financing statement under [Article Nine,] and a security interest in property subject to the statute or treaty can be perfected only by compliance therewith. . . ." UCC § 9302(4).[8]

As discussed above, section 205(a) of the Copyright Act clearly does establish a national system for recording transfers of copyright interests, and it specifies a place of filing different from that provided in Article Nine. Recording in the Copyright Office gives nationwide, constructive notice to third parties of the recorded encumbrance. Except for the fact that the Copyright Office's indices are organized on the basis of the title and registration number, rather than by reference to the identity of the debtor, this system is nearly identical to that which Article Nine generally provides on a statewide basis.[9] And, lest there be any doubt, the drafters of the UCC specifically identified the Copyright Act as

---

[8] [FN9] According to the official commentary to section 9302:

> Subsection (3) exempts from the filing provisions of this Article transactions as to which an adequate system of filing, state or federal, has been set up outside this Article and subsection (4) makes clear that when such a system exists perfection of a relevant security interest can be had only through compliance with that system (i.e., filing under this Article is not a permissible alternative).
>
> . . . .
>
> Perfection of a security interest under a . . . federal statute of the type referred to in subsection (3) has all the consequences of perfection under the provisions of [Article Nine].

UCC § 9302, Official Comment ¶¶ 8, 9.

[9] [FN10] Moreover, the mechanics of recording in the Copyright Office are analogous to filing under the UCC. In order to record a security interest in the Copyright Office, a creditor may file either the security agreement itself or a duplicate certified to be a true copy of the original, so long as either is sufficient to place third parties on notice that the copyright is encumbered. *See* 17 U.S.C. §§ 205(a), (c); 37 C.F.R. § 201.4(c)(1). Accordingly, the Copyright Act requires that the filed document "specifically identif[y] the work to which it pertains so that, after the document is indexed by the Register of Copyrights, it would be revealed by a reasonable search under the title or registration number of the work." 17 U.S.C. § 205(c); *see also* Compendium of Copyright Office Practices II ¶¶ 1604-1612; Circular 12, at 8035-4.

That having been said, it's worth noting that filing with the Copyright Office can be much less convenient than filing under the UCC. This is because UCC filings are indexed by owner, while registration in the Copyright Office is by title or copyright registration number. *See* 17 U.S.C. § 205(c). This means that the recording of a security interest in a film library such as that owned

establishing the type of national registration system that would trigger the section 9302(3) and (4) step back provisions:

> Examples of the type of federal statute referred to in [UCC § 9302(3)(a)] are the provisions of [Title 17] (copyrights). . . .

UCC § 9302, Official Comment ¶ 8; *see* G. Gilmore, *Security Interests in Personal Property* § 17.3, at 545 (1965) ("[t]here can be no doubt that [the Copyright Act was] meant to be within the description of § 9-302(3)(a)").

The court therefore concludes that the Copyright Act provides for national registration and "specifies a place of filing different from that specified in [Article Nine] for filing of the security interest." UCC § 9302(3)(a). Recording in the U.S. Copyright Office, rather than filing a financing statement under Article Nine, is the proper method for perfecting a security interest in a copyright.

. . .

CONCLUSION

The judgment of the bankruptcy court is reversed. The case is ordered remanded for a determination of which movies in NPI's library are the subject of valid copyrights. The court shall then determine the status of Cap Fed's security interest in the movies and the debtor's other property. To the extent that interest is unperfected, the court shall permit NPI to exercise its avoidance powers under the Bankruptcy Code [allowing the company to disregard the security interest and make an alternate disposition of the intellectual property interests involved].

IT IS SO ORDERED.

NOTES & QUESTIONS

1. Some federal courts have not followed (or have severely limited) the court's holding in *Peregrine*, ruling instead that filing a security interest in accordance with state law standards is sufficient to perfect a security interest in a copyright. For example, the court in *In re C Tek Software, Inc.,* 117 B.R. 762 (Bankr. D.N.H. 1990), applied state UCC filing requirements to determine whether a security interest in copyrighted software was properly perfected.

---

by NPI will involve dozens, sometimes hundreds, of individual filings. Moreover, as the contents of the film library changes, the lienholder will be required to make a separate filing for each work added to or deleted from the library. By contrast, a UCC-1 filing can provide a continuing, floating lien on assets of a particular type owned by the debtor, without the need for periodic updates. *See* UCC § 9204.

This technical shortcoming of the copyright filing system does make it a less useful device for perfecting a security interest in copyright libraries. Nevertheless, this problem is not so serious as to make the system unworkable. In any event, this is the system Congress has established and the court is not in a position to order more adequate procedures. If the mechanics of filing turn out to pose a serious burden, it can be taken up by Congress during its oversight of the Copyright Office or, conceivably, the Copyright Office might be able to ameliorate the problem through exercise of its regulatory authority. *See* 17 U.S.C. § 702.

Taking a less extreme view, the court in *In re World Auxiliary Power Co.,* 303 F.3d 1120 (9th Cir. 2002), limited the sweep of the *Peregrine* rule by holding that a copyright must be registered before a filing with the Copyright Office becomes the exclusive means to perfect a security interest in that copyright. Under this approach, filing a UCC-1 financing statement in the relevant state office would be a sufficient means to perfect a security interest in an unregistered copyright. *See id.* at 1126-29.

2. With respect to patents, federal courts have reached diverse conclusions about the need for federal filings to perfect a security interest in a patent. Confusion on this point stems from provisions of the Patent Act which specify means to record and establish the priority of patent assignments over subsequently created interests, but which do not indicate whether these provisions are applicable to security interests in patents. The relevant statutory provisions are as follows:

> Subject to the provisions of this title, patents shall have the attributes of personal property.

> Applications for patent, patents, or any interest therein, shall be assignable in law by an instrument in writing. The applicant, patentee, or his assigns or legal representatives may in like manner grant and convey an exclusive right under his application for patent, or patents, to the whole or any specified part of the United States.

> A certificate of acknowledgment under the hand and official seal of a person authorized to administer oaths within the United States, or, in a foreign country, of a diplomatic or consular officer of the United States or an officer authorized to administer oaths whose authority is proved by a certificate of a diplomatic or consular officer of the United States, or apostille of an official designated by a foreign country which, by treaty or convention, accords like effect to apostilles of designated officials in the United States, shall be prima facie evidence of the execution of an assignment, grant or conveyance of a patent or application for patent.

> An assignment, grant or conveyance shall be void as against any subsequent purchaser or mortgagee for a valuable consideration, without notice, unless it is recorded in the Patent and Trademark Office within three months from its date or prior to the date of such subsequent purchase or mortgage.

35 U.S.C. § 261. The last paragraph of this provision clearly specifies that the recording of a patent assignment will cut off a subsequent attempt by the assignor to create a further security interest or "mortgage" involving the same patent. However, this does not resolve the question of whether a security interest is a recordable interest to be treated like a patent assignment for purposes of these provisions.

Many courts have concluded that security interests were not intended by Congress to be recordable interests under these provisions and that, hence, compliance with federal requirements for filing patent assignments is not required to perfect a security interest in a patent. For example, the court in *In re Cybernetic Services, Inc.,* 239 B.R. 917 (B.A.P. 9th Cir. 1999), *aff'd,* 252 F.3d

1039 (9th Cir. 2001), *cert. denied,* 534 U.S. 1130 (2002), considered whether the provisions of the Patent Act compel a party seeking to perfect a security interest in a patent to file a notice of the interest with the United States Patent and Trademark Office (PTO). The court concluded that, unlike the Copyright Act, the Patent Act does not contain express provisions regarding security interests and liens. While the Patent Act specifies means for filing patent assignments, the Act defines that nature of such assignments and this definition does not appear to encompass security interests or liens. The court concluded that:

> A security interest is not an "assignment, grant or conveyance" of a patent. Patent law adheres to strict concepts of title, in order to protect the ownership of new inventions. It therefore distinguishes "assignments" of patents (of which "grants" and "conveyances" are specific types) from all other transfers (which are called "licenses"). William C. Hillman, *Documenting Secured Transactions* 2-19 to 2-20 (1998) (footnotes omitted).

239 B.R. at 921. The court held that, in the absence of clearer language or other indications of Congressional intent to provide for an exclusive means to perfect a security interest in a patent, the Patent Act should not be seen as stating any criteria for the perfection of such an interest and state laws should govern the proper procedure. *See also In re Cybernetic Services, Inc.,* 252 F.3d 1039, 1052 (9th Cir. 2001) (the Patent Act's "text, context, and structure, when read in the light of Supreme Court precedent, compel the conclusion that a security interest in a patent that does not involve a transfer of the rights of ownership is a 'mere license' and is not an 'assignment, grant or conveyance' within the meaning of 35 U.S.C. § 261. And because § 261 provides that only an 'assignment, grant or conveyance shall be void' as against subsequent purchasers and mortgagees, only transfers of ownership interests need to be recorded with the PTO."), *cert. denied,* 534 U.S. 1130 (2002); *In re Pasteurized Eggs Corp.,* 296 B.R. 283, 291 (Bankr. N.H. 2003) (perfection of a security interest in a patent requires a filing of a financing statement in accordance with UCC standards; recording with the USPTO is insufficient to perfect such a security interest).

In contrast, the court in *Peregrine* argued in dicta that a party seeking to perfect a security interest in a patent would need to file a notice of this interest with the PTO and that courts which have held otherwise have misconstrued the provisions of the UCC recognizing the primacy of federal recording standards. The court in *Peregrine* explained its logic as follows:

> In reaching [the conclusion that federal Copyright Law compels a filing with the Copyright Office in order to perfect a security interest in a copyright], the court rejects *City Bank & Trust Co. v. Otto Fabric, Inc.,* 83 B.R. 780 (D.Kan. 1988), and *In re Transportation Design & Technology Inc.,* 48 B.R. 635 (Bankr. S.D.Cal. 1985), insofar as they are germane to the issues presented here. Both cases held that, under the UCC, security interests in patents need not be recorded in the U.S. Patent and Trademark Office to be perfected as against lien creditors because the federal statute governing patent assignments does not specifically provide for liens:

Applications for patent, patents, or any interest therein, shall be assignable in law by an instrument in writing. The applicant, patentee, or his assigns or legal representatives may in like manner grant and convey an exclusive right under his application for patent, or patents, to the whole or any specified part of the United States.

. . . .

An assignment, grant or conveyance shall be void as against *any subsequent purchaser or mortgagee* for a valuable consideration, without notice, unless it is recorded in the Patent and Trademark Office within three months from its date or prior to the date of such subsequent purchase or mortgage.

35 U.S.C. § 261 (emphasis added).

According to *In re Transportation*, because section 261's priority scheme only provides for a "subsequent purchaser or mortgagee for valuable consideration," it does not require recording in the Patent and Trademark Office to perfect against lien creditors. *See* 48 B.R. at 639. Likewise, *City Bank* held that "the failure of the statute to mention protection against lien creditors suggests that it is unnecessary to record an assignment or other conveyance with the Patent Office to protect the appellant's security interest against the trustee."[10]

These cases misconstrue the plain language of UCC section 9104, which provides for the voluntary step back of Article Nine's provisions *"to the extent* [federal law] governs the rights of [the] parties." UCC § 9104(a) (emphasis added). Thus, when a federal statute provides for a national system of recordation or specifies a place of filing different from that in Article Nine, the methods of perfection specified in Article Nine are supplanted by that national system; compliance with a national system of recordation is equivalent to the filing of a financing statement under Article Nine. UCC § 9302(4). Whether the federal statute also provides a priority scheme different from that in Article Nine is a separate issue. . . . Compliance with a national registration scheme is necessary for perfection regardless of whether federal law governs priorities. Cap Fed's security interest in the copyrights of the films in NPI's library and the receivables they have generated therefore is unperfected.[11]

---

10 [FN12] The district court in *City Bank* further held that, if Congress intended to preempt the field of filing and to require perfection in the Patent and Trademark Office, it could have explicitly said so. *See* 83 B.R. at 782. However, under UCC § 9302(3), the proper inquiry is not whether Congress has preempted state law — for Article Nine's provisions clearly could not apply then — but rather whether Congress has established a regulatory scheme governing secured interests that is sufficiently comprehensive to supersede all or part of Article Nine by virtue of section 9104(a).

11 [FN14] The court also finds two trademark cases, *TR-3 Indus. v. Capital Bank (In re TR-3 Indus.),* 41 B.R. 128 (Bankr.C.D.Cal.1984), and *Roman Cleanser Co. v. National Acceptance Co. (In re Roman Cleanser Co.),* 43 B.R. 940 (Bankr.E.D.Mich.1984), *aff'd mem.* (E.D.Mich.1985), 802 F.2d 207 (6th Cir.1986), to be distinguishable. Both cases held that security interests in trademarks

In re Peregrine Entertainment Ltd. v. Capitol Federal Savings & Loan of Denver, 116 B.R. 194, 203-04 (C.D. Cal. 1990).

3. The means to perfect security interests in trademarks are somewhat clearer. Common law trademarks established through trademark use and governed by state laws can be the subject of security interests which can be perfected by filing a financing statement in accordance with UCC standards. *See In re Together Dev. Corp.,* 227 B.R. 439 (Bankr. D. Mass. 1998). Because federal trademark laws have been interpreted as establishing a recording system that does not apply to security interests and which, accordingly, does not supersede UCC requirements, security interests in federally registered trademarks can also be perfected by filings in accordance with UCC standards. *See id.*

The role of federal trademark laws in defining the proper means to prefect security interests in federally registered trademarks was examined in detail in *In re TR-3 Industries,* 41 B.R. 128 (Bankr. C.D. Cal.). In that case, TR-3 Industries, Inc., and TR-3 Chemical Corporation borrowed money from a bank and executed security agreements to secure repayment. The agreements granted the bank a security interest in the companies' trademark and trade name TR-3. The bank filed a UCC-1 financing statement in California but did not record the security agreements with the United States Patent and Trademark Office (PTO).

The companies filed for bankruptcy and sought to sell their assets including rights to the TR-3 mark. To clarify their ability to transfer these rights, the companies sought a ruling from the relevant bankruptcy court confirming that the bank did not have a perfected security interest in the TR-3 mark.

The issue before the court was whether the bank was required to file its security interest with the PTO, in which case its California filing was insufficient to create a perfected interest. The court concluded that:

> 1. Federal trademark laws enacted in the Lanham Act (15 U.S.C. Sections 1051 through 1127) contain no statutory provision for the registration, recording, or filing of any instrument or document asserting a security interest in any trademark, trade name, or application for the registration of a trademark; and

> 2. Congress' goals in passing the Lanham Act did not include providing a method for the perfection of security interests in trademarks, trade names, or applications for the registration of the same or a method for giving notice of the existence of claims of security interests in trademarks, trade names, or related applications for registration.

---

need not be perfected by recording in the United States Patent and Trademark Office. However, unlike the Copyright Act, the Lanham Act's recordation provision refers only to "assignments" and contains no provision for the registration, recordation or filing of instruments establishing security interests in trademarks. *See Li'l Red Barn, Inc. v. Red Barn System, Inc.,* 322 F.Supp. 98, 107 (N.D.Ind.1970) (mere agreement to assign mark in the future is not an "assignment" and therefore may not be recorded). The Copyright Act authorizes the recordation of "transfers" in the Copyright Office, and defines transfers as including "mortgages," "hypothecations" and, thus, security interests in copyrights.

Id. See also In re 199Z, Inc., 137 B.R. 778 (Bankr. C.D. Cal. 1992) (declining to extend the *Peregrine* rule to trademarks).

4. Trade secrets, as products of state laws, do not involve the same sorts of potential conflicts between federal and state laws that arise in connection with security interests related to federally-defined patents, copyrights, and trademarks. State laws should unquestionably govern the proper means for perfecting security interests in trade secrets. However, since the value of trade secrets can be destroyed through disclosures and such disclosures typically become more likely over time, the long-term value of trade secrets is often tenuous, making many trade secrets poor candidates for security interests tied to long-term loan payment obligations or other performance duties extending over substantial periods.

D. TAX CONSIDERATIONS IN ALLOCATING INTELLECTUAL PROPERTY OWNERSHIP AND LICENSING AMONG BUSINESS ENTITIES

Deborah Diehl, Whiteford, Taylor & Preston L.L.P., Is the IP Holding Company Dead?
Maryland Bar Journal
January/February 2004*

Over the last 10 to 15 years, many national retailers and other companies with multistate business operations have adopted the practice of setting up intellectual property holding companies, also known as trademark protection companies, in jurisdictions such as Delaware where royalty income is not taxed. The structure generally used for these intellectual property holding companies has been for the operating company to transfer patents, trademarks and other valuable intellectual property assets to the affiliated holding company and then to license back the right to use the assets in return for a royalty payment. At least in theory, the royalty payment is then a deductible expense for state income tax purposes by the entity making the payment, and the royalty income is not taxable income for the holding company receiving the payment. In practice, the royalty income is then frequently returned by the holding company in the form of a nontaxable loan or dividend to the operating entity from which it came.

Based on several recent studies, corporate tax receipts have plummeted over the past decade as a share of states' total tax revenues. For example, the Multistate Tax Commission, which represents several state revenue agencies, reports that the average effective state income tax rate for corporations has declined from 9.6 percent in 1980 to about 5.2 percent in 2002. In recent years, with the budget pressures many states are currently experiencing, and the recognition by the states of the "income shifting" from the use of intellectual property holding companies, the holding company structure has come

---

* This article is reproduced with the permission of the Maryland Bar Journal, published by the Maryland State Bar Association.

under increasing attack in many jurisdictions . . . in an effort by these states to recoup the taxes on this income. Some states have asserted that a holding company is subject to tax in the states in which the operating company is taxable. These efforts by the states appear to be increasing and [attempts to establish holding companies for intellectual property] are expected to decrease without resolution in favor of the holding companies of the federal constitutional issue raised by the attempt to tax the income of entities without the traditional nexus created by a physical presence in the taxing jurisdiction.

This constitutional issue, whether the taxation by a state of the income of an entity with no physical presence in the state violates the Commerce Clause of the United States Constitution, does not appear to exist in those jurisdictions . . . which either tax multistate entities on a unitary combined basis (with various apportionment formulas on which to determine the amount of taxable income) or in states which, pursuant to statute, disallow deductions for royalties paid to affiliates. . . .

A look at the recent decision by the Maryland Court of Appeals in *Comptroller of the Treasury v. Syl, Inc. and Comptroller of the Treasury v. Crown Cork & Seal Company (Delaware), Inc.*, 375 Md. 78 (2003), is helpful in understanding the constitutional issue which these cases raise. The *Syl* and *Crown Delaware* cases involve, respectively, an intellectual property holding company subsidiary of the national clothing retailer Syms and of a worldwide manufacturer and seller of metal cans, crowns and closures for bottles, can filling machines and plastic bottles and containers. Each holding company was incorporated in the State of Delaware and received a transfer from the parent company of the intellectual property assets used by the parent company and other affiliates in their operations in the State of Maryland and elsewhere. In each case, a license agreement existed between the parent company and the holding company pursuant to which the parent company paid the holding company a royalty based on the parent company's sales, and the amount of the royalty paid was based on a third party valuation of the intellectual property assets. Further, in each case, the holding company did not own or lease tangible property in Maryland, had no employees in Maryland, maintained no bank accounts in Maryland, did not sell or lease goods or services in Maryland, did not advertise in Maryland, and engaged in no mailings or solicitations to persons or entities in Maryland; however, each parent company had extensive business contacts in Maryland and filed Maryland corporate income tax returns.

The decision of the Maryland Court of Appeals in *Syl and Crown Delaware* to tax the royalty income of the holding companies appears to be based on the Court's finding that both companies had "no real economic substance as separate business entities." Interestingly, the Maryland Tax Court (Tax Court) had found that both holding companies were entities of substance and not phantoms entities. Although Maryland appellate courts are required to defer to factual findings by the Tax Court, the Court of Appeals of Maryland determined that the basic facts of the two cases were undisputed and, therefore, the Tax Court's legal conclusion based on those facts should be treated as an issue of law subject to reconsideration. In addition, the Court of Appeals of Maryland determined that even if viewed as a finding of fact, the Tax Court's conclusion was unsupported by substantial evidence. By "no real economic substance," the Court of Appeals was referring to its conclusions that "neither subsidiary had a full time employee, and the ostensible part time "employees" of each subsidiary were in reality officers or employees of independent "nexus-service" companies . . . the annual wages paid to these "employees" by the subsidiaries were miniscule . . . the so-called offices in Delaware were little more than mail drops . . . the subsidiary corporations did virtually nothing; whatever was done was performed by officers, employees, or counsel for the parent corporations . . . with respect to the operations of the parents and the protections of the trademarks, nothing changed after the creation of the subsidiaries." 315 Md. 78, (2003). The Court of Appeals also concluded that in both cases the predominant reason for the creation of the holding companies was sheltering income despite the conclusions of the Tax Court that the holding companies were established for non-tax reasons. Based on these conclusions, the Maryland Court of Appeals held that a portion of the holding companies' income, based upon their parent corporations' Maryland business, is subject to Maryland income tax and remanded the cases to the Tax Court for further proceedings consistent with its opinion.

What is not clear, based on the somewhat murky rationale set forth by the Court of Appeals, is whether the result would have been different had there been more "economic substance" to the holding companies and, if so, how much "economic substance" is necessary to avoid state taxation of a holding company. For example, it is impossible to determine whether the court would have found differently if the holding company had full time employees in the State of Delaware whose responsibilities included the protection, management and development of the intellectual property assets and if the salaries of these employees and the expenses incurred by them in performing these functions had been paid by the holding company. Also, it is unclear why the Court found it important that the predominant reason for the creation of the holding companies was sheltering income, because the United States Supreme Court has made it clear in a number of cases that this is a permissible basis for a corporate restructuring. *See, e.g., Gregory v. Helvering*, 293 U.S. 465 (1935).

Further, the *Syl and Crown Delaware* decision that nexus is present in Maryland seems to directly present the constitutional issue since the Court's rationale is clearly based on an assertion of jurisdiction over a holding company with no physical presence in the State. This appears to be directly contrary to the United States Supreme Court's rulings in *National Bellas Hess, Inc. v. Department of Revenue of Ill.*, 386 U.S. 753 (1967), and *Quill Corp. v. North Dakota*, 504 U.S. 298 (1992), which held (in the context of state use taxes) that physical presence is required to satisfy the substantial nexus requirement adopted by the United States Supreme Court in *Complete Auto Transit, Inc. v. Brady*, 430 U.S. 274 (1946). . . .

It is also helpful to review the decisions of other states in considering the taxation of intellectual property holding companies such as Syl and Crown Delaware with no physical presence in the taxing jurisdiction. One of the earliest decisions is *Geoffrey, Inc. v. South Carolina Tax Commission,* 313 S.C. 15 (1993), which involved the intellectual property holding company subsidiary of Toys R Us, Inc. Like *Syl and Crown Delaware,* Geoffrey involved a Delaware corporation which held valuable intellectual property used by its parent company in the State of South Carolina and elsewhere; it had no employees, no offices and no tangible property in the State. In 1990, without any full time employees, Geoffrey had income of approximately $55 million and paid no income taxes to any state.

Initially, the South Carolina Tax Commission disallowed the deduction taken by the parent company for the royalty payments made to Geoffrey from its South Carolina income, but later determined that the parent was entitled to the deduction and that Geoffrey was required to pay the income tax on the royalty income and was required to pay the South Carolina corporate license fee. The Supreme Court of South Carolina affirmed the trial court's judgment upholding the State Tax Commission's assessment of both income tax against Geoffrey's royalty income and the corporate license fee. The South Carolina Supreme Court's decision was based on a finding that Geoffrey had the minimum connection with the State of South Carolina that was required for due process and had a "substantial nexus" with the State required by the Commerce Clause, because it licensed its trademarks and trade names for use by the parent company in the State and received income in exchange for their use, and because of the presence of its intangible property in the State.

Interestingly, the change in position by the State Tax Commission permitted it to avoid the statute of limitations applicable if it disallowed the deduction taken by the parent company, thus having the ability to assess taxes against Geoffrey for a longer period of time. However, the strategy used in South Carolina required its Supreme Court to directly take on the constitutional issues. As mentioned above, the United States Supreme Court declined to hear the *Geoffrey* case.

Of particular concern to legal experts is the conclusion reached by the South Carolina Supreme Court that the mere use and presence of intellectual property in the State and deriving of income from such use gives the state jurisdiction for income tax purposes over the owner of such intellectual property. A logical extension of this result of this would be taxation by a jurisdiction of the income of an author whose books are sold in the jurisdiction when the individual has never been in the jurisdiction, or the taxation of the income of the owner of other intellectual property acquired over the internet by a resident of the jurisdiction. Tax practitioners have noted that the State of Maryland has followed a similar procedural strategy to that of South Carolina by choosing to tax the foreign entity, with no statute of limitations, rather than disallowing the royalty payment deduction and having a relatively short statute of limitations (in Maryland, there is no statute of limitations applicable where no return has been filed, and a three year limitations period generally applies where a return was filed). The citation by the Maryland Court of Appeals in the *Syl* and *Crown Delaware* decision to the Geoffrey case has caused concern that Maryland might ultimately take the position, like South Carolina, that the mere "presence" of intellectual property assets in the State, and the deriving of income from the use of such assets in the State, give the State jurisdiction to tax the income of the owner of such intellectual property.

Other cases with respect to the taxation of intellectual property holding companies include two Massachusetts cases, *Syms Corp. v. Commissioner of Revenue*, 436 Mass. 505 (2002), and *The Sherwin Williams Company v. Commissioner of Revenue*, 438 Mass. 71 (2002). In the *Syms* case, the Supreme Judicial Court of Massachusetts upheld the disallowance of the deduction taken by the parent company for royalty payments made to its intellectual property holding company subsidiary (i.e., Syl, the same entity involved in the Maryland case) on the basis that, pursuant to the sham transaction doctrine, the trademark transfer and license back had no practical economic effect other than the creation of tax benefits, tax avoidance was the clear motivating factor and its only business purpose, and the royalty expense was not an ordinary and necessary business expense, but a camouflaged assignment of income.

However, in the *Sherwin Williams* case, the Supreme Judicial Court of Massachusetts found that the reorganization, including the transfer to and licensing back of trademarks from two Delaware holding company subsidiaries, had economic substance in that it resulted in the creation of viable business entities engaging in substantive business activity, and that the transfer and license back of the trademarks was not a sham and the royalty payments were necessary and ordinary expenses of the corporation. The court stated that "all corporate formalities were meticulously observed" and differentiated the facts in the case from those in the *Syms* case, specifically noting that there was no evidence that the reorganization was specifically devised as a tax avoidance scheme, the revenue earned by the subsidiaries was retained and invested as part of their ongoing business operation, the license agreements were nonexclusive, and the subsidiaries assumed and paid the expenses of maintaining and defending their trademark assets.

There are other similar cases either recently decided or pending in various jurisdictions. For example, there is a major case pending in New Mexico relating to Kmart. The New Mexico Taxation and Revenue Department held that Kmart's intellectual property holding company's royalty income is subject to the state's gross receipts tax, which the New Mexico Court of Appeals affirmed in an unpublished decision. The Supreme Court of New Mexico has granted certiorari. In North Carolina and elsewhere similar cases are pending, relating to Limited Brands Inc. The states of New Jersey, Iowa and New York are pursuing the issues in administrative and court proceedings. In addition, some jurisdictions have considered and will likely continue to consider changes in their corporate income tax codes, such as legislating a unitary combined tax system like California's or changes denying deductions for royalty payments paid to affiliates. . . .

Where does this leave the business lawyer in advising a client which already has an intellectual property holding company or is considering forming one? In the case of clients with existing holding companies, . . . preparing for battle on the nexus issue in jurisdictions which have not yet considered the issue, and hoping that the holding company has "meticulously observed" all corporate formalities. In jurisdictions like Massachusetts, it may also mean hoping the holding company has economic substance. Specific ideas for observing corporate formalities and supporting a conclusion of economic substance should include having employees who manage, use and defend the intellectual property assets become employees of the holding company and paying their salaries and the legal and other expenses incurred in carrying out their responsibilities with respect to those assets directly from the holding company. In the case of a client considering the formation of a new intellectual property holding company (if there are any such brave souls), it is critical to advise the client to observe all corporate formalities and give economic substance to the holding company and to make sure the client is aware of the risks of proceeding given the current state of uncertainty.

NOTES & QUESTIONS

1. The brief discussion in the previous reading of taxation issues sometimes motivating companies to create special corporations for intellectual property ownership and licensing is presented here to illustrate how legal pressures and considerations other than corporate law issues may influence business formation decisions. The treatment of intellectual property interests under tax laws is addressed in greater detail in Chapter 1.

2. The types of taxation considerations addressed in the previous reading are only one of several types of business formation and intellectual property allocation issues that may motivate companies to create new business enterprises and to carefully allocate business operations and intellectual property ownership among those enterprises. Other considerations that may justify the separation of business activities into different corporate subunits include 1) a desire to develop a corporate business unit in a corporate subsidiary in preparation for spinning off the business unit through a sale of the stock of the subsidiary to another party, 2) operation of a portion of a business unit in a separate subsidiary because the unit must comply with state licensing standards in order to conduct certain business activities and it would be difficult to qualify the whole corporate enterprise under the relevant licensing standards, or 3) establishing shared ownership of a joint venture by multiple contributors who each own a fraction of the stock of a corporation that carries forward the venture. As these examples suggest, allocations of business activities and the ownership of assets including intellectual property among particular corporate subunits can be a flexible and highly useful means for shaping the externally perceived characteristics of the entities conducting particular business activities and the ownership structures underlying those entities.

E. FIDUCIARY DUTIES OF CORPORATE OFFICERS REGARDING INTELLECTUAL PROPERTY DEVELOPMENT AND MANAGEMENT

State corporation laws impose duties on corporate officers and directors that restrict how these corporate leaders can develop, protect, and manage corporate intellectual property. Two types of duties are relevant in this regard: first, a duty of care obligating a corporate officer or director to exercise reasonable care in gathering relevant factual information and in making decisions about important corporate matters such as the development, use, and disposition of valuable intellectual property, and, second, a duty of loyalty requiring a corporate officer or director to act as a fiduciary with respect to her corporation and thereby put the interests of the corporation ahead of those of the individual officer or director where these interests conflict.

This last type of fiduciary obligation has figured in a number of disputes in which corporate leaders have acquired personal interests in intellectual property and then sought to manipulate the intellectual property in ways that are detrimental to their corporations. The following cases describe some of the ways that these types of conflicts over intellectual property can arise, the fiduciary standards governing such conflicts, and the often sweeping relief that courts will grant in order to force an individual who has breached his fiduciary duties to his corporation to forfeit any resulting personal gains to the corporation involved.

FARWELL v. PYLE-NATIONAL ELECTRIC HEADLIGHT CO.
Supreme Court of Illinois
289 Ill. 157, 124 N.E. 449, 10 A.L.R. 363 (1919)

DUNN, C.J.

. . .

The Pyle-National Electric Headlight Company was incorporated in 1897 under the laws of New Jersey to manufacture and deal in electric headlights, and on February 9, 1897, George C. Pyle and Frank H. Ewers, who were the owners of four patents for steam turbines and three patents for electric lamps, of which Pyle was the inventor, entered into a written contract whereby they granted to the company an exclusive license to manufacture and sell patented articles and devices for all purposes for which such patented articles or devices, or parts thereof, could be utilized under the patents so assigned, or any patents or improvements that might thereafter be made to accomplish the same or similar purposes. The consideration for this agreement was $500 cash, $4,500 to be paid February 1, 1898, the issue to the owners of the patents of all capital stock of the corporation, of the par value of $700,000, except 10 shares, and the agreement of the corporation to pay monthly a royalty of 5 percent of the gross receipts derived from sales made under the license, such royalty to be not less than $150 for each calendar month from January 1, 1898. The president of the corporation was Royal C. Vilas, and the secretary Perry Trumbull.

. . .

In the latter part of 1898 or beginning of 1899 Granger Farwell became a director of the Pyle-National Electric Headlight Company at the request of Royal C. Vilas, who gave Farwell 10 shares of stock to qualify him for that position. Farwell afterward purchased more stock and continued to be a director until January, 1912, except for the period from February 7 to May 2, 1900, during which time no directors' meeting was held. On June 5, 1899, he obtained from Pyle and Ewers an assignment of their contract of February 9, 1897, with the Pyle-National Electric Headlight Company as well as of the legal title to the patents mentioned in that contract, and an agreement for the assignment of two other patents when issued upon applications then on file in the Patent Office — one for a rotary engine governor and the other for an arc lamp — of which patents the Pyle-National Electric Headlight Company would become the exclusive licensee by virtue of the agreement of February 9, 1897. These patents were subsequently issued and duly assigned to Farwell. The consideration of these assignments was $14,473.10, which Farwell paid. At the time of the assignment the payment of $4,500, which had been extended to January 1, 1900, and the royalties accruing since October 1, 1898, the payment of which had been extended to the same date, were unpaid, and they were afterward paid to Farwell. The purchase of the patents and all the contracts was made by Farwell for the joint benefit of Vilas and himself. Vilas soon after sold to Perry Trumbull one-third of his one-half interest.

. . .

On May 14, 1912, Farwell filed this bill for himself, the heirs of Vilas, and the executor of Trumbull's will, alleging that the company had manufactured and sold large quantities of the articles mentioned in the contract under the patents and by virtue of its license, and had built up a large, lucrative, and prosperous business, but that for large quantities of the articles so made and sold it had not paid the royalties provided in the agreement. The defendant filed an answer, which was afterward amended, admitting the execution of the agreements and assignments alleged in the bill, averring that it had for many years paid royalties on the basis of the total sales of the electric headlight equipments embodying the inventions covered by the patents, insisting that upon a proper construction of the agreement it was not liable to pay royalties on the basis claimed by the complainant, alleging that it had discontinued the use of all the inventions covered by the patents in the construction of its electric headlight equipments, and denying that any royalties were due under the terms of the contract.

. . .

The directors of a corporation are entrusted with the management of its business and property for the benefit of all the stockholders, and occupy the position of trustees for the collective body of stockholders in respect to such business. They are subject to the general rule, which prevails in regard to trusts and trustees, that they cannot use the trust property, or their relation to it, for their own personal gain. It is their duty to administer the corporate affairs for the common benefit of all the stockholders, and exercise their best care, skill, and judgment in the management of the corporate business solely in the interest of the corporation. They cannot have or acquire any personal or pecuniary interest in conflict with their duty as such trustees. . . . In *Nowak v. National Car Coupler Co.*, 260 Ill. 260, 103 N. E. 222, the question of the disqualification of a director to purchase property of the corporation was considered, and, citing previous cases, it was said:

> The general rule to be derived from the decisions is that a director of
> a solvent corporation may trade with, borrow money from, or loan

money to the corporation, or purchase its property, but in doing so he must act fairly, and be free from all fraud and oppression, and must impose no unfair or unreasonable terms. While a director is not disabled from purchasing the property of his corporation, the transaction will be subjected to the closest scrutiny by a court of equity, and if it was not conducted with the utmost fairness, to the end that the full value of the property should be obtained, the court will set it aside.

There is here no purchase of property from or by the corporation, or contract between the director and the corporation, which is sought to be set aside; but the rule in regard to the duty of directors, as trustees for the stockholders, reaches further than to transactions occurring directly between the directors and the corporation. In *Gilman, Clinton & Springfield Railroad Co. v. Kelly*, 77 Ill. 426, it was stated that the same rule applies to directors as to all persons acting in a fiduciary capacity, which requires the utmost fidelity to the interests of the cestui que trust; that it is a breach of duty for the directors to place themselves in a position where their own individual interests would prevent them from acting for the best interests of those they represent; and that the rule embraces every relation in which there may by any possibility arise a conflict between the duty to the person with whom the trustee is dealing or on whose account he is acting and his own individual interest.

The general rule stands upon our great moral obligation to refrain from placing ourselves in relations which ordinarily excite a conflict between self-interest and integrity. * * * In this conflict of interest the law wisely interposes. It acts not on the possibility that, in some cases, the sense of that duty may prevail over the motives of self-interest, but it provides against the probability in many cases, and the danger in all cases, that the dictates of self-interest will exercise a predominant influence, and supersede that of duty.

Michoud v. Girod, 4 How. 503, 11 L. Ed. 1076.

. . .

The contract of the corporation with Pyle and Ewers was not a liquidated demand against the corporation. It was an executory contract, continuing during the life of the patents, calling, not for the payment of certain sums of money at stated times, but for the payment, monthly, of 5 percent of the gross receipts from sales made by virtue of the contract. The interest of Pyle and Ewers was necessarily adverse to that of the corporation, and, under the principles which have been referred to, a director of a corporation could not acquire that interest for himself, unless he could make it appear that his act was for the interest of the corporation. The conflict of the individual interest of Farwell with that of the corporation, which it was his duty as a director to protect, is illustrated by the fact that he is claiming in this suit that he is entitled to royalties on sales of whole electric headlight equipments, and also on all sales of repairs and replacement parts, while the corporation contends that the royalties are payable only on the separate lamps, turbines, and governors, and not on the whole equipment, and not on repair and replacement parts. Royalties had been paid on the whole equipments, and not upon repair or replacement parts, and the court held that they should have been paid, not upon the whole equipment, but upon the patented articles and devices, and upon repair or replacement parts. These are not the only differences of construction, but are merely illustrative. In becoming the owner of the contract with Pyle and Ewers, Farwell placed himself in a position where his individual interest was in conflict with his duty to the corporation of which he was a director. He had no right to buy the contract for his own profit, but the corporation was entitled to the benefit of his bargain. It was solvent, and there is nothing to indicate that it was unable to purchase the contract. Farwell has been repaid many times over. The directors were bound to give the corporation the benefit of the royalties, instead of taking it to themselves.

. . .

The judgment of the Appellate Court is affirmed.

VENDO COMPANY v. STONER
Supreme Court of Illinois
58 Ill. 2d 289, 321 N.E.2d 1 (1974)

SCHAEFER, Justice

This appeal is the outgrowth of litigation which commenced in 1965 with the filing of a complaint in the circuit court of Kane County by plaintiff, The Vendo Company, against Harry B. Stoner and Stoner Investments, Inc., a company of which Stoner is the president and whose sole stockholders are Stoner and his wife.

The case was tried without a jury and resulted in a judgment against Stoner in the amount of $250,000 and a judgment against Stoner and Stoner Investments, Inc., of $1,100,000. An appeal was taken by defendants to the Appellate Court for the Second District, and that court reversed the judgment in part and remanded the cause for further hearings with respect to the amount of damages properly recoverable by the plaintiff. Plaintiff filed a petition for leave to appeal which was denied by this court.

Following the hearings on remand the circuit court entered a judgment against Stoner for $170,835 and a judgment against both defendants for $7,345,500. The case was again appealed to the appellate court by defendants. That court affirmed the judgment awarding damages against Stoner individually, but it reversed the judgment rendered against the two defendants jointly for $7,345,500, and remanded the cause for additional hearings as to the amount of damages. Each party filed a petition for leave to appeal, and each petition was allowed.

The intricate and prolonged litigation now before us concerns the development and marketing of a new and successful type of candy-vending machine by a concern called Lektro-Vend, allegedly with the active support of each defendant, during the period when Stoner was an employee and a director of plaintiff. Before discussing the two decisions hitherto rendered and the contentions now made by the parties, it is necessary to review various events which took place in 1959 and thereafter.

In April of 1959 the defendant Harry B. Stoner was the president and the controlling owner of Stoner Manufacturing Corporation, an Illinois corporation with its principal place of business in Aurora, Illinois, and a predecessor of the corporate defendant here. Stoner Manufacturing Corporation had been engaged for many years in the business of making and selling candy-vending machines throughout the United States. The plaintiff, a Missouri corporation located in Kansas City, Missouri, was at that time engaged in the business of manufacturing and selling vending machines designed to handle beverages, ice cream, and various other products. It did not make a machine for vending candy, but at least as early as 1958 it had considered the possibility of making a candy-vending machine, and had undertaken some research into that matter.

In April, 1959, plaintiff and Stoner Manufacturing Corporation entered into a contract for the purchase by plaintiff of the assets of the corporation, including inventions, patents, drawings, designs, and research and development work. Plaintiff's purpose in making the acquisition was in part to add a candy-vending machine to its line. So far as Harry B. Stoner was concerned, the motive for the sale appears to have arisen from a concern that the poor state of his health would prevent him from continuing in the active direction of his company.

Under the sale agreement plaintiff was to pay the Stoner Manufacturing Corporation $3,400,000 in cash and to deliver to it 60,000 shares of plaintiff's stock. The land and the property constituting the Stoner Manufacturing Corporation plant was leased to plaintiff at a stipulated rental for 10 years with an option of renewal for a like period. Plaintiff was also given an option to purchase the property on or after December 31, 1961.

Plaintiff agreed to pay annually, for a period of 10 years or until such time as it might exercise its option to purchase the plant, all profits in excess of $250,000 realized from the use of the assets being purchased. Any amount theretofore paid by plaintiff out of profits was to be credited upon the purchase of the plant. Plaintiff further agreed to pay, for a period of 10 years, 25% of the income received from foreign sales realized from the use of the assets being purchased.

The corporation agreed to use its best efforts to preserve its business organization intact, and to keep available to plaintiff the services of its present officers and employees.

The sales contract contained several restrictions on competition by the selling corporation. The contract specified:

> From and after the closing, the Company (i.e., Stoner Manufacturing Corporation) will not own, directly or indirectly, manage, operate, join, control or participate in the ownership, management, operation or control of, or be connected in any manner with, any business engaged in the manufacture and sale of vending machines under any name similar to the Company's present name, and, for a period of ten (10) years after the closing, the Company will not in any manner, directly or indirectly, enter into or engage in the United States or any foreign country in which Vendo or any affiliate or subsidiary is so engaged, in

the manufacture and sale of vending machines or any business similar to that now being conducted by the Company. The Company also
agrees that during its corporate existence it will, without incurring
any financial obligation, co-operate with Vendo to prevent the use by
others of the names 'Stoner' and 'Stoner Mfg. Corp.' in connection with
any business similar to that now carried on by the Company and also
agrees not to disclose to others, or make use of, directly or indirectly
any formulae or process now owned or used by the Company.

On June 1, 1959, Stoner executed an employment contract with plaintiff.
The contract recited plaintiff's desire to employ Stoner's services, and it stated
that the value of his services consisted of his 'advice and counsel in the operation of the Aurora, Illinois, facility, and his know-how, experience and reputation in the vending machine field.'

A paragraph of the employment contract also contained a limitation on competition. It provided:

> 5. During the term of this agreement and for a period of five (5) years
> following the termination of his employment hereunder, whether by
> lapse of time or by termination as hereinafter provided, Stoner shall
> not directly or indirectly, in any of the territories in which the
> Company (I.e., the Vendo Company) or its subsidiaries or affiliates is
> at present conducting business and also in territories which Stoner
> knows the Company or its subsidiaries or affiliates intends to extend
> and carry on business by expansion of present activities, enter into or
> engage in the vending machine manufacturing business or any branch
> thereof, either as an individual on his own account, or as a partner or
> joint venturer, or as an employee, agent or salesman for any person,
> firm or corporation or as an officer or director of a corporation or oth-
> erwise, provided however that the Company, its subsidiaries and affil-
> iates shall be excluded from the restrictions hereof and provided also
> that Stoner shall be permitted to own, hold, acquire and dispose of
> stocks and other securities which are traded in the investment secu-
> rity market whether on listed exchanges or over the counter.

The candy-vending machine which was being manufactured by Stoner
Manufacturing Corporation at the time it sold its assets to plaintiff in 1959
was a model which is called a 'drop shelf' machine in the jargon of the trade.
The 'Lektro-Vend' model subsequently developed by the Lektro-Vend
Company possessed three significant advantages over the drop-shelf model
which made it popular and successful with companies, known as 'operators,'
who purchase and service vending machines. The first of these advantages
was that the machine could sell candy bars in the same order in which it had
been stocked, a method called 'FIFO,' standing for first-in, first-out. The FIFO
design produced savings to the operator by reducing the risk of having to vend
or to discard stale items, and reducing the frequency of service calls to restock
the machine. The second advantage of the Lektro-Vend model was that it
permitted a continuous visible display of the item which was next to be
vended. Thirdly, the Lektro-Vend employed a type of construction which permitted more than one type of product to be stocked on a single conveyor, thus
eliminating the need to exhaust one product line before replacing it with a sec-

ond. While each of these traits had been in existence for some years, Lektro-Vend was the first to combine all of them in a single machine having a practical design.

As the result of research into the possibility of developing a vending machine of this character, plaintiff, in August, 1959, had built two developmental models, sketches of which were shown to Stoner. Representatives of plaintiff, while agreeing on the desirability of developing a machine with such capabilities, considered this particular prototype to be defective in certain mechanical respects and also as being too expensive to produce. The research project for the machine was accordingly shelved.

In mid-1960, two engineering employees of plaintiff, Rod Phillips and his son William, each of whom had been employed by the Stoner Manufacturing Corporation prior to the date of the sale of its assets to plaintiff, became dissatisfied with their job situation with plaintiff and resigned. At this time certain disagreements had developed between Stoner and plaintiff as to Stoner's role in plaintiff's operations, which Stoner considered should be more than the merely advisory function to which plaintiff had, in his view, assigned him.

. . .

Shortly before December 18, 1962, on which date plaintiff's board of directors was to meet, Stoner asked the chairman, Elmer Pierson, to be released from his employment contract, stating that he had an opportunity to invest in the manufacture and sale of the Lektro-Vend machine. Stoner did not disclose that he had already been giving support to the development of Lektro-Vend.

Plaintiff refused to release Stoner from his contract. A letter dated January 2, 1963, from Pierson explained the refusal in the following language:

> I have always felt that one of the major advantages of the Stoner acquisition contract, from our standpoint, was the fact that it guaranteed that your design genius and experience would never be coupled with our money to put a new and most formidable competitor into the business against Vendo. I can assure you that nothing has happened in recent years to change our position on this matter in any way. I am sure you will understand.

. . .

The Lektro-Vend Corporation was formed in September. Its original stockholders were Rod Phillips and William Phillips, certain other employees, and Mrs. Netrey, who held 50% of the stock. Neither Stoner personally nor Stoner Investments was a stockholder at that time.

. . .

Stoner's contract of employment terminated June 1, 1964, and it was not renewed. Although the appellate court in its first opinion states that Stoner remained on the board of plaintiff until the spring of 1965, defendants refer us to testimony by Stoner that he ceased being a director in March or April of 1964, and that testimony was corroborated by testimony of plaintiff's secretary.

On June 10, 1964, Lektro-Vend issued 5,000 shares of stock to Mrs. Stoner, and on July 15 it issued 5,000 shares of stock to Stoner Investments. In the years of 1965 and 1966, loans exceeding $350,000 were made to Lektro-Vend by Stoner Investments or another company controlled by Stoner.

In March, 1965, Stoner sent a letter to 50 vending machine operators in which he identified himself as the longtime former president of the old Stoner Manufacturing Corporation, and stated that he was now interested in Lektro-Vend. The letter contained the following passage:

> I believe that I can lay claim to having personally initiated the design and production of more vending machines still in use than any other one man in the history of vending. I believe that vending machines of my design still in use are making operators better than a million dollars a week right now and I am willing to risk my reputation as a vending machine designer and manufacturer to say that the LEKTRO-VEND products will set new highs in earnings to operators and will be the standard of comparison for the next 50 years.

The letter was plainly intended not only to associate Lektro-Vend with Stoner, but to convey to a reader the impression that Lektro-Vend would receive the benefits of the skill and reputation which Stoner had enjoyed as the head of Stoner Manufacturing Corporation.

. . .

Quite apart from any liability which may be predicated upon a breach of the covenants against competition contained in the sales agreement and the employment contract, it is clear that Stoner violated his fiduciary duties to plaintiff during the period when he was a director and an officer of plaintiff. Beginning in 1960 or 1961 and continuing up until just before he ceased to be employed by plaintiff he contributed substantial financial support, either directly or through Stoner Investments, Inc., to the development of a superior machine which would be competitive with the older and less satisfactory model produced by plaintiff. Stoner testified that up until a date shortly before the Lektro-Vend was publicly exhibited he did not see the models, and Phillips's testimony confirms this. Stoner also testified that until that time he did not even know that Phillips was working on such a machine. This latter testimony, however, was contradicted both by testimony given by Stoner on his deposition and by Phillips. In view of the substantial amounts which he was spending on Phillips's research project, moreover, Stoner's testimony that he never inquired as to Phillips's activities or visited the plant to inspect the work in progress is highly implausible. We conclude, as the trial court must have concluded, that Stoner was fully aware of the nature of the device which was being developed and also of its competitive potential. Indeed, Stoner himself testified that when he first observed the finished Lektro-Vend he called it "the vending machine of the future," and predicted that it would render other models obsolete.

Stoner was hired by plaintiff on the basis of the skill and experience which he could bring to plaintiff. Defendants contend that plaintiff did not take advantage of Stoner's talents and gave him the role of a mere figurehead. Assuming that plaintiff, whether prudently or imprudently, failed to make the best use of Stoner's abilities, such a failure certainly did not release Stoner from his duty not to assume a position which would be adverse to that of his employer.

In addition to his prior and subsequent support of Phillips's development of Lektro-Vend, Stoner's actions in respect to plaintiff's unsuccessful attempts in late 1962 and early 1963 to purchase the design violated his fiduciary obligations. In view of Stoner's prior expression of a desire to leave plaintiff's employment so that he could become associated with Phillips, it was perhaps naive of plaintiff to assign Stoner himself as its intermediary. Had he disclosed the extent of his financial involvement in the Lektro-Vend, it may be doubted whether plaintiff would have done so, rather than dealing with Phillips directly or through some other agent.

Stoner had a foot in each camp. Not only did his undisclosed individual interest in controlling the further development and ultimately the manufacture and sale of the Lektro-Vend create the possibility of his taking an unfair advantage of plaintiff, but the evidence gives strong indication that he actually misled plaintiff while he was purportedly acting as plaintiff's agent with regard to plaintiff's possible acquisition of the Lektro-Vend. The information given plaintiff that Phillips wanted a price of $1,500,000 for the Lektro-Vend came only from Stoner. Whether Phillips might have been willing to sell at a lower figure acceptable to plaintiff is unknown.

We recently had occasion in *Kerrigan v. Unity Savings Association* (1974), 58 Ill.2d 39 N.E.2d 317, to consider the obligation upon a director or officer to make full disclosure to his corporation. In that case, involving the appropriation of a business opportunity, the defense was made that the plaintiff, a savings and loan association, lacked the legal power to engage in the business which defendants were carrying on, which was the operation of an insurance agency. We rejected that defense for the reason that the association had never been given the opportunity to decide that question for itself. We said:

> . . . if the doctrine of business opportunity is to possess any vitality, the corporation or association must be given the opportunity to decide, upon full disclosure of the pertinent facts, whether it wishes to enter into a business that is reasonably incident to its present or prospective operations. If directors fail to make such a disclosure and to tender the opportunity, the prophylactic purpose of the rule imposing a fiduciary obligation requires that the directors be foreclosed from exploiting that opportunity on their own behalf. 58 Ill.2d at 28, 317 N.E.2d at 43-44.

. . .

Plaintiff was not, as defendants urge, limited to the recovery of the profits which accrued to Lektro-Vend. The limitation on a plaintiff's recovery proposed by defendants would mean that a fiduciary could violate his duty without incurring any risk. For if his misconduct were discovered the most that he could lose would be the profit gained from his illegal venture; the law would have operated only to restore him to the same position he would have been in had he faithfully performed his duties.

Defendants repeatedly state that the failure of plaintiff to develop a FIFO-type machine showed a lack of interest on its part. We have reviewed the testimony and we conclude that plaintiff did have and retained an interest in having such a machine. Its failure to develop one itself initially rested on problems in the design of the particular model which had been developed. The instances in which plaintiff, after 1962, failed to develop such a machine seem in part to be explained by a concern that several other companies had by then developed similar machines and that it might be too late for plaintiff to successfully enter the market. We are not called on here to review the business prudence of plaintiff's decisions, however, and we cannot say that plaintiff would have declined an offer to purchase the Lektro-Vend, with its advanced technology, or to seek to develop such a machine itself had a genuine opportunity to do so been extended to it.

. . .

Defendants also urge that the plaintiff has impermissibly changed the theory of its case from that on which it relied in the first trial. We think that defendants' contention represents an artificial analysis. In some situations there could be, of course, a violation of a covenant not to compete without the breach of a fiduciary duty, as would be the case if Stoner had not been an officer and director of plaintiff. In the present case, however, the acts of defendants in misappropriating the Lektro-Vend and their use of it to compete against plaintiff are intertwined, the latter being, so to speak, the means by which the former was brought to bear against plaintiff.

. . .

Various challenges are made by defendants to the evidence of damages which was adduced by plaintiff with respect to the $7,345,000 judgment entered against both defendants jointly. To a large extent defendants' objections represent no more than a rejection of the underlying theory of liability which we have held is applicable, namely, that plaintiff is entitled to be compensated for the difference between the profits which it could reasonably be expected to make if it had been the owner of the Lektro-Vend and the profits which it did in fact earn from the sale of candy-vending machines.

In our consideration of this facet of the appeal we are mindful of two limiting factors. The first is that the loss of profits, whether past or future, claimed to arise out of exclusion from a market is customarily not susceptible of detailed or direct proof, and that unless proof of an inferential character is permitted, the result would be to immunize a defendant from the consequences of his wrongful acts. That principle has been frequently enunciated by the Supreme Court of the United States in the context of actions to recover damages resulting from violations of the Federal antitrust laws. The principle is equally applicable where the claim of lost profits arises from a violation of fiduciary obligations or breach of contract.

The second limiting factor is that, as noted in [*Schatz v. Abbott Laboratories, Inc.*, 51 Ill.2d 143, 149 (1972)], the assessment of damages by a trial court sitting without a jury will not be set aside unless it is manifestly erroneous.

The judgment of $7,345,000, according to the trial court, was the sum of the profits lost to plaintiff between 1962 and June, 1969, during the period of defendants' breach ($2,135,000), and the diminution in the value of plaintiff's business as of June, 1969, attributable to defendants' activities ($5,210,500).

The former figure was derived from data showing the sales of vending machines, obtained from surveys conducted for plaintiff, corporate records of plaintiff, and publications of the United States Department of Commerce.

The sales data showed that plaintiff, after acquiring the assets of the Stoner Manufacturing Corporation, had a share of the candy-vending market, calculated in terms of the dollar amount of sales, of about 31% And that for the 10-year period from 1959 to 1969 plaintiff had approximately the same share of the market for vending machines other than those used for vending candy. Between 1962, just before the Lektro-Vend machine came on the market, and 1969, plaintiff's share in the candy-vending-machine market shrank to slightly over 16%, whereas its share of the noncandy-vending-machine market remained stable. Plaintiff's actual sales of candy-vending machines in 1962 amounted to about $5,400,000. In 1969 they were $4,166,000. By way of contrast the sales of Lektro-Vend rose from $48,000 realized in 1963, its first year of production, to $2,298,000 in 1969. Its sales for the entire period aggregated about $7,000,000.

The theory on which plaintiff proceeded was based on the proposition that if plaintiff had had the Lektro-Vend, it would have continued to hold the same market share that it had before defendants entered the market. By way of illustration plaintiff estimated that it had lost sales of $18,490,000 over the period from 1962 to 1969. After calculating the difference between the sales volume which could be anticipated on that assumption and the actual sales volume, a profit ratio was then applied so as to arrive at the lost profits.

The second component of the judgment, referred to as the diminution in the value of plaintiff's business as of June, 1969, was intended to reflect the fact that after June, 1969, a number of years would be required for plaintiff to regain its former market position. One of plaintiff's expert witnesses calculated this element of plaintiff's damages by making a comparison between the future sales which could be anticipated with plaintiff's share restored and the sales which could be anticipated without such restoration. A profit ratio was then applied to translate the sales figures into lost profits, and the latter figure was discounted so as to reflect present value. A second expert witness employed a somewhat different method whereby he capitalized the amount of what he determined to be the average annual lost profits prior to 1969.

. . .

[These types of evidence of the plaintiff's recoverable damages were properly considered in formulating the circuit court's damage award].

For the reasons discussed in this opinion the judgment of the appellate court is reversed and that of the circuit court is affirmed.

HENDERSON v. AXIAM, INCORPORATED

Superior Court of Massachusetts
1999 Mass. Super. LEXIS 580 (June 22, 1999)

FINDINGS OF FACT, RULINGS OF LAW AND ORDERS FOR JUDGMENT

Joseph A. Grasso, Jr., Justice.

This case involves a bitterly fought battle for control of a closely held corporation. The action was commenced in December of 1996 with the filing of a Complaint in which a number of plaintiffs, individually and derivatively on behalf of the corporation, sought declaratory and injunctive relief, an accounting, and damages allegedly suffered as a result of various alleged breaches of contract, breaches of fiduciary duty, conversion of corporate assets and opportunities, and unfair and deceptive trade acts or practices by the individual defendants, Phillip E. Holt ("Holt") and Debbra Holt (or, alternatively, "Mrs. Holt") in both their individual and representative capacities. The [plaintiffs'] claims against Holt and Mrs. Holt assert that by violating their fiduciary and good faith duties to plaintiffs and by converting and misappropriating the assets, income, resources and properties of Axiam, Inc. ("Axiam") for their own personal accounts they have violated G.L.c. 93A, § 11. The Holts, as plaintiffs-in-counterclaim, contend that one of the plaintiffs, G.L. Cabot Henderson ("Cabot Henderson" or "Henderson"), during his tenure as a director of the corporation, violated his fiduciary duties to Axiam and its shareholders. The factual predicate for the claims and the counterclaims centers around the dealings and relationships of a number of individuals with the defendant Axiam during the period from 1992 to the present.

. . .

An understanding of the matters in controversy requires a brief understanding of Axiam's genesis, its corporate history prior to the Holts' arrival at Axiam, and its products, including certain intellectual property which may or may not be patentable and which may or may not have significant value. Axiam is a closely held corporation, with fewer than thirty shareholders and approximately ten employees. Axiam was incorporated in Massachusetts on April 4, 1983. Axiam was founded by Clinton Rule ("Rule") and Robert M. Lee ("Lee"). Over the course of his involvement with Axiam, Rule invested almost $3,000,000 in the corporation. Rule's initial investment consisted of monies Rule had received upon the sale of his stock in Rule Industries, as well as a $900,000 loan secured by a mortgage on his personal residence in Gloucester.

Axiam is a high technology company, manufacturing and selling products that measure the roundness and geometry of parts of high-speed rotating devices. Axiam's products measure the roundness of objects in millionths of an inch. The precision with which Axiam's products can both measure the roundness of the parts and balance the assembled parts is of great value, especially in the manufacture of jet engines. Axiam's major business is assembly process control, including reduction and elimination of rotor vibration, for high-speed rotating devices, such as jet engines, wheels and shafts, as well as the space shuttle. Axiam's products consist of both hardware and the computer software which controls the hardware.

Axiam's first product was the RGS-640, which is used in the quality control process by manufacturers of jet engines and other high speed rotating devices subject to vibration to perform biplane deviation calculations, a significant measurement of vibration. The RGS-640 was conceived and developed by Rule and Lee as employees of Axiam. Following the RGS-640, Axiam's next generation product was the GMS 4000, which was (as the initials suggest) a geometric measuring system addressing issues of balance and vibration, as well as roundness. The GMS system was also developed and sold by Axiam prior to Holt's joining Axiam in 1992.

From its formation until 1992, Axiam was managed principally by its founders, Rule and Lee, each of whom served as president of the company at various times and each of whom served on the Board of Directors throughout that period. Prior to Holt's joining Axiam in 1992, and in response to a customer communication, Axiam had developed a product designed to eliminate vibration caused by the failure to align stacks of rotor disks vertically during assembly of high speed engines, such as jet engines. This product came to be known as Axiam's SmartStack system. This product was invented by employees of Axiam, with assistance from an M.I.T. professor, Dr. Kamal Yousef-Toumi ("Dr. Toumi"), who, under contract with Axiam, assisted in developing the mathematical algorithms for the computer software.

The Hiring of Holt and Mrs. Holt

Axiam hired Holt in January 1992 to provide day-to-day management and assist with the "turnaround" of Axiam. Holt served initially as general manager, becoming Senior Vice President and then, effective April 7, 1994, President of Axiam. His hiring was precipitated by Rule, who had met Holt a number of years earlier. Rule was impressed with Holt's computer expertise, and even more impressed with Holt's maverick style of cutting through bureaucracy. In hindsight, Holt's maverick style resulted in his taking control of Axiam in ways never envisioned at his hiring.

. . .

The Newco Strategy and the Attempt to Strip Axiam of its Intellectual Property, including SuperStack

[Concomitant with his attempt to obtain control over other aspects of Axiam's corporate affairs through improper means,] Holt also had set about to obtain for himself the benefits of Axiam's intellectual property, including SuperStack, to the detriment of Axiam's shareholders and the convertible noteholders. To understand the perceived value of Axiam's intellectual property requires some background.

Development of SmartStack into SuperStack

In early 1994, Pratt & Whitney, Canada, an Axiam customer, had discussed with Lee the desirability of adding geometric balancing capabilities to the engine stacking technology of SmartStack. Beginning in January of 1995,

Axiam employees, principally Ron Doss ("Doss"), Steve Kokkins ("Kokkins"), Fred Kastner ("Kastner") and Lee began developing this next generation of Axiam technology, known as the SuperStack system.

SuperStack is a technology that provides geometric balancing of rotors to permit an engine manufacturer to design the best overall assembly of the rotors in an engine to eliminate vibration. Geometric balancing involves assembly of rotor stacks to achieve the best possible stacking, with external weights to compensate for weight imbalances. SuperStack adds to Axiam's SmartStack technology the ability to determine where the weight distribution is on a rotor. As conceived, SuperStack would compensate for any weight imbalances, including banana shapes, which are a problem in rotors.

Upon becoming Director of Engineering in February 1995, Doss oversaw the entire SuperStack project. Under contract with Axiam, Dr. Toumi had developed mathematical algorithms to predict imbalances left by SmartStack and to decide where the counterbalances should go. Kastner then developed a software code, and wrapped it around the algorithms developed by Toumi. He took Toumi's developments (source code) and provided software interfaces, making them compatible with Axiam's products. Lee (and Kokkins after him) worked on defining inputs and outputs, or real life examples. By May 31, 1995, the SuperStack code had been completed.

Prior to his resignation from Axiam, Lee had also developed a master device to test it. The master device which Lee had designed to test SuperStack was essentially a dummy rotor with known imperfections for use in measurement. Prior to resigning from Axiam in April of 1995, Lee had sent his paper designs for the master device to a machine shop for fabrication, and had made arrangements for Axiam to rent time on a balancing machine for purposes of testing SuperStack. Once completed, the master device would permit testing of SuperStack. The master device itself had not yet been received from the machine shop by June 11, 1996, when Doss resigned from Axiam. However, by June 1996, the SuperStack software had undergone preliminary testing and was ready for second level testing.

The battle over SuperStack, its present and future state of development, is at the core of much of the dispute in this action. As he had done in connection with SmartStack, Dr. Toumi had developed the mathematical algorithms for SuperStack under contract with Axiam. Holt did not contribute at all in any of the development work on SuperStack. Only Kastner touched the source code as developed by Toumi. In July of 1995, Holt instructed Doss to cease work on SuperStack. Although Holt professed to Doss that expected funding from a Pratt & Whitney, Canada contract had not materialized, I infer that, at least in good part, the reason also related to Holt's desire to take all of the benefits of SuperStack for himself.

Holt was concerned that time was of the essence in developing SuperStack, which he called Axiam's "next generation product." In April 1995, he wrote a letter to Shea an investor that: "If we lose this window of opportunity, we shall have made a major mistake." In 1995, he told Pratt & Whitney, with whom

Axiam was attempting to establish a strategic alliance for development of SuperStack: "If you loved SmartStack, you will be mad about SuperStack." However, not only did Holt not enter into agreement with Pratt & Whitney, he also instructed Doss to cease work on SuperStack.

In early 1996, Holt instructed Doss to recommence work on SuperStack, asserting that he had spoken with Pratt & Whitney, Canada and expected a contract to be forthcoming. However, Holt had also decided that SuperStack was too valuable to share with Lee and other of Axiam's initial developers. Holt wanted to establish a new and separate corporation, in which he had the majority interest, both to rid himself of Axiam's debt and its founders and to reap the benefits of its technology as a reward for his own hard work. As a result, Holt began to consider how he could siphon off Axiam's intellectual property so that he would profit, while others such as Rule, Lee, Eissner [Axiam's largest shareholders] would not. His answer was what came to be known as the Newco strategy. When the Newco strategy later foundered on the unwillingness of the other shareholders and of the convertible noteholders to convert their debt to equity, thus releasing the lien on Axiam's intellectual property, Holt resorted to a back-up plan, seizing control of Axiam by seizing control of the majority of Axiam's shares.

Holt's Attempt to Spin Off Axiam's Intellectual Property for His Own Benefit

Beginning in early 1996, Holt began to develop a strategy to spin off Axiam's intellectual property into a separate corporation for his own personal benefit. Recognizing that any such plan would be vulnerable to legal challenge, at the same time Holt planned to move Axiam to California, believing that through "time and distance" he could avoid legal challenge. To Holt, time and distance meant that with the passage of sufficient time to orchestrate his plan and with a base of Axiam's operations in California, a lawsuit by the minority shareholders or convertible noteholders would be more difficult and less likely.

By November of 1996, when it became apparent that he would not be able to get cooperation from the convertible noteholders or the Board, and fearing that he was going to be fired by Guild and Cabot Henderson (whose allegiance had clearly shifted), Holt seized control of Axiam through an illegal stock transaction and commenced implementation of his strategy without Board, noteholder or shareholder approval.

Newco

Beginning in the early spring of 1996, Holt commenced steps to establish a new corporation which he controlled as the vehicle for developing Axiam's next generation product (SuperStack). Believing correctly that Cabot Henderson was eager to profit as well from such a development, Holt initially charged Henderson with developing the strategy to accomplish his goal: to develop SuperStack in an entirely new corporation controlled by Holt. This became the "Newco strategy."

Holt intended to have at least a majority interest in the new company, and he intended to exclude Axiam's shareholders, especially Lee and Eissner, from the new company. Illustrative of his enmity was Holt's announcement at a May 1996 staff meeting discussing Newco that part of the reason for setting up Newco was to prevent the "assholes who were no longer around from reaping the benefits of our hard work."

On April 26, 1996, Holt wrote a memorandum to Cabot Henderson, which he copied to his other allies, George Moker and Debbra Holt, setting forth certain aspects of a potential Newco strategy. In his memorandum, Holt discussed forming Newco "ASAP," with the same officers and directors as Axiam, but with the ultimate ownership to be determined. Regarding ownership of Newco, Holt asked Cabot Henderson to develop by the next Board meeting an offer to Axiam's convertible noteholders, seeking to have them exercise their right to convert their debt in Axiam to equity in return for "suitable incentive," which Holt suggested might include "participation in Newco." Holt did so because he was fearful that the convertible noteholders, whose debt was secured by Axiam's intellectual property, could otherwise thwart his plans.

In an April 27, 1996 memorandum, Holt suggested that he meet with the convertible noteholders to tell them about Newco. He also stated that "Newco and its staff are now the owners of SuperStack — it's a product that I do not wish Oldco to develop." Oldco unmistakably refers to Axiam. In a handwritten note on the memorandum, referring to himself Holt added, "peh is the 'inventor' of SmartStack, it goes where I go." Holt later amended his handwritten note to read in pertinent part "peh is the inventor of SuperStack. It goes where I go."

In May 1996, mindful both that Cabot Henderson desired to share in the riches of Axiam's intellectual property and that the Henderson family owned considerable positions in convertible notes and bridge loans, Holt charged Henderson with helping develop the Newco strategy. He gave Cabot Henderson the title of Vice President for Finance and Special Projects. On May 8, 1996, Holt and Cabot Henderson met with two attorneys Penman and Baldiga of Brown, Rudnick, Freed & Gesmer concerning the Newco strategy. This meeting with counsel heightened Holt's and Cabot Henderson's concerns that the strategy was subject to legal challenge. In a follow-up memorandum regarding the meeting from Henderson to Holt dated May 10, 1996, Henderson identified several issues that needed to be resolved pertaining to a potential Newco strategy, including: "The key legal question . . . why license the technology to Newco and what benefits are there to Oldco?"; the need for Axiam shareholder and convertible noteholder approval; the need for establishing the fair market value of Axiam's intellectual property by independent appraisal; how to establish a "bright line" between Axiam's intellectual property and "software upgrades" that a Newco would perform; and how to transfer business of Axiam to Newco without leaving Axiam open to legal attack.

Wanting answers rather than questions, Holt responded angrily: He made a note at the top of the Henderson memorandum instructing Henderson to "read and return" the memorandum and not to make copies. He also wrote a note to his assistant, Ellen Fernandes ("Ms. Fernandes"), asking her to ensure that there were no copies of the memorandum. One of Holt's repeated criticisms of Henderson's May 10 memorandum was that it contained questions and "academic bullshit," not answers or strategies. Holt's handwritten comments questioned whether Axiam's shareholders should be allowed to vote on the transfer of Axiam's intellectual property to Newco. He dismissed Henderson's suggestion that the fair market value of Axiam's intellectual property should be established by independent appraisal, asking instead what would happen if the independent appraisal came back at $10,000,000. He obviously did not want to share such wealth with Axiam's shareholders or the convertible noteholders.

. . .

Failure to Seek Patent Protection

As part of his scheme to spin off Axiam's valuable intellectual property into a separate corporation, Holt deliberately caused Axiam to delay pursuing the possibility of patent protection for its next generation product, SuperStack, and for enhancements of SmartStack. Whether SuperStack was patentable, or is patentable, has not been proven, and was not central to determination of the issues in this trial. Whether patentable or not, SuperStack was and is clearly an asset of *Axiam* not of Holt. Despite Holt's view, such as that contained in his April 27, 1996 memo to Henderson and George Moker in which he wrote "I want to be unequivocal here and to all concerned. PEH is the 'inventor' of SuperStack. It goes where I go." Holt is not the inventor of Axiam's SuperStack technology. This technology was developed by Lee, Doss, Kastner, and others at Axiam, using the algorithms devised by Toumi under contract to Axiam.

Holt also caused development of SuperStack within Axiam to be stopped, or delayed, for a variety of reasons, only some of which had to do with finances and the availability of finding a strategic partner with which to develop SuperStack. First and foremost, Holt wanted to complete the technology and market it through a new corporation which he controlled. Additionally, he wanted to make certain that lawyers' concerns about articulating a sound business reason for developing his Newco strategy did not interfere with his plans to pay as little as possible for Axiam's intellectual property should it be sold to Newco.

Axiam's intellectual property, including SmartStack and SuperStack, was believed by all of the so-called stakeholders in Axiam, both shareholders and convertible noteholders, to have very significant value. In the beginning of 1996, Holt directed Henderson, then Axiam's Vice President for Operations, to investigate obtaining patent protection for SuperStack and for enhancements to SmartStack. Henderson thereafter interviewed a number of patent law firms in order to select patent counsel. On February 21, 1996, Henderson reported in a memorandum to Holt that he had interviewed two law firms. On February 28, 1996, Henderson met with attorney Bruce Sunstein of the firm Bromberg & Sunstein, and provided him with product literature. On February 28, 1996, Henderson and Doss met with attorney Sunstein to discuss Axiam's intellectual property and the possibility of seeking patent protection for SuperStack. Attorney Sunstein subsequently visited Axiam, met with Axiam's engineers, and reviewed Axiam's technology.

On March 15, 1996, Henderson wrote a memo to Holt reporting on attorney Sunstein's visit to Axiam. Henderson stated that there were two main considerations in constructing Axiam's patent strategy: 1) patenting SuperStack to protect Axiam going forward and 2) patenting enhancements to SmartStack that had not been offered for sale within the past year. Henderson further reported that the goal was to file a provisional patent application for SuperStack as soon as possible. On March 15, 1996, attorney Sunstein sent a proposed engagement letter to Henderson. Sunstein estimated the cost of filing a provisional patent application for SuperStack to be approximately $10,000. Henderson told Holt of the engagement letter and asked for permission to engage Sunstein to begin the process of obtaining patent protection for Axiam's technology. Holt refused to permit Henderson to sign the engagement letter. Holt told Henderson that he could not sign the engagement letter because Holt did not want SuperStack to be patented in Axiam but in "Newco."

Although not a finished product at Axiam, clearly SuperStack exists in the development stage, and in fact was ready for testing at the second level when Doss left Axiam in June of 1996. All it needed was the master designed by Lee. Holt himself recognized this in his July 11, 1996 note to the SuperStack file that the "Software [was] ready to try."

Notwithstanding the importance to Axiam of completing SuperStack and protecting its intellectual property, to preserve his own opportunity to spin this intellectual property off into another corporation for his own personal benefit, Holt suspended Axiam's work on SuperStack during 1996 and refused to permit Axiam to engage the services of patent counsel to protect the intellectual property. This breach of fiduciary duty, however, is but a part of the larger breach of attempting to divert Axiam's corporate opportunities to himself.

. . .

It is well settled in Massachusetts that the directors and officers of a corporation stand in a fiduciary relationship to the corporation. *Demoulas v. Demoulas Super Markets, Inc.,* 424 Mass. 501, 528 (1997); *Durfee v. Durfee & Canning, Inc.,* 323 Mass. 187, 196 (1948). They owe to the corporation and its shareholders a duty of care and a "paramount duty of loyalty." *Demoulas,* 424 Mass, at 528; *Spiegel v. Beacon Participations, Inc.,* 297 Mass. 398, 410-11 (1937) ("They are bound to act with absolute fidelity and must place their duties to the corporation above every other financial or business obligation . . . They cannot be permitted to serve two masters whose interests are antagonistic"). In the case of a close corporation, which resembles a partnership, duties of loyalty extend to shareholders, who owe one another substantially the same duty of utmost good faith and loyalty in the operation of the enterprise that partners owe to one another, a duty that is even stricter than that required of directors and shareholders in corporations generally. *Demoulas,* 424 Mass. at 529; *Donahue v. Rodd Electrotype Co. of New England, Inc.,* 367 Mass. 578, 592-94 (1975).

As Chairman of the Board, President, and significant shareholder of Axiam, a close corporation, Holt owes Axiam a duty of "utmost good faith and loyalty." *Demoulas,* 424 Mass. at 529. "Not honesty alone, but the punctilio of an honor the most sensitive, is then the standard of behavior." *Donahue,* 367 Mass, at 594. As a purported director, Treasurer and shareholder of Axiam, Mrs. Holt owes Axiam the same duty of utmost good faith and loyalty.

. . .

The duty of loyalty requires that a director or officer of the corporation not take for personal benefit an opportunity or advantage that belongs to the corporation.

Demoulas, 424 Mass. at 529. Under the corporate opportunity doctrine, an officer seeking to pursue a corporate opportunity must disclose material details and then either gain assent of disinterested directors or show the decision is fair to the corporation. *Hanover Ins. Co. v. Sutton,* 46 Mass.App.Ct. 153, 166 (1999).

Plaintiffs allege . . . that Holt engaged in a theft of corporate opportunity by making a presentation of the SuperStack technology for his own benefit in the name of his separate corporation. Holt failed to disclose the details of this presentation. It is incontrovertible that Holt's purpose in doing so was inappropriately to benefit himself rather than Axiam or its shareholders. To the contrary, Holt's goal was to siphon off to Newco Axiam's intellectual property. Such conduct constitutes a breach of his duty of loyalty.

. . .

In claiming inventorship and ownership of SuperStack, failing to seek intellectual property protection for Axiam's intellectual property, and attempting to market SuperStack through his own separate corporation, ZeroVibe, Holt acted self-interestedly, wasted corporate assets, and breached his duty of loyalty. Holt's intentional failure to seek patent protection for SuperStack so that he could use that technology for his own benefit constitutes a breach of his fiduciary duty. The ZeroVibe presentation furthered no valid *Axiam* corporate purpose and was unfair to Axiam and its shareholders. Accordingly, Holt breached his fiduciary duty in making a presentation of Axiam's technology on ZeroVibe's behalf to an Axiam customer. Holt's failure to disclose to the Board that he made a SuperStack presentation on behalf of ZeroVibe, a company he solely owned at the time, is evidence of his bad faith. His use of Axiam's resources, including its technology, to make the ZeroVibe presentation is evidence that the presentation was an Axiam corporate opportunity. See *Demoulas,* 424 Mass. 501, 536 (1997) (use of corporate resources to support other companies owned and controlled by defendant directors "indicates that they were wrongfully diverted corporate opportunities"), *citing* 1 J.D. Cox & T.L. Hazen, *Corporations* § 11.7, at 11.33, 11.39 (1995) (fiduciary's use of corporate assets or personnel to acquire or nurture opportunity indicates breach of duty of loyalty).

. . .

As a consequence of the Holts' numerous violations of fiduciary duty, the shareholders are entitled to equitable relief designed to remove the Holts from the position of control they illegally obtained and to unwind the self-interested transactions in which they caused Axiam to engage while they were in control. It is well established that the courts of the Commonwealth have broad equitable powers to remedy breaches of fiduciary duty. *See Coggins,* 397 Mass. at 532 (awarding rescissory damages for directors' violations of fiduciary duty). This is especially true in cases involving bad faith of a director in a closely held corporation. *See Demoulas v. Demoulas,* 428 Mass. 555, 591 (1998) (affirming trial court's award of equitable relief for violations of fiduciary duty that "essentially restructured [the corporation's] corporate makeup"). "A court exercising its equitable power has no limit on its 'flexibility in devising a variety of remedies and shaping them to fit the circumstances of a particular case.' A lack of precedent, or mere novelty in incident should not be an obstacle." *Demoulas v. Demoulas,* 1996 WL 511519 *8 (Mass.Super.1996), *aff'd,* 428

Mass. 555 (1998), *quoting Brenner v. Berkowitz,* 617 A.2d 1225, 1233 (N.J.Super A.D.1992).

. . .

There is no adequate remedy at law to compensate the shareholders for the Holts' conduct. Under the Holts' control, Axiam has been looted of much value. Only an order restoring the balance between the shareholders, removing the Holts from their position of control, and securing the return of Axiam's intellectual property and its development can adequately remedy the wrongs committed by defendants .

. . .

[P]laintiff shareholders seek a declaratory judgment that Axiam, not Holt, owns the SuperStack technology and any other technology related to Axiam's business developed by Holt while he was an officer or director of Axiam. Under G.L. c. 231, § 1, this Court is empowered to "make binding declarations of right, duty, status and other legal relations sought thereby, either before or after a breach or violation thereof has occurred in any case in which an actual controversy has arisen and is specifically set forth in the pleadings and whether any consequential judgment or relief is or could be claimed at law in equity or not . . ."

Declaratory relief is appropriate where: 1) an actual controversy has arisen in the case presented; 2) the plaintiffs have an interest therein; and 3) and the granting of declaratory relief will terminate the controversy. These three requirements are met here. There is an actual controversy between the shareholders, who assert that Axiam owns the SuperStack technology, and Holt, who asserts, somewhat inconsistently, that he owns it and that it does not exist. The shareholders have an obvious interest in confirming Axiam's ownership rights in its technology, since that technology constitutes Axiam's principal asset. Moreover, the shareholders are bringing this suit in a representative capacity to vindicate the interests of the corporation with respect to its technology. *Baker v. Allen,* 292 Mass. 169, 171 (1935) ("A suit in equity by minority stockholders in a representative capacity against directors for wrongs committed by them against the corporation is not in vindication of any personal rights . . . The interests of the corporation alone are immediately concerned"). Axiam clearly has an interest in protecting its own technology. Finally, granting this relief will terminate the controversy and remove the uncertainty as to the ownership rights of the SuperStack technology.

In the course of the trial, the defendants contended that SuperStack was a mere idea and, as such, Axiam is not entitled to any ownership rights in it.[12]

---

[12] [FN39] Defendants also argue that this Court lacks the power to hear plaintiffs' claims with respect to SuperStack because it will require the Court to make "determinations as to the patentability of technology . . . [and] those matters are outside the subject matter jurisdiction of this Court." Def. Trial. Br. at 6. Defendants are wrong. Plaintiffs are not seeking a declaratory ruling that SuperStack is patentable. Plaintiffs are claiming that SuperStack is an invention and are seeking a declaratory judgment that Axiam, not Holt, owns this invention. Federal courts do not have exclusive jurisdiction over issues of ownership of, or rights of use in, inventions, confidential information or trade secrets. *Steranko v. Inforex, Inc.,* 5 Mass.App.Ct. 253, 269 (1977) (discussing Massachusetts common law principles relating to employer's entitlement to the inventions of employees).

Under Massachusetts law, an idea becomes an invention when it is put into practice or embodied in some tangible form. *Nat'l Development Co. v. Gray,* 316 Mass. 240, 249 (1944). From the facts found, it is clear that SuperStack fits that description. It is equally clear from the evidence that Holt did not invent SuperStack. He is neither the inventor nor the owner of it. Accordingly, the shareholders are entitled to a declaration that Axiam owns the SuperStack technology and any derivative of that technology. See, e.g., *Wireless Specialty Apparatus Co. v. Mica Condenser Co.,* 239 Mass. 158, 161 (1921) (former employee, who planned to take advantage of secret processes, machines, and other confidential information of plaintiff corporation, and who, in furtherance of the plan, formed a corporation whose officers and agents acted with notice, was enjoined from the use or disclosure of such processes and inventions).

The shareholders are also entitled to a declaration that Axiam owns all technology developed or under development at Axiam during the period of Holt's employment based on Holt's status as a fiduciary of Axiam. As found, Holt was not an inventor of Axiam's SmartStack or SuperStack technology. Even if he had been, where an inventor is more than a mere employee and occupies a special relationship of trust and confidence to the business, courts have consistently held that it is inequitable for the individual inventor to retain for himself a right which more properly belongs to the company. In such instances, the fiduciary is compelled to assign the technology rights to the corporation. *Kennedy v. Wright,* 676 F.Supp. 888, 891-92 (C.D.Ill.1988); *cf. Wireless Specialty Apparatus Co.,* 239 Mass. at 163 (employee who had relation of trust and confidence with the corporation and who, in the course of his employment, received confidential information was estopped from claiming as his own property inventions made in the course of his work even though there was no express agreement or understanding that inventions were to be the employer's property).

As a director, officer and significant stockholder of Axiam, Holt stands in a fiduciary relationship with the corporation. See *Demoulas,* 424 Mass. at 529; *Durfee,* 323 Mass. at 196; *Donahue,* 367 Mass. at 592-93. Accordingly, any rights he may claim to have in any inventions related to Axiam's business developed while he was an Axiam fiduciary belong to the corporation.

REXFORD RAND CORP. v. ANCEL
United States Court of Appeals for the Seventh Circuit
58 F.3d 1215 (1995)

FLAUM, Circuit Judge

This diversity case requires us to consider whether a minority shareholder's duty of loyalty to a closely held corporation continues after he has been "frozen out." Rexford Rand Corporation ("Rexford Rand") is a closely held corporation registered in Illinois.[13] Gregory Ancel ("Gregory") owns 25% of the corporation's

---

[13] [FN1] Rexford Rand was not organized under the Illinois Close Corporation Act. Under common law principles, however, Rexford Rand qualifies as a close corporation because it is a family-run business with only three shareholders. *See Galler v. Galler,* 32 Ill.2d 16, 203 N.E.2d 577, 583 (1964); *Hagshenas v. Gaylord,* 199 Ill.App.3d 60, 145 Ill.Dec. 546, 551-52, 557 N.E.2d 316, 321-22

stock. Albert Ancel ("Albert"), Gregory's brother, also owns 25%, and Selwyn Ancel ("Selwyn"), Albert and Gregory's father, owns the remaining 50%. Albert serves as President, Chief Executive Officer, Treasurer, and as a director of Rexford Rand. Selwyn is the Chairman of the Board of Directors.

From the corporation's inception in 1983 until December, 1991, Gregory served as Vice President and Treasurer of Rexford Rand. He also managed a sales group for the company, and his salary from Rexford Rand was his sole source of income. On December 3, 1991, Gregory was fired from his positions as Vice President, Treasurer, and employee. The reasons for Gregory's termination are in dispute. Gregory claims that he was "frozen out" by Albert and Selwyn;[14] Albert testified that Gregory was fired because of his job performance. Since he was fired, Gregory has received neither salary nor benefits. Rexford Rand has never paid a dividend to its shareholders.

In 1993, Rexford Rand neglected to file its annual report with the state of Illinois. As a result, the corporation was administratively dissolved. *See* 805 ILCS 5/12.35. The corporation's dissolution caused the names "Rexford Rand Corporation" and "Daxcel Corporation" (another trade name used by Rexford Rand) to become available. Gregory discovered that the corporation had been dissolved, but he did not inform Albert or Selwyn. Instead, Gregory reserved the names "Rexford Rand Corporation" and "Daxcel Corporation" and secured a corporate charter in the name of "Rexford Rand Corporation." This action prevented Rexford Rand from re-incorporating under its original name. *See* 805 ILCS 5/12.45(b)(2).[15] Rexford Rand brought suit claiming that Gregory breached his fiduciary duty as a shareholder in a close corporation by depriving the corporation of the use of its name. Following a bench trial, the district court ordered the return of the original name to the corporation and permanently enjoined Gregory from conducting business under the names "Rexford Rand Corporation" and "Daxcel Corporation." On appeal, Gregory argues that any fiduciary duty he owed to Rexford Rand ended when Albert and Selwyn froze him out in 1991. Because we believe that Gregory continued to owe Rexford Rand a duty of loyalty, we affirm.

As an initial matter, Gregory argues that this case is not properly in federal court because the $50,000 amount in controversy requirement has not been satisfied.

. . .

(1990), *appeal denied,* 133 Ill.2d 556, 149 Ill.Dec. 321, 561 N.E.2d 691 (1990); 1 *Principles of Corporate Governance* § 1.06 (ALI1994) (" 'Closely held corporation' means a corporation the equity securities . . . of which are owned by a small number of persons, and for which securities no active trading market exists.").

[14] [FN3] The term "freeze-out" refers to "the use of corporate control vested in the statutory majority of shareholders or the board of directors to eliminate minority shareholders from the enterprise or reduce their voting power or claims on corporate assets to relative insignificance. A freeze-out implies a purpose to force upon the minority shareholder a change which is not incident to any other corporate business goal." *Fleming v. International Pizza Supply Corp.,* 640 N.E.2d 1077, 1080 n. 4 (Ind.App.1994) (citation omitted).

[15] [FN4] A corporation that is administratively dissolved for failure to file its annual report may be reinstated within five years of dissolution. 805 ILCS 5/12.45(a).

Rexford Rand seeks equitable relief — the return of its corporate name — rather than damages. In an equitable action, "the amount in controversy is measured by the value of the object of the litigation." The object of this suit is the name "Rexford Rand Corporation." Rexford Rand seeks a federal forum, so it bears the burden of establishing jurisdiction.

Gregory challenges Rexford Rand's assertion that the value of its corporate name exceeds $50,000. If uncontested, the courts will accept the plaintiff's good faith allegation of the amount in controversy unless it "appear[s] to a legal certainty that the claim is really for less than the jurisdictional amount." Where, as here, a defendant challenges the plaintiff's allegation of the amount in controversy, the plaintiff must support its assertion with "competent proof." Competent proof means "'proof to a reasonable probability that jurisdiction exists.'" We believe that Rexford Rand has met this burden.

Rexford Rand, a chemical manufacturing firm, has approximately 30 employees and sells "over 200 products to approximately 6,800 customers in many states." The corporation has annual sales of approximately $1.75 million and has fixed assets of $500,000. Albert testified that the name "Rexford Rand" appears on the corporation's "[b]usiness cards, product literature and labels, containers and packaging, invoices, letterheads, envelopes, advertising, novelties, [and] on the buildings themselves." In addition, Albert stated that Rexford Rand sells primarily to repeat customers and "is dependent upon service to customers who then return to buy more product or additional product." Consequently, Rexford Rand argues that name recognition is very important to its survival and the loss of the Rexford Rand name would substantially impair the value of the business.[16] For a company with $1.75 million in annual sales that depends heavily on name recognition, we conclude that at least a "reasonable probability" exists that the value of the corporate name exceeds $50,000. Thus, the district court did not commit clear error by holding that the amount in controversy requirement was satisfied.

Next, we turn to the merits. Under Illinois law, a shareholder in a close corporation owes a duty of loyalty to the corporation and to the other shareholders. Shareholders must "deal with the utmost good faith, fairly, honestly, and openly with their fellow stockholders." *In re Dearborn Process Service, Inc.,* 149 B.R. 872, 880 (Bankr.N.D.Ill.1993). This duty is necessary, the *Hagshenas* court reasoned, because while a closely held corporation embodies the corporate form, it in many ways resembles a partnership. Thus, "the mere fact that a business is run as a corporation rather than a partnership does not shield the business venturers from a fiduciary duty similar to that of true partners." [*Hagshenas v. Gaylord,* 145 Ill.Dec. 546, 552, 557 N.E.2d 316, 3222 (1990)].[17]

---

[16] [FN5] Albert testified that the value of the business would be economically impaired by "80 percent" without the "Rexford Rand" name. Rexford Rand presented no other evidence, however, that would support the accuracy of this assertion.

[17] [FN7] In a partnership, the extent of the fiduciary duty owed by one partner to another varies from case to case depending on the circumstances; "a court must examine the relationship between the parties in each case so as to ascertain the standard to be applied to determine whether there has been a breach of a partner's fiduciary duty." *Saballus v. Timke,* 122 Ill.App.3d 109, 77 Ill.Dec. 451, 456, 460 N.E.2d 755, 760 (1983).

Generally, imposing a fiduciary duty on shareholders in a close corporation shields minority shareholders from oppressive conduct by the majority. Shareholders in close corporations have often invested a "substantial percentage" of their assets in the corporation, *see Donahue v. Rodd Electrotype Co.,* 367 Mass. 578, 328 N.E.2d 505, 514 (1975), and their position in the corporation may provide them with their only source of income. Minority shareholders are vulnerable to "freeze-outs" or "squeeze-outs," where the majority, for personal rather than legitimate business reasons, deprives the minority shareholder of his office, employment, and salary.[18] Moreover, because no active market exists for the corporation's stock (and prospective purchasers may be wary of buying into a small enterprise where dissension has already occurred), the minority stockholder most likely will not be able to sell his shares for any sum approaching their fair value. Consequently, an oppressed shareholder in a close corporation may seek a judicial remedy, including dissolution of the corporation.[19]

In addition, minority shareholders owe a duty of loyalty to a close corporation in certain circumstances. Minority shareholders have an obligation as *de facto* partners in the joint venture not to do damage to the corporate interests. If a minority shareholder harms the corporation through "unscrupulous and improper 'sharp dealings'" with the majority, he has breached his duty of loyalty.[20] "Conduct by any shareholder which is intended to be detrimental to the welfare of the enterprise . . . is a breach of a duty of loyalty which all shareholders owe to the common venture." J.A.C. Heatherington, *The Minority's Duty of Loyalty in Close Corporations,* 1972 DUKE L.J. 921, 945. Rexford Rand contends that Gregory acted unscrupulously and thus breached his duty of loyalty by reserving the Rexford Rand name for himself rather than informing Selwyn and Albert that Illinois was preparing to administratively dissolve the corporation.

Gregory acknowledges that, under normal circumstances, he would have owed a duty of loyalty to Rexford Rand. He argues, however, that his duty terminated after the alleged freeze-out, which deprived him of his position in the corporation as well as the benefits of his stock ownership. The Illinois courts have never decided whether a freeze-out terminates a minority shareholder's duty of loyalty to a close corporation. Generally, a shareholder's fiduciary duty continues after he resigns as an officer, director, or employee of a close corporation. *Hagshenas,* 145 Ill.Dec. at 553, 557 N.E.2d at 323 (50% shareholder

---

[18] [FN8] Close corporations often compensate their shareholders with salaries rather than dividends. Thus, loss of salary from a close corporation may be equivalent to the denial of dividends by a publicly held corporation. *Landorf v. Glottstein,* 131 Misc.2d 432, 500 N.Y.S.2d 494, 499 (1986), *aff'd,* 127 A.D.2d 1016, 511 N.Y.S.2d 776 (1987).

[19] [FN9] If dissolution is warranted, the court will appoint a receiver to oversee the liquidation of the corporate assets. *See* 805 ILCS 5/12.60. The proceeds will then be distributed to the shareholders after the claims of creditors have been satisfied. *Dubey v. Abam Building Corp.,* 266 Ill.App.3d 44, 203 Ill.Dec. 176, 179, 639 N.E.2d 215, 218 (1994).

[20] [FN10] In addition, a minority shareholder owes a fiduciary duty to the corporation when his interests are controlling on a particular issue. *Smith v. Atlantic Properties, Inc.,* 12 Mass.App. 201, 422 N.E.2d 798, 802-03 (1981) (25% shareholder owed fiduciary duty to close corporation where 80% vote required to declare dividends).

who resigned as officer and director still owed fiduciary duty because he retained his voting rights, which gave him 50% control over the corporation); *In re Dearborn,* 149 B.R. at 880 ("Resignation by a shareholder from the position of officer and director does not relieve that person of a fiduciary duty to the fellow shareholders."). Neither *Hagshenas* nor *Dearborn,* however, discussed the effect of a freeze-out on a shareholder's duty. Thus, we must attempt to determine how the Illinois courts would resolve this issue.

Our research indicates that only one court has addressed the question of whether a freeze-out terminates a shareholder's fiduciary duty to a close corporation. In *J Bar H, Inc. v. Johnson,* 822 P.2d 849 (Wyo.1991), the Supreme Court of Wyoming stated that "where a shareholder/director/employee of a close corporation has been wrongfully terminated from employment with the corporation and has been unjustly prevented from fulfilling her function as a director or officer, she can no longer be considered to act in a fiduciary capacity for the corporation." *Id.* at 861. The court reasoned that "the fiduciary duty not to compete depends on the ability to exercise the status which creates it." *Id.* A minority shareholder who has been frozen out no longer exercises the influence over corporate affairs that gives rise to a fiduciary duty. Consequently, no fiduciary duty should remain after a freeze-out. *Id.; cf. Tulumello v. W.J. Taylor Intl. Construction Co., Inc.,* 84 A.D.2d 903, 446 N.Y.S.2d 673 (1981) (employee of close corporation who was only a nominal officer because corporation was completely controlled by owner did not breach fiduciary duty by starting competing business).

While we understand the reluctance of the *J Bar H* court to place a fiduciary duty on a shareholder who has been frozen out, we do not believe that *J Bar H* achieves the optimal result. Gregory may have been the victim of oppressive activity, and he may have believed that reserving the Rexford Rand name for his own use would induce Albert and Selwyn to buy out his stock at a fair price. Gregory's desire to obtain a fair buyout is not itself objectionable; in fact, courts will occasionally order forced buyouts as a remedy for oppression.[21] The method by which he sought to induce a settlement, however, is troubling. By appropriating the corporate name, Gregory threatened to cause serious damage to the well-being of the corporation and to imperil Selwyn and Albert's investment as well as his own. The freeze-out did not deprive Gregory of his status as a shareholder and as a shareholder in a close corporation, Gregory should have placed the interests of the corporation above his personal interests. *Hagshenas,* 145 Ill.Dec. at 553, 557 N.E.2d at 323 (a partner may not enhance his "personal interests at the expense of the interests of the enterprise").

Even if Gregory was the victim of an improper "freeze-out," we do not believe that the Illinois courts would grant him the right to appropriate the corporate name in an attempt to gain a favorable settlement. Illinois allows oppressed shareholders to seek a judicial remedy, and Gregory should have relied on his suit against Albert and Selwyn seeking damages or dissolution of the

---

[21] [FN12] In addition, if an oppressed shareholder brings an action for dissolution, the parties will often settle by negotiating a buyout rather than dissolve a profitable business. Heatherington, *supra,* at 942-43.

corporation. If shareholders take it upon themselves to retaliate any time they believe they have been frozen out, disputes in close corporations will only increase. Rather, if unable to resolve matters amicably, aggrieved parties should take their claims to court and seek judicial resolution. Thus, the decision of the district court returning the name to the corporation and permanently enjoining Gregory from doing business under the names "Rexford Rand Corporation" and "Daxcel Corporation" is

AFFIRMED.

NOTES & QUESTIONS

1. In what respects may the development or management of intellectual property be particularly susceptible to improper self-dealing by a corporate officer or shareholder who breaches his fiduciary duties by administering company activities to benefit himself at the expense of his company or fellow company owners? What aspects of intellectual property assets may make such misconduct unusually easy to accomplish or to conceal?

2. Why should corporate laws establish duties of corporate officers and shareholders leading to personal liability for breaches of fiduciary obligations rather than leaving the definition of such obligations and risks of liability to the contracting of a corporation with its officers or among the co-owners of a corporate enterprise? Should the irreducible duties of corporate officers specified by statute be weaker or stronger for executives in companies that rely heavily on the development or use of intellectual property than for executives in other types of companies?

3. Under what circumstances should a party who was a corporate officer in a company when that company developed new intellectual products be able to establish or work for a second concern that seeks to rely on the same intellectual products? Does the answer depend only on whether the second concern's use of the intellectual products is infringing under intellectual property law standards? Or should corporate fiduciary duties to the first concern impose more demanding requirements on the former corporate officer in these circumstances, obligating the former officer not to use the first company's intellectual products to the private advantage of the former officer and to the disadvantage of the individual's former company?

CHAPTER 3

MISSTATEMENTS IN STOCK SALES REGARDING INTELLECTUAL PROPERTY INTERESTS

PROBLEM

Soon after the founding of Digital Ignition, the company's senior executives realized that further investment from parties other than the initial owners would be needed to finance the company's operations while it engaged in initial product development and marketing efforts. The goal of this financing would be to bring the company to the stage where it was ready for either an acquisition by another company or for an initial public offering of stock.

To generate this needed financing, Dr. See contacted William Elias, a local dentist with whom See had had some social contacts and who had expressed interest in possibly investing some of his considerable wealth in Digital Ignition. In order to convince Elias to invest in Digital Ignition, See described the assets and business potential of the company in highly favorable terms. See gave Elias a detailed written description of the digital ignition systems technology that See had developed and brought to the company, the patents covering this technology which were now held by Digital Ignition, the predicted attractiveness of the patented technology to a broad range of automobile owners, and the reasons why Digital Ignition's patents should assure the company of exclusive business opportunities and growth potential related to the marketing of products based on the new technology.

In summarizing the importance of the company's patents to Digital Ignition's future business activities, the documents provided to Elias indicated that "Dr. See and Digital Ignition have developed and patented major advances in automobile ignition system technology that promise to provide car owners with significant increases in automobile gas mileage and performance. We anticipate significant profit potential in future sales to both consumers using ignition systems based on the new technology to retrofit their existing vehicles and to new car manufacturers using the systems in newly manufactured vehicles. As the holder of patents on the key components of this new ignition systems technology, Digital Ignition is in a position to capture the full business potential of this exciting new technology over the life of these patents." Based on these representations and other information about Digital Ignition provided to him in discussions with See, Elias made an investment of $200,000 in Digital Ignition and is now one of the company's major shareholders.

Prior to his discussions with Elias, See told several executives at Digital Ignition that he was concerned about several digital ignition system products being developed and marketed by VF Industries. VF had hired Mary Jones, a former coworker of See's when both served as engine products designers for the International Motors Corporation. VF was developing digital ignition systems to be sold in the same markets that Digital Ignition was targeting for its products. An early version of one of VF's products demonstrated at a trade show appeared to incorporate some of Digital Ignition's patented technology. When See spoke to Elias, he was aware of this possible patent infringement by VF and the potential impact of VF's product sales on Digital Ignition's business prospects, but neither See nor any other Digital Ignition executive had yet evaluated the desirability of a patent infringement suit against VF or the likelihood of Digital Ignition's success in such a suit. Dr. See did not discuss VF's activities with Elias.

Six months after Elias' investment in the company, Digital Ignition filed a patent infringement action against VF asserting that VF's manufacturing and sales of digital ignition systems were covered by one of Digital Ignition's patents. Digital Ignition sought a preliminary injunction stopping VF from further product development, manufacturing, and marketing activities regarding products incorporating the patented technology. However, in an unexpected ruling, Digital Ignition was denied the preliminary injunction it sought. The district court involved cited what it felt to be two independently sufficient grounds for refusing to grant the preliminary injunction: first, Digital Ignition had not demonstrated a likelihood of success in establishing that VF's products were within the scope of Digital Ignition's patent claims and, second, VF had demonstrated a likelihood of invalidity of the patent in question on the ground that See had failed to properly name a co-inventor in the relevant patent application. The case is still pending and these issues of patent validity and infringement are expected to be more fully litigated at trial.

Elias was outraged upon hearing of the result in this preliminary injunction action. By the time this result was announced, Elias had learned through discussions with other Digital Ignition officers that See had been aware of the possible patent infringement by VF and the potential competitive impacts of the latter's products before Elias had invested in Digital Ignition. Elias felt that See had overstated the strength and significance of Digital Ignition's patents when Elias was considering an investment in the company.

Elias has filed a suit in federal court raising claims for damages under federal and state laws. His federal claims assert that the stock sales to him were accomplished through misleading statements violating SEC Rule 10b-5. Pursuant to these claims, Elias is seeking recovery for the loss in the value of his Digital Ignition stock due to recent publicity about the possible invalidity of the company's patents. In addition, Elias has filed state law claims asserting common law fraud by Digital Ignition officials in connection with Elias' purchase of Digital Ignition stock. Based on this fraud, Elias is seeking to rescind the purchase contract and to recover his $200,000. Because Elias' stock purchase agreement was entered into while he was at his winter home in Florida and many of the key representations at issue were made there, the law of the state of Florida will apply to these fraud claims.

You have been asked to provide a preliminary evaluation of the merits of Elias' suit, paying particular attention to whether it is likely that he will be able to establish that any misstatements made to him in connection with the disputed stock sales transaction involved material information. Please identify the major considerations affecting this aspect of his claims and identify what further information you would like to know in order to conduct a more thorough assessment of this case.

FOCUS OF THE CHAPTER

Assertions of misstatements to shareholders about company assets or business potential are common types of claims concerning new businesses, particularly where the businesses encounter unexpected business risks or difficulties. In the present case, responding to Elias' suit will require a careful consideration of the circumstances leading to the asserted misstatements about Digital Ignition's intellectual property and an evaluation of both federal and state laws governing fraud in general and securities fraud in particular.

Pressures surrounding the attraction of new investors can encourage company founders to overstate or misstate the strength of intellectual property interests. Raising capital for a new venture based on unproven intellectual property and related products or services is often challenging. Investors must be convinced to trust in both the business potential of a company's projected products or services and in the strength of the legal protections that will determine if the company has an exclusive opportunity to commercialize those products or services. To the extent that a particular company's business model depends on a complex chain of steps involving technological developments, new product designs, original marketing efforts, and the assertion of unproven legal protections, the chances that one of the critical steps needed for business success will go astray may appear high to many potential investors, causing substantial numbers of persons to choose investments in more established companies or technological fields.

The initial excerpt from the article on "Vaporware" describes the securities fraud standards that govern private claims by injured investors where companies or their executives have misrepresented the characteristics of company operations, products, or legal interests. It considers these standards in the context of misstatements about high-tech start-up companies.

The remaining readings are court opinions addressing the materiality of misrepresentations about intellectual property interests and the impacts of those interests in protecting valuable product marketing opportunities.

Pommer v. Medtest Corporation concerns a misrepresentation about the scope of patent rights covering a key company asset. A company official made a statement that the company possessed a patent covering its sole substantial asset, a proprietary testing process that the company hoped to market. However, no such patent had issued.

Alna Capital Assocs. v. Wagner analyzes a misstatement concerning efforts to perfect an intellectual property interest. A company president represented that a product incorporating the company's new refrigerant-enhancer invention was producing substantial profits and that these profits were likely to continue because a patent would soon issue to protect the company's exclusive marketing of products based on that invention. However, the initial product was not producing substantial profits and the Patent and Trademark Office had rejected the company's patent application for the invention because at least four different inventors had previously produced equivalent items.

Gompper v. VISX, Inc. involves an issued patent and a misstatement regarding the status of patent litigation. In a period when the company involved was announcing positive statements about its business and its patent portfolio, company managers were aware of litigation developments in which several of the company's key patents were held invalid and not infringed by an important competitor. Securities holders sued, arguing that company officials put forth the misleading profit projections in order to artificially inflate the company's stock price. The thrust of the complaint was that these statements about projected profits were false or misleading because the defendants knew there was no basis for the company's core patent claims and thus, no basis for the corporate officials' highly positive revenue projections.

Nathenson v. Zonagen, Inc., involves asserted misstatements about the scope and impact of an issued patent. A patent covering a method of application of a drug was described in a company press release as covering the formulation of the drug. Since a patent covering the latter would be much more valuable than one covering only a particular method of using the drug, shareholders asserted that the press release involved a material misstatement by the company and its officials. This case illustrates the continuing threat of liability for misstatements that attaches to statements by company officials about intellectual property interests from the early stages of company founding and growth to later settings where a mature company is trying to tout a new technological development.

Finally, *Zirn v. VLI Corp.* considers a misstatement about the content of legal advice from a company's patent counsel. The case involved an asserted use of fraudulent misstatements to encourage shareholders to undervalue their shares. Shareholders of the company involved claimed that company officials presented shareholders with an overly pessimistic view of the status of a company patent in order to lower the expectations of shareholders about the value of their shares and thereby convince the shareholders to vote for a proposed merger calling for low per share payments to the shareholders. The company officials had announced to the shareholders that the reinstatement of a particular patent which had inadvertently lapsed was unlikely even though patent counsel had advised the company's directors that reinstatement of the patent was likely and that the company had "an excellent case on the merits." This case examines not only the materiality under federal law standards of the asserted misstatements, but also the circumstances under which the making of material misstatements to shareholders may breach the duties of corporate officers and violate procedural and equitable dealing requirements imposed under state corporation laws.

READINGS

A.   STANDARDS GOVERNING SECURITIES FRAUD

Robert A. Prentice & John H. Langmore, Beware of Vaporware: Product Hype and the Securities Fraud Liability of High-Tech Companies
8 Harv. J.L. & Tech. 1 (1994)*

. . .

II.   THE ELEMENTS OF A SECTION 10(b)/RULE 10b-5 SUIT

Section 10(b) makes it unlawful "[t]o use or employ, in connection with the purchase or sale of any security any manipulative or deceptive device or contrivance in contravention of such rules and regulations as the Commission may prescribe as necessary or appropriate in the public interest or for the protection of investors." Rule 10b-5, of course, is the most significant of those rules and regulations promulgated by the SEC over the years.

A.   False Statement or Omission

The first element that must be established by a plaintiff alleging a violation of Section 10(b) and Rule 10b-5 is that the defendant engaged in some form of fraudulent, deceptive or manipulative conduct. The actionability of an outright false statement is fairly easy to understand, but many cases involve more difficult questions. This subsection addresses three of those more difficult issues: (1) What does "misleading" mean? (2) What about inaccurate projections and forecasts? (3) What about misleading omissions rather than positive misstatements?

1.   What Does "Misleading" Mean?

The simplest corporate misstatement cases involve obviously false statements, such as "Our new computer responds to voice-activated commands," when it does no such thing. Just as apparent are patently misleading omissions, such as neglecting to disclose that a high percentage of units sold have burst into flame. Both consumers and investors are misled in such instances.

More difficult questions are presented when the information is "soft" — subjective and perhaps forward-looking. When marketing hype is repeated in SEC-mandated disclosures, securities lawyers are typically alert enough to include various disclaimers regarding the risks that vaporware will not be promptly actualized in order to avoid misleading readers. However, securities

---

liability can flow from any public statement and marketing efforts too often go unscrutinized by attorneys.

In the Apple litigation, [*In re Apple Computer Sec. Litig.,* 886 F.2d 1109, 1115 (9th Cir. 1989), *cert. denied,* 496 U.S. 936 (1990),] Apple Computer produced affidavits from several market experts indicating that the vaporware phenomenon is well known, that "when a computer industry product is announced for future availability, the market fully understands that the product is still in the development stage." In other words, Apple was arguing that a preannounced product is merely vaporware, and everyone knows it, and therefore no one could be misled.

However, as the Ninth Circuit stated in response to this argument, "[t]here is a difference between knowing that any product-in-development may run into a few snags, and knowing that a particular product has already developed problems so significant as to require months of delay." A statement that production is progressing smoothly when significant problems have already arisen is obviously misleading. In other words, disclosure of the potential complications that all hardware and software manufacturers may encounter is not required. Disclosure of problems that have already been encountered and undermine previous expressions of optimism is required.

Additionally, statements, although literally true, may be misleading if they make up part of a "mosaic" of information that conveys a misleading impression. Thus, a statement which discloses most relevant facts might still be misleading if it is presented in such a manner that reasonable investors (or consumers) cannot assemble an accurate picture of the whole. This is often termed the "buried facts" doctrine. For example, a company might disclose a good deal of information regarding the features of its new computer and the speed with which the computer performs its tasks, failing to mention the total lack of reliability the computer has demonstrated in internal testing.

In a related vein, half-truths may also be considered misleading. For this reason, as noted above, Rule 10b-5 prohibits companies from "omit[ting] to state a material fact necessary in order to make the statements made, in light of the circumstances under which they were made, not misleading." Thus, if a product press release announced that a company's new line of computers was on schedule to be released on January 1, 1996, but failed to mention that development of the new software needed to operate the computers was behind schedule and would not be ready until July 1, 1996, a misleading half-truth has been told. The hardware is little more than vaporware if there is no software with which to operate it. Disclosure must generally be complete with respect to material facts.

At the same time, the law does not mean that by revealing one fact about a product, one must reveal all other facts that might be interesting to the stock market. One need reveal only such additional facts, if any, that are needed to ensure that what was revealed would not be "so incomplete as to mislead." Thus, a product press release touting a new printer's speed of operation would not necessarily be misleading if it failed to mention that the printer did not have color capacity.

2.   What About False and Misleading Projections?

A projection or forecast is not a statement of historical fact. Persons who hear or read a forward-looking statement, perhaps regarding a new computer that is in development, can generally understand that predictions do not always come true. No company must, or could, guarantee the accuracy of its predictions. Therefore, no one expects all vaporware announcements to be realized on schedule.

However, that does not mean that vaporware announcements are never actionable. In the *Apple* case, Apple officers made statements such as "Lisa is going to be phenomenally successful." In fact, Lisa turned out to be a nearly unmitigated flop. The key issue in terms of liability is the good faith and reasonable basis of the prediction, not its ultimate accuracy. As the Ninth Circuit noted in *Apple*:

> A projection or statement of belief contains at least three implicit factual assertions: (1) that the statement is genuinely believed, (2) that there is a reasonable basis for that belief, and (3) that the speaker is not aware of any undisclosed facts tending to seriously undermine the accuracy of the statement. A projection or statement of belief may be actionable to the extent that one of these implied factual assertions is inaccurate.

[886 F.2d at 1113].

Thus, when companies make vaporware announcements about the future availability and projected features of their products, just as when they make financial forecasts regarding gross income or profit margin, securities fraud liability may attach if the statements are not genuinely believed or have no reasonable basis.

In *Apple*, the court found that the company's statements that it had "unequalled strength, experience and expertise," that its new product was "a significant breakthrough," that "success should continue," and that its forecasting process had been "refined," were generally accurate and certainly believed in good faith. Apple, indeed, was a successful company with a good track record and for a time it believed in its Lisa and Twiggy products, even though they ultimately did not pan out as hoped. Therefore, the trial court held, and its holding was affirmed on appeal, that these statements were not actionable.

Courts generally have been careful to prevent plaintiffs from alleging "fraud by hindsight," a phrase used by the District Court of Massachusetts in dismissing claims arising from a series of infamous vaporware announcements by Lotus Development Corp. In that case, the court held that plaintiffs' claims that the software was not released as scheduled was only a claim of fraud by hindsight: "Especially where, as here, a product is understood to be in development, plaintiffs may not assert merely that, because the product did not come out when projected, plans for an earlier release were false." Again, the true test is the good faith and reasonableness of the company's previous public projections.

On the other hand, if a company predicts an important release date for particular vaporware, and does not publicly revise that date in light of known problems, then the prediction may become actionable. The *Apple* facts discussed above regarding Twiggy's development problems are an obvious example. Another example occurred in *Bharucha v. Reuters Holdings PLC* [810 F. Supp. 37 (E.D.N.Y. 1993)]. When Reuters touted the release of a new product, "Dealing 2000," which was to provide automatic matching facilities for foreign exchange transactions, and predicted that the new product would provide a major new source of revenue in 1990 and 1991, Reuters' ADRs rose from $25-3/4 to $70-5/8. However, when Reuters announced in October, 1990 that problems had occurred and Dealing 2000 would not be introduced for at least six months, Reuters' ADR price dropped to $ 32-5/8. A subsequent shareholders' complaint alleged that defendant officers knew or should have known that the predicted release date was misleading because the product had experienced development problems as early as May 1, 1989, and had not even reached the point where it could be released for beta testing. These allegations that the forward-looking statements had not been made in good faith enabled the complaint to survive a motion to dismiss.

As noted earlier, the actionability of a disclosed prediction does not turn on whether or not the prediction in fact proves to be inaccurate. This is particularly the case where a projection "bespeaks caution." Under the "bespeaks caution" doctrine, a properly qualified vaporware announcement will not be actionable. However, the adequacy of the caution given will be decided on a case-by-case basis. The caution must be precise rather than broad boilerplate and, obviously, will not immunize forward-looking statements known to be false when made.

For example, the plaintiffs in *In re Storage Technology Corp. Securities Litigation*, [804 F. Supp. 1368 (D. Colo. 1992),] alleged that defendant company had made unduly optimistic claims for its new advanced storage and retrieval computer (the "Iceberg"). Company officers and directors represented that Iceberg had a two- to three-year technological advantage over the competition. These statements naturally excited consumers and investors alike. When problems with Iceberg's production were eventually disclosed, the stock price plunged and plaintiff investors sued under, inter alia, Section 10(b) and Rule 10b-5. Storage Technology defended by claiming that its overly optimistic predictions were mixed with statements of caution. The court denied Storage Technology's motion to dismiss, concluding that its vaporware announcements had not been sufficiently qualified to avoid misleading investors:

> [T]he unmistakable message conveyed by defendants' pre-April 20, 1992 public statements was that Iceberg would be in production by 1992, Storage Technology would enjoy a competitive advantage because it would be the first to reach the market with this new product and Storage Technology would earn large profits in 1992 as a result of Iceberg. Although some of the comments were tempered with caution, I cannot say as a matter of law at this juncture that they are too cautious to be actionable. "Not every mixture with the true will neutralize the deceptive."

[*Id.* at 1373.]

In the case *In re Marion Merrell Dow, Inc. Securities Litigation,* [[1993 Transfer Binder] Fed. Sec. L. Rep. (CCH) ¶ 97,776 (W.D. Mo. Oct. 4, 1993),] plaintiffs evaded a motion to dismiss based on the "bespeaks caution" doctrine because the challenged statements and omissions (relating to adverse effects of defendants' drug) did not contain "repeated specific warnings of significant risk factors." Broad, generic warnings were deemed inadequate to "bespeak caution."

Still, when risk factors are clearly disclosed in a detailed fashion, investors will not be allowed to argue that they were misled when projections known to be contingent fail to materialize. For example, in *In re Convergent Technologies Securities Litigation,* [948 F.2d 507 (9th Cir.1991),] plaintiff investors complained that Convergent and its officers misled them by concealing from the market certain cost and production problems regarding the company's next generation ("NGEN") workstation product line. Product life cycle decisions are among the most difficult marketers have to make, because in the high technology field new products must continually be developed, but their development always poses technical problems and their marketing often diminishes the sales of the company's predecessor products.

The Ninth Circuit held, inter alia, that the market was not misled regarding the diminished sales of Convergent's earlier workstation product line because "[a]s a general matter, investors know of the risk of obsolescence posed by older products forced to compete with more advanced rivals," and that the risks regarding the development and marketing of NGEN had been particularized and emphasized.

3.   What About Mere Omissions of Fact?

Suppose that while a company is in the process of developing a new line of software, its engineers run into several technical roadblocks and it becomes unlikely that they will be able to meet the company's stated performance goals. This is certainly a common if not universal occurrence in high-tech product development, but must the company voluntarily disclose to the market whenever such roadblocks are encountered? In other words, when does a company have the duty to disclose news (usually bad news) to the market?

Of course, if the news is already known to the public or to the plaintiffs, there is no duty to disclose. Further, the general rule is that the simple fact that a company possesses nonpublic, material information does not mean that it automatically has a duty to disclose that information. Absent a duty to disclose, an omission is generally not deemed misleading or deceptive.

According to several recent court decisions, there are three basic situations giving rise to a duty to disclose: (a) when insider trading is occurring, (b) when specific statutes or regulations require disclosure, and (c) when a company should correct "inaccurate, incomplete, or misleading prior disclosures." Each of these will be discussed in turn.

a. Duty to Disclose Arising Because of Insider Trading

The insider trading cases are fairly clear-cut, although they are properly viewed as the major component of a larger subset of cases — those where a fiduciary relationship exists. Assume, for example, that officers of a small computer company that has recently gone public learn that their only product has developed so many technical glitches that it will probably never be anything more than vaporware. If those officers begin unloading their stock in the company without disclosing the technical glitches, an insider trading violation of Section 10(b), actionable by contemporaneous purchasers of the stock, occurs.

Insider trading is often alleged in securities fraud cases arising out of high-tech industries, because many such companies in their formative years reward officers and other employees with stock options. When stock prices drop, plaintiff shareholders often claim that the defendants had been making overly optimistic statements about the company's products or financial prospects in order to buoy the company's stock price for their own personal trading profit. Therefore, for purposes of the corporate disclosure cases discussed in this article, insider trading serves primarily as the wellspring for a duty to disclose by the company and as evidence of scienter, indicating a possible motivation behind misleading statements and omissions.

b. Duty to Disclose Arising from Statute or Regulation

A duty to speak out also arises when SEC rules and regulations require disclosure, as in the filing of annual or quarterly reports. One category of relevant cases deals with projections, forward-looking statements, and other "soft information." A pressing concern for public companies centers on the imposition of liability for not disclosing soft information. What if, for example, a company has a practice of making formal but internal projections as to the date its new products will be issued, and updates these internal projections every quarter? Certainly investors (as well as consumers) would be interested in such projections. Although, as noted earlier, such matters receive certain "safe harbor" protection if they are disclosed, SEC rules and regulations typically do not require that they be disclosed.

On the other hand, despite recent judicial reluctance to widen the corporate duty to disclose, the SEC's 1989 Interpretive Release on Management Discussion and Analysis ("MD&A") seemingly requires disclosure of some forward-looking information, complicating the disclosure picture. Thus, the MD&A disclosure provisions arguably require a company to disclose, for example, major development problems regarding a key product it hopes to produce. SEC action in the MD&A area certainly merits close monitoring by corporate counsel, for the SEC seems to be requiring more in the way of predictive information from companies than are the courts.

Similarly, NYSE-listed companies must consider Exchange Manual Rule ¶ 202.05 which provides that listed companies are "expected to release quickly to the public any news or information which might reasonably be expected to materially affect the market for its securities." Good and bad information about major products (not mere vaporware) would seem to meet these criteria.

c. Duty to Disclose in Order to Correct Prior Disclosures

An understanding of this third category of duty initially requires that a distinction be drawn between historical information and forward-looking information, and between the duty to correct and the duty to update. An examination of three hypothetical scenarios will illustrate the key distinctions drawn by most courts.

Scenario #1: Assume, first, that the McCoy Computer Co. product manager announces at a trade fair that McCoy's engineers have just completed a technological breakthrough enabling McCoy's soon-to-be-released computer to be equally compatible with both IBM-style PCs and Apple-style Macs. Assume that McCoy's officers truly believe this to be true, but six weeks later McCoy's engineers learn that they had overlooked a serious technical problem which will prevent the promised compatibility from occurring. This development means that the trade fair announcement contained an inaccurate statement of historical fact. The misstatement is actionable. Furthermore, McCoy would have an affirmative duty to correct this inaccuracy.

The seminal duty to correct case is perhaps *Ross v. A.H. Robins Co., Inc.*, [465 F. Supp. 904 (S.D.N.Y.), *rev'd on other grounds*, 607 F.2d 545 (2d Cir.1979), *cert. denied*, 446 U.S. 946 (1980),] in which A.H. Robins made optimistic statements in 1970 and 1971 about the safety, efficacy, and marketability of its intrauterine contraceptive devices. In 1972, an unpublished research report demonstrated that the device was not as safe as previously represented, and Robins was found potentially liable under Section 10(b) and Rule 10b-5 for neither correcting nor modifying its previous statements which had been revealed to be inaccurate statements of historical fact.

Another case involving product marketing is *In re Pfizer, Inc. Securities Litigation*, [[1990-1991 Transfer Binder] Fed. Sec. L. Rep. (CCH) ¶ 95,710 (S.D.N.Y. Dec. 21, 1990),] wherein plaintiffs alleged that Pfizer had been aggressively marketing its Shiley heart valve without disclosing its internal corporate knowledge of serious problems in manufacturing and quality assurance procedures. Pfizer alleged that it had no obligation to disclose its conjecture about these problems or about the tremendous legal liability to which they might give rise as the heart valves failed. The court disagreed, holding that plaintiffs' assertions that Pfizer had known as far back as 1980 that the Shiley heart valve had design flaws but had nonetheless continued to aggressively market and positively describe the valve, adequately stated a claim. Pfizer's marketing claims constituted inaccurate statements of historical fact crying out for correction.

To complicate our first hypothetical scenario slightly, assume that the inaccurate statement of historical fact was contained in a computer magazine article written by an analyst who regularly follows McCoy. Would McCoy have a duty to correct that statement? Inaccurate statements in such sources can affect market price and possibly lead to securities law liability. Companies should not, of course, be generally liable for the statements of third parties and have no duty to police the trade magazines to find inaccuracies that are not attributable to the companies. However, companies are liable for misstatements of their own employees appearing in the trade press and for third parties' misstatements if they have somehow placed their imprimatur upon those misstatements.

Scenario #2: Assume that McCoy's product manager had announced at a January 1993 trade fair that McCoy had sold 10,000 personal computers in 1992, and announced at a January 1994 trade fair that McCoy had sold 20,000 personal computers in 1993. If McCoy really sold these computers, these are accurate statements of historical fact. Assume further that on February 15, 1994, McCoy learns that due to competitive pressures it will probably sell no more than 3,000 personal computers in 1994. No statement needs correction, and most courts would hold that there is no free-standing duty to update an accurate statement of historical fact. In this case, there is no duty to speak, even though the situation, once accurately reported, has changed.

Scenario #3: Assume, finally, that McCoy's product manager states at the January 1994 trade fair that McCoy had sold 10,000 computers in 1992, 20,000 in 1993, and expects to sell 30,000 in 1994. Assume further that this forward-looking statement was made in good faith and with reasonable belief, but on February 15, 1994, McCoy learns that due to competitive pressures it is unlikely that it will sell more than 10,000 units in 1994. Here there is no duty to correct a historical inaccuracy, but a duty to update does exist. A statement, correct at the time, may have a forward connotation upon which readers or listeners may be expected to rely. If it becomes clear that the forward-looking statement was the product of a defective crystal ball, further disclosure may be called for. Thus, companies must update opinions and projections if they have become misleading as a result of intervening events.

In re Convergent Technologies Securities Litigation, [948 F.2d 507 (9th Cir. 1991),] involved several claims of misstatement and omission. One objection was to Convergent's statement that "[o]ur growth in the [first] quarter [of 1983] was the result of increases in shipments to our large OEM customers." Despite plaintiffs' claim that this statement misled investors by implying that the upward trend would continue, the court concluded that no duty to correct arose when Convergent learned that the upward tick in shipments was only temporary because the statement was an accurate statement of historical fact. Nor was there a duty to update, because the statement was not forward-looking.

On the other hand, in *Alfus v. Pyramid Technology Corp.*, [764 F. Supp. 598 (N.D. Cal.1991),] plaintiffs alleged that defendant corporation fed information to financial analysts for inclusion of the analysts' reports. Those reports were optimistic regarding Pyramid's financial prospects and its MIServer product line, which would purportedly become available in February 1989 and contribute to revenues in the quarter ending in March. These forward-looking statements allegedly were rendered misleading by the fact that the manufacture and initial marketing of the MIServer family of products were plagued by serious and persistent problems causing at least a seven-month delay in their introduction. The court held that because these omissions rendered the previous forward-looking vaporware announcements inaccurate, those announcements should have been updated.

Unfortunately, the duty to update is one of the murkiest areas of federal securities law. Such a duty generally seems to arise when a development occurs that renders a prior forward-looking statement no longer accurate. In other words, a duty to update exists if such a prior statement would be a misstatement or half-truth if it were republished currently. Because a duty to update exists only if forward-looking statements, accurate when made, remain alive and have become false or misleading as a result of subsequent events, it is arguably just a variation of the "duty to correct."

One difficulty often lies in knowing how long a prior statement remains "alive," i.e., how long investors could reasonably rely on the statement. Courts have not set forth clear guidelines regarding the "shelf life" of forward-looking statements. If, for example, on January 1, 1995, the ABC Computer Co. announces that its engineers are working hard on developing software to perform a particular task, may investors reasonably rely on that statement on January 1, 1996? How about January 1, 1997? Because there are no firm answers to these questions, forward-looking statements regarding vaporware (as well as regarding financial conditions) should be made with caution and only with respect to products in the advanced stages of development. To do otherwise, while not necessarily creating Section 10(b)/Rule 10b-5 liability, may create a continuing duty to update.

Another difficulty involves the question of timing. If a company begins to suspect that one of its vaporware products is going to be very late, when must it inform the market? The courts have held that material information may be withheld from the market if there is a good business reason to do so. However, while courts often find good business reasons for the delay of disclosure of "good" information, such as a favorable mineral strike or the obtaining of a major contract, they rarely find a good business reason for the delay of "bad" information, such as the fact that a new product line will not be released on the date previously announced. About the most that can be claimed is a good faith delay sufficient for the company to verify the accuracy of the bad news.

B. Materiality

A second basic element of a Section 10(b)/Rule 10b-5 claim is materiality. The false or misleading statement or omission must be as to a "material" fact in order to be actionable. Matters of only niggling consequence do not affect investment decisions and should not give rise to liability. Classic examples of material facts include major mineral strikes, a substantial dividend reduction, and a large decline in earnings. As discussed earlier, vaporware announcements touting new products aimed at consumers can also influence investors and thereby be material.

Of course, not all product-related misstatements are material. Thus, if a product manager stated that the company's next generation computer would be on the market by July 1 of the following year, when, in fact, she believed that it would not be on the market until July 5 of that year, the inaccuracy would probably be immaterial. Misstatements regarding a line of products accounting for only a small fraction of a company's sales and profits would also most likely not be material.

The difficulty, of course, is drawing the line in that gray area between the obviously material and the obviously immaterial. The Supreme Court has established a test of materiality keyed to whether there is a "substantial likelihood" that a misstated fact had, or disclosure of an omitted fact would have, "significantly altered the 'total mix' of information made available" in the eyes of a reasonable investor. A fact can be material, however, even if it would not have changed the plaintiff's decision on whether to consummate the transaction in question so long as it would have assumed actual significance in a reasonable investor's deliberations.

The Supreme Court has also stated that in some instances materiality is gauged by multiplying the probability that an event will occur by the magnitude of the event. The Supreme Court made its pronouncement in the context of a takeover that was being negotiated but had not yet been consummated, holding that the magnitude of the deal multiplied by the likelihood that it would be consummated might well make it material before negotiations had advanced to the point that the "price and structure" of the transaction had been fixed. It is easy to see the analogy to product development. Information about the development of a particularly significant product could be deemed material before that product was ready for market if there was a reasonable likelihood that it would become ready. Deciding when in the long evolution of a high-tech product the "probability times magnitude" formula provides a conclusion regarding materiality is obviously problematic.

In one case involving a product representation, *Pommer v. Medtest Corp.*, [961 F.2d 620 (7th Cir. 1992),] evidence indicated that the sellers of a company with but a single asset — the intellectual property in a self-administered cervicovaginal cytology testing process — sold the company's stock to a buyer and, in so doing, represented that the process was patented. In fact, it was not patented. Even though the process was ultimately patented two years later, the court concluded that the misstatement was material by applying the Supreme Court's formula:

> West [an attorney owning 26% of Medtest stock] told [buyers] that Medtest had a patent, doubtless recognizing that in selling stock as in other endeavors a bird in the hand is worth two in the bush. Counsel's belief that the process is patentable is a fair distance from a patent. The examiner may disagree or insist that the applicant limit the claims in a way that affects the commercial value of the invention. If we take counsel's belief as signifying an 80% chance that Medtest will obtain a patent on the central claims, still the difference is material. Even a small probability of a bad event may be material, if that event is grave enough.

[*Id.*]

A more concrete indication of materiality than the Supreme Court's "probability times magnitude" formula is, where applicable, actual market response. Given the premise that American securities markets are essentially efficient and respond accurately to new information, a large movement (up or down) of the market in response to a company's news (good or bad) is strong evidence of the materiality of the information. As noted earlier, the announcement that Apple Computer intended to discontinue the development and production of its Twiggy vaporware precipitated a 25% drop in the price of Apple's stock in a single day. This drop indicates that the information was clearly material, although the announcement was made concurrently with public disclosure of a negative report on quarterly earnings.

Similarly, in *In re U.S. Bioscience Securities Litigation*, [806 F. Supp. 1197 (E.D. Pa.1992),] plaintiffs alleged that the company treasurer made a claim that a drug produced by the company might be marketed during the latter half of a specified year, pending FDA approval, knowing that getting the drug to market so quickly was not realistic. When securities analysts learned the truth, they concluded that the news "severely undermined the credibility of both the drug and [Bioscience]." This response by analysts, whose role is critical to providing information upon which investors in public companies make their pricing decisions, was deemed by the trial judge to be evidence of materiality.

"Puffing," the defensive concept that renders overly favorable descriptions of products immaterial in a consumer's fraud suit, is also occasionally successful in an investor's Section 10(b)/Rule 10b-5 suit. For example, an investor sued Commodore International claiming, inter alia, that in press releases Commodore promised that its new product — CDTV (a new interactive compact disc television system for the home) — would do far more than it ultimately did. [*See Vosgerichian v. Commodore Int'l*, 832 F. Supp. 909 (E.D. Pa. 1993).] The trial court dismissed the investor's lawsuit on the same grounds that it might have dismissed a disappointed consumer's fraud suit:

> All of Commodore's statements about CDTV either constitute unactionable "puffing" (CDTV is "revolutionary," it can "change the world," could "be what VCR's were to the 1980's"), or they are not misleading. Commodore promised only that it would have 50 titles "in (its) introductory phase," not that it would have them immediately. Mr. Gould announced that CDTV represented a "major potential opportunity" — which could only be taken as a doubly qualified advertisement, not any kind of promise at all.

[*Id.* at 916.]

C. Scienter

Although many lower courts once held that mere negligence was sufficient to create a violation of Section 10(b) and Rule 10b-5, the Supreme Court in *Ernst & Ernst v. Hochfelder*, [425 U.S. 185 (1976),] held that in a private cause of action a "mental state embracing intent to deceive, manipulate or defraud" is a necessary element to establishing liability under Section 10(b) and Rule 10b-5. The scienter requirement need not entail a desire to deceive; it may mean only that defendant knowingly made a false statement and appreciated that it would likely mislead investors. As in other areas of the law, securities class action defendants are presumed to intend the natural consequences of their actions.

Although the Supreme Court has never spoken on the issue, most lower courts have held that "recklessness" may be sufficiently condemnable conduct to satisfy the scienter standard. Although courts have not been completely consistent in defining recklessness, one court recently described the concept as:

> [A] highly unreasonable omission, involving not merely simple, or even inexcusable negligence, but an extreme departure from the standard of ordinary care, and which presents a danger of misleading buyers or

sellers that is either known to the defendant or is so obvious that the actor must have been aware of it.

[*Hollinger v. Titan Capital Corp.*, 914 F.2d 1564, 1569 (9th Cir.1990).]

Scienter is a convoluted doctrine that raises difficult problems of both a legal and factual nature. Because plaintiffs cannot read defendants' minds, plaintiffs are typically allowed to establish scienter by inference. But plaintiffs must allege particular facts that give rise to an inference that defendants actually knew (or were reckless in their ignorance) of fraudulent conduct. The Second Circuit, for example, recognizes two primary means for plaintiffs to adequately plead scienter. First, plaintiffs "may allege facts establishing a motive to commit fraud and an opportunity to do so." Second, plaintiffs "may allege facts constituting circumstantial evidence of either reckless or conscious behavior."

In applying these concepts to product hyping, the first means of pleading scienter could be fulfilled by alleging that defendants' motive in prematurely announcing vaporware, as is commonly the case, was to discourage customers from buying competitors' products. It could also be fulfilled by alleging that defendant company officers sought to buoy the company's stock price with overly optimistic product announcements in order to profit personally by the exercise of stock options or other trading in the company's shares. Given the common practice of compensating officers and directors with share ownership, stock options, stock appreciation rights, and the like, plaintiffs often seize upon this "motive and opportunity" to fulfill the scienter requirement. As the Ninth Circuit noted in Apple, "[i]nsider trading in suspicious amounts or at suspicious times is probative of bad faith and scienter."

For example, in *In re RasterOps Corp. Securities Litigation*, [[1993 Transfer Binder] Fed. Sec. L. Rep. (CCH) ¶ 97,790 (N.D. Cal. Aug. 13, 1993),] plaintiffs claimed that the defendant company made misleadingly optimistic vaporware announcements. Plaintiffs survived a motion to dismiss on scienter grounds vis-à-vis individual officer defendants by alleging that defendants suppressed adverse information:

> [S]o that they could (1) protect and enhance their executive positions and the substantial compensation and prestige they obtained thereby; (2) enhance the value of their RasterOps stock holdings and their options to buy RasterOps stock; (3) sell shares of RasterOps stock they owned at inflated prices to obtain large profits; and (4) inflate the reported profits of the Company in order to obtain larger payments under RasterOps' incentive bonus compensation plan and/or via discretionary individual performance bonuses.

[*Id.* at 97,850.]

A second means of adequately establishing scienter in the vaporware context is by use of circumstantial evidence in the form of internal memoranda or the like indicating so many problems in product development that defendants could not have reasonably believed their optimistic product announcements. In Apple, for example, the product press release containing challenged Statements #4 and #5 regarding the Twiggy vaporware, was issued at a time when internal documents showed that Apple's tests indicated slowness and unreliability in Twiggy's information-processing capabilities; when the Apple division in charge of producing Lisa had warned top executives that its current unreliability would probably delay the introduction of Lisa by many months; and when Steven Jobs was expressing "virtually zero confidence" in the division in charge of developing Twiggy. The dissonance between Apple's external optimism and internal pessimism provided sufficient circumstantial evidence of scienter to warrant a jury trial, according to the Ninth Circuit.

Conversely, in *Berliner v. Lotus Development Corp.*, [783 F. Supp. 708 (D. Mass. 1992)], plaintiffs alleged that they bought Lotus stock at an artificially inflated price because Lotus kept announcing that the "1-2-3 Release 3.0" upgrade of its famous software package was about to be released when, in fact, it was nowhere near release. Plaintiffs first attacked a February 25, 1988 announcement that Release 3.0 would be available "late" in the second quarter of 1988, but the complaint alleged no facts or circumstances indicating that the projection was false when made. Absent such facts or circumstances, plaintiffs' allegations were insufficient as mere "fraud by hindsight."

Other pleadings were similarly rejected. On March 18, 1988, Lotus announced that although its senior vice president of software development had resigned, it had not yet changed its plans for introduction of Release 3.0. However, four days later, Lotus announced that the product would be delayed until the fourth quarter of 1988. That projection was repeated on March 29, July 18, August 9, August 12, and August 24. However, on October 7, 1988, Lotus rescheduled the release for the second quarter of 1989. Plaintiffs attempted to raise their claims above the level of fraud by hindsight by pointing to three "circumstances" probative of the falsehood of the later projections. First, plaintiffs alleged that five Lotus vice presidents resigned during the relevant period, but the court found several different reasons for the resignations and deemed them insufficient evidence that Lotus knew Release 3.0 would not meet its projected release dates. Second, plaintiffs alleged that Lotus did not begin beta testing until February 1989, urging the inference that because such testing is a prerequisite to commercial distribution of software, Lotus was reckless in projecting its earlier release dates. The court responded by pointing out that when Lotus announced on August 24, for example, that it was "aiming to" market Release 3.0 "late" in the fourth quarter, four months remained in the year, a period not alleged to be necessarily insufficient to complete beta testing. Finally, plaintiffs advanced a "motive and opportunity" type of argument that Lotus had an incentive to defraud the public in that (a) the company purportedly wished to dissuade customers from purchasing other products, and (b) Lotus insiders sold their Lotus shares during this time period. The court also rejected this third ground (and therefore dismissed the suit), stating in conclusory fashion that the insider sales, which were not alleged to have violated insider trading proscriptions, were not by themselves a sufficient basis for inferring that Lotus had repeatedly misrepresented the product's release date. However, the court never responded to plaintiffs' argument regarding Lotus' motive to dissuade customers from purchasing competitors' products — a motive which, as we have seen, often underlies vaporware announcements.

When, as is usually the case, individual defendants are included in a Section 10(b)/Rule 10b-5 complaint, many courts require very specific pleadings regarding the scienter of each. For example, in *In re Newbridge Network Securities Litigation*, [767 F. Supp. 275 (D. D.C. 1991),] part of the plaintiffs' complaint related to the defendants' alleged misrepresentations and omissions about problems with product quality. Regarding the scienter issue, the court held that where multiple individual defendants are sued, "the complaint must apprise each defendant of his or her participation in the fraud." Plaintiffs met that burden because their complaint specified the statements alleged to be misleading, adequately detailed when, where, and by whom they were made, and identified facts indicating conscious behavior by the individual defendants.

D. Reliance

Reliance by a plaintiff is "essential to a claim under Rule 10b-5 because it 'provides the requisite causal connection between a defendant's misrepresentation and a plaintiff's injury.'" As one court put it, reliance is "the subjective counterpart to the objective element of materiality."

Common law rules required that a plaintiff prove she had actually based decisions upon the defendant's misstatements or omissions. This traditional element of a common law fraud claim requiring a plaintiff to directly read or hear a misstatement and then rely on it has by necessity been altered in causes of action under Section 10(b) and Rule 10b-5.

The first such major alteration arose in *Affiliated Ute Citizens of Utah v. United States*, [406 U.S. 128 (1972),] wherein the Supreme Court held that plaintiffs need not establish reliance in an omission case. In other words, it makes little sense to ask plaintiffs to plead and prove reliance on facts that were hidden from them. Therefore, traditional reliance ("I saw, I read, I relied") need not be proved in omission cases. That the omitted information was material is sufficient to give rise to a presumption of reliance. Two other developments are of particular importance in recent 10b-5 cases.

1. "Fraud-on-the-Market"

In creating the "fraud-on-the-market" theory of reliance, lower courts reasoned that in cases of affirmative misrepresentation, reliance may be presumed even on the part of plaintiffs who did not see, read, or truly rely on misleading documents if they relied on the integrity of the market price. The Ninth Circuit, for example, reasoned that the purchaser of stock "relies generally on the supposition that the market price is validly set and that no unsuspected manipulation has artificially inflated the price, and thus indirectly on the truth of the representations underlying the stock price." This fraud-on-the-market theory equates an investor's reliance on market price with reliance upon statements made to the market. It changes the focus of the inquiry from whether the plaintiffs were misled to whether the market was misled. In *Basic, Inc. v. Levinson*, [485 U.S. 224, 247 (1988),] the Supreme Court accepted the fraud-on-the-market presumption, and the Efficient Capital Market Hypothesis (ECMH) upon which it is based.

Several cases involving statements about products have involved the fraud-on-the-market approach to reliance. One example is *DeVries v. Taylor*, [[1993 Transfer Binder] Fed. Sec. L. Rep. (CCH) ¶ 97,679 (D. Colo. June 28, 1993),] in which Thelma June DeVries (and others) sued Chemex Pharmaceuticals (and its officers and directors) alleging that they had misrepresented numerous aspects of Chemex's business and fraudulently concealed the truth about the development problems of one of its main products, a drug called Actinex. Defendants moved to dismiss on the reliance issue because DeVries candidly admitted that she was unaware of the facts on which the lawsuit was premised, had never read any of the documents allegedly containing misstatements and omissions, and had simply followed her husband Dale's recommendations in buying Chemex stock. On the other hand, Dale had worked in the securities business for 25 years and swore that he had relied on the securities markets to establish a fair price for Chemex stock. Given these facts, the court concluded that DeVries' reliance "on the alleged misrepresentations and omissions can be established via Dale's reliance on the same and the integrity of the marketplace."

Courts have recognized several basic rebuttals to the fraud-on-the-market presumption of reliance in a Section 10(b)/Rule 10b-5 case: (a) proof that the plaintiff did indeed know of the false statement or omission and traded in the stock anyway; (b) proof that the plaintiff would have made the purchase or sale even had she known of the false statement or omission; (c) proof that the market in question was not, in fact, efficient; (d) proof that the market price did not respond to the misrepresentation, indicating that the market was not misled; and (e) proof that "market makers" were privy to the truth in the case of a misrepresentation or omission, and, thus, the market price was not perversely affected by that misrepresentation or omission. This fifth category has evolved into what is currently known as the "truth-on-the-market" defense.

2. "Truth-on-the-Market"

The most interesting aspect of the fraud-on-the-market theory is the "truth-on-the-market" defense that has evolved from it. The essence of this defense is a claim by defendant companies in securities fraud cases that any inaccurate public announcements that they may have made were neutralized by corrections made by other sources that permeated throughout the efficient market. Clearly, if the market knew that a statement made by a corporate defendant was false or misleading, and the market priced the shares accordingly, a plaintiff's presumed reliance on a misleadingly high or low market price is severed. In essence, the company is arguing: "Yeah, we lied, but no one believed us."

Ironically, in vaporware cases the more spectacularly misleading the statement made by the company about its promised products, the more credible is its claim that the market was not defrauded because the truth was well known. This defense was used by Apple in its vaporware case involving Lisa and Twiggy. In *Apple*, the Ninth Circuit applied the truth-on-the-market defense in the following manner:

> The press portrayed Lisa as a gamble, with the potential for either enormous success or enormous failure. At least twenty articles stressed

the risks Apple was taking, and detailed the underlying problems producing those risks. Many of the optimistic statements challenged by plaintiffs appeared in those same articles, essentially bracketed by the facts which plaintiffs claim Apple wrongfully failed to disclose. The market could not have been made more aware of Lisa's risks.

[*In re Apple Computer Sec. Litig.*, 886 F.2d 1109, 1116 (9th Cir.1989).]

In almost the same breath that it recognized the truth-on-the-market defense, the *Apple* court stressed the limits of its holding:

> The investing public justifiably places heavy reliance on the statements and opinions of corporate insiders. In order to avoid Rule 10b-5 liability, any material information which insiders fail to disclose must be transmitted to the public with a degree of intensity and credibility sufficient to effectively counterbalance any misleading impression created by the insiders' one-sided representations.

[*Id.*]

Another product promotion case involving the truth-on-the-market defense is *Ballan v. Upjohn*, [814 F. Supp. 1375 (W.D. Mich. 1992),] in which plaintiffs claimed that in marketing and attempting to secure FDA approval for its drug Halcion, Upjohn hid data showing Halcion's negative side effects. Upjohn also omitted this data from its annual reports, quarterly reports, and other SEC filings. Upjohn argued that the market was well aware of the side-effects of Halcion, but the court denied Upjohn's motion to dismiss, quoting the Ninth Circuit's statement in *Apple* that unqualified exuberance from corporate insiders would typically be weighed heavily by the market and would not be overcome by "information [that] has received only brief mention in a few poorly-circulated or lightly-regarded publications." To prevail with the truth-on-the-market defense, defendant companies must prove that the corrective statements from other sources "credibly entered the market." The court also cited *In re Seagate Technology II Securities Litigation*, [802 F. Supp. 271 (N.D.Cal. 1992),] for the proposition that where the evidence of what the market knew consists of competing volumes of contradictory analysts' reports and contradictory articles published in the popular press, the truth-on-the-market defense is not established. Because the *Ballan* court could not "discern whether information concerning the side-effects of Halcion was credibly made available to the market by other sources," it could not summarily rule for defendants on the reliance issue.

E.   Causation

The causation element of a Section 10(b)/Rule 10b-5 claim is closely related to the reliance element. Indeed, for many years most courts were willing to assume that evidence of materiality plus reliance gave rise to a presumption of causation. After all, materiality is defined as the type of information which might well affect an investor's decision whether to invest. The Supreme Court itself, in *Affiliated Ute Citizens of Utah v. United States*, [406 U.S. 128 (1972),] pronounced that the "obligation to disclose and [the] withholding of a material fact established the requisite element of causation in fact." The ease of establishing reliance in both omission cases (through the *Ute* analysis) and in most misrepresentation cases (through the fraud-on-the-market theory) largely eliminated the causation requirement in securities fraud cases for a few years.

However, in a recent development of great benefit to defendants, many courts have split the causation requirement into two distinct elements, transaction causation and loss causation, and have required plaintiffs to establish both.

"Transaction causation" is a requirement of causation in fact which is largely a restatement of the reliance element, demanding that plaintiffs show that a securities violation directly caused them to enter into the challenged transaction. Plaintiffs must show that "but for" the fraud, they would not have entered into the transaction which ultimately resulted in a loss.

The more problematic causation aspect for plaintiffs is "loss causation," a concept that generally requires plaintiffs to show, additionally, that defendants' fraud proximately caused their economic loss. Loss causation acts to limit the damages stemming from a securities fraud and "in effect requires that the damage claimed be one of the foreseeable consequences of the misrepresentation." A strict application of this approach allows defendants to concede that they misrepresented but still escape liability if plaintiffs' economic losses were caused by other factors.

A leading case establishing the loss causation element is *Bastian v. Petren Resources Corp.*, [892 F.2d 680 (7th Cir.), *cert. denied*, 496 U.S. 906 (1990)]. Plaintiffs had the misfortune of investing in an oil and gas venture in 1981, the peak year for oil prices, before a steady decline caused virtually all of the oil and gas limited partnerships formed in that year to lose money. Plaintiffs claimed that they would not have invested in defendants' particular oil and gas limited partnership had they known certain facts about defendants' honesty or lack thereof. However, plaintiffs steadfastly refused to provide the court with evidence as to the cause of their loss. Because the court was convinced that plaintiffs, had they known the truth regarding defendants, would simply have invested in a different oil and gas limited partnership and lost their money anyway, it denied recovery on grounds that plaintiffs had failed to establish loss causation:

> If the alternative oil and gas limited partnerships to which these plaintiffs would have turned had the defendants leveled with them were also doomed, despite competent and honest management, to become worthless, the plaintiffs were not hurt by the fraud; it affected the place but not the time or amount of their loss.
>
> . . . .
>
> . . . No social purpose would be served by encouraging everyone who suffers an investment loss because of an unanticipated change in market conditions to pick through offering memoranda with a fine-tooth comb in the hope of uncovering a misrepresentation. Defrauders are a bad lot and should be punished, but Rule 10b-5 does not make them insurers against national economic calamities.

[*Id.* at 684-85.]

The promulgation of a high standard for establishing the separate element of loss causation has been strongly criticized as "an insuperable barrier to recovery." Fortunately for plaintiffs, some courts presume both transaction and loss causation if the plaintiff proves the elements of the fraud-on-the-market theory.

Causation has been an issue in several product promotion cases. Demonstrating transaction causation is not too onerous because of its coextensiveness with reliance. Loss causation is often more difficult to prove because of the many factors that might affect a stock's price. For example, on May 12, 1983, Fortune Systems announced that it was having problems with its new computer product which were causing it to lose orders and customers. Fortune's stock price dropped dramatically in wake of the announcement. Plaintiff shareholders attempted to recover for, inter alia, a stock price drop that had occurred in the two months preceding the announcement, claiming that the adverse product information had caused that loss. However, the court was convinced that defendant's evidence showed that other factors, including adverse stock market conditions, caused the pre-May 12 drop. [*See In re Fortune Sys. Sec. Litig.*, 680 F. Supp. 1360 (N.D.Cal. 1987).]

Plaintiffs fared better in *Ballan v. Upjohn Company*, [814 F. Supp. 1375 (W.D.Mich. 1992),] the case involving the drug Halcion discussed above. The following claims were deemed sufficient to allege loss causation:

> [Plaintiffs] have alleged that due to defendants' intentional and reckless concealment of true test results from regulatory agencies, Halcion, during the class period, became Upjohn's second biggest sales item. Plaintiffs have further alleged that Upjohn, in the face of charges regarding adverse reactions to Halcion, falsely denied those charges. Plaintiffs have alleged that Upjohn, when faced with the withdrawal of Halcion from the United Kingdom, falsely stated that there was no scientific or medical evidence that warranted such withdrawal. Plaintiffs claim to have purchased Upjohn securities at artificially inflated prices and were damaged when the market price of Upjohn stock fell at the end of the class period. . . . Plaintiffs have alleged that the drop in the value of Upjohn's stock was not due to the approaching patent expiration date of some sleeping drugs.

[*Id.* at 1384-85 (citations omitted).]

Similarly, in *Fujisawa Pharmaceutical Co. Ltd. V. Kapoor*, [814 F. Supp. 720 (N.D.Ill. 1993),] loss causation was adequately alleged when defendants sold all of the stock of Lyphomed Co. to plaintiff without disclosing that Lyphomed had filed false applications and information with the FDA in connection with Lyphomed's quest for FDA approval of new generic drugs. Defendants moved to dismiss for failure to allege loss causation, citing Bastian as precedent. The court denied the motion, responding:

> As [defendant] Kapoor's sole authority on loss causation, Bastian is a poor choice. The relationship between the plaintiffs' loss and the alleged fraud is much clearer in the present case. The Complaint alleged that Fujisawa would not have purchased Lyphomed had it known the truth about Lyphomed's shoddy testing and the ANDA

[Abbreviated New Drug Application] filings. It can also be inferred from the Complaint that Fujisawa's loss, in the form of the FDA restrictions and recalls, is a direct result of Kapoor's fraudulent statements and omissions which artificially inflated the price of Lyphomed stock and induced Fujisawa to purchase the company.

[*Id.* at 727 (citations omitted).]

F.   Purchase or Sale "In Connection with"

Because Section 10(b) prohibits fraud "in connection with a purchase or sale" of securities, plaintiffs must demonstrate (a) that a purchase or sale occurred, (b) that the alleged fraud occurred in connection with that purchase or sale, and (c) that the plaintiff was a purchaser or seller. The purchase or sale requirement derives from statutory language and is, generally speaking, broadly defined. The requirement that the plaintiff be a "purchaser or seller" is essentially a standing requirement. Unless a plaintiff bought or sold securities, he or she did not suffer the type of injury Section 10(b) and Rule 10b-5 are meant to remedy. For purposes of this article, these requirements simply mean that persons who bought, say, computers and software, because they were misled by statements regarding the characteristics of those products, can sue only on grounds of breach of warranty, common law fraud, consumer protection violations, and the like. Unless the persons were moved by the misrepresentations and omissions to buy the company's securities as well as its products, they would have no standing to bring a securities fraud suit under Section 10(b)/Rule 10b-5.

The most important aspect of this area of Section 10(b)/Rule 10b-5 doctrine, insofar as this article is concerned, is the "in connection with" requirement. Proper analysis of this element requires that the topic be divided into cases primarily involving relatively private representations made by defendants to individual plaintiffs, and cases primarily involving public representations made by defendants to the market generally. Vaporware preannouncements and other forms of product marketing often involve both types of representations.

1.   Private Representations

Courts traditionally construed the requirement that fraud be "in connection with" the purchase or sale of securities rather broadly in order to ease plaintiffs' pleading and proof burdens. The only Supreme Court case to address the matter, *Superintendent of Insurance of the State of New York v. Bankers Life and Casualty Co.*, [404 U.S. 6, 13 (1971),] announced that the requirement was satisfied by deceptive practices touching a purchase or sale of securities. A "touching" test ultimately proved too generous for the lower courts, which have searched for a more limiting principle.

Some courts have substantially equated the "in connection with" requirement to transaction causation. Other courts have examined the facts to determine whether a "nexus" existed between the defendant's fraud and plaintiff's investment decision, focusing on whether Section 10(b)'s purposes would be advanced by applying it to the particular transaction in question. The most restrictive view of the "in connection with" requirement demands that the fraudulent statement or omission complained of relate directly to the value of the security being sold or the consideration being offered therefor.

To illustrate the potential confusion caused by this array of approaches, consider the facts of *Brown v. Ivie.*, [661 F.2d 62 (5th Cir.), *cert. denied*, 455 U.S. 990 (1981)]. Plaintiff Brown and defendants Ivie and Lightsey were each officers, directors, and one-third shareholders of a small corporation. In 1979, defendants decided to oust plaintiff from the corporation and had a vehicle by which to do so — a 1976 shareholders' "buy-sell" agreement requiring any shareholder no longer employed by the corporation to sell his shares back to the corporation at book value. Unfortunately for defendants, the 1976 agreement was unenforceable because certain statutory formalities had not been observed in its drafting. Therefore, defendants used a pretense to induce plaintiff to sign a similar, enforceable agreement in 1979. As soon as plaintiff signed the agreement, defendants fired him from his position and invoked the buy-sell agreement to force plaintiff to sell his shares back to the corporation.

There is no doubt that defendants' fraud "touched" on the sale of plaintiffs' shares. Similarly, most courts would find transaction causation and a nexus between the defendants' fraud and plaintiff's sale. However, the defendants' lies (plaintiff was told that he had to sign the new agreement in order for the company to effectuate a change in insurance companies and to increase the amount of insurance held by the corporation on each shareholder) did not relate to either the value of the securities or the consideration given therefor. For that reason, courts taking the most limited view of the "in connection with" requirement would find that it was not met in this case, although the Fifth Circuit held that the "nexus" requirement applied and was met.

There will be some obvious cases where statements made to promote products will not under any approach be "in connection with" the purchase or sale of securities about which plaintiffs later complain. Consider *Jabend, Inc. v. Four-Phase Systems, Inc.*, [631 F. Supp. 1339 (W.D. Wash. 1986),] in which Grosenick had an idea to develop and market a computer hardware/software package for the insurance brokerage industry. Four-Phase assured Grosenick that its hardware was well-suited to Grosenick's purposes. Based on that assurance, Grosenick and Bender decided to pursue the venture. They chose the corporate form of business organization and formed Jabend, Inc. Naturally, they issued Jabend's stock to themselves in exchange for their capital investment. Four-Phase's product did not live up to representations, and Jabend ultimately went bankrupt. Grosenick sued Four-Phase under Section 10(b) and Rule 10b-5, claiming that he purchased Jabend stock in reliance on Four-Phase's representations about its computer hardware's abilities. The district court dismissed the suit for failing to meet the "in connection with" requirement because Four-Phase was trying to sell only computers and had nothing to gain by the sale of Jabend stock.

Under virtually all of the various approaches discussed above, the "in connection with" element would be missing in *Jabend*. The misrepresentations were not about the particular value of Jabend stock. Nor were the misrepresentations calculated to affect the price of Jabend stock, particularly since they were made before Jabend was ever formed. Because Four-Phase was seeking to sell computers rather than stock, there was no "nexus" between its representations and the subsequent sale of Jabend stock. Only an exceedingly liberal interpretation of the out-dated "touching" test could provide even the slightest grounds for an argument that the "in connection with" test was met in *Jabend*.

2.   Public Representations

The "in connection with" requirement is often at issue in class action securities fraud lawsuits under Section 10(b) and Rule 10b-5 that arise out of product representations, such as vaporware announcements, reaching the investing public in general. Fortunately for class action plaintiffs, in these situations courts generally find the "in connection with" requirement to be met where the misstatements or omissions are made in a setting reasonably calculated or reasonably expected to influence the investing public. If this is the test applied, most cases of misleading product marketing statements will satisfy the "in connection with" test.

For example, an optimistic vaporware announcement at a trade show or in the trade press will likely have a direct impact on the market price of the company's shares. As noted earlier in this article, such an announcement can be expected to, and is often calculated to, have a direct impact on the company's stock price. If the product representations made in the *Jabend* case, for example, had been communicated not to a single potential customer, but to the public at large, the "in connection with" requirement would no doubt have been met. The product press releases complained of in *Apple* clearly reached the investing public as could reasonably have been expected. Therefore, the "in connection with" requirement will not weed out too many plaintiffs' claims in the typical class action securities fraud suit.

G.   Damages

Lastly, plaintiffs in a Section 10(b)/Rule 10b-5 suit must demonstrate that they were damaged as a result of the fraud alleged. Because remediation is a primary goal of federal securities laws, compensatory damages provide the appropriate remedy in most 10b-5 securities fraud cases. Section 28(a) of the 1934 Act limits recoveries to "actual damages," but it is not always clear how those damages are to be computed.

The courts have developed several approaches to calculating damages, but in the vast majority of the suits brought under Section 10(b) and Rule 10b-5, courts borrow from the common law of torts, applying an "out of pocket" measure. In such cases, plaintiffs are entitled to recover the difference between the price paid and the actual value at the date of the transaction, plus interest. An important indicator of the "actual value" at the date of purchase (or sale) is the amount the market price drops (or rises) upon the public correction of a previous misleading statement or omission.

Before the *Apple* verdict was overturned by the trial judge, the jury had found that the individual defendants, Markkula and Vennard, were responsible for $2.90 of the $8.00 stock drop because of the Twiggy vaporware announcement. Lawyers estimated that 33 million shares were traded during the class period, implying damages of at least $96 million, plus interest.

Occasionally courts have found that the investors sustained damage when the defendant withheld "good news," resulting in the plaintiffs selling shares at a lower price than they would have had the truth been disclosed. However, when it comes to the product marketing statements that are the focus of this article, understatement seldom occurs. Overstatement is typically the order of the day.

Courts do consider other causes that might affect a stock's price drop. For example, in the *Apple* case, disappointing quarterly earnings were announced at the same time as the decision to discontinue Twiggy and were apparently the cause of $5.10 of the $8.00 stock drop, at least in the jury's eyes. Such issues were discussed in the loss causation section above.

B. EXAMPLES OF FRAUDULENT REPRESENTATIONS REGARDING INTELLECTUAL PROPERTY

POMMER v. MEDTEST CORPORATION
United States Court of Appeals for the Seventh Circuit
961 F.2d 620 (1992)

EASTERBROOK, Circuit Judge.

Medtest Corporation has a single asset: the intellectual property in a self-administered cervico-vaginal cytology testing process. Patrick Manning devised the process and together with Donald West, a lawyer, formed Medtest in December 1981 to obtain a patent and undertake development to make the process commercially attractive. Manning held 31% of the stock, West 26%, and the remainder was scattered among friends and relatives. In 1982 Manning sold some of his stock in Medtest to Robert and Anna Lisa Pommer: 250 shares in September for $25,000, and later another 2,750 shares for $175,000. The Pommers thus acquired 3% of Medtest's outstanding stock, which is valuable only to the extent the firm pays dividends, goes public, or is acquired by a third party.

None of these things has happened, and the Pommers believe that they are the victims of fraud. A jury agreed in this action under § 10(b) of the Securities Exchange Act of 1934, 15 U.S.C.§ 78j(b), and the SEC's Rule 10b-5, 17 C.F.R. § 240.10b-5. It awarded the Pommers more than $300,000 in damages, representing the purchase price of the stock plus interest. A magistrate judge, presiding by consent under 28 U.S.C. § 636(c), set aside the verdict and entered judgment for the defendants. She concluded that none of the representations made to the Pommers was materially false.

I

Given the verdict, we must take all of the evidence in the light most favorable to the Pommers. A jury could have concluded that West told the Pommers, while they were negotiating to buy the stock, that Medtest had a U.S. patent on the process and that a sale of Medtest to Abbott Laboratories, at a price between $50 million and $100 million, was imminent ("almost a finished deal"). A 3% interest in Medtest would have been worth between $1.5 million and $3 million had such a sale been consummated. In fact Medtest did not have a patent at the time. Counsel informed West in December 1981 that the process was patentable; the firm filed an application on September 30, 1982, and the patent issued on August 14, 1984. Medtest was not in the last stage of negotiation with Abbott Laboratories; it raised the subject with Abbott, and Abbott's employees mentioned a price in the $50 to $100 million range, but no details had been discussed, no hands had been shaken — and on October 28, 1982, Abbott sent Medtest a letter stating that it was not interested in acquiring Medtest. Since then Medtest has been developing the process on i`tions to sell Medtest to Abbott Laboratories. Until the last minute a deal may collapse, but some deals are more likely to close than others. Probabilities determine the value of stock. At a 90% chance of a buyout for $50 million, the Pommers' stock was worth $1.35 million; at a 10% chance it was worth $150,000. A jury could determine that West conveyed to the Pommers a substantially higher probability than the facts supported — that although West represented that the parties were just about to sign on the dotted line, actually there had been no more than superficial discussions, and Abbott had no serious interest in acquiring Medtest. There is "a substantial likelihood" that the Pommers (and any other "reasonable investor") would have viewed the truth about the negotiations with Abbott as "significantly alter [ing] the 'total mix' of information made available."

Defendants insist that until the parties agree on the price and structure of a transaction, the issuer may say what it pleases. For this proposition they cite *Flamm v. Eberstadt,* 814 F.2d 1169 (7th Cir. 1987), overlooking three important ("material") facts about *Flamm*. First, we discussed whether an issuer has a duty to speak even though it would prefer silence; Medtest was not silent. Second, the Supreme Court disapproved the price-and-structure approach when issuers make false statements about ongoing negotiations. Third, contemporaneously with *Flamm* we decided [*Jordan v. Duff and Phelps, Inc.*, 815 F.2d 429 (7th Cir. 1987)], which holds that the price-and-structure rule does not apply to closely held corporations such as Medtest. *Jordan* observed that in aftermarket transactions duties to disclose come from state law, and states regularly apply a special rule requiring disclosure when a manager of a closely held firm sells stock to (or buys it from) an outsider in a face-to-face transaction. Defendants do not address the effect of *Jordan,* or for that matter *Basic;* they cite neither case.

One could recast the magistrate judge's conclusion about the sale to Abbott as a finding that the Pommers knew enough of the truth that West's lies did not significantly affect their appreciation of the situation. An issuer that utters a mixture of truth and falsehood may have furnished the information necessary for an accurate appreciation of the securities' value — especially when the truth is written and the lie is oral. "While a misleading statement will not always lose its deceptive edge simply by joinder with others that are true, the true statements may discredit the other one so obviously that the risk of real deception drops to nil." *Virginia Bankshares, Inc. v. Sandberg,* 501 U.S. 1083, 111 S.Ct. 2749, 2760, 115 L.Ed.2d 929 (1991). Written disclosures of the truth are not only more compelling but also more verifiable. Memories may play tricks (or the parties may be less than candid about what they heard or said); writings are available for inspection. In shaping implied private rights of action, courts properly favor rules that simplify litigation, discourage unverifiable (and therefore irrefutable) claims, and reward issuers that commit their representations to writing.

The Pommers must have been aware that a deal with Abbott was not just around the corner. A substantial range of price implied that hard negotiations lay ahead. West told them that Medtest needed to secure foreign patents, and that with these in hand it would be an attractive acquisition candidate. As the magistrate judge remarked, foreign patents cannot be obtained in a flash. The Pommers waited more than a year before beefing; would they have sat quietly so long if they really thought they had been promised a bonanza in a few weeks? The price of the securities also implies that a sale was a long shot: Why would Manning sell 3% of Medtest to the Pommers for $200,000 if the stock soon would be worth $1.5 million and up? Even if Manning desperately needed to raise capital, better terms must have been available. Robert Pommer said at one point that he viewed the investment in Medtest as his chance to hit the Lotto — yet he persuaded the jury that the defendants sold him a sure thing.

Whether these things would be enough to neutralize the representations about Abbott we need not say. The falsehood about the patent remains. More, we have emphasized that an issuer needs to disclose the truth clearly before a lie becomes immaterial. It is not enough that the other party must have recognized a risk. Risks are ubiquitous. Disclosures assist investors in determining the magnitude of risks. Even savvy investors may recover when a bald lie understates the gravity of a known risk. A jury could find that defendants never told the truth. Although they direct us to an agreement between Manning and the Pommers, that two-page document contains no information beyond a boilerplate warning that Medtest's process "has only speculative value at the present time and may prove to be totally worthless, in which event the Shares purchased by Buyer pursuant hereto may also become worthless." Such generic warnings do not enlighten investors about the status of patent applications, negotiations to sell the business, and the like; they do nothing to disabuse an investor influenced by false oral statements purporting to describe the status of the firm's affairs. The truth, or an express disclaimer of reliance on oral representations protects a seller, but this record discloses neither.

II

Although defendants are not entitled to judgment notwithstanding the verdict, they sought a new trial in the alternative. The magistrate judge accepted their principal argument but did not formally grant the motion, deeming the subject moot. The Pommers ask us to disapprove the judge's conclusion, and thus avert any possibility of a new trial. Whether to grant a new trial is a question for the trial judge in the first instance, with deferential appellate review. The Pommers therefore must offer a compelling reason before we would forbid the magistrate judge from deciding on remand that a new trial would best serve the interests of justice.

The Pommers put before the jury Abbott's letter of October 28, 1982, disclaiming interest in Medtest. They contended that defendants' failure to show them this letter, while they were still paying for the stock, is an independent securities fraud. Defendants contended that the use of the letter should be restricted. The magistrate judge told the lawyers to argue their versions to the jury but after trial wrote that she should have kept the letter out of evidence, because the Pommers agreed to buy the stock before Abbott sent the letter. In contending that the judge's second thoughts are wrong, the Pommers again have an uphill contest, for our review of evidentiary matters is deferential.

The truth (or falsity) of defendants' statements, and their materiality, must be assessed at the time the statements are made, and not in the light of hindsight. We made exactly this point about the patent issued in 1984. The letter arrived after the Pommers agreed to purchase the stock. It was on this ground that the magistrate judge concluded that she should have restrained the Pommers' use of the document. Nonetheless, the Pommers contend, the judge was right the first time, because, if they had known that Abbott had broken off negotiations, they would have stopped paying.

If the Pommers were saying that they did not sign a contract to purchase the stock until after October 28, 1982, they would have a point. The statute of frauds is enforced rigorously in securities cases. If not bound by contract to pay for all 3,000 shares, the Pommers were making a fresh investment decision every time they sent a check. But the magistrate judge found that on October 19, 1982, they signed a note promising to pay $200,000 for the stock, and the Pommers do not rely on the statute of frauds.

Once they signed that note, the Pommers were committed under the law of contracts. There was no remaining investment decision. They might choose to balk and litigate, of course, but "[w]e have held repeatedly in recent years that the securities laws do not ensure that people will receive information sufficient to make correct decisions about filing or pursuing lawsuits."

According to the Pommers, *Goodman v. Epstein,* 582 F.2d 388, 409-14 (7th Cir.1978), required defendants to show them the letter of October 28. *Goodman* held that a partnership making a call for further capital must reveal current, material information because each new contribution is a fresh investment decision. As the ninth circuit properly observed in *Roberts,* however, *Goodman* depends on the fact that the partnership agreement did not compel the investors to comply with each request for funds. They had to decide, and to decide needed accurate information. The Pommers were not deciding anew to buy Medtest stock every time they wrote a check. They were deciding, instead, whether to keep or break their promise. They may have reasons to do either, but the nature of the asset covered by the contract — 3,000 shares of stock rather than, say, 3,000 crates of rutabagas — no longer matters. Once the written commitment is firm, we held in *LHLC,* the subject passes into the domain of contract law. The magistrate judge therefore acted within her discretion in concluding (on second thought) that the letter of October 28, reflecting an adverse turn of events after the sale of stock, should not have been used as substantive evidence. The judge may elect in her discretion to award the defendants a new trial on remand.

To say that withholding the letter from the Pommers is not an independent fraud is not (necessarily) to say that the letter is inadmissible. Although the parties stipulated that Medtest and Abbott conducted some negotiations, the letter may support an inference that these never became serious. Such an inference would assist the Pommers in demonstrating that the defendants acted with intent to defraud. Whether the letter may be used with appropriate cautions to the jury is a subject for the trial judge in the first instance.

. . .

REVERSED AND REMANDED

NOTES & QUESTIONS

To what extent does the materiality of a misstatement in conjunction with a stock sale turn on the particularity of the information that is misstated? Is a broadly stated misrepresentation — *e.g.,* a baseless assertion without having consulted counsel that "our company will gain patent protection for our new technology" — more likely to be seen as immaterial "puffing" than a more focused and precise misstatement of more particular information — *e.g.,* where no patent was obtained, a statement like that in *Pommer* that "our company presently possesses patent protection for our key technology"? Is the impact on potential investors of these two types of statements meaningfully different? Should the liability of corporate insiders or their companies for these two types of misstatements vary?

ALNA CAPITAL ASSOCIATES v. WAGNER
United States District Court for the Southern District of Florida
532 F. Supp. 591 (S.D. Fla. 1982), *aff'd in relevant part,*
758 F.2d 562 (11th Cir. 1985)

SPELLMAN, District Judge.

This securities fraud action is brought under § 10(b) of the Exchange Act of 1934, § 517.301 of the Florida Statutes, and Florida common law. Jurisdiction over the Rule 10b5 claim is based on Title 28 U.S.C. § 1331. The Court has heard the state claims on the basis of pendent jurisdiction. *United Mine Workers v. Gibbs*, 383 U.S. 715, 86 S.Ct. 1130, 16 L.Ed.2d 218 (1966).

The Plaintiff, Alna Capital Associates, is a limited partnership of which Albert Nahmad is the general partner. The only asset of the partnership is its stock in Watsco, Inc. Alna Capital Associates succeeded Alna Capital, Inc., a closely held corporation composed of the same investors as in Alna Capital Associates. Albert Nahmad was the president of the corporation and its only asset was the stock owned later by Alna Capital Associates. Albert Nahmad spearheaded the organization of both Alna Capital Associates and Alna Capital, Inc. for the purpose of buying a 38% block of the outstanding shares of Watsco, Inc. on December 29, 1972 from the defendant, William Wagner. William Wagner was president and chairman of the board of directors of Watsco, Inc. at the time of the stock sale.

The Plaintiff alleges that the Defendant Wagner fraudulently misrepresented material information and withheld material information which he had an obligation to disclose in connection with the sale to Nahmad and his associates of 300,000 shares of Wagner's personally-held stock in Watsco.

The alleged misrepresentations and omissions can be grouped into three categories: (1) Financial reports — misstatements in the public financial reports of Watsco; (2) Winslow — misstatements and omissions with regard to contracts entered into by the Winslow division of Watsco; and (3) Chargefaster — misstatements and omissions concerning the operation and patent status of "Chargefaster", a refrigeration product manufactured by Watsco.

. . .

Although the testimony was conflicting on many of the issues in this case, hereinafter set forth are the facts as the Court finds them in light of all the evidence submitted and considering the credibility of the witnesses.

The time frame of the allegedly actionable conduct was from August of 1972 until December 29, 1972. The events unfolded as follows. Albert Nahmad, a mechanical engineer with a Bachelor of Science degree from the University of New Mexico and a Master of Science degree in Industrial Administration from Purdue University, had been employed for several years by the accounting firm of Arthur Young and Company (hereafter "Arthur Young") in Indianapolis, Indiana. Subsequent to leaving Arthur Young, Nahmad went to New York City where he worked in the corporate acquisition department of W. R. Grace and Co. Nahmad left his job with W. R. Grace in 1971 and set about the task of finding a small manufacturing company to invest in and possibly manage. At the same time, William Wagner, the president of Watsco, was interested in selling his shares in the company and he hired brokers to effect a sale. One broker, Ted Murnick, contacted a Mr. Weiner, who in turn contacted his friend Albert Nahmad. Nahmad looked at Watsco financial reports and then decided to come to Hialeah, Florida to examine the Watsco business and speak to Wagner.

Nahmad spent three days with Wagner at the Watsco plant in August, 1972. Wagner asked $10.00 per share and Nahmad made a counteroffer of $8.50 per share. Wagner stated that he wanted a price of 15 times earnings while Nahmad suggested 12 times earnings. During the course of the meetings, Wagner had stated that Watsco's earnings for the year would be 70 cents per share.

Wagner also gave Nahmad a detailed description of Chargefaster, including the claim that the product transformed liquid refrigerant into saturated vapor, making it almost impossible for liquid to reach and damage the compressor of a cooling unit. Wagner explained that the marketing of Chargefaster had just begun and that a high profit margin would continue on the product because a patent would be obtained for Chargefaster.

Wagner described to Nahmad the marketing of the products manufactured by the Winslow division of Watsco, indicating that Winslow had oral wholesaling agreements.

After the meetings, Nahmad returned to New York. A few days later, a deal was agreed to by Nahmad and Wagner over the telephone whereby Nahmad and his associates would buy 300,000 shares from Wagner at $8.50 per share. Wagner's attorney, Carmen Accordino, prepared a draft agreement and sent it to Nahmad's attorney Michael Zuckerman in New York.

On September 26, 1972, an option agreement was signed by Nahmad and Wagner. Nahmad then hired Arthur Young & Co. in Miami, Florida to investigate and analyze the Watsco business as part of a pre-acquisition review, which that company undertook. Although the option agreement provided that Nahmad could request a physical inventory at his own expense, no such inventory was taken.

In October, Wagner and Nahmad discussed past litigation over Winslow distributorship agreements. Wagner did not mention the antitrust lawsuit filed by Clarence Firstenberg in Los Angeles or any other potential antitrust problems with Winslow's contracts.

Also in October, Wagner received a rejection from the United States Patent Office on his patent application for Chargefaster which was not communicated to Nahmad until long after the final closing.

As a result of the Arthur Young pre-acquisition review, Nahmad developed serious concerns about several matters, one of which was the inventory of Watsco, leading him to believe that the yearly profits of Watsco would be 64 cents instead of the projected 70 cents. Nahmad met with Wagner and informed him of his concerns about the inventory. Wagner reassured Nahmad that the inventory was fine, but Wagner did agree to lower the price per share to $8.00. As part of the renegotiation, Wagner's liability for a drop in shareholders' equity was reduced. Wagner also insisted that it was absolutely essential that the sale close by the end of the calendar year 1972.

Just prior to the signing of the November 27th agreement of sale, Watsco announced profits of 59 cents per share for the first three quarters of the fiscal year ending January 31, 1973. The November 27th agreement provided for Wagner to sell to Nahmad 300,000 shares of Watsco stock, which stock was registered and traded on the American Stock Exchange, for $8.00 per share. The contract provided for an initial cash payment of $700,000.00 plus 12 quarterly payments of approximately $141,666.00 plus 6% interest.

Section 3.16 of the contract provides that copies of all agreements to which Watsco was a party were attached to the contract of sale. Section 3.23 states that no amendments or terminations of agreements entered into by the company had occurred save those enumerated in Schedule E of the contract.

The sale closed on December 29, 1972. At the time of closing, Wagner was aware of Alna Capital, Inc., which was composed of Nahmad's associates.

Subsequent to closing, in early 1973, Arthur Young prepared the annual financial statement of Watsco. Arthur Young's initial version of the statement showed a 4th quarter loss of 9 cents per share, from 59 cents to 50 cents. The loss was occasioned by a combination of factors: a drop in the value of inventory due to obsolescence and shortages; a drop in the value of accounts receivable; and a recognition of a loss to Watsco in a "lease" transaction with Advanced Plastics Corporation. Arthur Young evaluated the striking change in the financial status of Watsco and determined that a restatement of the prior three quarterly reports was necessary to accurately reflect the financial condition of Watsco. Under the restatement, the quarterly earnings per share figures changed from

    1st Q - 17 cents to   1st Q - 13 cents
    2nd Q - 48 cents to   2nd Q - 37 cents
    3rd Q - 59 cents to   3rd Q - 45 cents

leaving the fourth quarter with 5 cents earnings per share.

Paul Manley of Arthur Young explained the restatement and its basis to the Defendant William Wagner at a meeting between the two. Wagner listened to the explanation by Manley and made no comment as to the significance or accuracy of the restatement.

The restatement was approved by the Watsco board of directors and was filed with the Securities Exchange Commission. With the public announcement of the restatement, the value of the market shares dropped from approximately $8.00 to approximately $4.00.

In the spring or summer of 1973, Nahmad became aware of written exclusive distributorship agreements between Watsco and the distributors of the Winslow hair spray products. Previously, Nahmad had been informed that Watsco merely had oral agreements with Winslow wholesalers. The undisclosed Winslow agreements had the effect of tying up the major national markets for distribution of Winslow products. In the summer of 1974, legal counsel to Watsco informed Nahmad that the Winslow distributorship agreements entailed serious antitrust problems.

Later in 1974, Nahmad became aware of certain problems relating to Chargefaster. Watsco had obtained a patent on Chargefaster in 1973 based on Wagner's renewed patent application, in which he claimed that the product converted all (100%) of liquid refrigerant into saturated vapor before it entered a cooling unit. Wagner had not yet informed Nahmad of the October, 1972 patent rejection or of its contents which stated that at least four other persons had previously produced devices capable of doing that which Chargefaster does.

When Wagner informed Nahmad that another manufacturer was infringing the Watsco Chargefaster patent, the company filed suit. The suit was subsequently dropped, partially on the basis of Wagner's advice. Subsequently, on advice of counsel and after the 1972 patent rejection became known to Nahmad, the Chargefaster patent was withdrawn by Watsco. Profits from Chargefaster had declined substantially since its first full year of sales.

In December of 1974, the present lawsuit was filed.

The complaint herein is founded on § 10(b) of the Exchange Act of 1934, 15 U.S.C. § 78j, on the Florida statutory version of Rule 10b5, F.S. § 517.301, and on Florida common law of fraud. 15 U.S.C. § 78j(b) reads as follows:

It shall be unlawful for any person, directly or indirectly, by the use of any means or instrumentality of interstate commerce or of the mails, or of any facility of any national securities exchange-

. . .

(b) To use or employ, in connection with the purchase or sale of any security registered on a national securities exchange or any security not so registered, any manipulative or deceptive device or contrivance in contravention of such rules and regulations as the Commission may prescribe as necessary or appropriate in the public interest or for the protection of investors.

Rule 10b5 reads as follows:

EMPLOYMENT OF MANIPULATIVE AND DECEPTIVE DEVICES

It shall be unlawful for any person, directly or indirectly, by the use of any means or instrumentality of interstate commerce, or of the mails, or of any facility of any national securities exchange,

(1) to employ any device, scheme, or artifice to defraud,

(2) to make any untrue statement of a material fact or to omit to state a material fact necessary in order to make the statements made, in the light of the circumstances under which they were made, not misleading, or

(3) to engage in any act, practice or course of business which operates or would operate as a fraud or deceit upon any person, in connection with the purchase or sale of any security.

Florida Statute § 517.301, practically identical to the substantive prohibitions of Rule 10b5, differs only in reaching securities transactions which have no interstate connection.

Although the Florida Statute is basically identical to Rule 10b5, the courts have interpreted the two provisions differently in two important regards. Both Statutes require proof of (1) a misrepresentation or omission, (2) of information that is material to the sale transaction, and (3) where the purchaser relied on such misrepresentation or omission. However, Rule 10b5 requires proof of fraudulent intent, knowledge, or reckless disregard of the falsity of the misrepresentation. In addition, a 10b5 case must be proven by clear and convincing evidence. F.S. § 517.301 has a less stringent scienter requirement, making negligent misrepresentations actionable. Also, there is no burden under Florida law to prove the claim by clear and convincing evidence. Punitive damages, which are unavailable under 10b5, may be obtained under Florida law.

Under Florida common law fraud, mere negligence satisfies the scienter requirement and the requirements are otherwise identical to those for F.S. § 517.301.

. . .

The third and final set of alleged misrepresentations concerns Chargefaster. Nahmad testified that Wagner never mentioned that Wagner's patent application for Chargefaster was initially rejected on the grounds that the product was not novel and that at least four different inventors had previously produced equivalent products. The Plaintiff also offered substantial evidence that Wagner falsely represented that Chargefaster converts into saturated vapor all of liquid refrigerant used to recharge cooling units. The evidence demonstrated that not all liquid refrigerant was converted by Chargefaster and that the product did not perform as advertised by Watsco under Wagner.

The Court finds that Wagner misrepresented the operation of Chargefaster to Nahmad. The sales history of Chargefaster subsequent to its first full year of sales confirms that it was not the revolutionary product Wagner claimed it to be. The tests conducted in the courtroom showed that the product did not convert all liquid refrigerant to saturated vapor but merely converted some of the liquid refrigerant into partially saturated vapor. Thus, Wagner misrepresented the performance of Chargefaster not only to the U.S. Patent Office, but also to Nahmad. Also, the evidence clearly shows that Wagner failed to state to Nahmad that the U.S. Patent Office had initially rejected his application for a Chargefaster patent in October, 1972.

MATERIALITY

The next pertinent inquiry with regard to the misrepresentations and omissions found by the Court is the question of materiality. The test of whether an omitted or misrepresented fact is material is whether a reasonable investor would have considered the fact important in deciding whether to invest. *S.E.C. v. Texas Gulf Sulphur Co.*, 401 F.2d 833 (2d Cir.1968); *T.S.C. Industries, Inc. v. Northway, Inc.*, 426 U.S. 438, 96 S.Ct. 2126, 48 L.Ed.2d 757 (1976); *Mills v. The Electric Auto-Lite Co.*, 396 U.S. 375, 90 S.Ct. 616, 24 L.Ed.2d 593 (1969).

. . .

The Chargefaster misrepresentations and omission were material. Chargefaster had become, almost overnight, a major contributor to the earnings of Watsco. It promised to continue to be profitable to the corporation if it could do what its inventor promised and could be patented. The non-disclosure of the patent rejection was thus highly material. Further, the misrepresentations as to the performance of the product were also material.

RELIANCE

After materiality, the next essential element of the Plaintiff's causes of action is reliance. With regard to omissions, the Supreme Court has stated that in a Rule 10b5 case, where there is an obligation to disclose and the Defendant fails to make disclosure, "positive proof of reliance is not a prerequisite to recovery. All that is necessary is that the facts withheld be material in the sense that a reasonable investor might have considered them important in the making of this decision." *Affiliated Ute Citizens v. United States*, 406 U.S. 128, 153-54, 92 S.Ct. 1456, 31 L.Ed.2d 741 (1972). Under *T.S.C.*

Industries, Inc. v. Northway, Inc., *supra*, the last part of that test would likely be altered to " . . . in the sense that a reasonable investor would have considered them important. . . ."

Simon v. Merrill, Lynch, Pierce, Fenner and Smith, Inc., 482 F.2d 880 (1973), gives weight to the proposition that the Plaintiff's "general reliance" on the non-disclosure by the Defendant must be shown in a 10b5 case. However, unlike the facts in *Affiliated Ute*, the claim in *Simon* did not arise out of a face to face transaction.

If general reliance is required for omissions in this face to face transaction, under the common law fraud, the Florida Blue Sky Law, or the 10b5 standards, it has been clearly demonstrated in the present case. Wagner was the ultimate source of information about Watsco. Nahmad evaluated and hired others to evaluate the business condition of Watsco, but he relied on Wagner's representations and omissions concerning Watsco.

With regard to misrepresentations, the reliance issue is whether or not the purchaser actually relied on the misrepresentations in deciding to purchase. Basically, the test is one of subjective materiality. Did the misrepresentations play a significant part in the decision to purchase? The test can also be viewed as one of causation in fact. Did the Defendant's misrepresentations induce or cause the Plaintiff to make his investment decision?

In this part of the case, a critical question to be asked in relation to each misrepresentation is: What did Nahmad know of the true facts and when did he know it?

. . .

Nahmad was aware prior to the November 27th agreement that there were serious problems with the quarterly financial statements of Watsco. The pre-acquisition review by Arthur Young alerted Nahmad to the faulty inventory control system of Watsco and the softness in accounts receivable, and gave him reason to question the validity of reported earnings and earnings projections. In fact, Nahmad renegotiated the contract of sale with Wagner due to his concern over the accuracy of the quarterly earnings statements. The pre-acquisition review led Nahmad to believe Watsco earnings for the year would be 6 cents less than projected by Wagner. Nahmad discussed with Wagner his concerns about inventory, but Wagner insisted that the earnings figures were correct and that Watsco would not have filed false public earnings statements since that would open them to a wide range of liability.

Nahmad was less than completely convinced by Wagner's protestations, and a renegotiation of the contract was worked out providing for a reduction in the purchase price of 50 cents per share and a substantial reduction in Wagner's potential liability for a drop in shareholders' equity.

The only fair conclusion to draw from the facts is that Nahmad relied substantially on the quarterly financial statements, even though he had real doubts that the company would live up to its earnings projection. The facts also indicate that Nahmad relied on the claims Wagner made regarding the performance of Chargefaster, which was, at that time, a major profits producer for Watsco.

SCIENTER

On the issue of scienter, the factual and legal questions become complex. Under the Florida common law claim, scienter may be satisfied by showing merely that the Defendant should have known that his misrepresentations were false. Otherwise stated, it is a mere negligence standard. That standard appears to be identical to the scienter requirement for violation of Florida Statute § 517.301.

The scienter requirement for a violation of Rule 10b5 is much more stringent. In *Ernst & Ernst v. Hochfelder*, 425 U.S. 185, 214, 96 S.Ct. 1375, 47 L.Ed.2d 668 (1976), the Supreme Court stated:

> When a statute speaks so specifically in terms of manipulation and deception, and of implementing devices and contrivances — the commonly understood terminology of intentional wrongdoing — and when its history reflects no more expansive intent, we are quite unwilling to extend the scope of the statute to negligent conduct.

In *G. A. Thompson and Co., Inc. v. Partridge*, 636 F.2d 945, 961 (5th Cir.1981), the Court held that proof of severe recklessness is sufficient to prove scienter in a 10b5 action.

The facts showed that Wagner had controlled Watsco (the Wagner Tool and Supply Company) since its origin in 1945. He operated the business in New York until 1956 when he moved the company to Hialeah. At all times through December 29, 1972, Wagner was the president and chairman of the board of directors of Watsco. In 1972, Wagner was making an active effort to sell Watsco. He had hired a broker to accomplish the sale.

Wagner's complete control of Watsco was emphasized by the fact that his son and his son-in-law occupied important, executive positions in the company. Wagner handled the daily business of the company. He examined all mail coming to or leaving Watsco. He used an intercom monitoring system at the plant to keep track of operations.

Wagner was actively involved in the many corporate acquisitions by Watsco over the eleven years preceding the sale to Nahmad. He reviewed all the raw financial figures and processed that information before sending it to his accountants, Bromberg & Aronow. In terms of financial decision-making, he had rejected a cost system for evaluating inventory and there was evidence that he was personally involved in the decision to treat the Advanced Plastics transaction as a lease. He was aware of major problems in the system of inventory control. He had a clear understanding of the positive effect overstating inventory value has on reported earnings. He also understood that the sale price of a corporation's stock by reference to a multiple of repeated earnings was a common practice.

When Paul Manley of Arthur Young & Co. confronted Wagner with the financial restatement and the reasons behind it, Wagner offered no explanation or contradiction. He merely acquiesced in the new figures.

Wagner admitted that he had direct knowledge of the Winslow contracts and the October, 1972 Chargefaster patent rejection. He knew of the

Firstenberg antitrust litigation and of the Winslow contract cancellations. It must also be inferred from the facts that he understood that Chargefaster did not perform as promised.

Wagner was shown to have made several misstatements as a witness at the trial of this case. These include his denying recognition of his own handwriting on a memo concerning the deterioration of Winslow and on a paper where he had indicated the sale price of Watsco stock by reference to a multiple of earnings.

Under the standards enunciated in *G. A. Thompson and Co., Inc. v. Partridge*, *supra*, and *Huddleston v. Herman and MacLean*, 640 F.2d 534 (5th Cir.1981), the Court finds that the scienter or fraud requirement has been satisfied by clear and convincing evidence. Conscious intent to defraud is obvious in the Winslow and Chargefaster misrepresentations. The accounting misrepresentations indicate that the Defendant must have known the true financial condition of the company. At a minimum, the monthly and quarterly financial statements were published with severe recklessness as to whether or not they were true.

The stringent 10b5 standard having been satisfied by the evidence in this case, the Court necessarily finds that the scienter requirements under the Florida Blue Sky Law and under common law fraud have been fully satisfied by the evidence.

. . .

NOTES & QUESTIONS

1. In order to form the basis for a securities fraud action under § 10(b) of the Exchange Act of 1934 and Rule 10b-5, a misrepresentation of material information must be made in connection with a purchase or sale of stock. However, federal courts have differed as to whether a purchase or sale of stock that is for a purpose other than making a traditional stock investment constitutes a purchase or sale of stock that is subject to federal anti-fraud provisions. For example, in *Alna Capital Associates v. Wagner*, 532 F.Supp. 591 (S.D.Fla. 1982), *aff'd in part*, 758 F.2d 562 (11th Cir. 1985), the purchase of stock was a means for acquiring ownership and control of the company involved rather than a means to gain a partial ownership interest and ongoing investment on the part of the stock purchaser. In these circumstances, some courts have held a stock transaction aimed at carrying out a corporate acquisition not be a purchase or sale of stock covered by 10b-5. If a court reaches this conclusion, even a material misstatement of information in connection with an acquisition of a company through a stock sale will not trigger liability under federal securities fraud standards.

Does this distinction make sense? Is there any reason why federal securities laws should protect the interest of a small scale investor acquiring a fractional stock interest in a company but not protect a party that buys a larger interest through a sufficient stock purchase to acquire complete ownership or practical control of the same company? How do the interests of a small scale investor in an intellectual property based business differ from a party acquiring future control over the business and do those differences justify greater securities law protections for the small scale investor?

2. Should the nature of a company's business activities affect whether federal securities laws are deemed to apply to particular misstatements? Should federal securities laws be interpreted to be especially protective against misstatements about intellectual property considerations where a company's business operations rely heavily on the protections of intellectual property interests like patents that may be hard to assess from outside the corporation by a present or potential shareholder? Should federal securities laws provide more or less protection to a stock buyer where the object of a stock purchase transaction is not a traditional investment goal but rather to take control over corporate assets like patents or other intellectual property interests held by the targeted company?

Even if federal securities laws do not apply because a stock sales transaction is not deemed to involve the type of investment-oriented transaction covered by federal anti-fraud standards, state securities laws or common law fraud standards may still provide relief. Thus, for example, in *Alna Capital* the Court of Appeals for the Eleventh Circuit noted that, while it doubted that the contested stock transaction in that case was subject to 10b-5 due to the fact that the transaction was aimed at acquiring the company involved, the purchaser of stock had been given materially misleading information and this was sufficient to establish a claim for recovery under the state common law fraud theory raised by the purchaser. *See* 758 F.2d at 563 & n. 3.

GOMPPER v. VISX, INC.
United States Court of Appeals for the Ninth Circuit
298 F.3d 893 (2002)

BRUNETTI, Circuit Judge.

The issue before us is whether the complaint in this securities fraud class action states a claim under the heightened pleading requirements of the Private Securities Litigation Reform Act of 1995 ("PSLRA"), 15 U.S.C. § 78u-4(b)(1), (2). The district court held that it did not, and dismissed the complaint without leave to amend. The plaintiffs appeal, and we affirm.

I. BACKGROUND

This action is brought under §§ 10(b), 20(a) and 20A of the Securities Exchange Act of 1934, 15 U.S.C. §§ 78j(b), 78t(a), 78t-1. Plaintiffs are individuals who purchased VISX, Inc. ("VISX") stock during the class period. The defendants are VISX, and various individuals who are either officers, directors, or both. We summarize the facts from the complaint, and assume these facts to be true for the purpose of our decision.

VISX develops and sells laser vision-correction devices. Prior to February 22, 2000, VISX charged a $250 fee for each use of its patented excimer laser system (the "per procedure fee"). In early 1999, Nidek, a Japanese competitor, obtained FDA approval to sell its products in the United States. Nidek did not charge a per procedure fee and therefore presented a tremendous competitive threat to VISX. In response, VISX immediately filed a patent infringement suit in the U.S. District Court for the Northern District of California.

Within days of filing that suit, VISX brought a similar action against Nidek before the International Trade Commission ("ITC"). After a two-week trial in August 1999, an ITC administrative law judge ruled in Nidek's favor. In an order entered in December 1999, the administrative law judge determined that Nidek's products did not infringe on VISX's patents, and further concluded that one of VISX's core patents was invalid because the patent applicant, Dr. Trokel, had failed to name a co-inventor, Dr. Srinivasan.

A little over two months later, on February 22, 2000, VISX publicly announced, that as part of a new business strategy, it was reducing its per procedure fee to $100. VISX's stock plummeted, and plaintiffs brought this action. Plaintiffs allege each defendant is liable for making false statements or for failing to disclose adverse facts while selling VISX stock and participating in a fraudulent scheme.

The class period begins on March 1, 1999, the date VISX announced anticipated First Quarter Fiscal Year 1999 results, and ends February 22, 2000, the date VISX announced it was reducing its per procedure fee. Plaintiffs argue that during this period defendants made positive statements about VISX's business and its patent portfolio in order to artificially inflate the stock price. The thrust of the complaint is that these statements were false or misleading because defendants knew there was no basis for their core patent claims and thus, the revenue projections. Without a valid patent portfolio, plaintiffs argue, VISX could not possibly maintain its lucrative per procedure fee, and, thus could not deliver on the stated revenue projections. The complaint alleges that defendants had this knowledge during the class period, but engaged in false public rhetoric in order to inflate stock prices and benefit from their own massive insider trading before the truth was revealed.

II. DISCUSSION

A. Standard of Review

We review de novo the district court's dismissal of a complaint for failure to state a claim under Federal Rule of Civil Procedure 12(b)(6). *See In re Silicon Graphics Inc. Sec. Litig.*, 183 F.3d 970, 983 (9th Cir.1999). On review, we accept the plaintiffs' allegations as true and construe them in the light most favorable to plaintiffs. Id.

B. Private Securities Litigation Reform Act of 1995

The PSLRA significantly altered pleading requirements in private securities fraud litigation by requiring that a complaint "plead with particularity both falsity and scienter." *Ronconi v. Larkin*, 253 F.3d 423, 429 (9th Cir.2001). A securities fraud complaint must now "specify each statement alleged to have been misleading, the reason or reasons why the statement is misleading, and, if an allegation regarding the statement or omission is made on information and belief, the complaint shall state with particularity all facts on which that belief is formed." 15 U.S.C. 78u-4(b)(1). Further, the complaint must "state with particularity facts giving rise to a strong inference that the defendant acted with the required state of mind." 15 U.S.C. 78u-4(b)(2) (emphasis added); *see also Silicon Graphics*, 183 F.3d at 974 (facts must come closer to demonstrating intent, as opposed to mere motive and opportunity). Thus, the complaint must allege that the defendants made false or misleading statements either intentionally or with deliberate recklessness. *See Silicon Graphics*, 183 F.3d at 985.

C.   Sufficiency of the Complaint under the PSLRA

As stated above, the gravamen of plaintiffs' cause is that defendants intentionally or recklessly misrepresented the truth when they made optimistic statements about VISX's future earnings and growth because they knew its patents were invalid, and, as a result, also knew that VISX could not possibly hope to maintain its current practice of charging $250 per procedure. Though the complaint adequately demonstrates the defendants were unquestionably aware of Dr. Srinivasan's claim against one of their core patents, in the end it fails to demonstrate the link between awareness of the claim and knowledge that the patents were therefore invalid. See Ronconi, 253 F.3d at 430 (no facts alleged that would support inference that corporation's optimistic predictions were known to be false or misleading at the time defendants made them); *accord City of Philadelphia v. Fleming Co.*, 264 F.3d 1245, 1265 (10th Cir.2001) (evidence in complaint must lead to the conclusion that company and officers must have known that litigation against it would be meritorious in the end).

To the contrary, the facts alleged in the complaint indicate that VISX and its officers fervently believed in the viability of the patent portfolio, and litigated its defense with ferocity. Thus, we agree with the district court's thorough analysis and ultimate conclusion that the facts alleged by plaintiffs are not sufficient to satisfy the strong inference of defendants' knowledge, as required by the PSLRA. See Ronconi, 253 F.3d at 430 (facts must show insiders knew, at the time they made the statements, about the negative event the complaint claims would occur in the future).

. . .

III.   CONCLUSION

For the reasons given above, we AFFIRM the district court's dismissal of the securities fraud class action against VISX and the individual defendants.

NOTES & QUESTIONS

1. As noted in *Gompper,* the Private Securities Litigation Reform Act of 1995 made a number of important changes in standards governing federal securities fraud claims by private parties. Some of these changes may impair plaintiffs' ability to raise claims based on misstatements of the future business significance of patents and other intellectual property interests.

Among other changes, the Act added several new pleading requirements for securities fraud claims. First, where a compliant alleges that a statement or omission is false or misleading, the complaint must specify which statement is misleading and the reasons why it is misleading. Second, when a complaint is submitted on information and belief, a plaintiff must state "with particularity all facts on which that belief is formed." Third, a plaintiff is required to "state with particularity facts giving rise to a strong inference that the defendant acted with the required state of mind." 15 U.S.C. § 78u-4(b)(1) & (2).

Since the passage of the Act, considerable confusion has arisen about the types of facts a plaintiff must plead to raise a "strong inference" that a defendant possessed the state of mind or "scienter" required for securities fraud liability. Some courts have asserted that the Act simply codifies standards applied in the Second Circuit before the passage of the Act. These standards required plaintiffs to meet the "burden of pleading circumstances that provide at least a minimal factual basis for their conclusory allegations of scienter." Such a burden could be met through allegations of a motive to deceive and access to accurate information. *See, e.g., Turkish v. Kasenetz*, 27 F.3d 23, 28-29 (2d Cir. 1994); *Connecticut National Bank v. Fluor Corp.*, 808 F.2d 957, 962 (2d Cir. 1987). At the opposite extreme, the Ninth Circuit has interpreted the Act to require more extensive allegations of scienter, obligating a plaintiff to plead strong circumstantial evidence of "deliberate recklessness." *In re Silicon Graphics Sec. Litig.*, 183 F.3d 970, 974 (9th Cir.1999). Most circuits have adopted intermediate approaches somewhere between the Second and Ninth Circuit approaches. *See* Michael A. Perino, *Did the Private Securities Litigation Reform Act Work?*, 2003 U. ILL. L. REV. 913, 925 (2003).

It is unclear how these changes may affect claims based on misrepresentations related to intellectual property interests. The complexity of insights held by corporate managers about the nature and business impacts of intellectual property interests may make it difficult or impossible for plaintiffs to detect and allege information needed to support securities fraud claims. Information about corporate executives' true insights about intellectual property interests and concerns affecting their businesses may not be shared beyond a few trusted corporate insiders, making it unlikely that this information will surface and be available to injured investors seeking to raise securities fraud claims. Absent this information, it may be very difficult for claimants to allege specific facts indicating that executives knew or were reckless about the inaccuracy of their representations concerning intellectual property interests. Even if fully disclosed and capable of proof, gaps between executives' personal understanding of intellectual property interests and their representations concerning those interests may seem so complex as to appear to be the product of mere negligence or over-confidence on the part of the executives involved. For these various reasons, the tightened pleading requirements applicable to federal fraud claims may prevent claimants from proceeding with some suits involving intellectual property misrepresentations that would have survived under prior pleading standards. However, even if this is the case, the same fraud actions may succeed under state securities laws or common law fraud theories where the special pleading requirements of the Act are not applicable.

2. The Private Securities Litigation Reform Act of 1995 also implemented important substantive changes by creating a "safe harbor" protecting corporations and their officials from liability for certain forward looking statements

about projected corporate performance. The forward looking statements given special protection include financial projections, statements concerning managements' plans or objectives, statements of future economic performance, and statements of the assumptions underlying the foregoing. *See* 15 U.S.C. §§ 77z-2(i)(1), 78u-5(i)(1) (2000). Under the safe harbor provisions of the Act, a forward looking statement, even if false, is not a basis for liability if it is identified as a forward looking statement and is "accompanied by meaningful cautionary statements identifying important factors that could cause actual results to differ materially from those in the forward-looking statement." 15 U.S.C. §§ 77z-2(c)(1)(A)(i), 78u-5(c)(1)(A)(i). In addition, a forward looking statement that is not properly identified or is not accompanied by the appropriate cautionary language still falls within the safe harbor if the statement is immaterial or if the plaintiff fails to prove that the defendant had "actual knowledge" that the forward-looking statement was false or misleading. 15 U.S.C. §§ 77z-2(c)(1)(B), 78u-5(c)(1)(B).

While the safe harbor provisions of the Act may make it harder for plaintiffs to assert liability based on forward looking statements about the anticipated impacts of patent interests on projected company performance, the safe harbor provisions of the Act will not protect defendants against claims based on representations of present conditions, such as a misrepresentation about the existence of a patent, the scope of an outstanding patent's claims, the nature of advice from patent counsel, and the status of patent enforcement litigation. Hence, while the safe harbor provisions may diminish claims that executives have overstated the future business significance of patents and other intellectual property protections, a broad range of misrepresentations regarding patents and patent rights will still form a substantial basis for private damage claims under federal securities laws. Furthermore, the Act has not limited state law claims based on materially misleading statements in stock sales transactions.

NATHENSON v. ZONAGEN, INC.
United States Court of Appeals for the Fifth Circuit
267 F.3d 400 (2001)

GARWOOD, Circuit Judge.

Plaintiffs-appellants James Nathenson and others (collectively, the plaintiffs) filed this putative class action in the court below against defendants-appellants Zonagen, Inc. (Zonagen), Zonagen chief executive officer and director Joseph Podolski (Podolski) and Zonagen outside directors and major shareholders Steven Blasnik (Blasnik) and Martin Sutter (Sutter) (collectively, the defendants). In their complaint, the plaintiffs sought class certification and alleged violations of sections 10(b) and 20(a) of the Securities Exchange Act of 1934 (1934 Act) and Rule 10b-5 of the Securities Exchange Commission (SEC). The defendants moved to dismiss the complaint under Fed.R.Civ.P. 12(b)(6). The district court granted the motion in a memorandum opinion and in a separate document rendered judgment that "this action is dismissed with prejudice." The plaintiffs now appeal. Finding sufficient merit in one of plaintiffs' complaints on appeal, we vacate and remand.

Facts and Proceedings Below

This is a private securities fraud action brought by nine putative class representatives on behalf of purchasers of common stock in Zonagen, a biopharmaceutical company based in The Woodlands, Texas. The plaintiffs allege that during the class period, February 7, 1996 through January 9, 1998, the defendants — Zonagen, its president and CEO, Podolski, and two of its outside directors and major shareholders, Blasnik and Sutter, the latter being Chairman of the Board — engaged in a scheme to defraud their shareholders by issuing a series of public misrepresentations about two of Zonagen's potential products in order to inflate artificially the value of Zonagen's stock and sell $67.5 million in stock in July 1997 at an inflated price. The two potential products in question are "Vasomax," an oral treatment for male erectile dysfunction (MED), and "Immumax," an adjuvant for the delivery of animal and human vaccines.

In order to market a drug in the United States, developers must first obtain the approval of the Food and Drug Administration (FDA). This approval process involves, among other things, conducting a series of clinical trials to establish the safety and efficacy of the drug. The maker of the drug then submits the results of these trials to the FDA as part of its New Drug Application (NDA). Phase I trials test the safety, dosage tolerance, and other pharmacokinetic properties of the drug; they also identify the primary side-effects, if any, that the drug may cause. During Phase II trials, researchers test the drug in a limited patient population to gather information about efficacy, optimal dosage levels, adverse effects, and safety risks. Phase III trials test the efficacy and safety of the drug in an expanded patient population at geographically dispersed trial sites.

The broad contours of the events in question are as follows. In 1995, Zonagen completed its Phase I trials for Vasomax in Ireland and reported the results of these trials in a Form 10-K filed with the SEC that year. The company then initiated Phase II trials in Germany; these trials concluded in March 1996. On February 7, 1996, the first day of the class period, Zonagen shares traded at $12 3/8. On February 7 and 14, 1996, before the completion of the Phase II trials, two news items appeared in which Podolski indicated that the "preliminary" results of the Phase II trials were positive. Similar statements were made to analysts on March 5 and in a March 14, 1996 press release (similar statements were also made in Zonagen's April 1, 1996 10K [report to the SEC] for the year ended December 31, 1995). The stock traded at $16 a share on March 13, 1996. On May 9 and 16, 1996, Zonagen issued press releases that described the Phase II results in positive terms, the May 9 release unmistakably implying and the May 16 release expressly stating that the Phase II trials produced statistically significant results. As the district court noted, Zonagen shares after March 13, 1996 "fell steadily until reaching . . . less than $10 per share in early August."

In press releases, as well as in its public filings with the SEC, Zonagen represented not only that the Phase II trials had positive results, but also that Zonagen had acquired the rights to a "method of use" patent, known as the Zorgniotti patent, which covered the administration of phentolamine, the active ingredient in Vasomax. In addition, Zonagen used its press releases and public filings of 1996-97 to state its belief that it had "discovered" a "new" adjuvant, which it called Immumax.

In November 1996, Zonagen began Phase III trials for Vasomax in the United States. Soon after, Zonagen began issuing press releases discussing these trials and expressing its hope that the results would enable Zonagen to file an NDA by June 1997. In its public filings with the SEC, it made similar statements about the Phase III trials in the United States. On November 14, 1996, Zonagen filed a Form S-3 with the SEC in connection with the proposed sale by some of its shareholders of Zonagen shares not previously publicly offered. In the Form S-3, Zonagen disclosed that the Phase II trials had not yielded statistically significant results and that the other patent (the Lowrey patent) it had hoped would cover Vasomax had been rejected in a non-final first office action by the United States Patent and Trademark Office.

In 1997, Zonagen's press releases and public filings noted the positive results of the Phase III trials. On June 11, 1997, Zonagen filed a Form S-3 with the SEC seeking registration of two million shares of Zonagen stock for sale by the company. The Form S-3 stated that the Phase III trials had yielded statistically significant results, and also discussed the "discovery" of Immumax and the Zorgniotti patent respecting Vasomax. On June 13, 1997, Zonagen issued a press release announcing the successful completion of its Phase III trials. On May 23, 1997, the last day of trading before the announcement, the price per share of Zonagen stock was $17 3/8. On May 27, the day of the announcement, the price per share rose to $24 1/2. On July 18, 1997, after no further announcements, Zonagen's share price closed at $32 1/4. On July 22, 1997, Zonagen filed a prospectus with the SEC which commenced its secondary offering of common stock. In a press release issued that same day, the company announced that it had raised $67.5 million in gross proceeds from the sale of 2.25 million shares sold at a price of $30 per share. Zonagen shares rendered a high of $44 3/8 on October 13, 1997. On January 12, 1998, the Monday following January 9, 1998, the last day of the class period, the stock closed at $13 15/16. The average closing price of Zonagen shares in the ninety days following the last day of the class period (January 9, 1998 through April 10, 1998) was $20 1/5. On June 2, 1998, the stock traded at $36 3/4 per share; by June 12, 1998, it had fallen to $24 3/4 per share.

On June 19, 1998, the plaintiffs filed their Consolidated Amended Complaint (complaint) seeking class certification and alleging that the defendants had violated section 10(b)[1] of the 1934 Act and Rule 10b-5[2] promulgated thereunder by

---

[1] [FN4] Section 10(b) provides in relevant part:

"It shall be unlawful for any person, directly or indirectly . . . (b) To use or employ, in connection with the purchase or sale of any security . . . any manipulative or deceptive device or contrivance in contravention of such rules and regulations as the [SEC] may prescribe as necessary or appropriate in the public interest or for the protection of investors." 15 U.S.C. § 78j(b).

[2] [FN5] Rule 10b-5 provides in relevant part:

"It shall be unlawful for any person, directly or indirectly . . .

(b) To make any untrue statement of a material fact or to omit to state a material fact necessary in order to make the statements made, in the light of the circumstances under which they were made, not misleading . . . in connection with the purchase or sale of any security." 17 C.F.R. 240.10b-5.

the SEC (an original complaint was filed March 9, 1998). The plaintiffs also contended that the three individual defendants were liable as "controlling persons" under section 20(a)[3] of the 1934 Act. As noted above, the complaint primarily charges that the defendants made a series of misrepresentations about their Vasomax and Immumax potential products in order to artificially inflate the company's share price, and then sold a large amount of stock at an inflated price. On August 3, 1998, the defendants moved to dismiss the complaint pursuant to Fed.R.Civ.P. 12(b)(6). On March 31, 1999, the district court granted the motion and dismissed the "action" with prejudice. The plaintiffs now appeal.

. . .

VI.   The Zorgniotti patent for Vasomax

Plaintiffs . . . allege that defendants made misleading statements concerning what is referred to as the Zorgniotti patent and its application to Vasomax. The rights to this patent application were acquired by Zonagen in April 1994, the patent was approved in June 1996 and was formally issued October 15, 1996.

The essence of plaintiffs' claim is that the Zorgniotti patent did not cover Vasomax because it was only a method of use patent covering, *inter alia,* phentolamine tablets or other items dissolved in the mouth *but excluding* those swallowed and dissolved in the stomach,[4] and that Vasomax was at all times intended to be administered only as a pill to be swallowed, and was hence affirmatively excluded from the patent so that "Vasomax was not covered or protected in any manner by this patent."

---

[3] [FN6] Section 20(a) of the 1934 Act provides in relevant part:

"Every person who, directly or indirectly, controls any person liable under any provision of this chapter . . . shall also be liable jointly and severally with and to the same extent as such controlled person." 15 U.S.C. § 78t(a).

[4] [FN21] The patent commences by stating that it is "directed to improved methods for modulating the human sexual response by administering vasodilator agents to the circulation of a human via transmucosal, transdermal, intranasal or rectal routes of administration that obviate 'first pass' deleterious effects on such agents." The application subsequently states "when an orally ingested drug reaches the intestine, it is absorbed into the portal circulation and delivered to the liver where it can be metabolized and inactivated. Hepatic inactivation following absorption of a drug from the gastrointestinal tract is referred to as 'first pass' effect . . . and, along with poor absorption and slow transit times through the gastrointestinal tract, functions to require larger oral doses of drugs than may be necessary with other routes of administration. This, in turn, can account for delays in the onset of the therapeutic effect of a drug." Later, the patent states that "[f]or purposes of the present invention, 'transmucosal delivery' generally refers to delivery of the drug to the oral or pharyngeal mucosa and includes buccal delivery, sublingual delivery, and delivery to the pharyngeal mucosa, *but not to the stomach*" (emphasis added). It gives as an example of a delivery covered by the patent "[v]asoactive agents . . . combined in a hard candy (which may be dissolved in the mouth) or in chewing gum to provide buccal or sublingual delivery to the oral mucosa." The patent also states that "[v]asodilating agents useful in the present invention include, but are not limited to, the group consisting of phentolamine mesylate, phentolamine hydrochloride . . . The presently preferred agent is phentolomine mesylate. The presently preferred administrative route is transmucosal, especially buccal." Vasomax uses phentolomine mesylate as the active pharmacologic agent. "Buccal" has been defined as "directed toward the cheek;" "of, relating to, involving, or lying within the mouth," "ORAL." Webster's Third New International Dictionary (1981) at 287.

The principle basis for plaintiffs' claim in this respect is Zonagen's June 24, 1996 press release stating, as alleged in paragraph 47 of the complaint, as follows:

> 47. On June 24, 1996, the Defendants issued a press release, stating, *inter alia:* Zonagen, Inc. announced today that it has received notification from the United States Patent and Trademark Office that the *patent covering its use of VASOMAX (TM) as a treatment for erectile dysfunction (impotency) has been allowed.*
> The Company noted the *approval was granted for the first of two separate applications associated with VASOMAX (TM).* The second, more recent application is still pending.
> 'The *approval of our U.S. patent,* the VASOMAX (TM) IND submission and the selection of our Phase III development team are crucial events in our commercialization strategy,' declared Joseph S. Podolski, President and CEO, Zonagen, Inc. . . .

(Emphases added).

If, as plaintiffs have alleged, Vasomax was at all times intended to be administered only as a pill or tablet to be swallowed and dissolved in the stomach, then it was plainly not covered by the Zorgniotti method of use patent which clearly and affirmatively excluded that method of use. It was hence false and misleading for the June 24, 1996 press release to state that "Zonagen, Inc. announced . . . that the patent *covering its use of Vasomax* (TM) as a treatment for erectile dysfunction (impotency) has been allowed" (emphasis added). The patent *did not* "cover" Zonagen's use of Vasomax, but rather affirmatively excluded that use.

Plaintiffs also complain of subsequent Zonagen statements concerning the Zorgniotti patent, namely statements in its November 14, 1996 S-3, March 31, 1997 10K, June 11, 1997 S-3 and July 22, 1997 Form 424B prospectus. Considered individually, none of these statements can of themselves reasonably be considered false or misleading in the same manner as the June 24, 1996 press release. However, the statements cannot be considered by themselves, for the statements in the above referenced June 24, 1996 press release — that the patent covered Zonagen's use of Vasomax — had never been retracted or modified and it had not been disclosed that the Zorgniotti patent did not cover Zonagen's use of Vasomax or did not extend to pills or tablets to be swallowed and dissolved in the stomach as Vasomax was. Hence, in the absence of other factors, a fact finder could determine that readers of these later statements could reasonably be assumed to have understood them as referring to the patent as described in the June 24, 1996 press releases, so that the representation of that press release was in effect carried forward to March, June and July 1997.

The district court held that scienter was not adequately pled as to the Zorgniotti patent statements made in 1997, but it considered those statements in isolation and not in light of the never retracted assertions of the June 24, 1996 press release. Although the question is a close one, we conclude that the necessary strong inference of scienter is pled as to Podolski, who was, and had been since July 1992, President and Chief Executive

Officer, as well as a director, of the corporation. We recognize that normally an officer's position with a company does not suffice to create an inference of scienter. However, there are a number of special circumstances here which, taken together, suffice to support a different result in the present case. To begin with, Zonagen was essentially a one product company, and that product was Vasomax. Thus, the November 1996 S-3, as well as the March 31, 1997 10K, the June 11, 1997 S-3, and the July 22, 1997 Form 424B, all reflect that "[s]ubstantially all of the Company's efforts and expenditures over the next few years will be devoted to Vasomax (TM)", and that "the Company's future prospects are substantially dependent on" Vasomax. Further, patent protection for Vasomax was obviously important. The June 11, 1997 S-3 states that "[t]he Company's ability to compete effectively with other companies is materially dependent on the proprietary nature of the Company's patents and technologies," and in the June 24, 1996 press release Podolski is quoted as describing the approval of the Zorgniotti patent as a "crucial event[s]." Additionally, the Company had acquired the Zorgniotti patent application in April 1994, so there was ample opportunity to become familiar with it prior to June 1996. In this connection, we also note that the Company is not large. As reflected by its 10Ks filed April 1, 1996 and March 31, 19979, the Company had only thirty-two full time employees in January 1996 and only thirty-five in January 1997. Finally, the Company's June 24, 1996 and November 6, 1996 press releases, which describe the Zorgniotti patent, both quote Podolski, and an article in the issue of *Fortune* distributed in mid-February 1998, states: "[i]n a recent interview, Podolski concedes, 'You can say today no patent specifically covers Vasomax;' he claims the company's issued patent 'broadly covers' the drug."

Taking all the above factors together we conclude that they suffice, if perhaps only barely so, to support the necessary "strong inference" of scienter on the part of Podolski and Zonagen with respect to the statement that the Zorgniotti patent covers Zonagen's use of Vasomax. The result, however, is otherwise as to Blasnik and Sutter, both of whom were outside directors, neither of whom is alleged to have made any statements or issued any press release about any patent (or Vasomax itself), and as to neither of whom is any other allegation made tending to support an inference of scienter in this respect. . . .

Conclusion

We have held that with one exception the district court did not err in holding that the allegations of the complaint were insufficient.

However, we have also held that the district court did err in holding insufficient the allegations of the complaint with respect to Zonagen having stated that the Zorgniotti patent covered Zonagen's use of Vasomax, so far as concerns Zonagen and Podolski, and in failing to address the potential section 20(a) liability of Blasnik and Sutter in that particular respect.

We accordingly vacate the district court's judgment of dismissal and remand for further proceedings not inconsistent herewith.

VACATED and REMANDED.

ZIRN v. VLI CORPORATION
Supreme Court of Delaware
681 A.2d 1050 (1995)

VEASEY, Chief Justice.

In this appeal, we follow and apply the law of partial disclosures. We hold that it is materially misleading to advise stockholders in a tender offer transaction of part, but only part, of the advice of the company's patent counsel as to the patent status of the company's most valuable asset. We also hold that the directors are exempt from liability for monetary damages for good-faith disclosure violations by virtue of the company's certificate of incorporation adopting the exemption authorized by 8 *Del.C. §* 102(b)(7).

We are asked to consider whether defendants below-appellees, VLI Corporation ("VLI"), the individual members of the VLI Board of Directors and American Home Products Corporation ("AHP") (collectively, the "Defendants"), breached their fiduciary duties in connection with the 1987 acquisition of VLI by AHP. On behalf of a class of similarly situated stockholders, plaintiff below-appellant, Marilyn Zirn ("Zirn"), contends, *inter alia,* that certain disclosures contained in the Schedule 14D-9 (the "14D-9"), disseminated by VLI in connection with AHP's tender offer for up to all of VLI's outstanding shares, were materially misleading absent further, related disclosures. Specifically, Zirn asserts that the 14D-9 materially misstated the views of VLI's special patent counsel concerning the prospects for reinstatement of a patent which inadvertently had been allowed to lapse. The patent at issue protected one of VLI's primary products, the Today® contraceptive sponge.

We hold that, in light of the attendant circumstances, VLI's 14D-9 was materially misleading in that it provided the VLI stockholders with a skewed impression of the prospects for patent reinstatement and, therefore, impeded the stockholders' ability to make an informed decision as to the merits of the VLI-AHP transaction. When VLI undertook to explain the risk that the patent might not be reinstated, it assumed a duty to disclose the correlative likelihood that the patent would be restored, so as to avoid painting an overly bleak picture of the situation with which VLI was faced. We find, however, that, by virtue of 8 *Del.C.* § 102(b)(7) and the amendment to VLI's Certificate of Incorporation extending the protection of that statutory provision to the VLI board of directors, there can be no liability for monetary damages imposed on the VLI director defendants. Accordingly, we AFFIRM the decision of the Court of Chancery entering judgment in favor of the Defendants.

The Facts

A detailed explication of the facts relevant to this appeal may be found in this Court's earlier, partial disposition of this matter. *Zirn v. VLI Corp.,* Del.Supr., 621 A.2d 773, 774-77 (1993) (*Zirn I*). Briefly stated, the case arises from the actions of the VLI Board of Directors and the interaction of VLI and AHP during the period from 1985 to 1988. In 1985, the VLI Board determined that the company could not be sustained as a profitable enterprise absent an infusion of new capital. After an extensive search for potential suitors, only AHP emerged as a willing and suitable partner. Negotiations began in late August 1987, culminating in a proposed change-of-control transaction tentatively structured around a $7.00 per share tender offer by AHP for up to all of VLI's outstanding shares.

Prior to the agreement being executed, however, VLI learned that the patent on its Today® contraceptive sponge, its most valuable asset, had inadvertently been allowed to lapse. Upon learning of this fact, AHP determined that only a merger with VLI would be acceptable. Although the consideration for the merger remained unchanged at $7.00 per share, AHP demanded and received the option to withdraw from the transaction if the patent was not successfully reinstated by March 1, 1988. This agreement was formalized on August 30, 1987, and the VLI Board promptly recommended the transaction to its stockholders.

On September 21, 1987, VLI's petition for patent reinstatement was rejected by the Patent and Trademark Office (the "PTO"). Subsequent events, including a substantial downturn in the stock market and an unexpected decline in sales of the Today® sponge, coupled with increased uncertainty about the likelihood of patent reinstatement, caused AHP to seek renegotiation of the transaction. On November 1, 1987, AHP proposed to change the form of the transaction from a merger to a tender offer/merger and to reduce the tender offer consideration from $7.00 per share to $6.25 per share. In exchange for these concessions, AHP offered to remove the patent reinstatement condition. On November 3, 1987, the VLI Board determined that, in light of the company's perceived need for capital and the absence of any other available suitors, the offer should be accepted.

On November 10, 1987, the VLI Board distributed to its stockholders: (1) a memorandum from VLI's Chief Executive Officer announcing the transaction; (2) a copy of VLI's Schedule 14D-9; and (3) a copy of AHP's Offer to Purchase. The 14D-9 included information concerning the circumstances surrounding the patent lapse and discussed the uncertain prospects for patent reinstatement. The 14D-9 also purported to provide the substance of patent counsel's advice to VLI concerning the likelihood of reinstatement and stated that:

> In July 1987, the Patent expired due to the Company's inadvertent failure to timely pay a maintenance fee. On September 21, 1987, the United States Patent and Trademark Office dismissed the Company's petition to reinstate the Patent. The Company has filed a petition requesting the Patent and Trademark Office to reconsider its dismissal. *The Company is unable to estimate when this petition for reconsideration will be decided by the Patent and Trademark Office and has been advised by special patent counsel that there is a significant possibility of the reconsideration petition not prevailing in the Patent and Trademark Office.*

(Emphasis supplied.) The 14D-9 did not, however, discuss the totality of patent counsel's advice. Specifically, patent counsel had indicated through correspondence to VLI that ultimate success in the PTO was likely and that VLI possessed "an excellent case on the merits." Moreover, contrary to the statement contained in the 14D-9, patent counsel had indicated that final PTO action could be expected by November 21, 1987.

AHP's tender offer closed on December 8, 1987 with 94.8 percent of VLI's outstanding shares having been tendered. The remaining 5.2 percent of the shares were acquired in a short-form merger on January 8, 1988. On the same date, AHP issued a Notice of Merger informing the non-tendering stockholders, including Zirn, that each of their shares had been converted into a right to receive $6.25. Pursuant to 8 *Del.C.* §§ 253 and 262, these individuals were informed of their appraisal rights and were instructed on the proper method of exercising those rights.

Procedural History and Disposition in the Court of Chancery

Prior to the short-form merger, on December 17, 1987, Zirn filed this class-action suit naming as defendants AHP, VLI and VLI's individual directors. In July of 1989, the Court of Chancery dismissed Zirn's claims relating to insider trading and conversion. The trial court, however, certified a class consisting of nearly all of VLI's stockholders of record as of November 16, 1987 and allowed the remaining claims of equitable fraud and breach of the duty of disclosure to proceed to trial. After trial concluded, the Court of Chancery granted judgment for the Defendants on all of Zirn's claims.

On appeal from that decision, this Court held that the Court of Chancery had applied the wrong standard of materiality, erroneously analyzing the subjective beliefs of the VLI directors. The Court then remanded the matter for further proceedings consistent with its 1993 opinion. On remand, the trial court reached its decision based on the record of the first trial, supplemented by additional discovery on the issue of patent counsel's opinion. Again, the trial court found for Defendants on all claims. This appeal followed.

In this appeal, Zirn contends that: (1) VLI's Board of Directors breached its fiduciary duty in connection with the disclosure of patent counsel's advice concerning the likelihood of patent reinstatement and the expected timing of reinstatement; (2) AHP breached its duty of disclosure in connection with the January 8, 1988 Notice of Merger by excluding from that document any discussion of patent counsel's advice; and (3) VLI and its directors are liable for equitable fraud. Since the Court of Chancery entered judgment for the Defendants and failed to reach the issue of damages, Zirn seeks from this Court an award of damages and prejudgment interest. We address these contentions *seriatim* below.

Disclosure Claims

Zirn contends that the VLI Board of Directors breached its fiduciary duty of disclosure when it prepared and distributed the 14D-9 and that the Court of Chancery erred in holding to the contrary.

The issues presented by Zirn involve mixed questions of law and fact. This Court's review is, therefore, *de novo.* In conducting this review,

> if the trial court's factual conclusions "are sufficiently supported by the record and are the product of an orderly and logical deductive process . . . we accept them, even though independently we might have reached opposite conclusions." *Levitt v. Bouvier,* Del.Supr., 287 A.2d 671, 673 (1972). Nevertheless, in an appropriate case, this Court may review *de novo* mixed questions of law and fact, such as determinations of materiality, *Zirn v. VLI Corp.,* Del.Supr., 621 A.2d 773, 777 (1993), and in certain

cases make its own findings of fact upon the record below, *Shell Petroleum, Inc. v. Smith,* Del.Supr., 606 A.2d 112, 114 (1992). The Court will affirm the trial court's legal rulings unless they represent an "err[or] in formulating or applying legal principles." *Gilbert v. El Paso Co.,* Del.Supr., 575 A.2d 1131, 1142 (1990).

Arnold v. Society for Sav. Bancorp., Del.Supr., 650 A.2d 1270, 1276 (1994) (*Arnold I*).

A.   Disclosure of Patent Counsel's Advice

Zirn argues that VLI's synopsis of patent counsel's advice was materially misleading absent further disclosure. Specifically, Zirn asserts that the discussion of patent counsel's advice contained in the 14D-9 was skewed in that it disclosed only a significant risk of the patent not being reinstated.

The Court of Chancery rejected this claim, however, holding that disclosure of a significant risk logically implies the corresponding possibility of the risk not being realized. We disagree and hold that the 14D-9 was materially misleading absent further disclosure of patent counsel's views. Once VLI undertook to discuss the import of patent counsel's advice, it assumed a duty to discuss that advice fully and fairly. To discharge this duty, it was necessary to include in the 14D-9 a discussion of the correlative probability of successful patent reinstatement.

It is well-established that the duty of disclosure "represents nothing more than the well-recognized proposition that directors of Delaware corporations are under a fiduciary duty to disclose fully and fairly all material information within the board's control when it seeks shareholder action." *Stroud v. Grace,* Del.Supr., 606 A.2d 75, 84 (1992). This duty inheres any time a corporate board of directors seeks stockholder action.

Our analysis therefore turns on whether or not the VLI Board disclosed all facts material to the decision faced by VLI's stockholders. The materiality standard is well understood:

> An omitted fact is material if there is a substantial likelihood that a reasonable shareholder would consider it important in deciding how to vote. . . . It does not require proof of a substantial likelihood that disclosure of the omitted fact would have caused the reasonable investor to change his vote. What the standard does contemplate is a showing of a substantial likelihood that, under all the circumstances, the omitted fact would have assumed actual significance in the deliberations of the reasonable shareholder. Put another way, there must be a substantial likelihood that the disclosure of the omitted fact would have been viewed by the reasonable investor as having significantly altered the "total mix" of information made available.

Rosenblatt v. Getty Oil Co., Del.Supr., 493 A.2d 929, 944 (1985) (quoting *TSC Indus., Inc. v. Northway, Inc.,* 426 U.S. 438, 449, 96 S.Ct. 2126, 2132, 48 L.Ed.2d 757 (1976) and adopting *TSC* materiality standard as Delaware law).

In addition to the traditional duty to disclose all facts material to the proffered transaction, directors are under a fiduciary obligation to avoid misleading partial disclosures. The law of partial disclosure is likewise clear: "[O]nce defendants travel[ ] down the road of partial disclosure . . . they . . . [have] an obligation to provide the stockholders with an accurate, full, and fair characterization of those historic events." *Arnold I,* 650 A.2d at 1280; *see also Lynch v. Vickers Energy Corp.,* Del.Supr., 383 A.2d 278, 281 (1977) (holding that defendants violated their disclosure obligations when they partially disclosed a reliable, "floor" asset valuation but did not disclose equally reliable "ceiling" values).

The Defendants argue with some force, however, that no aspect of patent counsel's advice standing alone was required to be disclosed.[5] We need not decide in the abstract whether the general subject matter of patent counsel's advice was material. Under *Arnold,* the disclosure of even a non-material fact can, in some instances, trigger an obligation to disclose additional, otherwise non-material facts in order to prevent the initial disclosure from materially misleading the stockholders.

VLI's Schedule 14D-9 simply stated that "[t]he Company . . . has been advised by special patent counsel that there is a significant possibility of the reconsideration petition not prevailing in the Patent and Trademark Office." This is certainly not an untrue statement. But, standing alone, it paints an unduly bleak picture of VLI's chances for success in the PTO. Patent counsel appeared to believe that the prospects for reinstatement were quite good. In a November 3, 1987 letter from patent counsel to the VLI Board of Directors, patent counsel expressed the view that, "[r]egarding the likely outcome of [patent counsel's] . . . efforts [to reinstate the patent], it is my opinion, and the opinion of other members of my law firm, that *we have an excellent case on the merits and there is a good chance that we will prevail in the PTO.*" (Emphasis supplied.) Patent counsel further stated that he was "confident that the VLI patent could ultimately be reinstated by one mechanism or another."

Thus, it is clear that VLI's partial disclosure failed to convey the totality of patent counsel's views and was thus materially misleading. VLI's stockholders were faced with a single decision: whether to tender their shares or retain them. In making this determination, one factor was particularly relevant, *viz.,* whether the AHP offer of $6.25 per share represented an adequate price given the aggregate value and prospects of the company. If a stockholder viewed the company's offer as inadequate, those shares would likely not have been tendered. Those who chose to tender despite an inadequate

---

[5] [FN1] Although determination of this issue is unnecessary to our decision in this case, it could be argued on the ground of attorney-client privilege that VLI was not required to disclose patent counsel's advice unless that privilege was waived by VLI. *Zirn v. VLI Corp.,* Del.Supr., 621 A.2d 773, 780 (1993) (*Zirn I*); *see also Tackett v. State Farm Fire & Casualty Ins. Co.,* Del.Supr., 653 A.2d 254, 259-60 (1995) (discussing circumstances which give rise to waiver of the privilege). Moreover, the subject matter of patent counsel's advice involved "soft" information and could be characterized as highly speculative. Nevertheless, "once defendants traveled down the road of partial disclosure . . . , they had an obligation to provide the stockholders with an accurate, full, and fair characterization" of patent counsel's advice. *Arnold v. Society for Sav, Bancorp, Inc.,* 650 A.2d 1270, 1280 (1994) (*Arnold I*).

price likely would have done so for extrinsic reasons (*e.g.*, personal financial needs, the likelihood of the company folding before an adequate offer came along or reluctance to pursue an appraisal remedy). Nevertheless, any misstatement contained in the 14D-9 which misled the stockholders concerning the value of the company would necessarily be material.

In light of the partial disclosure, the undisclosed advice of patent counsel was extremely relevant to a reasonable stockholder's valuation of the corporation. The patent provided protection for VLI's most valuable asset, the Today® contraceptive sponge. The failure accurately to convey the prospects for reinstatement was misleading in a material way, because it gave an unduly pessimistic assessment of VLI's chances for success in the PTO. This fact had a direct bearing on the individual stockholder's ability to value the corporation accurately and, consequently, this fact was one that a reasonable investor would want to know. In light of the partial disclosure of patent counsel's opinion, a more balanced disclosure thereof would have significantly altered the "total mix of information" available to the individual VLI stockholder. *TSC,* 426 U.S. at 449, 96 S.Ct. at 2132; *Rosenblatt,* 493 A.2d at 944.

The Court of Chancery rejected Zirn's claim of materiality, however, stating that the language of the Schedule 14D-9 was sufficiently tempered so as to avoid any misleading result. Essentially, the trial court held that the concept of a significant risk of failure implies a correlative probability of success. This analysis runs contrary to established precedent, however. For example, in *Lynch v. Vickers Energy Corporation,* this Court addressed a situation involving comparable facts. *Lynch,* 383 A.2d at 281. In *Lynch,* the Court held that disclosure of a floor value for the company's assets without the related disclosure of equally trustworthy ceiling estimates was materially misleading. In so holding, the Court reversed the determination of the Court of Chancery that qualifying language[6] in the tender offer materials was sufficient to avoid misleading the stockholders.

VLI argues at length that the holding we now reach will be tantamount to a rejection of the materiality requirement in cases of partial disclosure. This argument is plainly untenable. The partial disclosure rule is implicated only where the omission of a related fact renders the partially disclosed information *materially* misleading. Thus, the materiality standard announced by the United States Supreme Court in *TSC Industries v. Northway* and adopted by this Court in *Rosenblatt v. Getty Oil* is still controlling in this context. The only distinction between this case and the traditional disclosure context is that, in the partial disclosure setting, the initial disclosure may sometimes be voluntary rather than mandatory.

VLI further asserts that the holding we reach today will impose an undue burden on corporate fiduciaries and will force directors to disclose all historical

---

[6] [FN2] The disclosure materials at issue in *Lynch* stated that the "the Company's net asset value . . . is *not less* than $200,000,000 . . . and could be substantially greater." *Lynch v. Vickers Energy Corp.,* Del.Supr., 383 A.2d 278, 280 (1977). Although the Vickers board of directors had received estimates in the $200,000,000 range, they had also received estimates in the $250,000,000 to $300,000,000 range. Despite the presence of qualifying language, the Court held that failure to disclose the higher estimates was materially misleading.

information to which they have access. The result, it is argued, will be a deluge of information which will render it impossible for stockholders to determine what is and what is not significant. This is an equally untenable position.

VLI, of its own accord, determined to provide stockholders with only a one-sided portion of patent counsel's advice. One curative statement could have obviated the need for this litigation. Our holding here, as in *Arnold* and *Lynch,* does not compel disclosure of *all* information, it simply requires disclosure of enough information to avoid misleading the stockholders.

We also recognize, as the Court of Chancery did, that "[t]he goal of disclosure . . . is not to flood shareholders in a sea of related, but immaterial information that ripples endlessly away from the financial or governance core of the matter." The goal of disclosure is, however, to provide a balanced and truthful account of those matters which are discussed in a corporation's disclosure materials.

B.   Disclosure Relating to the Timing of Patent Reinstatement

In a related claim, Zirn contends that the Court of Chancery erred in holding that the misstatement of the VLI Board concerning the timing of possible patent reinstatement was immaterial. Zirn's claim arises from an obvious inconsistency between correspondence sent to VLI by patent counsel and the characterization of that information by the VLI Board. On November 3, 1987, patent counsel sent a letter to VLI indicating that "no final PTO action is expected until approximately November 21, 1987." In the 14D-9, issued on November 10, 1987, however, the VLI Board indicated that "[t]he Company is unable to estimate when this petition for reconsideration will be decided by the Patent and Trademark Office. . . ." In light of the above correspondence from patent counsel, the Court of Chancery concluded that the VLI Board misstated the information in its possession concerning the projected time frame for PTO action on the reinstatement petition. The Chancellor held that there was "no factual basis" for this statement and "one could conclude that the Schedule 14D-9 was misleading on this point." The Chancellor nevertheless held that this misstatement was not material and, therefore, not actionable.

Zirn argues that the Chancellor misapplied the materiality standard in reaching this determination. This argument, however, is without merit. The trial court correctly concluded that the information pertaining to reinstatement, while relevant to the Board's decision to renegotiate the original merger agreement and to accept the lower price of $6.25 per share, was not material to the VLI stockholders' decision to tender to AHP. The Court of Chancery correctly stated that the original, $7.00 per share transaction was no longer available. Thus, the stockholders were not faced with a decision of whether to hold out for the higher offer. Instead, the VLI stockholders were deciding whether to accept a $6.25 per share offer. Since information pertaining to the timing of the reinstatement was not relevant to a determination of the adequacy of the $6.25 per share offer, this information was not material. The Court of Chancery was correct in so holding.

C.   Disclosures Contained in AHP's Notice of Merger

Zirn contends that the Court of Chancery failed to address her claim that AHP breached its duty of disclosure in connection with the January 8, 1988 Notice of Merger. The crux of Zirn's claim is that AHP failed to disclose material information pertaining to patent counsel's opinion on the likelihood of patent reinstatement. VLI counters that the Court of Chancery considered all claims that were presented to it, that this claim was not fairly presented and that, in any event, the information was not material and need not have been disclosed.

In its opinion on remand, the Court of Chancery did not discuss Zirn's contention concerning AHP's failure to disclose the advice of patent counsel in the Notice of Merger. This fact is easily explained, however, by the remainder of the trial court's holding. Since the Court of Chancery deemed VLI's disclosures in the 14D-9 to be adequate on this point, duplication of this information in the Notice of Merger would have been superfluous. In light of our holding concerning VLI's partial disclosure of patent counsel's advice, this resolution of Zirn's claim is no longer adequate. Moreover, contrary to the assertions of VLI, the record reveals that this claim was fairly raised before the trial court. Accordingly, we reach the merits of Zirn's contention. Our standard of review is *de novo*.

The duty of an acquiror in AHP's position is clear. Having become the majority stockholder of VLI, AHP "bears the burden of showing complete disclosure of all material facts relevant to a minority shareholder's decision whether to accept the short-form merger consideration or seek an appraisal." The question presented is, therefore, one of materiality. The Court is mindful, however, of the context in which the alleged omission occurred.

As the Court of Chancery correctly held,

> [t]he purposes of the disclosure notifying the remaining shareholders of a short-form merger are two-fold. The first, of course, is to notify these shareholders of their right to cash. The second is to alert them to an event which may give rise to possible judicial remedies, most notably appraisal of the fair value of their shares.

A Notice of Merger filed pursuant to 8 *Del.C.* §§ 253 and 262 is primarily intended to notify the stockholders of action being taken by the parent corporation and to apprise the stockholders of their appraisal remedy. The statutory mechanism authorized by section 253 is intended to allow corporations holding a 90 percent or greater stake in another company to use an essentially summary procedure to effect a merger of the two entities. While voluminous disclosures may be included in the section 253 Notice of Merger, such elaboration is generally not required. Moreover, the short answer here is that there was no partial disclosure issue which was the central problem with VLI's 14D-9 at the tender offer stage.

In the instant case, however, disclosure was provided by both AHP and VLI in connection with the initial tender offer. Moreover, the terms of the tender offer were reached through arm's-length negotiations. In this context, the Notice of Merger need generally not be as detailed as in a context where the specter of intentional misinformation is present.

The tension between the summary nature of the section 253 procedure and the supplementary duties provided by common law is therefore clear. This apparent tension is resolved through an analysis of the factual circumstances of the case and an inquiry into the potential for deception or misinformation. In the instant case, AHP provided notice to VLI's stockholders adequate to inform them of their right to receive cash for their shares and their alternative right to an appraisal remedy. In furtherance of its common-law duties, AHP provided high and low bid quotations for VLI stock dating from the first quarter of 1985 until the fourth quarter of 1987. In addition, AHP provided the VLI stockholders with summary financial data and made reference to VLI's more complete filings with the Securities and Exchange Commission.

The omission of patent counsel's advice does not bear directly on the accuracy or other *bona fides* of the disclosure made by AHP. Rather, patent counsel's views would bear only indirectly on the value of the corporation.[7] Such information would be difficult to interpret and might well have confused the VLI stockholders in their efforts to digest the financial data included in the Notice of Merger. Moreover, this information is outside the purview of typical "soft information," which is generally limited to valuations of corporate assets and other appraisal-related information. *See, e.g., Weinberger v. Rio Grande Indus., Inc.,* Del.Ch., 519 A.2d 116, 127 (1986) (defining "soft" information as "valuation data based upon 'forward looking' information or estimates, including asset appraisals and income or cash flow projections").

The situation with which AHP was faced must also be viewed in contradistinction to that of VLI. AHP did not undertake to disclose only partially the advice of patent counsel or make any misleading disclosures concerning that advice. Moreover, unlike the situation encountered by VLI in connection with the 14D-9, AHP did not endeavor, nor was it required, to provide a detailed explanation of the motivations behind the short-form merger. Thus, the utility of disclosing patent counsel's advice in the Notice of Merger would be questionable at best. In addition, it is not clear to what extent AHP was privy to the confidential communications of patent counsel to VLI. The totality of the circumstances therefore indicates that disclosure should not be required in

---

[7] [FN5] *See Rio Grande Indus.,* 519 A.2d at 126-27, where the Court of Chancery applied the test enunciated by the Third Circuit Court of Appeals in *Flynn v. Bass Brothers Enters., Inc.,* 3d. Cir., 744 F.2d 978 (1984) to determine whether certain "soft" information should have been disclosed. As stated by the Court of Chancery:

> In *Flynn,* the Third Circuit held that the existence of a duty to disclose so-called "soft information" (*i.e.,* valuation data based upon "forward looking" information or estimates, including asset appraisals and income or cash flow projections) should be determined on a case-by-case basis ". . . by weighing the potential aid such information will give a shareholder against the potential harm, such as undue reliance, if the information is released with a proper cautionary note." 744 F.2d at 988.

> In making that determination, the *Flynn* court employed a balancing test which involves weighing ". . . the facts upon which the information is based; the qualifications of those who prepared or compiled it; the purpose for which the information was originally intended; its relevance to the stockholders' impending decision; the degree of subjectivity or bias reflected in its preparation; the degree to which the information is unique; and the availability to the investor of other more reliable sources of information." 744 F.2d at 988.

Rio Grande Indus., 519 A.2d at 126-27.

such a situation. Accordingly, we hold that, under the unique circumstances faced by AHP, the advice of patent counsel was not material.

Equitable Fraud

Zirn contends that the Court of Chancery erred in failing to hold VLI and its directors liable for equitable fraud. The Court of Chancery determined that no equitable fraud had been shown since the alleged misstatements and omissions were not material. In light of the analysis above, however, it is clear that this issue must be revisited. Nevertheless, a review of the facts presented reveals that, despite the presence of a material misstatement in the 14D-9, Zirn has failed to state a *prima facie* case for equitable fraud.

In *Gaffin v. Teledyne, Inc.,* Del.Supr., 611 A.2d 467, 472 (1992), this Court laid down the elements of common-law fraud as follows:

1) a false representation, usually one of fact, made by the defendant;

2) the defendant's knowledge or belief that the representation was false, or was made with reckless indifference to the truth;

3) an intent to induce the plaintiff to act or to refrain from acting;

4) *the plaintiff's action or inaction taken in justifiable reliance upon the representation;* and

5) damage to the plaintiff as a result of such reliance.

Id. (emphasis supplied) (quoting *Stephenson v. Capano Dev., Inc.,* Del. Supr., 462 A.2d 1069, 1074 (1983)). Unlike common law fraud, however, at equity "there is no requirement that the defendant have known or believed its statement to be false or to have made the statement in reckless disregard of the truth." *Stephenson,* 462 A.2d at 1074. Thus, equity provides a remedy for negligent or innocent misrepresentations.

To state a *prima facie* case for equitable fraud, plaintiff must therefore satisfy all the elements of common-law fraud with the exception that plaintiff need not demonstrate that the misstatement or omission was made knowingly or recklessly. Most significant among the elements stated above, at least for purposes of this appeal, is the requirement of justifiable reliance. As VLI properly points out, Zirn did not tender in response to VLI's 14D-9 and did not cash out her shares in response to AHP's Notice of Merger. Thus, on these facts, no reliance has been shown. Having failed to satisfy one of the elements required to demonstrate a *prima facie* case for equitable fraud, Zirn's claim must fail.

Moreover, the class action is a device ill-suited to the disposition of claims of equitable fraud: "A class action may not be maintained in a purely common law or equitable fraud case since individual questions of law or fact, particularly as to the element of justifiable reliance, will inevitably predominate over common questions of law or fact."

In light of our holding concerning the applicability of section 102(b)(7), it is also clear that no relief can be afforded to plaintiffs even if a *prima facie* case of equitable fraud could be shown. Pursuant to the amendment to VLI's Certificate of Incorporation extending to the VLI director defendants the protection authorized by section 102(b)(7), "the directors are free from personal financial liability whether monetary damages arise out of legal or equitable theories." *Arnold v. Society for Sav. Bancorp*, Del.Supr., *678 A.2d 533 (1996)* (*Arnold II*) (citing 8 *Del.C.* § 102(b)(7); *Arnold I,* 650 A.2d at 1290). As in *Arnold*, the VLI directors are not now subject to whatever injunctive relief might have been available at an earlier stage of the proceedings. Accordingly, there are no remedies for equitable fraud available to the plaintiff class.

Damages and Pre-Judgment Interest

In her final claim on appeal, Zirn contends that this Court should set the measure of damages in the case at bar so as to avoid another remand to the Court of Chancery. Since the Court of Chancery did not find the Defendants liable on any of Zirn's claims, the Chancellor did not reach the issue of damages. Zirn now contends that this Court should set the measure of damages at the difference between the original merger agreement price of $7.00 per share and the tender offer price of $6.25 per share. Defendants contend that VLI's Certificate of Incorporation provision, which extends the protection of 8 *Del.C.* § 102(b)(7) to VLI's directors [and which shields those directors from monetary damage liability for breaches of their duties of care undertaken in good faith], acts as a bar to the imposition of monetary damages against the VLI director defendants.

We agree with the Defendants and hold that the VLI directors are shielded from liability by 8 *Del.C.* § 102(b)(7) and the amendment to VLI's Certificate of Incorporation giving effect to that statutory provision. The record reveals that any misstatements or omissions that occurred were made in good faith. The VLI directors lacked any pecuniary motive to mislead the VLI stockholders intentionally and no other plausible motive for deceiving the stockholders has been advanced. A good faith erroneous judgment as to the proper scope or content of required disclosure implicates the duty of care rather than the duty of loyalty. *Arnold I,* 650 A.2d at 1287-88 & n. 36. Thus, the disclosure violations at issue here fall within the ambit of the protection of section 102(b)(7).

Had the stockholders of VLI acted at the appropriate time and demonstrated the disclosure violation found herein, they could have sought an injunctive remedy. *Arnold II,* 678 A.2d at 542. Unfortunately, the time for such action has passed. We recognize that our decision will leave the former stockholders of VLI without any redress. *Arnold II,* 678 A.2d at 541. This, however, is the result envisaged by section 102(b)(7). VLI's stockholders approved the amendment to the VLI Certificate of Incorporation with full knowledge of its import.

Conclusion

We hold that VLI's failure to disclose the portion of patent counsel's opinion dealing with the likelihood of successful patent reinstatement constituted a material omission in the context of the partial and inferentially pessimistic discussion in the 14D-9 of patent counsel's advice. When the VLI Board of Directors undertook to disclose a portion of patent counsel's views, it assumed a duty to do so fully and fairly. In order to discharge this duty, the VLI Board was obligated to disclose not only the possibility of failure but also the correlative possibility of successful patent reinstatement because that was the context of patent counsel's opinion. The absence of any further discussion rendered VLI's disclosure documents misleading and incomplete.

Nevertheless, the individual members of the VLI Board are effectively shielded from liability by the company's Certificate of Incorporation Amendment implementing the statutory protection allowed by 8 *Del.C.* § 102(b)(7). Thus, although we find that the VLI Board of Directors breached its fiduciary duty of disclosure, no relief may be afforded to plaintiff at this juncture. Moreover, whatever liability might have accrued to the directors cannot be treated as the vicarious responsibility of the corporation they served. *Arnold II,* 678 A.2d at 540. Accordingly, the decision of the Court of Chancery is AFFIRMED.

NOTES & QUESTIONS

1. In *Zirn*, the court suggested that the need for secrecy in order to retain attorney-client privilege protections regarding advice to a corporation by patent counsel might provide a ground for the corporation to withhold information about the patent counsel's advice from corporate shareholders. Under what circumstances should anti-fraud standards compel disclosures of legal advice by corporate officials even though attorney-client privilege standards would normally protect a corporation from forced disclosures? Is advice from patent counsel likely to be subject to forced disclosures with unusual frequency relative to other types of legal advice given the importance of patent rights in the business success of many high tech companies and the tendency of corporate executives to tout patent rights (actual or projected) as key business considerations in communications with potential shareholders?

2. The cases in this set of readings all involve misstatements about patents or patent rights in the context of partially commercialized products and services covered by the patents at issue. To what extent is the materiality of misstatements about patents dependent on the existence of at least some accumulated track record of marketing and profits of products and services covered by the misrepresented patents? Does it matter that representations about the profitability of patented products or services are made concurrently with misrepresentations about the patents or patent rights involved? Must the products or services covered by patents constitute a large percentage of a company's business in order for misrepresentations about related patents to be material? Where a promising, patented product or service has not yet been commercialized, how should the financial implications of a misstatement of patent rights be projected? Should the materiality of a misstatement about patent rights turn solely on the scope of the adverse financial implications of the misrepresentation or are there other factors which would be sufficient to establish the materiality of such a misrepresentation even if its financial implications were uncertain? When should a patent be considered a valuable corporate asset *per se* (perhaps because of its licensing value) such that an inaccurate description of the patent is a material misrepresentation?

3. What types of misstatements about intellectual property interests by company executives should be considered to be immaterial because shareholders already have curative information correctly describing the interests? Are there certain inherent risks associated with intellectual property interests and related business advantages which are so commonly understood that

contrary information in a statement by company executives should not be considered to be a material misrepresentation? For example, consider a case where a company official knows that a competitor possesses a non-infringing product with similar functionality, but nonetheless makes an unqualified statement to the effect that the company's patent portfolio will ensure continuing profits in sales to customers in a particular market because other competitors will be excluded from similar sales. In this setting, is the chance that a competitor will develop a superior, non-infringing product that will make a company's patented product worthless such a commonly understood possibility that it constitutes a source of curative information rendering the unbalanced misstatement about company profits immaterial? What about misstatements by company managers despite their knowledge that the information they are representing is incorrect for unusual reasons falling outside the normal range of risks of inaccuracy affecting that type of information? For example, should it matter in determining the materiality of an inherently speculative statement like "we are confident of our ability to gain a patent for our key technology" that the company executive making the statement knows that there is a specific reason not normally associated with typical risks surrounding patent applications which makes it highly unlikely that the company will obtain a patent?

CHAPTER 4

TRADE SECRETS

PROBLEM

Dr. See, the CEO of Digital Ignition Systems Corp. has come to you with a problem involving a leak of company trade secrets. The problem for Digital Ignition began when Jim Westphal, a disgruntled Digital Ignition marketing representative, emailed Edgar Sly, the CEO of Slick Auto, Inc. seeking employment with the company. Sly initially turned Westphal away, but Westphal begged him to reconsider and offered, "I will do *anything* to change your mind."

Sly, seeing a golden opportunity, replied to Westphal's email: "I will extend you an offer of employment if you demonstrate your true commitment to Slick Auto. My company has had trouble designing a digital ignition system. Any information about Digital Ignition's system would be of great interest to me. If you help us, we will help you."

Westphal replied, "As soon as I can get a hold of the information, I will mail it to you. As a bonus, I will also include a customer list in the package. The spy business is more stressful than I thought. I'm nervous about the confidentiality agreement I signed." Despite his reservations, two weeks after his last message, Westphal surreptitiously photocopied several files marked "confidential" and carried them home. He assembled a package for Slick Auto that contained among other things, photocopies of information regarding the software that controls non-patented portions of Digital Ignition's systems, as well as a list of Digital Ignition's customers. After downing several beers to celebrate his first successful spy mission, Westphal scrawled an address on a mailing label, did a victory dance, slapped the label on the package, and took off for the post office.

Unfortunately for the hapless disgruntled marketing representative, the post office delivered the misaddressed package to the offices of Auto Dynamic. Westphal discovered his error only after he received a letter from Auto Dynamic stating, "Mr. Westphal, we believe we have received your package by mistake. We are holding onto the package until we are given further instruction from you as to how to proceed."

The mistake made Westphal increasingly nervous about his deal with Slick Auto. After several sleepless nights, he decided to back out of the deal, hoping that if he ignored it, the mess would go away on its own. Westphal never responded to Auto Dynamic's letter and never brought the letter to the attention of Digital Ignition management. He mentioned the errant package to no one. Hearing nothing back from Westphal, Auto Dynamic chose to hold on to Westphal's package. Auto Dynamic did not inquire further or attempt to contact anyone else at Digital Ignition.

A few months later, Auto Dynamic began selling plug-compatible ignition systems similar to Digital Ignition's system to Digital Ignition customers. Previously, Auto Dynamic had only sold automobile air fresheners and had shown no expertise or interest in ignition systems or the ignition system market. Concerned by the sudden development, Dr. See asked his engineers at Digital Ignition to purchase and analyze Auto Dynamic's ignition system. Their analysis revealed that portions of the software incorporated into the Auto Dynamic system were suspiciously similar to software that controls non-patented portions of Digital Ignition's systems, though the Auto Dynamic system did not incorporate Digital Ignition's patented hardware designs, nor did it use Digital Ignition's patented method of ignition control. The engineers suspected that Auto Dynamic might have copied portions of Digital Ignition's product, based upon the similarity of the software, coupled with the apparent lack of special expertise of Auto Dynamic concerning ignition systems.

Dr. See and Digital Ignition have asked for your advice on pursuing claims against Westphal, Slick Auto, and Auto Dynamic. Please help Digital Ignition may make an informed decision on how to proceed by analyzing the possible theories that Digital Ignition might use in a lawsuit and the likelihood of success.

FOCUS OF THE CHAPTER

The readings in this chapter cover the intellectual property known as trade secrets. The first section of the chapter, Part A, defines the meaning of a trade secret under the Uniform Trade Secrets Act (UTSA), the Economic Espionage Act (EEA), and the Restatement of Torts. This section also touches upon the historical context for trade secret protection.

The next section, Part B, discusses civil protection for trade secrets, specifically the protection afforded under the Uniform Trade Secrets Act (UTSA) and the Restatement of Torts. *Learning Curve Toys, Inc. v. Playwood Inc.* describes the application of the UTSA. *DeGiorgio v. Megabyte Int'l, Inc.* and *Buffets, Inc. v. Klinke* examine the three elements of a trade secret necessary for information to qualify for trade secret protection. *E.I. duPont de Nemours & Co. v. Christopher* then provides an example of non-UTSA protection for trade secrets. Finally, defenses to misappropriation and rights against others are discussed.

The last section of the chapter, Part C, covers criminal protection for trade secrets. The section opens with a discussion of federal protection under the Economic Espionage Act (EEA). Continuing on, the section explores the liability arising from actual theft of trade secrets, as illustrated in *United States v. Lange.* Conspiracy to steal trade secrets is then covered in *United States v. Martin.* The section closes with an examination of state protection for trade secrets, as shown in *People v. Pribich,* and a comparison between state and federal trade secret protection.

READINGS

A. INTRODUCTION — WHAT IS A TRADE SECRET?

Trade secrets make up the bulk of intellectual property. Unlike patents, no novelty is required for a trade secret to receive legal protection — though otherwise-patentable technology may be held as a trade secret. Unlike copyrights, the protection extended to trade secrets is not limited to the expression of an idea — though something held as a trade secret may be copyrightable as well. A trade secret may be just about anything, from the formula for a popular soft drink, to the list of customers maintained by a small company.

There are a number of definitions available for what is a trade secret. The Uniform Trade Secret Act (UTSA), which governs civil litigation for trade secret misappropriation in most states, defines a trade secret as:

> "Trade secret" means information, including a formula, pattern, compilation, program device, method, technique, or process, that: (i) derives independent economic value, actual or potential, from not being generally known to, and not being readily ascertainable by proper means by, other persons who can obtain economic value from its disclosure or use, and (ii) is the subject of efforts that are reasonable under the circumstances to maintain its secrecy.

Uniform Trade Secrets Act § 1(4).

The federal Economic Espionage Act (EEA), which creates criminal sanctions for theft of trade secrets, has a slightly different definition of a trade secret:

> The term "trade secret" means all forms and types of financial, business, scientific, technical, economic, or engineering information, including patterns, plans, compilations, program devices, formulas, designs, prototypes, methods, techniques, processes, procedures, programs, or codes, whether tangible or intangible, and whether or how stored, compiled, or memorialized physically, electronically, graphically, photographically, or in writing if –
>
> > (A) the owner thereof has taken reasonable measures to keep such information secret; and
> >
> > (B) the information derives independent economic value, actual or potential, from not being generally known to, and not being readily ascertainable through proper means by, the public.

18 U.S.C. § 1839(3).

Both definitions feature common elements: trade secrets may be nearly any form of information, provided that (1) reasonable measures are taken to keep the information secret; and (2) the information has some economic value, through not being generally known by others.

NOTES & QUESTIONS

1. "Not Being Generally Known To" Whom?

Careful readers will note a slight variation in word choice between the UTSA and EEA definitions: the UTSA protects information that "derives independent economic value, actual or potential, from not being generally known to, and not being readily ascertainable by proper means by, *other persons who can obtain economic value from its disclosure or use*" (emphasis added); meanwhile, the EEA's protection extends to "information [that] derives independent economic value, actual or potential, from not being generally known to, and not being readily ascertainable through proper means by, *the public*" (emphasis added). This slight difference led to several pages of opinion in *U.S. v. Lange*, 312 F.3d 263 (7th Cir. 2002), appearing *infra*, as the court explored the gap between the two phrasings:

> The prosecutor's assumption is that the statutory reference in § 1839(3) to "the public" means the general public — the man in the street. Ordinary people don't have AutoCAD and 60-ton flywheels ready to hand. But is the general public the right benchmark? The statute itself does not give an answer: the word "public" could be preceded implicitly by "general" as the prosecutor supposes, but it also could be preceded implicitly by "educated" or "economically important" or any of many other qualifiers. Once we enter the business of adding words to flesh out the statute — and even the addition of "general" to "public" does this — it usually is best to ask what function the law serves. In criminal cases it also is important to inquire whether the unelaborated text is ambiguous, because if it is the language should be read to prevent surprises. . . .

> A problem with using the general public as the reference group for identifying a trade secret is that many things unknown to the public at large are well known to engineers, scientists, and others whose intellectual property the Economic Espionage Act was enacted to protect. This makes the general public a poor benchmark for separating commercially valuable secrets from obscure (but generally known) information. Suppose that Lange had offered to sell Avogadro's number for $1. Avogadro's number, 6.02×10^{23}, is the number of molecules per mole of gas. It is an important constant, known to chemists since 1909 but not to the general public (or even to all recent graduates of a chemistry class). We can't believe that Avogadro's number could be called a trade secret. Other principles are known without being comprehended. Most people know that $E = mc^2$, but a pop quiz of the general public would reveal that they do not understand what this means or how it can be used productively.

> One might respond that the context of the word "public" addresses this concern. The full text of § 1839(3)(B) is: "the information derives independent economic value, actual or potential, from not being generally known to, and not being readily ascertainable through proper means by, the public". Avogadro's number and other obscure knowledge is not "generally known to" the man in the street but might be deemed "readily ascertainable to" this hypothetical person. It appears in any number of scientific handbooks. Similarly one can visit a library and read Einstein's own discussion of his famous equation. Members of the general public can ascertain even abstruse information, such as Schrödinger's quantum field equation, by consulting people in the know — as high school dropouts can take advantage of obscure legal rules by hiring lawyers. But this approach uses the phrase "readily

available" to treat the "general public" as if it were more technically competent, which poses the question whether it would be better to use a qualifier other than "general" in the first place.

The court decided that, in this particular case, whether it was the "general" public, as opposed to wh`at they call the "economically relevant public" was immaterial to that case, as only scientists or engineers could derive economic benefit from the information at issue in *Lange*.

2. The Restatements

Before the passage of the UTSA, the definition of trade secrets was drawn from the Restatement of Torts (1939) § 757:

> A trade secret may consist of any formula, pattern, device or compilation of information which is used in one's business, and which gives him an opportunity to obtain an advantage over competitors who do not know or use it. It may be a formula for a chemical compound, a process of manufacturing, treating or preserving material, a pattern for a machine or other device, or a list of customers

Many state courts used the Restatement definition for years; several states still do. However, trade secrets as a subject was omitted from the Restatement (Second) of Torts (1978).

In 1995, the American Law Institute released the Restatement (Third) of Unfair Competition, which included trade secrets. This provided another definition of "trade secret":

> A trade secret is any information that can be used in the operation of a business or other enterprise and that is sufficiently valuable and secret to afford an actual or potential economic advantage over others.

Id. at § 39.

3. Historical Note: The Need for Trade Secret Protection

Some scholars follow trade secret protection as far back as the Greek and Roman empires, where a Roman cause of action, *action servi corrupti*, prohibited a slave from stealing the trade secret of his master and giving it to a competitor. Published cases dealing with the misappropriation of trade secret law appear in the early 19th century: an 1837 case from Massachusetts enforced the contractual promise of the seller of a chocolate mill not to disclose his recipe to any one else; an 1851 English case enjoined the manufacture of "Morison's Universal Medicine" by the defendant, who had come by the knowledge in violation of contract and in "breach of trust and confidence". Milton E. Babirak, Jr., *The Virginia Uniform Trade Secret Act: A Critical Summary of the Act and Case Law*, 5 VA. L.J. & TECH. 15 (2000).

B. CIVIL PROTECTION OF TRADE SECRETS

The civil protection of trade secrets is almost entirely a state-level issue. The states may be divided into two categories: those that have adopted the Uniform Trade Secrets Act (UTSA), and those who have not. An overwhelming majority of jurisdictions have adopted the UTSA, either as written or slightly modified, but those jurisdictions that have not are significant.

Also important to civil protection is the question of confidential disclosures: who may you disclose your secrets to, and under what conditions, while still protecting your secret?

The final topics for this section are the defenses against misappropriation, and the rights against other parties that stem from trade secrets.

1. Uniform Trade Secrets Act

a. Introduction

According to the prefatory note to the amended Uniform Trade Secrets Act (1985), the need for a standardized approach to trade secrets grew out of Supreme Court rulings holding that trade secrets are not barred by federal patent or copyright law, continuing technological and economic pressures, and the confused and inconsistent statutes and common law across many jurisdictions. Additionally, the Restatement (Second) of Torts, published in 1978, eliminated the sections that addressed trade secrets, upon which many state courts had relied for consistency.

The National Conference of Commissioners on Uniform State Laws elected to address this need, and released the original version of the Uniform Trade Secrets Act in 1979. An amended version followed in 1985, and has been widely adopted throughout the states. As of the time of writing, 44 states and the District of Columbia have enacted the Uniform Trade Secrets Act, either in the original 1979 form or with the amendments made in 1985. Several prominent jurisdictions have not, including Massachusetts, New York, and Texas.

b. Application of the UTSA

LEARNING CURVE TOYS, INCORPORATED v. PLAYWOOD TOYS, INCORPORATED
United States Court of Appeals for the Seventh Circuit
342 F.3d 714 (2003)

RIPPLE, Circuit Judge.

PlayWood Toys, Inc. ("PlayWood") obtained a jury verdict against Learning Curve Toys, Inc. and its representatives, Roy Wilson, Harry Abraham and John Lee (collectively, "Learning Curve"), for misappropriation of a trade secret in a realistic looking and sounding toy railroad track under the Illinois Trade Secrets Act, 765 ILCS 1065/1 et seq. The jury awarded PlayWood a royalty of "8% for a license that would have been negotiated [absent the misappropriation] to last for the lifetime of the product." Although there was substantial evidence of misappropriation before the jury, the district court did not enter judgment on the jury's verdict. Instead, it granted judgment as a matter of law in favor of Learning Curve, holding that PlayWood did not have a protectable trade secret in the toy railroad track. PlayWood appealed.

For the reasons set forth in the following opinion, we reverse the judgment of the district court and reinstate the jury's verdict.

Background

A. Facts

[In 1992, Robert Clausi and his brother-in-law Scott Moore began creating wooden toys under the name PlayWood Toys, Inc., a Canadian Corporation. Not having their own facilities, they contracted with Mario Borsato, who owned a wood-working facility, to manufacture toys based on PlayWood's specifications.

Clausi and Moore attended the New York Toy Fair in February, 1993, where they were approached by Roy Wilson, Learning Curve's toy designer, who explained that Learning Curve had a license to manufacture Thomas the Tank Engine ("Thomas") toys. Wilson liked PlayWood's prototypes, and raised the possibility of working together on the Thomas line. Harry Abraham, Learning Curve's vice president, and John Lee, Learning Curve's president, also stopped by and commented favorably on PlayWood's prototypes. The fair ended with the understanding that Abraham and Wilson would visit PlayWood in several days.]

On February 18, 1993, Abraham and Wilson visited PlayWood in Toronto as planned. The meeting began with a tour of Borsato's woodworking facility, where the prototypes on display at the Toy Fair had been made. After the tour, the parties went to the conference room at Borsato's facility. At this point, according to Clausi and Moore, the parties agreed to make their ensuing discussion confidential. Clausi testified:

> After we sat down in the board room, Harry [Abraham of Learning Curve] immediately said: "Look, we're going to disclose confidential information to you guys, and we're going to disclose some designs that Roy [Wilson of Learning Curve] has that are pretty confidential. If Brio were to get their hands on them, then we wouldn't like that. And we're going to do it under the basis of a confidential understanding."

> And I said: "I also have some things, some ideas on how to produce the track and produce the trains now that I've had a chance to look at them for the last couple of days, and I think they're confidential as well. So if we're both okay with that, we should continue." So we did.

> . . .

The parties' discussion eventually moved away from train production and focused on track design. Wilson showed Clausi and Moore drawings of Learning Curve's track and provided samples of their current product. At this point, Abraham confided to Clausi and Moore that track had posed "a bit of a problem for Learning Curve." Abraham explained that sales were terrific for Learning Curve's Thomas trains, but that sales were abysmal for its track. Abraham attributed the lack of sales to the fact that Learning Curve's track was virtually identical to that of its competitor, Brio, which had the lion's share of the track market. Because there was "no differentiation" between the two brands of track, Learning Curve's track was not even displayed in many of the toy stores that carried Learning Curve's products. Learning Curve had worked unsuccessfully for several months attempting to differentiate its track from that of Brio.

After detailing the problems with Learning Curve's existing track, Abraham inquired of Clausi whether "there was a way to differentiate" its track from Brio's track. Clausi immediately responded that he "had had a chance to look at the track and get a feel for it [over] the last few days" and that his "thoughts were that if the track were more realistic and more functional, that kids would enjoy playing with it more and it would give the retailer a reason to carry the product, especially if it looked different than the Brio track." Clausi further explained that, if the track "made noise and looked like real train tracks, that the stores wouldn't have any problem, and the Thomas the Tank line, product line would have its own different track" and could "effectively compete with Brio." Abraham and Wilson indicated that they were "intrigued" by Clausi's idea and asked him what he meant by "making noise."

Clausi decided to show Abraham and Wilson exactly what he meant. Clausi took a piece of Learning Curve's existing track from the table, drew some lines across the track (about every three-quarters of an inch), and stated: "We can go ahead and machine grooves right across the upper section . . . , which would look like railway tracks, and down below machine little indentations as well so that it would look more like or sound more like real track. You would roll along and bumpity-bumpity as you go along." Clausi then called Borsato into the conference room and asked him to cut grooves into the wood. . . . Based on the sound produced by the track, Clausi told Abraham and Moore that if PlayWood procured a contract with Learning Curve to produce the track, they could call it "Clickety-Clack Track". . . .

[When the meeting ended, Wilson took the piece of track with him. After several more meetings, PlayWood submitted a proposal, which Learning Curve rejected, saying their licensor wanted the Thomas products to be made in the United States.

In early 1994, PlayWood began to focus on the noise-producing track design. In December of 1994, Moore discovered that Learning Curve was marketing noise-producing track under the name "Clickety-Clack Track", very similar to the sample piece of track Wilson had taken from the meeting in February of 1993; Learning Curve was marketing its track as being the greatest recent innovation in wooden trains. Moore and Clausi were stunned.]

PlayWood promptly wrote a cease and desist letter to Learning Curve. The letter accused Learning Curve of stealing PlayWood's concept for the noise-producing track that it disclosed to Learning Curve "in confidence in the context of a manufacturing proposal." Learning Curve responded by seeking a declaratory judgment that it owned the concept.

Previously, on March 16, 1994, Learning Curve had applied for a patent on the noise-producing track. The patent, which was obtained on October 3, 1995, claims the addition of parallel impressions or grooves in the rails, which cause a "clacking" sound to be emitted as train wheels roll over them. The patent identifies Roy Wilson of Learning Curve as the inventor.

Clickety-Clack Track™ provided an enormous boost to Learning Curve's sales. Learning Curve had $20 million in track sales by the first quarter of 2000, and $40 million for combined track and accessory sales.

B. District Court Proceedings

[The case went to trial on PlayWood's claim against Learning Curve, Wilson, Abraham, and Lee, where the jury found for PlayWood. The judge declined to enter judgment for PlayWood.]

The district court granted Learning Curve's motion and entered judgment in its favor on the ground that PlayWood presented insufficient evidence of a trade secret. Specifically, the court determined that PlayWood did not have a trade secret in its concept for noise-producing toy railroad track under Illinois law because: (1) PlayWood did not demonstrate that its concept was unknown in the industry; (2) PlayWood's concept could have been easily acquired or duplicated through proper means; (3) PlayWood failed to guard the secrecy of its concept; (4) PlayWood's concept had no economic value; and (5) PlayWood expended no time, effort or money to develop the concept.

Discussion

A. Trade Secret Status

. . .

The parties agree that their dispute is governed by the Illinois Trade Secrets Act ("Act"), 765 ILCS 1065/1 et seq. To prevail on a claim for misappropriation of a trade secret under the Act, the plaintiff must demonstrate that the information at issue was a trade secret, that it was misappropriated and that it was used in the defendant's business. The issue currently before us is whether there was legally sufficient evidence for the jury to find that PlayWood had a trade secret in its concept for the noise-producing toy railroad track that it revealed to Learning Curve on February 18, 1993.

The Act defines a trade secret as:

> [I]nformation, including but not limited to, technical or non-technical data, a formula, pattern, compilation, program, device, method, technique, drawing, process, financial data, or list of actual or potential customers or suppliers, that:
>
> > (1) is sufficiently secret to derive economic value, actual or potential, from not being generally known to other persons who can obtain economic value from its disclosure or use; and
> >
> > (2) is the subject of efforts that are reasonable under the circumstances to maintain its secrecy or confidentiality.

765 ILCS 1065/2(d). Both of the Act's statutory requirements focus fundamentally on the secrecy of the information sought to be protected. However, the requirements emphasize different aspects of secrecy. The first requirement, that the information be sufficiently secret to impart economic value because of its relative secrecy, "precludes trade secret protection for information generally

known or understood within an industry even if not to the public at large." The second requirement, that the plaintiff take reasonable efforts to maintain the secrecy of the information, prevents a plaintiff who takes no affirmative measures to prevent others from using its proprietary information from obtaining trade secret protection.

Although the Act explicitly defines a trade secret in terms of these two requirements, Illinois courts frequently refer to six common law factors (which are derived from § 757 of the Restatement (First) of Torts) in determining whether a trade secret exists: (1) the extent to which the information is known outside of the plaintiff's business; (2) the extent to which the information is known by employees and others involved in the plaintiff's business; (3) the extent of measures taken by the plaintiff to guard the secrecy of the information; (4) the value of the information to the plaintiff's business and to its competitors; (5) the amount of time, effort and money expended by the plaintiff in developing the information; and (6) the ease or difficulty with which the information could be properly acquired or duplicated by others.

Contrary to Learning Curve's contention, we do not construe the foregoing factors as a six-part test, in which the absence of evidence on any single factor necessarily precludes a finding of trade secret protection. Instead, we interpret the common law factors as instructive guidelines for ascertaining whether a trade secret exists under the Act. The language of the Act itself makes no reference to these factors as independent requirements for trade secret status, and Illinois case law imposes no such requirement that each factor weigh in favor of the plaintiff. . . .

The existence of a trade secret ordinarily is a question of fact. As aptly observed by our colleagues on the Fifth Circuit, a trade secret "is one of the most elusive and difficult concepts in the law to define." In many cases, the existence of a trade secret is not obvious; it requires an ad hoc evaluation of all the surrounding circumstances. For this reason, the question of whether certain information constitutes a trade secret ordinarily is best "resolved by a fact finder after full presentation of evidence from each side." We do not believe that the district court was sufficiently mindful of these principles. The district court, in effect, treated the Restatement factors as requisite elements and substituted its judgment for that of the jury. PlayWood presented sufficient evidence for the jury reasonably to conclude that the Restatement factors weighed in PlayWood's favor.

1. Extent to which PlayWood's concept for noise-producing toy railroad track was known outside of PlayWood's business

PlayWood presented substantial evidence from which the jury could have determined that PlayWood's concept for noise-producing toy railroad track was not generally known outside of Playwood's business. It was undisputed at trial that no similar track was on the market until Learning Curve launched Clickety-Clack Track TM in late 1994, more than a year after PlayWood first conceived of the concept. Of course, as Learning Curve correctly points out, "[m]erely being the first or only one to use particular information does not in and of itself transform otherwise general knowledge into a trade secret." "If it did, the first person to use the information, no matter how ordinary or well known, would be able to appropriate it to his own use under the guise of a trade secret." However, in this case, there was additional evidence from which the jury could have determined that PlayWood's concept was not generally known within the industry.

First, there was substantial testimony that Learning Curve had attempted to differentiate its track from that of its competitors for several months, but that it had been unable to do so successfully.

[PlayWood's expert testified that PlayWood's concept was unique, and differentiated the design from the competition. Additionally, Learning Curve received a patent on the design, which required that it be novel. The court rejected Learning Curve's argument that PlayWood's design was not novel.]

2. Extent to which PlayWood's concept was known to employees and others involved in PlayWood's business

[The court held that this factor favored PlayWood.]

3. Measures taken by PlayWood to guard the secrecy of its concept

There also was sufficient evidence for the jury to determine that PlayWood took reasonable precautions to guard the secrecy of its concept. The Act requires the trade secret owner to take actions that are "reasonable under the circumstances to maintain [the] secrecy or confidentiality" of its trade secret; it does not require perfection. Whether the measures taken by a trade secret owner are sufficient to satisfy the Act's reasonableness standard ordinarily is a question of fact for the jury. Indeed, we previously have recognized that only in an extreme case can what is a 'reasonable' precaution be determined as a matter of law, because the answer depends on a balancing of costs and benefits that will vary from case to case.

Here, the jury was instructed that it must find "by a preponderance of the evidence that PlayWood's trade secrets were given to Learning Curve as a result of a confidential relationship between the parties." By returning a verdict in favor of PlayWood, the jury necessarily found that Learning Curve was bound to PlayWood by a pledge of confidentiality. The jury's determination is amply supported by the evidence. Both Clausi and Moore testified that they entered into an oral confidentiality agreement with Abraham and Wilson before beginning their discussion on February 18, 1993. . . . In addition to this testimony, the jury heard that Learning Curve had disclosed substantial information to PlayWood during the February 18th meeting, including projected volumes, costs and profit margins for various products, as well as drawings for toys not yet released to the public. The jury could have inferred that Learning Curve would not have disclosed such information in the absence of a confidentiality agreement. Finally, the jury also heard (from several of Learning Curve's former business associates) that Learning Curve routinely entered into oral confidentiality agreements like the one with PlayWood.

PlayWood might have done more to protect its secret. As Learning Curve points out, PlayWood gave its only prototype of the noise-producing track to Wilson without first obtaining a receipt or written confidentiality agreement from Learning Curve — a decision that proved unwise in hindsight. Nevertheless, we believe that the jury was entitled to conclude that PlayWood's reliance on the oral confidentiality agreement was reasonable under the circumstances of this case. First, it is well established that "[t]he formation of a confidential relationship imposes upon the disclosee the duty to maintain the information received in the utmost secrecy" and that "the unprivileged use or disclosure of another's trade secret becomes the basis for an action in tort." Second, both Clausi and Moore testified that they believed PlayWood had a realistic chance to "get in the door" with Learning Curve and to produce the concept as part of Learning Curve's line of Thomas products. Clausi and Moore did not anticipate that Learning Curve would violate the oral confidentiality agreement and utilize PlayWood's concept without permission; rather, they believed in good faith that they "were going to do business one day again with Learning Curve with respect to the design concept." Finally, we believe that, as part of the reasonableness inquiry, the jury could have considered the size and sophistication of the parties, as well as the relevant industry. Both PlayWood and Learning Curve were small toy companies, and PlayWood was the smaller and less experienced of the two. Viewing the evidence in the light most favorable to PlayWood, as we must, we conclude that there was sufficient evidence for the jury to determine that PlayWood took reasonable measures to protect the secrecy of its concept.

4. Value of the concept to PlayWood and to its competitors

There was substantial evidence from which the jury could have determined that PlayWood's concept had value both to PlayWood and to its competitors. It was undisputed at trial that Learning Curve's sales skyrocketed after it began to sell Clickety-Clack Track™. In addition, PlayWood's expert witness, Michael Kennedy, testified that PlayWood's concept for noise-producing track had tremendous value. Kennedy testified that the "cross-cuts and changes in the [track's] surface" imparted value to its seller by causing the track to "look different, feel different and sound different than generic track." Kennedy further testified that, in his opinion, the track would have commanded a premium royalty under a negotiated license agreement because the "invention allows its seller to differentiate itself from a host of competitors who are making a generic product with whom it is competing in a way that is proprietary and exclusive, and it gives [the seller] a significant edge over [its] competition."

[The trial court concluded that PlayWood's prototype had no economic value, as it was imperfect: the grooves were too deep to allow the train to roll smoothly. The appellate court rejected that conclusion, as PlayWood's expert testified that contracts in the toy industry were often negotiated using such imperfect prototypes, and the value in PlayWood's prototype was from the idea; the product could be perfected later, as indeed it was.]

It is irrelevant under Illinois law that PlayWood did not actually use the concept in its business. "[T]he proper criterion is not 'actual use' but whether the trade secret is 'of value' to the company."[1] Kennedy's testimony was more than sufficient to permit the jury to conclude that the concept was "of value" to PlayWood. It is equally irrelevant that PlayWood did not seek to patent its concept. So long as the concept remains a secret, i.e., outside of the public domain, there is no need for patent protection. Professor Milgrim makes this point well: "Since every inventor has the right to keep his invention secret, one who has made a patentable invention has the option to maintain it in secrecy, relying upon protection accorded to a trade secret rather than upon the rights which accrue by a patent grant." 1 Roger M. Milgrim, Milgrim on Trade Secrets § 1.08[1], at 1-353 (2002). It was up to PlayWood, not the district court, to determine when and how the concept should have been disclosed to the public.

5.   Amount of time, effort and money expended by PlayWood in developing its concept

PlayWood expended very little time and money developing its concept; by Clausi's own account, the cost to PlayWood was less than one dollar and the time spent was less than one-half hour. The district court determined that "[s]uch an insignificant investment is . . . insufficient as a matter of Illinois law to establish the status of a 'trade secret.' " We believe that the district court gave too much weight to the time, effort and expense of developing the track.

Although Illinois courts commonly look to the Restatement factors for guidance in determining whether a trade secret exists, as we have noted earlier, the requisite statutory inquiries under Illinois law are (1) whether the information "is sufficiently secret to derive economic value, actual or potential, from not being generally known to other persons who can obtain economic value from its disclosure or use;" and (2) whether the information "is the subject of efforts that are reasonable under the circumstances to maintain its secrecy or confidentiality." 765 ILCS 1065/2(d). A significant expenditure of time and/or money in the production of information may provide evidence of value, which is relevant to the first inquiry above. However, we do not understand Illinois law to require such an expenditure in all cases.

As pointed out by the district court, several Illinois cases have emphasized the importance of developmental costs. However, notably, none of those cases concerned the sort of innovative and creative concept that we have in this case. Indeed, several of the cases in Illinois that emphasize developmental costs concern compilations of data, such as customer lists. In that context, it makes sense to require the expenditure of significant time and money because there is nothing original or creative about the alleged trade secret. Given enough time and money, we presume that the plaintiff's competitors could compile a similar list.

---

[1] [FN6] Both the Uniform Trade Secrets Act and the Restatement (Third) of Unfair Competition expressly reject prior use by the person asserting rights in the information as a prerequisite to trade secret protection. See Unif. Trade Secrets Act § 1 cmt. (1990) ("The broader definition in the proposed Act extends protection to a plaintiff who has not yet had an opportunity or acquired the means to put a trade secret to use."); Restatement (Third) of Unfair Competition § 39 cmt. e (1995) ("Use by the person asserting rights in the information is not a prerequisite to protection under the rule stated in this Section," in part, because such a "requirement can deny protection during periods of research and development and is particularly burdensome for innovators who do not possess the capability to exploit their innovations.").

Here, by contrast, we are dealing with a new toy design that has been promoted as "the first significant innovation in track design since the inception of wooden train systems." Toy designers, like many artistic individuals, have intuitive flashes of creativity. Often, that intuitive flash is, in reality, the product of earlier thought and practice in an artistic craft. We fail to see how the value of PlayWood's concept would differ in any respect had Clausi spent several months and several thousand dollars creating the noise-producing track. Accordingly, we conclude that PlayWood's lack of proof on this factor does not preclude the existence of a trade secret.

6. Ease or difficulty with which PlayWood's concept could have been properly acquired or duplicated by others

Finally, we also believe that there was sufficient evidence for the jury to determine that PlayWood's concept could not have been easily acquired or duplicated through proper means. PlayWood's expert witness, Michael Kennedy, testified: "This is a fairly simple product if you look at it. But the truth is that because it delivers feeling and sound as well as appearance, it isn't so simple as it first appears. It's a little more elegant, actually, than you might think." In addition to Kennedy's testimony, the jury heard that Learning Curve had spent months attempting to differentiate its track from Brio's before Clausi disclosed PlayWood's concept of noise-producing track. From this evidence, the jury could have inferred that, if PlayWood's concept really was obvious, Learning Curve would have thought of it earlier.

[The trial court concluded that PlayWood's design was not a trade secret, because as soon as it appeared on the market, it could have been easily reverse engineered and duplicated, destroying any trade secret protection. The appellate court agreed that it may be easy to reverse engineer, but at the time the track was disclosed confidentially to Learning Curve, it had not been disclosed to the public, and so was still secret.]

. . .

Conclusion

For the foregoing reasons, the judgment of the district court is reversed, and the jury's verdict is reinstated. The case is remanded to the district court for a jury trial on exemplary damages and for consideration of attorneys' fees by the court. PlayWood may recover its costs in this court.

MANGREN RESEARCH AND DEVELOPMENT CORPORATION v. NATIONAL CHEMICAL COMPANY, INCORPORATED
United States Court of Appeals for the Seventh Circuit
87 F.3d 937 (1996)

ILANA DIAMOND ROVNER, Circuit Judge.

[This case was a diversity action, brought under the Illinois Trade Secrets Act (ITSA). Mangren contended that the defendants misappropriated its trade secrets in the course of developing and marketing a competing mold release agent. At trial, the jury found for Mangren, awarding $252,684.69 in compensatory damages and $505,369.38 in exemplary damages, to which the court added Mangren's attorneys' fees and costs. Defendants contend that Mangren did not have any protectable trade secrets, or that defendants did not misappropriate any secrets.]

I.

A.

Mangren's story is one of a grass-roots operation that made good. The company was founded in 1974 by Ted Blackman and Peter Lagergren while they were chemistry students at the University of Texas. Mangren initially manufactured dog shampoo and industrial cleaners and solvents in a garage that belonged to Blackman's father-in-law. Eventually, however, the company began to produce mold release agents. Rubber and plastics manufacturers apply such agents to the molds and presses they use in the manufacturing process. Typically, the end-product is formed by filling a mold or press with a liquefied rubber or plastic and then heating, which causes the liquid to solidify and to take the shape of the vessel containing it. The mold release agent is designed to prevent the solidifying substance from sticking to the mold during this process.

[In the mid-1970's, at the request of Masonite, a major consumer of mold release agents, Mangren began development of a mold release agent; after eighteen months of study, they found a chemical that suited their needs in a particular type of polytetrafluoroethylene ("PTFE"). This type of PTFE had three essential characteristics: (1) it was highly degraded; (2) it had a low molecular weight; and (3) it had low tensile strength. At the time of this discovery, PTFE was never used as the primary component of a mold release agent. Mangren's first product made use of TL-102, a PTFE; Masonite approved the product after much testing. The agent was cheap to produce, but so valuable that Mangren was able to price it high and earn a considerable profit.]

Having had considerable success selling to Masonite, Mangren decided to market its product to others as well. It first compiled a list of companies that produced molded rubber and plastic products. Yet, because not all of those manufacturers would have the equipment necessary to use Mangren's mold release agent, the company contacted each one individually, explaining its product and the equipment needed to use it. In this way, Mangren developed a list of potential customers, but only after devoting a considerable amount of time and effort to the project.

Even as its sales grew, Mangren remained a small company, never having more than six employees at any one time. Because its success depended on the uniqueness of its mold release agent, Mangren took a number of steps to ensure that its formula remained secret. First, all employees were required to sign a confidentiality agreement, and non-employees were not permitted in the company's laboratory. Once chemical ingredients were delivered to the company's premises, moreover, the labels identifying those ingredients were removed and replaced with coded labels understood only by Mangren employees. The company's financial and other records also referred to ingredients only by their code names.

B.

The seeds of the present lawsuit were planted when Mangren made two ill-fated hiring decisions in the 1980s. First, it hired Rhonda Allen in 1986 to be its office manager. Eventually, however, Allen became Mangren's sales manager, a position that provided her access to Mangren's customers and its pricing policies. In 1988, Mangren hired Larry Venable, an organic chemist, to help Blackman develop a chromium-free mold release agent. Although Venable did not have prior experience with PTFE-based mold release agents, he and Blackman succeeded in developing a chromium-free product that also used a highly degraded PTFE with low molecular weight and low tensile strength.

For reasons not relevant here, Mangren terminated the employment of Allen and Venable in 1989. After holding two intervening jobs, Venable met William Lerch early in 1990. Lerch had recently incorporated defendant National Chemical Company, Inc. ("National Chemical"), which was but one of a number of companies he then owned. Venable told Lerch about his Mangren experience and about an idea he had for developing a mold release agent to be used in the rubber industry. Lerch was excited about the prospect and inquired about the market for such a product. Venable responded that Masonite was a large user and therefore a potential customer.

The two discussed the possibility that they might be sued by Mangren if they developed a competing mold release agent. Venable was especially concerned because he realized that any product he could develop would be similar to Mangren's mold release agent. He knew, for example, that a mold release agent using TL–102 — the PTFE that Mangren used — would be "potentially troublesome" and probably would prompt a lawsuit. Lerch told Venable not to worry about a misappropriation suit and explained that he had once been accused of trade secret infringement but had won the case by changing one ingredient or proportion of ingredients in creating his product. Lerch laughed and said the same thing would happen here. Shortly thereafter, Lerch and Venable incorporated defendant National Mold Release Company to manufacture the mold release agent that National Chemical would sell.

[Venable developed a mold release agent, mostly using a PTFE designated as TL–10, though he occasionally used TL–102 as well. Venable also recommended that Lerch hire Allen to market the product, and Allen was hired as a vice president and placed in charge of developing a customer base. Allen approached Mangren customers she was familiar with from her time there with news of the new product and a slightly lower price than Mangren's. Masonite in particular was interested and purchased the product after some testing.]

Venable and Allen left defendants in April 1991. Venable began to work as a consultant for Bash Corporation ("Bash"), a Chicago-based construction supply company. Venable provided Bash with a mold release agent formula that was substantially derived from defendants' formula. Allen, whom Bash had hired on Venable's recommendation, then presented Bash's product to Masonite as the same high quality product she had sold on behalf of National Chemical. Indeed, in a letter notifying Masonite of her association with Bash, Allen represented that:

> This change will not affect Masonite in any way, except for the better. You can still expect the same quality coatings and service I have provided you with in the past. . . . The only change will be in my company name and address. Even the names of the coatings will not change.

Because of its similarity to defendants' mold release agent, Bash was quickly able to qualify its product for use at Masonite and to begin selling to that company. Early in 1992, however, Bash went out of business, prompting Allen to incorporate Bash Chemical Corporation ("Bash Chemical") in Texas. That company then continued to manufacture and market the same mold release agent previously sold by the Illinois-based Bash.

. . .

II.

. . .

A.

Under the ITSA, the term "trade secret" means

> information, including but not limited to, technical or non-technical data, a formula, pattern, compilation, program, device, method, technique, drawing, process, financial data, or list of actual or potential customers or suppliers, that:
>
> > (1) is sufficiently secret to derive economic value, actual or potential, from not being generally known to other persons who can obtain economic value from its disclosure; and
> >
> > (2) is the subject of efforts that are reasonable under the circumstances to maintain its secrecy or confidentiality.

This definition codifies two requirements for trade secret protection that had developed under the state's common law, both of which focus on the secrecy of the information sought to be protected. Defendants argue that Mangren failed to establish either element here.

Under the first statutory requirement, the information at issue "must be sufficiently secret to impart economic value to both its owner and its competitors because of its relative secrecy." This requirement precludes trade secret protection for information generally known within an industry even if not to the public at large. A plaintiff like Mangren must prove that the real value of the information "lies in the fact that it is not generally known to others who could benefit [from] using it." The evidence in this case presents a textbook example of information satisfying this requirement.

When Mangren first embarked on its mission to develop for Masonite a more effective mold release agent, Masonite was purchasing a product from DuPont that employed a flurotelemer as its primary ingredient. After eighteen months of intensive research and testing, Blackman and Lagergren found that a particular type of PTFE (one that was highly degraded and that had a low molecular weight and low tensile strength) would make their mold release agent more effective and less expensive than that of DuPont. When they made this discovery, the prevailing view was that such a PTFE was unsuited for the type of application that Blackman and Lagergren envisioned. Thus, Mangren was the first to successfully use this particular type of PTFE in a mold release agent. Although defendants are quick to point out that "[m]erely being the first or only one to use particular information does not in and of itself transform otherwise general knowledge into a trade secret", there was sufficient evidence for the jury to conclude that Mangren was not using general knowledge at all. A reasonable jury could find instead that Mangren had developed a distinctive formula based on information not generally known or accepted within the industry.

Mangren proved, moreover, that secrecy imparted considerable economic value to its new formula. Although its mold release agent was relatively inexpensive to produce, Mangren was able to exact a substantial price because of the product's value to the customers who used it. Masonite, in fact, attempted to find another supplier and even to develop its own mold release agent at one point, but was unable to find or to develop an equally effective product. Mangren, then, clearly satisfied the first of the statute's two requirements for a trade secret.

Defendants nonetheless contend that Mangren did not satisfy the second, as it did not make a reasonable effort to maintain the secrecy of its formula. They argue, for example, that all of Mangren's employees (of which there were never more than six at a time) knew Mangren's formula, that an observer of Mangren's premises could identify the formula's ingredients because Mangren did not replace existing labels with coded labels until ingredients had been delivered, and that Mangren could not produce signed agreements from Venable or Allen promising to maintain the confidentiality of its formula.

Arrayed against these purported deficiencies, however, is considerable evidence that the company made substantial efforts to protect the secrecy of its formula. Although Mangren was unable to produce confidentiality agreements for Venable and Allen, it presented to the jury signed agreements for other Mangren employees. Blackman testified, moreover, that each employee (including Venable and Allen) was required to sign a confidentiality agreement and that employees were further advised of the secret status of the company's mold release agent formula. Lagergren added that only Mangren employees were permitted in the company's laboratory. Mangren also demonstrated that it regularly replaced identifying labels with coded labels once ingredients were delivered to its premises. Those ingredients were then referred to in Mangren's financial and other records only by their code names. Even if Mangren could have taken further protective measures just in case, as defendants suggest, a devious potential competitor were to stake out its premises and attempt to identify the chemicals delivered there, whether or not the actions Mangren actually took were sufficient to satisfy the ITSA's reasonableness standard was a question for the jury. The evidence was certainly sufficient to enable reasonable jurors to conclude that Mangren made ample efforts to maintain the secrecy of its formula.

B.

Having determined that Mangren established a protectable trade secret in its mold release agent formula, we turn to the question of misappropriation. The ITSA defines a "misappropriation" in pertinent part as follows:

> [D]isclosure or use of a trade secret of a person without express or implied consent by another person who:
>
> . . .
>
> (B) at the time of disclosure or use, knew or had reason to know that knowledge of the trade secret was:
>
>> (I) derived from or through a person who utilized improper means to acquire it:
>>
>> (II) acquired under circumstances giving rise to a duty to maintain its secrecy or limit its use; or
>>
>> (III) derived from or through a person who owed a duty to the person seeking relief to maintain its secrecy or limit its use. . . .

Defendants argue that they did not "use" Mangren's trade secret under this definition because their mold release agent formula is not the same as Mangren's. Although they concede that the primary ingredient of their formula is also a highly degraded PTFE with a low molecular weight and low tensile strength, defendants emphasize that many of the other ingredients are different. Furthermore, the specific PTFE used in defendants' product is typically not the same as the one used by Mangren, although its essential characteristics are identical. Finally, defendants use a slightly smaller volume of PTFE in their mold release agent — twenty as opposed to twenty-three percent in Mangren's product. These differences, in defendants' view, should have precluded the jury from finding that they misappropriated Mangren's formula.

Defendants' argument, however, is inconsistent even with the jury instruction to which they agreed below. The jury was instructed that:

> In order for you to find that defendants misappropriated one of Mangren's trade secrets, you do not have to find that defendants copied or used each and every element of the trade secret. You may find that defendants misappropriated Mangren's trade secrets even if defendants created a new product if defendants could not have done so without use of Mangren's trade secret.

That instruction, as defendants apparently conceded below, is consistent with traditional trade secret law. We observed in *In re Innovative Constr. Sys.*, Inc., 793 F.2d 875, 887 (7th Cir. 1986), for example, that "the user of another's trade secret is liable even if he uses it with modifications or improvements upon it effected by his own efforts, so long as the substance of the process used by the actor is derived from the other's secret." Although that decision involved Wisconsin law, the law of Illinois is in accord. We have observed before, in fact, that if trade secret law were not flexible enough to encompass modified or even new products that are substantially derived from the trade secret of another, the protections that law provides would be hollow indeed.

Mangren emphasizes, moreover, that the trade secret misappropriated here was not necessarily its overall formula, but the essential secret ingredient — a highly degraded PTFE having a low molecular weight and low tensile strength, which had previously been considered unsuitable for such an application.[2] Defendants do not contest that they use a similar PTFE in their mold release agent and that it was Venable, the former Mangren employee, who revealed to them that such a PTFE could be used effectively. Once Venable let defendants in on the secret and defendants then used that secret to develop their own product, there plainly was a misappropriation even if defendants' product was not identical to Mangren's. In other words, reasonable jurors could conclude from the evidence in this case that defendants' mold release agent was substantially derived from Mangren's trade secret, for defendants could not have produced their product without using that secret. Defendants were not therefore entitled to judgment as a matter of law or to a new trial on the trade secret and misappropriation issues.

. . .

IV.

Because the trial evidence amply supports the jury's verdict, the district court properly denied defendants' renewed motion for judgment as a matter of law or for a new trial. The district court's judgment is therefore

Affirmed.

---

[2] [FN4] In their reply brief and again at oral argument, defendants stridently attacked this characterization of the trade secret:

> Mangren's argument seems to be that no one (at least not Venable, Allen or defendants) may ever use a PTFE similar to the one used by Mangren in its mold release formula. Mangren says this notwithstanding the fact that Blackman himself testified that Mangren used at least three different PTFEs which have the necessary characteristics for the mold release Mangren produced, and that there are dozens more of such PTFEs commercially available. If one is to take Mangren's argument literally, no one can ever use a highly degraded, low molecular weight, low tensile strength PTFE in a mold release agent without violating Mangren's alleged trade secret. Although such a conclusion makes bad law as well as bad sense, it is where Mangren's argument necessarily leads.

This hyperbolic argument misses the mark. Mangren has never suggested that because it was the first to develop a PTFE-based mold release agent, it has the exclusive right to produce and market such a product — as if it held a patent on the product, for example. Mangren would certainly have no claim for misappropriation if another company, after months of independent research and testing, developed a mold release agent using a similar PTFE. Under that scenario, of course, there would be no misappropriation at all because our hypothetical company would have developed its product in the same way that Mangren did — through its own ingenuity. But if, as Mangren proved to the jury's satisfaction in this case, the other company markets a PTFE-based mold release agent that it developed not through independent research and testing, but by using Mangren's trade secret, there was a misappropriation for which the law provides a remedy. That conclusion, which is actually where Mangren's argument leads, makes neither bad law nor bad sense.

NOTES & QUESTIONS

1. When Does a Claim Arise?

In *Cadence Design Systems, Inc. v. Avant! Corp.*, 253 F.3d 1147 (9th Cir. 2001), the Ninth Circuit certified the following question to be answered by the California Supreme Court:

Under the California Uniform Trade Secrets Act ("UTSA"), when does a claim for trade secret infringement arise: only once, when the initial misappropriation occurs, or with each subsequent misuse of the trade secret?

At issue was an earlier settlement between Cadence and Avant!, wherein Avant! was released from all liability for any then-existing causes of action. Avant! continued to use Cadence's trade secret after this settlement, and Cadence argued that the continual use created new causes of action.

The California Supreme Court responded that continued use of misappropriated trade secrets was part of a single claim, arising at the time of initial misappropriation. *See Cadence Design Systems, Inc. v. Avant! Corp.*, 127 Cal. Rptr. 2d 169 (2002).

2. Application of the UTSA: Interpretive Force of the Restatement

Before the release of the UTSA, the definition of a trade secret in the Restatement of Torts § 757, comment b (1939), was the sole uniformly recognized definition for a trade secret. Today, the UTSA has received wide spread adoption and all but a handful of states have adopted UTSA. Despite the UTSA's popular acceptance, the definition of the Restatement of Torts § 757 still has application, even in UTSA states. Courts often give weight to the old Restatement definition and refer to it to when applying the UTSA.

c. Elements of Trade Secrets

Trade secrets, under most definitions, consist of (i) information (ii) which is valuable through not being generally known to others (iii) which the holder has tried to keep secret.

i. Information

As noted by the UTSA definition, what "information" can make up a trade secret is an open-ended question: there is a wide range to be covered between designs for toys (*Learning Curve*) and chemical formulae (*Mangren*). One fairly common trade secret is the customer list.

DEGIORGIO v. MEGABYTE INTERNATIONAL, INC.
Supreme Court of Georgia
266 Ga. 539 (1996)

CARLEY, Justice.

[Megabyte is a distributor of computer hardware components. DeGiorgio was a salesman for Megabyte for several months before leaving to join

American Megabyte Distributors, Inc. (AMDI), a newly formed competitor. At trial, Megabyte produced evidence that their customer and vendor lists, entrusted to DeGiorgio, had been faxed to AMDI's president by DeGiorgio. Megabyte was granted an interlocutory injunction by the trial court, and DeGiorgio and AMDI appealed.]

. . .

2. Appellants further contend that the lists were not trade secrets which could support a grant of interlocutory injunctive relief under the Georgia Trade Secrets Act.

The lists at issue contained the identities of actual customers and vendors of Megabyte and specific information concerning them. Thus, the information on the lists was not readily ascertainable from any source other than Megabyte's business records. "Such a source would be improper if [Megabyte] had made a reasonable effort to maintain the secrecy of those customer [and vendor] lists." A review of the record reveals evidence from which the trial court could have found that Megabyte had made such a reasonable effort to maintain the secrecy of the customer and vendor lists which the trial court determined to be trade secrets. Accordingly, the trial court did not abuse its discretion in granting an interlocutory injunction under the Trade Secrets Act.

[The court then found that the injunction put in place by the trial court was overly broad, and reversed that portion of the lower court's holding, before remanding the case.]

ii. Value Through Secrecy

It is not enough that information be valuable; in order to qualify as a trade secret, the value must be derived through the secrecy of the information. Information that is widely known, or easily discoverable, is not protectable.

BUFFETS, INC. v. KLINKE
United States Court of Appeals for the Ninth Circuit
73 F.3d 965 (1996)

D.W. NELSON, Circuit Judge:

[Buffets Inc., doing business as Old Country Buffets (OCB), filed a complaint against the Klinkes for misappropriation of OCB's recipes and training manual, which OCB claimed as trade secrets. The district court, following a bench trial, entered judgment for the Klinkes.

Buffets, Inc. operates the nationwide chain of Old Country Buffet restaurants, serving all-you-can-eat food cafeteria-style for a fixed price. Dennis Scott, one of the founders of OCB, developed the menus and instituted the practice of "small batch cooking", which helps ensure freshness by only preparing small quantities at a time. Scott was an experience restaurateur, and adapted many of the recipes he was familiar with for this use. In 1989, Scott founded a new company, Evergreen Buffets, which began opening OCB restaurants. Scott's partner, Joel Brown, hired Mark Miller to work at one restaurant; Miller was later fired for alleged financial improprieties.]

In 1990, Scott met the Appellees Klinkes and gave them a tour of one of the OCB restaurants. The Klinkes were themselves successful restaurateurs, having operated a number of franchise restaurants for over 40 years. The Klinkes asked if they could buy an OCB franchise, but were told that OCB was not franchising. Paul Klinke, who was acquainted with Miller, later arranged for one of his former employees, Jack Bickle, to begin working at one of the OCB restaurants.

In March 1991, Scott, who had by now left OCB, again met with the Klinkes and told them that Miller might assist them in opening a buffet restaurant. Paul Klinke contacted Miller and Miller began working with him in April of 1991. Moreover, on March 19, 1991, Paul Klinke had dinner with Bickle and asked Bickle to provide him with OCB recipes and to get his son, Greg, a job as a cook at one of the OCB stores. Paul offered Bickle $60.00, but Bickle refused both the money and the opportunity to perform those services.

Between March 19, 1991 and April 2, 1991, Greg Klinke and Miller discussed the possibility of Greg's obtaining work at one of the OCB restaurants. On April 2, Greg applied for a job as a cook. On his application, however, he did not disclose either his true residence or his experience as a cook working for his parents. Nor did he reveal the fact that he was still on his parents' payroll.

That summer, Miller asked one of Scott's former administrative assistants to help him compile an employee's manual. Miller provided the bulk of the material for the manuals; the district court found that the new manuals were "almost exact copies of OCB position manuals." In August, Miller gave a licensed transcriber a box of recipes to retype and subsequently delivered to the Klinkes what the district court described as the "OCB recipes." The district court found that when the Klinkes first opened their buffet restaurant, Granny's, they used the copied position manuals to train their employees and the OCB recipes to prepare their dishes. . . After a bench trial, it held that neither the recipes nor the job manuals were trade secrets.

. . .

DISCUSSION

I.   TRADE SECRET STATUS OF THE RECIPES

[Washington defines a trade secret as] "information, including a formula, pattern, compilation, program, device, method, technique or process that:

(a) Derives independent economic value, actual or potential, from not being generally known to, and not being readily ascertainable by proper means by, other persons who can obtain economic value from its disclosure or use; and

(b) Is the subject of efforts that are reasonable under the circumstances to maintain its secrecy."

[T]he Washington Supreme Court makes the important distinction between copyright law and trade secrets law, noting that "[c]opyright does not protect an idea itself, only its particular expression. . . . By contrast, trade secrets law protects the author's very ideas if they possess some novelty and are undisclosed or disclosed only on the basis of confidentiality." OCB argues that novelty is not a requirement for trade secret protection; this contention, however, clearly contradicts Washington law. Moreover, contrary to OCB's assertions, the district court's finding that the recipes were more detailed than those of its competitors does not mandate a finding of novelty, for as is discussed below, the court held that even these detailed procedures were readily ascertainable.

Many of OCB's remaining arguments on appeal appear to misunderstand the logic of the district court's opinion. The district court did not hold, as OCB contends, that the recipes were not trade secrets merely because they had their origins in the public domain, but also because many of them were "basic American dishes that are served in buffets across the United States." This finding was certainly not erroneous. The recipes were for such American staples as BBQ chicken and macaroni and cheese and the procedures, while detailed, are undeniably obvious. Thus, this is not a case where material from the public domain has been refashioned or recreated in such a way so as to be an original product, but is rather an instance where the end-product is itself unoriginal.

Furthermore, OCB mischaracterizes the court's holding regarding the extent to which the recipes were readily ascertainable, suggesting that the court denied the recipes trade secret status merely because they could be reproduced. While this is not altogether incorrect, it was the reason that the recipes could be reproduced — namely, because they were little more than typical American fare — that led the court to conclude that they were readily ascertainable and thus not entitled to trade secret protection. There is thus no indication that the "defendant by an expenditure of effort might have collected the same information from sources available to the public."; rather, the alleged secrets here at issue were found to be so obvious that very little effort would be required to "discover" them.

OCB's contention that material may be protected by trade secret law even if its origins are in the public domain is thus irrelevant. Not only did the district court hold that the recipes and their procedures had their origins in well-known American cuisine, but it also maintained that in spite of their alleged innovative detail, they "[were] fairly basic" and could easily be discovered by others. A trade secrets plaintiff need not prove that every element of an information compilation is unavailable elsewhere. Trade secrets frequently contain elements that by themselves may be in the public domain but together qualify as trade secrets. The district court here found that the recipes themselves, and not merely their different components or any earlier formulations from which they may have been derived, were readily ascertainable.

The district court further held that the recipes had no independent economic value, a finding OCB fails to address adequately on appeal. OCB's argument focuses only on that portion of the district court's opinion that held that the recipes had no independent value because OCB had not proven that its food offerings were "superior in quality to that of its rivals." This, however, was not the sole basis for the court's holding. The court held that even though OCB food tasted better than that of its rivals and few of its rivals were succeeding, "OCB [had] failed to establish by a preponderance of the evidence that its rivals [were] not succeeding because of inferior food quality." The court thus notes that there was no demonstrated relationship between the lack of success of OCB's competitors and the unavailability of the recipes, i.e., OCB failed to provide that it necessarily derived any benefit from the recipes being kept secret. The court also noted that "limiting food costs is crucial to the profitability of a buffet" and explained that OCB failed to demonstrate that its recipes play a role in limiting costs.

Further weighing against any finding of economic value was the court's finding that OCB's recipes had to be simplified because of the limited reading skills of its cooks. Given this fact, it appears unlikely that the recipes themselves conferred any economic benefit upon OCB because it was from "translated" versions of these recipes, rather than the highly detailed versions now at issue, that OCB cooks prepared its well-celebrated food.

. . .

NOTES & QUESTIONS

1. What is Generally Known?

One issue that frequently arises in trade secrets cases is that of what is "generally known" by others, and what is therefore incapable of being "secret". In the *Buffets, Inc.* case, the trial court determined that recipes for such basic American staples as BBQ chicken and macaroni and cheese were generally known, and could not, therefore, be secret. But what about other information, such as a customer list for a particular product? One California court created an illustrative example of the problem:

> By way of illustration, consider a hypothetical market for widgets, supplied by five widget sellers. There are 100,000 businesses engaged in industries which have been known to use widgets in their operations; however, there is no way for the widget sellers to know for sure which of those individual businesses use widgets and which do not. Seller A has a list of 500 businesses to which he has sold widgets in the recent past. That list proves a fact which is unknown to his competitors: that those 500 businesses are consumers of widgets, the product they are trying to sell. Therefore, it has independent value to those competitors, because it would allow them to distinguish those proven consumers, who are definitely part of the widget market, from the balance of the 100,000 potential consumers, who may or may not be part of the market. With that list, they would know to target their sales efforts on those 500 businesses, rather than on 500 other businesses that might never use widgets.

> Now imagine the same facts, but assume that each of the other four sellers of widgets knows that the businesses on Seller A's customer list are proven widget consumers (although they do not know that those businesses buy their widgets from Seller A). Under those circumstances,

Seller A's customer list has no independent economic value, because the identities of those consumers are already known to his competitors.

In both situations, the identities of the businesses which bought widgets from Seller A are unknown. The distinguishing factor is whether it is also unknown that those businesses bought widgets at all. Thus, the customer list in the first hypothetical would be a protectable trade secret, while the list in the second hypothetical would not be.

Abba Rubber Co. v. Seaquist, 235 Cal. App. 3d 1 (App. Dist. 4, 1991).

2. Combination Trade Secret

Typically, information that is commonly known cannot qualify for trade secret protection. But what if the subject matter of an asserted trade secret is a combination of otherwise well-known principles? What if the elements of the asserted trade secret are available in the technical literature? Do you believe trade secret protection can be extended to a combination of otherwise commonly known facts?

In *Heyden Chemical Corp. v. Burrell & Neidig, Inc.,* the plaintiff chemical manufacturer claimed its processes of manufacturing formaldehyde and pentaerythritol as trade secrets. The court agreed that the processes were trade secrets:

Defendants say that the Heyden processes are not secret. The claim is that they have been known to the trade for years and are, in fact, in the public domain. In support of this assertion there were offered in evidence various essays, treatises and patents dealing with the manufacture of formaldehyde and pentaerythritol. In my opinion, these exhibits served to strengthen the plaintiff's claim. According to the testimony, there are to be found in the scientific literature some 800 to 1,000 references dealing with the production of formaldehyde and 500 to 600 references dealing with the production of pentaerythritol. Of the references on the subject of formaldehyde about 30 were offered in evidence. A like number dealing with pentaerythritol were introduced. In every one of the exhibits the systems discussed differed in major particulars from those used by Heyden. In some even the ingredients used were different. But regardless of how different the process described might be, if it contained a single element to be found in the Heyden system, the exhibit was offered to show a public disclosure of the Heyden process. Time and again while being examined on a particular exhibit, the witness would be asked to explain why an engineer, unfamiliar with the Heyden process, in setting up a formaldehyde or pentaerythritol plant, would select one element of the process described in the reference and discard the rest. A satisfactory answer to the question was never given.

The truth is, of course, that only a person who knew the Heyden process could make the selection of literature references which were offered in evidence. Dr. Elderfield of Columbia University, who appeared as an expert for the plaintiff and who was referred to as one of the leading authorities on organic chemistry, testified flatly that an engineer unfamiliar with the Heyden system could not duplicate that system by using the information contained in the literature without long and expensive research and experimentation.

Heyden Chem. Corp. v. Burrell & Neidig, Inc., 64 A.2d 465, 467 (1949).

iii. Reasonable Efforts Of Protection

Concurrent with the requirement of secrecy is the requirement that the user of a trade secret take reasonable efforts to maintain that secrecy. This can be accomplished through a combination of methods: in *Learning Curve*, PlayWood relied on confidentiality agreements with their outside contractor, as well as the small size of the company, to keep secret information secret; in *Mangren*, confidentiality agreements were paired with technological and physical protections, through the use of locked doors and coded ingredients. In both cases, the courts were satisfied by the efforts involved.

The *Buffets, Inc.* case continues:

II. TRADE SECRET STATUS OF THE JOB MANUALS

The district court held that the job manuals were not trade secrets as they were not the subject of reasonable efforts to maintain their secrecy. Commenting upon OCB's security measures, the court observed that "[g]iven the limited tenure of buffet employees, and the fact that they often move from restaurant to restaurant, a company which allows its employees to keep job position manuals cannot be heard to complain when its manuals fall into the hands of its rivals."

We see no error in the district court's ruling. In *Machen Inc. v. Aircraft Design, Inc.*, 65 Wash.App. 319, 828 P.2d 73 (1992), the Washington Court of Appeals cited the Uniform Trade Secrets Act for the proposition that "[r]easonable efforts to maintain secrecy have been held to include advising employees of the existence of a trade secret, limiting access to a trade secret on a 'need to know basis', and controlling plant access." The *Machen* court also notes that "general [protective] measures" may not be enough if they are not "designed to protect the disclosure of information." In this matter, the district court's finding that employees were allowed to take the job manuals home and keep them even though they were "supposed to be kept in the manager's office when not being used," directly addresses the reasonableness of OCB's security measures. Even if the manuals were loaned only on a "need-to-know" basis, as OCB claims, the fact that employees were advised of neither the manuals' status as secrets, nor of security measures that should be taken to prevent their being obtained by others, suggests that OCB's interest in security was minimal.

. . .

Finally, OCB argues that since the Klinkes illegally obtained the manuals, the question of whether the security measures taken to protect them were reasonable is irrelevant. This argument, however, misses the mark, as the issue of whether security measures were reasonable pertains to the preliminary question of whether the material is in fact a trade secret. If it is not, then the Klinkes may be liable for stealing something, but they cannot be liable for misappropriation of trade secrets. . . . Thus, we affirm the court's finding that the manuals were not trade secrets.

The judgment of the district court is AFFIRMED.

NOTES & QUESTIONS

1. Protecting Confidential Information

As is discussed later in the chapter, who you disclose your claimed trade secret to may have a significant impact on what protection you may have. In *Buffets, Inc.* the "secret" manual was available to all employees, and could be taken home if desired, a situation which the court held to be incompatible with any claim of secrecy.

In *Learning Curve*, PlayWood provided their "secret" design to Learning Curve, but under conditions that created a confidential relationship.

A similar situation arose in *Camp Creek Hospitality Inns, Inc. v. Sheraton Franchise Corporation, ITT*, 139 F.3d 1396 (11th Cir. 1998), where Camp Creek, operating a Sheraton franchise, provided secret marketing data to Sheraton Franchise under assurances from a representative that the data would be "kept in strict confidence". *Id.* at 1411. As such, the court found that Camp Creek had taken sufficient care with their information to allow them to proceed on their claims of misappropriation, when Sheraton Franchise provided the information to a competitor.

2. How Much Effort?

Courts require trade secret owners to take "reasonable" efforts to protect the secrecy of a trade secret. In the determination of what effort is "reasonable", courts consider the entirety of circumstances surrounding the owner's use of the trade secret. Often, trade secret owners must show that protective measures were taken to the extent possible under the circumstances.

Interestingly, the greater the extent to which a trade secret owner uses measures to protect his information, the more likely a court will conclude that the information is a trade secret. Efforts to maintain the secrecy of information are probative of the trade secret status of the information itself. Of course, even an extreme amount of protection cannot transform information that is in the public domain into a trade secret.

2. Non-UTSA Jurisdictions

As noted previously, a number of prominent jurisdictions have not enacted the Uniform Trade Secrets Act. In those states, which include Texas, Massachusetts, and New York, the courts often rely on common law factors, such as those considered by the Seventh Circuit in *Learning Curve, supra*. Most of the common law developed, in turn, from the Restatement of Torts (1939) definition.

E.I. DUPONT DENEMOURS & COMPANY, INC. v. CHRISTOPHER
United States Court of Appeals for the Fifth Circuit
431 F.2d 1012 (1970)

GOLDBERG, Circuit Judge:

This is a case of industrial espionage in which an airplane is the cloak and a camera the dagger. The defendants-appellants, Rolfe and Gary Christopher, are photographers in Beaumont, Texas. The Christophers were hired by an unknown third party to take aerial photographs of new construction at the Beaumont plant of E. I. duPont deNemours & Company, Inc. Sixteen photographs of the DuPont facility were taken from the air on March 19, 1969, and these photographs were later developed and delivered to the third party.

DuPont employees apparently noticed the airplane on March 19 and immediately began an investigation to determine why the craft was circling over the plant. By that afternoon the investigation had disclosed that the craft was involved in a photographic expedition and that the Christophers were the photographers. DuPont contacted the Christophers that same afternoon and asked them to reveal the name of the person or corporation requesting the photographs. The Christophers refused to disclose this information, giving as their reason the client's desire to remain anonymous.

Having reached a dead end in the investigation, DuPont subsequently filed suit against the Christophers, alleging that the Christophers had wrongfully obtained photographs revealing DuPont's trade secrets which they then sold to the undisclosed third party. DuPont contended that it had developed a highly secret but unpatented process for producing methanol, a process which gave DuPont a competitive advantage over other producers. This process, DuPont alleged, was a trade secret developed after much expensive and time-consuming research, and a secret which the company had taken special precautions to safeguard. The area photographed by the Christophers was the plant designed to produce methanol by this secret process, and because the plant was still under construction parts of the process were exposed to view from directly above the construction area. Photographs of that area, DuPont alleged, would enable a skilled person to deduce the secret process for making methanol. DuPont thus contended that the Christophers had wrongfully appropriated DuPont trade secrets by taking the photographs and delivering them to the undisclosed third party. In its suit DuPont asked for damages to cover the loss it had already sustained as a result of the wrongful disclosure of the trade secret and sought temporary and permanent injunctions prohibiting any further circulation of the photographs already taken and prohibiting any additional photographing of the methanol plant.

[The lower court denied motions to dismiss by the Christophers, as well as a motion for summary judgment, and granted DuPont's motion to compel the Christophers to disclose their client. The lower court allowed the Christophers' motion for interlocutory appeal.]

This is a case of first impression, for the Texas courts have not faced this precise factual issue, and sitting as a diversity court we must sensitize our

Erie antennae to divine what the Texas courts would do if such a situation were presented to them. The only question involved in this interlocutory appeal is whether DuPont has asserted a claim upon which relief can be granted. The Christophers argued both at trial and before this court that they committed no 'actionable wrong' in photographing the DuPont facility and passing these photographs on to their client because they conducted all of their activities in public airspace, violated no government aviation standard, did not breach any confidential relation, and did not engage in any fraudulent or illegal conduct. In short, the Christophers argue that for an appropriation of trade secrets to be wrongful there must be a trespass, other illegal conduct, or breach of a confidential relationship. We disagree.

It is true, as the Christophers assert, that the previous trade secret cases have contained one or more of these elements. However, we do not think that the Texas courts would limit the trade secret protection exclusively to these elements. On the contrary, in *Hyde Corporation v. Huffines*, 158 Tex. 566 (1958), the Texas Supreme Court specifically adopted the rule found in the Restatement of Torts which provides:

> One who discloses or uses another's trade secret, without a privilege to do so, is liable to the other if (a) he discovered the secret by improper means, or (b) his disclosure or use constitutes a breach of confidence reposed in him by the other in disclosing the secret to him. . . .

Thus, although the previous cases have dealt with a breach of a confidential relationship, a trespass, or other illegal conduct, the rule is much broader than the cases heretofore encountered. Not limiting itself to specific wrongs, Texas adopted subsection (a) of the Restatement which recognizes a cause of action for the discovery of a trade secret by any 'improper' means.

. . .

The question remaining, therefore, is whether aerial photography of plant construction is an improper means of obtaining another's trade secret. We conclude that it is and that the Texas courts would so hold. The Supreme Court of that state has declared that 'the undoubted tendency of the law has been to recognize and enforce higher standards of commercial morality in the business world.' That court has quoted with approval articles indicating that the proper means of gaining possession of a competitor's secret process is 'through inspection and analysis' of the product in order to create a duplicate. Later another Texas court explained:

> The means by which the discovery is made may be obvious, and the experimentation leading from known factors to presently unknown results may be simple and lying in the public domain. But these facts do not destroy the value of the discovery and will not advantage a competitor who by unfair means obtains the knowledge without paying the price expended by the discoverer.

We think, therefore, that the Texas rule is clear. One may use his competitor's secret process if he discovers the process by reverse engineering applied to the finished product; one may use a competitor's process if he discovers it by his own independent research; but one may not avoid these labors by taking the process from the discoverer without his permission at a time when he is taking reasonable precautions to maintain its secrecy. To obtain knowledge of a process without spending the time and money to discover it independently is improper unless the holder voluntarily discloses it or fails to take reasonable precautions to ensure its secrecy.

In the instant case the Christophers deliberately flew over the DuPont plant to get pictures of a process which DuPont had attempted to keep secret. The Christophers delivered their pictures to a third party who was certainly aware of the means by which they had been acquired and who may be planning to use the information contained therein to manufacture methanol by the DuPont process. The third party has a right to use this process only if he obtains this knowledge through his own research efforts, but thus far all information indicates that the third party has gained this knowledge solely by taking it from DuPont at a time when DuPont was making reasonable efforts to preserve its secrecy. In such a situation DuPont has a valid cause of action to prohibit the Christophers from improperly discovering its trade secret and to prohibit the undisclosed third party from using the improperly obtained information.

We note that this view is in perfect accord with the position taken by the authors of the Restatement. In commenting on improper means of discovery the savants of the Restatement said:

> f. Improper means of discovery. The discovery of another's trade secret by improper means subjects the actor to liability independently of the harm to the interest in the secret. Thus, if one uses physical force to take a secret formula from another's pocket, or breaks into another's office to steal the formula, his conduct is wrongful and subjects him to liability apart from the rule stated in this Section. Such conduct is also an improper means of procuring the secret under this rule. But means may be improper under this rule even though they do not cause any other harm than that to the interest in the trade secret. Examples of such means are fraudulent misrepresentations to induce disclosure, tapping of telephone wires, eavesdropping or other espionage. A complete catalogue of improper means is not possible. In general they are means which fall below the generally accepted standards of commercial morality and reasonable conduct.

Restatement of Torts § 757, comment f at 10 (1939).

In taking this position we realize that industrial espionage of the sort here perpetrated has become a popular sport in some segments of our industrial community. However, our devotion to free wheeling industrial competition must not force us into accepting the law of the jungle as the standard of morality expected in our commercial relations. Our tolerance of the espionage game must cease when the protections required to prevent another's spying cost so much that the spirit of inventiveness is dampened. Commercial privacy must be protected from espionage which could not have been reasonably anticipated or prevented. We do not mean to imply, however, that everything not in plain view is within the protected vale, nor that all information obtained through every extra optical extension is forbidden. Indeed, for our industrial competition to remain healthy there must be breathing room for observing a competing industrialist. A competitor can and must shop his competition for pricing and examine his products for quality, components, and methods of manufacture. Perhaps ordinary fences and roofs must be built to shut out incursive eyes, but we need not require the discoverer of a trade secret to guard against the unanticipated, the undetectable, or the unpreventable methods of espionage now available.

In the instant case DuPont was in the midst of constructing a plant. Although after construction the finished plant would have protected much of the process from view, during the period of construction the trade secret was exposed to view from the air. To require DuPont to put a roof over the unfinished plant to guard its secret would impose an enormous expense to prevent nothing more than a school boy's trick. We introduce here no new or radical ethic since our ethos has never given moral sanction to piracy. The market place must not deviate far from our mores. We should not require a person or corporation to take unreasonable precautions to prevent another from doing that which he ought not do in the first place. Reasonable precautions against predatory eyes we may require, but an impenetrable fortress is an unreasonable requirement, and we are not disposed to burden industrial inventors with such a duty in order to protect the fruits of their efforts. 'Improper' will always be a word of many nuances, determined by time, place, and circumstances. We therefore need not proclaim a catalogue of commercial improprieties. Clearly, however, one of its commandments does say 'thou shall not appropriate a trade secret through deviousness under circumstances in which countervailing defenses are not reasonably available.'

. . .

The decision of the trial court is affirmed and the case remanded to that court for proceedings on the merits.

NOTES & QUESTIONS

1. Process vs. Product

A not-uncommon occurrence in business is a secret process that creates an unprotected product. The *Christopher* case revolved around duPont's secret method for manufacturing methane. The protection for a secret process exists even where a product is unprotected, and may be reverse engineered. Consider *Phillips v. Frey*, 20 F.3d 623 (5th Cir. 1994). Phillips owned a business which made collapsible single-pole deer stands. These stands supported elevated seats used by individuals in gun or bow hunting. Phillips' product was not protected by a patent and any purchaser could reverse engineer the product to determine how it was made. What Phillips relied on was his secret process, as any attempt to duplicate the stand, without knowledge of the process involved, would be cost-prohibitive. Frey asserted that their product was made by reverse engineering Phillips work, but the court noted that while the *product* might have been obtained by reverse engineering, the *process* was not:

> Although it is likely appellants used reverse engineering for the design of [their competing stand], there was no evidence that the appellants used this method to acquire the manufacturing process employed by Ambusher. A process or device may be a trade secret even where others can gain knowledge of the process from studying the manufacturer's

marketed product. Although trade secret law does not offer protection against discovery by fair and honest means such as independent invention, accidental disclosure, or "reverse engineering," protection will be awarded to a trade secret holder against the disclosure or unauthorized use by those to whom the secret has been confided under either express or implied restriction of nondisclosure or by one who has gained knowledge by improper means.

Id. at 629.

2. Restatement of Torts § 757

The definitional starting point of non-UTSA states, also known as Restatement states, are the definitions described in section 757 of the first Restatement of Torts. Comment b of the Restatement of Torts § 757 defines the meaning of a trade secret:

> b. *Definition of trade secret.* A trade secret may consist of any formula, pattern, device or compilation of information which is used in one's business, and which gives him an opportunity to obtain an advantage over competitors who do not know or use it. It may be a formula for a chemical compound, a process of manufacturing, treating or preserving materials, a pattern for a machine or other device, or a list of customers. It differs from other secret information in a business (see § 759) in that it is not simply information as to single or ephemeral events in the conduct of the business, as, for example, the amount or other terms of a secret bid for a contract or the salary of certain employees, or the security investments made or contemplated, or the date fixed for the announcement of a new policy or for bringing out a new model or the like. A trade secret is a process or device for continuous use in the operation of the business. Generally it relates to the production of goods, as, for example, a machine or formula for the production of an article. It may, however, relate to the sale of goods or to other operations in the business, such as a code for determining discounts, rebates or other concessions in a price list or catalogue, or a list of specialized customers, or a method of bookkeeping or other office management.

> . . . .

RESTATEMENT OF TORTS § 757, cmt. b (1939).

The second edition of the Restatement of Torts intentionally omits the subject matter of § 757, reserving the topic instead for the Restatement of Unfair Competition §§ 38–49 (1995). Despite the widespread adoption of the Uniform Trade Secrets Act (UTSA), portions of §757 of the Restatement (First) of Torts have been cited approvingly in virtually every state, even non-Restatement states. This is especially true of *comment b*, which defines the meaning of a trade secret.

3. Defenses to Misappropriation and Rights Against Others

Now that your company has a trade secret, what happens when you discover that someone else is using it? The answer varies, depending on how your competitor came by the information. Unlike patent infringement, trade secret misappropriation is not a strict liability claim: what rights you have, and what liability your competitor may be subject to, is contingent upon the source of their knowledge.

a. The Honest Discoverer

Looking again to the Uniform Trade Secrets Act, we see that § 1(2) defines "Misappropriation":

> (2) "Misappropriation" means: (i) acquisition of a trade secret of another by a person who knows or has reason to know that the trade secret was acquired by improper means; or (ii) disclosure or use of a trade secret of another without express or implied consent by a person who (A) used improper means to acquire knowledge of the trade secret; or (B) at the time of disclosure or use knew or had reason to know that his knowledge of the trade secret was (I) derived from or through a person who has utilized improper means to acquire it; (II) acquired under circumstances giving rise to a duty to maintain its secrecy or limit its use; or (III) derived from or through a person who owed a duty to the person seeking relief to maintain its secrecy or limit its use; or (C) before a material change of his position, knew or had reason to know that it was a trade secret and that knowledge of it had been acquired by accident or mistake.

Inherent in this definition, and every other similar definition, is the requirement that the secret information be obtained by "improper means". The United States Supreme Court addressed the issue of trade secret laws in 1974, in *Kewanee Oil Co. v. Bicron Corp.*, 94 S.Ct. 1879. The Court held that federal patent laws did not preempt state trade secret laws on products that would otherwise be patentable subject matter. With respect to "improper means", the court noted that:

> The protection accorded the trade secret holder is against the disclosure or unauthorized use of the trade secret by those to whom the secret has been confided under the express or implied restriction of nondisclosure or nonuse. The law also protects the holder of a trade secret against disclosure or use when the knowledge is gained, not by the owner's volition, but by some 'improper means,' Restatement of Torts § 757(a), which may include theft, wiretapping, or even aerial reconnaissance. A trade secret law, however, does not offer protection against discovery by fair and honest means, such as by independent invention, accidental disclosure, or by so-called reverse engineering, that is by starting with the known product and working backward to divine the process which aided in its development or manufacture.

Id. at 1883.

Honest discovery is a complete defense to a claim of misappropriation of trade secrets. A competitor may develop the secret through their own inventive efforts, or through reverse engineering of a released product. This concept of free discoverability justifies trade secret protection: a competitor may pay you to license your secret, or may expend the effort to discover the secret for itself; neither side gains an undeserved edge in either case.

Theoretical independent development, that is the idea that a competitor *could have* independently developed the secret itself, is not a defense to misappropriation. That a product *could have been* reverse engineered does not excuse improper means of acquiring secret information. *See e.g. Boeing Co. v. Sierracin Corp.*, 108 Wash. 2d 38 (1987) (disallowing the use of evidence showing the hypothetical ease of reverse engineering).

b.   The Innocent Wrongful User

Returning to the UTSA definition of misappropriation, we see that the UTSA bans the use of a trade secret when the user "at the time of disclosure or use knew or had reason to know that his knowledge of the trade secret was (I) derived from or through a person who has utilized improper means to acquire it; (II) acquired under circumstances giving rise to a duty to maintain its secrecy or limit its use; or (III) derived from or through a person who owed a duty to the person seeking relief to maintain its secrecy or limit its use." This is a gap in the protections provided by trade secret laws: a company may innocently hire a competitor's former employee, and gain benefits from that employee's knowledge of the competitor's trade secrets, without being subject to liability for misappropriation (though the former employee may be). The Court of Appeals of New York phrased it as "the discoverer of a new process or trade secret. . . has no exclusive right to it against. . . one who in good faith acquires knowledge of it without breach of contract or of a confidential relationship with the discoverer." *Speedry Chem. Products, Inc. v. Carter's Ink Co.*, 206 F.2d 328 (C.A.N.Y. 1962).

The cure to this problem is notice. Upon learning of innocent wrongful use, the trade secret holder should immediately notify the user. The original Restatement of Torts (1939) addressed the issue of notice:

> One who learns another's trade secret from a third person without notice that it is secret and that the third person's disclosure is a breach of his duty to the other, or who learns the secret through a mistake without notice of the secrecy and the mistake,
>
> > (a) is not liable to the other for a disclosure or use of the secret prior to receipt of such notice, and
> >
> > (b) is liable to the other for a disclosure or use of the secret after the receipt of such notice, unless prior thereto he has in good faith paid value for the secret or has so changed his position that to subject him to liability would be inequitable.

Restatement of Torts § 758 (1939).

Practitioners should be aware of variations in the "Uniform" Trade Secrets Act throughout jurisdictions. Many states, in adopting the UTSA, made slight alterations to better conform with their own case law, or with their jurisdiction's view of trade secrets. In Virginia, for example, the language addressing this particular issue differs from the UTSA: the UTSA defines misappropriation, in part, to mean disclosure or use by a person who "before a material change of his position, knew or had reason to know that it was a trade secret and that knowledge of it had been acquired by accident or mistake"; the Virginia Act excludes the "material change" language. *See* Milton E. Babirak,

Jr., *The Virginia Uniform Trade Secret Act: A Critical Summary of the Act and Case Law*, 5 VA. L.J. & TECH. 15 (2000).

C. CRIMINAL PROTECTION FOR TRADE SECRETS

In addition to civil enforcement of trade secret ownership, there are criminal sanctions in place to prevent the misappropriation of trade secrets. These sanctions are divided between federal and state legislation.

1. Federal Protection

In 1996, the Economic Espionage Act (EEA) became law. This was the first federal statute that explicitly protected trade secrets, criminalizing the misappropriation, attempted misappropriation, or conspiracy to misappropriate trade secrets. Before the EEA's passage, any federal prosecution of the theft of trade secrets was conducted under the National Stolen Property Act or the mail and wire fraud statutes.

> Prior to the passage of the EEA, the only federal statute directly prohibiting economic espionage was the Trade Secrets Act, 18 U.S.C. § 1905, which forbids the unauthorized disclosure of confidential government information, including trade secrets, by a government employee. However, the Trade Secrets Act was of limited value, because it did not apply to private sector employees and it provided only minor criminal sanctions of a fine and not more than one year in prison.

> The government often sought convictions under the National Stolen Property Act ("NSPA"), 18 U.S.C. § 2314, or the mail and wire fraud statutes, 18 U.S.C. §§ 1341 and 1343. However, the NSPA was drafted at a time when computers, biotechnology, and copy machines did not even exist, and industrial espionage often occurred without the use of mail or wire. Consequently, it soon became clear to legislators and commentators alike that a new federal strategy was needed to combat the increasing prevalence of espionage in corporate America. Congress recognized the importance of developing a systematic approach to the problem of economic espionage, and stressed that only by adopting a national scheme to protect U.S. proprietary economic information can we hope to maintain our industrial and economic edge and thus safeguard our national security. The House and Senate thus passed the Economic Espionage Act, and the President signed the bill into law on October 11, 1996.

United States v. Hsu, 155 F.3d 189, 194-195 (3d Cir., 1998).

a. Economic Espionage Act of 1996

The Economic Espionage Act (EEA), 18 USCA §§ 1831-1839, makes it a crime to steal, attempt to steal, or conspire to steal trade secrets.

18 USCA § 1831 Economic Espionage

(a) In General. — Whoever, intending or knowing that the offense will benefit any foreign government, foreign instrumentality, or foreign agent, knowingly —

(1) steals, or without authorization appropriates, takes, carries away, or conceals, or by fraud, artifice, or deception obtains a trade secret;

(2) without authorization copies, duplicates, sketches, draws, photographs, downloads, uploads, alters, destroys, photocopies, replicates, transmits, delivers, sends, mails, communicates, or conveys a trade secret;

(3) receives, buys, or possesses a trade secret, knowing the same to have been stolen or appropriated, obtained, or converted without authorization;

(4) attempts to commit any offense described in any of paragraphs (1) through (3); or

(5) conspires with one or more other persons to commit any offense described in any of paragraphs (1) through (3), and one or more of such persons do any act to effect the object of the conspiracy, shall, except as provided in subsection (b), be fined not more than $500,000 or imprisoned not more than 15 years, or both.

(b) Organizations. — Any organization that commits any offense described in subsection (a) shall be fined not more than $10,000,000.

Section 1832 is nearly identical to § 1831, with somewhat reduced penalties for parties who are not acting as foreign agents. Section 1833 creates exceptions for law enforcement officials and "whistle blowers." Section 1834 addresses the forfeiture of any property derived from the theft of trade secrets. Section 1835 empowers the court to issue orders to preserve the confidentiality of trade secrets during prosecution. Section 1836 allows for civil actions to enjoin violations. Section 1837 extends the Act to violations committed by a citizen or permanent resident alien, or an organization organized under US or state laws. Section 1838 addresses the construction with other laws. Section 1839, as was noted earlier, is the definition section, including the EEA's definition of "trade secret."

NOTES & QUESTIONS

Critical Commentary

The passage of the EEA drew a significant amount of controversy, both for potential vagaries in the language and to criticize the intent behind the Act.

Some scholars had concerns with how various portions of the Act were going to be implemented by the Department of Justice, as well as with how various terms would be interpreted by courts.

> Arguably, the definition of "trade secret" set forth in the EEA is broader than state law definitions, including the definition of trade secret in the Uniform Trade Secrets Act ("UTSA"). However, in another sense, the EEA definition of "trade secret" is narrower than that of the UTSA. Specifically, the EEA only applies to trade secrets that are "related to or included in a product that is produced for or placed in interstate or foreign commerce." Because of the requirement that the trade secret at issue be "included in a product," there is some

question whether the EEA applies to trade secret information concerning services rather than products.

John R. Bauer et al., *Criminalization of Trade Secret Theft: On the Second Anniversary of the Economic Espionage Act*, 8-SUM CURRENTS: INT'L TRADE L.J. 59 (1999).

Other scholars were less concerned with the wording than with the purpose of the Act. Professor Rochelle Dreyfuss criticized the Act by noting that "something seems to have gone awry in the intellectual property bargain," in that companies were gaining more tools for the acquisition of exclusive rights in information that is not new.

> One alternative available to Congress was to use its Commerce Clause authority to criminalize violations of state civil law: that is, to create criminal liability for committing the tort of misappropriation as defined by state law. Perhaps that is what the EEA was intended to do, but that conclusion is by no means clear. On the one hand, the EEA appears to track the subject matter definitions of state law, and to prohibit "unauthorized appropriation" — a term not too different from the familiar "misappropriation" of state law. At the same time, however, the statute departs from state trade secrecy law in several important respects. Its definition of unauthorized appropriation is different from that found in the states. The statute also includes state-of-mind elements, including the intent to benefit another entity and to deprive the "owner" of the secret's value, which are unknown to state causes of action — as, indeed, is the concept of owner, as opposed to rights holder. Finally, the statute creates rights against interceptions that occur outside the United States, which state laws could probably never reach, and — given its criminal nature — also departs from state legislation by substituting punishment for remedial action.

> The result is something of a mongrel. The EEA's many novel provisions will provide courts with difficult questions to resolve, but since the Act is not based on federal intellectual property law, federal criminal law, or state intellectual property law, it is difficult to predict what case law and traditions courts will draw upon in resolving them.

Rochelle Cooper Dreyfuss, *Trade Secrets: How Well Should We Be Allowed to Hide Them? The Economic Espionage Act of 1996*, 9 FORDHAM INTELL. PROP. MEDIA & ENT. L.J 1, 7-8 (1998).

b. Actual Theft of Trade Secrets

UNITED STATES v. LANGE
United States Court of Appeals for the Seventh Circuit
312 F.3d 263 (2002)

EASTERBROOK, Circuit Judge.

[Matthew Lange was convicted of violating 18 USCA § 1832, for stealing trade secrets from his former employer, RAPCO, and attempting to sell them to a competitor. Lange denied the data met the statutory definition of a "trade secret."]

RAPCO is in the business of making aircraft parts for the aftermarket. It buys original equipment parts, then disassembles them to identify (and measure) each component. This initial step of reverse engineering, usually performed by a drafter such as Lange, produces a set of measurements and drawings. Because this case involves an effort to sell the intellectual property used to make a brake assembly, we use brakes as an illustration.

Knowing exactly what a brake assembly looks like does not enable RAPCO to make a copy. It must figure out how to make a substitute with the same (or better) technical specifications. Brakes rely on friction to slow the airplane's speed by converting kinetic energy to heat. Surfaces that do this job well are made by sintering — the forming of solid metal, usually from a powder, without melting. Aftermarket manufacturers must experiment with different alloys and compositions until they achieve a process and product that fulfils requirements set by the Federal Aviation Administration for each brake assembly. Completed assemblies must be exhaustively tested to demonstrate, to the FAA's satisfaction, that all requirements have been met; only then does the FAA certify the part for sale. For brakes this entails 100 destructive tests on prototypes, bringing a spinning 60-ton wheel to a halt at a specified deceleration measured by a dynamometer. Further testing of finished assemblies is required. It takes RAPCO a year or two to design, and obtain approval for, a complex part; the dynamometer testing alone can cost $75,000. But the process of experimenting and testing can be avoided if the manufacturer demonstrates that its parts are identical (in composition and manufacturing processes) to parts that have already been certified. What Lange, a disgruntled former employee, offered for sale was all the information required to obtain certification of several components as identical to parts for which RAPCO held certification. Lange included with the package — which he offered via the Internet to anyone willing to pay his price of $100,000 — a pirated copy of AutoCAD®, the computer-assisted drawing software that RAPCO uses to maintain its drawings and specifications data. One person to whom Lange tried to peddle the data informed RAPCO, which turned to the FBI. Lange was arrested following taped negotiations that supply all the evidence necessary for conviction — if the data satisfy the statutory definition of trade secrets.

[The court considered Lange's argument that RAPCO did not take "reasonable measures to keep such information secret," and rejected it. RAPCO stored all of its drawings and data in a locked, alarmed room, and the number of copies was kept minimal. Some of the information was coded, with few people knowing the codes, and all documents carried warnings of RAPCO's intellectual property rights. RAPCO also split work among subcontractors, to ensure that no subcontractor could replicate their product.]

The second ingredient is that "the information derives independent economic value, actual or potential, from not being generally known to, and not being readily ascertainable through proper means by, the public[.]" According to Lange, all data obtained by reverse engineering some other product are "readily ascertainable . . . by the public" because everyone can do what RAPCO did: buy an original part, disassemble and measure it, and make a copy. The prosecutor responds to this contention by observing that "the public" is unable to reverse engineer an aircraft brake assembly.

[The court examined the usage of the word "public" in § 1839(3), as discussed earlier in the chapter.]

Thus it is unnecessary here to decide whether "general" belongs in front of "public" — for even if it does, the economically valuable information is not "readily ascertainable" to the general public, the educated public, the economically relevant public, or any sensible proxy for these groups.

Another line of prosecutorial argument starts with the fact that § 1832(a)(4) makes it a crime to attempt to sell trade secrets without the owner's permission. Even if Lange did not have real trade secrets in his possession, the argument goes, he thought he did and therefore may be penalized for an attempted sale. The argument finds support in [*United States v. Hsu*, 155 F.3d 189 (3rd Cir. 1998)], which held that in order to avoid graymail — the threat that to obtain a conviction the prosecutor must disclose the secret by putting it in the trial record — a case may be based on § 1832(a)(4) without disclosing all details of the trade secret. We agree with the general approach of these decisions. *Hsu* analogized the attempted sale of information believed to be a trade secret to an attempt such as shooting a corpse, believing it to be alive, or selling sugar, believing it to be cocaine. Events of this sort underlie the maxim that factual impossibility is no defense to a prosecution for attempt. This does not mean, however, that the defendant's belief alone can support a conviction. All attempt prosecutions depend on demonstrating that the defendant took a substantial step toward completion of the offense, which could have been carried out unless thwarted. Although the American Law Institute recommends a definition of attempt linked closely to intent, the Supreme Court has not embraced this view and demands in cases under federal law that the prosecutor establish a probability of success. *See, e.g., Spectrum Sports, Inc. v. McQuillan*, 506 U.S. 447, 113 S.Ct. 884 (1993) ("dangerous probability" of success is an ingredient of attempted monopolization).

An attempted murder may be thwarted by substituting a sack of flour for the intended victim; a sale of drugs may be thwarted by substituting sugar for cocaine, or rock candy for crack. These situations present a good chance of success, but for the intervention. So does "the disgruntled former employee who walks out of his former company with a computer diskette full of engineering schematics" (*Hsu*, 155 F.3d at 201) — a fair description of Lange's conduct (though diskettes are obsolete). A sale of trade secrets may be thwarted by substituting a disk with the collected works of Shakespeare for the disk that the defendant believed contained the plans for brake assemblies, or by an inadvertent failure to download the proper file. The attempted sale of the disk is a culpable substantial step. But it is far less clear that sale of information already known to the public could be deemed a substantial step toward the offense, just because the defendant is deluded and does not understand what a trade secret is. Selling a copy of Zen and the Art of Motorcycle Maintenance is not attempted economic espionage, even if the defendant thinks that the tips in the book are trade secrets; nor is sticking pins in voodoo dolls attempted murder. Booksellers and practitioners of the occult pose no social dangers, certainly none of the magnitude of those who are tricked into shooting bags of sand that have been substituted for targets of assassination. Lange was more dangerous than our bookseller but much less dangerous than our hypothetical assassin. Perhaps data purloined from an ex-employer is sufficiently likely to contain trade secrets to justify calling the preparation for sale a substantial step toward completion of the offense, and thus a culpable attempt, even if the employee stole the wrong data file and did not get his hands on the commercially valuable information. We need not pursue the subject beyond noting the plausibility of the claim and its sensitivity to the facts — what kind of data did the employee think he stole, and so on. For it is not necessary to announce a definitive rule about how dangerous the completed acts must be in trade secret cases: the judge was entitled to (and did) find that Lange had real trade secrets in his possession.

Lange wants us to proceed as if all he tried to sell were measurements that anyone could have taken with calipers after disassembling an original-equipment part. Such measurements could not be called trade secrets if, as Lange asserts, the assemblies in question were easy to take apart and measure. But no one would have paid $100,000 for metes and bounds, while Lange told his customers that the data on offer were worth more than that asking price. Which they were. What Lange had, and tried to sell, were the completed specifications and engineering diagrams that reflected all the work completed after the measurements had been taken: the metallurgical data, details of the sintering, the results of the tests, the plans needed to produce the finished goods, everything required to get FAA certification of a part supposedly identical to one that had been approved. Those details "derive[d] independent economic value, actual or potential, from not being generally known to, and not being readily ascertainable through proper means by, the public[.]" Every firm other than the original equipment manufacturer and RAPCO had to pay dearly to devise, test, and win approval of similar parts; the details unknown to the rivals, and not discoverable with tape measures, had considerable "independent economic value . . . from not being generally known". A sensible trier of fact could determine that Lange tried to sell trade secrets. It was his customer's cooperation with the FBI, and not public access to the data, that prevented closing of the sale.

. . .

Affirmed.

c. Conspiracy to Steal Trade Secrets

UNITED STATES v. MARTIN

United States Court of Appeals for the First Circuit
228 F.3d 1 (2000)

TORRUELLA, Chief Judge.

[Dr. Stephen R. Martin and Caryn L. Camp were charged with ten counts of wire fraud, two counts of mail fraud, one count of conspiracy to steal trade secrets, one count of conspiracy to transport stolen goods, and one count of interstate transportation of stolen goods. Camp testified against Martin, and Martin was convicted on four counts of wire fraud, two counts of mail fraud, conspiracy to steal trade secrets, and conspiracy to transport stolen property in interstate commerce. The appeal challenged the sufficiency of the evidence.

Martin was a scientist. At the time he and Camp first came into contact, Martin was developing a company called "WDV." Sometime after they began conversing, Martin went to "Maverck." Camp was a chemist with IDEXX, which manufactured veterinary products. Martin had approached IDEXX previously with a proposal for research into HIV and feline immunodeficiency virus (FIV), which they rejected. As part of her employment, Camp had signed non-competition and non-disclosure agreements.

Camp found Martin in January, 1998, after becoming dissatisfied with her job. They began to correspond, first regarding the possibility of Camp working for WDV (and later Maverck), and then as pen-pals. During the course of this correspondence, Camp let slip minor confidential details of her work at IDEXX.]

II.   EVENTS BETWEEN MAY 1, 1998 AND JULY 18, 1998

The government's first six counts of wire fraud, on which Martin was acquitted, stem from correspondence occurring prior to July 18, 1998. One count of mail fraud, on which Martin was convicted, also stems from this period.

A.   Martin's Initial Requests

On May 1, in response to Camp's lengthy e-mail detailing her trip, Martin made his first explicit request for information, asking for "any info . . . on the HOT topics in veterinary diagnostics." Martin renewed his request in a May 3 e-mail in which he asked a number of questions about IDEXX prices, test composition, and test use. In a subsequent message, Martin outlined his ability to avoid patent infringement with IDEXX and noted that "IDEXX is going to be in trouble very soon." On May 3, Camp responded with answers to most of Martin's questions. Attached was a letter detailing problems with a particular IDEXX product. In reference to a previous discussion about flying planes, Martin began to refer to Camp as "Ace," a moniker which would become "Agent Ace" as their "spy" business heated up.

B.   Camp's Responses

On May 4, Camp wrote concerning IDEXX's legal problems. She also included "lots & lots of goodies for your next rainy day," including internal memoranda. Camp noted that the internal memoranda may have been confidential. "I feel like a spy," she commented. In a letter the next day, Camp regretted her actions, promising to "be good . . . and send no more dirty secrets from Idexx. . . ." Martin responded, claiming that he did "not want to know anything confidential about IDEXX," and asking only for "public information."

Despite Camp's repentance and Martin's denial of any desire for confidential or proprietary information, Camp continued to assemble and pass on information, an activity which she apparently viewed as ethically suspect.[3] Camp also relayed information on IDEXX's strategic plans, including a potential partnership with a company whose name, at least, was confidential. By late June, Camp appeared set on leaving IDEXX, as she commented that "I need to unload all of my stock options." Furthermore, Camp had received (and ignored) reminders of her non-compete and non-disclosure agreements; she forwarded these reminders to Martin, noting that "as a spy myself, I get a particular chuckle out of [them]," and that "my loyalty has ended." Camp and Martin began to formalize their plans for meeting at Lake Tahoe in early August, as well as for Camp's eventual move to Nevada.

. . .

E. The First Package

On July 12, Camp sent Martin a large package of information via Priority Mail, including various devices, product inserts, USDA course materials, information on her own projects, miscellaneous IDEXX product information, and "Examples of My Work," labeled "Confidential." Camp also promised to send an actual test kit, if Martin wished. The mailing and receipt of this package formed the basis of a mail fraud charge, of which Martin was ultimately convicted. After receiving the package, Martin once more praised Camp's aggressiveness, encouraged her to "keep on charging," to "keep on thinking about the competition, and how we can beat them," and promised that "lips are sealed."

III. EVENTS BETWEEN JULY 19, 1998 TO AUGUST 16, 1998

Correspondence during the next several weeks provided the basis for Martin's conviction on four counts of wire fraud.

A. More Questions and Answers

In several e-mails between July 19 and July 21, Camp outlined a proposal for customer-friendly additions and modifications to current IDEXX technology. Martin explained how such a test might be constructed, telling Camp that if it could be marketed successfully, she would receive "enough bonus money to buy [a] house for cash." Camp clearly understood that the proposal was for technology competitive with that of IDEXX, as she suggested the possibility that "[she and Martin would] own the whole market."

Camp's proposal also prompted Martin to ask about the relevance and applicability of x-Chek or similar software. Camp offered to send Martin a copy of

---

[3] [FN2] Camp's May 7 e-mail noted that "the fun part of my week has been putting together packages of information for you . . . " and celebrated "the intrigue of being Agent Ace." On June 22, she "couldn't resist playing Ace-the-Spy today . . . and so I am dropping a few more things in the mail." But her fun did not come without guilt: "I know I should be shot. But I just can't resist sending you this chain of internal Idexx e-mails regarding concern of a certain competitor;" "I am probably crossing the line with this [but] I've crossed lines worse than this one." However, Camp re-assured herself that she was doing nothing wrong, that she was forwarding "nothing proprietary" but simply the "dirty secrets of an IDEXX Livestock and Poultry weekly meeting."

the software IDEXX had developed for poultry and livestock testing. Martin responded the same day, writing that "he would like to play with the software you mentioned." Camp immediately replied, promising "lots of cool goodies," including the x-Chek disks. Camp also indicated that she was on the verge of "cleaning out her office" and leaving IDEXX; however, she noted that she was speaking to headhunters in addition to Martin.

Martin's response to this last message re-affirmed his intention to compete with IDEXX. Moreover, Martin acknowledged Camp's potentially illicit activity, and exhorted her to continue in her final few days at work. "Before you bag IDEXX (I am embarrassed to ask this), absorb as much information, physically and intellectually, as you can. I never had a spy before." Camp's answer bemoaned the constraints on her information gathering (because co-workers knew she was preparing to leave), detailed her continued efforts to take home both information and property, and admitted the illegality (or at least inappropriateness) of her actions. However, Camp noted that she had as of yet been unwilling to copy "confidential" documents, although she admitted that she had copied "semi-confidential" internal e-mail. The next day, Camp promised to send Martin additional kits as her last "secret agent" act.

B. The Second Package

In Camp's last several days at IDEXX, she continued to collect products and information, which she forwarded to Martin on July 24. The package included operating manuals, IDEXX marketing materials, research and development data, a sales binder prepared by an independent contractor, as well as a binder labeled "Competition."

C. Found Out

Unfortunately for Camp and Martin, Camp inadvertently sent her July 25 e-mail (acknowledging that July 24 was her last day and detailing the contents of her second package) to John Lawrence, the global marketing manager for Poultry/Livestock at IDEXX. Camp informed Martin of what she had done, and continued on her vacation. According to Camp, Martin later recommended that she lie to IDEXX, i.e., that she tell them that he was interested only in limited information unrelated to IDEXX core businesses. Upon her return to Maine, Camp was intercepted and interviewed by an FBI agent at the Portland airport. An August 9, 1998 search of Martin's home found the contents of Camp's second package, including the x-Chek software.

Discussion

. . .

II. CONSPIRACY TO STEAL TRADE SECRETS

The jury found Martin guilty of count 13, which charged him with conspiracy to steal trade secrets in violation of the Economic Espionage Act of 1996, specifically 18 U.S.C. § 1832(a)(5). In order to find a defendant guilty of conspiracy, the prosecution must prove (1) that an agreement existed, (2) that it had an unlawful purpose, and (3) that the defendant was a voluntary participant. The government must prove that the defendant possessed both the intent to agree and the intent to commit the substantive offense. In addition, the government must prove that at least one conspirator committed an "overt act," that is, took an affirmative step toward achieving the conspiracy's purpose.

The agreement need not be express, however, as long as its existence may be inferred from the defendants' words and actions and the interdependence of activities and persons involved. A so-called "tacit" agreement will suffice. Moreover, the conspirators need not succeed in completing the underlying act, nor need that underlying act even be factually possible.

As of yet, only the Third Circuit has had the opportunity to address § 1832(a), which specifically covers private corporate espionage. See *United States v. Hsu*, 155 F.3d 189 (3d Cir.1998). The statute criminalizes the knowing theft of trade secrets, as well as attempts or conspiracies to steal trade secrets. The Act defines a "trade secret" broadly, to include both tangible property and intangible information, as long as the owner "has taken reasonable measures to keep such information secret" and the information "derives independent economic value . . . from not being generally known to . . . the public." 18 U.S.C. § 1839(3). This definition of trade secret "protects a wider variety" of information than most civil laws; however, "it is clear that Congress did not intend . . . to prohibit lawful competition such as the use of general skills or parallel development of a similar product," *Hsu*, 155 F.3d at 196-97, although it did mean to punish "the disgruntled former employee who walks out of his former company with a computer diskette full of engineering schematics," *id.* at 201. In other words, § 1832(a) was not designed to punish competition, even when such competition relies on the know-how of former employees of a direct competitor. It was, however, designed to prevent those employees (and their future employers) from taking advantage of confidential information gained, discovered, copied, or taken while employed elsewhere.

Martin contends that the evidence is factually insufficient to establish a "meeting of the minds" or agreement to violate § 1832(a), because (1) insufficient evidence exists to establish an agreement between Martin and Camp; (2) insufficient evidence exists to prove that Martin had the necessary intent to commit an act prohibited by § 1832(a), i.e., injure the owner of the trade secret (IDEXX); and (3) the information provided by Camp to Martin did not meet the statutory definition of a trade secret under § 1839(3). As we explain below, none of these arguments are persuasive.

First, the evidence is sufficient for a reasonable jury to conclude that Martin and Camp formed an agreement regarding the theft of trade secrets. Martin's argument against the existence of an agreement relies on the facts that (a) his early e-mails specifically requested that Camp not send him confidential information, and (b) Camp did not seem to know the distinction between confidential information, proprietary information, and office gossip. However, while Martin's disclaimer and Camp's confusion indicate the lack of an explicit agreement at that time, they do not necessarily negate the existence of an agreement. A rational jury could have plausibly concluded on the basis of the evidence presented at trial that an agreement existed. By July 21, Martin had received extensive correspondence from Camp that she had either marked "confidential" or "proprietary," or had expressed some hesitation in forwarding.[4] Despite his previous protestations that he wanted nothing to do with IDEXX or its confidential information, Martin asked Camp on July 21 to "absorb as much information, physically and intellectually, as you can," and included a set of questions to direct Camp's research. Throughout June and July, Martin referred to Camp as "Agent Ace," or as his "spy." Given the type of information that Martin had already received, a reasonable jury could have concluded that, whatever Martin's original intentions, as of July 21, Camp and Martin had reached a tacit agreement by which she would send him items and information that potentially fell under the trade secret definition of 18 U.S.C. § 1839(3). In other words, sufficient evidence exists to show an agreement between Camp and Martin to violate § 1832(a).

Second, the evidence is sufficient to show that Martin intended to injure IDEXX by obtaining IDEXX trade secrets and competing against IDEXX. Although Martin consistently claimed that he had no interest in developing products that competed with IDEXX, and hence had no intention of injuring IDEXX economically, his correspondence with Camp detailed a plan of competition. Martin had, among other things, considered the possibility of starting a competing veterinary lab, and had asked Camp to think, in particular, about ways to compete with tests that IDEXX manufactured. A reasonable jury could have found that Martin intended to use the information gained from Camp, particularly information on IDEXX's costs and customer dissatisfaction with IDEXX, to create a more successful competitor with greater capability to injure IDEXX.

Third, Martin's final argument — that he actually received no trade secrets — even if true, is irrelevant. Martin has only been found guilty of a conspiracy to steal trade secrets, rather than the underlying offense. The relevant question to determine whether a conspiracy existed was whether Martin intended to violate the statute. *See Hsu*, 155 F.3d at 198 ("[T]he crimes charged — attempt and conspiracy — do not require proof of the existence of an actual trade secret, but, rather, proof only of one's attempt or conspiracy with intent to steal a trade secret."). The key question is whether Martin intended to steal trade secrets. A rational jury, considering the information Camp had already sent Martin, could have concluded that his further queries indicated such an intention.

A reasonable jury could therefore have concluded that Martin and Camp formed an agreement by which Camp conveyed information and property to Martin that potentially fell under the definition of a trade secret in 18 U.S.C. § 1839. As a result, sufficient evidence existed to convict Martin of conspiracy to steal trade secrets.

Conclusion

A careful reading of the seven-month e-mail communication between Dr. Stephen Martin and Caryn Camp could lead to the conclusion Martin and

---

[4] [FN8] Some of the information Martin received in their early correspondence clearly had the potential to fall within the § 1839 definition of trade secret: for example, cost information unavailable to the public included in Camp's message of May 2, a confidential IDEXX business plan included in Camp's June 8 message, and a customer list included in Camp's July 1 message.

his counsel urge — that this is simply a pen-pal relationship between a lonely Maine lab technician and a reclusive California scientist. However, the evidence could also lead a reader to the conclusion that something far more sinister was afoot: that an originally harmless communication mushroomed into a conspiracy to steal trade secrets and transport stolen property interstate, and that the electronic mail and U.S. mails were used to further a scheme to defraud IDEXX. Because we find there was sufficient evidence for a reasonable jury to conclude the latter beyond any reasonable doubt, we AFFIRM the defendant's conviction on all counts.

NOTES & QUESTIONS

1. Legal Impossibility Is No Defense

Both *Lange* and *Martin* make reference to *United States v. Hsu*, 155 F.3d 189 (3d Cir. 1998), the first appellate case to examine the provisions of the Economic Espionage Act. In *Hsu*, employees of Bristol-Meyer Squibb aided the FBI in conducting a "sting" operation against the defendants, who worked for a Taiwanese firm and were trying to procure secret procedures for the manufacture of a cancer drug. Because this was a sting operation, the actual trade secret was never in jeopardy. The defendants asserted, therefore, that there was no conspiracy to steal trade secrets. The court examined the argument within the scope of "legal impossibility":

> We hold that legal impossibility is not a defense to a charge of attempted misappropriation of trade secrets in violation of 18 U.S.C. § 1832(a)(4). We agree with the district court's conclusion that a charge of "attempt" under the EEA requires proof of the same elements used in other modern attempt statutes, including the Model Penal Code. A defendant is guilty of attempting to misappropriate trade secrets if, "acting with the kind of culpability otherwise required for commission of the crime, he . . . purposely does or omits to do anything that, under the circumstances as he believes them to be, is an act or omission constituting a substantial step in a course of conduct planned to culminate in his commission of the crime." Thus, the defendant must (1) have the intent needed to commit a crime defined by the EEA, and must (2) perform an act amounting to a "substantial step" toward the commission of that crime.

2. Companies as Criminals

The EEA includes provisions to charge organizations with the same crimes as individuals, and companies have been found guilty of attempted misappropriation of trade secrets. See *United States v. Yang*, 281 F.3d 534 (6th Cir. 2002), where the defendant and his corporation were charged with attempted theft of a trade secret and conspiracy to commit theft of a trade secret under § 1832. Both were convicted, and the company was originally sentenced to the statutory maximum fine of $5,000,000; the fine was vacated by the appellate court, as the trial judge did not provide his reasoning in imposing the maximum fine.

2. State Protection

Before the passage of the EEA and effective federal protection of trade secrets, a number of individual states addressed this issue, passing specific statutes to criminalize the theft of trade secrets. California's penal code is representative of the various state statutes.

California Penal Code § 499c(b):

(b) Every person is guilty of theft who, with intent to deprive or withhold the control of a trade secret from its owner, or with an intent to appropriate a trade secret to his or her own use or to the use of another, does any of the following:

> (1) Steals, takes, carries away, or uses without authorization, a trade secret.

> (2) Fraudulently appropriates any article representing a trade secret entrusted to him or her.

> (3) Having unlawfully obtained access to the article, without authority makes or causes to be made a copy of any article representing a trade secret.

> (4) Having obtained access to the article through a relationship of trust and confidence, without authority and in breach of the obligations created by that relationship, makes or causes to be made, directly from and in the presence of the article, a copy of any article representing a trade secret.

(c) Every person who promises, offers or gives, or conspires to promise or offer to give, to any present or former agent, employee or servant of another, a benefit as an inducement, bribe or reward for conveying, delivering or otherwise making available an article representing a trade secret owned by his or her present or former principal, employer or master, to any person not authorized by the owner to receive or acquire the trade secret and every present or former agent, employee, or servant, who solicits, accepts, receives or takes a benefit as an inducement, bribe or reward for conveying, delivering or otherwise making available an article representing a trade secret owned by his or her present or former principal, employer or master, to any person not authorized by the owner to receive or acquire the trade secret, shall be punished by imprisonment in the state prison, or in a county jail not exceeding one year, or by a fine not exceeding five thousand dollars ($5,000), or by both that fine and imprisonment.

PEOPLE v. PRIBICH
California Court of Appeal, Second District
27 Cal. Rptr. 2d 113 (1994)

Boris Pribich appeals after a jury convicted him of one count of the theft of trade secrets (Pen. Code § 499c, subd. (b)(2)) and found the offense to be a misdemeanor petty theft. The court suspended imposition of sentence, placed appellant on summary probation for three years, ordered him to pay restitution of $400, and stayed payment of a $1,000 fine. Appellant contends that the evidence was insufficient to support his conviction and that there were various jury instruction errors. We find the evidence insufficient as to a requisite element of the offense and reverse.

Facts

[In April of 1990, Hancock, an officer of Aquatec, a water cooler company, hired Boris Pribich to work on a freonless cooler, using a thermal chip. Aquatec held patents on methods of using such a chip in water cooler. Pribich fell behind his anticipated schedule, which concerned Aquatec, as they wanted to display the cooler at an October trade show. Aquatec wanted to give Pribich the chance to succeed, and provided staff, workspace, and permission to work at home on his own computer.]

Hancock was familiar with some of the information in appellant's computer at work, such as graphs and equations on the performance of thermal electric chips. This information was necessary to Aquatec's objective of improving the performance of the thermal electric chip. Hancock thus considered the information in appellant's computer at work to constitute trade secrets belonging to Aquatec, since the information dealt with Aquatec's product and was not available to the general public.

To protect such trade secrets, Aquatec did not allow nonemployees to go into the building without being escorted and required employees to sign a confidentiality agreement. Even the sales people employed at Aquatec who had confidentiality agreements with the company were not permitted to view appellant's work product because, as Hancock stated, "We didn't want our competitors tipped off, we did not want the people to know what we were working on. And Aquatec is a start up company and could easily be outdone by someone with a large amount of cash and no one was going in our engineering department without a confidential[ity] agreement." According to Hancock, the information in appellant's work computer "would be of great interest . . . to our competitors."

Appellant was repeatedly absent from work, fell behind schedule, and Hancock became increasingly concerned that appellant could not finish his project to enable Aquatec to have an operating unit of its new product to demonstrate at the trade show in October of 1990. On September 17 and 19, 1990, Hancock asked appellant to have all the documents he had on his project available at the plant and to bring all the Aquatec documents and computer files or programs that he had at home to the plant. On September 20, Hancock asked appellant whether he brought all the information that had been requested and reminded appellant of the confidentiality agreement that he had signed. Appellant advised Hancock that the computer program was his property and stated, "You are a prick, I can be a prick, too." Hancock requested appellant to go to his work area and show another employee, Yongky Muljadi, what he was doing on the computer so that Muljadi could be brought up to date on appellant's project.

Hancock then called the company's patent counsel to alert him of the events. Appellant was very upset at that time. He showed Muljadi the files on the computer screen and claimed they belonged to him. However, based on the code letters of the files, Muljadi concluded that some of them were not appellant's files. Appellant proceeded to delete the files he claimed were his. After deleting the files, appellant left the building and never came back to work.

Hancock thereafter hired a computer consultant, Robert Torchon, to retrieve the data in appellant's work computer. Torchon and Muljadi were unable to retrieve the data. Hancock then contacted appellant and demanded that all the computer files and programs and other materials be returned to Aquatec. Appellant refused to do so, unless Aquatec paid a fair or reasonable price for them. Aquatec did not produce for the October trade show any prototype of a water cooler using a thermal electric chip.

On October 12, 1990, a Los Angeles police officer served a search warrant at appellant's residence. The police found two computers, computer discs, programs and numerous papers. The police officer who served the warrant used a Turbo Basic program to obtain computer printouts generated from diskettes found in appellant's house. Most of the computer files found in appellant's house had "BAS" or "DWG" extension code letters, such as the code letters observed by Muljadi on the screen of appellant's work computer before appellant deleted the files.

According to Hancock, some of the documents obtained from appellant's home pertained to the work appellant was doing for Aquatec, constituted drawings of certain components that go into the coolers and certain information on the thermal electric cooler, and were deemed by Hancock to be proprietary documents or trade secrets of Aquatec. The documents included information about a heat exchanger, a heat problem in the thermal electric chip, and a bottle cap designed by Aquatec. A computer printout and computer programs, calculations, tests and graphs regarding the performance of Aquatec's new cooler were also discovered pursuant to the search warrant. Appellant was not supposed to have retained those items seized and should have returned them to Aquatec as Hancock had requested.

In appellant's defense at trial, Dr. Martin Balaban, a mechanical engineer employed by Union Carbide to design heat exchangers and a consultant for the Rand Corp., testified that none of the prosecution's documentary evidence obtained from appellant's computer at home included any original concepts which could have given Aquatec an advantage over competitors who did not know of those documents. Moreover, the prosecution evidence included a document which showed appellant's coefficient of performance for a week when he was sick, another document constituting a milestone chart in which appellant outlined his project schedule, and other documents reflecting concepts which were in the public domain, though the exact numbers and dimensions set forth in the documents were not generally available to the public. According to Balaban, based upon his professional engineering expertise, it is not possible to make a thermal electric water cooler for the home or office which would be energy efficient and marketable.

Appellant claimed that he did not erase the files at work which belonged to Aquatec. As a part of his employment with Aquatec, he was required to use two computer programs, Auto Cad and Turbo Basic. Before he left Aquatec, appellant removed his Turbo Basic program, of which he was the registered owner, and a game-type program which he had in his work computer. He removed the programs in Muljadi's presence. When Hancock contacted appellant at home and demanded the program which he had taken, appellant claimed that he owned the programs and he never offered to sell them to Hancock. Appellant merely offered to convert his files into stand alone files, which could be used without the Turbo Basic program. Appellant admitted that most of the documents seized by the police at his home dealt with Aquatec's New Century water cooler project.

The jury found appellant not guilty of one of the two charged offenses, the unauthorized deletion of computer data. (Pen.Code, § 502, subd. (c)(4).) However, appellant was found guilty of the theft of trade secrets as a misdemeanor. (Pen.Code, § 499c, subd. (b)(2).)

DISCUSSION

To satisfy the elements of the crime with which appellant was charged, the fraudulent appropriation of an article representing a trade secret entrusted to him, the prosecution must, of course, establish that the article appropriated represented a trade secret. Penal Code section 499c, subdivision (a)(9) defines a trade secret, in pertinent part, as "any scientific or technical information, design, process, procedure, formula, computer program or information stored in a computer . . . which is secret and is not generally available to the public, and which gives one who uses it an advantage over competitors who do not know of or use the trade secret; and a trade secret shall be presumed to be secret when the owner thereof takes measures to prevent it from becoming available to persons other than those selected by the owner to have access thereto for limited purposes." One of the requisite elements of a trade secret is lacking in the present case. Specifically, there is no evidence that any of the items allegedly fraudulently appropriated by appellant and retrieved from his computer at home would give "one who uses [any of the items] an advantage over competitors who do not know of or use the trade secret."

In the present case, Hancock testified that he was familiar with some of the information in appellant's computer at work, which included graphs and mathematical models relating to the performance of thermal electric chips, that he considered the items observed on appellant's computer at work as trade secrets and that the items in appellant's computer at work would be of "great interest" to a competitor. However, Hancock described the information in appellant's computer at work and not in his computer at home. It was the information in appellant's computer at home which had been appropriated and which was alleged to constitute trade secrets. Although Hancock indicated that a computer printout reflecting information retrieved from appellant's computer at home contained a proprietary or trade secret of Aquatec, he stated only that "a lot of it is very familiar" and "looks like material that I saw on the screen that [appellant] was working on and certain other graphs I have certainly seen." However, Hancock could not indicate "the exact coding" for the printout. Such testimony by Hancock insufficiently addresses the items purportedly fraudulently appropriated by appellant, i.e., the numerous items generated from appellant's computer at home.

Most significantly, Hancock did not establish that the items seized from appellant's computer at home could give "one who uses it an advantage over competitors." Hancock did indicate that one of the items retrieved from appellant's computer was a milestone chart or work schedule which was not a technical document but which he considered proprietary to Aquatec. Hancock would not have wanted anyone to know appellant's work schedule because it would have revealed where Aquatec was at any point in time regarding its product development. However, Hancock did not specifically allege any advantage a competitor could obtain by theoretical access to such information. For example, there was no indication that any unspecified company could or would have worked any faster or differently if it had access to appellant's work schedule.

. . .

Apart from whether a "substantial" competitive advantage is required for a violation of Penal Code section 499c, we find that the element of the offense that the prosecution establish the item appropriated give "one who uses it an advantage over competitors who do not know of or use the trade secret" requires more than merely conclusory and generalized allegations. Hancock asserted that the information in appellant's computer at work would be of "great interest" to a competitor and stated his desire not to have any competitors know appellant's work schedule, which was in appellant's computer at home. However, such statements do not reveal, except by an insufficient and generalized assumption, that any competitive advantage would specifically flow from the revelation of the information.

Indeed, it appears most unlikely that any competitive advantage could have been obtained by knowledge of appellant's work schedule or other information because, as indicated by the uncontradicted testimony of appellant's expert witness, it was impossible in light of known scientific principles to make a thermal electric water cooler for the home or office which would be energy efficient and marketable. Hancock himself acknowledged that one of the items retrieved from appellant's computer revealed appellant's opinion that the model under study was not suited for low-cost thermal electric modes and "was not working very well." Moreover, appellant's expert witness repeatedly stated during direct and cross-examination that none of the documents obtained from appellant's computer at home would give anyone who had them any advantage over competitors.

We note that in the prosecutor's argument to the jury, he belittled the defense expert's testimony regarding the lack of any advantage over competitors and urged that it was unrealistic to believe that no competitive advantage could ensue from the information, but the prosecutor pointed to no evidence at trial supporting this conclusion. Nor can we find in the record any substantial evidence as to this element of the offense.

Disposition

The judgment is reversed, and the trial court is directed to dismiss the information and to order any restitution and fine paid by appellant be remitted to him.

NOTES & QUESTIONS

1. Differences in Federal and State Law

In *Pribich*, the conviction was reversed because the prosecution failed to prove that the information taken met the definition of a trade secret. In both *U.S. v. Martin* and *U.S. v. Hsu*, discussed supra, the federal appellate courts held that, for the charge of conspiracy to steal trade secrets, whether or not the information sought was actually a trade secret was irrelevant. Do you see any conflict between these holdings, and if so, does it trouble you?

2. Does Federal Patent Law Preempt State Trade Secret Law?

In *Kewanee Oil Co. v. Bicron Corp.*, 416 U.S. 470, 483 (1974), the United States Supreme Court faced the question of "whether those items which are proper subjects for consideration for a patent may also have available the alternative protection accorded by trade secret law." The Court recognized that the federal patent scheme and the state trade secret scheme could coexist:

> Certainly the patent policy of encouraging invention is not disturbed by the existence of another form of incentive to invention. In this respect the two systems are not and never would be in conflict. Similarly, the policy that matter once in the public domain must remain in the public domain is not incompatible with the existence of trade secret protection. By definition a trade secret has not been placed in the public domain.

Kewanee, 416 U.S. at 484. Consequently, the Court held that the federal patent law did not preempt Ohio trade secret law and that subject matter that otherwise qualifies for protection under the federal patent regime could also enjoy trade secret protection under state law.

In *Bonito Boats v. Thunder Craft Boats,* 489 U.S. 141 (1989), the Supreme Court determined the "limits the operation of the federal patent system places on the States' ability to offer substantial protection to utilitarian and design ideas which the patent laws leave otherwise unprotected." In *Bonito Boats,* a Florida statute offered patent-like protection for boat hulls. The Court held that federal patent law preempted the Florida law:

> States may not offer patent-like protection to intellectual creations which would otherwise remain unprotected as a matter of federal law. Both the novelty and the nonobviousness requirements of federal patent law are grounded in the notion that concepts within the public grasp, or those so obvious that they readily could be, are the tools of creation available to all. They provide the baseline of free competition upon which the patent system's incentive to creative effort depends. A state law that substantially interferes with the enjoyment of an unpatented utilitarian or design conception which has been freely disclosed by its author to the public at large impermissibly contravenes the ultimate goal of public disclosure and use which is the centerpiece of federal patent policy. Moreover, through the creation of patent-like rights, the States could essentially redirect inventive efforts away from the careful criteria of patentability developed by Congress over the last 200 years.

Bonito Boats, 489 U.S. at 156-57. Can the holding of *Bonito Boats* be reconciled with the holding of *Kewanee Oil*?

3. State vs. Federal Protection

There has been some commentary on the differences between the state and federal protection schemes, and the difficulties inherent in the enforcement of the EEA. For example, Professor Rochelle Dreyfuss has commented that while the EEA "appears to track the subject matter definitions of state law," the federal law "departs from state trade secrecy law in several important respects." The differences between the state and federal law include the divergent definitions of "unauthorized appropriation"; the inclusion in the EEA of "state-of-mind elements" absent from the state law; and the reach of the EEA to include "interceptions that occur outside the United States, which state laws could probably never reach, and — given its criminal nature — also departs from state legislation by substituting punishment for remedial action." She describes the result of the EEA as "something of a mongrel," and warns that as a result, "it is difficult to predict what case law and traditions court will draw upon to resolve them." Rochelle Cooper Dreyfuss, *Trade Secrets: How Well Should We Be Allowed to Hide Them? The Economic Espionage Act of 1996,* 9 FORDHAM INTELL. PROP. MEDIA & ENT L.J. 1, 7-8 (1998).

4. Historical Note: The Rise of Specific Legislation

Early attempts to prosecute for theft of trade secrets under larceny laws were unsuccessful, and gave rise to new statutes, such as the California Penal Code section excerpted supra. Consider *Commonwealth v. Engleman*, 142 N.E.2d 406 (Mass. 1957), where Engleman, charged with larceny for the theft of trade secrets, had his conviction reversed by the Massachusetts Supreme Court. The Court held that the larceny statute Engleman was charged under was not broad enough to cover "trade secrets" as a type of property covered by the law. In response, the Massachusetts legislature passed M.G.L.A. 266 § 30, which made the theft of trade secrets a type of larceny.

CHAPTER 5

EMPLOYMENT ISSUES

PROBLEM

Before founding Digital Ignition, Dr. See worked as an engineer at International Motors Corporation. International Motors is a multinational corporation engaged in the design, manufacturing and marketing of automobiles and automotive equipment.

At International Motors, Dr. See worked with Dr. Paul Wilson, a fellow engineer in the electronic ignition systems design department. Dr. See and Dr. Wilson became good friends. Today, Dr. Wilson is the head of the department and is overseeing a project to improve the software incorporated in International Motors' ignition systems. The department conducts general research and development.

Dr. See wants to hire his friend, Dr. Wilson, to work for Digital Ignition. Dr. See has asked Dr. Wilson for the past six years to consider leaving International Motors. The prospect of working for a start-up appealed to the adventurous side of Dr. Wilson, but until this year he couldn't stomach the financial risk to his young family.

Yesterday, Dr. See met Dr. Wilson at a dinner at the house of a mutual acquaintance and jokingly suggested that Dr. Wilson join Digital Ignition. To his surprise, Dr. Wilson expressed interest in leaving International Motors for Digital Ignition. Dr. Wilson confided with Dr. See that two weeks ago, he had formulated an idea for an improved method for manufacturing digital ignition systems that he believes will drastically cut the cost of manufacturing digital ignitions by 50%. Dr. Wilson came up with the idea over the course of a weekend while working in his garage but has not yet put his idea down in writing. Dr. Wilson believes that the idea could be worth millions and wants to develop the concept at Digital Ignition.

The following day, Dr. See comes to you with a copy of Dr. Wilson's employment contract with International Motors and explains that he would like to hire Dr. Wilson away from International Motors. A review of Dr. Wilson's employment contract reveals several of its provisions place restrictions on Dr. Wilson's subsequent employment. One provision recites that Dr. Wilson, by accepting employment with International Motors, recognizes that he will be in a position to receive confidential information and that he agrees not to use or disclose the information on behalf of anyone but International Motors. Another provision prohibits exiting employees from soliciting customers or other employees upon the termination of employment with International Motors. Yet another provision states that Dr. Wilson agrees to assign rights to all intellectual property he creates during the term of employment to International Motors. There is no trailer or hold-over clause in Dr. Wilson's employment contract requiring him to assign rights in his post-employment inventions to International Motors.

Dr. See would like to offer Dr. Wilson a position with Digital Ignition and is excited about applying Dr. Wilson's idea to the manufacturing of Digital Ignition's product. He wishes to know whether any provisions in the Dr. Wilson's employment contract with International Motors will pose a problem for Digital Ignition as the new employer. Please advise Dr. See of any risk to Digital Ignition in the event of a suit by International Motors. Dr. See also wishes to know whether the provisions will pose a problem for his friend Dr. Wilson. In formulating your response, consider what claims International Motors might level against Dr. Wilson should it sue to enforce the terms of the employment contract. In addition, evaluate whether Dr. Wilson will be able to take his idea with him to Digital Ignition.

FOCUS OF THE CHAPTER

The readings in this chapter focus on intellectual property issues that arise in the context of the employment relationship. Absent a private agreement to the contrary, statutory default rules dictate the assignment of ownership of employee-created intellectual property. In some circumstances, the default rules favor employee ownership of employee-created intellectual property. Employers consequently have opted to secure ownership in intellectual property created out of an employment relationship through the use of private contracts in the form of employment contract terms.

In Part A, the focus of the readings centers upon the ownership of intellectual property rights. The first subsection of Part A discusses the statutory default rules that govern the ownership rights of intellectual property created by employees. First, the readings examine the statutory rules that govern the assignment of patent rights in employee inventions, including the concepts of shop right and one hired to invent. Second, the readings discuss the ownership rights in trade secrets produced by employee inventors, including the implied duties owed by an employee to his employer. Next, the readings discuss ownership of employee created works subject to copyrights. Finally, in the second subsection of Part A, the private adjustments to the default rules established by ownership assignment terms in an employment contract are considered.

After the termination of the employment relationship, issues can surface concerning the use or disclosure by an ex-employee of an employer's proprietary information. The readings in Part B of this chapter highlight the concerns that arise from transfers of intellectual property upon changes in employment. The first subsection discusses the enforceability of private agreements that place limits upon a former employee's ability to use and disclose the former employer's proprietary information. The readings illustrate the impact of measures such as nonuse and nondisclosure agreements, as well as covenants not to compete. The second subsection explores how employers may invoke the inevitable disclosure doctrine to restrict a former employee from using or disclosing information personal to the employee in subsequent employment. The last subsection then deals with the risks and liabilities a new employer may incur from hiring away inventive employees.

READINGS

A.   OWNERSHIP OF INTELLECTUAL PROPERTY

1.   Statutory Default Rules

a.   Patents

Employee inventors develop the overwhelming majority of inventions patented today. Under the default rules, an employee owns the subject matter of his invention even if the invention was conceived during the course of employment. Absent an agreement to the contrary, the patent statute's default rule confers the rights of a patent to the employee inventor and not to the employer.

The default rule of patent ownership reflects the old notion of invention as the fruit of individual genius, rather than the product of corporate machinery. The requirements of the patent statute itself suggest that the old romantic image of the individual inventor remains. For example, patents issue in the name of individuals and not in the name entities. Section 111 of the patent statute requires applicants to disclose the individual name of the true inventor. 35 U.S.C. § 111. Only when the inventor refuses to apply or cannot be reached after diligent effort can persons with sufficient proprietary interest in an invention — such as an employer — step in and submit an application for a patent. 35 U.S.C. § 118.

Even though an inventor generally owns the rights to an invention, the general rule is not without exception. An employee inventor's patent ownership rights may be subject to an obligation to assign the rights to his employer. Such is the case when an employee is "hired to invent." When an employee is hired for the purpose of employing his inventive abilities, the patent rights to his inventions belong entirely to the employer. Additionally, inventions may be subject to a "shop right," a compromise position that arises when the invention relates to employee duties or created with use of employer's time and resources. The shop right is a split entitlement that affords an employer a non-exclusive, nontransferable license to practice the invention, but retains the ownership of the patent in the employee inventor. Of course, independent inventions created by the employee without the use of employer time or resources and in a subject matter unrelated to the employee's duties belong solely to the employee.

i. Shop Right

MAX C. MCELMURRY AND WHITE RIVER TECH., INC. v. ARKANSAS POWER & LIGHT CO., ENTERGY CORP. AND MIDDLE SOUTH UTILITIES
United States Court of Appeals for the Federal Circuit
995 F.2d 1576 (1993)

RICH, Circuit Judge.

. . .

III. Shop Rights

A. Background

[Arkansas Power & Light Co. (AP&L)] hired Harold L. Bowman, the patentee, as a consultant on October 24, 1980, to assist in the installation, maintenance and operation of electrostatic precipitators at AP&L's White Bluff Steam Electric Station (White Bluff) located near Redfield, Arkansas. An electronic precipitator is a device which removes granular ash particles (fly ash) from the gasses emitted by coal-fired boilers used to generate steam. . . .

. . .

[While working as a consultant for AP&L, Bowman invented a new level detector to monitor the level of fly ash in the electronic precipitators. At his suggestion, AL&P installed the new level detector in one of its hoppers for testing purposes. When the invention proved successful, AL&P ordered that the level detector be installed at one hundred and twenty eight other hoppers at the AL&P's White Bluff site.] All costs associated with the installation and testing of the level detector on the one hundred and twenty eight (128) hoppers at White Bluff, including materials and working drawings, were paid by AP&L.

On October 24, 1982, Bowman moved from White Bluff to AP&L's Independence Steam Electric Station (ISES) located near Newark, Arkansas, to assist in the start-up, maintenance and operation of electronic precipitators at that facility. In November of 1982, Bowman formed White Rivers Technology, Inc. [WRT] with McElmurry and a Mr. Johnny Mitchum, to market certain inventions on which Bowman held patents or was planning to seek patent protection. Bowman filed a patent application on the level detector on February 18, 1983, and the patent-in-suit issued on July 9, 1985. At some point prior to its issuance, Bowman assigned his patent rights to WRT.

While at ISES, Bowman assisted another AP&L engineer, a Mr. Will Morgan, in installing the level detector on precipitator hoppers at that facility. . . . The level detectors had been installed and were in operation on all one hundred and twenty eight (128) precipitator hoppers by the end of 1984, prior to the issuance of the Bowman patent. Bowman's contract with ISES ended, however, in October of 1983 before completion of the project. All costs associated with the installation and testing of the level detectors at ISES, including materials and working drawings, were paid by AP&L even though some of the work was contracted out.

In 1985, based upon the success of the level detector on the precipitator hoppers at White Bluff and ISES, another AP&L engineer, a Mr. John Harvey, implemented a plan to install the level detector on fourteen (14) hydroveyer hoppers at ISES. Harvey informed Bowman of the plan to install the level detector on the hydroveyer hoppers, and Bowman indicated that he thought it was a good idea. Bowman also indicated that WRT would be interested in bidding on the project. AP&L ultimately awarded the contract, however, to another contractor because WRT was not the low bidder. In soliciting bids on the hydroveyer project, AP&L provided the contractors with specifications prepared by AP&L showing the work to be performed. The installation of the level detectors on the hydroveyor hoppers at ISES was completed in 1985, and all costs associated with their installation were paid by AP&L.

B.   District Court Litigation

On April 25, 1990, WRT brought suit against AP&L for patent infringement based on AP&L's solicitation of and contracting with a party other than WRT to install Bowman's patented level detector on the hydroveyer hoppers at ISES. The district court granted summary judgment in favor of AP&L on the basis that AP&L had acquired a "shop right" in the level detector claimed in the Bowman patent. AP&L argued and the court agreed that, as a matter of law, Bowman's development of the patented level detector at AP&L's facilities at AP&L's expense entitled AP&L, under the "shop rights" rule, to reproduce and use the level detector in its business. WRT then appealed to this court.

C.   Analysis

A "shop right" is generally accepted as being a right that is created at common law, when the circumstances demand it, under principles of equity and fairness, entitling an employer to use without charge an invention patented by one or more of its employees without liability for infringement. See generally D. Chisum, Patents, § 22.02[3] (1985 rev.); C.T. Dreschler, Annotation, Application and Effect of "Shop Right Rule" or License Giving Employer Limited Rights in Employee's Inventions and Discoveries, 61 A.L.R.2d 356 (1958); P. Rosenberg, Patent Law Fundamentals, § 11.04, 11–20 (1991). However, as recognized by several commentators, supra, the immense body of case law addressing the issue of "shop rights" suggests that not all courts agree as to the doctrinal basis for "shop rights," and, consequently, not all courts agree as to the particular set of circumstances necessary to create a "shop right."

For example, many courts characterize a "shop right" as being a type of implied license, and thus the focus is often on whether the employee engaged in any activities, e.g., developing the invention on the employer's time at the employer's expense, which demand a finding that he impliedly granted a license to his employer to use the invention. Other courts characterize a "shop right" as a form of equitable estoppel, and thus the focus is often on whether the employee's actions, e.g., consent or acquiescence to his employer's use of the invention, demand a finding that he is estopped from asserting a patent right against his employer. Neither characterization appears to be inherently better than the other, and the end result under either is often the same, given that the underlying analysis in each case is driven by principles of equity and fairness, and given that the courts often analyze a "shop right" as being a combination of the two even though they may characterize it in name as one or the other.

It is thus not surprising that many courts adopt neither characterization specifically, instead choosing to characterize a "shop right" more broadly as simply being a common law "right" that inures to an employer when the circumstances demand it under principles of equity and fairness. These courts often look to both the circumstances surrounding the development of the invention and the facts regarding the employee's activities respecting that invention, once developed, to determine whether it would be fair and equitable to allow an employee to preclude his employer from making use of that invention. This is essentially the analysis that most courts undertake regardless of how they characterize "shop rights."

In view of the foregoing, we believe that the proper methodology for determining whether an employer has acquired a "shop right" in a patented invention is to look to the totality of the circumstances on a case by case basis and determine whether the facts of a particular case demand, under principles of equity and fairness, a finding that a "shop right" exists. In such an analysis, one should look to such factors as the circumstances surrounding the development of the patented invention and the inventor's activities respecting that invention, once developed, to determine whether equity and fairness demand that the employer be allowed to use that invention in his business. A factually driven analysis such as this ensures that the principles of equity and fairness underlying the "shop rights" rule are considered. Because this is exactly the type of analysis that the district court used to reach its decision, we see no error in the district court's analysis justifying reversal.

To reach its decision, the district court looked to the discussion of "shop rights" set forth in the often-cited Dubilier case, in which the Court said:

> where a servant, during his hours of employment, working with his master's materials and appliances, conceives and perfects an invention for which he obtains a patent, he must accord his master a nonexclusive right to practice the invention. [citation omitted] This is an application of equitable principles. Since the servant uses his master's time, facilities and materials to attain a concrete result, the latter is in equity entitled to use that which embodies his own property and to duplicate it as often as he may find occasion to employ similar appliances in his business.

[*U.S. v. Dubilier Condenser Corporation*, 289 U.S. 178, 188–89]. The district court also accepted a discussion of "shop rights" set forth in one of WRT's briefs filed in the district court action as correctly summarizing several factors that may be considered in analyzing a "shop rights" case. At pages 9–10 of its opinion, the district court included the following excerpt from pages 6–8 of WRT's Memorandum Brief in Support of Response to Motion for Summary

Judgment:

> Because broad equitable principles are involved in determining whether shop rights in [an] invention arise, "the full nature of the parties' relationship must be examined to determine whether a shop right exists." Rosenberg, Patent Law Fundamentals, § 11.04, 11-20 (1991).

> The following factors have been considered: the contractual nature of the relationship between employer and employee, whether the employee consented to the employer's use of the invention, and whether the employee induced, acquiesced in, or assisted the employer in the use of the invention. . . . [footnote omitted].

> An employer will have shop rights in an invention in situations where the employer has financed an employee's invention by providing wages, materials, tools and a work place. Other factors creating shop rights include an employee's consent, acquiescence, inducement, or assistance to the employer in using the invention without demanding compensation or other notice of restriction. See Rosenberg, Patent Law Fundamentals § 11.04 (1991).

Applying Dubilier and the summary of the law set forth in WRT's own brief to the facts of this case, the district court properly found that AP&L had acquired a "shop right" in Bowman's patented level detector which entitled AP&L to duplicate the level detector for use in its business.

Bowman developed the patented level detector while working at AP&L and suggested it to AP&L as an alternative to the K-ray system. AP&L installed the level detector on one hundred and twenty eight (128) precipitator hoppers at White Bluff with Bowman's consent and participation. Bowman also consented to, and participated at least in part in, the installation of the level detector on one hundred and twenty eight (128) precipitator hoppers at ISES. In addition, the level detectors on half of the hoppers at ISES were installed by a contractor other than WRT, with Bowman's and WRT's knowledge and consent. All costs and expenses associated with the testing and implementation of the level detector on the hoppers at White Bluff and ISES were paid by AP&L.

Furthermore, Bowman never asserted that AP&L was precluded from using the level detector without his permission or that AP&L was required to compensate him for its use. Indeed, the record suggests that Bowman believed quite the opposite. As recognized by the district court at page 12 of its opinion, Bowman admitted in a deposition [footnote omitted] that he believed all along that AP&L would have shop rights. His patent attorney had informed him of that possibility and he subsequently shared the attorney's opinion with his partners in WRT. See Bowman deposition at 81–82.

WRT argues that Bowman's consent or acquiescence after he had assigned his rights in the Bowman application to WRT is irrelevant. Even if this were true, Bowman's actions at White Bluff prior to this assignment justify the district court's finding that a "shop right" was created. Nevertheless, WRT, of which Bowman was a part owner during the relevant time period, acquiesced both to AP&L's continued use of the level detector at White Bluff and ISES and to the installation of the level detector by outside contractors at ISES. This lends further support to the district court's decision.

WRT also argues that, even if AP&L had acquired a "shop right" to use the patented level detector, AP&L somehow exceeded the scope of that right when it allegedly "carelessly and casually disseminated the design and specifications of the patented device to private contractors." WRT argues that, by putting information of this nature on the open market, AP&L rendered the patent "worthless" and robbed Bowman of the "fruit of his labor." We find these arguments unpersuasive for two reasons.

First, WRT has failed to explain how AP&L's mere dissemination of specifications of the patented level detector constituted patent infringement. Clearly, it did not. The owner of a patent right may exclude others from making, using or selling the subject matter of a claimed invention. 35 U.S.C. §§ 154 and 271. AP&L's dissemination of information obviously does not fall into any of these categories. Even so, it is also unclear how disseminating specifications of the level detector after it was patented rendered the Bowman patent "worthless." The owner of the Bowman patent still retained the right to exclude all others than AP&L from practicing the claimed invention.

Second, we find no error in the district court's holding that AP&L's "shop right" entitled it to duplicate the level detector and to continue to use it in its business. Such a conclusion clearly finds support in the law. *H.F. Walliser & Co. v. F.W. Maurer & Sons Co.*, 17 F.2d 122, 124 (E.D. Pa. 1927); *see also Dubilier*, 289 U.S. at 188–89; *Thompson*, 174 F.2d at 778, 81 USPQ at 327–28; *Pure Oil Co. v. Hyman*, 95 F.2d 22, 25, 36 U.S.P.Q. (BNA) 306, 310 (7th Cir. 1938) ("shop right is co-extensive with the business requirements of the employer"). Furthermore, AP&L's "shop right" was not limited to AP&L's use of level detectors that AP&L itself had manufactured and installed. Quite to the contrary, we find that AP&L's "shop right" entitled it to procure the level detector from outside contractors. *Schmidt v. Central Foundry Co.*, 218 F. 466, 470 (D.N.J. 1914), *aff'd on other grounds*, 229 F. 157 (3d Cir. 1916).

Finally, WRT makes several arguments addressing the laws pertaining to the assignment of patent rights. However, AP&L has never asserted that it has any ownership rights in the Bowman patent. Rather, AP&L has merely claimed "shop rights" as a defense to WRT's patent infringement action. Accordingly, WRT's assignment arguments are considered irrelevant and thus unpersuasive.

AFFIRMED

ii. Hired to Invent

STANDARD PARTS CO. v. PECK
Supreme Court of the United States
264 U.S. 52 (1924)

Mr. Justice McKenna delivered the opinion of the Court.

Suit for injunction, preliminary and perpetual, and accounting for profits and damages, upon the ground of infringement of Letters Patent No. 1,249,473, issued to William J. Peck, respondent.

The bill is the usual one in patent cases. For answer to it the Standard Parts Company admits the use of the devices of the patent and alleges they were constructed under the supervision of Peck and under the terms and provisions of a contract dated August 23, 1915, by and between him and the Hess-Pontiac Spring and Axle Company, for and in behalf of the latter company and the Western Spring and Axle Company, and that it, the Standard Company, has succeeded to the entire assets, business and good will of those other companies, including all of their rights in said contract and devices. And the Standard Company avers that Peck was fully compensated for his connection with the devices.

. . .

On the case as thus presented, Peck's testimony and some other testimony was taken, and certain exhibits introduced, and the judgment of the District Court was . . . "that the property in the invention belonged to the employer" (the Hess-Pontiac Spring and Axle Company), and that this property passed to the Standard Parts Company when it acquired the assets of the Axle Company, and that Peck holds the legal title in trust for the Standard Company. A decree was directed to be entered requiring an assignment of the legal title to the latter Company.

. . .

The Circuit Court of Appeals reversed the decree of the District Court in so far as it decreed an assignment and transfer of the patent in suit and other patents and applications from Peck to the Standard Company.

. . .

The courts reached different rulings because of different readings of the cases. That of the District Court was, that while the mere fact that one is employed by another does not preclude him from making improvements in the machines with which he is connected, and obtaining patents therefor, as his individual property, yet, if he "be employed to invent or devise such improvements his patents therefor belong to his employer, since in making such improvements he is merely doing what he was hired to do."

The Circuit Court of Appeals rejected this test. It conceded, however, that the deduction of the District Court was sustained by *Solomons v. United States*, 137 U.S. 342; *McAleer v. United States*, 150 U.S. 424, and *Gill v. United States*, 160 U.S. 426, and if correct, required the affirmance of the decree of the District Court. And the court admitted that there was no later declaration than that of those cases, nor any criticism of it. The court, nevertheless, dissented from it, subordinating it to other cases and reasoning, they establishing, it was considered, "that an invention does not belong to the employer, merely by virtue of an employment contract, as well when that employment is to devise or improve a specific thing as when the employment is to devise improvements generally in the line of the employer's business." And considering further that Peck's employment was to devise or improve a specific thing, decided that his contract did not "of its own force, convey to the employer the equitable title to the patentable inventions" which he "might make in the course of its execution" but gave "to the employer a license only."

It is going very far to say that the declaration of *Solomons v. United States*, repeated in subsequent cases, and apparently constituting their grounds of decision, may be put aside or underrated — assigned the inconsequence of dicta. It might be said that there is persuasion in the repetition. It cannot be contended that the invention of a specific thing cannot be made the subject of a bargain and pass in execution of it. And such, we think, was the object and effect of Peck's contract with the Hess-Pontiac Spring and Axle Company. That company had a want in its business, a "problem," is Peck's word, and he testified that "Mr. Hess thought probably" that he, (Peck), "could be of some assistance to him [Hess] in working out" the "problem," and the "thought" was natural. Hess had previous acquaintance with Peck — his inventive and other ability, and approached him, the result being the contract of August 23, 1915, the material parts of which are as follows: "This agreement witnesseth, that second party is to devote his time to the development of a process and machinery for the production of the front spring now used on the product of the Ford Motor Company. First party is to pay second party for such services the sum of $300 per month. That should said process and machinery be finished at or before the expiration of four months from August 11, 1915, second party is to receive a bonus of $100 per month. That when finished, second party is to receive a bonus of $10 for each per cent of reduction from present direct labor, as disclosed by the books of first party."

By the contract Peck engaged to "devote his time to the development of a process and machinery" and was to receive therefore a stated compensation. Whose property was the "process and machinery" to be when developed? The answer would seem to be inevitable and resistless — of him who engaged the services and paid for them, they being his inducement and compensation, they being not for temporary use but perpetual use, a provision for a business, a facility in it and an asset of it, therefore, contributing to it whether retained or sold — the vendee (in this case the Standard Company) paying for it and getting the rights the vendor had (in this case, the Axle Company).

Other meaning to the contract would confuse the relation of the parties to it — take from the Axle Company the inducement the company had to make it — take from the company the advantage of its exclusive use and subject the company to the rivalry of competitors. And yet, such, we think, is the contention of Peck. He seems somewhat absorbing in his assertion of rights. He yields to the Axle Company a shop right only, free from the payment of royalty but personal and temporary — not one that could be assigned or transferred. Peck, therefore, virtually assets, though stimulated to services by the Hess Company and paid for them — doing nothing more than he was engaged to do and paid for doing — that the product of the services was so entirely his property that he might give as great a right to any member of the mechanical world as to the one who engaged him and paid him — a right to be used in competition with the one who engaged him and paid him.

NOTES & QUESTIONS

1. Shop Right

The "shop right" doctrine awards an employer a nontransferable, nonexclusive right to make use of an employee's invention without compensation.

A court typically bases its award of a shop right on the doctrines of estoppel, license implied in fact, and equity and fairness. The limited right awarded under the doctrine is not an ownership interest, but rather a defense against claims of infringement on the patent. An employer obtains nothing more than a right to use the employee invention without apprehension of an infringement suit. The employee inventor retains full ownership rights and may assign or license the patent rights to others.

2. A Beautiful Mind: An Employee Hired to Invent

Standard Parts Co. v. Peck marked the first time the United States Supreme Court held that an employee hired to apply his inventive ability owed a duty to assign patent rights to the employer. Notice that in *Standard Parts* the employee was directed to invent a specific improvement. Would the obligation to assign patent rights apply as well to an employee hired to conduct general research? What if the employer were the United States government? *See United States v. Dubilier Condenser Corp.,* 289 U.S. 178 (1933).

3. History of Default Patent Ownership

The default rule of patent ownership in the employment context has historically moved towards an increase in protection for employer's rights. Catherine Fisk, in the article, *Removing the "Fuel of Interest" from the "Fire of Genius": Law and the Employee-Inventor,* 65 U. CHI. L. REV. 1127 (1998), proposes that there are three overlapping periods in the development of employee inventor law. In the first period, during the early nineteenth century, the employee inventor exclusively owned the rights to their inventions. The ownership of inventions did not hinge upon the inventor's status as an employee. During this first period, "shop rights" were predicated on the doctrine of equitable estoppel rather than on the doctrine of employment law. The second period of the later nineteenth century saw a gradual shift towards awarding "shop rights" to employers on the basis of the employment relationship. In the third period, beginning at the turn of the twentieth century, the analysis of invention ownership was dominated by contract law, as employers increasingly relied upon employment contracts to protect valuable inventions developed during the employment relationship.

b. Trade Secrets

i. Introduction

The employer-employee relationship gives rise to the majority of trade secret disputes. The law of trade secrets balances the competing interests of the employer and the employee. Employers often invest substantial resources towards the development and maintenance of trade secrets. If competitors were free to bypass the cost of independent development by obtaining trade secrets by means of hiring away a company's employees, then employers may be reluctant to risk the cost of developing trade secrets and entrusting the knowledge to employees. The law protects investment in trade secrets by imposing a duty upon employees to not use or disclose their employer's trade secrets. On the other hand, the law recognizes that employees have a right to use their skill, knowledge, and experience in pursuing their chosen career. The public policy interest of employee mobility may therefore impose a limit on employer trade secret protection. Problems may arise when an employee's knowledge and skill are inextricably intertwined with the employer's claimed trade secrets. The following case illustrates the tension between the interests of the employer and that of the departing employee.

WEXLER v. GREENBERG
Supreme Court of Pennsylvania
160 A.2d 430 (1960)

COHEN, Justice.

Appellees, trading as Buckingham Wax Company, filed a complaint in equity to enjoin Brite Products Co., Inc., and its officers, Greenberg, Dickler and Ford, appellants, from disclosing and using certain formulas and processes pertaining to the manufacture of certain sanitation and maintenance chemicals, allegedly trade secrets. After holding lengthy hearings, the chancellor concluded that the four formulas involved are trade secrets which appellant Greenberg disclosed in contravention of his duty of nondisclosure arising from his confidential relationship with Buckingham. He decreed that appellants, jointly and severally, be enjoined permanently from disclosing the formulas or processes or any substantially similar formulas and from making or selling the resulting products. He also ordered an accounting for losses. After the dismissal by the court *en banc* of appellants' exceptions to the chancellor's findings of fact and conclusions of law, the chancellor's decree was made final and this appeal followed.

Buckingham Wax Company is engaged in the manufacture, compounding and blending of sanitation and maintenance chemicals. In March, 1949, appellant Greenberg, a qualified chemist in the sanitation and maintenance field, entered the employ of Buckingham as its chief chemist and continued there until April 28, 1957. In the performance of his duties, Greenberg consumed half of his working time in Buckingham's laboratory where he would analyze and duplicate competitors' products and then use the resulting information to develop various new formulas. He would change or modify these formulas for color, odor or viscosity in order that greater commercial use could be made of Buckingham's products. The remainder of his time was spent in ordering necessary materials and interviewing chemical salesmen concerning new, better or cheaper ingredients for the multitude of products produced by Buckingham so that costs could be lowered and quality increased. As a result of his activities Greenberg was not only familiar with Buckingham's formulas, he was also fully conversant with the costs of the products and the most efficient method of producing them.

Appellant Brite Products Co., Inc., is a Pennsylvania corporation. . . . [F]rom August, 1956, until August 20, 1957, the date of Brite's last order, Brite exclusively purchased Buckingham's manufactured products. These products were in turn distributed by Brite to its customers, mostly industrial users, marked with labels which identified said products as products of Brite. Brite's purchases of sanitation and maintenance products from Buckingham amounted annually to approximately $35,000.

. . . In August, 1957, Greenberg left Buckingham and went to work for Brite. At no time during Greenberg's employment with Buckingham did there exist between them a written or oral contract of employment or any restrictive agreement.

Prior to Greenberg's association with Brite, the corporation's business consisted solely of selling a complete line of maintenance and sanitation chemicals, including liquid soap cleaners, wax base cleaners, disinfectants and floor finishes. Upon Greenberg's arrival, however, the corporation purchased equipment and machinery and, under the guidance and supervision of Greenberg, embarked on a full-scale program for the manufacture of a cleaner, floor finish and disinfectant, products previously purchased from Buckingham. The formulas in issue in this litigation are the formulas for each of these respective products. The appellants dispute the chancellor's findings as to the identity of their formulas with those of Buckingham, but there was evidence that a spectrophometer examination of the respective products of the parties revealed that the formulas used in making these products are substantially identical. Appellants cannot deny that they thought the products sufficiently similar as to continue delivery of their own products to their customers in the same cans and drums and with the same labels attached which they had previously used in distributing the products manufactured by Buckingham, and to continue using the identical promotional advertising material. Appellees' formulas had been developed during the tenure of Greenberg as chief chemist and are unquestionably known to him.

The chancellor found that Greenberg did not develop the formulas for Brite's products after he left Buckingham, but rather that he had appropriated them by carrying over the knowledge of them which he had acquired in Buckingham's employ. The chancellor went on to find that the formulas constituted trade secrets and that their appropriation was in violation of the duty that Greenberg owed to Buckingham by virtue of his employment and the trust reposed in him. Accordingly, the relief outlined above was ordered.

We are initially concerned with the fact that the final formulations claimed to be trade secrets were not *disclosed to* Greenberg by the appellees during his service or because of his position. Rather, the fact is that these formulas had been developed by Greenberg himself, while in the pursuit of his duties as Buckingham's chief chemist, or under Greenberg's direct supervision. We are thus faced with the problem of determining the extent to which a former employer, *without the aid of any express covenant,* can restrict his ex-employee, a highly skilled chemist, in the uses to which this employee can put his knowledge of formulas and methods he himself developed during the course of his former employment because this employer claims these same formulas, as against the rest of the world, as his trade secrets. This problem becomes particularly significant when one recognizes that Greenberg's situation is not uncommon. In this era of electronic, chemical, missile and atomic development, many skilled technicians and expert employees are currently in the process of developing potential trade secrets. Competition for personnel of this caliber is exceptionally keen, and the interchange of employment is commonplace. One has but to reach for his daily newspaper to appreciate the current market for such skilled employees. We must therefore be particularly mindful of any effect our decision in this case might have in disrupting this pattern of employee mobility, both in view of possible restraints upon an individual in the pursuit of his livelihood and the harm to the public in general in forestalling to any extent widespread technological advances.

The principles outlining this area of the law are clear. A court of equity will protect an employer from the unlicensed disclosure or use of his trade secrets by an ex-employee provided the employee entered into an enforceable covenant so restricting his use, *Fralich v. Despar,* 165 Pa. 24, 30 Atl. 521 (1894), or was bound to secrecy by virtue of a confidential relationship existing between the employer and employee, *Pittsburgh Cut Wire Co. v. Sufrin,* 350 Pa. 31, 38 A. 2d 33 (1944). Where, however, an employer has no legally protectable trade secret, an employee's "aptitude, his skill, his dexterity, his manual and mental ability, and such other subjective knowledge as he obtains while in the course of his employment, are not the property of his employer and the right to use and expand these powers remains his property unless curtailed through some restrictive covenant entered into with the employer:" *Id.* at 35. The employer thus has the burden of showing two things: (1) a legally protectable trade secret; and (2) a legal basis, either a covenant or a confidential relationship, upon which to predicate relief.

Since we are primarily concerned with the fact that Buckingham is seeking to enjoin Greenberg from using formulas he developed without the aid of an agreement, we shall assume for the purpose of this appeal that the appellees have met their burden of proving that the formulas in issue are trade secrets. The sole issue for us to decide, therefore, is whether or not a confidential relationship existed between Greenberg and Buckingham binding Greenberg to a duty of nondisclosure.

The usual situation involving misappropriation of trade secrets in violation of a confidential relationship is one in which an employer *discloses to his employee* a pre-existing trade secret (one already developed or formulated) so that the employee may duly perform his work. In such a case, the trust and confidence upon which legal relief is predicated stems from the instance of the employer's *turning over to the employee* the preexisting trade secret. It is then that a pledge of secrecy is impliedly extracted from the employee, a pledge which he carries with him even beyond the ties of his employment relationship. Since it is conceptually impossible, however, to elicit an implied pledge of secrecy from the sole act of an employee turning over to his employer a trade secret which he, the employee, has developed, as occurred in the present case, the appellees must show a different manner in which the present circumstances support the permanent cloak of confidence cast upon Greenberg by the chancellor. The only avenue open to the appellees is to show that the nature of the employment relationship itself gave rise to a duty of nondisclosure.

The burden the appellees must thus meet brings to the fore a problem of accommodating competing policies in our law: the right of a businessman to be protected against unfair competition stemming from the usurpation of his trade secrets and the right of an individual to the unhampered pursuit of the occupations and livelihoods for which he is best suited. There are cogent - socio-economic arguments in favor of either position. Society as a whole greatly benefits from technological improvements. Without some means of post-employment protection to assure that valuable developments or improvements are exclusively those of the employer, the businessman could not afford to subsidize research or improve current methods. In addition, it must be recognized that modern economic growth and development has pushed the business venture beyond the size of the one-man firm, forcing the businessman to a much greater degree to entrust confidential business information relating to technological development to appropriate employees. While recognizing the utility in the dispersion of responsibilities in larger firms, the optimum amount of "entrusting" will not occur unless the risk of loss to the businessman through a breach of trust can be held to a minimum.

On the other hand, any form of post-employment restraint reduces the economic mobility of employees and limits their personal freedom to pursue a preferred course of livelihood. The employee's bargaining position is weakened because he is potentially shackled by the acquisition of alleged trade secrets; and thus, paradoxically, he is restrained, because of his increased expertise, from advancing further in the industry in which he is most productive. Moreover, as previously mentioned, society suffers because competition is diminished by slackening the dissemination of ideas, processes and methods.

Were we to measure the sentiment of the law by the weight of both English and American decisions in order to determine whether it favors protecting a businessman from certain forms of competition or protecting an individual in his unrestricted pursuit of a livelihood, the balance would heavily favor the latter. . . . The chancellor's finding that Greenberg, while in the employ of Buckingham, never engaged in research nor conducted any experiments nor created or invented any formula was undisputed. There is nothing in the record to indicate that the formulas in issue were specific projects of great concern and concentration by Buckingham; instead it appears they were merely the result of Greenberg's routine work of changing and modifying formulas derived from competitors. Since there was no experimentation or research, the developments by change and modification were fruits of Greenberg's own skill as a chemist without any appreciable assistance by way of information or great expense or supervision by Buckingham, outside of the normal expenses of his job. . . . [W]e hold that this information forms part of the technical knowledge and skill [Greenberg] has acquired by virtue of his employment with Buckingham and which he has an unqualified privilege to use. . . .

NOTES & QUESTIONS

1. Was Greenberg "Hired to Invent"?

Ownership of trade secrets in the employment setting depends upon three factors: (1) the nature of the work for which the employee was hired, (2) the degree to which the invention is related to the employer's business, and (3) the extent to which the employee used the employer's time and resources to develop the trade secret. When an employee is hired to invent, the product of his efforts belong to his employer. This is true even for a scientist hired to conduct general research and development, where the employer does not specify the thing or specific field in which the employee is to work. Nonetheless,

Wexler v. Greenberg illustrates that under certain situations, the employee is free to use his unpatented discoveries. One explanation for the result in *Wexler* is that Greenberg was not engaged in research and development. Instead, Buckingham hired Greenberg for his general skill in chemistry, to duplicate the preexisting formulas of competitor's cleaning products. The formulas duplicated by Greenberg for his former employer resulted directly from his skill and experience rather than from company-sponsored independent research and development. Greenberg therefore was free to use his skill, knowledge, and experience, as embodied in the formulas, in the service of subsequent employers.

Factual analysis of the trade secret issue reveals another way to look at the result in *Wexler*. Notice that the *Wexler* court merely "assumed for the purposes of the appeal . . . that the formulas in issue are trade secrets." Greenberg's role at Buckingham was to reverse engineer cleaning products owned by third parties. If the formulas for the cleaning products are readily susceptible of copying, then anyone who purchases the cleaning products from the third parties may determine the underlying formulas. Where an employer cannot prove that a former employer took information that was a trade secret, then without an express restrictive covenant to the contrary, the employee is free to use his knowledge and skill to pursue his living wherever he so chooses. Roger M. Milgrim, *Milgrim on Trade Secrets* § 5.02[3][e] (2005).

2. Post Employment Limits on Trade Secret Protection

After the termination of the employment relationship, an employee may use his skill, knowledge, and experience in subsequent employment so long as such use does not involve or threaten the disclosure of the former employer's trade secret or violate a restrictive covenant. An employer may not claim trade secret rights over the general knowledge of its employees. Such knowledge includes the employee's education, prior job experiences, and abilities, as well as any job-enhanced skills he gains during the term of employment.

In addition, once the employment relationship terminates, the employee is relieved of the implied duty not to compete with his former employer. An employee is free to improve himself and leverage his superior abilities at the conclusion of the employment relationship into a better job, even one in competition with his former employer. The law generally favors employee mobility and competition. The balance between the employer's interest in secrecy and the employee's rights to mobility is struck by distinguishing between the employer's unique confidential knowledge which the law protects, and the employee's own general knowledge and experience, which the law allows the employee to take with him.

3. Submission of Ideas by Employees

Every year, American employees submit ideas that save their employers millions of dollars. Submission of ideas by employees is generally governed by the common law of trade secrets, which gives an employer ownership rights to the trade secrets and ideas created by its employees. At minimum, if an idea is related to an employer's business and was developed on company time and using company resources, then the doctrine of shop right entitles the employer to use the idea without compensating the employee.

ii.   Implied Duties of Employees

When an employee accepts employment that places him in a position to gain knowledge of confidential information, he enters into a confidential relationship that implies a duty not to use or disclose an employer's trade secrets in competition with the employer. The law allows employers to divulge trade secrets to employees without jeopardizing trade secret protection. However, notice usually must be given prior to the disclosure of the confidential information to the employee. The form of the notice is unimportant so long as the notice ensures that the employee knows or has reason to know that the disclosure of information is made in confidence. It is with respect to the information that the employee knows or has reason to know is confidential that the implied duty of confidentiality arises.

HARRY R. DEFLER CORPORATION v. KLEEMAN
Supreme Court of New York, Appellate Division, Fourth Department
19 A.D.2d 396 (1963)

WILLIAMS, P. J.

. . . Since 1928, the plaintiff and its predecessor have engaged in the business of buying and selling industrial carbons, cokes, charcoal, graphite and other related products. Over a period exceeding 25 years Harry R. Defler, the founder of plaintiff's predecessor, developed a large number of customers for these various products and compiled a comprehensive catalogue of information in the form of office records. . . . Plaintiff's compilation of information was not available to the general public and could not have been duplicated by one who had not had the actual experience of Harry R. Defler. The value of this information was confirmed by the fact that on the death of Harry R. Defler, the assets of the original corporation, consisting primarily of its goodwill, name, outstanding contracts and business records, were sold to a purchaser who was himself familiar with the field, for $250,000. The physical assets of the corporation were of relatively slight value. The really substantial asset was Defler's property rights in the confidential information so transferred.

The purchaser organized the plaintiff corporation which continued doing business under the same name and in the same manner as in the past. On December 1, 1956 the plaintiff employed the defendant Francis S. Kleeman to serve as its general manager and elected him vice-president. As a necessary part of his employment as general manager, Kleeman, who had no previous experience in the type of business conducted by plaintiff, was furnished with free access to the business records containing all of such confidential information. There can be no question that this information was treated as confidential by the corporation and would not have been available to Kleeman if it were not essential for the performance of his duties as general manager. Kleeman was made aware of this when he entered plaintiff's employ.

Approximately one year after he became associated with the plaintiff, Kleeman hired the defendant Edward G. Schneider, Jr., to work for plaintiff as a salesman. Like Kleeman, Schneider had no previous experience in this particular type of business nor had he any knowledge of plaintiff's methods or of the information contained in its confidential records.

Sometime in the Spring of 1958 Kleeman and Schneider, although still in the plaintiff's employ and in violation of their duty of loyalty to the plaintiff's interests, embarked upon a course of action designed to divert to themselves the very business they had been employed to obtain and retain for the plaintiff. Mrs. Kleeman and Mrs. Schneider knowingly joined in the plan at a meeting in the Kleeman home, at which all four individual defendants were present, when it was agreed that the corporate defendant Carchem Products Corporation would be formed. The certificate of incorporation was executed on May 14, 1958. Thereupon Kleeman and Schneider ceased their efforts on behalf of their employer. Schneider, holding 50% of the stock of the new corporation, became its president, treasurer, chairman of the board and sole salesman. Virginia Kleeman purchased the remaining 50% for $500 with a check drawn on her joint bank account with her husband. She also became comptroller and Patricia Schneider became secretary. Kleeman loaned the corporation $5,000 from his personal bank account, thus providing the working capital which enabled the corporation to commence doing business.

The new corporation proved to be an immediate success. Schneider, who had not been able up to that time to develop any business for the plaintiff suddenly became extremely productive. He guided the new corporation with such acumen that within two months the $5,000 loan from Kleeman had been repaid in full and the corporation was able to pay a total of $1,750 per month under the guise of salaries to Virginia Kleeman and the Schneiders. At that time Virginia Kleeman worked a total of 10 hours each week. The corporation also paid her a $50 monthly rental for a space in the Kleeman home where the corporation's books were kept.

Unfortunately for the plaintiff, the new corporation's business success was attributable to the fact that it dealt almost exclusively with customers and suppliers of plaintiff. Defendants, during their employment by plaintiff and while disloyal to it, continued to enjoy all of the benefits of their relationship with plaintiff. They freely exploited plaintiff's confidential information as to the identity and particular needs of customers, solicited customers, vouched for Carchem's credit in plaintiff's name and even charged telephone and travel expenses to plaintiff although they were incurred in the interests of Carchem. Their audacity probably reached its peak when they paid, with plaintiff's funds, the legal fees incurred in connection with the incorporation of Carchem. Their conduct was not only reprehensible, but completely astounding.

The defendants' disloyalty continued apace after Schneider was discharged by the plaintiff on September 30, 1958. Kleeman not only acquiesced in Schneider's business transactions with plaintiff's customers and suppliers, in his wife's participation in the affairs of Carchem, and in the deposit of her salary in their joint bank account, but he withheld his knowledge of Schneider's activities from the other officers and directors of plaintiff. In some instances he actively diverted business to Carchem. Moreover, following his resignation from plaintiff's employment on February 25, 1960 he not only continued to divert business from plaintiff to Carchem but he procured business for himself in violation of a reasonable and valid noncompetition provision in his contract of employment.

The customers and suppliers of plaintiff, though perhaps well known in industrial fields, were not readily apparent as customers and suppliers for plaintiff's particular type of business. As we have observed, the information as to the availability of materials and the peculiar needs of plaintiff's customers was derived from the intimate knowledge acquired through years of experience by Defler. Therefore, the defendants by exploiting this information obtained an advantage not available to a stranger seeking to set himself up in fair competition with plaintiff. The actions of the defendants in this case amounted to a theft not only of customers which the plaintiff had discovered and developed but of the essential tools for serving such customers.

The conclusion is inescapable that the type of business piracy practiced by the defendants amounted to misconduct which the courts have not hesitated to restrain.

It has been well established that an employee, who has had entrusted to him confidential information pertaining to the conduct and clientele of his employer's business which he would not have obtained were it not for his status as a trusted employee and which affords him an advantage over other competitors to whom the information is not available, may not subsequently use that information to further his own ends. . . . This restriction arises because of the confidential nature of the employment relationship and is not dependent upon the presence in the employment agreement of a provision limiting activities after cessation of employment. . . . The courts have even extended this protective doctrine so that a former employee may not accomplish through indirect means, such as revealing the information to a third party, what he may not achieve directly. In such case the injunction may issue against the new employer attempting to use the information as well as against the former employee. There can be no question that the information which the defendants exploited falls well within the category of data to which protection has traditionally been accorded. "The principle of law, however, is not confined to secret processes of manufacture or methods of doing business, but has a much wider application. . . . The names of the customers of a business concern whose trade and patronage have been secured by years of business effort and advertising, and the expenditure of time and money, constituting a part of the good-will of a business which enterprise and foresight have built up, should be deemed just as sacred and entitled to the same protection as a secret of compounding some article of manufacture and commerce." (*Witkop & Holmes Co.* v. *Boyce, supra*, p. 131.). . . . The question of the extent to which protection may be accorded customer lists was thoroughly reviewed in *Town & Country Serv.* v. *Newbery* (3 N.Y. 2d 554). The criteria which the court relied upon in that case are equally applicable to the present case. It was stated (pp. 559, 560): "the plaintiff had obtained a customers list, the names of which 'could only be secured by the expenditure of a large amount of time, effort and money in gathering together such a vast list of consumers who desired to do business in this peculiar way. These customers were not classified as likely customers in any public directory. They were not discoverable by any public display of their willingness to deal.' . . . It would be different if these customers had been equally available to appellants and respondent, but, as has been related, these customers had been screened by respondent as considerable effort and expense, without which their receptivity and willingness to do business with this kind of a service organization could not be known."

Plaintiff is, therefore, entitled to an injunction permanently restraining the defendants from continuing their illegal activities. In addition, plaintiff is entitled to be compensated for the damages which it has sustained as a consequence of the defendants' unlawful acts (*Town & Country Serv.* v. *Newbery*, *supra; Duane Jones Co.* v. *Burke*, 306 N.Y. 172, *supra; Electrolux Corp.* v. *Val-Worth, Inc.*, 6 N Y 2d 556).

In cases of this nature an accounting for the profits realized by the defendants resulting from their illegal acts may furnish the most reliable method of computing the loss (see *Biltmore Pub. Co.* v. *Grayson Pub. Corp.*, 272 App. Div. 504; *Dad's Root Beer Co.* v. *Doc's Beverages*, 193 F. 2d 77 [C. A., 2d]). However, in view of the substantial and unnecessary expenses incurred by the defendants in the form of excessive salaries and otherwise, a bare accounting for the defendants' profits may not make the plaintiff whole. The accounting Justice should determine what the plaintiff's margin of net profit would have been if it had retained the business which the defendants diverted (see *Westcott Chuck Co.* v. *Oneida Nat. Chuck Co.*, 199 N. Y. 247; *Santa's Workshop* v. *Sterling*, 2 A D 2d 262). With respect to determining sales which the plaintiff could reasonably have expected to make but for defendants' disloyalties, there is in this case "a causal relation not wholly unsubstantial and imaginary, between the gains of the aggressor and those diverted from his victim". (*Underhill* v. *Schenck*, 238 N. Y. 7, 17.)

In view of the continuing nature of the damage sustained by the plaintiff and the fact that this proceeding is equitable in nature, the period of the accounting should extend to the date of the completion thereof, but without limiting plaintiff's right to future accountings. (Cf. *Duane Jones Co.* v. *Burke*, *supra*.)

An employee whose actions are disloyal to the interests of his employer forfeits his right to compensation for services rendered by him (*Lamdin* v. *Broadway Surface Adv. Corp.*, 272 N.Y. 133) and if he is paid without knowledge of his disloyalty he may be compelled to return what he has improperly received. . . . Therefore, the plaintiff may recover the amount of compensation paid to Kleeman and Schneider subsequent to May 14, 1958, the date on which the certificate of incorporation of Carchem was executed. . . . The defendants should also be required to account for any expenses of Carchem which were improperly charged to the plaintiff, and inasmuch as the defendant Francis S. Kleeman violated the provision in his employment agreement against competing with the plaintiff, directly or indirectly, for a period of three years following the termination of his employment, he should compensate the plaintiff for any damages sustained as the result.

NOTES & QUESTIONS

1. Duration of an Employee's Duty to the Employer

The duty not to use or disclose an employer's trade secret exists during the term of the employment and may endure past the termination of the employment relationship. During employment, there exists an implied duty not to compete, though some jurisdictions allow an employee to engage in activities in anticipation of leaving his current employer, including efforts in furtherance of forming a competing business. However, an employee who begins working for a rival company before leaving the first goes too far and breaches his fiduciary duty to the first employer.

2. Employer's Efforts to Maintain Secrecy

While the duty of confidentiality imposed upon employees exists even in the absence of an express confidentiality agreement, the extent to which the implied duties protect an employer's confidential information depends on the employer's efforts to keep the information secret. A lack of effort on the part of the employer to shield its information may jeopardize any implied protection for the information. In *Tyson Foods, Inc. v. Conagra, Inc.,* 79 S.W.3d 326 (Ark. 2002), the court held that Tyson's failure to guard the secrecy of the nutrient profile for its poultry feed defeated the company's attempt to invoke trade secret protection for the information.

> [I]t is the efforts taken by the *company* to safeguard the information that is critical, not the perception of individual officers. Absent clear corporate action to protect the nutrient profile as a trade secret, a subjective belief of an individual employee that the information is confidential or even had value seems largely irrelevant in our analysis.

Tyson, 79 S.W.3d at 483.

c. Copyrights

The copyright in a work initially vests in the author. 17 U.S.C. § 201(a). If more than one author prepares a work "with the intention that their contributions be merged into inseparable or interdependent parts of a unitary whole," then each of the authors owns an equal and undivided interest in the "joint work." 17 U.S.C. § 101.

In the employment context, an employer may commission and pay for a "work made for hire," defined in 17 U.S.C. § 101 as work "prepared by an employee within the scope of his or her employment." If an employee creates a work made for hire, then the employer is deemed the author and owns the copyright in the work. Unlike the laws governing patents and trade secrets, the legislative history of the Copyright Act reflects a rejection of the shop right doctrine. Instead of awarding the employer a mere shop right — a nonexclusive license to use the work — the Copyright Act awards outright ownership in the copyright to the employer. Not surprisingly, the determination of when a person qualifies as an employee has important consequences for proper assignment of the copyright in a work.

COMMUNITY FOR CREATIVE NON-VIOLENCE v. JAMES EARL REID
Supreme Court of the United States
490 U.S. 730 (1989)

MARSHALL, Justice.

In this case, an artist and the organization that hired him to produce a sculpture contest the ownership of the copyright in that work. To resolve this dispute, we must construe the "work made for hire" provisions of the Copyright Act of 1976 (Act or 1976 Act), 17 U.S.C. §§ 101 and 201(b), and in particular, the provision in § 101, which defines as a "work made for hire" a "work prepared by an employee within the scope of his or her employment" (hereinafter § 101(1)).

I

Petitioners are the Community for Creative Non-Violence (CCNV), a non-profit unincorporated association dedicated to eliminating homelessness in America, and Mitch Snyder, a member and trustee of CCNV. In the fall of 1985, CCNV decided to participate in the annual Christmastime Pageant of Peace in Washington, D. C., by sponsoring a display to dramatize the plight of the homeless. As the District Court recounted:

> Snyder and fellow CCNV members conceived the idea for the nature of the display: a sculpture of a modern Nativity scene in which, in lieu of the traditional Holy Family, the two adult figures and the infant would appear as contemporary homeless people huddled on a street-side steam grate. The family was to be black (most of the homeless in Washington being black); the figures were to be life-sized, and the steam grate would be positioned atop a platform 'pedestal,' or base, within which special-effects equipment would be enclosed to emit simulated 'steam' through the grid to swirl about the figures. They also settled upon a title for the work — 'Third World America' — and a legend for the pedestal: 'and still there is no room at the inn.' 652 F. Supp. 1453, 1454 (DC 1987).

Snyder made inquiries to locate an artist to produce the sculpture. He was referred to respondent James Earl Reid, a Baltimore, Maryland, sculptor. In the course of two telephone calls, Reid agreed to sculpt the three human figures. CCNV agreed to make the steam grate and pedestal for the statue. Reid proposed that the work be cast in bronze, at a total cost of approximately $100,000 and taking six to eight months to complete. Snyder rejected that proposal because CCNV did not have sufficient funds, and because the statue had to be completed by December 12 to be included in the pageant. Reid then suggested, and Snyder agreed, that the sculpture would be made of a material known as "Design Cast 62," a synthetic substance that could meet CCNV's monetary and time constraints, could be tinted to resemble bronze, and could withstand the elements. The parties agreed that the project would cost no more than $15,000, not including Reid's services, which he offered to donate. The parties did not sign a written agreement. Neither party mentioned copyright.

After Reid received an advance of $3,000, he made several sketches of figures in various poses. At Snyder's request, Reid sent CCNV a sketch of a proposed sculpture showing the family in a crËche like setting: the mother seated, cradling a baby in her lap; the father standing behind her, bending over her shoulder to touch the baby's foot. Reid testified that Snyder asked for the sketch to use in raising funds for the sculpture. Snyder testified that it was also for his approval. Reid sought a black family to serve as a model for the sculpture. Upon Snyder's suggestion, Reid visited a family living at CCNV's Washington shelter but decided that only their newly born child was a suitable model. While Reid was in Washington, Snyder took him to see homeless people living on the streets. Snyder pointed out that they tended to recline on steam grates, rather than sit or stand, in order to warm their bodies. From that time on, Reid's sketches contained only reclining figures.

Throughout November and the first two weeks of December 1985, Reid worked exclusively on the statue, assisted at various times by a dozen different people who were paid with funds provided in installments by CCNV. On a number of occasions, CCNV members visited Reid to check on his progress and to coordinate CCNV's construction of the base. CCNV rejected Reid's proposal to use suitcases or shopping bags to hold the family's personal belongings, insisting instead on a shopping cart. Reid and CCNV members did not discuss copyright ownership on any of these visits.

On December 24, 1985, 12 days after the agreed-upon date, Reid delivered the completed statue to Washington. There it was joined to the steam grate and pedestal prepared by CCNV and placed on display near the site of the pageant. Snyder paid Reid the final installment of the $15,000. The statue remained on display for a month. In late January 1986, CCNV members returned it to Reid's studio in Baltimore for minor repairs. Several weeks later, Snyder began making plans to take the statue on a tour of several cities to raise money for the homeless. Reid objected, contending that the Design Cast 62 material was not strong enough to withstand the ambitious itinerary. He urged CCNV to cast the statue in bronze at a cost of $35,000, or to create a master mold at a cost of $5,000. Snyder declined to spend more of CCNV's money on the project.

In March 1986, Snyder asked Reid to return the sculpture. Reid refused. He then filed a certificate of copyright registration for "Third World America" in his name and announced plans to take the sculpture on a more modest tour than the one CCNV had proposed. Snyder, acting in his capacity as CCNV's trustee, immediately filed a competing certificate of copyright registration.

Snyder and CCNV then commenced this action against Reid and his photographer, Ronald Purtee, seeking return of the sculpture and a determination of copyright ownership. The District Court granted a preliminary injunction, ordering the sculpture's return. After a 2-day bench trial, the District Court declared that "Third World America" was a "work made for hire" under § 101 of the Copyright Act and that Snyder, as trustee for CCNV, was the exclusive owner of the copyright in the sculpture. 652 F. Supp., at 1457. The court reasoned that Reid had been an "employee" of CCNV within the meaning of § 101(1) because CCNV was the motivating force in the statue's production. Snyder and other CCNV members, the court explained, "conceived the idea of a contemporary Nativity scene to contrast with the national celebration of the season," and "directed enough of [Reid's] effort to assure that, in the end, he had produced what they, not he, wanted." *Id.*, at 1456.

. . .

II

A

The Copyright Act of 1976 provides that copyright ownership "vests initially in the author or authors of the work." 17 U. S. C. § 201(a). As a general rule, the author is the party who actually creates the work, that is, the person who translates an idea into a fixed, tangible expression entitled to copyright protection. § 102. The Act carves out an important exception, however, for "works made for hire." If the work is for hire, "the employer or other person for whom the work was prepared is considered the author" and owns the copyright, unless there is a written agreement to the contrary. § 201(b). Classifying a work as "made for hire" determines not only the initial ownership of its copyright, but also the copyright's duration, § 302(c), and the owners' renewal rights, § 304(a), termination rights, § 203(a), and right to import certain goods bearing the copyright, § 601(b)(1). See 1 M. Nimmer & D. Nimmer, Nimmer on Copyright § 5.03 [A], pp. 5-10 (1988). The contours of the work for hire doctrine therefore carry profound significance for freelance creators — including artists, writers, photographers, designers, composers, and computer programmers — and for the publishing, advertising, music, and other industries which commission their works. Section 101 of the 1976 Act provides that a work is "for hire" under two sets of circumstances:

> (1) a work prepared by an employee within the scope of his or her employment; or
> (2) a work specially ordered or commissioned for use as a contribution to a collective work, as a part of a motion picture or other audiovisual work, as a translation, as a supplementary work, as a compilation, as an instructional text, as a test, as answer material for a test, or as an atlas, if the parties expressly agree in a written instrument signed by them that the work shall be considered a work made for hire.

Petitioners do not claim that the statue satisfies the terms of § 101(2). Quite clearly, it does not. Sculpture does not fit within any of the nine categories of "specially ordered or commissioned" works enumerated in that subsection, and no written agreement between the parties establishes "Third World America" as a work for hire.

The dispositive inquiry in this case therefore is whether "Third World America" is "a work prepared by an employee within the scope of his or her employment" under § 101(1). The Act does not define these terms. In the absence of such guidance, four interpretations have emerged. The first holds that a work is prepared by an employee whenever the hiring party retains the right to control the product. Petitioners take this view. A second, and closely related, view is that a work is prepared by an employee under § 101(1) when the hiring party has actually wielded control with respect to the creation of a particular work. This approach was formulated by the Court of Appeals for the Second Circuit, *Aldon Accessories Ltd.* v. *Spiegel, Inc.*, 738 F. 2d 548, cert. denied, 469 U.S. 982 (1984), and adopted by the Fourth Circuit, *Brunswick Beacon, Inc.* v. *Schock-Hopchas Publishing Co.*, 810 F. 2d 410 (1987), the Seventh Circuit, *Evans Newton, Inc.* v. *Chicago Systems Software*, 793 F. 2d 889, cert. denied, 479 U.S. 949 (1986), and, at times, by petitioners, Brief for Petitioners 17. A third view is that the term "employee" within § 101(1) carries its common-law agency law meaning. This view was endorsed by the Fifth Circuit in *Easter Seal Society for Crippled Children & Adults of Louisiana, Inc.* v. *Playboy Enterprises*, 815 F. 2d 323 (1987), and by the Court of Appeals below. Finally, respondent and numerous *amici curiae* contend that the term "employee" only refers to "formal, salaried" employees.

The starting point for our interpretation of a statute is always its language. *Consumer Product Safety Comm'n* v. *GTE Sylvania, Inc.*, 447 U.S. 102, 108 (1980). The Act nowhere defines the terms "employee" or "scope of employment." It is, however, well established that "[w]here Congress uses terms that have accumulated settled meaning under . . . the common law, a court must infer, unless the statute otherwise dictates, that Congress means to incorporate the established meaning of these terms." *NLRB* v. *Amax Coal Co.*, 453 U.S. 322, 329 (1981); see also *Perrin* v. *United States*, 444 U.S. 37, 42 (1979). In the past, when Congress has used the term "employee" without defining it, we have concluded that Congress intended to describe the conventional master-servant relationship as understood by common-law agency doctrine. See, *e. g.*, *Kelley* v. *Southern Pacific Co.*, 419 U.S. 318, 322–323 (1974); *Baker* v. *Texas & Pacific R. Co.*, 359 U.S. 227, 228 (1959) *(per curiam); Robinson* v. *Baltimore & Ohio R. Co.*, 237 U.S. 84, 94 (1915). Nothing in the text of the work for hire provisions indicates that Congress used the words "employee" and "employment" to describe anything other than " 'the conventional relation of employer and employee.' " *Kelley, supra*, at 323, quoting *Robinson, supra*, at 94; cf. *NLRB* v. *Hearst Publications, Inc.*, 322 U.S. 111, 124–132 (1944) (rejecting agency law conception of employee for purposes of the National Labor Relations Act where structure and context of statute indicated broader definition). On the contrary, Congress' intent to incorporate the agency law definition is suggested by § 101(1)'s use of the term, "scope of employment," a widely used term of art in agency law. See Restatement (Second) of Agency § 228 (1958) (hereinafter Restatement).

. . .

In contrast, neither test proposed by petitioners is consistent with the text of the Act. The exclusive focus of the right to control the product test on the relationship between the hiring party and the product clashes with the language of § 101(1), which focuses on the relationship between the hired and hiring parties. The right to control the product test also would distort the meaning of the ensuing subsection, § 101(2). Section 101 plainly creates two distinct ways in which a work can be deemed for hire: one for works prepared by employees, the other for those specially ordered or commissioned works which fall within one of the nine enumerated categories and are the subject of a written agreement. The right to control the product test ignores this dichotomy by transforming into a work for hire under § 101(1) any "specially ordered or commissioned" work that is subject to the supervision and control of the hiring party. Because a party who hires a "specially ordered or commissioned" work by definition has a right to specify the characteristics of the product desired, at the time the commission is accepted, and frequently until it is completed, the right to control the product test would mean that many works that could satisfy § 101(2) would already have been deemed works for hire under § 101(1). Petitioners' interpretation is particularly hard to square with § 101(2)'s enumeration of the nine specific categories of specially ordered or commissioned works eligible to be works for hire, e. g., "a contribution to a collective work," "a part of a motion picture," and "answer material for a test." The unifying feature of these works is that they are usually prepared at the instance, direction, and risk of a publisher or producer. By their very nature, therefore, these types of works would be works by an employee under petitioners' right to control the product test.

. . .

We therefore conclude that the language and structure of § 101 of the Act do not support either the right to control the product or the actual control approaches. The structure of § 101 indicates that a work for hire can arise through one of two mutually exclusive means, one for employees and one for independent contractors, and ordinary canons of statutory interpretation indicate that the classification of a particular hired party should be made with reference to agency law.

This reading of the undefined statutory terms finds considerable support in the Act's legislative history. . . .

. . .

In sum, we must reject petitioners' argument. Transforming a commissioned work into a work by an employee on the basis of the hiring party's right to control, or actual control of, the work is inconsistent with the language, structure, and legislative history of the work for hire provisions. To determine whether a work is for hire under the Act, a court first should ascertain, using principles of general common law of agency, whether the work was prepared by an employee or an independent contractor. After making this determination, the court can apply the appropriate subsection of § 101.

B

We turn, finally, to an application of § 101 to Reid's production of "Third World America." In determining whether a hired party is an employee under the general common law of agency, we consider the hiring party's right to control the manner and means by which the product is accomplished. Among the other factors relevant to this inquiry are the skill required; the source of the instrumentalities and tools; the location of the work; the duration of the relationship between the parties; whether the hiring party has the right to assign additional projects to the hired party; the extent of the hired party's discretion over when and how long to work; the method of payment; the hired party's role in hiring and paying assistants; whether the work is part of the regular business of the hiring party; whether the hiring party is in business; the provision of employee benefits; and the tax treatment of the hired party. See Restatement § 220(2) (setting forth a nonexhaustive list of factors relevant to determining whether a hired party is an employee). No one of these factors is determinative. See *Ward*, 362 U.S., at 400; *Hilton Int'l Co.* v. *NLRB*, 690 F. 2d 318, 321 (CA2 1982).

Examining the circumstances of this case in light of these factors, we agree with the Court of Appeals that Reid was not an employee of CCNV but an independent contractor. 270 U.S. App. D. C., at 35, n. 11, 846 F. 2d, at 1494, n. 11. True, CCNV members directed enough of Reid's work to ensure that he produced a sculpture that met their specifications. 652 F. Supp., at 1456. But the extent of control the hiring party exercises over the details of the product is not dispositive. Indeed, all the other circumstances weigh heavily against finding an employment relationship. Reid is a sculptor, a skilled occupation. Reid supplied his own tools. He worked in his own studio in Baltimore, making daily supervision of his activities from Washington practicably impossible. Reid was retained for less than two months, a relatively short period of time. During and after this time, CCNV had no right to assign additional projects to Reid. Apart from the deadline for completing the sculpture, Reid had absolute freedom to decide when and how long to work. CCNV paid Reid $15,000, a sum dependent on "completion of a specific job, a method by which independent contractors are often compensated." *Holt* v. *Winpisinger*, 258 U.S. App. D. C. 343, 351, 811 F. 2d 1532, 1540 (1987). Reid had total discretion in hiring and paying assistants. "Creating sculptures was hardly 'regular business' for CCNV." 270 U.S. App. D. C., at 35, n. 11, 846 F. 2d, at 1494, n. 11. Indeed, CCNV is not a business at all. Finally, CCNV did not pay payroll or Social Security taxes, provide any employee benefits, or contribute to unemployment insurance or workers' compensation funds.

Because Reid was an independent contractor, whether "Third World America" is a work for hire depends on whether it satisfies the terms of § 101(2). This, petitioners concede, it cannot do. Thus, CCNV is not the author of "Third World America" by virtue of the work for hire provisions of the Act. However, as the Court of Appeals made clear, CCNV nevertheless may be a joint author of the sculpture if, on remand, the District Court determines that CCNV and Reid prepared the work "with the intention that their contributions be merged into inseparable or interdependent parts of a unitary whole." 17 U.S.C. § 101. In that case, CCNV and Reid would be co-owners of the copyright in the work. See § 201(a).

For the aforestated reasons, we affirm the judgment of the Court of Appeals for the District of Columbia Circuit.

It is so ordered.

2. Private Adjustments Through Employment Contract Terms

a. Introduction

Statutory default rules that assign ownership in intellectual property as between employers and employees are gap-filling rules that come into play in the absence of an express agreement between the parties to the contrary. Parties may override the statutory default rules by entering into contractual agreements that expressly assign ownership in accordance with an agreement between the employer and employee. Because the default rules sometimes assign ownership in intellectual property to the employee, employers have increasingly turned to contracts to protect their proprietary information. Today, invention assignment provisions are commonplace in employment contracts for inventive employees.

Employers may use contracts not only to secure an invention assignment, but also to define other duties owed by an employee. Express agreements may extend the scope of the protection beyond those afforded by the duties implied by law. For example, a contract may impose restrictions on use and disclosure of information that does not qualify for trade secret protection, but which falls under the broader category of information that the employer deems confidential. The freedom to contract is not without limit. Covenants that restrict the use and disclosure of confidential information that is not a trade secret are strictly construed and covenants that restrain the communication of ideas in general are unreasonable and unenforceable.

Just as parties may agree to expand upon the employee's duties imposed by law, they may also covenant to relieve themselves of some of the duties. Parties may agree to expressly disclaim a confidential relationship. In *Anderson v. Century Prods. Co.,* 943 F. Supp. 137 (D.N.H. 1996), the defendant, Century, asserted that an agreement between it and the plaintiff disclaimed a confidential relationship between the parties. The *Anderson* court stated:

> A confidential relationship may arise by operation of law from the affiliation of the parties and the context in which the disclosures are offered. But courts hold that an implied confidential relationship can be defeated if the parties, by agreement, expressly disclaim any such relationship. As one treatise on the subject has noted:
>
>> A disclosure expressly received in confidence may create a confidential relationship. Conversely, express disclaimer by the disclosee of a confidential relationship from the outset will dispel the existence of such a relationship.
>
> R. Milgrim, *Trade Secrets* § 4.03 at 4–18 (1984). However, as it purports to waive tort liability, the language must clearly and explicitly indicate unwillingness to enter the relationship. This is the standard to which Century's waiver of confidential relationship must be held.

Anderson, 943 F. Supp. at 151. Express disclaimers negate the confidentiality obligations implied by law and permit the free use and disclosure of trade secrets acquired during the relationship. Since the law favors a strong policy of protecting trust, express disclaimers must use clear, unambiguous language. An agreement that ambiguously purports to disclaim a confidential relationship is considered ineffective.

b. Invention Assignments

In an invention assignment, an employee agrees to assign to the employer the rights to inventions created during the term of the employment relationship. Employers routinely use invention assignments to override the default rules that award ownership of inventions to employees. Courts enforce pre-invention assignment agreements according to their terms, subject to traditional contract doctrines. Valid invention assignments should be reasonable as to the scope of the matter assigned, should relate to the employer's business, and the time frame for assignment should be reasonable. An otherwise valid assignment agreement usually is enforceable despite a disparity in bargaining power between the employer and the employee and may be based on as little consideration as one dollar. Employers also often require a promise that an employee will assist in the prosecution of a patent application regarding the employee's invention and aid in perfecting the employer's title in the invention.

FREEDOM WIRELESS, INC. v. BOSTON COMMUNICATIONS GROUP, INC.
United States District Court for the District of Massachusetts
220 F. Supp. 2d 16 (2002)

HARRINGTON, Senior District Judge.

This case involves a patent infringement suit by Freedom Wireless, Inc. ("Freedom Wireless"). The two patents that are alleged to have been infringed in this case are U.S. Patent No. 5,722,067 (issued Feb. 24, 1998) and U.S. Patent No. 6,157,823 (issued Dec. 5, 2000), both of which were issued in the names of co-inventors Daniel Harned and Douglas Fougnies and assigned to Freedom Wireless by way of its predecessor company, Cellular Express, Inc. On June 3, 2002, Defendant Boston Communications Group, Inc., ("BCGI") filed a motion for summary judgment alleging that Freedom Wireless is not the owner of the two patents at issue and, therefore, lacks standing to sue for infringement. The Court heard argument on this issue on July 23, 2002.

It is a basic principle of patent law that a party who lacks legal ownership of a patent is without standing to sue for infringement of that patent. . . .

It is undisputed that Mr. Harned and Mr. Fougnies conceived of the invention claimed in the two patents at issue sometime between late 1993 and early 1994, when Mr. Harned was working for Orbital Sciences Corporation/ Space Data Division ("Orbital"). As part of his employment contract with Orbital, Mr. Harned had agreed to the following covenant:

> The Employee agrees that all inventions, innovations or improvements in the Company's methods of conducting business (including new contributions, improvements and discoveries) conceived or made by the Employee during his or her employment period belong to the Company. The Employee will promptly disclose such inventions, innovations or improvements to the Company and perform all actions reasonably requested by the Company to establish and confirm such ownership, including but not limited to cooperation in connection with the Company's obtaining patent and/or copyright protection.

BCGI argues that this agreement conveyed to Orbital an expectant interest in Mr. Harned's invention, which vested as a matter of law into full legal ownership at the moment Mr. Harned first conceived of his invention. Consequently, BCGI argues that Orbital is the owner of the patents at issue and that Mr. Harned's subsequent attempt to assign the invention to Freedom Wireless' predecessor company was a legal nullity.

The Court disagrees with BCGI's contention that the employment contract between Mr. Harned and Orbital created a valid assignment of Mr. Harned's invention. First, as a matter of contractual interpretation, this Court holds that under the terms of the contract Mr. Harned was only obligated to assign his rights to an invention if that invention was related to Orbital's methods of conducting business. This is because the agreement only applies to "inventions, innovations or improvements in the Company's methods of conducting business (including new contributions, improvements and discoveries)." Under ordinary rules of English usage, the prepositional phrase "in the Company's methods of conducting business" modifies all three nouns in the preceding series. *See, e.g., Pandol Bros., Inc. v. Indemnity Marine Assur. Co.,* 1996 U.S. App. LEXIS 23378, 1996 WL 498912, at **2 (9th Cir. Aug. 30, 1996) (unpublished) ("Giving this paragraph its most natural meaning, the prepositional phrase . . . modifies all that comes before it . . . [particularly where] no commas set off this phrase from what precedes it."). Thus, under the agreement, Mr. Harned was only under an obligation to assign his ownership to any "invention . . . in the Company's methods of conducting business" that was conceived of by him during his period of employment with Orbital.

This interpretation of the contract as covering only inventions related to Orbital's methods of conducting business is particularly appropriate in light of the strong public policy discouraging contracts that create an unreasonable restraint on trade. For over one hundred years, courts have looked skeptically upon employment contracts that require an employee to assign his inventions to his employer. *See, e.g., Bates Mach. Co. v. Bates,* 192 Ill. 138, 145, 61 N.E. 518 (1901); *Guth v. Minn. Min. & Mfg. Co.,* 72 F.2d 385, 388 (7th Cir. 1934); *Ingersoll-Rand Co. v. Ciavatta,* 110 N.J. 609, 624, 542 A.2d 879–86 (1988). Where such contracts are open-ended with respect to time limit or subject matter, they may be considered unenforceable as against public policy. *See Ingersoll-Rand,* 110 N.J. at 624 ("Courts, however, will not enforce invention assignment contracts that unreasonably obligate an employee in each and every instance to transfer the ownership of the employee's invention to the employer."); *see also* Cal. Lab. Code § 2870 (2002) (providing that invention assignment contracts that are open-ended with respect to time and subject matter are against public policy and therefore unenforceable). Thus, public policy supports an interpretation of the invention assignment contract between Mr. Harned and Orbital that limits the agreement to inventions that are within the subject matter of the employment relationship.

Having first held that the contract between Orbital and Mr. Harned is limited to inventions relating to Orbital's methods of conducting business, this Court further holds that Mr. Harned was not required to assign the invention claimed in the patents at issue in this case because the invention did not relate to Orbital's methods of conducting business. The two patents at issue in this case are for prepaid wireless telephone billing, which is a form of wireless telephone communications that allows users to pay in advance for cellular telephone service. *See Freedom Wireless, Inc. v. Boston Communications Group, Inc.,* 198 F. Supp. 2d 11 (D. Mass. 2002) (describing the technology of prepaid wireless billing). In its most generic embodiment, prepaid wireless billing utilizes some form of electronic signaling in conjunction with a computer database to charge a customer's prepaid account every time a cellular call is made or received. On the other hand, Orbital is a space technology company that develops satellite-based and space-based services, including personal satellite navigation services and guidance systems for rockets. Prepaid wireless billing does not relate to the methods of conducting a business dedicated to developing satellite-based and rocket-based services. Thus, because the invention claimed in the patents at issue is not sufficiently related to Orbital's methods of conducting business, Mr. Harned was not obligated to assign his rights to Orbital.

Finally, in addition to the subject matter limitation contained in the invention assignment agreement between Orbital and Mr. Harned, there is another reason why Freedom Wireless does not lack standing to sue for patent infringement. Freedom Wireless does not lack standing to sue because the invention assignment contract in this case was merely an agreement by Mr. Harned to assign his invention to Orbital at some point in the future and not an actual present assignment. *Arachnid, Inc. v. Merit Indus., Inc.* 939 F.2d 1574, 1580-81 (Fed. Cir. 1991). In order for a pre-invention assignment contract to create a present assignment of an expectant interest in an invention that automatically vests by operation of law into an actual assignment upon conception, the contract must contain words of present conveyance and must require "no further act once an invention [comes] into being." . . . The agreement in this case, which states that "all inventions belong . . . to the Company," and which requires future acts by the inventor such as "disclosing" the invention and "performing" actions necessary to establish ownership, is not sufficient to convey legal title to the invention. *Arachnid,* 939 F.2d at 1581 ("The *legal* title to an invention can pass to another only by a conveyance.") (quoting G. Curtis, A Treatise on the Law of Patents § 170 (4th ed. 1873). Thus, even if the contract between Mr. Harned and Orbital covered the invention claimed in the patents at issue, Freedom Wireless would still have legal title to the patent and standing to sue in this case because the employment contract did not contain terms sufficient to convey legal title to Orbital. *Arachnid,* 939 F.2d at 1581.

Because this Court rules that Freedom Wireless is the legal owner of the patents at issue in this case, BCGI's motion for summary judgment based on lack of standing is hereby denied.

NOTES & QUESTIONS

1. "Freedom to Create" Statutes

Parties may override of the common law default rules through use of contracts. Since the default rules assigning ownership rights favor employees, employers often seek to opt out of the rules by compelling assignment of inventions through contract. Eight states[1] have restricted the ability of employers to contract around the common law rules. These states have enacted so called "Freedom to Create" statutes that permit assignments of inventions only when the invention relates to the employer's business or results from work that the employee performed for the employer. An example of a typical "Freedom to Create" statute is section 2870 of the California Labor Code.

> § 2870. Application of provision that employee shall assign or offer to assign rights in invention to employer
>
> (a) Any provision in an employment agreement which provides that an employee shall assign, or offer to assign, any of his or her rights in an invention to his or her employer shall not apply to an invention that the employee developed entirely on his or her own time without using the employer's equipment, supplies, facilities, or trade secret information except for those inventions that either:
>
> > (1) Relate at the time of conception or reduction to practice of the invention to the employer's business, or actual or demonstrably anticipated research or development of the employer; or
> >
> > (2) Result from any work performed by the employee for the employer.
>
> (b) To the extent a provision in an employment agreement purports to require an employee to assign an invention otherwise excluded from being required to be assigned under subdivision (a), the provision is against the public policy of this state and is unenforceable.

2. Federal or State Law?

Patents are creatures of federal law, but ownership rights in patented inventions may fall under the governance of state law. How can this be? When the parties opt to contract around the default rules governing ownership rights to an invention, state contract laws apply. State laws therefore dictate the ownership rights between the employer and employee in the context of invention assignments. Only where state law creates a serious conflict with federal patent policy must state law yield to its federal counterpart.

---

[1] California, Delaware, Illinois, Kansas, Minnesota, North Carolina, Utah, and Washington.

B.　TRANSFERS OF INTELLECTUAL PROPERTY UPON CHANGES IN EMPLOYMENT

1.　Enforceability of Restrictions on Subsequent Employment for Parties Holding Trade Secrets

a.　Nonuse and Nondisclosure Agreements

Express agreements defining a confidential relationship are called restrictive covenants or confidentiality agreements. Such nonuse and nondisclosure agreements recite that an employee will receive confidential information and that the employee agrees not to use or disclose the information. Employers use contractual duties against use or disclosure to protect their secret information, which can include employee-created trade secrets. When employers use contract terms to protect trade secrets, the law usually construes such terms broadly. Because restrictions on use and disclosure are sometimes necessary to give meaningful protection to trade secrets, protection of trade secrets justifies permitting the restrictions. The justification does not apply when employers use contract terms to protect information that is confidential but not a trade secret. The law therefore strictly construes contract terms that limit use and disclosure of information that is confidential but not a trade secret. In general, courts refuse to enforce agreements that unreasonably restrain competition or unduly hinder an employee from pursuing a livelihood.

**UNION PACIFIC RAILROAD COMPANY v.
BRENT MOWER**

United States Court of Appeals for the Ninth Circuit
219 F.3d 1069 (2000)

FISHER, Circuit Judge:

Brent Mower is a former employee of Union Pacific Railroad Company ("UP"). UP obtained a broad injunction against Mower, prohibiting him from disclosing or revealing to third parties any confidential information he obtained while employed by UP. Mower appeals the issuance of that injunction. . . . We reverse and vacate the injunction.

FACTUAL AND PROCEDURAL BACKGROUND

A.　The Resignation Agreement

UP employed Mower from 1979 to 1992. During that time, Mower rose from a low-level claims adjuster position to Director of Occupational and Environmental Issues. In his management position, Mower's primary responsibility was the investigation and resolution of thousands of occupational illness claims filed against UP. Mower worked closely with UP's legal department on certain issues and, for a portion of his career, was considered a member of the legal department.

In 1992, UP asked Mower to resign, and the parties entered into a resignation and consulting agreement on November 20, 1992 (the "Resignation Agreement"). The Resignation Agreement provided that Mower would serve as a consultant to UP for a period of three years. The Resignation Agreement also stipulated that, from November 1992 until December 31, 1995, Mower would not (1) reveal UP's confidential and privileged information or any other information "harmful" to UP's best interests, (2) "communicate with anyone with respect to the business or affairs of [UP]," or (3) consult with any person asserting claims against UP. It is undisputed on appeal that Mower complied with the terms of the Resignation Agreement through December 31, 1995.

B. The Idaho Case

In May 1997, Mariano Ybarra filed a complaint against UP in Idaho, alleging that he had sustained personal injuries while employed at UP and that such injuries were the result of UP's negligence. Ybarra moved to supplement his witness list during March 1998 to add Mower as a witness. In a sworn affidavit, Mower stated that he would testify about a particular study he conducted during 1989, relating generally to Ybarra's type of injury, and about a position paper he prepared in connection with the study and presented to senior management at UP. UP objected, claiming that Mower's proffered testimony related to privileged information. The Idaho trial court deferred ruling on the issue to afford UP's counsel the opportunity to depose Mower.

C. The Injunction

In April 1998, while the issue of Mower's testimony was still pending in the Idaho case, UP filed its complaint for an injunction against Mower in the federal district court in Oregon. In its complaint, UP argued that, if allowed to testify in the Idaho case or in any other case, Mower would reveal UP's confidential information and trade secrets and would violate . . . Mower's fiduciary duty to preserve confidential information. In particular, UP protested Mower's intention to testify regarding the particular study and position paper discussed in Mower's affidavit in the Idaho case. UP alleged that it would suffer irreparable damage from Mower's disclosure of the position paper or any other confidential information, because such information "may be used . . . in a number of lawsuits against [UP]." UP asked the district court to enjoin Mower from disclosing confidential information in any lawsuit, in order to "prevent a multiplicity of litigation."

Mower objected to UP's complaint on several grounds. Mower argued, among other things, that the information in question — in particular, the study and position paper discussed in his affidavit — was neither confidential nor privileged. He emphasized the publicly available resources he had consulted during the study, including on-line databases and various professionals and academics who were not associated with UP. Mower also contended that the Resignation Agreement's expiration at the end of 1995 left him free to disclose such information, even if confidential or privileged.

The district court granted UP's motion for a preliminary injunction against Mower, finding that the information obtained by Mower during his employment was highly confidential and that Mower owed UP an implied duty of confidentiality. . . .

Following the district court's grant of the preliminary injunction, UP and Mower stipulated to the issuance of a substantially similar permanent injunction; however, Mower reserved his rights to object to the form of the injunction and to appeal. The district court entered the permanent injunction against Mower on October 14, 1998, and this appeal followed.

DISCUSSION

. . . On appeal, Mower argues that the district court erred in concluding that he owes a continuing duty of confidentiality to UP and in issuing an injunction on that basis. Mower also suggests that the district court erred in concluding that the information held by Mower, particularly the study and position paper, was entirely confidential. As explained below, we conclude that the injunction is inappropriate.

A.   The Implied Duty of Confidentiality and the Resignation Agreement

The district court issued the injunction against Mower based on its conclusion that, "after his employment and his services as a consultant terminated, defendant Mower remained under an implied duty not to disclose [UP's] confidential business information." The district court reasoned that Mower's duty of confidentiality "goes way beyond any express agreement that expired in 1995, but extends for his lifetime." The district court was correct only if Oregon law recognizes an implied duty of confidentiality and the Resignation Agreement either could not, as a matter of law, or did not, pursuant to its terms, serve to limit Mower's implied duty of confidentiality.[2]

Oregon law imposes on every employee a legal duty to protect an employer's trade secrets and other confidential information, an obligation that continues beyond the term of employment. In *McCombs v. McClelland*, 223 Ore. 475, 354 P.2d 311 (1960), the Oregon Supreme Court held that ex-employees are under "an implied obligation . . . not to use [their former employers'] trade secrets or confidential information for [their] own benefit or that of third persons. . . ." *Id.* at 483, 354 P.2d at 315-16 (noting that "the law is well settled" on this issue (quoting Annotation, *Implied Obligation of Employee Not to Use Trade Secrets or Confidential Information for His Own Benefit or That of Third Persons After Leaving the Employment*, 165 A.L.R. 1453, 1454 (1946)) (internal quotation marks omitted)). Thus, the district court properly concluded that Oregon law recognizes an implied duty of confidentiality.

However, Oregon also generally permits parties to alter by negotiation duties that would otherwise be governed by state law. In *Owings v. Rose*, 262 Ore. 247, 497 P.2d 1183 (1972), for example, the Oregon Supreme Court held that, "where the parties have made an express contract of indemnity[,] its terms will control" despite Oregon's recognition of indemnity actions based on implied contract. *Id.* at 263, 497 P.2d at 1190; *see also Eggiman v. Mid-Century Ins. Co.*, 134 Ore.

---

[2] [FN4] Because UP filed its complaint in Oregon district court and based its claim against Mower on that state's common law implied duty of confidentiality, we apply Oregon law to evaluate whether the district court's issuance of the injunction on that basis was appropriate. However, . . . Nebraska law governs our interpretation of the terms of the Resignation Agreement.

App. 381, 385-86, 895 P.2d 333, 335 (1995) (implied covenant of good faith and fair dealing applies unless altered by the express terms of an agreement); *White's Elecs., Inc. v. Teknetics, Inc.*, 67 Ore. App. 63, 67, 677 P.2d 68, 70-71 (1984) ("Absent an agreement to the contrary," an employee has a duty to assign patent rights to an employer.). Therefore, the general rule in Oregon appears to be that parties can "contract out" of implied duties.

Nor is there any indication that the outcome should be different with respect to the particular duty at issue in this case — the implied duty of confidentiality. In *McCombs*, the Oregon Supreme Court gave no indication that the duty of confidentiality should be regarded as inviolate. In fact, in recognizing the existence of this implied duty under Oregon law, the *McCombs* court relied on an American Law Reports annotation that suggests the contrary. *See McCombs*, 223 Ore. at 483, 354 P.2d at 315-16. The annotation notes that "the question as to the obligation of a former employee not to reveal . . . confidential information, *where there was an express contract in that regard*, is not within the scope of the annotation." Annotation, 165 A.L.R. at 1454 (emphasis added).

We conclude that, under Oregon law, parties have the power to alter the implied duty of confidentiality. The existence of an express agreement is relevant both in determining whether a particular employee is bound by a duty of confidentiality and in defining the scope of that duty. The remaining issue, therefore, is whether the Resignation Agreement affected Mower's implied duty of confidentiality. We believe it did.

The Resignation Agreement provided in relevant part:

4. *From now until December 31, 1995*:

(a) You will take no action, nor make any statement which, in the reasonable judgment of [UP's] management, would be harmful or otherwise detrimental to the best interests of [UP], any of its subsidiaries or its stockholders and, subject to your obligations to any future employer, you will use your best efforts to promote the business and affairs of [UP] and all of its subsidiaries in all reasonable ways at your disposal.

(b) You will make no statement or otherwise communicate with anyone with respect to the business or affairs of [UP] or any of its subsidiaries, except as may be (i) approved in writing by [UP] or (ii) required by any judicial or regulatory authority having jurisdiction over the subject matter. . . .

(c) You will remove no documents or other written materials, including copies of any kind, pertaining to the business or affairs of [UP] or any of its subsidiaries from the premises of [UP] and will promptly return to [UP] all such documents or materials now or hereafter in your possession.

5. *From now until December 31, 1995*, you agree that you will not . . . engage in any business of, . . . or consult with, directly or indirectly, any person, firm, corporation or other entity, which is engaged in the

business or practice relating to the assertion of claims or lawsuits against [UP]. . . . You and [UP] agree and acknowledge that you have acquired special knowledge and expertise in the claims and litigation defense strategy used by [UP]. It is the purpose and intention of this agreement to protect [UP's] trade secrets and privileged communications and claims and litigation strategies which you have learned during the course of your employment. It is not the intention of this agreement to restrict your ability to work for a competing railroad or other transportation company, but to protect [UP's] privileged information and strategies from disclosure.

6. This agreement is not a "noncompetition" agreement and shall not prohibit an employment or consulting relationship between you and any railroad, firm or other entity engaged in the business of defending claims and suits, including investigation and negotiation.

(Emphases added).

Although the Resignation Agreement was drafted broadly to prevent Mower from revealing a wide range of information about UP — regardless of whether such information was properly considered "confidential" — it is clear that an intention to protect any confidential or privileged information held by Mower was at the core of the Resignation Agreement and its restrictions on Mower's activities. Surely, if the events spawning this litigation had occurred before the expiration of the Resignation Agreement, UP would have argued that Mower was prohibited (under both paragraphs 4 and 5 of the Resignation Agreement) from discussing the substance of his study and the resulting position paper or probably from even disclosing their existence.

Just as clearly, however, the Resignation Agreement limited its protection of such information to a distinct period of time, ending December 31, 1995. The unambiguous meaning of the Resignation Agreement was that, after that date, Mower's obligation to conduct his affairs in accordance with that agreement terminated and he would no longer be subject to its nondisclosure requirements.

UP does not suggest that the terms of the Resignation Agreement were ambiguous. Rather, UP argues that — even if, as we hold today, the implied duty of confidentiality can be altered by contract — the Resignation Agreement merely *supplemented* Mower's pre-existing duty without affecting the protections afforded UP by that duty. UP suggests that to find otherwise would be to add to the agreement rather than to construe it in accordance with its terms.

UP's argument is contrary to applicable principles of contract interpretation. We must give effect to the unambiguous time limitation established by the parties. Under Nebraska law, "a written contract which is expressed in clear and unambiguous language is not subject to interpretation or construction"; and "the meaning of an unambiguous contract presents a question of law." *Lueder Constr. Co. v. Lincoln Elec. Co.*, 228 Neb. 707, 710, 424 N.W.2d 126, 128-29 (1988) (citations omitted). Moreover, "[a] contract must be construed as a whole and, if possible, effect must be given to every part thereof." *Husen v. Husen*, 241 Neb. 10, 13, 487 N.W.2d 269, 272 (1992) (quoting *Crowley v. McCoy*, 234 Neb. 88, 91, 449 N.W.2d 221, 224 (1989)) (internal quotation marks omitted).

In effect, UP's contention is that the Resignation Agreement cannot be read to alter Mower's implied duty of confidentiality because the company would not have entered into the Resignation Agreement if it had known that, by doing so, it restricted what would otherwise have been a perpetual duty imposed by law. That may or may not be so, but UP's argument neither changes our interpretation of the unambiguous terms of the Resignation Agreement nor overcomes the inappropriateness of the injunction issued against Mower. UP apparently concluded that the value of the information in question would diminish after several years and opted for a blanket, extremely broad prohibition for a term of years as opposed to an indefinite protection against the dissemination of only that specific information properly deemed "confidential" under Oregon law. The fact that UP's choice may have proved unwise does not alter the legal effect of the bargain it made. *See Husen*, 241 Neb. at 14, 487 N.W.2d at 272 ("Although the respondent may be dissatisfied with the bargain [it] made, it is not for this court to rewrite the contract [it] executed.").

We hold, as a matter of law, that the Resignation Agreement supplanted — rather than supplemented — Mower's implied duty of confidentiality. By the terms of the Resignation Agreement, Mower's duty of confidentiality terminated as of December 31, 1995.

CONCLUSION

Mower's implied duty of confidentiality — whatever its original scope — was superseded by the unambiguous terms of the Resignation Agreement. The Resignation Agreement limited Mower's duty of confidentiality to a distinct time frame, which has since passed. Finding no alternative basis upon which to uphold the injunction, we conclude that the injunction must be REVERSED and VACATED.

NOTES & QUESTIONS

1. Enforceability Requirements

A nonuse and nondisclosure agreement is enforceable if it (1) exists at the time of the confidential disclosure, (2) is reasonable in scope, and (3) uses language that is clear and unambiguous. If an agreement places too onerous of a burden on an employee, the agreement may be invalidated.

When determining whether the agreement imposes too great a burden on the employee, the court looks to whether the agreement creates a nondisclosure obligation, which is presumptively enforceable, or whether it compels restrictions on competition in general, which is disfavored. In addition, some jurisdictions require that agreements be reasonable as to the duration of the agreement. Limitations may also be placed on the protected subject matter, requiring that the information underlying the covenant qualify as a trade secret. In general, the law disfavors agreements that tie the employee's hands too far into the future or too broadly limits the scope of useable information.

2. Maintaining a Trade Secret

To be a trade secret, information must be protected from uncontrolled disclosure. Failure to guard the secrecy of information underlying a trade secret can result in loss of trade secret status. To protect the information underlying a trade secret, employers are allowed to limit the employee's ability to disclose the information to others. Use of nonuse and nondisclosure agreements may be necessary to give meaningful protection to trade secrets, especially when a knowledgeable employee exits the company. Not surprisingly, protection of a trade secret is per se justification for use of such restrictive agreements.

b.   Covenant Not to Compete

i.   Generally

Employers may also impose future restrictions that prevent departing employees from competing with the employer. Covenants not to compete protect the goodwill of the former employer's business. Courts enforce noncompete covenants so long as the scope, time, and territory covered are restricted to what is reasonably needed to protect the employer. Since courts regard covenants that impose restrictions on competition as restraints on trade, they are not as readily enforced as nonuse and nondisclosure agreements.

NIKE, INC. v. EUGENE MCCARTHY
United States Court of Appeals for the Ninth Circuit
379 F.3d 576 (2004)

FISHER, Circuit Judge:

In this case we must determine the validity of a noncompete agreement under Oregon law. Eugene McCarthy left his position as director of sales for Nike's Brand Jordan division in June 2003 to become vice president of U.S. footwear sales and merchandising at Reebok, one of Nike's competitors. Nike sought a preliminary injunction to prevent McCarthy from working for Reebok for a year, invoking a noncompete agreement McCarthy had signed in 1997 when Nike had promoted him to his earlier position as a regional footwear sales manager. Under Oregon law, which governs here, a noncompete agreement generally is void and unenforceable unless agreed to "upon" either the employee's initial employment or — relevant here — the "subsequent bona fide advancement of the employee with the employer." Or. Rev. Stat. § 653.295(1)(b) (2004). McCarthy's promotion to regional footwear sales manager was undisputedly an "advancement"; the critical issues are *when* the advancement occurred and whether Nike obtained McCarthy's agreement not to compete "*upon*" that advancement. Construing the Oregon statute and reviewing the circumstances surrounding McCarthy's promotion and the execution of the noncompete agreement, we hold that the agreement meets the statutory requirements to be enforceable. We also hold that Nike has a legitimate interest in enforcing the agreement, because there is a substantial risk that McCarthy — in shaping Reebok's product allocation, sales and pricing strategies — could enable Reebok to divert a significant amount of Nike's footwear sales given the highly confidential information McCarthy acquired at

Nike. Thus, we affirm the district court's preliminary injunction enforcing the agreement.

I.   FACTUAL AND PROCEDURAL BACKGROUND

McCarthy began working for Nike in 1993 and became a key account manager in 1995. During the spring of 1997, Nike undertook a major, national reorganization. Out of this came McCarthy's promotion to eastern regional footwear sales manager — and the present dispute as to when that promotion actually occurred. On February 28, John Petersen, McCarthy's supervisor, called McCarthy and asked, "How would you like to be the regional footwear sales manager for the eastern region?" McCarthy answered, "Absolutely, yes." Petersen mentioned there would be an increase in pay but did not say what the salary would be.

In the following weeks, McCarthy continued to perform some of his old duties while assuming some of the duties of his new position, including leading meetings and preparing a report. In order to perform these duties, McCarthy obtained confidential information he had not seen before that described the top-selling styles in the eastern region. During the week of March 10, Petersen announced to a group of employees that McCarthy was the new regional footwear sales manager. During the remainder of March, McCarthy took several business trips, which were expensed to the cost center for the regional footwear sales manager position.

On March 27, McCarthy received a letter from Petersen confirming the offer for the regional footwear sales manager position ("Offer Letter"). The letter indicated that the "start date" for the new position was April 1, 1997. According to several Nike executives, it is not unusual for an employee to begin to perform the duties of a new position prior to the start date, in order to ensure a smooth transition once he or she "officially" starts in the new position. The Offer Letter also specified that McCarthy's salary would be $110,000, which became effective April 1. Before that date, McCarthy's salary was charged to the cost center for the key account manager position.

In addition, the Offer Letter required McCarthy to sign an attached covenant not to compete and nondisclosure agreement as a condition of acceptance of the offer. The covenant not to compete contained the "Competition Restriction" clause at issue here, stating in relevant part:

> During EMPLOYEE'S employment by NIKE . . . and for one (1) year thereafter, (the "Restriction Period"), EMPLOYEE will not directly or indirectly . . . be employed by, consult for, or be connected in any manner with, any business engaged anywhere in the world in the athletic footwear, athletic apparel or sports equipment and accessories business, or any other business which directly competes with NIKE or any of its subsidiaries or affiliated corporations.

McCarthy signed the agreement that day. It is this noncompete agreement that Nike now seeks to enforce.

Two years later, McCarthy was again promoted, this time to the position of director of sales for the Brand Jordan division, the position he held until he resigned from Nike in June 2003. He was not asked to sign a new noncompete agreement. During the spring of 2003, McCarthy accepted a position with Reebok as vice president of U.S. footwear sales and merchandising and tendered his resignation in June. McCarthy began working at Reebok on July 22, 2003.

On August 18, 2003, Nike filed suit in Oregon circuit court, claiming breach of contract and seeking a declaratory judgment that McCarthy's employment with Reebok violated the covenant not to compete. . . .

. . .

A.   Oregon Revised Statute § 653.295(1)

We first address the merits of Nike's claims. McCarthy contends that the covenant not to compete is void under Oregon Revised Statute § 653.295(1). . . . As applied to McCarthy's situation, the statute requires that (1) there was a "bona fide advancement" of McCarthy and (2) that the noncompete agreement was "entered into upon" that bona fide advancement. *Id.* Although the parties agree that McCarthy's promotion to regional footwear sales manager involved an advancement within Nike, they disagree as to *when* the advancement occurred. McCarthy contends Nike did not obtain his consent to the noncompete agreement "upon" his advancement but well after it had already been implemented, and thus the agreement came too late to be enforceable under the statute. Understanding what the statute contemplates by way of a bona fide advancement will help shed some light on how to determine when an employee's advancement has occurred so as to justify an employer securing a noncompete agreement.

1.   Meaning of bona fide advancement

. . .

Although Oregon courts have interpreted section 653.295 before, they have not yet construed the meaning of "bona fide advancement." In the absence of a controlling interpretation by the Oregon Supreme Court, we must construe the term as we believe the Oregon Supreme Court would.

. . .

The text and context of section 653.295(1)(b) do not clearly indicate what constitutes a bona fide advancement. The statute does not define the term, nor does it appear in other provisions of the same statute or other related statutes. Therefore, we look to the plain, natural and ordinary meaning of the words. "Bona fide" is defined as "made or carried out in good faith; sincere." The American Heritage College Dictionary 158 (3d. ed. 2000). An "advancement" is "[a] forward step; an improvement," "[a] promotion, as in rank." *Id.* at 19.

Obviously, these definitions leave room for debate about what constitutes a bona fide advancement. In resolving this ambiguity, we find some helpful indicators of legislative intent in the statute's legislative history. In 1977, the Oregon legislature enacted section 653.295, which at that time provided that noncompete agreements were void unless entered into only at the time of initial hiring. . . .

Apparently responding to concerns that foreclosing non-compete agreements later in an employee's career created undesirable results for employers and employees, the Oregon legislature amended section 653.295 in 1983 to permit non-compete agreements to be entered "upon the subsequent bona fide advancement" of an employee within the company. Testimony before the Oregon Senate Committee on Business and Consumer Affairs explained that, under the proposed bill, "the employer still could not surprise the old employee with a new requirement, but the employer could impose the non-competition agreement as a condition of advancing to a higher position in which there is a real need and justification for a noncompete obligation." . . .

In light of this history, it is apparent that the legislature intended to permit employers to require existing employees to agree to a noncompete agreement, so long as the employee's job content and responsibilities materially increased and the employee's status within the company likewise improved. Otherwise, the employer would merely be imposing a new condition for the "same job." *Id.* Thus, an advancement would ordinarily include such elements as new, more responsible duties, different reporting relationships, a change in title and higher pay.

In McCarthy's case, his promotion included all of these elements. He received a new title of regional footwear sales manager and was presented to other employees as such. He undertook new duties associated with the new position, assumed a new supervisory role over other sales representatives and received a higher salary of $110,000. The issue remains, however, as to when his "advancement" occurred for purposes of triggering Nike's limited opportunity to obtain a binding noncompete agreement "upon" McCarthy's advancement.

2. Meaning of "upon . . . the advancement"

McCarthy's advancement consisted of multiple elements that played out over several weeks, with his promotion not being formalized until he received his Offer Letter with the accompanying noncompete agreement on March 27, 1997, and his pay increase not effective until April 1. In such circumstances, the question arises as to when a noncompete agreement must be entered into relative to this process of advancement. All the statute tells us is that the agreement must be "entered into upon the . . . bona fide advancement of the employee with the employer." Or. Rev. Stat. § 653.295(1).

McCarthy argues that a noncompete agreement must be entered into as soon as the employee takes on any of the duties of the new position. Such an inflexible rule, however, would put employers at risk of losing their noncompete option during a period of "auditioning" an employee for possible promotion and thus could hinder the advancement of employees from within a company, a concern that prompted the state legislature to amend the statute in 1983.

On the other hand, the statute and its legislative history make clear the process is not open-ended. The legislative history suggests that the employer and employee would likely come to some agreement or understanding on the terms and conditions of the new job, in the process of which the employer would inform the employee of the need for a non-compete agreement as a condition of the advancement. This would be consistent with affording employees the intended protection against "surprise" and imposition of "new conditions." For similar reasons, the legislative history implies that an employer should not spring a noncompete agreement on an employee long after the commencement of the advancement process — for instance by unreasonably delaying a pay increase or title change, or deferring consummation of the employer's and employee's agreement on the terms and conditions of the new job. In short, although a noncompete agreement need not be entered into at the first instance that the employee assumes any elements of the new job, including new duties, neither does the window of opportunity to ask for a noncompete agreement remain open until the employer sees fit formally to finalize the advancement process.

. . . McCarthy's noncompete agreement would be enforceable under section 653.295. McCarthy signed the noncompete agreement on March 27 in conjunction with reaching a final agreement on the terms and conditions of his new job, and his pay increase did not take effect until April 1. Moreover, McCarthy's advancement evolved over a reasonably short period of time, with no unreasonable delays by Nike in finalizing the process. For these reasons, we conclude that the district court did not err in finding that McCarthy's noncompete agreement was "entered into upon" his bona fide advancement.

B.   Protectible interest

Even if the covenant not to compete is not void under section 653.295, it is a contract in restraint of trade that must meet three requirements under Oregon common law to be enforceable:

> (1) it must be partial or restricted in its operation in respect either to time or place; (2) it must be on some good consideration; and (3) it must be reasonable, that is, it should afford only a fair protection to the interests of the party in whose favor it is made, and must not be so large in its operation as to interfere with the interests of the public.

Eldridge v. Johnston, 195 Ore. 379, 245 P.2d 239, 250 (Or. 1952). To satisfy the reasonableness requirement, the employer must show as a predicate "that [it] has a 'legitimate interest' entitled to protection." *North Pac. Lumber Co. v. Moore*, 275 Ore. 359, 551 P.2d 431, 434 (Or. 1976). McCarthy argues that Nike has failed to show such a legitimate interest in this case.

McCarthy's general skills in sales and product development as well as industry knowledge that he acquired while working for Nike is not a protectible interest of Nike's that would justify enforcement of a noncompete agreement. "It has been uniformly held that general knowledge, skill, or facility acquired through training or experience while working for an employer appertain exclusively to the employee. The fact that they were acquired or developed during the employment does not, by itself, give the employer a sufficient interest to support a restraining covenant, even though the on-the-job training has been extensive and costly." *Rem Metals Corp. v. Logan*, 278 Ore. 715, 565 P.2d 1080, 1083 (Or. 1977).

Nonetheless, an employer has a protectible interest in "information pertaining especially to the employer's business." *Id.*

Nike has shown that McCarthy acquired information pertaining especially to Nike's business during the course of his employment with Nike. As Brand Jordan's director of sales, McCarthy obtained knowledge of Nike's product launch dates, product allocation strategies, new product development, product orders six months in advance and strategic sales plans up to three years in the future. This information was not general knowledge in the industry. For instance, McCarthy was privy to information about launch dates — the date Nike plans to introduce a product in the marketplace — for Brand Jordan shoes up through the spring of 2004. According to the undisputed testimony of one of Nike's executives, if a company knew its competitor's launch dates, it could time the launch dates of its own products to disrupt the sales of its competitor.

Nevertheless, McCarthy argues that acquisition of confidential information alone is insufficient to justify enforcement of a noncompete agreement. . . .

. . .

An employee's knowledge of confidential information is sufficient to justify enforcement of the noncompete if there is a "substantial risk" that the employee will be able to divert all or part of the employer's business given his knowledge. *See Volt Servs. Group v. Adecco Employment Servs., Inc.*, 178 Ore. App. 121, 35 P.3d 329, 334 (Or. Ct. App. 2001) (stating that customer contacts "can create a protectible interest when the nature of the contact is such that there is a substantial risk that the employee may be able to divert all or part of the customer's business"). Given the nature of the confidential information that McCarthy acquired at Nike and his new position with Reebok, there is a substantial risk that Reebok would be able to divert a significant part of Nike's business given McCarthy's knowledge. McCarthy had the highest access to confidential information concerning Nike's product allocation, product development and sales strategies. As vice president of U.S. footwear sales and merchandising for Reebok, McCarthy would be responsible for developing strategic sales plans, providing overall direction for product allocation and shaping product lines, including how products are priced. Thus, McCarthy could help choose product allocation, sales and pricing strategies for Reebok that could divert a substantial part of Nike's footwear sales to Reebok based on his knowledge of information confidential to Nike without explicitly disclosing this information to any of Reebok's employees. Accordingly, the potential use of confidential information by McCarthy in his new position with Reebok is sufficient to justify enforcing the noncompete agreement. We conclude that Nike has demonstrated a likelihood of success as to the enforceability of its noncompete agreement with McCarthy.

V. BALANCE OF HARDSHIPS

McCarthy contends that the district court erred in ruling that the balance of harm tipped in favor of Nike because the only harm that Nike would have suffered is "fair competition." Contrary to McCarthy's contention, Nike has shown potential harm from unfair competition due to McCarthy's knowledge of confidential information peculiar to Nike's products.

On the other side of the scale, a number of factors mitigate the potential harm to McCarthy from the preliminary injunction. First, Nike is obligated under the covenant not to compete to pay McCarthy his full salary during the restriction period. Second, Reebok has agreed to pay health and medical benefits for McCarthy and his family. Third, Reebok has agreed to keep the job offer to McCarthy open for a year. McCarthy, however, testified that the athletic footwear and apparel business is a fast-moving industry and that if he is forced to sit out for a year, he would have to do a lot of "catching up" after he returns to the industry. Nevertheless, the potential disruption to Nike's sales and products outweighs any harm that the injunction would cause McCarthy in the intermediate or long term. Thus, we conclude that the balance of harm tips in favor of Nike.

AFFIRMED.

NOTES & QUESTIONS

1. Protecting an Employee's Interest in Pursuing a Living

Courts, sensitive to an employee's interest in moving freely from one job to another, refuse to enforce covenants that unduly hinder an employee from pursuing his chosen livelihood. One court, facing the dilemma of whether to enforce restrictions on a person's ability to pursue a career stated the issue so:

> [T]he right of an individual to follow and pursue the particular occupation for which he is best trained is a most fundamental right. Our society is extremely mobile and our free economy is based upon competition. One who has worked in a particular field cannot be compelled to erase from his mind all of the general skills, knowledge and expertise acquired through his experience. . . . Restraints cannot be lightly placed upon his right to compete in the area of his greatest worth.

AMP, Inc. v. Fleischhacker, 823 F.2d 1199, 1202 (7th Cir. 1987) (quoting the Illinois Supreme Court in *ILG Industries v. Scott*, 273 N.E.2d at 396). The law favors mobility and disfavors covenants that place unreasonable burdens on an individual's ability to make a living.

2. Enforceability

Covenants not to compete are not enforceable unless their terms are reasonable. Courts look to several factors when determining whether a noncompete agreement is reasonable. First, the restrictions must further a legitimate business purpose or agreement. Second, the business must own a trade secret or other legally protectable interest. Third, the covenant must not be overly inclusive as to the subject matter encompassed, the duration of the protection, and the geographic territory affected. Finally, the employer must give adequate consideration in return for the employee's agreement not to compete. Even when a covenant meets the requirements for enforceability, courts often strictly construe the terms of the contract. Some states, most notably California, refuse to enforce post employment covenants not to compete altogether.

3. "Blue Penciling" of Overbroad Covenants Not to Compete

Courts may refuse to enforce covenants not to compete where no legitimate business interest justifies an employer's use of the restrictions, where the covenant prevents competition for longer than necessary to protect a business interest, and where the territorial scope of the covenant encompasses an area broader than needed to protect the employer. Some jurisdictions allow a court to salvage an overbroad covenant not to compete by modifying the terms of the agreement and enforcing the covenant as modified, a practice known as blue penciling.

4. Noncompete Agreements Must be Supported by Consideration

When an employer extracts a promise from an employee to refrain from post-employment competition with the employer's business, the employer must give consideration in exchange for imposing this limit on the employee's future employment opportunities. The Washington Supreme Court in *Labriola v. Pollard Group, Inc.*, 100 P.3d 791 (Wash. 2004), held that a noncompete agreement signed by an employee, five years after he was hired, was not supported by consideration when the employer offered no additional benefits or promises to the employee in exchange for his promise.

> Consideration is a bargained-for exchange of promises. A comparison of the status of the employer before and after the noncompete agreement confirms that the 2002 noncompete was entered into without consideration. Employer did not incur additional duties or obligations from the noncompete agreement. Prior to execution of the 2002 noncompete agreement, Employee was an "at will" Employee. After Employee executed the noncompete agreement, he still remained an "at will" employee terminable at Employer's pleasure. We hold that continued employment in this case did not serve as consideration by Employer in exchange for Employee's promise not to compete.

Labriola, 100 P.3d at 836. Since the employer gave no independent consideration at the time Labriola signed the noncompete agreement, no enforceable contract was formed between the parties.

ii.   Hold-Over/Trailer Clauses

INGERSOLL-RAND CO. v. ARMAND CIAVATTA
Supreme Court of New Jersey
542 A.2d 879 (1988)

GARIBALDI, J.

The issue in this appeal is the enforceability of an employee invention "holdover" agreement. Specifically, the issue presented is whether a "holdover" clause requiring an employee to assign a post-termination invention that does not involve an employer's trade secret or proprietary information is enforceable. The products relevant to this dispute are a new type of friction stabilizer, which defendant invented and patented, and a split-set friction stabilizer, manufactured and distributed by plaintiff. Both devices are used in the mining industry to prevent the fall of rock from the roof and walls of underground mines. The Appellate Division reversed the Chancery Division's ruling in favor of plaintiff. 216 *N.J. Super.* 667 (1987). We affirm.

I

. . .

Ciavatta joined the Millers Falls Division of Ingersoll-Rand as Director of Engineering and Quality Control in 1972. From 1972 to 1974, Ciavatta was responsible for quality control and materials management in the production of hand and electric tools. In the fall of 1974, the company terminated his employment in the Millers Falls Division, at which time he became Program Manager with Ingersoll-Rand Research, Inc. As a condition of his employment with Ingersoll-Rand Research, he executed an "Agreement Relating to Proprietary Matter" (Proprietary Agreement) in which he agreed, in pertinent part:

> 1. To assign and I hereby do assign, to the COMPANY, its successors and assigns, my entire right, title and interest in and to all inventions, copyrights and/or designs I have made or may hereafter make, conceive, develop or perfect, either solely or jointly with others either

> (a) during the period of such employment, if such inventions, copyrights and/or designs are related, directly or indirectly, to the business of, or to the research or development work of the COMPANY or its affiliates, or

> (b) with the use of the time, materials or facilities of the COMPANY or any of its affiliates, or

> (c) within one year after termination of such employment if conceived as a result of and is attributable to work done during such employment and relates to a method, substance, machine, article of manufacture or improvements therein within the scope of the business of the COMPANY or any of its affiliates.

Additionally, in Paragraph 4 of the Agreement, Ciavatta agreed:

> 4. Not to divulge, either during my employment or thereafter to any person, agency, firm or corporation, any secret, confidential or other proprietary information of the COMPANY or any of its affiliates which I may obtain through my employment without first obtaining written permission from the COMPANY.

Ciavatta signed this Agreement on October 1, 1974, and at that time he had read and understood its terms.

While employed by Ingersoll-Rand Research as a Program Manager from October 1974 through March 1978, Ciavatta worked on a variety of development projects, other than those relevant to this litigation, including a tunneling device and the development of coal haulage machinery. As a result of his participation in these development projects, Ciavatta became interested in underground mining and read extensively the industry literature on the subject. From 1974 to 1978, Ciavatta never was formally involved in or assigned to research or development relevant to the friction stabilizer. Nevertheless, Dr. McGahan, the Director of Research, encouraged the research staff to be creative, to discuss ideas for projects or potential projects beyond those to which they had been assigned. These ideas were to be submitted on disclosure forms. Through 1975, Ciavatta submitted thirteen patent disclosures to his employer for mining technology and instrumentation. Five of the thirteen proposals were for devices to support or stabilize roofs of underground mines. Four of the five invention disclosures were not friction stabilizers, but one was an improvement to Ingersoll-Rand's split-set. Ciavatta's work during this period was his first exposure to mining support equipment. Ingersoll-Rand chose not to pursue any of his concepts. Thereafter, defendant claims, he lost his motivation to invent and did not originate any additional concepts while employed by Ingersoll-Rand.

In March 1978, the company transferred Ciavatta to the Split Set Division of Ingersoll-Rand Equipment Corp. While there, he served as Manufacturing Manager and Quality Control Manager. . . . During this period, the company did not employ Ciavatta to design, invent, or modify the basic configuration of its Split Set roof stabilizer, and in fact he did not do so. Ciavatta did, however, have access to Ingersoll-Rand's manufacturing drawings, materials, and specifications. Ingersoll-Rand considers all of that information confidential, although the information had been published in industry trade publications. At the Ingersoll-Rand Research Center the company maintains a security system in order to ensure the confidentiality of its information. Drawings are stamped proprietary, visitors are escorted while in the Ingersoll-Rand Research Center, vendors must sign proprietary information agreements, and all employees must enter into a Proprietary Master Agreement similar to that at issue in this case.

[In June 1979, Ingersoll-Rand terminated Ciavatta's employment.]

After his termination, Ciavatta circulated more than one hundred resumes seeking employment with other engineering firms. From February to July 1980, he briefly obtained employment as general manager of a bankrupt company located in Michigan.

Ciavatta asserts, and the trial court found, that he first conceived of the invention in dispute in the summer of 1979 while unemployed and off the Ingersoll-Rand payroll. Apparently, he was installing a light fixture in his home when he first conceived of his invention, an elliptical metal tube designed to stabilize the roofs of mines. While searching for employment following his discharge from Ingersoll-Rand, Ciavatta intermittently worked on his design. He completed his first sketch of the stabilizing device on August 25, 1979, approximately two months after Ingersoll-Rand fired him. Ciavatta's stabilizer differs from Ingersoll-Rand's in two respects: its tubular portion is closed rather than split, and the tube is elliptical in shape.

As he continued to develop the stabilizing device, Ciavatta consulted a patent attorney to determine his rights with regard to the device. At his attorney's request, Ciavatta obtained a copy of the Ingersoll-Rand employee Proprietary Agreement he had signed when beginning his employment with Ingersoll-Rand Research. He did not inform Ingersoll-Rand of his activities with respect to his roof support system. By letter dated October 24, 1979, his attorney advised Ciavatta that "this invention is yours and Ingersoll has no enforceable claim thereto."

After his brief employment with the bankrupt company in Michigan, Ciavatta returned to his work on the stabilizing device and began refining the system in a more systematic manner. Although still looking for employment, he "started to go through significantly more calculations," and obtained sample tubing to run experimental tests. In March 1980, nine months after his termination, Ciavatta filed for a United States patent on the device and was awarded U.S. Patent No. 4,316677 in February 1982. Subsequently, in March 1982, Ciavatta received a second patent, U.S. Patent No. 4322183, which involved an improvement to the roof stabilizer protected by Ciavatta's first patent.

In July 1980, Ciavatta prepared a business plan and solicited venture capital from a number of firms, including Kerr McGee Co. and United Nuclear Corp. These financing efforts failed, however, and Ciavatta used his life savings and borrowed over $125,000 from his brother and a bank to take his invention to the marketplace. Ciavatta exhibited his now-patented invention at a trade show in October 1982, and sales of his product then began. He made his first sale in January 1983. Sales for 1983 totaled approximately $30,000. By the time that the trial of this case commenced in June 1985 his total sales approximated $270,000. Ciavatta's stabilizer sells for approximately 15% less than Ingersoll-Rand's stabilizer. The trial court observed "[t]he market place has begun to accept defendant's product and his device appears to be a competitive threat to plaintiff's device." 210 *N.J. Super.* at 344.

The parties disagree on when Ingersoll-Rand learned of Ciavatta's invention. The company acknowledges that it had learned of the model for his invention by December 1981 or early 1982. In July 1982, Ciavatta received a letter from Ingersoll-Rand's patent counsel requesting that he assign his patent to the company. Ciavatta communicated to Ingersoll-Rand that his lawyer had advised him that he was not obligated to assign his patent to his former employer. Simultaneously, Ingersoll-Rand employees prepared several internal memoranda analyzing the feasibility of Ciavatta's product and its potential competitive impact. Ingersoll-Rand, now aware of the challenge posed by Ciavatta's invention, began to consider competitive responses to the introduction of the invention in the market.

In September 1983, after Ciavatta had sold his product to several Ingersoll-Rand customers, the company decided to lower the price of its split set stabilizer and to commence this lawsuit.

. . .

Paragraph 1(c) of Ciavatta's Proprietary Agreement with Ingersoll-Rand comprises a one-year so-called "holdover" agreement under which the employee promises to assign his or her "entire right, title and interest" in any invention he or she creates during a one-year period following termination of employment if that invention is "conceived as a result of and is attributable to work done during such employment." The central question presented in this case is the enforceability of that covenant.

The common law regards an invention as the property of the inventor who conceived, developed, and perfected it.... The Supreme Judicial Court of Massachusetts accurately summarized the common-law position in *National Development Co. v. Gray*, 316 Mass. 240, 246, 55 N.E.2d 783, 786 (1944):

> One by merely entering an employment requiring the performance of services of a noninventive nature does not lose his rights to any inventions that he may make during the employment . . . and this is true even if the patent is for an improvement upon a device or process used by the employer or is of such great practical value as to supersede the devices or processes with which the employee became familiar during his employment. . . . The law looks upon an invention as the property of the one who conceived, developed and perfected it, and establishes, protects and enforces the inventor's rights in his invention unless he has contracted away those rights.

Thus, employment alone does not require an inventor to assign a patent to his employer. Absent a specific agreement, an employed inventor's rights and duties with respect to an invention or concept arise from the inventor's employment status when he actually designed the invention.

Generally, where an employer hires an employee to design a specific invention or solve a specific problem, the employee has a duty to assign the resulting patent. Where the employee is not hired specifically to design or invent, but nevertheless conceives of a device during working hours with the use of the employer's materials and equipment, the employer is granted an irrevocable but non-exclusive right to use the invention under the "shop right rule." A shop right is an employer's royalty or fee, a non-exclusive and non-transferable license to use an employee's patented invention.

Since the common-law doctrines are vague and ambiguous in defining the rights of employers and employees in employees' inventions, most employers use written contracts to allocate invention rights. Such contracts requiring an employee to assign to the employer inventions designed or conceived during the period of employment are valid. The contractual allocation of invention rights between employers and employees is especially critical given the fact that 80% to 90% of all inventions in the United States are made by employed inventors. The United States is not alone in this regard. In West Germany, 60% to 75% of all inventions come from employed inventors; in France the figure is 70% to 75%. In both countries, 90% of all *useful* inventions are made by employees. Most large, technologically advanced companies today require their employees by contract to assign their patents to their employers. Courts, however, will not enforce invention assignment contracts that unreasonably obligate an employee in each and every instance to transfer the ownership of the employee's invention to the employer. Additionally, several states have recently adopted legislation that delimits employer-employee invention assignment agreements. Those statutes restrict the instances in which employers may compel the assignment of employee inventions. All of these statutes provide that any employee invention assignment agreement that purports to give employers greater rights than they have under the statute is against public policy and, consequently, unenforceable.

In the instant case, the contract involves the assignment of future or post-employment inventions. Contractual provisions requiring assignment of post-employment inventions are commonly referred to as "trailer" or "holdover" clauses. The public policy issues involved in the enforceability of these holdover clauses reflect the dichotomy of our views on the rights of an inventor and rights of an employer. Our society has long recognized the intensely personal nature of an invention and the importance of providing stimulation and encouragement to inventors. Some commentators believe that the existing patent system does not present sufficient motivation to an employee-inventor. These commentators allege that the United States is in danger of losing its position as technology leader of the world. They cite for support that America is experiencing a declining patent balance and is less patent-productive than many foreign countries. More and more United States patents are not issued to United States citizens and companies but to foreigners. Interestingly, Japan, which began tying employed inventors' compensation to the market value of the invention in 1959, has witnessed a dramatic increase in the number of inventions generated by employed inventors.

To encourage an inventor's creativity, courts have held that on terminating his employment, an inventor has the right to use the general skills and knowledge gained through the prior employment. Moreover, an employee may compete with his former employer on termination. Nonetheless, it is acknowledged that the inventive process is increasingly being supported and subsidized by corporations and governments. It is becoming a more collective research process, the collective product of corporate and government research laboratories instead of the identifiable work of one or two individuals. Employers, therefore, have the right to protect their trade secrets, confidential information, and customer relations. Thus, employees and employers both have significant interests warranting judicial attention.

In view of the competing interests involved in holdover agreements, courts have not held them void *per se*. Rather, the courts apply a test of reasonableness. Moreover, courts strictly construe contractual provisions that require assignment of post-employment inventions; they must be fair, reasonable, and just. Generally, a clause is unreasonable if it: (1) extends beyond any apparent protection that the employer reasonably requires; (2) prevents the inventor from seeking other employment; or (3) adversely impacts on the public. . . .

. . .

Regardless of the results reached in the individual cases, all courts recognize the competing interests at stake. That is, the question of the enforceability of holdover covenants clearly presents the interest of the employee in enjoying the benefits of his or her own creation, on the one hand, and the interest of the employer in protecting confidential information, trade secrets, and, more generally, its time and expenditures in training and imparting skills and knowledge to its paid work force, on the other. Moreover, courts recognize that the public has an enormously strong interest in both fostering ingenuity and innovation of the inventor and maintaining adequate protection and incentives to corporations to undertake long-range and extremely costly research and development programs.

IV

The cases thus support the enforceability of holdover agreements if they are reasonable. . . . By applying the reasonableness test, the judicial analysis of holdover agreements will parallel the judicial analysis of contracts requiring an employee to assign to the employer inventions made or conceived of by an employee *during* his or her employment. We have held such contracts to be enforceable when reasonable. Likewise, we will enforce holdover agreements to the same extent that we will enforce similar post-employment restrictive agreements, giving employers "that limited measure of relief within the terms of the noncompetitive agreement which would be reasonably necessary to protect his 'legitimate interests,' would cause 'no undue hardship' on the employee, and would 'not impair the public interest.' " *Whitmyer Bros., Inc. v. Doyle, supra,* 58 *N.J.* at 35; *Solari Indus., Inc. v. Malady, supra,* 55 *N.J.* at 585.

The first two parts of the [reasonableness] test focus on the protection of the legitimate interests of the employer and the extent of the hardship on the employee. Plainly, the court must balance these competing interests. In cases where the employer's interests are strong, such as cases involving trade secrets or confidential information, a court will enforce a restrictive agreement. Conversely, in cases where the employer's interests do not rise to the level of a proprietary interest deserving of judicial protection, a court will conclude that a restrictive agreement merely stifles competition and therefore is unenforceable. Courts also recognize that knowledge, skill, expertise, and information acquired by an employee during his employment become part of the employee's person. "They belong to him as an individual for the transaction of any business in which he may engage, just the same as any part of the skill, knowledge and information received by him before entering the employment." von Kalinowski, "Key Employees and Trade Secrets," 47 *Va.L.Rev.* 583, 586 (1961). An employee can use those skills in any business or profession he may choose, including a competitive business with his former employer. Courts will not enforce a restrictive agreement merely to aid the employer in extinguishing competition, albeit competition from a former employee. Ultimately, the consuming public would suffer from judicial nurturing of such naked restraints on competition.

At the same time, we recognize that employers have a right to protect their trade secrets and other confidential information. Initially, of course, employers can rely on the patent laws and their common law derivatives as a foundation for protecting their patented goods and trade secrets. Beyond such protections, employers may protect themselves contractually from the misappropriation of other company information by former employees. Through contract, an employer may protect its legitimate interest in preventing employees from using the thoughts and ideas generated by the employee and fellow workers while being paid by and using the resources of the employer to invent a product that directly competes with the employer's product.

Most courts have limited the legitimate protectible interests of an employer "to trade secrets and other proprietary information . . . and customer relations." *See, e.g., Solari Indus., Inc. v. Malady, supra; Whitmyer Bros., Inc. v. Doyle, supra.* The rationale offered for such a limitation is the broad definition of trade secret and other confidential information. There is no exact definition of a trade secret. Generally, cases rely on the broad definition of trade secret found in the *Restatement of Torts* § 757 comment b (1939):

> b. Definition of trade secret. A trade secret may consist of any formula, pattern, device or compilation of information which is used in one's business, and which gives him an opportunity to obtain an advantage over competitors who do not know or use it. It may be a formula for a chemical compound, a process of manufacturing, treating or preserving materials, a pattern for a machine or other device, or a list of customers.

The Restatement also lists six factors to determine whether a given idea or information is a trade secret: (1) the extent to which the information is known outside of the business; (2) the extent to which it is known by employees and others involved in the business; (3) the extent of measures taken by the owner to guard the secrecy of the information; (4) the value of the information to the business and to its competitors; (5) the amount of effort or money expended in developing the information; and (6) the ease or difficulty with which the information could be properly acquired or duplicated by others. *Restatement of Torts* § 757 comment b. In sum, a trade secret need not be novel, inventive, or patentable, and may be a device that is clearly anticipated in the prior art or one that is merely a mechanical improvement that a good mechanic can make. However, it may not be part of the general knowledge or information of an industry or a matter of public knowledge.

Ciavatta urges that holdover agreements also should be enforced only when the former employee has used the trade secrets or confidential information of the employer in developing his post-termination invention. Since it is undisputed that he did not do so in inventing his stabilizer, he argues, paragraph 1(c), the holdover clause, should not be enforced against him.

Ingersoll-Rand, however, argues that it is inequitable to limit an employer's "protectable interest" solely to trade secrets and other confidential information. Today, large corporations maintain at great expense modern research and development programs that involve synergistic processes. Such "think tanks" require the free and open exchange of new ideas among the members of a research staff using the employer's body of accumulated information and experiences. This creative process receives its impetus and inspiration from the assimilation of an employer's advanced knowledge and a spontaneous interaction among colleagues, co-employees, and superiors. Ingersoll-Rand argues that it maintains this creative atmosphere in its research and development effort at great expense and that it should be allowed to protect itself against a former employee who invents a unique, competing concept attributable to such brainstorming. Ingersoll-Rand contends that such creative brainstorming enriched Ciavatta and led to his invention and therefore that paragraph 1(c) of the proprietary agreement should be enforced.

We agree with Ingersoll-Rand that the protection afforded by holdover agreements such as the one executed by the parties in this lawsuit may under certain circumstances exceed the limitation of trade secrets and confidential information. We recognize that employers may have legitimate interests in protecting information that is not a trade secret or proprietary information, but highly specialized, current information not generally known in the industry, created and stimulated by the research environment furnished by the employer, to which the employee has been "exposed" and "enriched" solely due to his employment. We do not attempt to define the exact parameters of that protectable interest.

We expect courts to construe narrowly this interest, which will be deemed part of the "reasonableness" equation. The line between such information, trade secrets, and the general skills and knowledge of a highly sophisticated employee will be very difficult to draw, and the employer will have the burden to do so. Nevertheless, we do not hesitate to recognize what appears to us a business reality that modern day employers are in need of some protection against the use or disclosure of valuable information regarding the employer's business, which information is passed on to certain employees confidentially by virtue of the positions those employees hold in the employer's enterprise.

Courts, however, must be aware that holdover agreements impose restrictions on employees. Such agreements clearly limit an employee's employment opportunities and in many instances probably interfere with an employee securing a position in which he could most effectively use his skills, at the same time depriving society of a more productive worker. How restrictive the clause is on a particular employee depends, of course, on the facts and circumstances of the case. Indeed, in many instances, the employee may have little choice but to sign a holdover agreement in order to secure employment. Conversely, some very talented or experienced individuals, pursued by several corporations, may bargain for highly lucrative positions in exchange for their promise to be bound by a holdover agreement. Accordingly, courts must evaluate the reasonableness of holdover agreements in light of the individual circumstances of the employer and employee. Courts must balance the employer's need for protection and the hardship on the employee that may result.

The third prong of the [reasonableness] test relates to the public interest. Throughout this opinion, we have analyzed the relevant competing public interests. We reiterate that the public has a clear interest in safeguarding fair commercial practices and in protecting employers from theft or piracy of trade secrets, confidential information, or, more generally, knowledge and technique in which the employer may be said to have a proprietary interest. The public has an equally clear and strong interest in fostering creativity and invention and in encouraging technological improvement and design enhancement of all goods in the marketplace. The competing public interests are also evident from the current debate raging in the scientific community about the effect of secrecy in scientific research arising from increased ties between scientists, commercial enterprises, and the government, and the effect of such secrecy on the long term progress of scientific programs and innovations.

In sum, we conclude that holdover agreements are enforceable when reasonable, and that in determining if the post-termination restriction is reasonable, we will apply the three-prong test of *Solari/Whitmyer*. Thus, resolution of each case will depend on its own facts and circumstances. Courts must not go too far in construing holdover agreements to insulate employers from competition from former employees. That courts should not be overly zealous in protecting employers should not, however, dissuade a court from analyzing the reasonableness of a holdover covenant or from enforcing it where it is reasonable. Thus, here, we must balance the interests of Ingersoll-Rand and Ciavatta on the basis of the facts to determine whether the enforcement of the holdover agreement in this instance would be reasonable.

VI

We conclude that on the facts of this case, Ingersoll-Rand is not entitled to an assignment of the patent on Ciavatta's friction stabilizer. We find that Ingersoll-Rand has not substantiated that Ciavatta invented his friction stabilizer in violation of his contractual obligation under the holdover clause. Ingersoll-Rand has not established that Ciavatta "conceived" of his invention as a result of his employment at Ingersoll-Rand. The facts convince us that the holdover clause does not apply here however liberally we are willing to construe the protection afforded employers by such clauses. Furthermore, we also find that enforcement of the holdover agreement in this case would be unreasonable even if the contract by its terms applied to Ciavatta's invention.

NOTES & QUESTIONS

1. Why Would an Employer Need a Hold-Over/Trailer Clause?

In a hold-over clause, also known as a trailer clause, an employee agrees to assign to the employer the rights to inventions created for a time following the termination of the employment relationship. Hold-over clauses developed in response to cases which held that, in the absence of an express contract to the contrary, a departing employee's invention did not belong to the employer unless the employee conceived of the idea during the term of employment. Employee inventors who did not wish to hand over an invention idea to the employer could postpone conception of the invention and depart the employment relationship with the inchoate idea of the invention. If an employee delays on refining the concept and writing it down in tangible form, the employee leaves no evidence of conception until after the termination of employment. Without objective evidence of conception, there is no proof of invention to trigger pre-invention assignment agreements, and the employee may take with him an invention that should rightfully have belonged to the employer.

Hold-over clauses allow employers to close the loophole by extending the period in which an employee is obligated to assign rights to an invention beyond the term of the employment relationship. The extended period serves to catch inventions in development during the time of the employee's departure and prevents exiting employees from violating their obligation to assign rights to the former employer.

2. Competing Policy Interests

Some employer most valuable asset resides in the knowledge held by individual employees. Covenants not to compete allow employers to protect these assets by restricting employees' use of the employers' proprietary knowledge. In contrast to information recorded on paper or on a computer, protection for information that is inseparable from an individual's knowledge necessarily impinges upon the individual's freedom of mobility in employment. However, without protection for their investments, employers may be reluctant to train employees for fear that employees privy to the employer's trade secret may one day turn and use the information against them. Courts recognize the interest of employers in protecting their investments and tolerate some degree of restraint on competition in permitting the use of covenants not to compete. Balanced against the employer's rights to secrecy are the rights of employees in mobility.

Some scholars have suggested that permitting employee mobility may enhance knowledge spillover and foster rapid progress in an industry. Specifically, when employees are free to move, they may serve as a conduit through which new ideas and developments disseminate. Scholars[3] have attributed the success of Silicon Valley as a high-technology industrial district and the decline of Boston's counterpart in Route 128 to California's refusal to recognize covenants not to compete[4] and Massachusetts's willingness to enforce noncompete agreements.

iii. Nonsolicitation Agreements

By securing a nonsolicitation agreement, an employer may restrict an exiting employee from enticing customers or employees away from the employer. Nonsolicitation agreements that prohibit solicitation of customers are enforceable if the employer can show that, if not for his association with the employer, the employee would not have come in contact with the customers. However, an

---

[3] Annalee Sexenian, Regional Advantage: Culture and Competitions in Silicon Valley and Route 128 (1994). *See also* Ronald J. Gilson, *The Legal Infrastructure of High Technology Industrial Districts: Silicon Valley, Route 128, and Covenants Not to Compete*, 74 N.Y.U.L. Rev. 575 (1999).

[4] California in effect bars most non-compete agreements: "every contract by which anyone is restrained from engaging in lawful profession. . . is to that extent void." Cal. Bus. & Prof. Code §16600.

employee is free to socially contact persons befriended before the commencement of the employment relationship.

PALMER & CAY OF GEORGIA, INC. v. LOCKTON COMPANIES, INC.
Court of Appeals of Georgia
615 S.E.2d 752 (2005)

ANDREWS, Presiding Judge.

This case arose when Hutcherson, Varner, and Holley left their jobs at Palmer & Cay, a professional services firm providing insurance and employee benefits services, to work for Lockton, a competitor. They filed this declaratory judgment action seeking clarification of their obligations under their employment contract with Palmer & Cay, specifically [two nonsolicitation of customers' covenants, a nonsolicitation of employee's covenant, and a nondisclosure covenant].

As stated, the trial court upheld two of the covenants and struck down two. In Case Number A05A0272, Palmer & Cay appeals from the trial court's determination that the two nonsolicitation of customers' covenants are overbroad. In Case Number A05A0273, Lockton appeals from the court's determination that the nonsolicitation of employees and nondisclosure covenants are enforceable.

Case No. A05A0272

The two nonsolicitation of customers' covenants at issue in this case provide that for a period of two years after leaving the company:

> The Employee will not, in any way, directly or indirectly, except as an employee of the Company, solicit, divert, or take away, or attempt to solicit, divert or take away, the insurance or employee benefit plan business of any of the customers of the Company which were served by the Employee during the term of his employment with the Company, or any prospective customers of the Company which the Employee solicited for the Company within one year prior to his termination of employment, for the purpose of selling to or servicing for any such customer or prospective customer any insurance or employee benefit product or service which was provided or offered by the Company during his employment; and

> The Employee will not, directly or indirectly, cause or attempt to cause any of the foregoing customers or prospective customers of the Company to refrain from maintaining or acquiring from or through the Company any insurance or employee benefit plan product or service which was provided or offered by the Company during his employment, and will not assist, directly or indirectly, any other person or persons to do so; . . .

The trial court found this nonsolicitation agreement to be overbroad for three reasons. First, the court held that it prohibited the employees from servicing or selling to a client of the company a product that the employee never sold or serviced while employed by the company; for instance, employee benefit plans. Second, the employees were prohibited from contacting clients regardless of how long it had been since they sold to these clients and regardless of whether that client had severed its relationship with the company in the interim. Third, the court found the covenant to be overbroad because it prohibited the employee from servicing or selling to the company's clients a product that the company may no longer offer.

. . .

Georgia courts have traditionally applied close scrutiny to employment contracts containing restrictive covenants and have upheld them only when the covenant is strictly limited in time, territorial effect, and activities prohibited.

> While a contract in general restraint of trade or which tends to lessen competition is against public policy and is void (1983 Ga. Const., Art. III, Sec. VI, Par. V (c); OCGA § 13-8-2), a restrictive covenant contained in an employment contract is considered to be in partial restraint of trade and will be upheld if the restraint imposed is not unreasonable, is founded on a valuable consideration, and is reasonably necessary to protect the interest of the party in whose favor it is imposed, and does not unduly prejudice the interests of the public. Whether the restraint imposed by the employment contract is reasonable is a question of law for determination by the court, which considers the nature and extent of the trade or business, the situation of the parties, and all other circumstances. A three-element test of duration, territorial coverage, and scope of activity has evolved as a helpful tool in examining the reasonableness of the particular factual setting to which it is applied.

W. R. Grace & Co. [v. Mouyal, 262 Ga. 464, 465, 422 S.E.2d 529 (1992)].

Here, the agreement prohibits the employees from soliciting for business any customer of the company that they served during their employment. Holley, Varner and Hutcherson were with Palmer & Cay for periods of eleven, ten, and five years, respectively. The employees argued below that a covenant with no geographic restriction and no limitation on the type of product or service that may be provided, which also prohibits them from doing business with a customer that they may have served 11 years ago, is overbroad. We agree.

In a similar case, *Gill v. Poe & Brown of Georgia, Inc.*, 241 Ga. App. 580 (524 S.E.2d 328) (1999), this Court struck down a clause prohibiting the employee from soliciting any customers for a period of 18 months after terminating employment. The court found that the covenant applied to a list of customers created over four years before the employee left the job; therefore, the employer had no legitimate business interest in preventing the employee's solicitation of clients who may have long since severed their relationship with the employer. *Id.* at 583.

Likewise, the covenant at issue here provides no time restriction, and the length of time is considerably longer than the four years disapproved of in *Gill*. On the other hand, this Court has upheld employment agreements which limit the time of customer contact to a certain period before the termination of employment. . . .

Accordingly, we hold this nonsolicit clause is overbroad and unenforceable. Further, the trial court correctly held that both nonsolicit clauses were unenforceable." [I]n restrictive covenant cases strictly scrutinized as employment contracts, Georgia does not employ the blue pencil doctrine of severability." *Advance Technology Consultants, supra* at 320. Therefore, if one nonsolicit clause is unenforceable, they are all unenforceable. *Id.*

Case No. A05A0273

In this case, Lockton argues that the trial court erred in upholding the nonsolicitation of employees clause. . . . The nonsolicitation of employees covenant provides that, for two years after leaving the company, "the Employee will not, directly or indirectly, attempt in any manner to cause or otherwise encourage any employee of the Company to leave the employ of such corporation." The trial court found this covenant was enforceable because it contained language almost identical to covenants previously upheld by this Court. Lockton argues that this clause is overbroad because it lacks a territorial restriction, prohibits solicitation of employees that the plaintiff employees never met, and prohibits encouraging employees to leave regardless of the reason.

As to the lack of a territorial restriction, "requiring an express geographic territorial description in all cases is not in keeping with the reality of the modern business world in which an employee's 'territory' knows no geographic bounds, as the technology of today permits an employee to service clients located throughout the country and the world." *W. R. Grace, supra* at 467. The type of business at issue in this case, selling insurance and employee benefit plans, is the type of business which has no geographic bounds.

. . .

Therefore, for the reasons discussed above, the trial court did not err in upholding the nonsolicitation of employees and nondisclosure covenants. Accordingly the trial court correctly denied in part and granted in part both parties' motions for summary judgment.

2. Inevitable Disclosures of Trade Secrets as a Basis for Preemptive Employment Limitations

a. Generally

The doctrine of inevitability arises when an employee's knowledge and skills are inseparable from an employer's trade secrets such that the employee cannot avoid using of the trade secret for a subsequent employer. Under this circumstance a court may award an injunction restricting an employee's post-employment ability to using something that is conceptually a part of himself despite the absence of a covenant not to compete.

PEPSICO, INC. v. WILLIAM E. REDMOND, JR., AND THE QUAKER OATS COMPANY
United States Court of Appeals for the Seventh Circuit
54 F.3d 1262 (1995)

FLAUM, Circuit Judge.

Plaintiff PepsiCo, Inc., sought a preliminary injunction against defendants William Redmond and the Quaker Oats Company to prevent Redmond, a former

PepsiCo employee, from divulging PepsiCo trade secrets and confidential information in his new job with Quaker and from assuming any duties with Quaker relating to beverage pricing, marketing, and distribution. The district court agreed with PepsiCo and granted the injunction. We now affirm that decision.

I.

The facts of this case lay against a backdrop of fierce beverage-industry competition between Quaker and PepsiCo, especially in "sports drinks" and "new age drinks." Quaker's sports drink, "Gatorade," is the dominant brand in its market niche. . . . Quaker also has the lead in the new-age-drink category. . . . Both companies see 1995 as an important year for their products: PepsiCo has developed extensive plans to increase its market presence, while Quaker is trying to solidify its lead by integrating Gatorade and Snapple distribution. . . .

William Redmond, Jr., worked for PepsiCo in its PepsiCola North America division ("PCNA") from 1984 to 1994. Redmond became the General Manager of the Northern California Business Unit in June, 1993, and was promoted one year later to General Manager of the business unit covering all of California, a unit having annual revenues of more than 500 million dollars and representing twenty percent of PCNA's profit for all of the United States.

Redmond's relatively high-level position at PCNA gave him access to inside information and trade secrets. Redmond, like other PepsiCo management employees, had signed a confidentiality agreement with PepsiCo. That agreement stated in relevant part that he

> would not disclose at any time, to anyone other than officers or employees of [PepsiCo], or make use of, confidential information relating to the business of [PepsiCo] . . . obtained while in the employ of [PepsiCo], which shall not be generally known or available to the public or recognized as standard practices.

Donald Uzzi, who had left PepsiCo in the beginning of 1994 to become the head of Quaker's Gatorade division, began courting Redmond for Quaker in May, 1994. Redmond met in Chicago with Quaker officers in August, 1994, and on October 20, 1994, Quaker, through Uzzi, offered Redmond the position of Vice President — On Premise Sales for Gatorade. Redmond did not then accept the offer but continued to negotiate for more money. Throughout this time, Redmond kept his dealings with Quaker secret from his employers at PCNA.

On November 8, 1994, Uzzi extended Redmond a written offer for the position of Vice President — Field Operations for Gatorade and Redmond accepted. Later that same day, Redmond called William Bensyl, the Senior Vice President of Human Resources for PCNA, and told him that he had an offer from Quaker to become the Chief Operating Officer of the combined Gatorade and Snapple company but had not yet accepted it. Redmond also asked whether he should, in light of the offer, carry out his plans to make calls upon certain PCNA customers. Bensyl told Redmond to make the visits.

Redmond also misstated his situation to a number of his PCNA colleagues, including Craig Weatherup, PCNA's President and Chief Executive Officer, and Brenda Barnes, PCNA's Chief Operating Officer and Redmond's immediate superior. As with Bensyl, Redmond told them that he had been offered the position of Chief Operating Officer at Gatorade and that he was leaning "60/40" in favor of accepting the new position.

On November 10, 1994, Redmond met with Barnes and told her that he had decided to accept the Quaker offer and was resigning from PCNA. Barnes immediately took Redmond to Bensyl, who told Redmond that PepsiCo was considering legal action against him.

True to its word, PepsiCo filed this diversity suit on November 16, 1994, seeking a temporary restraining order to enjoin Redmond from assuming his duties at Quaker and to prevent him from disclosing trade secrets or confidential information to his new employer. The district court granted PepsiCo's request that same day but dissolved the order *sua sponte* two days later, after determining that PepsiCo had failed to meet its burden of establishing that it would suffer irreparable harm. The court found that PepsiCo's fears about Redmond were based upon a mistaken understanding of his new position at Quaker and that the likelihood that Redmond would improperly reveal any confidential information did not "rise above mere speculation."

From November 23, 1994, to December 1, 1994, the district court conducted a preliminary injunction hearing on the same matter. At the hearing, PepsiCo offered evidence of a number of trade secrets and confidential information it desired protected and to which Redmond was privy. First, it identified PCNA's "Strategic Plan," an annually revised document that contains PCNA's plans to compete, its financial goals, and its strategies for manufacturing, production, marketing, packaging, and distribution for the coming three years. Strategic Plans are developed by Weatherup and his staff with input from PCNA's general managers, including Redmond, and are considered highly confidential. The Strategic Plan derives much of its value from the fact that it is secret and competitors cannot anticipate PCNA's next moves. PCNA managers received the most recent Strategic Plan at a meeting in July, 1994, a meeting Redmond attended. PCNA also presented information at the meeting regarding its plans for Lipton ready-to-drink teas and for All Sport for 1995 and beyond, including new flavors and package sizes.

Second, PepsiCo pointed to PCNA's Annual Operating Plan ("AOP") as a trade secret. The AOP is a national plan for a given year and guides PCNA's financial goals, marketing plans, promotional event calendars, growth expectations, and operational changes in that year. The AOP, which is implemented by PCNA unit General Managers, including Redmond, contains specific information regarding all PCNA initiatives for the forthcoming year. The AOP bears a label that reads "Private and Confidential — Do Not Reproduce" and is considered highly confidential by PCNA managers.

In particular, the AOP contains important and sensitive information about "pricing architecture" — how PCNA prices its products in the marketplace. Pricing architecture covers both a national pricing approach and specific price points for given areas. Pricing architecture also encompasses PCNA's objectives for All Sport and its new age drinks with reference to trade channels, package sizes and other characteristics of both the products and the customers at which the products are aimed. Additionally, PCNA's pricing architecture outlines PCNA's customer development agreements. These agreements between PCNA and retailers provide for the retailer's participation in certain merchandising activities for PCNA products. As with other information contained in the AOP, pricing architecture is highly confidential and would be extremely valuable to a competitor. Knowing PCNA's pricing architecture would allow a competitor to anticipate PCNA's pricing moves and underbid PCNA strategically whenever and wherever the competitor so desired. PepsiCo introduced evidence that Redmond had detailed knowledge of PCNA's pricing architecture and that he was aware of and had been involved in preparing PCNA's customer development agreements with PCNA's California and California-based national customers. Indeed, PepsiCo showed that Redmond, as the General Manager for California, would have been responsible for implementing the pricing architecture guidelines for his business unit.

PepsiCo also showed that Redmond had intimate knowledge of PCNA "attack plans" for specific markets. Pursuant to these plans, PCNA dedicates extra funds to supporting its brands against other brands in selected markets. To use a hypothetical example, PCNA might budget an additional $500,000 to spend in Chicago at a particular time to help All Sport close its market gap with Gatorade. Testimony and documents demonstrated Redmond's awareness of these plans and his participation in drafting some of them.

Finally, PepsiCo offered evidence of PCNA trade secrets regarding innovations in its selling and delivery systems. Under this plan, PCNA is testing a new delivery system that could give PCNA an advantage over its competitors in negotiations with retailers over shelf space and merchandising. Redmond has knowledge of this secret because PCNA, which has invested over a million dollars in developing the system during the past two years, is testing the pilot program in California.

Having shown Redmond's intimate knowledge of PCNA's plans for 1995, PepsiCo argued that Redmond would inevitably disclose that information to Quaker in his new position, at which he would have substantial input as to Gatorade and Snapple pricing, costs, margins, distribution systems, products, packaging and marketing, and could give Quaker an unfair advantage in its upcoming skirmishes with PepsiCo. Redmond and Quaker countered that Redmond's primary initial duties at Quaker as Vice President — Field Operations would be to integrate Gatorade and Snapple distribution and then to manage that distribution as well as the promotion, marketing and sales of these products. Redmond asserted that the integration would be conducted according to a pre-existing plan and that his special knowledge of PCNA strategies would be irrelevant. This irrelevance would derive not only from the fact that Redmond would be implementing pre-existing plans but also from the fact that PCNA and Quaker distribute their products in entirely different ways: PCNA's distribution system is vertically integrated (i.e., PCNA owns the system) and delivers its product directly to retailers, while Quaker ships its product to wholesalers and customer warehouses and relies on independent distributors. The defendants also pointed out that Redmond had signed a confidentiality agreement with Quaker preventing him from disclosing "any confidential information belonging to others," as well as the Quaker Code of Ethics, which prohibits employees from engaging in "illegal or improper acts to acquire a competitor's trade secrets." Redmond additionally promised at the hearing that should he be faced with a situation at Quaker that might involve the use or disclosure of PCNA information, he would seek advice from Quaker's in-house counsel and would refrain from making the decision.

PepsiCo responded to the defendants' representations by pointing out that the evidence did not show that Redmond would simply be implementing a business plan already in place. On the contrary, as of November, 1994, the plan to integrate Gatorade and Snapple distribution consisted of a single distributorship agreement and a two page "contract terms summary." Such a basic plan would not lend itself to widespread application among the over 300 independent Snapple distributors. Since the integration process would likely face resistance from Snapple distributors and Quaker had no scheme to deal with this probability, Redmond, as the person in charge of the integration, would likely have a great deal of influence on the process. PepsiCo further argued that Snapple's 1995 marketing and promotion plans had not necessarily been completed prior to Redmond's joining Quaker, that Uzzi disagreed with portions of the Snapple plans, and that the plans were open to re-evaluation. Uzzi testified that the plan for integrating Gatorade and Snapple distribution is something that would happen in the future. Redmond would therefore likely have input in remaking these plans, and if he did, he would inevitably be making decisions with PCNA's strategic plans and 1995 AOP in mind. Moreover, PepsiCo continued, diverging testimony made it difficult to know exactly what Redmond would be doing at Quaker. Redmond described his job as "managing the entire sales effort of Gatorade at the field level, possibly including strategic planning," and at least at one point considered his job to be equivalent to that of a Chief Operating Officer. Uzzi, on the other hand, characterized Redmond's position as "primarily and initially to restructure and integrate our — the distribution systems for Snapple and for Gatorade, as per our distribution plan" and then to "execute marketing, promotion and sales plans in the marketplace." Uzzi also denied having given Redmond detailed information about any business plans, while Redmond described such a plan in depth in an affidavit and said that he received the information from Uzzi. Thus, PepsiCo asserted, Redmond would have a high position in the Gatorade hierarchy, and PCNA trade secrets and confidential information would necessarily influence his decisions. Even if Redmond could somehow refrain from relying on this information, as he promised he would, his actions in leaving PCNA, Uzzi's actions in hiring Redmond, and the varying testimony regarding Redmond's new responsibilities, made Redmond's assurances to PepsiCo less than comforting.

On December 15, 1994, the district court issued an order enjoining Redmond from assuming his position at Quaker through May, 1995, and permanently from using or disclosing any PCNA trade secrets or confidential information. The court entered its findings of fact and conclusions of law on January 26, 1995, *nunc pro tunc* December 15, 1994. The court, which completely adopted PepsiCo's position, found that Redmond's new job posed a clear threat of misappropriation of trade secrets and confidential information that could be enjoined under Illinois statutory and common law. The court also emphasized Redmond's lack of forthrightness both in his activities before accepting his job with Quaker and in his testimony as factors leading the court to believe the threat of misappropriation was real. This appeal followed.

II.

Both parties agree that the primary issue on appeal is whether the district court correctly concluded that PepsiCo had a reasonable likelihood of success on its various claims for trade secret misappropriation and breach of a confidentiality agreement. We review the district court's legal conclusions in issuing a preliminary injunction de novo and its factual determinations and balancing of the equities for abuse of discretion. *SEC v. Cherif,* 933 F.2d 403, 408 (7th Cir. 1991), *cert. denied,* 502 U.S. 1071, 117 L. Ed. 2d 131, 112 S. Ct. 966 (1992); *Somerset House, Inc. v. Turnock,* 900 F.2d 1012, 1014 (7th Cir. 1990).

A.

The Illinois Trade Secrets Act ("ITSA"), which governs the trade secret issues in this case, provides that a court may enjoin the "actual or threatened misappropriation" of a trade secret. 765 ILCS 1065/3(a) . . . . A party seeking an injunction must therefore prove both the existence of a trade secret and the misappropriation. The defendants' appeal focuses solely on misappropriation; although the defendants only reluctantly refer to PepsiCo's marketing and distribution plans as trade secrets, they do not seriously contest that this information falls under the ITSA.

The question of threatened or inevitable misappropriation in this case lies at the heart of a basic tension in trade secret law. Trade secret law serves to protect "standards of commercial morality" and "encourage invention and innovation" while maintaining "the public interest in having free and open competition in the manufacture and sale of unpatented goods." [2 Melvin F. Jager, Trade Secrets Law § IL.03 at IL-12 (Clark Boardman Callaghan, rev. ed. 1994)]. Yet that same law should not prevent workers from pursuing their livelihoods when they leave their current positions. *American Can Co. v. Mansukhani,* 742 F.2d 314, 329 (7th Cir. 1984). . . . This tension is particularly exacerbated when a plaintiff sues to prevent not the actual misappropriation of trade secrets but the mere threat that it will occur. While the ITSA plainly permits a court to enjoin the threat of misappropriation of trade secrets, there is little law in Illinois or in this circuit establishing what constitutes threatened or inevitable misappropriation. Indeed, there are only two cases in this circuit that address the issue: *Teradyne, Inc. v. Clear Communications Corp.,* 707 F. Supp. 353 (N.D.Ill 1989), and *AMP Inc. v. Fleischhacker,* 823 F.2d 1199 (7th Cir. 1987).

In *Teradyne,* Teradyne alleged that a competitor, Clear Communications, had lured employees away from Teradyne and intended to employ them in the same field. In an insightful opinion, Judge Zagel observed that "threatened misappropriation can be enjoined under Illinois law" where there is a "high degree of probability of inevitable and immediate . . . use of . . . trade secrets." *Teradyne,* 707 F. Supp. at 356. . . .

In *AMP*, we affirmed the denial of a preliminary injunction on the grounds that the plaintiff AMP had failed to show either the existence of any trade secrets or the likelihood that defendant Fleischhacker, a former AMP employee, would compromise those secrets or any other confidential business information. AMP, which produced electrical and electronic connection devices, argued that Fleishhacker's new position at AMP's competitor would inevitably lead him to compromise AMP's trade secrets regarding the manufacture of connectors. *AMP*, 823 F.2d at 1207. In rejecting that argument, we emphasized that the mere fact that a person assumed a similar position at a competitor does not, without more, make it "inevitable that he will use or disclose . . . trade secret information" so as to "demonstrate irreparable injury." *Id.*

. . .

The ITSA, *Teradyne,* and *AMP* lead to the same conclusion: a plaintiff may prove a claim of trade secret misappropriation by demonstrating that defendant's new employment will inevitably lead him to rely on the plaintiff's trade secrets. *See also* 1 Jager, *supra,* § 7.02[2][a] at 7-20 (noting claims where "the allegation is based on the fact that the disclosure of trade secrets in the new employment is inevitable, whether or not the former employee acts consciously or unconsciously"). The defendants are incorrect that Illinois law does not allow a court to enjoin the "inevitable" disclosure of trade secrets. Questions remain, however, as to what constitutes inevitable misappropriation and whether PepsiCo's submissions rise above those of the *Teradyne* and *AMP* plaintiffs and meet that standard. We hold that they do.

PepsiCo presented substantial evidence at the preliminary injunction hearing that Redmond possessed extensive and intimate knowledge about PCNA's strategic goals for 1995 in sports drinks and new age drinks. The district court concluded on the basis of that presentation that unless Redmond possessed an uncanny ability to compartmentalize information, he would necessarily be making decisions about Gatorade and Snapple by relying on his knowledge of PCNA trade secrets. It is not the "general skills and knowledge acquired during his tenure with" PepsiCo that PepsiCo seeks to keep from falling into Quaker's hands, but rather "the particularized plans or processes developed by [PCNA] and disclosed to him while the employer-employee relationship existed, which are unknown to others in the industry and which give the employer an advantage over his competitors." *AMP,* 823 F.2d at 1202. The *Teradyne* and *AMP* plaintiffs could do nothing more than assert that skilled employees were taking their skills elsewhere; PepsiCo has done much more.

Admittedly, PepsiCo has not brought a traditional trade secret case, in which a former employee has knowledge of a special manufacturing process or customer list and can give a competitor an unfair advantage by transferring the technology or customers to that competitor. . . . PepsiCo has not contended that Quaker has stolen the All Sport formula or its list of distributors. Rather PepsiCo has asserted that Redmond cannot help but rely on PCNA trade secrets as he helps plot Gatorade and Snapple's new course, and that these secrets will enable Quaker to achieve a substantial advantage by knowing exactly how PCNA will price, distribute, and market its sports drinks and new age drinks and being able to respond strategically. . . . This type of trade secret problem may arise less often, but it nevertheless falls within the realm of trade secret protection under the present circumstances.

Quaker and Redmond assert that they have not and do not intend to use whatever confidential information Redmond has by virtue of his former employment. They point out that Redmond has already signed an agreement with Quaker not to disclose any trade secrets or confidential information gleaned from his earlier employment. They also note with regard to distribution systems that even if Quaker wanted to steal information about PCNA's distribution plans, they would be completely useless in attempting to integrate the Gatorade and Snapple beverage lines.

The defendants' arguments fall somewhat short of the mark. Again, the danger of misappropriation in the present case is not that Quaker threatens to use PCNA's secrets to create distribution systems or co-opt PCNA's advertising and marketing ideas. Rather, PepsiCo believes that Quaker, unfairly armed with knowledge of PCNA's plans, will be able to anticipate its distribution, packaging, pricing, and marketing moves. Redmond and Quaker even concede that Redmond might be faced with a decision that could be influenced by certain confidential information that he obtained while at PepsiCo. In other words, PepsiCo finds itself in the position of a coach, one of whose players has left, playbook in hand, to join the opposing team before the big game. Quaker and Redmond's protestations that their distribution systems and plans are entirely different from PCNA's are thus not really responsive.

The district court also concluded from the evidence that Uzzi's actions in hiring Redmond and Redmond's actions in pursuing and accepting his new job demonstrated a lack of candor on their part and proof of their willingness to misuse PCNA trade secrets, findings Quaker and Redmond vigorously challenge. The court expressly found that:

> Redmond's lack of forthrightness on some occasions, and out and out lies on others, in the period between the time he accepted the position with defendant Quaker and when he informed plaintiff that he had accepted that position leads the court to conclude that defendant Redmond could not be trusted to act with the necessary sensitivity and good faith under the circumstances in which the only practical verification that he was not using plaintiff's secrets would be defendant Redmond's word to that effect.

The facts of the case do not ineluctably dictate the district court's conclusion. Redmond's ambiguous behavior toward his PepsiCo superiors might have been nothing more than an attempt to gain leverage in employment negotiations. The discrepancy between Redmond's and Uzzi's comprehension of what Redmond's job would entail may well have been a simple misunderstanding. The court also pointed out that Quaker, through Uzzi, seemed to express an unnatural interest in hiring PCNA employees: all three of the people interviewed for the position Redmond ultimately accepted worked at PCNA. Uzzi may well have focused on recruiting PCNA employees because he knew they were good and not because of their confidential knowledge. Nonetheless, the district court, after listening to the witnesses, determined otherwise. That conclusion was not an abuse of discretion.

. . . Thus, when we couple the demonstrated inevitability that Redmond would rely on PCNA trade secrets in his new job at Quaker with the district court's reluctance to believe that Redmond would refrain from disclosing these secrets in his new position (or that Quaker would ensure Redmond did not disclose them), we conclude that the district court correctly decided that PepsiCo demonstrated a likelihood of success on its statutory claim of trade secret misappropriation.

. . .

C.

For the same reasons we concluded that the district court did not abuse its discretion in granting the preliminary injunction on the issue of trade secret misappropriation, we also agree with its decision on the likelihood of Redmond's breach of his confidentiality agreement should he begin working at Quaker. Because Redmond's position at Quaker would initially cause him to disclose trade secrets, it would necessarily force him to breach his agreement not to disclose confidential information acquired while employed in PCNA. . . .

III.

Finally, Redmond and Quaker have contended in the alternative that the injunction issued against them is overbroad. They disagree in particular with the injunction's prohibition against Redmond's participation in the integration of the Snapple and Gatorade distribution systems. The defendants claim that whatever trade secret and confidential information Redmond has, that information is completely irrelevant to Quaker's integration task. They further argue that, because Redmond would only be implementing a plan already in place, the injunction is especially inappropriate.

While the defendants' arguments are not without some merit, the district court determined that the proposed integration would require Redmond to do more than execute a plan someone else had drafted. It also found that Redmond's knowledge of PCNA's trade secrets and confidential information would inevitably shape that integration and that Redmond could not be trusted to avoid that conflict of interest. If the injunction permanently enjoined Redmond from assuming these duties at Quaker, the defendants' argument would be stronger. However, the injunction against Redmond's immediate employment at Quaker extends no further than necessary and was well within the district court's discretion.

For the foregoing reasons, we affirm the district court's order enjoining Redmond from assuming his responsibilities at Quaker through May, 1995, and preventing him forever from disclosing PCNA trade secrets and confidential information.

AFFIRMED.

NOTES & QUESTIONS

1. History of the Inevitable Disclosure Doctrine

Before the Seventh Circuit's decision in *PepsiCo, Inc. v. Redmond*, inevitable disclosure cases involved the situation where a plaintiff holds a trade secret that the defendant competitor has tried but failed to independently develop. In an effort to obtain the trade secret, the defendant then hires away one of the plaintiff's employees who is privy to the trade secret. Typically, the plaintiff is the market leader in its field while the defendant is a competitor who has a smaller share of the market. Under these circumstances, the court assumes that the exiting employee cannot avoid using the knowledge of plaintiff's trade secret for his new employer, the defendant. *E.I. Du Pont de Nemours v. American Potash & Chemical Corp.*, 200 A.2d 428 (Del. Ch. 1964), is a good example of what commentators have called a "true" inevitable disclosure case. In the case, Du Pont brought an action to enjoin a former employee from disclosing Du Pont's secret process for manufacturing titanium dioxide pigments to American Potash. American Potash had tried unsuccessfully to obtain a license to use Du Pont's process and subsequently hired away one of Du Pont's managers who had knowledge of the process. The court denied American Potash's motion for summary judgment, holding that the record did not preclude a jury from finding that there was an imminent threat of a breach of the employee's fiduciary duty to Du Pont.

After *Pepsico*, an employer may potentially obtain injunctive relief against an employee for "virtually *any* competitive employment taken by an individual who had held any kind of position . . . of responsibility with plaintiff but had not entered into a restrictive covenant and accordingly not been given any consideration for restricting his postemployment opportunities." Roger M. Milgrim, *Milgrim on Trade Secrets* § 5.02[3][d] (2005). Injunctive relief is no longer predicated on evidence of actual or threatened trade secret misappropriation.

2. Framing the Dispute

Case law favors employee ownership in situations where an invention conception is completed after an employee's exit. Absent a hold-over or trailer clause, the exiting employee owns an invention conceived after the termination of the employment relationship. A dispute framed as an issue of ownership of an inchoate invention therefore favors the employee.

All disputes involving inchoate inventions may potentially be recast as trade secret misappropriation disputes, where the invention idea is the trade secret. By framing the issue as one of trade secret misappropriation, an employer can replace pro-employee case law governing ownership of inchoate inventions with more employer-friendly case law governing trade secret misappropriation.

When the issue is reframed as a trade secret dispute, an employer may use the doctrine of inevitable disclosure to enforce what is in effect a covenant not to compete.

b. Hazards of Applying the "Inevitable Disclosure" Doctrine

The inevitable disclosure doctrine can impose the equivalent of an after-the-fact noncontractual covenant not to compete. Unlike a noncompete agreement which must meet a contractual test for reasonableness, the doctrine of inevitability provides no frame of reference for courts aside from the uncertain standard of "inevitability." The doctrine in essence shifts the bargaining power to employers without giving employees the benefit of negotiations.

WILLIAM LEJEUNE v. COIN ACCEPTORS, INC.
Court of Appeals of Maryland
849 A.2d 451 (2004)

BATTAGLIA, J.

. . . William LeJeune appeals from a preliminary injunction issued by the Circuit Court for Anne Arundel County, enjoining him from working for Mars Electronics, Inc. (hereinafter "Mars") in a number of specified industries. The Circuit Court found that, if LeJeune were permitted to work in those industries, his former employer and Mars' principal competitor, Coin Acceptors, Inc. (hereinafter "Coinco"), would suffer irreparable injury because LeJeune had misappropriated trade secrets that would give Mars an unfair competitive advantage. We conclude that the evidence supports a finding of trade secret misappropriation. We also conclude, however, that the Circuit Court erred in relying on the theory of "inevitable disclosure" when ruling on the preliminary injunction. Therefore, we vacate the injunction and remand this case to the Circuit Court for further proceedings consistent with this Opinion.

I. Background

A. Facts

Coinco is a Missouri corporation in the business of designing, manufacturing, and servicing coin acceptors, coin changers, bill validators, and similar machines. Coinco divides its efforts to market and sell these machines into three separate "channels": "Vending," which includes beverage bottlers such as Coke and Pepsi; "Amusement," which includes video game manufacturers and distributors; and "Specialty Markets," which includes transit or transportation companies or companies that offer "self-check-out" services.

. . .

While employed with Coinco, LeJeune never entered into a non-compete or confidentiality agreement with Coinco. He worked in sales and was not involved in manufacturing or research and development. He did, however, develop an extensive understanding of Coinco's products through his service and sales experience. He also learned of Coinco's pricing, pricing strategies, marketing and business initiatives, and selling strategies but was not privy to all information relating to Coinco's contracts with customers. LeJeune worked from his home in Annapolis, where he regularly received company documents.

Considering new employment in May and June of 2003, LeJuene had several interviews with Mars, Coinco's primary competitor in the currency acceptor industry. During an introductory telephone interview in May 2003, LeJeune described his work experience with Coinco and mentioned to the interviewer, Chris Mumford, that "Coinco recently added Money Controls products to [its] portfolio to call on retail/kiosk accounts east of the Mississippi." He also stated that Coinco was concerned that Conlux, a sister company of Mars, was cutting into Coinco's sales. LeJeune later traveled to Lancaster, Pennsylvania, where he interviewed with several other Mars personnel. LeJeune discussed his experience at Coinco and explained why he sought employment with Mars. One of the interviewers, Mary Rampe, twice explained to LeJeune that no confidential Coinco information should be discussed during the interview. On July 7, 2003, LeJeune signed a job-offer letter from Mars and accepted a position as an Amusement OEM (Original Equipment Manufacturer) Manager. The new position would require LeJeune to focus on selling to the amusement industry, although he would have some contact with "full line distributors" that serve both the amusement and vending markets.

On July 14, 2003, LeJeune informed his supervisor, William Morgan, that he was leaving Coinco to work for Mars. On July 16, 2003, Morgan and LeJeune met for several hours to review the status of LeJeune's accounts. Morgan asked LeJeune to continue to work for Coinco for two weeks so that LeJeune could introduce Coinco's clients to LeJeune's successor. During his conversations with Morgan, LeJeune stated that he would be in a "unique" position at Mars because of his experience at Coinco. Morgan understood this to mean that LeJeune intended to use his knowledge of Coinco's business strategies. LeJeune stated that the reference to his "unique" position described his situation as one with extensive experience in the vending industry entering a job with a focus on the amusement market. That same day, LeJeune returned his laptop computer to Morgan along with a box of Coinco documents and materials.

Prior to this meeting with Morgan, LeJeune, on three separate occasions, had transferred or "burned" digital copies of numerous documents from his Coinco laptop to a compact disc ("CD"). On July 8, LeJeune copied, among other documents, Coinco's Executable Budgeting Software, which includes Coinco's manufacturing costs and profit margins. LeJeune conducted a second "burn" on July 8, transferring numerous personal files that had been saved on the Coinco laptop. On July 16, LeJeune again copied various files from the laptop, one of which contained pricing information related to Coinco's Specialty Markets Strategic Plan. Sometime after copying all of the files onto the CD, LeJeune created a second copy of the disc.

LeJeune explained that he had done this because he wanted to retain personal files, such as wedding photographs, that had been saved under the "My Documents" file on the laptop. He stated that, for the sake of simplicity and because he did not know how to save individual files onto a CD, he had "burned" the entire "My Documents" folder and captured some of Coinco's business documents. LeJeune stated that he had not saved any Coinco documents with the intent to use those documents in his work with Mars. An expert in computer forensics testifying on behalf of Coinco, however, stated that, when LeJeune copied the Executable Budgeting Software, that file was not part of the "My Documents" folder. The expert also discovered that LeJeune had erased information from the Coinco laptop in an effort to hide the downloads. The erased information was recovered by computer forensic specialists.

In addition to the computer files, LeJeune also retained hard copies of a number of other Coinco documents. Included among those documents were Coinco's price and cost information, Coinco's service pricing, a list of Coinco's preferred distributors, and detailed technical specifications relating to a Coinco's amusement product, the MC2600, and a Coinco vending product, the Bill Pro Validator. The pricing and cost information is sensitive because Coinco uses a tiered-pricing system.

Coinco's efforts to maintain the confidentiality of company information included limiting access to company documents to only personnel who needed to know the information. To this end, Coinco guarded the computer files on its mainframe computer with a password system, which allowed Coinco to control the employees' access to company information. Coinco also negotiates "non-disclosure" agreements with many of its clients to ensure that those clients do not share pricing information with other Coinco customers or Coinco competitors. In addition, Coinco's "Employee Handbook" states that its business methods are "proprietary," and employees should protect such information as confidential. Many of Coinco's pricing documents and other strategic information, including information at issue in this case (i.e., the Specialty Markets Strategic Plan, pricing and cost documents, and Bill Pro Validator specifications), were marked "confidential."

LeJeune stated that he did not discuss proprietary Coinco information, such as Coinco's price list, customer list, or strategic plan, with anyone at Mars. According to LeJeune, he did not know that Coinco was concerned about his knowledge of confidential information until he learned of Coinco's suit against him, at which time he returned all of the alleged confidential Coinco documents and files.

. . .

III.   Discussion

1.   Coinco's Trade Secrets

[The court determined that the documents and information that LeJeune retained without Coinco's permission qualified as trade secrets under the Maryland Uniform Trade Secrets Act (MUTSA).]

2. Misappropriation

Coinco is not entitled to injunctive relief unless it has established that LeJeune misappropriated its trade secrets, including Coinco's Executable Budgeting Software, Specialty Markets Strategic Plan, hard-copy pricing and cost lists, and specifications of the MC2600 and Bill Pro Validator. LeJeune contends that the only basis for granting an injunction under MUTSA is a finding of "actual or threatened" misappropriation. The evidence admitted at the preliminary injunction hearing, LeJeune argues, does not establish any "actual or threatened" misappropriation of a trade secret. LeJeune maintains that he did not acquire any information improperly because Coinco voluntarily provided him with all retained documents and then did not ask for their return until the start of this litigation. Additionally, LeJeune argues that Coinco did not present any evidence that he had used or disclosed trade secrets or that he intended to do so.

In response, Coinco urges that the evidence does support a finding that LeJeune misappropriated trade secrets. Coinco also claims that the evidence demonstrates that LeJeune misappropriated this information by copying selected confidential files from the Coinco laptop onto a CD and by retaining hard-copy documents after allegedly telling Coinco that he had returned everything.

. . . Section 11-1201(c) of MUTSA defines "misappropriation" as follows:

"Misappropriation" means the:

(1) Acquisition of a trade secret of another by a person who knows or has reason to know that the trade secret was acquired by improper means; or

(2) Disclosure or use of a trade secret of another without express or implied consent by a person who:

    (i) Used improper means to acquire knowledge of the trade secret; or

    (ii) At the time of disclosure or use, knew or had reason to know that the person's knowledge of the trade secret was:

        1. Derived from or through a person who had utilized improper means to acquire it;

        2. Acquired under circumstances giving rise to a duty to maintain its secrecy or limit its use; or

        3. Derived from or through a person who owed a duty to the person seeking relief to maintain its secrecy or limit its use; or

    (iii) Before a material change of the person's position, knew or had reason to know that it was a trade secret and that knowledge of it had been acquired by accident or mistake.

Section 11-1201(c) of MUTSA. This section describes two general types of misappropriation: (1) acquisition of a trade secret by improper means or (2) disclosure of a trade secret. We must consider this definition in conjunction with the terms of Section 11- 1202(a) of MUTSA, which provides an injunction for "actual" or "threatened" misappropriation. A court, therefore, can issue an injunction to prevent either of the following: (1) the actual or threatened acquisition of a trade secret by improper means or (2) the actual or threatened disclosure of a trade secret.

a. Acquisition of a Trade Secret by Improper Means

The Circuit Court was persuaded that the evidence was sufficient that LeJeune had acquired trade secrets by improper means. Both parties agree that LeJeune possessed documents and files belonging to Coinco, and we determined that several of these documents (i.e., the budgeting software, Specialty Markets Strategic Plan, pricing and cost documents, and MC2600 and Bill Pro Validator specifications) qualified as trade secrets. MUTSA states that a trade secret is acquired by "improper means" when it has been acquired by "theft, bribery, misrepresentation, breach or inducement of a breach of duty to maintain secrecy, or espionage through electronic or other means." Section 11-1201(b) of MUTSA.

. . .

. . . Coinco did not give LeJeune permission to transfer trade secrets from the company laptop to a CD. In an attempt to justify his actions, LeJeune stated that he transferred the "My Documents" folder from the company laptop to retain personal files, such as wedding photographs, and in the process, captured numerous Coinco documents. Coinco's expert testified, however, that LeJeune did not download only the "My Documents" folder, but he also transferred selected, specific Coinco files containing trade secrets. Considering this evidence, the trial judge apparently did not believe LeJeune's version of the events, and we see no reason here to upset the fact-finder's credibility determination.

. . .

[T]he trial court found and we agree that the information at issue is sensitive trade secret information. Moreover, . . . on the last day of his employment, LeJeune selected specific, confidential Coinco documents and actively transferred them from the Coinco laptop to a CD that he intended to keep for his personal use. After transferring the files, LeJeune then erased over four hundred files from the laptop. This suggests that LeJeune was attempting to hide his conduct and was aware that transferring the files was improper. LeJeune again demonstrated an intent to hide his possession of trade secrets when he told his supervisor that "everything" had been returned, although numerous hard-copy trade secrets remained in LeJeune's possession. The evidence in this case is sufficient to support the Circuit Court's finding that LeJeune acquired Coinco's trade secrets by improper means.

b. Inevitable Disclosure / Threatened Disclosure

Concluding that LeJeune misappropriated trade secrets by acquiring them improperly does not end our inquiry with respect to whether the Circuit Court's injunction was appropriate in this case. Injunctive relief, by its nature, addresses only what could happen in the future and cannot remedy misconduct, such as the improper acquisition of trade secrets, which occurred in the past. In fact, the injunctive remedies of Section 11-1202(a) of MUTSA provide no remedy at all for the past misappropriations. In other words, if LeJeune already had misappropriated the trade secrets and returned them, the court cannot craft an injunction to reverse time and erase whatever harm LeJeune caused by taking the trade secrets without consent.

Nevertheless, MUTSA's injunctive remedies could serve to protect Coinco if the evidence demonstrates a likelihood of some *future* misappropriation. As we stated previously, MUTSA permits a court to enjoin either (1) actual or threatened acquisition of a trade secret by improper means or (2) actual or threatened disclosure of trade secrets. With respect to the first category, the evidence clearly is insufficient to support a finding that LeJeune continues to acquire trade secrets improperly or that he has threatened other acquisition of Coinco's trade secrets by improper means. As to the second category, the record does not reveal any evidence that LeJeune actually had disclosed Coinco's trade secrets and that an injunction is necessary to stop that conduct. The sole question in the case at bar, therefore, is whether any threatened future disclosure or use of a trade secret justifies an injunction at this stage of the proceedings.[5]

The Circuit Court, however, did not make a finding of "threatened disclosure" of Coinco's trade secrets. Rather, it decided to issue the preliminary injunction based on a theory known as "inevitable disclosure." In making its ruling, the trial judge stated:

> I know I don't have to make a final ruling on whether the inevitable disclosure doctrine applies or not, but it is the court's position that with the knowledge that [LeJeune] has, it would be inconceivable to the court how he could do his job as the national accounts representative for the amusement industry without considering or weighing or taking into consideration the information that he acquired while he was employed with Coinco, and so for that reason, I do believe . . . that [Coinco] will suffer irreparable injury.

The theory of "inevitable disclosure" has been applied in courts outside of Maryland to enjoin a departing employee from working for a competitor when the court is persuaded that it is inevitable that the departed employee will use or disclose trade secrets in his or her work for the competitor. [Milton E. Babirak, Jr., *The Maryland Uniform Trade Secrets Act: A Critical Summary of the Act and Case Law*, 31 U. BALT. L. REV. 181, 198 (2002)]. Put another way, "inevitable

---

[5] [FN8] We have identified some evidence in the record suggesting that LeJeune has threatened disclosure of Coinco's trade secrets. When LeJeune met with his supervisor after announcing his resignation, he mentioned that he would be in a "unique" position at Mars, suggesting that he might use confidential Coinco information in his new employment. This comment raises suspicion particularly because, as we determined above, LeJeune had acquired trade secrets improperly by copying Coinco files onto his CD and by saving certain hard-copy trade secrets after he informed his supervisor "everything" had been returned. Further evidence of LeJeune's threatened disclosure comes from the discovery that not only did he burn one CD, but he also placed Coinco trade secrets on a second CD. If there is a second CD filled with trade secrets, it would come as no surprise that LeJeune had made a third or fourth CD to maintain for future reference. Even LeJeune's interview with Mars indicates his willingness to share trade secrets. When interviewing face-to-face with Mars personnel, he was reminded twice that confidential information should not be disclosed. One could infer from these reminders that LeJeune, in fact, had displayed some propensity to disclose trade secrets. Based on this evidence, we hold that Coinco will likely succeed on the merits of its claim of threatened misappropriation by disclosure of trade secrets.

disclosure" cases are so named because they are based on the original employer's claim that a former employee who is permitted to work for a competitor will — even if acting in the utmost good faith — inevitably be required to use or disclose the former employer's trade secrets in order to perform the new job.

. . . Another commentator explained that the doctrine arises often when the former employee did not sign a non-compete agreement:

> Significantly, the inevitable disclosure doctrine is utilized in cases where the employee has not signed, or has even refused to sign, a non-competition agreement or non-disclosure of proprietary information agreement with his prior employer, and where the employee has not threatened, directly or indirectly, to use or disclose the trade secrets of his former employer to his new employer.

Babirak at 198.

LeJeune claims that, because this Court has not recognized the theory of "inevitable disclosure," the Circuit Court erred in using it as a ground for issuing the preliminary injunction limiting his employment at Mars. LeJeune argues, however, that, even if this Court decides to adopt "inevitable disclosure," it should not be applied to his case. According to LeJeune, any trade secrets that LeJeune may have acquired while working in the Vending Channel at Coinco would not be useful to him while working in the Amusement Channel at Mars. Disclosure of the vending trade secrets, therefore, is not inevitable in LeJeune's opinion.

According to Coinco, however, "inevitable disclosure," although not expressly recognized in Maryland, was correctly applied in this case because it is a form of "threatened" misappropriation under MUTSA. Coinco claims that LeJeune inevitably would disclose his extensive knowledge about Coinco's business strategies while working for Mars, giving his new employer an unfair competitive advantage. This is so, in Coinco's view, because LeJeune has demonstrated a lack of candor and a willingness to use or disclose trade secrets. Coinco believes, therefore, that the theory of "inevitable disclosure" is appropriate in this case because LeJeune understands Coinco's strategic plan for the Amusement Channel, the market on which he would focus at Mars as a National Accounts Representative for the Amusement Industry. We disagree with Coinco and decline to adopt the theory of "inevitable disclosure" under the present circumstances.

Long before the adoption of the Uniform Act, the first reported cases applying "inevitable disclosure" involved extraordinary situations in which a company tried to guard the secrecy of some technology that had propelled the company into industry leadership. *See Allis-Chalmers Manufacturing Co. v. Continental Aviation & Engineering Corp.*, 255 F. Supp. 645 (E.D. Mich. 1966); *E.I. duPont de Nemours & Co. v. American Potash & Chemical Corp.*, 41 Del. Ch. 533, 200 A.2d 428 (Del. Ch. 1964); *B.F. Goodrich Co. v. Wohlgemuth*, 117 Ohio App. 493, 192 N.E.2d 99 (Ohio Ct. App. 1963).

Since the Uniform Act's adoption and widespread recognition by the states, the most notable case involving "inevitable disclosure" is *Pepsico, Inc. v. Redmond*, 54 F.3d 1262 (7th Cir. 1995). In that case, Pepsico sought to enjoin one of its former senior executives, Redmond, from working for Quaker Oats Company, Pepsico's rival in the sports beverage market. *Id.* at 1264. While at Pepsico, Redmond had access to confidential marketing strategies and "pricing architecture." *Id.* at 1265. Redmond continued to work for Pepsico while he secretly negotiated for employment with Quaker. Redmond accepted a senior sales position at Quaker and, when he informed Pepsico of that decision, misrepresented the nature of his new position. *Id.* Pepsico sued and obtained a preliminary injunction, barring Redmond from "assuming any duties with Quaker relating to beverage pricing, marketing, and distribution." *Id.* at 1263.

On appeal before the Seventh Circuit, Pepsico argued that Redmond would "inevitably disclose" trade secrets acquired at Pepsico because, at Quaker, he would be involved significantly in the marketing, pricing, and distribution of sports beverages. *Id.* at 1266. The court of appeals agreed, affirming the injunction and holding that "a plaintiff may prove a claim of trade secret misappropriation by demonstrating that defendant's new employment will inevitably lead him to rely on the plaintiff's trade secrets." *Id.* at 1269. The appellate court accepted the district court's reasoning that "unless Redmond possessed an uncanny ability to compartmentalize information, he would necessarily be making decisions about [Quaker's beverages] by relying on his knowledge of [Pepsico's] trade secrets." *Id.*

No court interpreting the provisions of MUTSA has applied the theory of "inevitable disclosure." Among other courts, including those interpreting other versions of the Uniform Act, the theory remains the subject of considerable disagreement. The court in *Whyte v. Schlage Lock Co.*, 101 Cal. App. 4th 1443, 125 Cal. Rptr. 2d 277 (Cal. Ct. App. 2002) recently presented a comprehensive discussion of the theory within the context of California law. Schlage Lock Company competed with Kwikset Corporation in the business of manufacturing and selling locks and related products to retailers. *Id.* at 1447. The Home Depot, one of the largest retailers of these products, accounted for a large percentage of Schlage's sales. As Schlage's vice-president of sales, Whyte was responsible for sales to several large retailers, including The Home Depot. *Id.* Although Whyte had signed a confidentiality agreement as to Schlage's proprietary information, he had not signed a covenant not to compete. Whyte was lured to join Kwikset, and Schlage sued, seeking an injunction based on the theory of inevitable disclosure. *Id.* at 1448. After surveying the cases that have considered the doctrine, the court opted to join those jurisdictions that have rejected it:

> The decisions rejecting the inevitable disclosure doctrine correctly balance competing public policies of employee mobility and protection of trade secrets. The inevitable disclosure doctrine permits an employer to enjoin the former employee without proof of the employee's actual or threatened use of trade secrets based upon an inference (based in turn upon circumstantial evidence) that the employee will use his or her knowledge of those trade secrets in the new employment. *The result is not merely an injunction against the use of trade secrets, but an injunction restricting employment.*

Id. at 1461-62 (emphasis added). The application of the doctrine, the court stated, " 'creates a de facto covenant not to compete' and 'runs counter to the strong public policy in California favoring employee mobility.'" *Id.* at 1462 (quoting *Bayer Corp.*, 72 F. Supp. 2d at 1120). The court continued:

> The chief ill in the covenant not to compete imposed by the inevitable disclosure doctrine is in its after-the-fact nature: The covenant is imposed *after* the employment contract is made and therefore alters the employment relationship without the employee's consent. When, as here, a confidentiality agreement is in place, the inevitable disclosure doctrine "in effect converts the confidentiality agreement into such a covenant [not to compete]. Or, as another federal court put it, "a court should not allow a plaintiff to use inevitable disclosure as an after-the-fact noncompete agreement to enjoin an employee from working for the employer of his or her choice."

Id. at 1462-63 (citations omitted); *see also EarthWeb*, 71 F. Supp. 2d at 311 ("Such retroactive alterations [as a result of applying inevitable disclosure] distort the terms of the employment relationship and upset the balance which courts have attempted to achieve in construing non-compete agreements."). The court was disturbed that the inevitable disclosure doctrine could "rewrite[ ] the employment agreement" by providing the employer with "the benefit of a contractual provision it did not pay for, while the employee is bound by a court-imposed contract provision with no opportunity to negotiate terms or consideration." *Id.* at 1463.

We find this reasoning persuasive, especially as applied to the circumstances in the case before us. Maryland has a policy in favor of employee mobility similar to that of California. Furthermore, Coinco decided not to enter into a confidentiality agreement or a covenant not to compete with LeJeune. To recognize "inevitable disclosure" in this case would allow Coinco the benefit of influencing LeJeune's employment relationship with Mars even though Coinco chose not to negotiate a restrictive covenant or confidentiality agreement with LeJeune. *See International Business Mach. Corp. v. Seagate Technology, Inc.,* 941 F. Supp. 98, 101 (D. Minn. 1992) ("A claim of trade secret misappropriation should not act as an ex post facto covenant not to compete."). Adopting the theory also would tend to permit a court to infer some inevitable disclosure of trade secrets merely from an individual's exposure to them. *See H & R Block Eastern Tax Servs. Inc. v. Enchura,* 122 F. Supp. 2d 1067, 1076 (W.D. Mo. 2000) (stating that no inference of inevitable disclosure can flow from exposure to trade secrets). For these reasons, we conclude that the theory of "inevitable disclosure" cannot serve as a basis for granting a plaintiff injunctive relief under MUTSA.

3. Risks to New Employers from Hiring Experienced High Tech Employees

a. Misappropriation: Wrongful Use or Disclosure

i. Acts Giving Rise to Third Party Liability

Employers may hold third parties who are strangers to the employer-employee relationship liable for improperly acquiring, using, or disclosing a trade secret. Liability for improper means of acquiring another's trade secret can arise from causing an exiting employee to breach a duty to maintain secrecy. Section 1 of the Uniform Trade Secrets Act defines improper means to include a "breach or inducement of a breach of duty to maintain secrecy"; similarly, the definition of improper means in section 43 of the Restatement (Third) of Unfair Competition includes "inducement of or knowing participation in a breach of confidence." Third parties may also incur liability for using or disclosing information after receiving notice of its trade secret status. Actual notice of trade secret status is not necessary. It is enough that the third party knew or should have known that the party disclosing the information did not have authority to disclose it, or was breaching a contractual or fiduciary duty by disclosing, or that the information was disclosed by accident.

COLGATE-PALMOLIVE CO. v. CARTER PRODUCTS
United States Court of Appeals for the Fourth Circuit
230 F.2d 855 (1956)

PARKER, Circuit Judge.

This is an appeal in a case involving patent infringement and appropriation of trade secrets. The patent in suit is United States Patent No. 2,655,480 issued October 13, 1953 to one Spitzer and others relating to a pressurized shaving cream. The plaintiffs in the court below, appellees here, were Spitzer and his partner Small, holders by assignment from the other patentees, and Carter Products Inc., manufacturer of drugs and cosmetics and the holder of an exclusive license under the patent. The defendants below, appellants here, were the Colgate-Palmolive Company, the manufacturer of a pressurized shaving cream alleged to infringe, the Stalfort Pressure-Pak Corporation and John C. Stalfort & Sons, Inc., who packaged pressurized shaving cream alleged to infringe the patent for the Mennen Company, and the Read Drug & Chemical Company, Inc., which sold the pressurized shaving cream for Colgate and Mennen. Plaintiffs claimed infringement of only eight claims of the patent. Defendants admitted infringement if these claims were valid but denied their validity and asked judgment declaring them as well as all other claims of the patent invalid.

The trial court held the patent valid, and enjoined infringement thereof as well as the use of a trade secret held to have been wrongfully appropriated by Colgate. It also ordered Colgate to assign to plaintiffs rights under patent applications found to have been based upon the trade secret. The case was referred to a special master to determine and report as to damages resulting from infringement and also as to damages and profits for which Colgate should be required to account because of misappropriation of trade secrets and to make recommendations as to whether the damages on account of patent infringement should be increased as allowed by statute, reserving, however, for future determination the question as to whether increased damages should be awarded. Judgment was entered that plaintiffs recover their costs and taxable disbursements to date, including against Colgate reasonable attorneys' fees, and the special master was directed to include in his report a recommendation as to the amount of attorneys' fees to be allowed. Three principal questions are presented by the appeal: (1) Is the patent valid? (2) Should the findings of the trial court as to misappropriation of trade secrets be sustained? And (3) Is the decree proper?

1. The Validity of the Patent.

Spitzer, one of the patentees, in the year 1948 conceived the idea of developing a shaving lather which, like the lather produced by machines in barber shops, could be used as it came from the container without being worked up on the face. He employed Foster D. Snell, Inc., consulting chemists, to work out his idea for him in terms of a mixture that could be enclosed in a small container and, upon the opening of a valve, would emerge in the form of a durable lather, which, without whipping up or other agitation, could be used for shaving purposes. Snell put to work on the project two chemists, Reich and Fine, who after several months of work and experimentation developed an emulsion consisting of an aqueous soap solution mixed with certain gases liquefied by pressure, which they enclosed in a container. When the valve of the container was opened the pressure of the gases extruded the emulsion and, as it came from the can, the particles of gas expended into minute bubbles covered with soap which was the shaving lather desired. Patent, applied for November 2, 1949, was issued to Spitzer, Reich and Fine October 13, 1953. In the meantime an exclusive license had been granted to Carter and the product was being marketed under the trade name of 'Rise'. It achieved at once outstanding commercial success. Sales of 'Rise' in 1950 amounted to $400,000, in 1951 to $800,000, in 1952 to $1,800,000 and in 1953 to $2,600,000. The sales of Colgate's infringing product in 1954 amounted to $5,000,000.

There was, of course, nothing novel in the use of soap to make lather, nor in the use of a can as a container, nor in the use of a gas liquefied by pressure and mixed with another liquid to spray the mixture from the can. What was novel was to get a mixture of the right gases, with the right soaps in the right proportions, confined in a container under the right pressure, so that a lather satisfactory for shaving purposes would be produced when the mixture was allowed to emerge. In producing such a mixture many problems were encountered and the record shows that their solution took many months. . . . Finally, after much experimentation, sodium soaps were eliminated and the soap solution adopted was a combination of 80 parts of TEA (triethanolamine) stearate and 20 parts of TEA cocoate, to prevent jelling. The proper propellant was found after much inquiry and experiment by mixing Freon-114 (1, 2 dichlor 1, 1, 2, 2 tetrafluorethane) with Freon-12. . . .

. . .

The defendant Colgate-Palmolive became interested in a pressurized shaving cream when 'Rise' came on the market; but although it had 200 or more chemists in its service and although it purchased packages of 'Rise' and had them analyzed, the record shows that it was unable to develop a satisfactory product until it had employed Fine, who had been working for Snell in the development of 'Rise'. He gave Colgate the formula which brought success to its efforts and which embodied the formula of 'Rise' in combination with a formula which Colgate had theretofore not found successful. He gave Colgate, also, the benefit of knowledge obtained at Snell's with respect to improving the

'Rise' formula by superfatting so as to produce a smoother lather and one which gives the feeling on the skin produced by the so-called brushless shaving creams. Colgate had Fine to file applications for patents covering this improved lather. Notwithstanding this experience and attempts to obtain patents in its own behalf on the subject matter, Colgate argues that the patent here in suit is lacking in invention and is anticipated by both domestic and foreign patents and by prior use.

[The court determined that the 'Rise' patent was valid.]

. . . What we have here is a new and useful composition of matter produced after lengthy experimentation, in which the various elements combine to produce a new and useful result. To the presumption that the finding of the District Judge as to validity is correct, a finding based upon lengthy evidence and the testimony of experts must be added the presumptions of validity arising from the fact that the patent was issued by the Patent Office, from the fact that the patented product entered at once into wide public use and achieved outstanding commercial success, and from the fact that it was copied by an infringer who was one of the largest soap manufacturers of the country and who had been trying in vain to develop a similar product but had been unable to do so until the knowledge of one of the patentees was obtained.

2.   The Trade Secrets.

. . .

We agree with the District Judge that Colgate must be held to liability for the appropriation and use of the 'Rise' formula in developing its shaving cream. That formula had been developed in the confidential work of Snell for Spitzer. Fine as an employee of Snell was under contract with Snell not to disclose information obtained in the course of this work. Colgate knew of Fine's employment and of his work on the development of 'rise', which Colgate had been unable to produce even after purchasing it on the market and having it analyzed. Although Colgate had twice before this refused to employ Fine, and although it knew of the confidential nature of his employment with Snell, it proceeded to employ him while it was engaged in the effort to develop a pressurized shaving cream and, within a month of his employment, put him to work on the problem, which he solved immediately by using the 'Rise' formula in combination with a formula which Colgate had found unsuccessful.

With respect to the superfatting, it appears that this was worked out at Snell's to give the lather a 'brushless effect' after the patent in suit had been applied for. It also appears that Fine, who had developed the superfatting process in the course of his work at Snell's, suggested it to Colgate and that Colgate adopted the process and caused an application for a patent covering it to be filed by Fine.

On these facts, there can be no question but that Colgate used the knowledge of Fine in producing its pressurized shaving cream or that this knowledge related to matters which were trade secrets of Spitzer and his associates. That Colgate did not enter into an open bargain with Fine to disclose this confidential information is no defense. Nor is it a defense that Fine upon his employment was entitled to use his skill in Colgate's interest. He was not entitled to give to Colgate the benefit of business secrets which had been disclosed to him at Snell's; and Colgate could not close its eyes to facts which clearly indicated that this was what he was doing, even if he had not been employed for that express purpose. One may not escape liability for appropriating the business secrets of another by employing one who has been entrusted with the secrets and permitting him to make use of them. With respect to this the District Judge said:

> . . . it is not necessary to, nor do we find that Colgate's employment of Fine was originally arranged for the specific purpose of having him divulge confidential information about the 'rise' patent that he had acquired at Snell's. The basis of our decision that Colgate's action was wrongful is that Colgate knew, or must have known by the exercise of fair business principles, that the precise character of Fine's work with Snell was, in all likelihood, covered by the agreement which Fine had with Snell not to divulge trade secrets, and that, therefore, Colgate was obligated to do more than it did towards ascertaining the extent to which Fine was, in fact, restricted in what he might disclose to Colgate. That it was wrong for Colgate not to go further than it did in this respect is confirmed by the very status of Fine when he came to Colgate. At that time Fine was a joint inventor and patentee of 'Rise.' In other words, Fine was willing to be, and was knowingly placed by Colgate in work that was in direct competition with the work in which Fine had shared at Snell's, resulting ultimately in his own patent. The very fact that Fine would do this should, per se, have raised in the minds of the representatives of Colgate, who arranged the employment of Fine, a feeling that he was entering upon a rather strange employment under the circumstances. It, therefore, was not enough for Colgate to say that they would see that Fine lived up to the limitations imposed by his contract with Snell. The weight of the credible evidence discloses that Colgate was far from being sufficiently avid to ascertain what those limitations really were, and to have Fine live up to them.

The principles of law applicable are well settled and are well stated in section 757 of the A.L.I. Restatement of Torts as follows:

> One who discloses or uses another's trade secret, without a privilege to do so, is liable to the other if

> (c) he learned the secret from a third person with notice of the facts that it was a secret and that the third person discovered it by improper means or that the third person's disclosure of it was otherwise a breach of his duty to the other, ...

In [*Herold v. Herold China & Pottery Co.*, 6 Cir., 257 F. 911, 913 (6th Cir. 1919)], Judge Knappen, speaking for the Court of Appeals of the Sixth Circuit, stated the rule as follows:

> The rule is well settled that secret formulas and processes, such as are claimed to be involved here, are property rights which will be protected by injunction, not only as against those who attempt to disclose

or use them in violation of confidential relations or contracts express or implied, but as against those who are participating in such attempt with knowledge of such confidential relations or contract, though they might in time have reached the same result by their own independent experiments or efforts.

We do not think that the finding, 12(b), with respect to the annealing of the polyethylene tubes by dipping them in hot water can be sustained. While Fine learned of this at Snell's and communicated his knowledge to Colgate, the process was one which was well known and cannot be treated as a trade secret or a confidential disclosure. *American Potato Dryers v. Peters*, 4 Cir., 184 F.2d 165, 172; A.L.I. Restatement of Torts, sec. 757, Comment (b) pp. 5-6. This, however, is not material since no injunctive relief is granted with respect thereto and the damages, whether based on the use of the original 'Rise' formula or the superfatted formula, would not be affected thereby.

NOTES & QUESTIONS

1. Notice as a Source of Fault for Trade Secret Misappropriation

Notice plays a role as a source of fault in trade secret misappropriation disputes. Without actual or constructive notice of the trade secret status of information, a third party to an employment relationship cannot be held liable for misappropriation of the trade secret. The privilege which shields a person who in good faith pays value for title in information is analogous to that found in patent, trademark, and copyright laws, and derives from the concept of voidable title. For example, in *Conmar Prods. Corp. v. Universal Slide Fastener Co.*, 172 F.2d 150 (2d Cir. 1949), the plaintiff brought an action which alleged that the defendants had induced plaintiff's employees to disclose a method for producing zippers. The defendant, ignorant of the fact that the employees were bound by a secrecy contract with plaintiff, had obtained the information innocently when it hired the employees. In an opinion by Judge Learned Hand, the court found that:

> the situation is proper for the application of the doctrine that a bona fide purchaser takes free from a trust. The act of inducing the breach is the wrong, and the inducer's ignorance is an excuse only because one is not ordinarily held liable for consequences which one could not have anticipated. Although it is proper to prevent any continued use of the secret after the inducer has learned of the breach, the remedies must not invade the inducer's immunity over the period while he was ignorant.

Conmar, 172 F.2d at 156. The timing of the notice matters. A party does not incur liability for misappropriation of a trade secret if notice was given after they have already innocently used or disclosed the information. "Having acquired the secrets innocently, [the defendants] were entitled to exploit them till they learned that they had induced the breach of the contract." *Id.* at 157.

Where the third party has notice that information was acquired through misappropriation but disregards the notice, the third party may be held liable to the trade secret owner for misappropriation. Once a party is put on notice, they have a duty to inquire as to the authority of the transferor to disclose the information, as well as a duty not to further use or disclose the information.

2. Material Changes in Position and Detrimental Reliance

A third party who knows or should have known of the trade secret status of the information he relys on to materially change his position is liable for trade secret misappropriation. However, a third party is absolved of liability if he materially changed his position prior to discovering the nature of the information upon which he relied.

In *Vantage Point, Inc. v. Parker Bros.*, 529 F. Supp. 1204 (E.D.N.Y. 1981), the plaintiff, Vantage Point, sought damages from Milton Bradley for misappropriating its idea for a three-dimensional oil exploration game. The creator of the game had unsuccessfully shopped the idea around to several game companies, among them Parker Brothers. A game developer who had access to the plaintiff's game idea while at Parker Brothers quit his job and joined two other men to form a partnership that created and sold game and toy ideas. The group developed an oil exploration game, called "King Oil," that was strikingly similar to Vantage Point's, and pitched it to Milton Bradley. Milton Bradley, unaware of any misconduct on the part of any member of the group, expressed an interest in the game. The record showed that Milton Bradley had no access to plaintiff's game idea prior to this time, and that by the time it received notice of possible misappropriation, it had materially changed its position.

> By May 1974 Milton Bradley had already changed its position by incurring costs in bringing King Oil to market. Harris testified that if Milton Bradley had pulled King Oil off the market immediately after [receiving notice], the company would have lost costs already incurred for tooling and other production components, for advertising and possibly some inventory. In these circumstances, "(t)he issue is whether the imposition of (a) duty" not to use the idea after notice of its improper disclosure, "would be inequitable under the circumstances." Restatement, Torts, § 758, comment on clause (b), subsec. (e) at 22. The Court concludes that imposition of the duty plaintiff desires would be inequitable. It is plain that prior to receipt of notice, Milton Bradley "paid value for the secret or made other investments in connection with it." *Id.* at 21. Thus, imposition of the duty "would subject (it) to loss" for actions taken when there was no such duty. *See id.*

Vantage Point, 529 F. Supp. at 1215. Detrimental reliance may be an absolute bar to liability, or may be considered an "exceptional circumstance" for the purpose of determining injunctive relief. Courts award damages only if unauthorized use continues after the defendant receives notice of the trade secret status of the information; retrospective damages for use that occurred prior to notice are not allowed.

Sometimes third parties who have detrimentally relied upon a trade secret wish to continue to use the information. Some courts refuse to impose a duty not to use the information where imposition of such a duty would burden a defendant with a loss for action taken when he was subject to no duty. Other courts take a different approach and fashion a restitution-based remedy where the trade secret owner is awarded limited restitution based on the stranger's savings from not needing to independently develop the information, in exchange for allowing the third party to continue using the information. Courts may require the payment of reasonable royalties for future use of the trade secret.

3. Vicarious Liability

Under the doctrine of respondeat superior, a new employer may be held vicariously liable for misappropriation of a trade secret by a new employee. The Indiana Supreme Court considered this issue in its decision in *Infinity Prods. Inc. v. Quandt,* 810 N.E.2d 1028 (Ind. 2004) reh'g denied (Jan. 27, 2005). The plaintiff, Infinity, alleged that its former employee, Quandt, misappropriated customer information, which Infinity held as a trade secret. The court concluded that Quandt was liable for misappropriating Infinity's trade secrets but that his new employer, Fabri-Tech, was not:

> The trial court held that Fabri-Tech was not liable for Quandt's acts under the doctrine of respondeat superior. Infinity contends this was error, as Quandt made use of Fabri-Tech's information while acting within the scope of his employment with Infinity, thus creating liability for his principal under the common law of torts. Fabri-Tech replied that respondeat superior is unavailable in an action covered by the Trade Secrets Act.

> This debate turns in the first instance on the scope of the act as adopted by the General Assembly in 1982. The legislature has left us some direction on this point.

> Indiana's statute is based on the Uniform Trade Secrets Act and we are one of some forty states that have adopted it. The legislature announced its purpose in adopting the uniform act and provided some guidance on its general construction: "This chapter shall be applied and construed to effectuate its general purpose to make uniform the law with respect to the subject matter of this chapter among states enacting the provisions of this chapter." Ind. Code Ann. § 24-2-3-1(b) (West 1995). The General Assembly has also told us: "The chapter displaces all conflicting law of this state pertaining to the misappropriation of trade secrets, except contract and criminal law." Ind. Code Ann. § 24-2-3-1(c). . . .

> As Infinity correctly points out, respondeat superior is a common law doctrine under which liability is imposed by law upon the master for acts done by the servant, regardless of the master's complicity in the acts. Indeed, it may impose liability even when the master directed the servant to the contrary. Appellant's Br. at 22. Surely, this doctrine must be thought of as conflicting with the uniform act's requirements that a claimant demonstrate that the defendant "knows or has reason to know" that the trade secret at issue was acquired by improper means. Ind. Code Ann. § 24-2-3-2 (West 1988). It is thus displaced by the provisions of the uniform act.

> Of course, the uniform act affords fulsome avenues of relief for persons who believe that secrets belonging to them have wrongly been misappropriated. It supplies a remedy for money damages

under a standard of proof that is, at first blush, less onerous that the common law usually requires. It also authorizes injunctive relief both to shut down actual misappropriation and to thwart threatened misappropriation. Ind. Code Ann. § 24-2-3-3. And it authorizes the award of attorney's fees upon conditions more liberal than most parts of our code. Ind. Code Ann. § 24-2-3-5.

We conclude that the trial court correctly held that Fabri-Tech could not be held liable absent the proof of scienter required by the uniform act.

Infinity Prods., 810 N.E.2d at 1033-34.

4. Liability of Corporate Shareholders and Directors

Shareholders and directors of a corporation who know of trade secret misappropriation by the corporation have an affirmative duty to take action to stop those activities. Shareholders and directors can be held personally liable if they fail to stop known acts of misappropriation.

b. Intentional Interference with Contractual or Fiduciary Relationship

i. Generally

When a third party induces a departed employee to breach a confidentiality agreement, the employer may be subject to liability for intentional interference with a contractual or fiduciary relationship. The Restatement (Second) of Agency, § 312, states, "A person who, without being privileged to do so, intentionally causes or assists an agent to violate a duty to his principal is subject to liability to the principal." Even when there is no express confidentiality agreement, a party who induces an agent to violate an implied duty to his former employer is liable to that former employer. Liability for intentional interference with contractual or fiduciary duties evinces an overlap between contractual obligations between parties and tort-based duties in conduct adversely affecting third parties. Inducement of a new employee to violate a special relationship not only serves as a form of improper means in trade secret cases, but is also a tort in and of itself.

The Restatement (Second) of Torts, §§ 766-767 list the elements of the tort of intentional interference with contractual relationship, which are: (a) intentional and (b) improper (c) interference with the (d) performance of a contract or other economic relations (e) causing pecuniary loss.

REEVES v. HANLON
Supreme Court of California
95 P.3d 513 (2004)

Baxter, J., expressing the unanimous view of the court.

. . .

Plaintiffs Robert L. Reeves and Robert L. Reeves & Associates, A Professional Law Corporation, brought the instant lawsuit against defendants Daniel P. Hanlon,

Colin T. Greene, and Hanlon & Greene, A Professional Corporation (H&G). The operative complaint included the following allegations: In 1995, Reeves's law firm, which emphasized immigration law and litigation, employed Hanlon as an attorney. In 1997, the firm employed Greene as an associate attorney. In 1998, Reeves entered into an agreement with Hanlon whereby Hanlon could earn an equity position in a law firm to be formed; thereafter, the firm's name was changed to "Reeves and Hanlon, Professional Law Corporation." On or about June 30, 1999, both Hanlon and Greene resigned from Reeves's firm without notice or warning. They improperly persuaded plaintiffs' employees to join H&G, personally solicited plaintiffs' clients to discharge plaintiffs and to instead obtain services from H&G, misappropriated plaintiffs' trade secrets, destroyed computer files and data, and withheld plaintiffs' property, including a corporate car. . . .

. . .

Trial of the matter commenced in January 2001. Following the presentation of briefing, evidence, and arguments, the trial court issued a statement of decision concluding that Hanlon and Greene had assumed fiduciary duties to plaintiffs and that they had engaged in interference with contracts and prospective business opportunity, and misappropriation of trade secrets. The court determined that, for more than five months prior to their departure, Hanlon and Greene had accessed plaintiffs' password-protected computer database to print out confidential name, address, and phone number information on 2,200 clients and had fomented dissatisfaction among plaintiffs' personnel. Although Greene had been chair of plaintiffs' litigation department and Hanlon had been responsible for over 500 client matters when they abruptly resigned without notice, they left no status reports or lists of matters or deadlines on which they had been working. Nor did they attempt to cooperate with plaintiffs on a notice to clients. Shortly before resigning, Greene intentionally erased extensive computer files in plaintiffs' computer server containing client documents and form files used by plaintiffs. The evening of their resignations, defendants personally solicited plaintiffs' key employees. As a result, plaintiffs lost nine employees over the next 60 days, six of them joining defendants' new firm. Defendants also began a campaign to solicit plaintiffs' clients, contacting at least 40 clients by telephone without offering them a choice of counsel. All of this had been "intentionally done . . . to disrupt [plaintiffs'] ongoing business." Although historically, plaintiffs typically lost only one or two clients a month, plaintiffs lost 144 clients to defendants over the next 12 months.

. . .

Discussion

A. Intentional Interference with At-will Employment Relations

What is disputed is the Court of Appeal's legal conclusion that "an employer may recover for interference with the employment contracts of its at-will employees by a third party when the third party does not show that its conduct in hiring the employees was justifiable or legitimate." Relying primarily on *GAB Business Services, Inc. v. Lindsey & Newsom Claim Services, Inc.* (2000) 83 Cal.App.4th 409 [99 Cal. Rptr. 2d 665] (*GAB*), defendants argue California law does not and should not recognize a cause of action in favor of an employer against another employer for interference with contractual relations by virtue of an offer of employment to an at-will employee.

We start by observing that, in California, the law is settled that "a stranger to a contract may be liable in tort for intentionally interfering with the performance of the contract." To prevail on a cause of action for intentional interference with contractual relations, a plaintiff must plead and prove (1) the existence of a valid contract between the plaintiff and a third party; (2) the defendant's knowledge of that contract; (3) the defendant's intentional acts designed to induce a breach or disruption of the contractual relationship; (4) actual breach or disruption of the contractual relationship; and (5) resulting damage. To establish the claim, the plaintiff need not prove that a defendant acted with the primary purpose of disrupting the contract, but must show the defendant's knowledge that the interference was certain or substantially certain to occur as a result of his or her action.

May the tort of interference with contractual relations be predicated upon interference with an at-will contract? Historically, the answer is yes. A third party's "interference with an at-will contract is actionable interference with the contractual relationship" because the contractual relationship is at the will of the parties, not at the will of outsiders.

More specifically, may such tort be based on interference with an at-will employment relationship? Again, historically, the answer is yes.

As reflected in our decisional and statutory law, however, it has long been the public policy of our state that "[a] former employee has the right to engage in a competitive business for himself and to enter into competition with his former employer, even for the business of . . . his former employer, provided such competition is fairly and legally conducted." Consistent with this policy favoring competition, decisions involving parties in competition readily indicate that certain competitive conduct is nonactionable when it interferes with the at-will contract relations of another. *Buxbom v. Smith* (1944) 23 Cal.2d 535 [145 P.2d 305] (*Buxbom*), for example, explained that "where the means of interference involve no more than recognized trade practices such as advertising or price-cutting, the plaintiff's loss as a result of the competitive strife is deemed *damnum absque injuria*."

More to the point here, *Buxbom* observed that "it is not ordinarily a tort to hire the employees of another for use in the hirer's business." (*Buxbom, supra,* 23 Cal.2d at p. 547.) As *Buxbom* explained, however, this general rule is subject to one significant limitation: "This immunity against liability is not retained . . . if unfair methods are used in interfering in such advantageous relations." (*Ibid.*) In *Buxbom*, the record established that the defendant gained an unfair advantage over the plaintiff through "deceptive dealings" (*ibid.*) and "false promises" made in connection with a distribution contract between the parties that the defendant had no intention of performing (*id.* at p. 548). He "deliberately induced the plaintiff to build up his distributing organization" to perform the contract and in a matter of weeks became the plaintiff's sole customer. (*Id.* at p. 547.) Once the defendant acquired this strategic position, he breached the distribution contract "to cut off the work required to sustain plaintiff's organization" and "to prevent plaintiff from competing effectively for the retention of [his] employees." (*Id.* at p. 548.)

Buxbom first indicated that the defendant's breach of the distribution contract was "a wrong and in itself actionable," but then proceeded to find the breach also constituted "an unfair method of interference with advantageous relations." (*Buxbom, supra,* 23 Cal.2d at p. 548.) Its reasoning was this: "Although defendant's conduct may not have been tortious if he had merely broken the contract and subsequently decided to hire plaintiff's employees," he was "guilty of a tortious interference in the relationship between the plaintiff and his employees" because he "intentionally utilized" the breach of the distribution contract "as the means of depriving plaintiff of his employees." (*Ibid.*)

Subsequent to *Buxbom*, the court in *Diodes, Inc. v. Franzen* (1968) 260 Cal. App. 2d 244 [67 Cal. Rptr. 19] (*Diodes*) reiterated the so-called privilege of competition, as applied in the context of employment relations, as follows: "Even though the relationship between an employer and his employee is an advantageous one, no actionable wrong is committed by a competitor who solicits his competitor's employees or who hires away one or more of his competitor's employees who are not under contract, so long as the inducement to leave is not accompanied by unlawful action." (*Id.* at p. 255.) "However, if either the defecting employee or the competitor uses unfair or deceptive means to effectuate new employment, or either of them is guilty of some concomitant, unconscionable conduct, the injured former employer has a cause of action to recover for the detriment he has thereby suffered." (*Ibid.*; see also *Metro Traffic Control, Inc. v. Shadow Traffic Network* (1994) 22 Cal.App.4th 853, 860 [27 Cal. Rptr. 2d 573] (*Metro*) ["[a]s a competitor of Metro, absent a showing of unlawful purpose or means, Shadow is privileged and not liable for inducing Metro's employees to leave and move to Shadow"].)

Strictly speaking, the foregoing authorities did not address the matter of competition in suits involving causes of action for intentional interference with at-will employment relations; rather, those cases involved breach of fiduciary duty claims (*Diodes*), claims for injunctive relief based on contractual non-compete clauses and trade secrets allegations (*Metro*), or claims for damages sustained in conjunction with a breach of contract (*Buxbom*).

Nonetheless, the same considerations support similar limitations for actions alleging interference with an at-will employment relation. Where no unlawful methods are used, public policy generally supports a competitor's right to offer more pay or better terms to another's employee, so long as the employee is free to leave. As Judge Learned Hand observed long ago, if the law were to the contrary, the result "would be intolerable, both to such employers as could use the employe[e] more effectively and to such employe[e]s as might receive added pay. It would put an end to any kind of competition." (*Triangle Film Corp. v. Artcraft Pictures Corp.* (2d Cir. 1918) 250 F. 981, 982.) Or as *Diodes* put it: "The interests of the employee in his own mobility and betterment are deemed paramount to the competitive business interests of the employers, where neither the employee nor his new employer has committed any illegal act accompanying the employment change." (*Diodes, supra*, 260 Cal. App. 2d at p. 255.)

Moreover, the economic relationship between parties to contracts that are terminable at will is distinguishable from the relationship between parties to other legally binding contracts. We have explained the policy generally protecting contracts this way: "The courts provide a damage remedy against third party conduct intended to disrupt an existing contract precisely because the exchange of promises resulting in such a formally cemented economic relationship is deemed worthy of protection from interference by a stranger to the agreement. Economic relationships short of contractual, however, should stand on a different legal footing as far as the potential for tort liability is reckoned." (*Della Penna v. Toyota Motor Sales, U.S.A., Inc.* (1995) 11 Cal.4th 376, 392 [45 Cal. Rptr. 2d 436, 902 P.2d 740].)

But as the Restatement Second of Torts explains, if a party to a contract with the plaintiff is free to terminate the contractual relation when he chooses, "there is still a subsisting contract relation; but any interference with it that induces its termination is primarily an interference with the future relation between the parties, and the plaintiff has no legal assurance of them. As for the future hopes, he has no legal right but only an expectancy; and when the contract is terminated by the choice of [a contracting party] there is no breach of it. The competitor is therefore free, for his own competitive advantage, to obtain the future benefits for himself by causing the termination. Thus, he may offer better contract terms, as by offering an employee of the plaintiff more money to work for him or by offering a seller higher prices for goods, and he may make use of persuasion or other suitable means, all without liability." (Rest.2d Torts, § 768, com. i.) Under this analysis, an interference with an at-will contract properly is viewed as an interference with a prospective economic advantage, a tort that similarly compensates for the loss of an advantageous economic relationship but does not require the existence of a legally binding contract.

We observe that in California, both of these torts protect the public interest in stable economic relationships and both share the same intent requirement. (*Korea Supply, supra*, 29 Cal.4th at p. 1157 [defendant must know that interference was certain or substantially certain to occur as a result of its action].) But while many of the elements of the two torts are similar, a plaintiff seeking to recover for interference with prospective economic advantage must also plead and prove that the defendant engaged in an independently wrongful act in disrupting the relationship. (*Korea Supply, supra*, 29 Cal.4th at p. 1158.) In this regard, "an act is independently wrongful if it is unlawful, that is, if it is proscribed by some constitutional, statutory, regulatory, common law, or other determinable legal standard." (*Ibid.*, fn. omitted.)

Consistent with the decisions recognizing that an intentional interference with an at-will contract may be actionable, but mindful that an interference as such is primarily an interference with the future relation between the contracting parties, we hold that a plaintiff may recover damages for intentional interference with an at-will employment relation under the same California standard applicable to claims for intentional interference with prospective economic advantage. That is, to recover for a defendant's interference with an at-will employment relation, a plaintiff must plead and prove that the defendant engaged in an independently wrongful act — i.e., an act "proscribed by some constitutional, statutory, regulatory, common law, or other determinable legal standard" (*Korea Supply, supra,* 29 Cal.4th at p. 1159) — that induced an at-will employee to leave the plaintiff. Under this standard, a defendant is not subject to liability for intentional interference if the interference consists merely of extending a job offer that induces an employee to terminate his or her at-will employment.

. . .

We now address whether application of the principles we announce today calls for affirmance of the $20,009.19 award against defendants. We conclude it does. Here, it is undisputed that Hanlon and Greene engaged in unlawful and unethical conduct in mounting a campaign to deliberately disrupt plaintiffs' business. Greene had been chair of plaintiffs' litigation department, and Hanlon had been responsible for over 500 client matters, and both had assumed fiduciary duties to plaintiffs. When the two abruptly resigned without notice, they left no status reports or lists of pending matters or deadlines on which they were working. Not only did they leave without providing such information, they acted unlawfully to delete and destroy plaintiffs' computer files containing client documents and forms. Additionally, Hanlon and Greene misappropriated confidential information, improperly solicited plaintiffs' clients, and cultivated employee discontent. While the computer files and the confidential information all appear to have pertained to plaintiffs' clients, not their employees, and while Hanlon and Greene waited until after their resignations to offer jobs to plaintiffs' employees, we cannot conclude the trial court abused its discretion in finding that defendants' unlawful and unethical actions were designed in part to interfere with and disrupt plaintiffs' relationships with their key at-will employees.

In short, defendants did not simply extend job offers to plaintiffs' at-will employees. Rather, defendants purposely engaged in unlawful acts that crippled plaintiffs' business operations and caused plaintiffs' personnel to terminate their at-will employment contracts. Accordingly, the Court of Appeal properly upheld the award of $20,009.19 for damages attributable to that wrongful conduct.

. . .

Disposition

The judgment of the Court of Appeal is affirmed.

ii. When is Interference Considered Improper?

Interference by a third party employer is generally improper if the third party does not act to protect its own financial interest or if it uses improper means. Courts look to the motive and means when determining whether interference is improper. For example, luring away an employee from a competitor is proper motive, even if it deprives the former employer of the employee's services; inducing an employee to violate duties to his former employer, on the other hand, is an example of improper motive. Even if the objectives are legitimate, liability can arise if the means used are improper, but courts disagree as to which means may be properly used.

Section 767 of the Restatement (Second) of Torts provides factors for determining whether interference is improper. These factors are as follows: (1) nature of defendant's conduct, (2) defendant's motive, (3) interests of the other with which the defendant's conduct interferes, (4) social and contractual interests, (5) interests pursued by the defendant, and (6) the relations between the parties.

STORAGE TECHNOLOGY CORP. V. CISCO SYSTEMS, INC.
United States Court of Appeals for the Eighth Circuit
395 F.3d 921 (2005)

GIBSON, Circuit Judge.

Storage Technology Corporation appeals the district court's entry of summary judgment against it on its various claims against Cisco Systems, Inc. arising out of the hiring of a number of Storage Technology's employees by Cisco's predecessor, NuSpeed Internet Systems, Inc. The district court held that Storage Technology's claims for interference with contractual relations, inducing breach of contract, conversion, and breach of fiduciary duties failed because Storage Technology did not come forward with any evidence of recoverable damages. The district court held that Minnesota has not recognized a claim for "corporate raiding," or hiring away another firm's employees. The district court held that the remaining claim, for misappropriation of trade secrets, was not supported by evidence that satisfied the requirements of Fed. R. Civ. P. 56(e). We affirm the judgment of the district court.

In November 1999, Mark Cree and Clint Jurgens founded NuSpeed Internet Systems, Inc., a new computer technology company. Cree and Jurgens's plan was to develop a product to link computers at one location to data storage networks at other locations through the Internet or other Wide Area Network using Internet Protocols. On December 2, Cree and Jurgens offered employment to Mark Schrandt, an engineer at Storage Technology, which was developing data storage networking products. Schrandt accepted NuSpeed's offer and gave Storage Technology oral notice on or about December 3 that he was leaving. He later gave a written resignation effective at the end of December. Schrandt began work for NuSpeed in January 2000. In December, while Schrandt was still at Storage Technology, he told four other Storage Technology engineers, Mark Bakke, Ed Fiore, Tim Kuik, and Dave Thompson, that he was going to work for NuSpeed, and they expressed interest in following Schrandt. Schrandt met with them outside of work to discuss NuSpeed, and by mid-December, these four Storage Technology employees had signed on with NuSpeed. Through November 2000, NuSpeed hired twenty-two more engineers who were or had been employed at Storage Technology, as NuSpeed grew to employ seventy-eight people.

In February 2000, a new open Internet protocol was published, called iSCSI (for "Internet, Small Computer Systems Interface"). NuSpeed quickly began working on incorporating iSCSI in its product, the SN 5420, which linked storage area networks over the Internet. In April 2000, NuSpeed announced that it was developing a device to transmit data using the iSCSI protocol. NuSpeed aspired to be the first company to bring such a product to market. Cisco Systems, Inc. acquired NuSpeed in September 2000 in a stock-for-stock transaction in which

NuSpeed's shareholders received $450 million in Cisco stock. Although the SN 5420 was indeed the first iSCSI device to market, Cisco never made a profit on NuSpeed, or the "Storage Router Business Unit," as it was called after the acquisition; as of January 2003, Cisco's operating losses for the unit stood at $50 million.

Storage Technology brought this suit against Cisco, alleging that NuSpeed had engaged in "corporate raiding" by hiring Schrandt, Bakke, Fiore, Kuik and Thompson, and the other former Storage Technology employees, alleging that the employees had gained knowledge at Storage Technology of a device for joining disparate and otherwise incompatible computer networks and NuSpeed had used that knowledge to develop a product based on Storage Technology's device. Storage Technology also alleged claims for interference with contractual relations for hiring away persons with whom Storage Technology had employment contracts; for inducing breach of contracts; for conversion of confidential information; for encouraging breach of fiduciary duties by former Storage Technology employees; and for misappropriation of trade secrets.

Cisco moved for summary judgment. Cisco denied that NuSpeed misappropriated any trade secret information or acted improperly in hiring Storage Technology engineers.

The district court granted summary judgment to Cisco. . . .

. . .

II.

Under Minnesota law, the elements of tortious interference with contract are (1) the existence of a contract, (2) the tortfeasor's knowledge of the contract, (3) the tortfeasor's intentional causation of a breach of the contract, (4) a lack of justification for the tortfeasor's action, and (5) damages resulting from the breach. *Bouten v. Richard Miller Homes, Inc.*, 321 N.W.2d 895, 900 (Minn. 1982). The tort of inducing a breach of contract, which Storage Technology pleads in a separate count, requires the same elements. *Aslakson v. Home Sav. Ass'n*, 416 N.W.2d 786, 788 (Minn. Ct. App. 1987).

We turn to the question of whether Storage Technology adduced any evidence to prove its damages for the alleged tortious interference with its employment contracts.

A.

The district court focused on the nature of damages in a tortious interference with contract case. Storage Technology has declined to prove damages to its own business and instead only attempted to establish a right to restitution in the amount of Cisco's alleged unjust enrichment. Cisco contends, and Storage Technology does not deny, that Cisco lost money on the NuSpeed product. At the deposition of Timothy Schulte, Storage Technology's counsel expressly denied that Storage Technology claims or has proven lost profits. Instead, Storage Technology contends it is entitled to $450 million, which was the price Cisco paid for NuSpeed. The district court held that "damages for interference with contract are limited to those that might have been recovered for a breach of the contract itself." The court held that because Storage Technology failed to prove what damages NuSpeed caused, Storage Technology had not made a showing sufficient to resist summary judgment.

The usual remedy provided by Minnesota law for interference with contract is to compensate the victim for the damages that resulted from the loss of the contract. The early case of *Swaney v. Crawley*, 133 Minn. 57, 157 N.W. 910, 911 (Minn. 1916), stated the principle that the "injured party is limited, as a general rule, to such damages as might have been recovered for a breach of the contract itself." *Potthoff v. Jefferson Lines, Inc.*, 363 N.W.2d 771, 777 (Minn. Ct. App. 1985), modified this statement by allowing the award of damages for emotional distress in an interference with contract suit, whereas such damages would not be available in a suit on the contract itself. *Potthoff* observed that the trial court had relied on the Restatement (Second) of Torts § 774A (1979), which allows loss of the benefits of contract, consequential losses, and damages for emotional distress, all of which focus on loss to the aggrieved party. See also *Kallok v. Medtronic, Inc.*, 573 N.W.2d 356, 363-64 (Minn. 1998) (holding recovery for tortious interference can include costs of litigation to enforce contract).

However, breach of some covenants and duties attendant on the employment relation entitles the aggrieved employer to restitution. An employee who breaches a noncompetition or nondisclosure covenant can be required to account for his profits. *Cherne Indus., Inc. v. Grounds & Assoc., Inc.*, 278 N.W.2d 81, 94-95 (Minn. 1979). The remedy for breach of the fiduciary duty of loyalty is also restitutionary. *See Miller v. Miller*, 301 Minn. 207, 222 N.W.2d 71, 78 (Minn. 1974) (remedy for breach of fiduciary duty of loyalty is imposition of constructive trust).

Therefore, where the defendant has not merely enticed a competitor's employees to leave their employment, but also induced them to breach a fiduciary duty of loyalty or restrictive covenant, the remedy must reflect the underlying wrong. When the underlying wrong would have supported a claim of restitution, so should a claim for inducing that wrong. In *Cherne*, an employee of Cherne left and formed a corporation, Grounds & Associates, which hired away two other employees. 278 N.W.2d at 87. All three former employees had signed non-competition and non-disclosure-of-confidential-information covenants, *id.* at 86, which they breached in the service of the new corporation. *Id.* at 88-91. Grounds & Associates argued that the proper remedy was award of Cherne's lost profits, rather than a restitutionary award of Grounds's profits. The Minnesota Supreme Court held:

> Although damages for breach of contract are traditionally measured by the nonbreaching party's loss of expected benefits under the contract, where an employee wrongfully profits from the use of information obtained from his employer, the measure of damages may be the employee's gain. Also, this court has specifically found that the violator of a covenant not to compete may be required to account for his profits, and such illegal profits may properly measure the damages.

Id. at 94-95 (internal citations omitted). *Cherne* did not expressly discuss the fact that it was holding a third party liable for the employees' breach of the noncompetition covenants, but in a later case the Minnesota Supreme Court referred to Cherne as implicitly holding that "third-party interference with [a] noncompete agreement is a tort." *Kallok*, 573 N.W.2d at 361. Thus, where the interference alleged is inducement of breach of restrictive covenants or fiduciary duties, the remedy should mirror the restitutionary remedy available for the breach of the covenant or fiduciary duty.

Storage Technology's interference with contract theory is not clear from its complaint. The complaint's "interference with contractual relations" count only alleges that Storage Technology had employment contracts with its employees and that NuSpeed hired the employees without justification, knowing that they would then terminate their contracts with Storage Technology. It also alleges that NuSpeed accomplished the hiring by using knowledge about Storage Technology's pay structure, etc., but it does not pursue this theory before us. Thus, the count in the complaint appears to allege only hiring of plaintiff's at-will employees. However, Storage Technology pleads in separate counts that NuSpeed induced Schrandt, Fiore, Kuik, and Bakke to breach fiduciary duties to Storage Technology by disclosing confidential information and soliciting Storage Technology employees to leave Storage Technology. In its brief, it contends that Schrandt breached his duty of loyalty by recruiting Storage Technology employees for NuSpeed while still in Storage Technology's employ. In its reply brief, Storage Technology contends that it had a noncompetition agreement with Schrandt, which he violated. Storage Technology therefore appears to be pursuing a theory that NuSpeed induced Storage Technology's employees to breach noncompetition and nondisclosure covenants and to breach their fiduciary duty of loyalty to Storage Technology.

We conclude that Minnesota courts would allow a restitutionary remedy in a case in which the interference alleged was inducing an employee's breach of noncompetition and nondisclosure covenants and fiduciary duties. We further conclude that Storage Technology is alleging NuSpeed induced such breaches by Storage Technology's employees. We therefore must ascertain whether Storage Technology has made a sufficient showing of unjust enrichment to survive summary judgment.

B.

Storage Technology's entire evidentiary basis for a restitutionary remedy consisted of the report of its expert, George Norton, that "Cisco's valuation of NuSpeed (basically, its key people and storage technology expertise) was $450 million and represents a proper valuation of the damages to Storage Technology and due to it for the trade secret appropriation, corporate raiding, and breach of contract and fiduciary responsibilities promulgated." The district court rejected Norton's opinion as "rank speculation."

The first and most apparent problem with Norton's testimony is that he attributed the entire value of the NuSpeed acquisition to employees and trade secrets wrongfully appropriated from Storage Technology, even though NuSpeed had other assets and employees. Norton did not attempt to value the people or the technology supposedly belonging to Storage Technology by any means other than by ascertaining what price Cisco paid for NuSpeed. The undisputed evidence shows that a crucial aspect of the acquisition was Cisco's desire to obtain NuSpeed's product incorporating the iSCSI protocol, which had nothing to do with Storage Technology.

Norton opined, "The value inherent in the price Cisco paid for NuSpeed was in the key employees of NuSpeed who embodied the storage expertise technology Cisco sought." But Norton testified at his deposition that he did not know what the technology was. Norton later contended that the value of NuSpeed to Cisco was in the fifteen key employees named in the acquisition documents. Of these, five are listed as having come from firms other than Storage Technology. Norton did not know what percentage of NuSpeed's total employees were from Storage Technology at the time Cisco acquired the company. He did not know if the deal would have gone forward if the people listed had not agreed to go to Cisco. Norton testified that he did not take into account the terms of the employees' contracts with Storage Technology. See *Nordling v. N. State Power Co.*, 478 N.W.2d 498, 505 (Minn. 1991) ("The fact that the contract is terminable at will . . . is to be taken into account in determining the damages that the plaintiff has suffered by reason of its breach.") (quoting Restatement (Second) of Torts § 766, comment g (1979)).

Norton was unwilling or unable to answer questions exploring what proportion of the acquisition price was attributable to what NuSpeed assets. His deposition was singularly uninformative. . . . Moreover, there is crucial evidence, which Norton does not take into account, that the reason Cisco was interested in NuSpeed was that NuSpeed had begun work on using iSCSI to access stored data. . . . Nobody contends that Storage Technology had anything to do with the idea of using software incorporating the iSCSI standard for storage networking. Storage Technology admitted that no software was ever written for the "SAN Appliance" — which it contends was the idea for a storage networking product that NuSpeed stole from Storage Technology. In fact, iSCSI did not even exist until February 2000, after Schrandt, Bakke, Thompson, Kuik and Fiore had already left Storage Technology. Norton did not take into account any value that may have resulted from the incorporation of the iSCSI standard in the SN 5420. . . .

. . .

Storage Technology's failure to produce evidence substantiating any amount of damages or restitution is fatal to its claim for tortious interference with contractual relations, as well as to each of its other claims.

We affirm the judgment of the district court.

NOTES & QUESTIONS

1. An Independent Tort

Under the tort of trade secret misappropriation, cases following the UTSA and Restatement consider inducement of a breach of a duty of confidentiality as one of the improper means of acquiring another's trade secrets (the other improper means being conversion, theft, misrepresentation, and industrial espionage). A finding of intentional interference with contractual or fiduciary duties therefore supports a finding of liability for the tort of misappropriation of a trade secret.

Notice however that the act of intentional interference with contractual or fiduciary duties is an independent tort in and of itself. RESTATEMENT (SECOND) OF TORTS § 766 (1979); Restatement (Second) of Agency § 312. An aggrieved party need not rely solely on the tort of trade secret misappropriation alone to seek redress for a competitor's act of inducing a former employee to breach a duty of confidentiality.

2. What About Independent Contractors?

What results if a former employee bound by a confidentiality agreement is an independent contractor? Can a competitor who hires the former employee be liable for intentional interference with the confidentiality agreement when the former employee is an independent contractor? Does the status of a former employee as an independent contractor negate the possibility of liability for those that hire him? *See Curtis 1000, Inc. v. Pierce*, 905 F. Supp. 898 (D. Kan. 1995).

3. Former Employee as Plaintiff

The plaintiff in an intentional interference action is typically a former employer seeking to prevent a competitor from inducing the breach of a former employee's confidentiality agreement. Though this is the typical case, a former employee may very well be a plaintiff in an intentional interference action. Former employees accused of misappropriating trade secrets may claim that the former employer's actions to prevent use and disclosure of information interferes with a new contract of employment. Since the former employer is tying the employee's hands, the former employee may claim that the former employer is improperly interfering with his contract of employment for a new employer.

CHAPTER 6

LICENSING IN BUSINESS ORGANIZATIONS

PROBLEM

Digital Ignition Systems Corporation (Digital Ignition) entered into a nonexclusive licensing agreement with Advanced Electronics, Inc. (AEI), a manufacturer of electrical devices. The license granted AEI, the licensee, permission to manufacture and sell products based on three patents owned by Digital Ignition. Digital Ignition offered the three patents as a package at a discount rate lower than what each patent would have cost if licensed individually. AEI accepted the patent package.

In addition to the three patents, the license included a transfer of trade secret know-how as well as trade secret information about an as yet unpatented improvement on the patented technology. Patent applications were pending for the licensed improvement, but a patent ultimately never issued. The trade secret know-how was transferred in the form of a printed manual. The royalty provisions in the licensing agreement separately allocated the royalties for the trade secrets and the patents. A confidentiality agreement was also included that barred the use and disclosure of any Digital Ignition trade secrets by AEI.

Because AEI felt that its company was relatively unknown in the automotive and racing markets, it also negotiated and received the right to sell the licensed product under the Digital Ignition trademark. A provision in the license agreement permits AEI to use the Digital Ignition trademark. The license sets standards for quality control over the product produced in association with the trademark and AEI agreed to allow Digital Ignition to supervise AEI's use of the mark.

For two years, AEI manufactured and sold digital ignition systems in accordance with its license with Digital Ignition without incident. Midway through the third year, AEI stopped paying royalties on the licensed patents and trade secrets. When contacted by Digital Ignition to provide an explanation for the delinquency, AEI claimed that it believed one of the patents in the package was invalid. Because of this, AEI assumed that it was no longer under an obligation to pay royalties on the patents or trade secrets.

At about the same time, Digital Ignition also became aware of AEI's use of Digital Ignition's trademark on a line of men's watches sold by AEI. The watches in question sported a racing car design with Digital Ignition's logo prominently displayed on the face of the watches. When questioned, AEI claimed that it has a license to use Digital Ignition's trademark.

The last problem arising out of the AEI licensing agreement was brought to the attention of Digital Ignition when it discovered that AEI was offering a how-to manual for sale to other manufacturers. The AEI manual excerpted whole sections of the Digital Ignition know-how manual. The AEI manual appeared to claim that the ideas described in the manual came from AEI.

Dr. See, the founder and CEO of Digital Ignition, has approached you for advice. He wants to know what action he should take against AEI in light of the alarming discoveries above. What advice would you give Dr. See? Would any additional information from Digital Ignition be helpful in making your recommendation? If so, what information?

FOCUS OF THE CHAPTER

This chapter focuses on the licensing of intellectual property and offers a survey of issues that arise concerning patent, trade secret, trademark, and copyright licensing.

The first section of the chapter, section A, considers licensing in the context of patents. This section covers the right of licensees to sue for infringement of the licensed patent (*Abbott Labs. v. Diamedix Corp.*), challenges to patent validity by licensees and third parties as those challenges impact upon licensing agreements (*Blonder-Tongue Labs v. Univ. of Ill. Found.* and *Lear Inc. v. Adkins*), and the duration of licensees' obligation to pay royalties (*Brulotte v. Thys Co.* and *Aronson v. Quick Point Pencil Co.*). The section also discusses implied transfers of patent rights as they affect a patent owner's right to enforce his exclusive rights to make, use, sell, and offer to sell the patented technology (*Jazz Photo Corp. v. ITC*). The section then discusses patent cross-licensing (*Texas Instruments, Inc. v. Hyundai Elec. Indus.*), patent pools (*Matsushita Elec. Indus. Co. v. Cinram Int'l, Inc.*), patent packages (*Wells Surveys, Inc. v. Perfo-Log, Inc.*), and licensing of university-created technology.

The second section of this chapter, section B, discusses licensing of trade secrets. The section provides an introduction to trade secret licensing and then explores the implications of the indefinite term of trade secret protection in defining a licensee's obligation to pay royalties on a licensed trade secret (*Warner-Lambert Pharm. Co. v. John J. Reynolds, Inc.*). Hybrid licensing of trade secrets in conjunction with patents is also discussed.

The next section, section C, explores the issues that arise in trademark licensing. First, the section discusses the rule against "naked licensing" — the licensing of a trademark without a transfer of an already established product reputation or "good will" — and the nature of the required good will (*Int'l Cosmetics Exch. Inc. v. Gapardis Health & Beauty, Inc.*). Next, the section describes the type of control a licensor must maintain over the nature and quality of the goods or services offered in association with a licensed mark (*Dawn Donut Co. v. Hart's Food Stores, Inc.*). The section closes by considering antitrust concerns that arise from trademark licensing (*Principe v. McDonald's Corp.*).

Section D deals with copyright licensing. This section offers an introduction to the rights that may be transferred through copyright licensing (*Silvers v. Sony Pictures Entm't, Inc.*), including the scope of the use authorized under the license (*Boosey & Hawkes Music Publishers, Ltd. v. Walt Disney Co.*). The section also touches upon the performance rights organizations ASCAP and BMI.

The last section of the chapter, section E, discusses the licensing of multiple forms of intellectual property. Specifically, the section looks at problems that arise from hybrid licensing of patents with trade secrets and patents with trademarks.

READINGS

A. PATENT LICENSING

A license is a contract whereby the owner of a patented invention authorizes the use of the information without liability, in exchange for payment. The rights of a licensee of a patent depend on the type of license, whether exclusive or nonexclusive, that he or she obtains from the licensor. The right of a licensee to sue for infringement of a licensed patent is discussed in the following case.

1. The Right to Sue for Infringement

ABBOTT LABORATORIES v. DIAMEDIX CORPORATION
United States Court of Appeals for the Federal Circuit
47 F.3d 1128 (1995)

BRYSON, Circuit Judge.

Diamedix Corporation appeals from an order denying its motion to intervene in a patent infringement action. The action was brought by Abbott Laboratories, which held a license from Diamedix, against a third party, Ortho Diagnostic Systems, Inc. We conclude that the district court should have permitted Diamedix to join the lawsuit as a party-plaintiff. The order of the district court denying the motion to intervene is therefore reversed.

I

United States Patents Nos. 4,474,878 (the '878 patent) and 4,642,285 (the '285 patent) were issued in 1984 and 1987, respectively, and assigned to appellant Diamedix Corporation. The two patents relate to immunoassay systems used to test blood for the presence of the hepatitis virus.

Prior to 1988, Diamedix granted eight non-exclusive licenses under the '878 and '285 patents. In August 1988, following a dispute with appellee Abbott Laboratories over alleged infringement of the patents, Diamedix entered into a "license agreement" with Abbott. In exchange for annual royalty payments, Abbott received a worldwide license to make, use, and sell products incorporating the inventions claimed in the patents. The license was exclusive to Abbott and its affiliates, but was subject to the rights previously granted to Diamedix's other licensees. In addition, the agreement reserved to Diamedix the right to make and use products that exploited the patents, as well as the right to sell such products to Diamedix's previous licensees, to Abbott's sublicensees, to end users, and to certain other parties to fulfill Diamedix's existing contractual obligations. The agreement was to remain in effect for the life of the patents unless Abbott decided to terminate it earlier. The agreement was not assignable by either party without the consent of the other.

In January 1994, Abbott filed an action in the United States District Court for the Northern District of Illinois charging appellee Ortho Diagnostic Systems, Inc., with infringing the '878 and '285 patents. Ortho denied the allegations of infringement, asserted as an affirmative defense that the patents are invalid, and claimed that Abbott is barred from seeking relief because of its delay in bringing suit.

Because Abbott did not join Diamedix as a party to the lawsuit, Diamedix promptly filed a motion to intervene and a complaint as plaintiff-intervenor alleging that Ortho had infringed its rights under the two patents. In its motion, Diamedix argued that it was entitled to intervene under Fed. R. Civ. P. 24(a)(2) based on its rights as legal owner of the patents. In the alternative, Diamedix moved to be permitted to intervene under Fed. R. Civ. P. 24(b). Diamedix also suggested that as the holder of legal title to the patents, it might be required to participate in order to give the district court jurisdiction over the suit. Ortho supported Diamedix's motion to intervene, on the ground that Diamedix retained a significant interest in the patents-in-suit under its agreement with Abbott and might be an indispensable party under Fed. R. Civ. P. 19(b).

Diamedix took an immediate appeal from the order denying its motion to intervene. This court stayed the action in the district court pending the resolution of the appeal.

II

A

The Patent Act of 1952 provides that a civil action for infringement may be brought by "a patentee." 35 U.S.C. § 281. The statute defines "patentee" to include the party to whom the patent was issued and the successors in title to the patent, 35 U.S.C. § 100(d), and has been interpreted to require that a suit for infringement ordinarily be brought by a party holding legal title to the patent. Parties not holding title to the patent have been accorded the right to sue (or "standing") in certain circumstances, but only upon joining or attempting to join the patent owners.

In *Waterman v. Mackenzie,* 138 U.S. 252, 34 L. Ed. 923, 11 S. Ct. 334 (1891), the Supreme Court addressed the question of the right to sue for infringement under a predecessor patent statute. The Court stated that an assignment by the patent owner of the whole of the patent right, or of an undivided part of the right, or of all rights in a specified geographical region, gives an assignee the right to bring an action for infringement in his own name. Any less complete transfer of rights, the Court explained, is a license rather than an assignment. If the patent owner grants only a license, the title remains in the owner of the patent; and suit must be brought in his name and never in the name of the licensee alone, unless that is necessary to prevent an absolute failure of justice, as where the patentee is the infringer, and cannot sue himself. Any rights of the licensee must be enforced through or in the name of the owner of the patent, and perhaps, if necessary to protect the rights of all parties, joining the licensee with him as a plaintiff. *Id.* at 255.

Thirty-five years later, in *Independent Wireless Tel. Co. v. Radio Corp. of Am.*, 269 U.S. 459, 70 L. Ed. 357, 46 S. Ct. 166 (1926), the Supreme Court applied the teaching of *Waterman* in a case in which an exclusive licensee sought to enforce the patent rights against an alleged infringer. The Court rejected the argument that the licensee could sue for infringement without joining the patent owner. "The presence of the owner of the patent as a party is indispensable not only to give jurisdiction under the patent laws," the Court held, "but also, in most cases, to enable the alleged infringer to respond in one action to all claims of infringement for his act, and thus either to defeat all claims in the one action, or by satisfying one adverse decree to bar all subsequent actions." 269 U.S. at 468.

The Court recognized an exception to that rule for cases in which the owner of a patent refuses or is unable to be joined as a co-plaintiff with the exclusive licensee in an infringement action. In such a case, the Court held, "the licensee may make [the patent owner] a party defendant by process and he will be lined up by the court in the party character which he should assume." 269 U.S. at 468. A patentee, the Court explained, "holds the title to the patent in trust for [the exclusive] licensee, to the extent that he must allow the use of his name as plaintiff in any action brought at the instance of the licensee in law or in equity to obtain damages for the injury to his exclusive right by an infringer or to enjoin infringement of it." *Id.* at 469. The Court emphasized, however, that before the exclusive licensee can sue in the patent owner's name, the patent owner must be given an opportunity to join the infringement action. *Id.* at 473-74.

Based on the analysis in *Waterman and Independent Wireless Tel. Co.*, this court has recognized the following principles: The right to sue for infringement is ordinarily an incident of legal title to the patent. A licensee may obtain sufficient rights in the patent to be entitled to seek relief from infringement, but to do so, it ordinarily must join the patent owner. And a bare licensee, who has no right to exclude others from making, using, or selling the licensed products, has no legally recognized interest that entitles it to bring or join an infringement action.

Abbott does not take issue with these principles. Rather, it argues that Diamedix is not required to be joined in this action because the agreement between Abbott and Diamedix transferred all substantial rights under the patents to Abbott. We disagree. Although the agreement effected a broad conveyance of rights to Abbott, Diamedix retained substantial interests under the '878 and '285 patents, and Abbott therefore does not have an independent right to sue for infringement as a "patentee" under the patent statute.

Diamedix retained the right to make and use, for its own benefit, products embodying the inventions claimed in the patents, as well as the right to sell such products to end users, to parties with whom Diamedix had pre-existing contracts, and to pre-existing licensees. Abbott's exclusive license was also made subject to prior licenses granted by Diamedix. Moreover, although Abbott was given the right of first refusal in suing alleged infringers, the agreement provides that if Diamedix asks Abbott to bring suit against an alleged infringer and Abbott declines to do so, Diamedix has the right to prosecute its own infringement action; thus, although Abbott has the option to initiate suit for infringement, it does not enjoy the right to indulge infringements, which normally accompanies a complete conveyance of the right to sue. In addition, even if Abbott exercises its option to sue for infringement, it is obligated under the agreement not to "prejudice or impair the patent rights in connection with such prosecution or settlement." Finally, the parties appear to have contemplated that Diamedix could participate in a suit brought by Abbott, because the agreement provides that Diamedix is "entitled to be represented therein by counsel of its own selection at its own expense."

In light of the various rights that Diamedix retains under the agreement, Abbott must be considered a licensee, not an assignee. Under *Waterman* and its successors, Abbott therefore may not sue on its own for infringement.

In arguing to the contrary, Abbott relies principally on this court's decision in *Vaupel Textilmaschinen KG v. Meccanica Euro Italia S.P.A.*, 944 F.2d 870, 20 U.S.P.Q.2D (BNA) 1045 (Fed. Cir. 1991). In that case, the court found that the patent grantee, Marowsky, did not have to be joined as a party to the infringement suit brought by Vaupel. The court reached that conclusion, however, only after finding that Marowsky had transferred all substantial rights under the patent to Vaupel.

The *Vaupel* court emphasized that Marowsky had granted Vaupel not only an exclusive license to make, use, and sell the licensed products, but also the exclusive right to sue for infringement of the patent rights. The court found that the transfer of the exclusive right to sue was "particularly dispositive" of the question whether Vaupel was authorized to bring suit without joining Marowsky.

In this case, Diamedix has retained a significantly greater interest in the patents than Marowsky retained in *Vaupel*. Unlike in *Vaupel,* Diamedix retained a limited right to make, use, and sell products embodying the patented inventions, a right to bring suit on the patents if Abbott declined to do so, and the right to prevent Abbott from assigning its rights under the license to any party other than a successor in business.

Those retained rights are the sort that are commonly held sufficient to make a patent owner who grants an exclusive license a necessary party to an infringement action brought by the licensee. We therefore conclude that Abbott does not have a sufficient interest in the '878 and '285 patents to sue, on its own, as the "patentee" entitled by 35 U.S.C. § 271 to judicial relief from infringement.

B

While Diamedix's joinder is required as a matter of statutory standing, it is consistent with the policies underlying Fed. R. Civ. P. 19, the federal joinder rule. Rule 19(a) provides that a person who can be joined as a party should be joined if (1) the person's absence would make it impossible to grant complete relief to the parties, or (2) the person claims an interest in the subject matter of the action and is so situated that the disposition of the action in his absence could impede his ability to protect that interest or leave any of the parties subject to a substantial risk of incurring multiple or inconsistent obligations.

Diamedix retains interests in the patents, and the disposition of Abbott's suit against Ortho could either prejudice Diamedix's interests or expose Ortho to the risk of multiple litigation or obligations, depending in part on whether Diamedix would be held to be in privity with Abbott and thus bound by any judgment against Abbott. Moreover, Abbott may labor under some disadvantages, not applicable to Diamedix, that would make its defense of the patents more difficult. For example, Diamedix may not be chargeable either with Abbott's delay in bringing suit, which Ortho has pleaded as a defense, or with the statements of Abbott's agent in urging the invalidity of the '878 and '285 patents before the PTO, which might compromise Abbott's defense of the patents in this lawsuit. The purpose of Rule 19 — to avoid multiple suits or incomplete relief arising from the same subject matter — is thus served by joinder, which permits Diamedix's dispute with Ortho to be adjudicated along with Abbott's.

That is not to say that if a patentee in Diamedix's position declines to participate, the action cannot go forward. A patentee that does not voluntarily join an action prosecuted by its exclusive licensee can be joined as a defendant or, in a proper case, made an involuntary plaintiff if it is not subject to service of process. For purposes of this case, however, we need only decide that when a patent owner retains a substantial proprietary interest in the patent and wishes to participate in an infringement action, the court must allow it to do so.

NOTES & QUESTIONS

1. Who Brings the Infringement Suit?

Typically, the best interest of both the licensor and the licensee are served by halting the conduct of a party that infringes the subject matter of a patent license. The licensor has an interest in prohibiting unlicensed use of his patented subject matter because each infringing act by the accused party costs the licensor a royalty. The licensee has an interest in halting the infringing conduct since the accused party is a potential competitor. An infringing party is unburdened by the obligation to pay royalties and may therefore stand at a competitive advantage to undercut the sales of the licensee.

There is no definitive answer as to which party to a licensing agreement should bring suit. Arguably the larger entity, which has the benefit of deeper pockets and more experience in litigation, should decide whether to file an infringement action. A party's motivation to defend the validity of a licensed patent is another consideration. A licensor has more to lose if a patent underlying a licensing agreement is declared invalid and unenforceable. The interests of the licensor and licensee in protecting the validity of a licensed patent are divergent. For example, in *Abbott*, the licensor Diamedix feared that the licensee Abbott "ha[d] an incentive not to defend the validity of the patents with great vigor, since a decision invalidating the patents would free Abbott from its royalty obligations." A licensee may stand to benefit whether the patent is declared invalid and unenforceable, thus freeing him from the obligation to pay royalties, or whether the patent is enforced against the infringer. In addition to motivation, the licensor, as owner of the patent, may be in the best position to access and provide the information needed to defend the validity of a patent.

As *Abbott* illustrates, a party chosen to bring suit usually is given the right of first refusal, rather than an exclusive right to bring an infringement action. The other party in the agreement typically may step in, or initiate suit itself, if the chosen party declines.

2. Who Controls the Litigation?

A licensor has the most to lose if a patent is declared invalid. Given that a licensee has incentives to not vigorously defend the validity of a patent, a licensor may be justified in doubting the commitment of the licensee as defender of the patent. A licensor should therefore reserve the right to intervene and defend the patent should the licensee fail to competently direct litigation.

Where a licensee controls litigation, a licensor may also wish to require a licensee to obtain its consent before entering into any settlement agreement. Additionally, a licensor who is named as a party to an infringement suit may be exposed to sanctions incurred during a botched litigation. For this reason, an agreement permitting a licensee to name the licensor as a party in an infringement suit may also include an indemnity clause to protect the licensor from the licensee's mishandling of litigation.

2. Challenges to Patent Validity

a. Res Judicata

BLONDER-TONGUE LABORATORIES, INC. v. UNIVERSITY OF ILLINOIS FOUNDATION
Supreme Court of the United States
402 U.S. 313 (1971)

Mr. Justice White delivered the opinion of the Court.

Respondent University of Illinois Foundation (hereafter Foundation) is the owner by assignment of U.S. Patent No. 3,210,767, issued to Dwight E. Isbell on October 5, 1965.

The patent has been much litigated since it was granted, primarily because it claims a high quality television antenna for color reception. One of the first infringement suits brought by the Foundation was filed in the Southern District of Iowa against the Winegard Co., an antenna manufacturer. Trial was to the court, and after pursuing the inquiry mandated by *Graham* v. *John Deere Co.*, 383 U.S. 1, 17-18 (1966), Chief Judge Stephenson held the patent invalid. . . . On appeal, the Court of Appeals for the Eighth Circuit unanimously affirmed Judge Stephenson. . . .

In March 1966, well before Judge Stephenson had ruled in the *Winegard* case, the Foundation also filed suit in the Northern District of Illinois charging a Chicago customer of petitioner, Blonder-Tongue Laboratories, Inc. (hereafter B-T), with infringing two patents it owned by assignment. . . .

Trial was again to the court, and on June 27, 1968, Judge Hoffman held that the Foundation's patents were valid and infringed. [The Seventh Circuit affirmed.]

B-T sought certiorari, assigning the conflict between the Courts of Appeals for the Seventh and Eighth Circuits as to the validity of the Isbell patent as a primary reason for granting the writ.

I

In *Triplett* v. *Lowell*, 297 U.S. 638 (1936), this Court held:

> Neither reason nor authority supports the contention that an adjudication adverse to any or all the claims of a patent precludes another suit upon the same claims against a different defendant. While the earlier decision may be comity be given great weight in a later litigation and thus persuade the court to render a like decree, it is not *res adjudicata* and may not be pleaded as a defense.

297 U.S. at 642.

> The holding in *Triplett* has been at least gently criticized by some judges.

. . .

III

Some litigants — those who never appeared in a prior action — may not be collaterally estopped without litigating the issue. They have never had a chance to present their evidence and arguments on the claim. Due process prohibits estopping them despite one or more existing adjudications of the identical issue which stand squarely against their position. Also, the authorities have been more willing to permit a defendant in a second suit to invoke an estoppel against a plaintiff who lost on the same claim in an earlier suit than they have been to allow a plaintiff in the second suit to use offensively a judgment obtained by a different plaintiff in a prior suit against the same defendant. But the case before us involves neither due process nor "offensive use" questions. Rather, it depends on the considerations weighing for and against permitting a patent holder to sue on his patent after it has once been held invalid following opportunity for full and fair trial.

A

Starting with the premise that the statutes creating the patent system, expressly sanctioned by the Constitution, represent an affirmative policy choice by Congress to reward inventors, respondents extrapolate a special public interest in sustaining "good" patents and characterize patent litigation as so technical and difficult as to present unusual potential for unsound adjudications. Although *Triplett* made no such argument in support of its holding, that rule, offering the unrestricted right to re-litigate patent validity, is thus deemed an essential safeguard against improvident judgments of invalidity.

We fully accept congressional judgment to reward inventors through the patent system. We are also aware that some courts have frankly stated that patent litigation can present issues so complex that legal minds, without appropriate grounding in science and technology, may have difficulty in reaching decision. . . . But assuming a patent case so difficult as to provoke a frank admission of judicial uncertainty, one might ask what reason there is to expect that a second district judge or court of appeals would be able to decide the issue more accurately. Moreover, as *Graham* also indicates, Congress has from the outset chosen to impose broad criteria of patentability while lodging in the federal courts final authority to decide that question. In any event it cannot be sensibly contended that all issues concerning patent validity are so complex and unyielding. Non-obviousness itself is not always difficult to perceive and decide and other questions on which patentability depends are more often than not no more difficult than those encountered in the usual non-patent case.

Even conceding the extreme intricacy of some patent cases, we should keep firmly in mind that we are considering the situation where the patentee was plaintiff in the prior suit and chose to litigate at that time and place. Presumably he was prepared to litigate and to litigate to the finish against the defendant there involved. Patent litigation characteristically proceeds with some deliberation, and with the avenues for discovery available under the present rules of procedure, there is no reason to suppose that plaintiff patentees would face either surprise or unusual difficulties in getting all relevant and probative evidence before the court in the first litigation.

Moreover, we do not suggest, without legislative guidance, that a plea of estoppel by an infringement or royalty suit defendant must automatically be accepted once the defendant in support of his plea identifies the issue in suit as the identical question finally decided against the patentee or one of his privies in previous litigation. Rather, the patentee-plaintiff must be permitted to demonstrate, if he can, that he did not have "a fair opportunity procedurally, substantively and evidentially to pursue his claim the first time." This element in the estoppel decision will comprehend, we believe, the important concerns about the complexity of patent litigation and the posited hazard that the prior proceedings were seriously defective.

Determining whether a patentee has had a full and fair chance to litigate the validity of his patent in an earlier case is of necessity not a simple matter. In addition to the considerations of choice of forum and incentive to litigate mentioned above, certain other factors immediately emerge. For example, if the issue is non-obviousness, appropriate inquiries would be whether the first validity determination purported to employ the standards announced in *Graham* v. *John Deere Co., supra*; whether the opinions filed by the District Court and the reviewing court, if any, indicate that the prior case was one of those relatively rare instances where the courts wholly failed to grasp the technical subject matter and issues in suit; and whether without fault of his own the patentee was deprived of crucial evidence or witnesses in the first litigation. But as so often is the case, no one set of facts, no one collection of words or phrases, will provide an automatic formula for proper rulings on estoppel pleas. In the end, decision will necessarily rest on the trial courts' sense of justice and equity.

We are not persuaded, therefore, that the *Triplett* rule, as it was formulated, is essential to effectuate the purposes of the patent system or is an indispensable or even an effective safeguard against faulty trials and judgments. Whatever legitimate concern there may be about the intricacies of some patent suits, it is insufficient in and of itself to justify patentees re-litigating validity issues as long as new defendants are available. This is especially true if the court in the second litigation must decide in a principled way whether or not it is just and equitable to allow the plea of estoppel in the case before it.

B

An examination of the economic consequences of continued adherence to *Triplett* has two branches. Both, however, begin with the acknowledged fact that patent litigation is a very costly process.

This statement . . . must be assessed in light of the fact that they are advanced by patentees contemplating action as plaintiffs, and patentees are heavily favored as a class of litigants by the patent statute. Section 282 of the Patent Code provides, in pertinent part:

> A patent shall be presumed valid. The burden of establishing invalidity of a patent shall rest on a party asserting it.

If a patentee's expense is high though he enjoys the benefits of the presumption of validity, the defendant in an infringement suit will have even higher costs as he both introduces proof to overcome the presumption and attempts to rebut whatever proof the patentee offers to bolster the claims.

As stated at the outset of this section, the expense of patent litigation has two principal consequences if the *Triplett* rule is maintained. First, assuming that a perfectly sound judgment of invalidity has been rendered in an earlier suit involving the patentee, a second infringement action raising the same issue and involving much of the same proof has a high cost to the individual parties. The patentee is expending funds on litigation to protect a patent which is by hypothesis invalid. These moneys could be put to better use, such as further research and development. The alleged infringer — operating as he must against the presumption of validity — is forced to divert substantial funds to litigation that is wasteful.

The second major economic consideration is far more significant. Under *Triplett*, only the comity restraints flowing from an adverse prior judgment operate to limit the patentee's right to sue different defendants on the same patent. In each successive suit the patentee enjoys the statutory presumption of validity, and so may easily put the alleged infringer to his expensive proof. As a consequence, prospective defendants will often decide that paying royalties under a license or other settlement is preferable to the costly burden of challenging the patent.

The tendency of *Triplett* to multiply the opportunities for holders of invalid patents to exact licensing agreements or other settlements from alleged infringers must be considered in the context of other decisions of this Court. Although recognizing the patent system's desirable stimulus to invention, we have also viewed the patent as a monopoly which, although sanctioned by law, has the economic consequences attending other monopolies. A patent yielding returns for a device that fails to meet the congressionally imposed criteria of patentability is anomalous. . . .

One obvious manifestation of this principle has been the series of decisions in which the Court has condemned attempts to broaden the physical or temporal scope of the patent monopoly. . . .

A second group of authorities encourage authoritative testing of patent validity. In 1952, the Court indicated that a manufacturer of a device need not await the filing of an infringement action in order to test the validity of a competitor's patent, but may institute his own suit under the Declaratory Judgment Act. Other decisions of this type involved removal of restrictions on those who would challenge the validity of patents.

Two Terms ago in *Lear, Inc.* v. *Adkins*, 395 U.S. 653 (1969), we relied on both lines of authority to abrogate the doctrine that in a contract action for unpaid patent royalties the licensee of a patent is estopped from proving "that his licensor was demanding royalties for the use of an idea which was in reality a part of the public domain." The principle that "federal law requires that all ideas in general circulation be dedicated to the common good unless they are protected by a valid patent," found support in . . . the first line of cases discussed above. The holding that licensee estoppel was no longer tenable was rooted in the second line of cases eliminating obstacles to suit by those disposed to challenge the validity of a patent. Moreover, as indicated earlier, we relied on practical considerations that patent licensees "may often be the only individuals with enough economic incentive to challenge the patentability of an inventor's discovery."

To be sure, *Lear* obviates to some extent the concern that *Triplett* prompts alleged infringers to pay royalties on patents previously declared invalid rather than to engage in costly litigation when infringement suits are threatened. *Lear* permits an accused infringer to accept a license, pay royalties for a time, and cease paying when financially able to litigate validity, secure in the knowledge that invalidity may be urged when the patentee-licensor sues for unpaid royalties. Nevertheless, if the claims are in fact invalid and are identical to those invalidated in a previous suit against another party, any royalties actually paid are an unjust increment to the alleged infringer's costs. Those payments put him at a competitive disadvantage *vis-à-vis* other alleged infringers who can afford to litigate or have successfully litigated the patent's validity.

This has several economic consequences. First, the alleged infringer who cannot afford to defend may absorb the royalty costs in order to compete with other manufacturers who have secured holdings that the patent is invalid, cutting the profitability of his business and perhaps assuring that he will never be in a financial position to challenge the patent in court. On the other hand, the manufacturer who has secured a judicial holding that the patent is invalid may be able to increase his market share substantially, and he may do so without coming close to the price levels that would prevail in a competitive market. Because he is free of royalty payments, the manufacturer with a judgment against the patent may price his products higher than competitive levels absent the invalid patent, yet just below the levels set by those manufacturers who must pay royalties. Third, consumers will pay higher prices for goods covered by the invalid patent than would be true had the initial ruling of invalidity had at least the potential for broader effect. And even if the alleged infringer can escape royalty obligations under *Lear* when he is able to bear the cost of litigation, any royalty payments passed on to consumers are as a practical matter unrecoverable by those who in fact paid them. Beyond all of this, the rule of *Triplett* may permit invalid patents to serve almost as effectively as would valid patents as barriers to the entry of new firms — particularly small firms.

Economic consequences like these, to the extent that they can be avoided, weigh in favor of modification of the *Triplett* mutuality principle. Arguably, however, the availability of estoppel to one charged with infringement of a patent previously held invalid will merely shift the focus of litigation from the merits of the dispute to the question whether the party to be estopped had a full and fair opportunity to litigate his claim in the first action. It would seem sufficient answer to note that once it is determined that the issue in both actions was identical, it will be easier to decide whether there was a full opportunity to determine that issue in the first action than it would be to re-litigate completely the question of validity. And, this does not in fact seem to have been a problem in other contexts, where strict mutuality of estoppel has been abandoned.

It has also been suggested that 35 U.S.C. § 285, which allows a court to award reasonable attorney's fees to a prevailing party "in exceptional cases," and 35 U.S.C. § 288, under which a patentee forfeits his right to recover costs even as to the valid claims of his patent if he does not disclaim invalid claims before bringing suit, work to inhibit repetitious suits on invalid patents. But neither of these provisions can operate until after litigation has occurred, and the outlay required to try a lawsuit presenting validity issues is the factor which undoubtedly forces many alleged infringers into accepting licenses rather than litigating. If concern about such license agreements is proper, as our cases indicate that it is, the accused infringer should have available an estoppel defense that can be pleaded affirmatively and determined on a pre-trial motion for judgment on the pleadings or summary judgment. Fed. Rules Civ. Proc. 8 (c), 12 (c), and 56.

D

It is clear that judicial decisions have tended to depart from the rigid requirements of mutuality. In accordance with this trend, there has been a corresponding development of the lower courts' ability and facility in dealing with questions of when it is appropriate and fair to impose an estoppel against a party who has already litigated an issue once and lost. . . .

When these judicial developments are considered in the light of our consistent view — last presented in *Lear, Inc.* v. *Adkins* — that the holder of a patent should not be insulated from the assertion of defenses and thus allowed to exact royalties for the use of an idea that is not in fact patentable or that is beyond the scope of the patent monopoly granted, it is apparent that the uncritical acceptance of the principle of mutuality of estoppel expressed in *Triplett* v. *Lowell* is today out of place. Thus, we conclude that *Triplett* should be overruled to the extent it forecloses a plea of estoppel by one facing a charge of infringement of a patent that has once been declared invalid.

NOTES & QUESTIONS

1. Patent Invalidity and Res Judicata: A One-Way Street

A final adjudication of *validity* of a patent is not binding on subsequent infringers who are not party to an action, even if a subsequent action relies upon identical grounds of attack. A patentee may therefore face several challenges to the validity of his patent, with no benefit of prior actions serving as precedent in subsequent litigation. Contrast this to the final adjudication of *invalidity* of a patent. A single final adjudication of invalidity is binding on the patent holder in other litigation and results in the termination of the patent.

2. Licensor's Reluctance to Sue?

While a licensee may not be the most committed to vigorously defend a licensed patent once an infringement suit is initiated, a licensor may have an incentive not to initiate a timely suit against an infringing party. A common defense raised when an action is brought against an accused infringer is an assertion that the patent at issue is invalid. Attacks on the validity of a patent can deter licensors from bringing suit against an infringer. This is because royalties stop once a patent is declared invalid. Since royalties paid prior to a judgment of invalidity are not subject to refund, a licensor may delay filing suit against an infringing party in order to push off the termination of licensees' royalty payment obligations. For this reason, a licensee may wish to include a provision in a licensing agreement that assures the timely filing of an infringement suit. In light of res judicata in the finding of invalidity of a patent, can you think of another reason that patentees shy away from bringing suit?

b.   Estoppel

LEAR, INC. v. ADKINS
Supreme Court of the United States
395 U.S. 653 (1969)

MR. JUSTICE HARLAN delivered the opinion of the Court.

In January of 1952, John Adkins, an inventor and mechanical engineer, was hired by Lear, Incorporated, for the purpose of solving a vexing problem the company had encountered in its efforts to develop a gyroscope which would meet the increasingly demanding requirements of the aviation industry. The gyroscope is an essential component of the navigational system in all aircraft, enabling the pilot to learn the direction and attitude of his airplane. With the development of the faster airplanes of the 1950's, more accurate gyroscopes were needed, and the gyro industry consequently was casting about for new techniques which would satisfy this need in an economical fashion. Shortly after Adkins was hired, he developed a method of construction at the company's California facilities which improved gyroscope accuracy at a low cost. Lear almost immediately incorporated Adkins' improvements into its production process to its substantial advantage.

The question that remains unsettled in this case, after eight years of litigation in the California courts, is whether Adkins will receive compensation for Lear's use of those improvements which the inventor has subsequently patented. At every stage of this lawsuit, Lear has sought to prove that, despite the grant of a patent by the Patent Office, none of Adkins' improvements were sufficiently novel to warrant the award of a monopoly under the standards delineated in the governing federal statutes. Moreover, the company has sought to prove that Adkins obtained his patent by means of a fraud on the Patent Office. In response, the inventor has argued that since Lear had entered into a licensing agreement with Adkins, it was obliged to pay the agreed royalties regardless of the validity of the underlying patent.

The Supreme Court of California unanimously vindicated the inventor's position. While the court recognized that generally a manufacturer is free to challenge the validity of an inventor's patent, it held that "one of the oldest doctrines in the field of patent law establishes that so long as a licensee is operating under a license agreement he is estopped to deny the validity of his licensor's patent in a suit for royalties under the agreement. The theory underlying this doctrine is that a licensee should not be permitted to enjoy the benefit afforded by the agreement while simultaneously urging that the patent which forms the basis of the agreement is void."

I.

At the very beginning of the parties' relationship, Lear and Adkins entered into a rudimentary one-page agreement which provided that although "all new ideas, discoveries, inventions, etc., related to . . . vertical gyros become the property of Mr. John S. Adkins," the inventor promised to grant Lear a license as to all ideas he might develop "on a mutually satisfactory royalty basis." As soon as Adkins' labors yielded tangible results, it quickly became apparent to the inventor that further steps should be taken to place his rights to his ideas on a firmer basis. On February 4, 1954, Adkins filed an application with the Patent Office in an effort to gain federal protection for his improvements. At about the same time, he entered into a lengthy period of negotiations with Lear in an effort to conclude a licensing agreement which would clearly establish the amount of royalties that would be paid.

These negotiations finally bore fruit on September 15, 1955, when the parties approved a complex 17-page contract which carefully delineated the conditions upon which Lear promised to pay royalties for Adkins' improvements. The parties agreed that if "the U.S. Patent Office refuses to issue a patent on the substantial claims [contained in Adkins' original patent application] or if such a patent so issued is subsequently held invalid, then in any of such events

Lear at its option shall have the right forthwith to terminate the specific license so affected or to terminate this entire Agreement. . . ."

As the contractual language indicates, Adkins had not obtained a final Patent Office decision as to the patentability of his invention at the time the licensing agreement was concluded. Indeed, he was not to receive a patent until January 5, 1960. This long delay has its source in the special character of Patent Office procedures. [Review of the patent application by the Patent Office may include several rounds of rejection and amendments.] Thus, when Adkins made his original application in 1954, it took the average inventor more than three years before he obtained a final administrative decision on the patentability of his ideas, with the Patent Office acting on the average application from two to four times.

The progress of Adkins' effort to obtain a patent followed the typical pattern. In his initial application, the inventor made the ambitious claim that his entire method of constructing gyroscopes was sufficiently novel to merit protection. The Patent Office, however, rejected this initial claim, as well as two subsequent amendments, which progressively narrowed the scope of the invention sought to be protected. Finally, Adkins narrowed his claim drastically to assert only that the design of the apparatus used to achieve gyroscope accuracy was novel. In response, the Office issued its 1960 patent, granting a 17-year monopoly on this more modest claim.

During the long period in which Adkins was attempting to convince the Patent Office of the novelty of his ideas, however, Lear had become convinced that Adkins would never receive a patent on his invention and that it should not continue to pay substantial royalties on ideas which had not contributed substantially to the development of the art of gyroscopy. In 1957, after Adkins' patent application had been rejected twice, Lear announced that it had searched the Patent Office's files and had found a patent which it believed had fully anticipated Adkins' discovery. As a result, the company stated that it would no longer pay royalties on the large number of gyroscopes it was producing at its plant in Grand Rapids, Michigan (the Michigan gyros). Payments were continued on the smaller number of gyros produced at the company's California plant (the California gyros) for two more years until they too were terminated on April 8, 1959.

II.

Since the California Supreme Court's construction of the 1955 licensing agreement is solely a matter of state law, the only issue open to us is raised by the court's reliance upon the doctrine of estoppel to bar Lear from proving that Adkins' ideas were dedicated to the common welfare by federal law. In considering the propriety of the State Court's decision, we are well aware that we are not writing upon a clean slate. The doctrine of estoppel has been considered by this Court in a line of cases reaching back into the middle of the 19th century.

. . .

III.

The uncertain status of licensee estoppel in the case law is a product of judicial efforts to accommodate the competing demands of the common law of contracts and the federal law of patents. On the one hand, the law of contracts forbids a purchaser to repudiate his promises simply because he later becomes dissatisfied with the bargain he has made. On the other hand, federal law requires that all ideas in general circulation be dedicated to the common good unless they are protected by a valid patent. *Sears, Roebuck* v. *Stiffel Co., supra; Compco Corp.* v. *Day-Brite Lighting, Inc., supra.* When faced with this basic conflict in policy, both this Court and courts throughout the land have naturally sought to develop an intermediate position which somehow would remain responsive to the radically different concerns of the two different worlds of contract and patent. The result has been a failure. Rather than creative compromise, there has been a chaos of conflicting case law, proceeding on inconsistent premises. Before renewing the search for an acceptable middle ground, we must reconsider on their own merits the arguments which may properly be advanced on both sides of the estoppel question.

A.

It will simplify matters greatly if we first consider the most typical situation in which patent licenses are negotiated. In contrast to the present case, most manufacturers obtain a license after a patent has issued. Since the Patent Office makes an inventor's ideas public when it issues its grant of a limited monopoly, a potential licensee has access to the inventor's ideas even if he does not enter into an agreement with the patent owner. Consequently, a manufacturer gains only two benefits if he chooses to enter a licensing agreement after the patent has issued. First, by accepting a license and paying royalties for a time, the licensee may have avoided the necessity of defending an expensive infringement action during the period when he may be least able to afford one. Second, the existence of an unchallenged patent may deter others from attempting to compete with the licensee.

Under ordinary contract principles the mere fact that some benefit is received is enough to require the enforcement of the contract, regardless of the validity of the underlying patent. Nevertheless, if one tests this result by the standard of good-faith commercial dealing, it seems far from satisfactory. For the simple contract approach entirely ignores the position of the licensor who is seeking to invoke the court's assistance on his behalf. Consider, for example, the equities of the licensor who has obtained his patent through a fraud on the Patent Office. It is difficult to perceive why good faith requires that courts should permit him to recover royalties despite his licensee's attempts to show that the patent is invalid.

Even in the more typical cases, not involving conscious wrongdoing, the licensor's equities are far from compelling. A patent, in the last analysis, simply represents a legal conclusion reached by the Patent Office. Moreover, the legal conclusion is predicated on factors as to which reasonable men can differ widely. Yet the Patent Office is often obliged to reach its decision in an *ex parte* proceeding, without the aid of the arguments which could be advanced by parties interested in proving patent invalidity. Consequently, it does not seem to us to be unfair to require a patentee to defend the Patent Office's judgment when his licensee places the question in issue, especially since the licensor's case is buttressed by the presumption of validity which attaches to his patent. Thus, although licensee estoppel may be consistent with the letter of contractual doctrine, we cannot say that it is compelled by the spirit of contract law, which seeks to balance the claims of promisor and promisee in accord with the requirements of good faith.

Surely the equities of the licensor do not weigh very heavily when they are balanced against the important public interest in permitting full and free competition in the use of ideas which are in reality a part of the public domain. Licensees may often be the only individuals with enough economic incentive to challenge the patentability of an inventor's discovery. If they are muzzled, the public may continually be required to pay tribute to would-be monopolists without need or justification. We think it plain that the technical requirements of contract doctrine must give way before the demands of the public interest in the typical situation involving the negotiation of a license after a patent has issued.

B.

The case before us, however, presents a far more complicated estoppel problem than the one which arises in the most common licensing context. The problem arises out of the fact that Lear obtained its license in 1955, more than four years before Adkins received his 1960 patent. Indeed, from the very outset of the relationship, Lear obtained special access to Adkins' ideas in return for its promise to pay satisfactory compensation.

Thus, during the lengthy period in which Adkins was attempting to obtain a patent, Lear gained an important benefit not generally obtained by the typical licensee. For until a patent issues, a potential licensee may not learn his licensor's ideas simply by requesting the information from the Patent Office. During the time the inventor is seeking patent protection, the governing federal statute requires the Patent Office to hold an inventor's patent application in confidence. If a potential licensee hopes to use the ideas contained in a secret patent application, he must deal with the inventor himself, unless the inventor chooses to publicize his ideas to the world at large. By promising to pay Adkins royalties from the very outset of their relationship, Lear gained immediate access to ideas which it may well not have learned until the Patent Office published the details of Adkins' invention in 1960. At the core of this case, then, is the difficult question whether federal patent policy bars a State from enforcing a contract regulating access to an unpatented secret idea.

Adkins takes an extreme position on this question. The inventor does not merely argue that since Lear obtained privileged access to his ideas *before 1960*, the company should be required to pay royalties accruing *before 1960* regardless of the validity of the patent which ultimately issued. He also argues that since Lear obtained special benefits before 1960, it should also pay royalties during the entire patent period (1960-1977), without regard to the validity of the Patent Office's grant. We cannot accept so broad an argument.

Adkins' position would permit inventors to negotiate all important licenses during the lengthy period while their applications were still pending at the Patent Office, thereby disabling entirely all those who have the strongest incentive to show that a patent is worthless. While the equities supporting Adkins' position are somewhat more appealing than those supporting the typical licensor, we cannot say that there is enough of a difference to justify such a substantial impairment of overriding federal policy.

Nor can we accept a second argument which may be advanced to support Adkins' claim to at least a portion of his post-patent royalties, regardless of the validity of the Patent Office grant. The terms of the 1955 agreement provide that royalties are to be paid until such time as the "patent . . . is held invalid," and the fact remains that the question of patent validity has not been finally determined in this case. Thus, it may be suggested that although Lear must be allowed to raise the question of patent validity in the present lawsuit, it must also be required to comply with its contract and continue to pay royalties until its claim is finally vindicated in the courts.

The parties' contract, however, is no more controlling on this issue than is the State's doctrine of estoppel, which is also rooted in contract principles. The decisive question is whether overriding federal policies would be significantly frustrated if licensees could be required to continue to pay royalties during the time they are challenging patent validity in the courts.

It seems to us that such a requirement would be inconsistent with the aims of federal patent policy. Enforcing this contractual provision would give the licensor an additional economic incentive to devise every conceivable dilatory tactic in an effort to postpone the day of final judicial reckoning. We can perceive no reason to encourage dilatory court tactics in this way. Moreover, the cost of prosecuting slow-moving trial proceedings and defending an inevitable appeal might well deter many licensees from attempting to prove patent invalidity in the courts. The deterrent effect would be particularly severe in the many scientific fields in which invention is proceeding at a rapid rate. In these areas, a patent may well become obsolete long before its 17-year term has expired. If a licensee has reason to believe that he will replace a patented idea with a new one in the near future, he will have little incentive to initiate lengthy court proceedings, unless he is freed from liability at least from the time he refuses to pay the contractual royalties. Lastly, enforcing this contractual provision would undermine the strong federal policy favoring the full and free use of ideas in the public domain. For all these reasons, we hold that Lear must be permitted to avoid the payment of all royalties accruing after Adkins' 1960 patent issued if Lear can prove patent invalidity.

C.

Adkins' claim to contractual royalties accruing before the 1960 patent issued is, however, a much more difficult one, since it squarely raises the question whether, and to what extent, the States may protect the owners of *unpatented* inventions who are willing to disclose their ideas to manufacturers only upon payment of royalties. The California Supreme Court did not address itself to this issue with precision, for it believed that the venerable doctrine of estoppel provided a sufficient answer to all of Lear's claims based upon federal patent law. . . . Consequently, we have concluded, after much consideration, that even though an important question of federal law underlies this phase of the controversy, we should not now attempt to define in even a limited way the extent, if any, to which the States may properly act to enforce the contractual rights of inventors of unpatented secret ideas. Given the difficulty and importance of this task, it should be undertaken only after the state courts have, after fully focused inquiry, determined the extent to which they will respect the contractual rights of such inventors in the future. Indeed, on remand, the California courts may well reconcile the competing demands of patent and contract law in a way which would not warrant further review in this Court.

NOTES & QUESTIONS

1. Licensee Estoppel and Royalty Payment Obligations

Courts will not enforce an agreement not to challenge the validity of a licensed patent if the licensor obtained the promise from a licensee in order to shield the licensed patent from challenges to its validity. *Lear v. Adkins* made it clear that licensees have standing to challenge the validity of a patent. Moreover, a licensee may stop paying royalties during the time that the challenge is pending.

In *Studiengesellschaft Kohle m.b.H v. Shell Oil*, 112 F.3d 1561 (Fed. Cir. 1997), the licensee, Shell Oil, sought to have the licensed patents declared invalid and unenforceable in response to an action brought by the licensor SGK, seeking relief for breach of contract and patent infringement. Shell alleged patent invalidity only after it was faced with a suit by SGK for failing to pay royalties as agreed to in its licensing agreement with the licensor. The court addressed the question of whether Shell was obligated to pay royalties on the challenged patent:

> [T]his court detects no significant frustration of federal patent policy by enforcing the 1987 license agreement between Shell and SGK, to the extent of allowing SGK to recover royalties until the date Shell first challenged the validity of the claims. First, . . . Shell executed a contractual agreement which produced significant benefits for the corporation and attested to the worth of the patent. Under the agreement (with its provision for Shell to notify SGK of all polypropylene production), Shell had the benefits of producing polypropylene insulated from unlicensed competition, insulated from investigations of infringement, and even insulated from royalties (until SGK's discovery of the Seadrift Process). To these benefits, Shell now seeks to add the benefit of abrogating its agreement and avoiding its breach of the contract. . . . [T]his court must prevent the injustice of allowing Shell to exploit the protection of the contract and patent rights and then later to abandon conveniently its obligations under those same rights.

Just as important, however, Shell's apparent breach of its duty to notify under the agreement is itself more likely to frustrate federal patent policy than enforcement of the contract. As already noted, *Lear* focused on the "full and free use of ideas in the public domain." *Lear*, 395 U.S. at 674. By abrogating its notification duty, Shell delayed a timely challenge to the validity of the '698 patent and postponed the public's full and free use of the invention of the '698 patent. Shell enjoyed the protection of the license from 1987 until SGK became aware of the Seadrift Process. Upon SGK's discovery of its Seadrift process, Shell suddenly seeks the protection of the *Lear* policies it flaunted for many years. However, a licensee, such as Shell, cannot invoke the protection of the Lear doctrine until it (i) actually ceases payment of royalties, and (ii) provides notice to the licensor that the reason for ceasing payment of royalties is because it has deemed the relevant claims to be invalid. Other circuits addressing this issue have arrived at the same conclusion.

In this factual setting, therefore, enforcement of the license according to its terms, even if this entails a determination of whether the Seadrift process infringes a now-invalidated patent, does not frustrate federal patent policy. Accordingly, this court remands this case to the district court for enforcement of the license (prior to the date Shell first challenged the validity of the claims) and, if necessary, computation of back royalties.

Studiengesellschaft, 112 F.3d at 1568.

2. Assignor Estoppel

Related to the doctrine of licensee estoppel is the doctrine of assignor estoppel. Assignor estoppel prevents an inventor who has assigned her rights to a patent to subsequently challenge the validity of that assigned patent as a defense to infringement of the patent. The Federal Circuit addressed the issue for the first time in *Diamond Scientific Co. v. Ambico*, 848 F.2d 1220 (Fed. Cir. 1988). In this case, the inventor-assignor left the employ of the assignee, Diamond, and started Ambico, a competing company:

Assignor estoppel is an equitable doctrine that prevents one who has assigned the rights to a patent (or patent application) from later contending that what was assigned is a nullity. . . .

The four most frequently mentioned justifications for applying assignor estoppel are the following: "(1) to prevent unfairness and injustice; (2) to prevent one [from] benefiting from his own wrong; (3) by analogy to estoppel by deed in real estate; and (4) by analogy to a landlord-tenant relationship." Although each rationale may have some utility depending on the facts presented by the particular case, our concern here is primarily with the first one.

Courts that have expressed the estoppel doctrine in terms of unfairness and injustice have reasoned that an assignor should not be permitted to sell something and later to assert that what was sold is worthless, all to the detriment of the assignee. Justice Frankfurter's dissent in *Scott Paper* explained that the doctrine was rooted in the notion of fair dealing. "The principle of fair dealing as between assignor and assignee of a patent whereby the assignor will not be allowed to say that what he has sold as a patent was not a patent has been part of the fabric of our law throughout the life of this nation." *Scott Paper Co. v. Marcalus Mfg. Co.*, 326 U.S. 249, 260, 90 L. Ed. 47, 66 S. Ct. 101

(Frankfurter, J., dissenting). "The essence of the principle of fair dealing which binds the assignor of a patent in a suit by the assignee, even though it turns out that the patent is invalid or lacks novelty, is that in this relation the assignor is not part of the general public but is apart from the general public." *Id.* at 261-62. In other words, it is the implicit representation by the assignor that the patent rights that he is assigning (presumably for value) are not worthless that sets the assignor apart from the rest of the world and can deprive him of the ability to challenge later the validity of the patent. To allow the assignor to make that representation at the time of the assignment (to his advantage) and later to repudiate it (again to his advantage) could work an injustice against the assignee.

IV.

Our holding is that this is a case in which public policy calls for the application of assignor estoppel. We are, of course, not unmindful of the general public policy disfavoring the repression of competition by the enforcement of worthless patents. Yet despite the public policy encouraging people to challenge potentially invalid patents, there are still circumstances in which the equities of the contractual relationships between the parties should deprive one party (as well as others in privity with it) of the right to bring that challenge.

. . .

We note first that Dr. Welter assigned the rights to his inventions to Diamond in exchange for valuable consideration (one dollar plus other unspecified consideration — presumably his salary over many years and other employment benefits). Dr. Welter also executed an inventor's oath, which stated his belief, *inter alia*, that he was the first and sole inventor, that the invention was never known or used before his invention and that it was not previously patented or described in any publication in any country. Furthermore, Dr. Welter apparently participated actively in the patent application process, including drafting the initial version of the claims and consulting on their revision.

Appellants would now defend against accusations of infringement by trying to show that the three patents in issue are invalid because the inventions either were inadequately disclosed by the specifications, lacked novelty, or would have been obvious to one of ordinary skill at the time the inventions were made. If appellants are permitted to raise these defenses and are successful in their proof, Dr. Welter will have profited both by his initial assignment of the patent applications and by his later attack on the value of the very subjects of his earlier assignment. In comparison, Diamond will have given value for the rights to Dr. Welter's inventions only to have him later deprive Diamond of the worth of those assigned rights.

Diamond, 848 F.2d at 1224-25. A more recent case dealing with the issue of assignor estoppel is *Mentor Graphics Corp. v. Quickturn Design Systems*, 150 F.3d 1374 (Fed. Cir. 1998). Relying on *Diamond*, the Federal Circuit once again reaffirmed that an assignee is estopped from challenging the validity of its patent as a defense to an infringement claim by the assignee:

> Due to the intrinsic unfairness in allowing an assignor to challenge the validity of the patent it assigned, the implicit representation of validity contained in an assignment of a patent for value raises the presumption that an estoppel will apply. Without exceptional circumstances (such as an express reservation by the assignor of the right to challenge the validity of the patent or an express waiver by the assignee of the right to assert assignor estoppel), one who assigns a patent surrenders with that assignment the right to later challenge the validity of the assigned patent.

Mentor, 150 F.3d at 1378.

3.   Duration of Obligation to Pay Royalties

Generally, the obligation of a licensee to pay royalties for a patent license is limited in duration to the term of the patent. The expiration of a patent terminates the obligation to pay royalties on the patented invention. The patent policy in favor of free use and competition regarding a patented invention once the relevant patent expires weighs against licensors' use of licensing contracts and state contract law to extend the term of the patent protection beyond its statutory scope.

a.   Post Patent Expiration Royalties

BRULOTTE v. THYS CO.
Supreme Court of the United States
379 U.S. 29 (1964)

MR. JUSTICE DOUGLAS delivered the opinion of the Court.

Respondent, owner of various patents for hop-picking, sold a machine to each of the petitioners for a flat sum and issued a license for its use. Under that license there is payable a minimum royalty of $500 for each hop-picking season or $3.33 1/3 per 200 pounds of dried hops harvested by the machine, whichever is greater. The licenses by their terms may not be assigned nor may the machines be removed from Yakima County. The licenses issued to petitioners listed 12 patents relating to hop-picking machines; but only seven were incorporated into the machines sold to and licensed for use by petitioners. Of those seven all expired on or before 1957. But the licenses issued by respondent to them continued for terms beyond that date.

Petitioners refused to make royalty payments accruing both before and after the expiration of the patents. This suit followed. One defense was misuse of the patents through extension of the license agreements beyond the expiration date of the patents. The trial court rendered judgment for respondent and the Supreme Court of Washington affirmed. The case is here on a writ of certiorari.

We conclude that the judgment below must be reversed insofar as it allows royalties to be collected which accrued after the last of the patents incorporated into the machines had expired.

The Constitution by Art. I, § 8 authorizes Congress to secure "for limited times" to inventors "the exclusive right" to their discoveries. Congress exercised that power by 35 U.S.C. § 154 which provides in part as follows:

> Every patent shall contain a short title of the invention and a grant to the patentee, his heirs or assigns, for the term of seventeen years, of the right to exclude others from making, using, or selling the invention throughout the United States, referring to the specification for the particulars thereof. . . .

The right to make, the right to sell, and the right to use "may be granted or conferred separately by the patentee." But these rights become public property once the 17-year period expires. As stated by Chief Justice Stone, speaking for the Court in *Scott Paper Co.* v. *Marcalus Co.*, 326 U.S. 249, 256:

> . . . any attempted reservation or continuation in the patentee or those claiming under him of the patent monopoly, after the patent expires, whatever the legal device employed, runs counter to the policy and purpose of the patent laws.

The Supreme Court of Washington held that in the present case the period during which royalties were required was only "a reasonable amount of time over which to spread the payments for the use of the patent." But there is intrinsic evidence that the agreements were not designed with that limited view. As we have seen, the purchase price in each case was a flat sum, the annual payments not being part of the purchase price but royalties for use of the machine during that year. The royalty payments due for the post-expiration period are by their terms for use during that period, and are not deferred payments for use during the pre-expiration period. Nor is the case like the hypothetical ones put to us where non-patented articles are marketed at prices based on use. The machines in issue here were patented articles and the royalties exacted were the same for the post-expiration period as they were for the period of the patent. That is peculiarly significant in this case in view of other provisions of the license agreements. The license agreements prevent assignment of the machines or their removal from Yakima County *after*, as well as before, the expiration of the patents.

Those restrictions are apt and pertinent to protection of the patent monopoly; and their applicability to the post-expiration period is a telltale sign that the licensor was using the licenses to project its monopoly beyond the patent period. They forcefully negate the suggestion that we have here a bare arrangement for a sale or a lease at an undetermined price, based on use. The sale or lease of *unpatented* machines on long-term payments based on a deferred purchase price or on use would present wholly different considerations. Those arrangements seldom rise to the level of a federal question. But patents are in the federal domain; and "whatever the legal device employed" a projection of the patent monopoly after the patent expires is not enforceable. The present licenses draw no line between the term of the patent and the post-expiration period. The same provisions as respects both use and royalties are applicable to each. The contracts are, therefore, on their face a bald attempt to exact the same terms and conditions for the period after the patents have expired as they do for the monopoly period. We are, therefore, unable to conjecture what the bargaining position of the parties might have been and what resultant arrangement might have emerged had the provision for post-expiration royalties been divorced from the patent and nowise subject to its leverage.

In light of those considerations, we conclude that a patentee's use of a royalty agreement that projects beyond the expiration date of the patent is unlawful *per se*. If that device were available to patentees, the free market visualized for the post-expiration period would be subject to monopoly influences that have no proper place there.

     . . . .

A patent empowers the owner to exact royalties as high as he can negotiate with the leverage of that monopoly. But to use that leverage to project those royalty payments beyond the life of the patent is analogous to an effort to enlarge the monopoly of the patent by tying the sale or use of the patented article to the purchase or use of unpatented ones. The exaction of royalties for use of a machine after the patent has expired is an assertion of monopoly power in the post-expiration period when, as we have seen, the patent has entered the public domain. We share the views of the Court of Appeals in *Ar-Tik Systems, Inc.* v. *Dairy Queen, Inc.*, 302 F.2d 496, 510, that after expiration of the last of the patents incorporated in the machines "the grant of patent monopoly was spent" and that an attempt to project it into another term by continuation of the licensing agreement is unenforceable.

Reversed.

b.   License Royalties on Unpatented, Publicly-Disclosed Products

ARONSON v. QUICK POINT PENCIL CO.
Supreme Court of the United States
440 U.S. 257 (1979)

MR. CHIEF JUSTICE BURGER delivered the opinion of the Court.

We granted certiorari, 436 U.S. 943, to consider whether federal patent law pre-empts state contract law so as to preclude enforcement of a contract to pay royalties to a patent applicant, on sales of articles embodying the putative invention, for so long as the contracting party sells them, if a patent is not granted.

(1)

In October 1955 the petitioner, Mrs. Jane Aronson, filed an application, Serial No. 542677, for a patent on a new form of key holder. Although ingenious, the design was so simple that it readily could be copied unless it was protected by patent. In June 1956, while the patent application was pending,

Mrs. Aronson negotiated a contract with the respondent, Quick Point Pencil Co., for the manufacture and sale of the key holder.

The contract was embodied in two documents. In the first, a letter from Quick Point to Mrs. Aronson, Quick Point agreed to pay Mrs. Aronson a royalty of 5% of the selling price in return for "the exclusive right to make and sell key holders of the type shown in your application, Serial No. 542677." The letter further provided that the parties would consult one another concerning the steps to be taken "[in] the event of any infringement."

The contract did not require Quick Point to manufacture the key holder. Mrs. Aronson received a $750 advance on royalties and was entitled to rescind the exclusive license if Quick Point did not sell a million key holders by the end of 1957. Quick Point retained the right to cancel the agreement whenever "the volume of sales does not meet our expectations." The duration of the agreement was not otherwise prescribed.

A contemporaneous document provided that if Mrs. Aronson's patent application was "not allowed within five (5) years, Quick Point Pencil Co. [would] pay . . . two and one half percent (2 1/2%) of sales . . . so long as you [Quick Point] continue to sell same."[1]

In June 1961, when Mrs. Aronson had failed to obtain a patent on the key holder within the five years specified in the agreement, Quick Point asserted its contractual right to reduce royalty payments to 2 1/2% of sales. In September of that year the Board of Patent Appeals issued a final rejection of the application on the ground that the key holder was not patentable, and Mrs. Aronson did not appeal. Quick Point continued to pay reduced royalties to her for 14 years thereafter.

The market was more receptive to the key holder's novelty and utility than the Patent Office. By September 1975 Quick Point had made sales in excess of $7 million and paid Mrs. Aronson royalties totaling $203,963.84; sales were continuing to rise. However, while Quick Point was able to pre-empt the market in the earlier years and was long the only manufacturer of the Aronson key holder, copies began to appear in the late 1960's. Quick Point's competitors, of course, were not required to pay royalties for their use of the design. Quick Point's share of the Aronson key holder market has declined during the past decade.

(2)

In November 1975 Quick Point commenced an action in the United States District Court for a declaratory judgment, pursuant to 28 U.S.C. § 2201, that

---

[1] [FN**] In April 1961, while Mrs. Aronson's patent application was pending, her husband sought a patent on a different key holder and made plans to license another company to manufacture it. Quick Point's attorney wrote to the couple that the proposed new license would violate the 1956 agreement. He observed that

> your license agreement is in respect of the disclosure of said Jane [Aronson's] application (not merely in respect of its claims) and that even if no patent is ever granted on the Jane [Aronson] application, *Quick Point Pencil Company is obligated to pay royalties in respect of any key holder manufactured by it in accordance with any disclosure of said application.* (Emphasis added.)

the royalty agreement was unenforceable. Quick Point asserted that state law which might otherwise make the contract enforceable was pre-empted by federal patent law. This is the only issue presented to us for decision.

(3)

On this record it is clear that the parties contracted with full awareness of both the pendency of a patent application and the possibility that a patent might not issue. The clause de-escalating the royalty by half in the event no patent issued within five years makes that crystal clear. Quick Point apparently placed a significant value on exploiting the basic novelty of the device, even if no patent issued; its success demonstrates that this judgment was well founded. Assuming, *arguendo*, that the initial letter and the commitment to pay a 5% royalty was subject to federal patent law, the provision relating to the 2 1/2% royalty was explicitly independent of federal law. The cases and principles relied on by the Court of Appeals and Quick Point do not bear on a contract that does not rely on a patent, particularly where, as here, the contracting parties agreed expressly as to alternative obligations if no patent should issue.

Commercial agreements traditionally are the domain of state law. State law is not displaced merely because the contract relates to intellectual property which may or may not be patentable; the states are free to regulate the use of such intellectual property in any manner not inconsistent with federal law. *Kewanee Oil Co.* v. *Bicron Corp.*, 416 U.S. 470, 479 (1974); see *Goldstein* v. *California*, 412 U.S. 546 (1973). In this as in other fields, the question of whether federal law pre-empts state law "involves a consideration of whether that law 'stands as an obstacle to the accomplishment and execution of the full purposes and objectives of Congress.' . . . " If it does not, state law governs.

In *Kewanee Oil Co.*, we reviewed the purposes of the federal patent system. First, patent law seeks to foster and reward invention; second, it promotes disclosure of inventions to stimulate further innovation and to permit the public to practice the invention once the patent expires; third, the stringent requirements for patent protection seek to assure that ideas in the public domain remain there for the free use of the public.

Enforcement of Quick Point's agreement with Mrs. Aronson is not inconsistent with any of these aims. Permitting inventors to make enforceable agreements licensing the use of their inventions in return for royalties provides an additional incentive to invention. Similarly, encouraging Mrs. Aronson to make arrangements for the manufacture of her key holder furthers the federal policy of disclosure of inventions; these simple devices display the novel idea which they embody wherever they are seen.

Quick Point argues that enforcement of such contracts conflicts with the federal policy against withdrawing ideas from the public domain and discourages recourse to the federal patent system by allowing states to extend "perpetual protection to articles too lacking in novelty to merit any patent at all under federal constitutional standards," *Sears, Roebuck & Co.* v. *Stiffel Co.*, 376 U.S. 225, 232 (1964).

We find no merit in this contention. Enforcement of the agreement does not withdraw any idea from the public domain. The design for the key holder was not in the public domain before Quick Point obtained its license to manufacture it. In negotiating the agreement, Mrs. Aronson disclosed the design in confidence. Had Quick Point tried to exploit the design in breach of that confidence, it would have risked legal liability. It is equally clear that the design entered the public domain as a result of the manufacture and sale of the key holders under the contract.

Requiring Quick Point to bear the burden of royalties for the use of the design is no more inconsistent with federal patent law than any of the other costs involved in being the first to introduce a new product to the market, such as outlays for research and development, and marketing and promotional expenses. For reasons which Quick Point's experience with the Aronson key holder demonstrate, innovative entrepreneurs have usually found such costs to be well worth paying.

Finally, enforcement of this agreement does not discourage anyone from seeking a patent. Mrs. Aronson attempted to obtain a patent for over five years. It is quite true that had she succeeded, she would have received a 5% royalty only on key holders sold during the 17-year life of the patent. Offsetting the limited terms of royalty payments, she would have received twice as much per dollar of Quick Point's sales, and both she and Quick Point could have licensed any others who produced the same key holder. Which course would have produced the greater yield to the contracting parties is a matter of speculation; the parties resolved the uncertainties by their bargain.

(4)

No decision of this Court relating to patents justifies relieving Quick Point of its contract obligations. We have held that a state may not forbid the copying of an idea in the public domain which does not meet the requirements for federal patent protection. Enforcement of Quick Point's agreement, however, does not prevent anyone from copying the key holder. It merely requires Quick Point to pay the consideration which it promised in return for the use of a novel device which enabled it to pre-empt the market.

In *Lear, Inc.* v. *Adkins*, 395 U.S. 653 (1969), we held that a person licensed to use a patent may challenge the validity of the patent, and that a licensee who establishes that the patent is invalid need not pay the royalties accrued under the licensing agreement subsequent to the issuance of the patent. Both holdings relied on the desirability of encouraging licensees to challenge the validity of patents, to further the strong federal policy that only inventions which meet the rigorous requirements of patentability shall be withdrawn from the public domain. Accordingly, neither the holding nor the rationale of *Lear* controls when no patent has issued, and no ideas have been withdrawn from public use.

Enforcement of the royalty agreement here is also consistent with the principles treated in *Brulotte* v. *Thys Co.*, 379 U.S. 29 (1964). There, we held that the obligation to pay royalties in return for the use of a patented device may not extend beyond the life of the patent. The principle underlying that holding was simply that the monopoly granted *under a patent* cannot lawfully be used to "negotiate with the leverage of that monopoly." The Court emphasized that to "use that leverage to project those royalty payments beyond the life of the patent is analogous to an effort to enlarge the monopoly of the patent. . . ." *Id.* at 33. Here the reduced royalty which is challenged, far from being negotiated "with the leverage" of a patent, rested on the contingency that no patent would issue within five years.

No doubt a pending patent application gives the applicant some additional bargaining power for purposes of negotiating a royalty agreement. The pending application allows the inventor to hold out the hope of an exclusive right to exploit the idea, as well as the threat that the other party will be prevented from using the idea for 17 years. However, the amount of leverage arising from a patent application depends on how likely the parties consider it to be that a valid patent will issue. Here, where no patent ever issued, the record is entirely clear that the parties assigned a substantial likelihood to that contingency, since they specifically provided for a reduced royalty in the event no patent issued within five years.

This case does not require us to draw the line between what constitutes abuse of a pending application and what does not. It is clear that whatever role the pending application played in the negotiation of the 5% royalty, it played no part in the contract to pay the 2 1/2% royalty indefinitely.

Our holding in *Kewanee Oil Co.* puts to rest the contention that federal law pre-empts and renders unenforceable the contract made by these parties. There we held that state law forbidding the misappropriation of trade secrets was not pre-empted by federal patent law. We observed:

> Certainly the patent policy of encouraging invention is not disturbed by the existence of another form of incentive to invention. In this respect the two systems [patent and trade secret law] are not and never would be in conflict. 416 U.S. at 484.

Enforcement of this royalty agreement is even less offensive to federal patent policies than state law protecting trade secrets. The most commonly accepted definition of trade secrets is restricted to confidential information which is not disclosed in the normal process of exploitation. *See* Restatement of Torts § 757, Comment *b*, p. 5 (1939). Accordingly, the exploitation of trade secrets under state law may not satisfy the federal policy in favor of disclosure, whereas disclosure is inescapable in exploiting a device like the Aronson key holder.

Enforcement of these contractual obligations, freely undertaken in arm's-length negotiation and with no fixed reliance on a patent or a probable patent grant, will

> encourage invention in areas where patent law does not reach, and will prompt the independent innovator to proceed with the discovery and exploitation of his invention. Competition is fostered and the

public is not deprived of the use of valuable, if not quite patentable, invention. (Footnote omitted.) 416 U.S. at 485.

The device which is the subject of this contract ceased to have any secrecy as soon as it was first marketed, yet when the contract was negotiated the inventiveness and novelty were sufficiently apparent to induce an experienced novelty manufacturer to agree to pay for the opportunity to be first in the market. Federal patent law is not a barrier to such a contract.

Reversed.

MR. JUSTICE BLACKMUN, concurring in the result.

For me, the hard question is whether this case can meaningfully be distinguished from *Brulotte* v. *Thys Co.*, 379 U.S. 29 (1964). There the Court held that a patent licensor could not use the leverage of its patent to obtain a royalty contract that extended beyond the patent's 17-year term. Here Mrs. Aronson has used the leverage of her patent application to negotiate a royalty contract which continues to be binding even though the patent application was long ago denied.

The Court . . . asserts that her leverage played "no part" with respect to the contingent agreement to pay a reduced royalty if no patent issued within five years. Yet it may well be that Quick Point agreed to that contingency in order to obtain its other rights that depended on the success of the patent application. The parties did not apportion consideration in the neat fashion the Court adopts.

In my view, the holding in *Brulotte* reflects hostility toward extension of a patent monopoly whose term is fixed by statute, 35 U.S.C. § 154. Such hostility has no place here. A patent application which is later denied temporarily discourages unlicensed imitators. Its benefits and hazards are of a different magnitude from those of a granted patent that prohibits all competition for 17 years. Nothing justifies estopping a patent-application licensor from entering into a contract whose term does not end if the application fails. The Court points out, that enforcement of this contract does not conflict with the objectives of the patent laws. The United States, as *amicus curiae*, maintains that patent-application licensing of this sort is desirable because it encourages patent applications, promotes early disclosure, and allows parties to structure their bargains efficiently.

On this basis, I concur in the Court's holding that federal patent law does not pre-empt the enforcement of Mrs. Aronson's contract with Quick Point.

NOTES & QUESTIONS

1. Royalties Prior to the Issuance of a Patent

Patent protection does not commence until the issuance of a patent. During the pendency of a patent application, the subject matter of the patent application may instead be protected under trade secret law. Any monetary consideration paid prior to the issuance of a patent therefore is not technically a patent royalty. Despite this fact, parties negotiating a licensing contract concerning a patent that is expected to result from a pending patent application may agree to the payment of a pre-issuance royalty.

Prior to the issuance of a patent, a licensor may characterize pre-issuance royalties as payment for the option to take a patent license once the patent issues, or as consideration in exchange for disclosure of the matter. By granting two separate contractual rights in the licensing contract, a licensor may avoid challenges by the licensee over the obligation to pay pre-issuance royalties.

2. Right to Elect Trade Secret Protection

So long as the subject matter of a patent application is maintained a secret, trade secret protection covers the period prior to patent issuance. Of course, inventors may choose to rely entirely on trade secret protection and elect not to patent their invention at all. Even if an inventor chooses to apply for a patent, certain aspects of the invention may be retained as a trade secret, so long as the best mode and written description requirements of patent law are met. Trade secret licensing is discussed later in Section B of this chapter.

4. Implied Transfers

a. Patent Exhaustion and the First Sale Doctrine

JAZZ PHOTO CORP. v. INTERNATIONAL TRADE COMMISSION
United States Court of Appeals for the Federal Circuit
264 F.3d 1094 (2001)

NEWMAN, Circuit Judge.

. . . Fuji Photo Film Co. charged twenty-seven respondents, including the appellants Jazz Photo Corporation, Dynatec International, Inc., and Opticolor, Inc., with infringement of fifteen patents owned by Fuji. The charge was based on the respondents' importation of used "single-use" cameras called "lens-fitted film packages" (LFFP's), which had been refurbished for reuse in various overseas facilities. . . .

The Commission determined that twenty-six respondents, including the appellants, had infringed all or most of the claims in suit of fourteen Fuji United States patents, and issued a General Exclusion Order and Order to Cease and Desist. This court stayed the Commission's orders during this appeal.

. . .

DISCUSSION

. . .

I

The Patented Inventions

The LFFP is a relatively simple camera, whose major elements are an outer plastic casing that holds a shutter, a shutter release button, a lens, a viewfinder, a film advance mechanism, a film counting display, and for some models a flash assembly and battery. The casing also contains a holder for a roll of film, and a container into which the exposed film is wound. At the factory a roll of film is loaded into the camera. The casing is then sealed by ultrasonic welding or light-tight latching, and a cardboard cover is applied to encase the camera.

LFFPs are intended by the patentee to be used only once. After the film is exposed, the photo-processor removes the film container by breaking open a pre-weakened portion of the plastic casing which is accessed by removal of the cardboard cover. Discarded LFFPs, subsequently purchased and refurbished by the respondents, are the subject of this action.

. . .

It is not disputed that the imported refurbished cameras contain all of the elements of all or most of the claims in suit.

The Accused Activities

The appellants import used LFFPs that have been refurbished by various overseas entities (called "remanufacturers" in the ITC proceeding). Some of the remanufacturers refused discovery entirely or in part, and some presented evidence that the [administrative law judge (ALJ)] found incomplete or not credible. The Commission explains: "Since so little was known about the accused infringing processes, the ALJ considered the common steps that each participating respondent admitted during the hearing were part of their processes." The ALJ summarized these common steps as follows:

- removing the cardboard cover;
- opening the LFFP body (usually by cutting at least one weld);
- replacing the winding wheel or modifying the film cartridge to be inserted;
- resetting the film counter;
- replacing the battery in flash LFFPs;
- winding new film out of a canister onto a spool or into a roll;
- resealing the LFFP body using tape and/or glue;
- applying a new cardboard cover.

The Commission held that these activities constitute prohibited reconstruction. In view of this holding, it was not material to the Commission's ruling that the full extent of various respondents' activities was not made known, for in all events the importation would be infringing and unlawful.

The appellants argue that they are not building new LFFPs, but simply replacing the film in used cameras. They argue that the LFFPs have a useful life longer than the single use proposed by Fuji, that the patent right has been exhausted as to these articles, and that the patentee can not restrict their right to refit the cameras with new film by the procedures necessary to insert the film and reset the mechanism. Unless these activities are deemed to be permissible, infringement of at least some of the patents in suit is conceded.

. . .

The Law of Permissible Repair and Prohibited Reconstruction

The distinction between permitted and prohibited activities, with respect to patented items after they have been placed in commerce by the patentee, has been distilled into the terms "repair" and "reconstruction." The purchaser of a patented article has the rights of any owner of personal property, including the right to use it, repair it, modify it, discard it, or resell it, subject only to overriding conditions of the sale. Thus patented articles when sold "become the private individual property of the purchasers, and are no longer specifically protected by the patent laws." *Mitchell v. Hawley*, 83 U.S. (16 Wall.) 544, 548, 21 L. Ed. 322 (1872). The fact that an article is patented gives the purchaser neither more nor less rights of use and disposition. However, the rights of ownership do not include the right to construct an essentially new article on the template of the original, for the right to make the article remains with the patentee.

While the ownership of a patented article does not include the right to make a substantially new article, it does include the right to preserve the useful life of the original article. It is readily apparent that there is a continuum between these concepts; precedent demonstrates that litigated cases rarely reside at the poles wherein "repair" is readily distinguished from "reconstruction." Thus the law has developed in the body of precedent, illustrating the policy underlying the law as it has been applied in diverse factual contexts.

The principle of the distinction between permissible and prohibited activities was explained in *Wilson v. Simpson*, 50 U.S. (9 How.) 109, 13 L. Ed. 66 (1850), where the Court distinguished the right of a purchaser of a patented planing machine to replace the machine's cutting-knives when they became dull or broken, from the patentee's sole right to make or renew the entire machine. The Court observed that the knives had to be replaced every 60-90 days whereas the machines would last for several years, explaining, "what harm is done to the patentee in the use of his right of invention, when the repair and replacement of a partial injury are confined to the machine which the purchaser has bought?" *Id.* at 123.

This principle underlies the application of the law. It was elaborated by the Court in *Aro Manufacturing Co. v. Convertible Top Replacement Co.,* 365 U.S. 336, 5 L. Ed. 2d 592, 81 S. Ct. 599 (1961), where the patented combination was a fabric convertible top and the associated metal support structure. The Court explained that replacement of the worn fabric top constituted permissible repair of the patented combination, and could not be controlled by the patentee. The Court restated the principles that govern the inquiry as applied to replacement of unpatented parts of a patented article:

> The decisions of this Court require the conclusion that reconstruction of a patented entity, comprised of unpatented elements, is limited to such a true reconstruction of the entity as to "in fact make a new article," *United States v. Aluminum Co. of America,* [148 F.2d 416, 425 (2d. Cir. 1945)], after the entity, viewed as a whole, has become spent. In order to call the monopoly, conferred by the patent grant, into play for a second time, it must, indeed, be a second creation of the patented entity, as, for example, in *American Cotton Tie Co. v. Simmons,* [106 U.S. 89, 27 L. Ed. 79, 1 S. Ct. 52 (1882)]. Mere replacement of individual unpatented parts, one at a time, whether of the same part repeatedly or different parts successively, is no more than the lawful right of the owner to repair his property.

365 U.S. at 346.

This right of repair, provided that the activity does not "in fact make a new article," accompanies the article to succeeding owners. In *Wilbur-Ellis Co. v. Kuther,* 377 U.S. 422, 141 U.S.P.Q. (BNA) 703, 12 L. Ed. 2d 419, 84 S. Ct. 1561 (1964), the Court dealt with the refurbishing of patented fish-canning machines by a purchaser of used machines. The Court held that the fairly extensive refurbishment by the new owner, including modification and resizing of six separate parts of the machine, although more than customary repair of spent or broken components, was more like repair then reconstruction, for it extended the useful life of the original machine. Precedent has classified as repair the disassembly and cleaning of patented articles accompanied by replacement of unpatented parts that had become worn or spent, in order to preserve the utility for which the article was originally intended. In *General Electric Co. v. United States,* 215 Ct. Cl. 636, 572 F.2d 745, 198 U.S.P.Q. (BNA) 65 (Ct. Cl. 1978), the court held that the Navy's large scale "overhauling" of patented gun mounts, including disassembly into their component parts and replacement of parts that could not be repaired with parts from other gun mounts or new parts, was permissible repair of the original gun mounts. The court explained that the assembly-line method of reassembly, without regard to where each component had originated, was simply a matter of efficiency and economy, with the same effect as if each gun mount had been refurbished individually by disassembly and reassembly of its original components with replacement of a minor amount of worn elements. Similarly, in *Dana Corp. v. American Precision Co.,* 827 F.2d 755, 3 U.S.P.Q.2D (BNA) 1852 (Fed. Cir. 1987), the court held that the "rebuilding" of worn truck clutches, although done on a commercial scale, was permissible repair. The defendants in *Dana Corp.* acquired worn clutches that had been discarded by their original owners, disassembled them, cleaned and sorted the individual parts, replaced worn or defective parts with new or salvaged parts, and reassembled the clutches. Although the patentee stressed that some new parts were used and that the rebuilding was a large scale commercial operation, the activity was held to be repair. *Id.* at 759, 3 U.S.P.Q.2D (BNA) at 1855. The court also observed that in general the new parts were purchased from Dana, the original manufacturer of the patented clutches, and that repair of used clutches was contemplated by the patentee. The court rejected the argument that the complete disassembly and production-line reassembly of the clutches constituted a voluntary destruction followed by a "second creation of the patented entity," invoking the phrase of *Aro Manufacturing*, 365 U.S. at 346.

"Reconstruction," precedent shows, requires a more extensive rebuilding of the patented entity than is exemplified in *Aro Manufacturing*, *Wilbur-Ellis*, *General Electric*, and *Dana Corp.* Underlying the repair/reconstruction dichotomy is the principle of exhaustion of the patent right. The unrestricted sale of a patented article, by or with the authority of the patentee, "exhausts" the patentee's right to control further sale and use of that article by enforcing the patent under which it was first sold. In *United States v. Masonite Corp.*, 316 U.S. 265, 278, 86 L. Ed. 1461, 62 S. Ct. 1070 (1942), the Court explained that exhaustion of the patent right depends on "whether or not there has been such a disposition of the article that it may fairly be said that the patentee has received his reward for the use of the article." Thus when a patented device has been lawfully sold in the United States, subsequent purchasers inherit the same immunity under the doctrine of patent exhaustion. However, the prohibition that the product may not be the vehicle for a "second creation of the patented entity" continues to apply, for such re-creation exceeds the rights that accompanied the initial sale.

Fuji states that some of the imported LFFP cameras originated and were sold only overseas, but are included in the refurbished importations by some of the respondents. The record supports this statement, which does not appear to be disputed. United States patent rights are not exhausted by products of foreign provenance. To invoke the protection of the first sale doctrine, the authorized first sale must have occurred under the United States patent. Our decision applies only to LFFPs for which the United States patent right has been exhausted by first sale in the United States. Imported LFFPs of solely foreign provenance are not immunized from infringement of United States patents by the nature of their refurbishment.

Application of the Law

In the Commission's Initial Determination the administrative judge . . . held that the remanufacturers had made a new LFFP after the useful life of the original LFFP had been spent. Thus, the ALJ ruled that the remanufacturers were engaged in prohibited reconstruction. The Commission adopted the ALJ's findings and conclusions. . . . The Commission ruled that the respondents were not simply repairing the LFFP in order to achieve its intended life span, but created a new single use camera that would again be discarded by its purchaser after use.

Although the Commission's conclusion is supported by its reasoning and reflects concern for the public interest, for there was evidence of imperfections and failures of some refurbished cameras, precedent requires that these cameras be viewed as repaired, not reconstructed. In *Dana Corp.*, for example, the truck clutches had lived their intended lives as originally produced, yet the court ruled that the "rebuilding" of the used clutches was more akin to repair than to reconstruction. The activities of disassembly and rebuilding of the gun mounts of *General Electric* were similarly extensive, yet were deemed to be repair. *Aro Manufacturing* and the other Supreme Court decisions which underlie precedent require that infringing reconstruction be a "second creation" of the patented article. Although the Commission deemed this requirement met by the "remanufactured" LFFPs, precedent places the acts of inserting new film and film container, resetting the film counter, and resealing the broken case — the principal steps performed by the remanufacturers — as more akin to repair.

The Court has cautioned against reliance on any specific set of "factors" in distinguishing permissible from prohibited activities, stating in *Aro Manufacturing* that "While there is language in some lower court opinions indicating that 'repair' or 'reconstruction' depends on a number of factors, it is significant that each of the three cases of this Court, cited for that proposition, holds that a license to use a patented combination includes the right 'to preserve its fitness for use. . . .'" 365 U.S. at 345. Indeed, this criterion is the common thread in precedent, requiring consideration of the remaining useful capacity of the article, and the nature and role of the replaced parts in achieving that useful capacity. The appellants stress that all of the original components of the LFFP except the film and battery have a useful remaining life, and are reused. The appellants state that but for the exposed roll of film and its container, any portion of the case that was broken by the photo processor, and the winding wheel in certain cameras, the refurbished LFFP is substantially the original camera, for which the patent right has been exhausted.

The Commission placed weight on Fuji's intention that the LFFP not be reused. . . . However, the patentee's unilateral intent, without more, does not bar reuse of the patented article, or convert repair into reconstruction.

. . . As discussed in *Aro Manufacturing*, the replacement of unpatented parts, having a shorter life than is available from the combination as a whole, is characteristic of repair, not reconstruction. On the totality of the circumstances, the changes made by the remanufacturers all relate to the replacement of the film, the LFFP otherwise remaining as originally sold.

Several of the Fuji patents in suit are directed to specific components of LFFPs. . . . The ruling of reconstruction as to these patents is incorrect, because the remanufacturing processes simply reuse the original components, such that there is no issue of replacing parts that were separately patented. If the claimed component is not replaced, but simply is reused, this component is neither repaired nor reconstructed.

License

Fuji alternatively contends that the right to repair the patented cameras is impliedly limited by the circumstances of sale, pointing to the instructions and warnings printed on the covers of the LFFPs, and arguing that these constituted a license limited to a single use. *See Mallinckrodt, Inc. v. Medipart, Inc.,* 976 F.2d 700, 709, 24 U.S.P.Q.2D (BNA) 1173, 1180 (Fed. Cir. 1992) (the conditions of sale of a "single-use" medical device may contractually restrict further use). The administrative law judge found that:

> A Fuji flash QuickSnap single use camera is in a box and both the box and the outer cardboard cover of the camera have statements instructing the purchaser to not remove the film and return the camera to the photo-processor and further cautioning the purchaser about the risk of electrical shock if opened by the purchaser. . . . [The packaging also] instructs the purchaser that the single use camera will not be returned to the purchaser after processing. Similar notations are on [other cameras].

A license is governed by the laws of contract. It was undisputed that no express conditions of sale, license terms or restrictions attended the sale of these cameras. There was no express contractual undertaking by the purchaser. The administrative judge observed that any issue of implied contract or license was mooted by the finding of infringement based on reconstruction, and made no findings on the issues of contract or license.

Determinations of express or implied license or contract are matters of law. As stated in *Hewlett-Packard*, "A seller's intent, unless embodied in an enforceable contract, does not create a limitation on the right of a purchaser to use, sell, or modify a patented product as long as a reconstruction of the patented combination is avoided." 123 F.3d at 1453, 43 U.S.P.Q.2D (BNA) at 1658. We do not discern an enforceable restriction on the reuse of these cameras based on the package statements. These statements are instructions and warnings of risk, not mutual promises or a condition placed upon the sale. These package instructions are not in the form of a contractual agreement by the purchaser to limit reuse of the cameras. There was no showing of a "meeting of the minds" whereby the purchaser, and those obtaining the purchaser's discarded camera, may be deemed to have breached a contract or violated a license limited to a single use of the camera. *See Hercules, Inc. v. United States*, 516 U.S. 417, 424, 134 L. Ed. 2d 47, 116 S. Ct. 981 (1996) ("An agreement implied in fact is 'founded upon a meeting of minds, which, although not embodied in an express contract, is inferred, as a fact, from conduct of the parties showing, in the light of the surrounding circumstances, their tacit understanding.'") (quoting *Baltimore & Ohio R.R. Co. v. United States*, 261 U.S. 592, 67 L. Ed. 816, 43 S. Ct. 425 (1923)). We conclude that no license limitation may be implied from the circumstances of sale.

. . .

CONCLUSION

The judgment of patent infringement is reversed with respect to LFFPs for which the patent right was exhausted by first sale in the United States, and that were permissibly repaired. Permissible repair is limited, as discussed herein, to the steps of removing the cardboard cover, cutting open the casing, inserting new film and film container, resetting the film counter, resealing the casing, and placing the device in a new cardboard cover. Included in permissible repair is replacement of the battery in flash cameras and the winding wheel in the cameras that so require. For these products the Commission's orders are vacated.

LFFPs whose prior sale was not in the United States, or LFFPs remanufactured by procedures more extensive than those we hold to constitute repair, or whose remanufacturing procedures were withheld or insufficiently disclosed to the Commission, remain subject to the Commission's orders. For these products the Commission's orders are affirmed.

NOTES & QUESTIONS

1. Scope of an Implied License

In *Carborundum v. Molten Metal*, 72 F.3d 872 (Fed. Cir. 1995), the defendant, MMEI sold pumps that allowed customers to practice the plaintiff's patented process for purifying metals. MMEI's patent infringement liability turned, in part, on the scope of the patent license given by the plaintiff patent holder to its customers in connection with the plaintiff's sales of related, unpatented equipment:

> MMEI argues that [the plaintiff] Metaullics' sale of the pumps, which had no other use than in the '584 gas injection apparatus, resulted in an unrestricted implied license to practice the invention for the entire term of the '584 patent. MMEI further asserts that restrictions on an implied license cannot be implied, but must be express. Because Metaullics placed no express restrictions on the use of the pumps, MMEI posits that Metaullics' customers obtained an unrestricted implied license to practice the invention. Thus, according to MMEI, customers who replaced a Metaullics pump with an MMEI pump could not be direct infringers under the unrestricted implied license. Absent direct infringement, MMEI argues that it could not contribute to or induce infringement. Although we agree with MMEI that Metaullics' customers had an implied license to practice the invention claimed in the '584 patent, we disagree as to the scope and meaning of that license.
>
> . . .
>
> Here, Metaullics sold an unpatented pump; the only use of the pump was in the metal purification apparatus of the '584 patent. Metaullics did not place any express restrictions on its customers as to the use of the pump. The circumstances of such a sale plainly indicate that a license should be implied under the apparatus patent. Metaullics and

its customers are presumed to have intended that at the time the customer purchased the pump, the customer was free to use it for its intended purpose to practice the invention claimed in the '584 patent. . . . Otherwise, the pump was worthless because it had no other practical use. Moreover, once Metaullics sold the pump without restriction, the parties to the sale were presumed to have intended that the purchaser was free to repair it with parts obtained from any source. However, Metaullics and its customers cannot be presumed to have intended that under these circumstances the implied license extended beyond the life of the pump. Unless the circumstances indicate otherwise, an implied license arising from sale of a component to be used in a patented combination extends only for the life of the component whose sale and purchase created the license.

Carborundum, 72 F.3d at 878-79.

2. Contracting Around the First Sale Doctrine

Under the first sale doctrine, the earliest unconditioned sale of an article "exhausts" a patent owner's rights as to that article. By authorizing the unconditioned sale of the article, the patent owner grants to the buyer an implied license to use and sell the article and relinquishes the patent owner's control over the purchaser's use or subsequent sale of that article. To avoid triggering exhaustion under the first sale doctrine, transfers of rights may be couched in terms of a licensing agreement. An express license agreement obviates the implied license under the first sale doctrine and allows a patent holder to impose restrictions on a purchaser's use of an item. Expressing the transfer of rights in terms of a license rather than in terms of an outright sale gives the patent owner greater leeway to enforce use and sale restrictions on a purchaser.

Agricultural biotechnology is one field where use of such licensing is prevalent. Patented plants present the patent holder with the unique problem of being self-replicating inventions. "Plant innovation is borne in seeds, and at least in the case of self-pollinating plants (such as soybeans), seeds make hundreds of copies of themselves in the natural growth process. From the standpoint of a producer of innovation, the notion of a self-replicating invention presents as compelling a case for intellectual property intervention as can be imagined." Mark D. Janis & Jay P. Kesan, *U.S. Plant Variety Protection: Sound and Fury . . . ?*, 39 HOUS. L. REV. 727, 730 (2002). Producers of patented seeds turn to "bag-tag" licenses to place restrictions on a grower's use of the seed, thus shielding the seed from being the "subject of any unconditional sale" and "allowing seed companies to assert that the patent law exhaustion doctrine should not be triggered." *Id.* at 771 n.156. In *Monsanto Co. v. McFarling*, 302 F.3d 1291 (Fed. Cir. 2002), a farmer, McFarling, purchased patented genetically modified soybeans from Monsanto under a licensing agreement. He planted and harvested a crop, and saved the seeds for planting in the next season. McFarling argued that, by purchasing the seed from Monsanto, he had acquired the right to produce additional seeds for planting under the doctrines of patent exhaustion and first sale. The Federal Circuit disagreed:

The restrictions in the [parties' agreement] are within the scope of the patent grant, for the patents cover the seeds as well as the plants. The "first sale" doctrine of exhaustion of the patent right is not implicated, as the new seeds grown from the original batch had never been sold. The price paid by the purchaser "reflects only the value of the 'use' rights conferred by the patentee." (Citation omitted). The original sale of the seeds did not confer a license to construct new seeds, and since the new seeds were not sold by the patentee they entailed no principle of patent exhaustion.

Monsanto, 302 F.3d at 1298-99. The principle of exhaustion under the first sale doctrine does not apply to expressly conditioned sales or licenses and furthermore cannot "turn a conditioned sale into an unconditioned one." *Pioneer Hi-Bred Int'l, Inc. v. Ottawa Plant Food, Inc.*, 283 F. Supp. 2d 1018, 1033 (N.D. Iowa 2003) (quoting *Mallinckrodt, Inc. v. Medipart, Inc.*, 976 F.2d 700 (Fed. Cir. 1992)). "Bag-tag" licenses protect a patent owner by conferring less than all of the rights in a patented plant, and disclaiming an unconditioned sale of the entire material.

Software is another field where use of licensing agreements has attained widespread use. It is more common for software "sales" to be licenses rather than outright sales. Copyright law, like patent law, has a first sale doctrine. Form licenses for software were first developed to avoid the copyright first sale doctrine, which allowed an owner of a copy of a work to "sell or otherwise dispose of" the copy without the copyright holder's consent. *Step-Saver Data Systems, Inc. v. Wyse Technology*, 939 F.2d 91, 96 n.7 (3d Cir. 1991) (quoting Bobbs-Merrill Co. v. Straus, 210 U.S. 339 (1908)). Copying of the work was a great concern for software producers:

Under [the first sale] doctrine, one could purchase a copy of a computer program, and then lease it or lend it to another without infringing the copyright on the program. Because of the ease of copying software, software producers were justifiably concerned that companies would spring up that would purchase copies of various programs and then lease those to consumers. Typically, the companies, like a videotape rental store, would purchase a number of copies of each program, and then make them available for over-night rental to consumers. Consumers, instead of purchasing their own copy of the program, would simply rent a copy of the program, and duplicate it. This copying by the individual consumers would presumably infringe the copyright, but usually it would be far too expensive for the copyright holder to identify and sue each individual copier. Thus, software producers wanted to sue the companies that were renting the copies of the program to individual consumers, rather than the individual consumers. The first sale doctrine, though, stood as a substantial barrier to successful suit against these software rental companies, even under a theory of contributory infringement. By characterizing the original transaction between the software producer and the software rental company as a license, rather than a sale, and by making the license personal and non-transferable, software producers hoped to avoid the reach of the first sale doctrine and to establish a basis in state contract law for suing the software rental companies directly.

Step-Saver 939 F.2d at 96 n.7. The cost of software development, coupled with the ease of copying encouraged software producers to protect their program by licensing their material, rather than subjecting it to an outright sale. With a license, the software producer may prohibit the consumer from making and selling unauthorized copies of the program.

b. Compulsory Licenses

A compulsory license is a license forced upon a patent holder or other intellectual property owner by statute or court order. In the United States, compulsory licenses for patents are rarely awarded by courts or imposed by statutes. Even if a patentee refuses to license her patent to others, she usually may not be forced to do so against her will. The owner of a patent is not required to license the patent and is allowed to unilaterally refuse to grant a license.

Under limited circumstances, a court may award a mandatory license or dedicate the patent to the public. These circumstances include when a patentee is found to have engaged in illegal or injurious conduct beyond a mere refusal to grant a license; when the patentee is found to have violated antitrust laws; and when public health, public safety, or some other public interest is implicated. Compulsory licensing most commonly appears in fields that impact public health or safety, justified by "public necessity."

Besides judicially awarded compulsory licenses, Congress may enact statutes that permit use of a patented invention without the patent owner's consent. Congress has passed mandatory licensing statutes that require patentees to license their inventions. Examples include, the Clean Air Act of 1970, 42 U.S.C. § 1857h-6; the Plant Variety Protection Act, 7 U.S.C. § 2402; and the Helium Act, 50 U.S.C. § 1678. In addition, the United States government may take and use patented inventions. When the United States government uses a patented invention without the permission of the patent owner, Title 28 of the United States Code, Section 1498 restricts the remedy of the patent owner to "action against the United States in the United States Court of Federal Claims for the recovery of his reasonable and entire compensation for such use and manufacture." 28 U.S.C. § 1498.

The pharmaceutical industry is a favorite target of proposed mandatory licensing statutes. Congress has proposed bills that, for example, would have allowed the FTC to order the "unrestricted, unconditional compulsory licensing of patents and trademarks related to prescription pharmaceuticals." *See* H.R. 9276, 94th Cong., 1st Sess. ("Prescription Drug Patent Licensing Act"). Another bill would have imposed what would have amounted to a compulsory trademark and trade dress license by barring protection under the Lanham Act for distinctive colors and pharmaceutical product configurations. See H.R. 6840, 97th Cong., 2d Sess. None of these proposals have been enacted into law. The most recent threat of pharmaceutical compulsory licensing by the United States government arose in the aftermath of the tragedies of September 11, 2001. From October 4 to November 20, 2001, the United States faced a national crisis after twenty-two cases of anthrax were reported on the East Coast, resulting in five fatalities.

The drug approved to combat anthrax, ciprofloxacin (commonly known as Cipro), became the target of a threat of compulsory licensing by Secretary of Health and Human Services, Tommy Thompson. Secretary Thompson threatened to disregard the patent covering Cipro, owned by the German drug company Bayer, if the drug manufacturer would not reduce its drug price. Bayer quickly complied.

Internationally, the World Trade Organization's agreement on Trade Related Intellectual Property Rights (TRIPS) established minimum standards of protection for intellectual property but also provided exceptions to override patent rights for public health reasons. Article 27(2) of the TRIPS agreement allows members to exclude patent protection to the extent "necessary to protect ordre public or morality, including to protect human, animal, or plant life or health or to avoid serious prejudice to the environment." Some have noted that the doctrine of "ordre public" may allow member countries to suspend patent protection for certain patents. In addition, article 31 of the TRIPS agreement expressly permits compulsory licensing. Member nations must first unsuccessfully attempt to obtain a voluntary license from the patent holder before compulsorily licensing the patent. However, the requirement for applying for a voluntary license is waived for "national emergency or other circumstances of extreme urgency or in cases of public non-commercial use." Further, for pharmaceuticals, Article 31(f) permits a country that lacks drug-manufacturing capabilities to import compulsorily licensed pharmaceuticals from another country.

5.   Cross-Licensing

a.   Why Enter Into a Cross-Licensing Agreement?

TEXAS INSTRUMENTS v. HYUNDAI ELECTRONICS INDUSTRIES
United States District Court for the Eastern District of Texas
49 F. Supp. 2d 893 (1999)

HEARFIELD, District Judge.

On May 1, 1998, Texas Instruments sued Hyundai for patent infringement in this Court and in several other courts across the nation and, eventually, around the world. Simultaneously, Hyundai sued Texas Instruments for declaratory judgment and, eventually, patent infringement.

Seven cases between Texas Instruments and Hyundai eventually ended up in this Court; this case (the "74 Case") was the first set for trial on Monday, March 8, 1999. . . . After approximately two days of deliberations, the jury returned a verdict of infringement against Hyundai and in favor of Texas Instruments assessing damages at twenty-five million, two-hundred thousand United States dollars ($ 25,200,000.00). The jury further found that Hyundai willfully infringed Texas Instruments' patents. After the jury returned a verdict of infringement against Hyundai and in favor of Texas Instruments, this Court tried the remaining defense of patent misuse. . . .

I. FINDINGS OF FACT

1. Article 5.2(A)(ii) — The Sales Cap Provision That Won't Go Away

So Article 5.2(A)(ii), we meet again. Article 5.2(A)(ii) is the "sale cap" termination provision that automatically terminates the parties' License Agreement when Hyundai's worldwide sales of royalty bearing products reaches three billion eight hundred ninety-five million United States dollars ($3,895,000,000.00). The parties fell into a dispute over the proper interpretation of this unique provision. Texas Instruments argued that "royalty bearing products" included *all* products sold by Hyundai regardless whether those particular products were "covered by" a valid Texas Instruments patent — products which practiced a Texas Instruments patent, in force at the time the product is sold, in the country in which the sale occurs (the "TI Countries"). Hyundai disagreed. Hyundai argued that "royalty bearing products" were limited to products "covered by" a valid Texas Instruments patent — that is, products which practiced a Texas Instruments patent, in force at the time the product is sold, in the country in which the sale occurs.

. . .

3. A Primer on Patent Portfolio Cross-License Agreements

. . . Texas Instruments has over four thousand (4,000) patents and files between seven hundred (700) and eight hundred (800) patent applications each year. Just last year, Texas Instruments had six hundred and eleven (611) new patents issued. Hyundai has over one thousand two hundred (1,200) patents in the United States with a large number of pending applications. Large companies like Texas Instruments and Hyundai literally have thousands of patents around the world. With so many patents worldwide, it is quite possible for Texas Instruments and Hyundai to have multiple patents maturing and expiring every day.

A party to a license agreement covering only a single patent would have to determine before selling its product in a different country whether its sales would infringe any patents of the other party. This patent-specific determination would have to be done continually since new patents are constantly being issued. Moreover, these searches would also have to be done every time a party made a change in an existing product or came up with a new product. This patent-specific endeavor is extremely expensive and time-consuming. The product in question would have to be examined in detail and compared to the elements of the claims of the patent in question. Depending on the type of product, this product examination could take several months and costs tens of thousands of dollars — all to evaluate a single product against a single patent.

For parties with large semiconductor patent portfolios like Texas Instruments and Hyundai, what is the solution? Enter the patent portfolio cross-license agreement. The portfolio license is widely used in the semiconductor industry because it is almost impossible on a patent-by-patent, country-by-country, product-by-product basis to determine whether someone is using a company's patents in a given country and provide protection for patents not yet issued. First, under a patent-specific license agreement, the parties have an extremely difficult time tracking the sales that should be included in the royalty base. This difficulty arises from the fact that the holder of a patent is entitled to receive royalties for items sold both directly and indirectly into the country where the patent exists. Parties to license agreements track indirect sales in order to receive full and fair value for their patents. If parties look only at direct sales, they are not receiving fair value for their patents. Tracking sales that come into a specific country is exceedingly difficult, for the party trying to track indirect sales has to know not only where the other party is selling its products, but also the identity of the purchasers in order to determine the likelihood that those products would come into a country where the other party has patents. Second, worldwide license rights are necessary in the semiconductor market because the semiconductor market is a worldwide market. Companies in the semiconductor market do not have the luxury of selling only in one country. Third, for parties with large patent portfolios like Texas Instruments and Hyundai, it is impossible to examine the entire portfolio on a patent-by-patent, country-by-country basis for all possible products. Finally, it is impossible to determine whether a specific product is "covered by" a patent without litigation. By using this expansive cross-license agreement mechanism — the portfolio license — mammoth companies in the semiconductor industry like Texas Instruments and Hyundai avoid the costly and inefficient endeavor of a patent-by-patent licensing scheme.

4. This License Agreement Was a Portfolio Cross-License Agreement

The 1993 License Agreement was a portfolio cross-license agreement because Hyundai wanted "as broad as possible [a] license under [Texas Instruments'] patents." Hyundai's Mr. M. B. Chung specifically asked for a ten-year license that included Texas Instruments' entire portfolio, worldwide in scope, including all of Hyundai's products. Having just completed a license agreement with Samsung, Texas Instruments offered Hyundai a license with the same terms. Hyundai refused and requested Texas Instruments first demonstrate its patents would be of value to Hyundai. This is not a cheap endeavor. Indeed, Texas Instruments spent tens of thousands of dollars and several months complying with Hyundai's request. Due to the expense and time involved in this endeavor, Texas Instruments used only a very few of its patents as a proxy for the value of its entire portfolio.

After Hyundai started to bite and the cork started to bob, Texas Instruments offered Hyundai the same terms previously accepted by Samsung — a "running royalty" of nine (9) percent on sales of DRAMs ("dynamic random access memory" products) in the United States, and three (3) percent on sales of DRAMs in Japan. Texas Instruments proposed the "running royalty" agreement because it is the easiest way to accurately measure royalties. With a "running royalty," if sales go up, so does the total royalty payment. Conversely, if sales go down, so does the total royalty payment. Simply put, a running royalty is self-correcting.

Hyundai absolutely refused to discuss any running royalty; instead, Hyundai insisted on a fixed (or lump-sum) approach. In April 1991, and again in June 1991, Texas Instruments offered Hyundai a running-royalty rate of nine (9) percent on United States DRAM sales, and three (3) percent on Japan DRAM sales. Why did Texas Instruments" running-royalty proposal focus on DRAM sales in the United States and Japan? At that time, Texas Instruments' negotiations with other semiconductor companies had established the reasonableness of Texas Instruments' proposed royalties, and because most DRAMs initially were sold into these two countries. Nonetheless, tracking sales into the United States and Japan remained an extremely difficult task because many companies were selling products into those countries F.O.B. ("free on board") at a foreign country. Further, tracking indirect sales requires pouring over licensee's books to see where and to whom products are being sold. There remains the task of contacting the licensee's customers to determine the quantity of DRAMs placed into a product delivered to the United States. All of this is virtually impossible; and the best a party can do is estimate the level of indirect sales.

Between April 1992 and September 1992, the parties underwent further negotiations. Not surprisingly, negotiations failed.

So, in September 1992, Texas Instruments filed a lawsuit against Hyundai in this very Court asserting Hyundai infringed a number of Texas Instruments' patents relating to the production of semiconductor memory chips. . . .

After the filing of the September 1992 lawsuit, Texas Instruments and Hyundai held two face-to-face meetings in October 1992 — one in San Francisco and the other in Phoenix. Texas Instruments' initial objective during these and other negotiations was to obtain a running royalty from Hyundai's sale of semiconductor products. . . . At the other end of the spectrum, Hyundai's initial objective during these and other negotiations was to obtain a fixed (or lump-sum) royalty.

In October of 1992, Texas Instruments and Hyundai reached an agreement that Hyundai would pay one hundred and nine million, nine hundred ninety-two thousand United States dollars ($ 109,992,000.00) for a fixed ten (10) year license to Texas Instruments' patents to be paid over the life of the license. At Texas Instruments' request, these payments were structured as maximum annual royalties also known as "royalty caps." But a problem remained. This lump sum was not self-correcting like the running royalty often used by Texas Instruments. That is, if Hyundai experienced extraordinary growth during the term of the license, the fixed sum would not take that unexpected growth (and thus sales) into account. . . .

Enter the sales-cap termination clause. For the License Agreement, Texas Instruments would accept one hundred and ten million United States dollars ($ 110,000,000.00) for a certain *volume* of license rights. When Hyundai consumed those license rights, the License Agreement would automatically terminate. If Hyundai did not consume those license rights, the License Agreement would continue until December 31, 2000. In other words, this sales-cap termination clause simply the converse of a running royalty. In a running royalty the term is fixed and the payment floats. Under this License Agreement and its sales-cap termination clause, the payment is fixed and the term floats. It was a rather clever solution.

. . . Hyundai offered an additional five million United States dollars ($5,000,000.00) in royalties from 1997 through 2001 to address Texas Instruments' concerns about Hyundai's potential for extraordinary growth. These additional five million United States dollars ($ 5,000,000.00) in royalties would be forthcoming if Hyundai's growth rate from 1997 to 2001 exceeded a factor of 1.811.

But what if Hyundai's growth exceeded that? Well, under Hyundai's proposal, the risk of Hyundai's extraordinary growth fell on Texas Instruments since Texas Instruments would be limited to the five million United States dollars ($5,000,000.00) should that risk become a reality. By shoving the risk of its own growth onto Texas Instruments, Hyundai, through its own extraordinary growth, would profit from the License Agreement at the expense of Texas Instruments. If Hyundai experienced extraordinary growth, Texas Instruments would be denied a fair return on its intellectual property. Indeed, if Texas Instruments had agreed to Hyundai's proposal and Hyundai had indeed experienced extraordinary growth, Texas Instruments' ability to negotiate licenses with other companies would become much more difficult. Companies often discover what others pay for licenses, which in turn sets a ceiling on what these companies would be willing to pay in the next round of negotiations. The next company sitting across the table from Texas Instruments would want a similar deal *at Texas Instruments' expense*. Simply put, the next guy would want too sweet of a deal from Texas Instruments. The net result would be to deprive Texas Instruments of a fair return on its intellectual property and its investment in research and development. For these and various other reasons, Texas Instruments rejected Hyundai's proposal.

From November 1992 to March 1993 both Texas Instruments and Hyundai struggled to negotiate a compromise. . . . Texas Instruments would agree to a running royalty of eight and a half percent (8.5%) *after* the [sales cap] had been reached. . . . Hyundai responded to Texas Instruments' suggestion by proposing that the License Agreement terminate (instead of providing for a running royalty) [once the sales cap had been reached].

Article 5.2(A)(ii) contains the unique sales-cap termination clause. Hyundai argues that this unique sales-cap termination clause operates to "tie-out" Hyundai's sales, and, consequently, subject Texas Instruments to the defense of patent misuse. First, the sales-cap provision does not restrict Hyundai's sales. The obvious purpose of the provision was to satisfy Hyundai's desire for a definite and certain royalty obligation while also satisfying Texas Instruments' desire for protection from Hyundai's potential for extraordinary growth. Texas Instruments feared Hyundai's potential for extraordinary growth; running royalty was the common cure for such fear. Hyundai apparently had some aversion to the running royalty; instead, Hyundai desired a definite and more certain royalty obligation than the running royalty afforded. Thus, the parties worked together to create a unique solution; give Hyundai the lump sum it wanted but limit the life of the License Agreement to a certain amount of worldwide sales — Article 5.2(A)(ii). This provision picks up where the lack of a running royalty leaves off — it measures Hyundai's growth over the life of the agreement. If Hyundai indeed experiences extraordinary growth, Texas Instruments will not suffer under the License Agreement's fixed (lump) sum royalty since Article 5.2(A)(ii) will automatically terminate the License Agreement prior to Texas Instruments' failing to receive a fair return on its intellectual property.

Prior to the start of negotiations for a new license agreement, Hyundai never asserted any view of Article 5.2(A)(ii) that differed from Texas Instruments' view of this provision. Indeed, a March 25, 1993 Hyundai document reveals that Hyundai had exactly the same view as Texas Instruments. In that Hyundai memorandum from Mr. M.B. Chung to the Chairman of Hyundai, Mr. M.B. Chung told Hyundai's chairman that "our side" has proposed the termination cap and that Mr. M.B. Chung understood that, assuming sixteen percent (16%) growth by Hyundai, the License Agreement would expire in the first quarter of 1999. Indeed, in making that determination, Mr. M.B. Chung himself performed his calculation on Hyundai's worldwide sales of integrated circuits (IC).

Texas Instruments' fear of Hyundai's potential for "extraordinary growth" was soon realized. Since negotiating the License Agreement, Hyundai manufactured so many more DRAMs than originally expected that Hyundai moved from being in the top twenty-five (25) world DRAM manufacturers before the agreement to number two (2) in the world by 1998.

Article 5.2(A)(ii) — the unique sales-cap termination clause — does not penalize Hyundai. The cap merely reflects a compromise between the parties — a unique way to measure Hyundai's sales growth based on the administratively convenient measure of worldwide sales. Texas Instruments did not force or coerce Hyundai into entering into the License Agreement containing the termination cap.

NOTES & QUESTIONS

1. Blocking Patents

Blocking patents are present where two or more parties hold patents that do not permit each party to practice its patent without obtaining permission from the other. This situation may arise, for example, when an inventor patents an improvement on a patented technology but does not hold the patent to the underlying technology. The holder of improvement's patent cannot practice the improvement without permission from the patentee of the underlying technology. In this situation, the two patents block each other such that permission from both patent holders is required to practice the improvement. Facing such a conundrum, parties may enter into a cross-licensing agreement.

Cross-licensing eliminates an otherwise existing blockage by allowing parties to covenant not to sue for infringement on certain patents. Parties are then free to practice the patented technologies separately without fear of having to defend against an infringement suit. When cross-licenses are employed to eliminate blocking patents by allowing parties to use patented technology without being held up by other patent holders, the practice of using cross-licenses is considered productive, pro-competitive, and not in violation of antitrust laws.

2. Use of Cross-Licensing in Resolution of Patent Litigation

Notice that Texas Instruments and Hyundai entered into a cross-licensing agreement only after Texas Instruments had filed an action of infringement against Hyundai. Cross-licensing may be used to settle or avoid infringement actions. When a cross-licensing agreement is entered into as part of a settlement agreement to unblock conflicting patent claims, the use is not considered anticompetitive and does not run afoul of antitrust laws. In *Dunlap Corp. v. Deering Milliken, Inc.,* 540 F.2d 1215 (4th Cir. 1976), the court noted:

> [T]he settlement of patent litigation, in and of itself, does not violate the antitrust laws. It is well established that "where there are legitimately conflicting [patent] claims or threatened interferences, a settlement by agreement, rather than by litigation, is not precluded by the [Sherman] Act." . . . It is only when settlement agreements are entered into in bad faith and are utilized as part of a scheme to restrain or monopolize trade that antitrust violations may occur.

Id. at 1220. What amounts to a use of cross-licensing in settlement agreements that violates the law? Cross-licensing agreements run afoul of antitrust laws if they are a means to carry out conduct that constitutes patent misuse, such as price fixing, tying, or market division.

3. Use in Joint R&D

In areas of developing technology, parties may enter into cross-licensing agreements in order to foster joint research and development (R&D) efforts. In 1984, Congress passed the National Cooperative Research Act (NCRA). The NCRA eliminated the per se rule of illegality for joint R&D ventures under state and federal law. Instead, cross-licensing agreements are judged on the basis of the rule of reason, where the purpose of the agreement is unlawful only if the agreement is used to accomplish the following:

(i)   Preserve the parties' dominant or monopoly market share;

(ii) Exclude competitors from the market;

(iii) Block the issuance of further licenses without mutual consent from the parties;

(iv) Fix prices;

(v)   Allocate customers or geographic markets — it is also unlawful for competitors limited to agree to cross-licenses in a particular field of use, which has the effect of allocating customers or markets.

The NCRA also grants joint researchers immunity from treble damage liability for conduct in the course of the joint venture if the researchers notify the DOJ and Federal Trade Commission and publish a notice of the joint venture in the Federal Register. Additionally, the NCRA provides joint researchers additional protection by permitting recovery of attorneys' fees from claimants who unsuccessfully bring actions for damages against the joint venture's conduct.

Recovery of the fees is limited to the extent that the claim was "frivolous, unreasonable, without foundation, or in bad faith."

4. Unique Industry Practices

In some industries, the sheer number of patents and the difficulty of determining infringement among industry participants make cross-licensing an indispensable part of unique industry practices. Without cross-licenses, threats of infringement suits impede the conduct of business by industry members. One well-known example where cross-licensing has become a regular and highly important industry practice is the semiconductor device industry.

To resolve the patent blockage problem, dominant parties in an industry may create a form license agreement on behalf of the entire industry. The agreement often requires patent cross-licensing arrangements. Royalty arrangements in the form license may call for royalty-free licenses, or may alternatively require equal percentage royalties from all participants, with the party having the largest sales paying a "balancing" payment to the other participants for sales in excess of the other participant's sales. Industry licensing agreements usually cover patents that have issued, patents applied for up to the date of the agreement, and future patents that issue during a defined period, typically five years, after the date of the agreement.

A drafter of an industry form licensing agreement must take care to assure the clarity of the license, especially if they are the sole author of the agreement. Critically, in some jurisdictions, any ambiguity in an agreement is automatically resolved against its drafter. For example, in *Intel Corp. v. VIA Techs., Inc.*, 319 F.3d 1357 (Fed. Cir. 2003), an ambiguity in a cross-licensing agreement drafted solely by Intel was resolved against Intel without reference to extrinsic evidence.

5. Grant Back Provisions

A grant-back provision is a condition in a licensing agreement that requires a licensee to grant to the licensor any improvements made upon the invention. A grant-back provision may require a patentee to grant a licensee a license to use unpatented improvements on the patented invention. Improvements can come from the patentee or from a licensor, with an agreement that the licensee communicates the improvement to the licensor, who then communicates it to other licensees.

Grant-back provisions are permitted when used to legitimately protect a licensor's position of competition in the market by allowing the licensor to keep current with improvements on her patented inventions. Such use is justified because, if not for the basic license, a licensee would not have been able to compete with the licensor. Courts frown upon grant-back provisions if they are used to extend the scope of the patentee's statutory monopoly for the purpose of creating a position of market control. Such use violates the provisions of the Sherman Act.

b. Antitrust Considerations and Patent Misuse: The *Texas Instrument* Saga Continues

TEXAS INSTRUMENTS v. HYUNDAI ELECTRONICS INDUSTRIES
United States District Court for the Eastern District of Texas
49 F. Supp. 2d 893 (1999)

HEARTFIELD, District Judge.

. . .

II. CONCLUSIONS OF LAW

1. The Life and Death of Per Se Patent Misuse Due to Tying

"Patent misuse is an affirmative defense to an accusation of patent infringement, the successful assertion of which 'requires that the alleged infringer show that the patentee has impermissibly broadened the "physical or temporal scope" of the patent grant with anticompetitive effect.'" All that a successful defense of patent misuse means is that a court of equity will not lend its support to enforcement of a misuser's patent. Patent misuse? Where did that come from? Apparently, it developed, in part, from salt tablets.

In 1942 the United States Supreme Court faced an attempt by G.S. Suppiger to make "use of its patent monopoly to restrain competition in the marketing of unpatented articles, salt tablets for use with the patented machines, and is aiding in the creation of a limited monopoly in the tablets not within that granted by the patent." *Morton Salt Co. v. G.S. Suppiger Co.,* 314 U.S. 488, 491 (1942). That is, the patentee G.S. Suppiger permitted the licensee to use with Suppiger's patented, salt-tablet-dispensing machines *only those salt tablets sold by the patentee.* Don't bother passing us the Suppiger salt, opined the Supreme Court as it affirmed the district court's dismissal of Suppiger's complaint "for want of equity[]." . . . That is, the Supreme Court would not maintain an infringement suit by Suppiger since it was engaged in patent misuse.

But what about *per se* patent misuse? Where did that come from? The rule was first enunciated in *International Salt Co. v. United States,* 332 U.S. 392, 396 (1947), and has been endorsed by this Court many times since. More important, does *per se* patent misuse still live? Texas Instruments says it is dead — laid to rest by Congress' passage of the 1988 Patent Misuse Act:

(d) No patent owner otherwise entitled to relief for infringement of a patent shall be denied relief or deemed guilty of misuse or illegal extension of the patent right by reason of his having done one or more of the following:

. . . (5) conditioned the license of any rights to the patent or the sale of the patented product on the acquisition of a license to rights in another patent or purchase of a separate product, unless, in view of the circumstances, the patent owner has market power in the relevant market for the patent or patented product on which the license or sale is conditioned.

35 U.S.C. § 271(d)(5).

First, this Court specifically notes that the Federal Circuit merely recognized that the courts have *historically* identified tying practices as constituting *per se* patent misuse — something the Supreme Court itself has done before: "It is far too late in the history of our antitrust jurisprudence to question the proposition that certain tying arrangements pose an unacceptable risk of stifling competition and therefore are unreasonable 'per se'". . . . Moreover, § 271(d)(5) specifically notes that patent misuse-tying analysis is to be considered "in view of the circumstances, " strongly suggesting that rule-of-reason analysis — not *per se* analysis — applies. According to the Supreme Court, when conducting a rule-of-reason analysis, "the factfinder weighs *all of the circumstances of a case* in deciding whether a restrictive practice should be prohibited as imposing an unreasonable restraint on competition." Indeed, the legislative history of the 1988 Patent Misuse Reform Act supports the death of *per se* patent misuse due to tying: "The relevant legislative history consists of formal statements made on the House and Senate floors by Senator DeConcini, chairman of the Subcommittee on Patents, Copyrights and Trademarks, Senator Leahy, chairman of the Subcommittee on Technology and the Law, and Representative Kastenmeier, chairman of the Subcommittee on Courts, Civil Liberties and the Administration of Justice." 6 *Chisum on Patents* § 19.04[1], at 19-295 (1997). "The 'tying' provision was extensively discussed in both the House and Senate." *Id.*

In the House of Representatives, Rep. Kastenmeier discussed the intent to eliminate *per se* rules due to tying: "The underlying principle being advanced by this proposal is the elimination of any vestiges of a per se or automatic inference of patent misuse from certain tying practices," Rep. Kastenmeier further remarked that Congress's decision to require a specific assessment of market power "in view of the circumstances" was "used in this context in order to permit the courts to reasonably assess the potential for anticompetitive effect of a particular practice." Congress intended for the courts to evaluate business justifications for certain licensing practices (like tying practices) under a rule-of-reason analysis. In words strikingly on point for this case, Rep. Kastenmeier stated:

> It is also our intention to avoid the use of inflexible rules once a court has found that market power exists. There may be circumstances in which there is market power and a tie-in, but where a finding of misuse would be inappropriate. One example would be where the patent owner has a business justification for the licensing practice. In real world situations where the only practical way to meter output is to tie the sale of a patented product to the sale of another separate product, then such a practice would be legitimate, unless such a practice — on balance — has a generally anticompetitive effect.

In the Senate, Senators DeConcini and Leahy made clear that *per se* rules due to tying were being abolished by Section 271(d)(5), and that showings of unreasonableness and anticompetitive effect would be required before misuse based on tying would be found. . . . No contrary statement appears in the legislative history of Section 271(d)(5). Although there may still be *per se* patent misuse lurking out there somewhere, it does not exist for patent misuse due to tying. This Court holds that the Patent Misuse Reform Act of 1988 removed the doctrine of *per se* patent misuse due to tying.

Assuming *arguendo* that *per se* patent misuse somehow survived the 1988 Patent Misuse Reform Act (and it did not), it is of no consequence in this particular case. First, "it is only after considerable experience with certain business relationships that courts classify them as per se violations. . ." Both parties admit that the Article 5.2(a)(ii) — the "sales-cap" termination clause — is a unique provision. When queried by the Court whether either party knew of any misuse case that involved an arrangement identical or similar to the sales-cap provision at issue here, counsel for both Texas Instruments and Hyundai candidly admitted that they were aware of no such case. Moreover, the License Agreement and its unique sales-cap provision was the result of a settlement. Indeed, the parties entered into the April 26, 1993 License Agreement to settle litigation pending in this very court. In *Speed Shore Corp. v. Woudenberg Enterprises* the Ninth Circuit faced a similar situation. 605 F.2d 469 (9th Cir.1979). There, defendants had previously admitted manufacturing shoring devices that infringed the plaintiff's patent. The parties negotiated a settlement and entered into a license agreement. Later, the defendants argued that the negotiated license agreement fostered patent misuse:

> It is well recognized that settlement agreements are judicially favored as a matter of sound public policy. Settlement agreements conserve judicial time and limit expensive litigation. The defendants seem to argue, however, that the equitable doctrine of patent misuse prevails over the policy of favoring the settlement or disputes. In this case we disagree. . . We feel that to allow a subversion of the deeply-instilled policy of settlement of disputes by applying the doctrine of inequitable conduct, in the manner contended for by the defendants, would have the effect of stripping good-faith settlements of any meaning. We do not believe that the doctrine of inequitable conduct was intended to extend so far.

Speed Shore, 605 F.2d at 473-74. Similarly, Texas Instruments and Hyundai negotiated a settlement and entered into the License Agreement — including the sales-cap provision that Hyundai now contends is an improper tie-out. Both parties literally invented the sales-cap provision as a compromise between Texas Instruments' desire for a running royalty and Hyundai's insistence on a lump sum. In this very Court Hyundai settled pending litigation by helping invent a unique sales-cap provision and entering the fifty-five (55) page License Agreement. Now, Hyundai wants to void that License Agreement with the very same provision — a provision Hyundai helped invent. That is, Hyundai wants this Court to exercise its *equitable* power to void a provision Hyundai helped create. Finally, and most important, this Court finds that even if *per se* patent misuse were still alive (and it is not), Hyundai has failed to establish facts necessary to support even that defunct doctrine.

2. Analysis

As Hyundai points out in its brief, "to establish [a now defunct] *per se* misuse through a tie-out, Hyundai must show that: (1) two separable items are involved in the tying arrangement; (2) the tied item is capable of substantial non-infringing use; and (3) the two items actually are tied. . . . Finally, Hyundai must show (4) that TI has market power in a relevant market encompassing the tying item."

A. Hyundai's "Separable Items" Should Be "Separate Products" — And There Are None

One of the fundamental requirements of a tying violation is that there be two *separate products* to tie together. Hyundai argues that the separate products (or "separable items" to borrow Hyundai's term) are: 1) "the right to make, use or sell products which are covered by TI's portfolio, patent portfolio"; and 2) "the unfettered right of Hyundai to make, use or sell those products which are entirely outside the scope of TI's patents." Hyundai does not contend that identifiably separate products are tied under the License Agreement. Hyundai admits that no customer ever walked into Hyundai's shop and asked to buy a "covered DRAM" as opposed to an "uncovered DRAM." DRAMs are DRAMs. Hyundai's theory of "separateness" or "separability" attempts to artificially separate *the same product* into two different "categories" based on legal status — specifically, whether a Texas Instruments patent "covers" the product in the place where the product is initially sold.

This Court holds that Hyundai has failed to show that separate products are tied by the License Agreement. . . . Hyundai's artificial division of products into "covered" and "uncovered" categories overlooks the critical fact that, in the real world, the "covered" or "uncovered" legal status of a Hyundai product is indeterminate absent patent-by-patent, product-by-product, country-by-country litigation. This is precisely why mammoth companies in the semiconductor industry, like Texas Instrument and Hyundai enter into portfolio cross-licenses like the License Agreement at issue here.

In truth, when Hyundai signed the License Agreement, it purchased one "product" — a unitary covenant that Texas Instruments would not sue Hyundai over any integrated circuit (IC), anywhere, during the term of the agreement. Under the License Agreement, Hyundai enjoyed complete freedom of operation. The License Agreement relieved Hyundai from the onerous burden of constantly monitoring whether Texas Instruments had obtained new patents (and in what countries), whether existing products infringed on existing patents or on those new patents, and whether newly developed products infringed any Texas Instruments patent. As this Court noted in its February 4, 1999 *Memorandum and Opinion Order* interpreting the License Agreement, this result could not have been reached through a patent-by-patent licensing scheme, even if the patent-by-patent license encompassed all of Texas Instruments' extant patents at the time the agreement was signed. Nor could it have been reached by limiting the license to products that were "covered" when sold, since that would have left unlicensed the many Hyundai products that, although "uncovered" by a Texas Instruments patent when sold, eventually made their way into a country where Texas Instruments had patents. The License Agreement provided a single protection to all Hyundai integrated circuits — it provided every integrated circuit manufactured by Hyundai with the freedom to be moved anywhere in the world with full protection from Texas Instruments claims of infringement. . . .

B. Texas Instruments Does Not Have Market Power in a Relevant Market

Hyundai also fails to establish that Texas Instruments has market power in a relevant market. Market power requires that Hyundai show that Texas Instruments has the power "to force [Hyundai] to do something it would not do in a competitive market." . . . Hyundai's allegation of market power is simply that the United States government has granted Texas Instruments the legitimate right to exclude others from Texas Instruments' patented technology. But antitrust law dictates this is not impermissible market power.

Hyundai relies heavily on the fact that Texas Instruments has licensed its portfolio of patents related to the manufacture of DRAMs . . . to most, if not all of the major manufacturers throughout the world, including Hyundai. Moreover, argues Hyundai, Texas Instruments considers the . . . patents "very important" to the "manufacturing of DRAMs in the United States." Indeed, Texas Instruments' own witnesses testified that the . . . patents are "key process patents" and "the lock to the door" with respect to the manufacturing of semiconductor DRAMs. So what? Once again, anti-trust law holds this not impermissible market power.

Moreover, Hyundai's representative . . . and economic expert . . . urged that Texas Instruments' market power was measured by whether or not Texas Instruments has "blocking patents." Blocking patents? A blocking patent, in the case of a DRAM, would be a patent without which a DRAM could not be made. While Hyundai presented testimony that Texas Instruments believes [its] patents to be very important for the manufacture of DRAMs, Hyundai itself specifically testified it does not believe Texas Instruments has any blocking patents. . . .

Moreover, Hyundai has failed to show coercion. If, as Hyundai admitted, it did not believe Texas Instruments had blocking patents, how could it have been coerced?

C. Equity Does Not Lie With Hyundai

Patent misuse is an equitable defense. As such, Hyundai must be equitably entitled to invoke that defense. "'It is one of the fundamental principles upon which equity jurisprudence is founded, that before a complainant can have a standing in court he must first show that not only has he a good and meritorious cause of action, but he must come into court with clean hands.'"

Hyundai comes to this Court with unclean hands. Let's recap what Hyundai has done thus far. First, Hyundai approaches Texas Instruments in order to enter into a patent portfolio cross-license agreement. Texas Instruments, fearful of Hyundai's potential for extraordinary growth, suggests the self-correcting, oft-used "running royalty" which would accurately track Hyundai's sales and fairly compensate Texas Instruments for its intellectual property. Hyundai refuses to entertain the notion of a running royalty. Rather, Hyundai insists on paying a fixed (or lump) sum. If the parties use Texas Instruments' running royalty suggestion, the risk and expense of Hyundai's extraordinary growth falls on Hyundai, which must pay royalties on its unexpected, increased sales. Conversely, if the parties use Hyundai's fixed (or lump) sum suggestion, the risk and expense of Hyundai's extraordinary growth falls on Texas Instruments, which must sacrifice a fair return on its intellectual property as Hyundai's sales shoot through the roof and overshadows the fixed (or lump) sum.

So what did the parties do? What they should have done — they negotiated a compromise. Texas Instruments suggests a type of sales-cap termination clause that would measure the life of the License Agreement by the volume of Hyundai's sales. In response to this suggestion, Hyundai voluntarily helped create and refine a "sales-cap termination clause" — Article 5.2(A)(ii), the very sales-cap termination clause currently accused of generating patent misuse. This Court finds, as a matter of fact, that Hyundai *at the very least* helped draft and create the very sales-cap termination clause it now insists amounts to patent misuse. Hyundai signed the License Agreement with the sales-cap termination clause and Texas Instruments dismissed its pending lawsuit against Hyundai. All was well until. . . .

On January 20, 1998 — roughly five years after the contract was signed — Hyundai injected a never before mentioned interpretation of Article 5.2(A)(ii) into the discussion — the "TI Country Concept." Why? Because Hyundai is trying to avoid the consequences of its own extraordinary growth. Rather than honor Article 5.2(A)(ii) — the sales-cap termination clause it helped create — Hyundai tries like the dickens to force the risk and expense of its own extraordinary growth onto Texas Instruments — *precisely what Article 5.2(A)(ii) was designed to avoid.* Much like its strained interpretation of the parties' License Agreement, it gets worse.

Hyundai carries its "TI Country Concept" into this Court and urges a strained interpretation of Article 5.2(A)(ii) contrary to what the extrinsic evidence now shows. Indeed, relying on New York law's inadmissibility of extrinsic evidence for the interpretation of unambiguous contracts, Hyundai actually urged an interpretation *opposite* to that of a patent portfolio cross-license. Despite being unable to consider the extrinsic evidence *which clearly shows this License Agreement to be a portfolio cross-license agreement*, this Court nonetheless rejected Hyundai's "TI Country Concept" and, for all practical purposes, held the License Agreement to be a portfolio cross-license agreement.

Then, six (6) days before the jury trial of this case, Hyundai amends its answer to include this defense of patent misuse. Despite a twenty-five million and two-hundred thousand United States dollar ($ 25,200,000.00) jury verdict in its favor, Texas Instruments must undergo further delay as it prepares for this subsequent bench trial. And prepare for what? The re-appearance of Hyundai's "TI Country Concept." Hyundai's defense of patent misuse relies upon the "TI Country Concept's" "covered" versus "uncovered" artificiality already rejected by this Court.

Ever since it introduced its "TI Country Concept" on January 20, 1998, Hyundai has consistently done one thing: try to avoid the risk and expense of its own extraordinary growth. Rather than honor Article 5.2(A)(ii) — the sales-cap provision designed to insure the risk of Hyundai's extraordinary growth would fall on Hyundai *and not Texas Instruments* — Hyundai consistently tried to deflect the consequences of its extraordinary growth onto Texas Instruments.

Finally, it would be inequitable, and contrary to all notions of fairness, to allow Hyundai to claim that counting "uncovered" products toward the termination cap results in misuse, when Hyundai itself proposed a construction of the License Agreement that did the same thing.

Suffice it to say that Hyundai does not come to this Court with clean hands — just the opposite. Accordingly, equity does not lie with Hyundai.

D.   The License Agreement is Terminated — TERMINATED

It was with a tremendous amount of deja vu that this Court undertook this patent misuse defense discussion. In its February 4, 1999 *Memorandum and Opinion Order*, this Court ruled that the License Agreement terminated according to the automatic triggering of Article 5.2(A)(ii) — the sales-cap provision. In that opinion, this Court specifically rejected Hyundai's "covered" versus "uncovered" theory (the "TI Country Concept") with respect to the definition of "royalty bearing products" and, consequently, calculation of Hyundai's worldwide sales applicable to the sales-cap calculation. This Court thought it had lain to rest Hyundai's strained, artificial parsing of the License Agreement's language by rejecting Hyundai's "TI Country Concept" and finding that the contract had, in fact, terminated.

But nestled within that fifty-five (55) page, dead License Agreement (that Hyundai helped draft), Hyundai managed to discover (a mere six (6) days before trial) this defense of patent misuse. We've passed the point of beating a dead horse — now we're tenderizing it. It is time, once and for all, for Hyundai to come to grips with the death of the License Agreement — a death brought about by Hyundai's own extraordinary growth.

III.   CONCLUSION

Hyundai's *per se* patent misuse defense fails for a variety of reasons. First, there is no such thing as *per se* patent misuse due to tying. Congress' passage of the Patent Misuse Reform Act of 1988 eliminated *per se* patent misuse due to tying. Hyundai's reading of the Federal Circuit's subsequent Virginia Panel case mirrors its strained interpretation of the parties' License Agreement. This Court does not read Virginia Panel for the proposition that Congress failed to eliminate *per se* patent misuse due to tying. Second, assuming *arguendo* that *per se* patent misuse still exists (and it does not), Hyundai fails as a matter of fact to establish there are separate products; Hyundai fails to show these "separable" products are tied; and Hyundai fails to establish that Texas Instruments has power in a relevant market. Finally,

Hyundai comes to this Court with the same, tired "TI Country Concept" already rejected by this Court in its interpretation of the parties' License Agreement. Rather than honor Article 5.2(A)(ii) — the sales-cap termination clause — and assume the risk and expense of its own extraordinary growth, Hyundai resurrects its previously rejected "TI Country Concept" to bolster its patent misuse defense. Well, this Court puts it down again. Hyundai does not come to this Court with unclean hands. Accordingly, even assuming Hyundai had established *per se* patent misuse or just plain patent misuse, this Court refuses to lend the support of equity to a party with such unclean hands.

In sum, Hyundai has significantly failed to make out the essential elements of its equitable patent-misuse defense. In light of this failure, and for the reasons set out above, this Court DISMISSES Hyundai's Sixth Affirmative Defense.

IT IS SO ORDERED.

6. Patent Pools

MATSUSHITA ELECTRICAL INDUSTRIAL CO., LTD. v. CINRAM INTERNATIONAL, INC.
United States District Court for the District of Delaware
299 F. Supp. 2d 370 (2004)

ROBINSON, Chief Judge.

I.   INTRODUCTION

Matsushita Electric Industrial Co., Ltd ("MEI") filed an action against Cinram International, Inc. ("Cinram") . . . for patent infringement . . . related to optical discs, including digital versatile discs ("DVDs"). Cinram filed . . . antitrust counterclaims against MEI. . . . Cinram specifically charges that MEI has conspired to restrain trade by participating in the non-exclusive DVD 6C Licensing Agency (the "6C Pool") in violation of Section 1 of the Sherman Act, 15 U.S.C. § 1. Cinram also alleges that MEI and other members of the 6C Pool have conspired, attempted, and committed the offense of monopolization in violation of Section 2 of the Sherman Act, 15 U.S.C. § 2. Cinram alleges that it has experienced harm to its business and properties and been forced to pay excessive patent royalties as a result of MEI's illegal actions. It also alleges that it is unable to license and exercise patents related to DVD technology on competitive terms. To redress these injuries, "Cinram seeks to have MEI license 6C Pool members and independent licensees, through the 6C Pool and individually, on non-discriminatory terms, so that pool members and independent licensees pay the same royalties (while each pool member receives a share of pool royalties collected based on its patent contribution). In short, Cinram . . . [seeks] to level the unlevel playing field."

II. BACKGROUND

. . .

2. The 6C Pool

The DVD Forum is an international association of companies that are engaged in the research, development, manufacture, and/or sales related to DVD technology. The DVD Forum was founded in 1995 by MEI under the name "DVD Consortium." Around 1995, the DVD Forum agreed on specifications for the recording, production, replication, and use of both DVDs and DVD equipment (the "DVD Standard Specification").

After establishing the DVD Standard Specification, six members of the DVD Forum, namely MEI, Hitachi, Mitsubishi, Toshiba, JVC, and AOL-Time Warner, organized the "6C Pool" and entered an agreement to manage the intellectual property rights around their DVD patented technology (the "6C Pool Formation Agreement").[2] Under the terms of the 6C Pool Formation Agreement, each member of the 6C Pool contributed one or more of its patents related to DVD technology to the pool to form a collection of patents "essential" to DVD production. Each pool member acquired a cross-license to the other members' "essential" patents in exchange for its contribution. The members agreed as part of formation to offer a non-exclusive, non-transferable license to these pooled patents to non-member companies interested in replicating DVDs in compliance with the DVD Standard Specification ("independent replicator"). To this end, the members drafted a standard license agreement to facilitate licensing the pooled patents (the "6C Pool License"). Section 2.1 of the 6C Pool License specifically recites:

> Licensor hereby grants to Licensee and its Affiliates a non-exclusive, non-transferable license to make, have made, use, sell, and otherwise dispose of DVD Products under the DVD Patents or any of their claims pursuant to the Conditions of Exhibit 3.

Also as part of formation, each member consented to offer individual licenses to its "essential" DVD patents on a non-exclusive basis to interested third party licensees as an alternative to the 6C Pool License. The members incorporated this option into the 6C Pool License to notify potential licensees of a separate means of acquiring licenses for "essential" patents. Section 2.3 of the 6C Pool License specifically recites:

> Instead of dealing with Licensor to obtain licenses for DVD patents of the members of the Group, Licensee shall have the option to negotiate and take a license under any DVD Patents and other related patents owned by each member of the Group pursuant to separate negotiations with each of the members on fair, reasonable, and non-discriminatory terms, whether or not Licensee intends to manufacture and/or sell DVD Products in conformity with the DVD Standard Specifications.

---

[2] [FN2] IBM has since joined the 6C Pool.

In view of Sections 2.1 and 2.3 of the 6C Pool License, an independent replicator who wishes to make DVDs without infringing any DVD patent, therefore, has the option of approaching either the 6C Pool for a 6C Pool License or each member of the 6C Pool for individual licenses.

The 6C Pool initially charged independent replicators $0.075 per disc under the 6C Pool License. The members later lowered the price to $0.065 or $0.05 per disc, depending upon when the independent replicator negotiated its 6C Pool License. MEI serves as the licensing agent to the Americas on behalf of the 6C Pool.

In addition to owning patents relating to DVD technology, MEI, JVC, AOL-Time Warner, and Mitsubishi commercially replicate DVDs. These four pool members, consequently, are in competition with independent replicators who must take either a 6C Pool License or individual licenses to avoid patent infringement. Indeed, MEI is a direct competitor of Cinram in the market for wholesale production of DVDs in the DVD-Video and DVD-ROM formats. Moreover, MEI may practice DVD technology in compliance with the DVD Standard Specification without owing the same per disc license fees that Cinram must pay as a 6C Pool licensee; MEI only pays a $0.0015 per disc royalty whereas Cinram must pay a $0.05 per disc royalty.

3. Business Review Letter from the United States Department of Justice

In October 1998, the 6C Pool requested a Business Review Letter from the United States Department of Justice ("DOJ"). . . . The 6C Pool specifically asked for a statement of the DOJ's antitrust enforcement intentions with respect to the 6C Pool's plan to assemble and offer a package license to "essential" patents, to manufacture products in compliance with the DVD-ROM and DVD-Video formation, and to distribute royalty income to members of the 6C Pool. . . .

Based on [the representations offered by the 6C Pool], the DOJ issued a Business Review Letter on June 10, 1999 indicating that it would not initiate an enforcement action. The DOJ found that the 6C Pool was "likely to combine complementary patent rights, thereby lowering the costs of manufacturers that need access to them in order to produce discs, players and decoders in conformity with the DVD-Video and DVD-ROM formats." The DOJ concluded that the 6C Pool was not likely to violate antitrust laws.

IV.   DISCUSSION

Under Section 1 of the Sherman Act, "every contract, combination . . . conspiracy, in restraint of trade or commerce . . . is hereby declared to be illegal." 15 U.S.C. § 1 (2003). Section 2 of the Sherman Act also makes it illegal for any person to "monopolize, or attempt to monopolize, or combine or conspire with any other person or persons, to monopolize any part of the trade or commerce." 15 U.S.C. § 2 (2003). The Supreme Court has advised that "the Sherman Act has always been discriminatingly applied in the light of economic realities." In addition, the Supreme Court has stated that "there are situations in which competitors have been permitted to form joint selling agencies or other pooled activities, subject to strict limitations under the antitrust laws to guarantee against abuse of the collective power thus created."

In determining whether a pooled activity violates antitrust laws, courts must consider whether to employ a per se or a rule of reason analysis. The per se approach treats certain practices as being so plainly anti-competitive and without redeeming virtue as to be per se unreasonable. The rule of reason approach, in contrast, broadly examines the business practices and related market factors to determine whether the questioned practice imposes an unreasonable restraint on competition. The Supreme Court has recognized that patent pools should be addressed under the rule of reason analysis, except for arrangements where the only apparent purpose is naked price fixing. In this context, the rule of reason analysis predominantly focuses on identifying pro-competitive benefits and balancing them against potential anti-competitive effects. Patent pooling arrangements may serve valid competitive objectives, especially in situations involving "blocking" and "complementary" patents. For example, where patents 'block' one another in the sense that neither can be used without infringing the other, pooling becomes necessary to remove the stalemate and facilitate exploitation of the patents. Similarly, if multiple patents complement each other to protect related but separate parts of a larger product or process, then pooling may be needed to produce a complete item. Pooling likewise may be justified as the best way of solving a patent interference or infringement dispute.

On the other hand, courts have recognized that certain types of pooling arrangements may significantly hurt competition. This is especially true when patents protect substitute goods that compete against each other in the marketplace. In these situations, patent pools should be scrutinized for naked price-fixing, output restraints, exclusionary practices, and foreclosure of competition in downstream or related markets. Trade is restrained, sometimes unreasonably, when the rights to use individual copyrights or patents may be obtained only by payment for a pool of such rights, but that the opportunity to acquire a pool of rights does not restrain trade if an alternative opportunity to acquire individual rights is realistically available. However, an antitrust plaintiff is not obliged to pursue any imaginable alternative, regardless of cost or efficiency, before it can complain that a practice has restrained competition. The true issue in situations involving a pool of rights is whether the antitrust plaintiff lacked a "realistic opportunity" as a "practical matter" to obtain individual licenses from individual owners as opposed to a single license from the pool. If the antitrust plaintiff has the opportunity to license independently, then the pool of rights does not restrain trade in violation of Section 1 of the Sherman Act. It likewise does not violate Section 2 of the Sherman Act because Section 2 requires proof of an anti-competitive act to acquire or maintain a monopoly.

MEI argues that the 6C Pool members each contractually agreed when they formed the 6C Pool to offer individual licenses for their "essential" patents to interested parties on fair, reasonable, and non-discriminatory terms as an alternative to the 6C Pool License. MEI points out that both the 6C Pool Formation Agreement and the actual 6C Pool License contain provisions reciting this obligation. In light of its contractual duties, MEI asserts that it is willing to grant an individual license to any company interested in its individual "essential" patents.

MEI maintains that it repeatedly notified prospective licensees of the availability of individual licenses. Specifically, MEI contends that it sent a letter, press release, application form for a 6C Pool License, and brochure of "essential" patents to Cinram as early as July 1999. It also contends that it sent additional letters to Cinram on January 19, 2001, April 23, 2001, and April 30, 2001. MEI further avers that Mr. Lewis Ritchie, Chief Financial Officer, Executive Vice President of Finance and Administration, and Corporate Secretary of Cinram, attended a 6C Pool presentation on July 13, 2000 and was informed of the availability of individual licenses. Thereafter on July 14, 2002, MEI claims that it even provided Mr. Ritchie with a copy of the standard 6C Pool License which explains that individual licenses are available as an alternative to the 6C Pool License. MEI argues that Cinram did not respond to any of these notifications, nor did it seek to negotiate an individual license or ask for individual licensing rates, even though it met with 6C Pool representatives on seven occasions from August 2000 to February 2002. Moreover, MEI points out that Cinram did not approach other 6C Pool members to inquire about individual licenses. On this basis, MEI asserts that Cinram cannot meet its burden to establish that individual licenses are not a realistic alternative.

To counter MEI's argument, Cinram asserts that MEI's contractual obligation to offer individual licenses is illusory because, in reality, it does not offer such licenses on fair, reasonable, and non-discriminatory terms. To this end, Cinram maintains that the structure of the 6C Pool discourages individual licenses because such licenses would undercut the pool price. As well, Cinram charges that as its direct competitor in the DVD manufacturing area, MEI is less inclined to offer low individual licensing fees because it does not want to help the competition.

Cinram also argues that the terms for individual licenses are cost-prohibitive. Cinram explains that the cost for individual licenses from four of the six 6C Pool members totaled $0.11. Cinram points out that this total substantially exceeds the $0.05 per disc royalty that it currently pays for a 6C Pool License, thereby making individual licenses entirely impractical. Cinram substantiates its argument by noting that DOCdata, Quanta, Metatec, Asustek Computer Inc., Wistron Corp., CMC Magnetics Corp., Cyberlink, Richoh, and Nippon Columbia all explored the possibility of individual licenses with 6C Pool members, but abandoned efforts in favor of a 6C Pool License. Cinram further validates its position by noting that MEI told Mr. Ritchie on two separate occasions that individual licenses would be "more costly" than a 6C Pool License and not a realistic alternative.

Finally, Cinram maintains that MEI and other 6C Pool members purposefully delayed in responding to inquiries regarding individual licenses. Cinram points out that Metatac contacted MEI and the other 6C Pool members for individual licensing terms in August 1999, but only received feedback from JVC and Hitachi after several months of delay. Particularly, JVC waited until June 2000 to respond, but did not quote any terms. JVC then took an additional ten months until April 2001 to provide a rate quote. Hitachi delayed fourteen months to provide its quotation to Metatec. With regard to MEI, Metatec renewed its request several times in 2001 and finally received a term sheet from MEI two and one-half years after its initial request. Similarly, Cinram notes that DOCdata approached MEI and the other 6C Pool members regarding individual licenses in early November 2000. Hitachi provided a response on December 12, 2000; JVC provided a response on December 25, 2000; Mitsubishi provided a response on December 1, 2000, and Toshiba provided a response on March 16, 2001. Despite three written reminders, MEI did not acknowledge this inquiry until March 2001. At that time, MEI apologized for the delay and requested additional time to respond. MEI finally responded to DOCdata's request after a total lag of one year, but did not quote the price for an individual license to its essential patents. Likewise, AOL-Time Warner deferred responding for six months and then informed DOCdata that it had not yet formulated a specific policy for granting individual licenses, but that any individual offer would necessarily be at a rate greater than its share of the 6C Pool royalties.

Viewing the evidence of record and all reasonable inferences to be drawn therefrom in a light most favorable to Cinram as the non-moving party, the court finds that there are no genuine issues of material fact regarding whether individual licenses are a realistic alternative to the 6C Pool License. While this court previously recognized in *Broadcast Music, Inc., v. Moor Law, Inc.,* 484 F. Supp. 357, 367 (D. Del. 1980) (citations omitted) that a plaintiff is not required to attempt individual licensing negotiations before suing under antitrust law when it is clear that such gesture would be futile, the court concludes that Cinram realistically could avail itself of individual licenses to "essential" DVD patents. Cinram was presented with a plethora of information regarding individual licensing terms from MEI through letters, brochures, and a direct presentation; it simply chose to pursue a 6C Pool License instead. Additionally, the court concludes that MEI did not seek to entirely avoid discussions with independent replicators about individual licensing terms. Rather, the court finds that MEI showed a willingness to discuss such terms based upon its two conversations with Mr. Ritchie. While MEI's slowness could be construed as purposeful delay as suggested by Cinram, the court understands that communications often proceed very slowly and deliberately in the business world, particularly when such communications occur on a global scale as in the instant case.

Moreover, despite the fact that numerous independent replicators approached MEI for individual licenses but eventually settled on a 6C Pool License, the court is not persuaded that MEI merely gave lip service to the option of individual licenses. The 6C Pool License is the simplest way to acquire a license to all the "essential" DVD patents. It likewise is the most economical approach, given that (1) the cost of a 6C Pool License is less than the cost of obtaining multiple individual licenses and (2) the per disc royalty under the 6C Pool License is $0.05 whereas the per disc royalty under individual licenses exceeds $0.11. The Second Circuit has stated that the only valid test to prove that an alternative is too costly to be a realistic alternative is whether the price for such a license, in an objective sense, is higher than the value of the intellectual property rights being conveyed. In accord with this reasoning, the court concludes that the per disc royalty differential only causes the individual licensing option to be an unrealistic alternative if it is higher than the value of the DVD rights conveyed. The court finds that the facts at bar do not show this to be the case.

Furthermore, the court does not overlook the fact that the DOJ issued a Business Review Letter concluding that the 6C Pool was not likely to violate antitrust laws. The court appreciates the DOJ's familiarity and experience analyzing complex pooling arrangements and is strongly persuaded by the DOJ's conclusions. In light of these considerations, the court finds that there is enough evidence of record to enable a jury to reasonably decide that individual licenses present a realistic alternative to the 6C Pool License and that the 6C Pool, in turn, does not violate antitrust laws. Accordingly, the court concludes that summary judgment is appropriate and grants MEI's motion as to Cinram's antitrust claims.

V.   CONCLUSION

For the reasons stated, MEI's motion for summary judgment as to Cinram's antitrust claims (D.I. 156) is granted.

U.S. PHILIPS CORPORATION v. INTERNATIONAL TRADE COMMISSION
United States Court of Appeals for the Federal Circuit
2005 U.S. App. LEXIS 20202 (Sept. 21, 2005)

BRYSON, Circuit Judge.

U.S. Philips Corporation appeals from a final order of the United States International Trade Commission, in which the Commission held six of Philips's patents for the manufacture of compact discs to be unenforceable because of patent misuse. The Commission ruled that Philips had employed an impermissible tying arrangement because it required prospective licensees to license packages of patents rather than allowing them to choose which individual patents they wished to license and making the licensing fee correspond to the particular patents designated by the licensees. . . . We reverse and remand.

I

Philips owns patents to technology for manufacturing recordable compact discs ("CD-Rs") and rewritable compact discs ("CD-RWs") in accordance with the technical standards set forth in a publication called the Recordable CD Standard (the "Orange Book"), jointly authored by Philips and Sony Corporation. Since the 1990s, Philips has been licensing those patents through package licenses. Philips specified that the same royalty was due for each disc manufactured by the licensee using patents included in the package, regardless of how many of the patents were used. Potential licensees who sought to license patents to the technology for manufacturing CD-Rs or CD-RWs were not allowed to license those patents individually and were not offered a lower royalty rate for licenses to fewer than all the patents in a package.

Initially, Philips offered four different pools of patents for licensing: (1) a joint CD-R patent pool that included patents owned by Philips and two other companies (Sony and Taiyo Yuden); (2) a joint CD-RW patent pool that included patents owned by Philips and two other companies (Sony and Ricoh); (3) a CD-R patent pool that included only patents owned by Philips; and (4) a CD-RW patent pool that included only patents owned by Philips. After 2001, Philips offered additional package options by grouping its patents into two categories, which Philips denominated "essential" and "nonessential" for producing compact discs compliant with the technical standards set forth in the Orange Book.

In the late 1990s, Philips entered into package licensing agreements with [Princo, GigaStorage, and Linberg]. Soon after entering into the agreements, however, Princo, GigaStorage, and Linberg stopped paying the licensing fees. Philips filed a complaint with the International Trade Commission that Princo, GigaStorage, and Linberg, among others, were violating section 337(a)(1)(B) of the Tariff Act of 1930, 19 U.S.C. § 1337(a)(1)(B), by importing into the United States certain CD-Rs and CD-RWs that infringed six of Philips's patents.

. . .

II

Patent misuse is an equitable defense to patent infringement. It "arose to restrain practices that did not in themselves violate any law, but that drew anticompetitive strength from the patent right, and thus were deemed to be contrary to public policy." Mallinckrodt, Inc. v. Medipart, Inc., 976 F.2d 700, 704 (Fed. Cir. 1992). The purpose of the patent misuse defense "was to prevent a patentee from using the patent to obtain market benefit beyond that which inheres in the statutory patent right." . . . .

This court summarized the principles of patent misuse as applied to "tying" arrangements in Virginia Panel Corp. v. MAC Panel Co., 133 F.3d 860, 868-69 (Fed. Cir. 1997). The court there explained that because of the importance of anticompetitive effects in shaping the defense of patent misuse, the analysis of tying arrangements in the context of patent misuse is closely related to the analysis of tying arrangements in antitrust law. The court further explained that, depending on the circumstances, tying arrangements can be viewed as per se patent misuse or can be analyzed under the rule of reason. Id. The court noted that certain specific practices have been identified as constituting per se patent misuse, "including so-called 'tying' arrangements in which a patentee conditions a license under the patent on the purchase of a separable, staple good, and arrangements in which a patentee effectively extends the term of its patent by requiring post-expiration royalties." Id. at 869 (citations omitted). If the particular licensing arrangement in question is not one of those specific practices that has been held to constitute per se misuse, it will be analyzed under the rule of reason. Id. We have held that under the rule of reason, a practice is impermissible only if its effect is to restrain competition in a relevant market. Monsanto Co. v. McFarling, 363 F.3d 1336, 1341 (Fed. Cir. 2004); Windsurfing Int'l, 782 F.2d at 1001-02.

The Supreme Court's decisions analyzing tying arrangements under antitrust law principles are to the same effect. The Court has made clear that tying arrangements are deemed to be per se unlawful only if they constitute a "naked restraint of trade with no purpose except stifling of competition" and "always or almost always tend to restrict competition and decrease output" in some substantial portion of a market. Broad. Music, Inc. v. Columbia Broad. Sys., Inc., 441 U.S. 1, 19-20, 60 L. Ed. 2d 1, 99 S. Ct. 1551 (1979). The Supreme Court has applied the per se rule only when "experience with a particular kind of restraint enables the Court to predict with confidence that the rule of reason will condemn it. . . ." [citations omitted].

While the doctrine of patent misuse closely tracks antitrust law principles in many respects, Congress has declared certain practices not to be patent misuse even though those practices might otherwise be subject to scrutiny under antitrust law principles. In 35 U.S.C. § 271(d), Congress designated several specific practices as not constituting patent misuse. The designated practices include "conditioning the license of any rights to the patent or the sale of the patented product on the acquisition of a license to rights in another patent or purchase of a separate product," unless, in view of the circumstances, the patent owner "has market power for the patent or patented product on which the license or sale is conditioned." Id. § 271(d)(5). Because the statute is phrased in the negative, it does not require that patent misuse be found in the case of all such conditional licenses in which the patent owner has market power; instead, the statute simply excludes such conditional licenses in which the patent owner lacks market power from the category of arrangements that may be found to constitute patent misuse.

Although section 271(d)(5) does not define the scope of the defense of patent misuse, but merely provides a safe harbor against the charge of patent misuse for certain kinds of conduct by patentees, the statute makes clear that the defense of patent misuse differs from traditional antitrust law principles in an important respect, as applied to tying arrangements involving patent rights. In the case of an antitrust claim based on a tying arrangement involving patent rights, this court has held that ownership of a patent on the tying good is presumed to give the patentee monopoly power. Section 271(d)(5) makes clear, however, that such a presumption does not apply in the case of patent misuse. To establish the defense of patent misuse, the accused infringer must show that the patentee has power in the market for the tying product.

Philips argues briefly that it lacks market power and that it is thus shielded from liability by section 271(d)(5). Based on detailed analysis by the administrative law judge, however, the Commission found that Philips has market power in the relevant market and that section 271(d)(5) is therefore inapplicable to this case. We sustain that ruling.

Philips contends that at the time Philips and Sony first created their package license arrangements, CDs had significant competition among computer data storage devices and thus Philips lacked market power in the market for computer data storage discs. However, Philips first created the package licenses long before GigaStorage and Princo entered into their agreements. According to the administrative law judge, the patent package arrangements were instituted in the early 1990s. Yet Princo did not enter into its agreement until June of 1997, and GigaStorage did not enter into its licensing agreement until October of 1999. Thus, any lack of market power that Philips and its co-licensors may have had in the early 1990s is irrelevant to the situation in the late 1990s, when the parties entered into the agreements at issue in this case. At that time, according to the administrative law judge's well-supported finding, compact discs had become "unique products [with] no close practice substitutes." Philips's argument about lack of market power is therefore unpersuasive, and for that reason section 271(d)(5) does not provide Philips a statutory safe haven from the judicially created defense of patent misuse.

Apart from its specific challenge to the Commission's ruling on the market power issue, Philips launches a more broad-based attack on the Commission's conclusion that Philips's patent licensing policies constitute per se patent misuse. . . .

In its brief, the Commission argues that it is "hornbook law" that mandatory package licensing has been held to be patent misuse. While that broad characterization can be found in some treatises, see 6 Donald S. Chisum, Chisum on Patents § 19.04[3] (2003), cited in C.R. Bard, Inc., 157 F.3d at 1373; 8 Ernest B. Lipscomb III, Lipscomb's Walter on Patents § 27 28: (3d ed. 1989 & Supp. 2003), Philips invites us to consider whether that broad proposition is sound. Upon consideration, we conclude that the proposition as applied to the circumstances of this case is not supported by precedent or reason.

In its opinion, the Commission acknowledged that the Virginia Panel case and many other patent tying cases "involve a tying patent and a tied product, rather than a tying patent and a tied patent." (emphasis in original). The Commission nonetheless concluded that "finding patent misuse based on a tying arrangement between patents in a mandatory package license is a reasonable application of Supreme Court precedent." In so ruling, the Commission relied primarily on two Supreme Court cases: United States v. Paramount Pictures, Inc., 334 U.S. 131, 156-59, 92 L. Ed. 1260, 68 S. Ct. 915 (1948), and United States v. Loew's, Inc., 371 U.S. 38, 44-51, 9 L. Ed. 2d 11, 83 S. Ct. 97 (1962). Those cases condemned the practice of "block-booking" movies to theaters (in the Paramount case) and to television stations (in the Loew's case) as antitrust violations.

. . .

We do not agree with the Commission that the decisions in Paramount and Loew's govern this case. In Paramount, the district court held that the defendant movie distributor had engaged in unlawful conduct because it offered to permit exhibitors to show the films they wished to license only if they agreed to license and exhibit other films that they were not interested in licensing. The Supreme Court affirmed that ruling. The Court held that block-booking was illegal because it "prevents competitors from bidding for single features on their individual merits," and because it "adds to the monopoly of a single copyrighted picture that of another copyrighted picture which must be taken and exhibited in order to secure the first." 334 U.S. at 156-57. The result, the Court explained, "is to add to the monopoly of the copyright in violation of the principle of the patent cases involving tying clauses." Id. at 158.

Because the block-booking arrangement at issue in Paramount required the licensee to exhibit all of the films in the group for which a license was taken, the Paramount block-booking was more akin to a tying arrangement in which a patent license is tied to the purchase of a separate product, rather than to an arrangement in which a patent license is tied to another patent license. Indeed, all of the patent tying cases to which the Supreme Court referred in Paramount involved tying arrangements in which, as the Court described them, "the owner of a patent [conditioned] its use on the purchase or use of patented or unpatented materials." 334 U.S. at 157. Because the arrangement in the Paramount case was equivalent in substance to a patent-to-product tying arrangement, Paramount does not stand for the proposition that a pure patent-to-patent tying arrangement, such as Philips's package licensing agreement, is per se unlawful.

Philips gives its licensees the option of using any of the patents in the package, at the licensee's option. Philips charges a uniform licensing fee to manufacture discs covered by its patented technology, regardless of which, or how many, of the patents in the package the licensee chooses to use in its manufacturing process. In particular, Philips's package licenses do not require that licensees actually use the technology covered by any of the patents that the Commission characterized as nonessential. In that respect, Philips's licensing agreements are different from the agreements at issue in Paramount, which imposed an obligation on the purchasers of package licenses to exhibit films they did not wish to license. That obligation not only extended the exclusive right in one product to products in which the distributor did not have exclusive rights, but it also precluded exhibitors, as a practical matter, from exhibiting other films that they may have preferred over the tied films they were required to exhibit. Because Philips's package licensing agreements do not compel the licensees to use any particular technology covered by any of the licensed patents, the Paramount case is not a sound basis from which to conclude that the package licensing arrangements at issue in this case constitute patent misuse per se.

In the Loew's case, the district court determined that the licensee television stations were required to pay fees not only for the feature films they wanted, but also for additional, inferior films. As in Paramount, the fact that the package arrangement required the television stations to purchase exhibition rights for the package at a price that was greater than the price attributable to the desired films made the tying arrangement very much like a tying arrangement involving products. . . .

In this case, unlike in Loew's, there is no evidence that a portion of the royalty was attributable to the patents that the Commission characterized as nonessential. . . . There is therefore no basis for conjecture that a hypothetical licensing fee would have been lower if Philips had offered to license the patents on an individual basis or in smaller packages.

Aside from Paramount and Loew's, the Commission relies on cases involving tying arrangements in which the patent owner conditions the availability of a patent license on the patentee's agreement to purchase a staple item of commerce from the patentee. . . . Those cases, however, are readily distinguishable because of the fundamental difference between an obligation to purchase a product and the extension of a nonexclusive license to practice a patent.

A nonexclusive patent license is simply a promise not to sue for infringement. The conveyance of such a license does not obligate the licensee to do anything; it simply provides the licensee with a guarantee that it will not be sued for engaging in conduct that would infringe the patent in question.

In the case of patent-to-product tying, the patent owner uses the market power conferred by the patent to compel customers to purchase a product in a separate market that the customer might otherwise purchase from a competitor. The patent owner is thus able to use the market power conferred by the patent to foreclose competition in the market for the product.

By contrast, a package licensing agreement that includes both essential and nonessential patents does not impose any requirement on the licensee. It does not bar the licensee from using any alternative technology that may be offered by a competitor of the licensor. Nor does it foreclose the competitor from licensing his alternative technology; it merely puts the competitor in the same position he would be in if he were competing with unpatented technology.

A package license is in effect a promise by the patentee not to sue his customer for infringing any patents on whatever technology the customer employs in making commercial use of the licensed patent. That surrender of rights might mean that the customer will choose not to license the alternative technology offered by the patentee's competition, but it does not compel the customer to use the patentee's technology. The package license is thus not anticompetitive in the way that a compelled purchase of a tied product would be.

Contrary to the Commission's characterization, the intervenors were not "forced" to "take" anything from Philips that they did not want, nor were they restricted from obtaining licenses from other sources to produce the relevant technology. Philips simply provided that for a fixed licensing fee, it would not sue any licensee for engaging in any conduct covered by the entire group of patents in the package. By analogy, if Philips had decided to surrender its "nonessential" patents or had simply announced that it did not intend to enforce them, there would have been no way for the manufacturers to decline or reject Philips's decision. Yet the economic effect of the package licensing arrangement for Philips's patents is not fundamentally different from the effect that such decisions would have had on third parties seeking to compete with the technology covered by those "nonessential" patents. Thus, we conclude that the Commission erred when it characterized the package license agreements as a way of forcing the intervenors to license technology that they did not want in order to obtain patent rights that they did.

The Commission stated that it would not have found the package licenses to constitute improper tying if Philips had offered to license its patents on an individual basis, as an alternative to licensing them in packages. The Commission's position, however, must necessarily be based on an assumption that, if the patents were offered on an individual basis, individual patents would be offered for a lower price than the patent packages as a whole. If that assumption were not implicit in the Commission's conclusion, the Commission would be saying in effect that it would be unlawful for Philips to charge the same royalty for its essential patents that it charges for its patent packages and to offer the nonessential patents for free. Yet that sort of pricing policy plainly would not be unlawful. See Directory Sales Mgmt. Corp. v. Ohio Bell Tel. Co., 833 F.2d 606, 609-10 (6th Cir. 1987).

To the extent that the Commission's decision is based on an assumption that individual licenses would necessarily be available for a lower price than package licenses, that assumption is directly contrary to the evidence and even to the administrative law judge's findings of fact. As noted above, the administrative law judge found that the royalty rate under Philips's package licenses depended on the number of discs the manufacturer produced under the authority of the license, not the number of individual patents the manufacturer used to produce those discs. That is, the royalty rate did not vary depending on whether the licensees used only the essential patents or used all of the patents in the package. Thus, it seems evident that if Philips were forced to offer licenses on an individual basis, it would continue to charge the same per unit royalty regardless of the number of patents the manufacturer chose to license. That alteration in Philips's practice would have absolutely no effect on the would-be competitors who wished to offer alternatives to the technology represented by Philips's so-called nonessential patents, since those patents would effectively be offered for free, and the competitors would therefore still have to face exactly the same barriers — the availability of a free alternative to the technology that they were trying to license for a fee.

More generally, the Commission's assumption that a license to fewer than all the patents in a package would presumably carry a lower fee than the package itself ignores the reality that the value of any patent package is largely, if not entirely, based on the patents that are essential to the technology in question. A patent that is nonessential because it covers technology that can be fully replaced by alternative technology that is available for free is essentially valueless. A patent that is nonessential because it covers technology that can be fully replaced by alternative technology that is available through a license from another patent owner has value, but its value is limited by the price of the alternative technology. Short of imposing an obligation on the licensor to make some sort of allocation of fees across a group of licenses, there is no basis for the Commission to conclude that a smaller group of the licenses — the so-called "essential" licenses — would have been available for a lower fee if they had not been "tied to" the so-called nonessential patents.

It is entirely rational for a patentee who has a patent that is essential to particular technology, as well as other patents that are not essential, to charge what the market will bear for the essential patent and to offer the others for free. Because a license to the essential patent is, by definition, a prerequisite to practice the technology in question, the patentee can charge whatever maximum amount a willing licensee is able to pay to practice the technology in question. If the patentee allocates royalty fees between its essential and nonessential patents, it runs the risk that licensees will take a license to the essential patent but not to the nonessential patents. The effect of that choice will be that the patentee will not be able to obtain the full royalty value of the essential patent. For the patentee in this situation to offer its nonessential patents as part of a package with the essential patent at no additional charge is no more anticompetitive than if it had surrendered the nonessential patents or had simply announced a policy that it would not enforce them against persons who licensed the essential patent. In either case, those offering technology that competed with the nonessential patents would be unhappy, because they would be competing against free technology. But the patentee would not be using his essential patent to obtain power in the market for the technology covered by the nonessential patents. This package licensing arrangement cannot fairly be characterized as an exploitation of power in one market to obtain a competitive advantage in another.

Aside from the absence of evidence that the package licensing arrangements in this case had the effect of impermissibly broadening the scope of the "essential" patents with anticompetitive effect, Philips argues that the Commission failed to acknowledge the unique pro-competitive benefits associated with package licensing. Philips points to the federal government's guide lines for licensing intellectual property, which recognize that patent packages "may provide pro-competitive benefits by integrating complementary technologies, reducing transaction costs, clearing blocking positions, and avoiding costly infringement litigation. By promoting the dissemination of technology, cross-licensing and pooling arrangements are often pro-competitive." U.S. Department of Justice and Federal Trade Commission, Antitrust Guidelines for the Licensing of Intellectual Property § 5.5 (1995); see also Herbert Hovenkamp, IP and Antitrust § 34.2c, at 34-7 (2004).

Philips introduced evidence that package licensing reduces transaction costs by eliminating the need for multiple contracts and reducing licensors' administrative and monitoring costs. [citation omitted]. Package licensing can also obviate any potential patent disputes between a licensor and a licensee and thus reduce the likelihood that a licensee will find itself involved in costly litigation over unlicensed patents with potentially adverse consequences for both parties, such as a finding that the licensee infringed the unlicensed patents or that the unlicensed patents were invalid. See Steven C. Carlson, Patent Pools and the Antitrust Dilemma, 16 Yale J. on Reg. 359, 379-81 (1999). Thus, package licensing provides the parties a way of ensuring that a single licensing fee will cover all the patents needed to practice a particular technology and protecting against the unpleasant surprise for a licensee who learns, after making a substantial investment, that he needed a license to more patents than he originally obtained. Finally, grouping licenses in a package allows the parties to price the package based on their estimate of what it is worth to practice a particular technology, which is typically much easier to calculate than determining the marginal benefit provided by a license to each individual patent. In short, package licensing has the pro-competitive effect of reducing the degree of uncertainty associated with investment decisions.

The package licenses in this case have some of the same advantages as the package licenses at issue in the Broadcast Music case. The Supreme Court determined in that case that the blanket copyright package licenses at issue had useful, pro-competitive purposes because they gave the licensees "unplanned, rapid, and indemnified access to any and all of the repertory of [musical] compositions, and [they gave the owners] a reliable method of collecting for the use of the their copyrights." 441 U.S. at 20. While "individual sales transactions [would be] quite expensive, as would be individual monitoring and enforcement," a package licensing agreement would ensure access and save costs. Id. Hence, the Supreme Court determined that such conduct should fall under "a more discriminating examination under the rule of reason." Id. at 24.

In light of the efficiencies of package patent licensing and the important differences between product-to-patent tying arrangements and arrangements involving group licensing of patents, we reject the Commission's conclusion that Philips's conduct shows a "lack of any redeeming virtue" and should be "conclusively presumed to be unreasonable and therefore illegal without elaborate inquiry as to the precise harm they have caused or the business excuse for their use." N. Pac. Ry. Co. v. United States, 356 U.S. 1, 5, 2 L. Ed. 2d 545, 78 S. Ct. 514 (1958). We therefore hold that the analysis that led the Commission to apply the rule of per se illegality to Philips's package licensing agreements was legally flawed.

B

In the alternative, Philips argues that the Commission's finding of per se patent misuse was not justified by the facts of this case. In particular, Philips contends that the evidence did not show that there were commercially viable alternatives to the technology covered by the so-called "nonessential" patents in the Philips licensing packages that any of its licensees would have preferred to use.

In order to show that a tying arrangement is per se unlawful, a complaining party must demonstrate that it links two separate products and has an anticompetitive effect in the market for the second product. The Supreme Court explained that the "essential characteristic" of an invalid tying arrangement lies in the seller's exploitation of its control over the tying product to force the buyer in to the purchase of a tied product that the buyer either did not want at all, or might have preferred to purchase elsewhere on different terms. When such "forcing" is present, competition on the merits in the market for the tied item is restrained. . . . The Commission found that the "nonessential" patents . . . constituted separate products from the "essential" patents in the package and that the package licensing agreements adversely affected competition in the market for the nonessential technology. The Commission's analysis of that factual issue was flawed, however.

Patents within a patent package can be regarded as "nonessential" only if there are "commercially feasible" alternatives to those patents. See Int'l Mfg. Co. v. Landon, 336 F.2d 723, 729 (9th Cir. 1964). If there are no commercially practicable alternatives to the allegedly nonessential patents, packaging those patents together with so-called essential patents can have no anticompetitive effect in the marketplace, because no competition for a viable alternative product is foreclosed. In such a case, the only effect of finding per se patent misuse is to give licensees a way of avoiding their obligations under the licensing agreements, with no corresponding benefit to competition in any real-world market.

The Department of Justice has recognized that the availability of commercially viable alternative technology is relevant to the analysis of package licensing agreements. In particular, the Department has stated that patent packages do not have the undesirable effects of tying if they include patents to technology for which there is no practical or realistic alternative. See, e.g., Business Review Letter, U.S. Department of Justice, Antitrust Division (Dec. 16, 1998). That principle is consistent with the main purpose of the separate-products inquiry in tying cases generally, which is to ensure that conduct is not condemned as anticompetitive "unless there is sufficient demand for the purchase of [the tied product] separate from the [tying product] to identify a distinct product market in which it is efficient to offer [the tied product]." Jefferson Parish, 466 U.S. at 21-22; see Mallinckrodt, 976 F.2d at 704 (tying is misuse only when the patentee uses its patent to obtain "market benefit" beyond that conferred by the patent).

In this case, the evidence did not show that there were commercially viable substitutes for the ["nonessential"] patents that disc manufacturers wished to use in making compact discs compliant with the Orange Book standards. There was thus insufficient evidence that including the four "nonessential" patents in the Philips patent packages had an actual anticompetitive effect. That is, the evidence did not show that there were commercially viable substitutes for those four "nonessential" patents that disc manufacturers wished to use in making compact discs compliant with the Orange Book standards.

   . . .

Beyond the absence of factual support for the Commission's findings, the Commission's analysis of the four "nonessential" patents demonstrates a more fundamental problem with applying the per se rule of illegality to patent packages such as the ones at issue in this case. If a patent holder has a package of patents, all of which are necessary to enable a licensee to practice particular technology, it is well established that the patentee may lawfully insist on licensing the patents as a package and may refuse to license them individually, since the group of patents could not reasonably be viewed as distinct products. See Landon, 336 F.2d at 729. Yet over time, the development of alternative technology may raise questions whether some of the patents in the package are essential or whether, as in this case, there are alternatives available for the technology covered by some of the patents. Indeed, in a fast-developing field such as the one at issue in this case, it seems quite likely that questions will arise over time, such as what constitutes an "essential" patent for purposes of manufacturing compact discs compliant with the Orange Book standard. [citation omitted]. Under the Commission's approach, an agreement that was perfectly lawful when executed could be challenged as per se patent misuse due to developments in the technology of which the patentees are unaware, or which have just become commercially viable. Such a rule would make patents subject to being declared unenforceable due to developments that occurred after execution of the license or were unknown to the parties at the time of licensing. Not only would such a rule render licenses subject to invalidation on grounds unknown at the time of licensing, but it would also provide a strong incentive to litigation by any licensee, since the reward for showing that even a single license in a package was "nonessential" would be to render all the patents in the package unenforceable. For that reason as well, we reject the Commission's ruling that package agreements of the sort entered into by Philips and the intervenors must be invalidated on the ground that they constitute per se patent misuse.

III

In the alternative, the Commission held that Philips's package licensing agreements constituted patent misuse under the rule of reason. The Commission's analysis under the rule of reason largely tracked the analysis that led it to conclude that the package licensing agreements constituted per se patent misuse.

. . .

Under the rule of reason, the finder of fact must determine if the practice at issue is "reasonably within the patent grant, i.e., that it relates to subject matter within the scope of the patent claims." . . .

The Commission's rule of reason analysis is flawed for two reasons. Most importantly, its conclusion was largely predicated on the anticompetitive effect on competitors offering alternatives to the four so-called nonessential patents in the Philips patent packages. Yet, as we have already held, the evidence did not show that including those patents in the patent packages had a negative effect on commercially available technology. The Commission assumed that there was a foreclosure of competition because compact disc manufacturers would be induced to accept licenses to the technology covered by [two of the "nonessential"] patents and therefore would be unwilling to consider alternatives. As noted, however, there was no evidence before the Commission that any manufacturer had actually refused to consider alternatives to the technology covered by those patents or for that matter that any commercially viable alternative actually existed.

In addition, as in its per se analysis, the Commission did not acknowledge the problems with licensing patents individually, such as the transaction costs associated with making individual patent-by-patent royalty determinations and monitoring possible infringement of patents that particular licensees chose not to license. The Commission also did not address the problem, noted above, that changes in the technology for manufacturing compact discs could render some patents that were indisputably essential at the time of licensing arguably nonessential at some later point in the life of the license. To hold that a licensing agreement that satisfied the rule of reason when executed became unreasonable at some later point because of technological development would introduce substantial uncertainty into the market and displace settled commercial arrangements in favor of uncertainty that could only be resolved through expensive litigation.

Finally, the Commission failed to consider the efficiencies that package licensing may produce because of the innovative character of the technology at hand. Given that the technology surrounding the Orange Book standard was still evolving, there were many uncertainties regarding what patents might be needed to produce the compact discs. As noted, package license agreements in which the royalty was based on the number of units produced, not the number of patents used to produce them, can resolve in advance all potential patent disputes between the licensor and the licensee, whereas licensing patent rights on a patent-by-patent basis can result in continuing disputes over whether the licensee's technology infringes certain ancillary patents owned by the licensor that are not part of the group elected by the licensee.

We therefore conclude that the line of analysis that the Commission employed in reaching its conclusion that Philips's package licensing agreements are more anticompetitive than pro-competitive, and thus are unlawful under the rule of reason, was predicated on legal errors and on factual findings that were not supported by substantial evidence. For these reasons, we cannot uphold the Commission's decision that Philips's patents are unenforceable because of patent misuse under the rule of reason.

. . .

REVERSED AND REMANDED.

NOTES & QUESTIONS

1. Valid Objective for Creation of a Pooling Arrangement

Patent pools arise when two or more patent owners agree to exchange licenses in their patents. Participants in pools have access to each other's patents, freeing them to commercialize technology that might otherwise be blocked by a conflicting patent or otherwise raise an infringement claim. In some industries, overlapping patents cloud a field to such an extent that a patentee in the industry finds it difficult in light of the existing patents held by others to discern his right to make, use, or sell his product. Not surprisingly, multiple infringement actions within an industry often spark the creation of a patent pool.

Use of a pooling arrangement to avoid or resolve an infringement action among patent holders is recognized as a reasonable and pro-competitive practice. While pooling arrangements are especially common with patents, pools may also involve other forms of intellectual property.

2. Concerns Regarding Patent Pools

a. *Antitrust* — Pooling arrangements necessarily involve joint action, often between parties that are in competition. If parties to a pooling agreement consent to more than pure cross-licensing, antitrust risks arise. *See Hartford-Empire Co. v. U.S.,* 323 U.S. 386 (1945). For example, competitors that pool their patents together in order to facilitate price-fixing engage in an activity that is seen as exclusionary and anticompetitive. Another example of an anticompetitive arrangement is present when a patent pool collectively dominates a market and licensing arrangements are used to implement territorial or field of use allocations of business activities among the patent pool's members. Such a practice may be seen as achieving a horizontal allocation of markets in violation of antitrust laws.

b. *Invalid Patents* — Because a challenge to the validity of a patent pool fails if even one patent in the pool is valid, the cost and risks for a party wishing to mount a challenge to the validity of a patent increases when the patent is included in a pool. A patent pool may therefore shield an invalid patent from challenges of invalidity. The shielding effect of a pool may inhibit innovation in the field occupied by an invalid patent.

Challenges to a patent included in a patent pool should be limited to the patents owned by the licensor who is the addressee of the challenge, and not overreach to the patents owned by other licensors in the pool.

3. Standard Setting Organizations

A Standard Setting Organization (SSO) is an industry group that sets common standards on behalf of an industry. SSOs are most often found in network industries, where network effects require interoperability between products of competitors.

When an SSO proposes technology owned by one or more companies as an industry standard, the owner of the proprietary standard can prevent the industry from adopting the standard by withholding his permission. SSOs allow industry participants to contract around the effect of overlapping intellectual property rights by requiring members to license their patented technology and agree to nondiscriminatory terms. Most SSOs allow their members to own intellectual property rights, but require members to license their rights and forgo injunctive relief. Licensing terms must be "reasonable and nondiscriminatory." Ownership of intellectual property rights, though permitted, is usually discouraged by SSOs.

While licensing arrangements established by SSOs bear similarities to patent pools, the two are not the same. First, SSOs are organized around technical outcomes while pools are organized around patents. Second, SSO agreements are drafted ex ante, even before some patents are actually granted, while pools are agreed to ex post. As a result, SSO rules tend to be more evenhanded in their approach. Finally, SSOs are more concentrated in network industries, while pools are more randomly distributed across industries. For a detailed examination of SSOs, see Mark A. Lemley, *Intellectual Property Rights and Standard–Setting Organizations*, 90 Cal. L. Rev. 1889 (2002).

7.   Patent Packages

When a license includes several of a licensor's patents, the license is known as a "patent package." It is not uncommon for a company that is a pioneer in its field to obtain multiple related patents. The scope of the inventive company's patent portfolio may be so broad as to dominate the field. A licensor interested in operating in the field consequently might be interested in obtaining a patent package in order to gain access to the full scope of the licensor's patents.

WELL SURVEYS, INC. v. PERFO-LOG, INC.
United States Court of Appeals for the Tenth Circuit
396 F.2d 15 (1968)

BREITENSTEIN, Circuit Judge.

Appellant-plaintiff Well Surveys, Inc., sued appellee-defendant Perfo-Log, Inc., for infringement of the Swift Patent No. 2,554,844 and the Peterson

Patent No. 2,967,994. Perfo-Log denies infringement and asserts patent misuse as a defense. The trial court granted summary judgment for Perfo-Log on the ground of misuse of the Swift patent.

This litigation is an episode in the prolonged controversy between WSI and McCullough Tool Co. over the Swift patent. In *McCullough Tool Co. v. Well Surveys, Inc.,* we upheld the validity of the Swift patent and said that WSI had purged itself of misuse in 1956 by the adoption of different licensing practices. WSI brought further proceedings against McCullough which have been disposed of in our recently filed opinion. McCullough is admittedly assisting Perfo-Log in the present suit.

The Swift patent covers a system of measuring radiation from the earth formations around a well casing and, at the same time, locating the collars of the casing as a positive indication of the depth at which particular radiation is measured. The expiration date of the Swift patent is May 29, 1968.

The Peterson patent relates to a type of collar locator which can be used with the Swift system. It expires January 10, 1978. Various other collar locators can be used for the same purpose as Peterson.

The district court found that licensees under the immunity agreements could not terminate until after the expiration of the Swift patent; and that there was no provision for change in royalty base or for diminution in royalty after the expiration of the Swift patent. On the basis of these findings the court held that WSI had misused the Swift patent and granted the Perfo-Log motion for summary judgment. The WSI motion for partial summary judgment was denied.

The courts withhold aid to a party who has used his patent right contrary to the public interest. A patentee is not entitled to continue to receive "the benefit of an expired monopoly." In our first *McCullough* decision we reviewed the principle of misuse and the package licensing of patents. We concluded that package licensing was not misuse in the absence of coercion and said: ". . . in order to constitute a misuse, there must be an element of coercion, such as where there has been a request by a prospective licensee for a license under less than all of the patents and a refusal by the licensor to grant such a license."

In the second *McCullough* decision we considered claims that WSI had misused its patents through monopolization of the well-logging industry, improper extension of its patent monopoly, and unfounded infringement threats and litigation. We held that the showing made was insufficient to establish a change in the licensing practices which we approved in the first McCullough decision and rejected the claims of misuse.

Perfo-Log says that the licenses which it submitted in support of a summary judgment motion establish per se a misuse of the Swift patent. Prime reliance is had on eight agreements which covered both the Swift and the Peterson patents. These agreements were not terminable at the will of the licensee until the lapse of varying periods after the expiration of the Swift patent. The uniform royalty rate of 5% was not diminished after the expiration of Swift. The royalty provision reads thus:

3.02 Company agrees to pay DII [WSI] as royalty on each Radioactivity Well Surveying operation conducted by Company, which, if unlicensed, would infringe the Patent Rights of DII [WSI] during the term of this agreement an amount equal to five per cent (5%) of the gross charge (exclusive of mileage) made for the survey so conducted or a sum of ten dollars ($10.00), whichever is greater.

The literal language does not exact a royalty on an expired patent because payment is required only for operations which infringe a patent right of WSI. There can be no infringement of an expired patent.

Although the royalty rate does not change, the base for that rate changes because after the expiration of Swift, no royalty is payable unless the Peterson patent is used in the logging operations. The lack of diminution in royalty rate for the use of Peterson without Swift and the provisions for termination do not of themselves establish coercion. The question is whether the licensee was forced to enter into a package arrangement. Perfo-Log offered nothing on this point but relied on the agreements. WSI submitted the affidavits of two officers to show a continuation of the license practices approved in our first McCullough decision. One of the affidavits stated:

> Every prospective licensee was offered a license under any of the radioactivity well surveying patents of Dresser Industries, Inc. and/or Well Surveys, Inc. which it desired, individually or collectively, upon negotiated reasonable terms. No licensee or prospective licensee was ever coerced to pay royalty on or for any operations covered by any expired patent.

To support its argument that the licenses per se establish patent misuse, Perfo-Log relies on the decision in *Rocform Corp. v. Acitelli-Standard Concrete Wall, Inc.*, 6 Cir., 367 F.2d 678. That case concerned patents, one of which was of basic importance, for pouring concrete basement walls. The license agreement covered several patents and provided no royalty reduction after the expiration of the basic patent. The Sixth Circuit held that the lack of diminution in royalty and the absence of an appropriate termination clause established misuse. One judge dissented on the basis of our first *McCullough* decision. *Id.* at 682. In its statement of facts the Sixth Circuit said that Rocform offered to license only under its standard package agreement. In the case at bar, the affidavits submitted by WSI show a willingness to license any or all patents under reasonable, negotiated terms. If the *Rocform* decision is taken as holding that a package license, including both important and unimportant patents, is misuse per se when there is no diminution in royalty, or provision for termination, after the expiration of an important patent, we respectfully disagree and adhere to our decision in the first *McCullough* case. The relative importance of patents has no significance if a licensee is given the choice to take a patent alone or in combination on reasonable terms. Freedom of choice is the controlling question.

Perfo-Log argues that the district judge drew a permissible inference of misuse from the licenses and that under United States v. United States Gypsum Co., 333 U.S. 364, this inference is binding on the appellate court unless clearly erroneous. The difficulty is that the inference was drawn on a motion for summary judgment. In such a situation "the inferences to be drawn from the underlying facts . . . must be viewed in the light most favorable to the party opposing the motion." Here the inference runs contrary to the uncontroverted showing by WSI that it offered to license any or all of its patents on reasonable, negotiated terms. In such circumstances the inference is not controlling. At the most it establishes a genuine issue as to a material fact and, under the provisions of Rule 56(c), F.R. Civ. P., precludes the grant of a summary judgment.

WSI urges that summary judgment on the misuse issue should have been given in its favor. Although we are convinced that the showing by WSI's affidavit of readiness to license any or all of its patents on reasonable terms is sufficient to defeat the Perfo-Log motion for summary judgment, we cannot say that such showing entitles WSI to the relief it seeks. The fact finder must weigh the provisions of the license agreements against the facts surrounding the grant of those licenses. In our opinion this is not a case for the use of the summary judgment procedure.

The judgment is reversed and the case is remanded for trial on the merits.

NOTES & QUESTIONS

1. Concerns Relating to the Component Patents

A licensor of a patent package must be conscious of the fact that the individual patents in a package may expire on different dates, and some may become more valuable than others over time. One arrangement that addresses this problem is to offer a package of patents at a rate less than the cost of all of the patents individually. The license agreement should explicitly state the arrangement, or it should be reflected in the royalty allocation. In addition, a licensor can give the licensee the option to terminate the agreement when a patent expires and invite renegotiation or provide for renegotiation upon expiration of a patent, with an arbitration provision for dispute settlement.

2. Antitrust Concerns

A licensor may not condition a license of a patent, which a licensee desires, on the licensing of patents that the licensee does not want. A package license that forces licensees to pay for the licensing of unwanted patents runs afoul of antitrust laws. *See Zenith Radio Corp. v. Hazeltine Research Inc.*, 395 U.S. 100 (1969). Packages for mutual convenience, however, are permissible. *Automatic Radio Mfg. v. Hazeltine Research, Inc.*, 339 U.S. 827 (1950). Parties are allowed to mutually agree to a license that includes multiple patents, provided that the arrangement achieves some administrative advantage or other convenient result for the parties.

8.   University Licensing

The licensing of patents resulting from university research and development has become big business at major universities. In 2003, for example, one university relied on licensing royalties to fund a quarter of its 2003 operating budget. This section examines the unique concerns that apply to university licensing.

One concern a licensee must keep in mind when pursuing a license from a university is the role of government funding in creation of the invention. For some universities, up to ninety percent of research conducted by the university is funded by a government agency. As a consequence of accepting government funding, the Bayh-Dole Act and related federal regulations impose restrictions on universities' ability to transfer the rights in innovation created through government-funded research. Typically, the government obtains a nonexclusive license to use the invention while the university maintains title to the inventions. A licensor should keep in mind the government's nonexclusive license in the patent when seeking a license and negotiating its terms.

Another concern that arises in university licensing involves the common university policy of encouraging the free dissemination of information. In *University of Colo. Found., Inc. v. Am. Cyanamid Co.*, 342 F.3d 1298 (Fed. Cir. 2003), two professors at the University of Colorado conducted a series of experiments as a favor to a colleague working for the pharmaceutical company Cyanamid. At the conclusion of the studies, the professors immediately wrote up their findings in an article entitled "Inadequate Iron Absorption from Many Prenatal Multivitamin-Mineral Supplements," and submitted a manuscript for publication in the New England Journal of Medicine. Though the findings of the studies ultimately resulted in a patentable improvement to the formulation of a prenatal multivitamin/mineral supplement, the professors did not apply for a patent concerning their discoveries but rather intended that the discoveries be dedicated to the public. The court awarded damages to the professors and the university for Cyanamid's improper use of the journal manuscript to obtain a patent over their discovery. The court recognized that journal publication, in the academic realm, "provides another incentive separate and apart from the patent laws." In light of the academic policy of encouraging free dissemination of information, a licensee must reconcile any confidentiality clause in the licensing agreement with the university's policy of information dissemination.

B. TRADE SECRET LICENSING

1. Introduction

Trade secret protection requires only that an owner safeguard the information underlying a trade secret to prevent unauthorized use and disclosure. Unlike patent protection, the owner of the underlying subject matter need not meet high inventive standards or file disclosures to secure trade secret protection. The trade-off for lower requirements for obtaining protection is that trade secret protection only prevents the use or disclosure of the secret by those standing in a special relationship to the trade secret owner and those who utilized improper means to acquire the information. Trade secret protection does not protect the trade secret owner from independent discoverers.

A key right of a trade secret owner in the context of licensing is the right to control the disclosure of a trade secret. To maintain trade secret protection, however, a trade secret owner must show reasonable diligence in safeguarding the secrecy of the matter disclosed, even with disclosures to licensees. A licensor entering into negotiations involving the disclosure of trade secrets should ensure that the subject matter of the disclosure and the rights and duties of each party are clearly defined in a contractual agreement. Clearly defined duties are in the best interest of the licensee as well. Absent an express agreement, the confidential relationship arising as a consequence of the negotiations and disclosure between the licensor and licensee may subject the licensee to comparatively ill-defined duties that arise as a matter of law. Of course, the subject matter of a trade secret license must be a trade secret. The licensing agreement is revocable on the theory of mutual mistake of fact if the subject matter of a trade secret license is later determined to be otherwise.

The ability of a trade secret transferor to control the use, disclosure, and reverse engineering of the trade secret subject matter by a transferee depends on whether the negotiated transaction is a sale or a license. An outright sale of a trade secret limits a transferor's ability to enforce restrictions on the transferee as compared to a license. Since a transferor of a license has greater leeway to control the conduct of the transferee, many trade secret owners, like software manufacturers, turn to licensing to protect the trade secrets embodied in their programs. *See ProCD, Inc. v. Zeidenberg*, 86 F.3d 1447 (7th Cir. 1996); *Step-Saver Data Systems, Inc. v. Wyse Technology*, 939 F.2d 91 (3d Cir. 1991). To decide whether a transaction embodied in an agreement is a license or an outright sale, courts examine the substance of the contract. A contract may be characterized as providing for a sale if the terms exceed the transferred product's life, the agreement cannot be terminated except in the case of reverse engineering, there is no negotiated, signed licensing agreement, and the product is acquired from a retail sales outlet or by mail order.

NOTES & QUESTIONS

1. Confidentiality & Post-Termination Clauses

A trade secret licensing agreement should include a confidentiality clause that clearly defines the steps the licensee must take to safeguard the secrecy of the trade secret. Specifically, an agreement should explicitly state the confidentiality requirements the licensee is expected to meet and make them binding. A licensor also needs to protect the secrecy of a trade secret after the termination of a licensing agreement. To accomplish this goal, an agreement may include a provision that requires the return of tangible embodiments of a trade secret at the end of a period of licensing and may extend the secrecy requirements binding upon the licensee beyond the end of the licensing period and beyond the entry of the trade secret into the public domain.

2. Multiple Trade Secrets

It is not uncommon for trade secret licenses to involve more than one trade secret. Licensing of multiple trade secrets, however, can give rise to Sherman § 2 monopolization and Clayton § 7 asset acquisition issues under the antitrust laws. Licensors must pay careful attention to the concerns arising from the component trade secrets in a multiple trade secret license. Trade secret protection has the potential to endure indefinitely, so long as the information remains a secret. However, once information becomes generally known, the trade secret status of the information ends, and the value of that information decreases. Licensors should account for the uncertain duration of trade secret protection by either assigning separate royalty rates for each individual trade secret, or by including a means of adjusting the royalty rate when a trade secret enters the public domain.

2.   Duration of Trade Secret Royalties

WARNER-LAMBERT PHARMACEUTICAL COMPANY v. JOHN J. REYNOLDS, INC.
United States District Court for the Southern District of New York
178 F. Supp. 655 (1959)

BRYAN, J.

Plaintiff sues under the Federal Declaratory Judgment Act, 28 U.S.C. §§ 2201 and 2202, for a judgment declaring that it is no longer obligated to make periodic payments to defendants based on its manufacture or sale of the well known product 'Listerine', under agreements made between Dr. J. J. Lawrence and J. W. Lambert in 1881, and between Dr. Lawrence and Lambert Pharmacal Company in 1885. Plaintiff also seeks to recover the payments made to defendants pursuant to these agreements since the commencement of the action.

Plaintiff is a Delaware corporation which manufactures and sells Listerine, among other pharmaceutical products. It is the successor in interest to Lambert and Lambert Pharmacal Company which acquired the formula for Listerine from Dr. Lawrence under the agreements in question. Defendants are the successors in interest to Dr. Lawrence.

Jurisdiction is based on diversity of citizenship.

For some seventy-five years plaintiff and its predecessors have been making the periodic payments based on the quantity of Listerine manufactured or sold which are called for by the agreements in suit. The payments have totaled more than twenty-two million dollars and are presently in excess of one million five hundred thousand dollars yearly.

. . .

In the early 1880's Dr. Lawrence, a physician and editor of a medical journal in St. Louis, Missouri, devised a formula for an antiseptic liquid compound which was given the name 'Listerine'. The agreement between Lawrence and J. W. Lambert made in 1881, and that between Lawrence and Lambert Pharmacal Company made in 1885, providing for the sale of the Lawrence formula, were entered into in that city. Lambert, and thereafter his corporation, originally engaged in the manufacture and sale of Listerine and other pharmaceutical preparations on a modest scale there. Through the years the business prospered and grew fantastically and Listerine became a widely sold and nationally known product. The Lambert Pharmacal Company . . . continued the manufacture and sale of Listerine and other preparations until March 31, 1955, when it was merged into Warner-Hudnut, Inc., . . . and the name of the merged corporation was changed to Warner-Lambert Pharmaceutical Company, Inc.

The plaintiff in this action is the merged corporation which continues the manufacture and sale of Listerine.

Plaintiff's second amended complaint in substance alleges the following:

Prior to April 20, 1881 Dr. Lawrence furnished Lambert with an unnamed secret formula for the antiseptic compound which came to be known as "Listerine," and on or about that date Lambert executed the first of the documents with which we are concerned here. This document, in its entirety, reads as follows:

> Know all men by these presents, that for and in consideration of the fact, that Dr. J. J. Lawrence of the city of St Louis Mo has furnished me with the formula of a medicine called Listerine to be manufactured by me, that I Jordan W Lambert, also of the city of St Louis Mo, hereby agree for myself, my heirs, executors and assigns to pay monthly to the said Dr. J. J. Lawrence his heirs, executors or assigns, the sum of twenty dollars for each and every gross of said Listerine hereafter sold by myself, my heirs, executors or assigns. . . .

On or about May 2, 1881 Lambert began the manufacture of the formula and adopted the trademark "Listerine." The agreed payments under the 1881 agreement were reduced on October 21, 1881 . . . [and again on March 23, 1883 by letters addressed to Lambert by Lawrence to the amount of six dollars per gross amount of sales].

Thereafter Lambert assigned his rights to Listerine and other Lawrence compounds to the Lambert Pharmacal Company and this company on January 2, 1885 executed an instrument assuming Lambert's obligations under these agreements with Lawrence and other obligations on account of other formulas which Lawrence had furnished. . . .

The agreements between the parties contemplated, it is alleged, "the periodic payment of royalties to Lawrence for the use of a trade secret, to wit, the secret formula for" Listerine. After some modifications made with Lawrence's knowledge and approval, the formula was introduced on the market. The composition of the compound has remained the same since then and it is still being manufactured and sold by the plaintiff.

It is then alleged that the "trade secret" (the formula for Listerine) has gradually become a matter of public knowledge through the years following 1881 and prior to 1949, and has been published in the United States Pharmacopoeia, the National Formulary and the Journal of the American Medical Association, and also as a result of proceedings brought against plaintiff's predecessor by the Federal Trade Commission. Such publications were not the fault of plaintiff or its predecessors.

The complaint recites the chains of interest running respectively from Lambert to the present plaintiff and from Lawrence to the defendants, and concludes with a prayer for a declaration that plaintiff is "no longer liable to the defendants" for any further "royalties."

Despite the mass of material before me the basic issue between the parties is narrow. The plaintiff claims that its obligation to make payments to the defendants under the Lawrence-Lambert agreements was terminated by the public disclosure of the Listerine formula in various medical publications. The defendants assert that the obligation continued and has not been terminated.

(1).

The plaintiff seems to feel that the 1881 and 1885 agreements are indefinite and unclear, at least as to the length of time during which they would continue in effect. I do not find them to be so. These agreements seem to me to be plain and unambiguous.

In the 1881 agreement Lambert, for himself, his heirs, executors or assigns, agrees to pay Lawrence, his heirs, executors and assigns, "twenty dollars for each & every gross of said Listerine hereafter sold by myself my heirs executors or assigns." By the 1885 agreement the Lambert Pharmacal Company "agrees and contracts for itself & assigns to pay . . . J. J. Lawrence, his heirs executors & assigns, six dollars on each & every gross of Listerine . . . manufactured or sold by the said Lambert Pharmacal Co. or its assigns. . . ."

There is no ambiguity or uncertainty in this language. Nor can I ascertain any alternative or hidden meanings lurking within it.

The payments to Lawrence and his successors are conditioned upon the sale (in the 1881 agreement) and the manufacture or sale (in the 1885 agreement) of the medical preparation known as Listerine which Lawrence conveyed to Lambert. The obligation to pay on each and every gross of Listerine continues as long as this preparation is manufactured or sold by Lambert and his successors. It comes to an end when they cease to manufacture or sell the preparation. There is nothing which compels the plaintiff to continue such manufacture and sale. No doubt Lambert and his successors have been and still are free at any time, in good faith and in the exercise of sound business discretion, to stop manufacturing and selling Listerine. The plain meaning of the language used in these agreements is simply that Lambert's obligation to pay is co-extensive with manufacture or sale of Listerine by him and his successors.

(2).

The plaintiff, however, claims that despite the plain language of the agreement it may continue to manufacture and sell without making the payments required by the agreements because the formula which its predecessors acquired is no longer secret. To sustain this position plaintiff invokes the shade, if not the substance, of the traditional common law distaste for contractual rights and duties unbounded by definite limitations of time and argues that absent a construction that the obligation to pay is co-extensive only with the secrecy of the formula, it must be a forbidden "perpetuity" which the law will not enforce. I find no support for the plaintiff's theory either in the cases which it cites or elsewhere.

The word "perpetuity" is often applied very loosely to contractual obligations. Indiscriminate application of the term serves only to confuse. The mere fact that an obligation under a contract may continue for a very long time is no reason in itself for declaring the contract to exist in perpetuity or for giving it a construction which would do violence to the expressed intent of the parties.

. . .

Contracts which provide no fixed date for the termination of the promisor's obligation but condition the obligation upon an event which would necessarily terminate the contract are in quite a different category and it is in this category that the 1881 and 1885 Lambert Lawrence agreements fall. On the face of the agreements the obligation of Lambert and its successors to pay is conditioned upon the continued manufacture or sale or Listerine. When they cease manufacturing or selling Listerine the condition for continued payment comes to an end and the obligation to pay terminates. This is the plain meaning of the language which the parties used.

Moreover, this is not a case in which the promisor's obligation will cease only on the occurrence of some fortuitous event unrelated to the subject matter of the contract. The obligation here is conditioned upon an event arising out of the very arrangement between the parties which is the subject matter of the contract.

. . .

In the case at bar the obligation to continue payments as long as Lambert or his successors continue to manufacture or sell Listerine is plain from the language of the agreements and is implicit in their terms. There is no need to "construe" these contracts so as to import a condition or date of termination other than that expressed by the parties themselves in the agreements which they made. Courts must "concern (themselves) with what the parties intended, but only to the extent that they evidenced what they intended by what they wrote." An attempt to write new terms into this plain and simple agreement would be unwarranted and gratuitous. "We may not now imply a condition which the parties chose not to insert in their contract. . . ." Nor is there any need to resort to extrinsic evidence in order to ascertain what the intention of the parties was, or what the termination date of the obligation to pay would be, for the agreements themselves indicate the condition upon which the obligation terminates.

There is nothing unreasonable or irrational about imposing such an obligation. It is entirely rational and sensible that the obligation to make payments should be based upon the business which flows from the formula conveyed. Whether or not the obligation continues is in the control of the plaintiff itself. For the plaintiff has the right to terminate its obligation to pay whenever in good faith it desires to cease the manufacture or sale of Listerine. This would seem to end the matter.

(3).

However, plaintiff urges with vigor that the agreement must be differently construed because it involved the conveyance of a secret formula. The main thrust of its argument is that despite the language which the parties used the court must imply a limitation upon Lambert's obligation to pay measured by the length of time that the Listerine formula remained secret.

. . .

In [ ] patent and copyright cases the parties are dealing with a fixed statutory term and the monopoly granted by that term. This monopoly, created by

Congress, is designed to preserve exclusivity in the grantee during the statutory term and to release the patented or copyrighted material to the general public for general use thereafter. This is the public policy of the statutes in reference to which such contracts are made and it is against this background that the parties to patent and copyright license agreements contract.

Here, however, there is no such public policy. The parties are free to contract with respect to a secret formula or trade secret in any manner which they determine for their own best interests. A secret formula or trade secret may remain secret indefinitely. It may be discovered by someone else almost immediately after the agreement is entered into. Whoever discovers it for himself by legitimate means is entitled to its use. But that does not mean that one who acquires a secret formula or a trade secret through a valid and binding contract is then enabled to escape from an obligation to which he bound himself simply because the secret is discovered by a third party or by the general public. I see no reason why the court should imply such a term or condition in a contract providing on its face that payment shall be co-extensive with use. To do so here would be to rewrite the contract for the parties without any indication that they intended such a result.

It may be noted that here the parties themselves made no reference to secrecy in either the 1881 or the 1885 agreements. The word "secret" is not used anywhere in either of them. It is true that I have assumed during this discussion that the plaintiff is correct in its contention that what Lambert bargained for was a "secret" formula. But that in no way justifies the further assumption that he also bargained for continuing secrecy or that there would be failure of consideration if secrecy did not continue.

The argument that there was failure of consideration in 1931 after the agreement had been in force for some forty-five years because of disclosure then, is wholly devoid of merit. The plaintiff does not question that the conveyance to it of the "secret formula" furnished consideration for the contract. Once a contract is supported by consideration its terms are up to the parties. Whether the consideration is adequate or not is no concern of the court. The parties are free to fix their own terms and they have done so here. Plaintiff's argument goes only to adequacy of consideration. There is no question of failure of consideration.

One who acquires a trade secret or secret formula takes it subject to the risk that there be a disclosure. The inventor makes no representation that the secret is non-discoverable. All the inventor does is to convey the knowledge of the formula or process which is unknown to the purchaser and which in so far as both parties then know is unknown to any one else. The terms upon which they contract with reference to this subject matter are purely up to them and are governed by what the contract they enter into provides.

If they desire the payments or royalties should continue only until the secret is disclosed to the public it is easy enough for them to say so. But there is no justification for implying such a provision if the parties do not include it in their contract, particularly where the language which they use by fair intendment provides otherwise.

The case at bar illustrates what may occur in such cases. As the undisputed facts show, the acquisition of the Lawrence formula was the base on which plaintiff's predecessors built up a very large and successful business in the antiseptic or germicide field. Even now, twenty-five or more years after it is claimed that the trade secret was disclosed to the public, plaintiff retains more than 50% of the national market in these products.

Plaintiff lays stress on the large sums which have been spent in advertising and promoting the product, and there is no doubt that this and the business acumen of plaintiff's predecessors have contributed greatly to the success of the business. But it may be noted that the advertising and promotional material is primarily based on what are claimed to be the extraordinary merits of the formula for Listerine which plaintiff's predecessors acquired from Dr. Lawrence. Plaintiff and its predecessors have proclaimed for many years through the widest variety of advertising and promotional media the unique, indeed, almost magical properties of the formula from which Listerine is still made which is the formula conveyed by Lawrence to Lambert.

At the very least plaintiff's predecessors, through the acquisition of the Lawrence formula under this contract, obtained a head start in the field of liquid antiseptics which has proved of incalculable value through the years. There is nothing novel about business being transacted only in a small way at the outset of a contract relationship and thereafter growing far beyond what was anticipated when the contract was made. Because the business has prospered far beyond anticipations affords no basis for changing the terms of the contract the parties agreed upon when the volume was small.

There is nothing in this contract to indicate that plaintiff's predecessors bargained for more than the disclosure of the Lawrence formula which was then unknown to it. Plaintiff has pointed to no principle of law or equity which would require or permit the court gratuitously to rewrite the contract which its predecessors made for these considerations.

If plaintiff wishes to avoid its obligations under the contract it is free to do so, and, indeed, the contract itself indicates how this may be done. The fact that neither the plaintiff nor its predecessors have done so, and that the plaintiff continues to manufacture and sell Listerine under the Lawrence formula with great success, indicates how valuable the rights under the contract are and how unjust it would be to permit it to have its cake and eat it too.

Thus, I hold that under the agreements in suit plaintiff is obligated to make the periodic payments called for by them as long as it continues to manufacture and sell the preparation described in them as Listerine.

NOTES & QUESTIONS

1. Enforcement in Perpetuity

The holding of *Warner-Lambert* teaches that if parties to a trade secret license agree to royalty payments for use of the information, the royalties on the trade secret may be enforced in perpetuity. The result in *Warner-Lambert* is controversial. Some jurisdictions have followed the Restatement (Third) of Unfair Competition, which takes the position that an agreement is unenforceable as an unreasonable restraint of trade if it purports to protect information that is in the public domain. Restatement (Third) of Unfair Competition § 41 cmt. d.

2. Hybrid License

An inventor has the right to elect either patent or trade secret protection for subject matter that qualifies for protection under both regimes. The owner of the subject matter is also permitted to use both forms of protection simultaneously for different aspects of their invention. For instance, matter not described or disclosed in a patent may be retained as a trade secret, so long as the invention has been completely described and the best mode disclosed. Licenses that cover trade secrets and patents must clearly distinguish trade secret royalties from patent royalties, otherwise royalties for both become unenforceable once the patent term runs out. *See Brulotte v. Thys Co.,* 379 U.S. 29 (1964). The consideration for the trade secret should be stated separately from the consideration for the patent. Additionally, to avoid antitrust issues, the licensor should not require the licensee to take the trade secret as a condition for obtaining a license on the patent.

C. TRADEMARK LICENSING

Trademarks and service marks identify the source of goods or services. Marks help consumers distinguish the goods or services of one provider from the goods or services of another provider. When consumers associate a mark with high quality, desirable goods or services, the mark may become a thing of value in and of itself. The licensing of trademarks allows owners of marks to benefit from the value accrued in their mark and also forms the backbone of the franchising industry.

1. Requirement of Good Will: Prohibition Against "Bare" or "Naked" License

INTERNATIONAL COSMETICS EXCHANGE, INC.v. GAPARDIS HEALTH & BEAUTY, INC.
United States Court of Appeals for the Eleventh Circuit
303 F.3d 1242 (2002)

BIRCH, Circuit Judge:

I. BACKGROUND

CLM, a French corporation, manufacturers and sells ethnic cosmetic products in France and Europe under its trademark "FAIR & WHITE." CLM's President, Xavier Tancogne, is a chemist with a doctorate in pharmacy and created the formula for the "FAIR & WHITE" products.

ICE, a United States company founded by Michael Aini, is engaged in the purchase, importation, sale and distribution of ethnic cosmetic products. Aini is also the owner of four "Home Boys" stores in Brooklyn, New York, which are discount stores selling health and beauty aids to the African-American community. While in France, Michael's brother Jacob ("Jack") became interested in "FAIR & WHITE." In 1998, Jack purchased small quantities of "FAIR &

WHITE" products from CLM to test United States market acceptance. These products were sold in the "Home Boys" stores and were well received.

Thereafter, ICE and CLM entered into contract negotiations to continue "to develop, market and promote the "FAIR & WHITE" brand name in the United States." The Agreement stated that CLM was the owner of the "FAIR & WHITE" trademark in France and Europe, and that ICE was "the owner and holder of all rights, title and interest in the mark 'FAIR & WHITE' in the United States, Canada and Caribbean Islands." In return, the Agreement obligated ICE to sell $250,000 for the first year and use its best efforts to increase sales by 20 percent per year over the next five years. However, there were no provisions as to purchase or manufacture of the products. In the fall of 1999, ICE purchased approximately $125,000 of "FAIR & WHITE" product from CLM. ICE applied to register the mark with the United States Patent and Trademark Office in early 2000.

Meanwhile, . . . Gapardis, a distributor of ethnic products in Miami, became interested in "FAIR & WHITE" products and contacted Tancogne. On 13 April 2000, . . . Gapardis became the exclusive distributor in the United States for CLM's cosmetics bearing the "FAIR & WHITE" mark.

At some point, Tancogne became aware that counterfeit "FAIR & WHITE" goods were being sold in the United States. He believed that ICE was responsible and stopped providing ICE with product in April of 2000. ICE then took immediate steps to procure substitute "FAIR & WHITE" products from a Spanish manufacturer, Jabones Pardo. ICE provided Pardo with samples of "FAIR & WHITE" products and the formula of its active ingredients. Thereafter, ICE distributed non-CLM manufactured goods bearing the "FAIR & WHITE" mark and the associated trade names in the United States.

II. DISCUSSION

First, we affirm the ruling that the ICE/CLM Agreement was enforceable. CLM argues that the Agreement was an invalid "'assignment in gross,' which at minimum assigned the mark to ICE only in conjunction with the sale of genuine CLM-manufactured products." CLM maintains that ICE was only interested in owning the mark and did not purchase its formula or any assets. However, it is well-settled law that "the transfer of a trademark or trade name without the attendant good-will of the business which it represents is, in general, an invalid, 'in gross' transfer of rights." Although an assignment must be accompanied by the attendant good-will, there need not be any transfer of tangible assets. "An assignment of United States trademark rights by a foreign manufacturer to its United States distributor ordinarily will not be regarded as an assignment in gross, even if the transfer occurs after the designation has acquired trademark significance in this country." J. Thomas McCarthy, McCarthy on Trademarks and Unfair Competition § 29:8 (4th ed. 2002) (citation omitted).

As the district court correctly notes, the Agreement clearly recognizes the prior efforts of ICE with respect to "FAIR & WHITE" product:

> I.C.E. has developed, distributed and marketed the "FAIR & WHITE" brand name in connection with the Products in the United States . . . and as a result of I.C.E.'s efforts, the "FAIR & WHITE" brand name has achieved wide-spread popularity, recognition and awareness, and has become known to retailers and consumers in the United States . . . .

Thus, at the time the Agreement was created, the assignment was not in gross because it continued the association of the "FAIR & WHITE" trademark with the very goods which created its reputation. Thus, we agree with the district court that the Agreement was enforceable. Having established that the Agreement was enforceable, we analyze the appropriateness of injunctive relief.

"The grant or denial of a preliminary injunction is within the sound discretion of the district court and will not be disturbed absent a clear abuse of discretion." A party seeking a preliminary injunction for trademark infringement must establish four elements: "(1) a substantial likelihood of success on the merits; (2) a substantial threat of irreparable injury if the injunction were not granted; (3) that the threatened injury to plaintiffs outweighs the harm an injunction may cause the defendant; and (4) that granting the injunction would not disserve the public interest."

A. *ICE's Entitlement to Injunctive Relief*

The evidence supports the finding that there was an Agreement between CLM and ICE, and that ICE made an initial order for approximately $125,000 of product in August of 1999. CLM and ICE agreed that ICE would use its best efforts to sell $250,000 of "FAIR & WHITE" product within the first year of the Agreement and 20 percent more within the next five years. CLM failed to supply ICE with "FAIR & WHITE" product, and therefore, breached the Agreement. In addition, the district court concluded that CLM's contract with Gapardis further violated the Agreement, which granted ICE exclusive distribution rights in the United States as well as exclusive ownership of the "FAIR & WHITE" mark.

Since ICE had no right to continue using the "FAIR & WHITE" mark after losing access to the trademarked product, it also had no right to prevent CLM from using the trademark on the grounds that by doing so would confuse consumers. Any confusion is due to ICE's palming off another product as "FAIR & WHITE." Consequently, ownership rights to the "FAIR & WHITE" mark in the United States reverted back to CLM. Therefore, ICE is not entitled to injunctive relief because it has no longer has a property interest in the trademark.

B. *CLM's Entitlement to Injunctive Relief*

The district court found that when ICE began selling counterfeit product, it caused a likelihood of confusion regarding the "FAIR & WHITE" mark and that subsequent sales by [another party] added to the confusion. "While the trademark laws could not provide a basis for relief unless there was a breach of contract," CLM established that ICE breached the Agreement and thus trademark law is applicable to claims of unauthorized use of the mark. In order to succeed on the merits of a trademark infringement claim, CLM must show that the ICE used the mark in commerce without its consent and "that the unauthorized use was likely to deceive, cause confusion, or result in mistake." There can be no dispute that the parties' concurrent use of the "FAIR & WHITE" mark poses a substantial likelihood of confusion among consumers. The district court further decided that CLM demonstrated a substantial threat of irreparable injury if injunctive relief was not granted. It is clear from the evidence that ICE and [a third party] were selling counterfeit "FAIR & WHITE" product in the United States. Furthermore, as stated by the district court, "the threatened injury to CLM, by confusion in the market regarding the F&W Mark, outweighs any harm to ICE in preventing it from selling product supplied by third parties, particularly in light of the Court's finding that ICE is no longer the exclusive distributor."

AFFIRMED.

NOTES & QUESTIONS

1. Why Require a Transfer of Good Will?

Prevention of consumer confusion and deception is the rationale behind the rule against assignments in gross. Over time, consumers associate particular goods or services with a mark. Through use in the market, a mark develops good will. The rule against a bare or naked license protects consumers' expectation by safeguarding the association between a mark and the underlying assets, or good will. Transfer of a trademark divorced from its good will is an assignment in gross and is an invalid transfer. A licensor who transfers a bare license without its good will may find that his mark is unenforceable against alleged infringers. Additionally, the licensor may face a charge of abandonment and lose ownership in the mark.

For a mark to have good will, the mark must be used in a market and not have been abandoned. The licensor of the mark must own the good will in the market. If the mark is not used in a market, then it has no good will in that market and cannot be transferred.

In order to avoid an assignment in gross, a trademark owner wishing to license his mark must transfer the good will associated with the mark along with the mark itself. Transfer of good will along with a mark is a requirement of 15 U.S.C. § 1060. Under the original strict interpretation of this rule, courts determined whether a trademark license transferred good will by looking for evidence that assets associated with the licensor's business were assigned along with the mark. *See Pepsico v. Grapette Co.*, 416 F.2d 285 (8th Cir. 1969). Today the requirement has relaxed and courts look for evidence that the license is used with a product or service that is sufficiently similar to that of the licensor's.

2. Good Will, Where Have You Gone?

More recently, courts have extended the scope of trademark protection to include a broadening array of uses. The extended scope of protection has spurred licensing activities. Some uses of a mark trigger non-source associations, such as the encouragement of team loyalty when a sports team licenses its name for use on apparel. Such uses of a mark for purposes other than source identification rarely impair the mark's potential for legal protection. A party who would otherwise be liable for infringement for selling apparel bearing the sports team's name will generally sign a licensing agreement with the owner for the use of the mark. Is this transfer not a form of naked licensing? How can this accepted practice be reconciled with the requirement that a licensor must transfer good will along with a mark?

3. Strategic or Defensive Transfer of Trademarks

Companies acquire trademarks for strategic or defensive purposes, as for example when a company launching a new product purchases another company's similar related mark in order to establish an earlier use date or to avoid conflicting marks. Even though such acquisitions may run counter to the prohibition against naked licensing, strategic acquisition of trademarks is an accepted and commonplace transaction. *See Money Store v. Harriscorp Finance Inc.*, 689 F.2d 666 (7th Cir. 1982); *Glamorene Products Corp. v. Proctor & Gamble Co.*, 538 F.2d 894 (CCPA 1976).

2.   Control Over the Mark

A licensor must maintain control over the quality of the goods or services offered under the licensed trademark. The validity of a trademark license depends on the control over the "nature" and "quality" of the goods or services offered by the licensee. A licensor's failure to exercise control has severe repercussions. Without control over the licensee's use, the mark may lose its significance and cease to function as a trademark. Once this occurs, the licensor loses his rights in the mark.

DAWN DONUT COMPANY v. HART'S FOOD STORES, INC.
United States Court of Appeals for the Second Circuit
267 F.2d 358 (1958)

LUMBARD, Circuit Judge.

. . .

Plaintiff, Dawn Donut Co., Inc., of Jackson, Michigan since June 1, 1922 has continuously used the trademark "Dawn" upon 25 to 100 pound bags of doughnut mix which it sells to bakers in various states, including New York, and since 1935 it has similarly marketed a line of sweet dough mixes for use in the baking of coffee cakes, cinnamon rolls and oven goods in general under that mark. In 1950 cake mixes were added to the company's line of products. Dawn's sales representatives call upon bakers to solicit orders for mixes and the orders obtained are filled by shipment to the purchaser either directly from plaintiff's Jackson, Michigan plant, where the mixes are manufactured, or from a local warehouse within the customer's state. For some years plaintiff maintained a warehouse in Jamestown, New York, from which shipments were made, but sometime prior to the commencement of this suit in 1954 it discontinued this warehouse and has since then shipped its mixes to its New York customers directly from Michigan.

Plaintiff furnishes certain buyers of its mixes, principally those who agree to become exclusive Dawn Donut Shops, with advertising and packaging material bearing the trademark "Dawn" and permits these bakers to sell goods made from the mixes to the consuming public under that trademark. These display materials are supplied either as a courtesy or at a moderate price apparently to stimulate and promote the sale of plaintiff's mixes.

The district court found that with the exception of one Dawn Donut Shop operated in the city of Rochester, New York during 1926-27, plaintiff's licensing of its mark in connection with the retail sale of doughnuts in the state of New York has been confined to areas not less than 60 miles from defendant's trading area. The court also found that for the past eighteen years plaintiff's present New York state representative has, without interruption, made regular calls upon bakers in the city of Rochester, N.Y., and in neighboring towns and cities, soliciting orders for plaintiff's mixes and that throughout this period orders have been filled and shipments made of plaintiff's mixes from Jackson, Michigan into the city of Rochester. But it does not appear that any of these purchasers of plaintiff's mixes employed the plaintiff's mark in connection with retail sales.

The defendant, Hart Food Stores, Inc., owns and operates a retail grocery chain within the New York counties of Monroe, Wayne, Livingston, Genesee, Ontario and Wyoming. The products of defendant's bakery, Starhart Bakeries, Inc., a New York corporation of which it is the sole stockholder, are distributed through these stores, thus confining the distribution of defendant's product to an area within a 45 mile radius of Rochester. Its advertising of doughnuts and other baked products over television and radio and in newspapers is also limited to this area. Defendant's bakery corporation was formed on April 13, 1951 and first used the imprint 'Dawn' in packaging its products on August 30, 1951. The district court found that the defendant adopted the mark 'Dawn' without any actual knowledge of plaintiff's use or federal registration of the mark, selecting it largely because of a slogan 'Baked at midnight, delivered at Dawn' which was originated by defendant's president and used by defendant in its bakery operations from 1929 to 1935. Defendant's president testified, however, that no investigation was made prior to the adoption of the mark to see if anyone else was employing it. Plaintiff's marks were registered federally in 1927, and their registration was renewed in 1947. Therefore by virtue of the Lanham Act, 15 U.S.C.A. § 1072, the defendant had constructive notice of plaintiff's marks as of July 5, 1947, the effective date of the Act.

. . .

The final issue presented is raised by defendant's appeal from the dismissal of its counterclaim for cancellation of plaintiff's registration on the ground that the plaintiff failed to exercise the control required by the Lanham Act over the nature and quality of the goods sold by its licensees.

We are all agreed that the Lanham Act places an affirmative duty upon a licensor of a registered trademark to take reasonable measures to detect and prevent misleading uses of his mark by his licensees or suffer cancellation of his federal registration. The Act, 15 U.S.C.A. § 1064, provides that a trademark registration may be cancelled because the Trademark has been "abandoned." And "abandoned" is defined in 15 U.S.C.A. § 1127 to include any act or omission by the registrant which causes the trademark to lose its significance as an indication of origin.

Prior to the passage of the Lanham Act, many courts took the position that the licensing of a trademark separately from the business in connection with which it had been used worked an abandonment. The theory of these cases was that:

> A trade-mark is intended to identify the goods of the owner and to safeguard his good will. The designation if employed by a person other than the one whose business it serves to identify would be misleading. Consequently, 'a right to the use of a trade-mark or a trade-name cannot be transferred in gross.'

Other courts were somewhat more liberal and held that a trademark could be licensed separately from the business in connection with which it had been used provided that the licensor retained control over the quality of the goods produced by the licensee. *E. I. DuPont de Nemours & Co. v. Celanese Corporation of America,* 1948, 167 F.2d 484, 35 CCPA 1061, 3 A.L.R.2d 1213; *see also* 3 A.L.R.2d 1226, 1277-1282 (1949) and cases there cited. But even in the DuPont case the court was careful to point out that naked licensing, viz. the grant of licenses without the retention of control, was invalid.

The Lanham Act clearly carries forward the view of these latter cases that controlled licensing does not work an abandonment of the licensor's registration, while a system of naked licensing does. 15 U.S.C.A. § 1055 provides:

> Where a registered mark or a mark sought to be registered is or may be used legitimately by related companies, such use shall inure to the benefit of the registrant or applicant for registration, and such use shall not affect the validity of such mark or of its registration, provided such mark is not used in such manner as to deceive the public.

And 15 U.S.C.A. § 1127 defines "related company" to mean "any person who legitimately controls or is controlled by the registrant or applicant for registration in respect to the nature and quality of the goods or services in connection with which the mark is used."

Without the requirement of control, the right of a trademark owner to license his mark separately from the business in connection with which it has been used would create the danger that products bearing the same trademark might be of diverse qualities. If the licensor is not compelled to take some reasonable steps to prevent misuses of his trademark in the hands of others the public will be deprived of its most effective protection against misleading uses of a trademark. The public is hardly in a position to uncover deceptive uses of a trademark before they occur and will be at best slow to detect them after they happen. Thus, unless the licensor exercises supervision and control over the operations of its licensees the risk that the public will be unwittingly deceived will be increased and this is precisely what the Act is in part designed to prevent. Clearly the only effective way to protect the public where a trademark is used by licensees is to place on the licensor the affirmative duty of policing in a reasonable manner the activities of his licensees.

The critical question on these facts therefore is whether the plaintiff sufficiently policed and inspected its licensees' operations to guarantee the quality of the products they sold under its trademarks to the public. The trial court found that: "By reason of its contacts with its licensees, plaintiff exercised legitimate control over the nature and quality of the food products on which plaintiff's licensees used the trademark 'Dawn.' Plaintiff and its licensees are related companies within the meaning of Section 45 of the Trademark Act of 1946." It is the position of the majority of this court that the trial judge has the same leeway in determining what constitutes a reasonable degree of supervision and control over licensees under the facts and circumstances of the particular case as he has on other questions of fact; and particularly because it is the defendant who has the burden of proof on this issue they hold the lower court's finding not clearly erroneous.

I dissent from the conclusion of the majority that the district court's findings are not clearly erroneous because while it is true that the trial judge must be given some discretion in determining what constitutes reasonable supervision of licensees under the Lanham Act, it is also true that an appellate court ought not to accept the conclusions of the district court unless they are supported by findings of sufficient facts. It seems to me that the only findings of the district judge regarding supervision are in such general and conclusory terms of to be meaningless. In the absence of supporting findings or of undisputed evidence in the record indicating the kind of supervision and inspection the plaintiff actually made of its licensees, it is impossible for us to pass upon whether there was such supervision as to satisfy the statute. There was evidence before the district court in the matter of supervision, and more detailed findings thereon should have been made.

Plaintiff's licensees fall into two classes: (1) those bakers with whom it made written contracts providing that the baker purchase exclusively plaintiff's mixes and requiring him to adhere to plaintiff's directions in using the mixes; and (2) those bakers whom plaintiff permitted to sell at retail under the "Dawn" label doughnuts and other baked goods made from its mixes although there was no written agreement governing the quality of the food sold under the Dawn mark. The contracts that plaintiff did conclude, although they provided that the purchaser use the mix as directed and without adulteration, failed to provide for any system of inspection and control. Without such a system plaintiff could not know whether these bakers were adhering to its standards in using the mix or indeed whether they were selling only products made from Dawn mixes under the trademark "Dawn."

The absence, however, of an express contract right to inspect and supervise a licensee's operations does not mean that the plaintiff's method of licensing failed to comply with the requirements of the Lanham Act. Plaintiff may in fact have exercised control in spite of the absence of any express grant by licensees of the right to inspect and supervise.

The question then, with respect to both plaintiff's contract and non-contract licensees, is whether the plaintiff in fact exercised sufficient control.

Here the only evidence in the record relating to the actual supervision of licensees by plaintiff consists of the testimony of two of plaintiff's local sales representatives that they regularly visited their particular customers and the further testimony of one of them, Jesse Cohn, the plaintiff's New York representative, that "in many cases" he did have an opportunity to inspect and observe the operations of his customers. The record does not indicate whether plaintiff's other sales representatives made any similar efforts to observe the operations of licensees.

Moreover, Cohn's testimony fails to make clear the nature of the inspection he made or how often he made one. His testimony indicates that his opportunity to observe a licensee's operations was limited to "those cases where I am able to get into the shop" and even casts some doubt on whether he actually had sufficient technical knowledge in the use of plaintiff's mix to make an adequate inspection of a licensee's operations.

The fact that it was Cohn who failed to report the defendant's use of the mark "Dawn" to the plaintiff casts still further doubt about the extent of the supervision Cohn exercised over the operations of plaintiff's New York licensees.

Thus I do not believe that we can fairly determine on this record whether plaintiff subjected its licensees to periodic and thorough inspections by trained personnel or whether its policing consisted only of chance, cursory examinations of licensees' operations by technically untrained salesmen. The latter system of inspection hardly constitutes a sufficient program of supervision to satisfy the requirements of the Act.

Therefore it is appropriate to remand the counterclaim for more extensive findings on the relevant issues rather than hazard a determination on this incomplete and uncertain record. I would direct the district court to order the cancellation of plaintiff's registrations if it should find that the plaintiff did not adequately police the operations of its licensees.

But unless the district court finds some evidence of misuse of the mark by plaintiff in its sales of mixes to bakers at the wholesale level, the cancellation of plaintiff's registration should be limited to the use of the mark in connection with sale of the finished food products to the consuming public. Such a limited cancellation is within the power of the court. Section 1119 of 15 U.S.C.A. specifically provides that "In any action involving a registered mark the court may . . . order the cancellation of registrations, in whole or in part. . . ." Moreover, partial cancellation is consistent with § 1051(a)(1) of 15 U.S.C.A., governing the initial registration of trademarks which requires the applicant to specify "the goods in connection with which the mark is used and the mode or manner in which the mark is used in connection with such goods. . . ."

The district court's denial of an injunction restraining defendant's use of the mark "Dawn" on baked and fried goods and its dismissal of defendant's counterclaim are affirmed.

NOTES & QUESTIONS

1. Quality Control

An owner of a trademark may transfer the rights to a mark, so long as the licensor maintains control over its use. One of the first cases to allow trademark licensing over the objection of abandonment was *E.I. du Pont de Nemours & Co. v. Celanese Corp. of America*, 167 F.2d 484 (C.C.P.A. 1948). In *Celanese*, the court refused to cancel Celanese's trademark even though the company licensed off its mark to another party. Cancellation was inappropriate because Celanese maintained control over the quality standards for the product produced under the licensed mark. In light of the rationale for the rule against assignments in gross, why would control over a mark be the key inquiry for cancellation of a mark?

Courts determine on a case-by-case basis whether a licensor has exerted sufficient control over the quality of the goods and services produced under a licensed trademark. The control exerted over the licensee must guarantee the quality of the goods and services produced. A licensor may rely on third parties to conduct product testing, but sole reliance on third parties to enforce quality control standards may not be sufficient.

In a trademark licensing agreement, a licensor is well advised to specify which products and services the licensor authorizes the licensee to use in connection with the mark and define the requirements governing the quality of the goods or services to be produced. A licensor who fails to supervise a licensee's use of a mark may face a charge of abandonment of the mark. Specifically, if a licensor acquiesces to the use of a mark by a licensee who is unwilling or unable to abide by the quality control requirements set forth in a licensing agreement, the licensor risks abandonment of his rights in the mark. The licensor has an affirmative duty to act when he discovers a licensee's deviations from the quality control standards specified in a licensing agreement.

2. Enforcement of the Quality Control Requirement

Courts do not always strictly enforce the quality control requirement over a licensed trademark. Under certain circumstances, sufficient control can be found even without actual control or express provisions of control in a licensing contract. *Taco Cabana v. Two Pesos*, 932 F.2d 1113 (5th Cir. 1991), provides an example of such a circumstance:

> The purpose of the quality-control requirement is to prevent the public deception that would ensue from variant quality standards under the same mark or dress. Where the particular circumstances of the licensing arrangement persuade us that the public will not be deceived, we need not elevate form over substance and require the same policing rigor appropriate to more formal licensing and franchising transactions. Where the license parties have engaged in a close working relationship, and may justifiably rely on each party's intimacy with standards and procedures to ensure consistent quality, and

no actual decline in quality standards is demonstrated, we would depart from the purpose of the law to find an abandonment simply for want of all the inspection and control formalities.

The history of the Stehling brothers' relationship warrants this relaxation of formalities. Prior to the licensing agreement at issue, the Stehling brothers operated Taco Cabana together for approximately eight years. Taco Cabana and TaCasita do not use significantly different procedures or products, and the brothers may be expected to draw on their mutual experience to maintain the requisite quality consistency. They cannot protect their trade dress if they operate their separate restaurants in ignorance of each other's operations, but they need not maintain the careful policing appropriate to more formal license arrangements.

Taco Cabana, 932 F.2d at 1121-1122. Moreover, courts do not require bilateral quality monitoring on the part of licensors. In other words, there is no need for equivalent policing of the licensor's and licensee's operations; the law only requires consistent quality.

3. Licensor's Ownership Arising From Use by a Licensee

If a licensee makes first use of a mark, does the licensee's use create ownership rights in the licensor? Under the old view, trademarks had to be used in order to become subject to ownership rights. Until a licensor used a mark, he did not own the mark and therefore had no right to transfer it. More recent decisions do not require that a licensor make first use of the mark before he licenses it.

Use by a licensee may create or maintain ownership of the mark in the licensor. Section 5 of the Lanham Act provides that the use of a mark by a "related company" inures to the benefit of the licensor. A licensor may rely on a licensee's use of the mark for any purpose, including first use of a mark, so long as the licensor controls the nature and quality of the goods or services. Section 45 of the Lanham Act defines the term "related company" to mean any person whose use of a mark is supervised by the owner of the mark for the purpose of ensuring the nature and quality of the products. So long as a licensor retains control over the mark, use by the licensee will be considered a use by the licensor.

4. Degree of Control: Franchisee Distinguished from Licensee

The franchising system was made possible by controlled trademark licensing. A franchise relationship arises where a trademark owner exercises "significant control or assistance" over the activities of a franchisee related to the franchisee's entire method of operation. "Significant control or assistance" under § 5 of Federal Trade Commission Act is greater involvement than merely assisting a transferee in selling the trademarked product or service. Control necessary to protect a trademark owner's rights in a mark does not constitute "significant" control or assistance that gives rise to a franchise relationship. A licensor is permitted to exercise a degree of supervision and control over licensees in order to protect its trademark. Moreover, control for trademark protection purposes does not make the licensee the licensor's agent.

3. Antitrust Concerns: Tying

Tying in the context of trademark licensing occurs when a trademark owner forces a licensee to purchase ingredients or other products from the licensor or restricts the licensee to purchase only from licensor-approved suppliers as a condition for obtaining the license. Another version of tying involves multiple trademarks, as when an owner conditions licensing of one mark on the licensing of another.

Trademark licensing practices that otherwise run afoul of antitrust laws prohibiting tying might be justified under certain circumstances. The first justification for tying involves the licensor's duty to police the quality and nature of the goods and services produced in association with the licensed mark. For unique products or those that embody secret formulas or trade secrets, a licensor is permitted to require licensees to purchase products or product components from the licensor or an approved source. On the other hand, for non-unique products for which the licensor can furnish product specifications or instructions, the licensor cannot require purchases by the licensee. A second circumstance in which otherwise illegal tying practices are tolerated is in infant industries. For a short time, a licensor may require the purchase of a product if the tied product is new and previously unknown. Another circumstance that justifies tying practices involves franchising agreements. The goal of franchising is to establish a standard identity of all franchisees in the public's mind. In a franchise relationship, the trademark of the franchisor serves as a unifying element that assures consumers that products or services offered under the mark meet a uniform standard of quality. Courts accept that in order to form a unitary identity in the minds of consumers, a franchisor may need to require a franchisee to license multiple related marks.

PRINCIPE v. MCDONALD'S CORPORATION
United States Court of Appeals for the Fourth Circuit
631 F.2d 303 (1980)

PHILLIPS, Circuit Judge.

This appeal presents the question of whether a fast food franchisor that requires its licensees to operate their franchises in premises leased from the franchisor is guilty of an illegal tying arrangement in violation of § 1 of the Sherman Act, 15 U.S.C. § 1. On the facts of this case, we hold it does not and affirm the directed verdict for the defendants.

II

McDonald's is not primarily a fast food retailer. While it does operate over a thousand stores itself, the vast majority of the stores in its system are operated by franchisees. Nor does McDonald's sell equipment or supplies to its licensees. Instead its primary business is developing and collecting royalties from limited menu fast food restaurants operated by independent business people.

McDonald's develops new restaurants according to master plans that originate at the regional level and must be approved by upper management.

Regional administrative staffs meet at least annually to consider new areas into which McDonald's can expand. Once the decision is made to expand into a particular geographic area, specialists begin to search for appropriate restaurant sites.

As part of the planning process, McDonald's decides what type of store to build on each site and where to locate it on the land. Differences in lot size and shape necessitate adjustments in store and parking lot configurations. Projected market size dictates dining room size. Land elevation, sign restrictions, store visibility and local set back requirements control restaurant placement.

As constructed, McDonald's restaurants are finished shells; they contain no kitchen or dining room equipment. Furnishing store equipment is the responsibility of the operator. . . . McDonald's does provide specifications such equipment must meet, but does not sell the equipment itself.

Having acquired the land, begun construction of the store and selected an operator, McDonald's enters into two contracts with the franchisee. Under the first, the franchise agreement, McDonald's grants the franchisee the rights to use McDonald's food preparation system and to sell food products under the McDonald's name. The franchise pays a $12,500 franchise fee and agrees to remit three per cent of his gross sales as a royalty in return. Under the second contract, the lease, McDonald's grants the franchisee the right to use the particular store premises to which his franchise pertains. In return, the franchisee pays a $15,000 refundable security deposit (as evidence of which he receives a twenty year non-negotiable non-interest bearing note) and agrees to pay eight and one half per cent of his gross sales as rent. These payments under the franchise and lease agreements are McDonald's only sources of income from its franchised restaurants. The franchisee also assumes responsibility under the lease for building maintenance, improvements, property taxes and other costs associated with the premises. Both the franchise agreement and the lease generally have twenty year durations, both provide that termination of one terminates the other, and neither is available separately.

III

The Principes argue McDonald's is selling not one but three distinct products, the franchise, the lease and the security deposit note. The alleged antitrust violation stems from the fact that a prospective franchisee must buy all three in order to obtain the franchise.

. . .

IV

"There is, at the outset of every tie-in case, including the familiar cases involving physical goods, the problem of determining whether two separate products are in fact involved." *Fortner Enterprises, Inc. v. United States Steel Corp.*, 394 U.S. 495, 507, 89 S. Ct. 1252, 1260, 22 L. Ed. 2d 495 (1969) (Fortner I). Because we agree with McDonald's that the lease, note and license are not separate products but component parts of the overall franchise package, we hold on the facts of this case there was no illegal tie in. Accordingly, we affirm the summary judgment and directed verdict for McDonald's on the tying claims.

Given the realities of modern franchising, we think the proper inquiry is not whether the allegedly tied products are associated in the public mind with the franchisor's trademark, but whether they are integral components of the business method being franchised. Where the challenged aggregation is an essential ingredient of the franchised system's formula for success, there is but a single product and no tie in exists as a matter of law.

Applying this standard to the present case, we hold the lease is not separable from the McDonald's franchise to which it pertains. McDonald's practice of developing a system of company owned restaurants operated by franchisees has substantial advantages, both for the company and for franchisees. It is part of what makes a McDonald's franchise uniquely attractive to franchisees.

First, because it approaches the problem of restaurant site selection systematically, McDonald's is able to obtain better sites than franchisees could select. Armed with its demographic information, guided by its staff of experts and unencumbered by preferences of individual franchisees, McDonald's can wield its economic might to acquire sites where new restaurants will prosper without undercutting existing franchisees' business or limiting future expansion. Individual franchisees are unlikely to possess analytical expertise, undertake elaborate market research or approach the problem of site selection from an area wide point of view. Individual franchisees benefit from the McDonald's approach because their stores are located in areas McDonald's has determined will produce substantial fast food business and on sites where that business is most likely to be diverted to their stores. Because McDonald's purposefully locates new stores where they will not undercut existing franchisees' business, McDonald's franchisees do not have to compete with each other, a substantial advantage in the highly competitive fast food industry.

Second, McDonald's policy of owning all of its own restaurants assures that the stores remain part of the McDonald's system. McDonald's franchise arrangements are not static: franchisees retire or die; occasionally they do not live up to their franchise obligations and must be replaced; even if no such contingency intervenes, the agreements normally expire by their own terms after twenty years. If franchisees owned their own stores, any of these events could disrupt McDonald's business and have a negative effect on the system's goodwill. Buildings whose architecture identified them as former McDonald's stores would sit idle or be used for other purposes. Replacement franchisees would have to acquire new and perhaps less desirable sites, a much more difficult and expensive process after the surrounding business area has matured. By owning its own stores, McDonald's assures its continued presence on the site, maintains the store's patronage even during management changes and avoids the negative publicity of having former McDonald's stores used for other purposes. By preserving the goodwill of the system in established markets, company store ownership produces attendant benefits for franchisees.

Third, because McDonald's acquires the sites and builds the stores itself, it can select franchisees based on their management potential rather than their real estate expertise or wealth. Ability to emphasize management skills is important to McDonald's because it has built its reputation largely on the consistent quality of its operations rather than on the merits of its hamburgers. A store's quality is largely a function of its management. McDonald's policy of owning its own stores reduces a franchisee's initial investment, thereby broadening the applicant base and opening the door to persons who otherwise could not afford a McDonald's franchise. Accordingly, McDonald's is able to select franchisees primarily on the basis of their willingness to work for the success of their operations. Their ability to begin operating a McDonald's restaurant without having to search for a site, negotiate for the land, borrow hundreds of thousands of dollars and construct a store building is of substantial value to franchisees.

Finally, because both McDonald's and the franchisee have a substantial financial stake in the success of the restaurant, their relationship becomes a sort of partnership that might be impossible under other circumstances. McDonald's spends close to half a million dollars on each new store it establishes. Each franchisee invests over $100,000 to make the store operational. Neither can afford to ignore the other's problems, complaints or ideas. Because its investment is on the line, the Company cannot allow its franchisees to lose money. This being so, McDonald's works with its franchisees to build their business, occasionally financing improvements at favorable rates or even accepting reduced royalty payments in order to provide franchisees more working capital.

All of these factors contribute significantly to the overall success of the McDonald's system. The formula that produced system wide success, the formula that promises to make each new McDonald's store successful, that formula is what McDonald's sells its franchisees. To characterize the franchise as an unnecessary aggregation of separate products tied to the McDonald's name is to miss the point entirely. Among would be franchisees, the McDonald's name has come to stand for the formula, including all that it entails. We decline to find that it is an illegal tie in.

NOTES & QUESTIONS

1. The Single Product Defense

The practice of tying, disfavored by the courts as anticompetitive, is defined as the conditioning of the sale of one product upon the purchase of a different (tied) product. The single product defense is premised on the principle that there can be no unlawful tying where there is only one product. The court in *Principe v. McDonald's Corp.*, 631 F.2d 303 (4th Cir. 1980), relies on the single product defense in ruling in favor of McDonald's. The court states, "Where the challenged aggregation is an essential ingredient of the franchised system's formula for success, there is but a single product and no tie in exists as a matter of law." *Id.* at 309.

2. Territorial Limitations

The United States Supreme Court in *United States v. Topco Associates, Inc.*, 405 U.S. 596 (1972), held that horizontal territorial divisions used as schemes to suppress competition were illegal per se under the Sherman Act. In *Topco,* the government alleged that a cooperative supermarket association's horizontal territorial limitations over its members were illegal as anti-competitive horizontal territorial restraints. The Court agreed and struck down the scheme.

The result in *Topco* has been widely criticized because business practices like the one in *Topco* may be viewed as pro-competitive. The *Topco* cooperative allowed its members, independent small grocery stores, to pool their purchasing strength together and compete against much lager chain stores. The ruling in *Topco* effectively denied the independent grocery stores a workable scheme, without which they were at a competitive disadvantage compared to the larger grocery chain stores.

D. COPYRIGHT LICENSING

1. Introduction

Historically, the doctrine of indivisibility under the Copyright Act of 1909 held that the bundle of exclusive rights associated with copyrights could not be assigned or transferred in parts. Today, owners of copyrights may divide up the rights in the copyright bundle and assign or license each separately. The current Copyright Act expressly recognizes the divisibility of a copyright: "Any of the exclusive rights comprised in a copyright, including any subdivision of any of the rights specified in section 106, may be transferred . . . and owned separately. The owner of any particular exclusive right is entitled, to the extent of the right, to all of the protection and remedies accorded to the copyright owner by this title." 17 U.S.C. § 201(d)(2) (2005).

NANCEY SILVERS v. SONY PICTURES ENTERTAINMENT, INC.
United States Court of Appeals for the Ninth Circuit
402 F.3d 881 (2005)

GRABER, Circuit Judge

May an assignee who holds an accrued claim for copyright infringement, but who has no legal or beneficial interest in the copyright itself, institute an action for infringement? After analyzing the 1976 Copyright Act and its history, as well as the scant, although persuasive, precedent that is available in analogous situations, we answer that question "no." Accordingly, we reverse the ruling of the district court, which allowed this action by the assignee to proceed.

FACTUAL AND PROCEDURAL BACKGROUND

Nancey Silvers wrote the script of a made-for-television movie called "The Other Woman." Although Silvers wrote "The Other Woman" script, she did not hold the copyright, because "The Other Woman" was a work-for-hire that Silvers completed for Frank & Bob Films II, aka Von Zerneck/Sertner Films ("Frank & Bob Films"). Frank & Bob Films was the original owner of the copyright to "The Other Woman," and remains so today.

About three years after "The Other Woman" aired on a broadcast network, Sony Pictures Entertainment, Inc., released the motion picture "Stepmom." After the release of "Stepmom," Frank & Bob Films executed an "Assignment of Claims and Causes of Action" in favor of Silvers. Frank & Bob Films retained ownership of the underlying copyright to "The Other Woman" script, but assigned to Silvers "all right, title and interest in and to any claims and causes of action against Sony Pictures Entertainment, Inc., Columbia TriStar, and any other appropriate persons or entities, with respect to the screenplay *The Other Woman* . . . and the motion picture *Stepmom.*"

Silvers then filed a complaint against Sony for copyright infringement, alleging that the movie "Stepmom" was substantially similar to the script for "The Other Woman." Sony moved to dismiss on the ground that Silvers lacked standing to bring an action for copyright infringement in the absence of some legal or beneficial ownership in the underlying copyright. The district court denied the motion and certified the issue for interlocutory appeal.

DISCUSSION

A. *The Statute*

Article I, section 8, clause 8, of the Constitution states: "The Congress shall have Power . . . To promote the Progress of Science and useful Arts by securing for limited Times to Authors . . . the exclusive Right to their . . . Writings. . . ." As is clear from its text, that clause of the Constitution grants no substantive protections to authors. Rather, Congress is empowered to provide copyright protection.

Copyright, therefore, is a creature of statute, and the only rights that exist under copyright law are those granted by statute. As the Supreme Court wrote 170 years ago:

> This right [in copyright] . . . does not exist at common law — it origi-nated, if at all, under the acts of congress. No one can deny that when the legislature is about to vest an exclusive right in an author or an inventor, they have the power to prescribe the conditions on which such right shall be enjoyed. . . .

Accordingly, our starting point is the statute.

Section 501(b) of the 1976 Copyright Act establishes who is legally autho-rized to sue for infringement of a copyright:

> The *legal or beneficial owner of an exclusive right under a copyright* is entitled, subject to the requirements of section 411, to institute an action for any infringement of that particular right committed while he or she is the owner of it.

17 U.S.C. § 501(b) (emphasis added). The meaning of that provision appears clear. To be entitled to sue for copyright infringement, the plaintiff must be the "legal or beneficial owner of an exclusive right under a copyright."

Section 106 of the 1976 Copyright Act, in turn, defines "exclusive rights":

(1)   to reproduce the copyrighted work in copies or phonorecords;

(2)   to prepare derivative works based upon the copyrighted work;

(3)   to distribute copies or phonorecords of the copyrighted work to the public by sale or other transfer of ownership, or by rental, lease, or lending;

(4)   in the case of literary, musical, dramatic, and choreographic works, pantomimes, and motion pictures and other audiovisual works, to perform the copyrighted work publicly;

(5)   in the case of literary, musical, dramatic, and choreographic works, pantomimes, and pictorial, graphic, or sculptural works, including the individual images of a motion picture or other audiovisual work, to display the copyrighted work publicly; and

(6)   in the case of sound recordings, to perform the copyrighted work publicly by means of a digital audio transmission.

17 U.S.C. § 106. The right to sue for an accrued claim for infringement is not an exclusive right under § 106. Section 201(d) refers to exclusive rights and provides:

(1)   The ownership of a copyright may be transferred in whole or in part by any means of conveyance or by operation of law, and may be bequeathed by will or pass as personal property by the applicable laws of intestate succession.

(2)   Any of the exclusive rights comprised in a copyright, including any subdivision of any of the rights specified by section 106, may be transferred as provided by clause (1) and owned separately. The owner of any particular exclusive right is entitled, to the extent of that right, to all of the protection and remedies accorded to the copyright owner by this title.

17 U.S.C. § 201(d). Exclusive rights in a copyright may be transferred and owned separately, but § 201(d) creates no exclusive rights other than those listed in § 106, nor does it create an exception to § 501(b).

Section 501(b) must also be read in conjunction with § 501(a), which provides that one who "violates any of the exclusive rights of the copyright owner as provided by sections 106 through 122 . . . is an infringer." The definition of an infringer in subsection (a) is parallel to the definition of a proper plaintiff in subsection (b). Common to both subsections is an exclusive copyright interest.

In addition, when a copyright interest is transferred it must be recorded to protect the copyright holder's right to bring an infringement suit. 17 U.S.C. § 205(d). This requirement ensures that prospective buyers or transferees have notice of the copyright interests owned by others. By contrast, the recording statute does not contemplate a transfer of anything other than an ownership interest in the copyright, along with the concomitant exclusive rights.

Returning to the operative section, under § 501(b) the plaintiff must have a legal or beneficial interest in at least one of the exclusive rights described in § 106. Additionally, in order for a plaintiff to be "entitled . . . to institute an action" for infringement, the infringement must be "committed while he or she is the owner of" the particular exclusive right allegedly infringed. 17 U.S.C. § 501(b).

The statute does not say expressly that *only* a legal or beneficial owner of an exclusive right is entitled to sue. But, under traditional principles of statutory interpretation, Congress' explicit listing of who *may* sue for copyright infringement should be understood as an *exclusion of others* from suing for infringement. The doctrine of *expressio unius est exclusio alterius* "as applied to statutory interpretation creates a presumption that when a statute designates certain persons, things, or manners of operation, all omissions should be understood as exclusions."

There are two particularly important reasons to apply such a presumption here. First, we are mindful of the principle with which we began our discussion: Copyright is a creature of statute, so we will not lightly insert common law principles that Congress has left out. Second, the durational limitation in § 501(b) shows that Congress restricted even the legal or beneficial owner of a copyright; the owner is not entitled to sue unless the alleged infringement occurred "while he or she [was] the owner of it." In other words, Congress' grant of the right to sue was carefully circumscribed.

We think the meaning of § 501(b) is clear, but we recognize that its omission explicitly to address the present question may create an ambiguity. Therefore, we consult legislative history.

B. *Legislative History*

The 1976 Copyright Act was the result of 15 years of drafting, deliberations, and compromise. The House Report suggests strongly that Congress intended to limit the class of persons who may sue for infringement:

> Subsection (b) of section 501 enables *the owner of a particular right* to bring an infringement action in that owner's name alone, while at the same time insuring to the extent possible that *the other owners* whose rights may be affected are notified and given a chance to join the action.

> The first sentence of subsection (b) empowers the "legal or beneficial owner of an exclusive right" to bring suit for "any infringement of that particular right committed while he or she is the owner of it." A "beneficial owner" for this purpose would include, for example, an author who had parted with legal title to the copyright in exchange for percentage royalties based on sales or license fees.

Non-owners claiming a bare right to sue, such as Silvers, are not entitled to notice or joinder, which suggests that Congress did not envision their existence, or that the right to sue was a right severable from ownership of one of the authorized exclusive rights.

In other words, Congress wanted to ensure that an *owner* of *any exclusive right* in the copyright was entitled to bring a suit for infringement. Congress foresaw a permissible division of exclusive rights; the owner of any one of those exclusive rights may sue, with other owners being entitled to notice and joinder. In this sense, Congress intended to "unbundle" the exclusive rights.

Under the 1909 Copyright Act, which was the predecessor of the Copyright Act of 1976, a copyright "proprietor" was the *only* individual who had standing to sue for an infringement. Courts interpreted the 1909 statute as providing a proprietor with an indivisible bundle of rights arising from a copyright — rights that could not be assigned piecemeal. This enforced unity of rights created serious hardships for copyright holders who were interested in assigning the various property rights arising from a copyright separately, for instance selling the motion picture rights in a novel separately from the right to print the novel in book form. Congress, aware of these constraints on commercial dealings, largely dispensed with the doctrine of indivisibility in the Copyright Act of 1976. Although Congress allowed for divisibility of *ownership* interests under a copyright, it did not alter the requirement that *only owners* of an exclusive right in the copyright could bring suit.

The legislative history makes clear, too, that the list of exclusive rights found in § 106 is exhaustive. The House Report states:

> The exclusive rights accorded to a copyright owner under section 106 are "to do and to authorize" any of the activities specified in the five numbered clauses.

If a right is not "specified," then it is not one of the exclusive rights granted by Congress. The House Report that deals with the exclusive rights provided in § 106 also explains that "each of the five enumerated rights may be subdivided indefinitely and, . . . in connection with section 201 [governing transfer of rights], *each subdivision* of an exclusive right may be *owned and enforced* separately." In other words, exclusive rights may be chopped up and owned separately, and each separate owner of a subdivided exclusive right may sue to enforce that owned portion of an exclusive right, no matter how small. For instance, A may own the copyright in a book, while B may own the right to develop the book into a screenplay. A may sue an infringer of the book; B may sue an infringer of the screenplay. But only owners of an exclusive right in a copyright may sue. For instance, neither A nor B in the example above could assign an accrued claim for copyright infringement to C if C had no legal or beneficial interest in the copyright.

C. *Patent Law*

We have long noted the strong connection between copyright and patent law: "Where precedent in copyright cases is lacking, it is appropriate to look for guidance to patent law 'because of the historic kinship between patent law and copyright law.'" Although the Supreme Court has not addressed the issue at hand, it has addressed the question whether a bare assignment can give rise to a cause of action in the context of patent law.

The Patent Act of 1952 provides that "[a] patentee shall have remedy by civil action for infringement of his patent." 35 U.S.C. § 281 (1988). Like the 1976

Copyright Act, the Patent Act does not explicitly forbid an assignment of causes of action separate from an assignment of substantive rights in the protected work. Nonetheless, the Supreme Court has interpreted the Patent Act to provide that *only* a holder of patent rights may sue.

Courts continue to read the patent statute to mean that, in general, only a patentee (or an exclusive licensee who possesses all substantial rights in the patent) may institute an action for infringement. We should interpret the Copyright Act consistently with the requirement of the Patent Act. Despite the differences between patents and copyrights, and between the statutes governing them, the common question is whether a substantive, exclusive right to intellectual property may be divorced from a cause of action for infringement of that substantive right. Under both copyright and patent law, substantive rights are assignable; the question whether those rights are severable from the entitlement to sue someone for infringing those rights requires a similar analysis.

CONCLUSION

The bare assignment of an accrued cause of action is impermissible under 17 U.S.C. § 501(b). Because that is all Frank & Bob Films conveyed to Silvers, Silvers was not entitled to institute and may not maintain this action against Sony for alleged infringement of the copyright in "The Other Woman."

Reversed.

NOTES & QUESTIONS

1. Exclusive Versus Nonexclusive Licenses

The rights enjoyed by a copyright licensee are dictated in part by the exclusive or nonexclusive nature of a license. In general, an exclusive license must be conveyed in writing to be valid. Such a license is treated as a transfer of ownership because it conveys a part of a copyright holder's rights to the licensee. Consequently, an exclusive license grants the licensee standing to sue for infringement of the particular right covered by the license. A nonexclusive license, in contrast, allows a copyright holder to convey the same rights to more than one licensee and may be granted orally or implied from conduct. A licensee holding a nonexclusive license has no standing to sue and may be restricted in his ability to resell the licensed right. 1 MELVILLE B. NIMMER & DAVID NIMMER, NIMMER ON COPYRIGHT § 10.02[4].

2. Implied Transfers

A license of a right to a copyrighted work may entail a concomitant transfer of collateral rights needed to permit the full enjoyment of the license. For example, a license to record a musical work implies a right to distribute and sell the musical work, and a license to make copies in a work implies that ownership of the copies produced shall be in the licensee.

In addition to the implied transfer of collateral rights, an owner of a copyright may be compelled by statute to grant a license in his work. Compulsory licensing includes licenses for secondary transmissions over cable television, for making ephemeral recordings, for playing of works in jukeboxes, for public broadcasting, for satellite retransmissions, for digital subscription transmissions of sound recordings, for making and distributing phonorecords, and for digital phonorecord deliveries.

3. Duration of the License

Generally, if a licensing contract does not expressly state the period or duration of the agreement, the license is assumed to be effective for the extent of the then existing copyright term of the work. Once transferred, a license without an express term limit allows the licensee to enjoy the right transferred for the duration of the copyright.

One exception to this assumption is a license for publication. A license for publication of a work may automatically terminate before the end of the copyright term. For a publication license, termination of the license is triggered when the work ceases to be published. After termination, the licensee cannot thereafter use the work.

A licensee's duty to pay royalties does not end until either the copyright expires or the license expires, whichever occurs first.

4. Statutory Termination of Transfers and Nonexclusive Licenses

Copyright protection for a work of authorship lasts for the life of the author plus 70 years. An author of a copyrighted work initially owns the rights in the work but may transfer any or all of his rights to others through assignment or licensing. Typically, if the license does not explicitly state the period or duration of the licensing agreement, the license term is assumed to extend for the remaining duration of the copyright term.

Statutory termination permits authors to reclaim their rights in a work before the end of the copyright term. Under 17 U.S.C. § 203, an author may effect termination during a 5 year period starting 35 years from the date of the grant. For a right of publication of a work, the period begins at 35 years from the date of publication, or 40 years from the date of the execution of the grant, whichever term ends earlier. To effect termination, written notice must be provided to the grantee and to the U.S. Copyright Office. Notice must be served "not less than two or more than ten years" before the effective date of the termination. 17 U.S.C. § 203(a)(4)(A). Works created before 1976 may be terminated pursuant to § 304.

Statutory termination allows a copyright grant to revert back to the author. Unless terminated, a grant continues unchanged. 17 U.S.C. § 203(b). Derivative works are an exception to the statutory termination of a grant. 17 U.S.C. § 304(c)(6)(A). Derivative works prepared under the authority of a grant may still be used after termination of the grant. Termination does, however, bar the creation of new derivative works. The derivative works exception is illustrated by Mills Music, Inc. v. Snyder, 469 U.S. 153 (1985). In *Mills Music*, the author's heirs terminated the author's grant of a copyright to a music publisher. Before the termination of the grant, the music publisher had awarded licenses to third parties to produce derivative works of the author's song pursuant to the author's grant. The publisher received royalties from the derivative works. The Court held that the derivative works exception permitted use of derivative works to continue under the terms of the grant after the grant's termination. The royalty-bearing licenses for the derivative works therefore remained in force even after the heir's termination of the author's grant.

2. Scope of the Use: Unforeseen Uses

BOOSEY & HAWKES MUSIC PUBLISHERS, LTD. v. THE WALT DISNEY COMPANY

United States Court of Appeals for the Second Circuit
145 F.3d 481 (1997)

LEVAL, Circuit Judge:

Boosey & Hawkes Music Publishers Ltd., an English corporation and the assignee of Igor Stravinsky's copyrights for "The Rite of Spring," brought this action alleging that the Walt Disney Company's foreign distribution in video cassette and laser disc format ("video format") of the film "Fantasia," featuring Stravinsky's work, infringed Boosey's rights. In 1939 Stravinsky licensed Disney's distribution of The Rite of Spring in the motion picture. Boosey, which acquired Stravinsky's copyright in 1947, contends that the license does not authorize distribution in video format.

I. BACKGROUND

During 1938, Disney sought Stravinsky's authorization to use The Rite of Spring (sometimes referred to as the "work" or the "composition") throughout the world in a motion picture. Because under United States law the work was in the public domain, Disney needed no authorization to record or distribute it in this country, but permission was required for distribution in countries where Stravinsky enjoyed copyright protection. In January 1939 the parties executed an agreement (the "1939 Agreement") giving Disney rights to use the work in a motion picture in consideration of a fee to Stravinsky of $6000.

. . .

Disney released Fantasia, starring Mickey Mouse, in 1940. The film contains no dialogue. It matches a pantomime of animated beasts and fantastic creatures to passages of great classical music, creating what critics celebrated as a "partnership between fine music and animated film." The soundtrack uses compositions of Bach, Beethoven, Dukas, Schubert, Tchaikovsky, and Stravinsky, all performed by the Philadelphia Orchestra under the direction of Leopold Stokowski. As it appears in the film soundtrack, The Rite of Spring was shortened from its original 34 minutes to about 22.5; sections of the score were cut, while other sections were reordered. For more than five decades Disney exhibited The Rite of Spring in Fantasia under the 1939 license. The film has been re-released for theatrical distribution at least seven times since 1940, and although Fantasia has never appeared on television in its entirety, excerpts including portions of The Rite of Spring have been televised occasionally over the years. Neither Stravinsky nor Boosey has ever previously objected to any of the distributions.

In 1991 Disney first released Fantasia in video format. The video has been sold in foreign countries, as well as in the United States. To date, the Fantasia video release has generated more than $360 million in gross revenue for Disney.

Boosey brought this action in February 1993. The complaint sought (1) a declaration that the 1939 Agreement did not include a grant of rights to Disney to use the Stravinsky work in video format; (2) damages for copyright infringement in at least 18 foreign countries; (3) damages under the Lanham Act for false designation of origin and misrepresentation by reason of Disney's alteration of Stravinsky's work; (4) damages for breach of contract, alleging that the video format release breached the 1939 Agreement; and (5) damages for unjust enrichment.

II. DISCUSSION

A. Declaratory Judgment on the Scope of the License.

1. Whether the "motion picture" license covers video format. Boosey contends that the license to use Stravinsky's work in a "motion picture" did not authorize distribution of the motion picture in video format, especially in view of the absence of an express provision for "future technologies" and Stravinsky's reservation of all rights not granted in the Agreement. Disputes about whether licensees may exploit licensed works through new marketing channels made possible by technologies developed after the licensing contract — often called "new-use" problems — have vexed courts since at least the advent of the motion picture.

In *Bartsch v. Metro-Goldwyn-Mayer, Inc.,* [391 F.2d 150 (2nd Cir.), *cert. denied,* 393 U.S. 826 (1968),] we held that "licensees may properly pursue any uses which may reasonably be said to fall within the medium as described in the license." We held in *Bartsch* that a license of motion picture rights to a play included the right to telecast the motion picture. We observed that "if the words are broad enough to cover the new use, it seems fairer that the burden of framing and negotiating an exception should fall on the grantor," at least when the new medium is not completely unknown at the time of contracting.

The 1939 Agreement conveys the right "to record [the composition] in any manner, medium or form" for use "in [a] motion picture." We believe this language is broad enough to include distribution of the motion picture in video format. At a minimum, Bartsch holds that when a license includes a grant of rights that is reasonably read to cover a new use (at least where the new use was foreseeable at the time of contracting), the burden of excluding the right to the new use will rest on the grantor. The license "to record in any manner, medium or form" doubtless extends to videocassette recording and we can see no reason why the grant of "motion picture" reproduction rights should not include the video format, absent any indication in the Agreement to the contrary. If a new-use license hinges on the foreseeability of the new channels of distribution at the time of contracting — a question left open in *Bartsch* — Disney has proffered unrefuted evidence that a nascent market for home viewing of feature films existed by 1939. The *Bartsch* analysis thus compels the conclusion that the license for motion picture rights extends to video format distribution.

We recognize that courts and scholars are not in complete accord on the capacity of a broad license to cover future developed markets resulting from new technologies. The Nimmer treatise describes two principal approaches to the problem. According to the first view, advocated here by Boosey, "a license of rights in a given medium (e.g., 'motion picture rights') includes only such uses as fall within the unambiguous core meaning of the term (e.g., exhibition of motion picture film in motion picture theaters) and exclude any uses that lie within the ambiguous penumbra (e.g., exhibition of motion picture on television)." Under this approach, a license given in 1939 to "motion picture" rights would include only the core uses of "motion picture" as understood in 1939 — presumably theatrical distribution — and would not include subsequently developed methods of distribution of a motion picture such as television videocassettes or laser discs.

The second position described by Nimmer is "that the licensee may properly pursue any uses that may reasonably be said to fall within the medium as described in the license." Nimmer expresses clear preferences for the latter approach on the ground that it is "less likely to prove unjust."

We acknowledge that a result which deprives the author-licensor of participation in the profits of new unforeseen channels of distribution is not an altogether happy solution. Nonetheless, we think it more fair and sensible than a result that would deprive a contracting party of the rights reasonably found in the terms of the contract it negotiates. This issue is too often, and improperly, framed as one of favoritism as between licensors and licensees. Because licensors are often authors — whose creativity the copyright laws intend to nurture — and are often impecunious, while licensees are often large business organizations, there is sometimes a tendency in copyright scholarship and adjudication to seek solutions that favor licensors over licensees. Thus in *Cohen*, 845 F.2d at 854, the Ninth Circuit wrote that a "license must be construed in accordance with the purpose underlying federal copyright law," which the court construed as the granting of valuable, enforceable rights to authors and the encouragement of the production of literary works. Asserting that copyright law "is enacted for the benefit of the composer," the court concluded that it would "frustrate the purposes of the [copyright] Act" to construe the license as encompassing video technology, which did not exist when the license was granted.

In our view, new-use analysis should rely on neutral principles of contract interpretation rather than solicitude for either party. Although *Bartsch* speaks of placing the "burden of framing and negotiating an exception . . . on the grantor," it should not be understood to adopt a default rule in favor of copyright licensees or any default rule whatsoever. What governs under *Bartsch* is the language of the contract. If the contract is more reasonably read to convey one meaning, the party benefited by that reading should be able to rely on it; the party seeking exception or deviation from the meaning reasonably conveyed by the words of the contract should bear the burden of negotiating for language that would express the limitation or deviation. This principle favors neither licensors nor licensees. It follows simply from the words of the contract.

The words of Disney's license are more reasonably read to include than to exclude a motion picture distributed in video format. Thus, we conclude that the burden fell on Stravinsky, if he wished to exclude new markets arising from subsequently developed motion picture technology, to insert such language of limitation in the license, rather than on Disney to add language that reiterated what the license already stated.

Other significant jurisprudential and policy considerations confirm our approach to new-use problems. We think that our view is more consistent with the law of contract than the view that would exclude new technologies even when they reasonably fall within the description of what is licensed. Although contract interpretation normally requires inquiry into the intent of the contracting parties, intent is not likely to be helpful when the subject of the inquiry is something the parties were not thinking about. Nor is extrinsic evidence such as past dealings or industry custom likely to illuminate the intent of the parties, because the use in question was, by hypothesis, new, and could not have been the subject of prior negotiations or established practice. Moreover, many years after formation of the contract, it may well be impossible to consult the principals or retrieve documentary evidence to ascertain the parties' intent, if any, with respect to new uses. On the other hand, the parties or assignees of the contract should be entitled to rely on the words of the contract. Especially where, as here, evidence probative of intent is likely to be both scant and unreliable, the burden of justifying a departure from the most reasonable reading of the contract should fall on the party advocating the departure.

Nor do we believe that our approach disadvantages licensors. By holding contracting parties accountable to the reasonable interpretation of their agreements, we encourage licensors and licensees to anticipate and bargain for the full value of potential future uses. Licensors reluctant to anticipate future developments remain free to negotiate language that clearly reserves the rights to future uses. But the creation of exceptional principles of contract construction that places doubt on the capacity of a license to transfer new technologies is likely to harm licensors together with licensees, by placing a significant percentage of the profits they might have shared in the hands of lawyers instead.

Neither the absence of a future technologies clause in the Agreement nor the presence of the reservation clause alters that analysis. The reservation clause stands for no more than the truism that Stravinsky retained whatever he had not granted. It contributes nothing to the definition of the boundaries of the license. And irrespective of the presence or absence of a clause expressly confirming a license over future technologies, the burden still falls on the party advancing a deviation from the most reasonable reading of the license to insure that the desired deviation is reflected in the final terms of the contract. As we have already stated, if the broad terms of the license are more reasonably read to include the particular future technology in question, then the licensee may rely on that language.

Bartsch therefore continues to articulate our "preferred" approach to new-use questions, and we hold that the district court properly applied it to find that the basic terms of Disney's license included the right to record and distribute Fantasia in video format.

3. Performance Rights Organizations: ASCAP & BMI

Collective rights organizations facilitate commerce in copyrighted content by allowing transactions to proceed without the roadblock of individual owners asserting their rights to their works. One area where collective rights organizations have developed is the area of performance rights in music. The owners of copyrights in musical works formed the performance rights organizations ASCAP (American Society of Composers, Authors, and Publishers) and BMI (Broadcast Music Inc.).

Both ASCAP and BMI act as centralized organizations for the management of copyrights in music. The origins of ASCAP and BMI are summarized by Justice White in *BMI v. CBS*, 441 U.S. 1 (1979):

> In 1914, Victor Herbert and a handful of other composers organized ASCAP because those who performed copyrighted music for profit were so numerous and widespread, and most performances so fleeting, that as a practical matter it was impossible for the many individual copyright owners to negotiate with and license the users and to detect unauthorized uses. 'ASCAP was organized as a "clearing-house" for copyright owners and users to solve these problems' associated with the licensing of music. 400 F.Supp. 737, 741 (S.D.N.Y. 1975). As ASCAP operates today, its . . . members grant it nonexclusive rights to license non-dramatic performances of their works, and ASCAP issues licenses and distributes royalties to copyright owners in accordance with a schedule reflecting the nature and amount of the use of their music and other factors.

> BMI, a nonprofit corporation owned by members of the broadcasting industry, was organized in 1939, is affiliated with or represents . . . publishing companies and . . . authors and composers, and operates in much the same manner as ASCAP. Almost every domestic copyrighted composition is in the repertory either of ASCAP . . . or of BMI. . . .

> Both organizations operate primarily through blanket licenses, which give the licensees the right to perform any and all of the compositions owned by the members or affiliates as often as the licensees desire for a stated term. Fees for blanket licenses are ordinarily a percentage of total revenues or a flat dollar amount, and do not directly depend on the amount or type of music used. Radio and television broadcasters are the largest users of music, and almost all of them hold blanket licenses from both ASCAP and BMI.

BMI, 441 U.S. at 4-5. Together, ASCAP and BMI account for 95% of the United States market for performance rights to musical compositions. The performance rights organizations issue licenses and collect and distribute royalty fees for members under an agreed formula. The organizations also play a copyright policing role by monitoring public performances and bringing actions against alleged infringers.

E. LICENSING MULTIPLE TYPES OF INTELLECTUAL PROPERTY: HYBRID LICENSING

Licenses involving more than one kind of intellectual property have become the norm. It is common for a license to include two patents rather than one and for a license covering a patent to also cover trade secrets or know-how. Special problems arise when a license transaction includes two or more kinds of intellectual property. Each form of intellectual property confers different rights, has a different duration of protection, and requires compliance with different procedures. Parties negotiating a license involving more than one kind of intellectual property must take great care to address the unique demands of each.

1. Patent and Trade Secret Licensing

The most common form of hybrid licensing involves patents and trade secrets. A licensor may be both a patentee and owner of trade secrets related to the patent. Moreover, patent license may include a provision whereby the licensor is obligated to convey to the licensee trade secret information about improvements to the patented invention.

A license involving both patents and trade secrets should specify royalties related to the patents separately from royalties related to the trade secrets. An obligation to pay royalties related to a patent terminates upon the expiration of the patent. In contrast, the obligation to pay royalties concerning a trade secret may last indefinitely since the term of trade secret protection lasts so long as the information is maintained as a trade secret. Since the term of protection for a patent usually ends before the term for a trade secret, a licensor risks losing royalties altogether when a patent expires if a license covering both the patent and related trade secrets does not separately define royalties for licensing the patent and for licensing the trade secrets. *See Bloggild v. Kenner Prods.*, 776 F.2d 1315 (6th Cir. 1985) (license that included both patent and trade secret was held invalid since the license was entered into before patents issued and required payment of royalties after the patents expired); *Pitney Bowes, Inc. v. Mestre*, 701 F.2d 1365 (11th Cir. 1983) (hybrid agreement licensing patent rights and trade secrets unenforceable beyond date of expiration of patent).

2. Patent and Trademark Licensing

Dual licenses involving patents and trademarks are common in industrial property licensing. Processes may be patented, with the resultant product being sold and marketed under a specific trademark. Licensing arrangements may be undertaken to transfer both rights to make and sell the patented invention and to use the related trademark. However, problems may arise from hybrid licenses of patents and trademarks.

One problem is the blurring of the licensor's permissible activities in controlling the activities of the licensee. A licensor of a trademark must control the quality and nature of the goods and services associated with the mark. To effectuate this type of control, a licensor is permitted to supervise a licensee's use of the mark; however, such supervision may make the licensor privy to the licensee's improvements on the patented invention. The licensor may open himself to accusations of misappropriating the licensee's technology if he has no right to the improvements. To avoid unwitting misappropriations of information from the licensee, the parties need to develop a clear and workable confidentiality provision.

Another problem that may arise with a license involving a patented process and a trademark occurs when a licensee proposes to abandon the patented process in favor of another process while continuing to use the trademark. If the alternative process produces a product that meets trademark quality control standards under the license, the licensee may argue that the licensor is illegally attempting to condition the continued licensing of the mark on the use of the patented process.

A further problem may occur if a licensee, once having obtained a license to produce a patented product and to use a trademark, desires to discontinue using the licensor's mark and to manufacture the same product under licensee's own mark. Such an action on the part of the licensee may be viewed by the former licensor as a form of free riding, whereby the licensee trades off the good will established under the former licensor's mark. The licensor in such a situation may insist on a long-term license for the mark.

CHAPTER 7

INTELLECTUAL PROPERTY ASSETS AND THE TERMINATION OF A BUSINESS

PROBLEM

Digital Ignition has licensed its patented plug-in technology to Colonel Motors, a mid-sized automotive company that specializes in the manufacture of elite, upscale automobiles. Digital Ignition also licenses some patented technology from Spintel, a microchip company. During a sharp downturn in the economy, both Colonel Motors and Spintel file for bankruptcy. Because of what is perceived to be the unfavorable terms of its license with Digital Ignition, Spintel seeks to reject the license in hopes of entering into a better deal with another automotive company. Colonel Motors also seeks to reject its license with Digital Ignition in hopes of finding a cheaper supplier of substitutes for the patented plug-in technology. Because of the downturn, Digital Ignition is also considering the termination and restructuring of one of its subsidiary companies, responsible for research and development in improving its plug-in technology. The subsidiary holds title jointly with Digital Ignition in many of its patents and trade secrets.

You are general counsel for Digital Ignition and are asked to assess the legal issues that these facts pose for your client. Specifically, you are asked for advice on how best to protect your client's business interests as Colonel Motors and Spintel undergo bankruptcy and as Digital Ignition's subsidiary is terminated.

FOCUS OF THE CHAPTER

An unfortunate truth of any business is the possibility that it might come to an end. The end may occur voluntarily as the owners decide to shift their capital investment into other ventures, or it may occur involuntarily as debts and economic downturns force the owners of the business to file for bankruptcy. As with any business contingency, many of the negative implications of business termination can be mitigated by foreseeing business issues and planning accordingly. This chapter focuses on the legal issues affecting intellectual property that arise when a business terminates, whether voluntarily or involuntarily.

Whether as a business attorney or an intellectual property attorney, you should pay special attention to the challenges for business termination planning posed by intellectual property. In the context of bankruptcy, you need to be aware of how intellectual property becomes a part of the bankruptcy estate, how bankruptcy proceedings can stay ongoing or pending intellectual property litigation, and, most importantly, how intellectual property licenses are treated in bankruptcy. Many of these problems raise questions of valuation and securitizing intellectual property that have been addressed in previous chapters. Terminating a business voluntarily can also raise questions of valuation and intellectual property ownership. Many of these questions can be addressed by careful drafting of business documents, such as the articles of incorporation, the partnership agreement, or contracts. Drafting these documents requires an understanding of the background legal principles presented in this chapter.

The materials in this chapter focus on what happens to the intellectual property assets of a business when it terminates. There are two ways in which a business can come to an end. The first is when a business entity becomes insolvent and goes through bankruptcy proceedings to obtain a fresh start. The second is through a decision by the pertinent members of a business entity to end the business as a going concern and liquidate the assets. Each of these situations raises unique intellectual property issues.

In intellectual property practice, you should be aware of the possibility of bankruptcy as you draft intellectual property licenses and structure assignments of intellectual property interests. Intellectual property is also an increasingly important asset for the purposes of finance. Patents, copyrights, and trademarks as well as intellectual property intensive goods like software and movies serve as collateral for many businesses, both high and low tech. This sort of collateral is affected by bankruptcy law, which has special rules to deal with how to distribute assets among creditors and other parties who have a claim to the assets. These issues are discussed in the section entitled "The Bankruptcy Estate." Furthermore, ongoing intellectual property litigation may be affected by bankruptcy law, particularly its automatic stay provisions, which are used to pause judicial proceedings. These issues are discussed in the section entitled "The Automatic Stay." Finally, the Bankruptcy Code has special rules treating intellectual property licenses which allow the debtor to either assume or reject the obligations under these licenses. These special rules provide difficult traps for the unwary in both bankruptcy and intellectual property practice and are discussed in the section entitled "The Intellectual Property License in Bankruptcy."

Termination outside of bankruptcy also raises special questions for intellectual property. For example, when a partnership terminates, decisions have to be made about how intellectual property assets and licenses will be divided among the former owners of the partnership. In general, whenever a business winds down, intellectual property assets are affected and questions have to be answered about the ownership and transfer of these assets. Many of these questions are answered by general contract and business law and are addressed in the section "Termination Outside of Bankruptcy."

READINGS

A. TERMINATION THROUGH BANKRUPTCY

Bankruptcy law allows insolvent debtors to obtain a fresh start either by allowing them to liquidate their assets and satisfy creditors under Chapter 7 of the Bankruptcy Code or by reorganizing their business structure in order to meet their obligations under Chapter 11 of the Bankruptcy Code. This section provides an overview of the bankruptcy processes that arise regardless of whether a debtor decides to liquidate or to reorganize. The focus will be on three issues: (1) the bankruptcy estate, (2) the automatic stay, and (3) the treatment of intellectual property licenses.

When a debtor enters bankruptcy, the court assigns a bankruptcy trustee to manage the debtor's estate. The role of the trustee is to put together the assets that comprise the estate in order to maximize its value. Assets can include property, contracts, and other obligations owed to the debtor, such as legal claims. The cases on the bankruptcy estate illustrate the types of intellectual property issues that arise in determining the bankruptcy estate.

Section 362 of the Bankruptcy Code states that the filing of a bankruptcy petition acts as a stay of various judicial, administrative, or other proceedings against the debtor. This automatic stay provision allows the debtor to pause ongoing or postpone prospective litigation. The cases on the automatic stay and intellectual property litigation illustrate the effect of Section 362 on pending or prospective infringement suits.

The most complicated and important provisions of the Bankruptcy Code deal with the treatment of intellectual property licenses and other so-called executory contracts. Often the debtor will be subject to continuing contractual obligations after filing for bankruptcy. For example, he may be leasing real or personal property or licensing a copyright or patent. These continuing contractual obligations are called executory contracts. Under Section 365, the bankruptcy trustee has the power to decide how to handle the obligations under executory contracts. The trustee has three options: to reject the contract, to assume the contract, or to assume and assign the contract. If the trustee rejects the contract, then the debtor is in breach and the other party has a claim for breach of contract against the bankruptcy estate. If the trustee assumes the contract, then the estate is under the continuing obligations of the contract. If the trustee assumes and assigns, then the continuing obligations and benefits of the contract are transferred to someone else.

Section 365 raises special concerns for debtors who are party to an intellectual property license. If the debtor is the licensor, then the licensee may be put in the position of not being able to use the intellectual property if the trustee chooses to reject the license. Section 365(n) was enacted in 1988 to protect the licensee by allowing the licensee to continue using the intellectual property in the situation where the debtor/licensor rejects the license. There are two important caveats to section 365(n). First, since the Bankruptcy Code does not include trademarks in the definition of intellectual property, section 365(n) does not protect licensees of trademarks when the debtor/trademark owner rejects trademark licenses. Second, section 365(n) does not apply to the situation where the licensee is the debtor and elects to reject the license. This latter scenario is particularly troubling when the debtor/licensee elects to assume the license and assign it to a competitor of the licensor. The cases on the intellectual property in bankruptcy illustrate this problem and other issues raised by section 365(n).

1. The Bankruptcy Estate

PATRICK A. CASEY, P.A. v. JOEL S. HOCHMAN, M.D.
United States Court of Appeals for the Tenth Circuit
963 F. 2d. 1347 (1992)

HOLLOWAY, Circuit Judge.

On January 21, 1982, Dr. Joel Hochman, a psychiatrist, and his wife Darrellyn, a housewife, filed a Chapter 11 petition for bankruptcy . . .

The Hochmans acted as debtors-in-possession under Chapter 11 from January 21, 1982, until May 3, 1984, when motions of creditors to convert the bankruptcy into a Chapter 7 liquidation were granted. In the interim, Dr. Hochman had created the device in question in early 1983. A specific finding to this effect was made by the bankruptcy judge, and this is not disputed. At the time of conversion of the bankruptcy case to a Chapter 7 proceeding, Dr. Hochman had unsuccessfully attempted to have the device patented.

The bankruptcy judge made extensive subsidiary historical findings of fact. These findings are not specifically attacked. As noted, this appeal challenges only the ruling of the bankruptcy judge determining that the device, the patent and income from the licensing agreement were part of the bankruptcy estate, which ruling was affirmed by the district judge on appeal. Further facts relating to the device will be detailed below.

The original Chapter 11 proceeding was commenced by the Hochmans on January 21, 1982. Well after the 1984 conversion of the proceeding into Chapter 7, three scheduled creditors filed a complaint in July 1988 under 11 U.S.C. § 727. They objected to a discharge in bankruptcy of the Hochmans, alleging acts calculated to defraud creditors by the concealment and misappropriation of assets of the bankruptcy estate. After a five-day trial the bankruptcy judge found that the Hochmans intentionally concealed rents from a ranch and other properties and proceeds and the patent and license fees paid on the Tamponator device. These actions were found to be in violation of § 727 and a discharge in bankruptcy was denied by the bankruptcy judge.

The Hochmans appealed to the district court, arguing that they had not had a fair trial and that the bankruptcy judge erred in his ruling that the Tamponator was part of the bankruptcy estate, inter alia. The district judge rejected an argument that the trial in the bankruptcy court was unfair. He also held that the determination that the device was part of the bankruptcy estate was "not clearly erroneous."

A notice of appeal to this court was timely filed. On this appeal the Hochmans raise only the issue concerning whether the Tamponator device, the patent, and income from the license agreement and other income related to the device are part of the Chapter 7 estate. This central argument is presented in two parts: (1) the Hochmans claim that the findings and consideration below as to whether the device was part of the bankruptcy estate were not adequate; and (2) the determination that the device, the patent, income from the license agreement and related income were part of the bankruptcy estate was error. . . .

We turn now to the merits of the rulings that the Tamponator device, the patent, and income from the licensing agreement and related efforts of the Hochmans were part of the bankruptcy estate. The findings of the bankruptcy judge were stated in his opinion in detail and we summarize them below.

The Hochmans commenced the bankruptcy case in Chapter 11 on January 21, 1982. The bankruptcy judge found that when the debtors filed a motion for reconsideration of conversion of their case to Chapter 7, they explained to the court and creditors that Dr. Hochman had obtained initial approval of a patent of a medical device "with an enormous income potential." The judge said that the transcript shows that Dr. Hochman knew and understood that the patentable medical device "was property of the estate." Significantly for our purposes, the judge found that "Dr. Hochman had created the device in early 1983." *Id.* Hochman filed a patent application, # 069740196, through a patent attorney on February 28, 1983. The patent office acted on the application on April 12, 1984, rejecting the sixteen claims and giving the debtors three months from April 12, 1984, to respond. The patent examiner noted that claims 11 through 15 were "free of the art of record." The bankruptcy judge found that the Hochmans did respond to the patent office just prior to expiration of their deadline and that on May 7, 1985, Patent No. 40515167 was issued for the invention.

The bankruptcy judge found that the "invention known as the tampenator [sic] was property acquired by the debtors during the chapter 11 case and was property of the estate." The patent application made on February 28, 1983, and the rights thereunder "were property acquired by the debtors during the case and were property of the estate." The judge found that the debtors "knew that the invention and the patent were property of the estate" which they concealed.

It was found that on July 23, 1984, 81 days after conversion to Chapter 7, Dr. Hochman entered into two agreements with Hancock, Newton & Thomas concerning the invention. Dr. Hochman signed a licensing agreement giving this group the right to license, manufacture, use, sell and commercialize the invention for a license fee of $150,000 and royalties equivalent to six per cent of the selling price of each licensed product. $5,000 had already been paid to Dr. Hochman. Dr. Hochman represented that he was owner of the patent and had the right to grant an exclusive license. The agreement provided that Dr. Hochman would do all things necessary to obtain letters patent. The license agreement had been contingent upon Dr. Hochman securing the patent by December 12, 1984. . . .

The defendants-appellants, Dr. and Mrs. Hochman, challenge the rulings below that the Tamponator device, the patent thereof, and payments on the licensing agreement were within the Chapter 7 bankruptcy estate. They argue that 11 U.S.C. § 541(a) provides that commencement of a bankruptcy case creates the estate; the estate is comprised of all legal and equitable interests of the debtor in property as of the commencement of the case; and that when a Chapter 11 case is converted to a Chapter 7 case, the original filing date of the petition under Chapter 11 establishes the commencement of the case and the basis for determining the assets comprising the bankruptcy estate in accordance with 11 U.S.C. § 348(a). They say that § 348(a) makes it clear that the conversion to a Chapter 7 proceeding "does not effect a change in the date of the filing of the petition or the commencement of the case."

Further the defendants-appellants argue that the appellees fail to address the question whether an asset was acquired by the estate or by the debtors; that the appellees have blurred the distinction between property acquired by the estate and by the debtor. They conclude that since the device was invented in 1983, and the patent and payments in question followed, these were property acquired by the debtors.

We must agree. In these circumstances, upon conversion the assets which are the property of the Chapter 7 estate are determined with reference to the date of filing of the original Chapter 11 petition. . . . The bankruptcy judge found that the device was invented in early 1983 by Dr. Hochman. This finding is not questioned and there is no suggestion by the appellees that the device existed earlier. This was a year after the commencement of the first bankruptcy proceeding on January 21, 1982, with the filing of the Chapter 11 case. The basic rule is laid down by 11 U.S.C. § 541(a):

> (a)   The commencement of a case under section 301, 302, or 303 [voluntary, involuntary, and joint cases] of this title creates an estate. Such estate is comprised of all the following property, wherever located:
>
> > (1)   Except as provided in subsections (b) and (c)(2) of this section, all legal or equitable interests of the debtor in property as of the commencement of the case. . . .

The effect of § 541(a) is clearly stated in L. King, 4 Collier on Bankruptcy ¶ 541.05 at 541-24:

> As previously stated, under section 541(a) the estate is normally comprised only of property and interests therein belonging to the debtor at the time the petition is filed. In general, property not then owned but subsequently acquired by the debtor does not become property of the estate, but becomes the debtor's, clear of all claims that are discharged by the bankruptcy proceedings.

The basic principles stated in the treatise are clearly recognized in decisions under the Bankruptcy Act. In *Everett v. Judson,* 228 U.S. 474 (1913), the Supreme Court stated:

> We think that the purpose of the law was to fix the line of cleavage with reference to the condition of the bankrupt estate as of the time at which the petition was filed and that the property which vests in the trustee at the time of adjudication is that which the bankrupt owned at the time of the filing of the petition. . . .

The appellants place their reliance on § 541(a)(6) and (7) as making the device, the patent and proceeds property of the Chapter 7 bankruptcy estate. Those subsections provide, inter alia, for inclusion in the estate of

> (6)   Proceeds, product, offspring, rents, and profits of or from property of the estate, except such as are earnings from services performed by an individual debtor after the commencement of the case.

(7) Any interest in property that the estate acquires after the commencement of the case.

The argument of the appellees confuses property acquired by the debtors and property acquired by the estate. In this connection we note that the bankruptcy judge made a finding that the "invention known as the Tamponator was property acquired by the debtors during the chapter 11 case and was property of the estate." The judge further found, as noted, that Dr. Hochman developed the invention in 1983. We are persuaded that the facts found clearly establish that the device, the patent and proceeds from the licensing agreement were property acquired by the debtors, but we do not agree with the judge's conclusion that they were "property of the estate."

The appellees argue that property acquired post-petition is generally within the bankruptcy estate and that there are only two exceptions to this rule, those provided by § 541(a)(6) concerning proceeds, product, rents and profits from property of the estate. They also point to the 180-day limitation in §541(a)(5) which places in the estate an interest in particular types of property (inheritances, property settlements, etc.) that would have been property of the estate if such interest had been an interest of the debtor on the date of filing of the petition, and if the debtor acquires or becomes entitled to it within 180 days after such date. The appellees simply have the general rule backwards; under § 541(a)(1) the general rule is that the estate includes interests of the debtor in property as of the commencement of the case. Both of these provisions relied on (§ 541(a)(5) and (6)) are actually exceptions from the general rule that post-petition acquisitions are property of the debtor — exceptions specially provided to include particular property within the bankruptcy estate.

PENICK PHARMACEUTICAL, INC. AND UNOFFICIAL COMMITTEE OF EQUITY HOLDERSOF PENICK PHARMACEUTICAL, INC. v. MCMANIGLE
United States Bankruptcy Court for the Southern District of
New York
227 B.R. 229 (1998)

On June 9, 1994 (the "Petition Date"), the Debtors filed chapter 11 petitions in this court. . . . Both pre- and post-petition, the Debtor has been engaged in the manufacture and sale of pharmaceutical products and in research and development with respect thereto.

On March 17, 1998, the Committee filed its complaint herein seeking a declaration that a certain new process relating to the manufacture of opium derivatives (the "Process") is not the property of the bankruptcy estate of the Debtor but is rather the property of the Debtor, free and clear of all claims of the Trustee, creditors and any other entity. . . .

The Process is the invention of Bao-Shan Huang ("Dr. Huang"), Yansong Lu ("Mr. Lu"), Ben-Yi Ji. ("Dr. Ji" and together with Dr. Huang and Mr. Lu, the "Employee Inventors") and Aris P. Christodoulou ("Dr. Christodoulou" and together with the Employee Inventors, the "Inventors"). Dr. Christodoulou was, at all relevant times until May 9, 1997, when he resigned, an officer and director of the Debtor. He is a shareholder of PPI and a member of the Committee. Dr. Huang was employed by the Debtor as a consultant to work in its research and development department (the "R & D Department") in 1994. In connection therewith, on May 10, 1994 he signed an Employee Confidentiality and Invention Assignment Agreement containing provisions in the following terms:

> 2. Employee shall disclose promptly to Employer any and all INVEN-TIONS conceived or made by him/her during his/her employment with Employer, whether or not made during his/her hours of employment or with the use of Employer facilities, materials, or personnel, and whether made solely or jointly with others, and hereby assigns all of his/her entire right, title and interest in any such INVENTIONS to Employer. As used herein, the term INVENTIONS means any and all developments, innovations, discoveries, improvements and ideas, whether patentable or not.

> 3. Employee shall, whenever requested to do so by Employer, execute any applications, confirmatory assignment documents, or other instruments which Employer shall consider necessary, to apply for and obtain Letters Patent in the United States, or any foreign country, and shall take such other action at Employer's expense as Employer deems necessary to protect Employer's interests in the INVENTIONS.

The agreement was signed by Dr. Christodoulou, as director, on behalf of the Debtor. In December of that year, Dr. Huang formulated certain synthetic routes for the Process. In June 1995, Dr. Huang was hired by the Debtor as an employee in the R & D Department and in that capacity, in January 1996, conducted the first laboratory test of the Process. In October 1996, Dr. Ji and Mr.Lu were hired by the Debtor, initially as consultants and then as employees in the R & D Department. Both signed Employee Confidentiality and Invention Assignment Agreements containing terms identical to those in Dr. Huang's Employee Confidentiality and Invention Assignment Agreement set forth above. Again, these agreements were signed by Dr. Christodoulou, as director, on behalf of the Debtor. Dr. Ji and Mr. Lu developed certain intermediate synthetic routes used in the Process. The respective fees and salaries of the Employee Inventors were paid by the Debtor's bankruptcy estate and laboratories, chemicals and equipment belonging to such estate were used in researching and developing the Process. Dr. Christodoulou's part in the invention of the Process was to conceptualize the use of morphine as a starting material for the preparation of certain opium derivatives.

The Debtor filed the first provisional application for the Process with the United States Patent & Trademark Office (the "PTO") on July 26, 1996, the second provisional patent application for the Process with the PTO on April 29, 1997 and the regular patent application for the Process with the PTO on July 11, 1997. The Debtor's basic patent application was allowed by the PTO and the Debtor is awaiting a response from the PTO with respect to six divisional patent applications arising from the regular patent application. The Debtor paid all costs and expenses in connection with such applications, including in respect of the hiring of special patent counsel, Burgess, Ryan &

Wayne, whose appointment as special counsel to the Trustee was approved by this court on July 22, 1997.

Meanwhile, by an Assignment of Application for Patent (the "Assignment") dated July 8 and 9, 1997, "in consideration of . . . $1.00 . . . and other valuable consideration," the Inventors assigned to "Penick Corporation" their interest in the Process and the patent application and Letters Patent relating thereto, in the case of the Employee Inventors, in accordance with the terms of their respective Employee Confidentiality and Invention Assignment Agreements.

Discussion

When a debtor files for bankruptcy protection, a bankruptcy estate is created. Under section 541(a)(1) of the Bankruptcy Code, the estate includes "all legal or equitable interests of the debtor in property as of the commencement of the case." 11 U.S.C. § 541(a)(1)(1994). Property of the estate also includes "[p]roceeds, product, offspring, rents, or profits of or from property of the estate, except such as are earnings from services performed by an individual debtor after the commencement of the case," 11 U.S.C. § 541(a)(6) (1994), and "[a]ny interest in property that the estate acquires after commencement of the case." 11 U.S.C. § 541(a)(7) (1994). Thus, the estate does not remain static.

The Trustee, on the one hand, argues that the Process belongs to the bankruptcy estate of the Debtor pursuant to section 541(a)(6) or (7) of the Bankruptcy Code. The Committee, on the other hand, contends that the Process is not "property of the estate" under section 541(a)(6) because it is derived not from property of the estate but from "the minds and intellectual activity of [the Inventors]," nor under section 541(a)(7) because it was acquired not by the estate pursuant to the Assignment but by the "post-petition Debtor".

The parties have extensively briefed the question of whether a corporate debtor may hold property as non-estate property, the Trustee arguing, in essence, that post-petition property acquisitions necessarily constitute estate property under section 541(a)(6) or (7). For purposes of this motion, however, this court need not resolve the theoretical question because it is clear on the undisputed facts that the Process was derived from property of the estate so as to bring it within section 541(a)(6) and/or acquired by the estate so as to bring it within section 541(a)(7).

Upon the filing of a voluntary chapter 11 petition, a debtor automatically becomes "debtor in possession." As such, it occupies the shoes of a bankruptcy trustee in every major way. As a de jure trustee, it holds its powers in trust for the benefit of creditors. Specifically, in the case of an inanimate debtor in possession such as a corporation, the fiduciary duties borne by a trustee for a debtor out of possession fall on the debtor's directors, officers and managing employees, who have a duty to maximize the value of the estate, and who are burdened to ensure that the resources that flow through the debtor in possession's hands are used to benefit the unsecured creditors and other parties in interest. Thus, upon filing its petition, the Debtor became debtor in possession and, through its management, including Dr. Christodoulou, was burdened with the duties and responsibilities of a bankruptcy trustee.

In addition, however, as debtor in possession and de jure trustee, the Debtor had certain statutory powers. Most importantly, it was authorized to operate its business pursuant to section 1108 of the Bankruptcy Code. Pursuant to section 363(c)(1) of the Bankruptcy Code, as debtor in possession, the Debtor was permitted to conduct its business in the ordinary course. As was the case outside of bankruptcy, the Debtor then acted through its directors and officers, including Dr. Christodoulou, who continued to operate its business.

Thus, in the course of the operation of the Debtor's business by the Debtor as debtor in possession, the Employee Inventors were employed by the Debtor on behalf of the Debtor's estate. When Dr. Christodoulou signed Dr. Ji and Mr. Lu's respective Employee Confidentiality and Invention Assignment Agreements on behalf of the Debtor, he did so as agent of the Debtor as debtor in possession and in furtherance of his aforementioned fiduciary duties. These Employee Confidentiality and Invention Assignment Agreements gave the Debtor, as debtor in possession, on behalf of the estate, certain rights in the inventions of the Employee Inventors. These rights became property of the estate pursuant to section 541(a)(7) of the Bankruptcy Code. The benefit of Dr. Huang's Employee Confidentiality and Invention Assignment Agreement, which predated the filing of the petition, was estate property pursuant to section 541(a)(1). The Employee Inventors' salaries were paid by the estate and when the Employee Inventors rendered their services, it was to the Debtor as debtor in possession. The laboratories, chemicals and equipment used by the Employee Inventors were property of the estate either because they were property of the Debtor at the Petition Date, see 11 U.S.C. § 541(a)(1) (1994), or were acquired by the estate using funds derived from the Debtor's continuing operation of its business and therefore property of the estate pursuant to section 541(a)(7). When the Employee Inventors entered into the Assignment, it was in furtherance of their respective obligations to the Debtor as debtor in possession under the Employee Confidentiality and Invention Assignment Agreements and in exchange for consideration provided by the estate. Similarly, Dr. Christodoulou assigned his interest in the Process in exchange for consideration provided by the estate. Finally, the application for patent protection of the Process was, until the appointment of the Trustee, prosecuted on behalf of the Debtor as debtor in possession, financed by estate funds. Upon the appointment of the Trustee, the Debtor's management was displaced and the Trustee assumed management of the operation of the Debtor's business for the estate. The patent application continued to be prosecuted on behalf of the estate.

Nobody would seriously doubt that the tangible product of a debtor manufactured by its employees' "hands" post-petition and pre-confirmation were property of the estate and the Process is no different merely by virtue of its being intangible and the product of an intellectual process. In fact, development of the Process was apparently not the product of a purely intellectual exercise as it required physical testing using estate property. While the Inventors' minds might not have been property of the estate, their work product indubitably was. To the extent that the Process does not constitute product of or from property of the estate within section 541(a)(6), it was acquired by the estate pursuant to the Assignment, and therefore property of the estate pursuant to section 541(a)(7) of the Bankruptcy Code.

[In *Casey v. Hochman*, 963 F.2d 1347 (10th Cir. 1992)], the court held that the patent on a device invented by a debtor after the filing of his chapter 11 petition was not included in property of the estate. However, there the debtor was an individual who was not bound by any agreement or fiduciary duty to deliver up his invention to the estate. In contrast, here, the Employee Inventors were employed by the debtor in possession on behalf of the estate and bound by the terms of their employment to assign their inventions to their employer and, in fact, did so. Dr. Christodoulou was similarly bound by reason of his fiduciary obligations.

SIMPLIFIED INFORMATION SYSTEMS, INC. v. CANNON

United States Bankruptcy Court for the Western
District of Pennsylvania
89 B.R. 538 (1988)

GERALD J. WEBER, District Judge.

Debtor has asserted that the computer software, created by Cannon, is property of the estate. Cannon argues that Debtor merely possesses an exclusive license to use the software for the life of the corporation, with reversion to Cannon upon corporate dissolution. Cannon bases this assertion upon his claim that Barthalow and he made an oral contract to that effect.

With the exception of certain factors not presently relevant, property of the estate includes ". . . all legal or equitable interests of the [D]ebtor in property as of the commencement of the case." 11 U.S.C. § 541(a). This also includes both intangible and transitory property. Therefore, software ownership can be property of the estate. However, the parameters of Debtor's interest are determined by state and federal non-bankruptcy law. In the instant case we must turn to federal copyright law in order to determine ownership of the software design.

The right of copyright is statutorily created, and is based upon Article I, § 8, cl. 8 of the U.S. Constitution. Section 102(a) of the Copyright Act states in pertinent part:

> 102(a). Copyright protection subsists in accordance with this title, in original works of authorship fixed in any tangible medium of expression, now known or later developed, from which they can be perceived, reproduced or otherwise communicated, either directly or with the aid of a machine or device. Works of authorship include the following categories:
>
> > (1) literary works; . . .

A computer program is a work of authorship and is classified as a literary work for the purpose of obtaining copyright protection.

Section 201(a) of the Copyright Act states that "[c]opyright in a work . . . vests initially in the author or authors," and, "[i]n the case of a work made for hire, the employer or other person for whom the work was prepared is considered the author . . . [and] owns all of the rights comprised in the copyright" unless otherwise expressly agreed in writing. Clearly then, the ownership of the copyright depends upon the identity of the statutory "author", which in turn depends upon whether the "work" is a "work made for hire".

A "work made for hire" is "a work prepared by an employee within the scope of his or her employment . . ." 17 U.S.C. § 101. Under the Copyright Act, one may be an employee without regard to the method of payment, i.e., salary, piecework, royalty, or gratis. The employer's president may also be considered an employee. Furthermore, the "work made for hire" doctrine is not avoidable merely by performing the work in a separate location, or on non-work time.

This doctrine does not prevent the employer and employee from forming an agreement to the contrary; the "work made for hire" doctrine creates a presumption in favor of its validity, which can be rebutted only by express written agreement of the parties.

In the case at bar, Cannon's claim to the software cannot be sustained. The whole purpose for the corporation's formation was the creation and marketing of a computer process which would assist doctors' staffs in their various clerical duties, such as scheduling, charting, and billing. The program written by Cannon was intended to perform these functions.

Cannon was the Debtor's President when he wrote the program; that he wrote it during "off" hours, or at his other business facility is not relevant. Cannon's employment contract required him to devote his time and attention, and his best effort ". . . to the discharge of his duties." His duty regarding the corporation was to create this software. From August 1981 to June 1982 Cannon received $400.00 per week, to sustain him and his family while he worked on the program. The Board of Directors even consented to his outside employment, so long as it did not interfere with the Debtor's business purpose — the development and marketing of the software for use in physicians' offices.

Cannon asserts that an oral agreement to the contrary was reached, creating authorship in Cannon, and an exclusive licensure with the Debtor; however, the Copyright Act requires a written agreement between the parties in order to rebut the "work for hire" presumption. There exists no such agreement in this case. To the contrary, the credible evidence presented leads to the conclusion that this software constitutes "work made for hire." As such, the statutory authorship of same goes to the Debtor corporation. Therefore, upon the filing of the bankruptcy petition, said software became and is property of the Debtor's estate.

C TEK SOFTWARE, INC. v. NEW YORK STATE BUSINESS VENTURE PARTNERSHIP
United States Bankruptcy Court for the District of New Hampshire
127 B.R. 501 (1991)

JAMES E. YACOS, Bankruptcy Judge.

Debtor, C Tek Software, Inc., initiated an adversary proceeding against certain creditors to determine the validity, extent, or priority of certain liens. In an earlier opinion, I decided that New York State Business Venture Partnership ("NYSBVP") had a perfected security interest in the computer software ClienTrak. *See In re C Tek Software, Inc.*, 117 B.R. 762 (Bankr.D.N.H. 1990). However, I left for a further trial the question of "the extent of the security interest NYSBVP has in the source code in light of the enhancements made after the security interest was taken." *Id*. at 763 n. 1. A trial was held on this matter on October 10, 1990, and I then took the matter under submission.

Findings of Fact

1. C Tek is the owner of computer software known as "ClienTrak." This software is sold to companies in the financial services industry, principally banks and insurance companies. The software stores information and generates correspondence.

2. On October 26, 1987, NYSBVP took and perfected a security interest in some pieces of hardware owned by C Tek as well as "[t]he source code and all ownership rights to the computer software ClienTrak including copyrights 1983, 1984, 1985, 1986 and 1987."

3. On June 17, 1988, C Tek entered into a Master Distribution Agreement ("MDA") with Intelligent Investment Systems ("IIS"). The MDA is a ten year licensing agreement which gives IIS the exclusive worldwide right to sell and develop the software ClienTrak. Under the MDA, IIS promised to pay C Tek royalties, which would decrease in amount over time as IIS made changes to the software. Most importantly, paragraph 2.1(f) of the MDA gave IIS the right "to produce, copy, distribute and market derivative versions of the software and documentation without limitation."

4. At the time the MDA was executed, the software ClienTrak was at version 3.7.2B. It would have taken a group of programmers about five years to independently produce comparable software.

5. On April 6, 1989, C Tek filed a chapter 11 petition in this court. On August 31, 1989, NYSBVP got a default order vacating the automatic stay but without prejudice to C Tek's rights to initiate this adversary proceeding.

6. IIS made revisions to thousands of lines of source code after receiving its licensing rights under the MDA. IIS employed several programmers to make the changes and assist users. The software is currently at version 4.1.8. The differences between this source code and the prior version delivered to IIS at the time the MDA was executed are of three types. First, the overwhelming majority of changes were the elimination of "bugs" i.e., minor defects in the source code so the software does not operate as intended. Second, some minor "cosmetic" changes were made to make the display and controls more user-friendly. Third, three major changes were made to the import function, the report customizer, and the communications message exchange. This last group of changes is the only ones a programmer would call "enhancements." No new "modules" were added to the five modules existing in version 3.7.2B.

The Issue

IIS is not now contending that it has rights to market the software through version 3.7.2B after foreclosure. The dispute concerns who owns the changes made to the software after that point up to version 4.1.8. IIS recognizes that copyrights of a derivative work cover only the original matters added and not the underlying work.

There is little room to question IIS' right to attempt to copyright any derivative software it may develop under paragraph 2.1(f) of the MDA. NYSBVP argues that the MDA did not expressly say IIS had copyright rights in its derivative product only that IIS could produce derivative works. Yet, any other construction of this contractual provision would be contrary to the logical inference of this provision and the spirit and intent of the MDA. Also, it seems plain that if there was no agreement as to who owns copyrightable material it should be the author of such material.

NYSBVP also argues that paragraph 4.2(b) of the MDA provides that upon termination of the agreement C Tek will step into the shoes of IIS. However, this provision has nothing to do with copyrights in derivative works. Rather, it concerns sublicenses and subdistributorship agreements of the original software.

The only substantive question before me is whether some or all of the changes IIS made to the source code were significant enough to meet the "originality" requirement for copyright protection for a "derivative work".

Copyright Law

A derivative work is defined by statute as follows:

A work based upon one or more preexisting works, [in] any . . . form in which a work may be recast, transformed, or adapted. A work consisting of editorial revisions, annotations, elaborations, or other modifications which as a whole represent an original work of authorship, is a "derivative work."

I start with the proposition established by the U.S. Supreme Court [in *Stewart v. Abend* 495 U.S. 207 (1990)] that:

[t]he aspects of a derivative work added by the derivative author are that author's property, but the element drawn from the pre-existing work remains on grant from the owner of the pre-existing work.

In order to qualify as a derivative work, and thus qualify for copyright protection, the work must be "original." . . . "The test of originality is concededly one with a low threshold." All that is needed to satisfy both the Constitution and the statute is that the "author" contributed something more than a "merely trivial" variation, something recognizably "his own." Originality in this context "means little more than a prohibition of actual copying." No matter how poor artistically the "author's" addition, it is enough if it be his own.

Works substantially derived from prior works, whether the preexisting works are copyrighted or in the public domain, are also subject to copyright protection so long as the derivative work itself is original. The original aspects of the derivative work must themselves be nontrivial, and the copyright in the derivative work does not affect the copyright protection in the underlying work.

Unfortunately, that case involved a comparison of dolls which does not provide much guidance to this court. However, the language used did say originality is an easy concept to meet, and the court would not allow summary judgment against the derivative author even where it found the "[n]ontrivial differences between the . . . dolls are indeed difficult, if not impossible, to discern."

The [First Circuit has] stated:

> It is axiomatic that the designation "original" is not intended to be lim-
> ited to works that are novel or unique. Rather, the word "original,"
> which was "purposely left undefined" by Congress refers to works that
> have been "independently created by an author," regardless of their
> literary or aesthetic merit, or ingenuity, or qualitative value.

I find this point meaningful because NYSBVP has in part belittled the "bug"
work as not being important enough to warrant protection. The law simply
does not support this contention.

To answer completely the question of what is the test for originality in
"knowledge" cases, I must look to a series of four Eighth Circuit cases.

The Eighth Circuit has issued a series of "knowledge" copyright cases that
provide considerable guidance as to what constitutes originality in a "knowledge" case. The first case is *Hutchinson Tel. Co. v. Fronteer Directory Co. of
Minnesota, Inc.*, 770 F.2d 128 (8th Cir.1985). In this case, the Court held that
the creation of a white pages telephone directory was an original work of
authorship. The Court explained:

> "Originality" under the prior construction did not connote novelty or
> uniqueness but simply that the work be independently created. If a
> work is similar to preexisting works, it must show more than trivial
> variation from those works.
>
> . . .
>
> Hutchinson's records are gathered and maintained for many purposes,
> including publication of a directory. The proper focus is not whether
> Hutchinson's sole motivation for maintaining the records is the publi-
> cation of a directory, but whether the directory itself is derived from
> information compiled and generated by Hutchinson's efforts.

Thus, the court was focusing on the independent effort of the author in
deeming the work original. The Court [in *The Toro Co. v. R & R Products Co.*,
787 F.2d 1208 (8th Cir. 1986)] held that a lawn care manufacturer's parts
numbering system lacked even a low threshold of originality and commented:

> Under originality case law a work need not be artistic or novel to
> achieve protection. *Mazer v. Stein,* 347 U.S. 201 [74 S.Ct. 460, 98 L.Ed.
> 630] (1954). Originality denotes only enough definite expression so
> that one may distinguish authorship.
>
> . . .
>
> If the disputed work is similar to a pre-existing protected work or one
> in the public domain, the second work must contain some variation
> recognizable as that of the second author.
>
> . . .
>
> The undisputed evidence below shows that appellant's "system" is com-
> posed of arbitrarily assigning to a particular replacement part a ran-
> dom number when appellant creates the part. Appellant's Vice

President for Distribution testified that once a part is created "an arbitrary number is assigned" to the part to identify it. Appellant's counsel, when moving for a new trial, told the court that "it was undisputed at trial that Toro's parts numbering system was arbitrary and random." There was no evidence that a particular series or configuration of numbers denoted a certain type or category of parts or that the numbers used encoded any kind of information at all. In short, numbers were assigned to a part without rhyme or reason. This record establishes that appellant's parts numbering "system" falls short of even the low threshold of originality. The random and arbitrary use of numbers in the public domain does not evince enough originality to distinguish authorship. The expression itself is nothing more than the public domain numbers. There is no variation, other than the trivial hyphen, to establish authorship. Also, it is clear that no effort or judgment went into this selection or composition of the numbers, which distinguishes this case from the telephone directory cases. We are left, then, with the accidental marriage of a part and a number. We do not believe that such a marriage produces an original work of authorship. Appellant simply has not added enough to its parts numbers to make them original and remove them from the public domain. This is not to say that all parts numbering systems are not copyrightable. A system that uses symbols in some sort of meaningful pattern, something by which one could distinguish effort or content, would be an original work. Originality is a very low threshold, but still a threshold.

The next Eighth Circuit case on this issue is *West Publishing Co. v. Mead Data Central, Inc.,* 799 F.2d 1219, 1223 (8th Cir.1986). In this case, the court held that the arrangement of page numbers by a legal publishing company was original. (The Court distinguished Toro on the grounds that the arrangement took some effort.) Thus, a competing computer legal research service could not appropriate the page numbering. This decision is obviously on the fringe end of originality requirements. Regardless, its definition of originality is highly instructive. The court stated:

> The standard for "originality" is minimal. It is not necessary that the work be novel or unique, but only that the work have its origin with the author — that it be independently created. Little more is involved in this requirement than "a prohibition of actual copying."

> To be the original work of an author, a work must be the product of some "creative intellectual or aesthetic labor." However, "a very slight degree of such labor[,] . . . almost any ingenuity in selection, combination or expression, no matter how crude, humble or obvious, will be sufficient" to make the work copyrightable.

Thus, the Court was once again looking at independent effort or judgment to deem something an original creation. In [*Applied Innovations, Inc. v. Regents of the University of Minnesota,* 876 F.2d 626 (8th Cir. 1989)], the court held that psychological test statements that were "independently created" are original and copyrightable. It also held that revisions to the questions "are recognizable as the work of the authors and thus are sufficiently original."

Applying these Eighth Circuit cases to my case I believe all of the efforts of IIS in revising the source code, when considered collectively, are original work entitled to copyright protection. The changes the IIS programmers made to the source code required independent effort and judgment. Even NYSBVP's own expert admitted that it is more difficult to modify another programmer's source code than to create one's own. IIS has created something that is recognizably its own in the source code. Admittedly, most of the changes are not important modifications to the functionality of the source code, but that is not the test under copyright law. IIS' changes are not "trivial" in the copyright sense; they required more than token independent effort or judgment. . . .

Finally, I find support in my decision if I look to the purpose of copyright law and the originality requirement. The purpose of copyright law is to encourage creative activity by granting a limited monopoly. What IIS did is socially useful work. NYSBVP's own expert said most of the work — the debugging work — was "warranty work." This is valuable work and should be encouraged.

Nor will the purpose of the originality requirement be thwarted. In a seminal opinion on originality, *L. Batlin & Sons, Inc. v. Snyder,* 536 F.2d 486 (2d Cir.1976), the court explained that the originality requirement is designed to prevent someone from making "minuscule variations", *id.* at 492, to monopolize preexisting work. One commentator has explained why courts should be particularly careful in assessing the originality requirement for derivative works:

The requirement of originality is significant chiefly in connection with derivative works, where, if interpreted too liberally, it would paradoxically inhibit rather than promote the creation of such works by giving the first creator a considerable power to interfere with the creation of subsequent derivative works from the same underlying work.

IIS is not trying to monopolize preexisting work. It merely seeks copyright protection for its own derivative work, which is severable from the preexisting work.

Accession

Having determined that IIS has a copyright in changes from source code version 3.7.2B to 4.1.8, I am left with the question of how NYSBVP can foreclose on the source code. The testimony clearly established that IIS could return version 3.7.2B to the creditor. Therefore, under the law of accession this is all NYSBVP could get. A case illustrating this principle is *AMCA Int'l Finance Corp. v. Interstate Detroit Diesel Allison, Inc.,* 428 N.W.2d 128 (Minn.Ct.App. 1988). In this case the debtor replaced the engine of an excavator subject to a security interest, and was allowed to give the creditor the original engine when the creditor repossessed. The court explained:

The only way, therefore, that [creditor] would have a security interest would be through the doctrine of accession. Accession is defined as follows:

We think the general rule is quite well settled that, where the articles later attached to an automobile or other principal article of personal property became so closely incorporated with the principal article that they cannot be identified and detached therefrom without injury to the automobile or principal article, such articles become part of the machine or principal article to which they are so attached and will pass by accession to one having a chattel mortgage or other lien upon the principal article, if the lien is enforced. But when the articles added can be readily identified and detached without injury to the principal machine or article, they do not pass by accession to the one having a prior chattel mortgage or lien on the principal article.

Conclusion

IIS had a license from the debtor to copyright derivative software. The software IIS developed is copyrightable because it meets the originality requirements of copyright law. Thus, since the changes to the source code can be severed from the underlying work, IIS owns those changes free and clear of any lien of NYSBVP.

NOTES & QUESTIONS

1. Bankruptcy law allows a financially distressed business (or person) to start over by liquidating all assets and satisfying creditors. The law also offers the alternative for a company to reorganize and restructure its debt. Under a liquidation, the business' assets are assembled to create the bankruptcy estate, which is managed by a court-designated trustee whose decisions are reviewed by a bankruptcy judge. The assets are valued, and the estate is used to settle the business' debts, some of which are discharged as a result of the bankruptcy. Under a reorganization, the business changes its business form and the terms of its financial obligations are restructured.

2. Most companies and financial institutions treat patents as a valuable asset that can be bought and sold as well as licensed. Companies use patents as collateral securitizing debt obligations much like a company or an individual might mortgage land or a building. In addition, licensing revenues are not only an important part of a company's cash flow but also an alternative form of collateral for obtaining loans.

While collateralizing a patent and licensing revenues provides an important means to access credit, using either a patent or its licenses as collateral exposes the company to several risks. First, creditors can, in the event of default, foreclose on the patent much in the same way as it would foreclose on a house. Patent foreclosures have been rare, partly because the patent is often more valuable in the hands of the company, which has the know-how to effectively market and use the patent, than in the hands of the financial institution, which typically does not. Second, creditors often might have a say in the terms of how a patent is licensed in order to protect its financial interests. Often, the patent owner and creditor or a purchaser of a patent may create business entities whose sole function is to hold the patent as an asset.

3. Once patents are recognized as a business asset, patent owners, licensees, and creditors can adopt business strategies to protect their interests in bankruptcy. One tactic is to put the patent in a trust that is usually exempted from the bankruptcy estate under law. The Biopharma Royalty Trust, used by

Bristol Meyers Squib for securitizing its license of the HIV/AIDS drug Zerit from Yale Medical Colleges, the patent owner, provides a model. While this trust has not been tested in bankruptcy, the use of a trust mechanism also permits the securitization of patents, or the selling of financial interests in the profit stream generated by a patent. The Biopharma Royalty Trust is the first pharmaceutical royalty rated by Standards & Poor's and consists of $ 57.15 million worth of royalty notes, maturing on June 6, 2006.

A trust is an example of a "bankruptcy remote entity." Another example is the creation of a subsidiary corporation or some other separate business entity which would be the actual owner of the patent. This entity's sole purpose is to hold the patent and serve as the party through which royalties pass from the licensee to the original patent owner. In the event of bankruptcy, if the entity has been created correctly, the patent and the license will be sheltered from the estate.

4. Bankruptcy law allows the debtor business to manage its debts and effectively use its debts to satisfy the interests of the creditors and the business as a going concern. The bankruptcy court judge and the trustee play a crucial role in meeting these goals.

When a debtor enters into a business transaction while in bankruptcy, the trustee and bankruptcy judge oversee the negotiations to ensure that the debtor is obtaining maximum value. In the 1999 bankruptcy of National Health and Safety, Corp., the debtor entered into a sales transaction with Mednet Healthcare Network. The purpose of the sale was to transfer rights in National Health's intellectual property to Mednet, a company that could more effectively use and license the intellectual property within its network of healthcare providers. National Health's primary assets consisted of software copyrights, customer lists, and business methods associated with its network of uninsured customers that were sold access to health care services through National Health's plan.

This deal illustrates a common problem raised by intellectual property in bankruptcy: determining the value of the patents owned by the debtor. Sophisticated financial models are sometimes used to place a dollar value on these patents, but this approach is limited because of the uniqueness of each patent. Another way valuation issues are handled is by compensating the patent owner with a share of all future royalties earned by an assignee of the patent. The problem with this approach is that the assignee may not always effectively license the patent and may make a future transfer of the patent, potentially cutting off any rights of the original owner of the patent.

In the case of National Health, the debtor did retain the right to receive a share of the royalties. In addition, the debtor used an auction method to determine the value of the patents in this case, essentially transferring the patents to the highest bidder. The bankruptcy court approved the use of the auction method and also approved the royalty sharing agreement after imposing obligations on Mednet to report and account for all royalties earned by licensing the patents.

5. Domain Names. Courts are split on whether domain names are intellectual property that are part of the bankruptcy estate. In *Online Partners.Com Inc. v. AtlanticNet Media Corp.*, 2000 U.S. Dist. LEXIS 783 (N.D. Cal. 2000),

the court held that domain names are intellectual property and become part of the bankruptcy estate. However, in *Network Solutions, Inc., v. Umbro Int'l, Inc.,* 529 S.E. 2d 80 (Va. 2000), the Supreme Court of Virginia held that a domain name is not a property interest, but represents the contractual right to use the services of a domain name registrar.

6. Secured versus unsecured claims. Creditors can take security interests in intellectual property. Security interests in intellectual property have to be properly recorded and perfected. The steps needed to perfect security interests in intellectual property are discussed in detail in Chapter 2. If a security interest has not been properly recorded and perfected, the bankruptcy trustee has the right to set aside the security interest, rendering the creditor an unsecured creditor. An unsecured creditor is one who does not have a security interest in collateral backing the debt obligation.

In the distribution of assets among creditors, secured creditors have the right to receive the value of the collateral securing the debt before any unsecured creditors. Secured creditors can be forced to pay administrative expenses that the court deems to be "reasonable, necessary costs and expenses of preserving, or disposing of, such property to the extent of any benefit" to the secured creditor under section 506(c). Unsecured creditors are paid out of any assets remaining from the collateral after the secured creditors have been compensated and from all assets that do not serve as collateral. There are, however, nine levels of priority that receive payment before unsecured creditors. The nine levels of priority, as described in Section 507, are, in order: (i) administrative expense claims; (ii) claims in the ordinary course of business; (iii) certain claims for wages, salaries, and commissions; (iv) certain claims for contributions to employee benefit plans; (v) certain special claims in the grain and fishing industries; (vi) certain individual claims for deposits for purchase, lease or rental of property or services; (vii) alimony and child support claims; (viii) tax claims of governmental units; and (ix) claims to government agencies to maintain capital of insured depository institutions.

2.   The Automatic Stay and Intellectual Property Litigation

CHECKERS DRIVE-IN RESTAURANTS, INC. v. COMMISSIONER OF PATENTS AND TRADEMARKS
Court of Appeals for the District of Columbia
51 F.3d 1078 (1995)

HARRY T. EDWARDS, Chief Judge:

This appeal concerns the scope of the automatic stay provision under the Bankruptcy Code. This provision, which is found at 11 U.S.C. § 362(a) (1988), generally operates to block legal actions that could affect the property of a debtor in bankruptcy, and it serves both to shelter the debtor from harassment and to prevent creditors from engaging in a race to liquidate the estate's assets.

Appellant, Checkers Drive-In Restaurants, Inc., ("Checkers"), claims the automatic stay barred it from filing an affidavit as normally required to maintain its federal service mark registration pursuant to section 8 of the Lanham Trademark Act, 15 U.S.C. § 1058 (1988) ("Lanham Act"). Under section 8 of the Lanham Act, a service mark registration is canceled at the end of six years following the date of registration, unless the registrant files an affidavit (between the fifth and sixth years) setting forth his or her current use of the mark. Checkers's section 8 filing came due while it was pursuing a petition to cancel a competing service mark registration of a debtor in bankruptcy. Checkers failed to file the required affidavit during the statutory period, allegedly on the assumption that the Bankruptcy Code's automatic stay provision barred the required filing. The United States Patent and Trademark Office then canceled Checkers's service mark registration. Checkers appealed to the Commissioner of Patents and Trademarks ("Commissioner"), arguing that, because the automatic stay barred it from filing the affidavit, its failure to do so did not warrant the cancellation of its service mark registration under the Lanham Act. Rejecting this reasoning, the Commissioner denied Checkers's appeal. When Checkers challenged this decision in the District Court, the trial judge granted the Commissioner's motion for summary judgment. Checkers now appeals from that decision.

We affirm the judgment of the District Court. Although the Bankruptcy Code's automatic stay provision is broad in scope, it does not reach as far as Checkers would stretch it here. Checkers asserts that the section 8 filing requirement was stayed by operation of either of two subsections of the automatic stay provision. The first stays the continuation of any judicial, administrative, or other action against the debtor if the action was begun before the debtor filed its petition for bankruptcy. The second stays any act to take possession of, or exercise control over, property held by the bankrupt's estate. We find neither to apply. Checkers's filing of a section 8 affidavit was not part of its claim against the debtor, nor would it have affected the debtor's property. Rather, it would have merely maintained the status quo with respect to Checkers's own property. Accordingly, we hold that the Commissioner properly canceled Checkers's registration.

I.   BACKGROUND

This case arises from a dispute between two owners of federally registered service marks, both of which employed the word "Checkers" in their design. Checkers owned, by assignment, a service mark for use in connection with its marketing of restaurant services. Checkers's mark was registered pursuant to the Lanham Act on October 23, 1984. By virtue of this registration, Checkers gained a number of benefits, for federal registration of a trademark or service mark constitutes "prima facie evidence of the validity of the registered mark and of the registration of the mark, of the registrant's ownership of the mark, and of the registrant's exclusive right to use the registered mark in commerce on or in connection with the goods or services specified in the [registration] certificate." Moreover, the Lanham Act provides registrants with the opportunity to recover treble damages for violations of their rights, and, after five years of continuous use, permits registrants to make their rights "incontestable" — i.e., to transform their registration into conclusive evidence of their rights — by filing an affidavit setting forth certain information.

However, section 8 of the Lanham Act provides that, to maintain these benefits, all registrants must file, between the fifth and sixth years after initial registration, an affidavit setting forth the continued use of the registered mark in commerce "on or in connection with" the goods or services listed in the registration statement for the mark, or providing an adequate explanation for nonuse of the mark. If a registrant fails to file the required affidavit, the Commissioner by law must cancel its registration at the end of the sixth year. Thus, Checkers was required to file its section 8 affidavit no later than October 23, 1990, to maintain the registration of its service mark.

On March 16, 1988, another service mark registrant, Checkers Restaurant Group, Inc., ("CRG"), petitioned the Trademark Trial and Appeal Board ("TTAB") to cancel Checkers's registration pursuant to 15 U.S.C. § 1064 (1988), which provides for the filing of such a cancellation petition "by any person who believes that he is or will be damaged by the registration of a mark on the principal register." In support of its petition, CRG argued, inter alia, that Checkers's registration interfered with CRG's federally guaranteed right to use its service mark "in other than its existing geographic area." Checkers answered this cancellation petition and counterclaimed, seeking to cancel CRG's own service mark on essentially the same grounds.

In August 1989, before these competing cancellation claims could be resolved, CRG filed a petition for relief under Chapter 11 of the federal Bankruptcy Code, in the United States Bankruptcy Court for the Eastern District of New York. In so doing, CRG triggered the application of the automatic stay provision, which provides that the filing of a bankruptcy petition "operates as a stay, applicable to all entities," of eight different categories of conduct encompassing a wide swath of legal actions, including litigation, lien enforcement, and administrative proceedings, that could affect or interfere with the property of the bankrupt's estate. Accordingly, on January 8, 1990, CRG petitioned the TTAB to stay all proceedings relating to the cross-cancellation petitions filed by itself and Checkers. The TTAB responded on February 16, 1990, with an order staying the cancellation proceeding "since petitioner's registration is the subject of a counterclaim."

Checkers and CRG then negotiated a settlement agreement by which CRG transferred all rights to its service mark to Checkers in exchange for $42,500, and Checkers granted CRG a license to use its service mark at CRG's two existing restaurants in New York City. On November 30, 1990, the Bankruptcy Court approved this settlement. Accordingly, on December 19, 1990, Checkers moved the TTAB to lift the stay it had imposed on the cancellation proceedings, dismiss those proceedings as moot, and accept a section 8 affidavit filed concurrently. In response, the TTAB dismissed the parties' cancellation petitions with prejudice, and forwarded Checkers's section 8 affidavit to the Post-Registration Section of the Patent and Trademark Office for consideration.

However, because Checkers filed the affidavit after October 23, 1990, that Office's Affidavit/Renewal Examiner rejected it as untimely and canceled

Checkers's service mark registration. Checkers sought relief from the Commissioner, arguing that the automatic stay imposed by 11 U.S.C. § 362(a) prevented it from filing a section 8 affidavit during the pendency of the cancellation proceedings, and that, after the stay was lifted, its section 8 affidavit was timely filed pursuant to 11 U.S.C. § 108(c) (1988), which extends periods fixed by non-bankruptcy law "for commencing or continuing a civil action in a court other than a bankruptcy court on a claim against the debtor" until 30 days after a stay is terminated, if the period fixed by non-bankruptcy law already has run. The Commissioner rejected Checkers's argument, reasoning that

> this petitioner was not the party in bankruptcy and the filing of a Section 8 affidavit in relation to its [service mark registration] would not have been an exercise of control over a debtor in bankruptcy nor would it have furthered any claim against the debtor. The Section 8 filing would have spoken only to the petitioner's own continued use of its own registration.

Checkers sought judicial review of the Commissioner's decision by filing suit in the District Court. On January 7, 1994, the District Court granted summary judgment for the Commissioner, holding that the Bankruptcy Code did not stay Checkers's obligation to file a timely section 8 affidavit.

II. ANALYSIS

On appeal, Checkers claims the District Court erred in rejecting its argument that the automatic stay provision blocked the filing of a section 8 affidavit while Checkers was pursuing its cancellation petition against a debtor in bankruptcy. Specifically, Checkers claims that either of two subsections of the automatic stay provision operated to bar the required filing. The first stays "the commencement or continuation, including the issuance or employment of process, of a judicial, administrative, or other action or proceeding against the debtor that was or could have been commenced before the commencement of the" bankruptcy. The second stays "any act to obtain possession of property of the estate or of property from the estate or to exercise control over property of the estate." We review de novo the District Court's grant of summary judgment on this issue.

In the words of the Congress that enacted it, the automatic stay . . . "is one of the fundamental debtor protections provided by the bankruptcy laws." It gives the debtor a breathing spell from his creditors. It stops all collection efforts, all harassment, and all foreclosure actions. It permits the debtor to attempt a repayment or reorganization plan, or simply to be relieved of the financial pressures that drove him into bankruptcy.

The automatic stay also offers important protection for creditors. Without it, certain creditors would be able to pursue their own remedies against the debtor's property. Those who acted first would obtain payment of the claims in preference to and to the detriment of other creditors. Bankruptcy is designed to provide an orderly liquidation procedure under which all creditors are treated equally. A race of diligence by creditors for the debtor's assets prevents that.

To effectuate these congressional purposes, section 362(a) generally must be construed broadly. Its breadth is not unlimited, however. As the Ninth Circuit has stated, "while seemingly broad in scope, the automatic stay provisions should be construed no more expansively than is necessary to effectuate legislative purpose." Thus, we have held that, although the automatic stay blocks many legal actions against the debtor, it does not similarly bar claims brought by the debtor against other parties.

Checkers here asserts a construction of section 362(a) that would extend that provision "well beyond Congress's purpose." The policies underlying the automatic stay — those of sheltering the debtor from the demands of creditors and preserving the bankrupt's estate pending orderly distribution by a trustee — are not implicated by an act, such as Checkers's filing of a section 8 affidavit, that has no effect upon a claim against the debtor or the property of the estate, but rather maintains the status quo with respect to the property of an entity engaged in litigation with the debtor. We therefore reject Checkers's contention that the filing required by section 8 of the Lanham Act in this case would have constituted either the "continuation" of an "action or proceeding against the debtor" within the meaning of subsection 362(a)(1), or an act "to exercise control over property of the estate" within the meaning of subsection 362(a)(3).

A.   Subsection 362(a)(1)

Checkers first claims that its filing of a section 8 affidavit was stayed by subsection 362(a)(1), which bars legal actions that continue a pre-petition claim against the debtor. Checkers rests its argument on that portion of its cancellation petition alleging that CRG's registration interfered with Checkers's right to use its service mark outside of its existing geographic area. Checkers contends that, because this claim alleged interference with a right guaranteed to Checkers by virtue of the federal registration of its service mark, its maintenance of federal registration was necessary to its ability to bring the claim. Thus, Checkers argues, any act to maintain its federal registration — such as the filing of a section 8 affidavit — constituted the "continuation" of its claim against the debtor within the meaning of subsection 362(a)(1). This is a specious claim.

Subsection 362(a)(1) stays the continuation of "a judicial, administrative, or other action or proceeding against the debtor." Checkers's interpretation of this provision would extend the automatic stay to encompass not only actions against the debtor, but also acts that maintain the status quo within which such actions exist. In this case, the action against the debtor was Checkers's cancellation claim against CRG. Checkers's filing of a section 8 affidavit constituted no part of that claim. Rather, the filing served merely to maintain the status quo with respect to Checkers's own pre-existing service mark registration. We discern nothing in the automatic stay provision nor in its underlying policy to suggest that Congress intended it to block actions that maintain the status quo between a debtor and its legal adversary. To the contrary, our review of the legislative history reveals precisely the opposite intent — for, as already mentioned, Congress included section 362(a) in the Bankruptcy Code to ensure the preservation of the status quo between a debtor and its creditors

The cases cited by Checkers are not to the contrary. Checkers relies on cases from the bankruptcy courts holding that the automatic stay barred filings required to revive a pre-petition judgment lien. While we express no view as to the merits of these decisions, we find each distinguishable from the present case for the simple reason that each involved a filing necessary to renew a legal action — be it a lien, an assignment of assets, or an attachment of property — operating directly against the debtor. Here, by contrast, Checkers's section 8 filing would have operated not to renew or sustain its cancellation petition against CRG — the action against the debtor — but, as we have said, merely to maintain the status of its own property.

We recognize that Checkers's filing of a section 8 affidavit could, in some attenuated sense, be deemed necessary to the maintenance of part of Checkers's cancellation petition against CRG. Without a valid federal registration, Checkers might not have had standing to pursue that portion of its cancellation petition claiming injury from CRG's alleged interference with rights guaranteed to Checkers by federal law. However, to acknowledge that the section 8 filing was tangentially related to Checkers's ability to litigate a portion of its claim against CRG is not to bring that filing within the scope of section 362(a). Any construction of section 362(a) that would reach the filing at issue here would extend the power of the bankruptcy courts into a whole host of activities far removed from the concerns addressed by the Bankruptcy Code. For example, under Checkers's construction of the provision, a homeowner involved in an action to quiet title against a debtor in bankruptcy could claim that section 362(a) stayed his payment of property taxes imposed by state law. Such payment certainly is in some sense necessary to the maintenance of good title in the property, and, therefore, could be described as the "continuation" of a claim against the debtor. However, not only does such a sweeping construction of section 362(a) have the potential to raise serious constitutional questions regarding the scope of the jurisdiction that may permissibly be exercised by non-Article III bankruptcy courts, but it is not even remotely necessary to the achievement of the provision's twin goals — namely, creating a "breathing spell" for the debtor and preventing a "race of diligence" by creditors. For these reasons, we reject it. . . .

B. Subsection 362(a)(3)

Checkers next argues that its filing of a section 8 affidavit was stayed by subsection 362(a)(3), which bars acts to exercise control over property of the bankrupt's estate. As Checkers sees it, by filing an affidavit necessary to maintain its own service mark registration, Checkers would have taken an act to exercise control over the right to use the "Checkers" service mark, in derogation of CRG's own claim to that right. Central to Checkers's theory is the notion that, by virtue of their cross-cancellation claims, Checkers and CRG each were vying for the single and exclusive federal right to use a service mark employing the word "Checkers" in interstate commerce. Thus, in Checkers's view, any act that served to maintain its own claim to that right was an act to "exercise control over" property of the bankrupt's estate within the meaning of subsection 362(a)(3).

Checkers misunderstands the nature of the right created by federal registration under the Lanham Act. We recognize that federal registration constitutes prima facie evidence of the registrant's "exclusive right to use the registered mark in commerce." However, we also note that each federal registration constitutes such evidence. In this case, therefore, the federal registrations of both Checkers and CRG constituted prima facie evidence that each enjoyed the exclusive right to utilize its respective service mark in commerce. While the cross-cancellation proceeding might ultimately have established that protection of the rights of one registrant required cancellation of the service mark of the other, each held an independent property right in its own service mark until that decision was made, if ever. Thus, contrary to Checkers's theory, its filing of a section 8 affidavit would have affected only its own property, not the property of CRG. Accordingly, the required filing was not stayed by subsection 362(a)(3).

C. Cancellation of a Registration Under Section 8 of the Lanham Act

Because we find that neither subsection 362(a)(1) nor subsection 362(a)(3) stayed Checkers's filing of a section 8 affidavit in this case, we hold that the Commissioner properly canceled Checkers's service mark. In so holding, we recognize that the circumstances of this case do not present the paradigmatic situation that prompted Congress to enact section 8 of the Lanham Act. Congress intended that section "to remove from the register automatically marks which are no longer in use. Failure of registrants to file affidavits results in removal of such deadwood." Nevertheless, in establishing cancellation as the penalty for failure to file the required affidavit, Congress made no exception for the innocent or the negligent. Thus, the Commissioner had no discretion to do other than cancel Checkers's service mark registration in this case.

Moreover, while the application of the section 8 filing requirement may appear harsh in this case, Checkers failed to avail itself of a simple means of avoiding this result. Checkers neglected to take the prudential step of seeking clarification from the bankruptcy court, or even from the Commissioner, as to whether its section 8 filing obligation was stayed. Checkers had ample time to make such an inquiry; CRG filed its petition for bankruptcy approximately two months before the first day of the year-long "window" during which Checkers was required to file its section 8 affidavit. By failing to inquire, Checkers assumed the risk that the required filing was not stayed. That gamble did not pay off, and accordingly, Checkers's service mark was canceled at the conclusion of the filing period.

IN RE: THE SINGER COMPANY
United States Bankruptcy Court for the Southern District of
New York
46 Collier Bankr. Cas. 2d. 962 (2000)

BURTON R. LIFLAND, Bankruptcy Judge.

The Singer Company B.V. (Singer B.V.) and Singer do Brasil Industria e Comercio Ltda ("Singer Brasil") (collectively "the Plaintiffs") commenced the instant adversary proceeding against Groz Beckert KG ("Groz") and Dyno Corporation ("Dyno") (collectively "the Defendants"), seeking a judgment . . . declaring that an action commenced by the Defendant Groz in the Southern District of Florida (the "Florida Action") prior to the effective date of the Debtor's plan of reorganization violates the automatic stay.

BACKGROUND

The Parties

On September 12 and 13, 1999, the Singer Company N.V. and certain of its affiliates (collectively the "Debtors"), filed voluntary petitions for relief under chapter 11 of the Bankruptcy Code. On August 24, 2000, this Court entered an order confirming the Debtors' Joint Plan of Reorganization (the "Plan"). The Plan provided, among other things, that the automatic stay would remain in effect until the effective date of the Plan which occurred on September 14, 2000 (the "Effective Date"). Singer B.V. and Singer Brasil are Reorganized Debtors under the Plan.

Defendant Groz is a German corporation and is the plaintiff in the Florida action. Defendant Dyno is a Delaware corporation and is the defendant in the Florida Action. Dyno is the exclusive distributor in the United States of sewing machine needles manufactured by Singer Brasil.

Singer Spezialnadelfabric GmbH ("Singer Germany"), a former affiliated company, is a German corporation that was engaged in the business of manufacturing needles. Singer Germany is also subject to an insolvency proceeding in Germany (the "German Case") which is still pending.

The Dispute

The dispute between the parties centers around a U.S. patent for a sewing machine needle that was issued by Singer U.S. in 1985. In the Florida Action, Groz seeks to enjoin Dyno, Singer's distributor in the United States, from selling needles produced by Singer Brasil pursuant to the U.S. patent.

The Patent

In 1983, Singer Germany sold to Singer Brasil the specially designed equipment for manufacturing the then patent-pending needle (the "Equipment"). United States Patent and Trademark Office issued the '330 patent to Singer U.S. in May 1985. The '330 patent covers a certain needle for use in a sewing machine having a one-way needle clamp. Seven months after the patent application was granted, Singer U.S. assigned the '330 Patent to Singer Germany. Both prior to and after the assignment, Singer Germany provided Singer Brasil support for the installation, utilization and repair of the Equipment. Since 1983, Singer Brasil has openly manufactured the needles using the technology claimed in the '330 Patent. The Plaintiffs assert that, in light of the foregoing facts, Singer Brasil has an implied license to the '330 Patent which constitutes its estate property under section 541(a) of the Bankruptcy Code. There is substantial currency to the implied license argument from the facts presented.

Furthermore, since 1994, Dyno has exclusively distributed Singer Brasil's needles in the United States. Sales of the allegedly infringing needles represent almost 8.5% of Singer Brasil's aggregate sales.

The Florida Action

In November 1999, Groz purchased certain assets of Singer Germany in the course of the German case. Among those assets was the '330 Patent. On August 10, 2000, nearly nine months after purchasing the '330 Patent and two weeks before the scheduled hearing on confirmation of Singer's Plan, Groz commenced the Florida Action, alleging that Dyno's sale of needles manufactured abroad by Singer Brasil infringes the '330 Patent and seeking injunctive relief and damages to remedy the alleged infringement and stop the distribution of the needles. On September 11, 2000, Singer B.V. and Singer Brasil commenced the instant adversary proceeding against Groz and Dyno and filed a motion seeking to enjoin the Florida Action. On October 13, 2000, Groz filed a motion to dismiss the instant adversary proceeding.

DISCUSSION

As a threshold matter, Groz challenges the subject matter jurisdiction of this Court to enjoin its Florida Action against Dyno. However, one of the issues before this Court is an allegation that Groz violated the automatic stay when it commenced the Florida Action. Allegations concerning stay violations are claims arising under the Bankruptcy Code and give rise to core proceedings. Under this broad grant of subject matter jurisdiction, there can be no question that this Court now has jurisdiction to issue an injunction to stay Groz's action against Dyno. As discussed in more detail below, the Florida Action is inextricably related to the Singer bankruptcy proceedings and thus falls within the subject matter jurisdiction of this Court.

Groz violated Section 362(a)(1) of the Bankruptcy Code

Section 362(a)(1) of the Bankruptcy Code provides, in pertinent part that, when a bankruptcy petition is filed, "the commencement or continuation. . . of a judicial, administrative, or other action or proceeding against the debtor that was or could have been commenced before the commencement of the case under this title, or to recover a claim against the debtor that arose before the commencement of the case under this title" is stayed. 11 U.S.C. § 362(a)(1). Although the plain language of section 362 limits the extension of the automatic stay to a proceeding against the debtor, under specific circumstances non-debtors may be protected by the automatic stay. Several courts, for example, have held that actions are subject to the automatic stay even when the debtor is not a defendant, in situations where the debtor is the real party in interest and the action is merely a design to circumvent the automatic stay. The Plaintiffs contend that Groz's Florida Action, by not technically naming Singer Brasil a defendant, is not only an end run attempt to exercise control over Singer Brasil's implied license but is a violation of the automatic stay since Singer Brasil is the real party in interest. Groz argues that the Florida Action is merely a commercial lawsuit between two non-debtors seeking to prevent "allegedly unlawful conduct", specifically Dyno's sale of allegedly infringing needles manufactured by Singer Brasil. Groz also argues that even if Singer Brasil was the real party in interest and that the Florida Action was commenced while the automatic stay was still in effect, it is now moot because the Effective Date has now occurred and section 362 has ceased to have any application in this case.

With respect to the Effective Date argument, Groz seems to believe that, even if it did violate the automatic stay by commencing the Florida Action a few weeks before the Effective Date, it was only a "brief violation." Just like one cannot be slightly "enceinte", the same applies to a violation of the automatic stay. A violation of the automatic stay is just that, a violation of the automatic stay — there is no such thing as a slight violation. The occurrence of the Effective Date after such a violation has taken place does not somehow moot the violation.

Groz's assertion that the Florida Action is nothing more than a commercial dispute between two non-debtors is also without merit. It is painstakingly clear that Dyno's interests with respect to the Florida Action are so inextricably intertwined with the Debtors, that actions against them could be seen essentially as actions against the estate. The core of the Florida Action involves the '330 Patent. Dyno is merely Singer's distributor. Singer Brasil is the purported owner of the implied license to exploit the '330 Patent. It follows that Singer Brasil is the real party defendant for patent infringement. In effect, the Florida Action is nothing more than an effort to circumvent section 362 by suing Dyno when the real party in interest is Singer Brasil. Accordingly the commencement of Groz's action in the Southern District of Florida clearly violated the essence of section 362 of the Bankruptcy Code.

Groz violated section 362(a)(3) of the Bankruptcy Code

Section 362(a) of the Bankruptcy Code stays "any act to obtain possession of the property of the estate or of property from the estate or to exercise control over property of the estate." 11 U.S.C. § 362(a)(3). Courts have construed property of the estate so as to include all legal or equitable interests of the debtor in property, both tangible and intangible, including exempt property, as of the date the case is commenced. Singer Brasil asserts that it has an interest in the '330 Patent in the form of an implied license and that the Florida Action attempts to strip any value of Singer Brasil's license to the '330 Patent by, among other things, effectively preventing the distribution of Singer Brasil's needles in the United States. Whereas the applicable non-bankruptcy law determines the extent of an interest in property, absent an overriding federal policy, bankruptcy law determines whether that interest is "property of the estate."

In patent law, an implied license merely signifies a patentee's waiver of the statutory right to exclude others from making, using, or selling the patented invention. The burden of proving that an implied license exists is on the party asserting an implied license as a defense to infringement. The Supreme Court has held that:

> No formal granting of a license is necessary in order to give it effect. Any language used by the owner of the patent, or any conduct on his part exhibited to another from which that other may properly infer that the owner consents to his use of the patent in making or using it,

or selling it, upon which the other acts, constitutes a license and a defense to an action for a tort.

The Federal Circuit has noted that the sale of unpatented equipment which is used to conduct a patented process may itself constitute the grant of an implied license to conduct such process. When a party argues that the sale of a device carries with it an implied license to use that device in practicing a patented invention, that party has the burden to show that, inter alia, the purchased device has no non-infringing uses and that the circumstances of the sale plainly indicated that the grant of a license should be inferred.

In order to imply that a license was given to Singer Brasil, Singer Brasil must demonstrate that the '330 Patent for which the implied license was sought was explicitly necessary to make use of an explicitly granted right. Singer argues that Singer Germany's sale of the specialized equipment, which had no other use than for the manufacturing of the needles utilizing the '330 Patent, resulted in an implied license for the '330 Patent. This argument is persuasive. Not only did Singer Germany sell Singer Brasil the specialized Equipment, but they both installed and, when necessary, repaired the Equipment for Singer Brasil. Furthermore, Singer Brasil has been openly manufacturing these needles for seventeen years. Based upon the facts at hand, it appears that the Plaintiffs have a substantial likelihood of success in proving that Singer Germany granted Singer Brasil an implied license for the '330 Patent. Consequently, Singer Brasil has an interest in the '330 Patent which constitutes property of the estate.

Furthermore, a purchaser of a patent takes it encumbered by prior licenses, including implied licenses. Groz allegedly purchased the '330 Patent in November 1999. It is the duty of the purchaser to inform himself of the nature of the licensee's ownership and the extent of his right. Since Singer Brasil has been openly manufacturing these needles for the past seventeen years and has been the sole manufacturer of these needles, it is highly unlikely that Groz did not know, or was unable to learn about the implied license given to Singer Brasil. Consequently, if it is found at a later date that Singer Brasil does indeed have an implied license, then Groz will be encumbered by it.

In light of the foregoing facts, I find that the Florida Action is a clear attempt to exercise control over property of Singer's Bankruptcy estate, specifically the interest Singer Brasil has in the '330 Patent, and that the commencement of that action prior to the Effective Date was a violation of the automatic stay.

NOTES & QUESTIONS

1. Under section 362(a) of the Bankruptcy Code, the commencement of a bankruptcy case invokes the automatic stay, which stops virtually all collection efforts on account of pre-petition obligations of the debtor, including any foreclosure proceedings. The purpose of the automatic stay is to ensure that all disputes over the debtor's assets are adjudicated within the bankruptcy proceedings and to prevent a free for all as creditors attempt to assert their rights through individual lawsuits against the debtor. The stay gives the debtor a

"breathing spell" as he attempts to reorganize his assets and satisfy all the creditors. Exceptions are available from the stay under section 362(b). Creditors can ask the court to lift the stay in two narrow situations: (i) when the creditor's interest in the property of the estate is not adequately protected by the bankruptcy proceeding or (ii) when the debtor has no equity in property that is not necessary for successful reorganization.

2. In light of the policies underlying the automatic stay, the decision in *Checkers* should not be surprising. The filing of the Section 8 affidavit by Checkers is not a claim against the debtor's estate that would affect the plan of reorganization. Put another way, the filing with the USPTO is not an end run around the bankruptcy court to liquidate assets of the bankruptcy estate. Checkers' failure to file the section 8 affidavit is an example of bad planning and confusion over the scope of the stay. While it is true that the cancellation proceedings were stayed by the filing of the bankruptcy proceedings, Checkers was not stayed from filing the requisite affidavit in order to maintain its own service mark. Do you see why the cancellation proceeding was stayed by the filing of the bankruptcy proceeding? The outcome of the proceedings would have affected the debtor's estate and could have resulted in a creditor (namely Checkers) obtaining a benefit from the estate outside the formal bankruptcy proceedings.

3. Does the reasoning discussed in note 2 apply to the facts of *Singer*? The litigation was between Groz and a licensee of Singer, not Singer itself. Why should this litigation that does not include Singer be resolved in light of Singer's bankruptcy petition? The court describes Groz's lawsuit against Dyno as an end run to affect control over Singer's interest in the '330 patent. Make sure you understand the analysis. Is this an equitable argument or a legal argument based on the text of the Bankruptcy Code? Suppose the case involved a trademark and not a patent and that Dyno was a franchisee of Singer, the trademark owner. Would a lawsuit against the franchisee be stayed if the franchisor filed a bankruptcy petition?

4. Courts have held that the automatic stay provisions do not apply to a preliminary injunction against the debtor in a patent infringement suit. *See Seiko Epson Corp. v. Nu-Kote Int'l, Inc.*, 190 F. 3d 1360, 1364-65 (Fed. Cir. 1999) ("the statutory stay of proceedings . . . did not free [debtor] of the contempt orders and the injunctions upon which the contempt was based"). For a similar result in the context of trademark, see *In re Cinnabar 2000 Haircutters, Inc.*, 20 B.R. 575, 577 (Bankr. S.D.N.Y. 1982) (automatic stay not "a haven for contumacious conduct in violation of a party's judicially determined tradename rights").

3.   The Intellectual Property License in Bankruptcy

a.   Statutory Background

Bankruptcy Code

Section 365. Executory contracts and unexpired leases

(a)   . . . . the trustee, subject to the court's approval, may assume or reject any executory contract or unexpired lease of the debtor.

. . .

(n)(1)   If the trustee rejects an executory contract under which the debtor is a licensor of a right to intellectual property, the licensee under such contract may elect —

    (A)   to treat such contract as terminated by such rejection if such rejection by the trustee amounts to such a breach as would entitle the licensee to treat such contract as terminated by virtue of its own terms, applicable non-bankruptcy law, or an agreement made by the licensee with another entity; or

    (B)   to retain its rights (including a right to enforce any exclusivity provision of such contract, but excluding any other right under applicable non-bankruptcy law to specific performance of such contract) under such contract and under any agreement supplementary to such contract, to such intellectual property (including any embodiment of such intellectual property to the extent protected by applicable non-bankruptcy law), as such rights existed immediately before the case commenced, for —

        (i)   the duration of such contract; and

        (ii)   any period for which such contract may be extended by the licensee as of right under applicable non-bankruptcy law.

(2)   If the licensee elects to retain its rights, as described in paragraph (1)(B) of this subsection, under such contract —

    (A)   the trustee shall allow the licensee to exercise such rights;

    (B)   the licensee shall make all royalty payments due under such contract for the duration of such contract and for any period described in paragraph (1)(B) of this subsection for which the licensee extends such contract; and

    (C)   the licensee shall be deemed to waive —

        (i)   any right of setoff it may have with respect to such contract under this title or applicable non-bankruptcy law; and

        (ii)   any claim allowable under section 503(b) of this title arising from the performance of such contract.

(3)   If the licensee elects to retain its rights, as described in paragraph (1)(B) of this subsection, then on the written request of the licensee the trustee shall —

    (A)   to the extent provided in such contract, or any agreement supplementary to such contract, provide to the licensee any intellectual property (including such embodiment) held by the trustee; and

(B)   not interfere with the rights of the licensee as provided in such contract, or any agreement supplementary to such contract, to such intellectual property (including such embodiment) including any right to obtain such intellectual property (or such embodiment) from another entity.

(4)   Unless and until the trustee rejects such contract, on the written request of the licensee the trustee shall —

(A)   to the extent provided in such contract or any agreement supplementary to such contract —

(i)   perform such contract; or

(ii)   provide to the licensee such intellectual property (including any embodiment of such intellectual property to the extent protected by applicable non-bankruptcy law) held by the trustee; and

(B)   not interfere with the rights of the licensee as provided in such contract, or any agreement supplementary to such contract, to such intellectual property (including such embodiment), including any right to obtain such intellectual property (or such embodiment) from another entity.

Section 101. Definitions

In this title —

. . .

(35A) "intellectual property" means —

(A) trade secret;

(B) invention, process, design, or plant protected under title 35;

(C) patent application;

(D) plant variety;

(E) work of authorship protected under title 17; or

(F) mask work protected under chapter 9 of title 17;

to the extent protected by applicable non-bankruptcy law.

NOTES & QUESTIONS

1. Section 365(a) applies to all executory contracts and unexpired leases in bankruptcy. Under 365(a), the trustee has the power, with the approval of the court, to assume or reject an executory contract or unexpired lease of the debtor. If the contract or lease is assumed, then it becomes part of the estate and both parties to the contract or lease are still subject to its terms. The trustee upon assumption must make adequate assurances to the other side of

continuing performance and cure any defaults under the contract. If the trustee rejects, however, the rejection constitutes a breach of the contract or lease and the other party has a claim against the estate for contract breach. Except for non-residential real estate leases, the contract or lease must be assumed or rejected within 60 days after the order for relief in a Chapter 7 proceeding and anytime prior to the confirmation of a reorganization plan in a Chapter 11 proceeding. In addition, the non-debtor can file a motion with the court to compel the trustee to assume or reject in either type of proceeding.

2. What is an executory contract? Most courts have adopted the definition developed by Professor Vern Countryman in his article *Executory Contracts in Bankruptcy,* 57 MINN. L. REV. 439 (1973). According to Professor Countryman, an executory contract is "a contract in which the obligation of both the bankrupt and the other party to the contract are so far unperformed that the failure of either to complete performance would constitute a material breach excusing the performance of the other." *Id.* at 460. Some courts have adopted a definition that requires only one party to have unperformed obligations. *See, e.g., In re Tonry,* 724 F. 2d 467 (5th Cir. 1984). Yet other courts adopt a balancing of the equities approach that treats a contract as executory to the extent that such treatment is consistent with the policies of bankruptcy law. *See, e.g., In re Fox,* 83 B.R. 290 (Bankr. E.D. Pa. 1988).

3. Why does it matter if a contract is executory? The practical importance has to do with the trustee's ability to assume or reject the contract. As we will see in the discussion below, such a power can be very important in defining the scope of the bankruptcy estate and the ability of the debtor to operate the estate in bankruptcy.

4. Executory contracts involving intellectual property. In general, intellectual property licenses are deemed to be executory contracts as long as both licensor and licensee have ongoing obligations under the license. One court, however, denied executory contract treatment when a licensor of intellectual property had no obligations and only had the role of receiving royalty payments. *See In re Learning Publications, Inc.,* 94 B.R. 763 (Bankr. M.D. Fla. 1988). *See also Microsoft Corp. v. DAK Industries, Inc.,* 66 F. 3d 1091 (9th Cir. 1995) (construing a software license as a sale since licensor Microsoft had no continuing obligations except the receipt of royalties); *In re Gencor,* 298 B.R. 902 (Bankr. M.D. Fla. 2003) (patent settlement agreement not executory). All courts recognize that the characterization of a contract as executory rests on the extent and type of remaining obligations and not on whether the licensor or the licensee is the debtor. Special issues arise, however, depending upon whether the debtor is the licensor or the licensee.

5. If the debtor is the licensor, section 365(n) places limitations on the trustee's ability to reject the license. Upon rejection by the trustee, the non-debtor licensee can elect to treat the rejection as a termination of the agreement or to retain its rights under the license. If the non-debtor licensee retains his rights under the license, the licensee has the right to use the intellectual property as it existed at the time of the filing of the bankruptcy petition and

must continue to make royalty payments. The trustee must provide the intellectual property to the licensee and must not interfere with the licensee's rights under the license.

6. Section 365(n) was enacted in 1988 and is known as the Intellectual Property Bankruptcy Protection Act. Congress enacted the provision in response to the court's decision in *Lubrizol Enters., Inc. v. Richmond Metal Finishers, Inc.,* 756 F. 2d 1043 (4th Cir. 1985) (excerpted below). The Lubrizol decision was viewed as an inequitable to non-debtor licensees who, absent the protections of section 365(n), would be denied access to intellectual property when the licensor entered bankruptcy.

7. Notice that the definition of "intellectual property" in the Bankruptcy Code does not include "trademarks." The implication is that the protections of section 365(n) do not apply to trademark licensees. Congress deemed that trademarks should be excluded because the quality control issues raised by trademark licensing could not readily be resolved by section 365(n). For a critical discussion of the exclusion of trademarks, see Xuan-Thao N. Nguyen, *Bankrupting Trademarks,* 37 U.C. DAVIS LAW REVIEW 1267 (2004) (arguing that the exclusion hurts business goodwill that trademark law is designed to protect). The one court to address the treatment of trademarks under section 365(n) extended the provisions protections to trademark licensees under equitable grounds. *See In re Matusalem,* 158 B.R. 514 (Bankr. S.D. Fla. 1993).

8. If the debtor is the licensee, then section 365(n) does not apply. The debtor licensee has the right under 365(a) to either assume or reject the license. If the debtor licensee rejects, then the debtor loses all rights to use the intellectual property and the non-debtor licensor can sue for any contractual breach claims. The difficult question is the ability of the debtor licensee to assign the licensee upon assumption. Section 365(f)(1) permits such assignments subject to the limitations of section 365(c)(1). We will discuss the special problem of assignments by debtor licensees below. What is important to understand before reading the cases is the different treatment of exclusive versus non-exclusive licenses for the purposes of assignment.

In general, an assignment of a license by a debtor licensee is barred if the assignment is prohibited by applicable non-bankruptcy law and if the licensor does not consent to the assignment. If a license is non-exclusive, then the licensee in general does not have the ability to assign the license since a non-exclusive intellectual property license is viewed as personal to the licensee. If the license is exclusive, however, then the license might be assignable depending upon whether copyrights, patents, or trademarks are at issue. Under copyright law, for example, an exclusive license is viewed as a transfer of a property right and therefore the debtor licensee of a copyright can assign the copyright to someone else. Patent law and trademark law, however, do not treat exclusive licenses as transfers of property rights, and as a result the assignability of exclusive patent and trademark licenses is an open question. We will discuss these issues in greater detail below.

b. Licensor as Debtor

IN RE: CELLNET DATA SYSTEMS, INC.
United States Court of Appeals for the Third Circuit
327 F.3d 242 (2003)

NYGAARD, Circuit Judge.

This appeal presents us with an issue of first impression involving elections under 11 U.S.C. § 365(n). CellNet Data Systems, Inc. sold its intellectual property to Schlumberger Resource Management Services, Inc., which specifically excluded the assets and liabilities of certain licensing agreements under the terms of the sale. After CellNet rejected those licensing agreements under 11 U.S.C. § 365(a) of the bankruptcy code, the licensee exercised its rights under § 365(n) to continue to use the intellectual property, subject to the royalty payments due under the original license. Both CellNet, as party to the contract, and Schlumberger, as holder of the intellectual property, claim the right to receive the royalty payments. The District Court determined that Schlumberger had expressly severed the royalties from the intellectual property by the terms of the purchase agreement and that the royalties remained in CellNet's estate. Although CellNet then rejected the license, the licensee, by operation of § 365(n), elected to enforce the license and thus the District Court concluded that the royalties due under the revived contract belonged to CellNet. We will affirm.

The essential facts are not in dispute, rather how those facts operate is at issue. In 1997, CellNet, a developer of a wireless data network for meter reading, now in bankruptcy, entered into a joint venture with Bechtel Enterprises, Inc., forming a company called BCN Data Systems LLC. As part of the joint venture, CellNet entered into several licensing agreements with BCN, that provided BCN with an exclusive license to use CellNet's intellectual property outside the United States. In return, CellNet received a royalty payment equal to three percent of BCN's gross revenues. The License Agreements also contained a covenant that CellNet would provide technological support to BCN during the lifetime of the Agreements.

Three years later, with CellNet on the verge of bankruptcy, Appellant, Schlumberger, proposed the sale of CellNet's assets. Schlumberger and CellNet entered into a Proposal Letter under which Schlumberger would purchase "all or substantially all of the assets and business operations of [CellNet] and its subsidiaries." The January 31, 2000 Proposal Letter also provided that Schlumberger "would acquire all assets of [CellNet] free and clear of all liens other than certain liens to be agreed (the 'Assets'), other than the Excluded Assets (as defined below), used in, held for use in, or related to the business and operations of [CellNet]." Thus, the proposal contemplated that certain assets of CellNet would not be subject to the ultimate purchase agreement. However, the term "Excluded Assets" was left open for future agreement by the parties.

CellNet filed for bankruptcy on February 4, 2000. On March 1, 2000, Schlumberger and CellNet entered into an Asset Purchase Agreement that mirrored the intent of the Proposal Letter, in that Schlumberger would purchase all of CellNet's assets, subject only to certain excluded assets. This time, however, the agreement included language that explained:

> At any time prior to March 25, 2000, [Schlumberger] shall be entitled unilaterally to amend this Agreement, including without limitation Schedules 1.01(a)(i) (Stock Acquired), 1.01(b) (Excluded Contracts) and 1.01(e) (Excluded Assets) attached hereto, solely for the purpose of excluding any or all of the stock, assets, liabilities and agreements of [CellNet] pertaining to [CellNet's] joint venture with Bechtel Enterprises, Inc., or its affiliates, (collectively, the "BCN Assets and Liabilities") from the stock, assets, liabilities and agreements being acquired or assumed by [Schlumberger] hereunder.

Thus, the Purchase Agreement provided that Schlumberger would purchase all of CellNet's intellectual property, etc., but would be able to specifically exclude all stocks, assets, liabilities, and agreements pertaining to CellNet's venture with BCN. Pursuant to a letter by counsel on March 24, 2000, Schlumberger elected to exercise its right to exclude the BCN assets and liabilities. The letter went on to specifically designate the License Agreements between CellNet and BCN as assets and liabilities excluded from the purchase under the heading "Excluded Contracts."

Despite excluding the License Agreements, Schlumberger asserted a right to the royalties under the Agreements prior to the approval of the Asset Purchase Agreement by the bankruptcy court. This was based on the belief that CellNet would have to reject the Agreements under § 365(a) as executory contracts that it could not fulfill and that Schlumberger would then be entitled to the royalties as owner of the underlying intellectual property. CellNet believed otherwise, but in an effort to complete the sale of its assets, agreed to reject the License Agreements and preserve the right of the parties to contest ownership of the royalties. The parties memorialized the decision to reject the License Agreements under § 365(a) in an additional section of the Asset Purchase Agreement. The new section read:

> Schlumberger] has elected not to assume the License and Consulting Services Agreement between [CellNet] and BCN Data Systems, L.L.C. ("BCN"), dated January 1, 1997, the [OCDB License Agreement] between [CellNet] and BCN dated January 1, 1997 . . . (collectively, the "BCN License Agreements"). [CellNet] shall obtain an order from the Bankruptcy Court pursuant to Section 365(a) of the Bankruptcy Code rejecting the BCN License Agreements. The parties hereto acknowledge that if BCN elects to retain its rights under the BCN License Agreements in accordance with Section 365(n)(1)(B) of the Bankruptcy Code, then the rights and obligations of the parties with respect to the License Agreements, including without limitation any royalty rights thereunder, are disputed by the parties. Each party reserves all rights under this Agreement with respect to the BCN License Agreements, and neither this Amendment nor any action taken in connection herewith, including the filing of any modified Sale Order, shall be deemed to be a waiver or admission of any matter related to the dispute between [CellNet] and [Schlumberger] regarding the BCN License Agreements.

Under this agreement, CellNet agreed to reject the License Agreements pursuant to § 365(a), but both parties acknowledged that a dispute over royalties would remain if BCN elected to retain its rights under § 365(n). On May 4, 2001, the Bankruptcy Court approved the Asset Purchase Agreement with both the addition, as well as additional language that further expressed that the sale did not alter the rights of CellNet, Schlumberger, or BCN regarding the License Agreements and the royalties due thereunder.

Following approval of the sale, CellNet moved to reject the License Agreements under § 365(a). Section 365(a) provides that "the trustee, subject to the court's approval, may assume or reject any executory contract or unexpired lease of the debtor." 11 U.S.C. § 365(a). CellNet was permitted to act as the trustee because it was a debtor-in-possession pursuant to 11 U.S.C. §1107(a). The Bankruptcy Court approved the motion and CellNet informed BCN of its election. BCN, in turn, chose to retain its rights under § 365(n). Section 365(n) provides that "[i]f a trustee rejects an executory contract under which the debtor is a licensor of a right to intellectual property, the licensee under such contract may elect" to either terminate the contract or retain certain rights under the license. Specifically, the licensee may elect:

> to retain its rights (including a right to enforce any exclusivity provision of such contract, but excluding any other right under applicable non-bankruptcy law to specific performance of such contract) under such contract and under any agreement supplementary to such contract, to such intellectual property . . . as such rights existed immediately before the case commenced. . . .

If a licensee elects to retain its rights, section 365(n)(2)(B) of the Code requires it to "make all royalty payments due under such contract for the duration of such contract. . . ." By its election, and operation of § 365(n), BCN was permitted to continue to use the intellectual property originally licensed from CellNet, but was required to pay the royalties due under that license.

Rather than remain in a joint venture, CellNet and Bechtel agreed that Bechtel would acquire all of the assets and liabilities of BCN and make one lump sum payment to CellNet that would encompass the future royalty payments due under the License Agreements. The Bankruptcy Court approved the sale to Bechtel, and the negotiated amount of $2,250,000 for the future royalties was placed in escrow pending resolution of who was entitled to the royalties.

Both the Bankruptcy Court and the District Court found that CellNet was entitled to the royalties. In its opinion, the District Court addressed the same arguments now raised before us. Schlumberger argued that the Asset Purchase Agreement and its later rejection of the License Agreement did not operate to separate the right to the royalties from the underlying ownership of the intellectual property. Alternatively, Schlumberger asked the District Court to look past the original exclusion and find that because it owns the intellectual property and CellNet subsequently rejected the license under §365(a), it has superior rights to the royalties.

In affirming the decision of the Bankruptcy Court in favor of CellNet, the District Court thoroughly analyzed the Asset Purchase Agreement and subsequent exclusion of License Agreements. After finding that the Purchase

Agreement was not ambiguous, the District Court looked at the "express reservation" requirement necessary for the separation of royalties from intellectual property and decided that the Purchase Agreement could only be interpreted to separate the royalties due under the license from the intellectual property. The District Court also addressed Schlumberger's contention that it had superior rights under § 365 because it owned the intellectual property and CellNet had rejected the license pursuant to § 365(a). The District Court agreed with CellNet that the election of BCN pursuant to § 365(n) renewed certain obligations related to the license. The District Court found that under the License Agreements, the royalty payments were due to CellNet and that because Schlumberger had excluded those License Agreements from its purchase, CellNet "remains entitled to receive the BCN royalties pursuant to statutory authority even if it rejected the License Agreements and is not technically a party to them."

III. Discussion

A.   The Effects of the Asset Purchase Agreement:

Schlumberger's first argument is that the Purchase Agreement and letter of March 2000 did not operate to sever the royalties from ownership of the intellectual property. Both the Bankruptcy Court and District Court disagreed and found that Schlumberger had separated ownership from its rights by the plain language of the Purchase Agreement and March Letter Amendment. These findings are clearly correct.

On appeal, Schlumberger points to two cases from the bankruptcy court that would require an express reservation to separate the components. In *Chemical Foundation, Inc. v. E.I. du Pont De Nemours & Co.,* 29 F.2d 597 (D.Del.1928) the court discussed the effects of assigning a patent on the right to receive royalties for that patent:

> Yet, as an assignment of a patent, without more, does not transfer to the assignee the right to recover damages or profits for prior infringements, although royalties to accrue and damages and profits for future infringements are incident to and accompany the patent unless separated by express reservation, and as a patentee may after assigning the patents sue and recover for past infringements, it would seem obvious that an assignor of a patent would have like rights with respect to royalties accrued at the time of the assignment. But the right to recover accrued royalties or damages and profits for past infringements may likewise be assigned.

Chemical espouses the proposition that royalties were inherent in ownership of a patent and flowed accordingly, although they could be divorced by an express reservation. This idea was expanded in *Crom v. Cement Gun Co.,* 46 F.Supp. 403 (D.Del. 1942), where the court discussed the ownership of a patent. After quoting much of the above language in *Chemical,* the court found that:

> Where an assignment conveys all the assignor's right, title and interest, if the right to receive royalties is to be severed from the beneficial

ownership of the patent and remain in the assignor, there must be an express reservation or some agreement to that effect. I do not think that the mere retention of the 'license'. . . is sufficient to make the severance, particularly where, as in the present case, it is merely for the purpose of protecting a supposed but nonexistent shop right and is in contravention of the understanding of the parties.

Unlike the cases Schlumberger cites, the unambiguous Purchase Agreement and March Letter Amendment present here did expressly sever the royalties. This conclusion has support in a straightforward reading of the documents. The Purchase Agreement permitted Schlumberger "unilaterally to amend this Agreement . . . solely for the purpose of excluding any or all of the stock, assets, liabilities and agreements of [CellNet] pertaining to [CellNet's] joint venture with Bechtel Enterprises, Inc." Beyond this language, the Purchase Agreement also explained that "[n]otwithstanding anything herein to the contrary, the Purchaser shall not purchase or acquire, and shall have no rights or liabilities with respect to, any Excluded Asset." The Purchase Agreement further defined "Excluded Assets" to include "all rights of the Sellers under any Excluded Asset" and "all proceeds from any Excluded Asset."

These sections must be read in concert with the March 24, 2000 Letter, which sought to specify those items excluded from the Purchase Agreement. In that letter, Schlumberger "elect[ed] to amend the Asset Purchase Agreement to exclude the BCN Assets and Liabilities from the stock, assets, liabilities and agreements of the Sellers being acquired or assumed under the Asset Purchase Agreement." The letter went on to specifically enumerate the various License Agreements between CellNet and BCN as excluded assets. Thus, Schlumberger expressly sought to exclude all rights and liabilities under the License Agreements, including its rights to all proceeds under those Agreements.

Schlumberger now attempts to argue that the Purchase Agreement and March Letter (both of which it drafted) are ambiguous and that extrinsic evidence is necessary to decide whether the Purchase Agreement contemplated severance of the royalties. This argument is unpersuasive. As the District Court correctly noted:

> The Asset Purchase Agreement and March 24 letter contain no ambiguities and, by those documents, Schlumberger excluded the License Agreements from the assets it was acquiring. While Schlumberger has argued that, under this pattern of events, it is entitled to receive the royalties from BCN, either as a matter of contract law or under the Bankruptcy Code, both parties agree the Asset Purchase Agreement and March 24 letter accurately represent the parties' intentions. Thus, it is only the legal effect of the transaction that Schlumberger challenges.

Under New York law, "ambiguity does not exist 'simply because the parties urge different interpretations.'" When Schlumberger elected to exclude "all the proceeds from [the BCN License Agreements]" it expressly excluded the royalties from these agreements from the intellectual property it was purchasing. The effect of this exclusion is that the License Agreements remain in CellNet's estate.

Schlumberger also finds fault with the District Court's holding that "[b]ecause the right to royalties arises only from the License Agreements, Schlumberger's exclusion of those agreements (and the royalties they set forth) was unambiguous and effective. Instead, Schlumberger argues that the right to the royalties derives from ownership of the intellectual property and not from the License Agreements. As a general proposition, Schlumberger is correct that it is the intellectual property that creates the right to royalties-as an owner may parcel out its "bundle of rights." However, this argument does not alter our analysis under these factual circumstances. At the time the License Agreements were created, CellNet owned the intellectual property and thus could license the right of exclusivity outside the United States to BCN in exchange for royalties. This separation of rights from the "bundle" was memorialized in the License Agreements. When Schlumberger purchased the intellectual property owned by CellNet, the license already existed and, pursuant to § 365(n), would likely continue to exist. Based on Schlumberger's acceptance that they would be purchasing CellNet's intellectual property subject to BCN's rights, and that BCN's rights existed solely from the excluded licenses, what Schlumberger bought was less than the full "bundle of rights" associated with ownership.

Thus, the initial right to royalties arose from the ownership of the intellectual property, but after Schlumberger elected to exclude the License Agreements, it severed those rights from the bundle it was purchasing. Once the royalties were divorced from the intellectual property, the only authority for their existence was the License Agreement. Because Schlumberger had excluded the Agreements, CellNet remained a party to those Agreements and would be entitled to the royalties thereunder.

Finding that CellNet would be otherwise rightfully entitled to the royalties once Schlumberger separated the royalties from the intellectual property that it purchased, we now turn to the question of how CellNet's rejection of the License Agreements under 11 U.S.C. § 365(a) and BCN's subsequent revival under § 365(n) affects the rights of the parties.

B. After the 11 U.S.C. § 365(n) Election, Who is Entitled to the Royalties?

Under the Bankruptcy Code, a trustee may elect to reject or assume its obligations under an executory contract. This election is an all-or-nothing proposition — either the whole contract is assumed or the entire contract is rejected. Pursuant to its Purchase Agreement with Schlumberger, CellNet, as trustee, rejected the License Agreements under 365(a). Normally in bankruptcy, this would end the obligations between the contracting parties and relegate the non-breaching party to an unsecured creditor. . . . Congress, however, altered this system by passing an amendment that added § 365(n). Section 365(n) only applies to intellectual property and grants the licensee of intellectual property certain rights not enjoyed by other contracting parties. Specifically, if a trustee rejects an executory contract under § 365(a), the licensee of intellectual property may elect either:

(A)   to treat such contract as terminated by such rejection if such rejection by the trustee amounts to such a breach as would entitle the licensee to treat such contract as terminated by virtue of its own terms, applicable non-bankruptcy law, or an agreement made by the licensee with another entity; or

(B)   to retain its rights (including a right to enforce any exclusivity provision of such contract, but excluding any other right under applicable non-bankruptcy law to specific performance of such contract) under such contract and under any agreement supplementary to such contract, to such intellectual property (including any embodiment of such intellectual property to the extent protected by applicable non-bankruptcy law), as such rights existed immediately before the case commenced, for —

(i)   the duration of such contract; and

(ii)   any period for which such contract may be extended by the licensee as of right under applicable non-bankruptcy law.

Looking to the facts before us, Schlumberger excluded the License Agreements from its purchase, and then CellNet rejected the Agreements under § 365(a). In turn, BCN elected to retain its rights and was thus obligated to "make all royalty payments due under such contract for the duration of such contract." Schlumberger argues that because CellNet rejected the contract, it has not assumed the benefits of the contract and thus has no rights under the contract. Schlumberger then posits that because it owns the underlying intellectual property, it has superior rights to the royalties — despite not purchasing the License Agreements. We disagree.

The District Court found that CellNet was entitled to the royalties because "§ 365(n) of the Bankruptcy Code renews certain obligations related to the license." Despite Schlumberger's argument that because "§ 365(n)(2) does not designate that the payment of royalties must be made to any particular party," it should be entitled to the royalties, the District Court focused instead on the language stating that the "licensee shall make all royalty payments due under such contract." The District Court concluded "that Congress intended the language 'due under the contract' to provide both the quantity of the royalty payments and the designation of the party intended to receive those payments, whether the debtor or its contractual assignee." Because Schlumberger excluded the contract from its purchase, "CellNet remains entitled to receive the BCN royalties pursuant to statutory authority even if it rejected the License Agreements and is not technically a party to them." The District Court concluded that "royalty payments made pursuant to § 365(n)(2)(B) of the Bankruptcy Code are the property of the licensor, even though the licensor may have transferred its intellectual property assets during the bankruptcy."

Schlumberger makes essentially three arguments related to the effects of § 365(n). First, Schlumberger claims that CellNet has no rights because it rejected the contract under § 365(a). To support this conclusion, Schlumberger cites our opinion in In Re Bildisco, 682 F.2d 72, 82 (3d Cir.1982), where we held that "as a matter of law, a debtor-in-possession is '[a] new entity . . . created with its own rights and duties, subject to the supervision of the bankruptcy court.'" Schlumberger claims that this demonstrates that the License Agreements were not part of the estate because they were never assumed by CellNet as debtor-in-possession.

Schlumberger is incorrect. In NLRB v. Bildisco, 465 U.S. 513, 104 S.Ct. 1188, 79 L.Ed.2d 482 (1984), the Supreme Court affirmed our previously cited opinion. The Court, however, stated that:

> Obviously if the [debtor-in-possession] were a wholly 'new entity,' it would be unnecessary for the Bankruptcy Code to allow it to reject executory contracts, since it would not be bound by such contracts in the first place. For our purposes, it is sensible to view the debtor-in-possession as the same 'entity' which existed before the filing of the bankruptcy petition, but empowered by virtue of the Bankruptcy Code to deal with its contracts and property in a manner it could not have done absent the bankruptcy filing.

This implies that the License Agreements were property of the bankruptcy estate after Schlumberger excluded them and before CellNet rejected them. Schlumberger contends that the act of rejection serves to remove the contract from the bankruptcy estate and points to *In Re Access Beyond Technologies, Inc.,* 237 B.R. 32, 47 (D.Del.1999), for the proposition that "[a]n executory contract does not become an asset of the estate until it is assumed pursuant to § 365(a) of the Code." That case however, is factually distinguishable from ours. In *Access,* the debtor attempted to assign its rights under a patent cross-license agreement. The debtor characterized the transaction as a sale under 11 U.S.C. § 363, but the court held that the debtor must first assume the agreement in order to transfer it. The court noted that otherwise, "[i]f the debtor does not assume an executory contract, it is deemed rejected. Thus, if a debtor does not assume an executory contract before he sells it . . . , the buyer may be purchasing an illusion: the executory contract will disappear on conclusion of the bankruptcy case." *Access* did not deal with our situation, which involves an executory contract after an election by a licensee under § 365(n). We need not specify the exact status of the contract. For our purposes it is suffice to say that after a licensee has resorted to § 365(n), the rights of the contract as they existed pre-petition and pre-rejection are in force.

The plain language of § 365(n)(2)(B) indicates that the renewed royalties are directly linked to the rejected contract, not the intellectual property. The section specifically provides that the "licensee shall make all royalty payments due under such contract for the duration of such contract." Thus, the contract is the primary mechanism for determining where the royalties flow. Although Schlumberger is correct that § 365(n)(2)(B) does not specify that the royalties must be paid to the trustee, the immediately proceeding section says that "trustee shall allow the licensee to exercise such rights," and the next section deals with the rights of the licensee against the trustee. The several sections of § 365(n)(2) make sense only in contemplation of an ongoing relationship between the licensee and the licensor/trustee.

Schlumberger next argues that the legislative history of § 365(n) favors awarding it the royalties. It notes that the legislative history of § 365(n) explains that the subsection parallels § 365(h), which deals with real estate and allows a similar retention of rights by holders of real estate leases. With this link in place, Schlumberger analogizes that its position in this case would be the equivalent of where a purchaser bought a shopping center, but did not assume the lease of an occupying tenant. Under § 365(h), the tenant could choose to remain in possession and pay rent, but the rent would belong to the new owner. According to Schlumberger, the position taken by CellNet and the District Court would alter the above situation and provide that the tenant could still remain in possession, but would pay rent to the former owner of the shopping center.

Although this analogy is powerful, and the logic deceptively simple, Schlumberger's reasoning is specious because it rests on a flawed comparison of the parties. Although both sections of the Bankruptcy Code discuss their respective elections as being limited by non-bankruptcy law, the concept of tenants remaining in possession when a new landlord gains control is fraught with state law property principles not applicable in the intellectual property context. We find that there is no relationship between Schlumberger and the License Agreements-which it specifically did not purchase-that can be equated with the relationship of possessory control by a new landlord over a tenant remaining in possession.

Schlumberger's final argument is that the long-standing principle that the benefits of a contract should accompany the burden dictates that they should retain the royalties. Its argument, however, is trumped by the facts. It is true that the burden of the License Agreements falls on Schlumberger, who cannot use the intellectual property outside the United States and that the benefit to that burden is the royalty payments. However, state law allows the severance of the benefit from the burden and Schlumberger has done just that by excluding the License Agreement from its purchase and not contracting with CellNet for the royalties.

LUBRIZOL ENTERPRISES, INC. v. RICHMOND METAL FINISHERS, INC.
United States Court of Appeals for the Fourth Circuit
756 F.2d 1043 (1985)

James Dickson Phillips, Circuit Judge:

The question is whether Richmond Metal Finishers (RMF), a bankrupt debtor in possession, should have been allowed to reject as executory a technology licensing agreement with Lubrizol Enterprises (Lubrizol) as licensee. The bankruptcy court approved rejection pursuant to 11 U.S.C. § 365(a), but the district court reversed on the basis that within contemplation of § 365(a), the contract was not executory and, alternatively, that rejection could not reasonably be expected substantially to benefit the bankrupt debtor. We reverse and remand for entry of judgment in conformity with that entered by the bankruptcy court.

I

In July of 1982, RMF entered into the contract with Lubrizol that granted Lubrizol a nonexclusive license to utilize a metal coating process technology owned by RMF. RMF owed the following duties to Lubrizol under the agreement: (1) to notify Lubrizol of any patent infringement suit and to defend in such suit; (2) to notify Lubrizol of any other use or licensing of the process, and to reduce royalty payments if a lower royalty rate agreement was reached with another licensee; and (3) to indemnify Lubrizol for losses arising out of any misrepresentation or breach of warranty by RMF. Lubrizol owed RMF reciprocal duties of accounting for and paying royalties for use of the process and of canceling certain existing indebtedness. The contract provided that Lubrizol would defer use of the process until May 1, 1983, and in fact, Lubrizol has never used the RMF technology.

RMF filed a petition for bankruptcy pursuant to Chapter 11 of the Bankruptcy Code on August 16, 1983. As part of its plan to emerge from bankruptcy, RMF sought, pursuant to § 365(a), to reject the contract with Lubrizol in order to facilitate sale or licensing of the technology unhindered by restrictive provisions in the Lubrizol agreement. On RMF's motion for approval of the rejection, the bankruptcy court properly interpreted § 365 as requiring it to undertake a two-step inquiry to determine the propriety of rejection: first, whether the contract is executory; next, if so, whether its rejection would be advantageous to the bankrupt.

Making that inquiry, the bankruptcy court determined that both tests were satisfied and approved the rejection. But, as indicated, the district court then reversed that determination on the basis that neither test was satisfied and disallowed the rejection. This appeal followed.

II

We conclude initially that, as the bankruptcy court ruled, the technology licensing agreement in this case was an executory contract, within contemplation of 11 U.S.C. § 365(a). Under that provision a contract is executory if performance is due to some extent on both sides. This court has recently adopted Professor Countryman's more specific test for determining whether a contract is "executory" in the required sense. By that test, a contract is executory if the " 'obligations of both the bankrupt and the other party to the contract are so far unperformed that the failure of either to complete the performance would constitute a material breach excusing the performance of the other.' " This issue is one of law that may be freely reviewed by successive courts.

Applying that test here, we conclude that the licensing agreement was at the critical time executory. RMF owed Lubrizol the continuing duties of notifying Lubrizol of further licensing of the process and of reducing Lubrizol's royalty rate to meet any more favorable rates granted to subsequent licensees. By their terms, RMF's obligations to give notice and to restrict its right to license its process at royalty rates it desired without lowering Lubrizol's royalty rate extended over the life of the agreement, and remained unperformed. Moreover, RMF owed Lubrizol additional contingent duties of notifying it of suits, defending suits and indemnifying it for certain losses.

The unperformed, continuing core obligations of notice and forbearance in licensing made the contract executory as to RMF. In *Fenix Cattle Co. v. Silver (In re Select-A-Seat Corp.)*, 625 F.2d 290, 292 (9th Cir. 1980), the court found that an obligation of a debtor to refrain from selling software packages under an exclusive licensing agreement made a contract executory as to the debtor notwithstanding the continuing obligation was only one of forbearance. Although the license to Lubrizol was not exclusive, RMF owed the same type of unperformed continuing duty of forbearance arising out of the most favored licensee clause running in favor of Lubrizol. Breach of that duty would clearly constitute a material breach of the agreement.

Moreover, the contract was further executory as to RMF because of the contingent duties that RMF owed of giving notice of and defending infringement suits and of indemnifying Lubrizol for certain losses arising out of the use of the technology. Contingency of an obligation does not prevent its being executory under § 365. Until the time has expired during which an event triggering a contingent duty may occur, the contingent obligation represents a continuing duty to stand ready to perform if the contingency occurs. A breach of that duty once it was triggered by the contingency (or presumably, by anticipatory repudiation) would have been material.

Because a contract is not executory within the meaning of § 365(a) unless it is executory as to both parties, it is also necessary to determine whether the licensing agreement was executory as to Lubrizol. We conclude that it was.

Lubrizol owed RMF the unperformed and continuing duty of accounting for and paying royalties for the life of the agreement. It is true that a contract is not executory as to a party simply because the party is obligated to make payments of money to the other party. Therefore, if Lubrizol had owed RMF nothing more than a duty to make fixed payments or cancel specified indebtedness under the agreement, the agreement would not be executory as to Lubrizol. However, the promise to account for and pay royalties required that Lubrizol deliver written quarterly sales reports and keep books of account subject to inspection by an independent Certified Public Accountant. This promise goes beyond a mere debt, or promise to pay money, and was at the critical time executory. Additionally, subject to certain exceptions, Lubrizol was obligated to keep all license technology in confidence for a number of years.

Since the licensing agreement is executory as to each party, it is executory within the meaning of § 365(a), and the district court erred as a matter of law in reaching a contrary conclusion.

III

There remains the question whether rejection of the executory contract would be advantageous to the bankrupt. Courts addressing that question must start with the proposition that the bankrupt's decision upon it is to be accorded the deference mandated by the sound business judgment rule as generally applied by courts to discretionary actions or decisions of corporate directors.

As generally formulated and applied in corporate litigation the rule is that courts should defer to — should not interfere with — decisions of corporate directors upon matters entrusted to their business judgment except upon a finding of bad faith or gross abuse of their "business discretion." Transposed to the bankruptcy context, the rule as applied to a bankrupt's decision to reject an executory contract because of perceived business advantage requires that the decision be accepted by courts unless it is shown that the bankrupt's decision was one taken in bad faith or in gross abuse of the bankrupt's retained business discretion.

In bankruptcy litigation the issue is of course first presented for judicial determination when a debtor, having decided that rejection will be beneficial within contemplation of § 365(a), moves for approval of the rejection. The issue thereby presented for first instance judicial determination by the bankruptcy court is whether the decision of the debtor that rejection will be advantageous is so manifestly unreasonable that it could not be based on sound business judgment, but only on bad faith, or whim or caprice. That issue is one of fact to be decided as such by the bankruptcy court by the normal processes of fact adjudication. And the resulting fact determination by the bankruptcy court is perforce then reviewable up the line under the clearly erroneous standard.

Here, the bankruptcy judge had before him evidence not rebutted by Lubrizol that the metal coating process subject to the licensing agreement is RMF's principal asset and that sale or licensing of the technology represented the primary potential source of funds by which RMF might emerge from bankruptcy. The testimony of RMF's president, also factually uncontested by Lubrizol, indicated that sale or further licensing of the technology would be facilitated by stripping Lubrizol of its rights in the process and that, correspondingly, continued obligation to Lubrizol under the agreement would hinder RMF's capability to sell or license the technology on more advantageous terms to other potential licensees. On the basis of this evidence the bankruptcy court determined that the debtor's decision to reject was based upon sound business judgment and approved it.

On appeal the district court simply found to the contrary that the debtor's decision to reject did not represent a sound business judgment. The district court's determination rested essentially on two grounds: that RMF's purely contingent obligations under the agreement were not sufficiently onerous that relief from them would constitute a substantial benefit to RMF; and that because rejection could not deprive Lubrizol of all its rights to the technology, rejection could not reasonably be found beneficial. We conclude that in both of these respects the district court's factual findings, at odds with those of the bankruptcy court, were clearly erroneous and cannot stand.

A

In finding that the debtor's contingent obligations were not sufficiently onerous that relief from them would be beneficial, the district court could only have been substituting its business judgment for that of the debtor. There is nothing in the record from which it could be concluded that the debtor's decision on that point could not have been reached by the exercise of sound (though possibly faulty) business judgment in the normal process of evaluating alternative courses of action. If that could not be concluded, then the business judgment rule required that the debtor's factual evaluation be accepted by the court, as it had been by the bankruptcy court.

B

On the second point, we can only conclude that the district court was under a misapprehension of controlling law in thinking that by rejecting the agreement the debtor could not deprive Lubrizol of all rights to the process. Under 11 U.S.C. § 365(g), Lubrizol would be entitled to treat rejection as a breach and seek a money damages remedy; however, it could not seek to retain its contract rights in the technology by specific performance even if that remedy would ordinarily be available upon breach of this type of contract.

Even though § 365(g) treats rejection as a breach, the legislative history of § 365(g) makes clear that the purpose of the provision is to provide only a damages remedy for the non-bankrupt party. For the same reason, Lubrizol cannot rely on provisions within its agreement with RMF for continued use of the technology by Lubrizol upon breach by RMF. Here again, the statutory "breach" contemplated by § 365(g) controls, and provides only a money damages remedy for the non-bankrupt party. Allowing specific performance would obviously undercut the core purpose of rejection under § 365(a), and that consequence cannot therefore be read into congressional intent.

IV

Lubrizol strongly urges upon us policy concerns in support of the district court's refusal to defer to the debtor's decision to reject or, preliminarily, to treat the contract as executory for § 365(a) purposes. We understand the concerns, but think they cannot control decision here.

It cannot be gainsaid that allowing rejection of such contracts as executory imposes serious burdens upon contracting parties such as Lubrizol. Nor can it be doubted that allowing rejection in this and comparable cases could have a general chilling effect upon the willingness of such parties to contract at all with businesses in possible financial difficulty. But under bankruptcy law such equitable considerations may not be indulged by courts in respect of the type of contract here in issue. Congress has plainly provided for the rejection of executory contracts, notwithstanding the obvious adverse consequences for contracting parties thereby made inevitable. Awareness by Congress of those consequences is indeed specifically reflected in the special treatment accorded to union members under collective bargaining contracts, and to lessees of real property. But no comparable special treatment is provided for technology licensees such as Lubrizol. They share the general hazards created by § 365 for all business entities dealing with potential bankrupts in the respects at issue here.

The judgment of the district court is reversed and the case is remanded for entry of judgment in conformity with that entered by the bankruptcy court.

NOTES & QUESTIONS

1. The *Cellnet* and *Lubrizol* cases illustrate the treatment of intellectual property and technology licenses by debtor licensors when section 365(n) applies and when it does not. Work through the details of *Cellnet* to obtain a

sense of the logic of sections 365(a) and 365(n). Schlumberger's argument is that as purchaser of Cellnet's intellectual property it has the rights to the royalties once the licensee decides to retain its rights under the license and pay royalties. Cellnet's argument is that Schlumberger's rights are limited to what it acquired via contract, which severed the royalty rights. The court agreed with Cellnet. Who has the better argument in your opinion? Is this a case about poor contract drafting or about bankruptcy policy favoring the debtor licensor?

2. The *Lubrizol* case was the impetus for Congress to enact section 365(n) as a protection for non-debtor licensees. Absent section 365(n), how could the licensee have protected itself in *Lubrizol*? One option would have been language in the license that limited the licensor's ability to reject in the event of bankruptcy. Another option would have been to purchase the intellectual property outright rather than to license it. Are these feasible options for licensees? Would they have been feasible under the facts of *Lubrizol*? Is a statutory solution such as section 365(n) a better option?

3. Notice that the holding of the *Lubrizol* case will apply whenever section 365(n) does not. Specifically, section 365(n) does not apply to trademarks or trade names. Therefore, drafters of license agreements in these contexts need to be especially wary of the possibility of bankruptcy by the licensor. There is one other situation where section 365(n) protections would not apply, and the *Lubrizol* trap may arise: foreign copyrights. The definition of intellectual property includes "works of authorship protected under Title 17," a reference to copyright law. If the work of authorship, such as software, was created outside of the US or a country with which the US has a treaty agreement, then the work may not be "protected under Title 17." This situation is unusual and would apply, for example, to a foreign company that is licensing its copyright to a United States licensee. If the foreign company files for bankruptcy in the United States, the company as debtor may be able to reject the license like the debtor in *Lubrizol*.

4. One contingency that the non-debtor licensee needs to be aware of is a sale of intellectual property by the debtor licensor free and clear of any interest to a third party. If the sale goes through, then the third party purchaser would obtain the intellectual property free of any licenses. The debtor licensor has the right to initiate such a transaction under section 365(f), but the court must approve it. In such an eventuality, the debtor has the right to object to the sale before the bankruptcy court. Notice that section 365(n) protections do not apply to the debtor licensor's decision to sell the intellectual property, but only to the decision to reject the license. Therefore, it is up to the non-debtor licensee to convince the court not to approve the proposed sale given the equities of the situation or at the least to obtain adequate protection for its interests if the sale is approved. Although there is no precedent involving intellectual property transferred under these circumstances, there is some precedent involving the sale of real estate free and clear of existing leases. See the discussion in *Precisions Industries, Inc. v. Qualitech Steel SBQ,* 327 F. 3d 537 (7th Cir. 2003) (allowing the sale of real estate free and clear of existing leases). With this problem in mind, reconsider Schlumberger's argument about real property transfers in the *Cellnet* case. Do you think the court's

distinction between real property and intellectual property for the purposes of section 365(a) and non-debtor licensee protection makes sense?

5. One lesson to draw from this material is the importance of good drafting in protecting one's interests in intellectual property and licenses, particularly in the shadow of bankruptcy. One example of creative lawyering to deal with these problems is provided by the "source code escrow," a common tool to protect a software licensee's rights in the event of a licensor's bankruptcy. A source code escrow is an agreement among a licensor, a licensee and a third party escrow agent. Under the terms of the agreement, the agent secretly retains the source code, which may be released to the licensee in the event of certain contingencies such as the licensor's failure to perform maintenance obligations under the terms of the license. For a discussion, see N. Neville Reid & Sajida Mahdi, *Intellectual Property and Bankruptcy — Salient Issues,* 862 PLI/COMM 313 (April-May, 2004).

c. Licensee as Debtor

INSTITUTE PASTEUR v. CAMBRIDGE BIOTECH CORPORATION
United States Court of Appeals for the First Circuit
104 F.3d 489 (1997)

CYR, Circuit Judge.

Unsuccessful in their intermediate appeal to the district court, Institut Pasteur and Pasteur Sanofi Diagnostics [collectively: "Pasteur"] again appeal from the bankruptcy court order which confirmed the chapter 11 reorganization plan ("Plan") proposed by debtor-in-possession Cambridge Biotech Corporation ("CBC"), the holder of two licenses to utilize Pasteur patents. The Plan provision central to the present dispute calls for the sale of all CBC stock to a subsidiary of bioMerieux Vitek, Inc. ("bioMerieux"), a major competitor of appellant Pasteur. Finding no error, we affirm.

I

BACKGROUND

CBC manufactures and sells retroviral diagnostic tests for detecting the human immunodeficiency virus (HIV) associated with AIDS. Its HIV diagnostics division annually generates approximately $14 million in revenues. Institut Pasteur, a nonprofit French foundation engaged in AIDS-related research and development, owns various patented procedures for diagnosing HIV Virus Type 2 ("HIV2 procedures"). Pasteur Sanofi Diagnostics holds the exclusive right to use and sublicense Institut Pasteur's patents.

In October 1989, CBC and Pasteur entered into mutual cross-license agreements, whereby each acquired a nonexclusive perpetual license to use some of the technology patented or licensed by the other. Specifically, CBC acquired the right to incorporate Pasteur's HIV2 procedures into any diagnostic kits sold by CBC in the United States, Canada, Mexico, Australia, New Zealand and elsewhere.

Each cross-license broadly prohibits the licensee from assigning or sublicensing to others. ("[N]o other person shall acquire or have any right under or by virtue of this Agreement."). Nevertheless, either Pasteur or CBC was authorized to "extend to its Affiliated Companies the benefits of this Agreement so that such party shall remain responsible with regard [to] all [license] obligations." "Affiliated Company" is defined as "an organization which controls or is controlled by a party or an organization which is under common control with a party."

CBC filed its chapter 11 petition on July 7, 1994, and thereafter continued to operate its retroviral diagnostic testing business as debtor-in-possession. Its reorganization plan proposed that CBC assume both cross-licenses, continue to operate its retroviral diagnostics division utilizing Pasteur's patented HIV2 procedures, and sell all CBC stock to a subsidiary of bioMerieux, a giant French biotechnology corporation and Pasteur's direct competitor in international biotechnology sales. Pasteur previously had licensed bioMerieux to use its HIV2 procedures, but the earlier license related to a single product manufactured by bioMerieux (i.e., bioMerieux's VIDAS automated immunoassay test system), and applied only to VIDAS sales in markets other than the United States, Canada, Mexico, Australia, and New Zealand, markets expressly encompassed within the CBC cross-licenses.

Not surprisingly, in due course Pasteur objected to the Plan. Citing Bankruptcy Code § 365(c), 11 U.S.C. § 365(c), it contended that the proposed sale of CBC's stock to bioMerieux amounted to CBC's assumption of the patent cross-licenses and their de facto "assignment" to a third party in contravention of the presumption of non-assignability ordained by the federal common law of patents, as well as the explicit non-assignability provision contained in the cross-licenses. Isabelle Bressac, Pasteur's licensing director, attested that Pasteur would not have granted its competitor, bioMerieux, or a subsidiary, a patent license under the terms allowed CBC.

The bankruptcy court authorized CBC to assume the cross-licenses over Pasteur's objection. It ruled that the proposed sale of CBC stock to bioMerieux did not constitute a de facto "assignment" of the cross-licenses to bioMerieux, but merely an assumption of the cross-licenses by the reorganized debtor under new ownership, and that Bankruptcy Code § 365(c) enabled CBC to assume the cross-licenses as debtor-in-possession because the pre-petition licensing relationship between Pasteur and CBC was neither "unique" nor "something in the category of a personal services contract." The district court upheld the bankruptcy court ruling on intermediate appeal.

II

DISCUSSION

. . . Pasteur argues that the CBC Plan effects a de facto assignment of its two cross-licenses to bioMerieux, contrary to Bankruptcy Code § 365(c)(1) which provides as follows:

The trustee [viz., CBC] may not assume or assign any executory contract . . . , whether or not such contract . . . prohibits or restricts assignment of rights or delegation of duties, if —

(1)(A) applicable law excuses a party[ ] other than the debtor[ ] [viz., Pasteur] to such contract . . . from accepting performance from or rendering performance to an entity other than the debtor or the debtor in possession, whether or not such contract . . . prohibits or restricts assumption or assignment; and

(B) such party [viz., Pasteur] does not consent to such assumption or assignment. . . .

11 U.S.C. § 365(c)(1).

Pasteur argues that in order to encourage optimum product innovation the federal common law of patents presumes that patent licensees, such as CBC, may not sublicense to third parties absent the patent holder's consent. This federal common law rule of presumptive non-assignability thus qualifies as an "applicable law," within the meaning of Bankruptcy Code § 365(c)(1)(A), which precludes Pasteur from being compelled to accept performance from any entity other than CBC — e.g., bioMerieux's subsidiary — and therefore prevents CBC from either assuming or assigning these cross-licenses. Further, says Pasteur, even assuming that section 365(c) might allow a debtor simply to assume the cross-licenses without a subsequent assignment to a third party, CBC formally structured this Plan transaction as an assumption by the debtor-in-possession, whereas in substance it was an assignment of the cross-licenses to bioMerieux, a complete stranger to the original cross-licensing agreements.

These contentions are foreclosed by our decision in *Summit Inv. & Dev. Corp. v. Leroux (In re Leroux)*, 69 F.3d 608 (1st Cir.1995), which analyzed and interpreted companion Bankruptcy Code subsections 365(c) and (e) and their relevant legislative history. As in the present case, in *Leroux* we were urged to interpret subsections 365(c) and (e) as mandating a "hypothetical test." Under such an approach, the chapter 11 debtor would lose its option to assume the contract, even though it never intended to assign the contract to another entity, if either the particular executory contract or the applicable non-bankruptcy law purported to terminate the contract automatically upon the filing of the chapter 11 petition or to preclude its assignment to an entity not a party to the contract.

We rejected the proposed hypothetical test in *Leroux,* holding instead that subsections 365(c) and (e) contemplate a case-by-case inquiry into whether the non-debtor party (viz., Pasteur) actually was being "forced to accept performance under its executory contract from someone other than the debtor party with whom it originally contracted." *Id.* Where the particular transaction envisions that the debtor-in-possession would assume and continue to perform under an executory contract, the bankruptcy court cannot simply presume as a matter of law that the debtor-in-possession is a legal entity materially distinct from the pre-petition debtor with whom the non-debtor party (viz., Pasteur) contracted. Rather, "sensitive to the rights of the non-debtor party (viz., Pasteur)," the bankruptcy court must focus on the performance actually to be rendered by the debtor-in-possession with a view to

ensuring that the non-debtor party (viz., Pasteur) will receive "the full benefit of [its] bargain."

Given the pragmatic "actual performance" test adopted in Leroux, the ultimate findings of fact and conclusions of law made by the bankruptcy court
below did not constitute error. CBC simply does not occupy the same position
as the debtor in *CFLC, Inc.*, 89 F.3d 673 (9th Cir.1996), upon which Pasteur
relies most heavily. The Plan in *CFLC, Inc.* unmistakably provided for an outright assignment of the debtor's patent license to an entirely different corporation with which the patent holder Cadtrak Corporation had never
contracted. By contrast, CBC all along has conducted, and proposes to continue, its retroviral diagnostic enterprise as the same corporate entity which
functioned pre-petition, while utilizing Pasteur's HIV2 procedures in that
same pre-petition endeavor.

Pasteur nonetheless insists that the reorganized CBC is different than the
pre-petition entity, not due merely to its chapter 11 filing but because it is now
owned by a different legal entity than before — namely, bioMerieux's subsidiary qua CBC shareholder. Pasteur's contention finds no support, however,
either in Massachusetts law, see supra note 1, or in the cross-license provisions it negotiated.

Stock sales are not mergers whereby outright title and ownership of the
licensee-corporation's assets (including its patent licenses) pass to the acquiring corporation. Rather, as a corporation, CBC "is a legal entity distinct from
its shareholders." Absent compelling grounds for disregarding its corporate
form, therefore, CBC's separate legal identity, and its ownership of the patent
cross-licenses, survive without interruption notwithstanding repeated and
even drastic changes in its ownership. Pasteur cites no apposite authority to
the contrary.

Furthermore, Pasteur's position finds no support in the negotiated terms of its
cross-licenses. As the patent holder — and given CBC's corporate form and the
governing Massachusetts law, supra — Pasteur was free to negotiate restrictions
on CBC's continuing rights under the cross-licenses based on changes in its stock
ownership or corporate control. Nevertheless, these cross-licenses contain no provision either limiting or terminating CBC's rights in the event its stock ownership were to change hands. The generic non-assignability provisions found in
these cross-licenses ("This Agreement . . . has been made solely for the benefit of
the parties hereto" and "no other person shall acquire or have any right under or
by virtue of this Agreement.") plainly do not address the circumstance presented
here. Rather, these non-assignability provisions simply beg the essential question, which is whether bioMerieux's subsidiary, by virtue of its acquisition of
CBC stock, terminated CBC 's rights under the cross-licenses. Interpreted as
Pasteur proposes, CBC's own rights under the cross-licenses would terminate
with any change in the identity of any CBC stockholder.

Other cross-license provisions directly undercut Pasteur's interpretation as
well. These cross-licenses explicitly authorize CBC to share its license rights
with any "affiliated company," which on its face presumably encompasses a

parent corporation such as bioMerieux's subsidiary (defining "Affiliated Company" as "an organization which controls . . . a party or an organization which is under common control with a party"). Yet more importantly, CBC insisted upon a provision which would afford it the unilateral right to terminate any sublicense Pasteur might extend to a company called Genetic Systems "if control of Genetic Systems shall . . . be acquired, directly or indirectly, by any person or group of connected persons or company not having such control at the date hereof, by reconstruction, amalgamation, acquisition of shares or assets or otherwise." Taken together, these provisions persuade us that Pasteur foresaw, or reasonably should have foreseen, that CBC might undergo changes of stock ownership which would not alter its corporate legal identity, but nonetheless chose not to condition the continued viability of its cross-licenses accordingly.

III

CONCLUSION

As CBC remains in all material respects the legal entity with which Pasteur freely contracted, Pasteur has not made the required individualized showing that it is or will be deprived of "the full benefit of [its] bargain," under the ruling challenged on appeal. Accordingly, the district court judgment is affirmed and costs are awarded to appellee.

IN RE CATAPULT ENTERTAINMENT, INC.
United States Court of Appeals for the Ninth Circuit
165 F.3d 747 (1999)

FLETCHER, Circuit Judge.

Appellant Stephen Perlman ("Perlman") licensed certain patents to appellee Catapult Entertainment, Inc. ("Catapult"). He now seeks to bar Catapult, which has since become a Chapter 11 debtor in possession, from assuming the patent licenses as part of its reorganization plan. Notwithstanding Perlman's objections, the bankruptcy court approved the assumption of the licenses and confirmed the reorganization plan. The district court affirmed the bankruptcy court on intermediate appeal. Perlman appeals that decision. We are called upon to determine whether, in light of § 365(c)(1) of the Bankruptcy Code, a Chapter 11 debtor in possession may assume certain nonexclusive patent licenses over a licensor's objection. We conclude that the bankruptcy court erred in permitting the debtor in possession to assume the patent licenses in question.

I.

Catapult, a California corporation, was formed in 1994 to create an online gaming network for 16-bit console videogames. That same year, Catapult entered into two license agreements with Perlman, wherein Perlman granted to Catapult the right to exploit certain relevant technologies, including patents and patent applications.

In October 1996, Catapult filed for reorganization under Chapter 11 of the Bankruptcy Code. Shortly before the filing of the bankruptcy petition, Catapult entered into a merger agreement with Mpath Interactive, Inc. ("Mpath"). This agreement contemplated the filing of the bankruptcy petition, followed by a reorganization via a "reverse triangular merger" involving Mpath, MPCAT Acquisition Corporation ("MPCAT"), and Catapult. Under the terms of the merger agreement, MPCAT (a wholly-owned subsidiary of Mpath created for this transaction) would merge into Catapult, leaving Catapult as the surviving entity. When the dust cleared, Catapult's creditors and equity holders would have received approximately $14 million in cash, notes, and securities; Catapult, in turn, would have become a wholly-owned subsidiary of Mpath. The relevant third party creditors and equity holders accepted Catapult's reorganization plan by the majorities required by the Bankruptcy Code.

On October 24, 1996, as part of the reorganization plan, Catapult filed a motion with the bankruptcy court seeking to assume some 140 executory contracts and leases, including the Perlman licenses. Over Perlman's objection, the bankruptcy court granted Catapult's motion and approved the reorganization plan. The district court subsequently affirmed the bankruptcy court. This appeal followed.

II.

Section 365 of the Bankruptcy Code gives a trustee in bankruptcy (or, in a Chapter 11 case, the debtor in possession) the authority to assume, assign, or reject the executory contracts and unexpired leases of the debtor, notwithstanding any contrary provisions appearing in such contracts or leases. See 11 U.S.C. § 365(a) & (f). This extraordinary authority, however, is not absolute. Section 365(c)(1) provides that, notwithstanding the general policy set out in § 365(a):

> (c) The trustee may not assume or assign any executory contract or unexpired lease of the debtor, whether or not such contract or lease prohibits or restricts assignment of rights or delegation of duties, if
>
> > (1)(A) applicable law excuses a party, other than the debtor, to such contract or lease from accepting performance from or rendering performance to an entity other than the debtor or the debtor in possession, whether or not such contract or lease prohibits or restricts assignment of rights or delegation of duties; and
> >
> > (B) such party does not consent to such assumption or assignment. . . .

Our task, simply put, is to apply this statutory language to the facts at hand and determine whether it prohibits Catapult, as the debtor in possession, from assuming the Perlman licenses without Perlman's consent.

While simply put, our task is not so easily resolved; the proper interpretation of § 365(c)(1) has been the subject of considerable disagreement among courts and commentators. On one side are those who adhere to the plain statutory language, which establishes a so-called "hypothetical test" to govern the assumption of executory contracts. On the other side are those that forsake the statutory language in favor of an "actual test" that, in their view, better accomplishes the intent of Congress. [T]oday we hold that we are bound by the plain terms of the statute and join the Third and Eleventh Circuits in adopting the "hypothetical test."

III.

We begin, as we must, with the statutory language. The plain language of § 365(c)(1) "link[s] non-assignability under 'applicable law' together with a prohibition on assumption in bankruptcy." In other words, the statute by its terms bars a debtor in possession from assuming an executory contract without the non-debtor's consent where applicable law precludes assignment of the contract to a third party. The literal language of § 365(c)(1) is thus said to establish a "hypothetical test": a debtor in possession may not assume an executory contract over the non-debtor's objection if applicable law would bar assignment to a hypothetical third party, even where the debtor in possession has no intention of assigning the contract in question to any such third party.

Before applying the statutory language to the case at hand, we first resolve a number of preliminary issues that are either not disputed by the parties, or are so clearly established as to deserve no more than passing reference. First, we follow the lead of the parties in assuming that the Perlman licenses are executory agreements within the meaning of § 365. Second, it is well-established that § 365(c)'s use of the term "trustee" includes Chapter 11 debtors in possession. Third, our precedents make it clear that federal patent law constitutes "applicable law" within the meaning of § 365(c), and that nonexclusive patent licenses are "personal and assignable only with the consent of the licensor."

When we have cleared away these preliminary matters, application of the statute to the facts of this case becomes relatively straightforward:

> (c) Catapult may not assume . . . the Perlman licenses, . . . if
>
> > (1)(A) federal patent law excuses Perlman from accepting performance from or rendering performance to an entity other than Catapult . . .; and
> >
> > (B) Perlman does not consent to such assumption. . . .

Since federal patent law makes nonexclusive patent licenses personal and non-delegable, § 365(c)(1)(A) is satisfied. Perlman has withheld his consent, thus satisfying § 365(c)(1)(B). Accordingly, the plain language of § 365(c)(1) bars Catapult from assuming the Perlman licenses.

IV.

Catapult urges us to abandon the literal language of § 365(c)(1) in favor of an alternative approach, reasoning that Congress did not intend to bar debtors in possession from assuming their own contracts where no assignment is contemplated. In Catapult's view, § 365(c)(1) should be interpreted as embodying an "actual test": the statute bars assumption by the debtor in possession only where the reorganization in question results in the non-debtor actually having to accept performance from a third party. Under this reading of § 365(c), the debtor in possession would be permitted to assume any executory contract, so long as no assignment was contemplated. Put another way, Catapult suggests that, as to a debtor in possession, § 365(c)(1) should be read to prohibit assumption and assignment, rather than assumption or assignment.

Catapult has marshaled considerable authority to support this reading. The arguments supporting Catapult's position can be divided into three categories: (1) the literal reading creates inconsistencies within § 365; (2) the literal reading is incompatible with the legislative history; and (3) the literal reading flies in the face of sound bankruptcy policy. Nonetheless, we find that none of these considerations justifies departing from the plain language of § 365(c)(1).

A.

Catapult first argues that a literal reading of § 365(c)(1) sets the statute at war with itself and its neighboring provisions. Deviation from the plain language, contends Catapult, is necessary if internal consistency is to be achieved. We agree with Catapult that a court should interpret a statute, if possible, so as to minimize discord among related provisions. However, the dire inconsistencies cited by Catapult turn out, on closer analysis, to be no such thing.

Catapult, for example, singles out the interaction between § 365(c)(1) and § 365(f)(1) as a statutory trouble spot. Subsection (f)(1) provides that executory contracts, once assumed, may be assigned notwithstanding any contrary provisions contained in the contract or applicable law:

> (f)(1) Except as provided in subsection (c) of this section, notwithstanding a provision in an executory contract or unexpired lease of the debtor, or in applicable law, that prohibits, restricts, or conditions the assignment of such contract or lease, the trustee may assign such contract or lease under paragraph (2) of this subsection. . . .

The potential conflict between subsections (c)(1) and (f)(1) arises from their respective treatments of "applicable law." The plain language of subsection (c)(1) bars assumption (absent consent) whenever "applicable law" would bar assignment. Subsection (f)(1) states that, contrary provisions in applicable law notwithstanding, executory contracts may be assigned. Since assumption is a necessary prerequisite to assignment under § 365, a literal reading of subsection (c)(1) appears to render subsection (f)(1) superfluous. In the words of the Sixth Circuit, "[S]ection 365(c), the recognized exception to 365(f), appears at first to resuscitate in full the very anti-assignment 'applicable law' which 365(f) nullifies." Faced with this dilemma, one district court reluctantly concluded that the "[c]onflict between subsections (c) and (f) of § 365 is inescapable."

Subsequent authority, however, suggests that this conclusion may have been unduly pessimistic. The Sixth Circuit has credibly reconciled the warring provisions by noting that "each subsection recognizes an 'applicable law' of markedly different scope." Subsection (f)(1) states the broad rule — a law that, as a general matter, "prohibits, restricts, or conditions the assignment" of executory contracts is trumped by the provisions of subsection (f)(1). Subsection (c)(1), however, states a carefully crafted exception to the broad rule — where applicable law does not merely recite a general ban on assignment, but instead more specifically "excuses a party . . . from accepting performance from or rendering performance to an entity" different from the one with which the party originally contracted, the applicable law prevails over subsection (f)(1). In other words, in determining whether an "applicable law" stands or falls under § 365(f)(1), a court must ask why the "applicable law" prohibits assignment. Only if the law prohibits assignment on the rationale that the identity of the contracting party is material to the agreement will subsection (c)(1) rescue it. We agree with the Sixth and Eleventh Circuits that a literal reading of subsection (c)(1) does not inevitably set it at odds with subsection (f)(1).

Catapult next focuses on the internal structure of § 365(c)(1) itself. According to Catapult, the literal approach to subsection (c)(1) renders the phrase "or the debtor in possession" contained in § 365(c)(1)(A) superfluous. In the words of one bankruptcy court, "[i]f the directive of Section 365(c)(1) is to prohibit assumption whenever applicable law excuses performance relative to any entity other than the debtor, why add the words 'or debtor in possession?' The [hypothetical] test renders this phrase surplusage."

> A close reading of § 365(c)(1), however, dispels this notion. By its terms, subsection (c)(1) addresses two conceptually distinct events: assumption and assignment. The plain language of the provision makes it clear that each of these events is contingent on the non-debtor's separate consent. Consequently, where a non-debtor consents to the assumption of an executory contract, subsection (c)(1) will have to be applied a second time if the debtor in possession wishes to assign the contract in question. On that second application, the relevant question would be whether "applicable law excuses a party from accepting performance from or rendering performance to an entity other than . . . the debtor in possession." Consequently, the phrase "debtor in possession," far from being rendered superfluous by a literal reading of subsection (c)(1), dovetails neatly with the disjunctive language that opens subsection (c)(1): "The trustee may not assume or assign. . . ."

A third potential inconsistency identified by Catapult relates to § 365(c)(2). According to Catapult, a literal reading of subsection (c)(1) renders subsection (c)(2) a dead letter. Subsection (c)(2) provides:

> (c) The trustee may not assume or assign any executory contract or unexpired lease of the debtor, whether or not such contract or lease prohibits or restricts assignment of rights or delegation of duties, if

>   . . .

>> (2) such contract is a contract to make a loan, or extend other debt financing or financial accommodations, to or for the benefit of the debtor, or to issue a security of the debtor. . . .

According to Catapult, the contracts encompassed by subsection (c)(2) are all non-assignable as a matter of applicable state law. As a result, a literal reading of subsection (c)(1) would seem to snare and dispose of every executory contract within subsection (c)(2)'s scope. Perlman, however, persuasively rebuts this argument, noting that even if the state law governing the assignability of loan agreements and financing contracts is relatively uniform today, Congress by enacting subsection (c)(2) cemented nationwide uniformity in the bankruptcy context, effectively ensuring creditors that these particular contracts would not be assumable in bankruptcy. Put another way, it is the national uniformity of applicable state law that has rendered subsection (c)(2) superfluous, not the terms of subsection (c)(1).

In any event, subsection (c)(1) does not completely swallow up subsection (c)(2). Subsection (c)(1) by its terms permits assumption and assignment of executory loan agreements so long as the non-debtor consents. Subsection (c)(2), in contrast, bans assumption and assignment of such agreements, consent of the non-debtor notwithstanding. Accordingly, contrary to Catapult's assertion, subsection (c)(1) does not necessarily catch upriver all the fish that would otherwise be netted by subsection (c)(2). Once again, the "inconsistency" identified by Catapult proves evanescent under close scrutiny. We see no reason why these two provisions cannot happily coexist.

We conclude that the claimed inconsistencies are not actual and that the plain language of § 365(c)(1) compels the result Perlman urges: Catapult may not assume the Perlman licenses over Perlman's objection. Catapult has not demonstrated that, in according the words of subsection (c)(1) their plain meaning, we do violence to subsection (c)(1) or the provisions that accompany it.

B.

Catapult next urges that legislative history requires disregard of the plain language of § 365(c)(1). First off, because we discern no ambiguity in the plain statutory language, we need not resort to legislative history.

We will depart from this rule, if at all, only where the legislative history clearly indicates that Congress meant something other than what it said. Here, the legislative history unearthed by Catapult falls far short of this mark. [T]here exists no contemporaneous legislative history regarding the current formulation of subsection (c)(1). Catapult, however, argues that the language as ultimately enacted in 1984 had its genesis in a 1980 House amendment to an earlier Senate technical corrections bill. The amendment was accompanied by "a relatively obscure committee report." In explaining the amendment, the report stated:

> This amendment makes it clear that the prohibition against a trustee's power to assume an executory contract does not apply where it is the debtor that is in possession and the performance to be given or received under a personal service contract will be the same as if no petition had been filed because of the personal service nature of the contract.

However, since the report relates to a different proposed bill, predates enactment of § 365(c)(1) by several years, and expresses at most the thoughts of only one committee in the House, we are not inclined to view it as the sort of clear indication of contrary intent that would overcome the unambiguous language of subsection (c)(1).

C.

Catapult makes the appealing argument that, as a leading bankruptcy commentator has pointed out, there are policy reasons to prefer the "actual test." That may be so, but Congress is the policy maker, not the courts.

Policy arguments cannot displace the plain language of the statute; that the plain language of § 365(c)(1) may be bad policy does not justify a judicial rewrite. And a rewrite is precisely what the actual test requires. The statute expressly provides that a debtor in possession "may not assume or assign" an executory contract where applicable law bars assignment and the non-debtor objects. The actual test effectively engrafts a narrow exception onto § 365(c)(1) for debtors in possession, providing that, as to them, the statute only prohibits assumption and assignment, as opposed to assumption or assignment.

V.

Because the statute speaks clearly, and plain language does not produce a patently absurd result or contravene any clear legislative history, we must "hold Congress to its words." Accordingly, we hold that, where applicable non-bankruptcy law makes an executory contract non-assignable because the identity of the non-debtor party is material, a debtor in possession may not assume the contract absent consent of the non-debtor party. A straightforward application of § 365(c)(1) to the circumstances of this case precludes Catapult from assuming the Perlman licenses over Perlman's objection. Consequently, the bankruptcy court erred when it approved Catapult's motion to assume the Perlman licenses, and the district court erred in affirming the bankruptcy court.

NOTES & QUESTIONS

1. A lot hinges on whether a specific intellectual property license is characterized as exclusive or nonexclusive. In general, nonexclusive licenses are deemed to be personal to the licensee and hence non-assignable. If they are non-assignable, then they will be non-assumable under section 365(a) when the licensee files for bankruptcy. *See In re CFLC, Inc.,* 89 F. 3d 673 (9th Cir. 1996). The treatment of exclusive licenses is a little bit more uncertain. Exclusive copyright licenses are viewed as transfers of property rights and therefore are more likely to be assignable and hence assumable. *See In re Golden Books Family Entertainment, Inc.,* 269 B.R. 311 (Bankr. D. Del. 2001). But despite the statutory characterization of exclusive copyright licenses as transfers of property rights, one court has found that a specific exclusive license was not assignable. *See Gardner v. Nike,* 279 F. 3d 774 (9th Cir. 2002). Exclusive patent and trademark licenses have in general been found to be non-assignable. *See In re Hernandez,* 285 B.R. 435 (Bankr. D. Ariz. 2002) (patent license); *Tap Publ'n, Inc. v. Chinese Yellow Pages (New York), Inc.,* 925 F. Supp. 212 (S.D.N.Y. 1996) (trademark license).

2. Much also rests on the drafting of the license. If the licensor is concerned about the assumption and assignment of the license by a debtor licensee, he can protect his interests through creative drafting. The licensor should make sure that the license will not be construed as a sale by avoiding conveyance

and granting language as well as by imposing some continuing obligations upon himself. The licensor can also incorporate section 365(n)-like language into the license to protect himself in the event of the licensee's bankruptcy.

3. Can you think of one simple drafting trick that could have avoided the problem in *Institut Pasteur*? Note that the problem is that under the terms of the reorganization the debtor is owned by the licensor's competitor who owns a controlling share of the debtor licensee. By assuming the license, the debtor licensee would be shifting effective control over the intellectual property to the licensor's competitor. Hence, the uproar. Of course, a similar problem could have occurred outside of bankruptcy if the competitor had acquired the licensee. In either case, the licensor could have protected himself by including a clause in the license that terminated the license in the event of a change in corporate control of the licensee.

4. There is currently a circuit split over the correct standard for determining when a nonexclusive licensee of intellectual property can assume a license in bankruptcy. The First Circuit adopts an "actual test," which looks to see if the debtor licensee will assign the assumed license in derogation of applicable law against assignments. The Third, Ninth, and Eleventh Circuits adopt a "hypothetical test," which looks to see if the debtor licensee could, upon assumption, assign the license in derogation of applicable law against assignments. How would *Catapult*, the Ninth Circuit case, have come out under the actual test? How would *Institut Pasteur*, the First Circuit case, have come out under the hypothetical test? Is there a substantive difference between the two tests?

5. One difference between these tests is that the hypothetical test tends towards a categorical rule that bases assumability on the nature of the license. In *Catapult*, the court denies assumption largely on the fact that the license was nonexclusive. The actual test tends to be more case by case and contextual and less rule-like. In *Institut Pasteur*, the court allows assumption of a nonexclusive license because there is no evidence that it would be assigned improperly. Despite its reliance on a test based on actual assignment, does the First Circuit ignore the business realities of allowing the assumption of an intellectual property license by an entity whose controlling shareholder is the licensor's competitor? The First Circuit's decision arguably rests on a formalistic notion of an assignment. On the other hand, a corporation is a distinct entity from its shareholders, and there is no actual assignment from CBC to bioMerieux. Do you think the hypothetical test would have treated the assumption by CBC when it was controlled by bioMerieux the same as an outright assignment from CBC to bioMerieux?

B.   TERMINATION OUTSIDE OF BANKRUPTCY

HAPGOOD v. HEWITT
Supreme Court of United States
119 U.S. 226 (1886)

BLATCHFORD, J.

[Hapgood & Co., a Missouri corporation,] was in existence from before August 1, 1873, to January 1, 1880, when it was dissolved. At the latter date the three trustees constituted its board of directors, and [Charles H.] Hapgood was president. By virtue of the laws of Missouri, Hapgood and the other two persons became trustees of the corporation, with power to settle its affairs, and recover the debts and property belonging to it. Hapgood was the president of the corporation during its entire existence, and had the control and management of its business. All the officers and employees were under his direction. He had power to hire and discharge all agents and employees of every grade, to determine the classes and kinds of goods that should be manufactured, and the general way in which the business should be conducted. The corporation employed a large number of manual laborers, and various employees of higher grades, among them a superintendent, a secretary, a foreman, and a traveling salesman, all of whom had charge of different departments, but were under the control and direction of the president, as chief executive officer. The duties of the superintendent were to having general charge of the manufacturing department, subject to the discretion of the president, and to devise and get up such new devices, arrangements, and improvements in the plows manufactured as should adapt them to the market, and as should be needed, from time to time, to suit the wants of customers.

Shortly before August 1, 1873, Hewitt represented to the corporation that he was a man of large experience in mechanical pursuits; that he had been for several years immediately preceding engaged with Avery & Sons, plow manufacturers in Louisville, and had been since 1868 familiar with the manufacturing of plows and agricultural implements; that he had been instrumental in devising and getting up the best plows manufactured by Avery & Sons; that the most valuable improvements in the plows manufactured by them had been devised by him, and adopted at his suggestion and instigation; that since 1869 he had given his undivided attention to the manufacture of plows, and understood thoroughly the different kinds of plows in the market, and the classes of plows needed for the trade; and that he could and would give to any manufacturer who should secure his services the benefit of his experience in devising and making improvements in the plows manufactured. In consequence of these representations, and relying upon them, the corporation employed Hewitt to devote his time and services to getting up, improving, and perfecting plows and other goods, and to introducing the same; and, that he might be more fully identified with the corporation, he purchased one share of its stock, and was elected vice-president. At some time in 1874, Hewitt increased his interest in the company by purchasing one-half of the shares owned by the president. As a part of the same transaction, it was agreed between Hewitt and the corporation that from that date Hewitt should fill the position of superintendent of the manufacturing department, and, as such, not only exercise a general supervision over that department, subject to the president, but also devote his time and services to devising improvements in, and getting up and perfecting, plows adapted to the general trade of the corporation. He accepted the position, and held it until the fall of 1877, when his connection with the corporation ceased.

He agreed, in such new position, to use his best efforts, and devote his knowledge and skill, in devising and making improvements in the plows manufactured by the corporation, and in getting up and perfecting plows and other agricultural implements adapted to its trade. In view of the expected value of his services in this latter direction, the corporation was induced to pay him, and did pay him, a salary of $3,000 a year. It was manufacturing a plow known as a sulky or riding plow, so arranged that the plow was carried on a frame supported by wheels, and that the driver of the horses rode on the frame. Down to the year 1876 this sulky plow had a wooden frame. During that year it was thought desirable by the officers of the corporation that a change should be made by the substitution of an iron frame for the wooden one. The officers, including Hewitt, had frequent conversations during the winter of 1875-76 with reference to such change. In those conversations, and in personal conversations with Hewitt, the president stated that he was anxious to retain in the iron sulky all the essential features of the wooden sulky, so far as was consistent with the use of an iron frame, and suggested other features which he thought it important to adopt in the new plow, and Black, a salesman, urged the importance of having an iron axle of an arched form.

As the result of these conversations and deliberations, Hewitt was, early in the summer of 1876, directed by the president to proceed at once to devise and build an iron sulky plow according to the suggestions so made; that is, that he should retain in the new plough all the valuable features of the wooden sulky which the corporation had been manufacturing, should construct the plow of wrought and malleable iron, should adopt the other features suggested by the president and the arch suggested by Black, and should add such additional features as might seem advantageous to him (Hewitt). He was directed to proceed with the work without delay, so that the corporation might be ready to manufacture the new plow for the season of 1877. In accordance with those directions, Hewitt devised and constructed a sulky plow, in wrought and malleable iron, and, after some delays, about the first of April, 1877, produced a plow satisfactory to the president. During all the time that he was engaged in devising and constructing the new plow he was in the employ of the corporation, and drawing a salary of $3,000 a year. The time during which he was so engaged was the regular working hours in the factory. The men who did the manual labor on the new plow were all employees of and paid by the corporation, and all the materials used in its construction were bought and paid for by the corporation. The work, as it progressed, was under the general superintendence of Hewitt, but the work in the respective departments was also under the special superintendence of the respective foremen of those departments, who were also paid by the corporation. During the whole time of the construction of the plow it was understood by all the parties engaged therein, and by those at whose instance its construction was commenced, that it was being devised and constructed for the use and benefit of the corporation, and as a model for the future construction of sulky plows by it.

After the plow was completed, and been accepted by the president as satisfactory, the latter directed Hewitt to go to Chicago and have the necessary malleable castings made for the construction of plows after the model. Hewitt did so, obtaining at Chicago castings, moulds, and other things necessary for the future building of plows after the model. During the time so spent he was drawing his regular salary; and all his expenses, as well as the price of the models, castings, and other things obtained by him, were paid by the corporation During the time Hewitt remained in its employ he never made any claim of property in any of the devices and improvements made or suggested by him in the new plow, and never stated or claimed that he was entitled to a patent on any of said improvements, or that he had any rights adverse to the corporation in any of said improvements or devices; and never, during the term of his employment, asserted any right to a patent in his own name for such improvements or devices, or any of them. After his connection with the corporation had ceased, and after he had made an arrangement with the president, whereby the latter bought back all his (Hewitt's) stock in the corporation, and after the corporation had been for many months, with the knowledge of Hewitt, engaged in the manufacture of such plows, Hewitt, on January 14, 1878, applied for a patent on the improvements in the plow, and on the twenty-sixth of March, 1878, a patent was granted to him, covering certain parts of the plow; being devices which had been theretofore used by the corporation, with his knowledge and consent. After this patent was issued he, for the first time, claimed, as he has since claimed, that he had and has an exclusive right to manufacture such parts of the plow as are covered by the patent, and has threatened to enforce his rights under the patent, as against the corporation, its representatives, successors, and assigns, and to hold them liable in damages for any infringement of the same.

The bill also alleges that, in devising and constructing the plow, Hewitt was only performing his duty as an employee of the corporation, and carrying out his contract with it; that he was doing only what he was hired and paid to do; that the result of his labors belonged to the corporation; that it became, in equity and good conscience, the true and rightful owner of the right to manufacture the plow; that, if there is any part thereof which is patentable, the patent belonged to the corporation as equitable assignee of Hewitt and that he was and is bound, in equity and good conscience, to make an assignment of the patent to the corporation, or to its trustees.

The bill also alleges that, upon the dissolution of the corporation of Hapgood & Company, the stockholders thereof organized another corporation, under the laws of Illinois, under the name of the Hapgood Plow Company, one of the plaintiffs; that the Hapgood Plow Company succeeded to the business of the prior corporation, and became, by assignment from it, the owner of all the latter's assets, whether legal or equitable, including the rights in the patent, issued to Hewitt, which such prior corporation had, or was entitled to, whether legal or equitable, and its right to manufacture a sulky plow in accordance with the model plow made by Hewitt, including all the devices covered, or claimed to be covered, by the patent; and that all the rights in the premises which the prior corporation had, have been fully transferred to and vested in the new corporation. The bill then alleges a refusal by Hewitt to assign the patent to the plaintiffs, and that he claims to hold it adversely to them.

The prayer of the bill is for a decree directing the defendant to make an assignment of the patent, or of such interest as he may have therein, and of all his rights thereunder, to the Hapgood Plow Company, assignee of Hapgood & Company, or to the trustees of Hapgood & Company, in trust for the

Hapgood Plow Company, vesting the title to the patent, or to the defendant's rights thereunder, in the Hapgood Plow Company, or in said trustees in trust for that corporation, and that he be enjoined and restrained from maintaining any action at law or in equity for any infringement of the patent by Hapgood & Company, or for the use by that corporation of any of the devices or improvements covered by the patent.

The decision of the circuit court was placed on the ground (1) that Hewitt was not expressly required, by his contract, to exercise his inventive faculties for the benefit of his employer, and there was nothing in the bill from which it could be fairly inferred that he was required or expected to do so; (2) that whatever right the employer had to the invention by the terms of Hewitt's contract of employment was a naked license to make and sell the patented improvement as a part of its business, which right, if it existed, was a mere personal one, and not transferable, and was extinguished with the dissolution of the corporation.

We are of opinion that the views taken of the case by the circuit court were correct. There is nothing set forth in the bill as to any agreement between the corporation and Hewitt that the former was to have the title to his inventions, or to any patent that he might obtain for them. The utmost that can be made out of the allegations is that the corporation was to have a license or right to use the inventions in making plows. It is not averred that anything passed between the parties as to a patent. We are not referred to any case which sustains the view that, on such facts as are alleged in the bill, the title to the invention, or to a patent for it, passed. . . .

Whatever license resulted to the Missouri corporation, from the facts of the case, to use the invention, was one confined to that corporation, and not assignable by it. . . . The Missouri corporation was dissolved. Its stockholders organized a new corporation under the laws of Illinois, which may naturally have succeeded to the business of the prior corporation; but the express averment of the bill is that it took, by assignment, the rights it claims in this suit. Those rights, so far as any title to the invention or patent is concerned, never existed in the assignor. As to any implied license to the assignor, it could not pass to the assignee.

As to so much of the prayer of the bill as asks that Hewitt be enjoined from maintaining any action at law or in equity for any alleged infringement of the patent by the prior corporation, or for its use of any of the devices or improvements covered by the patent, which is all there is left of the prayer of the bill, any suit to be brought would not be a suit against the corporation, for it is dissolved; and could not be a suit in equity against its trustees, for they are not alleged to be using the invention. It could only be a suit at law against the trustees or the stockholders of the old corporation for infringement by it while it existed. The theory of the bill is that there is a perfect defense to such a suit. In such a case a court of equity, certainly a circuit court of the United States, will not interfere to enjoin even a pending suit at law, much less the bringing of one in the future.

Decree affirmed.

PAV-SAVR CORP. v. VASSO CORP.
Appellate Court of Illinois for the Third District
493 N.E. 2d 423 (1986)

Justice BARRY delivered the opinion of the court.

The matter before us arises out of the dissolution of the parties' partnership, the Pav-Saver Manufacturing Company. The facts are not in dispute, and only those needed to explain our disposition on the issues on appeal will be stated.

Plaintiff, Pav-Saver Corporation ("PSC") is the owner of the Pav-Saver trademark and certain patents for the design and marketing of concrete paving machines. Harry Dale is the inventor of the Pav-Saver "slip-form" paver and the majority shareholder of PSC, located in Moline, Illinois. H. Moss Meersman is an attorney who is also the owner and sole shareholder of Vasso Corporation. In 1974 Dale, individually, together with PSC and Meersman formed Pav-Saver Manufacturing Company for the manufacture and sale of Pav-Saver machines. Dale agreed to contribute his services, PSC contributed the patents and trademark necessary to the proposed operation, and Meersman agreed to obtain financing for it. The partnership agreement was drafted by Meersman and approved by Attorney Charles Peart, president of PSC. The agreement contained two paragraphs which lie at the heart of the appeal and cross-appeal before us:

> 3. The duties, obligations and functions of the respective partners shall be:
>
> > A. Meersman shall provide whatever financing is necessary for the joint venture, as required.
> >
> > B. (1) PAV-SAVER shall grant to the partnership without charge the exclusive right to use on all machines manufactured and sold, its trade mark 'PAV-SAVER' during the term of this Agreement. In order to preserve and maintain the good will and other values of the trademark PAV-SAVER, it is agreed between the parties that PAV-SAVER Corporation shall have the right to inspect from time to time the quality of machines upon which the licensed trademark PAV-SAVER is used or applied on machines for laying concrete pavement where such machines are manufactured and/or sold. Any significant changes in structure, materials or components shall be disclosed in writing or by drawings to PAV-SAVER Corporation.
> >
> > > (2) PAV-SAVER grants to the partnership exclusive license without charge for its patent rights in and to its Patent # 3,377,933 for the term of this agreement and exclusive license to use its specifications and drawings for the Slip-form paving machine known as Model MX 6-33, plus any specifications and drawings for any extensions, additions and attachments for said machine for said term. It being understood and agreed that same shall remain the property of PAV-SAVER and all copies shall be returned to PAV-SAVER at the expiration of this partnership.

Further, PAV-SAVER, so long as this agreement is honored and is in force, grants a license under any patents of PAV-SAVER granted in the United States and/or other countries applicable to the Slip-Form paving machine.

. . .

11. It is contemplated that this joint venture partnership shall be permanent, and same shall not be terminated or dissolved by either party except upon mutual approval of both parties. If, however, either party shall terminate or dissolve said relationship, the terminating party shall pay to the other party, as liquidated damages, a sum equal to four (4) times the gross royalties received by PAV-SAVER Corporation in the fiscal year ending July 31, 1973, as shown by their corporate financial statement. Said liquidated damages to be paid over a ten (10) year period next immediately following the termination, payable in equal installments.

In 1976, upon mutual consent, the PSC/Dale/Meersman partnership was dissolved and replaced with an identical one between PSC and Vasso, so as to eliminate the individual partners.

It appears that the Pav-Saver Manufacturing Company operated and thrived according to the parties' expectations until around 1981, when the economy slumped, sales of the heavy machines dropped off significantly, and the principals could not agree on the direction that the partnership should take to survive. On March 17, 1983, Attorney Charles Peart, on behalf of PSC, wrote a letter to Meersman terminating the partnership and invoking the provisions of paragraph 11 of the parties' agreement.

In response, Meersman moved into an office on the business premises of the Pav-Saver Manufacturing Company, physically ousted Dale, and assumed a position as the day-to-day manager of the business. PSC then sued in the circuit court of Rock Island County for a court-ordered dissolution of the partnership, return of its patents and trademark, and an accounting. Vasso counterclaimed for declaratory judgment that PSC had wrongfully terminated the partnership and that Vasso was entitled to continue the partnership business, and other relief pursuant to the Illinois Uniform Partnership Act. Other related suits were filed, but need not be described as they are not relevant to the matters before us. After protracted litigation, the trial court ruled that PSC had wrongfully terminated the partnership; that Vasso was entitled to continue the partnership business and to possess the partnership assets, including PSC's trademark and patents; that PSC's interest in the partnership was $165,000, based on a $330,000 valuation for the business; and that Vasso was entitled to liquidated damages in the amount of $384,612, payable pursuant to paragraph 11 of the partnership agreement. Judgment was entered accordingly.

Both parties appealed. PSC takes issue with the trial court's failure to order the return of its patents and trademark or, in the alternative, to assign a value to them in determining the value of the partnership assets. Further, neither party agrees with the trial court's enforcement of their agreement for liquidated damages. In its cross-appeal, PSC argues that the amount determined by the formula in paragraph 11 is a penalty. Vasso, on the other hand, contends in its appeal that the amount is unobjectionable, but the installment method of pay-out should not be enforced.

In addition to the afore-cited paragraphs of the parties' partnership agreement, the resolution of this case is controlled by the dissolution provision of the Uniform Partnership Act . The Act provides:

(2). When dissolution is caused in contravention of the partnership agreement the rights of the partners shall be as follows:

(a) Each partner who has not caused dissolution wrongfully shall have

. . .

II. The right, as against each partner who has caused the dissolution wrongfully, to damage for breach of the agreement.

(b) The partners who have not caused the dissolution wrongfully, if they all desire to continue the business in the same name, either by themselves or jointly with others, may do so, during the agreed term for the partnership and for that purpose may possess the partnership property, provided they secure the payment by bond approved by the court, or pay to any partner who has caused the dissolution wrongfully, the value of his interest in the partnership at the dissolution, less any damages recoverable under clause (2a II) of this section, and in like manner indemnify him against all present or future partnership liabilities.

(c) A partner who has caused the dissolution wrongfully shall have:

. . .

II. If the business is continued under paragraph (2b) of this section the right as against his co-partners and all claiming through them in respect of their interests in the partnership, to have the value of his interest in the partnership, less any damages caused to his co-partners by the dissolution, ascertained and paid to him in cash, or the payment secured by bond approved by the court and to be released from all existing liabilities of the partnership; but in ascertaining the value of the partner's interest the value of the good will of the business shall not be considered.

Initially we must reject PSC's argument that the trial court erred in refusing to return Pav-Saver's patents and trademark pursuant to paragraph 3 of the partnership agreement, or in the alternative that the court erred in refusing to assign a value to PSC's property in valuing the partnership assets. The partnership agreement on its face contemplated a "permanent" partnership, terminable only upon mutual approval of the parties. It is undisputed that PSC's unilateral termination was in contravention of the agreement. The wrongful termination necessarily invokes the provisions of the Uniform Partnership Act so far as they concern the rights of the partners. Upon PSC's notice terminating the partnership, Vasso elected to continue the business pursuant to section 38(2)(b) of the Uniform Partnership Act. As correctly noted by Vasso, the statute was enacted "to cover comprehensively the problem of dissolution ... [and] to stabilize business." Ergo, despite the parties' contractual direction that PSC's patents would be returned to it upon the mutually approved expiration of the partnership, the right to possess the partnership property and continue in business upon a wrongful termination must be derived from and is controlled by the statute. Evidence at trial clearly established that the Pav-Saver machines being manufactured by the partnership could not be produced or marketed without PSC's patents and trademark. Thus, to continue in business pursuant to the statutorily-granted right of the party not causing the wrongful dissolution, it is essential that paragraph 3 of the parties' agreement — the return to PSC of its patents — not be honored.

Similarly, we find no merit in PSC's argument that the trial court erred in not assigning a value to the patents and trademark. The only evidence adduced at trial to show value of this property was testimony relating to good will. It was unrefuted that the name Pav-Saver enjoys a good reputation for a good product and reliable service. However, inasmuch as the Uniform Partnership Act specifically states that "the value of the good will of the business shall not be considered," we find that the trial court properly rejected PSC's good will evidence of the value of its patents and trademark in valuing its interest in the partnership business.

Next, we find no support for PSC's argument that the amount of liquidated damages awarded to Vasso pursuant to the formula contained in paragraph 11 of the parties' agreement is a "penalty." The test for determining whether a liquidated damages clause is valid as such or void as a penalty is stated in Section 356 of the Restatement (Second) of Contracts:

> (1) Damages for breach by either party may be liquidated in the agreement but only at an amount that is reasonable in the light of the anticipated or actual loss caused by the breach and the difficulties of proof of loss. A term fixing unreasonably large liquidated damages is unenforceable on grounds of public policy as a penalty.

The burden of proving that a liquidated damages clause is void as a penalty rests with the party resisting its enforcement.

PSC has not and does not argue that the amount of liquidated damages was unreasonable. (Significantly, neither party purported to establish that actual damages suffered by Vasso were either more or less than $384,612.) PSC now urges, however, that "[t]he ascertainment of the value of the Pav Saver partnership for purposes of an accounting are [sic] easily ascertained. The accountants maintain detailed records of accounts payable and receivable and all equipment." In advancing this argument, PSC misconstrues the two-part test of a penalty: 1) whether the amount fixed is reasonable in light of the anticipated or actual loss caused by the breach; and 2) the difficulty of proving a loss has occurred, or establishing its amount with reasonable certainty. The difficulty or ease of proof of loss is a matter to be determined at the time of contracting — not, as PSC suggests, at the time of the breach.

It appears clear from the record that Meersman, with some insecurity about his partner's long-term loyalty to the newly-formed partnership, insisted on a liquidated damages provision to protect his financial interests. Nonetheless the record discloses that the agreement was reviewed by Peart and not signed until it was acceptable to both parties. As of December 31, 1982, the date of its last financial statement prior to trial, Pav-Saver Manufacturing Company carried liability on notes owed to various banks amounting to $269,060. As of December 31, 1981, the loans outstanding amounted to $347,487. These loans, the record shows, were obtained primarily on the basis of Meersman's financial ability to repay and over his signature individually. The amount of liquidated damages computed according to the formula in the parties agreement — $384,612 — does not appear to be greatly disproportionate to the amount of Meersman's personal financial liability. As earlier stated, the slip-form Pav-Saver machines could not be manufactured and marketed as such without the patents and trademark contributed by Pav-Saver Corporation. Likewise, the services of Dale were of considerable value to the business.

In sum, we find there is no evidence tending to prove that the amount of liquidated damages as determined by the formula was unreasonable. Nor can we say based on the evidence of record that actual damages (as distinguished from a mere accounting) were readily susceptible to proof at the time the parties entered into their agreement. Suffice it to say, the liquidated damages clause in the parties' agreement appears to have been a legitimate matter bargained for between parties on equal footing and enforceable upon an unilateral termination of the partnership. We will not disturb the trial court's award of damages to Vasso pursuant to the liquidated damages formula.

We turn next to Vasso's arguments urging reversal of the trial court's decision to enforce paragraph 11 of the parties' agreement with respect to the manner of paying out the amount of damages determined by the formula. The paragraph provides for the liquidated sum to be paid out in equal installments over a 10-year period. The trial court held that the $384,612 owed by PSC should be paid in 120 monthly installments of $3205.10 each commencing with March 17, 1983. In support of its argument that it was entitled to a set-off of the full amount of liquidated damages, including the unaccrued balance, Vasso argues that the doctrine of equitable set-off should apply on these facts and further urges that such set-off is required by statute.

In considering whether the liquidated damages formula contained in paragraph 11 of the partnership agreement was enforceable, we necessarily scrutinized the totality of the agreement — not merely the dollar figure so determined. Certainly at first blush the formula appears to yield a suspiciously high amount that is not directly related to any anticipated damages that either party might incur upon a wrongful termination of the agreement by the other. The manner of pay-out however — equal installments over a 10-year period — appears to temper the effect that the amount of liquidated damages so determined would have on the party who breached the agreement. In our opinion, the validity of the clause is greatly influenced by the pay-out provision. What might have been a penalty appears to be a fairly bargained-for, judicially enforceable liquidated damages provision. While, in hindsight, Vasso may sense the same insecurity in enforcement of the paragraph in toto that Meersman had hoped to avoid by insisting on the provision in 1974 and 1976, Vasso's concerns of PSC's potential insolvency are neither concrete nor sufficiently persuasive to entitle it to a right of set-off.

The primary authority cited in support of Vasso's equitable set-off argument (*North Chicago Rolling Mill Co. v. St. Louis Ore & Steel Co.,* 152 U.S. 596, 14 S.Ct. 710, 38 L.Ed. 565 (1894)) is inapposite. There, the debtor was insolvent. In this case, PSC has been shown to have relatively little in operating finances, but has not been proved incapable of paying its creditors. Were PSC obliged to pay out the full amount of liquidated damages at this point, PSC's insolvency would be a certainty. However, PSC's assets and financial condition were known to Vasso at the time the parties agreed to become partners. Vasso cannot contend that its partner's potential insolvency in the event of a wrongful termination by it was unforeseeable at the time of contracting. We do not find that the equities so clearly favor Vasso as to require application of the doctrine of equitable set-off in disregard of the parties' agreement for installment payments.

Further, our reading of section 38(2) of the Uniform Partnership Act fails to persuade us that the statute requires a set-off of the liquidated damages. That section permits the partner causing the dissolution (PSC) to have the value of its interest in the partnership, less "any damages recoverable [by Vasso]" (sub-paragraph (b)) or "any damages caused [by PSC]" (sub-paragraph (c)), paid in cash. It does not require a cash set-off, however, in the unusual event (this case) wherein damages exceed the value of the terminating partner's interest.

Where, as here, a valid liquidated damages clause is enforceable, that clause may be implied into the statute to the extent that it does not violate the legislative intent of the Act. We do not believe that the legislative purpose of stabilizing business (Kurtzon) is frustrated by limiting Vasso's statutory set-off to past accrued damages and enforcing the pay-out terms of the parties' agreement. Under the circumstances, we perceive of no compelling grounds, legal or equitable, for ignoring or rewriting paragraph 11 of the parties' agreement. Therefore, all statutory references to "damages" recoverable by Vasso are supplanted by the parties' agreement for liquidated damages. As the trial court properly ruled, enforcement of the agreement results in a judgment for PSC in the amount of its share of the value of the partnership assets ($165,000) set off by past due installments of liquidated damages accrued from the date of the partnership's termination (March 17, 1983), and an ongoing obligation to pay out the balance monthly during the 10- year period which would end in March of 1993.

For the foregoing reasons, we affirm the judgment of the circuit court of Rock Island County.

Affirmed.

Justice STOUDER concurring in part — dissenting in part.

I generally agree with the result of the majority. I cannot, however, accept the majority's conclusion the defendant is entitled to retention of the patents.

The Uniform Partnership Act is the result of an attempt to codify and make uniform the common law. Partners must act pursuant to the provisions of the Act which apply when partners have not agreed how they will organize and govern their ventures. These UPA provisions are best viewed as "default" standards because they apply in the absence of contrary agreements. The scope of the Act is to be determined by its provisions and is not to be construed to extend beyond its own proper boundaries. When the partnership contract contains provisions, imposing on one or more of the partners obligations differing from those which the law ordinarily infers from the partnership relation, the courts should strive to construe these provisions so as to give effect to the honest intentions of the partners as shown by the language of the contract and their conduct under it.

The plaintiff (PSC) brought this action at law seeking dissolution of the partnership before expiration of the agreed term of its existence. Under the Uniform Partnership Act where dissolution is caused by an act in violation of the partnership agreement, the other partner(s) are accorded certain rights. The partnership agreement is a contract, and even though a partner may have the power to dissolve, he does not necessarily have the right to do so. Therefore, if the dissolution he causes is a violation of the agreement, he is liable for any damages sustained by the innocent partner(s) as a result thereof. The innocent partner(s) also have the option to continue the business in the firm name provided they pay the partner causing the dissolution the value of his interest in the partnership.

The duties and obligations of partners arising from a partnership relation are regulated by the express contract as far as they are covered thereby. A written agreement is not necessary but where it does exist it constitutes the measure of the partners' rights and obligations. While the rights and duties of the partners in relation to the partnership are governed by the Uniform Partnership Act, the uniform act also provides that such rules are subject to any agreement between the parties. It is where the express contract does not cover the situation or question which arises that they are determined under the applicable law, The Uniform Partnership Act.

> The partnership agreement entered into by PSC and Vasso in pertinent part provides:

> 3.B.(2) [PSC] grants to the partnership exclusive license without charge for its patent rights . . . for the term of this agreement. . . . [I]t being understood and agreed that same shall remain the property of [PSC] . . . and shall be returned to [PSC] at the expiration of this partnership. . . .

The majority holds this provision in the contract is unenforceable. The only apparent reason for such holding is that its enforcement would affect defendant's option to continue the business. No authority is cited to support such a rule.

> The partnership agreement further provides:

> 11. . . . If either party shall terminate or dissolve said [partnership], the terminating party shall pay to the other party as liquidated damages . . . [$384,612].

This provision becomes operative at the same time as the provision relating to the return of the patents.

Partnership agreements are governed by the same general rules of construction as are other written agreements. If their provisions are explicit and unambiguous and do not violate the duty of good faith which each partner owed his co-partners, the courts should carry out the intention of the parties. The Uniform Partnership Act should not be construed to invalidate an otherwise enforceable partnership agreement entered into for a legitimate purpose.

Here, express terms of the partnership agreement deal with the status of the patents and measure of damages, the question is settled thereby. I think it clear the parties agreed the partnership only be allowed the use of the patents during the term of the agreement. The agreement having been terminated, the right to use the patents is terminated. The provisions in the contract do not conflict with the statutory option to continue the business and even if there were a conflict the provisions of the contract should prevail. The option to continue the business does not carry with it any guarantee or assurance of success and it may often well be that liquidation rather than continuation would be the better option for a partner not at fault.

As additional support for my conclusion, it appears the liquidated damages clause was insisted upon by the defendant because of earlier conduct of the plaintiff withdrawing from a former partnership. Thus, the existence of the liquidated damages clause recognizes the right of plaintiff to withdraw the use of his patents in accordance with the specific terms of the partnership agreement. Since liquidated damages depends on return of the patents, I would vacate that part of the judgment providing defendant is entitled to continue use of the patents and provide that use shall remain with plaintiff.

SOUTHWEST WHEY INC. v. NUTRITION 101, INC.
United States District Court for the Central District of Illinois
117 F. Supp. 2d 770 (2000)

RICHARD MILLS, District Judge.

If you do not want another to tell your secrets, you must not tell them yourself.

Seneca: Phaedra

I. BACKGROUND

On May 10, 1989, Plaintiff Southwest Whey, Inc., ("Southwest Whey") and Defendant Nutrition 101, Inc., ("Nutrition 101") entered into a written agreement to operate a joint venture. Southwest Whey agreed to obtain whey from dairies and Nutrition 101 agreed to market whey to hog farmers in the region east of the Mississippi River and in other areas by mutual agreement. The joint venture was dissolved by Southwest Whey on September 16, 1993.

For most of the 1980's, Southwest Whey's business largely consisted of obtaining and selling whey west of the Mississippi River. Jack Muse ("Muse"), Southwest Whey's president, wanted to expand the business geographically. However, his efforts to obtain contracts with dairies or pork producers east of the Mississippi prior to the commencement of the joint venture produced little, if any, success.

Nutrition 101 was owned and operated by Ross Peter ("Peter"). Nutrition 101 primarily sold feed to pork producers. Peter was experienced in marketing feed to farmers and had an extensive customer base of pork producers. Peter and Muse began discussions which led to the formation of the joint venture on May 13, 1989. A written agreement was included "to guide the joint venture." Southwest Whey "agreed to procure whey from dairies and Nutrition 101 agreed to market whey to hog farmers in the region east of the Mississippi River." The agreement did not specifically include a non-compete restrictive covenant to govern the parties' actions or competition following dissolution.

Neither Southwest Whey nor Nutrition 101 had a written compilation of claimed trade secrets prior to or during the joint venture. The farmer and dairy contracts used by the parties did not contain any confidentiality or non-disclosure provisions. Moreover, Southwest Whey did not impose any confidentiality restrictions upon the dairies to prevent the disclosure of information learned by them from the joint venture regarding the sale, storage, transfer, or delivery of whey. Similarly, no confidentiality restrictions were imposed upon the truck drivers who transported the whey regarding any knowledge they had or may acquire because of their dealings with the joint venture.

By late 1992, a conflict had arisen between the partners to the joint venture. Southwest Whey suggested to Nutrition 101 that the parties consider shutting down the business. In January 1993, the parties met to discuss a proposed buy-sell agreement to wind up the joint venture. Nutrition 101's proposal was not acceptable to Southwest Whey. Southwest Whey's proposal included a restrictive covenant preventing Nutrition 101 from competing with them for ten years. This proposal was rejected by Nutrition 101. The parties were unable to agree to any of the proposals.

By the summer of 1993, Muse began to inform dairies of his plan to end Nutrition 101's interest in the joint venture. Muse visited farmers who purchased whey from the joint venture in St. Louis, Missouri, during the first week of September of 1993. He inquired as to whether farmers would continue to purchase whey at the same terms and prices if the joint venture ended and Southwest Whey ended up with the business. Muse indicated that each farmer agreed that they would continue to purchase from Southwest Whey.

On September 16, 1993, Southwest Whey informed Nutrition 101 that it had decided to cease operations as a joint venture, and that Nutrition 101 would no longer have access to whey from dairies under contract with the joint venture. One month later, Southwest Whey notified the customers of the dispute and solicited their continued business. Southwest Whey had no written contracts with pork producers who had no obligation to continue to take whey and could at any time "come and go."

This case was originally filed on September 11, 1998. On March 31, 2000, Southwest Whey filed its eight-count amended complaint against Nutrition 101, alleging (I) Breach of Contract; (II) Interference with Prospective Advantage; (III) Violation of Illinois Trade Secrets Act ("ITSA"); (IV) Violation of Illinois Trade Secrets Act — Exemplary Damages; (V) Conversion; (VI) Breach of Fiduciary Duty; (VII) Breach of Fiduciary Duty — Exemplary Damages; and (VIII) Breach of Good Faith and Fair Dealing.

Nutrition 101 has moved for summary judgment on [Counts II, III, IV, and VIII].

. . .

IV. Trade Secrets (Counts III and IV)

Southwest Whey alleges that it has developed and used certain trade secrets in connection with the marketing and distribution of whey as a hog feed element. Following the dissolution of the joint venture, Southwest Whey alleges that Nutrition 101's efforts in connection with the marketing and distribution of whey as a hog feed element constitute the misappropriation of trade secrets of Southwest Whey in violation of ITSA. Nutrition 101 moves for summary judgment on Counts III and IV.

In Illinois, a trade secret is defined as:

information, included but not limited to, technical or non-technical data, a formula, pattern, compilation, program, device, method, technique, drawing, process, financial data, or list of actual or potential customers or suppliers, that:

(1) is sufficiently secret to derive economic value, actual or potential, from not being generally known to other persons who can obtain economic value from its disclosure or use; and

(2) is the subject of efforts that are reasonable under the circumstances to maintain its secrecy or confidentiality.

In order to establish improper use of trade secrets, there must be a showing that the information at issue was (1) secret (not generally known in the industry); (2) misappropriated; and (3) used in the appropriator's business.

Southwest Whey essentially alleges that it brought several methods, techniques, and practices into the joint venture which is the basis of its trade secrets claim. Specifically, in an answer to an interrogatory, Southwest Whey identified the following thirty-one methods, techniques, and practices which constitute trade secrets in connection with the marketing and distribution of whey as a hog feed element: (1) Contract language with farmers; (2) Contract language with dairies; (3) Allowable distance for hauling whey from dairy to farmer for freshness; (4) Allowable distance for hauling whey from dairy to farmer for profit; (5) Techniques for hook ups at dairies; (6) Tank cleaning techniques; (7) Tank configurations, including the pumping equipment and appurtenances; (8) Pricing strategies; (9) How to prevent the whey from destroying concrete; (10) Knowledge of feed characteristics of whey; (11) Knowledge of whey sources generally; (12) Knowledge that farmers would pay for whey; (13) Routes from dairies to the farmers; (14) Customer lists; (15) Vendor lists; (16) Techniques for identifying suppliers and customers; (17) Marketing methods for farmers; (18) Marketing methods for dairies; (19) How to mix and/or dilute whey to make it an effective supplemental feed source; (20) Studies on the nutritional value of whey; (21) Handling plants and managers to minimize inconvenience with truckers; (22) Siting of loading operations; (23) Use tracking at farms to maximize sales and ensure continued customer care; (24)

Confinement and location techniques and procedures for use at farms; (25) Development of on-farm delivery system; (26) Use of cone bottom tanks; (27) Recirculation techniques and the need for them; (28) Tank agitation techniques; (29) Screening techniques; (30) Gauge for tank management; and (31) Use of elevator buckets and other products for delivery of whey at farms.

Southwest Whey asserts that it attempted to protect the thirty-one "trade secrets" by not giving them to anyone in their entirety other than Nutrition 101. Thus, they contend that even if some or most of the thirty-one enumerated elements do not constitute trade secrets, "the whole package put together" is a trade secret. Specifically, the various elements combine to form the "overall trade secret" which Southwest Whey has acquired after years of trial and error that has come at great expense.

The Court first notes that a "trade secret" "may include a compilation of confidential business and financial information." The key inquiry in ascertaining whether information is a trade secret under the ITSA is on the secrecy of the information sought to be protected. Specifically, courts look at how easily information can be duplicated without involving substantial time, effort, or expense. Factors in determining whether information constitutes a trade secret include the following: (1) The extent to which the information is known outside the business; (2) The extent to which it is known by others involved in the business; (3) The extent that measures have been taken to guard the secrecy of the information; (4) The value of the information to the party and his competitors; (5) The amount of money or effort expended by the party in developing the information; and (6) The ease or difficulty with which the information at question could be obtained or duplicated by others.

The Court notes that the statutory protection afforded trade secrets reflects the balancing of social and economic interests. An individual who has put forth the time, money, and effort to obtain a secret advantage should be protected from a party who obtains the secret through improper means. Nevertheless, in a competitive market, a party is entitled to utilize the general knowledge and skills acquired through experience in pursuing his chosen occupation.

Moreover, merely being the first or only one to use certain information does not alone turn what is otherwise general knowledge into a trade secret. Otherwise, no matter how ordinary or well known the information, the first person to use it would be able to obtain the protection of the statute. Additionally, "generalized confidential business information" does not constitute a protectable trade secret. Specifically, the mere legwork in acquiring this information cannot be the basis for a claim. Any other result would mean that a party who learns the basics of an industry from an individual would be precluded from entering the business at all in a competitive relationship. Such a result is contrary to a free market economy.

Southwest Whey basically asserts that it is the total process gained over the years that is the trade secret at issue in this case. Southwest Whey has alone on a large scale been able to transform this process into a workable, profitable enterprise. Southwest Whey contends that it has taken sufficient measures to protect its trade secrets. Specifically, although certain aspects of the process were revealed to the dairies, truckers, farmers or supply vendors, only that which was necessary for the process to function was revealed at any time. Muse indicated that only Southwest Whey and Nutrition 101 knew the entire process of marketing and delivering whey. Therefore, the trade secret in the "whole package" was protected.

Moreover, the record reveals that Nutrition 101 is Southwest Whey's only competitor on a major scale in the procurement and selling of whey. There have been, however, a few individual truckers or farmers in the same geographical area engaging in this process on a much smaller scale. These instances are basically limited to the occasional farmer or trucker who hauls whey for the price of freight alone on nothing more than an individual dairy basis. No other entity in the area has engaged in the procurement and selling of whey on such a large scale.

One of the factors in determining whether information constitutes a trade secret involves an analysis of the measures taken to protect the secrecy of the information. Southwest Whey asserts that it never revealed the entire process to any individual or group. Rather, the dairies, farmers, truckers, and supply vendors would learn only that which was needed to fulfill their duties. Thus, although the different segments would learn parts of the overall process, only Nutrition 101 was told everything regarding Southwest Whey's enterprise. However, none of the contracts with the other segments contained confidentiality or non-disclosure clauses.

The parties in the instant action dispute whether there was a non-compete clause between them. Paragraph (13) of the Joint Venture agreement reads "101 personnel to sign agreement not to pass information or data to non involved parties or be involved in any aspect of whey marketing other than as representatives of 101." Southwest Whey contends that this language constitutes a non-compete clause. Nutrition 101 alleges that this language merely means that if an employee were to leave Nutrition 101, he could not use this information further. This provision only involved Nutrition 101 because only they had employees. Moreover, Nutrition 101 contends that the fact that the parties discussed a possible restrictive covenant when they discussed the buy/sell arrangement of the joint venture is evidence that there was not a non-compete clause in the original agreement.

Southwest Whey also alleges that when the agreement was made, the parties contemplated that no termination would occur. "It's either for life or we won't do it." Therefore, the agreement contains no provision detailing what Nutrition 101 could do following a termination. Nutrition 101 contends that because the agreement does not provide for a dissolution date or event, it could be terminated by either party at any date. Moreover, it was Southwest Whey who eventually terminated the agreement.

The Court will now address whether each of the statutory prongs is met.

(A) Sufficiently Secret to Derive Economic Value

Pursuant to the statute, the Court must determine first whether the information sought to be protected as a trade secret is sufficiently secret to derive economic value from not being generally known. Certainly, the affidavit and deposition testimony of Jack Muse is important to this inquiry. Muse indicated that Southwest Whey alone was engaged in the business on a major scale. Moreover, they were the first to engage in the process of successfully marketing and delivering whey on such a scale. These facts indicate that Southwest Whey was engaged in a profitable enterprise. However, the fact that a party was the first or only entity to utilize certain information does not turn what is otherwise general information into a trade secret. As Nutrition 101 contends, some of the individual "secrets" that make up the whole package do seem to constitute general information that can be readily ascertained. For example, the individual secrets that relate to Southwest Whey's knowledge of whey characteristics could be construed as general knowledge that has long been available to the public.

Moreover, Southwest Whey alleges that its process of hauling whey from a dairy to a farmer while maintaining the freshness and making a profit is also a trade secret. However, as Nutrition 101 notes, farmers had been doing this since before the joint venture began, albeit on a smaller scale. Southwest Whey contends that because this has only been done on a smaller scale, issues of freshness and profits are more applicable to their transportation of whey. The fact that these farmers did this on a smaller scale does not mean that issues of profits and freshness were not important. The farmers were no less trying to maintain the freshness and make a profit.

Moreover, some of what are alleged to constitute a portion of the trade secret appear to amount to nothing more than Muse's legwork in establishing his business. Mere legwork in identifying the basics of the industry cannot serve as the basis for a claim under the Act. Muse contends that one component of the overall trade secret is his pricing strategy. His basic strategy has been to charge $4 a ton margin over the cost of freight. This appears to be the result of Muse's legwork in identifying how much he could charge while still making a good profit within the industry. As Nutrition 101 contends, it cannot be true that anyone who employs a similar pricing strategy in seeking to make a profit on whey is violating a trade secret.

Nonetheless, Southwest Whey maintains that it is the "whole package" which constitutes a trade secret. The first prong of the statute requires the Court to assess whether the relevant information was sufficiently secret to derive economic value. At this stage, the Court must view the evidence in the light most favorable to Southwest Whey. It is undisputed that Southwest Whey's only competitor on a major scale is Nutrition 101. Although there may have been individual truckers or farmers engaged in the business on a much smaller scale, there were no other participants in the industry of the same magnitude as Southwest Whey. This is instructive in determining whether Southwest Whey's collection of information acquired over the years is sufficiently secret to derive economic value. It is true that some of the items that constitute a portion of the trade secret are not trade secrets. However, the fact that only Southwest Whey has engaged in the business at this level at least raises a material fact as to the first prong of the statute. Specifically, there is a material issue as to whether the entire package is sufficiently secret to derive economic value.

(B) Reasonable Efforts to Maintain Secrecy

The second prong involves the efforts of the owner to maintain the secrecy of the alleged trade secret. Nutrition 101 alleges that Southwest

Whey has failed to take any affirmative measures to protect its trade secret.

The record reveals that no restrictive covenant was signed between the parties to the action. However, it is important to note that a restrictive covenant or confidentiality agreement is not a prerequisite to recovery under the ITSA. Nonetheless, some affirmative step must be taken to maintain the trade secret. Southwest Whey contends that the language in Paragraph 13 of the written agreement constitutes a restrictive covenant: "101 personnel to sign agreement not to pass information or data to non involved parties or to be involved in any aspect of whey marketing other than as representatives of 101." However, the Court finds that this language was included in the agreement to prevent employees of Nutrition 101 from entering the market on their own. The Court notes that the parties discussed the possibility of entering into a restrictive covenant when they discussed terminating the joint venture. This indicates that there was no restrictive covenant from the outset. Thus, the language in the agreement does not constitute a restrictive covenant.

Southwest Whey attempts to get around this by arguing that their agreement with Nutrition 101 was an agreement to do business forever. Muse indicated that he would not have entered into the agreement if it had an end to it. However, the written agreement between the parties does not specify a definite term or a particular undertaking. According to Illinois partnership law, "dissolution is caused . . . by the expressed will of any partner when no definite term or particular undertaking is specified." Therefore, Southwest Whey's argument that the partnership was an agreement to do business forever is without merit.

The record is clear that there was no written record of trade secrets at any time prior to or during the joint venture. Nonetheless, Southwest Whey alleges that Nutrition 101 would not have been exposed to their trade secrets and allowed into the partnership unless it was for life. However, because the partnership agreement did not specify a particular amount of time, it was subject to dissolution at any time. Therefore, the Court rejects Southwest Whey's contention that their means of protecting their trade secrets was to form a partnership for life.

Moreover, neither the farmer nor the dairy contracts used by the joint venture contained any confidentiality or non-disclosure provisions. Southwest Whey imposed no restrictions upon the dairies in their negotiation of contracts regarding the disclosure of information about the joint venture regarding the sale, storage, transfer, or delivery of whey. Similarly, no restrictions were placed on the truck drivers who hauled the whey regarding any knowledge they had or might acquire because of their relationship with the joint venture. In short, Southwest Whey did not insist on any non-disclosure clauses. This is true despite the fact that such clauses were not uncommon in the industry.

Southwest Whey responds by noting that Nutrition 101 was the only other entity which knew everything about the process of successfully marketing and delivering whey. Muse's approach was to keep the different segments of his business separate. Moreover, he did not tell his clients about his business or reveal its contract terms with the farmers to the dairies. Thus, although the various entities could learn bits and pieces, only Nutrition 101 was exposed to the whole process.

The Court is not persuaded that Southwest Whey used reasonable efforts to maintain the secrecy of its trade secrets. The record does not reveal any affirmative steps taken by Southwest Whey to protect its trade secrets.

Southwest Whey did not insist upon Nutrition 101 signing a restrictive covenant at any time before, during, or after the joint venture. Moreover, they did not require any of the truckers, farmers, dairies, or other parties to sign non-disclosure clauses. The argument that no specific entity other than Nutrition 101 was exposed to the entire process does not constitute a reasonable effort to maintain the secrecy. This merely means that Southwest Whey did not reveal all of the thirty-one enumerated secrets that make up the entire package except to Nutrition 101. However, some of the trade secrets deal specifically with a particular industry. The Court notes that it would only make sense that the secrets related to the dairy industry would only be revealed to those in the dairy industry, not in the farming industry. Thus, the twelve secrets that may be classified as involving the dairy industry were revealed only to those in the dairy industry. Nothing prevented those in the dairy industry from sharing these secrets. The fact that these dairy secrets may not have been revealed to those in the transportation industry is not a reasonable effort to maintain the secrecy. Similarly, Southwest Whey took no reasonable steps to prevent the truckers from revealing the secrets that pertain to the transportation industry. Nothing prevented these truckers from sharing the secrets. The fact that these secrets may not have been revealed to those in the dairy industry does not constitute a reasonable effort to maintain the secret.

Accordingly, even when viewing the evidence in the light most favorable to Southwest Whey, there is no genuine issue of material fact that they failed to take any reasonable efforts to maintain the secrecy of the trade secrets. This is a prerequisite under the Trade Secrets Act. Therefore, summary judgment is allowed as to Counts III and IV.

Because Southwest Whey has failed to establish the existence of a trade secret pursuant to the statute, the Court need not address whether any trade secret was misappropriated by Nutrition 101.

Ronald S. Laurie, Intellectual Property Allocation Strategies in Joint Ventures, Inflexion Point Strategy, LLC
Practising Law Institute, Patents, Copyrights, Trademarks, and Literary Property Course Handbook Series PLI. No. 5923, (March, 2005)*

I. INTRODUCTION

The term "joint venture" is commonly used to mean "an association of economically independent business entities . . . for a common commercial purpose

---

of defined scope and duration, by contract or in the form of a new business entity, and by means of which the [v]enturers pool resources and share risks, rewards and control." Typically, each joint venturer contributes a unique attribute (e.g., technology, capital, management expertise, or product distribution and marketing) toward a shared common objective and acceptance of risk. Other terms that are commonly used to describe joint ventures include "strategic alliance," and "partnership."

. . .

III. IP ALLOCATION GENERALLY

In order to operate the joint venture — whether under the contractual, entity-based or two-stage models — the joint venturers and/or the JV entity will need to either own, or be licensed under, IP rights related to their business to operate. The choice of ownership versus licensing depends on a variety of factors. One factor is whether the IP arose independently of the JV (e.g., pre-existing or created by one of the joint venturers outside of the JV) or arose from operation of the JV. The former is often referred to as "Background IP," whereas the latter is often referred to as "Foreground IP."

Another factor is whether the JV is contractual, entity-based or established pursuant to the two-stage model. If the JV is entity-based or follows from the two-stage model, the relevant IP either can be owned by the JV, owned by one or both of the joint venturers and licensed to the JV, or some combination of the foregoing. For example, background IP might be owned by its creator (one of the joint venturers) and licensed to the JV entity, or even assigned to the JV entity. Similarly, foreground IP (which in this instance would have been created by the JV entity) could be owned by the JV entity, or allocated to the joint venturers individually, who would then grant appropriate licenses to the JV entity. If the JV is contractually based, both the foreground and background IP must be owned by one (or both) of the joint venturers and licensed to the other. Nevertheless, many other variations are also possible.

A.   Default Allocation Paradigm: Joint Ownership

In situations where IP is to be owned by the joint venturers themselves (under either the contractual, entity or two-stage models), the most common form of IP allocation is some form of "joint ownership." For example, foreground IP is often allocated as follows: IP developed solely by one joint venturer is solely owned by that joint venturer, while IP developed jointly by the joint venturers is owned jointly by those joint venturers. Indeed, even if the joint venturers fail to expressly allocate IP ownership under the contractual JV model, this type of IP allocation will arise under default law, because (at least in the United States) ownership initially vests with the creators of the subject matter in question.

1.   Conflicting Rights Under Default Laws

The default rights of joint owners (to exploit and/or to enforce) are governed by respective national laws applicable to the type of IP asset in question.

a)   Right to Exploit

For example, consider U.S. patent rights. Absent an agreement to the contrary, the default rule is that each joint owner can exploit the patent without the permission of the other and without any duty to share royalties. Further, the joint owner's right to exploit includes the right to license third parties. The freedom to license without accounting enables a savvy prospective patent licensee to play the joint owners against one another other to maximize favorable deal terms for the licensee.

The situation becomes even more complicated when dealing with multiple IP types. For example, while U.S. patent law imposes no duty of accounting among exploiting joint owners, U.S. copyright law does impose such a duty.

b)   Right to Enforce

The counterpart of exploitation is enforcement and, here as well, joint ownership presents pitfalls for the unwary. Again taking U.S. patent law as an example, normally, each joint owner must join in a suit to enforce the patent against a third party. This requirement protects a defendant from defending against multiple suits on the same patent and an absent joint owner from a finding of invalidity or unenforceability negatively affecting his rights. Consequently, any joint owner can hinder an offensive patent infringement action by refusing to join as a plaintiff.

Thus, joint owners of a U.S. patent find themselves in a situation where each joint owner can freely license without obligation to the other, but where each joint owner can prevent the other from suing by refusing to join the suit. In such a case, the rewards of licensing go to the joint owner who either grants a license first, or undercuts another joint owner's offer with a more favorable deal. It is no wonder that courts have characterized patent joint owners as being "at the mercy of each other."

A non-litigant joint owner can grant the defendant a license — even after initiation of the action — which will cut off part or all of the relief the litigant joint owner may obtain by exercising its unilateral right to sue. Specifically, a nonexclusive license (even post-suit) will prevent the litigant joint owner from obtaining injunctive relief, and will also protect the defendant from liability for post-grant (but not pre-grant) damages. But if the non-litigant joint owner grants the defendant an exclusive license (even post-suit), the non-litigant joint owner no longer can consent to join the suit as a joint owner of the patent, and the suit must be dismissed.

c)   International Considerations

Further complexity as to joint owners' rights ensues because different countries have different default laws. For example, consider the copyright joint ownership laws of three major industrialized countries: the United States, the United Kingdom, and Japan. Under U.S. law, joint owners of a copyright can freely exploit for themselves. Under U.K. law, the joint owners cannot exploit for themselves without consent of the other joint owners. Under Japanese law, the joint owners cannot exploit without consent, but such consent cannot be unreasonably withheld.

Indeed, parties in different countries — looking at joint ownership through the prism of their individual national laws — may have entirely different expectations of what it means to be a joint owner. Based on the example above, American and British joint owners of a copyright might have had entirely different expectations regarding their individual rights to exploit. Some lawyers have been called to renegotiate joint ownership agreements when it became apparent, years after execution, that the joint owners had no meeting of the minds on their respective rights to exploit and enforce jointly developed subject matter.

2.   Enforceability of Contractual Provisions

a)   Against Third Parties

The previous two sections demonstrate the considerable variation in the default rules for the different types of intellectual property, as well as under the different national laws. An astute joint owner therefore will negotiate provisions in the JV agreement setting forth, in detail, the joint owners' respective rights and obligations. For example, such provisions might include covenants regarding unilateral exploitation, licensing of competitors, sharing of royalties, joining suits, and sharing of enforcement costs and proceeds. However, the effectiveness of these covenants remains uncertain as they may not always be enforceable.

Consider, for example, that the joint owners have agreed not to unilaterally exploit a jointly owned IP asset for the benefit of third parties. Such a covenant may be unenforceable against a third party who is held by a court to be a bona fide purchaser for value ("BFP") from one of the joint owners.

b)   Against Joint Owners Themselves

Unlike the uncertainty surrounding contractual covenants with respect to third parties, such agreements should be enforceable against the joint owners themselves. For example, breach of a joint owner's covenant not to use for itself should be enforceable against that joint owner. However, this may prove untrue in some situations.

For example, where a joint owner goes bankrupt, the bankruptcy court (or trustee) generally has the power either to assume or reject a contract held by the bankrupt party. If the court rejects the JV agreement, the non-bankrupt joint owner may lose the benefit of the contractual provisions restricting the activity of the bankrupt joint owner. Conversely, the court might assume the JV agreement, but assign it to a third party (typically in connection with a sale of the joint ownership interest). In this scenario, the court would effectively divest the bankrupt joint owner of its joint ownership rights and vest those rights in a new joint owner (i.e. the third party) — perhaps even a competitor.

3.   Recommendations

Joint ownership is fraught with pitfalls and should be avoided wherever possible. However, joint ownership may sometimes be unavoidable. For example, one joint venturer may oppose the formation of the joint venture on any other terms. In such a situation, the joint venturers must think through all issues and carefully plan for all contingencies. The joint owners cannot simply rely on default rules because, as discussed above, the rights to exploit and enforce vary with the type of intellectual property and applicable national laws. Such variation makes it impossible for the joint owners to effect an integrated and consistent plan for development, use and distribution of the subject matter covered by the jointly owned IP. Instead, the joint venturers should use the contractual or JV agreement to override the hodgepodge of inconsistent default laws by clearly allocating all the rights and responsibilities of the joint owners.

There are many possible alternatives to joint ownership, all of which involve some form of allocating IP ownership to individual parties (whether the joint venturers or the JV entity), who would then grant appropriate licenses to other parties as needed. In the next section, we explore some of these IP allocation possibilities.

B.   Preferred IP Allocation Strategies

1.   IP Ownership: Background, Non-Derivative Foreground and Derivative Foreground IP

In order to properly allocate ownership of IP under the preferred approach, the first step is to classify the IP based on the nature of the IP. Indeed, the election of a JV structural model and an associated IP allocation strategy are interdependent and, in turn, the IP allocation strategy is contingent on whether the IP asset represents Background, Non-Derivative Foreground or Derivative Foreground technology.

Background IP includes both IP in technology developed by the joint venturers prior to the formation of the JV ("Pre-existing Background IP") and in technology developed during the existence of the JV, but not pursuant to it ("New Background IP"). Specifically, Pre-existing Background IP comprises IP in technology created by each joint venturer prior to JV formation, that is necessary or useful in conducting the business of the contemplated joint venture, or required to commercially exploit the Foreground IP (as defined below). New Background IP also constitutes IP in technology necessary or useful in conducting the business of the joint venture, or required to commercially exploit the Foreground IP; but the difference lies in its development taking place during the JV and yet not pursuant to the JV development activity. The concept of New Background IP becomes more relevant in the case where one or more joint venturers is a large enterprise having multiple groups doing similar developments.

In contrast, Foreground IP describes IP associated with technology developed pursuant to the JV by the joint venturers, either individually or jointly, and in furtherance of the JV. Derivative Foreground IP is a subset of Foreground IP comprising IP developed pursuant to the JV that extends the core technology of one (and only one) joint venturer.

2.   Optimizing Rights to Use of the Non-IP Owning Joint Venturers

a)   Licenses: Exclusivity, Field of Use and Royalties

Once IP ownership is allocated, the rights of the other (non-owning) joint venturers to use such IP are defined under appropriate license provisions. These licenses include licenses among joint venturers, from a joint venturer to the new JV entity ("NewCo") if applicable, or from NewCo to the joint venturers. In this respect, many combinations of licensing parameters are possible and the joint venturers should decide at the outset which is suitable to their relationship. These licensing parameters include, e.g., whether the license is exclusive or non-exclusive, whether it is limited to a specific field of use, and whether it is royalty-bearing or royalty-free. The parameters are used in various combinations to prescribe (i.e., enable and/or restrict) permissible competitive use of the Background and Foreground IP by the joint venturers and NewCo with respect to one another.

b)   Non-Competition Covenants

Non-competition covenants are a useful adjunct to IP licenses in terms of restricting competitive activity among the joint venturers on the one hand, and between the joint venturers and NewCo on the other. Non-competition covenants can be both more restrictive and less restrictive than IP licenses. They are less restrictive because they typically have a shorter term. Thus, while the IP licenses may extend during the existence of the JV (and possibly beyond), non-competition covenants are typically for a much shorter term, e.g. several years. They are more restrictive because they extend beyond use of the licensed IP by proscribing all competitive activity within a defined field. The scope of the non-compete is usually co-extensive with the area outside of any field-limited licenses. . . .

V.   EXIT STRATEGIES

This section examines the disposition of the IP assets under different exit strategies available for the unwinding of the joint venture business. Possible exit strategies include merger or acquisition, dissolution, and bankruptcy. The IP assets of concern include owned IP (e.g., patents, trademarks and copyrights for which the JV itself is the registered owner, and trade secrets), and licensed-in IP (e.g., inbound IP licenses from the joint venturers and from third parties).

For convenience, the disposition of IP assets will be discussed in the context of a separate JV entity, although many of the concepts will be equally applicable to rights held by an individual joint venturer for the benefit of itself and its partners in the joint venture.

A.   Merger or Acquisition of the JV Entity

If the joint venturers wish to allow for the possibility of merger or acquisition of the independent JV entity, they should negotiate appropriate provisions at the time of forming the JV entity. For example, all inbound licenses should be negotiated and drafted to facilitate their transfer to a potential acquirer of the JV business.

Also, a joint venturer might wish to be protected in the event the JV is acquired by a competitor, for example, by a provision automatically terminating any inbound license from such joint venturer upon a change of control of the JV to a competitor of the minority joint venturer. These competitors may be expressly identified or not. Or, if the license is not terminated, its scope can be "frozen," limiting it to the portion of the acquirer's business represented by the JV before the acquisition. These provisions ensure that, after the acquisition of the JV entity by a competitor of a joint venturer, any inbound licenses from such joint venturer to the JV entity do not accrue (or only accrue in a limited way) to the benefit of the competitor.

B.   Dissolution of the JV Entity

Dissolution of the JV entity as an exit strategy must be analyzed in terms of three distinct considerations: IP owned by the JV entity, IP licensed from third parties, and IP licensed from the joint venturers.

1.   IP Owned by the JV Entity

The analysis of the disposition of the owned IP further must be divided into two competing objectives: protecting the joint venturers' right to use and preventing the joint venturers' continued right to use such IP.

Where the joint venturers wish to continue to make use of the IP owned by the JV following its dissolution, assignment of the IP to the joint venturers as joint owners should be avoided because doing so raises the problems of joint ownership already discussed in III A above. Instead, ownership of the IP assets should vest in one joint venturer with grantback licenses flowing to the other former joint venturers. Alternatively, the joint venturers can choose to maintain the JV solely as an IP holding company (i.e. a shell company) where the joint venturers in turn have a license under the IP. The latter alternative of establishing an IP holding company is especially advantageous for enforcing the joint venture's IP rights against third parties and for the further licensing of the IP to third parties if so desired by the joint venturers. In either case, the scope of any licenses to the former joint venturers (e.g., term of the license grant, exclusivity provision, right to sublicense, field of use, royalty payment, etc.) should be negotiated at the time of forming the JV entity.

Another option is to structure the JV agreement to prohibit grantback licenses. This has the benefit of discouraging dissolution of the JV in the first instance. However, the IP assets risk being wasted unless a third party buyer can be found. Alternatively, the JV agreement could provide that a specified joint venturer has the right to buy out the other joint venturers upon dissolution of the JV, and thus to gain sole ownership of the owned IP. The proceeds from the owned IP will be distributed to the joint venturers in accordance with their original equity stakes in the JV.

2.   Inbound Licenses from Third Parties

Inbound licenses from third parties represent an asset of the JV just like the owned IP and thus will be treated in a similar manner. Issues relating to the inbound licenses, such as their transferability, divisibility and sublicensing, should be specified at the time these licenses are negotiated.

3.   Inbound Licenses from Joint Venturers

Joint venturers' inbound licenses typically cover background IP of the joint venturers closely related to their individual fields of business. Thus, upon dissolution, these licenses usually revert back to the granting joint venturer. However, in some instances, the licensor subsequently may grant equivalent field of use licenses to the other former joint venturers under separate license agreements. Again, these options should be contemplated at the time of JV formation.

4.   Outbound Licenses from JV entity

The JV also may have granted licenses to third parties (i.e., outbound licenses). Upon dissolution, such licenses can either be: (i) left with the JV to be disposed of as part of the corporate unwinding process; or (ii) transferred to an entity that obtains ownership of the underlying (IP, technological and/or human) assets related to the subject matter of the license. If the license is a "naked" license that includes no obligations on the part of the licensor (i.e., the JV), option (i) is acceptable. But if the license imposes any such obligations (e.g., support, updates, maintenance, further development, etc.), then choice (ii) is appropriate (and the licensee will so insist).

VI.   CONCLUSION

IP allocation represents one of the most important strategic assessments when considering a joint venture and should be addressed in the JV agreement itself at the time of formation. Preferably, the joint venturers are advised to avoid joint ownership of the developed IP in favor of one of the alternate IP allocation models presented in this paper or otherwise. In these alternative models, ownership of each distinct IP asset is granted to an individual party (e.g., joint venturer or the JV entity), with appropriate licenses to other parties as needed. It is also important to plan in advance for possible dissolution of the JV, so that ownership and rights to use the JV's IP assets are appropriately distributed among the former joint venturers.

NOTES & QUESTIONS

1. Many of the issues raised by these materials will be explored again in the context of mergers and acquisitions, which often involve the termination of

some business enterprise. Especially keep in mind the drafting and other contractual issues raised by these cases. As is often the case, a successful termination of a business enterprise rests on developing meaningful exit strategies.

2. The *Hapgood* case provides a colorful illustration of employment issues that affect the ownership of intellectual property. The Court may have been motivated by a desire to protect the employee inventor against the corporation in this case. Note the discussion of assignments and compare it with the discussions in the bankruptcy cases. Contractually the problem posed by the case could be addressed by including a term in the initial license or assignment that would make the patent fully assignable or transferable upon a change in corporate structuring, especially upon as simple an event as a corporate name change.

3. The *Pav-Saver* and *Southwest Whey* cases illustrate the problems of intellectual property ownership and allocation in joint ventures. The decisions in *Pav-Saver* demonstrate the importance of partnership agreement drafting in resolving disputes over intellectual property ownership in partnerships. Did the majority interpret the partnership agreement correctly? How could *Pav-Saver* have retained more effective control over its patents in the event of partnership termination? Note that the dissent bases its analysis on the provisions in the Uniform Partnership Act regarding the termination of partnerships. To what extent does the Uniform Partnership Act deal with the special ownership issues raised by intellectual property?

4. The *Southwest Whey* decision provides a review of trade secret law and may appear to say little about the law of business enterprises. Note that the court avoids the business questions by finding that there was no trade secret here. Is the court's analysis convincing? If there was a trade secret, how would you envision that that the business issues would have been resolved in light of *Pav-Saver* and the discussion in the Laurie reading?

5. The Laurie reading provides an overview of intellectual property issues in the context of joint ventures. Many of the issues addressed in this reading also arise in connection with transfers of intellectual property in mergers and acquisitions. These transfers are discussed in detail in Chapter 8.

CHAPTER 8

INTELLECTUAL PROPERTY ISSUES IN MERGERS AND ACQUISITIONS

PROBLEM

Dr. Y.L. See, Chief Executive Officer (CEO) of Digital Ignition Systems Corporation, has been approached by the CEO of Automated Rotary Systems, Incorporated (ARS) to discuss the possibility of a transaction to pool the two companies' efforts in developing and marketing engine parts for automobiles, motorboats, and small jets. Dr. See is interested in working with ARS because of the possibilities of expanding the market for Digital Ignition's products and obtaining access to proprietary software and customer lists owned by ARS. Dr. See is considering several possible arrangements. One is to organize a joint venture between the two companies for product development. Since this type of project raises significant antitrust concerns, Dr. See has deferred consideration of this arrangement until later (see Chapter 13). The second possibility is a merger of the two businesses to produce a bigger entity, perhaps still called Digital Ignition Systems Corporation, with the combined management and assets of the two businesses. The third possibility is a straight purchase by Digital Ignition Systems of the principal assets of ARS. Dr. See has asked you, his general counsel, to assess the relative merits of the last two possibilities. Specifically, he would like an analysis of the potential liabilities associated with each type of transaction and the benefits and costs of these alternative transactional structures.

FOCUS OF THE CHAPTER

A desire to capture intellectual property value often motivates executives to consider the merger of two companies or the acquisition of one company by another. If two companies utilize the same technology or engage in similar research and development projects, executives of the two companies may find it desirable to pool their assets in order to take advantage of synergies that may arise from complementary intellectual property. Alternatively, one company may acquire the intellectual property and operational capabilities of the other by buying all of its assets. Mergers or acquisitions undertaken to pool or transfer assets in these ways often raise complex corporate and securities law issues. When intellectual property is involved in such transactions, special attention must be paid to how intellectual property ownership and infringement liability questions will be resolved for the surviving entities.

In order to assist clients with these sorts of arrangements, transactional and intellectual property attorneys must understand not only the law of mergers and acquisitions, but also the way in which the arrangements should be structured. Attorneys' efforts in these contexts often focus on the drafting of key transactional documents, such as the merger agreement specifying the terms on which two companies will be combined. Successful drafting of these sorts of documents typically requires a deep understanding of the details of a business combination transaction, including the impact of the transaction on assets and rights associated with the affected companies' intellectual property portfolios. As with any complex legal transaction, due diligence is of central importance, and the well-trained attorney needs to be attentive to the details of what a company purports to own and how assets will be transferred. The final case in this chapter involving a multi-million dollar judgment against the Weyerhaeuser Company provides a harsh lesson about what can happen when attorneys fail to investigate or fail to disclose the details of an intellectual property portfolio.

The questions discussed in this chapter are fundamental. They pertain to issues of property ownership, liability risks, and contract rights, the basic building blocks of many legal transactions. While the factual contexts addressed in some of the materials are quite complex, by focusing your attention on these three types of issues you will be able to interpret and understand the complicated fact patterns. Pay special attention to how descriptions of the intellectual property and transactions at stake affect the results.

The materials in this chapter are divided into five parts. Part A provides a general overview of basic concepts and legal standards pertaining to mergers and the sale of corporate assets. This part focuses on the corporate law of Delaware (the most important state for business incorporations) as the source of examples of relevant legal standards. With this background, we turn to four types of issues that are frequently raised by intellectual property in mergers and acquisitions: (1) ownership; (2) liability; (3) transfer; and (4) due diligence.

Part B addresses issues of intellectual property ownership in mergers and acquisitions. The article by David Kennedy provides a helpful overview of the reallocation of intellectual property rights resulting from a merger or sale of assets. Kennedy also discusses the transfer of licensing rights in the context of a merger. The Kennedy reading is followed by three cases that illustrate the types of intellectual property ownership issues that can arise when a company transfers its assets to or merges with another company. The cases emphasize the importance of contract drafting in securing and clarifying the allocation of rights.

Part C addresses the following question: Once corporate property and activities are reallocated through a merger or other acquisition, does pre-existing liability for intellectual property infringement follow? The first case in this part discusses the concept of successor liability, a central doctrine for determining liability in the context of a merger or acquisition. The second case presents an application of the doctrine of successor liability in the context of a dispute involving trade secrets and other confidential data.

Part D presents a case that demonstrates the problems that can arise in drafting transfer documents in a merger or acquisition. The case illustrates the role of contractual remedies, particularly remedies for breaches of warranties.

Part E continues this discussion through a major decision involving the Weyerhaeuser Company's liability for breaches of warranties made in the transfer of intellectual property rights to its subsidiary. This final case offers a fairly deep discussion of the important intellectual property considerations surrounding a particular corporate acquisition transaction and a review of concepts from the chapters on bankruptcy and due diligence.

READINGS

A. SOME BASIC TERMINOLOGY

This section provides some general background on the two types of corporate transactions that are the subject of this chapter: mergers and acquisitions. Courses in mergers and acquisitions or advanced corporate law will provide greater depth on these topics. Our goal here is to familiarize you with the basic concepts so that you can understand the cases in this chapter and the intellectual property issues that arise in mergers and acquisitions.

A merger is a legal transaction joining together two corporate entities. The resulting combined entity bears the name of one of the original companies and is treated as a legal continuation of that company. In a second, related type of transaction called a consolidation, the combined entity is a new corporation, with a new name but many of the characteristics of the original corporations. Because of the frequent benefits of continuing the name and reputation of one of the combined entities, mergers are far more common than consolidations and the remainder of our discussions here will address mergers rather than consolidations. In general, the legal standards governing mergers and consolidations are the same, although you should note that the Delaware Corporations Code, as excerpted below, refers to mergers and consolidations separately.

In a merger, the corporation that continues to exist is called the acquiring or surviving company. The other concern is called the target or disappearing company.

For tax or regulatory reasons, a merger may take a more complicated form called a triangular merger. A triangular merger is so named because it involves three entities: an acquiring company, its subsidiary, and a target. The subsidiary is a company whose stock is owned at the outset of the merger by the acquiring company. One type of triangular merger is called a forward triangular merger. This type of merger involves the merger of the subsidiary into the target so that the subsidiary is the surviving company. You can envision the situation as follows:

The other type of triangular merger is called a reverse triangular merger. This type of merger involves the target merging into the subsidiary so the target is the surviving company. You can envision the situation as follows:

An acquiring company may adopt a triangular merger form in order to keep some distance between itself and the target company for tax or regulatory purposes. The choice between a reverse and forward triangular merger will depend in part on the characteristics of the subsidiary and target companies and whether it is legally advantageous to have one or the other be the surviving entity (for example, because one of the companies has already qualified for business licenses, but the licenses will only continue in force if that entity survives the merger and continues in existence). The choice between a reverse and forward triangular merger will also sometimes depend on tax considerations (such as different taxation standards applicable to the subsidiary and target companies in their respective states of incorporation) or corporate law considerations (such as differences in the state laws applicable to the subsidiary and target companies regarding how to properly structure shareholder voting and managerial decision making needed to approve a merger). Notice that in both a reverse and forward triangular merger the acquiring company stays the same except that as the result of the merger it owns stock in an entity that is a combination of the subsidiary and the target with the name of either the subsidiary or target depending upon whether the merger is undertaken in the reverse or forward format.

Procedures for mergers are governed primarily by state laws although, as you will see in the materials below, federal law — particularly federal securities law — can come into play. Delaware Corporations Code § 251, the major sections of which are reprinted below, provides an overview of the major steps that must be followed in completing a merger involving a Delaware corporation:

§ 251. Merger or consolidation of domestic corporations and limited liability company.

(a) Any 2 or more corporations existing under the laws of this State may merge into a single corporation, which may be any 1 of the constituent corporations or may consolidate into a new corporation formed by the consolidation, pursuant to an agreement of merger or consolidation, as the case may be, complying and approved in accordance with this section.

(b) The board of directors of each corporation which desires to merge or consolidate shall adopt a resolution approving an agreement of merger or consolidation and declaring its advisability. The agreement shall state: (1) The terms and conditions of the merger or consolidation; (2) the mode of carrying the same into effect; (3) in the case of a merger, such amendments or changes in the certificate of incorporation of the surviving corporation as are desired to be effected by the merger, or, if no such amendments or changes are desired, a statement that the certificate of incorporation of the surviving corporation shall be its certificate of incorporation; (4) in the case of a consolidation, that the certificate of incorporation of the resulting corporation shall be as is set forth in an attachment to the agreement; (5) the manner, if any, of converting the shares of each of the constituent corporations into shares or other securities of the corporation surviving or resulting from the merger or consolidation, or of canceling some or all of such shares, and, if any shares of any of the constituent corporations are not to remain outstanding, to be converted solely into shares or other securities of the surviving or resulting corporation or to be cancelled, the cash, property, rights or securities of any other corporation or entity which the holders of such shares are to receive in exchange for, or upon conversion of such shares and the surrender of any certificates evidencing them, which cash, property, rights or securities of any other corporation or entity may be in addition to or in lieu of shares or other securities of the surviving or resulting corporation; and (6) such other details or provisions as are deemed desirable, including, without limiting the generality of the foregoing, a provision for the payment of cash in lieu of the issuance or recognition of fractional shares, interests or rights, or for any other arrangement with respect thereto, ... Any of the terms of the agreement of merger or consolidation may be made dependent upon facts ascertainable outside of such agreement, provided that the manner in which such facts shall operate upon the terms of the agreement is clearly and expressly set forth in the agreement of merger or consolidation. The term "facts," as used in the preceding sentence, includes, but is not limited to, the occurrence of any event, including a determination or action by any person or body, including the corporation.

(c) The agreement required by subsection (b) of this section shall be submitted to the stockholders of each constituent corporation at an annual or special meeting for the purpose of acting on the agreement. Due notice of the time, place and purpose of the meeting shall be mailed to each holder of stock, whether voting or nonvoting, of the corporation at the stockholder's address as it appears on the records of the corporation, at least 20 days prior to the date of the meeting. The notice shall contain a copy of the agreement or a brief summary thereof, as the directors shall deem advisable. At the meeting, the agreement shall be considered and a vote taken for its adoption or rejection. If a majority of the outstanding stock of the corporation entitled to vote thereon shall be voted for the adoption of the agreement, that fact shall be certified on the agreement by the secretary or assistant secretary of the corporation. If the agreement shall be so adopted and certified by each constituent corporation, it shall then be filed and shall become effective, . . . In lieu of filing the agreement of merger or consolidation required by this section, the surviving or resulting corporation may file a certificate of merger or consolidation, . . . which states:

(1) The name and state of incorporation of each of the constituent corporations;

(2) That an agreement of merger or consolidation has been approved, adopted, certified, executed and acknowledged by each of the constituent corporations in accordance with this section;

(3) The name of the surviving or resulting corporation;

(4) In the case of a merger, such amendments or changes in the certificate of incorporation of the surviving corporation as are desired to be effected by the merger, or, if no such amendments or changes are desired, a statement that the certificate of incorporation of the surviving corporation shall be its certificate of incorporation;

(5) In the case of a consolidation, that the certificate of incorporation of the resulting corporation shall be as set forth in an attachment to the certificate;

(6) That the executed agreement of consolidation or merger is on file at an office of the surviving corporation, stating the address thereof; and

(7) That a copy of the agreement of consolidation or merger will be furnished by the surviving corporation, on request and without cost, to any stockholder of any constituent corporation.

Many of the rights and responsibilities of the companies involved in a merger will be determined by the merger agreement between the companies. This agreement will often address the ownership of intellectual property and other assets as well as liabilities of the companies with respect to intellectual property and other property rights.

The second type of corporate transaction we will focus on in this section is the acquisition of all or substantially all of the assets of a corporation. In many ways, this should be a more familiar transaction. An acquisition of this type entails one company, the acquirer, purchasing a substantial share of the assets of another company, the target. The acquisition is structured through an asset purchase contract, but is also subject to corporate law limitations. The Delaware Corporations Code contains the following provision regarding these sorts of corporate asset acquisitions:

§ 271. Sale, lease or exchange of assets; consideration; procedure.

(a) Every corporation may at any meeting of its board of directors or governing body sell, lease or exchange all or substantially all of its property and assets, including its goodwill and its corporate franchises, upon such terms and conditions and for such consideration, which may consist in whole or in part of money or other property, including shares of stock in, and/or other securities of, any other corporation or corporations, as its board of directors or governing body deems expedient and for the best interests of the corporation, when and as authorized by a resolution adopted by the holders of a majority of the outstanding stock of the corporation entitled to vote thereon or, if the corporation is a nonstock corporation, by a majority of the members having the right to vote for the election of the members of the governing body, at a meeting duly called upon at least 20 days' notice. The notice of the meeting shall state that such a resolution will be considered.

(b) Notwithstanding authorization or consent to a proposed sale, lease or exchange of a corporation's property and assets by the stockholders or members, the board of directors or governing body may abandon such proposed sale, lease or exchange without further action by the stockholders or members, subject to the rights, if any, of third parties under any contract relating thereto.

Sometimes a target company may dissolve after selling substantially all of its assets to an acquirer. In such a situation, the result may look much like a merger since the target company is gone and the acquirer has assumed the assets of the target. Because of the similarity between the two transactions, the acquisition of the target followed by its dissolution is sometimes referred to as a de facto merger and subjected to the requirements applicable to a merger. Although the doctrine is somewhat out of favor, particularly in Delaware, the concept is important to be aware of and arises in some of the materials below.

Intellectual property poses several special problems for both mergers and acquisitions. We will focus on four questions:

(1) Who owns intellectual property after a merger or acquisition?

(2) Who is liable for intellectual property infringement after a merger or acquisition?

(3) How is intellectual property transferred in a merger or acquisition?

(4) How is the transfer of intellectual property made effective through due diligence in a merger or acquisition?

We will consider materials addressing each of these questions

B. OWNERSHIP ISSUES

David H. Kennedy, Intellectual Property Issues Arising Out of Acquisitions
Practicing Law Institute, Patents, Copyrights, Trademarks, and Literary Property Course Handbook Series
PLI. No. 6056 (March-May 2005)*

I. ALLOCATION OF IP RIGHTS IN CONNECTION WITH SALE OF BUSINESS UNIT

A.   Summary Comparison of Ownership vs. License Rights

1.   Sole Ownership

Sole ownership of IP has the following elements:

- Unfettered discretion to use, distribute to third parties and commercially exploit the IP in any m anner (including through sublicensing and assignment);

- Permanent, non-terminable rights; and

- Ability to solely control the enforcement of rights against infringing or misappropriating third parties.

2. Joint Ownership

Subject to any applicable agreement of the joint owners, a party that jointly owns IP rights generally will have the same rights as apply in the context of sole ownership, except as follows:

- A single joint owner will not have the power to grant exclusive licenses to third parties without the agreement of the other joint owner (nor will a joint owner be able to assign outright the entirety of the IP rights in question);

- The joint owners usually will agree as to whether and to what extent each has any obligation to account to the other for profits realized from the exploitation of the jointly-owned IP (depending on the nature of the IP, joint owners may or may not have an obligation to account to each other);

- The ability of a joint owner to enforce the IP rights against infringing third parties may be constrained depending on the applicable arrangements agreed to by the joint owners (problems may arise if the joint owners disagree regarding the manner in which an action is prosecuted against a third party infringer or whether an action should be brought against a given suspected infringer); and

- The protection and maintenance of jointly-owned IP is more complex because arrangements must be agreed by the joint owners with respect to (i) whether a patent should be sought for a particular invention (or whether trade secret protection should be relied on instead), and (ii) allocation of responsibility for prosecution of patent applications and for payment of fees and the other administrative activities required to maintain in effect patents and other "registered" intellectual property.

3. Exclusive License

An exclusive license to IP rights includes the following elements (in contrast to ownership rights):

- Rights that are exercisable are only those specifically granted (which may be limited in nature);

- In the case of an exclusive license within a defined field of use of the IP rights in question, an exclusive license would be tantamount to sole ownership in the field of use as to which the exclusivity is applicable, except to the extent that the license would be terminable or there would be limitations imposed on sublicensing or assignment;

- Exclusive licensees can be given the right to enforce the licensed IP rights against third party infringers in the field of use to which the exclusivity applies (although for standing reasons, the exclusive licensee may be required to join the IP owner as a party to any enforcement action);

- In contrast to ownership, an exclusive (or non-exclusive) license usually is terminable (for breach or other specified reasons) or expires at the end of a specified license term;

- An exclusive license (again, in contrast to the rights inherent in ownership) may not be freely assignable or sublicensable; and

- Exclusive licensees usually have no role in determining how to protect IP (patent vs. trade secret), in prosecuting patent applications that are included in the licensed IP and in many cases the licensor will not be willing to covenant to maintain in effect licensed patents or other "registered" IP, although it would not be unusual in this context for an exclusive licensee to be given the right, at its option and expense, to maintain in force patents or to continue the prosecution of patent applications that the licensor determines to abandon.

4. Non-Exclusive License

A non-exclusive license generally has the same elements as an exclusive license (other than the licensed rights are not exclusively licensed) subject to the following:

- A non-exclusive licensee has no right to enforce the licensed rights against suspected third party infringers;

- A licensor generally will have no obligation to enforce the licensed IP against third parties (in some cases, however, a non-exclusive licensee is entitled to an adjustment in the royalty rate if the licensor fails to bring, at the licensee's request, an enforcement action against unlicensed competitor of the licensee);

- A non-exclusive licensee generally has no role in the prosecution of pending patent applications or the maintenance in force of licensed patents; and

- A non-exclusive patent and copyright licensee that enters bankruptcy proceedings may not be able to retain its rights (without the agreement of the licensor) even in the context of a successful reorganization.

B. Allocation of Ownership of Seller IP in a Sale of a Business Unit

The allocation rule that applies to the Seller's intellectual property to be transferred to the Buyer will be the same rule that applies to the other assets to be transferred in the transaction.

The most often applied rule for determining what assets are to be included in the sale of a division or other business unit of a Seller is one based on whether the intellectual property or other asset of the Seller "primarily relates to the Business" or is "used primarily in connection with the Business", with the term "Business" being defined to consist of the business unit of Seller that is being purchased by the Buyer (oftentimes with express reference to the principal products of the business unit in question).

Infrequently, the ownership allocation test may be based on whether an asset is "used exclusively in connection with the Business" or is "used in connection with Business" (in each case, subject to specific exceptions).

Regardless of the ownership allocation rule that is utilized, patents and patent applications are usually reviewed on a patent-by-patent basis with a view to the Seller and Buyer agreeing on a specific list of which patents are to be transferred to the Buyer (which the parties may or may not agree is exhaustive).

It usually will not be practicable to specifically identify the trade secrets and copyrights to be transferred and, therefore, the general allocation rules are used to specify what trade secrets and copyrights are to be transferred, although the parties may seek to describe the trade secrets and copyrights through high level descriptions (difficulties in identifying and segregating trade secrets and copyrights may make the parties more inclined to agree to joint ownership or for one side or the other to settle for broad license rights instead of ownership).

Third party license agreements generally need to be reviewed on a case-by-case basis to determine whether the licensed third party technology is used principally in the Business purchased by the Buyer or the businesses retained by the Seller.

- Generally there will be no ability to transfer third party technology by sublicense to the Buyer (with the Seller retaining rights as a licensee) or for the underlying agreement to be assigned subject to the Seller retaining rights in the third party technology on a sublicensing basis (thus, in the case of third party technology that is used by both the transferred Business and the retained businesses, one side or the other will need to assume the cost of obtaining replacement licenses from the respective third party licensors).

- Consent to assign to the Buyer any third party license agreements usually will be required.

[T]he "Business" [for purposes of these provisions] is usually defined to be the business in question, as conducted by the Seller as of the Closing Date.

- The definition may or may not expressly refer to predecessor operations and discontinued operations of such businesses and operations.

- The definition may also expressly refer to products in development to make explicit that the concept of taking a "snapshot" of the business at the Closing does not operate to limit the business to the shipping products to the exclusion of products in development.

The concept of primarily relating to the Business usually is not fleshed out with further definition or otherwise given further content. Application of this test to a particular intellectual property asset could be considered to include the following factors:

- Does the intellectual property asset in question cover or protect any products of the Business (and, conversely, does it cover or protect any products of the businesses being retained by the Seller) or is it otherwise actively used in connection with the Business as well as the businesses being retained by the Seller?

- What are the respective revenues of the Business and of the Seller's retained businesses from products that are covered or protected by the intellectual property asset and how significant are these revenues in relation to the Seller's and Buyer's respective total revenues?

- Was the inventor or developer of the intellectual property asset employed by the Business at the time the intellectual property asset was created or developed (or, if multiple inventors or developers were involved, which side of the business employed a majority of the inventors/developers)?

- Which business unit actually funded the development of the intellectual property asset in question?

- What is the overall size of the market for products sold by the retained business of the Seller that are covered or protected by the intellectual property asset relative to the overall size of the market for products sold by the Business that are covered or protected by the intellectual property asset?

C. Selected Discussion Issues for License Agreements Relating to Sale of Business Unit

Scope of Licenses. The initial issue to be addressed is the scope of the license rights to be granted by the Seller to the Buyer and from the Buyer to the Seller.

- Internal Use Rights. As to some technology, the rights licensed by one side or the other may be limited to a license for internal use purposes only

- Distribution Rights. Usually the licenses that are negotiated in this context include distribution or other commercial exploitation rights.

  - If distribution rights are granted and the products in question are software, the respective agreements should specify whether the licensee party is authorized to provide only object code to its customers.

  - If software products are involved, it may be necessary for the licensee party to be granted the right to establish customary source code escrows and to license API's in connection with licensing software that will be integrated in an OEM's product (and, depending on the licensee party's business model, broader source code licensing rights may be required).

- Sublicenses. The extent of each party's sublicensing rights should be clearly specified.

  - If software is involved, the licensee party will require sublicensing rights to the extent necessary to distribute its products to its customers.

  - It would not be unusual for consultants and other independent contractors who are working on development with the licensee party to be permitted to have access to and use the licensed IP and for the licensee party to be permitted to sublicense wholly owned subsidiaries (and sometimes majority-owned subsidiaries).

- The licensee party also might require broad sublicensing rights in connection with technology partnering arrangements and joint ventures or in connection with the co-development of a joint or bundled product.

- Sublicensing rights are more problematic in the case of patent licenses: "naked" patent sublicensing often is not permitted.

- In the case of patent rights, the licensor party often will desire to include "anti-foundry" or "anti-patent laundering" provisions in an non-exclusive license to prevent an infringer of the licensor party's patents from seeking to avoid infringement by having the licensee party make or sublicense products for or to the infringing third party.

Extent of Exclusive Rights. Will the license under the retained IP granted by Seller to Buyer (the "Seller License") or the license granted back by Buyer to Seller under the purchased IP (the "Buyer License") be exclusive (in a specified field) or non-exclusive?

- It is not unusual for the seller of a division or other business unit who is retaining IP that is used in the retained businesses to grant an exclusive license within the field of use applicable to the transferred business, which may be supplemented with a general non-compete covenant by the Seller for a duration that typically runs between three and five years.

    - If the Seller License is non-exclusive in all respects, the Seller would be permitted to exercise or authorize others to exercise the right to utilize the retained IP to make, sell, etc., products the are the same or similar to the products sold by the transferred business.

    - Sometimes, given the similarity of the Seller's retained business and the Business being sold to the Buyer and/or the overlapping of target markets of the Seller and Buyer, it is very difficult to define a field in which the Seller is willing to give exclusive rights to the Buyer under the Seller's retained IP.

- If the Seller License is to be exclusive, it would not be unusual for the Buyer License to be exclusive as well in the field(s) of the Seller's retained businesses.

Improvements: New Developments.

- Ownership. Usually agreements in this context provide that the Buyer will own any improvements it makes to the technology licensed to it under the Seller License and Seller will own any improvements made by Seller with regard to the technology licensed to it under the Buyer License (and of course the developing party would own any new developments it might create).

    - Sometimes agreements in this context provide that the owner of the underlying technology on which the improvement is based will own all improvements to such technology, whether made by the Buyer or the Seller (note that such provisions may raise concerns under antitrust laws).

- Inclusion in License Grant. The transaction could provide either for (i) no disclosure to the other party of improvements by the party making the improvement or (ii) disclosure to the other party of material improvements at reasonable periodic intervals by the party making the improvement.

    - The rule could be different depending on whether the improvement is made by a licensor or a licensee (e.g., a license agreement could provide for disclosure to the licensor of improvements made by the licensee but not any disclosure by the licensor of improvements made by it).

    - The license agreement could provide for no obligation to disclose any improvements, but still provide for a license of improvements so that: (i) if there is any voluntary disclosure by one side to the other, the other automatically is licensed to use the disclosed improvement within its field to use or (ii), in the case of patentable improvements, one side would not be able fence in the other with new patents that block off independent developments by the other side.

    - In some contexts, a Buyer and a Seller may negotiate broad patent cross licenses or covenants not to sue that apply to all new developments (and not just improvements) to ensure that neither side is in a position to acquire and enforce patents against the other.

- Sometimes this license or covenant not to sue is limited to patents that would be infringed by the existing products or services of the other party that are shipping or being provided at the time of closing; in other cases, the license or covenant not to sue may be extended to cover enhancements, new versions or successor products or services developed after the sale closing date sometimes being (this is intended to give comfort to each side that it would be free of interference from the other side with respect to its existing products, as enhanced, for a specified "breathing period").

- Such licenses or covenants not to sue may be further limited by excluding any new products or services with substantial additional functionality or features (this is intended to ensure that potentially valuable new developments covered by a Seller's retained IP that have application to existing products and services of the business being sold are not incorporated into the products or services by the Buyer after the Closing without appropriate compensation being given to the Seller).

Termination; Irrevocability. Should the Seller License and Buyer License be terminable for breach or upon the occurrence of specified events?

- Where there are no ongoing payment obligations, the parties may prefer to provide for perpetual and irrevocable licenses (if the Buyer is a new company that is obtaining funding in connection with the purchase of the business from the Seller, any right of the Seller to terminate the license granted to Buyer may be problematic).

- Where one side or the other is very concerned about the possibility of the other party exercising rights beyond the scope of the license grant, a termination for breach may be desired (with a covenant included to the effect that the licensee party will not exercise rights outside the scope of the license).

- Some licensors insist on retaining the right to terminate by reason of a breach of a confidentiality covenant or the transfer of the license agreement by the licensee in violation of any applicable limitations on transfer such as an attempt to transfer the license to a competitor of the licensing party.

Assignability. Generally licenses will be non-transferable without the prior written consent of the licensing party. In some cases, a significant amount of negotiations take place as to whether the licensee party is permitted to transfer the license in connection with the sale of all or substantially all of its business, whether by stock purchase, merger or asset purchase.

- The licensor party may be concerned about a competitor acquiring the other party and thereby gaining access to the license granted by the licensor and also may be concerned about a party with whom it is engaged, or is about to be engaged, in IP or other litigation acquiring the licensee party to gain the benefit of the license.

    - The licensor party might agree to allow the transfer of the license in connection with the sale of the licensee party's business subject to the prior written consent of the licensor party, which the licensor party might agree not to unreasonably delay or withhold (and the licensee party perhaps acknowledging that the withholding of consent by the licensor party shall be deemed to be reasonable if the proposed assignee is a competitor of the licensor party).

    - Alternatively, the agreement might prohibit assignment in connection with the sale of the business if the proposed assignee is a competitor of the licensor party. The definition of competitor of the licensor party could be based on a list of competitors attached at the time of signing, together with any successor or affiliate thereof. The licensor party will desire to have future competitors included as well, either automatically (with the licensing party having a duty to check with licensor to find out who the then relevant competitors are for this purpose or the licensor party instead having the right to update the list of competitors from time to time in its reasonable discretion).

- The licensor party also may be troubled with the notion of a broad field of use patent license being transferable to a large company that acquires the licensee party without any additional consideration being payable to the licensor party.

- The acquiror could, e.g., be a company with products that infringe the licensor party's patents and that is engaged in cross-licensing negotiations or litigation with the licensor party; in this case, the ability of the infringing third party to acquire the licensee party and thereby acquire the shelter of the licensee party's license could dramatically affect the "balance of power" between the licensor party and the infringing third party.

- In order to limit the value available to an infringing third party that seeks to acquire a broad field of use license from the licensee party, in some contexts the license granted to the licensee party is "frozen" in connection with the sale of the licensee party's business (including in connection with a change of control by stock purchase or merger) so that the licensed rights thereafter can only be utilized with respect to any then commercially launched products but not for any new or significantly improved products.

Enforcement of IP. If an exclusive license is provided for, it would not be unusual for the exclusive licensee to be granted the right to enforce the licensed IP against infringers in the field of use of the exclusive license, with any recoveries in such field of use being retained by the exclusive licensee.

- The licensee party may not have standing to sue third party infringers of the licensed IP and it would be customary to include provisions obligating the licensor party, at the licensee party's request and expense, to become a named party in any enforcement action and otherwise to cooperate with licensee party in taking enforcement action against infringers that licensee party requests.

- In a purely non-exclusive license context, it generally is not workable for there to be any arrangements by which the licensed IP can be enforced against the licensee party's competitors for the benefit of the licensee party (this whole notion is contrary to the concept of a non-exclusive license).

- In unusual cases (such as a spinoff of a subsidiary), the licensor may agree to "rent" a patent to the licensee party for use as a defensive weapon in infringement litigation commenced against the licensee party by one of its competitors.

- In some cases, a non-exclusive licensee may be given the right to request the licensor party to bring infringement actions against non-licensed competitors, but licensors generally insist in the context of a non-exclusive license that they be given absolute discretion with regard to the conduct of enforcement actions.

Maintenance of Patents/Assignment of Rights upon Abandonment. Agreements in this context sometimes may provide for any obligation on the part of the respective licensor either to continue to prosecute diligently any patent applications included in the licensed IP or to maintain in force any licensed patents, but in many cases licensors retain absolute discretion in this regard.

- Where there is no covenant on the part of the licensor party to continue to prosecute diligently any patent applications included in the licensed IP or to maintain in force any licensed patents, the licensee party may desire to include an obligation on the part of the licensor party to notify the licensee party if maintenance fees are not going to be paid and a patent is going to be abandoned or if prosecution of a pending patent application is going to be abandoned.

- Where the licensor party has the obligation to give notice to the licensee of any such abandonment, the licensee party, at its election and at its cost, may be given the rights to step in and continue the prosecution process or to pay any maintenance fees owing, in either case with the licensing party assigning ownership to the other party subject to an irrevocable non-exclusive license in favor of the abandoning party in the relevant field of use.

II. LICENSES AND MERGERS

As the creation and commercialization of intellectual property has come to play an increasingly important role in the modern economy, intellectual property considerations have moved from peripheral to central in determining the structures of business transactions. Multi-billion dollar companies more and more frequently have their origins in a set of ideas, and the entire life cycles of world-leading enterprises are governed by the legal relationships created between inventors, investors, producers and consumers of intellectual property.

Lawyers who assume the responsibility for advising participants in an economy driven by advances in the creation of intellectual property need to have a broad perspective on how the structure of transactions entered into at various stages of the capitalization and commercialization of intellectual property will impact the future value of the property. For example, the form of a security interest granted to an early-stage lender may have important ramifications in an emerging company's ability to secure future financing or to be sold. The failure to make provision for the occurrence of certain future events, such as a merger or bankruptcy by or of one of the parties, may result in lost opportunities or crippling litigation. Similarly, decisions made in structuring merger or workout transactions will impact the ability of companies acquiring intellectual property assets to exploit those assets through future financing or licensing transactions.

The following contains a discussion of structural issues arising at the confluence of the laws governing licensing and merger transactions and bankruptcy.

Although mergers and bankruptcies are often considered by creators and licensors of intellectual property as eventualities so remote that they needn't be given serious consideration during the negotiation of license agreements or other intellectual property transactions, attorneys advising such clients should give full consideration to merger and bankruptcy issues and not merely adopt boilerplate contractual provisions that may or may not protect their clients' interests. While there continues to be some uncertainty in the governing law, the structure of a license agreement may determine whether or not the license will survive a merger or bankruptcy event.

As the Ninth Circuit Court of Appeals recognized in *Linney v. Cellular Alaska Partnership*, 151 F.3d 1234, 1241 (9th Cir. 1998), "the legal status of a merger under an anti-assignment clause is 'less than clear'" (citing *Star Cellular Telephone Company, Inc. v. Baton Rouge CGSA, Inc.*, 1993 Del. Ch. LEXIS 158 (July 30, 1993), *aff'd* 1994 Del. LEXIS 190 (1994). Because of this uncertainty in the underlying law, the parties to a license agreement are well advised to include provisions specifically addressing the issue of future mergers, in addition to general provisions prohibiting or permitting assignment of the license.

Merger transactions are generally governed by state corporate law. The assignment of copyright licenses and transfer of copyright ownership, however, is governed by federal law, which preempts conflicting state law. *See Everex Sys., Inc. v. Cadtrak Corp. (In re CFLC, Inc.)*, 89 F.3d 673, 677-680 (9th Cir. 1996); *Mai Systems Corp. v. Peak Computer, Inc.*, 991 F.2d 511, 518-519 (9th Cir. 1993); *DSC Communications Corp. v. Pulse Communications, Inc.*, 170 F.3d 1354, 1360-1362 (Fed. Cir. 1999). "The enforcement of a copyright license raises issues that lie at the intersection of copyright and contract law, an area of law that is not yet well developed." *Sun Microsystems, Inc. v. Microsoft Corp.*, 188 F.3d 1115, 1122 (9th Cir. 1999). The rules of contract construction embodied in state law control the interpretation of license agreements, "provided that such rules do not interfere with federal copyright law and policy." (*Id.* quoting *S.O.S., Inc. v. Payday, Inc.*, 886 F.2d 1081, 1088 (9th Cir. 1989).

Although the Ninth Circuit has recognized the uncertainty in the law in its *Linney* decision, 151 F.3d at 1241, and has also noted the conflicting policy goals of state laws and policies favoring the transferability of property and federal patent and copyright laws and policies favoring retention of control over their intellectual property by inventors and authors, *see, e.g., Everex*, 89 F.3d at 677-80; *Cohen*, 845 F.2d at 853, there is at present no clearly controlling authority which establishes whether a merger transaction, and in particular the widely used reverse triangular merger structure, results in a transfer by the acquired company of its rights under license agreements. Although the U.S. District Court for the Northern District of California, in the case of *SQL Solutions, Inc. v. Oracle Corp.*, 1991 U.S. Dist. LEXIS 21097 (N.D. Cal. Dec. 18, 1991), expressly held that under California law a transfer of rights occurred as a result of a reverse triangular merger through which SQL became a wholly owned subsidiary of Sybase, the opinion is of questionable precedential value. It may have been reversible error for the court to fail to expressly consider the relevant merger statute, and other aspects of the court's analysis may fairly be criticized as lacking a sound basis.

The SQL Solutions opinion has not been affirmed or cited by any appellate court, and has only been cited (in passing and not for its primary holding) by two lower courts during the twelve years since its issuance. Moreover, in a comprehensive and persuasive opinion that was affirmed by the Delaware Supreme Court and cited by the Ninth Circuit in *Linney*, the Delaware Court of Chancery in *Star Cellular Telephone Company, Inc. v. Baton Rouge CGSA, Inc.*, 1993 Del. Ch. LEXIS 158 (July 30, 1993), *aff'd* 1994 Del. LEXIS 190

(1994), concluded that a change of control in a merger transaction would not be deemed to result in a transfer of a federally-issued cellular telephone license. Other courts have also reached or suggested the conclusion that no legally significant transfer of property rights occurs as a result of a reverse triangular merger. *See, e.g., TXO Production Co. and Marathon Oil Co. v. M.D. Mark, Inc.*, 999 S.W. 2d 137 (Tex. App. 14th Dist. 1999) (in merger of a subsidiary into a parent, Texas Court of Appeals found that no prohibited transfer occurred under Texas merger statute); *International Paper Company v. Ernest Broadhead*, 662 So. 2d 277 (Ala. Civ. App. 1995) (finding that a merger did not constitute a transfer or assignment).

Delaware Corporations Code Section 259 provides that all property rights of constituent corporations "shall be vested" in the corporate entity surviving or resulting from the merger, and there is ample case law establishing that in general, the property rights of the constituent corporations continue to reside in the surviving corporation after a merger. *See, e.g., Texaco Ref. & Mktg., Inc. v. Delaware River Basin Comm'n*, 824 F.Supp. 500 (D. Del. 1993), aff'd 30 F.3d 1488 (3d Cir. 1994). Similarly, California Corporations Code Section 1107 provides that "[u]pon merger pursuant to this chapter, the separate existence of the disappearing corporations ceases and the surviving corporation shall succeed, without other transfer, to all the rights and property of each of the disappearing corporations and shall be subject to all the debts and liabilities of each in the same manner as if the surviving corporation had itself incurred them." Courts applying Section 1107 and its predecessors have found that property rights arising under state law, e.g. rights pertaining to real property, are generally not affected by merger transactions and continue to reside with the corporate entity surviving the transaction. *See, e.g., Treadaway v. Camellia Convalescent Hospitals, Inc.*, 43 Cal. App. 3d 189 (1974).

A licensee, however, cannot assign a non-exclusive copyright license without the express authorization of the licensor. *Everex*, 89 F.3d at 677-80; *Harris v. Emus Records Corp.*, 734 F.2d 1329, 1333-1335 (9th Cir. 1984). *See also S.O.S.*, 886 F.2d at 1088 (under federal copyright policy, "copyright licenses are assumed to prohibit any use not authorized"); *Cohen v. Paramount Pictures Corp.*, 845 F.2d 851, 853 (9th Cir. 1988) (licenses must be analyzed to determine what use they affirmatively permit); 17 U.S.C. § 204(a) (transfer of copyright ownership must be in writing). Although the "first sale doctrine" permits the owner of a copy of a copyrighted computer program to sell or otherwise transfer ownership of that copy without the authority of the copyright owner, the conditions under which a possessor of a copy of a copyrighted program will be deemed an "owner" for purposes of the first sale doctrine are strictly limited. *See Adobe Systems, Inc. v. One Stop Micro, Inc.*, 84 F.Supp.2d 1086, 1089-1092 (N.D. Cal. 2000); *DSC Communications*, 170 F.3d at 1360-1362; *Mai Systems*, 991 F.2d at 518-519.

Other than *SQL Solutions*, there does not appear to be any case which squarely addresses the issue of whether an expressly non-assignable copyright license will survive a reverse triangular merger transaction. The *SQL Solutions* opinion cites two principal cases as the grounds for its conclusion that "[m]ore fully reasoned cases have held that a transfer of rights is no less a transfer because it occurs by operation of law in a merger." 1991 WL 626458 at * 4. The court characterized the two cases as follows:

> *Koppers Coal & Transportation Co. v. U.S.*, 107 F.2d 706, 708 (3d Cir. 1939) (interpreting the Delaware merger statute and criticizing as "metaphysical" the notion, based on the theory of corporate continuity, that no transfer occurs); *PPG Industries, Inc. v. Guardian Industries Corp.*, 597 F.2d 1090, 1096 (6th Cir. 1979), cert. denied 444 U.S. 930 (1979) (interpreting the Ohio merger statute).

There are a number of reasons why the *SQL Solutions* court's conclusion regarding transfers by operation of law is questionable.

First, the court may have erred by failing to expressly take into consideration the provisions of California Corporations Code Section 1107. *See U.S. v. Oil Resources, Inc.*, 817 F.2d 1429, 1432 (9th Cir. 1987) (remanding for further proceedings because district court erred by failing to consider applicable statutes in finding shareholders personally liable for corporate taxes under "trust fund" theory articulated in *Trubowitch*, 30 Cal.2d at 345). Second, the 1939 *Koppers Coal & Transportation* decision (which is also the primary authority relied upon by the 6th Circuit in its 1979 *PPG Industries* decision) does not appear to be a reliable source for ascertaining the present state of Delaware law regarding the issue of whether a transfer occurring by operation of law in a merger is distinguishable from a sale, gift or other active transfer of property.

In *Star Cellular Telephone Company*, it was held that a contractual prohibition against assignments did not prohibit a transfer of a federally-issued cellular telephone license which occurred by operation of law in a merger. Although a complete discussion of the basis for the *Star Cellular* holding is beyond the scope of this discussion, the court attempted to ascertain the intent of the parties at the time they entered into the agreement as to whether the licensed rights would be prohibited from surviving a merger transaction. The court first examined the provisions of the contract addressing transferability, then the other recitals and provisions of the contract, then extrinsic evidence. Finding it impossible to determine the parties' actual intent, the Court attempted to determine the parties' likely intent by lastly resorting to an interpretation of the transferability provisions "grounded on principles fundamental to the law of assignments."

PPG INDUSTRIES, INC. v. GUARDIAN INDUSTRIES CORP.
Court of Appeals for the Sixth Circuit
597 F.2d 1090 (1979)

LIVELY, Circuit Judge.

The question in this case is whether the surviving or resultant corporation in a statutory merger acquires patent license rights of the constituent corporations. The plaintiff, PPG Industries, Inc. (PPG), appeals from a judgment of the district court dismissing its patent infringement action on the ground that the defendant, Guardian Industries, Corp. (Guardian), as licensee of the patents in suit, was not an infringer. Guardian cross-appeals from a holding by the district court that its alternate defense based on an equipment license agreement was ineffective.

I

Prior to 1964 both PPG and Permaglass, Inc., were engaged in fabrication of glass products which required that sheets of glass be shaped for particular uses. Independently of each other the two fabricators developed similar processes which involved "floating glass on a bed of gas, while it was being heated and bent." This process is known in the industry as "gas hearth technology" and "air float technology"; the two terms are interchangeable. After a period of negotiations PPG and Permaglass entered into an agreement on January 1, 1964 whereby each granted rights to the other under "gas hearth system" patents already issued and in the process of prosecution. The purpose of the agreement was set forth in the preamble as follows:

> WHEREAS, PPG is desirous of acquiring from PERMAGLASS a world-wide exclusive license with right to sublicense others under PERMAGLASS Technical Data and PERMAGLASS Patent Rights, subject only to reservation by PERMAGLASS of non-exclusive rights thereunder; and
> WHEREAS, PERMAGLASS is desirous of obtaining a nonexclusive license to use Gas Hearth Systems under PPG Patent Rights, excepting in the Dominion of Canada.

This purpose was accomplished in the two sections of the agreement quoted below:

SECTION 3. GRANT FROM PERMAGLASS TO PPG

3.1 Subject to the reservation set forth in Subsection 3.3 below, PERMAGLASS hereby grants to PPG an exclusive license, with right of sublicense, to use PERMAGLASS Technical Data in Gas Hearth Systems throughout the United States of America, its territories and possessions, and all countries of the world foreign thereto.

3.2 Subject to the reservation set forth in Subsection 3.3 below, PERMAGLASS hereby grants to PPG an unlimited exclusive license, with right of sublicense, under PERMAGLASS Patent Rights.

3.3 The licenses granted to PPG under Subsections 3.1 and 3.2 above shall be subject to the reservation of a non-exclusive, non-transferable, royalty-free, world-wide right and license for the benefit and use of PERMAGLASS.

SECTION 4. GRANT FROM PPG TO PERMAGLASS

4.1 PPG hereby grants to PERMAGLASS a non-exclusive, non-transferable, royalty-free right and license to heat, bend, thermally temper and/or anneal glass using Gas Hearth Systems under PPG Patent Rights, excepting in the Dominion of Canada, and to use or sell glass articles produced thereby, but no license, express or implied, is hereby granted to PERMAGLASS under any claim of any PPG patent expressly covering any coating method, coating composition, or coated article.

Assignability of the agreement and of the license granted to Permaglass and termination of the license granted to Permaglass were covered in the following language:

SECTION 9. ASSIGNABILITY

9.1 This Agreement shall be assignable by PPG to any successor of the entire flat glass business of PPG but shall otherwise be non-assignable except with the consent of PERMAGLASS first obtained in writing.

9.2 This Agreement and the license granted by PPG to PERMAGLASS hereunder shall be personal to PERMAGLASS and non-assignable except with the consent of PPG first obtained in writing.

SECTION 11. TERMINATION

11.2 In the event that a majority of the voting stock of PERMAGLASS shall at any time become owned or controlled directly or indirectly by a manufacturer of automobiles or a manufacturer or fabricator of glass other than the present owners, the license granted to PERMAGLASS under Subsection 4.1 shall terminate forthwith.

Eleven patents are involved in this suit. Nine of them originated with Permaglass and were licensed to PPG as exclusive licensee under Section 3.2, Supra, subject to the non-exclusive, non-transferable reservation to Permaglass set forth in Section 3.3. Two of the patents originated with PPG. Section 4.1 granted a non-exclusive, non-transferable license to Permaglass with respect to the two PPG patents. In Section 9.1 and 9.2 assignability was treated somewhat differently as between the parties, and the Section 11.2 provisions with regard to termination apply only to the license granted to Permaglass.

As of December 1969 Permaglass was merged into Guardian pursuant to applicable statutes of Ohio and Delaware. Guardian was engaged primarily in the business of fabricating and distributing windshields for automobiles and trucks. It had decided to construct a facility to manufacture raw glass and the capacity of that facility would be greater than its own requirements. Permaglass had no glass manufacturing capability and it was contemplated that its operations would utilize a large part of the excess output of the proposed Guardian facility.

The "Agreement of Merger" between Permaglass and Guardian did not refer specifically to the 1964 agreement between PPG and Permaglass. However, among Permaglass' representations in the agreement was the following:

(g) Permaglass is the owner, assignee or licensee of such patents, trademarks, trade names and copyrights as are listed and described in Exhibit "C" attached hereto. None of such patents, trademarks, trade names or copyrights is in litigation and Permaglass has not received any notice of conflict with the asserted rights of third parties relative to the use thereof.

Listed on Exhibit "C" to the merger agreement are the nine patents originally developed by Permaglass and licensed to PPG under the 1964 agreement which are involved in this infringement action.

Shortly after the merger was consummated PPG filed the present action, claiming infringement by Guardian in the use of apparatus and processes described and claimed in eleven patents which were identified by number and origin. The eleven patents were covered by the terms of the 1964 agreement. PPG asserted that it became the exclusive licensee of the nine patents which originated with Permaglass under the 1964 agreement and that the rights reserved by Permaglass were personal to it and non-transferable and non-assignable. PPG also claimed that Guardian had no rights with respect to the two patents which had originated with PPG because the license under these patents was personal to Permaglass and non-transferable and non-assignable except with the permission of PPG. In addition it claimed that the license with respect to these two patents had terminated under the provisions of Section 11.2, Supra, by reason of the merger.

One of the defenses pled by Guardian in its answer was that it was a licensee of the patents in suit. It described the merger with Permaglass and claimed it "had succeeded to all rights, powers, ownerships, etc., of Permaglass, and as Permaglass' successor, defendant is legally entitled to operate in place of Permaglass under the January 1, 1964 agreement between Permaglass and plaintiff, free of any claim of infringement of the patents. . . ."

After holding an evidentiary hearing the district court concluded that the parties to the 1964 agreement did not intend that the rights reserved by Permaglass in its nine patents or the rights assigned to Permaglass in the two PPG patents would not pass to a successor corporation by way of merger. The court held that there had been no assignment or transfer of the rights by Permaglass, but rather that Guardian acquired these rights by operation of law under the merger statutes of Ohio and Delaware. The provisions of the 1964 agreement making the license rights of Permaglass non-assignable and non-transferable were held not to apply because of the "continuity of interest inherent in a statutory merger that distinguishes it from the ordinary assignment or transfer case."

With respect to the termination provision in Section 11.2 of the 1964 agreement, the district court again relied on "the nature of a statutory merger in contrast to an outright sale or acquisition of stock" in holding that a majority of the voting stock of Permaglass did not become owned or controlled by Guardian.

II

Questions with respect to the assignability of a patent license are controlled by federal law. It has long been held by federal courts that agreements granting patent licenses are personal and not assignable unless expressly made so. This has been the rule at least since 1852 when the Supreme Court decided *Troy Iron & Nail v. Corning*, 55 U.S. (14 How.) 193, 14 L.Ed. 383 (1852). The district court recognized this rule in the present case, but concluded that where patent licenses are claimed to pass by operation of law to the resultant or surviving corporation in a statutory merger there has been no assignment or transfer.

There appear to be no reported cases where the precise issue in this case has been decided. At least two treatises contain the statement that rights under a patent license owned by a constituent corporation pass to the consolidated corporation in the case of a consolidation, W. Fletcher, Cyclopedia of the Law of Corporations s 7089 (revised ed. 1973); and to the new or resultant corporation in the case of a merger, A. Deller, Walker on Patents § 409 (2d ed. 1965). However, the cases cited in support of these statements by the commentators do not actually provide such support because their facts take them outside the general rule of non-assignability. Both texts rely on the decision in *Hartford-Empire Co. v. Demuth Glass Works, Inc.*, 19 F.Supp. 626 (E.D.N.Y.1937). The agreement involved in that case specified that the patent license was assignable and its assignability was not an issue. Clearly the statement in the Hartford-Empire opinion that the merger conveyed to the new corporation the patent licenses owned by the old corporation results from the fact that the licenses in question were expressly made assignable, not from any general principle that such licenses pass to the resultant corporation where there is a merger. It is also noteworthy that the surviving corporation following the merger in Hartford-Empire was the original licensee, whereas in the present case the original licensee was merged into Guardian, which was the survivor. Fletcher also cites *Lightner v. Boston & A. R. Co.*, 1 Low Dec. 338, 15 Fed.Cas. No. 8,343, p. 514 (C.C.Mass. 1869). In that case both of the constituent corporations had been licensed by the patent holder. Thus, the reason for the rule against assignability was not present; the patent holder had selected both as licensees. There was also language in one of the licensing agreements involved in Lightner which indicated to the court that a consolidation was anticipated and that use of the patented mechanism by the consolidated corporation was authorized. Again, this decision does not indicate that the general rule of non-assignability of patent licenses does not apply in merger situations.

Guardian relies on two classes of cases where rights of a constituent corporation have been held to pass by merger to the resultant corporation even though such rights are not otherwise assignable or transferable. It points out that the courts have consistently held that "shop rights" do pass in a statutory merger. A shop right is an implied license which accrues to an employer in cases where an employee has perfected a patentable device while working for the employer. Though the employee is the owner of the patent he is estopped from claiming infringement by the employer. This estoppel arises from the fact that the patent work has been done on the employer's time and that the employer has furnished materials for the experiments and financial backing to the employee.

The rule that prevents an employee-inventor from claiming infringement against a successor to the entire business and good will of his employer is but one feature of the broad doctrine of estoppel which underlies the shop right cases. No element of estoppel exists in the present case. The license rights of Permaglass did not arise by implication. They were bargained for at arms length and the agreement which defines the rights of the parties provides that Permaglass received non-transferable, non-assignable personal licenses. We do not believe that the express prohibition against assignment and transfer in a written instrument may be held ineffective by analogy to a rule based on estoppel in situations where there is no written contract and the rights of the parties have arisen by implication because of their past relationship.

The other group of cases which the district court and Guardian found to be analogous hold that the resultant corporation in a merger succeeds to the rights of the constituent corporations under real estate leases. The most obvious difficulty in drawing an analogy between the lease cases and those concerning patent licenses is that a lease is an interest in real property. As such, it is subject to the deep-rooted policy against restraints on alienation. Applying this policy, courts have construed provisions against assignability in leases strictly and have concluded that they do not prevent the passage of interests by operation of law. There is no similar policy which is offended by the decision of a patent owner to make a license under his patent personal to the licensee, and non-assignable and non-transferable. In fact the law treats a license as if it contained these restrictions in the absence of express provisions to the contrary.

We conclude that the district court misconceived the intent of the parties to the 1964 agreement. We believe the district court put the burden on the wrong party in stating:

> Because the parties failed to provide that Permaglass' rights under the 1964 license agreement would not pass to the corporation surviving a merger, the Court finds that Guardian succeeded to Permaglass' license pursuant to 8 Del.C. § 259, and Ohio Revised Code §§ 1701.81 and 1701.83.

The agreement provides with respect to the license which Permaglass granted to PPG that Permaglass reserved "a non-exclusive, non-transferable, royalty-free, world-wide right and license for the benefit and use of Permaglass." (emphasis added). Similarly, with respect to its own two patents, PPG granted to Permaglass "a non-exclusive, non-transferable, royalty-free right and license. . . ." Further, the agreement provides that both it and the license granted to Permaglass "shall be personal to PERMAGLASS and non-assignable except with the consent of PPG first obtained in writing."

The quoted language from Sections 3, 4 and 9 of the 1964 agreement evinces an intent that only Permaglass was to enjoy the privileges of licensee. If the parties had intended an exception in the event of a merger, it would have been a simple matter to have so provided in the agreement. Guardian contends such an exception is not necessary since it is universally recognized that patent licenses pass from a licensee to the resultant corporation in case of a merger. This does not appear to be the case. . . . We conclude that if the parties had intended an exception in case of a merger to the provisions against assignment and transfer they would have included it in the agreement. It should be noted also that the district court in *Packard*, supra, held that an assignment had taken place when the licensee was merged into another corporation.

The district court also held that the patent licenses in the present case were not transferred because they passed by operation of law from Permaglass to Guardian. This conclusion is based on the theory of continuity which underlies a true merger. However, the theory of continuity relates to the fact that there is no dissolution of the constituent corporations and, even though they cease to exist, their essential corporate attributes are vested by operation of law in the surviving or resultant corporation. It does not mean that there is no transfer of particular assets from a constituent corporation to the surviving or resultant one.

The Ohio merger statute provides that following a merger all property of a constituent corporation shall be "deemed to be Transferred to and vested in the surviving or new corporation without further act or deed. . . ." (emphasis added). Ohio Revised Code, (former) § 1701.81(A)(4). This indicates that the transfer is by operation of law, not that there is no transfer of assets in a merger situation. The Delaware statute, which was also involved in the Permaglass-Guardian merger, provides that the property of the constituent corporations "shall be vested in the corporation surviving or resulting from such merger or consolidation. . . ." 8 Del.C. § 259(a). The Third Circuit has construed the "shall be vested" language of the Delaware statute as follows:

> In short, the underlying property of the constituent corporations is Transferred to the resultant corporation upon the carrying out of the consolidation or merger. . . . *Koppers Coal & Transportation Co. v. United States*, 107 F.2d 706, 708 (3d Cir. 1939).

In his opinion in *Koppers*, Judge Biggs disposed of arguments very similar to those of Guardian in the present case, based on the theory of continuity. Terming such arguments "metaphysical" he found them completely at odds with the language of the Delaware statute. Finally, on this point, the parties themselves provided in the merger agreement that all property of Permaglass "shall be deemed transferred to and shall vest in Guardian without further act or deed. . . ." A transfer is no less a transfer because it takes place by operation of law rather than by a particular act of the parties. The merger was effected by the parties and the transfer was a result of their act of merging.

Thus, Sections 3, 4 and 9 of the 1964 agreement between PPG and Permaglass show an intent that the licenses held by Permaglass in the eleven patents in suit not be transferable. While this conclusion disposes of the license defense as to all eleven patents, it should be noted that Guardian's claim to licenses under the two patents which originated with PPG is also defeated by Section 11.2 of the 1964 agreement. This section addresses a different concern from that addressed in Sections 3, 4 and 9. The restrictions on transferability and assignability in those sections prevent the patent licenses from becoming the property of third parties. The termination clause, however, provides that Permaglass' license with respect to the two PPG patents will terminate if the ownership of a majority of the voting stock of Permaglass passes from the 1964 stockholders to designated classes of persons, even though the licenses themselves might never have changed hands.

Apparently PPG was willing for Permaglass to continue as licensee under the nine patents even though ownership of its stock might change. These patents originated with Permaglass and so long as Permaglass continued to use the licenses for its own benefit a mere change in ownership of Permaglass stock would not nullify the licenses. Only a transfer or assignment would cause a termination. However, the agreement provides for termination with respect to the two original PPG patents in the event of an indirect takeover of Permaglass by a change in the ownership of a majority of its stock. The fact that PPG sought and obtained a stricter provision with respect to the two patents which it originally owned in no way indicates an intention to permit transfer of licenses under the other nine in case of a merger. None of the eleven licenses was transferable; but two of them, those involving PPG's own development in the field of gas hearth technology, were not to continue even for the benefit of the licensee if it came under the control of a manufacturer of automobiles or a competitor of PPG in the glass industry "other than the present owners" of Permaglass. A consistency among the provisions of the agreement is discernible when the different origins of the various patents are considered.

III

The second issue in the case does not require detailed consideration. Guardian maintains that it was licensed to use four furnace units which are alleged to infringe the eleven patents in suit. This argument is based on an "Exclusive License Agreement" of February 24, 1969 between PPG and Permaglass which Guardian contends was an "equipment license" rather than a license for processes covered by the various patents. It argues that it was free to operate the four furnace units under either the 1964 or the 1969 agreement. PPG agrees that Guardian succeeded to whatever rights Permaglass had under the 1969 agreement, but maintains that this agreement merely licensed a different group of patents relative to the "air form development," an improved method which had recently been perfected. PPG states that it is not claiming infringement of any of the "air form" patents referred to in the 1969 agreement and that rights which Permaglass acquired under that agreement afford no defense to the present infringement action.

The district court attempted to determine whether the four units operated by Guardian are "licensed furnace units" under the agreement. This involved, among other things, the necessity of trying to decipher the meaning of "and/or" as used by the parties always a nettlesome task. However, if PPG's claim that none of the eleven patents in suit is covered by the 1969 agreement is correct, for purposes of this appeal the definition of "licensed furnace units" is immaterial. The district court did hold that the 1969 agreement was not intended to modify the 1964 agreement. This finding is fully supported by the evidence. It was the 1964 agreement which defined the rights of Permaglass with respect to the eleven patents in suit. We have held that the rights of Permaglass under the 1964 agreement terminated upon its merger into Guardian. Since the 1969 agreement was not intended to modify the 1964 agreement in any way, it cannot afford a defense as a matter of law to the claim of infringement. Though facts may be developed at trial which will require further consideration of this particular defense, the district court was correct in denying dismissal on the basis of the 1969 agreement.

The judgment of the district court is reversed on appeal and affirmed on cross-appeal, and the cause is remanded for further proceedings.

VERSON CORPORATION v. VERSON INTERNATIONAL GROUP, PLC
District Court for the Northern District of Illinois
899 F. Supp. 358 (1995)

MORAN, Senior District Judge.

Plaintiff Verson Corporation brought this lawsuit alleging that defendants Verson International Group, Verson Wilkins Limited, and Verson International Limited violated a license agreement for intellectual property. Before us now is defendants' motion to dismiss plaintiff's amended complaint. For the reasons set forth below, the motion is denied.

BACKGROUND

Verson Corporation (Verson), the successor to Verson Allsteel Press Company (VASP) and theF wholly-owned subsidiary of Allied Products Corporation, manufactures presses for the metal-forming industry. In the early 1980s VASP began experiencing financial difficulties. In order to ease through its financial downturn VASP and a group of its international managers entered into an agreement wherein the managers would buy out VASP's international operations with a newly formed independent company, Verson International Limited (collectively referred to herein, along with Verson Wilkins Limited and Verson International Limited, as "VIL"). VIL and VASP entered into a series of agreements to facilitate the management buyout (MBO), the most important for our purposes being the VASP/VIL License Agreement (license agreement). In that agreement VASP agreed to turn over to VIL its patents and non-patented trade secrets, and allowed VIL to use this know-how. The license agreement called for both parties to turn over all newly developed know-how to the other for a period of five years. The parties also agreed to a series of restrictive covenants that gave VASP the exclusive right to market its products in the United States and Canada and gave VIL the exclusive right to market its products in the rest of the world. Both territorial restrictions were to last five years.

In the first lawsuit between the parties VIL sued VASP alleging that VASP had violated the license agreement's restrictive covenants and seeking an injunction requiring Verson to turn over certain know-how. VASP argued that the territorial and durational restrictions violated state and federal antitrust laws. We enforced the restrictions only in part, finding that VIL was barred only from the use of VASP know-how in the United States and Canada, and that VASP was barred only from marketing its products in Europe. Verson Wilkins Ltd. v. Allied Products Corp., 723 F.Supp. 1, 20

(N.D.Ill. 1989). We also required VASP to turn over the know-how covered under the license agreement. In 1990 the parties executed a settlement agreement disposing of the remaining disputes regarding exchange of the know-how.

Soon thereafter VIL entered into an agreement with Enprotech Mechanical Services, Inc. (Enprotech), a direct competitor of Verson in the North American market. In this agreement VIL turned over know-how it received from VASP in the 1985 license agreement and granted Enprotech the exclusive right to use this know-how to manufacture replacement parts for Verson presses. This arrangement spawned the present lawsuit. In its complaint Verson alleged that VIL violated Article 16 of the 1985 license agreement which required VIL to obtain VASP's approval before licensing the know-how to another party, by turning over VASP know-how to Enprotech. Defendants moved to dismiss the complaint, claiming that Article 16 did not survive the termination of the agreement. We granted that motion on December 30, 1994. Verson moved for reconsideration of our order and for leave to amend its complaint, arguing that the Enprotech agreement, which Verson claims is an assignment, violated the license agreement's restriction on VIL's right to assign the know-how. Although this constituted a new line of attack for Verson, we allowed it to amend its complaint to more fully make out this claim. Verson has since amended its complaint to incorporate the assignment argument. Before us now is VIL's motion to dismiss the amended complaint. VIL argues that the 1990 settlement agreement prevents Verson from maintaining this action; that it is the co-owner of the know-how, not a licensee, and thus had the right to assign it to Enprotech; that the right to assign the know-how was implicit in the 1985 licensing agreement; that a perpetual ban on assignability would be an unreasonable restraint of trade; and that its transaction with Enprotech is a sublease rather than an assignment. We will examine each of these arguments in turn.

DISCUSSION

A. The 1990 Settlement Agreement

VIL argues that a settlement agreement executed in connection with the earlier case involving these parties bars Verson's action here. In the first lawsuit VIL obtained an injunction requiring Verson to turn over various types of know-how related to the licensing agreement. The case was still pending, however, because the parties disputed what documents needed to be produced and who was to pay for the copying. The parties entered into a settlement in which VIL accepted some of the disputed know-how in complete satisfaction of any claim for know-how it might have had under the licensing agreement, and Verson agreed not to challenge VIL's right to use this know-how. VIL argues that this action challenging VIL's assignment (or sublease) of the know-how to Enprotech is a restriction on the use of the know-how and thus violates the settlement agreement. Verson responds that VIL's right to assign or transfer the know-how remained as it was under the licensing agreement.

We agree with Verson that the 1990 settlement agreement does not prevent it from attempting to restrict VIL's right to assign the know-how. In settlements, as in all contracts, every effort should be made to give force to the words employed by the parties and to not imply words that the parties could have used but did not. Through the settlement Verson agreed only not to restrict VIL's use of the know-how. The word "use" does not ordinarily also include sale, transfer, or assignment. This is especially so when dealing with the right to use intellectual property. One can use know-how, trade secrets, or patents freely, but still not transfer or assign that information. The right to the know-how at issue here could easily be separated into the right to use the know-how and the right to sell, transfer, or assign the know-how, and the parties' selection of the word "use" provides support for the view that they did not intend for the settlement agreement to grant VIL a right to assign the know-how that was not already granted under the terms of the license agreement. The parties could have added "transfer or assign" to "use," and the fact that they did not is probative of the issue.

Other sections of the settlement also provide some support for that view. Under a section entitled "Reservation of Rights," both parties reserved the right to sue each other for any breach of the licensing agreement. The fact that both parties sought to preserve their rights under the licensing agreement arguably indicates that the settlement was intended only to resolve the dispute as to what know-how Verson was required to turn over and who was to pay for the copying costs. VIL's reading of the reservation-of-rights clause, that the parties intended only to prevent public disclosure of the know-how, is strained, given that the parties could have easily drafted the clause to reflect that intent but did not. Therefore, we hold that the 1990 settlement agreement was not an unambiguous waiver of Verson's right to challenge VIL's assignment of the know-how.

B.   Is VIL a Co-Owner of the Know-How Or Only a Licensee?

The premise behind Verson's complaint is that VIL is a non-exclusive licensee of the know-how. In earlier orders we expressed some doubt regarding this proposition and left open the question whether VIL is a co-owner of the know-how. VIL seizes upon this language and presses the argument here.

The starting place for determining whether VIL is a co-owner of the know-how is the 1985 license agreement. The agreement states that "[u]pon expiration of the term of this Agreement, subject to [confidentiality provisions], Licensee shall have the non-exclusive perpetual royalty free right to continue to exercise, use or practice the rights granted Licensee under Section 2.01 without limitation as to Territory. . . ." As we indicated above, the use of know-how can be readily distinguished from the ownership of the know-how. Thus, one meaning of the license agreement grants VIL only the right to use the know-how to compete with Verson worldwide. The language of this provision, or the other provisions in the agreement, does not necessarily indicate the parties intended for VIL to become co-owner of the know-how at the termination of the five-year period.

Despite the lack of any express provision in the license agreement granting it co-ownership of the know-how, VIL presents four arguments to support its claim: first, that the amount it paid in connection with the MBO indicates that VIL would become co-owner of the know-how; second, that it developed some of the know-how itself; third, that the clear intent of the MBO and license agreement was to make VIL and Verson head-to-head competitors after five years; and, fourth, that VIL acquired property rights to the know-how when it acquired VASP's international operations.

We find that none of these four arguments helps VIL's cause here, even if we can entertain them in support of a motion to dismiss. First, the amount VIL paid in connection with the MBO does not by itself demonstrate anything about the parties' intent. The license agreement was just one part of a series of agreements executed in connection with the MBO. It is impossible to say as a matter of law that the consideration paid by VIL was to acquire ownership rights to the know-how after five years. VIL may be able to present evidence that the true value of what it received in the MBO could not come near the $8 million it actually paid if ownership of the know-how were not included, and in such a situation we could find the consideration paid to be probative of the parties' intent. However, we cannot make that determination on a motion to dismiss.

Second, Verson disputes VIL's claim that it developed part of the know-how at issue here. It is clear that whether or not VIL did develop this know-how is a disputed question of fact that cannot be resolved on a motion to dismiss. Such a determination must await further development by the parties.

Third, we have repeatedly recognized that the goal of the MBO in general, and the license agreement in particular, was to place VIL and Verson as head-to-head competitors at the end of five years, as VIL argues. That proposition does not, however, establish VIL's ownership of the know-how. At the end of the agreement, VIL had every right to compete with Verson in any market in the world. In that respect the two firms were head-to-head competitors. Limiting VIL to the right to use, instead of assign, the know-how does not appear to frustrate this goal. All VIL is prevented from doing is assigning or selling the know-how to a competitor. This limitation has no effect on VIL's ability to compete with Verson in the manufacture, sale, or repair of presses.

Finally, it is not clear at this point what rights VIL acquired in the MBO when it took over VASP's international operations. Until now we have never been faced with determining exactly what rights VIL acquired in the MBO. Verson has submitted a number of the agreements involving VASP and its many subsidiaries, which purportedly demonstrate that VIL acquired only licensing rights, not ownership rights, to the know-how. VIL has not contradicted Verson's recitation of the corporate history. Accepting Verson's allegation that no ownership rights were transferred in the MBO — an allegation supported by the submitted documents — we hold that Verson has properly alleged that VIL was a mere licensee, not a co-owner, of the know-how.

C. Implied Right of Assignability

VIL does not dispute that there is no provision in the license agreement granting it an explicit post-termination right to assign the know-how. Yet it argues that despite this lack of express authority, authority to assign its rights under the agreement must be inferred from the circumstances and the parties' conduct.

Under well-established law the holder of a nonexclusive patent license may not assign its license unless the right to assign is expressly provided for in the license agreement. Under . . . longstanding federal case law, patent licenses are treated as personal to the licenseholder and therefore are presumed to be not assignable. *Id.*

VIL argues that his presumption against assignability may be overcome by the circumstances and the conduct of the parties. We seriously doubt whether [the cases cited] survive the later developed line of cases refusing to imply a right of assignability of patent licenses. Even if some vestige of Farmland and Bowers remains, we cannot overlook decades of precedent to the contrary. Therefore, we feel bound to require compelling evidence of the parties' intent before implying a right to assign. Such evidence is not presented here, nor may it be considered to resolve a motion to dismiss.

VIL points to two aspects of the parties' conduct to support its claim that a right of assignment should be inferred. First, it argues that the fact that the license agreement gave it broad authority to sublicense its rights without Verson's approval establishes conclusively that the parties did not believe that the patented rights were highly personable and therefore could be assigned. We disagree. VIL seeks to bootstrap its negotiated right to sublicense into a right to assign. Were VIL correct, every license granting a right to sublicense would also implicitly contain a right of assignment. That is clearly not the case. On the contrary, under the axiom of expressio unius, the presence of the provision on sublicensing indicates that the parties did not intend to allow assignments. Further, VIL cannot seriously maintain that Verson did not consider the know-how to be highly personable. The license agreement contained a strict confidentiality clause and every indication from the parties' conduct since the MBO is that the know-how is vital to successful competition in the industry. Therefore, it is clear that VIL's right to sublicense does not establish as a matter of law an intent to also allow it to assign its rights.

VIL also claims that Article 16 of the licensing agreement, which required VIL to first obtain Verson's approval before assigning its rights to a competitor, demonstrates that when the parties sought to restrict the right to assign they did so expressly, and the fact that there is no provision limiting VIL's right to assign post-termination establishes that no such limitations were intended by the parties. In addition, VIL argues that because our order of December 30, 1993, ruled that Article 16 did not survive the termination of the licensing agreement, preventing VIL from assigning its rights post-termination would mean that it had greater leeway to assign before the termination than after, which it asserts is an absurd result.

We are not persuaded that the presence of Article 16 overcomes the strong presumption against implying a right to assign licenses for intellectual property. Article 16 and a post-termination restriction on assignment are not, as VIL suggests, in hopeless conflict. It is reasonable for Verson to have allowed VIL greater leeway to assign its rights during the five-year period of the licensing agreement because VIL was prohibited by the agreement from competing with Verson in North America. After the termination of the agreement, however, VIL could compete directly with Verson in North America, which may have prompted Verson to restrict VIL's right to assign. In any event, we need not rule that this is what the parties intended. Rather, we conclude that the license agreement does not conclusively refute Verson's claim that the know-how cannot be assigned. . . .

[The court's discussion of VIL's restraint of trade is omitted here.]

E. Assignment or Sublicense

VIL's final argument is that its agreement with Enprotech is not an assignment at all, but rather is a sublicense, and since the license agreement granted VIL the authority to sublicense its rights, Verson's suit must fail.

Verson argues that intellectual property rights can be severed and assigned separately. That is, a patentee may assign the right to use a patent for sale of a product but retain the right to use the patent for other purposes. Support for this proposition can be found in tax cases, and in some of the cases dealing with who has standing to sue for patent infringement. Under this view the answer depends on whether the patentee has transferred all its rights in a particular market (an assignment) or has transferred only some of those rights, retaining others for itself (a license). During the course of this litigation VIL has retreated from its earlier opposition to this principle and now seems content to argue that, even if that were the law, the Enprotech agreement still cannot be considered an assignment.

Verson claims that the Enprotech agreement is an assignment rather than a sublicense because VIL transferred all the rights associated with the after-market for Verson presses. Specifically, the Enprotech agreement states:

> [VIL] (i) grants and assigns to [Enprotech] (1) the exclusive (as between Licensor and Licensee), royalty free right and license to utilize the Proprietary Rights in the Territory for the manufacture and sale of Verson Parts and for the rebuilding and modernization of Verson Presses and subject to the reserved rights of [VIL], the maintenance and repair of Verson Presses, and (2) the right and license to use the Trademark in connection with the manufacture and sale of Verson Parts and, subject to the review and consent of [VIL], which consent will not be unreasonably withheld, the maintenance, repair, rebuilding and modernization of Verson Presses and (ii) sells to Enprotech the Technical Information and Other Information subject to the terms and conditions of this Agreement.

The "territory" is defined to include certain countries in North America and Central America. "Proprietary rights" and "technical information" basically entail the Verson technology that VIL received under the licensing agreement.

VIL counters that it has retained sufficient rights to the after-market to render the Enprotech agreement a sublicense rather than an assignment. It identifies five such rights: (1) the right to make replacement parts in connection with the sale of new presses; (2) the exclusive right to provide service for the enhancement retrofit of Verson presses; (3) the exclusive right to provide service work for the maintenance and repair of Verson presses; (4) a fifty-year period for the agreement; and (5) a parts supply agreement requiring Enprotech to purchase spare parts from a corporation affiliated with VIL.

We can quickly dispense with VIL's argument that rights two and three render the agreement a sublicense. Those rights do not limit the agreement's grant to Enprotech of an exclusive right to manufacture replacement parts; the issue of repair service does not limit Enprotech's ability to use the know-how in the replacement parts market.

Similarly, the fifty-year period does not, as a matter of law, render the agreement a sublicense. Verson has alleged that the fifty-year period far exceeds the useful life of any of the know-how, given the normal rate of change in technology in the industry, and thus the fifty-year period does not serve as any practical restraint on Enprotech's rights under the agreement. Since VIL has not demonstrated that this well-pleaded allegation is incorrect as a matter of law, we must accept it as being true for the purposes of this motion to dismiss.

Nor does the parts supply agreement, as a matter of law, render the Enprotech agreement a sublicense. Although Enprotech is required to purchase certain products from a VIL-affiliated corporation, the agreement states that Enprotech's failure to abide by the parts supply agreement does not affect its exclusive rights granted elsewhere in the agreement. Therefore, the parts supply agreement need not be read to limit Enprotech's right to the use the know-how in the parts market.

That leaves the Enprotech agreement's provision granting VIL the right to manufacture replacement parts in connection with the sale of new presses. It is too early at this juncture to determine as a matter of law that VIL's retention of this right limits Enprotech's interest to a mere sublicense rather than an assignment. VIL may be able to demonstrate that its retained right to provide replacement parts as part of contracts for the sale of new presses represents a sufficiently large portion of the replacement part market to make the Enprotech agreement a sublicense, but we are not in a position to make that determination here. Since VIL has failed to demonstrate that the Enprotech agreement is a license as a matter of law, we must deny its motion to dismiss. VIL is free to renew this argument at a later stage if it can present extrinsic evidence clarifying the ambiguity in the Enprotech agreement.

[MOTION DENIED.]

MOTOROLA, INC. v. AMKOR TECHNOLOGY, INC.
Supreme Court of Delaware
849 A.2d 931 (2004)

HOLLAND, Justice:

The dispute involves third-party Citizen Watch Co., Ltd.'s ("Citizen") assignment of its Patent License Agreement ("PLA") with Motorola to Amkor.

Motorola contends that Motorola's and Citizen's intent in entering into the Agreement, as expressed in the plain terms of the PLA, precludes the assignment. Amkor claims that the assignment is valid. We conclude that, in the context of the PLA, the terms "license" and "assignment" are ambiguous and a material issue of fact exists, precluding summary judgment. Therefore, the judgment of the Superior Court must be reversed.

Facts

Amkor and Motorola are currently in the business of, among other things, developing and providing semiconductor assembly test services and products, commonly referred to as ball grid array packages ("BGA Packages"). BGA Packages are a housing apparatus for integrated circuit structures that are used to make semiconductor products. Both Motorola and Amkor hold patents relating to BGA Packages. Prior to selling its BGA Assembly Business Unit to Amkor on March 28, 2002, Citizen was also in this business and also held certain patents relating to BGA Packages.

On June 30, 1993, Motorola and Amkor entered into an Immunity Agreement, pursuant to which Motorola and Amkor provided each other with cross-releases and cross-licenses for their BGA Package patents. In consideration of Motorola's grant of a license to Amkor, the Immunity Agreement required Amkor to pay royalties to Motorola on a quarterly basis for use of Motorola's BGA Package patents. The royalty payments were based on Amkor's quarterly use of the technology covered by the patents. Amkor paid Motorola approximately $36.8 million under the Immunity Agreement for use of Motorola's technology. The Immunity Agreement expired by its own terms on December 31, 2002.

On January 25, 1996, Motorola entered into the PLA with Citizen. The PLA grants Citizen the right to use the same Motorola BGA Package patents that are the subject of the Immunity Agreement between Motorola and Amkor. The PLA grants at least two specific rights to Citizen that were not granted to Amkor. First, Motorola and Citizen cross-license their respective patents governing BGA packaging technology on a royalty-free basis. Second, the PLA with Citizen includes an assignment from Motorola to Citizen of an undivided one-half interest in two of Motorola's U.S. patents: Patent No. 5,241,133 (the "Mullin Patent") ; and Patent No. 5,216,278 (the "Lin Patent"). Amkor was required to pay Motorola for use of these two patents under the Immunity Agreement, and was granted no ownership interest in them.

The PLA also contains restrictions on Citizen's ability to transfer its royalty-free rights to third parties. These restrictions are set forth in Sections 4.1 and 5.1 of the PLA. Section 4.1 of the PLA expressly prohibits Citizen from entering into contracts with a set list of companies to license its royalty-free rights to the Mullin and Lin patents:

> CITIZEN agrees not to offer to enter into or to enter into a contract with current BGA licensees of MOTOROLA, including those listed in Appendix A [inter alia, Amkor], for a license to make, have made, or sell BGAs under U.S. Patent Nos. 5,241,133 [Mullin] and/or 5,216,278 [Lin].

Section 5.5 of the PLA limits Citizen's ability to transfer or assign its rights under the agreement, as follows:

> The rights or privileges provided for in this Agreement may be assigned or transferred by either party only with the prior written consent of the other party and with the authorization or approval of any governmental authority as then may be required, except to a successor in ownership of all or substantially all of the assets of the assigning party relating to the business unit employing the patents licensed hereunder but such successor, before such assignment or transfer is effective, shall expressly assume in writing to the other party the performance of all the terms and conditions of this Agreement to be performed by the assigning party.

On March 28, 2002, Amkor purchased substantially all of the assets of Citizen's BGA Assembly Business Unit. Concurrently with the sale of Citizen's business, Citizen and Amkor entered into an Intellectual Property Assignment Agreement ("IPAA") that "assigns" to Amkor Citizen's PLA with Motorola as well as Citizen's one-half interest in the Mullin and Lin Patents. The IPAA requires Citizen to gain the necessary consents for the alleged assignments from all relevant entities but "exclud[es] any consent that may be required from Motorola."

After the IPAA was executed, Amkor advised Motorola that Amkor had taken over Citizen's ownership rights in the Mullin and Lin Patents, and acquired a royalty-free license to the Motorola BGA patent portfolio under the PLA. Motorola informed both Citizen and Amkor that they were in material breach of their respective agreements with Motorola, and that the alleged transfers were invalid under Section 4.1. Amkor stopped paying royalties to Motorola for the second and third quarters of 2002, and stated that it would not pay royalties for the fourth quarter of 2002. . . .

The Superior Court noted that the PLA contained no definitions of the terms "license" or "assignment." Therefore, it looked to the "commonly accepted meanings" from Black's Law Dictionary, which defined an assignment as the "act of transferring to another all or part of one's property, interest, or rights." Black's defined a license as "a personal privilege to do some particular act or series of acts. . . ." Based on these definitions, the Superior Court rejected Motorola's claim that a license is subsumed in the definition of an assignment.

Instead, the Superior Court concluded that the terms license and assignment "are distinct and separate, as used in Section 4.1 and Section 5.5, involving different obligations and responsibilities." Consequently, the Superior Court held that "[a]lthough Motorola may not have intended to allow Citizen and Amkor to circumvent [Section] 4.1 by assigning the patents to Amkor via [Section] 5.5, that is what is permitted by the clear meaning of the language of the . . . PLA." Accordingly, the Superior Court granted Amkor's motion for summary judgment and denied Motorola's cross-motion. . . .

Illinois Contract Law

The PLA contract at issue in this case expressly provides that it is governed by the law of Illinois, under which "the primary goal in construing a contract is to give effect to the intent of the parties." In determining the parties' intent, the contract must be read as a whole. When the language of the contract is clear and unambiguous, the parties' intent must be determined solely from the plain language of the contract. If the contract language creates an ambiguity, however, extrinsic evidence is permissible and the interpretation of the language becomes a question of fact.

Illinois follows the general rule that a contract is not ambiguous merely because the parties disagree as to its meaning. Rather, "[a] contract is properly found ambiguous when the language used is susceptible to more than one meaning or is obscure in meaning through indefiniteness of expression." Therefore, if reasonable people may draw different inferences from the undisputed facts, an ambiguity exists and summary judgment is inappropriate.

Parties' Intent

In construing a contract, the primary objective for any court is to give effect to the parties' intent. Accordingly, in deciding on the interpretation of the PLA, the Superior Court's principal goal under Illinois law was to ascertain Citizen's and Motorola's intent in entering into the contract. Thus, the dispositive question in this litigation is what was the parties' intention?

In determining the parties' intent with regard to Section 4.1 and 5.5, Illinois law required the Superior Court to consider the contract as a whole and not focus on the sections as isolated provisions. Section 4.1 of the PLA explicitly precludes Citizen from "licensing" its rights to the Mullin and Lin Patents to Amkor. If an "assignment" to Amkor is allowed by Section 5.5, however, Motorola argues that such an assignment will render the restrictions of Section 4.1 meaningless.

Motorola argues that it intended to preclude current BGA licensees, such as Amkor, from obtaining royalty-free use of the BGA Package patents from Citizen. Section 4.1 of the PLA expressly prohibits Citizen from contracting for a license with "current BGA licensees" of Motorola. It is undisputed that Amkor was a current BGA licensee. Amkor concedes that Section 4.1 creates a bar to its agreement with Citizen.

Nevertheless, Amkor argues that Section 5.5 of the PLA creates a specific exception to the prohibition in Section 4.1. In support of this argument, Amkor points to the language of Section 5.5, which allows assignment of the BGA Package patents without the express written consent of Motorola if the acquiring party succeeds in ownership in "all or substantially all of the assets of the assigning party relating to the business unit employing the patents licensed hereunder. . . ." Accordingly, Amkor contends that the PLA restricts Citizen from sublicensing the technology for profit, but allows assignment of all of Citizen's rights that would be occasioned by a sale of all or substantially all of its relevant business unit assets.

Contract Ambiguous

Whether Motorola's or Amkor's interpretation of the parties' intent is correct is dependent on the meaning of the terms "license" and "assignment." Amkor argues that the plain meaning of those terms show that they are separate and distinct. Conversely, Motorola argues that a "license" is subsumed within an "assignment." Thus, under Amkor's reading of the contract, the PLA precludes a "license" but allows "assignment." Under Motorola's reading, by prohibiting Citizen from "licensing" the BGA Package Patents to current licensees such as Amkor, the PLA necessarily precludes an "assignment" as well.

Both Motorola's and Amkor's interpretations of the PLA contract language may be reasonable. Where more than one plausible construction of a contract exists or the contract is ambiguous because two or more key provisions conflict, an issue of material fact arises and summary judgment must be denied. A provision is "key" or "material" if a reasonable person would "attach importance to [it] . . . in determining his choice of action in the transaction in question. . . ."

The Superior Court held that the specific licensing restrictions of Section 4.1 do not modify the general assignment provisions of Section 5.5, with the result that as long as the requirements of Section 5.5 are met, the assignment is valid. To reach that conclusion, the Superior Court relied upon Black's Law Dictionary's definitions of the terms "license" and "assignment." The Superior Court held that, as long as the assignment provisions of Section 5.5 are met, the licensing prohibitions of Section 4.1 are irrelevant.

The Superior Court concluded that although "Motorola may not have intended to allow Citizen and Amkor to circumvent [Section] 4.1 by assigning the patents to Amkor via [Section] 5.5, that is what is permitted by the clear meaning of the Motorola/Citizen PLA." As a general rule, whenever it is possible, a court must preserve the reasonable expectations that form the basis of the parties' contractual relationship. In this case, contrary to that legal principle, the Superior Court held that the language in Section 5.5 bound Motorola to what may have been the unintended consequences that Section 4.1 prohibited. The Superior Court's construction of Section 5.5, in apparent isolation from Section 4.1, was contrary to the law of Illinois.

Contract terms are controlling when they establish the parties' common meaning so that a reasonable person in the position of either party would have no expectations inconsistent with the contract language. When the provisions in controversy are fairly susceptible of different interpretations or may have two or more different meanings, there is ambiguity. In those circumstances, the interpreting court must look beyond the language of the contract to ascertain the parties' intentions. In this case, the Superior Court should have, but did not, look to parol evidence to interpret the PLA.

To the extent that the parties' intent cannot be determined from the plain terms of the PLA or the parties' intent is open to more than one interpretation, the Superior Court should have considered parol evidence to resolve the ambiguity. The ambiguity in the meaning and the application of the contract language in the PLA created material issues of fact that required the Superior Court to admit and consider parol evidence. Those material issues of fact must be resolved by the trier of fact, and cannot be resolved by a summary judgment procedure.

[REVERSED.]

NOTES & QUESTIONS

1. The Kennedy reading points out that both mergers and bankruptcies raise questions about the treatment of third party licenses with respect to assignments and sublicensing. We discussed the bankruptcy treatment of third party licenses in Chapter 7. As we noted there, bankruptcy resolves the status of these licenses in accordance with section 365 of the Bankruptcy Code which provides for the assumption and assignment of executory contracts by a bankrupt debtor. As the Kennedy reading states, however, the solution in the merger context is far from clear. Because of this lack of clarity in statutory and case law, the resolution of questions about the treatment of third party licenses in a merger often rests with contract law and the ability of the parties to a merger or acquisition to clearly state their intentions with respect to the transferability of licenses. Notice what this means is that care must be taken in drafting both intellectual property license agreements to clearly state the parties' rights with respect to transfers and assignments and merger or corporate asset sales agreements to clearly describe what rights are transferred or assigned. The scope of potential liability if a party breaches should also be clearly stated in the respective documents.

2. The treatment of assignments of intellectual property licenses in mergers and acquisitions reflects a tension between state law, in favor of alienability, and federal intellectual property law, in favor of retaining control by the intellectual property owner. The California court's resolution of this tension in SQL Solutions, cited in the Kennedy reading, reflects a minority, and perhaps erroneous, viewpoint. Think about how bankruptcy law deals with this tension in Section 365. How is this tension different in the bankruptcy context than in the mergers and acquisitions context? Does the fact that rights stemming from bankruptcies, like many intellectual property rights, are matters of federal law remove the tension? Should there be a federal statute that addresses this ambiguity in the law? If so, which side should the statute favor, alienability or control?

3. The ambiguity highlighted by Kennedy concerning the treatment of assignments is illustrated by the three cases in this section. Each offers a different perspective on how courts can address the problem. In *PPG*, a case about which Kennedy expresses some skepticism, the court holds that intellectual property licenses are not transferred as part of a merger. Its reasoning rests on the reading of state corporate law which characterizes a merger as a transfer by operation of law. Since the license at issue prohibited all transfers of intellectual property rights, the new entity after the merger could not obtain any rights under the license. Does the court in *PPG* miss something? Should intellectual property be treated in the same way as other types of assets? The courts in *Verson* and *Motorola* take an approach that looks more closely at the underlying contracts. Do the courts interpret the relevant contracts correctly? Is there one contract that clearly memorializes the agreement? If not, how

does each court construct the intention of the parties? What lessons are to be drawn for the transactional or intellectual property attorney from these cases? Notice the distinction the court draws in Motorola between an assignment and a license. Why is that distinction relevant? Does the court get it right?

C. LIABILITY ISSUES

ED PETERS JEWELRY CO., INC. v.
C & J JEWELRY CO., INC.
United States Court of Appeals for the First Circuit
124 F.3d 252 (1997)

CYR, Circuit Judge.

[BACKGROUND: Peters was a sales agent for Anson, a financially strapped jewelry manufacturer in Rhode Island. Because of financial difficulties, Fleet, Anson's creditor, foreclosed on Anson's assets, selling them to C & J Jewelry, a corporation owned equally by Considine Family Trust and Jacobsen. Peters brought an action against Anson, Fleet, and C & J Jewelry to recover unpaid commissions. The excerpt from the opinion below addresses Peters' case against C & J.]

. . . Peters invokes the "successor liability" doctrine, by contending that C & J is simply Anson reorganized in another guise, and therefore answerable in equity for Anson's outstanding liabilities, including the $859,068 debt due Peters in sales commissions. *See H.J. Baker & Bro. v. Orgonics, Inc.,* 554 A.2d 196 (R.I. 1989).

Under the common law, of course, a corporation normally may acquire another corporation's assets without becoming liable for the divesting corporation's debts. But since a rigid non-assumption rule can be bent to evade valid claims, the successor liability doctrine was devised to safeguard disadvantaged creditors of a divesting corporation in four circumstances. An acquiring corporation may become liable under the successor liability doctrine for the divesting corporation's outstanding liabilities if: (1) it expressly or impliedly assumed the divesting entity's debts; (2) the parties structured the asset divestiture to effect a de facto merger of the two corporations; (3) the divesting corporation transferred its assets with actual fraudulent intent to avoid, hinder, or delay its creditors; or (4) the acquiring corporation is a "mere continuation" of the divesting corporation.

The district court dismissed the instant successor liability claim on the ground that Peters could not have been prejudiced, because Fleet had a legitimate right to foreclose and Peters did not prove the Anson assets were worth more than the total Anson indebtedness to Fleet. On appeal, C & J takes essentially the same position, but with the flourish that the successor liability doctrine is inapplicable per se where the divesting corporation's assets were acquired pursuant to an intervening foreclosure, rather than a direct purchase. We do not agree.

First and foremost, existing case law overwhelmingly confirms that an intervening foreclosure sale affords an acquiring corporation no automatic exemption from successor liability.

Second, by its very nature the foreclosure process cannot preempt the successor liability inquiry. Whereas liens relate to assets (viz., collateral), the indebtedness underlying the lien appertains to a person or legal entity (viz., the debtor). Thus, although foreclosure by a senior lienor often wipes out junior-lien interests in the same collateral. As one might expect, therefore, UCC § 9-504 focuses exclusively on the effect a foreclosure sale has upon subordinate liens, see R.I. Gen. Laws § 6A-9-504(4), supra, rather than any extinguishment of the underlying indebtedness. Whereas the successor liability doctrine focuses exclusively on debt extinguishment, be the debt secured or unsecured.

Following the October 1993 foreclosure sale by Fleet, the then-defunct Anson unquestionably remained legally obligated to Peters for its sales commissions, even if the lack of corporate wherewithal rendered the obligation unenforceable as a practical matter. True, Fleet might have sold the Anson assets to an entity with no ties to Anson, but that is beside the point, since the Peters successor liability claim alleges that C & J is Anson in disguise. As Peters simply seeks an equitable determination that C & J, as Anson's successor, is liable for the sales commissions Peters earned from Anson, its claim in no sense implicates any lien interest in any former Anson asset. Third, successor liability is an equitable doctrine, both in origin and nature. Moreover, the UCC, as adopted in Rhode Island, provides that generally applicable principles of equity, unless expressly preempted, are to supplement its provisions. Moreover, R.I. Gen. Laws § 6A-9-504 neither explicitly nor impliedly preempts the successor liability doctrine.

Finally, the fact that C & J acquired the Anson assets indirectly through Fleet, rather than in a direct sale from Anson, does not trump the successor liability doctrine as a matter of law, since equity is loath to elevate the form of the transfer over its substance, and deigns to inquire into its true nature. Thus, were C & J otherwise qualified as Anson's "successor" under Rhode Island law, because its principals acted with intent to evade the Peters claim, see infra, there would be no equitable basis for treating the asset transfer by foreclosure differently than a direct transfer from Anson to C & J. Consequently, we reject the contention that C & J's acquisition of Anson's assets through the Fleet foreclosure pursuant to R.I. Gen. Laws § 6A-9-504, warranted dismissal of the successor liability claim as a matter of law.

Thus, Peters was entitled to attempt to prove that C & J, as Anson's "successor," became liable for the Anson debt to Peters because C & J is a "mere continuation" of the divesting corporate entity. The "mere continuation" determination turns upon fact-finding inquiries into five emblematic circumstances: (1) a corporation transfers its assets; (2) the acquiring corporation pays "less than adequate consideration" for the assets; (3) the acquiring corporation "continues the [divesting corporation's] business"; (4) both corporations share "at least one common officer who [was] instrumental in the transfer"; and (5) the divesting corporation is left "incapable of paying its creditors."

(i)   "Transfer" of Assets

Anson transferred all its operating assets, thereby enabling C & J to continue the identical product line without interruption. C & J nonetheless contends that a cognizable "transfer" could not have occurred, because Anson did not convey all its assets to C & J; that is, it conveyed its real property to Little Bay Realty. We disagree.

[Under the first criterion], the plaintiff need only demonstrate "a transfer of corporate assets." That is, it is not necessary, as a matter of law, that a single corporation acquire all the divesting corporation's assets, though the relative inclusiveness of any such asset transfer may prove to be a very pertinent factual consideration which the fact finder would take into account in the overall mix.

Yet more importantly, however, this is not an instance in which the divesting corporation transferred its real estate to a third corporation which was beyond the de facto control of the principals of the corporation which acquired the operating assets. Considine and Jacobsen deliberately structured the overall transaction so as to keep the Anson operating assets and real property under the ownership of two separate entities, C & J and Little Bay Realty respectively, concurrently established and controlled by them. Once again, therefore, since the successor liability doctrine is equitable in nature, it is the substance of the overall transaction which controls, rather than its form. Thus, the fact that C & J leased the real property from Little Bay is not controlling, since C & J (through Considine and Jacobsen) retained de facto control of the former Anson real estate following its transfer to Little Bay. Accordingly, viewing the evidence in the light most favorable to Peters, we cannot conclude, as a matter of law, that no cognizable "transfer" occurred.

(ii)   "Inadequate Consideration"

Peters likewise adduced sufficient evidence from which a rational jury could conclude that the operating assets were transferred to C & J for "inadequate consideration." The second . . . factor rests on the theory that inadequate consideration is competent circumstantial evidence from which the fact finder reasonably may infer that the transferor harbored a fraudulent intent to evade its obligations to creditors. On the other hand, a valuable consideration negotiated at arm's-length between two distinct corporate entities normally is presumed "adequate," particularly if the divesting corporation's creditors can continue to look to the divesting corporation and/or the sales proceeds for satisfaction of their claims.

The total consideration for all Anson assets in this case was less than $500,000. Fleet effectively wrote off its outstanding balances ($10,628,000) on the Anson loan in 1993, and provided C & J and Little Bay Realty "new" financing totaling approximately $2.9 million. Thus, though normally loans obtained by buyers to finance asset acquisitions would be considered in calculating the total consideration paid, here the two newly-formed acquiring companies actually incurred no "new" indebtedness to Fleet. In fact, if the two companies were determined to be Anson's "successors," the asset sale would have gained them loan forgiveness approximating $7.728 million (i.e., $10,628,000, less new indebtedness of only $2.9 million), given their total exoneration from Anson's preexisting indebtedness to Fleet. Since the "new" Fleet loans cannot count as "consideration," at least as a matter of law, C & J and Little Bay paid a combined total of only $1 million in additional cash consideration for the Anson operating assets and real estate, of which $550,000 was immediately re-injected into the two acquiring companies for capital improvements and debt service. As a practical matter, therefore, C & J and Little Bay acquired all the Anson assets for only $450,000. Finally, the remaining $550,000 in new capital was directed back into the C & J and Little Bay coffers, where it served as an immediate benefit to Considine and Jacobsen, not a detriment.

Although Peters utterly failed to demonstrate that the Anson assets were worth as much as $12,738,000, it nevertheless adduced competent evidence as to their minimum value. Thus, the trial record would support a rational inference that the assets transferred by Anson had a fair value of just under $4 million. Fleet documents indicate that the book value of the operating assets approximated $5.2 million; Fleet's conservative estimate of their value approximated $2.11 million; and its conservative valuation of the real property was $1.78 million. Therefore, with a total minimum asset value just under $4 million, and a de facto purchase price below $500,000, a rational jury could conclude that C & J and Little Bay acquired the Anson assets at 12.5 cents on the dollar.

At these minimal levels, adequacy of consideration presents an issue for the fact finder. On the present record, therefore, it was error to determine as a matter of law that no rational fact finder could conclude that 12.5% of fair value was "inadequate" consideration for the Anson assets.

Moreover, even assuming arguendo that the circumstantial evidence of fraudulent intent presented by Peters, in the way of demonstrating "inadequate consideration," could not have survived the Rule 50(a) motion for judgment as a matter of law, Peters adduced competent direct evidence of actual fraudulent intent as well. Actual fraud is a successor liability test entirely independent of the circumstantial "mere continuation" test.

Peters adduced direct evidence that Considine and Jacobsen entered into the asset transfer with the specific intent to rid the business of all indebtedness due entities not essential to its future viability, including in particular the Peters sales commissions. Peters notified Anson in March 1993 that it intended to pursue Anson vigorously for payment of its sales commissions. The intention to evade the Peters debt is explicitly memorialized in Jacobsen's notes, and yet more explicitly in the May 5, 1993 memo from Considine to Fleet ("If Fleet can find a way to foreclose the company [viz., on its security interests in Anson's real estate and operating assets] and sell certain assets to our company that would eliminate most of the liabilities discussed above, then we would offer Fleet . . . $3,250,000."). Thereafter, Fleet presciently forewarned Considine that its counsel was "not convinced that you will be able to do this [i.e., shed the Peters debt] without inviting litigation," and then insisted on an indemnification clause from C & J should any such litigation eventuate. Moreover, it is immaterial whether Considine believed that this evasive maneuver was essential to ensure the solvency and success of the Anson business; fraudulent intent need not be malicious.

(iii) "Continuation of Business"

Furthermore, Peters proffered ample evidence on the third factor in the Baker test, by demonstrating that C & J did "continue [Anson's] business." Among the considerations pertinent to the business continuity inquiry are: (1) whether the divesting and acquiring corporations handled identical products; (2) whether their operations were conducted at the same physical premises; and (3) whether the acquiring corporation retained employees of the divesting corporation.

C & J was incorporated in October 1993 for the specific purpose of acquiring the assets of the then-defunct Anson. Peters adduced evidence that C & J not only continued manufacturing the same jewelry products as Anson, but conducted its manufacturing at the same physical premises and continued servicing Anson's principal customer, Tiffany's. Moreover, its uninterrupted continuation of the Anson manufacturing business was prominently announced to Anson's customers in an October 1993 letter from C & J. In its October 1993 letter, C & J stated that it had "acquired all of the assets of Anson," that it was its "intention to build on [Anson's '55-year heritage of quality'] to reestablish the Anson brand as the pre-eminent one [in the jewelry market]," and that C & J had therefore "retained all of the former Anson employees [including Anson's 'current retail sales representation'] — the core of any business." Finally, in order to facilitate the product-line continuation, C & J specifically assumed responsibility for, and paid off, all indebtedness due Anson's "essential" trade creditors. Thus, the Peters proffer handily addressed the third factor in the Baker inquiry.

(iv) Commonality of Corporate Officers

Fourth, Peters adduced sufficient evidence at trial that C & J and Anson had "at least one common officer [viz., Considine or Jacobsen] who [was] instrumental in the [asset] transfer." C & J responds, inappositely, that the respective ownership interests held by the principals in the divesting and acquiring corporations were not identical, as Considine owned 52% of the Anson stock, whereas Jacobsen and the Considine Family Trust were equal shareholders in C & J.

The present inquiry does not turn on a complete identity of ownership (i.e., shareholders), however, but on a partial identity in the corporate managements (i.e., "officers"). Thus, the fact that Jacobsen not only held a corporate office in both Anson and C & J but was instrumental in negotiating the asset transfer to C & J was sufficient in itself to preclude a Rule 50 dismissal under the fourth prong, even if he were not an Anson shareholder.

Further, the same result obtains even if we were to assume that the "one common officer" — referred to in Baker — must be a shareholder as well. Prior to *Baker*, the Rhode Island Supreme Court did not require complete identity between those who "controlled" the two corporations or the asset transfer, whether their "control" derived from stock ownership or from their management positions. For example, the court had upheld a judgment for plaintiff, following trial, even though the officers and incorporators of the divesting and acquiring corporations were not the same, on the ground that the principals involved in the sale "all had a[ ] [common] interest in the transaction." Considine easily fits the bill here. After all, "C & J" stands for something and Jacobsen conceded at trial that Considine "participates in the management of C & J Jewelry." Moreover, Considine admitted that no C & J decision could be taken without Considine's prior approval.

C & J heavily relies as well on the fact that Considine, individually, held no direct ownership interest in C & J, but instead had conveyed his interest to the Considine Family Trust. Once again, however, as equity looks to substance not form, the fact that Considine established a family trust to receive his ownership interest in C & J did not warrant a Rule 50 dismissal, especially in light of his concession that he actively participates in the management of C & J. See Fleet Credit Memo (10/14/93), at 1 ("[T]hese transactions will be considered a Troubled Debt Restructure ('TDR') because of Considine's effective control of the assets both before and after the contemplated transaction."); (noting that Considine would be a "Principal" of C & J, although his "involvement in day-to-day operations will be limited"). Moreover, such intra-family transfers may be nominal only, and thus may constitute circumstantial evidence of a fraudulent, manipulative intent to mask the continuity in corporate control. Focusing on the transactional substance, rather than its form, therefore, we cannot conclude that a rational fact finder could not decide that Considine used the family trust to camouflage his ultimate retention of control over the Anson jewelry manufacturing business which C & J continued to conduct, without interruption, after Anson's demise.

(v)   Insolvency of Divesting Corporation

Finally, C & J does not dispute that Anson is a defunct corporation, consequently unable to pay its debt to Peters. . . .

Accordingly, since the Peters proffer, at the very least, generated a trial worthy dispute under each of the five Baker factors, the motion [for judgment as a matter of law] was improvidently granted.

TXO PRODUCTION CO. & MARATHON OIL CO. v. M.D. MARK, INC.
Court of Appeals of Texas
999 S.W. 2d 137 (1999)

TXO was an oil and gas exploration company and a wholly-owned subsidiary of Marathon. PGI was a geophysical consulting firm which conducted seismic surveys. PGI and TXO entered into a series of contracts between 1979 and 1989 that allowed TXO to use certain seismic data. The contracts changed over the years, but each contained a confidentiality provision that the data "shall not be sold, traded, disposed of, or otherwise made available to third parties." Marathon eventually merged with TXO, and when TXO informed PGI of the merger and that the data would be automatically transferred to Marathon pursuant to the applicable merger statutes, PGI sought a $200 per mile transfer fee to allow Marathon to use the data. Marathon never paid the fee.

Mark subsequently acquired the rights to PGI's data and, based on Marathon's refusal to pay the transfer fee, sued appellants for breach of contract, conversion, and misappropriation of trade secrets. Appellants filed a motion for summary judgment, asserting the statute of limitations barred Mark's conversion and misappropriation claims. Mark filed a response to appellants' motion and its own motion for summary judgment on the breach of contract claim. The trial court found that (1) the merger was a transfer of the seismic data constituting a breach of the parties' agreements; (2) the conversion and misappropriation claims were barred by limitations; (3) Mark's damages were limited to the $200 per mile transfer fee.

Whether the Merger Violated the Non-Disclosure Agreements

In their first and second points of error, appellants contend the trial court erred in holding, as a matter of law, that their merger violated the non-disclosure agreements. They argue the court's construction of the contract conflicts with the majority of jurisdictions which have considered the issue.

We begin by noting that no case in Texas and or in any other jurisdiction has addressed this specific issue. However, courts in other jurisdictions have addressed the effect of a merger on other restrictive provisions. For example, courts have addressed the effect of a merger on a non-assignment clause in an insurance policy which called for termination of the contract in the event of an assignment to which the insurer did not consent. . . . Numerous courts also have addressed the effect of a merger on a non-assignment clause in a real estate lease. . . . An obvious basis for the outcome in the above cases is that courts disfavor forfeiture in insurance policies and leases. Courts, however, have been equally unwilling to find that merger breaches a non-assignment provision in other circumstances.

Mark cites to cases that have found a corporate merger violates an anti-assignment provision. Mark relies primarily on [*PPG Indus., Inc. v. Guardian Indus. Corp.*, 597 F.2d 1090, 1095 (6th Cir. 1979)]. In that case, PPG and Permaglass each independently developed a process to fabricate glass, and they agreed to grant each other rights to their patents. The agreement granting the rights contained a non-assignability provision, which PPG claimed Permaglass breached when it later merged with an unrelated third party. The court agreed, noting that if the parties desired an exception to their non-assignability provision in case of merger, they could have so provided. Since they did not, the provision of non-assignability prevailed.

We disagree with the reasoning and outcome of PPG and [*Nicolas M. Salgo Assocs. v. Continental Ill. Properties*, 532 F.Supp. 279 (D.D.C.1981)]. Furthermore, those cases are distinguishable because there, the corporations merged into unrelated entities. In . . . the present case, a subsidiary merged into a parent corporation. Because the change was merely one of corporate form, . . . the merger did not involve an increased risk to [a] non-merging party. By contrast, the non-merging parties in *PPG* and *Salgo* were obviously prejudiced as a result of the merger: in *PPG*, the third party into which Permaglass merged gained access to a patent right it would not otherwise have had absent the merger, and in *Salgo*, the non-merging party was forced to accept a partner with whom it did not agree to form a partnership. Finally, the holdings of both cases are contrary to the merger statutes, as addressed more fully below.

Appellants contend the court's order conflicts with the applicable merger statutes, i.e., the Delaware Code, the Ohio Code, and the Texas Business Corporation Act. In general, these statutes provide that all rights, privileges, and obligations belonging to the merging corporation vest in the surviving corporation upon merger. All of these merger statutes are based upon the Model Business Code, the comments to which explicitly state that a merger is not a conveyance or transfer and that the surviving corporation automatically becomes the owner of all real and personal property in the event of a merger.

According to appellants, the court's interpretation prevents the flow of TXO's contractual rights to Marathon, in violation of the statutes. We agree. Under the merger statutes it is clear that all of TXO's interests vested in Marathon immediately upon the merger. Further, under these provisions there is no transfer of the rights of the merging corporation; rather, the rights vest automatically and without further action. Accordingly, a requirement that the surviving corporation pay a fee in the event of a merger unnecessarily hinders the free flow of those rights to the surviving corporation.

The merger statutes also refute Mark's claim of harm resulting from the disclosure. Mark contends that the merger allowed Marathon to have access to seismic data that it would otherwise not have had. Furthermore, Mark notes that both Marathon and TXO were its customers prior to the merger, but the merger allowed two entities to have access to data for which only one paid a fee. To the contrary, the merger statutes make clear that, after a merger, there remains only one entity, and the separate existences of the merging corporations cease. Because Marathon did not have access to the seismic data until after the merger, and because after the merger only one entity existed, Mark cannot claim it was entitled to a fee from both entities and thus sustained a monetary loss.

We next look to the contracts themselves for guidance as to the effect of the merger on the non-disclosure provisions. A number of courts that have found mergers do not violate anti-assignment provisions have considered the parties' failure to expressly state that the provision is triggered by a merger. We also reiterate that the Texas Legislature intended by its amendments to the Business Corporations Act that a prohibited transfer would not be implied by merger but would only occur in the event the parties agreed that merger specifically violated an anti-assignment provision.

Here, the contracts provided that the data "shall not be sold, traded, disposed of, or otherwise made available to third parties." Arguably, the agreements' prohibitions on making the seismic data "available" could encompass statutory merger, which by operation of law makes all property of the merging corporation the property of the survivor, thereby making that property available to the survivor. However, the possibility of merger was certainly foreseeable under the circumstances. The parties could have easily specified that the non-disclosure provision was implicated by a statutory merger, but they chose not to do so. In accordance with the holdings of the cases cited above and the policy enunciated by the drafters of the Texas Corporations Business Act, we will not imply a violation of the non-disclosure agreement in light of the parties' failure to address this situation.

Conclusion

The trial court held that as a matter of law, the merger of Marathon and TXO constituted a transfer of the seismic data to a third party. This holding conflicts with the applicable merger statutes and the majority of cases which have considered similar issues. As such, we find Mark was not entitled to judgment as a matter of law, and the trial court erred in granting summary judgment in its favor. We further hold that, as a matter of law, the merger did not constitute a prohibited transfer or disclosure, and appellants were entitled to summary judgment.

NOTES & QUESTIONS

1. Look back at the provisions of Delaware Corporations Code Section 251 dealing with mergers. The surviving entity in a merger assumes the assets and liabilities of the merging companies, subject to any limitations in the merger agreement. This means that a merger will result in the surviving company being burdened by the liabilities of the merging companies, both contractual and tort, even if executives of the companies were not aware of the liabilities at the time of the merger.

2. The treatment of liabilities in acquisitions of corporate assets is different from the treatment in mergers. In general, a company that buys the assets of another company does not usually assume the selling corporation's liabilities. However, the doctrine of successor liability explained in *Peters* does transfer liabilities along with assets in some situations. These situations include (summarizing the standards mentioned in the *Peters* decision) acquisitions of corporate assets involving: (1) an express or implied assumption of liability; (2) a de facto merger; (3) the use of an acquisition to perpetrate fraud; and (4) a transaction producing an acquiring company that is a mere continuation of the asset seller's business. The *Peters* court also identifies five factors that are considered in determining if one business is a mere continuation of another: (1) the transfer of operating assets; (2) inadequate consideration paid for assets transferred; (3) the continuation of business activities; (4) a commonality of officers; and (5) the incapability of the selling company to pay ongoing obligations. The *Peters* case offers a good example of how these factors can be applied.

3. Think about how the doctrine of successor liability would apply when a company buys the intellectual property assets of another company, such as in the *Weyerhaeuser* case discussed below in Section E. Warranties in an asset

sales agreement may also establish liability of a seller of intellectual property, allowing a buyer to recover amounts which will offset successor liability. As we will see in the *Weyerhaeuser* case, if Company A buys the intellectual property of Company B, that property is warranted to be free of related infringement liability, and the use of that intellectual property in turn is infringing, then Company A may be liable for the infringement and have a cause of action for breach of warranty against Company B.

4. The *TXO* case is another example of how ownership of intellectual property is treated in the case of a merger. Note that the court takes an approach that is very different from the *PPG* court. While both courts appeal to state corporate law, the *TXO* court holds that the merger statute considered there did not provide for a transfer of assets but a transfer of corporate identity. Note that the *TXO* court also states that if the parties wanted to limit transferability of intellectual property through a merger, they could have expressed that intention in their merger contract. Therefore, the decision rests in part on the interpretation of the statute and in part on contract law. Is the fact that PGI was aware that TXO was subsidiary of Marathon at the time of the license relevant to the court's decision? Is that fact what distinguishes *TXO* from *PPG*?

D. TRANSFER ISSUES

BIOLIFE SOLUTIONS, INC. v. ENDOCARE, INC.
Court of Chancery of Delaware
838 A.2d 268 (2003)

LAMB, Vice Chancellor.

I.

The plaintiff sold assets to a competitor in return for a mixture of cash and shares of the competitor's publicly traded common stock. The purchaser later refused to perform its obligation under a related registration rights agreement to file a registration statement covering the shares so that they could be sold in compliance with the federal securities laws. Shortly afterwards, the market price of the shares plummeted, and, eventually, the shares were delisted after the seller's public accountants withdrew their report on its prior period financial statements.

The seller sought a variety of remedies for this breach of contract, including specific performance and, alternatively, money damages. The claim for money damages was tried beginning on March 31, 2003. In this post-trial opinion, the court concludes that the seller is entitled to damages measured by reference to the market price of the shares over a period of five consecutive trading days beginning when the seller could first have sold them had the necessary registration statement been filed in a timely manner.

II.

A.   The Parties

Plaintiff BioLife Solutions, Inc., which was formally named Cryomedical Sciences, Inc. ("CMS"), is a Delaware corporation with its principal place of business in Binghamton, New York. BioLife's current business is the development, manufacture and marketing of solutions for the preservation of cells, tissues and organs at low temperatures (the "Solutions Business"). Before June 24, 2002, BioLife also was engaged in developing, manufacturing and marketing minimally invasive cryosurgical devices for the ablation of tissues (the "Cryosurgical Business").

CMS was one of the first companies to perfect the use of cryosurgical devices for the treatment of prostate diseases. During the early 1990s, it had essentially 100% of the worldwide market for this application. CMS began to struggle thereafter, and was quickly passed in marketplace acceptance by Endocare, Inc. (and a competitor, Galil Medical Systems, Inc.), whose cryosurgical equipment was viewed as superior for the treatment of prostate cancer. By the spring of 2002, CMS was facing severe financial difficulties.

Defendant Endocare, is a Delaware corporation with its principal place of business in Irvine, California. Endocare is engaged primarily in the development, manufacture, and marketing of temperature-based, minimally invasive surgical devices and technologies designed to treat certain cancers. Endocare was a direct competitor of CMS. By the spring of 2002, Endocare had approximately 80% of the market share for cryosurgical equipment used for prostate cancer.

B.   The Transaction

In early 2002, BioLife and Endocare entered into negotiations regarding the acquisition of the Cryosurgical Business by Endocare. On May 28, 2002, BioLife and Endocare entered into an Asset Purchase Agreement (the "Agreement"). Closing on the Agreement occurred on June 24, 2002 (the "Closing"). Pursuant to the Agreement, Endocare acquired all of the tangible and intangible assets relating to BioLife's Cryosurgical Business. At the Closing, Endocare paid to BioLife $2,200,000 in cash, and provided BioLife with a stock certificate representing 120,022 shares of Endocare's common stock.

Included among the financial information provided in the Agreement was the Statement of Operations for the CMS business. This Statement showed that CMS's revenue for calendar year 2001 was approximately $954,000 (or an average of approximately $240,000 per quarter), while its revenue for the first three months of 2002 (the only quarter available as of either the signing of the Agreement or the Closing) had declined to $82,893.

At Closing, the parties also entered into a Registration Rights Agreement. Pursuant to Section 1.2 of the Registration Rights Agreement,

Endocare agreed, "as soon as reasonably practicable after the [June 24, 2002] Closing Date . . . but in no event more than 90 days thereafter" to file a registration statement on SEC Form S-3 and "as soon as reasonably practicable thereafter, effect all such qualifications and compliances as may be reasonably necessary and as would permit or facilitate the sale and distribution of" the stock transferred pursuant to the Agreement. Because the closing occurred on June 24, 2002, this 90-day period expired on September 22, 2002.

Section 1.2(a) of the Registration Rights Agreement also gave Endocare the right to delay filing the Form S-3, but only under the following limited circumstances:

1. where the "Form S-3 is not available for such offering;" or

2. until Endocare received "the consents and the financial statements and other financial information required by the [Securities] Act [of 1933] and the SEC to be included in such registration statement from the independent certified public accountants of both [Endocare] and [BioLife];"

3. "if [Endocare] shall furnish to [BioLife] a certificate signed by [Endocare's] Chief Executive Officer stating that in the good faith judgment of the Board, it would be seriously detrimental to [Endocare] and its stockholders for such Form S-3 Registration to be effected at such time, in which event [Endocare] shall have the right to defer the filing of the Form S-3 registration for a period of not more than 90 days after receipt of the request of [BioLife] under this Section 1.2;" or

4. where the filing of the registration statement or effecting qualification or compliance "in any particular jurisdiction" that would require Endocare "to qualify to do business or to execute a general consent to service of process in effecting such registration, qualification or compliance."

C.   Delivery Of The Assets

Pursuant to Section 2.1 of the Agreement, the assets sold to Endocare consisted for the most part of intellectual property, 47 pieces of tangible assets (primarily equipment), inventory and accounts receivable. According to Endocare, "[t]he primary assets sought . . . were the intangible assets held by BioLife — its patents, trademarks, and customer lists."

1. The "Primary Assets"

The intellectual property (the patents, trademarks, and copyrights) were delivered at Closing in the form of an Assignment of Patents, an Assignment of Servicemarks and Trademarks, and an Assignment of Copyrights. The customer lists were provided to Endocare on May 27, 2002, the day before the Agreement was signed.

In addition to the actual assignment of the patents, there were also patent files that BioLife was required to deliver to Endocare. These files, which were maintained by BioLife's patent attorneys, contained the material that had been collected in connection with the various patent applications-correspondence to the patent office and the client, and notes and memoranda to the file by the patent attorneys. There is no doubt that Endocare was entitled to receive those documents, and there is also no doubt that delivery of those documents occurred slowly.

On August 9, 2002, Lawrence Ginsberg, Endocare's intellectual property counsel, contacted the law firm of Pillsbury Winthrop, LLP, which had represented BioLife in connection with the Agreement. The purpose of this call was to ascertain why the patent files had not been transferred and when they would be transferred. Following that initial conversation, Ginsberg again made contact with Pillsbury, and was told by Glenn Perry, a Pillsbury attorney, that he would "set the wheels in motion." BioLife, through Pillsbury, forwarded what it believed were the correct patent files to Endocare on September 3, 2002. In fact, some of the files sent were not related to patents that had been assigned under the Agreement, and certain patent files that were assigned were not actually sent. On October 14, after recognizing this error, Ginsberg e-mailed Anthony Miele, BioLife's new patent attorney at the law firm of Palmer & Dodge, LLP, to inquire about transferring the proper patent files. Miele responded later that day, stating that the patent file transfers "were in the works" and that he would "push these along." On October 21, Ginsberg again e-mailed Miele to inquire about the status of the patent file transfers. Finally, on November 4, 2002, Ginsberg e-mailed Miele, reiterating Endocare's need to obtain the patent files.

On November 11, 2002, BioLife transferred what Endocare initially thought were the complete patent files. However, not all the patent files had in fact been transferred to Endocare. Several patent files were not turned over to Endocare until March 13, 2003.

John Baust, CMS's president and CEO at the time of the Agreement, testified at trial that the late delivery of these patent files was due to the actions of one of CMS's former patent firms. He stated:

> [t]here was an earlier firm we dealt with in the early nineties, Sherman & Shalloway, in Alexandria, who were retaining patent files that, frankly, neither of the other patent firms [that CMS utilized], to my knowledge knew about. Nor did I.

> And when we found out about that, we then asked Sherman & Shalloway to transfer those files to Mr. Miele, at Palmer Dodge, so that he could determine what was appropriate to forward to Endocare, because I had no idea what was in those files.

> That took some time. Sherman & Shalloway was reluctant to transfer. They felt there was an outstanding bill from the mid-nineties, and they were holding those files until that bill was satisfied. And so it took some months for them to be convinced to transfer the files.

Although Endocare argues that BioLife's failure to provide all the patent files constitutes a material breach of the Agreement, it is clear that Endocare was primarily concerned with one particular patent file. By the time of trial,

Endocare focused its argument in this regard almost exclusively on the patent file for the urethral warmer (Patent No. 5,437,673 ; the "673 Patent"). In particular, Paul Mikus, Endocare's former CEO and current chairman of its board, claimed at trial that Endocare's patent counsel needed the file related to the 673 Patent in order to perform proper due diligence on its contents before determining whether to commence an infringement action against one of Endocare's competitors (Galil). . . .

IV

. . .

B. Endocare Has Not Shown That Failure To Deliver Certain Assets Was Material To The Transaction

A party is excused from performance under a contract if the other party is in material breach thereof. "The converse of this principal is that a slight breach by one party, while giving rise to an action for damages, will not necessarily terminate the obligations of the injured party to perform under the contract." Non-performance by an injured party under such a circumstance operates as a breach of contract. "The question whether the breach is of sufficient importance to justify non-performance by the non-breaching party is one of degree and is determined by 'weighing the consequences in the light of the actual custom of men in the performance of contracts similar to the one that is involved in the specific case.' "

Section 241 of the Restatement (Second) of Contracts sets forth several factors to consider when determining whether "a failure to render . . . performance is material" (thus justifying repudiation of a contract). These factors include: (a) the extent to which the injured party will be deprived of the benefit which he reasonably expected; (b) the extent to which the injured party can be adequately compensated for the part of that benefit of which he will be deprived; (c) the extent to which the party failing to perform or to offer to perform will suffer forfeiture; (d) the likelihood that the party failing to perform or to offer to perform will cure his failure, taking account of all the circumstances including any reasonable assurances; and (e) the extent to which the behavior of the party failing to perform or to offer to perform comports with standards of good faith and fair dealing.

Endocare argues that even if it breached the Registration Rights Agreement, it was justified in doing so because BioLife had already materially breached its obligations under the Agreement. The first document that formally set forth Endocare's position regarding its refusal to file a registration statement was a letter dated September 12, 2002 from Endocare's outside attorneys to BioLife's Chief Executive Officer. That letter states that "[a]s of the date hereof, Endocare has not received any material portion of the Assets from Cryomedical." In its letter, Endocare did not mention any specific assets that had not been delivered. By trial, however, Endocare's claim regarding BioLife's failure to deliver assets had been essentially reduced to two categories: documents necessary for FDA compliance and the patent files.

1.   Documents Required To Be Maintained By The FDA

Endocare claims that it never received either (a) the FDA-required documents with respect to how to build the cryosurgical equipment it was acquiring from BioLife or (b) the service records with respect to that equipment. As discussed below, the failure to timely deliver these assets was not a material breach, and materially all of the assets were in fact delivered before Endocare was obligated to file a registration statement.

a.   Endocare Had No Real Interest In Acquiring An Ongoing Business

Evidence adduced at trial demonstrated that Endocare never intended to build new CMS cryosurgical equipment. Instead, its focus was on CMS's existing customer base transfer to Endocare's equipment.

The cryosurgical equipment acquired from CMS was a very different technology than Endocare's own. CMS's equipment "was a liquid nitrogen system." "Endocare took a different approach to their fundamental design, and they used what is called a Joule Thompson effect. They used a pressurized gas." Although CMS had been "the company that originally founded the commercial application for cryosurgery, . . . Endocare had come along with the next generation technology and . . . taken most of the market share away." Because of these radically different designs, the manufacturing process of these two systems was not similar. As a result, the two companies' cryosurgical equipment was not interchangeable. Thus, probes from one system could not be used with consoles from another.

It would be unreasonable to believe that Endocare meant to acquire CMS — in its view a second-rate system incompatible with its own — and then try to sell it to customers. Mikus's testimony supports the conclusion that Endocare's purchase of the Cryosurgical Business was done only to eliminate competition. For example, Endocare did little due diligence with respect to the Cryosurgical Business, as Mikus did not know if anyone had toured CMS's facilities before the Closing. Moreover, Endocare had no plans to hire any former CMS employees (with the possible exception of the former Chief Executive Officer). In addition, Mikus did not know how many active accounts CMS had as of the Closing.

Another example of Endocare's lack of interest in the continuation of the Cryosurgical Business relates to CMS's inventory of cryosurgical consoles. Although CMS had an inventory of cryosurgical consoles as of the Closing, Mikus did not know if CMS was still manufacturing consoles or when the last console had been made. Moreover, Mikus admitted that Endocare never intended to manufacture new CMS consoles. Cannon, who had been hired to continue a mobile services division, only used CMS's equipment for about six weeks after Closing, when he switched to Endocare's equipment.

With respect to cryosurgical probes, Mikus did not know if CMS was still manufacturing them as of the Closing, did not know how many probes were in CMS's inventory, and did not know, post-Closing, if all probes had been used. Moreover, Endocare had no intention of manufacturing new CMS probes.

According to Cannon, much of the equipment was "junked" because Endocare was not going to use it.

Endocare argues it entered into the Agreement "with the expectation that it would receive substantial revenue from BioLife's existing cryosurgical business." Endocare alleges "[t]he revenue from the cryosurgical business had been represented as approximately $1 million in 2001, and Endocare expected to realize revenues in that range going forward." The documentary evidence in the case suggests otherwise-specifically, one of the attachments to the Agreement was Part 3.3, which sets forth certain financial information of CMS (without its BioLife component). Included in this information was the Statement of Operations from the CMS business alone. This statement showed that CMS's revenue for calendar year 2001 was approximately $954,0000 (or an average of approximately $240,000 per quarter), while its revenue for the first three months of 2002 (the only quarter available as of the Closing) had declined to $82,923. Such a decline in revenue is startling, and it is simply not credible for Endocare to argue that it continues to expect $1 million in revenue per year based on these most recent results.

b.   All Necessary Documents Were Delivered

Although Endocare originally claimed, on September 12, 2002, that it had "not received any material portion of the Assets from Cryomedical," it has since conceded that most of the FDA-required documents "were ultimately collected through Charlie Cannon's efforts prior to September 20, 2002." The only specific FDA-required documents that Endocare claims were not produced are "the service records related to its mobile services business" citing to the deposition of Cannon at various places.

Cannon actually testified in a manner contrary to what Endocare implies. In particular, Cannon explained that he maintained his own equipment for the mobile services, and kept the service records for that equipment at his office in Jersey Shore, Pennsylvania. Moreover, Cannon testified that Dave Rust, an Endocare regional manager, "came down [to Jersey Shore] and collected copies of the shipping and mobile service records." Thus, the record evidence implies that Endocare actually does have these records in its possession. Finally, Cannon testified that Endocare never intended to continue the mobile services using CMS's equipment. Thus, Endocare would have had no use for service documents for equipment it had no intention of using, manufacturing, or supporting.

For all of these reasons, the court finds that to the extent certain physical assets (or documents related to those assets) were not delivered or were delivered late, such non-delivery or late delivery might have given rise to a damages claim by Endocare, but it did not give rise to a material breach of the Agreement thereby excusing Endocare from filing a registration statement pursuant to the Registration Rights Agreement.

2.   The Patent Files

BioLife does not dispute, because it cannot, that it failed to transfer certain patent files to Endocare by September 20, 2002, the last business day during the 90-day period under the Registration Rights Agreement. The undisputed evidence in the case demonstrates that BioLife transferred additional patent files on November 11, 2002, but that it was not until March 13, 2003 that it transferred what it now contends are all the remaining patent files. This late transfer of patent files, however, did not amount to a material breach of the Agreement sufficient to justify Endocare's refusal to file a registration statement.

First, the Agreement itself places no heightened emphasis on the patent files themselves. This is so despite the fact that Endocare now claims that the patent files, and particularly the patent file associated with the 673 Patent, were the cornerstone of its acquisition of CMS. Second, had those patent files been material to the Agreement, one would expect Endocare to have made arrangements to receive them at Closing or at least to specifically mention them by name in its September 12 letter when it relied on the alleged failure to deliver assets to justify its decision to refuse to file a registration statement. Instead, the September 12 letter merely stated, in a substantial overstatement, that "Endocare has not received any material portion of the Assets from [CMS]. . . ."

Finally, Endocare now has the patent files it complains it never received. Although Endocare may have suffered some damage as a result of the late delivery, such damage cannot be so material as to justify its refusal to file a registration statement. Endocare primarily sought the 673 Patent file to determine if another competitor (Galil) could be subject to a patent infringement lawsuit. Now that Endocare has the patent files associated with the 673 Patent, it can presumably reach a decision whether to pursue its lawsuit against Galil.

Endocare also complains about having never received a so-called "lab notebook" for the 673 Patent. Responding to questions regarding whether there were "any notebooks in existence at CMS that showed an early date of invention for the urethral warming system [the system covered by the 673 Patent]," Baust stated that this system was developed at Allegheny General Hospital between 1991 and 1993. He further testified that "[t]he development notebooks would have been maintained by either Doctor Onik, Doctor Reyes or Allegheny General. . . . We focused on the patent-related information and secured the patent, but those files, to my knowledge, were not with CMS."

For all these reasons, the court concludes that the failure to timely deliver patent files was not a material breach of the Agreement by BioLife, and that Endocare was not justified in refusing to satisfy its filing obligation under the Registration Rights Agreement.

[JUDGMENT FOR BIOLIFE.]

NOTES & QUESTIONS

1. The *Biolife Solutions* case illustrates some of the mechanics of acquisition transactions involving intellectual property. In analyzing the case, you should focus on the elements of the deal. What did each side want? What did each side have to do? Pay special attention to the asset transfer. How is intellectual property transferred from one party to another? Features of due diligence reviews of intellectual property interests and infringement risks are discussed in more detail in Chapter 9. In the context of mergers and acquisitions, these reviews typically focus on the validity and scope of intellectual property interests and the likely effectiveness of merger and acquisition agreements in transferring those interests.

2. The court at one point states that Endocare had no interest in acquiring an ongoing business. Why is this finding relevant? What does it say about the expectations of the parties and performance obligations under the contract? Why would Endocare have entered into this deal if it did not want to acquire an ongoing business? The court suggests that Endocare was primarily interested in the acquisition of the targeted company's customer lists. Is a corporate acquisition an expensive means for that end?

3. The case also discusses requirements for filing stock registration documents with the Securities and Exchange Commission. Note that part of the consideration to be received by BioLife in the disputed acquisition was stock. Whenever a company issues stock over a particular value, it must register the stock with the Securities and Exchange Commission before it can make the issuance. Since Endocare seemed to be delaying the registration process, BioLife had special reasons to be concerned about whether it would receive the consideration it expected from the transaction. Endocare, of course, was arguing that its performance obligation was excused because BioLife was in breach by not turning over its patent files and other assets.

4. Notice that the transfer of intellectual property assets occurs through assignments. The transfer of the patent files is incidental to the assignments, but part of the transaction. Why would Endocare want the patent files? The contents of these files describe the prosecution history of each of the patents and therefore are important for litigation as well as for other purposes. Do you think that a serious acquirer would have asked to see the files before the transaction was completed? Do you think Endocare had looked at the files before hand? Why would it be a good idea to look at the files? One answer is provided by the case discussed in Section E, which deals with due diligence.

E. IMPACTS OF INEFFECTIVE TRANSFERS AND INADEQUATE DILIGENCE

PARAGON TRADE BRANDS, INC. v. WEYERHAEUSER COMPANY

United States Bankruptcy Court for the Northern District of Georgia
324 B.R. 829 (2005)

MURPHY, BANKRUPTCY J.

. . .

II. FINDINGS OF FACT

A. Background of the Private-Label Baby Diaper Business Weyerhaeuser Transferred to Paragon in the IPO

. . .

5. Weyerhaeuser commenced a baby diaper business in 1972. This business consisted largely of selling a private-label diaper to large retail

establishments that placed their store names on the package and sold the diaper on their shelves at lower prices than the branded diapers sold by [Procter & Gamble (PG)], which sold the "Pampers" and "Luvs" brands, and [Kimberly-Clark Corporation (KC)], which sold the "Huggies" brand. The diaper was the primary product in Weyerhaeuser's Personal Care Products ("PCP") Division.

6. In the late 1980s, Weyerhaeuser embarked on a plan to refocus on its core businesses. Because the baby diaper business was not considered one of its core businesses, the diaper business was targeted for divestment. Weyerhaeuser informed the investment community about its refocusing and proceeded to move as quickly as possible to dispose of its baby diaper business (the "Business").

7. The Business had performed well in the early 1980s, earning pre-tax profits for Weyerhaeuser in 1983 and 1984 of $31 to $39 million. A key to Weyerhaeuser's success during these years was a "brand matching" practice, which included utilizing an elastic leg gather feature patented under PG's Buell '003 patent. This strategy gave Weyerhaeuser's private-label diaper an advantage over its competitors' private-label diapers.

8. In 1981, PG sued Weyerhaeuser for infringing the Buell patent, seeking an injunction against use of the patented feature, damages for a reasonable royalty, and enhanced damages for willful infringement. Weyerhaeuser asserted various invalidity defenses to PG's Buell patent, and elected to take the case to trial instead of removing the feature or re-designing its diaper to avoid the infringement claim. The jury found that Weyerhaeuser willfully infringed PG's Buell patent, and that a reasonable royalty would have been 1% of sales. The trial court rejected Weyerhaeuser's invalidity defenses. On July 2, 1985, the trial court entered judgment against Weyerhaeuser, permanently enjoining it from making its private-label diaper as it was then designed, and awarding PG reasonable royalty damages of $2.3 million, plus prejudgment interest and attorneys' fees.

. . .

12. [Weyerhaeuser sought to improve its diaper business.] The primary means for improvement was the addition of a newer feature known as the inner leg gather, or "ILG." An ILG, in layman's terms, is a second elasticized inner barrier cuff in the diaper that contains or channels effluent, and thus reduces leakage. Because leakage prevention is the primary purpose of a diaper, the ILG was the most important new feature for diapers ever incorporated in disposable diapers. Weyerhaeuser internally concluded that failure to add the ILG would negatively impact its sales volume by one million cases (1% of market share, or 1/12 its sales) in the first year and another 500,000 cases in the second through fourth years. Weyerhaeuser personnel believed that having the ILG on its Ultra diaper was essential for it to compete in the private-label diaper market. KC's ILG was marketed nationally in early 1990, and PG was expected to do so in September, 1990.

. . .

14. PG and KC, however, each had patent claims encompassing the ILG feature, under PG's "Lawson" patent and KC's "Enloe" patent. PG's Lawson patent described an ILG that was fluid impermeable or hydrophobic, and KC's Enloe patent described an ILG that was fluid pervious. For each day after March 1991 that Weyerhaeuser earned sales and profits using the ILG technology, its potential liability for patent infringement grew.

. . .

16. . . . Weyerhaeuser obtained patent opinions from outside counsel that the Lawson, Dragoo and Enloe patents were invalid based on certain cited prior art. Weyerhaeuser had received a similar invalidity opinion regarding Buell that was proven wrong at trial. These opinions did not guarantee success in litigation, but would help protect Weyerhaeuser against a willful infringement finding, which carried the threat of enhanced or treble damages. Weyerhaeuser knew that issued patents, such as Lawson, Dragoo and Enloe, are presumed valid, and that a party attacking validity has the burden of overcoming this presumption by clear and convincing evidence. The patent opinions Weyerhaeuser obtained did not assess the probability or likelihood that a court would find invalid the presumptively valid ILG patents of PG and KC, and Pat Coogan, Weyerhaeuser's in-house patent counsel with oversight responsibilities for the PCP Division, testified he did not request such an assessment from outside counsel. In what appears to have been a lengthy meeting held September 5, 1991, Mr. Coogan advised Weyerhaeuser's General Counsel, Bob Lane, that Weyerhaeuser's chance to succeed on an invalidity defense to PG's Lawson or KC's Enloe patent infringement claims was no better than "50/50."

17. In the year before launching its ILG diaper in March, 1991, Weyerhaeuser negotiated with PG to obtain a license to use its ILG feature, offering on many occasions to pay royalties or to trade licenses to various Weyerhaeuser patents for the right to use the ILG feature. These negotiations failed in May 1991 because PG demanded a 3% royalty to license the ILG feature, an amount Weyerhaeuser stated it could not afford to pay and remain competitive in the diaper market.

18. Also in 1991, PG and KC were litigating with each other in federal district court in Seattle, Washington (the "Seattle litigation" or "Seattle trial") over whose ILG invention was reduced to practice first and which had priority of invention. As issued on September 22, 1987, PG's Lawson patent made claims to both the generic ILG invention and ILGs made of impermeable materials. KC's Enloe patent, issued November 3, 1987, made claims to ILGs made of "fluid pervious" materials (referred to later as "Enloe I"). KC sought to establish Enloe's priority of invention to invalidate Lawson's claims and to establish a right to have Lawson's ILG claims transferred to an amended Enloe application filed with the Patent And Trademark Office ("PTO").

19. Weyerhaeuser expected that the Seattle litigation was of sufficient scope for the winner between PG and KC to be found to have a "likelihood of success" in a later action to enjoin Weyerhaeuser from making and selling its

private-label ILG Ultra diaper, and from using the ILG on any other product. In June 1991, trial of the Seattle litigation was conducted. Weyerhaeuser's in-house patent counsel Pat Coogan attended most of the trial.

20. In March 1991, a few months before the Seattle trial started, Weyerhaeuser's Investment Evaluation Department ("IED") commenced efforts to value the Business and determine how to sell it to obtain the best value. Weyerhaeuser also hired the investment banking firm of Morgan Stanley to advise on the Business's likely market value and likely buyers. In a report issued August 28, 1991, Weyerhaeuser's IED concluded that the Business's value was $90 million. Morgan Stanley's base case valuation of the Business was between $75 and $95 million. Neither the valuation of Morgan Stanley nor Weyerhaeuser's IED, however, assumed any royalty payable to KC or PG for the ILG technology, or payment of damages for past infringement. Morgan Stanley also reported to Weyerhaeuser an "unusually limited universe of buyers" for the Business and a significant risk that no transaction would result from a sale process.

21. In its valuation study, the IED reported that (i) each percentage point change in the Business's market share would change the Business's value by about $30 million; and (ii) a $1 change in the gross profit margin per standard case sold would change the Business value by $80 million. Assuming, however, a combined 5.5% royalty payable by the Business (which equaled PG's and KC's last demands before Weyerhaeuser closed the IPO, as discussed beginning at page 13, ¶ 29), Weyerhaeuser's gross profit margin per case would drop by $1.49, from $5.62 to $4.13. According to Weyerhaeuser's valuation analysis before the 1992-93 IPO, if paying these royalties, the Business would have zero or negative value. Notes prepared by a Weyerhaeuser IED officer of a meeting with Mr. Coogan, Mr. Robert Dowdy, and others August 20, 1991, reflect discussions over possibly putting the diaper division in a separate subsidiary to protect Weyerhaeuser from what was then stated to be a substantial and growing infringement liability. In November 1991, Chemical Bank, a bank with whom Weyerhaeuser had a relationship through its investment banking arm, advised Weyerhaeuser that the Business might not be saleable at anything better than a "fire sale" price. In early 1992, Weyerhaeuser also investigated disposing of the Business through a leveraged management buyout.

22. On September 10, 1991, while Weyerhaeuser was reviewing disposition of the Business, the decision in the Seattle litigation awarded priority of invention to KC's Enloe patent. As a result, Lawson's claims to generic ILGs were held invalid as obvious or anticipated in light of Enloe. The district court, however, held that Lawson's claims to impermeable, or hydrophobic, ILGs remained valid despite Enloe, given that Enloe's "fluid pervious" ILG patent taught away from Lawson's impermeable ILG design. The consequence of this decision was that Weyerhaeuser's largely impermeable ILG diaper stood squarely within Lawson patent claims of PG that did survive the Seattle trial, and Weyerhaeuser knew it. Weyerhaeuser had no solid non-infringement position against the surviving Lawson impermeable ILG patent claims. Mr. Coogan also realized that the Seattle court's decision meant Lawson's

generic claims to all ILGs (regardless of permeability) would, in due course, be transferred to Enloe and issue in an amended Enloe patent that would encompass all ILGs, including ILGs used on Weyerhaeuser's Ultra diaper. Mr. Coogan reported this expectation to nine different Weyerhaeuser officers and lawyers, including its CFO and CEO, in his September 13, 1991 memorandum sent three days after the Seattle decision issued.

23. The Seattle trial result put Weyerhaeuser in the predicament of having to license the technology to make and sell its impermeable ILG diaper from not just one, but two competitors: PG, holding Lawson's surviving impermeable ILG patent claims; and KC, which would be granted an amended Enloe patent claiming all ILGs, regardless of hydrophobicity. Weyerhaeuser expected the prevailing party in the Seattle litigation, which was on appeal, would demand royalties from Weyerhaeuser for use of the ILG feature, and if a license and royalty agreement could not be resolved, that one or the other — PG or KC — would sue to enjoin Weyerhaeuser from using the ILG and for damages, including lost profits and/or reasonable royalties. Weyerhaeuser representatives were aware during this period that its potential liability for infringing PG's ILG patents included damages for lost profits on sales Weyerhaeuser was taking from PG, and that such damages could be "enormous" because PG's profit margin on the Weyerhaeuser ILG diaper sales approached 30%.

24. In December 1991, PG formally notified Weyerhaeuser that its Ultra diaper infringed PG's Lawson and Dragoo patents. In a December 1991 meeting, Weyerhaeuser's General Counsel, Bob Lane advised Weyerhaeuser's auditor, Arthur Andersen, that the damages arising from such a PG claim could be "enormous" for Weyerhaeuser. On February 10, 1992, Mr. Lane reported to Weyerhaeuser's auditor, Arthur Andersen, that the PG claim could result in a 3% royalty payable and an injunction.

25. By early 1992, Weyerhaeuser had been unable to sell the Business through traditional means. In March 1992, Weyerhaeuser launched a plan to dispose of the Business through an initial public offering of 100% of stock of a newly-formed Weyerhaeuser subsidiary into which it would transfer the Business. Weyerhaeuser retained Merrill Lynch to be the lead underwriter for this offering. Merrill Lynch retained the Skadden Arps law firm as its counsel. Weyerhaeuser retained the Paul Weiss law firm to be its counsel. The newly-formed company, which became Paragon, had no separate counsel. Weyerhaeuser employees responsible for the Business were expected to become the managers of the newly-formed public company after the IPO. The Business had a successful year (on paper) in 1991, earning over $33 million in operating profit on net sales over $396 million. Its performance was up significantly from its $2 million operating profit in 1990 on net sales of about $286 million, and significantly better than the Business's performance the prior four years, 1986-89. The Business's successful results in 1991 and 1992 positioned Weyerhaeuser to pursue the IPO.

26. Weyerhaeuser incorporated Paragon Trade Brands, Inc. in June 1992 as its wholly-owned subsidiary, to own the business Weyerhaeuser planned to take public. Initially, the IPO was planned to close in late August or September 1992, but it was tabled in early September due to concerns over the

effect a PG diaper price reduction would have on the Business's narrow profit margin.

27. In August 1992, two separate events occurred that confirmed the problematic ILG patent predicament facing the Business. First, on August 14, 1992, the PTO decided in Enloe's (KC's) favor the pending interference action fought between PG and KC over ILG patent priority. Weyerhaeuser's in-house patent counsel, Mr. Coogan, knew that as a result, KC's Enloe patent would be amended to include the generic ILG claims originally granted to Lawson. This new patent, which would not be limited to "impermeable" or "fluid pervious" iterations, would squarely encompass Weyerhaeuser's Ultra ILG diaper.

28. The second event with impact on the ILG patent predicament facing Weyerhaeuser occurred August 26, 1992, when the Federal Circuit Court of Appeals affirmed the Seattle trial court's decision as to priority of invention in the Seattle litigation, again leaving PG's Lawson patent with valid claims to ILGs made of impermeable materials. Based on this ruling, Weyerhaeuser's ILG diaper remained squarely within the claims of what was now a litigation-tested Lawson patent of impermeable diaper ILGs. It was foreseeable by Weyerhaeuser and known within the patent law practice at the time of the IPO that a license can be required from two different parties in order to sell a particular product.

29. Weyerhaeuser expected that both PG and KC would seek royalties from Weyerhaeuser for use of the ILG or, failing an agreed payment, would sue for an injunction against use of the feature and damages. In fact, Weyerhaeuser conducted dual license negotiations with PG and KC in the months before closing the IPO transaction to obtain freedom to use the ILG feature. No license agreement with PG or KC was concluded before closing. PG's last demand before the IPO closed was for a 3% royalty on net sales of all ILG products in return for a license under Lawson and the companion ILG patent, Dragoo. No evidence shows that PG offered, before the IPO closed, to forgive past infringement as part of a license agreement. KC's last demand before the IPO closed was a 2.5% royalty on net sales of ILG products for seven and a half years in return for a license under Enloe I and the to-be-issued generic ILG patent (which later issued as Enloe III), which would be deemed fully paid after the 7.5 years. The proposed KC license did not contemplate a separate payment for past infringement. Both PG and KC rejected Weyerhaeuser's various counteroffers, which consisted of cross-licenses of various Weyerhaeuser diaper patents, or a royalty as low as 0.2%.

30. Weyerhaeuser could not have proceeded with the IPO had the Business been paying royalties in the range demanded by PG and KC. In the IPO Prospectus, which Weyerhaeuser and its attorneys drafted, Weyerhaeuser disclosed the existence of PG's and KC's ILG patent claims, but Weyerhaeuser did not disclose the level of royalties demanded or the severe impact the royalties would have on the Business if forced to pay them. Weyerhaeuser did not disclose that past attempts to license the feature from PG had failed; it downplayed the negotiations as "discussions"; and, the IPO Prospectus represented to the new public shareholders in at least three places that "the Company believes that any outcome with respect to these [ILG patent] matters will have no material adverse effect on its financial position or its results of operations."

A 5.5% royalty (the aggregate amount PG and KC were demanding) would have eliminated virtually all of the Business's 6% profit margin. A 4% royalty (approximately the amount the Business eventually agreed to pay in 1999 in the settlement agreements with PG and KC) would have eliminated approximately two-thirds of the Business's profit margin.

31. Weyerhaeuser had withheld needed capital from the Business in the years before the IPO. The plan was for Paragon, after the IPO, to use its profits to finance its four-year capital improvement program, which was designed to (i) make its operations more cost-efficient so it could survive anticipated pricing actions of the brands and its private-label competitors, (ii) add and improve product features to keep pace with expected continuing diaper improvements in the industry, and (iii) expand production capacity. Being forced to pay royalties in the range of 5% would have severely undermined, if not destroyed, the Business's ability to make the capital investments necessary to survive the pending and anticipated future diaper price wars. In fact, PG and KC did continue their price wars after the IPO, and diaper prices sharply declined by 15 to 22% within three years. Had the Business been forced to pay substantially all its profits to PG and KC in royalties to use the ILG feature, the Business would not have been a viable, on-going business after the IPO, and the IPO likely would not have occurred.

32. The evidence showed that the Business could not, and its managers did not expect it could, independently raise its diaper prices to recoup the extra costs of ILG royalties. As a private-label manufacturer, the Business was a known price follower of the branded manufacturers' (PG and KC) prices. No evidence was presented to show that any of its managers expected they could rely on PG and KC to raise their prices if the Business paid them royalties, thus allowing price increases to recoup the royalty costs. PG and KC, with aggregate market share of +−70%, had been chronically engaged in "fierce battles" inter se over market share, and were lowering prices. In addition to the pressures from PG and KC, Paragon faced, as Weyerhaeuser had, vigorous competition from its private-label competitors that further constrained its ability to raise prices.

33. At the time of the IPO, the Business had no alternative, market-tested design that could be used to replace the ILG feature for the Ultra diaper. Dropping the ILG feature from the Ultra diaper would have been disastrous to the Business, returning it to the "sick" condition from which the ILG feature had rescued it. The Ultra diaper, which was the Business's premium quality private-label diaper, represented approximately 84% of its net sales. The Business also produced and sold a line of economy diapers (the "Economy diaper") that had fewer features than the Ultra diaper. The Economy diaper, which represented about 14% of net sales in 1993 (15% in 1992), did not utilize an ILG feature when the IPO closed. At the time of the IPO, the Business had just introduced a training pant, which is a form of diaper used by older toddlers. The training pant did not then utilize an ILG and represented about 1% of the net sales of the Business at that time. Accordingly, as sold to the public through the IPO, the Business had essentially been built as, and was, a company with a single product — the Ultra ILG diaper — but with good potential for growth and expansion.

34. The consequences of not having the right to use the key ILG feature had been discussed within Weyerhaeuser as similar to the consequences it suffered from the 1985 Buell injunction. These consequences included an injunction requiring the Business to pull the Ultra diaper from retailer shelves, costs to develop a new diaper design, lost sales and profits from being forced to sell an inferior, non-ILG product, payment of the substantial royalties PG and KC were demanding for a license to continue using the ILG feature, and liability to PG and KC for their lost profits, which Weyerhaeuser knew could be substantial.

B. The IPO

36. At [the closing of the IPO of Paragon stock in 1993], Weyerhaeuser transferred the Business to Paragon by executing an Asset Transfer Agreement (ATA) and Intellectual Property Agreement (IPA) (together, the ATA and IPA are the "Transfer Agreements"). The ATA and IPA, as finally executed at the IPO closing, contained assumption of liabilities clauses, whereby Paragon assumed virtually all liabilities of Weyerhaeuser relating to operation of the Business, past and prospective (defined as the "Assumed Liabilities"), including patent liabilities. The Transfer Agreements, at ATA Section 11.02(a) and IPA Section 4.01, also contained certain provisions providing that Paragon would indemnify and defend Weyerhaeuser from the Assumed Liabilities, including any third party claims against Weyerhaeuser for patent infringement relating to operation of the Business. As discussed at length in the Summary Judgment Order entered October 30, 2002, assumption of liability and indemnity clauses existed in early drafts of these contracts, prepared months earlier than the February 2, 1993 actual closing. Later, however, numerous warranties were added to the contracts. Plaintiff sued on four of the warranties. Two are found in the ATA, and were made with no limitation as to Weyerhaeuser's knowledge. In the final, signed ATA, these two warranties provide, in relevant part:

> 3.01(c): [Weyerhaeuser] has, and will transfer to [Paragon] at the Closing, good title to all of the other Assets [all assets other than Real Property] . . . free and clear of any and all mortgages, security interests, liens, claims, charges, options and encumbrances of any nature whatsoever, except for minor defects and irregularities in title or encumbrances that do not materially impair the use of any such Assets for the purposes for which they are held.

> 3.01(d): The Transferred Assets and the services and materials to be provided pursuant to the Related Agreements are sufficient to conduct the Business as now being conducted.

The other two warranties, in the IPA, provide that, "to the best of [Weyerhaeuser's] knowledge":

> 3.11(ii): "Schedules 3.01(a) and 3.01(b) are accurate and complete lists of all Patent Rights and Trademarks, as used in connection with the Business or the Products."

> 3.11(vii): "[T]he Primary Intellectual Property plus Trademarks and Secondary Intellectual Property are adequate for the continuation of the Business as currently conducted."

At closing of the IPO, Weyerhaeuser certified the warranties were true and correct. In Section 3.01(a) of the ATA, Weyerhaeuser represented and warranted to Paragon that the ATA warranties were enforceable on their terms. The IPA and ATA were each fully integrated contracts, which, pursuant to merger clauses in each, superseded all prior discussions between the parties over the subject matter of the agreements. The IPA and ATA were required to be, and were, filed with the SEC as "material contracts" and made a part of the Registration Statement for Paragon's newly issued common stock. Weyerhaeuser, in Section 11.02(b) of the ATA, agreed to indemnify Paragon for all losses, costs, expenses and damages arising from a breach of any of the four warranties at issue.

C. Paragon After The IPO

37. After the IPO, the Business now known as Paragon continued to make and sell the Ultra diaper with the same ILG feature Weyerhaeuser had used before the IPO. For infringement purposes, Paragon's ILG feature did not change from the feature on which Weyerhaeuser had built the Business. Paragon also continued to sell the Economy diaper and training pant. After the IPO, in the mid to late 1990s, Paragon added the ILG feature to the Economy diaper and to the training pant. Also after the IPO, Paragon began to sell a "Supreme" diaper. No credible evidence was introduced to show that this product ever had an ILG.

38. After the IPO, Paragon continued to employ the same outside patent counsel that Weyerhaeuser had used on diaper patent issues before the IPO. After the IPO and through at least 1996, Paragon's attorneys continued to consult Weyerhaeuser's in-house patent attorney, Pat Coogan, regarding the ILG patent matters. For the first two years after the IPO, PG and KC lowered their diaper prices by more than 20%, and Paragon was forced to respond by lowering its diaper prices accordingly.

39. After the IPO, the representations in the IPO Prospectus that "the Company believes any outcome of [the ILG patent] matters will have no material adverse effect" on the Business restrained Paragon from agreeing to licenses with PG and KC at royalty rates that would have so eroded Paragon's profits as to be a material adverse effect on Paragon's financial position. On January 20, 1994, PG sued Paragon in federal district court in Delaware for infringing PG's Lawson and Dragoo patents (the "Delaware Litigation"). In return for dismissal of the lawsuit, PG demanded that Paragon pay a 2.5% royalty. Paragon sought an alternative resolution by tendering several alternative diaper designs to PG, and asked PG to agree that the designs would not infringe its patents. On February 28, 1994, PG responded to Paragon's request, agreeing that two of the samples would not infringe Lawson or Dragoo. PG asserted, however, that even if Paragon elected to switch to one of these designs. Paragon would still be required to pay a 2.5% royalty on all past infringement of Lawson and Dragoo, back to 1991 (approximately $30 million), plus a 1% royalty on future net sales of the sample diaper for licenses under PG's Aziz and Buell patents, because PG claimed the sample diaper infringed Aziz and Buell.

40. Paragon rejected PG's offer. Paragon had not commercially tested the samples it had delivered to PG, and believed them to be inferior designs, which were not a commercially viable option. Paragon countered PG's offer by offering

to pay a 0.1% royalty for licenses of Lawson and Dragoo for three years, after which no further royalties would be due. Paragon's offer and position was consistent with the IPO Prospectus immateriality disclosure, and with the pre-IPO advice of Mr. Coogan as to what would be a "reasonable royalty" for PG's ILG patents. PG rejected Paragon's counteroffer, telling Paragon it believed the parties were at an impasse. Consequently, pretrial discovery proceeded.

41. During 1995, KC filed a lawsuit against Paragon in Dallas, Texas for infringing its Enloe and Enloe II ILG patents. By July 1996, after settlement discussions with PG had resumed, PG had lowered its royalty demand for Lawson and Dragoo licenses to 2%, but still demanded Paragon pay $30 million for past infringement back to 1991, when Weyerhaeuser had begun selling the ILG diaper. Even though this was PG's lowest settlement offer, Paragon believed it could not afford to pay PG a 2% royalty, given its competitive situation and the likelihood that this rate would become precedent for a royalty payable to KC for licensing KC's Enloe patents, which Paragon considered stronger, more defensible patents than Lawson. The pendency of the KC claims under Enloe, which would (soon) include a generic claim for all ILGs, materially limited Paragon's options in reaching a settlement with PG. From the time of the IPO through the February 1997 PG trial in Delaware, Paragon continued to study alternative designs to avoid paying any royalty, but found no viable alternative to the ILG design on its diaper. Removing the ILG altogether was not a viable option for Paragon.

42. Before the trial in Delaware and thereafter, Stephen Judlowe, Paragon's trial counsel who had originally been selected by Mr. Coogan, Weyerhaeuser's in-house patent counsel, was advising Paragon that the likelihood of Paragon's success at trial against PG's claims was very high, and as high as 80%, and that even if Paragon lost on PG's claims it would win on its counterclaim for PG's alleged infringement of Paragon's Pieniak patent and would, "at the end of the day walk away making money" on the litigation. Paragon relied on Mr. Judlowe's advice and rejected PG's settlement offer. PG and Paragon proceeded to trial.

. . .

44. When the patent infringement lawsuits were filed against Paragon, Paragon did not send Weyerhaeuser a formal written notice demanding that Weyerhaeuser defend it or indemnify it for liability. Weyerhaeuser had actual notice, however, that Paragon had been sued by PG for infringing Lawson and Dragoo: Mr. Coogan was consulted after the IPO by Paragon in-house counsel, and was deposed in the PG case. Mr. Abraham testified he instructed each of Paragon's general counsels to consult with Mr. Coogan on ILG claims and strategy. Susan Barley, Paragon's General Counsel from at least January 1994 through the summer of 1995, provided credible testimony that she kept Mr. Coogan up to date on the progress of the negotiations with PG while she was at Paragon, and that Mr. Coogan attended meetings with her and lawyers from Mr. Milnamow's firm to strategize about PG and KC ILG patent issues. Cathy Hasbrouck, who was hired as its General Counsel when Paragon moved from Seattle to Georgia in 1996 and remained in that position through conclusion of Paragon's bankruptcy case, provided credible testimony that she also discussed these patent issues with Mr. Coogan during the period leading to

trial, and received advice from him on the defense of the case that was consistent with the bullish advice received from Paragon's outside counsel. Mr. Coogan, while admitting receiving a call from a "woman in Georgia," claimed not to remember such a discussion. His denial was not credible.

D. Paragon Is Driven To Bankruptcy By Intellectual Property Inadequacies

45. The Delaware Court's December 30, 1997 judgment, entered January 6, 1998, against Paragon, held that its ILG feature infringed PG's Lawson and Dragoo patents and permanently enjoined Paragon from selling its primary product, the private-label "Ultra" diaper. The judgment also required Paragon to pay PG lost profits damages, royalty damages equal to 2% of past infringing sales, and enhanced damages for what had been Weyerhacuser's willful infringement of Dragoo equal to 100% of the damages award attributable to the March through December 1991 period. By order dated May 28, 1998, the damages portion of the judgment against Paragon was found to be $178,429,536.00.

46. The Delaware Court's judgment precipitated the filing of Paragon's Chapter 11 bankruptcy petition January 6, 1998. Ten days later the United States Trustee appointed an Official Committee of Unsecured Creditors ("Creditors' Committee"). Weyerhaeuser was appointed as one of nine creditors to serve on the Creditors' Committee. Weyerhaeuser served as a Creditors' Committee member throughout the duration of Paragon's case in this court. On November 2, 1998, the United States Trustee also appointed an Official Committee of Equity Security Holders (the "Equity Committee").

E. Paragon's Losses For Which Plaintiff Seeks Damages

[Paragon sought recovery from Weyerhaeuser for breach of warranties resulting in the following damages: 1) bankruptcy-related costs; 2) product redesign costs; 3) lost profits; 4) obligations incurred to PG and KC from the litigation; and 5) Paragon's losses from its inability to exercise options with a Mexican company because of the bankruptcy.]

F. Plan Confirmation and Proceedings in This Adversary Proceeding

71. Over Weyerhaeuser's opposition, the Equity Committee in Paragon's bankruptcy, on behalf of the Paragon Estate, commenced this breach of warranty adversary proceeding against Weyerhaeuser October 4, 1999, contending Weyerhaeuser breached the four ATA and IPA warranties (quoted above at page 17, ¶ 36). Following hearings on confirmation thereof, Paragon's Modified Second Amended Plan Of Reorganization (the "Plan") was confirmed by order entered January 13, 2000 (the "Confirmation Order"), and the effective date of the Plan was January 28, 2000. The Plan and Confirmation Order reaffirmed the reasonableness of and necessity for Paragon to settle with PG and KC. Pursuant to the Plan and Confirmation Order, Mr. Randall Lambert was appointed the Paragon Estate's Litigation Claims Representative to pursue this and other claims of the Estate. Accordingly, Mr. Lambert was substituted for the Equity Committee as Plaintiff in this action. Following the close of discovery, Plaintiff moved for partial summary judgment holding Weyerhaeuser liable for breaching the four warranties at issue. Weyerhaeuser

cross-moved for complete summary judgment or dismissal. In support of the summary judgment motions, the parties jointly submitted an extensive record of more than nine volumes of joint exhibit appendices and twenty-five deposition transcripts. Oral argument on the motions was heard June 24, 2002.

72. The Summary Judgment Order entered October 30, 2002, found Weyerhaeuser breached all four warranties as a matter of law on the grounds that Paragon's intellectual property was not adequate or sufficient at the IPO closing, so that Weyerhaeuser's warranties were not true. Because Paragon lacked the licenses then necessary to operate its business, the Delaware Judgment, the risks of continued litigation, the disruption to Paragon's business from its inability to sell the ILG diaper, and the allowed claims of and license fees to PG and KC — which were necessary for Paragon to incur to obtain rights to use the ILG technology it did not have at closing of the IPO — constituted a stark gap in Paragon's intellectual property, known to Weyerhaeuser and undisclosed in the IPO. As a result, Plaintiff is entitled to damages for the breaches. For the reasons set forth in the Summary Judgment Order, Weyerhaeuser's arguments — that Paragon's indemnity of Weyerhaeuser against intellectual property claims in IPA Section 4.01, and other assumption of liability promises in the ATA and IPA precluded Plaintiff's breach of warranty claims and entitlement to damages — were rejected.

73. Weyerhaeuser filed a motion for reconsideration of the Summary Judgment Order November 12, 2002. In its Reply to Plaintiff's response to its motion for reconsideration, Weyerhaeuser raised for the first time a new document and argument it had failed to raise either in the original proceedings or in its motion to reconsider: a U.S. Assignment And Assumption Agreement signed by Paragon at the IPO closing. Weyerhaeuser also raised for the first time the Tyco decision's issues discussed above, despite having notice of the trial and appellate court decisions at or near the time they issued, and despite entry of the Federal Circuit's Tyco decision over a year before oral argument on the summary judgment motions. Following oral argument on the motion for reconsideration, Weyerhaeuser's motion was denied. This matter was then set for trial only on damages.

74. During a fourteen-day damages trial conducted October 30 to November 6, November 24 and 25, and December 3 to 10, 2003, Plaintiff presented evidence and argument on the issue of damages for Weyerhaeuser's breach of warranties.   Plaintiff argued three alternative common law measures of damages: a "cost to cure" measure, a "difference in value" measure, and a "destruction of business" measure, plus consequential damages under the first two measures. Alternatively, Plaintiff argued for damages pursuant to the indemnity provision in ATA Section 11.02(b), in which Weyerhaeuser promised to pay Paragon for all "Losses" arising from or relating to a breach of warranty. Plaintiff also seeks prejudgment interest and attorneys' fees under each remedy as well.

75. Weyerhaeuser contends Plaintiff is limited to the ATA Section 11.02(b) indemnity remedy for its breach of warranties, to the exclusion of a common law remedy customarily available for breach of warranty. Weyerhaeuser contends Plaintiff is entitled to no damages under the purportedly exclusive ATA Section 11.02(b) remedy because (i) given that Paragon settled, Plaintiff did

not establish Paragon was actually liable to PG or KC for patent infringement, and (ii) Paragon and Plaintiff did not provide Weyerhaeuser sufficient notice of the PG and KC actions to be entitled to indemnity, and Weyerhaeuser was actually prejudiced from the lack of notice. Weyerhaeuser also argues that Paragon's agreements to indemnify and defend Weyerhaeuser from certain intellectual property liabilities under ATA Section 11.02(a) and IPA Section 4.01 require Paragon to repay to Weyerhaeuser any liability Weyerhaeuser owes Paragon for breach of Weyerhaeuser's warranties.

76. Finally, Weyerhaeuser contends that under Washington law, the only proper common law measure of damages is difference in value at the time of sale. Weyerhaeuser argues that under that measure, Plaintiff's damages are limited to what the missing PG and KC licenses hypothetically would have cost Paragon, both reduced to after-tax dollars and discounted to present value as of February 2, 1993, and then further reduced by Weyerhaeuser's assumption that Paragon would have raised prices and recouped much of the increased royalty costs to acquire the licenses. Plaintiff responds that it is not limited to a difference in value measure, and may recover all damages and losses necessary to put Paragon in the position it would have occupied if it had received Weyerhaeuser's baby diaper business in its as-warranted condition — that is, with sufficient intellectual property to conduct the ILG diaper business. Plaintiff submits the measure that best accomplishes that goal is an equivalent to a "cost to cure" measure.

77. Among other contentions, Weyerhaeuser contends that the consequential damages Plaintiff seeks are not recoverable under Washington law, that Plaintiff's damages should be limited for Paragon's alleged failure to mitigate damages, and that no damages should be allowed for KC-related losses because of the Tyco decision. Weyerhaeuser also asserts Plaintiff is not entitled to pre-judgment interest on any damage element. The parties have stipulated, however, to Plaintiff's entitlement to recover a certain amount of Plaintiff's attorneys fees and costs upon being awarded damages.

[Judge Murphy levied a judgment of $458 million against Weyerhaeuser. Paragon had been seeking $700 million in damages. Judge Murphy stated: "The gravamen of Weyerhaeuser's liability, is that, in addition to the funds that Weyerhaeuser received in connection with the IPO, the primary benefit of the bargain to Weyerhaeuser was divorcing itself from what it knew to be an enormous potential patent infringement liability that was substantially certain to occur. Additionally, Weyerhaeuser was able to reap the benefit of an unpredictably successful IPO. To reward Weyerhaeuser's strategic divestment by limiting damages . . . would encourage other large corporations to evade liabilities by transferring assets to a subsidiary and divesting themselves of their liability-laden subsidiaries."]

NOTES & QUESTIONS

1. Review Paragraph 16 of the preceding reading which describes Weyerhaeuser's use of opinion letters from outside counsel. In 2004, the Federal Circuit ruled that no adverse inference for willfulness could be made from a litigant's failure to obtain an opinion letter or from the refusal to turn

over such a letter protected by attorney-client privilege. *See Knorr-Bremse v. Dana Corp.*, 383 F. 3d 1337 (Fed. Cir. 2004). The facts of the *Weyerhaeuser* case predated this important decision. Does the decision in *Knorr-Bremse*, as summarized here, seem sensible in light of cases like *Weyerhaeuser*? If the company could have claimed attorney-client privilege, should it have? Would refusal to turn over the opinion letter or the decision not to get one have been sensible under the facts of *Weyerhaeuser*? Notice that the *Knorr-Bremse* decision deals specifically with the question of willfulness in a patent infringement suit. A breach of warranty case might raise different concerns regarding the use of opinion letters.

2. Look at the discussion of valuation in Paragraph 20 of the preceding opinion. What method of valuation did Weyerhaeuser use here? Review the section on valuation in Chapter 1. For thorough discussions of valuation methods for intellectual property, see Richard Razgaitis, VALUATION AND PRICING OF TECHNOLOGY-BASED INTELLECTUAL PROPERTY (2003); Gordon V. Smith & Russell L. Parr, VALUATION OF INTELLECTUAL PROPERTY AND INTANGIBLE ASSETS (2000). Accounting issues are also critical to the careful consideration of intellectual property in mergers and acquisitions. *See* Andrew W. Carter, Accounting for Intellectual Property During Mergers and Acquisitions in Lanning Bryer & Melvin Simensky, eds., INTELLECTUAL PROPERTY ASSETS IN MERGERS AND ACQUISITIONS 5.1-5.11 (2002). An important question to think about is the need for better financial accounting standards for intellectual property. In reading the facts of *Weyerhaeuser*, would better, less manipulatable accounting standards have helped?

3. Consider the discussion of the P&G and Kimberly Clark patent litigation in paragraphs 22 and 23 of the preceding opinion as well as the discussion of the subsequent licensing negotiations in paragraph 29. To what extent did Weyerhaeuser's problems stem from an uncertain and unpredictable patent system? How would you, in advising companies like Weyerhaeuser, counsel a client about the risks of patent infringement litigation? Should Weyerhaeuser have intervened in the lawsuit? Should Weyerhaeuser have worked more to invent around the existing patents on the assumption that the patents were valid, even if ownership of the patents was uncertain?

4. Paragraphs 30 and 31 discuss disclosures made by Weyerhaeuser as part of the IPO of Paragon stock. Do these disclosures seem adequate? How would you have advised Weyerhaeuser both prospectively (before the case was decided) and retrospectively (after the case was decided)?

5. Look at the Asset Transfer Agreements and the Intellectual Property Agreements discussed in paragraph 36. These are standard agreements with standard terms. What does each agreement cover? What do each of the excerpted terms mean? Do the terms provide any basis for Weyerhaeuser to escape liability?

6. Paragraphs 38, 42, and 44 provide insights into what Weyerhaeuser's and Paragon's attorneys were doing in negotiating the IPO. The materials in Chapter 9 provide more information about due diligence reviews of intellectual property and potential infringement liability. How could due diligence

reviews have been better conducted here? Could purchasers of stock in the IPO have been more diligent in scrutinizing the transaction, perhaps insisting that Paragon have independent counsel? Can the uncertainties of the patent system discussed above in note 3 explain some of the behavior here?

7. Paragraph 71 offers a glimpse of the bankruptcy procedures which formed the background to the *Weyerhaeuser* case. Review the introductory materials to Chapter 7, which discuss bankruptcy proceedings. Could Paragon have impleaded Weyerhaeuser in the intellectual property litigation because Weyerhaeuser was obligated to indemnify Paragon regarding its liabilities determined in the litigation? Was there an advantage to litigating and settling and then suing Weyerhaeuser for breach of warranty?

8. The judge adopted the cost to cure measure of damages, advocated by Paragon, over the difference in value measure, advocated by Weyerhaeuser. The difference in value measure was based on the difference between the value of the business as actually delivered to Paragon and the value of the business as warranted. The cost to cure measure, on the other hand, included the costs to Paragon of the infringement lawsuit, the costs of bankruptcy, and consequential damages such as business operating losses and costs of product redesigns. Attorney's fees and costs would be in addition to these damages. The following is a breakdown of the damages awarded to Paragon by the court:

Element of Damage	Dollar Amount
Damages related to infringement of P&G patent (consisting of settlement payments and litigation expenses)	$219, 100, 000
Damages related to infringement of KC patent (consisting of settlement payments and litigation expenses)	$158, 300, 000
Product redesign costs (consequential damages including prejudgment interest)	$14, 982, 556
Bankruptcy retention bonuses (consequential damages including prejudgment interest)	$7, 002, 301
Bankruptcy fees and costs (consequential damages including prejudgment interest)	$40, 773, 293
Lost profits (consequential damages)	$17, 700, 000

The damages totaled $457,858,150, to which the court added attorney's fees and costs of $3,017,210. By way of comparison, the court calculated damages under a difference in value measure of $284,625,000.

CHAPTER 9

INTELLECTUAL PROPERTY DUE DILIGENCE PRECEDING PUBLIC SALES OF STOCK

PROBLEM

Digital Ignition is preparing for an initial public offering (IPO) of its stock. The company has developed a group of popular consumer products in its plug-compatible ignition systems, but is unable to meet consumer demand for these products through its present manufacturing and distribution channels. Digital Ignition's executives believe that a public offering of Digital Ignition stock will aid the company in expanding its manufacturing and product distribution operations concerning its consumer products.

As part of its preparation for this IPO, Digital Ignition has engaged your law firm to address a number of intellectual property issues related to the proposed offering. The attorneys at your firm working on this matter are Todd Alvarez, a partner with extensive experience concerning securities law and intellectual property issues in IPOs of high tech companies, and you, Sue Kim, a third-year associate working under Alvarez's direction.

You and Alvarez have met with Digital Ignition's general counsel and senior executives and have a general idea of the type of offering that the company is planning. The tentative plan is to offer 4,000,000 shares of company stock at an initial price of approximately $10.00 per share to generate approximately $40 million dollars in new financing. Further financial details regarding the proposed stock offering are being developed by the financial executives at Digital Ignition, with assistance from the investment bankers who are aiding the company in defining the features of the offering and the underwriters who will handle the offering. These financial details are not the concern of your firm; rather, you have been engaged to ensure that Digital Ignition properly identifies and discloses its operating risks as required by securities laws governing offerings of stock in public markets.

The legal team at your firm has started to develop some of the disclosure documents that will need to be filed with the federal Securities and Exchange Commission (SEC) at the outset of the IPO and that will ultimately become part of the publicly available prospectus describing Digital Ignition and its IPO. As part of the disclosures in these documents, company officials will need to describe the company's present and planned business activities and the impact of intellectual property interests in aiding or limiting these business activities.

In order to properly identify and disclose these intellectual property impacts, your law firm will conduct a "due diligence" review of Digital Research's intellectual property interests and the intellectual property interests held by other parties that may limit Digital Research's planned activities.

This review should entail reasonable fact finding and analysis to support the representations that Digital Research will ultimately make in its disclosure documents about the company's future business plans and prospects and the projected impact of intellectual property interests on these aspects of business performance.

Alvarez has asked you to develop a plan for collecting information about Digital Research's intellectual property interests and associated operating risks as part of the due diligence review of the company preceding its IPO. Based on initial discussions with Digital Ignition's executives and counsel, Alvarez wrote the attached draft memorandum summarizing several intellectual property features of Digital Ignition's operations which should be scrutinized in the due diligence review. Alvarez would like you to address the following three questions:

1) Are there any other types of intellectual property interests or risks beyond those mentioned in the memorandum that are likely to enhance or impede Digital Ignition's operations and that should be considered in the due diligence review?

2) Regarding the intellectual property interests mentioned in Alvarez's memorandum or others you may identify as relevant, what types of practical business risks or advantages may these interests create for Digital Ignition?

3) Given these potential risks and advantages, what types of factual inquiries and sources of information at Digital Ignition should be pursued in the due diligence review of the company to reasonably clarify the impact of intellectual property interests on the company's operations and to form the basis for disclosure statements to be filed in connection with the company's IPO?

In addressing these questions, you are not expected to provide a detailed description of the intellectual property-based risks and advantages associated with the IPO. Rather, the goal of your answers should be to define an initial plan for gathering information on the intellectual property aspects of the company's business activities, specifying the types of information to be obtained and the evaluations to be conducted. You should consider the materials and cases in the readings describing the features of reasonable due diligence reviews under federal securities laws, the beneficial defenses to liability that such reviews may support, and the special handling that privileged materials may require in the course of a due diligence review.

———

TO: Sue Kim

FROM: Todd Alvarez

SUBJECT: Initial IP Considerations in Due Diligence Review of Digital Ignition

Based on our initial consultations with Digital Ignition's management, I want to start planning for the due diligence review of the company's intellectual property interests in connection with its proposed IPO. The company's business is strongly influenced by its own intellectual property interests and may be constrained by the interests of other companies. The relevant intellectual property interest will generally fall into one of the following four categories:

1) Intellectual property created by Digital Ignition that may provide the company with a competitive advantage by establishing domains of exclusive business activity;

2) Intellectual property acquired by Digital Ignition that may provide the company with a competitive advantage by establishing domains of exclusive business activity;

3) Intellectual property that Digital Ignition may license to others to create sources of income; and

4) Intellectual property of other parties that may conflict with the planned business activities of Digital Ignition.

While there may be other important sources of concern, based on the description of the company's business we were given, the due diligence review of Digital Ignition should consider at least the following:

1) Patents and related trade secret know how concerning the company's core digital ignition technology developed by Dr. See in the early 1980s;

2) Further patents on improvements to that technology developed and patented in the 1990s;

3) Trademarks under which the company has initiated marketing of its consumer products;

4) Trade secrets which Dr. See or other employees of Digital Ignition may have brought to the company, intentionally or inadvertently, from their prior employers in the automobile ignition field or allied engineering areas;

5) Patents held by other concerns in the ignition equipment field that may limit Digital Ignition's ability to manufacture and sell its devices;

6) Copyrights on software from other companies that was used to create Digital Ignition's products, portions of which copyrighted software may have been included in the software controls embedded in Digital Ignition's products;

7) Patents held by Ignition Horizons, Inc., another innovative concern that has developed advances that complement the advances covered by Digital Ignition's patents. Digital Ignition has licensed exclusive rights under Ignition Horizons' patents to make plug-compatible replacement ignition systems containing features covered by Ignition Horizons' designs. These components significantly enhance the performance of the ignition systems and Digital Ignition's executives feel that their company's exclusive ability to offer ignition systems with these licensed features will be an important marketing advantage for the company.

FOCUS OF THE CHAPTER

Due diligence reviews of intellectual property interests are conducted in a variety of settings where a party needs to assess the future business prospects of a concern and to take intellectual property impacts into account in making these assessments. Settings in which businesses commonly conduct due diligence reviews of intellectual property include merger transactions (in which the focus of a due diligence review is typically the intellectual property of the target company being acquired), transactions involving the sale of a corporate subsidiary or other business unit (in which the focus of a due diligence review is the value of the business unit being sold off and the impact of intellectual property interests on that value), and initial public stock offerings (in which the focus of a due diligence review is the impact of intellectual property interests on the future business prospects of the company which is making the offering). The common feature of due diligence reviews of intellectual property in these settings is the need to project how intellectual property interests held by the company under scrutiny may enhance the business potential of that company and how the intellectual property interests of other parties may limit the company's actions or create expensive infringement liability.

The scope of a reasonable due diligence review depends on both the nature of the legal risks involved and the features of the business under scrutiny:

> It is imperative that the metes and bounds of intellectual property due diligence be carefully defined in advance. When establishing such parameters, one must strike a commercially reasonable balance between assuring that the investigation is broad enough in scope to identify that which is material to the transaction, but not so extensive as to be wasteful of time and resources. Moreover, the results of the defining process provide a guide for the intellectual property due diligence team and a checklist to assure thoroughness. The due diligence team must have a basic understanding of the target company's primary product lines, business environment, and future plans so that it can focus on the intellectual property assets that are relevant to the business. It is also important to remember that because the intellectual property due diligence is normally conducted as part of a total transactional investigation, the objectives of the intellectual property investigation must be consistent with the overall objectives (and, of course, budget) of the total due diligence activity, and coordinated with the responsible attorney and the project's diligence attorney.

Gary M. Lawrence, Due Diligence in Business Transactions § 13.03 (2005).

Due diligence reviews of intellectual property and other business features are particularly important in connection with initial public offerings (IPOs) of stock. An IPO is typically a major corporate event for several reasons. The offering often recognizes the early success and promise of the firm involved. A public offering can generate the levels of investor support needed to propel a concern into significant expansion of existing operations and new activities not previously possible. The offering may also produce substantial wealth for company founders and early stage managers and co-owners. The public offering will also mark the company's entry into a new period of required public disclosures about company activities and prospects and expanded regulatory oversight regarding securities matters. A public offering that distributes corporate ownership among numerous shareholders may also reduce management accountability to shareholders, most of whom will hold too small a fractional ownership interest to be motivated to carefully monitor corporate activities and insufficient share voting power to influence corporate affairs.

Although other factors may also influence the timing of an IPO, a company will frequently seek to offer its stock to the public when (1) initial investors have backed the company with the full measure of funds they are likely to invest and are seeking a return on their investment and (2) the company has a sufficient early-stage success and potential for expansion to make an IPO attractive to numerous shareholders. A company may conduct an IPO to produce additional funds for research and development, new product introductions, or expansions in existing operations.

At least four types of intellectual property interests may aid or limit the future success of an IPO candidate. First, a company's own intellectual property interests may define attractive manufacturing and marketing opportunities for products or services that can only be pursued by the intellectual property holder. Second, intellectual property interests held by competitors or other parties may limit a company's potential business activities and constrain its profit making opportunities. Third, IP interests of suppliers may affect the availability and price of key components incorporated in company products. Fourth, a company's intellectual property may provide profitable opportunities for licensing, either as a means to pursue business activities that the licensor can not address directly or as a means to transfer technologies into new business domains and generate corresponding new licensing revenues.

Individuals such as corporate officers making or verifying particular factual statements about a company in disclosure documents filed with the SEC in connection with an IPO will generally bear personal liability for making or verifying materially misleading statements. However, these individuals will avoid such liability if they rely in good faith on reasonable investigations as the basis for their statements. These sorts of "due diligence" defenses to liability indirectly shape the process of formulating prospectuses and other IPO-related disclosure documents. In order to maximize the protections for the individuals involved, careful due diligence reviews will generally precede the completion of factual disclosure documents submitted to the SEC by company officials.

Due diligence reviews of intellectual property interests often involve the handling and consideration of information sources (such as patent validity opinion letters) which are covered by attorney-client privilege protections. These reviews may also involve the generation of new documents (such as reports of due diligence findings) which are themselves privileged. Efforts to gain or keep privilege protections in the course of due diligence reviews can place significant procedural limitations on those reviews. Furthermore, the circumstances in which the results of due diligence reviews are released to additional parties may undercut previously existing privilege protections by constituting an implied waiver of the attorney-client privilege. While such a waiver may be warranted in order to gain some advantage from a disclosure of due diligence results to additional parties, choices to make these types of disclosures should be made with the applicable privilege waiver implications in mind.

The readings below describe the features and legal advantages of due diligence reviews of intellectual property risks and benefits associated with an IPO. The first article by Diane J. Kasselman describes the legal justifications for due diligence reviews of intellectual property interests in connection with an IPO, as well as some of the strategic considerations in conducting such reviews. The second article by Mary J. Hildebrand and Jacqueline Klosek provides further tips on means for conducting intellectual property due diligence reviews. The *Feit* case presents a judicial evaluation of the minimum features of a reasonable due diligence review. While the due diligence review in this case did not involve evaluations of intellectual property interests, the legal standards and policy considerations described in this opinion are directly applicable to due diligence reviews of intellectual property interests and define the proper scope of a due diligence review preceding an IPO. The *Knogo Corporation* case, while arising outside the context of an IPO, provides a detailed description of the types of information submitted to counsel about intellectual property interests that may qualify for attorney-client privilege protections. Such protections may later figure in preparations for an IPO as the prior work of counsel is shared with parties other than the corporate client (such as underwriters) in the course of a due diligence review or where the work of counsel is relied upon by corporate officials as the basis for representations in disclosure documents about the enforceability or scope of intellectual property interests. Finally, the article by Eric K. Steffe, W. Blake Coblentz, and Jessica Parezo describes how shared interests among the parties conducting due diligence reviews can provide a basis for continuing privilege protections of information shared in due diligence reviews of intellectual property interests.

READINGS

A. FEATURES OF DUE DILIGENCE REVIEWS OF INTELLECTUAL PROPERTY

Diane J. Kasselman,
Intellectual Property Due Diligence in Businesss Transactions
Practising Law Institute
Patents, Copyrights, Trademarks, and Literary Property Course Handbook Series No. G0-011U (October, 2002)*

I.   Introduction

Conducting intellectual property due diligence is like participating in an archeological dig. You must sift through many layers of information to discover accurate details relating to a company's intellectual property assets. This article discusses: (i) why we conduct intellectual property due diligence; (ii) the components of intellectual property due diligence; and (iii) the issues that may arise based on the findings of intellectual property due diligence.[1]

II.   Intellectual Property Due Diligence

Black's Law Dictionary defines "due diligence" as

> [s]uch a measure of prudence, activity or assiduity as is properly to be expected from and ordinarily exercised by a reasonable and prudent man under the particular circumstances; not measured by any absolute standard but depending upon the relative facts of the special case.

In the context of mergers, acquisitions, joint ventures or public or private offerings, "due diligence" involves an evaluation of a company's assets as they relate to the operation of the business, or businesses, contemplated in the proposed transaction.

A.   What is Intellectual Property Due Diligence?

Just as corporate due diligence identifies the corporate assets implicated in a proposed business transaction (e.g. receivables, real estate, inventory, etc.), intellectual property due diligence ("IP Due Diligence") focuses specifically on the intellectual property assets. These include: trademarks, service marks, patents, copyrights, Internet domain names, software, trade secrets and any agreements granting or obtaining rights in intellectual property.

Many believe that IP Due Diligence is necessary only in connection with "high-tech" industries. This could not be further from the truth. Virtually all companies, in every industry, own and/or use intellectual property in the operation of their businesses. IP Due Diligence is required in order to identify and assess the company's intellectual property in light of the proposed transaction.

B.   Why Perform Due Diligence?

Would you buy a house without knowing whether there is clear title to the property; whether there is a Certificate of Occupancy for the addition the seller put on last year; or whether the neighbor has an easement on the property? Of course not! Similarly, no business transaction should be completed

---

[1] [FN1] This article generally addresses due diligence concerns from the buyer's perspective. However, sellers apply the same diligence methods to ensure that representations and warranties are true. Independent of proposed business transactions, periodic IP Due Diligence is a useful tool to keep a company's intellectual property assets "in order."

without determining what is being sold (all corporate assets and goodwill) and whether is it worth the price. Intellectual property assets are identified and scrutinized to determine:

- the importance of intellectual property within the framework of the deal;

- the commercial advantage of the company's intellectual property portfolio; and

- the potential liabilities associated with the company's intellectual property portfolio or in the use of intellectual property in the operation of the business.

IP Due diligence will reveal whether those assets can pass to the buyer "free and clear," or whether there are problems that must be corrected before the completion of the transaction. It is always good business practice to perform adequate due diligence for proposed transactions. In the context of acquisitions, the diligence effort is ultimately a business decision. Conversely, public offerings subject issuers to strict liability under securities law for material nondisclosure or misrepresentations in the offering. However, a "due diligence defense" is available to experts (including attorneys and accountants), underwriters, etc. if they exercised the appropriate level of due diligence.[2]

C.   What is the Scope of Due Diligence?

The scope and level of scrutiny of the IP Due Diligence depends on the structure of the business transaction. There are different considerations for an asset deal, a merger, a stock purchase and public or private offering. For example, in an asset purchase, diligence should determine transferability of the intellectual property owned and licensed by the company from third parties, and in a stock sale, diligence may uncover issues related to restrictive change-of-control provisions.

III.   Components of Intellectual Property Due Diligence

IP Due Diligence consists of the following steps:

- Understand the business

- Review documents

- Conduct searches

- Conduct interviews

- Identify issues

- Report findings

Each step is an important part of the overall due diligence process. The information gathered and analyzed during IP Due Diligence joins with the

---

[2] [FN2] See sections 11 and 12 of the Securities Act of 1933.

results of corporate's, and other specialty areas', diligence efforts to determine the continued viability of the proposed transaction.

A.   Understand the Business

The first step in IP Due Diligence is to understand the nature and operation of the business under scrutiny. Although virtually every business has intellectual property to evaluate (e.g. trademarks, copyrights, patents, licenses), the particular industry may generate a more detailed level of scrutiny. For example, aerospace companies may have used government funding that requires a license back to the government of the developed intellectual property; a pharmaceutical company considers patents in light of abbreviated new drug applications to the United States Food and Drug Administration; the film industry usually implicates issues with respect to rights of publicity and software providers may raise issues with respect to open source code and export restrictions.

Once there is a clear understanding of: (i) the nature of the business (with any industry-specific nuances), (ii) the structure of the deal and (iii) the value of the intellectual property in relation to the deal, the researcher can develop an IP Due Diligence plan to find the answers.

B.   Review Documents

Documents and information about the company (including intellectual property-related documents and information) are usually provided in response to the potential buyer's document request list. All transactions are not alike, and, because there are so many distinct factors that make deals different, a due diligence request list should be tailored to reflect the proposed transaction. Generally, in performing IP Due Diligence, the diligence team will want to ask for and review the following genre of documents, including:

- Schedules of registered, applied-for and material unregistered intellectual property (including Internet domain name registrations), along with underlying documentation (e.g. certificates of registration, copies of applications, etc.)

- Licenses or other agreements granting or obtaining rights in intellectual property (ask for descriptions of any oral agreements)

- Assignment of intellectual property by or to the company

- Other agreements affecting the company's use of intellectual property including, consulting, research and development, joint venture, prior acquisitions, consent to use, covenants not to sue, etc.

- Confidentiality, non-disclosure, non-compete and employee/consulting agreements covering rights in intellectual property (e.g. assignment of inventions, discoveries, improvements, works of authorship, etc.)

- List of software (proprietary and third party)

- Summary description of subject matter held as trade secrets

- Opposition, reexamination, interferences or other adversarial proceedings before any intellectual property registry

- Intellectual property-related claims and correspondence, including pending and threatened claims, cease-and-desist letters and contacts. . . .

A sample Intellectual Property Due Diligence Request List is attached [at the end of this article].

In reviewing the documents, identify the extent of the company's rights in existing intellectual property and in intellectual property not yet developed. For example:

- whether a license grants exclusive or non-exclusive rights?

- what is the field of use?

- what is the territory?

- what is the duration of the license?

In addition, in determining the extent, if any, of a company's copyright protection in an original work of authorship created for the company by an independent consultant, IP Due Diligence will reveal whether it qualifies as a "work-for-hire" under U.S. copyright law.

C.   Conduct Searches

One of the most critical aspects of IP Due Diligence is to determine what intellectual property the company owns. Even if the company provides detailed schedules in response to the diligence request, it is important to conduct independent searches.

On-line Searches. Online searches[3] are simple and relatively inexpensive methods to verify, and possibly augment, a company's disclosed schedule. You can search: (i) by scheduled intellectual property; and (ii) by company name.

- *By Scheduled Intellectual Property.* Generally, searches using the number listed on the schedule will locate record(s) in the database. However, information with respect to U.S. patent applications is not available to the public,[4] and trademark information is not available for every country where trademark protection exists.[5]

---

[3] [FN3] [These online searches can be conducted through] Dialog's databases, e.g., Inpadoc, Derwent, Trademarkscan, Patfull, US Copyrights and LitAlert, and Thomson & Thomson's Saegis database.

[4] [FN4] Patents filed exclusively in the United States were generally held confidential until the patent issued. Effective in November 2000, patent applications are held in confidence for 18 months and then disclosed, unless the application qualifies for an exception to maintain secrecy.

[5] [FN5] These databases contain information with respect to trademarks registered or applied for in the United States (federal and state), Canada, Austria, Benelux (Belgium, Netherlands and Luxembourg), Denmark, Finland, France, Germany, Italy, Liechtenstein, Monaco, Norway, Spain, Sweden, Switzerland and the United Kingdom. Information is also available for Japan and Community Trademark applications consisting of 15 countries (Austria, Belgium, Germany, Denmark, Spain, Finland, France, U.K., Greece, Ireland, Italy, Luxembourg, Netherlands, Portugal and Sweden).

- *By Company.* A search in the name of the company and any subsidiaries and/or affiliates included in the transaction may reveal additional intellectual property that should be included in the disclosure schedules.

On-line searches can provide the following information:

- the "record owner" — the person who, in the records of that registry, is the current owner;

- the current status — whether the property is active, abandoned or expired;

- encumbrances — whether there are security interests granted in the property;

- oppositions, reexaminations and other adversarial proceedings; and

- litigation.

Information contained on-line is not always accurate and may not reflect the most current information. This may be due to backlogs in the registries, failure of the new owner of the intellectual property to record new information in the registries or typographical errors in recordation. For example, on-line records may not reflect that an issued patent is the subject of a reexamination, or that a bank's security interest in a trademark has been released. In addition, a slip of the finger during the recordation process at an intellectual property registry may result in the erroneous allocation of one company's intellectual property to another company![6]

Searches in the Registries. Because on-line searches do not always reflect the most current information and because there are frequently typographical errors in on-line records, it may be advisable to review the actual documents filed in the intellectual property registries. Even if the company has provided the "prosecution history" or "file wrapper" for the particular item of intellectual property, there is no way to ascertain its completeness without requesting the records from the applicable registries.

In the United States, records for applications for trademark registration, registered trademarks, and copyrights and issued patents may be ordered from the U.S. Patent and Trademark Office ("PTO") and United States Copyright Office without the consent of the owner. Files pertaining to patent applications may be obtained with the patent applicant's consent. Similarly, public records relating to state registrations of trademarks and perfected security interests in the intellectual property being reviewed can be obtained from the applicable Secretary of State. However, the fees associated with ordering information from intellectual property registries and Secretaries of State (and foreign registries, if applicable),[7] and the time spent reviewing such folders may translate into a sizeable expense.

---

[6] [FN6] To avoid this, carefully review the Notice of Recordation from all applicable intellectual property registries. In the U.S. Patent and Trademark Office and United States Copyright Office, errors made by those offices may be corrected without additional fees.

[7] [FN7] It may be advisable to retain local counsel when evaluating the company's rights in any foreign intellectual property.

Ultimately, the extent of the searches should be commensurate with the relative value of the company's intellectual property to the proposed transaction.

D.   Conduct Interviews

Interviews with the people familiar with the business put the proposed transaction into focus. Interviews can provide answers to questions that only an "insider" knows and will fill in the "missing pieces" from your review of the materials provided by the company or obtained independently. For example, the seemingly impressive portfolio of the company's patents, trademarks and copyrights may be given "short shrift" by key company business people who intend to abandon certain trademarks and to cease paying maintenance fees for certain patents. In most cases, there will be a "contact" person with whom you can speak. However, when secrecy cloaks the proposed transaction, the person who has the knowledge you seek may be unaware of the deal, and therefore, unavailable to you.

Whom Do You Interview? — Ideally, you want to speak with people familiar with the business and the intellectual property used in connection with the business. This could be any one, or combination of the following:

- the company's in-house counsel

- outside firm(s) — one or more firms that handle intellectual property prosecution and litigation (e.g. one firm for patent prosecution, another for trademark and copyrights, and yet another to handle intellectual property-related litigation)

- people in the company familiar with particular aspects of the business (e.g., research & development, information technology, marketing)

What Do You Ask? — The interview(s) should provide you with information regarding the company's:

- intellectual property portfolio (including how it was acquired)

- licensing of its own, and third party intellectual property (including inter-company licensing)

- use of intellectual property in the business

- information technology operations (including websites)

- marketing strategies

- research and development

- policies with respect to obtaining, maintaining and protecting intellectual property

- pending and threatened litigation or adversarial proceedings before intellectual property registries

- restrictions on intellectual property due to settlements, covenants not to sue, consents to use, cross licenses, licenses to the U.S. government or restrictive covenants in other agreements

E.   Identify The Issues

Throughout IP Due Diligence, the researcher must be alert to spot issues that could affect the transaction. For example, a diminished intellectual property portfolio (in material areas of the business) may lead to negotiations to adjust the purchase price. Similarly, flaws in title, shared intellectual property, ongoing litigation and unreleased liens may result in modifications to the representations, warranties, covenants and/or indemnification sections of the deal documents. These issues are addressed in Section IV, "Issues Arising from Intellectual Property Due Diligence".

F.   Report Your Findings

At the conclusion of IP Due Diligence the researcher should be able to identify:

- material intellectual property
  - who owns it
  - whether it is active
  - how it is used in the business (and in the company's other businesses)
- material third party agreements
- existing and potential liabilities
  - relating to owned or licensed intellectual property
  - with respect to the operation of the business

With this information at hand, the researcher will be able to produce a report that can be used to determine the benefits and risks associated with the proposed transaction.

Diligence reports can be narrow or comprehensive. This is generally dictated by the importance of intellectual property to the deal and the structure of the deal. Diligence reports can be presented in many formats, including:

- oral report
- e-mail report
- detailed written memorandum (with schedules)
- summary written reports featuring (i) material intellectual property assets (including agreements) and (ii) identifying key business points and potential problem areas

IV.   Issues Arising from Intellectual Property Due Diligence

A.   Status of Intellectual Property

In response to the IP diligence request, many companies list all intellectual property, regardless of its status. Therefore, IP Due Diligence may reveal that large portions of the company's IP assets are no longer active. Initially, this may cause concern until the reason for the early cancellation or abandonment is explained.

Often, a product that was marketed under a now abandoned brand name is no longer being manufactured and/or sold by the company. There would be no reason to continue to pay maintenance fees on trademarks that the company ceased using in commerce and intends not to use in the future.

Similarly, there would be no need to maintain a patent in a technology that is no longer "state-of-the-art" and that is no longer practiced.

However, to the extent that any material registered or issued intellectual property has expired, been abandoned or cancelled, the prospective buyer will need to determine a course of action. Abandoned or cancelled applications for trademarks and patents that have been identified as material to the business also need to be scrutinized to determine the reason the application was not pursued. Obtaining the prosecution history enables the researcher to review what objections the PTO raised against the trademark or patent and the company's responses.

In assessing a diminished intellectual property portfolio with respect to material items, the buyer may consider:

- whether the business remains viable without the intellectual property
- whether there are alternatives to the intellectual property
- if the intellectual property was issued or registered, whether it can be reinstated
- whether continued use of the intellectual property poses risks of litigation
- whether entry of the intellectual property into the public domain reduces the company's competitive edge

B. Ownership

Two ownership issues frequently occur as a result of IP Due Diligence: (i) the company is not listed in the applicable intellectual property's records as the "owner;" and (ii) there is a gap in the chain of title.

The Company is Not the Record Owner. The entity identified as the "owner" of the intellectual property listed on the schedule provided by the company is not the "current owner" according to the records of the applicable intellectual property registry. Common reasons include:

- the company's name change was never recorded
- intellectual property is in the name of an affiliated entity (parent, subsidiary or affiliate)
- the acquisition pursuant to which the company obtained rights in intellectual property was never recorded
- the inventor/author never assigned his/her rights in the intellectual property to the company
- the company no longer owns the intellectual property

Ideally, the researcher has a corporate structure chart and will be able to determine, based on the structure of the deal, whether the error is problematic. For example, if buyer will obtain the stock of the company and its subsidiaries (including the subsidiary that is the "record owner" of the intellectual property at issue), then ownership is not a problem. Conversely, if buyer is purchasing the assets of the company related to a particular business, then, if certain intellectual property necessary for the operation of the business is not in the company's name, the manner in which title will pass to the buyer may become a "deal issue."

If the discrepancy is not easily discerned from documents provided by the company, the researcher should request explanations from the company. In all cases, the researcher should request the copies of any underlying documents that demonstrate "beneficial" ownership in the company (e.g., certificate of name change, assignments, mergers, etc.).

Gap in the Chain of Title. Although the company can be traced as the most recent, and therefore is the "record owner," of the intellectual property, there are gaps in the chain of title. In other words, there is not a traceable path leading from the first registered owner to the company. For example:

- A patent issued to Company A in 1990.

- In 1993, Company A assigned all its right, title and interest in and to that patent to Company B.

- Company B never recorded the assignment in the PTO.

- In 1995, Company B assigned the patent to Company C.

- Company C recorded the assignment.

- In 2002, your client wants to acquire the assets of Company C, including this patent.

In this example, the records in the PTO indicate that Company C is the "record owner." However, the records reflect that a company without recorded ownership (Company B) assigned its rights in this patent to Company C. There is a gap in the chain linking Company A's interest in that patent to Company C.

The resolution of these discrepancies (e.g., whether to record the evidence closing the gap, whether to assign the intellectual property to a different entity, whether to obtain royalty-free licenses or whether to do nothing) and the obligation and expense of recordation to correct incomplete or incorrect records becomes a business point.

C.   Encumbrances

Companies seeking financing for acquisitions or other business loans routinely use intellectual property as collateral. Typically, the company seeking financing will grant to the financial institution a continuing security interest (until the loan is paid) in all existing and after-acquired intellectual property.

Financial institutions are usually diligent in recording liens on the individual intellectual property in intellectual property registries and in the states (through UCC filings). However, once the loan is paid off, evidence that the loan has been satisfied, usually a Release Letter from the bank, is often not recorded in the applicable intellectual property registry. Accordingly, IP Due diligence may reveal one or more unreleased lien in favor of different financial institutions. Inquiry into this matter often reveals that the loan has been paid off. In this case, the researcher should request written evidence of the pay-off. If no release was executed, it may be necessary to obtain releases from the financial institutions and record the releases in the applicable registries.

Another form of "encumbrance" is a limitation on, or an impediment to, one's ability to exploit its own intellectual property. For example:

- Licenses to the U.S. government due to government funds received by the company

- Exclusive licenses to third parties, precluding the company's use (even internal use) of the intellectual property

- Covenants not to sue.

D. Assignability/Change of Control

Anti-assignment clauses or change of control provisions that are triggered by the structure of the proposed transaction may become deal issues. This is most critical in asset deals where consents must be obtained and transfer fees paid. In connection with the proposed structure, there should be a clear understanding of:

- whether consents will be obtained

- who will obtain the consents

- who will bear the expenses related to consents

- when consents should be obtained

- the effect on the business if consent is denied

- the potential liabilities if consent is required but the company transferred the assets without requesting consent

E. Litigation

IP Due Diligence focuses on any active or threatened litigation relating to the company's material intellectual property. Usually, the company provides a brief summary of the claims and does not provide detailed documentation with respect to that claim. The researcher must speak with the person familiar with the litigation (this may be outside counsel) to determine the company's position on the merits. Depending on the materiality of the intellectual property, the researcher may want to review the intellectual property's underlying documents as well as the litigation file.

F. Shared Intellectual Property

IP Due Diligence may reveal that not all intellectual property is used exclusively in the business being acquired. In other words, after divesting itself of the business, seller will still require the use of certain intellectual property in its other businesses. Depending on who owns the intellectual property, the nature of the intellectual property and how it is to be used by both businesses, there are many choices, including:

- assignment of intellectual property to buyer with a license back to the seller

- buyer retains ownership of the intellectual property and licenses it to buyer

- seller retains ownership of intellectual property in all other fields of use, other than the fields of use used in the business[8]

- other creative solutions to be determined by the parties (e.g. joint ownership, assignment to a licensing entity that licenses the intellectual property to both buyer and seller, etc.)

- in the case of third party licensed intellectual property:

  - buyer retains the license and sublicenses to seller

  - buyer assigns the license to seller and becomes a sublicensee of seller

  - buyer covenants to assist seller in obtaining licenses from third party licensor on terms as favorable as seller's license

Naturally, the decision on how to handle shared intellectual property is a business point that will be a bargaining and/or negotiating tool in the deal.

V. Summary

A carefully planned and executed IP Due Diligence plan, that includes understanding the nature and operation of a company's business and using that understanding as a filter during the actual diligence process (e.g. searches, document review, interviews, issue spotting and diligence report), is a key element in the successful conclusion of a proposed business transaction.

Intellectual Property Due Diligence Request

A. SCHEDULES of all United States and foreign intellectual property owned by the Company [and its subsidiaries/affiliates], including:

1. <u>Patents and Patent Applications</u> (includes invention disclosures), identifying

- Title

- Patent number and/or application number

---

[8] [FN8] This solution may pose a risk of impermissible trademark splitting which could result in the abandonment of the trademark(s) at issue.

- Issue date and/or application date
- Country
- Record owner
- For invention disclosures, identify:
  - Title
  - Identification number
  - Subject matter

2. <u>Trademarks and Trademark Applications</u> (includes trademarks, service marks, collective marks, certification marks, material unregistered marks and trade names or other fictitious business names), identifying:

- Mark
- Registration number and/or application number
- Registration date and/or application date
- Country
- Record owner
- For material unregistered marks, identify:
  - Date of first use
  - Nature of goods and/or services

3. <u>Copyrights and Copyright Applications</u> (includes material unregistered copyrights), identifying:

- Title
- Nature of the work
- Registration number
- Registration date or date application sent
- Effective date of the registration
- Country
- Record owner
- Author(s)
- Type of ownership (e.g. single, joint, work for hire)

4. <u>Domain Names,</u> identifying:

- Domain name
- Registrant
- Registry
- Date of Registration

- Date of Expiration
- Contact information (technical and administrative)

5. <u>Material Software and Databases</u> (includes algorithms, toolkits, methodologies or code, whether independent or embodied in the company's products), identifying:

- Title (e.g. name, description, etc)
- Owner (if the company is not the owner, list the agreement in Section B, below)
- If the company is owner, indicate method of creation (e.g. authorship, work for hire (employee or consultant))
- Function/application

6. <u>Trade Secrets</u>, identifying:

- Summary description of the subject matter held as a trade secret

B.   AGREEMENTS RELATING TO INTELLECTUAL PROPERTY, including:

1. <u>Licenses and Other Agreements</u> (including assignments, settlement agreements, consents-to-use, inter-company (affiliate) agreements, joint venture, etc.) granting or obtaining rights in, or involving the ownership or use of, intellectual property (including patents, trademark, copyright, software, trade secret, rights of publicity, know-how, technology, database, etc), identifying:

- Title
- Parties
- Who is Licensor
- Who is Licensee
- Date of execution
- Subject matter

2. <u>Consulting or Development Agreements</u> related to the development of intellectual property by independent consultants, identifying:

- Title
- Parties
- Date of execution
- Subject matter

3. <u>Confidentiality Agreements relating</u> to the disclosure of confidential information, trade secrets, know-how, inventions and other proprietary information, identifying:

- Title
- Parties

- Date of execution

- Subject matter

4. <u>Employee Agreements</u> relating to the development and assignment of intellectual property to the company.

5. <u>Escrow Agreements</u> (including software and technology), identifying:

- Title

- Parties (include Escrow Agent)

- Date of execution

- Subject matter

6. <u>Web Site Agreements</u> (including, linking, hosting, connectivity, development, advertising and content provider agreements), <u>Service Agreements</u> (including software service, outsourcing, maintenance, on-line service etc.), and <u>E-Commerce Agreements</u> (including electronic data exchange, electronic mail, etc), identifying:

- Title

- Parties

- Date of execution

- Subject matter

- Web site involved

7. <u>Web Site Policies</u> (including, terms and conditions of use, privacy policies, etc.).

8. Provide copies of the agreements listed in Section B, 1 through 7, above.

C. CLAIMS, THREATENED CLAIMS AND RELATED MATTERS relating to intellectual property, including:

1. <u>Adversarial Proceedings</u> (includes litigation, interference, cancellation, opposition, reexamination or other adversarial proceedings pending before any court or intellectual property registry), provide:

- A schedule of all pending proceedings, identifying:

  - Caption, title or description of action

  - Forum

  - Nature of action (infringement, opposition, etc.)

  - Parties

  - Date commenced

  - Current status of action

- Copies of papers related to the scheduled pending proceedings (e.g. complaints, answers, correspondence, etc.)

2. <u>Threatened Actions</u> (includes cease-and-desist letters, oral communications) by or against the company, provide:

- A schedule of all Threatened Actions, identifying:

  - Party threatening action

  - Subject matter

  - Date of threatened action

- Copies of papers related to the scheduled threatened action

3. <u>Audit Requests</u> (from government agencies and intellectual property rights protection groups such as Business Software Alliance, ASCAP, BMI, etc.), provide:

- A schedule of all Audit Requests, identifying:

  - Requestor

  - Subject matter

  - Date of Request

- Copies of papers related to the scheduled Audit Request, including the Company's response.

4. <u>Legal Opinions.</u> Provide copies of all legal opinions provided to the Company within [ ] years.

5. <u>Agreements.</u> Provide copies of all judgments, consent decrees, orders, settlement agreements, covenants not to sue or other agreements that grant or prohibit the company's use of intellectual property

D.   MISCELLANEOUS, including:.

1. <u>"Form-of" Agreements</u> (including employee invention assignment and non-disclosure agreements, consultant agreements, confidentiality agreements).

2. <u>Intellectual Property Policies</u> related to the use, protection and maintenance of the company's intellectual property, provide:

- Copies of all written policies, or

- Description of such policies and practices

3. <u>Encumbrances.</u> For all company intellectual property in which there exists an unreleased security interest, lien or other encumbrance, provide documents granting encumbrance.

4. <u>Other Materials.</u> Copies of written materials describing the company, including its intellectual property (e.g. 10K, public or private offerings, sales materials, etc.)

E. CONTACTS. Provide the name and contact information for the following people, as applicable:

1. In-house counsel

2. Outside intellectual property counsel(s):

- Litigation

- Prosecution

3. Business contact(s):

- Marketing

- Research & development

- Information Systems

Mary J. Hildebrand & Jacqueline Klosek, Intellectual Property Due Diligence: A Critical Prerequisite to Capital Investment
http://library.findlaw.com/2003/Dec/1/133278.html
(last visited on May 15, 2005)*

Tips in Conducting Intellectual Property Due Diligence:

1. *Include intellectual property experts in the due diligence team.* Prior to commencing any intellectual property due diligence, effort should be directed to ensure that the proper team is in place. As a threshold matter, the legal team that undertakes to conduct intellectual property due diligence must have a basic understanding of the primary product lines, business environment and future plans of the target to ensure that the team remains focused primarily on the intellectual property assets that are relevant to the business. Since the intellectual property due diligence team will participate in the investor's evaluation of a proposed transaction, it is also essential that the team understand the relative importance of the proposed investment to the client. Early familiarity with these issues should enable the legal team to contribute to the entire process in a meaningful way.

2. *Ensure that the intellectual property due diligence plan reflects the importance of the deal.* Once the proper team has been assembled, a necessary step is to develop a well-drafted intellectual property due diligence request that will use questions that are designed to assist in identifying areas that merit further inquiry as evidenced by a positive response. By the same token, a negative response to certain questions permits the legal team to move on to areas of genuine concern that are relevant to the business and/or the specific transaction at issue.

---

3. *Take nothing on faith.* Our firm recently dealt with a matter in which a client was attempting to acquire a target whose main asset was a business method for processing insurance claims over the Internet. As part of our efforts, patent counsel did a search on the target's business method. Not only did we find that the target's invention might be infringing another patent, we also found that there was active litigation between an entity that was holding a patent on a similar method and another company using a method similar to the one used by the target. The target later admitted that they had discussed this issue with other attorneys. They did not, however, disclose it in response to the intellectual property due diligence request.

Depending on the nature of the responses, the deal and the business, further investigative activities may include (a) conducting searches in appropriate databases in all relevant jurisdictions to identify patent rights including pending and/or provisional patent applications, registered patents, registered copyrights and registered trademarks, (b) examination, analysis and verification of the results of such searches, (c) verification of claimed but unregistered intellectual property rights, (d) review and analysis of relevant provisions of executed agreements that could include licenses, consulting and confidentiality agreements, assignments and other documents, (e) interviews with key business and technology development staff at the target and, where the situation warrants, with previous employees and consultants, (f) examination and analysis of potentially infringing registrations and third-party intellectual property rights, and (g) other efforts appropriate to the situation.

4. *Confirm everything.* In another matter, our client was making a $50 million investment into a target company holding numerous patents that were of interest to our client. As part of our intellectual property due diligence, patent attorneys conducted a computerized search of the relevant patents. This search revealed that the ownership interests were not what we expected them to be. As is our custom, this initial computerized search was followed with a manual search. The manual search of the actual documentation revealed that the ownership interests were indeed as they were expected to be and that the computerized search was erroneous. In this case, the inaccuracy in the computerized search was the result of a secretarial error in preparing the filing documents. Consider, however, the results if the opposite had occurred, that is to say, that the computerized search appeared to be accurate but was not and no further manual search was performed. This highlights the importance of verifying information that is presented through more than one source.

5. *Understand the dynamic relationship between the documents and the core business.* While it is extremely important to examine all agreements, registrations, filings and other documents to ensure that they are valid, the legal team must clearly establish a relationship between such documentation and the relevant intellectual property assets. We recently represented a client that was interesting in acquiring a division of a target that held a large collection of patents. Prior to the investment, the target provided us with voluminous documentation purportedly pertaining to its patents. However, an inspection of the documentation revealed that the information provided concerned patents that had nothing to do with the target's core business.

6. *Foreign laws may impact the deal.* In recent years, the number of cross-border mergers and acquisitions has increased dramatically. This fact, combined with the reality that many individuals developing intellectual property assets for American companies are from outside of the United States, increases the likelihood that intellectual property due diligence will involve review and analysis of non-US intellectual property assets. When analyzing such assets, it must be recalled that few countries treat intellectual property in the exact same way and rights often depend on complex treaties and conventions executed by and among many different nations. Accordingly, it will be important to avoid making assumptions about such foreign assets based upon an understanding of US laws and procedures pertaining to intellectual property.

B. LEGAL TESTS FOR REASONABLE DUE DILIGENCE REVIEWS

FEIT v. LEASCO DATA PROCESSING EQUIPMENT CORPORATION

United States District Court for the Eastern District of New York
332 F. Supp. 544 (1971)

WEINSTEIN, District Judge.

This case raises the question of the degree of candor required of issuers of securities who offer their shares in exchange for those of other companies in take-over operations. Defendants' registration statement was, we find, misleading in a material way. While disclosing masses of facts and figures, it failed to reveal one critical consideration that weighed heavily with those responsible for the issue-the substantial possibility of being able to gain control of some hundred million dollars of assets not required for operating the business being acquired.

. . .

III. SURPLUS SURPLUS

A. Definition of Surplus Surplus

Reliance's surplus surplus is the central element in this litigation. Leasco's desire to acquire it provided much of the original impetus for the exchange offer. Lack of disclosure of facts relating to the amount of surplus surplus and Leasco's intentions concerning its use, as well as the materiality of those omissions provide the basis of plaintiff's complaint. Finally, the method and difficulty of ascertaining its amount is critical to the defendants' affirmative defense. We cannot proceed without examining the concept.

Reliance is a fire and casualty insurance company subject to stringent regulation by the Insurance Commissioner of Pennsylvania. Such a company is required by the regulatory scheme to maintain sufficient surplus to guarantee the integrity of its insurance operations. Such "required surplus" cannot be separated from the insurance business of the company. That portion of surplus not required in insurance operations has been referred to as surplus surplus. In a widely relied upon report to the New York Insurance Department, the matter was summed up as follows:

> The 'required surplus' is one that will be adequate to cover for a reasonable period of time any losses and expenses larger than those predicted and any declines in asset values, including all chance variations in the crucial factors of the operation. Any surplus beyond this cover is 'surplus surplus' which, by definition, is unneeded; it may be treated quite differently in the process of regulation.

. . .

IX. SECTION 11

Section 11(a) of the Securities Act of 1933 provides for civil liability for misstatements and omissions in a registration statement. 15 U.S.C. § 77k(a). It reads:

> (a) In case any part of the registration statement, when such part became effective, contained an untrue statement of a material fact or omitted to state a material fact required to be stated therein or necessary to make the statements therein not misleading, any person acquiring such security (unless it is proved that at the time of such acquisition he knew of such untruth or omission) may, either at law or in equity, in any court of competent jurisdiction, sue [to recover damages or obtain equitable relief].

. . .

In non-quantitative terms, a fact is "material" in a registration statement whenever a rational connection exists between its disclosure and a viable alternative course of action by any appreciable number of investors. Materiality is then a question of fact to be determined in the context of a particular case.

. . .

Our finding that by failing to include an estimate-or-range-of surplus surplus in the registration statement Leasco "omitted to state a material fact required to be stated therein or necessary to make the statements therein not misleading" establishes plaintiff's cause of action. 15 U.S.C. § 77k(a). All that remains is to consider the defenses provided by Section 11 and whether the defendants have sustained their respective burdens of proof with regard to those defenses.

. . .

D. Due Diligence of the Directors — Steinberg, Schwartz & Hodes

Before analyzing the due diligence defenses presented by these defendants we must consider whether they are all properly treated together. Steinberg and Schwartz are and were, respectively, Chief Executive Officer and President of

Leasco — clearly "inside" directors. Hodes is a partner in the law firm which represents Leasco; he held no management office.

The leading case of *Escott v. BarChris Construction Corp.*, 283 F.Supp. 643 (S.D.N.Y. 1968) drew a distinction between directors who were officers of BarChris and its director-lawyer, Grant, who occupied a position analogous to Hodes' at Leasco. Judge McLean treated Grant as an "outside" director despite the fact that he had been a director for eight months prior to the public offering in question and had prepared the registration statement. The court then held Grant to a very high standard of independent investigation of the registration statement because of his peculiar expertise and access to information and held him liable for failure to meet that standard.

The assignment of "outside director" status to the lawyer in *BarChris* represented the court's conclusions on the facts peculiar to BarChris. It does not preclude a finding that "in some cases the attorney-director may be so deeply involved that he is really an insider." Folk, *Civil Liabilities Under the Federal Securities Acts — the BarChris Case*, 1 SECURITIES L. REV. 3, 39 (1969) (reprinted from 55 VA. L. REV. 1 (1969)). This is the case presented by Hodes.

Hodes has been a director of Leasco since 1965-three years or more at the time of this registration statement. He participated extensively in the discussions leading up to the exchange offer for Reliance shares as early as the fall of 1967 and was constantly involved in the deal throughout both the preliminary and execution stages of the transaction. He, or a representative of his law firm, attended all meetings and was consulted on all matters pertaining to this acquisition. He was directly responsible for preparation of the registration statement and initiated all of the research regarding reorganization of Reliance and separation of its surplus surplus. He kept Leasco's Schwartz apprised of the progress on possible alternatives for Reliance. The testimony and exhibits at this trial make it clear that insofar as surplus surplus is concerned Hodes was so intimately involved in this registration process that to treat him as anything but an insider would involve a gross distortion of the realities of Leasco's management.

Section 11[b] (3) (A) provides a "due diligence" in investigation defense to all defendants but the issuer.

> (b) Notwithstanding the provisions of subsection (a) of this section no person, other than the issuer, shall be liable as provided therein who shall sustain the burden of proof
>
> . . .
>
> (3) that (A) as regards as part of the registration statement not purporting to be made on the authority of an expert, and not purporting to be a copy of or extract from a report or valuation of an expert, and not purporting to be made on the authority of a public official document or statement, he had, after reasonable investigation, reasonable ground to believe and did believe, at the time such part of the registration statement became effective, that the statements therein were true and that there was no omission to state a material required to be stated therein or necessary to make the statements therein not misleading;"

15 U.S.C. § 77k(b) (3) (A).

The defendant must establish (1) that he conducted a reasonable investigation and (2) that after such investigation he had reasonable ground to believe and did believe the accuracy of the registration statement. Thus, a defendant may fulfill his burden of investigation and still not have reasonable cause to believe in the completeness of the prospectus or he may simply fail in his duty to investigate. Liability will lie in either case.

The standard of reasonableness which applies is that of a reasonably prudent man managing his own property. As stated in Section 11(c):

> In determining, for the purpose of paragraph (3) of subsection (b) of this section, what constitutes reasonable investigation and reasonable ground for belief, the standard of reasonableness shall be that required of a prudent man in the management of his own property. 15 U.S.C. § 77k(c)

There is little judicial gloss on this defense. In fact, Judge McLean's opinion in *BarChris* is the only one we have found which treats the subject at any length. The key to reasonable investigation as expressed in that opinion is independent verification of the registration statement by reference to original written records. The facts in *BarChris* revealed a consistent pattern of directors and underwriters who relied on the oral word of management regarding the accuracy of the registration statement. They made little, if any, effort to verify management's representations by reference to materials readily available such as corporate minutes, books, loan agreements, and various other corporate agreements.

Judge McLean makes it plain that a completely independent and duplicative investigation is not required but, rather, that the defendants were expected to examine those documents which were readily available. Speaking of the attorney-director's contentions he noted:

> It is claimed that a lawyer is entitled to rely on the statements of his client and that to require him to verify their accuracy would set an unreasonably high standard. This is too broad a generalization. It is all a matter of degree. To require an audit would obviously be unreasonable. On the other hand, to require a check of matters easily verifiable is not unreasonable. Even honest clients can make mistakes. The statute imposes liability for untrue statements regardless of whether they are intentionally untrue. The way to prevent mistakes is to test oral information by examining the original written record. "There were things which Grant could readily have checked which he did not check. For example, he was unaware of the provisions of the agreements between BarChris and Talcott. He never read them." *BarChris, supra*, 283 F.Supp. at 690.

This theme of an obligation of reasonable verification is also reflected in the commentators' analysis of the *BarChris* case. The reasonable investigation-verification-requirement is simply one means of promoting the full disclosure policy of Section 11.

> The purpose of the civil liability imposed by section 11 is to protect the investor through full disclosure, and the standards of reasonable

investigation must be framed in light of this goal. They should also reflect the two criteria set forth in the legislative history: (1) the importance of the role played by each participant in the scheme of distribution and (2) the reliance that the investor is justified in placing upon each participant. These criteria seem to be satisfied by a requirement that some of the parties to the registration process play a more adverse role vis-à-vis management than they may have in the past. The less a participant relies on management, the more the investor may rely on the involvement of the participant in the registration process." Comment, *BarChris: Due Diligence Refined*, 68 COLUM. L .REV. 1411, 1419 (1968).

In *BarChris* the management directors were found to have known about the misrepresentation and therefore the only question of reasonable investigation arose in the context of non-insider verification of information provided by those inside directors. These standards nevertheless apply equally to insider verification of the accuracy and completeness of data and statements they propose to include in the registration statement. Inclusion or omission of an item without a reasonable investigation or verification will lead to liability for these inside directors just as surely as if they actually knew of the inaccuracy or had no reasonable belief in the accuracy.

What constitutes "reasonable investigation" and a "reasonable ground to believe" will vary with the degree of involvement of the individual, his expertise, and his access to the pertinent information and data. What is reasonable for one director may not be reasonable for another by virtue of their differing positions.

It was clear from the outset, however, that the duty of each potentially liable group was not the same. The House report on the bill that became the original Securities Act stated that the duty of care to discover varied in its demands upon the participants with the importance of their place in the scheme of distribution and the degree of protection that the public had a right to expect from them. It has been suggested that although inside directors might be better able to show that they undertook some investigation, the outside director could more easily demonstrate that the investigation he actually undertook was sufficient to sustain his defense." Comment, *BarChris: Due Diligence Refined*, 68 COLUM. L. REV. 1411, 1416 (1968).

Inside directors with intimate knowledge of corporate affairs and of the particular transactions will be expected to make a more complete investigation and have more extensive knowledge of facts supporting or contradicting inclusions in the registration statements than outside directors. Similarly, accountants and underwriters are expected to investigate to various degrees. Each must undertake that investigation which a reasonably prudent man in that position would conduct.

BarChris imposes such stringent requirements of knowledge of corporate affairs on inside directors that one is led to the conclusion that liability will lie in practically all cases of misrepresentation. Their liability approaches that of the issuer as guarantor of the accuracy of the prospectus.

This ruling suggests that an inside director who, either as an officer or in some other capacity, has intimate familiarity with the corporate affairs or handles major transactions, especially those as to which false statements or omissions appear in the prospectus, is least able to establish due diligence. *BarChris* indicates that for such an individual knowledge of the underlying facts precludes showing 'reasonable ground to believe' or belief in fact as to the truth of the non-expert statements. In substance, there is a strong though theoretically rebuttable presumption that he had no reasonable ground to believe or belief in fact that the registration statement was accurate. Since an individual so situated will also have difficulty showing an absence of reasonable grounds of belief or belief in fact that expertised portions contain no misleading statements or omissions, a similar although less weighty presumption is present there. It would be fair to say that this postulated presumption arises when the intimate connection of the individual with the affairs of the issuer is demonstrated. Such an individual comes close to the status of a guarantor of accuracy." Folk, *Civil Liabilities Under the Federal Securities Acts: The* BarChris *Case*, 1 SECURITIES L. REV. 3, 25 (1969) (reprinted from 55 VA .L. REV. 1 (1969)).

Comment, *BarChris: Due Diligence Refined*, 68 COLUM .L. REV. 1411, 1420 (1968). It is with this strict standard in mind that we must approach the question of whether these three inside directors have established their defenses.

As already indicated, defendants' principle claim is that they considered including an estimate and decided against such action because of the uncertainties of computation. Steinberg and Hodes were both convinced, according to their testimony, that the estimates they had obtained were not reliable and that a reliable one could not be achieved with the data available. The key to all of their arguments is the unavailability of Reliance's management and the Pennsylvania Insurance Commissioner. We find that the director-defendants failed to fulfill their duty of reasonable investigation and that they had no reasonable ground to believe that an omission of an estimate of surplus surplus was not materially misleading.

(1)   Lack of Belief in Surplus Surplus Estimates.

These defendants did not have reasonable grounds to believe that the estimates of $80, $100, and $125 million in their possession were so inaccurate that one or all of them could not have been included in the prospectus with a carefully drafted qualifying statement similar to the one accompanying the inclusion in the January 31, 1969 registration statement. Defendants argue that the $125 million figure included in that prospectus was more reliable because Roberts had been consulted and approved the figure. This contention is rejected as unbelievable on the basis of the entire situation and Roberts' own testimony that he himself brought up the subject of the figure included in the draft prospectus because he had never seen it before and was curious as to its origin.

Defendants also maintain that the Pennsylvania Insurance Commissioner had been consulted and approved the figure contained in the February prospectus. This is not true.

It appears that the estimates prepared by Netter and Gibbs were considered sufficiently reliable by those defendants to predicate major expenditures in time and money in mounting the takeover drive. The $125 million estimate was used as a working figure in the research concerning reorganization alternatives for Reliance during and after the tender period. The defendants did not have reasonable grounds to believe that the estimates they already had were so inaccurate as to warrant exclusion from the prospectus.

(2)   Hostility of Roberts.

Defendants also argue that the management of Reliance, particularly Roberts, was so hostile to the exchange offer that the information necessary to calculate surplus surplus accurately was unavailable throughout the entire exchange offer period. They further contend that this hostility denied them standing before the Insurance Commissioner and hence his approval of a meaningful approximation. The facts of Roberts' relationship with Leasco do not support this contention.

It is true that Roberts evinced considerable hostility to both the exchange offer and Leasco prior to August 1, 1968. Peace was made on that date at a considerable financial gain to Roberts and cooperation began at once and increased in intensity.

The Court can reach but one conclusion in the face of the facts [found in this case] — Roberts would have cooperated in the calculation of an amount of surplus surplus after August 1, 1968 if he had been asked. He testified that he could have arrived at an estimate "damn quickly" if necessary, and it is our finding based on his testimony, our observation of him on the stand, and the sense of the situation that he would have done so — or at least would have provided the information necessary for such a calculation.

. . .

The critical point of this analysis is that Leasco, and particularly the three inside defendants, knew of the rapprochement with Reliance and were cognizant of all its ramifications. Being able, aggressive businessmen they must be held to an understanding of the implications of Roberts's tacit abdication of his duty to his shareholders in return for personal benefits. It could not but have occurred to them that after August 1st he might have been receptive to inquiries about surplus surplus and other corporate information. By relying on a state of facts which existed in June and July they ignored the obvious potential source of invaluable information they had acquired by consummation of the August 1, 1968 contract.

We find that these three defendants did not have reasonable ground to believe that omission of an estimate of surplus surplus from the registration statement was justified on the ground that they did not have access to the pertinent data on Reliance or entre to the Insurance Commissioner. Roberts would have provided both had he been asked. They ignored this fact in concluding that an accurate estimate of surplus surplus could not be developed by Leasco. They failed to exercise that high degree of care imposed upon them by Section 11.

(3) Lack of Adequate Inquiry.

Even if both of our prior conclusions regarding the lack of reasonable ground to believe in the accuracy of the registration statement were in error, these insider-defendants have nevertheless failed in their duty to reasonably investigate the accuracy of the prospectus. The uncontroverted testimony of two of the defendants themselves — Steinberg and Hodes — was that neither they nor anyone else in Leasco ever attempted to obtain a computation of surplus surplus beyond those of Leasco's Gibbs.

Surplus surplus was a crucial element of the plan to acquire Reliance. Yet, no one connected with Leasco commissioned an estimate by an insurance consultant; no one asked any Leasco employee to calculate it; Hodes never ordered one of his law firm's associates to attempt to arrive at a figure; and certainly no one made inquiry of one man who would have easily produced a figure — Roberts.

These defendants proceeded on the assumption that they could not arrive at an accurate figure without making the attempt. They may have failed — although we do not believe they would have — but they were bound by their duties under Section 11 to attempt to verify their conclusion that it was not calculable. It is this sort of laxity and oversight to which the requirement of reasonable investigation is directed and which Judge McLean held unacceptable in *BarChris*. By assiduously proving that they never had figures other than those previously alluded to these defendants have persuaded the court that they failed to vindicate their responsibility of due diligence.

Nor can it be argued that they need not have attempted the computation or made any inquiry because such gestures would have been futile. Roberts testified that any one knowledgeable in the insurance field might have arrived at a considered figure. Section 11 requires an attempt to make use of such expertise. Hodes, Schwartz and Steinberg are liable along with the issuer, Leasco.

E. Due Diligence of the Dealer-Managers — White, Weld & Co. and Lehman Brothers.

Section 11 holds underwriters to the same burden of establishing reasonable investigation and reasonable ground to believe the accuracy of the registration statement. The courts must be particularly scrupulous in examining the conduct of underwriters since they are supposed to assume an opposing posture with respect to management. The average investor probably assumes that some issuers will lie, but he probably has somewhat more confidence in the average level of morality of an underwriter who has established a reputation for fair dealing. Judge McLean expressed the proper relationship between underwriters and management in *BarChris*:

> In a sense, the positions of the underwriter and the company's officers are adverse. It is not unlikely that statements made by company officers to an underwriter to induce him to underwrite may be self-serving. They may be unduly enthusiastic. *Escott v. BarChris Construction Corp.*, 283 F. Supp. 643, 696 (S.D.N.Y.1968).

In light of this adverse position they must be expected to be alert to exaggerations and rosy outlooks and chary of all assurances by the issuer. Their duty is to the investing public under Section 11 as well as to their own self-interest and that duty cannot be taken lightly.

> Such adversity is required since the underwriter is the only participant in the registration process who, as to matters not certified by the accountant, is able to make the kind of investigation which will protect the purchasing public. Management may be so hard pressed for cash and so incorrigibly optimistic that they will accept or undervalue the risk of civil liability. The directors, as noted above, are not free to assume an adverse role, and in any event they are not entirely free from the pressures on and optimism of management. The SEC simply does not have the staff to verify independently even the more dubious registration statements. Only the underwriter and the accountant are free to assume an adverse role, have little incentive to accept the risk of liability, and possess the facilities and competence to undertake an independent investigation. They may therefore reasonably be required to share the burden of verification.
>
> The duty of the underwriter, then, is not merely limited to listening to management's explanations of the company's affairs. Rather he must make an investigation reasonably calculated to reveal all of those facts which would be of interest to a reasonably prudent investor. If he undertakes such an investigation, he will not be liable for material misrepresentations which his efforts did not uncover. If he does not, he will be liable for all misrepresentations which such an investigation would have uncovered.
>
> It is difficult to speculate as to what would constitute an investigation reasonably calculated to reveal those facts which would be of interest to a reasonably prudent investor. Of course all would agree that the underwriter should read minutes and important contracts and check out any inconsistencies in the representations of management. But the spirit of Judge McLean's opinion undoubtedly requires something more." Comment, *BarChris: Due Diligence Refined*, 68 COLUM. L. REV. 1411, 1421 (1968).

Dealer-managers cannot, of course, be expected to possess the intimate knowledge of corporate affairs of inside directors, and their duty to investigate should be considered in light of their more limited access. Nevertheless they are expected to exercise a high degree of care in investigation and independent verification of the company's representations. Tacit reliance on management assertions is unacceptable; the underwriters must play devil's advocate.

We find that the dealer-managers have just barely established that they reasonably investigated the surplus surplus concept as it related to Reliance and that they had reasonable ground to believe that omission of a specific figure was justified.

The evidence indicates a thorough review of all available financial data by White, Weld & Co. and its counsel. They independently examined Leasco's audit and the report of an actuary on Reliance. They made searching inquiries of Leasco's major bank. Whitney, counsel to the dealer-managers, undertook a study of Leasco's corporate minutes, records and major agreements.

Regarding surplus surplus, the dealer-managers were particularly careful in their inquiries of Leasco. Stone of White, Weld had considerable prior experience with surplus surplus. He was fully aware of the complexity of the computation problem. The Netter Report, Gibbs' Memorandum and New York Insurance Department Report were all referred to at the due diligence meetings held late in June and early in July of 1968 in New York where representatives of Leasco and the dealer-managers reviewed the proposed registration statement line by line. Based on these reports and on his own expertise, Stone briefed Whitney, lead counsel for the underwriters.

Whitney and Stone were informed by Leasco that Roberts was hostile to the exchange offer — which, in fact, was the case in early July when these meetings were held; that he would not cooperate by providing either information or an estimate of his own; and that he would not verify the approximations they already had in their possession. This assertion was reinforced by Roberts' June 24, 1968 letter to his shareholders urging them "not to act in haste" and by his May 15, 1968 letter concerning his intention to form a holding company for Reliance. Counsel for White Weld was also aware of Hodes' June 24, 1968 telegram to Roberts requesting cooperation in the preparation of a registration statement and of Roberts' reply of July 1, indicating that Reliance would not then comply.

Based on the information supplied by Leasco and confirmed by examination of these documents, Whitney rightly concluded that as of July 5th Roberts would not cooperate either by providing an opinion, by furnishing the critical data, or by verifying the estimates included in the Netter Report and Gibbs' Memorandum. In his opinion surplus surplus could not then be calculated with any accuracy.

The underwriters did not themselves contact Roberts because they had ascertained to their satisfaction that he would not be cooperative. Throughout July, Whitney and Stone were in constant contact with Leasco representatives regarding the progress of the exchange offer. During this period they received yet further verification of Roberts' intransigence which reconfirmed Whitney's opinion and certainly could not have provided a reasonable ground to reject his earlier conclusion. First, they learned of the subsequent requests for information directed to Roberts on July 9 and July 12 and of his evasion of such inquiries on July 15. They were, of course, aware that Roberts had filed a law suit seeking to inhibit any exchange offer. Finally, any doubt which may have lingered regarding Roberts' attitude was dispelled by his July 23rd letter of opposition to his shareholders in which he discussed in detail the reasons why the offer should be rejected.

We find, therefore, that it is somewhat more probable than not that as of August 1, 1968 the dealer-managers had sufficient verification of their previous conclusion concerning the possibility of accurately computing surplus surplus. They still had reasonable ground to believe that omission of such a figure was not misleading.

The dealer-managers were, however, undoubtedly aware of the August 1st contract between the Reliance management and Leasco and absent any further verification, their failure to recognize the implications of this agreement might well create liability for the same reasons expressed in our discussion of the defenses of the directors. But Whitney was in continuous contact with Leasco after August 1st and was apparently never disabused of the notion that Roberts remained recalcitrant. This view was conclusively buttressed by receipt of a copy of a letter dated August 13, 1968 from Kenneth J. Bialkin of Wilkie, Farr & Gallagher to the SEC, set forth at page 562, supra, stating that Reliance officials "have . . . declined to furnish information." Receipt of this letter served to reconfirm Whitney's belief that neither data nor advice would be forth-coming from Roberts. The registration statement became effective six days later, on August 19, 1968.

Though the finding might have gone the other way, on balance we conclude that the dealer-managers conducted a reasonable investigation and reasonably verified Leasco's representations that access to Reliance's management was precluded by Roberts' attitude. We note in passing that neither of the underwriters had their names on the January, 1969 Leasco prospectus which did rely on the $125 million estimate of surplus surplus.

Both White, Weld & Co. and Lehman Brothers have established their due diligence defenses with regard to this registration statement.

. . .

XII.   CONCLUSIONS

Members of the plaintiff-class are entitled to recover money damages pursuant to Section 11 of the Securities Act of 1933. 15 U.S.C. § 77k. The failure to include an estimate of surplus surplus in the registration statement filed in conjunction with this exchange offer was an omission of a material fact required to be stated to prevent the statements from being misleading. The three individual director-defendants who have appeared, Hodes, Schwartz and Steinberg, failed to make a reasonable investigation with regard to inclusion of such an estimate and did not have a reasonable ground to believe that this failure was not an omission to state a material fact. The issuer, Leasco, and these three directors are jointly and severally liable to the class. 15 U.S.C. § 77k(f).

The two dealer-manager defendants — White, Weld & Co. and Lehman Brothers — performed a reasonable investigation with regard to the propriety of an inclusion of an estimate of surplus surplus and had a reasonable ground to believe and did believe that the failure to include such a figure was not an omission to state a material fact. Accordingly they have established their due diligence defense and are not liable to the class.

So ordered.

NOTES & QUESTIONS

1. In addition to establishing possible defenses to liability for misstatements, due diligence reviews of intellectual property interests and risks prior to public stock offerings serve significant business interests in structuring the

terms of the offerings and in encouraging investors to participate in the offerings. Due diligence reviews help potential purchasers of stock ensure that they are "getting what they pay for." The results of these reviews can affect not only key offering terms — such as the size of the offering and initial price of the securities involved — but also whether the prospects of the companies involved seem sound enough to support the type of investor trust and interest needed to complete a successful public stock offering.

In private placements of stock where new stock offerings are sold directly to purchasers, a buyer may either conduct his own due diligence review of a company's intellectual property interests or be given access to the results of the company's own review. In a public stock offering, underwriters, who set the price at which new stock will initially trade, serve as representatives for stock purchasers generally in assessing the strength of a company's intellectual property position and in appropriately valuing the company involved:

> In the context of a public offering, the underwriters serve as the surrogates of the ultimate investors with respect to conducting due diligence; the underwriters are putting their name and reputation on the line when they market an issuer to prospective purchasers, and it is crucial that they have conducted sufficient diligence to support their "promotion" of the issuer's business and prospects. For example, few underwriters will allow a public offering to go effective until they have evaluated the issuer's business by speaking directly with some of the issuer's principal customers. Similarly, in the case of a biotechnology company issuer, the underwriters and their counsel will want to verify that the issuer has sufficient patent protection for its new drug developments and is taking appropriate steps to obtain the requisite regulatory approvals, because failure in either case could have significant adverse consequences on the issuer's business.

Mitchell S. Bloom & Lawrence A. Gold, PUBLIC OFFERINGS AND PRIVATE PLACEMENTS § 1.1.2 (2000).

2. Systematic due diligence reviews of a company's intellectual property interests and risks are often critically important features of private sales transactions in which a company sells off a subsidiary or division to a particular buyer or group of buyers. The sales agreement covering such a transaction will typically involve provisions in which the seller warrants the transferred company's ownership of key intellectual property interests and the lack of known infringement of intellectual property rights of others. In addition, the seller may warrant that the intellectual property rights being transferred to the buyer or group of buyers are sufficient to support the business activities of the company being transferred. Reasonable due diligence reviews are important means to confirm the accuracy of the warranties being made in these contexts and the scope of contractual liability the seller may risk by agreeing to these sorts of warranty terms.

The following contract terms are excerpted from an agreement governing the sale of all of the stock of a subsidiary of gambling giant Harrah's Entertainment

Corporation. These terms illustrate the scope of intellectual property warranties that may be incorporated in a corporate sales agreement and, by implication, the types of due diligence reviews which should precede a seller's agreement to such terms:

> Section 3.10 Intellectual Property. The Company [for which ownership is transferred under the stock sales agreement] owns or has the defensible right to use, whether through ownership, licensing or otherwise, all material Intellectual Property used in the businesses of the Company and each Subsidiary of the Company in substantially the same manner as such businesses are conducted on the date hereof ("Material Intellectual Property"). Except as set forth in Section 3.10 of the Company Disclosure Letter and except as would not, individually or in the aggregate, reasonably be expected to have a material adverse impact on the validity or value of any Material Intellectual Property, (A) no written claim of invalidity or conflicting ownership rights with respect to any Material Intellectual Property has been made by a third party and no such Material Intellectual Property is the subject of any pending or, to the Company's knowledge, threatened action, suit, claim, investigation, arbitration or other proceeding, (B) no individual, corporation, limited liability company, partnership, association, trust, unincorporated organization, other entity or "group" (as defined in Rule 13d-5(b)(1) under the Exchange Act) (each, a "Person") has given written notice to the Company or any Subsidiary of the Company that the use of any Material Intellectual Property by the Company, any Subsidiary of the Company or any licensee is infringing or has infringed any domestic or foreign patent, trademark, service mark, trade name, or copyright or design right, or that the Company, any Subsidiary of the Company or any licensee has misappropriated or improperly used or disclosed any trade secret, confidential information or know-how, (C) the making, using, selling, manufacturing, marketing, licensing, reproduction, distribution, or publishing of any process, machine, manufacture or product related to any Material Intellectual Property, does not and will not infringe any domestic or foreign patent, trademark, service mark, trade name, copyright or other intellectual property right of any third party, and does not and will not involve the misappropriation or improper use or disclosure of any trade secrets, confidential information or know-how of any third party of which the Company has knowledge, (D) (i) neither the Company nor any Subsidiary of the Company has performed prior acts or is engaged in current conduct or use, or (ii) to the knowledge of the Company, there exists no prior act or current use by any third party, that would void or invalidate any Material Intellectual Property, and (E) the execution, delivery and performance of this Agreement and the Ancillary Agreement by the Company and the consummation of the transactions contemplated hereby and thereby will not breach, violate or conflict with any instrument or agreement that the Company is party to and that concerns any Material Intellectual Property, will not cause the forfeiture or termination or give rise to a right of forfeiture or termination of any of the Material Intellectual

Property or impair the right of [the acquiring company] to make, use, sell, license or dispose of, or to bring any action for the infringement of, any Material Intellectual Property. Pursuant to that certain Exclusive License Agreement dated as of July 2, 1998, by and between Horseshoe Gaming, L.L.C. and Horseshoe License (the "Intellectual Property License Agreement"), the Company has an exclusive, irrevocable, fully paid license to use the Property (as defined in the Intellectual Property License Agreement) in perpetuity anywhere in the world, except for the State of Nevada.

Richard A. Goldberg & Monique K. Moore, *Negotiating the Purchase Agreement* in A GUIDE TO MERGERS & ACQUISITIONS 2005 425, 692 (PLI 2005).

3. Beyond the role of due diligence reviews in preparing for public offerings of stock and other transfers of corporate ownership, systematic reviews of intellectual property interests can serve important management functions and avoid certain types of liability for management errors. For example, responsible monitoring of intellectual property interests and liabilities through due diligence reviews can aid corporate directors in meeting their corporate law duties and avoiding personal liability for corporate losses. In general, corporate board members must exercise due care in making decisions about corporate actions. As the strength and management of intellectual property interests become more important features of various types of businesses and threats posed by the intellectual property interests of others become more substantial risks, the significance of attention by corporate directors to intellectual property monitoring grows accordingly.

Where corporate directors know (or should have known through reasonable information gathering) about intellectual property risks that are likely to adversely affect planned corporate actions, yet the directors disregard these risks to the detriment of their corporations, the directors may face personal liability for the resulting corporate losses. *See generally In re Caremark International Inc. Derivative Litigation*, 698 A.2d 959, 1996 Del. Ch. LEXIS 125 (1996). Due diligence in monitoring intellectual property interests and risks has major importance in companies that base their business strategies on the strength of their intellectual property and on the lack of business barriers due to the intellectual property interests of others. *See* Steven E. Bochner & Susan P. Krause, *Intellectual Property Management and Board Liability*, PRACTIING LAW INSTITUTE, CORPORAE LAW AND PRACTICE COURSE HANDBOOK SERIES NO. B0-004Y 457-58 (August 1998). These issues are addressed further in Chapter 12.

4. Companies sometimes state a positive belief that they are not infringing the intellectual property rights of others. For example, the investor information web site of Agilent Technologies (a maker of a wide variety of communications, electronics, life sciences and chemical analysis products) contains the following representations about the company's activities and possible infringement of intellectual property rights of other concerns:

While we do not believe that any of our products infringe the valid intellectual property rights of third parties, we may be unaware of intellectual property rights of others that may cover some of our technology, products or services. Any litigation regarding patents or other intellectual property could be costly and time-consuming and could divert our management and key personnel from our business operations. The complexity of the technology involved and the uncertainty of intellectual property litigation increase these risks. Claims of intellectual property infringement might also require us to enter into costly license agreements. However, we may not be able to obtain license agreements on terms acceptable to us, or at all. We also may be subject to significant damages or injunctions against development and sale of certain of our products.

Agilent Technologies, *Risks, Uncertainties and Other Factors That May Affect Future Results*, http://investor.agilent.com/risk.cfm (last visited on May 19, 2005).

What type of self-scrutiny of claims or assertions of intellectual property infringement should a company be expected to make before representing that "we do not believe that any of our products infringe the valid intellectual property rights of third parties"? Is it sufficient that additional portions of the company's web site indicate that there may be intellectual property interests and acts of infringement that the company has not detected yet? Does the statement that "we do not believe" that there is infringement imply that this belief is based on a reasonable inquiry or is it enough if the executives making the statement were personally unaware of infringement? What should be the impact on corporate liability if persons at a middle management or operating employee level of the corporation had knowledge of the probable infringement of another party's intellectual property interest, but this knowledge had not risen upward in the corporation's hierarchy sufficiently to reach the executives who made the representation about the company's lack of infringement?

C. MAINTAINING AND WAIVING PRIVILEGE PROTECTIONS IN DUE DILIGENCE REVIEWS

The sharing of corporate information to facilitate due diligence reviews may raise questions about the scope and waiver of attorney-client privilege protections normally held by a corporate client. In the course of due diligence reviews of intellectual property interests and infringement threats by outsiders to a corporation such as corporate underwriters, corporate executives may choose to supply the outsiders with earlier, privileged evaluations of those interests and threats prepared by counsel. These evaluations may have been based on additional privileged submissions of factual information to counsel. While such disclosures may help the outsiders to assess the intellectual property interests and infringement threats at issue, these disclosures may also raise questions about whether the legal advice and related factual submissions to counsel have been disclosed outside the corporate client so as to waive the previously applicable privilege protections.

The following reading describes the types of attorney-client privilege protections that may attach to materials submitted to counsel in connection with obtaining a patent or in seeking an opinion of counsel regarding patent infringement. The next reading describes how these privilege protections may be waived through disclosures of legal evaluations during due diligence reviews of intellectual property interests and infringement threats in conjunction with IPOs and other major business transactions.

1.   The Scope of Privilege Protections

KNOGO CORPORATION v. UNITED STATES
United States Court of Claims, Trial Division
1980 U.S. Ct. Cl. LEXIS 1262; 213 U.S.P.Q. (BNA) 936 (1980)

COLAIANNI, Trial Judge.

I have before me a motion for the production of documents for inspection and copying. The third-party defendant, Checkpoint Systems, Inc. (hereinafter referred to as defendant), brings this motion under Rule 74 against plaintiff, Knogo Corporation. Plaintiff asserts the attorney-client privilege in opposing the production of the 12 documents which were identified in response to Government interrogatories. . . .

. . .

The 12 documents themselves, the affidavits of William Brunet, Esq., and Arthur Minasy, and the uncontested assertions of counsel are the bases of the background facts needed for resolution of the issues. Arthur Minasy, president of plaintiff Knogo Corporation, is the patentee of the patent in suit. William Brunet, Esq., is a member of the Bar of the State of New York dating from a time prior to the communications in question. Mr. Brunet is the attorney who prosecuted the patent in suit before the Patent and Trademark Office (hereinafter referred to as the Patent Office) on behalf of Mr. Minasy, who was the client of Mr. Brunet during the pertinent period of the communications. Mr. Eugene Novikoff, a neighbor and long-standing personal friend of Mr. Minasy, is an electrical engineer and the person who assisted Mr. Minasy in building the first experimental models of the invention which later became the subject of the patent in suit. Mr. Carroll Hamlet is a consultant who was paid by Mr. Minasy for services rendered in connection with the construction of a prototype of the invention.

The assertion of the attorney-client privilege will be evaluated on the basis of the requirements first expressed by Judge Wyzanski in *United States v. United Shoe Machinery Corp.*, 89 F.Supp. 357, 358-59, 85 USPQ 5, 6 (D. Mass. 1950):

(1) the asserted holder of the privilege is or sought to become a client;

(2) the person to whom the communication was made

    (a)   is a member of the bar of a court, or his subordinate and

    (b)   in connection with this communication is acting as a lawyer;

(3) the communication relates to a fact of which the attorney was informed

    (a)   by his client

    (b)   without the presence of strangers

    (c)   for the purpose of securing primarily

        (i)   an opinion on law or

(ii) legal services or

(iii) assistance in some legal proceeding, and not

(d) for the purpose of committing a crime or tort; and

(4) the privilege has been

(a) claimed and

(b) not waived by the client.

Defendant challenges the assertion of privilege over documents 1 through 4 on two grounds. The first questions the confidentiality of the communications and the second denies that the communications were the communications of the client. In terms of the *United Shoe* criteria, these come under (3)(b) and (4)(b) for the defendant's first objection and (3)(a) for the second.

Some of the most difficult discovery questions presented in patent litigation relate to the assertion of attorney-client privilege with respect to communications containing primarily or exclusively technical information.

Documents 1 and 2 are purely technical expositions of the invention in suit as a whole and of its component parts in particular. Documents 3 and 4 contain technical explanations of the general field of technology to which the invention in suit relates and comparisons from a technical standpoint between the invention in suit and other devices. None of the four documents contains an express request for legal advice or legal services.[9] However, it is clear that they were each prepared to provide the attorney with the information necessary to assess the invention's patentability, prepare and file a patent application which led to the patent in suit, and prosecute that patent application through the Patent Office.[10] With these facts in mind, attention initially turns to defendant's argument that documents 1-4 are not privileged because they are not the communications of the client.

There is nothing on the face of documents 1 through 4 to indicate that they were necessarily the communications of the client, Minasy. However, defendant's argument that these documents are not subject to the attorney-client privilege because they were not written by Minasy loses its force in light of the showing presented in the affidavit of Minasy and in statements of plaintiff's counsel. In addition to the background facts provided above, it is apparent that the four documents were prepared at the specific request of Minasy so that he might give them to his attorney for the purpose of rendering legal services to Minasy. The preparers of the four documents, though not the client personally, were either in the client's employ or were working in close concert with the client on the invention.

The law has long recognized that a privileged communication need not originate personally with the client in the sense that it was first written or first spoken by the client.

---

[9] [FN1] The request for legal advice or services need not be an express request, nor need the implied request necessarily appear on the face of the document for which the claim of privilege is made. *Hercules, Inc. v. Exxon Corp.*, 434 F.Supp. 136, 144, 196 USPQ 401, 406 (D. Del. 1977).

[10] [FN2] The court in *Eutectic Corp v. Metco, Inc.*, 61 F.R.D. 35, 41, 180 USPQ 570, 574 (E.D.N.Y. 1973), saw no good reason to distinguish between communications made for purposes of the preparation versus the prosecution of the patent application.

The client's freedom of communication requires a liberty of employing other means than his own personal action. The privilege of confidence would be a vain one unless its exercise could be thus delegated. A communication, then, by any form of agency employed or set in motion by the client is within the privilege.

Modern case law continues to apply this principle when dealing with corporate clients. The principle applies, a fortiori, in the case at bar where the client is an individual and the original preparers of the documents constituting the communications are special agents of the client in the sense that they were specifically authorized to prepare the documents for the specific purpose of furnishing information to the client's attorney. Thus, the four documents are the communications of the client for the purpose of claiming the privilege.

The most difficult issue presented by defendant's challenge to documents 1-4 relates to the confidentiality of the communications. The issue has two parts. The first focuses on the standard for determining the requisite confidentiality in the contest of the attorney-client privilege. The second asks whether a communication of technical information satisfies that standard as a matter of law or fact.

The intention of the client is the standard which determines whether the confidentiality required for the privilege is present. The client must make the communication with the intention that the attorney keep it confidential. There must be some expectation of confidentiality, and the fact that the communication consists entirely of information from the public domain does not defeat the privilege. The requisite confidential intent exists if the attorney was informed "without the presence of strangers."

The following cases are representative of those commonly cited for the proposition that communications consisting primarily of technical information are not invested with the confidentiality required to support the claim of attorney-client privilege: *Burlington Indus. v. Exxon Corp.*, 65 F.R.D. 26, 184 USPQ 651 (D. Md. 1974), and *Jack Winter, Inc. v. Koratron, Inc.*, 50 F.R.D. 225, 166 USPQ 295 (N.D. Cal. 1970). The *Jack Winter* line of cases refers to 35 U.S.C. §§ 111 and 112[11] and concludes that the patent applicant and his attorney are under a duty to disclose to the Patent Office how to make and use the invention and that this duty precludes any expectation of confidentiality with respect to communications containing primarily technical information provided to the attorney who prepares and prosecutes the patent application. Put another way, these cases proceed on the assumption that since the communication consists primarily of technical information, and since the client wants a patent application to be prepared and filed in the Patent Office, and since this application may ultimately be allowed and available to the public, that the client could not have intended that the information be held in confidence.

In opposition to the *Jack Winter* view are cases like: *Natta v. Hogan*, 392 F2d 686, 157 USPQ 183 (10th Cir. 1968), and *In re Amplicillin Antitrust Litigation*, [81 F.R.D. 377, 202 USPQ 134, 142-43 (D. D.C. 1978)]. The *Natta*

---

[11] [FN3] 37 C.F.R. § 1.56 (1979), entitled in part "Duty of disclosure" is a regulation which also appears pertinent.

line of cases concludes that the duty of a patent attorney who prepares and prosecutes patent applications is no greater than the duty of any attorney who represents a client before the courts or administrative bodies and that this duty need not override a patent applicant's confidential intent regarding communications consisting primarily of technical information about the invention.[12] A distinction can be made between the duty to disclose how to make and use the invention and the mere funneling of technical information from the client through the attorney to the Patent Office. The former is the job of the patent attorney, while the latter is an inaccurate, and uninformed characterization of the patent attorney's role in the preparation and prosecution of a patent application.

Careful consideration of the respective analyses which underlie the two conflicting lines of authority leads me to conclude that the confidentiality required for the successful assertion of the attorney-client privilege can exist in regard to communications which are primarily technical expositions. I therefore deny defendant's motion for the production of documents 1-4 on the basis of the plaintiff's showing of confidential intent.

The overriding concern in the tug-of-war between privilege and discovery is the maintenance of a fair balance between the promotion of candor in attorney-client communications and the discovery of all documents that might lead to admissible evidence. The application of the privilege always excludes relevant documents from discovery, but it does not necessarily prevent the party seeking discovery from learning the same facts that are reflected in the privileged documents. The privilege only applies to the communication that takes place between the attorney and the client. It does not apply to the technical information itself, so long as that technical information is sought by other discovery techniques outside of the context of the attorney-client communication. In other words, the client cannot assert the privilege if asked how the invention works, but he can assert the privilege if he is asked to recount what he told his attorney concerning how the invention works. The expectation of confidentiality applies to the communication, but not to the information contained in the communication. Thus, the instant decision does not place an undue burden upon the discovery process, and whatever the burden, it appears to be justified in light of the policy of preserving that degree of candor demanded by the guardians of adequate legal representation.

The conclusion reached by the authorities in the *Jack Winter* camp rests upon an oversimplification of the role performed by the patent attorney during the patent application process. The attorney is not a mere conduit for either the client's communications containing the technical information or the technical information itself. He does not file his client's communications with the Patent Office. He does not file transcripts of his conversations with the client regarding technical matters and then await the issuance of a

---

[12] [FN4] Communications containing technical information are to be distinguished from the communication which is nothing more than the affidavit of the client, e.g., a Rule 131 affidavit, an oath, or a declaration of the applicant. In these latter cases the requisite confidentiality is lacking as a matter of law because the communication is made with the intention that the attorney transmit the affidavit, oath, or declaration to the Patent Office.

patent, yet this is the impression one derives from a reading of the *Jack Winter* view.

The reality of the cooperative effort put forth by the inventor and the attorney is far different from the *Jack Winter* portrayal. The technical discussions between attorney and client enable the attorney to extract from this information one or more patentable inventions. The attorney then drafts one or more patent applications in accordance with the requirements of the federal statutes and regulations. The attorney "has no duty to transmit information which is not material to the examination of the application."[13] 37 C.F.R. § 1.56(b) (1979). The application for patent is reviewed by the client, and once approved, it is signed by the client and then filed in the Patent Office by the attorney on behalf of the client. The signed, sworn, and filed application might be considered a communication for relay and not for the attorney's ears alone, but the same cannot be said about the technical communications which preceded the signed, sworn, and filed patent application.

The fact that much of the technical information in one form or another finds its way into the patent application, to be made public when the patent issues, should not preclude the assertion of the privilege over the communication in which that information was disclosed to the attorney.

If an attorney-client communication could be discovered if it contained information known to others, then it would be the rare communication that would be protected and, in turn, it would be the rare client who would freely communicate to an attorney. In any attorney-client relation, the attorney necessarily takes actions that are based upon the information provided by the client. As a result of this action, the information may be asserted in a variety of public representations: written and oral, inter partes and ex parte, and before courts and administrative bodies alike.[14]

The situation is like that where a client gives general information to his lawyer so that the lawyer may prepare a complaint in any ordinary civil action. The fact that some of the information is thus publicly disclosed does not waive the privilege.

A hindsight evaluation to determine if a client has the necessary intention of keeping a given communication confidential can be a troublesome task. There is, for example, no inference of an intent to disclose anything to the Patent Office when the purpose of the communication by the client to the attorney is merely to elicit a legal opinion concerning the patentability of the invention. Some inference of an intent to disclose begins to arise when the filing of a patent application becomes the dominant purpose behind the communication of

---

[13] [FN5] "Such information is material where there is a substantial likelihood that a reasonable examiner would consider it important in deciding whether to allow the application to issue as a patent." 37 C.F.R. § 1.56(a) (1979).

[14] [FN6] The client does not waive the privilege by bringing a suit which places the validity of the patent in issue. *Burlington Indus. v. Exxon Corp.*, 65 F.R.D. 26, 35, 184 USPQ 651, 654 (D. Md. 1974). Waiver does not occur until the client places in issue the communication itself. This most frequently occurs in suits between a client and his attorney or where there is a prima facie case of fraud based upon the dealings between the client and his attorney.

the technical information. Since aspects of both purposes are inextricably present in most cases, it becomes unreliable at best, and an invitation for false swearing at worst, to ask the client to recall the dominant intent.

The practical test for determining whether the client intended the communication to be confidential is the one laid down in *United Shoe, supra*, by J. Wyzanski more than 30 years ago, namely, whether the communication was made "without the presence of strangers." This is often verifiable from the face of the document in question by inspecting it for any indication, such as a circulation list, that extraneous parties were intended to receive the same communication.

In the case at bar the client has repeatedly affirmed, through his own affidavit, the affidavit of the attorney to whom the communications were made, and the statements of the attorney of record in this suit, that documents 1-4 were shown only to counsel. The documents themselves bear no contradictory indicators. Defendant's objection that documents 1 and 2 were "typed by a secretary employed by another company" ignores common agency principles and the realities of modern businesses which contract for the services of temporary employees and consultants, the latter themselves often employing secretarial and other personnel.

NOTES & QUESTIONS

1. Technical information submitted to counsel like that at issue in *Knogo* may describe structural or operational differences (or the lack of them) between a new invention and a prior device. Information about these differences would be useful to counsel in drafting patent claims which emphasize the differences, as well as in providing legal advice to the inventor about the enforceability and scope of potential patent rights in the invention. Assuming that a patent is obtained for the invention and assigned to a company that later seeks to conduct an IPO, the same technical information — along with counsel's legal advice at the time a patent was applied for — might be revisited at a later point as persons conducting a due diligence review of the company seek to evaluate the validity and commercial value of the patent. As discussed in the next reading, the release of this information to the persons conducting the due diligence review may waive any applicable attorney-client privilege protections.

2. Where a previous legal analysis is not available and a corporation contemplating an IPO seeks an opinion of counsel regarding the validity and enforceable scope of a patent in order to have this opinion considered in a due diligence review of the corporation, counsel may collect the same type of technical information as was at issue in *Knogo*. Under the standards addressed in *Knogo*, this information, along with counsel's analysis of the patent, will typically be privileged when the resulting legal advice is rendered to the corporation. However, as with the use of a preexisting legal analysis, the forwarding of a specially obtained legal opinion to outside parties conducting a due diligence review may forfeit attorney-client privilege protections for that opinion and supportive factual information.

2. Maintaining Privilege Protections in Due Diligence Reviews

Eric K. Steffe*, W. Blake Coblentz & Jessica Parezo, The Common-Interest Doctrine and Intellectual Property Due Diligence
24 Biotechnology L. Rep. 1 (Feb. 2005)**

INTRODUCTION

Companies involved in intellectual property due diligence investigations are sometimes faced with situations in which business transactions would be facilitated by disclosing their attorney's legal impressions to a potential business partner. In the biotechnology and pharmaceutical industries, for example, vast resources and expertise are required to bring a product to market. Most biotechnology companies are focused on a specific portion of the product chain (e.g., identifying a drug candidate) and rely on numerous external collaborations and alliances with other biotechnology and pharmaceutical companies for further product development. Prior to entering an intercompany alliance, however, potential business partners need answers to complicated legal questions, including (1) whether intellectual property owned by third parties exists that may be infringed during the collaborative effort; and (2) whether the other company's own intellectual property sufficiently covers the product intended for commercialization. A potential business partner is faced with the choice of either retaining an attorney to perform due diligence investigations from scratch or, to save time and money, requesting that the other company turn over any relevant legal opinions that have already been prepared for its own use. However, absent applicability of an exception to the waiver rule, sharing legal opinions with another waives the attorney-client privilege.

Provided below is a discussion of the attorney-client privilege and exceptions to the waiver rule; a review of case law involving the common-interest doctrine in the context of transactions involving intellectual property; and considerations and recommendations for companies involved in due diligence investigations.

ATTORNEY-CLIENT PRIVILEGE AND EXCEPTIONS TO THE WAIVER RULE

The attorney-client privilege protects from disclosure confidential communications from client to lawyer during professional employment. The protection

---

* Mr. Steffe is a Director at Sterne, Kessler, Goldstein & Fox P.L.L.C. At the time of the preparation of this article, Mr. Coblentz was a summer associate and Ms. Parezo an associate at Sterne, Kessler. The content of this article reflects the thoughts of the authors and should not be attributed to Sterne, Kessler or any of its former, current, or future clients.

extends to "both information provided to the lawyer by the client and professional advice given by an attorney that discloses such information." With a few exceptions, discussed below, a client who discloses privileged information to a third party waives the privilege. Generally speaking, the scope of the waiver includes all documents and information in the client's hands that relate to the waived subject matter. Thus, if the privilege is waived — for example, because a company shared with a potential collaborator an opinion of counsel relating to a patent that is later asserted against the parties in an action for infringement — the opinion itself and all of the company's internal documents relating to the opinion may well have to be turned over to the plaintiff during discovery. Nonetheless, a company's need to conduct business may trump concerns about waiver of the privilege when a potential collaborator with leverage wants intellectual property assurances but refuses to commit the resources necessary to perform its own investigation.

Exceptions to the waiver rule that have been recognized by the courts include situations involving joint clients, joint litigants, and common interest arrangements. The joint client privilege applies where two or more clients seek representation from the same lawyer. Communications between such joint clients and their lawyer can remain privileged vis-à-vis third parties. However, such representations can raise conflicts of interest where a common lawyer represents joint clients whose interests may diverge in the future. The joint-litigant privilege preserves the attorney-client privilege for communications shared by co-parties in litigation even where those parties are represented by different counsel. The joint-litigant privilege is also limited, as, to be recognized, the information exchange must occur within the context of actual or threatened litigation. In contrast, the common-interest doctrine extends the joint-litigant privilege by allowing parties represented by different counsel to share information outside the context of the litigation. Parties having "an identical legal interest with respect to the subject matter of the communication" are permitted under the doctrine to share information without waiving the attorney-client privilege. The purpose of the doctrine is to encourage parties working under a common legal interest "to benefit from the guidance of counsel, and thus avoid the pitfalls that otherwise might impair their progress toward their shared objective."

CASE LAW TREATMENT OF THE COMMON-INTEREST DOCTRINE IN THE CONTEXT OF TRANSACTIONS INVOLVING INTELLECTUAL PROPERTY

Intellectual property cases applying the common-interest doctrine

Hewlett-Packard Co. v. Bausch & Lomb Inc., 115 F.R.D. 308, 309, 4 U.S.P.Q. 1673, 1673 (N.D. Cal. 1987).

In *Hewlett-Packard*, the District Court for the Northern District of California held that there was no waiver of the attorney-client privilege when the defendant, Bausch & Lomb, seeking to sell one of its divisions, voluntarily disclosed its patent attorney's opinion letter to a prospective purchaser, GEC. The opinion letter concerned Hewlett-Packard's patent, which was the patent in issue in the litigation. While acknowledging that forcing Bausch & Lomb to produce the document would contribute to ascertaining the truth at trial and that this was a "close case," the court focused on policy considerations to support its finding no waiver:

> [h]olding that this kind of disclosure constitutes a waiver could make it appreciably more difficult to negotiate sales of businesses and products that arguably involve interests protected by laws relating to intellectual property. Unless it serves some significant interest courts should not create procedural doctrine that restricts communication between buyers and sellers, erects barriers to business deals, and increases the risk that prospective buyers will not have access to important information that could play key roles in assessing the value of the business or product they are considering buying.

Id. at 311, 4 U.S.P.Q. at 1675.

Even though GEC subsequently decided not to buy the Bausch & Lomb division, the court held that Bausch & Lomb and GEC had a common interest because, at the time of the negotiations, it was "quite likely" that the parties would be identically aligned in any litigation against Hewlett-Packard. To further support its holding, the court stressed that Bausch & Lomb "did everything within its power to impress upon GEC the importance of maintaining the confidentiality of the opinion letter, and GEC, in turn, seemed to have undertaken to hold the letter in confidence."

Johnson Electric North America Inc. v. Mabuchi North America Corp., 1996 U.S. Dist. LEXIS 5227, at *9-10 (S.D.N.Y. October 29, 1996).

On facing a claim that it was infringing patents held by Mabuchi, Johnson Electric filed suit seeking a declaratory judgment that the patents were invalid. During discovery, Mabuchi's counsel traveled to Hong Kong to depose one of Johnson's customers, Dickson, and sought production of documents relating to communications between New York counsel for Johnson and Hong Kong counsel for Dickson.

The District Court for the Southern District of New York held that there had been no waiver of the attorney-client privilege because of the common interest of Johnson and Dickson. The court stated that the common interest doctrine "does not require that both, or indeed either, of the communicants be parties to a litigation." The court further noted that Johnson and Dickson were "de facto allies" because both faced a threat of liability if Mabuchi prevailed on its infringement theories. Moreover, "Johnson, as a supplier anxious to please its customer, had a strong economic incentive to avoid unnecessarily embroiling that customer in litigation that arose from Johnson's activities in marketing the assertedly infringing equipment."

United States v. A.S.C.A.P., 1996 U.S. Dist. LEXIS 16201, at *1 (S.D.N.Y. October 29, 1996).

In an action for determination of reasonable license fees, the American Society of Composers, Authors and Publishers (ASCAP) sought production of documents relating to a series of discussions held over a period of 6 years among cable suppliers and their counsel. The cable suppliers resisted on the grounds that the documents were protected under attorney-client privilege and the work-product rule. While stating that there was insufficient information in the record to determine if the work-product rule applied, the District Court for the Southern District of New York took the position that the cable providers' attorney-client privilege claim stood on firmer ground.

> [T]he discussions involved an assessment of legal issues, and indicate that the attorneys played an active role, either in reporting legal developments or in advising the companies on legal matters . . . [the companies] were conducting these discussions to serve a common legal and economic interest — the minimization of music performance rights fees. Thus, the statements made at the meetings would presumably be covered by the so-called common-interest extension of the attorney-client privilege.

1996 U.S. Dist. LEXIS 16201, at *3-4.

Tenneco Packaging Specialty and Consumer Products, Inc. v. S.C. Johnson & Son, Inc., 1999 U.S. Dist. LEXIS 15433, at *1 (N.D. Ill. September 9, 1999).

Tenneco Packaging Specialty and Consumer Products, Inc., is the holder of a patent claiming a rolling zipper on a plastic storage bag. In an asset-purchase agreement, S.C. Johnson & Son (SCJ) received the rights to a similar patent from Dowbrands and had bags with a rolling zipper manufactured on its behalf by KCL Corporation. Tenneco sued SCJ and KCL for patent infringement and sought to compel deposition testimony and production of an opinion of Dowbrands' counsel that SCJ withheld as falling under the attorney-client privilege.

The opinion, which had been drafted by Dowbrands' attorney to provide that company with legal advice concerning potential infringement of Tenneco's patent, was shown to SCJ while SCJ was performing due diligence for the asset-purchase agreement. In denying Tenneco's motion, the District Court for the Northern District of Illinois pointed out that access to the opinion was controlled by specific procedures designed to prevent dissemination of its contents, such as showing the opinion to only a limited number of SCJ representatives after they had acknowledged that it was subject to a confidentiality agreement. Moreover, the opinion was disclosed when the asset purchase deal was "largely locked up."

In re Regents of the University of California, 101 F.3d 1386, 1388-89, 40 U.S.P.Q.2d 1784, 1786 (Fed.Cir. 1996).

Shortly after filing a patent application in 1978, the Regents for the University of California entered into an exclusive option agreement that provided Eli Lilly with license rights to future issued U.S. and foreign patents. At trial before the District Court for the Southern District of Indiana, Genentech sought declaratory judgment that a U.S. patent arising out of this application was invalid, unenforceable, and not infringed by Genentech's human growth hormone product. The District Court granted Genentech's motion to compel testimony concerning certain communications between in-house counsel for Lilly and counsel for UC concerning prior art and errors in the patent which

Genentech contended were relevant to the issue of inequitable conduct. The University then filed a writ of mandamus to prevent "the wrongful exposure of privileged communications."

While acknowledging that the scope of the attorney-client privilege is narrowly drawn in the Seventh Circuit, the Federal Circuit overturned the District Court's holding by concluding that the legal interest between UC and Lilly was sufficiently identical for the common interest doctrine to apply. The Federal Circuit cited factors such as the potentially and ultimately exclusive nature of the license agreement (Lilly was "more than a nonexclusive licensee") and that the two parties had the same interest in obtaining valid patents.

Intellectual property cases not applying the common-interest doctrine

Libbey Glass, Inc. v. Oneida, Ltd., 197 F.R.D. 342 (N.D. Ohio 1999).

Libbey Glass, Inc., a glassware manufacturer, sued Oneida Ltd. for trade dress infringement. In an attempt to increase its presence in the glassware market, Oneida had contracted with Pasabahce Cam Sanayii VE Ticaret A.S., a Turkish manufacturer of glassware, to purchase several lines of glassware.

Because of concerns about the legal implications of similarities between the glassware Pasabahce manufactured for Oneida and Libbey's glassware, employees at Oneida disclosed to Pasabahce information from Oneida's counsel. Libbey argued that this disclosure constituted a waiver of the attorney-client privilege and sought discovery of all attorney-client communications relating to the transaction between Oneida and Pasabahce. The District Court for the Northern District of Ohio agreed with Libbey and rejected the "more expansive" view of the common-interest doctrine expressed in *Hewlett-Packard*.

Under the "more restrictive" view, information shared during a business undertaking loses its privileged status, "even though such sharing helped address or ameliorate bona fide concerns about the legal implications of some aspect of the business venture." The court pointed out that Pasabahce never consulted with their own counsel, and no steps had been taken by Oneida or Pasabahce to ensure that the shared information would remain confidential.

The burden belongs on the party claiming privilege to have avoided uncertainty, and to have taken effective steps to ensure that all participants were aware of the need to maintain confidentiality, and to show that mechanisms were in place to accomplish that objective before the information was shared.

However, even if steps had been taken to preserve confidentiality, the court found in the alternative "that the shared communications were ancillary to the negotiation of a business agreement" and thus would have still constituted a waiver of the attorney-client privilege. According to the court,

> Oneida sought commercial gain, not legal advantage, through disclosure of its lawyer's advice to Pasabahce. The parties were formulating not a "common legal" strategy, but a joint commercial venture.

Id. at 349; *see also Bank Brussels Lambert v. Credit Lyonnais (Suisse) S.A.*, 160 F.R.D. 437, 447 (S.D.N.Y).

Katz and MCI v. AT&T Corp., 191 F.R.D. 433, 435 n. 1 (E.D. Pa. 2000).

Ronald A. Katz, the owner a large number of patents related to telephonic interactive voice applications, formed an entity, Ronald A. Katz Technology Licensing, L.P. (RAKTL) to license his portfolio. RAKTL and MCI negotiated an agreement granting MCI a non-exclusive license to Katz's portfolio and an exclusive right to enforce the portfolio against AT&T.

RAKTL and MCI as joint plaintiffs then filed a patent infringement suit against AT&T. Because of the complexity of the case, the District Court for the Eastern District of Pennsylvania appointed a Special Master to manage discovery. During discovery, the Special Master granted AT&T's motion to compel discovery of documents relating to the negotiations between RAKTL and MCI that resulted in the licensing agreement.

RAKTL and MCI objected to the Special Master's order on the grounds that sharing documents during the negotiation phase did not waive the attorney-client privilege in view of the common legal interest of RAKTL and MCI. In particular, RAKTL and MCI argued that, before the documents were exchanged, they had "reached an agreement in principle to enforce the Katz patent portfolio against AT&T and, therefore, they had a common legal interest in enforcing the Katz patents."

Citing *Hewlett-Packard*, the court agreed that the common-interest doctrine can protect the attorney-client privilege even where information is exchanged prior to final agreement and even if the parties ultimately do not conclude an agreement. The district court nonetheless affirmed the Special Master, as the "Report reflects the determination by the Special Master that the plaintiffs failed to meet their burden of showing the requisite identity of interests required under the doctrine because the parties had not reached an agreement, final or otherwise, as to the licensing issues prior to the signing of the agreement. . . ." According to the court, during negotiations, the interests of the parties were adversarial and conducted at arm's length.

Concerning the existence of an identity of legal interest, the court found the record to be "sufficiently ambiguous as to the existence of an identity of interest to preclude overturning the decision of the Special Master as clearly erroneous."

CONSIDERATIONS AND RECOMMENDATIONS FROM THE CASE LAW

The common-interest doctrine allows parties to share otherwise privileged information without waiving the attorney-client privilege. However, as the case law illustrates, the doctrine's applicability depends primarily on the nature of the relationship between the parties at the time the information is shared. For example, the doctrine has been applied in more than one case where a licensee with exclusive rights and a licensor share otherwise-privileged information while jointly developing a patent portfolio. Similarly, the doctrine has been applied when information is exchanged during negotiation of asset-purchase agreements where there is concern about infringing third-party patents. However, sharing information during negotiation of more routine business transactions (such as between a manufacturer and a distributor or between a future licensee and licensor) has been viewed as waiving the privilege. Another important factor is whether at the time the information is shared the parties have in place an agreement that effectively maintains confidentiality and limits the number of individuals having access to the information.

Further, the geographic location of the court deciding whether the common interest doctrine applies can be determinative. For example, given the "more expansive" view enunciated by the District Court for the Northern District of California and the "more restrictive" view expressly adopted by the District Court for the Northern District of Ohio, presumably courts in the Ninth Circuit are more receptive to preserving the attorney-client privilege via the common-interest doctrine than are courts in the Sixth Circuit.

In light of these uncertainties, companies should consider resisting requests from potential business partners for otherwise-privileged information, especially during the arm's-length negotiation phase of a proposed business transaction. As an alternative, companies should offer to provide potential business partners with a list of public documents, such as, for example, third-party patents and published patent applications, which were considered during a freedom-to-operate study, without also sharing privileged legal analyses and conclusions. The potential business partner could then benefit from its own attorney's legal opinion concerning the relevance of the public documents to the proposed business transaction. While many business partners would rather not spend the time or money required to obtain such legal opinions on their own, it should be kept in mind that, if a waiver is found, corporate executives who participated in the information exchange may well be forced to testify concerning the details of the exchange in some future litigation. Thus, any such exchange should occur between the respective outside counsel for the parties as opposed to between executives of the two companies.

In situations where a company's need to conduct business trumps concerns about waiver of the attorney-client privilege when a potential business partner with leverage wants intellectual property assurances but refuses to perform its own due diligence study, the company should consider requiring the potential business partner to sign a common-interest agreement that recognizes the confidential nature of the information and strictly limits access to just a few individuals who agree to destroy or return any shared documents. While perhaps not always sufficient for routine business transactions, having such common-interest arrangements in place at the time the information is shared has been viewed with favor by the courts. As a caveat, however, a company having multiple potential customers who are all seeking assurances, for example, concerning potential infringement of the same third-party patent, may find it difficult to comply with the terms of a common-interest agreement.

In sum, relying on the common-interest doctrine is useful for companies who feel compelled to share otherwise-privileged information with a potential business partner. However, in light of the case law, companies relying on even the most carefully drafted common-interest agreements must accept some uncertainty concerning the risk of waiver.

NOTES & QUESTIONS

Should a corporation's sharing with co-participants in an IPO (such as underwriters) of legal analyses and associated information submitted to counsel be deemed to be a disclosure which forfeits otherwise applicable privilege protections? To what extent do a corporation and its underwriters — who determine the initial price for stock in a new public offering and who in some cases buy all of the newly offered stock from the corporation and resell the stock to investors — have a "common interest" in connection with an IPO? Is this a sufficient common interest in shared legal analyses to avoid a privilege waiver?

CHAPTER 10

DISCLOSURES OF INTELLECTUAL PROPERTY INTERESTS AND RISKS CONCERNING PUBLICLY TRADED COMPANIES

PROBLEM

Digital Ignition is continuing to prepare for its initial public offering (IPO). As discussed in Chapter 9, your law firm is involved in the due diligence review of intellectual property risks associated with Digital Ignition's present and planned activities. You, Sue Kim, are a third year associate working on this project under the direction of partner Todd Alvarez. In discussions with Digital Ignition executives, Alvarez has identified a trademark enforcement issue related to the company's plans for international marketing of its products. The issue appears to entail material risks for the company and will therefore probably need to be described in the company's disclosure document or "prospectus" filed with the federal Securities and Exchange Commission (SEC) and released to the public in connection with Digital Ignition's IPO. Alvarez is asking you for your assistance in developing the language to be included in the portion of the prospectus that will address this risk.

The risk at issue involves planned efforts of Digital Ignition to expand its marketing of consumer-oriented ignition systems in the United States and abroad. One of the company's business strategies is to market its ignition products for consumers under a brand name that consumers already recognize and respect. Accordingly, the company has concluded a licensing agreement with Hollywood Auto Parts, Inc., allowing Digital Ignition to market ignition products in this country and abroad under the "Hollywood Auto" trademark. Hollywood Auto has been a successful retailer of a broad range of consumer-oriented auto products for some years and has a generally favorable reputation for product quality among consumers. Hollywood Auto has used the "Hollywood Auto" trademark extensively both here and abroad, having regularly and systematically registered the mark for some years. The company's marketing efforts and trademark registrations have included the use of the "Hollywood Auto" trademark for various car ignition products.

An early draft of Digital Ignition's prospectus described the company's licensing arrangement with Hollywood Auto and Digital Ignition's plans for expanded marketing under the "Hollywood Auto" trademark as follows:

> Digital Ignition intends to utilize rights to market goods under the "Hollywood Auto" trademark to expand the global market penetration of all of its products, particularly in Latin America. As an established and well respected retailer of automobile products in this country and abroad, Hollywood Auto, Inc., has developed considerable consumer recognition for its brand name and achieved extensive marketing

success. Hollywood Auto's products are well known by consumers in the United States, Latin America, and other parts of the world. Products manufactured by Digital Ignition and sold under the "Hollywood Auto" trademark are expected to be marketed through a wide variety of distributors and retail stores. Digital Ignition believes that consumers' existing positive impressions of Hollywood Auto's products will carry over to Digital Ignition's newly introduced ignition systems for consumers. Digital Ignition's marketing of consumer-oriented ignition systems under the "Hollywood Auto" trademark should be of particular significance in aiding Digital Ignition's ability to target sales by sellers of auto supplies in Latin America, including mass merchandisers, wholesalers, warehouse clubs and online marketers. Overall, the company believes that the marketing of its goods under the "Hollywood Auto" brand name will be an important new source of sales revenues.

Todd Alvarez has asked you to review this language and revise it as necessary. He has raised several concerns about the present prospectus language quoted above and has stated that a revised section on Digital Ignition's plans for marketing under the "Hollywood Auto" trademark will probably need to be drafted. The specific concerns he sees with the present language include the failure to adequately describe business and legal risks associated with:

1) Hollywood Auto's possible failure to properly secure the trademark rights on which Digital Ignition plans to rely;

2) The possibility that Digital Ignition has not concluded agreements with Hollywood Auto that are sufficient to secure rights to market products in the full range of countries, business settings, and product domains where Digital Ignition hopes to market consumer-oriented ignition systems;

3) The scope of product quality requirements and associated policing arrangements that will be part of the trademark licensing relationship between Hollywood Auto and Digital Ignition and that may impose significant obligations and costs on Digital Ignition and reduce its freedom to control the nature and marketing of its products;

4) Grounds for breach of the licensing agreement between the firms and the associated possibility that Hollywood Auto will withdraw the right to use its mark if the terms of the licensing agreement are not met;

5) The possibility that, even if Digital Ignition successfully secures rights to use the "Hollywood Auto" trademark in the countries of interest, the laws of some of these countries or the weak enforcement of trademark rights in these countries may provide such poor protection to Digital Ignition that it may not achieve the exclusive marketing opportunities and related profits it indicates that it expects; and

6) The risk that, even if Digital Ignition successfully secures exclusive rights to the "Hollywood Auto" trademark in a particular jurisdiction, additional business activity limitations under the laws of that jurisdiction — for example, the requirement in some countries that

Digital Ignition or an applicable subsidiary must register and qualify to do business in those countries to sell its products even if Hollywood Auto has previously qualified — may preclude Digital Ignition making effective business use of its licensed trademark rights.

You have been asked to consider whether these and other trademark-related risks associated with Digital Ignition's proposed marketing under the "Hollywood Auto" trademark are adequately described in the prospectus language above. In particular, you should address three matters:

1) Are there any trademark-related risks other than those mentioned above that are raised by Digital Ignition's proposed marketing under the "Hollywood Auto" trademark?

2) Regarding the risks described above and any further ones that you have identified, are there any changes in Digital Ignition's licensing arrangements or proposed marketing practices that would significantly reduce the business risks associated with the company's use of the "Hollywood Auto" trademark and thereby avoid the need for disclosure of some of the material risks presently embodied in the proposed practices?

3) As to any remaining or unavoidable risks, what changes in the portions of Digital Ignition's prospectus quoted above should be made to adequately disclose the material trademark-related risks and heighten the likelihood that the company will be immune from securities fraud claims should Digital Ignition's efforts to market products under the "Hollywood Auto" trademark produce unfavorable corporate results?

FOCUS OF THE CHAPTER

Both at the time of its initial public offering of stock and periodically at later stages of the company's operations, a publicly traded company must file with the federal Securities and Exchange Commission (SEC) various disclosure documents that describe material risks raised by company activities. In general, a material risk is one that entails sufficient financial or operational risk for the company that a reasonable investor might be swayed at least somewhat in his or her opinion of the company by information about the risk and would wish to consider such information in deciding whether to buy or sell the company's stock. The nature of material corporate risks regarding intellectual property interests and related corporate activities was explored in Chapter 3.

Requirements for information disclosure at the point when a company undertakes an IPO are particularly stringent and are described in great detail in federal regulations. The readings in this chapter include the regulatory standards that compel a company conducting an IPO to address intellectual property risks and related business features in the disclosure statement or "prospectus" filed with the SEC upon initiation of the IPO. The readings also include examples of prospectus language reflecting attempts by several high tech companies to provide sufficient details about their intellectual property interests and infringement liability risks to meet the SEC's disclosure requirements.

The initial reading in this chapter describes the function and basic contents of a prospectus filed with the SEC in connection with an IPO. This reading places the prospectus in the context of the preliminaries to an IPO, discussing the objectives that influence the drafting of this type of specialized document, the personnel involved in the drafting process, and the types of business risks that may raise descriptive challenges. The reading focuses on portions of a prospectus that must address intellectual property interests and risks.

The second reading contains excerpts from the SEC's standards governing required disclosures of intellectual property interests and risks in a prospectus. These standards compel a company which is an IPO candidate to disclose major risks associated with its present and projected business activities (such as weaknesses in key intellectual property interests), major contracts (such as licensing agreements allowing the firm to make or sell particular products or to market products under protected trademarks), and material litigation (such as patent infringement litigation involving claims that an important business activity of the company infringes a patent held by another concern).

The third reading includes excerpts from a prospectus filed with the SEC by Santarus, Inc. This company is a specialty pharmaceutical company focused on acquiring, developing, and commercializing proprietary products for the prevention and treatment of gastrointestinal diseases and disorders. Santarus initiated a major drug development and marketing program based on patent licenses obtained from the University of Missouri and in reliance on having the exclusive rights to market its new drugs due to protections afforded to the company by its licensed patents. The company's prospectus describes the fundamental importance of patent rights to this concern's business model, as well as the many risks that might undercut those rights due to the company's own errors, those of its licensor, or factors — such as the discovery of new prior art rendering its licensed patents invalid — which are completely beyond the company's control.

The *Stac* case involves shareholder litigation by investors who claimed that competitive threats known to management were inadequately disclosed in a company's prospectus. The case illustrates how a company's failure to disclose a competitive risk stemming from the weakness of its intellectual property interests can render a prospectus inadequate. The disclosure claimed to be inadequate in this case involved the failure of a company mounting an IPO to disclose that it was aware that a much larger competitor was about to launch a product which would compete directly with the company's primary product and that the company's intellectual property interests might be insufficient to stop these potentially damaging marketing efforts by the competitor.

The *Sherleigh Associates* case deals with a company's failure to balance its positive statements in a prospectus about future foreign business operations with cautionary descriptions of trademark licensing issues that might limit those operations. The analysis in this case illustrates how glowing statements about projected business activities can create incremental liability risks where those statements are not balanced by cautionary warnings about known intellectual property problems that are likely to impede implementation of the anticipated activities.

In re Seachange International, Inc., involves shareholder claims that a company's prospectus overstated the strength of intellectual property protections for a key company product and omitted information held by management indicating that the company was infringing the intellectual property rights of another firm. The shareholders argued that the company implicitly asserted it held proprietary protections for the product when it did not or, if the company was deemed not to have made this sort of affirmative misstatement, its prospectus was nonetheless materially misleading because the company did not disclose information about outstanding patent infringement claims against it that would, if successful, disrupt the company's projected marketing program.

In re Alliance Pharmaceutical, Corp., illustrates some of the especially difficult disclosure problems that can arise in conjunction with the issuance of new stock and the filing of a prospectus in conjunction with the acquisition of one company by another. Shareholders in this case claimed that the acquiring company filed a materially misleading prospectus in that the company (1) failed to disclose known problems in the drug studies regarding one of its key products (thereby inflating the acquiring company's apparent value) and (2) concealed information about an agreement enhancing the marketing abilities of the company being acquired (thereby deflating the acquired company's apparent value). In the latter respect, the shareholders presented a rather unusual argument that disputed disclosures were materially misleading because they were overly negative and pessimistic about projected business activities.

The *Burstein* case involves a prospectus filed in connection with a company's acquisition of a division of a second concern. Shareholders challenged the company's description of the future business prospects of the acquired division and the company's failure to address trade secret problems that were likely to limit those prospects. In particular, the shareholders claimed that the company's rosy projections for the division failed to point out that the company was counting on business practices that would involve misappropriations of trade secrets held by another company and that the division's projected business practices would involve breaches of confidentiality agreements by certain employees hired in connection with the acquisition of the division. The court's analysis of these claims illustrates how positive statements about future business activities may be taken to imply parallel assertions about a company's planned reliance on the use of certain types of intellectual property. These types of implied representations about the importance of intellectual property may, in turn, give rise to related duties on the part of corporate executives to disclose known problems regarding the availability of the intellectual property.

READINGS

A. INTRODUCTION: GOALS AND REQUIRED CONTENTS OF A PROSPECTUS

1. Drafting a Prospectus for a Public Offering

In order to proceed with an initial public offering (IPO) of stock, a description of the company conducting the IPO (the "offeror" or "issuer" of new stock) and the offering transaction must be filed with the federal Securities and Exchange

Commission (SEC). The primary disclosure document is a "prospectus" that is initially reviewed by the SEC for informational sufficiency and then released to the public, at which point it becomes the main vehicle for investors to learn about the offeror and to consider whether to purchase stock in the IPO. In addition to specific information about the nature of the new stock interests the company conducting the IPO will issue, a prospectus must contain a broad range of background information on the financial and business condition of the company. This information must address both the present condition of the firm at the time of its public offering and the major considerations likely to affect the future of the company and its merit as a target of investment.

Drafting a prospectus is a collaborative process involving significant contributions from professionals such as legal counsel and underwriters and from company managers. Professionals ensure that disclosures in a prospectus are framed with the proper scope and form to gain SEC approval and to provide investors with an adequate basis to make investment decisions. Company managers provide much of the raw information about company characteristics and plans that is reshaped to comprise the descriptive contents of the prospectus. Considerable give and take between professionals drafting or reviewing portions of a prospectus and company officials supplying necessary information is typically needed before an adequate document is produced.

a. Goals in Drafting a Prospectus

Overall, a prospectus is both a disclosure and a marketing tool. As noted by one commentator:

> the extensive disclosure requirements in [federal securities laws] are designed to ensure that the issuer prepares and organizes a wide range of historical and prospective information regarding its business and operations. However, . . . the prospectus is also a "marketing tool," usually the issuer's first opportunity to describe and position itself and its business to the broader business and investment community. . . . Moreover, the type and format of disclosure in the IPO prospectus will become the basis for preparing future disclosure documents under [federal securities laws] and the issuer's widely disseminated annual report. Accordingly, it is quite important that the initial analysis of the issuer's strategic advantages at the time of the IPO be broad and thorough, and completed in a fashion which enables the issuer and its counsel to quickly identify areas of possible change during the period beyond the filing and effectiveness of the registration statement.

Alan S. Gutterman, *Strategic Business Planning Analysis and Marketing the High Technology Initial Public Offering Candidate*, 6 SANTA CLARA COMPUTER & HIGH TECH L.J. 197, 208 (1991).

b. Typical Contents of a Prospectus

A typical prospectus will include the following major sections and topics:

1) <u>Basic Offering Information</u> — A prospectus must contain a variety of descriptive information about the company involved and its proposed

offering of new stock to the public. Topics that must be addressed include the company's business and risk factors, the anticipated use of the proceeds of the stock sale, the dilution (that is, percentage decrease) in present stock ownership interests that will result if the sale is completed, the securities to be offered and the rights to be acquired by buyers, the plan for initial sales and distribution of the new stock, information about present securities holders, if any, who will participate in the offering by selling securities, and descriptions of experts and counsel who are aiding in the completion of the offering and the interests of these parties in the offeror.

2) <u>Description of Business, Products, and Legal Proceedings</u> — The prospectus must include a description of the offeror's recent business activities and results in order to provide a "baseline" for later disclosures about developments in the offeror's business. Topics that should be addressed include the offeror's primary products and services, customer base, research and development activities, and competitive environment. The disclosed information should also include a description of key corporate properties that are material to the company's business activities. While this portion of the prospectus may emphasize the "strategic advantages" that distinguish the offeror from its competitors, the analysis of the offeror's business strengths must not be one sided, but must instead also describe the legal or business factors that will constrain the future success of the company.

3) <u>Securities</u> — The prospectus must also address additional information about the characteristics of both the new securities to be offered and the company's existing securities. The description must include information on the market for the common stock of the issuer, as well as the past dividends for that stock and expected future policies regarding dividends.

4) <u>Financial Information</u> — The prospectus must describe a range of basic financial information about the issuer, as well as disclosing any disagreements with the company's accountants regarding the presentation of its accounting information or other matters.

5) <u>Management and Key Security Holders</u> — A prospectus must describe an offeror's directors and officers, the compensation of key executives, securities or other interests in the company held by key executives, and the scope of securities holdings by other parties who own a significant percentage of shares. The company must also disclose significant transactions and relationships between it and other parties who manage or otherwise control the company.

6) <u>Exhibits</u> — The prospectus must also include a summary of the contents of material contracts affecting the company's business or the terms of the offering. These contracts must be included with the prospectus as exhibits unless special "confidential treatment" is requested.

See SEC Rule S-K; Robert G. Heim, GOING PUBLIC IN GOOD TIMES AND BAD 224-25 (2002).

c. Disclosures in Prospectuses Regarding Intellectual Property

Discussions of intellectual property interests and their present or potential impact on the operations of a corporation preparing for an IPO may appear in portions of a prospectus describing the company's business, its assets, significant risks affecting future operations, legal proceedings related to enforcement of intellectual property interests, or material contracts for licensing intellectual property. For companies in which intellectual property is particularly important, such as many high tech concerns, intellectual property interests may be addressed in several of these portions of a prospectus. Discussions of intellectual property in these portions of a prospectus may include the following:

1) Description of the Offeror's Business: Where a company is relying heavily on intellectual property interests in order to secure an exclusive business opportunity for the concern, the description of its business in its prospectus will need to address the nature of its intellectual property interests and their impact on company operations and competitive threats. While intellectual property interests are often legitimate means to protect valuable business opportunities and can properly be identified as such in prospectus disclosures, descriptions of intellectual property protections and their beneficial impact on company operations must be carefully tailored so as to be balanced presentations, not just optimistic descriptions of hoped for results.

2) Profile of the Offeror's Assets: A company that has developed a new technology or business method will often count intellectual property interests protecting the new technology or business method among the company's most important assets. In many instances, the future attractiveness of the company as a potential target for takeover and buyout will depend on whether such an acquisition will include the transfer of valuable intellectual property rights. Furthermore, in the absence of such a buyout, the company's enforceable intellectual property rights may provide the means for the company to reserve certain business opportunities to itself. To the extent that a company expects to rely on intellectual property interests in these ways, these interests will generally be material assets of the company that should be addressed in the corresponding portions of the company's prospectus.

3) Risks Associated with the Offeror's Operations: Intellectual property interests may raise two types of risks in connection with an offeror's business activities: risks associated with the unexpected unenforceability or limited commercial impact of the company's own intellectual property interests and further risks that the company's present or projected activities infringe intellectual property interests of others. Particularly where a company has relied on the exclusivity of certain manufacturing or marketing opportunities as protected by intellectual property rights, the unenforceability of those rights after significant resources have been committed to pursuing related business opportunities may be very harmful to the company. Similarly, even if intellectual property rights remain enforceable, but competitors adopt means

to supply consumers with products or services without infringing the relevant intellectual property rights, the commercial impact of those rights may be drastically reduced leading to associated corporate losses. Finally, if the intellectual property rights of others are enforced against the company, particularly after the company has already devoted assets to activities that infringe the other party's rights, the company may be forced to pay significant damages for past infringement and to cease the affected operations or to obtain a license to use the related intellectual property at highly unfavorable royalty rates. These types of risks arising out of the company's ownership or use of intellectual property must be properly addressed in the discussions of business operation risks in the company's prospectus.

4) Legal Proceedings Affecting the Offeror: Where a company has already been subjected to or meaningfully threatened with legal proceedings which, if successful, will materially affect the ways that the company uses intellectual property and achieves value and profits from such property, the existence and status of these proceedings must be disclosed in the company's prospectus. For example, where a key patent that the company is relying on to establish a future business opportunity is slated by the United States Patent and Trademark Office for reexamination — meaning that the patent may be rendered invalid or diminished in scope — the existence of this pending proceeding must be disclosed. Similarly, where the company has been threatened with or subjected to infringement litigation under the patents of another party and the litigation will have a material impact on the company's business activities if successful, this type of litigation, its merit, and its potential impact on company operations should be disclosed.

5) Material Contracts: A company's material contracts may include at least two types of intellectual property licensing agreements. First, where the company is relying on using the intellectual property of another party in significant corporate activities, the key terms of the licensing agreement whereby the company has obtained the rights to use the specified intellectual property will probably be material and should be disclosed as part of the company's prospectus. The contracts under which intellectual property rights are licensed will be particularly important if a company is an exclusive licensee and is relying on this status to carve out corresponding business domains in which it will be the sole party able to offer a particular product feature or process. The absence of an enforceable licensing contract — or the company's failure to comply with the terms of that contract and loss of rights to use the corresponding intellectual property — may cause severe disruptions in company operations. Second, to the extent that the company plans to license its own intellectual property to others and to generate significant licensing revenues, the existence of the corresponding licensing agreements or means for forming these agreements, as well as the methods that the company plans to use to monitor licensees' actions required under the agreements and to bring enforcement actions against licensees who do not comply

with licensing terms, should be part of the company's discussions of material contracts in its prospectus.

These types of discussions of intellectual property interests in prospectuses will be subject to the overarching impact of the "bespeaks caution" doctrine. This doctrine places limits on the personal liability of persons making or verifying misleading statements in prospectuses and other public disclosures where the statements at issue are surrounded by qualifying or cautionary language that would indicate to the reasonable investor that the accuracy and implications of the statements should be taken with caution. In general,

> [t]he bespeaks caution doctrine provides a mechanism by which a court can rule as a matter of law (typically in a motion to dismiss for failure to state a cause of action or a motion for summary judgment) that defendants' forward-looking representations contained enough cautionary language or risk disclosure to protect the defendant against claims of securities fraud.

Donald C. Langevoort, *Disclosures that "Bespeak Caution"*, 49 BUS.LAW. 481, 482-83 (1994). The doctrine reflects a pragmatic interpretation of two of the requirements for liability under federal securities laws governing public disclosures of information about companies: the materiality of information that is misstated or incompletely disclosed and the need for some form of reliance of an investor on a misstatement or omission before a civil claim will lie. As noted by one court:

> The "bespeaks caution" doctrine . . . reflects a relatively recent, ongoing, and somewhat uncertain evolution in securities law, an evolution driven by the increase in and the unique nature of fraud actions based on predictive statements. In essence, predictive statements are just what the name implies: predictions. As such, any optimistic projections contained in such statements are necessarily contingent. Thus, the "bespeaks caution" doctrine has developed to address situations in which optimistic projections are coupled with cautionary language — in particular, relevant specific facts or assumptions — affecting the reasonableness of reliance on and the materiality of those projections. To put it another way, the "bespeaks caution" doctrine reflects the unremarkable proposition that statements must be analyzed in context.

Rubinstein v. Collins, 20 F.3d 160, 167 (5th Cir. 1994).

Courts are careful not to apply the bespeaks caution doctrine too broadly as this would undercut the deterrents created by federal securities laws regarding misleading statements. This would be the case because;

> an overbroad application of the doctrine would encourage management to conceal deliberate misrepresentations beneath the mantle of broad cautionary language. To prevent this from occurring, the bespeaks caution doctrine applies only to precise cautionary language which directly addresses itself to future projections, estimates or forecasts in a prospectus. By contrast, blanket warnings that securities involve a high degree of risk [are] insufficient to ward against a federal securities fraud claim.

In re Worlds of Wonder Securities Litigation, 35 F.3d 1407, 1414 (9th Cir. 1994) (quoting with approval *In re Worlds of Wonder Securities Litigation*, 814 F.Supp. 850, 858 (N.D.Cal. 1993)).

2. Regulatory Standards

SEC STANDARDS FOR PROSPECTUS CONTENTS REGULATION S-K (EXCERPTS)
United States Securities and Exchange Commission
17 C.F.R PART 229

[The following are selected portions of the SEC's standards governing the types of disclosures that a company must make in a prospectus in order to register newly issued securities and engage in a public offering of those securities. The company making the disclosures is referred to here as the "registrant." The portions of the standards presented here are those most likely to require disclosures about intellectual property interests and related business risks.]

§ 229.101 (Item 101) Description of business.

(a) General development of business. Describe the general development of the business of the registrant, its subsidiaries and any predecessor(s) during the past five years, or such shorter period as the registrant may have been engaged in business. Information shall be disclosed for earlier periods if material to an understanding of the general development of the business.

. . .

(c) Narrative description of business.

(1) Describe the business done and intended to be done by the registrant and its subsidiaries, focusing upon the registrant's dominant segment or each reportable segment about which financial information is presented in the financial statements. To the extent material to an understanding of the registrant's business taken as a whole, the description of each such segment shall include the information specified in paragraphs (c)(1)(i) through (x) of this section. The matters specified in paragraphs (c)(1)(xi) through (xiii) of this section shall be discussed with respect to the registrant's business in general; where material, the segments to which these matters are significant shall be identified.

(i) The principal products produced and services rendered by the registrant in the segment and the principal markets for, and methods of distribution of, the segment's principal products and services. In addition, state for each of the last three fiscal years the amount or percentage of total revenue contributed by any class of similar products or services which accounted for 10 percent or more of consolidated revenue in any of the last three fiscal years or 15 percent or more of consolidated revenue, if total revenue did not exceed $50,000,000 during any of such fiscal years.

(ii) A description of the status of a product or segment (e.g. whether in the planning stage, whether prototypes exist, the degree to which product design has progressed or whether further engineering is necessary), if there has been a public announcement of, or if the registrant otherwise has made public information about, a new product or segment that would require the investment of a material amount of the assets of the registrant or that otherwise is material. This paragraph is not intended to require disclosure of otherwise nonpublic corporate information the disclosure of which would affect adversely the registrant's competitive position.

. . .

(iv) The importance to the segment and the duration and effect of all patents, trademarks, licenses, franchises and concessions held.

. . .

(x) Competitive conditions in the business involved including, where material, the identity of the particular markets in which the registrant competes, an estimate of the number of competitors and the registrant's competitive position, if known or reasonably available to the registrant. Separate consideration shall be given to the principal products or services or classes of products or services of the segment, if any. Generally, the names of competitors need not be disclosed. . . . The principal methods of competition (e.g., price, service, warranty or product performance) shall be identified, and positive and negative factors pertaining to the competitive position of the registrant, to the extent that they exist, shall be explained if known or reasonably available to the registrant.

. . .

Instructions to Item 101:

1. In determining what information about the segments is material to an understanding of the registrant's business taken as a whole and therefore required to be disclosed, pursuant to paragraph (c) of this Item, the registrant should take into account both quantitative and qualitative factors such as the significance of the matter to the registrant (e.g., whether a matter with a relatively minor impact on the registrant's business is represented by management to be important to its future profitability), the pervasiveness of the matter (e.g., whether it affects or may affect numerous items in the segment information), and the impact of the matter (e.g., whether it distorts the trends reflected in the segment information). Situations may arise when information should be disclosed about a segment, although the information in quantitative terms may not appear significant to the registrant's business taken as a whole.

. . .

§ 229.103 (Item 103) Legal proceedings.

Describe briefly any material pending legal proceedings, other than ordinary routine litigation incidental to the business, to which the registrant or any of its subsidiaries is a party or of which any of their property is the subject. Include the name of the court or agency in which the proceedings are pending, the date instituted, the principal parties thereto, a description of the factual basis alleged to underlie the proceeding and the relief sought. Include similar information as to any such proceedings known to be contemplated by governmental authorities.

Instructions to Item 103:

. . .

  2. No information need be given with respect to any proceeding that involves primarily a claim for damages if the amount involved, exclusive of interest and costs, does not exceed 10 percent of the current assets of the registrant and its subsidiaries on a consolidated basis. However, if any proceeding presents in large degree the same legal and factual issues as other proceedings pending or known to be contemplated, the amount involved in such other proceedings shall be included in computing such percentage.

. . .

§ 229.503 (Item 503) Prospectus Summary, Risk Factors, and Ratio of Earnings to Fixed Charges.

The registrant must furnish this information in plain English.

. . .

  (c) Risk factors. Where appropriate, provide under the caption "Risk Factors" a discussion of the most significant factors that make the offering speculative or risky. This discussion must be concise and organized logically. Do not present risks that could apply to any issuer or any offering. Explain how the risk affects the issuer or the securities being offered. Set forth each risk factor under a subcaption that adequately describes the risk.

. . .

§ 229.601 (Item 601) Exhibits.

. . .

  (b) Description of exhibits. Set forth below is a description of each document listed in the exhibit tables.

   . . .

   (10) Material contracts—

    (i) Every contract not made in the ordinary course of business which is material to the registrant and is to be performed in whole or in part at or after the filing of the registration statement or report or was entered into not more than two years before such filing.

. . .

(ii) If the contract is such as ordinarily accompanies the kind of business conducted by the registrant and its subsidiaries, it will be deemed to have been made in the ordinary course of business and need not be filed unless it falls within one or more of the following categories, in which case it shall be filed except where immaterial in amount or significance:

. . .

(B) Any contract upon which the registrant's business is substantially dependent, as in the case of continuing contracts to sell the major part of registrant's products or services or to purchase the major part of registrant's requirements of goods, services or raw materials or any franchise or license or other agreement to use a patent, formula, trade secret, process or trade name upon which registrant's business depends to a material extent;

3. Examples of Intellectual Property Disclosures

S.E.C. FORM S-1
SANTARUS, INC (EXCERPTS)
Filed: March 31, 2004

<u>PROSPECTUS SUMMARY</u>

The following summary is qualified in its entirety by, and should be read together with, the more detailed information and financial statements and related notes appearing elsewhere in this prospectus. Before you decide to invest in our common stock, you should read the entire prospectus carefully, including the risk factors and the financial statements and related notes included in this prospectus.

<u>Santarus, Inc.</u>

We are a specialty pharmaceutical company focused on acquiring, developing and commercializing proprietary products for the prevention and treatment of gastrointestinal diseases and disorders. The primary focus of our current efforts is the development and commercialization of next generation proton pump inhibitor, or PPI, products — the most frequently prescribed drugs for the treatment of many upper gastrointestinal, or GI, diseases and disorders. The PPI market, including five delayed-release PPI brands, had U.S. sales of $12.9 billion in 2003, according to IMS Health, an independent pharmaceutical market research firm. Also, according to IMS Health, total

U.S. prescriptions for PPIs grew from 86.3 million in 2002 to 95.2 million in 2003 — a 10% increase.

We submitted our first new drug application, or NDA, in August 2003 for RapinexTM powder-for-suspension 20mg and our second NDA in February 2004 for Rapinex powder-for-suspension 40mg, which are immediate-release formulations of omeprazole, a widely prescribed PPI currently available for oral use only in delayed-release formulations.

. . .

RISK FACTORS

. . .

All of our product development and clinical research activities are currently dedicated to developing our Rapinex product candidates. Because each of the three Rapinex product candidates [Rapinex powder-for-suspension, Rapinex capsule and Rapinex chewable tablet], is derived from the same intellectual property rights licensed from the University of Missouri, each product candidate is vulnerable to substantially the same risks stemming from potential patent invalidity, misappropriation of intellectual property by third parties, reliance upon a third party for patent prosecution and maintenance and unexpected early termination of our license agreement.

. . .

The pharmaceutical industry is intensely competitive, particularly in the GI field, where currently marketed products are well-established and successful. Competition in our industry occurs on a variety of fronts, including developing and bringing new products to market before others, developing new technologies to improve existing products, developing new products to provide the same benefits as existing products at lower cost and developing new products to provide benefits superior to those of existing products. In addition, our ability and that of our competitors to compete in our industry will depend upon our and their relative abilities to obtain and maintain intellectual property protection for products and product candidates.

. . .

Risks Related to Our Intellectual Property and Potential Litigation

The protection of our intellectual property rights is critical to our success and any failure on our part to adequately secure such rights would materially affect our business.

Patents. Our commercial success will depend in part on the patent rights we have licensed or will license and on patent protection for our own inventions related to the product candidates that we intend to market. Our success also depends on maintaining these patent rights against third-party challenges to their validity, scope or enforceability. Our patent position is subject to the same uncertainty as other biotechnology and pharmaceutical companies. For example, the U.S. Patent and Trademark Office, or

PTO, or the courts may deny, narrow or invalidate patent claims, particularly those that concern biotechnology and pharmaceutical inventions.

We may not be successful in securing or maintaining proprietary or patent protection for our product candidates, and protection that we do secure may be challenged and possibly lost. Our competitors may develop products similar to ours using methods and technologies that are beyond the scope of our intellectual property rights. Other drug companies may be able to develop generic versions of our products if we are unable to maintain our proprietary rights. For example, although we believe that we have valid patent protection in the U.S. for our product candidates until at least 2016, it is possible that generic drug makers will attempt to introduce generic immediate-release omeprazole products similar to ours prior to the expiration of our patents. Any patents related to our Rapinex product candidates will be method and/or formulation patents and will not protect the use of the active pharmaceutical ingredient outside of the formulations described in the patents and patent applications licensed to us. In addition, our competitors or other third parties, including generic drug companies, may challenge the scope, validity or enforceability of our patent claims. As a result, these patents may be narrowed in scope or invalidated and may fail to provide us with any market exclusivity or competitive advantage even after our investment of significant amounts of money. We also may not be able to protect our intellectual property rights against third-party infringement, which may be difficult to detect. If we become involved in any dispute regarding our intellectual property rights, regardless of whether we prevail, we could be required to engage in costly, distracting and time-consuming litigation that could harm our business.

To date, four U.S. patents have been issued relating to technology we license from the University of Missouri and several U.S. and international or foreign counterpart patent applications are pending. The initial U.S. patent from the University of Missouri does not have corresponding international or foreign counterpart applications and there can be no assurance that we will be able to obtain foreign patent rights to protect our products. We consult with the University of Missouri in its pursuit of the patent applications that we have licensed, but the University of Missouri remains primarily responsible for prosecution of the applications. We cannot control the amount or timing of resources that the University of Missouri devotes on our behalf. It may not assign as great a priority to prosecution of patent applications relating to technology we license as we would if we were undertaking such prosecution ourselves. As a result of this lack of control and general uncertainties in the patent prosecution process, we cannot be sure that any additional patents will ever be issued.

Trade Secrets and Proprietary Know-how. We also rely upon unpatented proprietary know-how and continuing technological innovation in developing our product candidates. Although we require our employees, consultants, advisors and current and prospective business partners to enter into confidentiality agreements prohibiting them from disclosing or taking our proprietary information and technology, these agreements may not provide meaningful protection for our trade secrets and proprietary know-how. Further, people who are not parties to confidentiality agreements may obtain access to our trade secrets or know-how. Others may independently develop similar or equivalent trade secrets or know-how. If our confidential, proprietary information is divulged to third parties, including our competitors, our competitive position in the marketplace will be harmed and our ability to successfully penetrate our target markets could be severely compromised.

Trademarks. Our trademarks will be important to our success and competitive position. We have received U.S. and EU trademark registration for our corporate name, Santarus®, and we have applied for U.S. and EU trademark registration for Rapinex, and for various other names. However, there is no guarantee we will be able to secure any of our trademark registrations with the PTO or comparable foreign authorities. For example, our application for the trademark Rapinex has been opposed in the EU, and we have opposed a biotechnology company's applications for the marks 'Santaris' and 'Santaris Pharma' in the EU.

If we do not adequately protect our rights in our various trademarks from infringement, any goodwill that has been developed in those marks would be lost or impaired. We could also be forced to cease using any of our trademarks that are found to infringe upon the trademark or service mark of another company, and, as a result, we could lose all the goodwill which has been developed in those marks and could be liable for damages caused by any such infringement.

Our Rapinex product candidates depend on technology licensed from the University of Missouri and any loss of our license rights would harm our business and seriously affect our ability to market our products.

Each of our Rapinex product candidates is based on patented technology and technology for which patent applications are pending that we have exclusively licensed from the University of Missouri. A loss or adverse modification of our technology license from the University of Missouri would materially harm our ability to develop and commercialize our current product candidates, Rapinex powder-for-suspension, Rapinex capsule and Rapinex chewable tablet, and other product candidates based on that licensed technology that we may attempt to develop or commercialize in the future.

The licenses from the University of Missouri expire in each country when the last patent for licensed technology expires in that country and the last patent application for licensed technology in that country is abandoned. In addition, our rights under the University of Missouri license are subject to early termination under specified circumstances, including our material and uncured breach of the license agreement or our bankruptcy or insolvency.

Further, we are required to use commercially reasonable efforts to develop and sell products based on the technology we licensed from the University of Missouri to meet market demand. If we fail to meet these obligations in specified countries, after giving us an opportunity to cure the failure, the University of Missouri can terminate our license or render it nonexclusive with respect to those countries. To date, we believe we have met all of our obligations under the University of Missouri agreement. However, in the event that the University of Missouri is able to terminate the license agreement for one of the reasons specified in the license agreement, we would lose our rights to develop, market and sell our current Rapinex product candidates and we would not be able to develop, market and sell future product candidates based on those licensed technologies. We would also lose the right to receive potential milestone and royalty payments from [TAP Pharmaceutical Products Inc. (TAP)] based on its development of products under our sublicense to TAP of the University of Missouri technology. Our ability to market our products is subject to the intellectual property rights of third parties.

The product candidates we currently intend to market, and those we may market in the future, may infringe patent and other rights of third parties. In addition, our competitors, many of which have substantially greater resources than us and have made significant investments in competing technologies or products, may seek to apply for and obtain patents that will prevent, limit or interfere with our ability to make, use and sell products either in the U.S. or international markets. Intellectual property litigation in the pharmaceutical industry is common, and we expect this to continue. In particular, intellectual property litigation among companies targeting the treatment of upper GI diseases and disorders is particularly common and may increase due to the large market for these products.

. . .

If we or our third-party manufacturers are unsuccessful in any challenge to our rights to market and sell our products, we may be required to license the disputed rights, if the holder of those rights is willing, or to cease marketing the challenged products, or, if possible, to modify our products to avoid infringing upon those rights. If we or our third-party manufacturers are unsuccessful in defending our rights, we could be liable for royalties on past sales or more significant damages, and we could be required to obtain and pay for licenses if we are to continue to manufacture and sell our products. These licenses may not be available and, if available, could require us to pay substantial upfront fees and future royalty payments. Any patent owner may seek preliminary injunctive relief in connection with an infringement claim, as well as a permanent injunction, and, if successful in the claim, may be entitled to lost profits from infringing sales, attorneys' fees and interest and other amounts. Any damages could be increased if there is a finding of willful infringement.

Even if we and our third-party manufacturers are successful in defending an infringement claim, the expense, time delay and burden on management of litigation could have a material adverse effect on our business. We may be subject to damages resulting from claims that we or our employees have wrongfully used or disclosed alleged trade secrets of their former employers.

Many of our employees were previously employed at universities or other biotechnology or pharmaceutical companies, including our competitors or potential competitors. In addition, certain of our employees are parties to non-compete and non-disclosure agreements with their prior employers. Although no claims against us are currently pending, we may be subject to claims that these employees or we have inadvertently or otherwise breached these non-compete agreements or used or disclosed trade secrets or other proprietary information of their former employers. Litigation may be necessary to defend against these claims. Even if we are successful in defending against these claims, litigation could result in substantial costs and be a distraction to management. If we fail in defending such claims, in addition to paying money claims, we may lose valuable intellectual property rights or personnel. A loss of key research personnel or their work product could hamper or prevent our ability to commercialize product candidates, which could severely harm our business.

. . .

BUSINESS

. . .

Intellectual Property

Our goal is to obtain, maintain and enforce patent protection for our products and product candidates, compounds, formulations, processes, methods and other proprietary technologies invented, developed, licensed or acquired by us, preserve our trade secrets, and operate without infringing on the proprietary rights of other parties, both in the U.S. and in other countries. Our policy is to actively seek to obtain, where appropriate, intellectual property protection for our product candidates, proprietary information and proprietary technology through a combination of contractual arrangements and laws, including patents, both in the U.S. and elsewhere in the world. We regard the protection of patents, trademarks and other proprietary rights that we own or license as critical to our success and competitive position. Laws and contractual restrictions, however, may not be sufficient to prevent unauthorized use or misappropriation of our technology or deter others from independently developing products that are substantially equivalent or superior to our products.

Due to the length of time and expense associated with bringing new pharmaceutical products to market, we recognize that there are considerable benefits associated with developing, licensing or acquiring products that are protected by existing patents or for which patent protection can be obtained. Although we do not currently own any issued patents, all of the product candidates we currently intend to market will incorporate patented technology owned by others that we have licensed. In addition, we have applied and intend to continue to apply for patent protection for new technology we develop whenever we determine that the benefit of patent protection outweighs the cost of obtaining patent protection.

Our ability to assert our patents against a potential infringer depends on our ability to detect the infringement in the first instance. Many countries, including certain European countries, have compulsory licensing laws under which a patent owner may be compelled to grant licenses to third parties in some circumstances (for example, the patent owner has failed to 'work' the invention in that country, or the third party has patented improvements). In addition, most countries limit the enforceability of patents against government agencies or government contractors. In these countries, the patent owner may be limited to monetary relief and may be unable to enjoin infringement, which could materially diminish the value of the patent. Compulsory licensing of life saving drugs is also becoming increasingly popular in developing countries either through direct legislation or international initiatives. Such compulsory licenses could be extended to include some of our product candidates, which could limit our potential revenue opportunities. Moreover, the legal systems of certain countries, particularly certain developing countries, do not favor the aggressive enforcement of patents and other intellectual property protections, which makes it difficult to stop infringement.

Our success will also depend in part on our not infringing patents issued to others, including our competitors and potential competitors. If our product candidates are found to infringe the patents of others, our development, manufacture and sale of such potential products could be severely restricted or prohibited. For example, AstraZeneca may sue us for patent infringement in connection with the commercialization of our Rapinex product candidates. . . . Although we believe that we have meritorious defenses to any claims related to AstraZeneca's patents, AstraZeneca may nevertheless pursue litigation against us. The outcome of any such litigation is uncertain and defending such litigation would be expensive, time-consuming and distracting to management. It is likely that in the future we will encounter other similar situations which will require us to determine whether we need to license a technology or face the risk of defending an infringement claim.

Patent litigation can involve complex factual and legal questions and its outcome is uncertain. Any claim relating to infringement of patents that is successfully asserted against us may require us to pay substantial damages. Even if we were to prevail, any litigation could be costly and time-consuming and would divert the attention of our management and key personnel from our business operations. Furthermore, a patent infringement suit brought against us or any strategic partners or licensees may force us or any strategic partners or licensees to stop or delay developing, manufacturing or selling potential products that are claimed to infringe a third party's intellectual property, unless that party grants us or any strategic partners or licensees rights to use its intellectual property. In such cases, we may be required to obtain licenses to patents or proprietary rights of others in order to continue to commercialize our products. However, we may not be able to obtain any licenses required under any patents or proprietary rights of third parties on acceptable terms, or at all. Even if any strategic partners, licensees or we were able to obtain rights to the third party's intellectual property, these rights may be non-exclusive, thereby giving our competitors access to the same intellectual property. Ultimately, we may be unable to commercialize some of our potential products or may have to cease some of our business operations as a result of patent infringement claims, which could severely harm our business.

We also depend upon the skills, knowledge and experience of our scientific and technical personnel, as well as that of our advisors, consultants and other contractors. To help protect our proprietary know-how that is not patentable, and for inventions for which patents may be difficult to enforce, we rely on trade secret protection and confidentiality agreements to protect our interests. To this end, we require our employees, consultants, advisors and certain other contractors to enter into confidentiality agreements which prohibit the disclosure of confidential information and, where applicable, require disclosure and assignment to us of the ideas, developments, discoveries and inventions important to our business. Additionally, these confidentiality agreements require that our employees, consultants and advisors do not bring to us, or use without proper authorization, any third party's proprietary technology.

While we intend to take the actions that we believe are necessary to protect our proprietary rights, we may not always be successful in doing so. We may be dependent on the owners of the proprietary rights we license to protect those rights. Our current licensor remains, and any future licensors may remain, responsible for the prosecution of patent applications relating to the technology licensed from them. These licensors are not our employees and we cannot control the amount or timing of resources they devote on our behalf or the priority they place on prosecuting these patent applications. In addition, we and our licensors may face challenges to the validity and enforceability of proprietary rights and may not prevail in any litigation regarding those rights. As a result, these patents may be narrowed in scope, deemed unenforceable or invalidated and may fail to provide us with any market exclusivity or competitive advantage even after our investment of significant amounts of money.

We have received U.S. and EU trademark registration for our corporate name, Santarus, and have opposed a third-party biotechnology company's applications for the marks 'Santaris' and 'Santaris Pharma' in the EU. We have applied for U.S. and EU trademark registration for the name Rapinex and for various other names. Our application for the trademark Rapinex has been opposed in the EU. In addition, in connection with our initial NDA submission for Rapinex powder-for-suspension 20mg, the FDA indicated to us that it objects to our use of the Rapinex name for our product candidates. The FDA may object to a product name if it believes there is potential for confusion with other product names or if it believes the name implies medical claims. We have responded to the objection in an effort to preserve the name and the resources we have already devoted to the Rapinex trademark registration. However, we may not prevail or we may determine to adopt an alternative name for our initial product candidates in the interest of time or for other reasons. If we adopt an alternative name, we would lose the benefit of our existing trademark applications for Rapinex and may be required to expend significant additional resources in an effort to identify a suitable product name that would qualify under applicable U.S. and EU trademark laws, not infringe the existing rights of third parties and be acceptable to the FDA. Over time, we intend to introduce new trademarks, service marks and brand names and maintain registrations on trademarks that remain valuable to our business.

License Rights from the University of Missouri

In January 2001, we entered into an exclusive, worldwide license agreement with the University of Missouri for all of its patents and pending patent applications relating to specific formulations of PPIs with antacids and other buffering agents. Currently, four U.S. patents have been issued and several U.S. patent applications and international or foreign counterpart applications are pending and are subject to this license. The four issued patents, U.S. Patent Nos. 5,840,737, 6,489,346, 6,645,988 and 6,699,885, together generally cover pharmaceutical compositions combining PPIs with buffering agents, such as antacids, and methods of treating GI disorders by administering solid or liquid forms of such compositions. U.S. Patent Nos. 5,840,737, 6,489,346 and 6,645,988 expire in July 2016. We expect that U.S. Patent No. 6,699,885 and any patents that may be issued on pending patent applications will expire no earlier than July 2016.

Pursuant to the terms of the license agreement, we paid the University of Missouri a one-time licensing fee of $1.0 million in 2001 and a one-time $1.0 million milestone payment upon the filing of our first NDA in 2003. We are required to make additional milestone payments to the University of Missouri upon the achievement of certain regulatory events, and we are required to bear the costs of prosecuting and maintaining the licensed patents but our licensor remains responsible for prosecution of any applications. These future success-based development milestone payments may total up to $8.5 million in the aggregate, including $5.0 million upon approval in the U.S. of our first product based on the licensed technology. We are also required to make milestone payments based on first-time achievement of significant sales thresholds, up to a maximum of $86.3 million, and to pay royalties on net sales of our products. In addition, we issued to the University of Missouri 164,284 shares of our common stock in connection with the license agreement. Under the license agreement, we are permitted to sublicense our rights to third parties. We are obligated to pay to the University of Missouri a portion of any sublicense fees, milestone payments or royalties that we receive from any sublicense, including our sublicense to TAP. Under the license agreement, we are required to carry occurrence-based liability insurance with policy limits of at least $5.0 million per occurrence and a $10.0 million annual aggregate.

The license from the University of Missouri expires in each country when the last patent for licensed technology expires in that country and the last patent application for licensed technology in that country is abandoned, provided that our obligation to pay certain minimum royalties in countries in which there are no pending patent applications or existing patents terminates on a country-by-country basis on the 15th anniversary of our first commercial sale in such country. If we fail to meet diligence obligations in specified countries, the University of Missouri can terminate our license or render it non-exclusive with respect to those countries. Our rights under this license are also generally subject to early termination under specified circumstances, including our material and uncured breach or our bankruptcy or insolvency. We can terminate this agreement at any time, in whole or in part, with 60 days written notice.

B. MISSTATEMENTS IN PROSPECTUSES REGARDING INTELLECTUAL PROPERTY INTERESTS OR THEIR BUSINESS IMPLICATIONS

IN RE STAC ELECTRONICS SECURITIES LITIGATION
United States Court of Appeals for the Ninth Circuit.
89 F.3d 1399 (1996)

T.G. NELSON, Circuit Judge.

OVERVIEW

Timothy J. Anderson and other class representatives (collectively "Anderson") who purchased stock in Stac Electronics ("Stac") between May 7 and July 20, 1992, appeal the district court's dismissal of their class action under Sections 11 and 15 of the Securities Act of 1933, 15 U.S.C. §§ 77k, 77o, and Sections 10(b) and 20 of the Securities Exchange Act of 1934, 15 U.S.C. §§ 78j(b) and 78t. Anderson alleges that Stac, certain of its officers and directors, and its lead underwriters, Alex. Brown & Sons, Inc., and Montgomery Securities ("Alex. Brown" and "Montgomery," respectively; collectively, "Underwriters"), made material misrepresentations or omissions regarding Stac's initial public offering ("IPO") of May 7, 1992. We have jurisdiction under 28 U.S.C. § 1291, and we affirm.

FACTS AND PROCEDURAL HISTORY

This case arises from Stac's May 7, 1992, IPO of stock in its computer products company. Stac's most prominent product was the "Stacker," a data-compressing device which doubles storage capacity of disk drives in computers using Microsoft's MS-DOS and compatible systems.

> The district court related the following facts, which are not disputed by the parties:

> Before it went public, Stac's performance was mixed: it reported net losses per share in 1988, 1989, and 1990, and a net income per share of $.01 in 1991. It also reported revenues hovering around three quarters of a million dollars for 1988 and 1989, with increased revenues in 1990 (to $1.7 million) and 1991 (to $8.3 million).

> There was a pronounced move upward-in both revenues and earnings per share-immediately prior to the initial public offering of Stac stock. While Stac reported revenues of $2.3 million and a loss of $.04 per share in the six months prior to March 31, 1991, it reported revenues of $17 million and earnings of $.21 per share in the six months prior to March 31, 1992. The increased revenues and earnings for the 1992 six month period derived from sales of Stacker.

> On May 7, 1992, Stac went public, with an initial offering of 3,000,000 shares of common stock. The stock was sold to the public at $12.00 a share, with the individual named Defendants — except for Hoff, Finch and Robelen — selling some 508,000 shares. Neither Hoff, Finch, Robelen nor any of the venture capital Defendants is alleged to have sold any Stac stock during the class period [May 7 to July 20, 1992]. Defendants Alex. Brown & Sons, Inc. and Montgomery Securities acted as co-lead underwriters for the offering; they received substantial fees — some $2.5 million-for their services.

In connection with the IPO, Stac issued a Registration Statement and Prospectus ("Prospectus"), dated May 7, 1992, which included a four-page section on risk factors warning investors, inter alia, of Stac's competition, its dependence on Stacker, its reliance on distributors, its limited source of supply, and the potential volatility of its stock price. The Prospectus specifically discussed Microsoft's competitive threat, Stac's return policy and return allowances, and the possible effects on revenues of "channel fill," or heavy purchasing by distributors immediately following the introduction of a new product.

Apart from the Prospectus, information about Stac was disseminated to the public through "roadshow" presentations preceding the IPO and through analysts' reports and press statements by Stac officers and Underwriters following the IPO. All of these portrayed Stac as a good investment.

While these portrayals at first seemed accurate — Stac rose to $15 after the IPO — success was short-lived. Stac's stock price fell on July 2, 1992, on the heels of another computer software company's announcement of poor third quarter results.

Stac Director Gary Clow ("Clow") and both Underwriters made statements to Dow Jones News Wire distinguishing Stac from the faltering software company. While Alex. Brown continued to rate Stac highly, Montgomery reduced its rating and earnings estimate for Stac on July 6, 1992. On July 20, 1992, Stac disclosed a disappointing third quarter performance, and on July 21, 1992, Stac stock declined to $5.50 per share. Within two days, plaintiffs filed suit. This initial suit was consolidated in the First Amended Class Action Complaint ("the FAC"), filed December 4, 1992.

. . .

The complaint basically alleged that Stac went public knowing, but without disclosing, that Microsoft was about to come out with a competitive product (a new version of DOS incorporating Stacker-like data compression capabilities) that would take away Stac's market; that Stac engaged in sham licensing negotiations with Microsoft in order to stall introduction of its new product until Stac could make an IPO and unload stock; and that Stac insiders artificially inflated Stac's stock price prior to the IPO through channel "stuffing" and other fraudulent practices.

The district court dismissed the FAC with leave to amend in a detailed order dated September 17, 1993. *Anderson v. Clow*, Fed. Sec. L. Rep. (CCH) ¶ 97,807 at 97,994-95 (S.D.Cal. 1993). The district court held that plaintiffs had failed to state a claim against Stac, the Underwriters, or any other named defendant, primarily on the basis of its finding that, to the extent it was required to do so, Stac had adequately disclosed all purported omissions in its Prospectus in a way that rendered the Prospectus not misleading. The order also stayed discovery.

On November 18, 1993, the plaintiffs filed a Second Amended Complaint ("the SAC"), asserting the same claims as the FAC and adding nine new individual defendants. The district court dismissed the SAC with prejudice for failure to state a claim under Fed.R.Civ.P. 12(b)(6) and for failure to meet the particularity requirements of Fed.R.Civ.P. 9(b). Like the first order, the order appealed from is extremely thorough. Anderson's appeal was timely.

DISCUSSION

. . .

I

Primary Liability.

Anderson argues that by "falsifying" its financial statements and failing to disclose pertinent information in its possession regarding Microsoft's plans to include data compression in its newest version of DOS, Stac misled investors and violated Section 11 of the Securities Act of 1933, 15 U.S.C. § 77k(a), Section 10(b) of the Exchange Act of 1934, 15 U.S.C. § 78j(b), and Rule 10b-5 of the Securities and Exchange Commission ("SEC"), 17 C.F.R. § 240.10b-5. The district court held that the SAC failed to state a claim under Section 11, Section 10(b), or Rule 10b-5. It further held that the SAC failed to plead with sufficient particularity its Section 10(b) and Rule 10b-5 claims, as required by Fed.R.Civ.P. 9(b). We address the adequacy of Anderson's claims de novo.

On appeal, Anderson stresses the following: Stac and its officers: 1) failed to disclose imminent competition from Microsoft and deliberately stalled licensing negotiations with Microsoft in order to delay Microsoft's market entry; and 2) falsified its financial statements by artificially inflating reported results through channel "stuffing," accomplished by offering customers "special terms," including discounts and exceptional rights of return; understating its existing reserves; and failing to disclose Stac's "inevitable" impending decline.

Both Section 11 of the Securities Act and Section 10(b) of the Exchange Act require a plaintiff "adequately [to] allege a material misrepresentation or omission." Section 11 creates a private remedy for any purchaser of a security if any part of the registration statement,

> when such part became effective, contained an untrue statement of a material fact or omitted to state a material fact required to be stated therein or necessary to make the statements therein not misleading. . . .

15 U.S.C. § 77k(a). "The plaintiff in a § 11 claim must demonstrate (1) that the registration statement contained an omission or misrepresentation, and (2) that the omission or misrepresentation was material, that is, it would have misled a reasonable investor about the nature of his or her investment." "No scienter is required for liability under § 11; defendants will be liable for innocent or negligent material misstatements or omissions."

. . .

A.   Stac's Prospectus.

The district court found that all of the omissions alleged by Anderson were either actually disclosed, or need not have been disclosed, in Stac's prospectus. The "materiality" of an omission is a fact-specific determination that should ordinarily be assessed by a jury. "[O]nly if the adequacy of the disclosure or the materiality of the statement is so obvious that reasonable minds could not differ are these issues appropriately resolved as a matter of law."

1.   Microsoft's plans to include data compression.

The gravamen of Anderson's complaint concerns Stac's alleged failure to disclose its knowledge of Microsoft's plans to introduce data compression in its upcoming version of DOS. According to Anderson, Stac entered into "sham" licensing negotiations with Microsoft merely to stall Microsoft's introduction of its new product. In the SAC, Anderson also alleged that Stac's patents were inadequate to prevent others from using its technology to create competitive products. Prior to the district court's ruling, however, Stac won a $120 million judgment against Microsoft for patent infringement relating to Stacker. The district court properly took judicial notice of this judgment in determining that the proprietary and patent information provided in the Prospectus was not misleading. Anderson does not raise the patent issue on appeal.

Regarding the threat of Microsoft "looming," the district court correctly observed that the Prospectus makes detailed disclosures concerning the risk of competition. For instance, the Prospectus states that "[a] number of competitors offer products that currently compete with [Stac's] products" and that these companies "could seek to expand their product offerings by designing and selling products using data compression or other technology that could render obsolete or adversely affect sales of [Stac's] products." After noting Stac's dependence on sales of DOS-compatible products, the Prospectus observes that:

> One developer of a compatible operating system has licensed a competitive data compression product for incorporation into the latest version of the operating system. There can be no assurance that Microsoft . . . will not incorporate a competitive data compression technology in their products or that such a technology will not emerge as an industry standard.

Further, the Prospectus reveals that "[Stac] has licensed and intends to license portions of its core technology to others," a practice which it cautions could result in more competition and price reductions.

Anderson alleges that the "no assurance" language is inadequate and that Stac committed fraud because it knew that Microsoft was going to come out with a competitive product, but masked this knowledge as a contingency. Anderson quotes repeatedly the following statement: " 'To warn that the untoward may occur when the event is contingent is prudent; to caution that it is only possible for the unfavorable events to happen when they have already occurred is deceit.'"

We have rephrased this principle as follows: " 'There is a difference between knowing that any product-in-development may run into a few snags, and knowing that a particular product has already developed problems so significant as to require months of delay.' The latter scenario characterizes the situation we encountered in *Warshaw v. Xoma Corp.*, 74 F.3d 955 (9th Cir.1996). Corporate officers of Xoma, a biotech company which had yet to make a profit on its research, assured stockholders that FDA approval of its new drug was imminent, in spite of knowledge that the drug might not work and was unlikely to receive such approval. Anderson has not alleged any such contradictory statements here. In [*In re Convergent Technologies Sec. Litig.*, 948 F.2d 507, 515 (9th Cir.1991)], we proceeded to distinguish the case before us from the Fifth Circuit case quoted, noting that Convergent's prospectus "virtually overflow[ed]" with risk factors, and to hold that the defendant company was not obliged to disclose its internal projections because such projections are tentative. We cited as adequate multiple warnings in the Convergent prospectus stating that "there is no assurance" of financial success given a variety of named obstacles to production. We therefore cannot agree with Anderson's characterization of Stac's "no assurance" language as "misleading" or inadequate.

Anderson argues that Stac should have explicitly disclosed its ongoing negotiations with Microsoft and its knowledge that Microsoft intended to introduce data compression technology in its new version of DOS. In short, Anderson suggests that Stac was obliged not only to report on its own product line and marketing plans, but to report on and make predictions regarding Microsoft's intentions.

Stac counters, and we have held, that a company is not required to forecast future events or to caution "that future prospects [may not be] as bright as past performance." In *re Worlds of Wonder Sec. Litig.*, 35 F.3d 1407, 1420 (9th Cir. 1994) ("WOW") ("'Absent allegations that [the issuer] withheld financial data or other existing facts from which forecasts are typically derived, the alleged omissions are not of material, actual facts. Therefore, the forecasts need not have been disclosed, and the failure to make the omitted forecasts did not render the other statements that were made misleading.'").

We agree with Stac that another company's plans cannot be known to a certainty. Even assuming, as we must, that Microsoft had informed Stac that it planned to introduce data compression, Stac could not have known whether or not Microsoft would truly do so. As Stac points out, the contingency of the event is underscored by the fact that a competitive product was liable to violate Stacker's patent, as borne out by the state judgment against Microsoft. Also, the market already knew of the potential for Microsoft's inclusion of data compression technology, as Anderson alleged in the FAC.

. . .

For the reasons stated above, the district court's opinion is affirmed.

SHERLEIGH ASSOCIATES, LLC v. WINDMERE-DURABLE HOLDINGS, INC.
United States District Court for the Southern District of Florida
178 F. Supp. 2d 1255 (2000)

LENARD, District Judge.

I. Factual Background

This is a securities class action on behalf of all persons who purchased the publicly traded securities of Defendant Windmere-Durable Holdings, Inc. ("Windmere") between May 12, 1998 and September 22, 1998, including those who acquired Windmere common stock and 10% Senior Subordinated Notes in Windmere's July 22, 1998 public offering. This action alleges violations of the Securities Act of 1933 (the "'33 Act") and the Securities Exchange Act of 1934 (the "'34 Act").

As alleged in the Consolidated Amended Class Action Complaint (hereinafter "Amended Complaint"), Windmere is a diversified international manufacturer and distributor of small electrical kitchen appliances and other household items. On May 11, 1998, Windmere issued a press release, filed with the Securities and Exchange Commission ("SEC") in a Form 8-K and signed by Defendant Harry D. Schulman ("Schulman"), the Chief Operating and Financial Officer, announcing Windmere's acquisition of the Home Products Group ("HPG") of the Black & Decker Corporation ("Black & Decker"). According to the press release, the HPG purchase would give Windmere a license to use the valuable Black & Decker brand name in North and Latin American markets, and would increase Windmere's manufacturing and distribution capacity.

Windmere acquired HPG on June 26, 1998 for $315 million in cash. Windmere financed its purchase of HPG with a "bridge loan" from NationsBank. To repay the NationsBank bridge loan, Windmere, along with the lead underwriter, Defendant Montgomery, offered its debt and equity securities to investors in a public offering on July 22, 1998 (the "July Offering"). The July Offering commenced pursuant to a registration statement, which included the Prospectus and two Prospectus supplements (collectively, the "Registration Statement"), that the SEC declared effective on June 4, 1998. In the July Offering, Windmere offered $103 million of common stock, approximately three million shares at $34 per share, and $130 million of 10% Senior Subordinated Notes.

The Registration Statement stated that the proceeds of the offering would be used to pay, in part, the NationsBank bridge loan. The Registration Statement further explained that Windmere "intended to utilize the marketing and distribution channels acquired through HPG to expand global market penetration of its products, particularly in Latin America." The acquisition, the Registration Statement explained, offered "immediate growth opportunities" and "uniquely positioned [Windmere] to capitalize on growth opportunities" in the household appliance and personal care markets. The Registration Statement went on to describe Windmere's 50% ownership of NewTech Electronics Industries ("NewTech"), and that Windmere would recognize 50% of the net earnings and losses of NewTech.

As alleged in the Amended Complaint, Windmere, Montgomery, Schulman and Defendant David M. Friedson ("Friedson"), Windmere's Chairman and Chief Executive Officer, promoted and sold the Windmere securities by issuing positive statements in pre-offering road show presentations to investors between July 6, 1998 and July 21, 1998. During these road show presentations, Plaintiffs allege, Defendants represented that Windmere was enjoying substantial benefits from the "complimentary strengths" between Windmere's existing operations and those of the recently acquired HPG. Windmere further represented that it "continued to enjoy strong revenue growth with a decreasing cost structure."

During this period, several adverse material facts were allegedly concealed or not disclosed by Defendants. . . . Windmere did not have the requisite licenses required to operate HPG and to sell HPG products in various Latin

American countries and thus could not sell HPG products in these Latin American countries or even call on HPG's then-existing customer base, until such time as the licenses were obtained. Windmere allegedly knew as early as March, 1998 that, after the acquisition but prior to the July Offering, it was obligated by local law in each Latin American country to create a new company for HPG, and to register those entities with the authorities in each country. Windmere had not yet begun this complicated and time-consuming process, however. At the time of the July Offering and during the Class Period, Plaintiffs allege Windmere's failure to obtain such licenses was causing Windmere to experience declining international sales and undermining the business objectives that the HPG acquisition was intended to serve.

. . .

On September 23, 1998, eight weeks after the July Offering, Windmere issued a press release stating that it was experiencing weak international sales, particularly in Latin America, and that NewTech was experiencing lower than expected earnings. That day, Windmere's stock price dropped to $7.1875 per share, down $27 per share from the $34 July Offering price. Between September 23, 1998 and February 23, 1999, the price further declined from $7 per share to below $ 4 per share. Although Windmere had previously expected 1998 earnings per share to be $1.50, Windmere in actuality realized earnings of only $0.57 per share for 1998.

A.   Specific Allegations of False and Misleading Statements

1.   Statements Prior to the July Offering

Plaintiffs allege Windmere issued a series of false and misleading statements in connection with the July Offering. On May 11, 1998, Windmere issued a press release announcing the acquisition of HPG (the "May 11 Press Release").[1] This release stated, in part, "Windmere and Black & Decker have established a long-term licensing arrangement which will allow Windmere to continue to market products under the Black & Decker brand name in . . . North and Latin America . . . for a minimum of six and one-half years on a royalty-free basis[.] . . . The combined company will be uniquely positioned to capitalize on growth opportunities[.] Immediate growth opportunities will result from . . . [these] marketing capabilities[.]"

---

[1] [FN1] This press release and others referred to in the Amended Complaint are referenced or reproduced in part within the pleading, but not attached thereto. The entire press release documents are provided by the Windmere Defendants, however. The following excerpts of the May 11 Press Release appear at pages 13-14 of the Amended Complaint:

> Windmere-Durable Holdings, Inc., a diversified manufacturer and distributor of a broad range of consumer products, including personal care products for the home and professional salons, kitchen electric appliances and consumer electronics, today announced that it has signed a definitive agreement to acquire The Black & Decker Corporation's Household Products Group, which will include the Cooking, Garment Care, Food Preparation and Beverage categories.

Plaintiffs further allege that on May 12, 1998, Defendants Schulman and Friedson convened a nationwide conference call for large Windmere shareholders and potential shareholders, including hedge funds, stock traders, brokers and securities analysts ("the May 12 Conference Call"). During the May 12 Conference Call, Defendants allegedly stated: (1) the acquisition would "more than triple" Windmere's 1998 revenues; (2) the acquisition would be "accretive," allow Windmere to obtain substantial cost synergies, and allow Windmere to market its products using HPG's well-recognized brand name; and (3) that Windmere was on target to post revenue of $750 million and earnings per share of $1.50 for 1998.

Plaintiffs allege these statements were materially false and misleading. At the time of the May 11 Press Release and the May 12 Conference Call, Windmere allegedly did not have the licenses needed to conduct business in the Latin American countries in which it proposed to sell and market HPG products. The Latin American market was a linchpin, Plaintiffs allege, of Windmere's expected "immediate growth opportunities" that would result from the acquisition.

On May 15, 1998 Windmere filed a Form 10-Q for the first quarter of 1998, the period ending March 31, 1998, reporting sales of $55.3 million and net earnings of $1.136 million for the quarter. This Form 10-Q also reported Windmere's decision to purchase HPG and thereby obtain the purported ability to market products in North and Latin America. On June 10, 1998, Windmere issued a press release to announce management changes "that will successfully integrate the recent acquisition of [HPG]." (the "June 10 Press Release") The June 10 Press Release reported "Windmere-Durable's revenues for 1997 were $261.9 million, and with the pending acquisition of Black & Decker Corporation's Household Products Group, Windmere's annualized revenue rate will be approximately $750 million."

On June 23, 1998, Plaintiffs allege Windmere issued a press release (the "June 23 Press Release") relating to its acquisition, stating in pertinent part:

> We look for the integration of The Black & Decker Household Products Group to begin as soon as the transaction is completed," added Mr. Friedson. "We expect to benefit from the significant business growth and operating synergies created by this acquisition beginning in the first six months of the acquisition and continuing through the next several years.

Pursuant to the terms of the acquisition agreement, Windmere will purchase the assets of The Black & Decker Corporation's Household Products Group for $315 million in cash. In connection with the transaction, Windmere and Black & Decker have established a long-term licensing arrangement which will allow Windmere to continue to market products under the Black & Decker brand name in the Cooking, Garment Care, Food Preparation and Beverage categories in North and Latin America, excluding Brazil, for a minimum of six and one-half years on a royalty-free basis, with potential renewal periods upon mutual agreement.

. . .

The combined company will be uniquely positioned to capitalize on growth opportunities within the personal care and kitchen appliance categories. Immediate growth opportunities will result from the combination of innovative product development, marketing capabilities and manufacturing infrastructure.

After the May 12 Conference Call, analyst reaction was allegedly favorable, with one industry analyst, CIBC Oppenheimer, issuing a favorable rating based in part on "sales synergies" such as expanding into new categories and selling products in Latin America.

2.   The Road Show

During the pre-offering road show, from July 6, 1998 to July 21, 1998, Plaintiffs allege Defendants Montgomery, Schulman and Friedson "participated in oral presentations, including demonstrative presentations with graphs and diagrams, stressing the success that Windmere was having and would continue to have after the acquisition[.]" Plaintiffs state that "Defendants were under intense pressure to complete the offering as soon as possible, as the proceeds were needed to repay NationsBank for the bridge loan used to pay for the HPG acquisition."

3.   The Registration Statement

Plaintiffs assert the Registration Statement, effective June 4, 1998, materially misstated the nature of the acquisition, in that it did not adequately describe the requirements of Windmere's integration with HPG, and the specific financial, legal and logistical risks that were ongoing or were foreseeable at the time. The Registration Statement stated, "[t]he Company has combined top brand names and a reputation for quality and innovation with its efficient, low-cost, vertically integrated manufacturing capabilities. The Company expects to continue to achieve growth and increased profitability by pursing the following strategies[.]" Plaintiffs then highlight two strategic categories, "Leverage Manufacturing Capabilities," and "Expansion of the Company's International Presence." [Regarding international sales,] the Registration Statement states:

> The Company intends to utilize the marketing and distribution channels acquired through the HPG Acquisition to expand the global market penetration of all of its products, particularly in Latin America. As a result of the HPG Acquisition, the Company has acquired the leading market share in irons, and a smaller market presence in the blender category, in Argentina, Colombia, Ecuador, Puerto Rico, Venezuela, Chile, Mexico and the Caribbean. In addition to targeting mass merchandisers, wholesalers, warehouse clubs and government institutions in Latin America, the Company intends to pursue alternative channels of distribution in Latin America which it believes will continue to be important sources of sales. On a pro forma basis, after giving effect to the HPG Acquisition, the Company's international sales would have been $218.9 million in 1997, as compared to $82.1 million in international sales for Windmere-Durable alone in 1997.

Plaintiffs contend these facts were materially false and misleading, and that the true facts were:

a) On or prior to the effective date of the Prospectus, July 22, 1998, Windmere could not use Black & Decker's existing licenses to operate its business in Latin America. PG Latin America was not previously run as a separate entity by Black & Decker, but functioned as part of Black & Decker's Power Tools Division. When Windmere acquired HPG, it was required to undergo the complicated and time-consuming process of creating a new company for HPG in each Latin American country in which HPG operated and was required to register those entities to do business. Thus, Windmere could not even call on HPG's existing customers in Latin America for continued business because it lacked the proper licenses to sell HPG's produces in those foreign countries. Windmere had internally projected that these corporate entities would be organized between March and June 1998. Nevertheless, the corporate requirements had not been met prior to the Class Period or the July Offering. Thus, at the time the Company issued the above statements, it was unable to "utilize the marketing and distribution channels" of HPG to expand market penetration in Latin America until it had obtained the requisite licenses. In July 1998, a former HPG employee visited the Company's manufacturing plant in Queretaro, Mexico, and learned that Windmere could still not call on HPG's existing customers and was losing business as a result. Indeed, Windmere had not obtained the necessary licenses throughout the Class Period. In late July and August, Windmere's General Counsel sought to move the licensing process forward, but without success. As a result, throughout the Class Period, Windmere failed to meet the necessary corporate requirements and obtain the needed licenses to do business in Latin America. The Company would not be able to realize significant profits in Latin America until the legal requirements of doing business there had been met. The Company's lack of the necessary licenses prior to Windmere's takeover of the HPG business in Latin America constituted a principal cause for the Company's later revealed poor performance during the Class Period.

b) Moreover, in a summer 1998 senior-staff meeting, significant problems with the integration of HPG's Latin American Division were discussed. Soon after it acquired HPG on June 26, 1998, Windmere discovered that Latin American retailers' warehouses were overstocked with HPG products. As a result, Windmere could not sell product in Latin America competitively because retailers were saturated resulting from prior sales of HPG products to them at discounted prices or on other favorable terms. Windmere was fully aware of the excessive inventory build-up problem in Latin America at least as early as when the Company acquired HPG. By the time Windmere acquired HPG on June 26, 1998 and for almost a full month thereafter before the July 22, 1998 effective date of the Registration Statement, the inventories of Latin American retailers were bloated with HPG products and additional sales of HPG products to them at least throughout the remainder of 1998 would [be] very difficult to achieve until those inventories had been substantially sold off. Defendants . . . had begun operating HPG by June 26, 1998, when HPG was acquired. Indeed, Defendants themselves told the marketplace and investors during road show presentations that Windmere was already in the process of integrating the operations of HPG. There was thus a large build-up of HPG products on the shelves of HPG's Latin American retailers before the July Offering[.] Despite the severity of the sales problem for Windmere, the Company failed to disclose it to the investing public in the Registration Statement and instead emphasized the dramatic increase in sales which would purportedly result from the HPG acquisition.

Plaintiffs further allege Defendants made material misstatements in the section entitled, "Risks of International Operations and Expansion," describing certain international economic and political variables that could effect the company's business, including "the burdens and costs of compliance with a variety of foreign laws and, in certain parts of the world, political instability[.]" Plaintiffs claim this description was materially false and misleading because, at the time the statement was made, Windmere "was already materially reducing sales in Latin America because the Company could not do business with HPG's existing customers. In considering the HPG acquisition, the Company had internally projected that it would obtain the required licenses between March and June 1998, a period well before the issuance of the above statements." Thus, Plaintiffs allege, the discussion of risk in the Registration Statement was "but a generic warning containing no meaningful factual disclosure of the adverse facts which were then actually negatively impacting Windmere's business by at least July 22, 1998."

In addition, Plaintiffs contend, the "High Volume, Low-Cost Manufacturing Capabilities" section contained material misstatements. There, the Registration Statement states, "[t]he Company believes that its high volume, vertically integrated manufacturing capabilities provide the Company flexibility and cost advantages[.] The Company intends to take advantage of its capabilities as a multinational manufacturer to reduce operating costs and increase productivity." Plaintiffs allege these statements were false because certain manufacturing integration within the combined company "would take a significant amount of time, and Windmere would have to find its own companies to create HPG products. Windmere nevertheless told the public in its June 23, 1998 release . . . that it expected to enjoy the benefits and synergies from the HPG acquisition 'beginning in the fist six months of the acquisition.'"

. . .

III.   Discussion and Analysis

First analyzing the appropriate pleading standards for securities fraud claims under the '33 Act and the '34 Act, the Court analyzes the allegations in the Amended Complaint under the appropriate standard of review. Finding Plaintiffs have stated actionable securities fraud claims on all counts, except for Count IV as to Defendant Montgomery only, the Court determines that the Motion of the Windmere Defendants shall be denied in its entirety, and the Motion of Defendant Montgomery shall be granted as to Count IV only and denied in all other respects.

A.   Sections 11 and 12(a)(2) of the Securities Act of 1933

The allegations in Counts I and II claim all Defendants violated sections 11 and 12(a)(2) of the '33 Act by making material omissions or misstatements in connection with the July Offering. Section 11 allows any purchaser of a security to bring a cause of action based on material misstatements, if any part of the registration statement, when such part became effective, contained an untrue statement of a material fact or omitted to state a material fact required to be stated therein or necessary to make the statements therein not misleading. . . .

15 U.S.C. § 77k(a). A plaintiff may bring a section 11 claim against any person who signed the prospectus, the officers and board of directors of the issuing corporation, the underwriters of the securities offering, or any expert whose profession gives authority to that part of the registration statement he or she prepared.

In order to state a section 11 claim, the plaintiff "must demonstrate (1) that the registration statement contained an omission or misrepresentation, and (2) that the omission or misrepresentation was material, that is, it would have misled a reasonable investor about the nature of his or her investment." As the Supreme Court explained:

> Section 11 was designed to assure compliance with the disclosure provisions of the ['33] Act by imposing a stringent standard of liability on the parties who play a direct role in a registered offering. If a plaintiff purchased a security issued pursuant to a registration statement, he need only show a material misstatement or omission to establish his prima facie case. Liability against the issuer of the security is virtually absolute, even for innocent misstatements. Other defendants bear the burden of demonstrating due diligence.

Herman & MacLean, [459 U.S. 375, 381-82 (1983)].

Under section 12(a)(2), on the other hand, any person who "offers or sells a security . . . by means of a prospectus or oral communication" that "includes an untrue statement of a material fact or omits to state a material fact necessary in order to make the statements, in the light of the circumstances under which they were made, not misleading," shall be liable to any "person purchasing such security from him." 15 U.S.C. § 77l(a)(2). Thus, section 12(a)(2) liability may be based on oral as well as written communications.

Where a section 11 claim "sounds in fraud," the particularity requirements of Federal Rule of Civil Procedure 9(b) may apply. In such a case, Plaintiffs must allege: (1) the precise statements, documents, or misrepresentations made; (2) the time, place, and person responsible for the statement; (3) the content and manner in which these statements misled the plaintiffs; and (4) what the defendants gained by the alleged fraud. Yet, where particularity requirements are applied to such claims, "[a] balance must be struck between allowing bald allegations of material misstatements or omissions with little factual basis, on the one hand, and so tightening the requirements of pleading that Plaintiffs must plead evidence, on the other."

1. Plaintiffs Have Adequately Pled Section 11 and 12(a)(2) Claims for Material Omissions in the Registration Statement Against All Defendants.

The most significant of Plaintiffs' allegations are the assertions that at the time of the July Offering, "Windmere did not have the requisite licenses in place required to operate HPG and to sell HPG produces in Latin America and thus could not, until such time as the licenses were obtained, sell HPG products in Latin America or even call on HPG's then-existing customer base." Plaintiffs contend that the disclosures regarding the HPG acquisition triggered a duty to disclose, among other things, the risk that, after the acquisition, months could pass during which Windmere would be unable to move or sell products in Latin America until these license issues were resolved.

The Eleventh Circuit has stated that "[a] duty to disclose may . . . be created by a defendant's previous decision to speak voluntarily. Where a defendant's failure to speak would render the defendant's own prior speech misleading or deceptive, a duty to disclose arises." Similarly, the First Circuit has explained that "the obligations that attend the preparation of a registration statement and prospectus filed in connection with a public stock offering . . . embody nothing if not an affirmative duty to disclose a broad range of material information." Consequently, in connection with a public stock offering, "there is a strong affirmative duty of disclosure."

Here, the Registration Statement made a number of affirmative statements regarding Windmere's acquisition of HPG and the HPG's operations at that time. For example, the Registration Statement discussed HPG's "marketing and distribution channels" and "leading market share" in Latin America as well as the expectation of Windmere's international sales on a pro forma basis, including HPG's 1997 results. Additional facts relevant to this risk, but not disclosed by Defendants are: (1) alleged "stuffed channels" within the HPG's chain of distribution, such that prior to the acquisition Windmere should have disclosed these particular market conditions; (2) that certain specific difficulties with integrating HPG manufacturing facilities in Mexico with the remainder of Windmere's operations, amounted to a material risk that Windmere would not be able to sell products in Latin America until these obstacles were cleared; and (3) the "pro-forma" comparison of a combined Windmere-HPG organization was misleading given that at the time of the Registration Statement Windmere was not in a position to operate HPG in its Latin American markets.

The Windmere Defendants spoke voluntarily in the Registration Statement and the press releases about Windmere's intention to use the distribution channels acquired by purchasing HPG to expand the sales of its products, "particularly in Latin America." Further, the Company proclaimed that it intended "to pursue alternative channels of distribution in Latin America which it believes will continue to be important sources of sales."

2. The Registration Statement Does Not Disclose The Risk of Latin American Licensing or Distribution Problems.

In the section entitled "Risk Factors" at pages S-14 to S-24, the Registration Statement provides detailed information on certain risk factors accompanying any investment in Windmere securities and associated with the acquisition of HPG. Upon review of the numerous risk subsections, the Court finds four categories relate to national licensing agreements and distribution within Latin American markets: "Risks of International Operations and Expansion," "Dependence on International Trademarks," "Risks Associated with Integration of Black & Decker Household Products Group," and "Government Regulation."

After carefully reviewing the entire Registration Statement and these risk sections in particular, and comparing these with the factual allegations which the Court must take as true, the Court finds none of these risk sections or additional cautionary language in the Registration Statement adequately address the issue of renewed licenses in Latin American markets — the allegedly undisclosed material risk here — under the "meaningful cautionary language" standard discussed below. As related to certain, specifically alleged integration difficulties, the Registration Statement's risk discussion does not adequately cover the real or foreseeable risk that ongoing international sales of Windmere's products would or could be foreseeably jeopardized by the need to obtain such licenses. Further, as discussed below, the "cautionary language" attached to various press release statements also fails to meet the "meaningful cautionary language" standard that would allow a reasonable investor to understand these alleged material risks. The section entitled, "Risk of International Operations," for example, addresses issues relating to international sales and marketing in foreign jurisdictions, including Latin America. The section does state that, "[b]ecause the Company manufactures its products and conducts business in several foreign countries, the Company is affected by economic and political conditions in those countries, including . . . the burdens and costs of compliance with a variety of foreign laws and, in certain parts of the world, political instability." No mention is made, however, of the risk of licensing Windmere's operations subsequent to the HPG acquisition, or the specific requirement to seek licenses in various Latin American markets. Rather, the section focuses on currency, economic, and political considerations, particularly as they relate to the People's Republic of China.

The "Dependence on Trademarks" section, on the other hand, touts the fact that "[a]s part of the JPG Acquisition, the Company licensed the *Black & Decker* brand for use in marketing HPG products in North America, Central America, South America (excluding Brazil) and the Caribbean under a licensing arrangement with a minimum term of six and one-half years." This section describes the licensing arrangement between Windmere and Black & Decker, and goes on to describe risks relating to trademark exploitation, but does not substantively address Windmere's need to get approval of domestic governments or licenses to sell Black & Decker products after the acquisition was consummated.

Similarly, the "Patents and Protection of Proprietary Technology" section addresses "patent and design registration," and discusses the risks of creating new proprietary technology and patent registration once new technology is created. Again absent, however, is any mention of the need to get approval of domestic governments or licenses to sell Black & Decker products after the sale was consummated.

After reviewing the entire Registration Statement, the Court finds notably absent any section that addresses what would allegedly cause the significant gap in sales volume: risks relating to international intellectual property generally, risks relating to international licensing requirements specifically, or related risks due to uncertainty of various national licensing requirements.

. . .

4. Safe Harbor and Bespeaks Caution Doctrine Are Not Applicable

Defendants argue the challenged statements are forward looking in nature, are subject to the statutory safe harbor, and thus not actionable. The Private Securities Litigation Reform Act of 1995, Pub.L. No. 194-67 (hereinafter "Reform Act"), "provides a safe harbor from liability for certain 'forward-looking' statements." Pursuant to the safe harbor, "corporations and individual defendants may avoid liability for forward-looking statements that prove false if the statement is 'accompanied by meaningful cautionary statements identifying important factors that could cause actual results to differ materially from those in the forward-looking statement.'" Thus, the Court must discern whether any such statement is accompanied by "meaningful cautionary language." Yet the harbor has limits, for "a defendant can fully benefit from the safe harbor's shelter only when it has disclosed risk factors in a warning accompanying the forward-looking statement." The cautionary language must therefore meet a threshold of specificity. *See* [*Harris v. Ivax,* 182 F.3d 799, 807 (11th Cir. 1999)] (holding that "when an investor has been warned of risks of a significance similar to that actually realized, she is sufficiently on notice of the danger of the investment").

Moreover, where plaintiffs allege a "material omission," the cautionary language must be sufficiently "meaningful," such that it discloses "important factors that could cause actual results to differ materially from those in the forward-looking statement." The *Harris* court found general disclosures relating to a goodwill writedown, and consequential one-time charge to earnings, adequate for a reasonable investor to assess the risk associated with certain forward-looking statements, and thus an accompanying warning was "of a significance similar to that [risk] actually realized." The court concluded, "[i]n short, where an investor has been warned of risks of a significance similar to that actually realized, she is sufficiently on notice of the danger of the investment to make an intelligent decision about it according to her own preferences for risk and reward."

Here, the Court has analyzed the Registration Statement and additional documents for both general "boilerplate" cautionary language, and for specific cautionary language of risks relating to international licensing issues. Plaintiffs allege Defendants failed to reveal either known, present facts, or facts that should have been known through due diligence, regarding Windmere's lack of licenses to operate HPG. Plaintiffs further allege certain risk factors and cautionary statements were, themselves, materially misleading or devoid of material risk disclosures, and that therefore the statements cannot be within the safe harbor because the disclosures were inadequate. Plaintiffs argue that "to caution that it is only possible for the unfavorable events to happen when they have already occurred is deceit."

After comparing the Amended Complaint's factual allegations and the various cautionary statements within the ambit of the Reform Act's safe harbor provision, the Court finds the cautionary language, both in the aggregate and when analyzed for specifics, when cast against the alleged omissions and misstatements here, did not fairly and adequately warn potential investors of the alleged risks associated with investing in Windmere securities. Thus, the

Court finds the Reform Act's safe harbor provision does not apply to the allegations in the Amended Complaint.[2]

5. Material Omissions or Misstatements Amount to Actionable Claim

Taken together, the allegations of material misstatements and omissions in the Amended Complaint adequately state claims against all Defendants for violations of sections 11 and 12(a)(2) of the '33 Act. Plaintiffs have alleged through specific factual allegations: (1) that the registration statement contained omissions or misrepresentations; and (2) that the omissions or misrepresentations were material, that is, would have misled a reasonable investor about the nature of his or her investment. As such, the Court denies the motions to dismiss Counts I and II as to all Defendants.

IN RE SEACHANGE INTERNATIONAL, INC.
United States District Court for the District of Massachusetts
2004 U.S. Dist. LEXIS 1687 (Feb. 6, 2004)

WOODLOCK, District Judge.

Plaintiff shareholders of SeaChange International, Inc. ("SeaChange") bring this putative class action against SeaChange, two members of its management team, three of its directors, and the three lead underwriters of its January 28, 2002 secondary stock Offering (the "Offering"). The shareholders allege that the registration statement and prospectus SeaChange filed with the Securities and Exchange Commission ("SEC") in conjunction with the Offering contained material misrepresentations and omissions in violation of §§ 11, 12(a)(2), and 15 of the Securities Act of 1933 ("Securities Act"). Defendants now move through two separate motions — one by SeaChange, the management team defendants, and the director defendants; the other by the underwriters — to dismiss the case pursuant to Fed. R. Civ. P 12(b)(6) for failure to state a claim.

I. BACKGROUND

A. Facts

SeaChange is a Delaware-incorporated company with its principal executive offices in Maynard, Massachusetts. SeaChange is a leading developer, manufacturer, and marketer of video storage systems, which automate the management and distribution of video streams, such as feature-length movies and advertisements. SeaChange markets its systems to cable television

---

[2] [FN5] Defendants further argue the "bespeaks caution doctrine" applies to the challenged statements, and that certain cautionary language associated with the disclosures was "sufficient to render the alleged omissions or misrepresentations immaterial as a matter of law." *Saltzberg v. TM Sterling/Austin Assocs., Ltd.*, 45 F.3d 399, 400 (11th Cir. 1995). Here, the Defendants allegedly made present, known misrepresentations or omissions, as the Defendants knew or should have known the licensing requirement was not met but nonetheless failed to disclose the requirement, or failed to disclose the lack of licenses could result in drastically decreased revenue. *See, e.g., Stac Elecs.*, 89 F.3d at 1408 ("By definition, the bespeaks caution doctrine applies only to affirmative, forward-looking statements"). The Court will reserve final ruling on this issue pending fact discovery.

operators and broadcasters as a means to offer video-on-demand ("VOD") movies and programming, which allow viewers to watch content at any time with remote pause, rewind, and fast-forward features. SeaChange's ITV System, for example, digitally manages, stores, and distributes digital video, allowing cable operators and telecommunications companies to offer VOD and other interactive television services, including retrieval of internet content through the television. Additionally, SeaChange's SPOT System allows cable operators and broadcasters to insert targeted digital advertisements into cable programming, and its MediaCluster System, a grouping of several individual servers, allows broadcasters to directly transmit video content to viewers without the need for tape libraries and other storage and playback systems.

On January 9, 2002, SeaChange filed a final Form S-3 Registration Statement ("Registration Statement"), which included the Prospectus, with the SEC; and on January 29, 2002, SeaChange conducted the Offering. In the Offering, SeaChange and seven stockholders (including defendants William Styslinger, William Fiedler, and Martin Hoffman) sold 3,594,411 shares of its common stock at a price of $28.99 per share. The underwriters of the Offering exercised an over-allotment option and purchased an additional 539,162 common shares from SeaChange. The Offering netted total proceeds of $108,630,307 for SeaChange and $5,768,280 for the seven selling shareholders.

On March 5, 2002, SeaChange issued a news release, announcing its financial results for the fourth quarter, which ended on January 31, 2002, two days after the Offering. Although results for the quarter exceeded its prior projections, as evidenced by the company's 10-K form, SeaChange reported VOD segment sales of $10.3 versus analyst estimates of $12 million. In addition, on March 5 it became public that AOL Time Warner's cable unit had awarded the contract to provide VOD services in Manhattan to nCUBE, one of SeaChange's competitors. SeaChange's shares fell that day 17%, from $22.26 to $18.49, with a volume of 8.26 million shares traded, more than ten times the three-month daily average.

On May 28, 2002, nCUBE announced that a jury in the federal district court in the District of Delaware had returned a jury verdict against SeaChange in favor of nCUBE. The jury found that SeaChange had willfully infringed on nCUBE's patented VOD software and awarded nCUBE $2 million in damages and a 7% royalty on systems going back to February 1, 2002. In daytime trading on May 28, 2002, SeaChange shares fell 15% to $10.39, and in after-hours trading, the shares fell to $9.09.

On June 5, 2002, SeaChange reported a net loss of $21 million ($0 .82 per share) for the first fiscal quarter of the year. The losses included $14.4 million in one-time charges and adjustments related to the nCUBE litigation.

B.   Procedural History

On October 20, 2002, Leon and Rena Beylus filed a class action complaint against SeaChange, two members of its management team, three of its directors, and the three lead underwriters of the Offering. Shortly following the filing of the Beylus complaint, three additional sets of plaintiffs filed related complaints. Three of the plaintiffs in the cases made competing motions to consolidate the actions and for appointment as lead plaintiff. Subsequently, all sets of plaintiffs agreed by stipulation that the four actions would be consolidated in this action and that James A. Radley would serve as lead plaintiff. Additionally, they agreed under the stipulation that Bernstein Leibhard & Lifshitz, LLP would serve as lead plaintiffs counsel and Shapiro Haber & Urmy, LLP would serve as liaison counsel.

C. Parties

Lead plaintiff James Radley purchased common stock pursuant to or traceable to the allegedly false statements in the Registration Statement and the Prospectus. Radley represents a putative class of those who similarly bought stock in the Offering.

In addition to SeaChange, plaintiffs bring this action against: William Styslinger, who is SeaChange's chairman, president, and chief operating officer; William Fielder, who is SeaChange's chief financial officer; Martin Hoffman, Thomas Olson, and Carmine Vona, who are SeaChange directors; and Morgan Stanley & Co., Inc., Thomas Weisel Partners LLC, and RBC Dain Rauscher, Inc., the three lead underwriters for the Offering. For the remainder of this discussion, I refer to SeaChange and the individual defendants (Styslinger, Fielder, Hoffman, Olson, and Vona) collectively as "SeaChange defendants," and I refer to the three underwriter defendants as the "Underwriters."

D. Allegations

Plaintiffs allege that SeaChange defendants and the Underwriters made material misrepresentations or omissions in the Prospectus pertaining to five general circumstances. Specifically, plaintiffs allege that the Prospectus omitted information or contained misleading statements concerning the fact that SeaChange: (1) was willfully infringing an nCUBE VOD patent, (2) was operating at a competitive disadvantage because it could not provide the VOD capacity to compete in the largest metropolitan areas, (3) was at a competitive disadvantage because its SPOT system was analog and did not provide the digital applications that rival systems did, (4) had already been informed by AOL Time Warner that it would not be awarded the contract for Manhattan, and (5) had no reasonable expectation of achieving financial results in line with the consistent earnings projections they had been making for the five months prior to the Offering.

. . .

III. DISCUSSION

. . .

C. Misleading Material Statements

While in their complaint, plaintiffs tend to mix together allegations of material misrepresentations and allegations of material omissions, they identify a number of affirmative statements in the Prospectus that they contend either were false or, due to omissions of material facts, misleading. Plaintiffs point out five categories of such statements: statements concerning (1) demand for SeaChange products, (2) SeaChange's competitive position, (3) sources of revenue, (4) revenue growth, and (5) proprietary information and the nCUBE litigation. I find these allegations fail to state a claim under § 11 or § 12. First, statements in the first four categories were "forward-looking" within the meaning of the safe harbor provisions of the PSLRA and therefore cannot ground § 11 or § 12 liability. Second, the statements regarding proprietary information and the nCUBE litigation provided such disclosure of material information as was required.

. . .

(2) *Proprietary Information and nCUBE Litigation* — In addition to the statements from the "Risk Factors" section, plaintiffs allege that a number of statements in the Prospectus regarding SeaChange's proprietary information were materially misleading. Specifically, plaintiffs allege in the complaint that references to "our ITV System," "our video systems," and our "MediaCluster System" . . . were materially false and misleading because Defendants represented that SeaChange had full proprietary rights to the Mediaserver technology when, in fact, at the time the statements were made, SeaChange did not have proprietary rights to the technology and was willfully infringing upon nCUBE's patent on this technology.

Plaintiffs similarly allege that the following statements, from a section of the Prospectus entitled "Legal Proceedings," were materially false and misleading as to the nCUBE litigation:

> We responded on January 26, 2001, denying the claim of infringement. . . .

> We cannot be certain of the outcome of the foregoing litigation, but do plan to oppose the allegations against us and assert our claims against the other parties vigorously. [W]e are unable to estimate the impact to our business, financial condition and results of operations or cash flows.

Plaintiffs contend the statements were false and misleading because SeaChange was, at the time it made the statements, willfully infringing on nCUBE's patent. Thus, plaintiffs argue that SeaChange knew with a "high degree of certainty" that nCUBE would receive a jury verdict in its favor, which would adversely impact SeaChange's business.

The only factual allegation plaintiffs offer to support their contention that SeaChange knew the statements to be false or misleading is the jury verdict, subsequent to the Offering, which found that SeaChange had willfully infringed nCUBE's VOD system patent. I observe, as well, from the nCUBE litigation docket that the trial judge found the case to have been exceptional under 35 U.S.C. § 258 and awarded attorneys fees to nCUBE. Such a finding is generally reserved for cases involving willful infringement and the conduct of litigation asserting bad faith claims and defenses.

To be sure, willfulness in the context of patent infringement is not equivalent to actual knowledge. But it may be inferred, from the jury verdict of willful infringement and the judge's grant of attorneys fees against

SeaChange, that SeaChange knew it was infringing nCUBE's patent when generating the Prospectus and Registration Statement. This permissible inference is sufficient at the pleading stage to establish knowledge by SeaChange at the time of the registration statement that a loss in the nCUBE litigation was highly likely.

Given the permissible inference that SeaChange knew that it was infringing on nCUBE's patent — or, in the words of plaintiffs, that it "knew the suit [against it] was meritorious" — I turn to the question whether the statements made as part of the registration statement were affirmatively misleading.

It cannot seriously be disputed that the statements in the Prospectus concerning the nCUBE litigation were literally true; the statements merely described the litigation in very broad terms. Plaintiffs, however, cite *Roeder v. Alpha Industries, Inc.*, 814 F.2d 22, 26 (1st Cir. 1987), for the proposition that "[w]hen a corporation does make a disclosure — whether it be voluntary or required — there is a duty to make it complete and accurate." Accordingly, they argue that while SeaChange's statements about the nCUBE litigation might have been literally true, they were nevertheless incomplete and misleading because they did not disclose the patent infringing conduct.

The disclosure duty referred to in *Roeder,* however, is not so diffuse as plaintiffs suggest. While a company that chooses to reveal material information, even though it had no duty to do so, "must disclose the whole truth," *id.,* it need not disclose everything it knows; rather, the company is required only to make additional disclosures to keep the information from being materially misleading. As the First Circuit stated in *Backman v. Polaroid Corp.*, 910 F.2d 10 (1st Cir. 1990):

> Plaintiffs quote *Roeder* that even a voluntary disclosure of information that a reasonable investor would consider material must be "complete and accurate." This, however, does not mean that by revealing one fact about a product, one must reveal all others that, too, would be interesting, market-wise, but means only such others, if any, that are needed so that what was revealed would not be "so incomplete as to mislead."

Id. at 16.

Here, the Prospectus mentions the nCUBE litigation in general descriptive terms, as required by Item 103 of Regulation S-K. . . . The Prospectus stated that SeaChange was contesting nCUBE's claim of patent infringement, that it was not certain what the outcome of the litigation would be, and that it could not "estimate the impact" of the litigation. It contained no statements suggesting that SeaChange would prevail in the litigation or implying that the impact of the litigation on the company would be positive. Given that at the time of the Offering the jury had not yet returned a verdict, SeaChange was not obligated to predict the outcome or estimate the impact of the nCUBE litigation.

The information provided in the Prospectus was accurate, even considering knowledge of the patent infringing conduct. While the information may have been, in some predictive sense, incomplete, I find that, given the well understood vagaries of litigation, it was not so incomplete as to mislead investors.

D.   Omissions of Material Fact Required to be Stated

In addition to alleging that affirmative statements in the Prospectus were materially misleading, plaintiffs also contend that defendants violated § 11 by failing to disclose in the Prospectus or Registration Statement material facts known by SeaChange at the time of the Offering. In their amended complaint plaintiffs confusingly conflate allegations of omissions related to affirmative statements in the Prospectus with allegations of free-standing omissions unrelated to specific statements. However, in their summary judgment opposition, plaintiffs clarify that their allegations encompass the latter type of omission. In other words, plaintiffs contend that even if none of the affirmative statements in the Prospectus are actionable as misleading under § 11 or § 12, SeaChange nevertheless had a duty under § 11 to disclose information it possessed at the time of the Offering about (1) the nCUBE litigation, (2) the AOL Time Warner Manhattan contract, and (3) intra-quarter performance.

To avoid dismissal of a claim based on a free-standing omission of material fact — one not tied to a specific statement in the Prospectus — plaintiffs must sufficiently allege: (1) that the Prospectus contained an omission; (2) that the omission was material; (3) that defendants were under a duty to disclose the omitted information; and (4) that such omitted information existed at the time the Prospectus became effective. Considering in turn whether plaintiffs allegations of omissions satisfy these elements, I find that plaintiffs have failed to state a claim because they have not alleged facts which implicate any duty on the part of SeaChange to disclose the information plaintiffs contend was unlawfully omitted from the Prospectus. Even if omitted information is material, there can be no liability for the omission under the securities laws unless there is a duty to disclose the information. In other words, "[s]ilence, absent a duty to disclose, is not misleading." Here, plaintiffs have failed to identify any such duty as to any of the allegedly omitted information.

(1) *nCUBE Litigation* — Plaintiffs suggest that even if none of the statements in the Prospectus describing the nCUBE litigation were materially false or misleading, SeaChange nevertheless had, under § 11, the obligation to disclose the fact that it was likely to lose the litigation because SeaChange knew at the time of the Offering that it was infringing on nCUBE's patent. This allegation is closely-aligned with the allegation found deficient above, . . . but it is distinct in that it is not tied to any affirmative statements in the Prospectus.

Plaintiffs point to no duty — other than a generalized duty of disclosure . . . — that would require SeaChange to describe the nCUBE litigation differently or in more detail than it did in the Prospectus. The defendants fully complied with the disclosure duty imposed by Item 103 of Regulation S-K which requires registrants to:

> [d]escribe briefly any material pending legal proceedings, other than ordinary routine litigation incidental to the business, to which the registrant or any of its subsidiaries is a party or of which any of their property is the subject [and to include] the name of the court or agency in which the proceedings are pending, the date instituted, the principal parties thereto, a description of the factual basis alleged to underlie the proceeding and the relief sought.

17 C.F.R. § 229.103.

Item 103 marks the extent of a registrant's obligation to disclose information pertaining to pending litigation. In directing the required disclosure in Item 103 to the general contours of ongoing litigation, the SEC has deliberately chosen not to impose the type of duty of disclosure that plaintiffs contend defendants' breached. The disclosure required by Item 103 is meant to put potential investors on notice of pending litigation, not to force companies to predict a particular outcome in the litigation. Here, the Prospectus set forth information required in Item 103 and further stated that the company could not be certain of the outcome of the litigation and that it could face "significant liability for damages and invalidation of [its] proprietary rights." This disclosure was certainly enough to alert investors of the nCUBE litigation and to prompt them to make further inquiry directly about the litigation should they choose to do so.

Plaintiffs' citation of *Roeder,* is misguided. While plaintiffs may be correct that *Roeder* supports the conclusion that SeaChange's patent infringing conduct was material, the decision does not assist them in locating the source of a duty to disclose necessary to their claim. Indeed, the First Circuit in *Roeder* found that while the fact that the defendant company had paid a bribe to obtain a subcontract was material, plaintiff failed to state a claim for securities fraud because he did not allege facts that, if proved, established the defendant had a duty to disclose the bribe. The *Roeder* court stressed that "[a] duty to disclose 'does not arise from the mere possession of nonpublic market information," and endorsed "the prevailing view . . . that there is no [ ] affirmative duty of disclosure" in cases where "there is no insider trading, no statute or regulation requiring disclosure, and no inaccurate, incomplete, or misleading prior disclosures." *Roeder* applies here and requires dismissal of plaintiffs' nCUBE claims given their failure to allege facts which give rise to any affirmative duty of SeaChange to disclose its patent infringing conduct.

    . . .

III.   CONCLUSION

For the reasons set forth more fully above, defendants' motions to dismiss under Fed.R.Civ.P. 12(b)(6) are GRANTED as to all claims.

IN RE ALLIANCE PHARMACEUTICAL CORP. SECURITIES LITIGATION
United States District Court for the Southern District of New York
279 F. Supp. 2d 171 (2003)

McMahon, District Judge.

Plaintiffs, former shareholders of Molecular Biosystems, Inc. ("MBI"), bring this action against Alliance Pharmaceutical Corp. ("Alliance") and three of its officers — Duane J. Roth ("D. Roth), Theodore D. Roth ("T. Roth"), and Tim T. Hart ("Hart") — under Sections 11 and 12(a)(2) of the Securities Act of 1933 (15 U.S.C. §§ 77k, 77l). Plaintiffs also allege that the individual defendants, as control persons of Alliance, violated Section 15 of the Securities Act of 1933

(15 U.S.C. § 77o). Defendants move for summary judgment under Fed.R.Civ.P. 56 on all of the plaintiffs' claims.

Defendants' motion is granted in part and denied in part.

I. BACKGROUND

A. Factual History

The following facts, unless otherwise noted, are undisputed.

1. The Merger of Alliance and MBI and the Commencement of this Lawsuit

Defendant Alliance, a New York corporation, is a pharmaceutical research and development company. Alliance is the developer of Oxygent, a temporary oxygen carrier or blood substitute designed to reduce or eliminate the need for blood transfusions during surgery. MBI is the developer of Optison, an intravenous ultrasound contrast agent used in ultrasound examinations of the heart.

In October 2000, Alliance and MBI announced that they had entered into an agreement for Alliance to acquire MBI. Under the terms of the parties' merger agreement, Alliance would acquire all of MBI's stock in exchange for 770,000 shares of Alliance stock and MBI would become a wholly-owned subsidiary of Alliance. In connection with the proposed merger and stock exchange, Alliance filed a Registration Statement with the Securities and Exchange Commission on November 9, 2000 and two amendments thereto on November 22 and 29, 2000 (collectively the "Registration Statement"). The Registration Statement included a proxy statement-prospectus. The Registration Statement was declared effective by the SEC on November 29, 2000.

On December 29, 2000, at a special shareholder's meeting, the shareholders of MBI voted to approve the merger. On January 3, 2001, Alliance issued a press release announcing that it had completed its acquisition of MBI.

On January 8, 2001, Alliance issued a press release publicly disclosing that it had voluntarily suspended further patient enrollment in its Phase 3 study of Oxygent in cardiac surgery patients due to an imbalance in certain adverse events between the control group and the Oxygent treatment group.

Plaintiffs allege that this announcement had a devastating effect on the stock prices of both companies. On the day preceding the merger announcement, MBI common stock closed at $0.45 per share, while Alliance common stock closed at $13.50 per share. On January 3, the day the merger was announced, Alliance's common stock traded as high as $8.813 per share and closed at $8.625 per share. On January 8, when Alliance announced the suspension of the Oxygent trial, the price of Alliance common stock plunged 62% from the previous day's closing price of $7.50, to close at $2.375 per share. Plaintiffs allege that on January 22, 2001, Alliance issued a report stating that (1) it would reduce its workforce by approximately 20%; and (2) the bulk of the staff positions eliminated were those "involved in preparations for the anticipated near-term commercialization of Oxygent." Plaintiffs also allege that "[i]t was reported that contrary to the representations in the Registration Statement, the Company may not have sufficient cash to meets [sic] its working capital commitments for the current fiscal year."

On February 23, 2001, in response to the precipitous drop in the value of their stock, plaintiffs filed this action on behalf of all individuals — except defendants and related parties — who acquired common stock of Alliance pursuant to the merger between MBI and Alliance. Plaintiffs filed their second amended complaint on February 14, 2002. Plaintiffs allege that defendants failed to disclose (1) known problems in the Phase 3 study of Oxygent, (thereby inflating Alliance's value), and (2) information about an agreement between MBI and "its only viable competitor" for Optison sales in Japan, South Korea, and Taiwan (thereby deflating MBI's value).

. . .

3. The Optison Agreement

As previously noted, MBI is the developer of Optison, an intravenous ultrasound contrast agent used in ultrasound examinations of the heart. Prior to the merger, MBI had entered into collaborative agreements with Mallinckrodt, Inc. and Chugai Pharmaceutical Co. Ltd., pursuant to which the two companies assumed all development, manufacturing, and marketing responsibilities for Optison in their respective territories.

Mallinckrodt controlled the Optison business for all territories except Japan, South Korea, and Taiwan. At the time that the Registration Statement became effective, Optison had received regulatory approval and was being marketed by Mallinckrodt in the United States and Europe. MBI was entitled to royalties on Mallinckrodt's sales of Optison.

Chugai had a right to distribute Optison in Japan, South Korea, and Taiwan. At the time that the Registration Statement became effective, Chugai was conducting Phase 3 clinical trials of Optison in Japan. MBI was entitled to "milestone payments" from Chugai, based on Chugai's achievement of certain product development and regulatory goals, and royalties from Chugai on any future sales of Optison in its territories.

In May 2000, MBI and Mallinckrodt settled litigation brought by two of MBI's competitors (Sonus and Nycomed Amersham plc), who had alleged that Optison sales by MBI in the United States and Europe infringed their patents. Pursuant to the settlement, Sonus became entitled to royalties on sales of Optison by MBI and Mallinckrodt, with the exception of sales in certain Asian countries, including Chugai's territories.

On January 16, 2001, Sonus announced that it had entered into a patent licensing agreement with Chugai and MBI with respect to the development and marketing of Optison in Chugai's territories (referred to by the parties as the "Sonus License Agreement"). Pursuant to the Sonus License Agreement, Chugai and MBI received non-exclusive rights under certain Sonus patent applications and patents to develop, manufacture, and sell Optison in Chugai's territories. In addition, Chugai agreed to pay Sonus an initial $1 million license fee after the signing of the agreement and a second $1 million license fee (refundable under certain circumstances not relevant here) in June 2001. Chugai and MBI also agreed to pay royalties to Sonus on sales of Optison if and when it was approved for marketing in the Chugai territories. The Sonus License Agreement granted Chugai and MBI license rights under patent applications that Sonus had pending, rather than patents that had issued to Sonus; there was no guarantee that the applications would be granted.

Plaintiffs allege that the Sonus License Agreement was reached well before it was announced on January 16, 2001. Plaintiffs point to a September 13, 2000 letter from Bobba Venkatadri, President and CEO of MBI, to Ted Roth, President and COO of Alliance, informing him that MBI had "reached a handshake agreement for the terms of licensing Sonus patents in Chugai territory." Plaintiffs also note that the licensing agreement itself is dated "as of December 22, 2000."

Nevertheless, both plaintiffs and defendants admit that, as late as December 27 or 28, 2000, there were serious disagreements between the parties to the Sonus license agreement over the terms of the contract. It is undisputed that the possibility of reaching an agreement was threatened when Sonus refused to agree to a covenant not to sue proposed by Chugai; on December 27, 2000, at 10:02 p.m., Michael Martino of Sonus sent an e-mail to Joseph M. Connell, Executive Director of Marketing and Business Development at MBI that attached a "redlined" version of the draft agreement, with Chugai's comments, and that stated: "Given this apparent impasse over an asinine issue and Alliance's last minute comments, I have informed my Board that it is unlikely that this deal will be consummated. Frankly, my strategy is to enjoy the rest of the holiday with my family and reevaluate Sonus' options in the light of the new year."

Despite Martino's email, the parties continued negotiations until at least December 28, 2000. The covenant not to sue was revised as demanded by Sonus and, on December 29, 2000, Chugai faxed Sonus copies of the Sonus License agreement, signed by Chugai. Chugai requested that Sonus sign the agreement and send it to MBI for its signature; Sonus did so the same day.

When Sonus sent the signed agreement to MBI, it stated that it was aware, based on prior discussions, that Alliance had requested language in the agreement giving MBI the right to sublicense the Sonus patents in the event the licensing agreement between Chugai and MBI terminated. Sonus proposed that Sonus and MBI handle the issue in a side letter. MBI then signed a faxed copy of the Sonus License Agreement on December 29, 2000, but conditioned its delivery of the agreement on reaching a side agreement with Sonus. MBI also faxed a letter containing the terms of this side agreement and stating that the agreement was not to be considered delivered unless Sonus countersigned the side letter and returned it to MBI.

On January 2, 2001, Sonus returned the letter, signed, with an added term. Sonus requested that MBI initial the added term and return the letter to Sonus, or revise the letter to reflect the change and send it back to Sonus to be signed again. MBI agreed to the additional term and initialed the proposed change to the letter. Both parties concede that it is not clear from the record exactly when MBI initialed and agreed to the change, but they agree that it must have been some time between January 2, 2001 and January 16, 2001, when Sonus issued a press release announcing that it had entered into the Sonus License Agreement with Chugai and MBI.

. . .

D. Materiality of Alleged Omissions in Alliance's Statements

Plaintiffs allege that defendants violated Section 11 and Section 12(a)(2) by making four statements in the Registration Statement/Prospectus that were false and/or misleading due to material omissions. I consider each of these statements in turn. In evaluating each, I apply the standard . . . [requiring] that in order for an omission to meet the materiality requirement, "there must be a substantial likelihood that the disclosure of the omitted fact would have been viewed by the reasonable investor as having significantly altered the 'total mix' of information made available."

Materiality is a mixed question of law and fact. Only when the omissions are so obviously important or unimportant to a reasonable investor that "reasonable minds cannot differ on the question of materiality" is the issue appropriately resolved as a matter of law by summary judgment.

. . .

4. MBI's Optison Partnerships and Settlement of Patent Litigation

[I]n regard to Optison, plaintiffs allege that defendants failed to disclose the existence or terms of a material agreement between MBI and Sonus, its "only viable competitor in the Asian Countries." Plaintiffs allege that this omission made the statements in the Registration Statement material, because the Registration statement "painted a gloomy picture of Chugai's interest in developing Optison, and emphasized the risks of patent litigation." Specifically, the Registration Statement, under "Risk Factors" of MBI, stated:

> MBI HAS LIMITED CONTROL OVER ITS MARKETING PARTNERS AND THEIR ABILITY TO PRODUCE ROYALTY INCOME FOR MBI. MBI does not manufacture products and does not have and does not intend to develop its own marketing organization. MBI relies instead on its corporate partners to manufacture, market, and sell Optison. . . . Chugai has exclusive distribution rights for Optison in Japan, Taiwan and South Korea. [Chugai has] complete control over all aspects of product development, manufacturing and marketing of Optison in [its] territories. Therefore, MBI is dependent on [Chugai's] product development, regulatory and manufacturing capabilities, marketing efforts, resources and commitment to Optison. . . . Chugai may not market the licensed products effectively or at all. If MBI's partners were not able to alter Optison or their manufacturing processes to avoid conflicts with third-party patents, they would have to terminate the commercialization of Optison or pay royalties to the holders of the patents. Patent litigation can be very expensive and the result uncertain. MBI may not have the financial resources to resolve additional patent conflicts.

In addition, patent conflicts may cause Mallinckrodt [MBI's sales agent for the United States and Europe] or Chugai to divert resources away from developing and marketing Optison.

Plaintiffs contend that the "list of horribles" quoted above was false and misleading because defendants failed to disclose: "(a) that MBI cleared the way for the sale of Optison in the Far East Territories by entering into the Sonus Agreement; and (b) Chugai had demonstrated its continued commitment to development [sic] and market Optison by making two million dollar non-refundable license payments plus royalties to Sonus to develop and market Optison in the Far Eastern Territories."

Defendants respond to this allegation by arguing that: "Alliance had no duty to disclose the parties' discussions and negotiations regarding the Sonus License Agreement prior to the time that MBI consummated the agreement in early January 2001." But it is clear that the law does not require that a contract be finalized in order for it to be material. In *SEC v. Texas Gulf Sulphur Co.*, the Second Circuit held that material facts include those that "affect the probable future of the company and [that] may affect the desire of investors to buy, sell, or hold the company's securities." 401 F.2d 833, 849 (2d Cir. 1968) (en banc). An event need not be finalized to be material. "When contingent or speculative events are at issue, the materiality of those events depends on 'a balancing of both the indicated probability that the event will occur and the anticipated magnitude of the event in light of the totality of the company activity.'" So the fact that the Sonus License agreement was not finalized until early January 2001 is not, as defendants claim, "fatal" to plaintiffs' case.

Defendants argue in the alternative that, even if the Sonus License Agreement had existed as of the relevant date, the statement above was not rendered misleading because of the agreement. Defendants assert that there is no evidence in the record that, as a result of the agreement, (1) "MBI did not rely on its product partners with respect to Optison," (2) "there was any guarantee that [its product partners] would market Optison effectively," or (3) "there was not the possibility of future patent disputes regarding Optison." Defendants correctly observe that there is no evidence in the record of these facts or any other facts that would make the statement overtly false. Nevertheless, plaintiffs have raised a genuine issue of material fact as to whether the above statement was rendered misleading by the Sonus deal.

I agree with defendants' contention that plaintiffs overstate their case by referring to the warnings as a "parade of horribles." But defendants did provide relatively detailed information in the Prospectus about the relationship between MBI and Chugai, the hurdles faced by Chugai, and the threat of patent litigation. In light of the fact that MBI and Mallinckrodt had settled claims in May 2000 brought by Sonus and Nycomed Amersham plc for patent infringement based on MBI's sales of Optison in the United States and Europe, a reasonable investor could have been concerned, based in part on the statement above, that sales of Optison were threatened by the possibility that Sonus would bring a claim for patent infringement in other territories. While the Sonus License agreement did not forestall the possibility of all patent litigation regarding Optison in the Chugai territories, it did address the threat of a competitor with a known interest in bringing claims. And while receipt of any money under the agreement was conditioned on the successful completion of Sonus's pending patent applications, the fact that Chugai agreed to pay Sonus at least one million dollars before the patents were approved could suggest to a reasonable fact finder that the benefits conferred in the deal were valuable, even though Sonus could not guarantee successful marketing of Optison. Furthermore, a reasonable fact finder might conclude that the fact that Chugai had agreed to invest one to two million dollars in an effort to advance the marketing of Optison could render the statement that "Chugai may not market the licensed products effectively or at all" materially misleading.

There is no evidence in the record that negotiation of the Sonus License Agreement began before November 29, 2000, so there is no genuine issue of material fact as to (1) whether the balancing of the probability and the anticipated magnitude of the event weighs in favor of materiality; or (2) whether the statement was false or misleading at the time the Registration Statement became effective. There is thus no factual basis in the record before me for a Section 11 claim. I thus dismiss this claim.

But plaintiffs have raised a genuine issue of material fact as to whether, at some point before January 3, 2001, (1) the balancing of the probability and the anticipated magnitude of the event weighs in favor of materiality; and (2) the fact of the advanced negotiations of the Sonus License Agreement made the statement in the Prospectus about Chugai and the threat of patent infringement materially misleading. A reasonable investor might have found that the Sonus License Agreement significantly altered the total mix of information made available. The omission of this information is not so obviously unimportant to a reasonable shareholder that reasonable minds cannot differ on the question of materiality. Summary judgment is thus inappropriate as to plaintiffs' claim under Section 12(a)(2) based on this statement.

BURSTEIN v. APPLIED EXTRUSION TECHNOLOGIES, INC

United States District Court for the District of Massachusetts
150 F.R.D. 433 (1999)

COLLINGS, United States Magistrate Judge.

I. INTRODUCTION

Plaintiffs Richard I. Burstein ("Burstein") and David A. Bamel ("Bamel") have instituted the instant action on their own behalf and as representatives of a purported class against defendant Applied Extrusion Technologies, Inc. ("AET") and twelve individual defendants, each of whom was either a member of the Board of Directors of AET and/or served as a principal executive officer of that company during the relevant period. In their six-count consolidated and amended class action complaint, Burstein and Bamel allege that the defendants have violated the following federal securities laws: §§ 11 and 15 of the Securities Act of 1933, 15 U.S.C. §§ 77k and 77o (Count I); § 12(2) of the 1933 Act, 15 U.S.C. § 77l(2) (Count II); 10(b) of the Securities Exchange Act of 1934 and Rule

10b-5 promulgated thereunder, 15 U.S.C. § 78j(b) (Count III); and § 20(a) of the Exchange Act, 15 U.S.C. § 78t(a) (Count IV). Further it is alleged that the defendants are liable under state law for violation of Massachusetts General Laws Chapter 93A (Count V) and negligent misrepresentation (Count VI).

Pursuant to Rules 12(b)(6) and 9(b), Fed.R.Civ.P., the AET defendants have moved to dismiss the plaintiffs' amended and consolidated complaint in its entirety. The issues raised by the defendants' motion have been fully briefed, and oral argument was heard on June 30, 1993. With the record now complete, the defendants' disposition motion is in a posture for decision.

It is axiomatic that in the context of a motion to dismiss, the focus is upon the sufficiency of the complaint. The facts as alleged are accepted as true, and all reasonable inferences arising therefrom are viewed in a light favorable to the plaintiffs. In support of their claims, Burstein and Bamel allege the following facts in their amended and consolidated complaint.

Plaintiff Burstein is an individual who purchased two hundred (200) shares of the common stock of AET in an initial public offering of the company stock. Plaintiff Bamel is an individual who purchased varying numbers of shares of the common stock of AET on four different dates: three thousand (3,000) shares on August 1, 1991; two thousand (2,000) shares on August 14, 1991; fifteen hundred (1,500) shares on September 19, 1991; and fifteen hundred (1,500) shares on November 20, 1991. The prices Bamel paid for the AET common stock ranged from $9.50 per share to $11.50 per share.

AET, a Delaware corporation with a principal place of business in Massachusetts, is a company engaged in the development, manufacture and sales of a wide range of thermoplastic products. In December of 1990, AET paid eighteen million two hundred fifteen thousand dollars ($18,215,000.00), including the assumption of six million five hundred thousand dollars ($6,500,000.00) of debt, in order to acquire the Maynard Plastics Division of Chelsea Industries ("Maynard"). Maynard was described by AET as "one of the two principal manufacturers of monofilament, bioxially-oriented nets in the United States and one of the two domestic competitors for the Company's strong net products." AET had no experience in manufacturing strong nets before acquiring Maynard. Indeed, the Maynard acquisition was intended to complement AET's existing non-net thermoplastic product lines.

In order to extinguish certain corporate debt, including that incurred in acquiring Maynard six months earlier, AET conducted an initial public offering of its common stock pursuant to a Registration Statement and Prospectus dated June 6, 1991. According to the Prospectus, AET's business strategy was

> . . . to address rapidly growing niche markets and offer technologically advanced materials which improve the performance and competitive position of its customers' products. The Company has focused on developing an efficient, cost effective manufacturing process to enable it to supply these markets profitably.

The primary elements of this strategy were the provision of technologically superior products, the penetration of diverse, growing niche markets and the development of highly efficient manufacturing processes. AET considered its success "in part to depend upon its ability to effectively [sic] manage the integration of Maynard Plastics."

. . .

[T]he plaintiffs contend that the Prospectus was false or misleading [in its] suggestion that all the Maynard operation needed to be competitive and profitable was more effective, efficient management when, in reality, the defendants knew, should have known, or recklessly disregarded material facts or circumstances to the contrary. In this regard, the plaintiffs catalogue a variety of factors relating to the integration of Maynard that were purportedly either misstated in, or omitted from, the Prospectus. Inter alia, it is alleged that the Maynard operation had experienced ongoing quality problems with its products that could not be alleviated without major restoration and retooling of the production lines; that the Maynard operation was incapable of producing competitive extruded netting products absent complete disassembly and overhaul of the machinery; that the Maynard operation could not produce the square strong net products necessary to be competitive unless the production lines were revamped with new dies that could produce true square net; that AET would either itself have to develop the requisite die technology or it would have to utilize proprietary technical information wrongfully appropriated from its primary competitor; that the Maynard integration plan relied upon the technical expertise of persons hired by AET who were former employees of its competitor Leucadia, Inc., as well as the use of thousands of documents wrongfully appropriated from Leucadia, Inc. by those employees; that these former Leucadia, Inc. employees were bound by confidentiality agreements not to disclose the technology that AET needed; that absent the ability to utilize the proprietary information and documents from Leucadia, Inc., AET would suffer substantial delay and expense in its effort to make the Maynard lines efficient and competitive.

At the time of the initial public offering, a lawsuit filed by Leucadia, Inc. on November 20, 1990 against AET was pending. The existence of this litigation was disclosed in the Prospectus along with the following details:

> The Company (AET) and Leucadia are the only parties to the action, which seeks injunctive relief and damages based on allegations that the Company has engaged in actual or threatened misappropriation of Leucadia's alleged trade secrets and confidential business information relating to extruded and/or oriented plastic netting products. The Company has answered and counter-claimed, seeking injunctive relief and damages against Leucadia, Inc. for attempted monopolization and abuse of process.

AET further stated that "[m]anagement does not believe that any of these legal proceedings will have a material adverse effect on the financial condition or results of operations of the Company." In the notes to its financial statements, AET again referenced the pending litigation, noting the company's intent "to vigorously [sic] defend this action. At present, the litigation is in the preliminary stages, and management and legal counsel are presently unable to predict the outcome." AET then reiterated its belief that the lawsuit would not have a "material adverse effect" on its financial condition.

The plaintiffs allege that the Prospectus was false and misleading in that it failed to disclose that the Leucadia litigation was likely to have a material adverse effect on the success of the Maynard integration if AET was prohibited from using Leucadia proprietary information and the expertise of its former employees which were necessary to make the Maynard operation effective and profitable. It is further alleged that the defendants knew or recklessly failed to know that their employees had wrongfully misappropriated thousands of proprietary or trade secret documents from Leucadia and, consequently, that the litigation would be resolved on terms onerous to AET.

. . .

III.   THE MOTION TO DISMISS THE CLAIMS UNDER FEDERAL LAW

. . .

B.   Failure to Plead Fraud With Particularity

The defendants contend that the allegations of the consolidated and amended complaint fail to comply with Fed.R.Civ.P. 9(b) which requires that

> In averments of fraud or mistake, the circumstances constituting fraud or mistake shall be stated with particularity. Malice, intent, knowledge and other conditions of the mind of a person may be averred generally.

Rule 9(b), Fed.R.Civ.P.

There can be no doubt that in this Circuit, Rule 9(b) is applied to securities fraud claims with rigor. [*Romani v. Shearson Lehman Hutton,* 929 F.2d 875, 878 (1st Cir. 1991)]; *Royal Business Group Inc. v. Realist, Inc.,* 933 F.2d 1056, 1065-1066 (1st Cir. 1991). Indeed, the First Circuit has stated:

> It is well settled that Rule 9(b) requires the plaintiff in a securities fraud case to specify the time, place and content of an alleged false representation . . . The requirement that supporting facts be pleaded applies even when the fraud relates to matters peculiarly within the knowledge of the opposing party.

Romani v. Shearson Lehman Hutton, supra, 929 F.2d at 878 (citations omitted).

A general averment of knowledge of falsity will not suffice; the complaint must "*also* set( ) forth specific facts that make it reasonable to believe that defendant knew that a statement was materially false or misleading." *Greenstone v. Cambex Corporation,* 975 F.2d 22, 25 (1st Cir. 1992).

1.   The Prospectus

a.   The Integration Claim

The plaintiffs allege that AET knew or recklessly disregarded adverse facts and circumstances relating to the Maynard integration at the time of the initial public offering, but did not disclose them in the Prospectus. As factual support, it is alleged that Maynard had a history of continuing quality problems with its products and was incapable of producing competitive "high quality bioxially oriented monofilament extruded netting products." In order to alleviate these problems, the Maynard lines needed to be completely overhauled and revamped with new dies that could produce true strong net as opposed to diamond net, an inferior product. AET's plan to improve the Maynard production lines was dependent upon utilization of technical research, development and manufacturing expertise of former employees of its primary competitor who were bound by confidentiality agreements not to disclose the technology that AET needed. Further, AET contemplated using thousands of documents containing proprietary information of Leucadia to upgrade the Maynard lines so as to make them operate efficiently and competitively. The technology and proprietary information that AET needed was at the heart of the ongoing trade secrets lawsuit filed against AET by Leucadia. Without access to the Leucadia documents and former personnel, AET would face both significant delay and expense in making the Maynard production lines competitive because the requisite die technology would have to be independently developed.

AET had acquired Maynard six months prior to the initial public offering. It can reasonably be inferred that AET had assessed and evaluated what steps were necessary to make Maynard competitive and profitable. Indeed, the integration process was underway at the time the Prospectus was issued. Moreover, it can also be reasonably inferred that AET knew that it had hired former employees of its major competitor who were alleged to have wrongfully misappropriated thousands of documents containing proprietary technical information. The Leucadia litigation was instituted in November of 1990, approximately seven months before the offering.

There is no apparent dispute that the time, place and content requirements of Rule 9(b) are met with respect to all of the plaintiffs' claims. Moreover, with respect to the integration claim, the additional prerequisite of the rule is satisfied. These factual allegations are neither vague nor conclusory. Rather, they

> . . . would support a reasonable inference that adverse circumstances existed at the time (the statement or representation was made), and were known and deliberately disregarded by the defendants.

Romani v. Shearson Lehman Hutton, supra, 929 F.2d at 878. In short, this claim complies with the particularity requirements of Rule 9(b).

b.   The Litigation

In the Prospectus, AET stated that "[m]anagement does not believe that any of these legal proceedings [the Leucadia litigation] will have a material adverse effect on the financial condition or results of operations of the Company." The plaintiffs essentially claim that this statement was false or misleading in that the defendants knew or recklessly disregarded that the Leucadia litigation was in fact likely to have a material adverse effect on AET's integration plan for Maynard.

The factual allegations in support of this claim are as stated above. Again, the complaint details the inability of the Maynard production lines to produce true strong net products, a factor that substantially caused Maynard's unprofitable status. In order to become competitive, the Maynard operation had to be overhauled and updated, not merely made more efficient. It is specifically alleged that

> As defendants knew or were reckless in not knowing, AET was incapable of revamping the Maynard production lines with new dies that could produce true square net unless it utilized proprietary technical documents being made available to it by its newly-hired employees, who had wrongfully appropriated those documents from Leucadia, or unless and until AET was able to develop independently the die technology needed to make competitive square net products.

The Leucadia trade secrets action against AET had been ongoing for seven months at the time of the initial public offering, and it is alleged that the defendants had reason to know that the documents would have to be returned to Leucadia, that Leucadia had substantial grounds for seeking preliminary injunctive relief, and that these circumstances would cause expense and delay in the integration plan.

It is further alleged that the Leucadia litigation was settled in August of 1991, two months after the offering. The settlement terms included agreements by AET to return thousands of documents to Leucadia, to refrain from inducing former Leucadia employees from divulging proprietary or trade secret information and to refrain from using or developing any annular reciprocating piston or striker die process for a period of three years.

In challenging this claim, the defendants first take the position that as a matter of law they were under no duty to disclose corporate misconduct associated with the Leucadia litigation in the Prospectus. The case of *Roeder v. Alpha Industries, Inc.,* 814 F.2d 22 (1st Cir. 1987) is cited in support of this legal proposition. In *Roeder,* an investor alleged that the company in which he owned stock failed to disclose timely certain criminal activity by an officer of the corporation. Although the company knew of the bribery and the ongoing criminal investigation, the information was not announced until indictments appeared imminent. Affirming the district court's dismissal of the complaint, the First Circuit confirmed that a corporation is under no affirmative duty "to disclose all material information even if there is no insider trading, no statute or regulation requiring disclosure, and no inaccurate, incomplete or misleading prior disclosures." *Roeder v. Alpha Industries, Inc., supra,* 814 F.2d at 27.

The defendants argue that, because they complied with SEC reporting regulations in the Prospectus and there is no insider trading alleged, they had no further disclosure obligation. However, AET did more than describe the pending Leucadia litigation in the Prospectus. A further, affirmative statement was made that management did not believe the lawsuit would have a material, adverse effect on the operation of the company. The plaintiffs specifically allege that this statement was false and misleading. This fact distinguishes the present complaint from that in the *Roeder* case where no inaccurate or misleading voluntary disclosure was identified. *Roeder v. Alpha Industries, Inc., supra,* 814 F.2d at 26.

The *Roeder* court noted that

> When a corporation does make a disclosure — whether it be voluntary or required — there is a duty to make it complete and accurate. . . . "If

> . . . a company chooses to reveal relevant, material information even
> though it had no duty to do so, it must disclose the whole truth."

Roeder v. Alpha Industries, Inc., supra, 814 F.2d at 26 (citations omitted).

The plaintiffs have alleged sufficient facts to support a reasonable inference that the Leucadia lawsuit would have a material impact upon the Maynard integration. Having voluntarily chosen to make a positive statement with respect to the litigation, the defendants had a duty to make that disclosure "accurate and complete."

The defendants next argue that the decision in *Greenstone v. Cambex Corporation,* 975 F.2d 22 (1 Cir. 1992) is on all fours and thus clearly dispositive of the plaintiffs' claim. In *Greenstone,* an investor instituted a securities fraud claim against Cambex Corporation alleging that ". . . Cambex's financial statements, though literally true, were 'misleading' in 'light of the circumstances under which they were made,' for they failed to disclose Cambex's potential liability to IBM lessors." The Court determined that the complaint alleged "fraud by hindsight" and affirmed the dismissal of the action.

The facts in *Greenstone* can readily be distinguished in key respects from those alleged in the present complaint. At the outset, the lawsuit in the *Greenstone* case was filed after the allegedly misleading financial statements were released. The First Circuit pointed out that "[t]he bringing of the lawsuit tends to show its earlier likelihood. And, the existence of that likelihood helps support (in an evidentiary sense) an inference that defendants knew about that likelihood." *Greenstone v. Cambex Corporation, supra,* 975 F.2d at 26. Not only is it alleged in the instant complaint that the Leucadia lawsuit had been pending for seven months at the time of the initial offering, the subject matter and circumstances of Leucadia's claims are detailed. Leucadia's lawsuit is described as a trade secrets action seeking injunctive relief. It is alleged that AET had hired former employees of Leucadia and that the defendants knew or recklessly failed to know that those employees had wrongfully appropriated thousands of proprietary or trade secret documents from Leucadia. It was further alleged that AET was relying on the Leucadia proprietary information and the technical expertise of the former Leucadia employees in order to succeed in the Maynard integration. On these facts, it is reasonable to infer, as alleged, that it was "virtually impossible for AET to avoid the Leucadia litigation being resolved on terms onerous to AET." Accepting the plaintiffs' allegations as true, AET's potential liability was clear.

As in the *Greenstone* case, the plaintiffs herein allege that the Leucadia litigation was settled shortly, i.e., within two months, after the Prospectus issued. Moreover, the terms of the settlement, as alleged, were not favorable to AET. The First Circuit was of the view that such allegations help the plaintiffs, stating that the investor

> . . . can reasonably argue that it helps to support a chain of inferences:
> 1) that the suit was valid, 2) that its underlying assertion . . . was true,
> 3) that [the defendant] must have known this earlier, and 4) that [the
> defendant] therefore must have known earlier that a lawsuit (or the
> equivalent) was probable.

Greenstone v. Cambex Corporation, supra, 975 F.2d at 26-27.

True, the Court determined that "this single, factual cornerstone," was not enough to carry the day in *Greenstone*. However, added to the additional facts and circumstances alleged in the complaint at hand, the plaintiffs' litigation claim passes the Rule 9(b) hurdle.

NOTES & QUESTIONS

1. Disclosures in a prospectus or other company documents regarding intellectual property strengths or weaknesses may figure in claims against parties other than the company making the disclosures. For example, where a customer sued a brokerage firm asserting that she was improperly induced to hold previously purchased stock by a constant flow of favorable but untrue and misleading information from brokers at the firm, the contents of a prospectus provided to the shareholder by the brokers was deemed sufficient to put the shareholder on notice of certain patent infringement risks facing the company in which the customer held stock. *See Parsons v. Hornblower & Weeks-Hemphill*, 447 F. Supp. 482 (M.D.N.C. 1977). The district court in this case found that the following discussion in the company's prospectus adequately addressed the uncertain patent position of the corporation involved:

RISK FACTORS

10. Although the Company has filed a number of patent applications pertaining to various aspects of the CARTRIVISION system, it does not expect to obtain fundamental patent protection for the basic concept or design of its system. No assurance can be given that patent infringement claims will not be asserted which may adversely affect the Company or that any valid patent protection will be obtained by the Company. The Company may be required to obtain patent licenses in order to produce and market the CARTRIVISION system, but no assurance can be given that such licenses can be obtained.

HISTORY AND BUSINESS

Patents and Trademarks

There can, however, be no assurance that patents will issue on the Company's patent applications or on any application it files in the future or that patents issued to the Company will be enforceable, if litigated, nor does the Company believe that it has established a unique proprietary position.

Messrs. Townsend and Townsend do not know of any clearly valid adversary United States patents which can successfully be asserted against the Company's presently proposed recorder-playback unit and cartridge, although the prior art in the field discloses a number of patents which relate in varying degrees to the CARTRIVISION system and adversary claims could be made at any time by competitors of the Company.

A United States patent relating to a type of frequency modulation recording has been called to the Company's attention by a substantial United States patent owner in view of the proposed use of frequency modulation recording in the CARTRIVISION system. The validity of this patent has never been adjudicated.

Id. at 492.

2. Fast moving technological or business developments may rapidly reveal that earlier disclosures in a prospectus of a high tech company are inaccurate. For example, newly discovered prior art may call into question the validity of patents that were emphasized in prior disclosures as a basis for a key business initiative. Or product announcements of a competitor based on patented improvements which cannot be added to a company's own products may undercut the projected business value of a new line of business described in glowing terms in an initial disclosure. When should disclosures that were apparently accurate when made be required to be revised based on new information which indicates that the original disclosure, standing alone, may be materially misleading? Does the degree of any applicable duty to update prior disclosures depend on the scope of the positive statements made in the initial disclosures, with a broad set of disclosures aiding a company's efforts to raise funds implying an equally broad obligation to monitor the ongoing accuracy of the statements made and to correct those found to be inaccurate upon receipt of further information?

3. When are "boiler plate" provisions describing a company's potential intellectual property problems in general terms adequate to inform shareholders about the ongoing business risks associated with those problems and to preclude the shareholders from successfully claiming to have been mislead about the absence of the risks? For example, assume that a publishing company includes in its prospectus a general statement that its published works may inadvertently incorporate works that are copyrighted by other parties, thereby raising a risk of copyright infringement liability for the concern. Once the management of the company realizes that a particular book that it has published includes work plagiarized from another work and that the author of the other work is threatening to institute a major copyright infringement action, will the earlier notice to shareholders of the possibility of this type of suit and liability be a sufficient disclosure? Should it matter whether the author with the possible claim has filed suit as yet or whether management feels that the copyright claims, if filed, are likely to result in liability for the publisher? What probability or amount of copyright infringement liability should raise a need for further disclosures to shareholders?

CHAPTER 11

ADVANCED TECHNIQUES FOR MAXIMIZING INTELLECTUAL PROPERTY VALUE IN MATURE COMPANIES

PROBLEM

Digital Ignition has successfully developed and marketed automobile ignition products for twenty years. Company engineers have pursued an effective research program, with the result that the company has obtained a regular stream of new patents on advances in computer-controlled automobile ignition systems. Many of these patents protect commercially significant features of the company's products. However, some of the patents address technologies which have not proven useful in the company's products so far, but which may still be the basis for marketable products manufactured by Digital Ignition or other companies.

Recognizing that a balance between innovation, manufacturing, and marketing activities, as well as the full commercial use of the company's intellectual property, is important to Digital Ignition's continued success, the company has hired Duane Sawyer, an experienced computer industry executive, to serve as Digital Ignition's new Vice President of Technology Development. As one of his first tasks, Sawyer has been asked by Digital Ignition's Chief Executive Officer to undertake a broadly focused review of how the company is developing new technologies and utilizing those technologies to the company's commercial advantage.

This study will address not only the means whereby Digital Ignition allocates resources to the development and acquisition of new technologies (including how it obtains the rights to use such technologies), but also the steps the company takes to commercialize intellectual property and related rights which are generated in Digital Ignition's research programs. The aim of this review will be to suggest new ways that the company can maximize the value of its investments in technology development and the value of intellectual property resulting from these development efforts.

Broad ranges of potential business strategies are to be considered in the upcoming study, including Digital Ignition's decision-making processes for allocating resources between innovative (e.g., technology development) and non-innovative (e.g., product marketing) expenditures, the company's means for identifying new technologies that will be developed internally rather than being acquired from other sources, strategies for realizing the value of intellectual property rights beyond the simple marketing of related products and the licensing of others to do the same, and the circumstances, if any, in which the low cost licensing or relinquishment of the company's intellectual property rights to further research by others will aid Digital Ignition's ultimate commercial interests.

Questions about the best ways to protect Digital Ignition's intellectual property rights as research goes forward and about how to use those rights in marketing the company's existing products (including the types of issues addressed in Chapter 1), are not the focus of the new study. Digital Ignition's senior executives are convinced that careful attention to these matters over the years has produced generally effective intellectual property protection and product marketing practices for the company. Rather, top management is looking for new ideas about means that a well established, well organized, and well funded technology innovator such as Digital Ignition can use to focus its resources effectively on technology development and then use the resulting new technologies and intellectual property rights to the best advantage of the corporation.

Duane Sawyer is embarking on the first stages of this study. He has contacted your law firm — an experienced intellectual property firm that Sawyer worked with repeatedly in his former capacity as a computer industry executive — for ideas about the types of intellectual property development and administration strategies that he should consider and analyze in the course of his study. Sawyer wants your firm to develop a listing of new business management strategies that a company like Digital Ignition might use to improve its technology development and intellectual property administration. The listing should include brief descriptions of the benefits that are likely to be achieved through each of the new strategies, the risks or other detrimental features associated with each strategy, and the basic changes in business practices needed to implement each strategy.

Using this information, Sawyer will work with the company's executives and managers to determine which of the potential strategies will be beneficial to Digital Ignition as well as how to best implement those strategies within the company's existing operations. Because the implementation advantages and methods will be worked out later by corporate insiders having the relevant operating information, your firm need not worry about the detailed features of Digital Ignition's operations, but should rather focus on techniques and strategies that have a significant potential for success in firms like Digital Ignition.

Please provide Sawyer with an overview of advanced organizational management strategies that may aid Digital Ignition in making effective decisions about developing new intellectual property and maximizing the value of rights associated with that property.

FOCUS OF THE CHAPTER

The readings in this chapter describe a number of corporate management strategies that can aid an organization in improving technology development decisions and the organization's use of related intellectual property.

The first several readings address ways that corporations and other organizations can structure operations and related decision making processes to

FOCUS OF THE CHAPTER

improve their development and use of intellectual property. The initial reading by Professor George G. Triantis describes how operating a corporation in a multi-divisional structure or other similar arrangement can be used to clarify resource allocation decisions and improve the effectiveness of resource allocations to technology development.

The second reading by Professor Dan Burk explains how choices by corporate managers about whether to "make or buy" corporate resources (such as decisions about whether to develop a new technology internally or to acquire such a technology from outside sources) define the scope of internal corporate activities and are influenced by the nature of intellectual property rights. The third reading by Professor David McGowan describes how a combination of intellectual property rights and carefully crafted contractual licenses can be used to promote a multi-party, highly distributed effort to develop a new technology — in this case, the open source movement advancing the development of certain computer software systems.

The next several readings focus on tactical measures that an organization can use to increase the value of its intellectual property interests. The first of these readings describes a particular financing technique — intellectual property securitization in which royalties from intellectual property licenses are used to pay interest on related bonds — that has been used in a number of fields to realize immediate financial returns from intellectual property interests having proven value and royalty potential. The next reading analyzes the use of intellectual property enforcement insurance as a means to bolster the enforcement of intellectual property rights and to ensure that owners gain the full value of these interests. The *Jumpsport* case included at this point describes some of the reasons why firms may seek this type of insurance, as well as some of the problems (such as the creation of potentially discoverable, unprivileged self-studies of the insurance applicants) that companies may face in obtaining intellectual property enforcement insurance.

The next reading, focusing on the Supreme Court's decision in the *Tasini* case, examines the special problems that companies may encounter as long term users of intellectual property. Attempts to commercialize intellectual property over extended periods may raise unexpected problems as modes of use of such property and means of distribution change drastically. For example, the *Tasini* case involved content distribution problems encountered by the New York Times as it attempted to capitalize on new, computer-based services and products involving online databases and CD-ROMs. The article which follows the *Tasini* case describes how some corporations have responded to the problems raised by changing, partially unknown needs for future intellectual property use.

The last three readings in this chapter focus on potentially valuable dispositions of intellectual property. The particular dispositions explored here include auctions of intellectual property (either by intellectual property owners who are voluntarily shedding interests that they do not expect to use in their future business activities or by bankruptcy trustees who are seeking to realize the maximum sales price for intellectual property assets of bankrupt companies), contributions of intellectual property interests to charitable organizations to gain tax deductions, and low cost licensing or releases of intellectual property interests in order to spur technology development by other parties — such as open source software developers — whose efforts are expected to benefit the intellectual property owner at a later point.

READINGS

A. ALLOCATING BUSINESS RESOURCES TO INNOVATION

1. Multi-Divisional Corporations as Internal Capital Markets

Corporations adopting multi-divisional organizational structures or other arrangements facilitating shifts in resources to back various types of profit making activities can implement internal capital markets regarding the use of corporate resources. Allocations of limited operating resources to activities within portions of such companies are equivalents of capital investments by shareholders in smaller companies. By establishing competition among corporate subunits for additional corporate funds, these arrangements tend to allocate corporate resources to future projects — innovative or non-innovative — that promise the greatest returns on investments.

Because they have private information about the capabilities of corporate operating subunits and the probable value of particular new activities undertaken in the context of other corporate business operations, corporate managers allocating resources within internal capital allocation arrangements can often achieve greater returns on investments than their external counterparts. In the particular context of decisions about whether to back the development of new intellectual property, firms that use internal information to tailor the scope and timing of backing for innovative activities can maximize the value of their intellectual property by reducing costs of producing intellectual property and increasing the range of commercial applications for such property.

Internal capital markets can be means for firms to allocate resources between innovative and non-innovative profit-making activities. For example, a corporation may choose to allocate $1,000,000 to the development of new products or to the enhancement of marketing efforts for existing products, whichever is predicted to produce the most additional corporate profits per dollar spent. Similarly, within the range of available innovation efforts, corporate decision processes implementing internal capital markets can evaluate backing for alternative innovation efforts based on their perceived profit potential. In comparisons of innovative with non-innovative activities, as well as comparisons of the relative merit of different types of innovative activities, intellectual property protections and related projections of exclusive commercial opportunities are important means of clarifying the probable value of potential courses of action.

The following reading describes how large corporate organizations implement internal capital markets and the reasons why resulting investments of resources can be more profitable than equivalent investments by persons outside such organizations. While the focus of this reading is on investments in corporate activities generally rather than on allocations of corporate resources to innovative activities in particular, the principles discussed here apply to decisions about investments in innovative activities, explaining why large organizations such as major corporations can sometimes be especially efficient allocators of investments in the development of new intellectual property.

George G. Triantis, Organizations as Internal Capital Markets: The Legal Boundaries of Firms, Collateral, and Trusts in Commercial and Charitable Enterprises
117 Harv. L. Rev. 1102, 1105, 1109-15 (2004)*

. . .

[T]his Article presents a distinct . . . explanation of the legal boundaries of organizations. These boundaries define internal capital markets within which resources may be readily redeployed, but across which redeployment may occur only at some cost. Internal capital markets permit capital to move between projects; in the language of real options, they enhance the value of "switching options," or the ability to delay a capital allocation decision until more information becomes available. The distinction between external and internal capital markets is that capital moves between projects by contract in the former case and by authority or fiat in the latter. A corporate manager might finance a new venture by contracting with outside investors (external) or by shifting resources from an existing project within the firm (internal). For example, capital is redeployed through external markets when one firm distributes some of its assets to investors and another firm sells securities to those investors, or when two separate firms contract with each other to move capital between projects managed by each firm. If instead the two projects were contained in an internal capital market, the new project might be financed by diverting cash flow from the existing project, by liquidating some of that project's assets, or by borrowing against those assets.

Internal capital enables a firm to avoid the information asymmetry between a firm's managers and outside investors, or between two firms, that may impede or may raise the cost of external finance. Internal capital thereby reduces the cost of switching capital allocations and increases investment flexibility. There is a tradeoff, however, between this gain and the agency costs of having this flexibility managed by an agent who can exploit her private information for her own benefit. A manager may reallocate capital within internal markets to maximize her private benefits rather than firm value, and she may use her informational advantage to conceal from investors the shift in resources or its impact on firm value.

. . .

An internal capital market permits the reallocation of capital between projects at a lower cost than through external capital markets because project managers possess expertise and private information that cannot be efficiently communicated to outside investors. Managers of internal capital markets are

---

informed but self-interested agents. The internal capital markets thesis of organizational boundaries may be framed as addressing a balance between the benefits and the costs of leaving investment switching options in the hands of agents. Therefore, three factors define the optimal size (or boundaries) of an internal capital market: the value of the flexibility to adjust over time the allocation of capital among available projects, the value added by a competent and informed agent who manages that flexibility, and the incentive conflicts resulting from the agent's control over that flexibility.

Investment flexibility can be framed in terms of real options. In this context, a real option is the ability to adjust an investment decision when better information is obtained. In the realm of capital budgeting, real options include the ability to defer, abandon, accelerate, or decelerate projects. The ability to reallocate capital between projects may be viewed as a switching option — that is, the abandonment or deceleration of one project and the initiation, continuation, or acceleration of another project. For example, suppose an investor initially funds two ventures, V1 and V2, based on incomplete information. When new information is subsequently revealed, the investment mix may be changed, albeit at some cost. This switching option — the ability to adjust the investment mix with the benefit of new information — is valuable because the option will be exercised only if the reallocation of capital between the two projects increases the aggregate return. One might similarly view the ability to divert cash flow from one project to another as a switching option by presuming that the cash flow is reinvested in the source project unless the option to switch is exercised.

Real options analysis offers several important insights. First, the value of the switching option is a function of the correlation between the payoff distributions of the two projects. The less positively correlated and the more negatively correlated the distributions, the more valuable the option to switch between projects.

Second, a switching option is valuable and often worth incurring some cost to create and preserve. Suppose that the return from V1 is initially expected to exceed the return from V2. It may nevertheless be advisable to invest enough in V2 to keep alive the option of later engaging more fully in V2 by moving capital from V1, especially if the distributions of returns from the two projects are negatively correlated. The more valuable the option, the greater the return from investments to create and preserve it. Therefore, to the degree that internal capital markets increase the value of switching options, they also encourage the creation of such options.

Third, the value of an option depends on the proper timing of its exercise. Switching between projects is costly. Therefore, even when new information about the relative returns on the two projects justifies the partial liquidation of the first and the shifting of capital to the second, switching should be deferred until further information confirms the superior returns of the second project. As a general proposition, the costly exercise of an option should be deferred until the option matures; accordingly, the value of an option typically depends on the time until maturity. Several factors, however, may accelerate the optimal timing of the decision to switch: in particular, the costs of switching may increase over time if the salvage values of assets in the source project deteriorate, and the value of switching to the second project may be compromised by delay if competitors can enter the product market in the meantime.

If reallocation occurs through external capital markets, an organization must distribute capital from one project (perhaps from cash flow or partial liquidation of the project) to investors, who must then finance a second project in another organization. Alternatively, capital may move directly between firms without passing through the hands of investors, such as through inter-firm loans.

Reallocation through internal capital markets may occur by any of the following means. First, the cash flow from one project may be diverted to fund another. Second, assets of one project may be sold and the proceeds transferred to another project. Third, the firm may implicitly borrow against the assets of one project to finance another venture whenever liability is incurred by the organization as a whole, because all of its assets are available to satisfy the creditor. Indeed, the firm may enhance its cross-financing option by giving the new creditor a security interest — and therefore priority — in the assets of the first project, even though the loan proceeds fund the second project. Fourth, two projects may share common expenses, such as administrative overhead, and an organization can shift capital between projects by changing the portion of organizational overhead allocated to each project. Fifth, the projects may trade goods or services with each other at internally determined rates. As explained later in this Article, organizations are not required by law to use market or arm's-length prices for such transfers, and managers can reallocate capital between projects by selecting exchange terms in favor of one or the other project.

The advantage of an internal capital market is that it facilitates the delegation of control over switching options from investors to managers, who have superior expertise and access to information regarding available projects. The value of a switching option depends on the competence of decision-making with respect to the creation, preservation, and exercise of the option. The competence of such decision-making in turn relies on the quality of information about factors that affect the distribution of the projects' future payoffs — factors such as projected costs, revenues, technology, and competitors. A significant portion of this information may be unobservable or "soft," in the sense of being difficult to communicate to investors. The decisions of investors initially to determine the distribution of capital and subsequently to reinvest it are impaired by their inferior information about the expected returns from each project and the obstacles to effective disclosure by project managers (for example, the cost of revealing information to competitors or even government regulators). The greater the asymmetry of information and expertise between managers and investors, the greater the potential contribution by managers and the more significant the potential gain from an internal capital market. A similar information asymmetry also impedes the direct movement of capital from one firm to another (without passing through the hands of investors). Indeed, such obstacles to contracting between firms are compounded by the agency problems existing between each firm and its investors. Options that are effectively managed in this respect are more valuable, and accordingly, investors are more willing to invest ex ante to create and preserve such options. Specifically, investors are more likely to create an option to switch from V1 to V2 by investing a small amount in V2 if the option will be exercised subsequently by a competent manager.

. . .

The value of a switching option in the hands of an agent is impaired by incentive conflicts. In particular, an agent may switch (or abstain from switching) capital allocations in order to maximize her private benefits rather than the aggregate return to the enterprise. Managers enjoy private benefits that are not shared by other investors because of their control over decision-making. These benefits typically include opportunities to self-deal, build empires, entrench positions, enhance professional reputations, and consume perquisites. Whether managerial pursuit of private benefits conflicts with the interests of investors in the exercise of shifting options depends on the type of private benefit in question. Compare the following three examples. First, empire building is unlikely to skew switching incentives because, for any given firm size, a manager wants to maximize profitability. Second, private benefits from entrenchment or shirking may lead to suboptimal switching activity; some studies, for instance, find that managers are reluctant to abandon losing projects. Third, private benefits from social prestige or investment in portable human capital may respond to social fads and thereby induce excessive switching and overinvestment in the creation of options.

There is a range of well-known mechanisms that restrain the extraction of private benefits to some degree. If investors receive low payoffs at the end of one period, they will be reluctant to make new investments with the same manager in future periods. Therefore, managers may forego private benefits in the current period to raise the likelihood that the enterprise will continue. Tax authorities might also provide some discipline. Stockholders have legal rights to enforce the duties of loyalty owed by managers to the corporation. Shareholders can also vote to replace directors and thereby remove misbehaving managers, and in many cases, they can veto extraordinary decisions. Debtholders (and less frequently, stockholders) can seek to control by contract the appropriation of private benefits.

The ability of shareholders and debtholders to monitor managerial misbehavior is impaired by the fact that the information necessary to detect opportunistic switching is frequently not verifiable, even if observable. The suspect reallocation itself may be subtle and not apparent to the investor. For example, there may be little evidence that cash is commingled, that administrative burdens are shifted between projects, or that transfers occur between ventures at prices at odds with arm's-length terms. Indeed, the very expertise and informational advantage that investors wish to exploit in assigning to their managers the task of reallocating capital over time also undermine the ability of investors to monitor and discipline their managers' self-interested exercise of discretion. Incentive-based compensation such as stock ownership may align managerial incentives with those of their principals, but only at the cost of imposing risk on the managers and inducing risk-averse decision-making. Thus, even in the aggregate, these various constraints on the extraction of private benefits are not completely effective and leave residual agency conflicts. As such, internal capital markets may yield inefficient reallocation of capital and a consequent reduction in the value of investor interests. In these cases, investors may seek to control the switching authority of their managers.

Investors are unlikely to be able to specify ex ante optimal switching strategies because information asymmetries prevent investors from observing or verifying the efficiency of reallocations. Therefore, investors may instead seek to control ex ante the ability of their managers to move capital among projects, whether or not switching would be efficient. If managerial bias is against switching, investors may wish to compel periodic review of the allocation of capital, and . . . they may delegate the review to intermediaries. For example, investors may fund projects in stages or through short-term debt contracts that must be refinanced periodically. Conversely, if managers are prone to make inefficient reallocations, investors may seek to encumber their managers' discretion to switch by constraining the internal capital market.

. . .

B.   Decisions to "Make or Buy" New Intellectual Property

Where a company or organization is interested in producing new products or adopting new operating methods, intellectual property protections may influence whether the company seeks to develop a new advance internally or to acquire rights to a similar advance from an outside source. This choice is the equivalent in a product development context of decisions faced by organizations in other contexts about whether to "make or buy" needed resources. The results of these "make or buy" decisions define the scope of corporate activities: items sought to be produced internally imply a related range of corporate activities, while items sought to be acquired from outside imply only sets of acquisition activities by corporations in a variety of relevant markets.

A branch of economic analyses revolving around Ronald Coase's "Theory of the Firm" holds that these "make or buy" decisions about the proper scope of internal organizational activities will tend to be made in order to minimize the transaction costs associated with accomplishing some organizational task. Coase's conclusions about the scope of activities assumed by organizations reflect the following propositions:

> (1) the choice between firm and market organization is neither given, nor largely determined, by technology, but mainly reflects efforts to economize on transaction costs; (2) the study of transaction costs is preeminently a comparative institutional undertaking; and (3) this very same comparative approach in which microanalytic features are brought under scrutiny applies not merely to firm and market organization but also generalizes to the study of externalities, regulation, and other forms of complex economic organization.

Oliver E. Williamson, *Book Review,* 77 Cal. L. Rev. 223, 223-24 (1989) (reviewing R. H. Coase, THE FIRM, THE MARKET, AND THE LAW (1988)).

The theory of the firm explored by Coase has been seen by some analysts as a useful tool for assessing the scope of innovative activities maintained internally by large corporations having sufficient resources to be able to choose whether to produce or acquire new technologies. These analysts use the theory of the firm to interpret the impact of intellectual property protections on corporate and other organizational decision making. As noted by one observer:

> Intellectual property law is [a] field where the theory of the firm is beginning to make inroads. One important observation is that intellectual property is sometimes a substitute for vertical integration. In other words, a stronger intellectual property regime makes it profitable to move transactions to the market rather than keep them within the firm. Outsourcing research has been made easier by stronger patent rights. Research and invention make difficult subject matter for contract because unforeseen research developments are common, and the output of a research project is difficult to describe. Patents give rights to the patent owner that act as a substitute for usage terms that otherwise would have to be specified in a contract.

Michael J. Meurer, *Law, Economics, and the Theory of the Firm,* 52 BUFF. L. REV. 727, 746-47 (2004).

––––––––––

In the following reading, Professor Dan L. Burk extends this analysis further, contending that the theory of the firm should be a fundamental starting point for interpreting the proper scope of intellectual property rights so as to minimize transaction costs and facilitate efficient decisions by organizational personnel about means to develop and acquire innovative technologies.

Dan L. Burk, Intellectual Property and the Firm
71 U. Chi. L. Rev. 3 (2004)*

Since its articulation by Ronald Coase, the economic theory of the firm has generated an enormous body of literature in corporate law and related fields. That literature has become increasingly dominated by property-based theories of the firm that consider the allocation and disposition of institutional assets. Given this influence and direction, it is curious that the theory of the firm has received relatively little attention in intellectual property scholarship. In a so-called information age, where the most important assets of firms increasingly are intangible assets, one might expect that property-based theories of the firm would be readily applied to intellectual property.

While the dearth of such analysis might suggest that theories of the firm have little to tell us regarding intellectual property, this supposition is not only counterintuitive, but belied by scholarship employing these theories in the intellectual property context, which is now beginning to emerge. Some work in this regard has already been done by Robert Merges, considering the law of ownership applicable to inventions created by employees. Although Merges does not explicitly invoke the theory of the firm, his analysis has elements common to such theories. Merges has also explicitly applied the theory of the firm to consider the control of innovators over inputs into their production.

More recently, David McGowan has considered theories of the firm in relation to the licensing of copyrighted "open-source" software. He suggests that the purportedly decentralized open-source programming community operates more as an economic firm than romanticized visions of this community might suggest. McGowan's work in this context implies, though does not explicitly state, that intellectual property licensing may be a coordinating factor in the production function of economic firms. Likewise, D. Gordon Smith has considered fiduciary duties in light of property-based theories of the firm. Smith does not explicitly consider intellectual property, but his analysis clearly maps onto the law of trade secrecy.

This scholarship suggests that there are insights to be gained by considering intellectual property in light of theories of the firm. However, as indicated, much of the work to date only hints at the fruits that such an exercise might bear. Even where the conjunction of the two is explicit, the commentators tend to take the state of intellectual property doctrine as given. Both Merges and McGowan are interested in the theory of the firm primarily as a vehicle to evaluate the innovative practices of certain industries, rather than as a tool to assess the state of intellectual property law itself.

In this Essay I wish to employ the theory of the firm in this latter fashion. I offer a preliminary examination of the relationship between intellectual property and theories of the firm, considering whether intellectual property law has progressed in the way we might have predicted in light of the theory of the firm, and to the extent that it has not, asking whether the theory of the firm has any recommendation to make for its improvement. In particular, I examine whether existing intellectual property law provides for efficient allocation of intellectual property rights within firms in a manner that comports with property-based theories of the firm. I begin with a short overview of property-based theories of the firm, and then suggest how such theories might fit one conception of intellectual property law. Finally, I focus briefly on doctrines in several major areas of intellectual property that suggest themselves for consideration in light of theories of the firm.

I.   Theories of the Firm

Modern theories of the firm, particularly the property-based theories considered here, have evolved in order to explain and justify the presence of organizational hierarchies within free market systems. But, paradoxically, the economic theory of the firm has yet to include any commonly accepted definition of the organization contemplated, that is, the concept of the "firm." Certainly the term as used in this context is not synonymous with its meaning in everyday conversation or even in legal parlance; the economic firm is not necessarily a legally recognized organization, although some legally recognized firms are also economic firms. The economic literature on the firm generally uses the term to denote an area of economic activity characterized by hierarchical organization and command production, rather than by market negotiation. The production center thus denoted is generally conceived to encompass an entrepreneur controlling a variety of inputs, including employees, via a complex of relationships, usually contractual in nature.

This conception of the firm, derived from the early work of Coase and of F.H. Knight, exists to explain the presence of hierarchical organizations within free markets. Coase, in particular, developed his early theory of the firm to explain why firms should exist even though markets are considered an efficient mechanism to coordinate productive activity. As in much of Coase's other influential work, the answer depends largely upon an inefficiency of markets, transaction costs that attend negotiated bargains. Firms, Coase postulated, exist in order to lower such transaction costs. Under this model, the productive activities of the firm are directed by an entrepreneurial fiat, rather than being realized via negotiated market transactions. In some cases, hierarchical production may prove less costly than market production due to the transaction costs of the market. In such cases, competitive pressures will tend to compel the formation of firms, as market participants organize themselves to minimize inefficiencies or face displacement by competitors that have already done so.

This model predicts the emergence of firm organizations where the transaction costs of the market become too high. Commentators expanding upon Coase's insight have identified opportunism as one of the key transaction costs associated with bargaining in the marketplace and have introduced theories of incomplete contracting into the analysis. Parties to a transaction cannot anticipate all future contingencies and, as a consequence, any contract they negotiate will be incomplete. Thus, contracts will necessarily present opportunities for one or the other party to take advantage of unforeseen developments. In particular, a party to a contract may attempt to "hold up" the other party, extorting additional concessions once resources have been committed to a project and cannot be easily recommitted to another venture. Such relationship-specific resources, by virtue of their tailoring to a particular project, increase the efficiency of projects but also create this potential for opportunism. Generalized resources may be more easily recommitted to new uses but are less well suited to any given project. Thus, in the face of possible hold-ups, parties may face an undesirable incentive to avoid asset specificity.

The development of a firm, which organizes production by command rather than by negotiation, may be explained as an attempt to deter such hold-up problems by eliminating repeated negotiations. If production is organized by executive fiat rather than by negotiation, there may be fewer opportunities for hold-ups to occur. However, by integrating production into a hierarchical structure, hold-up problems may simply be moved within the firm. Employment relationships are themselves contractual, and the boundary between internal and external contracts may be difficult or impossible to define. Some commentators have suggested that the relationships that comprise the firm are subject to much the same incentives and characteristics as those between firms; other commentators have extended this concept, modeling the firm as a nexus of contractual relationships, where team production is organized through a web of contractual arrangements. At some point, these employment contracts spill over into arms-length relationships with independent contractors outside the firm. The resulting model portrays the firm in many ways as a microcosm of market relationships, reflecting in miniature the same contractual structures within and without the firm's boundary.

This suggests that the major transaction costs delineating the boundaries of the firm may be coordination and agency costs: the interests of employees may not be perfectly aligned with that of the entrepreneur directing firm activity, prompting opportunistic behavior. Employees may see opportunities to exploit situations not foreseen in their employment agreements, and, once assets have been devoted to a project, they may hold up the firm for additional concessions. Commentators analyzing this scenario have argued that opportunism can be deterred only by some form of "gap-filling" provision allocating control of resources in situations not contemplated by contract. The analysis suggested by these commentators places property rights into this role, effectively to serve as the default for incomplete contracts. Allocation of ownership rights to the firm is thus advanced to ameliorate the problem of opportunism within the firm; proprietary control of relationship-specific assets prevents employees from using them to hold up the firm. Thus, under a property-based model, the right to exclude, and the concomitant right to grant access to the assets of the firm, ultimately define the boundary of the firm.

The types of assets contemplated by developers of this property-based model appear to have been the largely traditional physical assets of production: buildings, machinery, furnishings, paper clips. Less tangible assets, such as specialized financial instruments, may also have been contemplated, and specific human capital has surely been a key consideration in the model's approach to hold-ups. But the assets of the modern firm are at least equally likely to accrue as intangible resources: ideas, know-how, information, inventions, goodwill, and the like. Thus, consonant with the transactional and property-based models reviewed here, the firm might be modeled as a nexus of intellectual property rights vested in entrepreneurs, together with actual or implied licenses based on those rights, permitting employees to use and modify the firm's intellectual property.

II. Proprietary Knowledge

In the United States, intellectual property systems have most often been characterized as instruments to induce investment in creative products that, in the absence of a proprietary right, might be under-produced. Creative products frequently display characteristics similar to those of "public goods," that is, goods that can be enjoyed by more than one individual simultaneously, and from which it is difficult to exclude consumers. Since consumers cannot easily be excluded from enjoying the good, they would be unlikely to pay for it, and creators, knowing this, will be unlikely to invest in producing it in the first place. Proprietary rights give the creator a legal right to exclude, which allows the creator to derive an income stream from selling access to the work, either by selling the work directly or by collecting royalties from others who sell the work.

Typically, then, intellectual property rights have been viewed as the basis for market negotiation; by assigning exclusive interests in creative works, intellectual property facilitates bargaining. In other words, intellectual property rights are conceived of primarily as mechanisms for coordinating activities between firms. However, as detailed above, the boundary of the firm is often indeterminate, and the distinction separating contractual relationships within the firm from contractual relationships between firms may be ambiguous.

Property-based theories of the firm suggest that the right to access and use dedicated resources must be allocated within the firm as well as beyond the firm. This means that, in addition to their recognized inter-firm functions, proprietary rights may also serve to coordinate resources within a firm.

This function of proprietary rights in the firm has not been the focus of the standard explanations for intellectual property. However, at least one theory of intellectual property has focused on the assignment of proprietary rights as a mechanism to coordinate development of the creative product. This "prospect theory" of intellectual property is most closely associated with the work of Edmund Kitch, who argued that the assignment of intellectual property places development of valuable innovation in the hands of an entrepreneur who can then coordinate development of that resource. Following this rationale, one may argue that by vesting firms with control of such intangible assets, the exclusive intellectual property rights found in patent, copyright, and trade secrecy may serve to prevent opportunism and promote coordination of intangible resources. Employees or potential licensees who wish to develop proprietary information must seek the permission of the rights-holding entrepreneur. This view of the "prospect" coordination rationale is also consonant with models of the firm as a nexus of contractual production. Employees routinely make, use, sell, offer for sale, reproduce, distribute, adapt, and otherwise make use of the firm's intellectual property in ways that would constitute infringement if the uses were unauthorized. We typically presume that such uses are authorized but may have given little thought to the source of the authorization — the license that allows employees to make use of the firm's intangible assets in the course of their employment.

On this model, firms may be reluctant to develop project-specific intellectual property if control is incompletely allocated, as this sets the stage for potential hold-up by employees. Allocation of rights may be relatively obvious where tangible property or monetary assets are concerned; the employee who converts or appropriates such assets to his own use is guilty of theft, embezzlement, or waste. But misappropriation of intangible assets such as know-how, concepts, inventions, or designs is more problematic because the nonrivalrous nature of the resource leaves the appearance that nothing has been "taken." Indeed, if rights to intangible assets are left inchoate, employees may be unable to distinguish their personal knowledge and creative resources from those developed under the auspices of the firm.

The point is perhaps most clear in the case of trade secrecy, which arises out of a complex pedigree of tort, contract, and equitable legal claims. Although trade secrecy disputes occasionally involve blatant industrial espionage, more typically they arise in cases of employee mobility, where a departing employee is purported to have taken proprietary information. Other typical cases involve instances of corporate divorce, where a former corporate ally is purported to have misused proprietary information after a joint venture or licensing relationship had gone sour. Resolving trade secrecy disputes is especially problematic in the case of employee departure, as courts are reluctant to curtail the mobility of labor. Society typically will benefit if workers are encouraged to acquire employable skills. But such general ability may be difficult to separate from the specific human capital in which an employer has invested for a particular project. Thus both employee and venture situations are characterized by the need to identify and allocate assets that were specifically dedicated to the particular relationship.

As such, much of trade secrecy law is concerned with demarcation of firm assets, designating incentives and methods for giving proper notice to employees, partners, or licensees of the business information considered to be proprietary and confidential. The substantive law reflects such attempts at demarcation. Trade secrecy is typified by a duty of confidentiality arising in a business relationship. Confidence cannot be imposed upon another party without that party's implied or express consent, so the circumstances giving rise to trade secrecy must be such that a party knew or should have known of the confidentiality obligation. Such obligations may arise from the formal statement of a written contract, or from a contract implied in fact based upon the behavior of the parties, or even from a contract implied in law based upon the general expectations of society. Firms are also expected to take "reasonable measures" to ensure secrecy of their proprietary information — for example, marking confidential information as confidential, password protecting or physically securing such information, and logging or monitoring use of the information.

Such measures signal to employees which assets are considered valuable and project-specific by the employer. Moreover, the additional investment in confidentiality measures is unlikely to be made in generalized assets that pose no danger of hold-up. Consonant with this principle, the law of trade secrecy excludes from protection information that is either generally known or readily ascertainable from information that is generally known. Neither does trade secrecy law protect against reverse engineering or independent discovery of the secret. Generally ascertainable knowledge, or knowledge that can be independently discovered at a low enough cost to make such re-creation feasible, is unlikely to be information that is project-specific, nor is such knowledge likely to represent enough of a project-specific investment to make hold-up likely.

Indeed, the remedies available for misappropriation of trade secrets might be characterized as designed to negate the benefits of hold-up, placing the opportunist monetarily or injunctively where he would have been without the benefit of the proprietary information. Courts may delay use of the misappropriated information for the period of time that it would have taken to reverse engineer or independently develop the secret, or deprive the wrongdoer of the profits gained by not having to expend resources on reverse engineering or independent development. Such head-start damages or head-start injunctions effectively place the opportunist where he would have been had he been operating wholly outside the boundaries of the firm. This characterization additionally implies that joint ventures or licenses that convey project-specific assets fall within the boundaries of the firm for purposes of the property-based theory, even though the entities involved may be separate actors for legal purposes.

Yet, paradoxically, trade secrecy does not confer a property right, or at best it confers an incomplete property right. Trade secrecy does not confer a right as against the world, but only as against a limited number of individuals that stand in a confidential relationship with the proprietor. Courts have displayed some confusion as to this quasi-property right, sometimes treating it as property and other times repudiating that label. But under a firm-based analysis, this incomplete propertization is not a problem; confidential information does not confer a right as against the world, but it need not, and public welfare dictates that it probably should not. A full discussion of the economic and constitutional limits of trade secrecy lies beyond the scope of this Essay, but for this discussion, it is enough to recognize that trade secrecy need only confer an allocative property right against opportunism as between the parties to the secret.

III. Copyright

The discussion to this point suggests that many aspects of trade secrecy are consonant with the need to distinguish project-specific from general assets and to allocate specific assets so as to avoid opportunism — thus trade secrecy law aligns fairly well with the property-based theory of the firm. At the same time, trade secrecy is costly, requiring cumbersome secrecy measures and detailed confidentiality agreements — in other words, requiring parties to an employment contract to largely foresee the conditions of possible opportunism. Allocation of more complete rights via patent or copyright avoids the need for cumbersome secrecy or for ex ante contractual obligations to establish proprietary rights in information insofar as these systems enable the firm to establish an exclusive right in intangible relationship-specific assets.

In the case of copyright, this outcome has been statutorily formalized under United States law via the work made for hire doctrine. Under this doctrine, individual employees who create copyrightable works while operating within the scope of their employment are not considered to be the authors of those works. Rather, the institution employing the creator becomes the legally recognized author. Thus, the key considerations determining whether a work is made for hire are the statutory criteria of "employee" and "scope of employment."

The Supreme Court has interpreted the statute to require that "employees" be distinguished from independent contractors on the basis of agency principles. The factors used to assess an individual's employment status may include the ability of the worker to accept or decline assignments, the provision of materials by the employer, the duration of the relationship, tax treatment of the worker, and provision of benefits. The test is flexible, with no particular factor designated as dispositive, although some lower courts have given greater weight to certain ubiquitous factors. The scope of employment criterion is similarly judged under agency principles. Relying upon the Restatement of Agency, courts have defined the scope of employment in terms of the type of work the individual was hired to perform, the temporal and locational boundaries of the employment, and the motivation for creating the copyrightable work. Under the third factor, the creative activity must have been motivated at least in part to serve the interests of the employer.

The work is considered by statutory default to be made for hire whenever these criteria obtain. This has several legal consequences, but for the present discussion, the most relevant consequence of work made for hire status is the default ownership of the work. Designating the employer as author means that ownership rests with the firm, subject to contractual transfer, rather than initial employee ownership subject to contractual transfer.

The copyright statute also allows designation of authorship for certain commissioned works. In certain statutorily defined situations, the employee and employer may designate by contract whether the work will be considered a work made for hire. Thus, both ownership and authorship are open to negotiation in these situations. There is a good deal of historical path dependence to the statutory list of commissioned works. Industry organizations must have sufficient political capital to have a type of commissioned work added to the list, or, as in the case of sound recordings' brief appearance on the list, sufficient political capital to effect removal.

But in general, the list contemplates subject matter that is highly collaborative or requires multi-party coordination: motion pictures, compilations, atlases. Such works are among the most likely to be subject to hold-up problems if property rights are fragmented. Such works are also most likely to involve negotiations on the border of the firm, where firms are engaged in recruiting contractors who may sometimes fall inside the firm's transactional boundaries and sometimes outside. In the latter case, market negotiations will be more efficient than entrepreneurial fiat. Some flexibility in adopting or eschewing the property default rule makes sense in these instances, as the parties will know best on which side of the firm boundary a contractor's activity falls.

Of course, copyrightable works created outside an agency relationship may always be assigned to an employer by means of an employment contract. This is the common practice in U.S. patent law, which lacks a work made for hire provision. But reliance on contractual assignment re-introduces the problem of indefiniteness. Copyright, in particular, may foster ambiguities, as the statute requires a signed writing to transfer exclusive rights in a work, purportedly in order to create certainty in transfers. Blanket assignment of works in advance of an individual's general employment may not satisfy this statutory requirement, as the contract would not contemplate the transfer of any specific work. Pre-assignment might be more viable where an individual is engaged to create a specifically contemplated work, and this is indeed the situation under the "commissioned works" categories. One can imagine that a duty to transfer or a nonexclusive license might also be implied from the employment relationship, as has commonly been the case in patent law. Indeed, an implied non-exclusive license would look like patent law's shop right. But all of these permutations create ambiguities that might prove opportune for hold-up.

Work made for hire sidesteps this possibility by creating an allocative default rule. In several dimensions, the conceptual structure of copyright's work made for hire doctrine appears a natural extension from the fiduciary-based principles of trade secrecy reviewed above. The doctrine has developed via application of agency principles, which, like fiduciary principles, have been identified as consonant with property-based theories of the firm. Tellingly, in the work made for hire situation, courts are not typically concerned with the classic agency situations — claims of third parties against a principal for actions of the purported agent or claims by principals against an agent for breach of a fiduciary duty. Rather, agency principles are used to allocate control of what Gordon Smith has called a "critical resource" in which the firm has invested, and in which we would wish to encourage specific investment.

This division appears roughly consonant with the criterion of "asset specificity" under a property-based theory of the firm. The factors and categories defining employee works made for hire, or commissioned works, will tend to define situations where we would want to encourage development of project-specific resources. However, the doctrine as currently constituted may also allocate some nonspecific assets to the control of the firm. This occurs when authorship, and not simply ownership, is allocated to the firm. By erasing the identity of the natural creator, work made for hire removes from the natural author a reputational interest that is otherwise specific to the natural person, and not the firm. This interest is recognized most strongly in nations with strong moral rights regimes and less so in U.S. copyright. But work made for hire denies the natural author even the limited U.S. moral rights regime of the Visual Artists Rights Act. Thus, an "asset specificity" approach suggests that authorship and ownership should perhaps be bifurcated under work made for hire, allocating the reputational interest to the natural author even while assigning default ownership of the work to the firm.

IV.   Patent Law

Unlike copyright law, U.S. patent law lacks a work made for hire provision. Although corporations or institutions can be authors, they cannot be inventors; only natural persons can be so designated. This is something of a puzzle, as the need for a default rule of institutional ownership might seem more pronounced in patent law than in copyright. With a few exceptions, such as large motion picture projects, creativity within the traditional subject matter of copyright tends to be relatively low-cost; a modest investment in pencil and paper may suffice. Patent development may sometimes be similarly inexpensive. But corporate research and development is typically expensive, nearly always collaborative, and frequently critical to a firm's survival. These factors should militate toward developing the sort of clear ownership rule that has emerged in copyright, but oddly has not in patent.

Of course, one might argue that patent law has no need for institutional inventors because a patent law work made for hire doctrine is rendered unnecessary by liberal application of contract law. As a matter of employment practice, sophisticated research operations routinely require employees, as part of their employment agreements, to assign patents or other invention rights to the employer. In theory, such "pre-assignment" contracts will create a duty for an employee to assign the rights to whatever may be discovered. But, as a practical matter, in a significant number of situations the contracts either are never executed or fail to anticipate the circumstances of invention, lending support to the concern regarding incomplete contracts. And, unlike copyright, the default rule for patent allocates property rights to the employee rather than to the firm.

In the absence of explicit contractual terms requiring an assignment, an implied duty to assign may be found. Courts have tended to recognize such an implied duty to assign patent rights in situations where an employee hired to solve a problem engages in research, and the invention relates to that effort. Initially, courts recognized this duty only where employees were hired to solve a specific problem, but the rule has evolved to apply to employees engaged to perform general research and development, as well as those engaged for specific research. In each case, invention was part of the employment duties undertaken, so a duty to assign the invention to the employer should come as no surprise to the employee.

In situations where an employee was not hired to engage in research, but developed an invention in which the employer has an interest, courts have assigned to the employer a nonexclusive license known as the "shop right." The shop right, in some cases, is characterized as a contract implied in fact, inferred to exist in situations where the inventor appeared to acquiesce to the employer's use of the invention. In other cases, it appears as a license implied in law, arising from an equitable sense that the employer is entitled to use an invention developed on the employer's time by means of the employer's materials. This implied license evolved into an independent right of the employer, although a limited one: the right is personal and nonexclusive and does not pass by license or assignment.

Although the shop right arises in situations involving non-research employees, inventions subject to the shop right must still relate to the employment. In determining the existence of the shop right, courts have taken into account whether the invention relates to the duties of the employee, whether the invention falls within the scope of the employer's business, and whether the invention was created with materials supplied by the employer or was developed during working hours. When the invention falls within these criteria, the employer enjoys the shop right. The employee need not convey the full interest in the invention, however, due to what the courts perceive as the "peculiar nature of the act of invention," which courts characterize as springing from the employee's own inventive genius, and not from the material contributions of the employer.

This characterization of the inventive process appears out of step with the reality of industrial research and development, but it does suggest a possible reason for the absence of a work made for hire doctrine in patent law: a romantic notion of the inventor inventing in an individual flash of genius may be exerting an even greater influence upon patent doctrine than that of the romantic author upon copyright law. The result of imposing the shop right is to effectively grant the employer a compulsory license at a zero royalty. The lack of exclusivity, however, leaves the employer at the mercy of the employee's residual control of the invention.

Professor Merges has suggested that these employee contract rules might be explained under contractual theories of "penalty defaults." These theories share with property-based theories of the firm a pedigree rooted in concepts of incomplete contract. The general argument suggests that in the face of incompleteness, contractual defaults can play an information-forcing role. Thus, the terms of the contract should be calibrated to penalize the party with the greatest informational advantage if that party is not forthcoming in the contracting process. In the specific case of employee inventions, the implication is that the employer, being the more sophisticated party to the contract, will be more forthcoming in negotiating invention assignments under the threat of a default rule that strips the employer of invention ownership.

But the information-forcing story is a largely unsatisfying explanation for the rules that have developed, supplying at best an incomplete justification of the employee ownership doctrine. There would seem to be relatively little information to force. The employment contract is signed at the beginning of the relationship between employer and employee, when the employer has relatively little information about the employee's abilities, creativity, or work habits. To be sure, the employer will have scrutinized the employee's references, resume, transcripts, and interview responses, but these are likely to provide little indication of the types of inventions the employee may develop, or the circumstances under which she may develop them. For that matter, invention is frequently serendipitous, defying premeditation and fostering the image of the romantic inventor. But we nonetheless would wish to encourage investment in the environment that fosters such serendipity, even if the employer has no advance information about the precise outcome.

The theory of the firm may supply a more complete explanation of employee ownership rules, setting default rules to ensure residual control rather than to force information disclosure. In developing employee ownership rules, courts have essentially dragooned doctrines of implied contract or fiduciary duty into bridging the gaps left by incomplete contracts. The doctrines play precisely the role contemplated by property rights under property-based theories of the firm. The criteria chosen for these employee rules suggest that courts are groping toward the demarcation line of asset specificity. Inventions created by employees specifically employed to do research are perhaps most likely to be those in which the firm has become irrevocably invested. Inventions created by non-research employees, even those using the firm's resources, may be those on which the firm is less likely to be dependent. As such, the latter inventions are less likely candidates for opportunism. As with copyright's work made for hire doctrine, an employee's activity within the "scope of employment" and use of firm resources are indicators of relationships lying within the boundaries of the firm, rather than out in the market.

At the same time, such judicial gap-filling is just that — attempts to fill gaps in incomplete contracts by inferring the existence of unarticulated agreements from the parties' actions, or creating obligations in law that appear to result in more-just outcomes. The solution itself is piecemeal, developed ad hoc, and riddled with discontinuity. While the case law tends toward stable designation of residual rights, it lacks the certainty of an actual property allocation.

This same uncertainty appears in the employment-related aspects of substantive patent law itself, especially in the concept of the "inventive entity." Inventive entities may be composed of a single individual inventor or a group of inventors. Inventive groups composed of different individuals constitute different inventive entities even if their memberships partially overlap. In other words, an inventive entity composed of Alice, Bob, and Carol is not the same inventive entity as that composed of Alice and Carol, or of Ted, Carol, and Bob. Because patent law recognizes natural individuals, and not juridical individuals, as inventors, firms are not typically considered inventive entities. Instead, research groups within a firm are considered inventive entities.

Inventions must be novel and non-obvious to qualify for patent protection. The novelty requirement is typically operationalized under the statute by requiring that the invention cannot have been known or used by "others" in the United States. But different inventive entities, even when including some of the same individuals, might constitute "others" for purposes of the statute. Thus, one research group could generate prior art that might interfere with the patentability of related inventions created by another research group composed of some of the same personnel. The inventive entity comprising Alice, Bob, and Carol might generate prior art against a related invention created by Bob, Carol, and Ted, or even by Bob and Carol. The common knowledge carried by natural persons into each of these inventive entities almost ensures overlapping discoveries, but any difference in membership causes that knowledge to be imputed to a different "inventor." Prior art generated by another overlapping entity could also be used to deny patents on grounds of obviousness, as prior art that qualifies for section 102 novelty purposes may also be used to measure obviousness.

Courts recognizing this problem began by carving out exceptions where the outcome of this rule seemed unduly harsh. Congress has addressed other parts of the problem through piecemeal legislation. For example, Congress has twice amended section 103 of the patent statute in order to exclude categories of subject matter from consideration as prior art if the subject matter and claimed invention were either commonly owned or subject to a common assignment. The statutory amendments track the general rule against an inventor defeating his own novelty. Public knowledge will generally be held as prior art against the inventor, but the rule excludes privately held, proprietary knowledge from the prior art category. This arrangement, as Professor Merges observes, will encourage the inventor to invest in such knowledge prior to the beginning of an inventive project. Such preliminary investigation may be useful in focusing or directing the actual project, making the conduct of the research proper more efficient. Translated into the nomenclature of theories of the firm, such knowledge constitutes a project-specific asset, a type of investment that should be encouraged.

But project-specific knowledge may also provide an opportunity for hold-up if the residual rights in the knowledge are not specifically allocated. The statutory amendments condition prior art consideration of commonly developed subject matter upon whether the invention is "owned by the same person or subject to an obligation of assignment to the same person." Thus the statute itself relies to some extent upon the nature of the employment agreement, and to the extent that such agreements may be incomplete, upon the courts' willingness to plug gaps in the agreement. Under the conditions of employee mobility most likely to lead to hold-up, the inventions of inventive entities with overlapping memberships may frequently not be subject to assignment to the same "person." This suggests a need to fully vest firms with residual inventive rights under a doctrine of "invention made for hire."

Conclusion

I have suggested in this Essay that certain intellectual property doctrines may be better understood when viewed through the lens of property-based theories of the firm, and that certain doctrines, such as work made for hire, might be adjusted in light of such theories. In doing so, I have focused primarily on doctrines of ownership allocating residual rights between employees and employers. Other relevant relationships in the intellectual property context, such as partnerships or joint ventures, may also be amenable to such analysis. Similarly, we might profit by analyzing other intellectual property doctrines, such as joint authorship in copyright or double patenting, in light of property-based theories of the firm. Additionally, because different forms of intellectual property likely entail different degrees of asset specificity, firm-based comparisons between different regimes of intellectual property may be fruitful for understanding the role of intellectual property in the firm. These possibilities suggest that the theory of the firm should be a useful tool in further examination of intellectual property law.

3. Allocations of Research Activities among Firms and Distributed Communities: The Open Source Experience

David McGowan,
Legal Implications of Open-Source Software
2001 U. Ill. L. Rev. 241, 242-45, 285-87 (2001)*

. . .

The production and distribution of open-source or "free" software presents an interesting case study of the relationships among the theory of the firm, intellectual property rights, and contract law. Firms such as Red Hat, Inc. have built businesses successful enough to win the approval of financial markets and maintain large market capitalizations even though they did not develop the software on which their work is based, do not employ the programmers who created and maintain it, do not control its future development, and cannot control any improvements they themselves make to it. One might explain all of this with a standard model in which firms make money on service, or by arguing that the capital markets for Internet firms have been irrational. But even if such explanations are true they tell only a part of the story. They do not explain how the operating system was produced in the first place.

The open-source program behind Red Hat's business model is an operating system that is a variant of Unix. The program consists of a kernel of Linux code and a shell of code developed by the GNU Project, which together I will refer to as the GNU/Linux operating system (OS). This operating system is not "owned" by anyone if we use that term in its conventional sense — to refer to the exclusion of consumers from using the owner's code as a means of inducing payment for use. The components of the GNU/Linux OS are copyrighted, and the rights are held by identifiable persons and firms. Under the open-source model of software production, however, these rights are used to enforce norms of the open-source community: Code may be freely copied, modified and distributed, but only if the modifications (derivative works) are distributed on these terms as well.

These restrictions are imposed in form agreements such as the GNU General Public License (GNU GPL). The licenses, and the GNU GPL in particular, represent an elegant use of contractual terms and property rights to create social conditions in which software is produced on a model of openness rather than exclusion. The licenses have not been tested in court, and some analysts question whether they create legally binding rights and obligations. It is therefore all the more remarkable that the social structure these licenses support has produced valuable software that is important to the operation of the Internet and, in the case of the GNU/Linux OS, presents a credible source of future competition for Microsoft's operating systems.

The development of the GNU/Linux OS presents an interesting case for exploring the theory of the firm. Following Coase, we often think of firms as institutions in which activity is arranged by authoritative command rather than negotiation. On this view, the firm consists of various inputs controlled by an entrepreneur; the scope of the firm is determined by the cost of in-house production compared to the cost of a market transaction with another firm. Viewing firms as areas of market-like activity organized hierarchically to minimize costs allows us to focus on persons within firms as individual economic agents. A rational actor assumption leads to the fear that these agents will try to do what is best for themselves rather than the firm — shirking work, appropriating opportunities, and the like.

Following Jensen and Meckling, we have given the name "agency costs" to the sum of the costs of agent misbehavior plus costs incurred to discover and stop such misbehavior. One implication of seeing the world in agency-cost terms is that we should expect firms to use various devices to align the interests of agents and firms, and such devices are in fact common. Monitoring agents is expensive for firms; that they are willing to incur such costs suggests that agent opportunism is a real and significant concern. Yet large numbers of programmers have spent time working to develop the GNU/Linux OS, and they generally have not been paid for this work. If conventional technology firms find it necessary to pay salaries and grant options to hire bright programmers who will work long hours designing and coding software, how is it that the GNU/Linux OS has become a commercially viable product that can sustain firms such as Red Hat?

These questions bring us quickly to property rights. The standard explanation for copyright is that it is a reward system in which creators are given a right to exclude others from their work, which allows them to earn returns by charging a fee for access. The reward model sees the revenue creators earn as necessary to induce them to create the work in the first place. The cost of excluding the public from use is tolerated on the assumption that it succeeds in inducing creation that would not otherwise occur. The optimal copyright system is therefore one in which the marginal gain in creativity induced by the rights exceeds the marginal cost of exclusion plus the cost of administering the system. The production of commercially viable software under a regime of free copying, modification, and distribution therefore deserves attention. We should study the case of open-source software production to see whether our existing legal rules could produce socially desirable results at a lower cost.

This case study seeks to answer these questions: How is it that the GNU/Linux OS was produced in the first place? Is the model in which this operating system was produced sustainable? Is it generalizable? What role, if any, does the law play in making such production possible? My answers, in brief, are as follows.

Open-source software production is not about the absence or irrelevance of intellectual property rights. Open-source production instead rests on the elegant use of contractual terms to deploy those rights in a way that creates a social space devoted to producing freely available and modifiable code. In open-source production, property rights are held in reserve to discipline possible violations of community norms. Open-source production therefore does not take place in a true commons, though the low cost of copying and using code combined with the broad grants of the relevant licenses creates a situation that resembles a commons in some respects.

Though individuals or firms may charge for open-source code, the ability of community members to copy and distribute the code severely constrains pricing for the code itself. In many cases, persons who wish to obtain the code without charge may do so. The right to exclude is not actively employed to secure payment for code. Open-source works may therefore be more widely and cheaply available than code produced in a conventional, exclusion-based model.

If other variables — such as the rate of innovation and production — can be held equal, then the social cost associated with open-source production will be lower than the cost associated with conventional production. Whether the rate of innovation and production in general can be held equal is an open question. In some cases open-source production might be slower than conventional production, while in others it might be faster. Rates of development might also vary within projects, with core technical problems being solved faster than problems related to making a program easier for non-expert consumers to use.

The licenses that enforce the property rights on which this structure rests are important to its success. The licenses provide a mechanism for enforcing norms, for distinguishing the open-source community from conventional software production and, in some cases, for providing incentives to programmers who require them. Although the agreements that define open-source code are sometimes said to create de facto property rights or "covenants running with the code," these agreements in fact create a nonexclusive permission to use the code subject to certain conditions. The relevant property right is copyright, which does run with the code, which is why the permissions granted by the licenses must run with the code as well.

"Open-source" or "free" software refers to a type of license and not to the economic characteristics of particular projects. These terms encompass projects involving a million lines of code and projects involving only a thousand lines of code. The Linux kernel and a network printer patch might both be "open-source" software, but that fact shows only that such labels do little analytical work on their own.

The social structures necessary to support production of large, complex projects are different from the structures, if any, necessary to support small projects. It is a mistake to speak generally of the incentives or motivations behind "open-source" or "free" software production. The costs of coordination and working on particular projects must be taken into account. Large, complex projects have to provide some form of reward to induce programmers to contribute their work while accepting the hierarchy necessary to coordinate production. Smaller, less complex projects need not incur coordination costs, and therefore have no need for such payoffs. Programmers may receive reputational payoffs from working on such projects, but they also may work on such projects for personal reasons, such as the sheer enjoyment of programming.

The importance of intellectual property rights and open-source licenses increases as the complexity of projects and the cost of coordinating them increases. Where significant costs have to be sunk to ensure success, more robust legal and social structures are required. Where no such costs are needed, production may succeed in more anarchic structures.

. . .

[T]he Internet made the open-source production model viable by lowering the costs of coordination. These costs include identifying a problem to be tackled, recruiting programmers, receiving and incorporating their input, and giving reputational or other forms of social returns to programmers who require them. Open-source production may therefore be seen as an example in which high coordination costs led to the creation of firms devoted to conventional production models — the expected Coasean result — but in which a reduction in those costs allowed the formation of less centralized, unconventional "firms" devoted to particular projects. Though hierarchy persists in these firms, the hierarchies appear to be very narrow bands sitting atop a relatively decentralized set of producing agents, a similarly expected Coasean result.

By making widespread distribution of code possible, technology also allows programmers who maximize reputation to reap greater returns from their work. Though programmers on these projects are not subject to fiat control by project maintainers, projects may command a degree of loyalty by providing a forum for programmers to develop their reputational capital or to satisfy an urge to create in a social context supporting that creation. The social structure of the projects themselves is therefore a large part of the point of open-source production. To some and perhaps many programmers, the community of a given project — including its hierarchy — may be as relevant a product of their work as the code itself. For open-source production, therefore, the social consequences of cost-reducing technology are as significant as the ability of such technology to lower the cost of production.

With respect to small projects that do not require extensive coordination, logic and experience to date suggest that the open-source model is sustainable. For interesting problems encountered by a large number of programmers — such as fixes to popular hardware or software — the model is likely to be quite robust. We cannot in the abstract say how sustainable or robust the model is for complex projects that require coordination and, therefore, some form of hierarchy. Complex projects are costlier to produce than simple ones and therefore require stronger supporting structures if production is to go forward. We may say that projects that are important to the community as a whole are more likely to succeed than niche projects; projects that compete with a dominant and aggressive firm are more likely to succeed than those that do not; projects that present interesting technical questions are more likely to succeed than projects that do not; and projects that attract large numbers of developers and provide them with reliable feedback and reputational payoffs are more likely to succeed than projects that do not. In each case, these variables relate to the conditions necessary for the formation of norms that support hierarchical production models outside the traditional firm context.

We may also say that the payoffs these variables provide will have to track, in at least a rough way, the complexity and cost of the project. Greater project complexity implies a more complex hierarchy, which is costlier to administer and carriers a greater risk of error. These factors may reduce some payoffs to programmers. The success of such projects will, in any event, depend on whether their maintainers can minimize coordination costs — importantly including the cost of processing and evaluating information — relative to conventional production. To the degree that software production becomes componentized, for example, coordination costs will decrease and open-source production of components will become more robust. Coordination and assembly of components will still be costly, of course. But Red Hat's viability to date is some evidence that even now firms can provide such services without the active use of exclusion to facilitate conventional software production.

NOTES & QUESTIONS

1. What are the features of complex software programs that make them suitable for development through open source processes? Are there technologies other than software that can be developed through similar open source communities linked in part by copyright interests and conditional licensing arrangements?

2. Can intellectual property interests other than copyrights — such as patents, trademarks, or trade secrets — be used with selective licensing arrangements to establish and administer open source technology development projects?

B. INTELLECTUAL PROPERTY SECURITIZATION

Intellectual property securitization involves the use of a stream of royalty payments generated by the licensing of intellectual property to pay interest amounts due on bonds. By selling bonds specifying that future interest payments will be made in this way, an intellectual property holder can realize the value of an intellectual property interest at the time of the bond sales rather than waiting for later royalty payments. The following reading describes the use of this technique in the music industry, as well as some of the complex business relationships and potential pitfalls involved.

Hewson Chen, Don't Sell Out, Sell Bonds: The Pullman Group's Securitization of the Music Industry
2 Vand. J. Ent. L. & Prac. 161 (2000)*

If opposites attract, then perhaps there is an explanation for the unlikely marriage between rock 'n roll and the bond market. One can only wonder what strange magnetism is powerful enough to wed the "youthful, wild and unpredictable" rock culture with the world of "dry, cautious, and mind-numbingly technical" investment finance. Indeed, some strange voodoo magic has luminaries like David Bowie, James Brown, and Holland-Dozier-Holland all singing the same tune, and "securitization" is its name.

Securitization is the selling of debt to investors. In general, securitization converts future income streams like credit card receivables or auto loan payments to present in-pocket cash. Notably, this transformation from future income to current wealth gives the issuer of the security immediate access to cash at less cost than other financing methods such as bank loans. In the 1970s, this technique was applied to the housing industry, and since then, securitization has evolved into greater varieties of income streams, including medical insurance, typhoon insurance, and unused airline tickets. The application of securitization in the entertainment industry, however, remains largely untested.

Is securitization a viable model for financing intellectual properties in the music industry? David Pullman, Founder, Chairman, and CEO of The Pullman Group, LLC, thinks so. In 1997, Pullman, as managing director of Fahnestock & Company's Structured Asset Sales Group, successfully orchestrated the issuance of $55 million in bonds backed by singer David Bowie's royalty and publishing income. To date, Pullman has proven the viability of this concept by issuing similar bonds for legendary artists like James Brown, Holland-Dozier-Holland, and Ashford & Simpson. These music legends are interested in securitizing because these deals promise several benefits to the established artist. The securitization deal is more attractive than a traditional royalty/advance agreement because the artist retains 100 percent of the copyright, generates an immediate monetary windfall, and saves money on taxes because the sale of the bonds is not treated as a taxable event. Securitization deals are more attractive than bank loans. Unlike bank loans, which are short-term in nature and involve a floating rate, Pullman's securities are fixed rate, non-recourse, and long-term in nature, translating into less risk for the artist. Also, bank loans typically only yield about one-tenth what the artist can get through securitization. According to the Pullman Group, the benefits of securitization translate into at least 20 percent extra income for the artist.

This increased amount of money up-front can result in additional indirect advantages. "By gaining control of the net sum of future royalties today, the artist can reinvest and diversify," making the artist's wealth less dependent on the success or failure of any specific market. Moreover, the ability to control

---

the net value of future royalties today facilitates estate planning, so the artist's heirs will have money available to pay taxes without being forced to sell off the artist's catalog.

As the innovator who first married securitization to star power, David Pullman is one of few financiers who can successfully structure such deals, and, in fact, such bonds bear his name in industry vernacular. The overall idea behind a "Pullman Bond" is that the artist makes money up front by selling bonds to investors. The interest on these bonds is then paid with the income stream resulting from certain assets, typically a catalog of songs.

A number of steps ensure that risks to the investor are minimized. The income producing assets are insulated from possible bankruptcy proceedings by transferring the assets temporarily from the artist to a special purpose vehicle ("SPV"). Credit enhancements such as cash reserve accounts, financial guarantees, letters of credit, or default insurance may be used to reduce the risk of default of payment on the bonds. Finally, an artist's works may be pooled with the works of other artists to diversify "the risk that a particular artist's popularity may decrease and affect future royalty payments negatively."

However, there are many critics who remain skeptical of entertainment securitization. Some of the banks that have tried to enter the entertainment securitization market now dismiss the deals to be "more about hype than value." Pullman regards these criticisms as grumblings from disgruntled competitors. "When I did the Bowie deal people thought I was crazy," he notes. "Three months after I started it, other people tried to copy me. Six months later, it was everyone else's idea. We keep going at it. Other people have tried and failed."

. . .

The main reason behind Pullman's heavy market share of the music bonds industry is that "the assets are complex." As he observes, it is a "world-wide industry" with "world-wide cash flows." For example, the Bowie deal took months to devise, cost over a million dollars, and resulted in a thousand pages of documentation. But even with the experience of numerous music securitization deals, Pullman notes that these transactions are still difficult to orchestrate: "I thought that after doing a series of these deals, things would get easier, and they haven't. So that's what's amazing about it all — that they don't become cookie cutter."

Indeed, the difficulty of creating deals and the few successes of music securitization may well limit music bonds to the fringes of the industry. Some commentators have said that music securities are "lousy investments," where "the seller is smarter than the buyer." This potential information asymmetry also raises policy concerns. Securitization shifts the risk of success or failure from the record company and publisher onto the investor, who is in arguably the worst position to assess the odds. Instead, the risk of a particular catalog is perhaps most efficiently allocated to record companies and publishers, who have ready access to income stream histories and industry tracking data. Pullman counters this criticism by pointing out that his focus is different from that of the average record company. "[We deal with] people who are already successful and are legends with a steady income stream, and, in general, the majority of artists in a record company's roster don't fit that example. We're dealing with a select few, the cream of the crop, in terms of artists that have longevity."

This focus on artists of legendary stature also allows Pullman to avoid the uncertainty of predicting the popularity of entertainers in a fickle market. With regard to songs that have achieved "classic" status, income streams are relatively stable. For example, "with Ziggy Stardust it's nearly 30 years later and we know if it's still producing income 30 years later — remember with artists, 90 percent of the income comes in the first 6 months after release — so if this song's producing this 30 years out, that's what it should do going forward."

But with business limited to artists of legendary status, some think that the real money to be made from intellectual property securitization lies outside of the music industry. In 1997, an attorney who worked with Pullman on the Bowie Bond deal observed that "the music business is a limited market. . . . But if you can get to the software companies, then this could be a huge business." However, Pullman remains optimistic about the future of music bonds. Despite the music industry's focus on short-term artists with one- to three-record careers and the implication that the pool of viable securitization candidates is dwindling, Pullman maintains:

> We're just at the beginning of [music securitization]. What [the increasing focus on short-term artists] is really doing is making catalogs like James Brown, David Bowie, Ashford and Simpson, or Holland-Dozier-Holland . . . more valuable, because there are fewer people creating catalogs that have standards, or that have long careers or that have created a new sound. So we think that's better, that we have these gems that don't really have to compete with a lot of the different artists that are out there. . . . James Brown doesn't compete against a new artist. In fact, James Brown, the Isley Brothers, these guys are sampled over and over again by [new artists]. So [are] Ashford and Simpson.

Furthermore, the slow adoption of music securitization should be no surprise. Pullman points out that traditional securities markets also encountered hesitation and skepticism in their infancy:

> I started when there was not one auto loan or credit card security. Asset-backed securities were brand new, [but] it kept evolving. Newer and newer asset classes. . . . Around 1990, not all banks did securitization, and a lot of banks questioned it. In the year 2000, there's not one bank that doesn't securitize its assets. They were all naysayers about securitization, the banks, just the way that they are about entertainment royalty securitization.

Over time, Pullman predicts, music securitization will become more commonplace, and there is some indication that Pullman has successfully raised awareness and acceptance about these more progressive bonds. Though the Bowie deal was partially guaranteed by EMI Records, the later Holland-Dozier-Holland deal was struck without any similar guarantee.

> I think that each year we move further and further down the line. So in terms of the first deal with Bowie, people said that we couldn't

repeat it . . . that it was a one-time event, and that it was unique, that he had his record masters and publishing and the writer's share. And now we're able to obtain ratings on deals that are just based on the writer's share, probably something that most artists still retain. . . . So, therefore, I think that each year we'll go further and further out on the curve. And then at some point in time meet with what the record companies and publishers have traditionally done as a business. Right now I think [record companies and entertainment bond firms] complement each other more. But the future is that, what I hear in terms of feed-back, is that artists would much rather do this deal than sell [their works]. And with the consolidation of the industry, artists want the flexibility to go where they can.

One of the reasons why securitization will likely be viewed with greater acceptance is that securitization provides a potential win-win opportunity for record companies as well. Specifically, as a result of securitization,

[record companies] have more money in their coffers to offer other artists, as opposed to all of their money going out to one artist . . . So if we're talking about a $30 million James Brown deal or a $55 million David Bowie deal, [obtaining that money from the sale of bonds instead of from record company advances] gives these companies more money to put out for new artists. Think of it this way: 55 million is the equivalent of 55 one million dollar advances, 550 hundred thousand dollar advances, and 5500 ten thousand dollar advances. So you can sign on more new artists. . . .

At least for now, the proponents of music securitization are in a dilemma. Securitization promises to revolutionize the music industry, yet it is still so obscure that only one firm, the Pullman Group, has been able to make it work. Even so, the pro-artist values advanced by music securitization should be encouraged in an industry where record companies of increasing size flex overwhelming bargaining power over artists. Securitization remains intensely specialized and somewhat untested in the music business. But does it also promote democracy and diversity in the recording industry? "Definitely," says David Pullman, the only man who, so far, seems to be able to make the bonds sing.

NOTES & QUESTIONS

1. Assuming that a securitization arrangement calls for payment of bond interest at a fixed rate (say 5%) out of an artist's song publishing royalties, what is the resulting allocation of risks and opportunities between the artist and the bond holders? Why do artists tend to prefer this type of arrangement over payments of cash for outright assignments of their royalty interests in particular works?

2. What features of an intellectual property interest make it a good candidate for securitization? Will securitization — which has thus far been used mostly for royalties from copyright licensing — work equally well with royalties from licensing other types of intellectual property interests?

C.   INTELLECTUAL PROPERTY ENFORCEMENT INSURANCE

Insurance payouts aiding intellectual property owners in pressing infringement claims can be important business tools in realizing the value of intellectual property interests. Intellectual property enforcement insurance (most commonly issued in the form of patent enforcement insurance) compensates insured parties for the costs of litigation needed to enforce infringement claims. Such insurance can ensure that the sometimes extreme burdens of infringement litigation will not cause intellectual property owners to hesitate in asserting infringement claims. Rather, with the support provided by intellectual property enforcement insurance, intellectual property owners can realize the full value of their interests by compelling infringers to stop undercutting the commercial activities of the intellectual property owner or to pay licensing fees for their infringing activities. Intellectual property enforcement insurance can also spread the costs of enforcement over extended periods during which insurance premiums are paid rather than imposing large litigation costs on an intellectual property owner in the particular period when litigation is brought.

Additional considerations affecting the desirability of intellectual property enforcement insurance include the following:

Advantages

1. Insurance will deter infringement because the owner of an intellectual property interest will be perceived as having the financial power to protect the interest;

2. Insurance reduces pressure on the interest owner to settle infringement suits to minimize litigation expenses;

3. Insurance may encourage investment in companies holding intellectual property interests by reducing shareholders' apparent risks; and

4. Insured interests may be easier to license because licensees will perceive that the interest holders will be likely to pursue infringers and that licensees are therefore obtaining opportunities to use the licensed intellectual property that will not be available to others absent similar licenses and associated royalty payments.

Disadvantages

1. Insurance premiums are often based on the number of intellectual property interests held rather than the likelihood of enforcement litigation;

2. Policyholders must periodically update their list of covered intellectual property interests or risk having uncovered litigation expenses related to uncovered interests;

3. Disputes may arise between policyholders and their insurers about the scope of coverage, leading to further litigation costs;

4. Insurance may encourage policy holders to litigate weak infringement claims; and

5. Money spent on premiums might better be spent on new product development and marketing.

See generally Bruce E. Burdick, *Patent Insurance, Is It Worth It?* (2002), http://members.tripod.com/burdicklawfirm/insurart.htm (last visited on 8/3/05).

The following reading describes the features of patent enforcement insurance and some of the intellectual property evaluations and related legal issues a company may encounter in obtaining such insurance.

JUMPSPORT, INC. v. JUMPKING, INC.
United States District Court for the Northern District of California
213 F.R.D. 329 (2003)

BRAZIL, United States Magistrate Judge.

. . .

The principal issue we address is whether plaintiff has shown that a document it inadvertently produced in response to a discovery request was "prepared in anticipation of litigation" as that phrase is used in Federal Rule of Civil Procedure 26(b)(3)("Rule 26(b)(3)") to fix the outer boundaries of the work product doctrine.

. . .

Plaintiff JumpSport is a small company engaged in the business of designing, manufacturing and selling trampoline enclosures, trampolines, and related games and accessories. It owns two United States patents for trampoline safety enclosures, U.S. Patent No. 6,053,845, issued on April 25, 2000 ("the 845 patent"), and U.S. Patent No. 6,261,207, issued on July 17, 2001 ("the 207 patent").

JumpSport began marketing its trampoline enclosure product in 1997, before filing its first patent application, and continued to market and sell trampoline enclosure products throughout the pendency of those applications. By the end of 1998, defendant Jumpking, Inc. ("Jumpking"), a large manufacturer of trampolines, began offering its own trampoline enclosure product. Thereafter, defendants Hedstrom Corporation ("Hedstrom") and Variflex, Inc. ("Variflex"), both large sporting goods manufacturers, also brought competing trampoline enclosure products to market.

At all times relevant to the instant motion, JumpSport believed that the trampoline enclosures sold by defendants were copied from JumpSport's product, and that defendants' products infringed its pending patent application for the 845 patent (and the subsequently filed continuing application for the 207 patent). On a few occasions in 1999 and 2000, prior to the issuance of the 845 patent, JumpSport management spoke with Jumpking management to discuss the possible formation of a business relationship between the two companies as a means of resolving the anticipated patent infringement dispute without the necessity of litigation.

While plaintiff was interested in negotiating business solutions with its competitors, it knew that it might be forced to sue in order to protect its intellectual property rights. It also knew that, as a modest sized start-up company, its resources would be considerably strained by the high cost of such litigation. With these high costs in mind, in February of 2000 JumpSport began preparing an application for "patent enforcement" or "patent pursuit" insurance coverage through a company called Litigation Risk Management, Inc. ("LRM"), which specializes in preparing the materials necessary to complete an application for this kind of insurance. Between February and October of 2000, JumpSport did not actively pursue the insurance application because of financial constraints. In October of 2000, when talks with Jumpking regarding a possible business relationship appeared to be going nowhere, JumpSport decided to go forward with the application.

JumpSport was required to submit several documents as part of its insurance application, including an assessment of the value of the company and of the patents it held, as well as an independent legal analysis of its patent rights by a lawyer with expertise in intellectual property. LRM required JumpSport to commission the first report (the financial assessment report) from the accounting and consulting firm Deloitte & Touche ("Deloitte"). Accordingly, in the late fall of 2000, JumpSport commissioned Deloitte to prepare a report assessing the value of JumpSport and its intellectual property.

At the end of January of 2001, Deloitte submitted the first draft of its report, entitled, "JumpSport, Inc. — Fair Market Value Of Invested Capital and Intellectual Property As Of November 15, 2000." This draft contains a brief description of the economy in the United States and of the sporting goods market, a company overview of JumpSport, a valuation of JumpSport's invested capital and its intellectual property, and a valuation synthesis and conclusion, including dollar estimates of potential damage settlements for alleged patent infringement. The report discloses no reasoning about law or litigation.

Because of the high cost of the patent litigation insurance, JumpSport ultimately chose not to proceed with its application. It did decide, however, to proceed with litigation. In December of 2001, JumpSport filed suit against defendants Jumpking, Hedstrom and Variflex for patent infringement and misrepresentation.

In late July of 2002, in response to discovery propounded by defendant Jumpking, plaintiff produced a large quantity of documents that inadvertently included the first draft of the Deloitte report. When it discovered this error in early November of 2002, JumpSport promptly asked Jumpking to return the document — contending that it was protected by the work product doctrine. Counsel for Jumpking, whose damages expert had examined the report before JumpSport sought its return, was not persuaded — and refused to return the document. JumpSport then filed this motion, asking the Court to order Jumpking to return the draft report. Thereafter, Jumpking's expert refined the opinions he was preparing for the damages phase of this litigation, citing the Deloitte draft twice in his lengthy rebuttal report.

. . .

To determine whether JumpSport has shown the draft Deloitte report was "prepared in anticipation of litigation" we examine both the nature of the document and our specific factual situation, in light of the policies that inform work product doctrine, to determine whether this document can fairly be said to have been prepared because of the prospect of litigation.

Our analysis will include two stages. In the first, we will consider whether the prospect of litigation was a substantial factor in the mix of considerations, purposes or forces that led to the preparation of the document. In the second stage, which we will reach only if JumpSport persuades us to answer the first inquiry in the affirmative, we will determine how much harm would be done to the policies that work product doctrine is intended to serve if we were to conclude that the draft report is entitled to no protection (or how much those policy objectives would be advanced if the document were found to fall within the reach of the rule). A finding that denying any protection to the document would risk substantial harm to objectives that the work product doctrine has been crafted to promote would support a conclusion that JumpSport has shown that it could "fairly be said" that the Deloitte report was prepared "because of the prospect of litigation."

We begin our application of the two stage test by examining the nature of the draft Deloitte report and the specific factual circumstances in which it was prepared.

A. The Nature of the Document

The draft report was not written by lawyers, but by two men with educations in business administration. The "Terms & Conditions" (imposed by Deloitte) under which the report was prepared announce that Deloitte "shall have no responsibility for any assumptions provided by the Client" and "no responsibility to address any legal matters or questions of law." In the cover letter transmitting the draft report to JumpSport its authors articulate their understanding "that management will use the results of our analysis for *internal* financial reporting and planning purposes in connection with its business and risk management activities. No other use of this document is intended or should be inferred." This understanding of purpose is repeated in the first section of the report.

The core product that the report provides consists of two estimates of fair market value: one of "Invested Capital" and the other of "certain Patents." Thus, much of the report consists of clearly discoverable financial information. The section devoted to anticipated future growth includes a conclusory (unsupported and unexplained) assertion, expressly attributed to JumpSport's management, that "other competitive enclosures currently sold in the United States allegedly infringe JumpSport's patented technology" and that the "Company is positioned to capture a significant market share when management begins to enforce its patent rights." This section also repeats assertions by management (again unexplained and unsupported) that the company's patent rights inspired (1) a decision by Sears to make JumpSport its sole supplier of trampolines and their enclosures and (2) a request by Jumpking in the late summer of 2000 to discuss "a potential alliance between the two companies."

The draft report also contains a description of the one patent that had been issued to JumpSport before the draft was written — but that description simply parrots verbiage from the published patent itself. It includes no independent analysis and discloses no legal reasoning. A separate paragraph that follows the description of the patent briefly identifies "two possibilities to design around the patent" that management passed along to the Deloitte authors. There is no reasoning in this short paragraph about why the identified designs would not infringe, and the only reasons given for the assertion that neither design would threaten JumpSport are practical (not legal).

In the section of its report entitled "Valuation Analysis," Deloitte opines that the company's most valuable assets are its intellectual property rights. Proceeding from the untested assumption (provided by management) that JumpSport would have a 100 percent market share for the next ten years, the authors examine publicly available data about royalty rates secured by other companies in other business settings to identify a range of royalty rates that JumpSport might command. In a separate section entitled "Other Valuation Issues" the Deloitte authors disclose that the bottom lines of their valuation estimates include figures for the potential value of damage settlements. These estimates of settlement value also were provided by management of JumpSport — and no basis for them is articulated. The report also discloses, with no elaboration, that JumpSport's management anticipates settling with Jumpking in 2002 and with its two other competitors, Hedstrom and Variflex, in 2003.

The only opinions about legal matters that are reflected in the report are completely conclusory assertions by JumpSport management that competitors' products infringe JumpSport's patents, that those competitors will settle for substantial sums when sued, and about what might constitute successful approaches to designing around the patents. The document discloses no legal analysis or reasoning by anyone. The few assertions that have legal predicates are not explained at all. There is no effort to assess the validity of the patents and no comparison of the patent claims with competitors' products. Nor is there any discussion of pros and cons of possible lawsuits, or any analysis of litigation that might ensue. No legal strategies or litigation tactics are discussed, no approaches or arguments are outlined, and no potential evidence or sources of evidence are disclosed.

B.   The Factual Situation

What do we find when we examine "the factual situation in the particular case"? In 1999 and early 2000, before the '845 patent issued in late April of 2000, JumpSport and Jumpking discussed the possibility of forming some kind of business alliance. These discussions were unproductive — so JumpSport realized that it might well be forced to initiate a lawsuit.

JumpSport also realized that prosecuting patent litigation could be very expensive — so it approached a broker, Litigation Risk Management, Inc. ("LRM"), to explore the possibility of acquiring insurance that would fund the attorneys' fees and other costs that such litigation would entail (so-called "patent enforcement" or "patent pursuit" insurance). In the late summer or fall of 2000 LRM advised JumpSport that it would need a "Known Occurrence Patent Enforcement Policy" because it already had identified three known infringers (the three companies that JumpSport eventually named in the complaint that launched the instant litigation). LRM also advised JumpSport that the application process would involve several elements. One was a valuation of the company and of the patents that would be the subject of litigation. According to JumpSport, LRM insisted that Deloitte be retained for this purpose. So JumpSport agreed to retain Deloitte for this purpose — and that agreement led to the preparation of the draft report.

The insurance application also included two other elements: a cost and risk assessment or summary by LRM, and an "evaluation of the patent portfolio by independent patent counsel selected by Litigation Risk Management." In the letter that set forth the terms of its engagement, LRM stated: "We recognize that the LRM Risk Assessment is performed at the request and direction of counsel to facilitate the legal opinions and litigation strategies developed on behalf of JumpSport in anticipation of litigation."

This assertion, apparently written to support a later claim to work product protection, is, of course, not binding on the court. It is additional evidence, however, that at the time JumpSport authorized the preparation of the Deloitte report it understood that there was a substantial likelihood that litigation between it and Jumpking would ensue. In fact, the decision to seek this particular kind of insurance, a "Known Occurrence Patent Enforcement Policy," constitutes substantial evidence that JumpSport anticipated a very real possibility that this litigation would be necessary. So even though the company continued to hope that it could strike a deal with its competitors, and even though it eventually decided, on cost-benefit grounds, not to acquire the policy, JumpSport clearly had "the prospect of litigation in mind when it directed the preparation" of the Deloitte report.

In March of 2001, LRM submitted to JumpSport a draft of the independent patent validity analysis by attorneys at Baker & Botts who had been retained for this purpose, a draft of a report by LRM itself, and a second draft of the valuation report by Deloitte. This second Deloitte report included new material reflecting "information obtained from discussions with independent patent counsel" and a new assertion that the purpose of the report was to provide "litigation risk assessment information to counsel and LRM relative to underwriting recommendations to be made by LRM. . . ."

None of these other draft reports are in issue here. The only document that is in issue is the first Deloitte draft report — initially submitted to JumpSport at the end of January of 2001. It is only that report that was inadvertently disclosed during JumpSport's document production. While we have no occasion to determine whether any of these other draft documents could qualify for protection as work product, as comments below will suggest, we would expect our analysis of the work product issues to take a different turn if we were considering the Baker & Botts legal analysis.

It also is instructive to note that a carrier that had issued an insurance policy of this kind apparently would decline to pay anything in response to a claim until it received yet another independent set of legal analyses from an independent counsel. When a carrier received a claim under this kind of policy it could insist, before funding its contractual share of the litigation costs, that it be provided an opinion letter from an independent and appropriately qualified intellectual property lawyer that concluded (with supporting analysis) that the accused products in fact infringed the insured's patents.

The fact that industry practices contemplate so much direct input from qualified patent lawyers, both before and after issuance of a policy like this, reinforces the notion, suggested by the content of the draft Deloitte report, that no participant in the application process looks to a report like the one Deloitte prepared as an independent source of any significant or reliable legal analysis or litigation strategy. The valuation report might pass along or accept as assumptions legal conclusions or legal reasoning that originated in independent patent counsel — but its authors (non-lawyers) would not be expected to engage in legal analysis on their own. We thus feel confident that the assumptions about infringement and settlement that surface in conclusory form in the first draft of the Deloitte report are not the product of any legal analysis by the authors of the report. That finding, coupled with the nakedness of the statements in the report that seem to reflect a legal conclusion by someone, encourage us to infer that all the participants in this insurance application process understood that the kind of general valuation of the business and its patent assets that we see in the draft Deloitte report was intended to serve purposes appreciably farther removed from litigation than the analyses by independent patent counsel — and thus was appreciably farther removed from the center of the work product universe.

Having now examined the nature of the draft report and the factual situation in which Deloitte produced it, it is time to apply the test for determining whether "the document can fairly be said to have been prepared or obtained because of the prospect of litigation."

C. Application of the test

(i) The First Stage of the Test: Was the Prospect of Litigation a Substantial Factor Leading to the Preparation of the Deloitte Report

We first consider whether JumpSport has shown that the prospect of litigation was a "substantial factor" in the mix of considerations and forces that led to the preparation of the report. We think JumpSport has made this showing. As we pointed out, by the time JumpSport decided to commission the report the prospect of litigation was in no sense remote or speculative. While at that point it was not inevitable that litigation would ensue, the likelihood that the parties would find themselves in the court system was quite substantial — especially given the failure, over a substantial period, of the talks that had been aimed at trying to avoid litigation by forming some kind of business alliance with Jumpking. So the odds that litigation would commence were high — and the time was near.

But that is not where our consideration of this question should stop. We also must take into account the nature and magnitude of the role that the prospect of litigation played in causing this report to be generated. One question we ask in this setting is whether there were other, non-litigation considerations or motives at work in the decision to commission the report — and, if so, how substantial they were. The evidence before us supports a finding that the most immediate reason for commissioning this report was to position the company to try to secure patent enforcement insurance coverage. At least in theory, however, a report from a major accounting firm that assesses the value of the company's invested capital and its intellectual property could be put to many different kinds of business purposes. Moreover, many of those same purposes could be advanced by a company having the kind of insurance that JumpSport was positioning itself to acquire. For example, having this kind of insurance could improve the company's ability to raise capital. It also might lubricate efforts to merge with or acquire another entity. Yet another purpose could be to increase the price the company might bring if it were offered for sale. Such insurance also might improve a company's chances of going public successfully, or of securing favorable terms from licensees.

The only evidence before the court that speaks to any of these possibilities is a statement in the Supplemental Declaration of Steven W. Moulton, Vice President and General Counsel of JumpSport. After describing the role that the report was to play in applying for the patent enforcement insurance policy, Mr. Moulton avers that "JumpSport intended to engage Deloitte to provide a separate valuation report that JumpSport could use for the business purpose of obtaining potential investors to help fund the patent enforcement insurance policy, and the report would be based upon the same information Deloitte had obtained during its analysis for the patent enforcement litigation. Ultimately JumpSport and Deloitte did not agree on the scope and use of any such report, and JumpSport did not obtain a report for this purpose."

While this evidence suggests that JumpSport contemplated the possibility of using the Deloitte report for more than one purpose, and while it is possible that JumpSport also understood that acquiring patent enforcement insurance might redound to its business benefit even if no litigation ensued, there is no evidentiary basis for a finding that any of these kinds of considerations was anything but peripheral. In other words, the record does not support a finding that any consideration or purpose other than positioning the company to acquire the insurance coverage would have been sufficient to cause JumpSport to commission the report that is in issue here. Nor does the record support a finding that JumpSport's interest in acquiring this kind of insurance was inspired to any appreciable extent by any motivation other than funding patent enforcement litigation.

In sum, we conclude, on the record before us, that the prospect of litigation to enforce its patent rights was the only significant factor underlying JumpSport's pursuit of the insurance — and that trying to meet the informational requirements of the prospective insurer was at least the primary factor that led JumpSport to commission the Deloitte report. In these circumstances, a conclusion that the prospect of litigation was "a substantial factor in the mix of considerations" that led to the preparation of the document is not foreclosed either by the fact that the connection between the report and the litigation was not immediate and direct (the report would support the acquisition of the insurance, then the insurance would support the litigation), or by the fact that one could characterize the interest that most directly inspired the company's pursuit of the coverage as a "business" or "financial" interest. Much of litigation, after all, is business — or about business. Stated differently, a "factor" can be "substantial" (as that term is used in this setting) even if more than one label might be attached to it (business and litigation), even if the causal connection between it and the prospect of litigation is in some measure indirect, and even if more than one interest motivated the preparation of the document.

Similarly, the fact that JumpSport ultimately decided not to purchase the insurance does not foreclose a finding that the prospect of litigation was a substantial factor leading to the preparation of the report. The time on which courts primarily should focus when addressing this issue is the time the party was making the decision to have the document prepared. It is the party's prospective mind set at that juncture that matters — for we are trying to determine what role the "prospect" of litigation played in the preparation of the document. Had JumpSport abandoned pursuit of the insurance because it abandoned the idea of initiating litigation we would have no occasion to struggle with this matter — but that is not the reason JumpSport elected not to buy the insurance. Moreover, the litigation that JumpSport had in mind when it commissioned the report in fact occurred.

Our conclusion that the prospect of litigation was not only a substantial factor, but the dominant consideration driving the decision to commission the Deloitte report is buttressed by the fact that no one has suggested that in the normal course of business, or for some other reason independent of the prospect of litigation, JumpSport would have had a report of this character prepared during this period. While not essential to a conclusion that the prospect of litigation was a substantial factor, this kind of finding is likely to be sufficient to support that conclusion when it is clear that the prospect of litigation was real and relevant to the decision to have the document prepared.

Given all these considerations, we hold that JumpSport has satisfied the first prong of the test for determining whether a document can fall within the reach of Rule 26(b)(3).

(ii)   The Second Stage of the Test: How Much Harm Would be Done to the Policy Objectives of the Work Product Doctrine if Protection is Not Available to the Deloitte Report?

We cannot conclude that the Deloitte report was "prepared in anticipation of litigation" unless JumpSport also satisfies the second prong of the test (something partially akin to the "proximate cause" or "legal cause" inquiry in the torts field). In the second stage of the test we focus on the policy objectives that the work product doctrine is intended to serve — then we determine how much (if any) harm they would suffer if the document was not protected (or how much those objectives would be advanced by a determination that the document falls within the reach of the Rule). In addressing these issues we again consider the nature of the document and the particular factual setting in which it was created.

In this case, it is the nature of the document that undermines most the contention that it should be deemed to fall within the ambit of the work product rule. As noted above, the Deloitte report contains no legal analysis, no discussion of legal strategies, no observations at all about the substantive or procedural matters that litigation might entail. Its authors expressly disclaim any "responsibility to address any legal matters or questions of law." They also expressly articulate, twice, their understanding of the limited purposes the document was intended to serve: "management will use the results of our analysis for *internal* financial reporting and planning purposes in connection with its business and risk management activities. No other use of this document is intended or should be inferred."

The primary objective of the report is to ascribe dollar value to JumpSport's invested capital and its intellectual property (which consisted, at the time, of one issued patent and some related pending applications). The vast majority of the verbiage in the document addresses business and financial matters — virtually all discoverable. There are instances in which the authors make assumptions (clearly ascribed to JumpSport's management) that have law-based predicates, e.g., that the patents are enforceable, and that competitors will recognize this fact and pay substantial sums to settle lawsuits that JumpSport might bring to enforce its rights. But these assumptions are neither explained nor defended. They are simply made.

The report's brief description of the one issued patent is taken directly from the language of the patent itself — a public document. That description includes no analysis of claims, no discussion of prior art or other bases for challenging validity, and no comparison of the claims with the products that might be accused of infringing. One paragraph identifies two "design around" possibilities, both suggested by JumpSport's management, but there is no discussion of why, under the law or the arguable scope of the claims, the alternative designs would not infringe. Nor do the authors identify or discuss evidence, or sources of evidence that might come into play in litigation. In fact, they say nothing about what might be involved in future litigation or how it might be prosecuted or defended. They simply assume, for purposes of valuing the company's assets, that JumpSport would be victorious in any such litigation. These superficial assumptions could not possibly reveal anything of real litigation value to any prospective party opponent.

Given the content of the report, would a refusal to extend protection to this document invade that "zone of privacy" that courts have assumed that lawyers and clients need if they are to think reliably, critically, and creatively about their litigation? Because the document reveals no legal reasoning and no thoughts about what might occur in litigation or how litigation might be handled, the answer must be no.

Alternatively, would a refusal to extend protection to this document damage the sets of incentives that are said to be essential to the effective functioning of the adversary system? Answering this question is a more complicated undertaking because the Deloitte report includes some information that might be relevant to litigating damages issues in an enforcement action. The report contains information (and some opinions) about the income, assets, and value of the company (as of late 2000), as well as about the value of its patent and what level of royalty rates the patent might support at that time.

Several observations about this information are in order. First, as noted above, virtually (perhaps literally) all of the data on which the report was based would be discoverable (in fact, according to plaintiff's counsel, this information already has been discovered in this case by defendant's counsel). And there is nothing in the way the Deloitte authors (non-lawyers) organized or packaged this material, or in the topics they decided to address and the categories of information they decided to describe, that would tend to reveal anything about litigation strategies or theories that JumpSport's lawyers might later decide to adopt. Because a party could foresee that at least the vast majority of the underlying data would be discoverable, and would know that a document like this (that was prepared by non-lawyers) would not disclose litigation strategies, the fact that the draft report might not be protected by the work product doctrine would not serve as a consequential deterrent to commissioning its preparation.

Second, by the time this case goes to trial, much of the information in the report (which was gathered in the latter half of 2000) will be at least somewhat dated. While some of the information in the report might remain relevant to some parts of the damages questions, the primary focus of damages litigation likely would be on information covering the intervening period. These facts also would be foreseeable at the time JumpSport decided to commission the report — and would help reduce the likelihood that JumpSport would be inhibited from having the report prepared by the possibility that it might in the future get into the hands of an adversary in litigation.

We acknowledge that Jumpking's damages expert has submitted a declaration in which he asserts that he relied to some extent on information in the Deloitte draft when he developed his rebuttal report. In some circumstances, how an adversary later uses a document in the litigation, or how he proposes to use it, could be relevant to the issues we address here — if that use was foreseeable at the time the decision was originally made to direct the preparation of the document. If, for example, it was foreseeable that a document of the kind in issue could be used tellingly by an adversary to gain litigation leverage on an important disputed issue, and if it was unlikely that the adversary could gain that same leverage through evidence, data, or analyses with other (accessible) sources, then a decision that the document could receive no protection under Rule 26(b)(3) might well inhibit a party from deciding to have such a document prepared in the first place.

. . . [W]e are not persuaded that any part of the Deloitte draft is likely to serve as a unique source of significant leverage on any issue of real consequence in this case. We also note that Jumpking's damages expert claims to have cited the draft only twice in a rebuttal report that is at least 26 pages long. And while part of the report would shed some light on some of the information that JumpSport's management had in late 2000 about arguably relevant royalty rates, there is no reason to believe management did not simultaneously have additional information in the same subject area.

. . .

Accordingly, we find that refusal to extend protection to this document does not damage the sets of incentives essential to the effective functioning of the adversary system. Because we find that disclosure of the Deloitte Report does not threaten the parties' "zone of privacy," or enable one side to borrow its adversaries' wits to any significant degree, we hold that JumpSport has not satisfied the second stage of the test.

. . .

Although JumpSport satisfied the requirements of the first stage of the test by persuading us that the prospect of litigation was a "substantial factor" leading to the preparation of the document, JumpSport has failed to demonstrate that extending protection to this draft report would advance appreciably any of the policy objectives that the work product doctrine has been developed to serve. In sum, the content of the Deloitte report, and the circumstances in which it was prepared, remove it too far from the heartland of work product sensitivity to justify ruling that it warrants protection under this doctrine. It follows that we cannot conclude that "the document can fairly be said to have been prepared or obtained because of the prospect of litigation."

Because we conclude that the draft Deloitte report does not fall within the ambit of Rule 26(b)(3) we deny JumpSport's motion for an order compelling Jumpking to return the document. We need not address the other grounds that Jumpking advances for reaching the same conclusion.

IT IS SO ORDERED.

D. CORPORATIONS AS LONG-TERM INTELLECTUAL PROPERTY USERS: ANTICIPATING NEW MODES OF USE AND DISTRIBUTION

Because they often hold or use intellectual property for extended periods, corporations can encounter unusual legal problems as modes of intellectual property use and distribution change with shifts in related technologies or social practices. New types of media and methods of distribution related to advances in computer technology have been particularly challenging for corporations holding limited rights to use works in physical media such as books or movies. Corporations have sometimes acquired limited intellectual property interests (usually through licenses) which were sufficient to meet their original commercial needs only to find that they were unready to pursue related commercial opportunities opened up by new technologies. To pursue these further opportunities, the corporations needed to go back to the holders of the relevant intellectual property interests and seek further rights to use the properties involved, often under circumstances where the corporations had strong needs for the rights in question and were consequently at a substantial negotiating disadvantage.

This type of problem confronted the New York Times Company in the following case as it sought to redistribute some of its newspaper stories through new, computer-facilitated media such as CD-ROM disks and online databases.

NEW YORK TIMES COMPANY, INC. v. TASINI
United States Supreme Court
522 U.S. 483 (2001)

GINSBURG, J.

This copyright case concerns the rights of freelance authors and a presumptive privilege of their publishers. The litigation was initiated by six freelance authors and relates to articles they contributed to three print periodicals (two newspapers and one magazine). Under agreements with the periodicals' publishers, but without the freelancers' consent, two computer database companies placed copies of the freelancers' articles — along with all other articles from the periodicals in which the freelancers' work appeared — into three databases. Whether written by a freelancer or staff member, each article is presented to, and retrievable by, the user in isolation, clear of the context the original print publication presented.

The freelance authors' complaint alleged that their copyrights had been infringed by the inclusion of their articles in the databases. The publishers, in response, relied on the privilege of reproduction and distribution accorded them by § 201(c) of the Copyright Act, which provides:

> Copyright in each separate contribution to a collective work is distinct from copyright in the collective work as a whole, and vests initially in the author of the contribution. In the absence of an express transfer of the copyright or of any rights under it, the owner of copyright in the collective work is presumed to have acquired only the privilege of reproducing and distributing the contribution as part of that particular collective work, any revision of that collective work, and any later collective work in the same series. 17 U.S.C. § 201(c).

Specifically, the publishers maintained that, as copyright owners of collective works, *i.e.,* the original print publications, they had merely exercised "the privilege" § 201(c) accords them to "reproduc[e] and distribut[e]" the author's discretely copyrighted contribution.

In agreement with the Second Circuit, we hold that § 201(c) does not authorize the copying at issue here. The publishers are not sheltered by § 201(c), we conclude, because the databases reproduce and distribute articles standing alone and not in context, not "as part of that particular collective work" to which the author contributed, "as part of . . . any revision" thereof, or "as part of . . . any later collective work in the same series." Both the print publishers and the electronic publishers, we rule, have infringed the copyrights of the freelance authors.

I

A

Respondents Jonathan Tasini, Mary Kay Blakely, Barbara Garson, Margot Mifflin, Sonia Jaffe Robbins, and David S. Whitford are authors (Authors).

Between 1990 and 1993, they wrote the 21 articles (Articles) on which this dispute centers. Tasini, Mifflin, and Blakely contributed 12 Articles to The New York Times, the daily newspaper published by petitioner The New York Times Company (Times). Tasini, Garson, Robbins, and Whitford wrote eight Articles for Newsday, another New York daily paper, published by petitioner Newsday, Inc. (Newsday). Whitford also contributed one Article to Sports Illustrated, a weekly magazine published by petitioner Time, Inc. (Time). The Authors registered copyrights in each of the Articles. The Times, Newsday, and Time (Print Publishers) registered collective work copyrights in each periodical edition in which an Article originally appeared. The Print Publishers engaged the Authors as independent contractors (freelancers) under contracts that in no instance secured consent from an Author to placement of an Article in an electronic database.

At the time the Articles were published, all three Print Publishers had agreements with petitioner LEXIS/NEXIS (formerly Mead Data Central Corp.), owner and operator of NEXIS, a computerized database that stores information in a text-only format. NEXIS contains articles from hundreds of journals (newspapers and periodicals) spanning many years. The Print Publishers have licensed to LEXIS/NEXIS the text of articles appearing in the three periodicals. The licenses authorize LEXIS/NEXIS to copy and sell any portion of those texts.

Pursuant to the licensing agreements, the Print Publishers regularly provide LEXIS/NEXIS with a batch of all the articles published in each periodical edition. The Print Publisher codes each article to facilitate computerized retrieval, and then transmits it in a separate file. After further coding, LEXIS/NEXIS places the article in the central discs of its database.

Subscribers to NEXIS, accessing the system through a computer, may search for articles by author, subject, date, publication, headline, key term, words in text, or other criteria. Responding to a search command, NEXIS scans the database and informs the user of the number of articles meeting the user's search criteria. The user then may view, print, or download each of the articles yielded by the search. The display of each article includes the print publication (e.g., The New York Times), date (September 23, 1990), section (Magazine), initial page number (26), headline or title ("Remembering Jane"), and author (Mary Kay Blakely). Each article appears as a separate, isolated "story" — without any visible link to the other stories originally published in the same newspaper or magazine edition. NEXIS does not contain pictures or advertisements, and it does not reproduce the original print publication's formatting features such as headline size, page placement (e.g., above or below the fold for newspapers), or location of continuation pages.

The Times (but not Newsday or Time) also has licensing agreements with petitioner University Microfilms International (UMI). The agreements authorize reproduction of Times materials on two CD-ROM products, the New York Times OnDisc (N.Y.TO) and General Periodicals OnDisc (GPO).

. . .

B

On December 16, 1993, the Authors filed this civil action in the United States District Court for the Southern District of New York. The Authors alleged that their copyrights were infringed when, as permitted and facilitated by the Print Publishers, LEXIS/NEXIS and UMI (Electronic Publishers) placed the Articles in the NEXIS, NYTO, and GPO databases (Databases). The Authors sought declaratory and injunctive relief, and damages. In response to the Authors' complaint, the Print and Electronic Publishers raised the reproduction and distribution privilege accorded collective work copyright owners by 17 U.S.C. § 201(c). After discovery, both sides moved for summary judgment.

. . .

We granted certiorari to determine whether the copying of the Authors' Articles in the Databases is privileged by 17 U.S.C. § 201(c). Like the Court of Appeals, we conclude that the § 201(c) privilege does not override the Authors' copyrights, for the Databases do not reproduce and distribute the Articles as part of a collective work privileged by § 201(c). Accordingly, and again like the Court of Appeals, we find it unnecessary to determine whether the privilege is transferable.

II

. . .

Section 201(c) [of the Copyright Act] both describes and circumscribes the "privilege" a publisher acquires regarding an author's contribution to a collective work:

> In the absence of an express transfer of the copyright or of any rights under it, the owner of copyright in the collective work is presumed to have acquired *only* the privilege of reproducing and distributing the contribution as part of that particular collective work, any revision of that collective work, and any later collective work in the same series. (Emphasis added.)

A newspaper or magazine publisher is thus privileged to reproduce or distribute an article contributed by a freelance author, absent a contract otherwise providing, only "as part of" any (or all) of three categories of collective works: (a) "that collective work" to which the author contributed her work, (b) "any revision of that collective work," or (c) "any later collective work in the same series." In accord with Congress' prescription, a "publishing company could reprint a contribution from one issue in a later issue of its magazine, and could reprint an article from a 1980 edition of an encyclopedia in a 1990 revision of it; the publisher could not revise the contribution itself or include it in a new anthology or an entirely different magazine or other collective work."

Essentially, § 201(c) adjusts a publisher's copyright in its collective work to accommodate a freelancer's copyright in her contribution. If there is demand for a freelance article standing alone or in a new collection, the Copyright Act allows the freelancer to benefit from that demand; after authorizing initial publication, the freelancer may also sell the article to others. It would scarcely "preserve the author's copyright in a contribution" as contemplated by Congress, H.R. Rep. 122, U.S.Code Cong. & Admin.News 1976, pp. 5659, 5738, if a newspaper or magazine publisher were permitted to reproduce or distribute copies of the author's contribution in isolation or within new collective works. See Gordon, Fine-Tuning *Tasini:* Privileges of Electronic Distribution and Reproduction, 66 Brooklyn L.Rev. 473, 484 (2000).

III

In the instant case, the Authors wrote several Articles and gave the Print Publishers permission to publish the Articles in certain newspapers and magazines. It is undisputed that the Authors hold copyrights and, therefore, exclusive rights in the Articles. It is clear, moreover, that the Print and Electronic Publishers have exercised at least some rights that § 106 initially assigns exclusively to the Authors: LEXIS/NEXIS' central discs and UMI's CD-ROMs "reproduce . . . copies" of the Articles, § 106(1); UMI, by selling those CD-ROMs, and LEXIS/NEXIS, by selling copies of the Articles through the NEXIS Database, "distribute copies" of the Articles "to the public by sale," § 106(3); and the Print Publishers, through contracts licensing the production of copies in the Databases, "authorize" reproduction and distribution of the Articles, § 106.

Against the Authors' charge of infringement, the Publishers do not here contend the Authors entered into an agreement authorizing reproduction of the Articles in the Databases. Nor do they assert that the copies in the Databases represent "fair use" of the Authors' Articles. Instead, the Publishers rest entirely on the privilege described in § 201(c). Each discrete edition of the periodicals in which the Articles appeared is a "collective work," the Publishers agree. They contend, however, that reproduction and distribution of each Article by the Databases lie within the "privilege of reproducing and distributing the [Articles] as part of . . . [a] revision of that collective work," § 201(c). The Publishers' encompassing construction of the § 201(c) privilege is unacceptable, we conclude, for it would diminish the Authors' exclusive rights in the Articles.

In determining whether the Articles have been reproduced and distributed "as part of" a "revision" of the collective works in issue, we focus on the Articles as presented to, and perceptible by, the user of the Databases. In this case, the three Databases present articles to users clear of the context provided either by the original periodical editions or by any revision of those editions. The Databases first prompt users to search the universe of their contents: thousands or millions of files containing individual articles from thousands of collective works (*i.e.,* editions), either in one series (the Times, in NYTO) or in scores of series (the sundry titles in NEXIS and GPO). When the user conducts a search, each article appears as a separate item within the search result. In NEXIS and NYTO, an article appears to a user without the graphics, formatting, or other articles with which the article was initially published. In GPO, the article appears with the other materials published on the same page or pages, but without any material published on other pages of the original periodical. In either circumstance, we cannot see how the Database perceptibly reproduces and distributes the article "as part of" either the original edition or a "revision" of that edition.

One might view the articles as parts of a new compendium — namely, the entirety of works in the Database. In that compendium, each edition of each periodical represents only a miniscule fraction of the ever-expanding Database. The Database no more constitutes a "revision" of each constituent edition than a 400-page novel quoting a sonnet in passing would represent a "revision" of that poem. "Revision" denotes a new "version," and a version is, in this setting, a "distinct form of something regarded by its creator or others as one work." Webster's Third New International Dictionary 1944, 2545 (1976). The massive whole of the Database is not recognizable as a new version of its every small part.

Alternatively, one could view the Articles in the Databases "as part of" no larger work at all, but simply as individual articles presented individually. That each article bears marks of its origin in a particular periodical (less vivid marks in NEXIS and NYTO, more vivid marks in GPO) suggests the article was *previously* part of that periodical. But the markings do not mean the article is *currently* reproduced or distributed as part of the periodical. The Databases' reproduction and distribution of individual Articles — simply as *individual Articles* — would invade the core of the Authors' exclusive rights under § 106.

The Publishers press an analogy between the Databases, on the one hand, and microfilm and microfiche, on the other. We find the analogy wanting. Microforms typically contain continuous photographic reproductions of a periodical in the medium of miniaturized film. Accordingly, articles appear on the microforms, writ very small, in precisely the position in which the articles appeared in the newspaper. The Times, for example, printed the beginning of Blakely's "Remembering Jane" Article on page 26 of the Magazine in the September 23, 1990, edition; the microfilm version of the Times reproduces that same Article on film in the very same position, within a film reproduction of the entire Magazine, in turn within a reproduction of the entire September 23, 1990, edition. True, the microfilm roll contains multiple editions, and the microfilm user can adjust the machine lens to focus only on the Article, to the exclusion of surrounding material. Nonetheless, the user first encounters the Article in context. In the Databases, by contrast, the Articles appear disconnected from their original context. In NEXIS and NYTO, the user sees the "Jane" Article apart even from the remainder of page 26. In GPO, the user sees the Article within the context of page 26, but clear of the context of page 25 or page 27, the rest of the Magazine, or the remainder of the day's newspaper. In short, unlike microforms, the Databases do not perceptibly reproduce articles as part of the collective work to which the author contributed or as part of any "revision" thereof.

Invoking the concept of "media neutrality," the Publishers urge that the "transfer of a work between media" does not "alte[r] the character of" that work for copyright purposes. That is indeed true. See 17 U.S.C. § 102(a) (copyright protection subsists in original works "fixed in any tangible medium of expression"). But unlike the conversion of newsprint to microfilm, the transfer of articles to the Databases does not represent a mere conversion of intact periodicals (or revisions of periodicals) from one medium to another. The Databases offer users individual articles, not intact periodicals. In this case, media neutrality should protect the Authors' rights in the individual Articles to the extent those Articles are now presented individually, outside the collective work context, within the Databases' new media.

For the purpose at hand — determining whether the Authors' copyrights have been infringed — an analogy to an imaginary library may be instructive. Rather than maintaining intact editions of periodicals, the library would contain separate copies of each article. Perhaps these copies would exactly reproduce the periodical pages from which the articles derive (if the model is GPO); perhaps the copies would contain only typescript characters, but still indicate the original periodical's name and date, as well as the article's headline and page number (if the model is NEXIS or NYTO). The library would store the folders containing the articles in a file room, indexed based on diverse criteria, and containing articles from vast numbers of editions. In response to patron requests, an inhumanly speedy librarian would search the room and provide copies of the articles matching patron-specified criteria.

Viewing this strange library, one could not, consistent with ordinary English usage, characterize the articles "as part of" a "revision" of the editions in which the articles first appeared. In substance, however, the Databases differ from the file room only to the extent they aggregate articles in electronic packages (the LEXIS/NEXIS central discs or UMI CD-ROMs), while the file room stores articles in spatially separate files. The crucial fact is that the Databases, like the hypothetical library, store and retrieve articles separately within a vast domain of diverse texts. Such a storage and retrieval system effectively overrides the Authors' exclusive right to control the individual reproduction and distribution of each Article, 17 U.S.C. §§ 106(1), (3).

The Publishers claim the protection of § 201(c) because users can manipulate the Databases to generate search results consisting entirely of articles from a particular periodical edition. By this logic, § 201(c) would cover the hypothetical library if, in response to a request, that library's expert staff assembled all of the articles from a particular periodical edition. However, the fact that a third party can manipulate a database to produce a non-infringing document does not mean the database is not infringing. Under § 201(c), the question is not whether a user can generate a revision of a collective work from a database, but whether the database itself perceptibly presents the author's contribution as part of a revision of the collective work. That result is not accomplished by these Databases.

. . .

IV

The Publishers warn that a ruling for the Authors will have "devastating" consequences. The Databases, the Publishers note, provide easy access to complete newspaper texts going back decades. A ruling for the Authors, the Publishers suggest, will punch gaping holes in the electronic record of history. The Publishers' concerns are echoed by several historians, see Brief for Ken Burns et al. as *Amici Curiae,* but discounted by several other historians, see

Brief for Ellen Schrecker et al. as *Amici Curiae;* Brief for Authors' Guild, Inc., Jacques Barzun et al. as *Amici Curiae.*

Notwithstanding the dire predictions from some quarters, it hardly follows from today's decision that an injunction against the inclusion of these Articles in the Databases (much less all freelance articles in any databases) must issue. See 17 U.S.C. § 502(a) (court "may" enjoin infringement); *Campbell v. Acuff-Rose Music, Inc.,* 510 U.S. 569, 578, n. 10, 114 S.Ct. 1164, 127 L.Ed.2d 500 (1994) (goals of copyright law are "not always best served by automatically granting injunctive relief"). The parties (Authors and Publishers) may enter into an agreement allowing continued electronic reproduction of the Authors' works; they, and if necessary the courts and Congress, may draw on numerous models for distributing copyrighted works and remunerating authors for their distribution. *See, e.g.,* 17 U.S.C. § 118(b); *Broadcast Music, Inc. v. Columbia Broadcasting System, Inc.,* 441 U.S. 1, 4-6, 10-12, 99 S.Ct. 1551, 60 L.Ed.2d 1 (1979) (recounting history of blanket music licensing regimes and consent decrees governing their operation). In any event, speculation about future harms is no basis for this Court to shrink authorial rights Congress established in § 201(c). Agreeing with the Court of Appeals that the Publishers are liable for infringement, we leave remedial issues open for initial airing and decision in the District Court.

. . .

Amy Terry Sheehan, Tasini Aftermath: The Consequences of the Freelancers' Victory
14 DePaul-LCA J. Art & Ent. L. 231 (2004)*

. . .

The freelancers' landmark victory in *Tasini* has proved to be empty of any actual concrete benefit to freelancers. The predictions in Justice John Paul Stevens' *Tasini* dissent have come true. Justice Stevens forecast that freelance material would be purged from electronic archival databases and that the freelancers would not see any actual financial gain from the majority's decision. The post-*Tasini* dealings between publishers and freelance authors have proven both calculations true. As Emily Bass explained:

> On one hand, the United States Supreme Court has said in unequivocal terms that digital rights belong to the freelance author and are his to exercise unless he or she consents to transfer or license them. On the other hand, there is the practical question of whether freelance authors can manage to hold on to their rights and, even if they can, whether they can then realize their value.

Justice Stevens explained that "the difficulties of locating individual freelance authors and the potential exposure to statutory damages may well have the effect of forcing electronic archives to purge freelance pieces from their databases." Also in explaining why freelancer authors will not benefit financially, the *Tasini* dissent pointed out that "[a]s counsel for petitioners represented at oral argument, since 1995, The New York Times has required freelance authors to grant them 'electronic rights' to articles. And the inclusion of such a term has had no effect on the compensation authors receive."

. . .

[A]fter *Tasini*, publishers set out to determine what material they did not have the rights to, and deleted that material from their electronic databases. The day the Court handed down its decision, Arthur Sulzberger Jr., chairman of The New York Times Company and publisher of The New York Times, said that the Times would "now undertake the difficult and sad process of removing significant portions from its electronic historical archive." The New York Times deleted freelance material from 1980-1995 for which it did not have contractual rights. Approximately 115,000 articles by 27,000 writers were affected. Other publishers such as Time Magazine took similar steps. These consequences would not have swayed Justice Ginsburg however. In the *Tasini* opinion, she points out that "speculation about future harms is no basis for this Court to shrink authorial rights Congress established in § 201(c)."

The New York Times made efforts both to prevent purging and to restore freelance authors' works. Before removing material from its electronic database, it gave freelance writers the opportunity through a phone line and website to sign a waiver giving the Times the necessary rights to retain the electronic versions of the articles. Current freelance contracts include a provision giving The New York Times a non-exclusive license "to reproduce, distribute, display, perform, translate, or otherwise publish . . . prior contributions." . . .

As a result of the restoration website, restoration hotline and the "previous works" provisions, The New York Times has restored approximately 20 percent of affected material. . . .

A. Freelancers' Contracts in the Post-*Tasini* World

Many publishers did not wait for the courts to rule on *Tasini*. They took proactive measures in order to protect themselves in case the verdict turned out as it did. Contracts between freelance authors and publishers began to change in the mid-1990s soon after the *Tasini* lawsuit was filed. The New York Times, as well as most other major publishers that use freelance work, began to require freelance authors to sign away their electronic republication rights. "[T]he practical implication of the *Tasini* decision was to grant a right under the Copyright Act that in many cases has proved valueless: Exploiters of works have enough bargaining power to obtain royalty-free licenses to make revisions of freelancers' copyrighted works." Because publishers had already taken action and because they had superior bargaining power, the *Tasini* decision had "little prospective importance in terms of changing current industry practice."

Many publishers currently use work-made-for-hire or all-rights provisions in contracts with freelance writers. For example, a standard New York Times freelance contract reads:

> The Times owns all right, title and interest, including copyright, in
> and to the Article(s), throughout the world (such material being com-
> missioned by the Times as a contribution to a work and therefore a
> "work made for hire" under the Copyright Act or, alternatively, if not
> a "work made for hire," then you hereby assign all such right, title,
> interest and copyright in and to the Article(s) to the Times).

Other publishers, such as the Tribune Company, whose publications include
the Chicago Tribune, the Los Angeles Times, Newsday, and the Baltimore Sun,
have similar freelance work for hire contracts for writers, photographers, and
illustrators. Publishers prefer work for hire agreements because they offer the
most protection and are simple to obtain because of their bargaining power.

. . .

NOTES & QUESTIONS

1. If the long term value of intellectual property in partially unknown future
uses lies at the heart of disputes like that in *Tasini*, how should this value be
allocated between intellectual property producers (such as the authors in
Tasini) and initial intellectual property distributors (such as the publishers in
Tasini)? Is this just a matter of risk and opportunity allocation that can be
resolved by contract provisions reserving rights related to future uses of intellectual property to one party or the other? Are there differences in the abilities of these parties to exert meaningful bargaining power in negotiating
intellectual property acquisition contracts that suggest that the allocation of
rights in future uses of such property should not be fully resolvable by contract
and that some sort of inalienable right to control currently unknown future
uses of intellectual property (or to at least share in the economic proceeds
resulting from such uses) should be preserved by statute in favor of intellectual property creators? Or would the preservation of such rights in authors
and other intellectual property creators simply set up undesirable future bargaining processes in which initially successful distributors of intellectual property are forced to pay large sums to realize the full commercial potential of
their initial success?

2. Does the proper resolution of the rights of authors and distributors
regarding new uses of previously transferred intellectual property depend on
the technological or transactional relationship between the initial and subsequent uses of the intellectual property and related efficiency benefits to the
public? For example, consider a case where there are clear transactional efficiencies that can be gained by letting a party, such as the New York Times,
extend its prior use of intellectual property from one media to another.
Greater familiarity with the distributed material or its users may allow an initial distributor to be far more efficient and effective in distributing that material in a new media than other parties who are capable of undertaking the
same distribution. Does the greater efficiency in additional modes of distribution that can be achieved by an initial intellectual property distributor provide
a basis for favoring additional uses of intellectual property by the initial distributor? Does this logic suggest that, where the relevant contracts are
ambiguous about whether future uses have been authorized as part of partial

transfers of intellectual property rights, the authorization of future uses by highly efficient distributors should be recognized as a matter of contract interpretation?

E. VALUABLE DISPOSITIONS OF INTELLECTUAL PROPERTY

1. Auctions

Where an intellectual property owner can not commercialize an interest through the production of related products — either because the interest falls outside of the owner's main line of business or because the owner has gone bankrupt and has terminated normal business operations — the owner may seek to dispose of the intellectual property interest through an auction aimed at obtaining the maximum price for an assignment of the interest. Auctions of intellectual property interests initiated by the interest owners are now conducted through a number of internet sites. *See, e.g.,* Patent Show, http://www.patentauction.com/ (last visited on 10/12/2005); Free Patent Auction, http://www.freepatentauction.com/ (last visited on 10/12/2005). Ocean Tomo, LLC, a merchant banking firm focusing on intellectual property assets, has announced that it will hold live patent auction events, with simulcasts on eBay Live Auctions. *See* Ocean Tomo Patent Auction, http://www.oceantomo.com/auctions.html (last visited on 10/12/2005) (describing these live auctions as means to "increase liquidity of patent transactions, thus unlocking significant value").

Bankruptcy trustees and courts have also shown interest in intellectual property auctions as means to maximize the sale value of a bankrupt firm's assets and thereby increase the amount of funds available to bankruptcy claimants. In one case where this technique was used, the patents and other business assets of e-business applications developer Commerce One, Inc., were separately auctioned off in late 2004. The patents realized $15.5 million, while the non-patent assets, sold to a different party, only realized $4.1 million. These results provide concrete evidence of the degree to which the value of intellectual property held by a high tech company can far exceed the value of other business assets. *See generally* Renee Boucher Ferguson, *Commerce One Patents Auctioned Off,* http://www.eweek.com/article2/0,1759,1737418,00.asp (Dec. 8, 2004) (last visited on 8/5/2005). However, at least one commentator has criticized this result as reflecting an improper trend toward viewing patents as weapons with disruptive value independent of associated product production capabilities. *See* Jason Schultz, *When Dot-Com Patents Go Bad: The Auction of Commerce One's Intellectual Property Demonstrates that Patents are Worth More Today as Weapons Than Anything Else. That's Wrong,"* http://www.salon.com/tech/feature/2004/12/13/patent_reform/index_np.html (Dec. 13, 2004) (last visited on 8/5/2005).

The reading below contains the order of the bankruptcy court authorizing the auctioning off of Commerce One's patents and describing the procedures to be followed in conducting the auction. The court's order specified two alternative procedures for the disposition of Commerce One's assets: one procedure to be used if the auction for the company's patents generated qualified bids and a second fallback procedure for selling the patents with the company's other assets if no qualifying bids were received for the patents alone.

IN RE: COMMERCE ONE INC.
United States Bankruptcy Court for the Northern
District of California
Case No. 04-32820 DM

DENNIS MONTALI, BANKRUPTCY Judge

ORDER APPROVIING OVERBID PROCEDURES AND RELATED MATTERS RE SALE OF CERTAIN ASSETS OF THE DEBTORS

The MOTION BY DEBTORS FOR ORDER APPROVING OVERBID PROCEDURES AND RELATED MATTERS RE SALE OF CERTAIN ASSETS OF THE DEBTORS (the "Motion") came on for hearing before this Court on October 21, 2004 at 1:30 p.m. Craig M. Prim of Murray & Murray, A Professional Corporation, appeared on behalf of Commerce One, Inc. and Commerce One Operations, Inc., the debtors and debtors in possession herein (collectively, the "Debtors"), Rick B. Antonoff of Greenberg Traurig appeared on behalf of Commerce Acquisition LLC, a Delaware limited liability company (the proposed Buyer), Roberto Kampfner of White & Case LLP appeared as proposed counsel to the Official Committee of Unsecured Creditors, Patricia Cutler appeared on behalf of the Office of the United States Trustee, and other appearances were as noted on the record.

The Court having reviewed the notice of hearing, the Motion, the evidence, and declarations filed in support thereof, having considered the objection filed by the Official Committee of Unsecured Creditors ("OCC") and the arguments from counsel at the hearing, and finding due and adequate notice of the relief requested by the Motion was given to all necessary parties, for the reasons set forth on the record, and that good cause appearing therefor,

IT IS HEREBY ORDERED THAT:

1. The Motion is granted as modified herein, and the objection by the OCC is overruled;

2. Bidding Procedures. The Debtors are authorized to propose the sale of their assets in accordance with the procedures set forth below:

A. Sale of Purchased Assets (excluding Web Services Patents)("Buyer Deal #2"): In order to allow the Debtors to separately market for sale their Web Services Patents, subject to the termination rights set forth at Paragraph 4 below, Buyer has agreed to modify its original offer to acquire the Purchased Assets (see Buyer Deal #1 below for original terms) as follows: (1) For a purchase price of $4.1 million representing the forgiveness of outstanding amounts owing by the Debtors to Secured Creditors plus up to $40,000 for the post-petition salaries and benefits of the Debtors' Conductor employees plus additional funds, as necessary, to make payments of the current obligations of the Debtors with respect to salaries and other employment benefits of employees of the Debtors retained during the pendency of the within Chapter 11 cases (if such payments are approved by the Court), Buyer will purchase substantially all of the assets of the Debtors other than (a) the Web Services Patents and (b) the Excluded Assets as set forth in the Purchase Agreement, except that Buyer will receive assignment of all of the Debtors' interest in the promissory note issued by eScout LLC and eScout Acquisition LLC in the principal amount of $2,000,183 which matures in February 2005 (the "eScout Note"); (2) Buyer or the Successful Bidder will also be responsible for paying any "cure" amounts owing under Section 365 of the Bankruptcy Code with respect to any executory contracts or unexpired leases to be assumed and assigned as part of the sale; (3) Buyer or the Successful Bidder will be provided a license to the Web Services Patents to operate the existing businesses as described in Paragraph 2-B below; and (4) Buyer will have an allowed general unsecured claim of $1 million representing its deficiency claim, provided any payment on such claim is capped at $500,000. The bidding procedures hereby approved by the Court and applicable to Buyer Sale #2 are set forth on Exhibit "A" attached hereto and incorporated herein by this reference [omitted].

B. Sale of Web Services Patents (the "Web Services Patents Sale"): Debtors may solicit bids for the sale of their Web Services Patents separate from the proposed sale to Buyer as proposed under the Purchase Agreement. Persons wishing to present a bid solely on the Web Services Patents may do so pursuant to the bidding procedures hereby approved by the Court and set forth on Exhibit "B" attached hereto and incorporated herein by this reference. The sale of the Web Services Patents will be subject to (1) the issuance to Buyer or the Successful Bidder of Buyer Deal #2 of a non-exclusive, perpetual, worldwide, royalty-free license to the Web Services Patents to allow Buyer or the Successful Bidder to operate the businesses and such additional terms as will be set forth more fully in the license to be issued to Buyer or the Successful Bidder prior to the closing of Buyer Deal #2, and (2) the prior license issued to Mitsubishi.

C. Sale of Purchased Assets (including Web Services Patents)("Buyer Deal #1"): In the event that no Qualified Bids are received with respect to the sale of the Web Services Patents, the Debtors may propose that the Court either approve Buyer Deal #2 (subject to Buyer's termination right as described at Paragraph 4 below) or that the Court approve the sale of the Purchased Assets in accordance with the terms of the original Purchase Agreement (herein referred to as Buyer Dealer #1) which provides for, among other things, the sale of substantially all of the assets of the Debtors (excluding cash, certain accounts and notes receivable, . . . and certain other miscellaneous assets), including the Web Services Patents, to Buyer in exchange for the reduction of the outstanding amounts owing to Secured Creditors of $4,100,000, which includes principal of $4,000,000 and all accrued interest to Secured Creditors, plus up to $40,000 for the post-petition salaries and benefits of Debtors' Conductor employees, plus additional funds, as necessary, to make payments of the current obligations of the Debtors with respect to salaries and other employment benefits, of employees of the Debtors retained during the pendency of the within Chapter 11 cases. . . . In the event Qualified Bids are received with respect to the Web Services Patents, the Debtors may proceed with Buyer Deal #2 as one auction and the Web Services Patents Sale as another auction. However, in the event that no Qualified Bids are received with respect to the Web Services Patents Sale, the Debtors will be authorized to propose the sale of the Purchased Assets in accordance with Buyer Deal #1. The bidding procedures hereby approved by the Court and applicable to Buyer Sale #1 are set forth on Exhibit "C" attached hereto and incorporated herein by this reference [omitted].

. . .

COMMERCE ONE, INC.

COMMERCE ONE OPERATIONS, INC.
Jointly Administered Chapter 11 Cases; Bankruptcy Case No. 04-32820-DM-11

EXHIBIT B: BIDDING PROCEDURES RE WEB SERVICES PATENTS

The following constitute the bidding procedures ("Bidding Procedures") established by the Court for persons wishing to present an offer with respect to the Purchased Assets comprised of the Debtors' Web Services Patents:

i. On or before November 12, 2004, by 5:00 p.m. prevailing Pacific time (the "Bid Deadline"), any bidder ("Bidder") must submit its bid ("Bid") providing an aggregate purchase price consisting of cash in an amount not less than $1,000,000. Bids may not be subject to any contingency for financing, due diligence or otherwise and must provide for a closing no later than the fifth (5th) business day following the date on which any agreed closing conditions have been satisfied or are waived (the "Closing Date").

ii. The Bid must be in writing setting forth all material terms and conditions of the Bid, and be addressed to [several specified attorneys] (the "Bid Notification Parties")[.]

Upon receipt of any Bid, Debtors' counsel shall also provide a copy of the Bid to any other bidders, to counsel for the creditors' committee ("Committee") formed in the cases, and if requested, to the Office of the United States Trustee.

iii. A Bid must be accompanied by a good faith cash deposit in the form of a cashier's check made payable to "Commerce One, Inc." in an amount not less than $100,000 which will be credited towards the Purchase Price if the sale is completed with the Bidder making the deposit.

iv. In the event of the approval of the Bid, such Bidder's deposit shall become non-refundable if (i) the Bid is accepted, (ii) the Bidder fails to close if and as required by the terms of such Bid, and (iii) the Debtors are otherwise ready, willing and able to close under the Bid and are not in default under the Bid. If the Debtors close a sale of the Purchased Assets to another Bidder, the deposit will be refunded within three (3) business days of such closing. In the event a dispute arises over whether a deposit is refundable or non-refundable, the Debtors shall hold the deposit pending a determination of the issue by the Court or written agreement of the Debtors and the Bidder who made the deposit.

v. Simultaneous with submission of the Bid, the Bidder must provide to the Debtors reasonably satisfactory evidence of its financial ability to fully and timely consummate the sale on the terms of the Bid.

vi. If the Bidder is an entity formed for the purpose of acquiring the Purchased Assets, the Bidder shall also provide to the Debtors current audited financial statements or other evidence satisfactory to the Debtors and the Committee and their respective advisors of the equity holder(s) of the Bidder who shall guarantee the obligation of the Bidder or such other form of financial disclosure and credit-quality support or enhancement acceptable to the Debtors.

vii. The Bidder must agree to keep its final and highest bid open pending a closing of a sale to an entity other than the Bidder. In the event a Bid is approved but not consummated by the Closing Date (or such later time as the Debtors and the Bidder shall mutually agree in writing), the next highest bid shall be approved without the necessity of further Court order.

viii. A bid from a bidder that delivers items i-vii above, whose financial information and credit quality support or enhancement demonstrate the financial capability of the bidder to consummate the sale, and that Debtors, in consultation with the Committee, determine is reasonably likely (based on availability of financing, experience and other considerations) to be able to consummate the sale if selected as the Successful Bidder (defined below), will be deemed to be a "Qualifying Bid."

ix. Debtors shall notify each bidder whether the bidder's bid is a Qualifying Bid by no later than November 15, 2004. Debtors will reserve the right under the Bidding Procedures to reject any Bidder's offer which, in its judgment after consultation with the Committee, is inadequate or insufficient or which is contrary to the best interests of the Debtors' bankruptcy estates. Debtors, in consultation with the Committee, will also notify all bidders submitting a Qualifying Bid of Debtors' determination of the highest and best offer. Each Qualifying Bidder must inform the Debtors whether it intends to participate in the auction (see section "x" immediately below)(the "Auction"). Only Qualifying Bidders who appear in person (through an authorized representative) will be eligible to participate in the Auction.

x. If Debtors receive Qualifying Bids, Debtors will conduct the Auction at the Sale Hearing. At the Auction, if Buyer or a bidder that submitted a Qualifying Bid elects to submit a subsequent competing bid after a Qualifying Bid has been accepted (a "Subsequent Competing Bid"), such Subsequent Competing Bid must be in an amount that exceeds the Initial Bid by not less than $25,000, and each bid made after a Subsequent Competing Bid, and each bid thereafter, must be in an amount that exceeds the previous high bid by not less than $25,000.

xi. Bidders will be required to execute appropriate nondisclosure or confidentiality agreements as may be reasonably required by the Company.

However, in order to obtain due diligence access or additional information from the Debtors, a prospective bidder must first advise the Debtors in writing of its preliminary (non-binding) proposal regarding (i) the assets sought to be acquired, (ii) the price proposed to be paid, (iii) the structure and financing of the transaction, (iv) any additional conditions to closing that it may wish to impose, and (v) the nature and extent of additional due diligence it may wish to conduct. If based on the preliminary proposal and such additional factors as Debtors determine are relevant, Debtors, in their business judgment, determine that the preliminary proposal is reasonably likely to result in a bona fide and serious higher and better offer for the Purchased Assets, Debtors shall afford the bidder due diligence access to the Company, provided, however, that any such bidder that is a competitor of the Company will be provided with certain customer and supplier information initially on an anonymous basis to maintain the confidential and proprietary customer and supplier information, pricing information, and marketing, sales and other business strategies, dissemination of which could compromise the value of the Purchased Assets. Such bidders will be provided full disclosure of customer and supplier identities only upon a determination of Debtors, after consultation with the Committee and advance notice to Buyer, that such bidder is a serious, bona-fide bidder prepared to submit a Qualifying Bid. Debtors will coordinate all reasonable requests for additional information and due diligence from such bidders. Any additional due diligence shall not continue after the Bid Deadline.

xii. The Debtors reserve the right, in consultation with the Committee, to adopt additional rules for bidding at the Auction that, in their business judgment, and subject to approval of the Court, will better promote the goals of the bidding process and that are not inconsistent with any of the provisions of the sale procedures, the Bankruptcy Code or any order of the Bankruptcy Court entered in connection therewith.

xiii. Immediately prior to the conclusion of the Auction, Debtors will, in consultation with the Committee, (i) review each Qualifying Bid on the basis of financial and contractual terms and the factors relevant to the sale process, including those factors affecting the speed and certainty of consummating the sale and (ii) identify the highest and best offer for the Purchased Assets of the Debtors at the Auction (the "Successful Bid") and notify all bidders at the Auction prior to its adjournment of the name or names of the maker of the Successful Bid, and the amount and other terms of the Successful Bid. The Successful Bidder will be required to complete and execute all agreements or other documents with the Debtors evidencing and containing the terms and conditions upon which the Successful Bid was made.

. . .

NOTES & QUESTIONS

1. In what ways are auctions in bankruptcy proceedings of debtors' intellectual property different than auctions in such proceedings of debtors' real or personal property? When will the auctioning of a company's patents separate from its other operating assets make sense as a means to maximize the value

of a bankruptcy estate and serve the interests of claimants in a bankruptcy proceeding?

2. What types of inquiries might potential bidders wish to make before submitting a bid in a patent auction like the one conducted in the Commerce One bankruptcy proceeding? If the bidders are potential competitors of other parties acquiring the physical or operating assets of the bankrupt concern, will there be confidentiality or competitive problems in disclosing business information related to the patents to the bidders in the patent auction?

3. How might a bankruptcy trustee disposing of an intellectual property interest in an auction (or a private intellectual property owner auctioning off an interest outside of a bankruptcy proceeding) take steps prior to the bidding to maximize the amounts obtained for the interest in the auction? Would disclosures of the bankrupt company's prior efforts in commercializing the interest at issue be enough to attract potential bidders? What other steps to clarify the enforceability and commercial significance of an intellectual property interest being sold at auction might increase the apparent value of the interest?

2. Donations to Charitable Organizations

Donations of intellectual property interests to charitable organizations can produce valuable tax deductions for the donors in the same manner as donations of other types of property. However, a number of special tax law issues have arisen in connection with donations of intellectual property, including questions about what types of donations of partial interests in intellectual property will warrant deductions, how intellectual property interests should be valued for purposes of determining the size of deductions, and how the potential of donated interests to produce future income should be taken into account in determining the proper size of deductions. For a thorough discussion of these and other tax law issues surrounding intellectual property, see generally Jeffrey A. Maine & Xuan-Thao N. Nguyen, INTELLECTUAL PROPERTY TAXATION: TRANSACTION AND LITIGATION ISSUES (2003).

Because the value of an intellectual property interest at the time of a donation may be unclear, the amount of deduction allowed for this type of donation has been the focus of numerous disputes. In most situations, the amount of a deduction for a charitable donation of property equals the fair market value of the property transferred, less any reciprocal benefits to the donor. However, in the context of intellectual property donations, such a fair market value measure has proven problematic. The suspicion of the Internal Revenue Service has been that intellectual property donors may tend to overstate the value of donated property in order to gain large tax deductions and that donees may cooperate with these overstatements because they want to aid major donors and have little reason to seek lower valuations. In addition, there is often no market or other neutral source of valuation information regarding donated intellectual property that might be used in challenging an asserted valuation of the property. Valuation estimates based on the potential of donated intellectual property to produce future income provide some means of characterizing the property and the proper size of a related deduction, but these estimates are often inaccurate since they are based on highly speculative views of future business developments. For an overview of the valuation and other problems surrounding charitable donations of intellectual property, see Don Macbean, *Better to Give Than to Receive: Evaluating Recent IP Donation Tax Policy Changes,* 2005 DUKE L. & TECH. REV. 19 (2005).

In 2004, Congress addressed these problems with legislation that significantly changed the treatment of intellectual property donations under federal tax laws. The new standards governing intellectual property donations apply to donations made on or after 6/3/04. In general, the new standards limit a deduction for a charitable donation of intellectual property to the donor's tax basis in the intellectual property, with a possible additional series of deductions determined from the income realized from the intellectual property by the donee. *See* 26 U.S.C. § 170(e)(1)(B)(iii) & (m).

These new standards promise to be problematic in part because they focus deduction determinations on an owner's tax basis in donated intellectual property. The initial basis for an intellectual property interest that is acquired from another party will typically be the acquisition price. However, where intellectual property is created by a corporation or other business, the initial basis will typically be the production cost, less portions of that cost that have already been deducted as business expenses. Determining this cost may involve complicated allocations of research and development expenses and other internal costs. Depreciation considerations may add to the complexity of determining the relevant basis figure for a donation of intellectual property. *See* generally Mary LaFrance, *Days of Our Lives: The Impact of Section 197 on the Depreciation of Copyrights, Patents, and Related Property,* 24 HOFSTRA L. REV. 317 (1995).

The following readings describe the old and new tax law standards governing deductions for donations of intellectual property.

GENERAL EXPLANATION OF TAX LEGISLATION ENACTED IN THE 108TH CONGRESS (2005)
Joint Committee on Taxation

. . .

AMERICAN JOBS CREATION ACT OF 2004 (PUBLIC LAW 108-357)

. . .

[Modification to] charitable contribution rules for donations of patents and other intellectual property (sec. 882 of the Act and secs. 170 and 6050L of the [Internal Revenue] Code)

Present and Prior Law

In general, under present and prior law, a deduction is permitted for charitable contributions, subject to certain limitations that depend on the type of taxpayer, the property contributed, and the donee organization.[1] In the case of non-cash contributions, the amount of the deduction generally

---

[1] [FN920] Charitable deductions are provided for income, estate, and gift tax purposes. [*See* Internal Revenue Code] Secs. 170, 2055, and 2522, respectively.

equals the fair market value of the contributed property on the date of the contribution.

Under present and prior law, for certain contributions of property, the taxpayer is required to reduce the deduction amount by any gain, generally resulting in a deduction equal to the taxpayer's basis. This rule applies to contributions of: (1) property that, at the time of contribution, would not have resulted in long-term capital gain if the property was sold by the taxpayer on the contribution date; (2) tangible personal property that is used by the donee in a manner unrelated to the donee's exempt (or governmental) purpose; and (3) property to or for the use of a private foundation (other than a foundation defined in section 170(b)(1)(E)).

Charitable contributions of capital gain property generally are deductible at fair market value. Capital gain property means any capital asset or property used in the taxpayer's trade or business the sale of which at its fair market value, at the time of contribution, would have resulted in gain that would have been long-term capital gain. Contributions of capital gain property are subject to different percentage limitations than other contributions of property. Under present and prior law, certain copyrights are not considered capital assets, in which case the charitable deduction for such copyrights generally is limited to the taxpayer's basis.[2]

In general, a charitable contribution deduction is allowed only for contributions of the donor's entire interest in the contributed property, and not for contributions of a partial interest.[3] If a taxpayer sells property to a charitable organization for less than the property's fair market value, the amount of any charitable contribution deduction is determined in accordance with the bargain sale rules.[4] In general, if a donor receives a benefit or quid pro quo in return for a contribution, any charitable contribution deduction is reduced by the amount of the benefit received. For contributions of $250 or more, no charitable contribution deduction is allowed unless the donee organization provides a contemporaneous written acknowledgement of the contribution that describes and provides a good faith estimate of the value of any goods or services provided by the donee organization in exchange for the contribution.[5]

In general, taxpayers are required to obtain a qualified appraisal for donated property with a value of $5,000 or more, and to attach the appraisal to the tax return in certain cases. Under Treasury regulations, a qualified appraisal means an appraisal document that, among other things, (1) relates to an appraisal that is made not earlier than 60 days prior to the date of contribution of the appraised property and not later than the due date (including extensions) of the return on which a deduction is first claimed under section 170;[6] (2) is prepared, signed, and dated by a qualified appraiser; (3) includes

---

[2] [FN921] See sec. 1221(a)(3), 1231(b)(1)(C).

[3] [FN922] Sec. 170(f)(3).

[4] [FN923] Sec. 1011(b) and Treas. Reg. sec. 1.1011-2.

[5] [FN924] Sec. 170(f)(8).

[6] [FN925] In the case of a deduction first claimed or reported on an amended return, the deadline is the date on which the amended return is filed.

(a) a description of the property appraised; (b) the fair market value of such property on the date of contribution and the specific basis for the valuation; (c) a statement that such appraisal was prepared for income tax purposes; (d) the qualifications of the qualified appraiser; and (e) the signature and taxpayer identification number ("TIN") of such appraiser; and (4) does not involve an appraisal fee that violates certain prescribed rules.[7]

Reasons for Change

The Congress believed that the value of certain intellectual property, such as patents, copyrights, trademarks, trade names, trade secrets, know-how, software, similar property, or applications or registrations of such property that is contributed to a charity often is highly speculative. Some donated intellectual property may prove to be worthless, or the initial promise of worth may be diminished by future inventions, marketplace competition, or other factors. Although in theory, such intellectual property may promise significant monetary benefits, the benefits generally will not materialize if the charity does not make the appropriate investments, have the right personnel and equipment, or even have sufficient sustained interest to exploit the intellectual property. The Congress understood that valuation is made yet more difficult in the charitable contribution context because the transferee does not provide full, if any, consideration in exchange for the transferred property pursuant to arm's length negotiations, and there may not be a comparable sales market for such property to use as a benchmark for valuations.

The Congress was concerned that taxpayers with intellectual property were taking advantage of the inherent difficulties in valuing such property and were preparing or obtaining erroneous valuations. In such cases, the charity would receive an asset of questionable value, while the taxpayer received a significant tax benefit. The Congress believed that the excessive charitable contribution deductions enabled by inflated valuations were best addressed by ensuring that the amount of the deduction for charitable contributions of such property may not exceed the taxpayer's basis in the property. The Congress noted that for other types of charitable contributions for which valuation is especially problematic-charitable contributions of property created by the personal efforts of the taxpayer and charitable contributions to certain private foundations-a basis deduction generally is the result under present and prior law.

Although the Congress believed that a deduction of basis was appropriate in this context, the Congress recognized that some contributions of intellectual property may be proven to be of economic benefit to the charity and that donors may need an economic incentive to make such contributions. Accordingly, the Congress believed that it was appropriate to permit donors of intellectual property to receive certain additional charitable contribution deductions in the future but only if the contributed property generates qualified income for the charitable organization.

Explanation of Provision

The Act provides that if a taxpayer contributes a patent or other intellectual property (other than certain copyrights or inventory) to a charitable

---

[7] [FN926] Treas. Reg. sec. 1.170A-13(c)(3).

organization, the taxpayer's initial charitable deduction is limited to the lesser of the taxpayer's basis in the contributed property or the fair market value of the property. In addition, the taxpayer is permitted to deduct, as a charitable deduction, certain additional amounts in the year of contribution or in subsequent taxable years based on a specified percentage of the qualified donee income received or accrued by the charitable donee with respect to the contributed property. For this purpose, "qualified donee income" includes net income received or accrued by the donee that properly is allocable to the intellectual property itself (as opposed to the activity in which the intellectual property is used).

The amount of any additional charitable deduction is calculated as a sliding-scale percentage of qualified donee income received or accrued by the charitable donee that properly is allocable to the contributed property to the applicable taxable year of the donor, determined as follows:

Taxable Year of Donor	Deduction Permitted for Such Taxable Year
1st year ending on or after contribution.	100 percent of qualified donee income
2nd year ending on or after contribution.	100 percent of qualified donee income
3rd year ending on or after contribution.	90 percent of qualified donee income
4th year ending on or after contribution.	80 percent of qualified donee income
5th year ending on or after contribution.	70 percent of qualified donee income
6th year ending on or after contribution.	60 percent of qualified donee income
7th year ending on or after contribution.	50 percent of qualified donee income
8th year ending on or after contribution.	40 percent of qualified donee income
9th year ending on or after contribution.	30 percent of qualified donee income
10th year ending on or after contribution.	20 percent of qualified donee income
11th year ending on or after contribution.	10 percent of qualified donee income
12th year ending on or after contribution.	10 percent of qualified donee income
Taxable years thereafter	No deduction permitted

An additional charitable deduction is allowed only to the extent that the aggregate of the amounts that are calculated pursuant to the sliding-scale exceed the amount of the deduction claimed upon the contribution of the patent or intellectual property.

No charitable deduction is permitted with respect to any revenues or income received or accrued by the charitable donee after the expiration of the legal life of the patent or intellectual property, or after the tenth anniversary of the date the contribution was made by the donor.

The taxpayer is required to inform the donee at the time of the contribution that the taxpayer intends to treat the contribution as a contribution subject to the additional charitable deduction provisions of the provision. In addition, the taxpayer must obtain written substantiation from the donee of the amount of any qualified donee income properly allocable to the contributed property during the charity's taxable year.[8] The donee is required to file an annual

---

[8] [FN927] The net income taken into account by the taxpayer may not exceed the amount of qualified donee income reported by the donee to the taxpayer and the IRS under the provision's substantiation and reporting requirements.

information return that reports the qualified donee income and other specified information relating to the contribution. In instances where the donor's taxable year differs from the donee's taxable year, the donor bases its additional charitable deduction on the qualified donee income of the charitable donee properly allocable to the donee's taxable year that ends within the donor's taxable year.

Under the Act, additional charitable deductions are not available for patents or other intellectual property contributed to a private foundation (other than a private operating foundation or certain other private foundations described in section 170(b)(1)(E)).

Under the Act, the Secretary may prescribe regulations or other guidance to carry out the purposes of the provision, including providing for the determination of amounts to be treated as qualified donee income in certain cases where the donee uses the donated property to further its exempt activities or functions, or as may be necessary or appropriate to prevent the avoidance of the purposes of the Act.

Effective Date

The provision is effective for contributions made after June 3, 2004.

CHARITABLE CONTRIBUTIONS; PATENTS
Internal Revenue Service
Revenue Ruling 2003-28 (Feb. 26, 2003)

Section 170. — Charitable, etc., Contributions and Gifts, 26 CFR 1.170-1: Charitable, etc., contributions and gifts; allowance of deduction.

. . .

ISSUES

(1) Is a taxpayer's contribution to a qualified charity of a license to use a patent deductible under § 170(a) of the Internal Revenue Code if the taxpayer retains any substantial right in the patent?

(2) Is a taxpayer's contribution to a qualified charity of a patent subject to a conditional reversion deductible under § 170(a)?

(3) Is a taxpayer's contribution to a qualified charity of a patent subject to a license or transfer restriction deductible under § 170(a)?

FACTS

Situation 1. X contributes to University, an organization described in § 170(c) (qualified charity), a license to use a patent, but retains the right to license the patent to others.

Situation 2. Y contributes a patent to University subject to the condition that A, a faculty member of University and an expert in the technology covered by the patent, continue to be a faculty member of University during the remaining life of the patent. If A ceases to be a member of University's faculty before the patent expires, the patent will revert to Y. The patent will expire 15 years after the date Y contributes it to University. On the date of the contribution, the likelihood that A will cease to be a member of the faculty before the patent expires is not so remote as to be negligible.

Situation 3. Z contributes to University all of Z's interests in a patent. The transfer agreement provides that University may not sell or license the patent for a period of 3 years after the transfer. This restriction does not result in any benefit to Z, and under no circumstances can the patent revert to Z.

LAW AND ANALYSIS

Issue (1)

Section 170(a) provides, subject to certain limitations, a deduction for any charitable contribution, as defined in § 170(c), payment of which is made within the taxable year.

Section 170(f)(3) denies a charitable contribution deduction for certain contributions of partial interests in property. Section 170(f)(3)(A) denies a charitable contribution deduction for a contribution of less than the taxpayer's entire interest in property unless the value of the interest contributed would be allowable as a deduction under § 170(f)(2) if the donor were to transfer the interest in trust.

Section 170(f)(2) allows a charitable contribution deduction, in the case of property that the donor transfers in trust, if the trust is a charitable remainder annuity trust, a charitable remainder unitrust, or a pooled income fund. Further, § 170(f)(2) allows a deduction for the value of an interest in property (other than a remainder interest) that the donor transfers in trust if the interest is in the form of a guaranteed annuity or the trust instrument specifies that the interest is a fixed percentage, distributed yearly, of the fair market value of the trust property (to be determined yearly) and the grantor is treated as the owner of such interest for purposes of applying § 671.

By its terms, § 170(f)(3)(A) does not apply to, and therefore does not disallow a deduction for, a contribution of an interest that, even though partial, is the taxpayer's entire interest in the property. If, however, the property in which such partial interest exists was divided in order to create such interest, and thus avoid § 170(f)(3)(A), a deduction is not allowed. Section 1.170A-7(a)(2)(i) of the Income Tax Regulations.

Sections 170(f)(3)(B)(ii) and 1.170A-7(b)(1) allow a deduction under § 170 for a contribution not in trust of a partial interest that is less than the donor's entire interest in property if the partial interest is an undivided portion of the donor's entire interest. An undivided portion of a donor's entire interest in property consists of a fraction or percentage of each and every substantial interest or right owned by the donor in such property and must extend over the entire term of the donor's interest in such property and in other property into which such property is converted. A charitable contribution in perpetuity of an interest in property not in trust does not constitute a contribution of an undivided portion of the donor's entire interest if the donor transfers some specific rights and retains other substantial rights.

In enacting § 170(f)(3), Congress was concerned with situations in which taxpayers might obtain a double benefit by taking a deduction for the present value of a contributed interest while also excluding from income subsequent receipts from the donated interest. In addition, Congress was concerned with situations in which, because the charity does not obtain all or an undivided portion of significant rights in the property, the amount of a charitable contribution deduction might not correspond to the value of the benefit ultimately received by the charity. The legislative solution was to guard against the possibility that such problems might arise by denying a deduction in situations involving partial interests, unless the contribution is cast in certain prescribed forms. The scope of § 170(f)(3) thus extends beyond situations in which there is actual or probable manipulation of the non-charitable interest to the detriment of the charitable interest, or situations in which the donor has merely assigned the right to future income.

Section 170(f)(3)(A) and § 1.170A-7(a)(1) treat a contribution of the right to use property that the donor owns, such as a contribution of a rent-free lease, as a contribution of less than the taxpayer's entire interest in the property. Similarly, if a taxpayer contributes an interest in motion picture films, but retains the right to make reproductions of such films and exploit the reproductions commercially, § 1.170A-7(b)(1)(i) treats the contribution as one of less than the taxpayer's entire interest in the property. In both cases, the taxpayer has not contributed an undivided portion of its entire interest in the property. Accordingly, neither contribution is deductible under § 170(a).

In Situation 1, X contributes a license to use a patent, but retains a substantial right, i.e., the right to license the patent to others. The license granted to University is similar to the rent-free lease described in § 1.170A-7(a)(1) and the partial interest in motion picture films described in § 1.170A-7(b)(1)(i), in that it constitutes neither X's entire interest in the patent, nor a fraction or percentage of each and every substantial interest or right that X owns in the patent. As a result, the contribution in Situation 1 constitutes a transfer of a partial interest, and no deduction under § 170(a) is allowable. The result would be the same if X had retained any other substantial right in the patent. For example, no deduction would be allowable if X had contributed the patent (or license to use the patent) solely for use in a particular geographic area while retaining the right to use the patent (or license) in other geographic areas.

Issue (2)

Section 1.170A-1(e) provides that if, as of the date of a gift, a transfer of property for charitable purposes is dependent upon the performance of some act or the happening of a precedent event in order for it to become effective, no deduction is allowable unless the possibility that the charitable transfer will not become effective is so remote as to be negligible. Similarly, under § 1.170A-7(a)(3), if, as of the date of a gift, a transfer of property for charitable purposes may be defeated by the performance of some act or the happening of some event, no deduction is allowable unless the possibility that such act or event will occur is so remote as to be negligible.

In Situation 2, Y's contribution of the patent is contingent upon A continuing as a member of University's faculty for an additional 15 years, the remaining life of the patent. On the date of the contribution, the possibility that A will cease to be a member of the faculty before the expiration of the patent is not so remote as to be negligible. Therefore, no deduction is allowable under § 170(a).

Issue (3)

. . .

In Situation 3, Z transfers to University all of Z's interests in the patent with the restriction that University cannot transfer or license the patent for a period of 3 years after the transfer. Unlike the conditional reversion in Situation 2, the restriction on transfer or license is not a condition that can defeat the transfer. Thus, Z's contribution is deductible under § 170(a), assuming all other applicable requirements of § 170 are satisfied, and subject to the percentage limitations of § 170.

. . .

HOLDINGS

Under the facts of this revenue ruling:

(1) A taxpayer's contribution to a qualified charity of a license to use a patent is not deductible under § 170(a) if the taxpayer retains any substantial right in the patent.

(2) A taxpayer's contribution to a qualified charity of a patent subject to a conditional reversion is not deductible under § 170(a), unless the likelihood of the reversion is so remote as to be negligible.

(3) A taxpayer's contribution to a qualified charity of a patent subject to a license or transfer restriction is deductible under § 170(a), assuming all other applicable requirements of § 170 are satisfied. . . .

NOTES & QUESTIONS

1. Present tax standards that limit the immediately available deduction for an intellectual property donation to the donor's tax basis in the intellectual property represent a substantial change from prior tax rules that allowed a deduction for the fair market value of most types of donated intellectual property. The impacts of this change may be very different for different types of intellectual property donations. For example, with respect to donated copyrights, the impact of this change may depend on whether a donated copyright interest resulted from the creative efforts of the donor or was acquired from a prior copyright owner. Under tax law standards existing before the change in deduction rules, a donation by the creator of a work of a valuable copyright in that work only produced a deduction equal to the creator's tax basis in the copyright. *See* I.R.C. § 1221(a) (3). The result is the same (at least as to the donor's immediately available deduction) under the current standards for intellectual property donations. However, a donation of a copyright by a bona fide purchaser of the copyright would previously have qualified for a charitable deduction equal to the fair market value of the copyright at the time of the donation. Following the change in deduction standards, the immediately available deduction for such a donation of an acquired copyright is limited to the

donor's tax basis in the copyright. Hence, at least with respect to a copyright that has increased in value since its acquisition and which therefore has a fair market value in excess of the owner's tax basis determined from the acquisition price, a party donating a previously acquired copyright will be adversely affected by the new tax standards limiting the immediately available deduction for a copyright donation to the tax basis of the donor. *See* William A. Drennan, *Charitable Donations of Intellectual Property: The Case for Retaining the Fair Market Value Tax Deduction,* 2004 UTAH L. REV. 1045, 1080-81 (2004).

An even more dramatic difference may result for donations of patents and trade secrets. Since a taxpayer can generally deduct all of its research and development costs in conducting a trade or business, *see* I.R.C. § 174(a), many firms pursue this option with respect to research and development leading to valuable new technologies and related patents or trade secrets. However, the deduction of these amounts leads to a zero basis in the related patents or trade secrets. Hence, the use of such a basis amount as the measure of the immediately available deduction for a donation of a patent or trade secret will mean that no immediate deduction will be available for donations of many patents or trade secrets, at least where the donor has produced the technology covered by the patents or trade secrets. A different result will apply to patents or trade secrets that have been acquired from another party and have a tax basis related to the acquisition price. *See id.* at 1081-83.

In light of these rules, innovators may find it desirable to sell copyrights or patents related to their creative efforts, pay the relevant taxes on the income realized, and then donate cash to charities, with the result that they will obtain deductions for the full cash amounts of the donations. *See id.* at 1092-83.

Of course, these considerations based on the initial, basis-dependant deduction available to a donor of intellectual property may be offset somewhat by the benefits of later, donee income-dependent deductions available to a donor under the current tax standards described in the readings above. Unfortunately, in assessing whether to donate intellectual property, interest owners may see these additional benefits as being highly contingent since the later deductions depend on the subsequent actions and commercialization success of a donee. Furthermore, even where a donee seems likely to produce substantial income related to a donated intellectual property interest, resulting in additional deductions for the donor as described in the readings above, the value of these later deductions will need to be discounted by their delayed availability since they will only arise as the income is produced in the years subsequent to a donation.

2. Current tax standards tying the potential scope of deductions for intellectual property donations to the revenues generated from that property by donees may encourage continuing post-donation relationships between intellectual property donors and donees. Donors of intellectual property now have a clear stake in the amount of revenues generated by donees in the first few years following a donation. Consequently, donors may seek to assist charitable donees in the effective licensing or other commercialization of donated intellectual property interests. This emphasis on post-donation revenues may also encourage intellectual property owners to emphasize donations of interests

with clear income producing potential and gifts to institutions that are enthusiastic about immediate commercialization of the intellectual property interests they receive. Donors might also wish to establish contractual arrangements with donees that obligate the latter to take specific steps to commercialize donated intellectual property interests. As noted by two observers:

> [A] patent donation in these circumstances may be a way for the patent holder to create or strengthen a relationship with a university, research institute, or other charitable donee, while creating a tax benefit at the same time. The deduction would now be tied to the charity's reported income amounts, avoiding the uncertainties inherent in determining fair market value at the time of contribution.
>
> Donors will need to conduct some due diligence on prospective donees of patents or other intellectual property, to ensure that the donee has the desire and capacity to exploit the intellectual property in the near future. For example, a written agreement with a donee might require the donee to honor existing royalty contracts or pursue a particular business plan with respect to the use of the intellectual property. If the charity fails to follow through, the donor might have a claim against the charity for the amount of the deductions that could have been taken had the charity honored its commitments. In these and other ways, the new intellectual property donation rules may have a significant impact on the relationship between donors and charitable donees.

Richard F. Riley, Jr. & Terri W. Cammaranom, *New Restrictions (and New Opportunities) in Donating Patents and Other Intellectual Property,* 8 VALUATION STRATEGIES 35 (May/June 2005).

3.   Releasing Intellectual Property to Enhance Open Source Product Development

Steve Seidenberg, Big Blue Discovers New Way to Leverage Patents: Open-Source Revolution Keeps IBM in the Black
Corporate Legal Times, p. 24 (April 2005)*

What do you call a company that spends vast sums on R&D to obtain new patents; then suddenly makes 500 of its patented inventions available to everyone else, including its competitors . . . for free? Do you call it misguided? Altruistic? Insane? Stupid?

No, you call it IBM.

On Jan. 11, the world's biggest patent owner made 500 of its patents available to the public for free. Valued at more than $10 million, these patents cover a broad spectrum of software technology, including dynamic link libraries, interfaces, multiprocessing and databases.

But there is a catch. The patented technology is freely available only to those who want to use it in open-source software (which is software that lets users see, copy and modify the code). Developers can't use it in proprietary software, such as Microsoft Windows.

Many experts are impressed by IBM's latest step in exploiting its intellectual property.

"They are right for business reasons, but I don't think it was an easy decision to make," says Jeffrey Matsuura, an expert in high-tech law and business at the Alliance Law Group, a Virginia-based law firm. "I think other companies should — and will — consider doing the same thing."

Open-Source Movement

Most companies use patents in three ways: to exclusively exploit their inventions in the marketplace, license patents to other companies for big bucks, and protect themselves against infringement claims. IBM definitely isn't turning its back on those strategies. But the company also is exploring a fourth way to leverage patents.

"We are trying to use patents in a way that companies haven't done before," says Manny Schecter, IBM's associate general counsel for IP law. "We are trying to foster more collaborative innovation and create a patent commons in the open-source software space."

The company's action was spurred, in part, by a December 2004 report issued by The Council on Competitiveness, "The National Innovation Initiative." The report's authors argued that traditional methods for exploiting IP are no longer enough to promote innovation.

"No single organization has the scale to build today's complicated [IT] systems," the report stated. The authors of the study believe companies need to move away from proprietary software regimes and embrace open standards to ensure compatibility between IT products.

Some experts say that open-source development helps large and small developers avoid a growing threat to innovation: the proliferation of exclusive patent rights. Eben Moglen, an expert in intellectual property law who teaches at Columbia Law School, describes this as the anti-commons problem: "When there are too many exclusive rights in an area, you have to negotiate with an unmanageable number of people to do research, and the transaction costs become too high," he argues. "This happened in the biotech area during the 1990s. It was hard to do research because one had to buy rights from 20 to 30 different inventors."

This same problem now may be interfering with software development. "Patent lawyers are telling me software patents are more trouble than they are worth," he says. "They create a whole series of problems with companies taking in each others' laundry."

Big companies can leverage their patent portfolios to negotiate necessary cross-licenses. However, small- and medium-sized software businesses usually don't own enough patents to press for similar deals. They must either pay hard-earned cash for patent licenses, spend time and money trying to design around patents, or simply give up on innovating in patent-infested areas.

Because of this, many smaller tech companies look askance on software patents. It also is the reason many companies in Europe have actively opposed a proposal to legalize software patents in the European Union. Open source advocates also have joined the chorus against the proposed EU software patents, claiming that such patents would hinder innovation and thus harm society.

Big Blue Consultant

Protecting innovation is an admirable goal. But what does IBM get out of it? How does the company benefit by promoting new open-source technologies it can't own?

First, IBM obtains a defensive benefit. When developers create open-source technologies, IBM's rivals can't exclusively exploit these technologies.

Second, new open-source technologies can help IBM sell its other services. As customers flock to open-source IT products, they will hire companies such as IBM to install, maintain and customize these products. For instance, Deutsche Bahn, which runs Germany's railway system, hired IBM to advise it on how best to switch from the proprietary Unix operating system, to Linux, an open-source alternative. And Deutsche Bahn is running its new Linux system on new IBM servers — which means more profit for Big Blue.

"What IBM understands is that its success in the 21st Century isn't in making low-end hardware; it isn't in its interest to make propriety products that have interoperability problems; and it isn't in its interest to license Microsoft products," Moglen says. Instead, he says, "IBM is turning itself into the most important information consultancy in the world."

IBM isn't unique. Many other companies can benefit by making some of their patents available to the open-source community.

"One class of companies want open source to flourish because their business model includes use of open-source code, and they sell services and hardware around it. For these companies, [IBM's] type of donation makes a lot of sense," says Kevin Rivette, an IP management consultant with The Boston Consulting Group and author of the popular IP management book, Rembrandts in the Attic.

And there are plenty of such companies. For instance, just days after IBM announced it was donating 500 patents to open source, Sun Microsystems followed suit by making available 1,600 of its patents. This donation was aimed at strengthening Sun's OpenSolaris opensource operating system.

Buzz Kill

Many other companies are firmly opposed to open-source. Microsoft, for example, has been waging a PR campaign to convince businesses that open-source software is not as safe, less powerful and more expensive than products such as Windows.

Yet experts argue even companies that are committed to selling proprietary software eventually will embrace open source.

"Slowly and quietly people will change their business models to adopt open source," Rivette says. "Open source is creeping into so many things. How can you avoid putting open source into your business model?"

Rivette sees only one thing that can stop the eventual success of open-source software: companies that make their living not by selling products, but enforcing their software patents against others. These companies may have key patents essential to open-source software, and no financial incentive to make their patents available to the open-source community.

Acacia Research, for example, produces no IT goods or services, but makes lots of money from its patents on methods for sending compressed audio and video over the Internet. Acacia has sued many companies for allegedly violating these patents, and the patent owner has reached remunerative settlements with more than 227 firms.

Yet even companies such as Acacia may wind up accepting open source. "They will come around because they are business people," Rivette says. "If they figure out how to make money off it, they will use it."

Matsuura also predicts a rosy future for open-source software, expecting more companies to use it and in more contexts. This will benefit software users, who will get high quality, customizable software at lower prices. It also will help IT companies that want to use open source to enhance the sales of their own products and services.

As for companies that stubbornly fight against open source, they could wind up in trouble. "Customers want products that are secure, interoperable, innovative — all features that are associated with open source," Schecter says. "If other companies don't participate in the open-source movement, they might get left behind."

NOTES & QUESTIONS

1. IBM's published statement about the non-enforcement of its patents against open source software developers was as follows:

IBM Statement of Non-Assertion of Named Patents against OSS

IBM is committed to promoting innovation for the benefit of our customers and for the overall growth and advancement of the information technology field. IBM takes many actions to promote innovation. Today, we are announcing a new innovation initiative. We are pledging the free use of 500 of our U.S. patents, as well as all counterparts of these patents issued in other countries, in the development, distribution, and use of open source software. We believe that the open source community has been at the forefront of innovation and we are taking this action to encourage additional innovation for open platforms.

The following is the text of our pledge. It is our intent that this pledge be legally binding and enforceable by any open source software developer, distributor, or user who uses one or more of the 500 listed U.S. patents and/or the counterparts of these patents issued in other countries.

<u>IBM's Legally Binding Commitment Not To Assert the 500 Named Patents against OSS</u>

The pledge will benefit any Open Source Software. Open Source Software is any computer software program whose source code is published and available for inspection and use by anyone, and is made available under a license agreement that permits recipients to copy, modify and distribute the program's source code without payment of fees or royalties. All licenses certified by opensource.org and listed on their website as of 01/11/2005 are Open Source Software licenses for the purpose of this pledge.

IBM hereby commits not to assert any of the 500 U.S. patents [listed in this notice], as well as all counterparts of these patents issued in other countries, against the development, use or distribution of Open Source Software.

In order to foster innovation and avoid the possibility that a party will take advantage of this pledge and then assert patents or other intellectual property rights of its own against Open Source Software, thereby limiting the freedom of IBM or any other Open Source Software developer to create innovative software programs, the commitment not to assert any of these 500 U.S. patents and all counterparts of these patents issued in other countries is irrevocable except that IBM reserves the right to terminate this patent pledge and commitment only with regard to any party who files a lawsuit asserting patents or other intellectual property rights against Open Source Software.

IBM Statement of Non-Assertion of Named Patents against OSS, http://www.ibm.com/ibm/ licensing/patents/pledgedpatents.pdf (last visited on 10/15/2005).

2. IBM's commitment not to enforce certain of its patents against open source developers was part of a broader reassessment of patent enforcement strategy within the company. IBM executives apparently concluded that the company's patent enforcement strategy warranted a number of changes aimed at enhancing collaborative software development. This change of strategy was seen as a means to encourage new modes and quantities of software development:

> I.B.M. executives say the company's new approach to intellectual property represents more than a rethinking of where the company's self-interest lies. In recent speeches, for example, Samuel J. Palmisano, I.B.M.'s chief executive, has emphasized the need for more open technology standards and collaboration as a way to stimulate economic growth and job creation.

On this issue, I.B.M. appears to be siding with a growing number of academics and industry analysts who regard open-source software projects as early evidence of the wide collaboration and innovation made possible by the Internet, providing opportunities for economies, companies and individuals who can exploit the new model.

'This is exciting,' said Lawrence Lessig, a professor at Stanford Law School and founder of the school's Center for Internet and Society. 'It is I.B.M. making good on its commitment to encourage a different kind of software development and recognizing the burden that patents can impose.'

Steve Lohr, *IBM to Give Free Access to 500 Patents,* NEW YORK TIMES, January 11, 2005, at C1.

3. IBM's pledge not to enforce certain patents against developers of open source software has been matched by several other companies. By August of 2005, Sun Microsystems, Novell, Red Hat and Nokia had joined IBM in promising not to use their patents against at least some open source developers. However, some of the pledges by these companies were narrowly focused.

For example, Nokia indicated that its commitment on May 25, 2005 not to enforce its patents only applied to then-current versions of the Linux Kernel, the central component of the Linux operating system. The company reserved the right to enforce its patents against updates to the Linux Kernel. *See Legally Binding Commitment Not to Assert Nokia Patents against the Linux Kernel,* http://www.nokia.com/P23405 (last visited on 10/15/2005).

Sun's promise only related to projects that adhere to the Common Development and Distribution License (CDDL), an open source license applied to software developed as part of the Sun-sponsored OpenSolaris project. *See Sun Grants Global Open Source Community Access to More than 1,600 Patents,* http://www.sun.com/smi/Press/sunflash/2005-01/sunflash.20050125.2.html (last visited on 10/15/2005). The OpenSolaris project seeks to produce software based on a subset of the source code for Sun's Solaris Operating System. By limiting its patent non-enforcement pledge to parties adhering to the CDDL, Sun provided encouragement to developers who agree to participate in the OpenSolaris project and to make their work available in accordance with the CDDL, while providing no reassurance to other open source developers. *See generally* Tom Sanders, *OSDL Launches Open Source Patent Protection* (August 10, 2005), http://www.vnunet.com/vnunet/news/2140955/osdl-launches-open-source (last visited on 10/12/2005).

4. Some advocates of open source software development have argued that the commitment of IBM and others not to enforce their patents concerning open source software development projects is not enough to spur open source software development since the companies involved were already supporters of open source software development and were unlikely to have enforced these patents even absent their commitments. The real source of threats to open source development, these critics argue, are companies like Microsoft which have strong business reasons to oppose certain open source projects (such as

the development of open source operating system software products like Linux which compete with Microsoft's Windows products) and have large patent arsenals to use against open source developers. The critics suggest that contributions of patents from IBM and others to create an opposing body of patents which are enforceable against Microsoft and others would be more useful in staving off patent enforcement threats and in reassuring open source developers. They see open source development as the equivalent of a Cold War battlefield where the only real protection lies in building up opposing patent positions that establish a state of "mutually assured destruction" in which large companies are deterred from asserting their patent rights and open source developers are correspondingly reassured in their efforts to produce new software that may infringe the patents of these companies. *See* Matthew Broersma, *Open Source Patent Pool Mooted and Booted* (8/15/2005), http://www.linuxworld.com.au/index.php/id;307230270;fp;512;fpid;123851584 6 (last visited on 10/15/2005).

CHAPTER 12

ADVANCED TECHNIQUES FOR MINIMIZING RISKS OF INTELLECTUAL PROPERTY INFRINGEMENT IN MATURE COMPANIES

PROBLEM

Digital Ignition's engineers have recommended a change in one of the company's computer-controlled ignition products that may raise new risks of copyright infringement liability for the company. For some time, Digital Ignition has successfully marketed a computer-based system for controlling ignition processes in consumer automobiles. The computer programming involved in the original version of this product was all produced by Digital Ignition's employees and the company holds the copyrights regarding the resulting software.

The proposed engineering change is to include "Linux," an open source software program, in Digital Ignition's product for consumer automobile ignition systems. Linux is a well-known software program developed through the open source process in which various programmers contribute components or improvements of a particular software program with the expectation that their work will be incorporated in the whole and distributed as part of subsequent versions of the software program. The change to a Linux-based system will allow Digital Ignition's product to be built with computer hardware commonly used in personal computer systems and will allow Digital Ignition's programmers to develop and test new software for the product using the wide array of software programming and testing tools already available for Linux-based systems.

The proposed redesign of Digital Ignition's product appears to have substantial engineering merit, but has raised some questions about new intellectual property infringement risks that the company may face if it markets products incorporating Linux. In particular, Dr. Y.L. See, Digital Ignition's chief executive officer, and several of the company's other senior officers are aware that a number of companies — including the International Business Machines Corporation (IBM) — have been sued based on claims of copyright infringement in connection with the use or marketing of Linux-based software products. These suits have been brought by parties claiming to have a copyright interest in portions of Linux and asserting that they have never granted a license allowing the use and distribution of their copyrighted material as part of Linux. Digital Ignition's executives are concerned that they will be opening their company up to similar claims by marketing the proposed new ignition system. Such claims might be based on direct infringement of copyrights in Linux as Digital Ignition produces copies of Linux for inclusion in its products or as Digital Ignition produces further derivative works based on

Linux for use in its products. Further infringement claims might also be based on the advertising and sales of Linux-based systems to consumers on the theory that such sales entail the illegal and infringing distribution of unlicensed copies of copyrighted Linux components.

Assuming that there is some likelihood (albeit small) of copyright infringement liability on one of these grounds, uncertainty about the identify and location of the programmers who have contributed to Linux and the corresponding difficulty of obtaining licenses from all of the relevant parties suggest that reducing the company's infringement risks through a systematic effort to gain copyright licenses is not a realistic option. Dr. See is seeking advice on further means (such as insurance or careful management responses to infringement claims) that will reduce the company's financial risks from infringement liability should the company go forward with marketing the proposed new ignition system based on Linux. Dr. See, Digital Ignition's Vice-President of Engineering, and the company's Vice-President of Marketing — all three of whom are both officers of Digital Ignition and members of the company's board of directors — also wish to know if they will face any risk of personal liability as company officers or directors if they authorize the production and marketing of the Linux-based product knowing that such activities may entail copyright infringement by Digital Ignition and associated losses to the company from infringement liability. Please provide the requested advice to Dr. See and the other Digital Ignition executives.

FOCUS OF THE CHAPTER

The readings in this chapter describe a particular intellectual property infringement threat facing many large, mature firms — the possibility that their use or incorporation in products of open source software may raise uncertain copyright infringement claims. The chapter also describes insurance and corporate management tools that companies can use to reduce corporate threats from these sorts of uncertain infringement risks.

The development processes for open source software were previously considered in Chapter 11. This chapter examines the intellectual property risks to users of open source software, including companies that wish to remarket open source software components within broader products.

The initial reading on open source software and related intellectual property issues specifies how intellectual property interests may constrain the distribution of products incorporating open source software components and how unexpected copyright infringement claims may arise where the interests of an author of a component of an open source work have not been properly taken into account in the software licensing and distribution process.

The next series of readings address insurance coverage for intellectual property infringement risks. These readings begin with an article providing an overview of the types of insurance policies that can help companies reduce the financial risks of unknown intellectual property infringement threats. This article is followed by several cases involving disputes concerning the scope of insurance protections for losses from intellectual property infringement. These cases describe the range of insurance protections against intellectual property infringement or misappropriation liability that are available under a variety of types of policies, including policies covering commercial general liability, losses of physical property, and losses stemming from management errors and omissions. These cases also illustrate, through the situations giving rise to the insurance claims in the cases, a number of types of corporate practices that can produce unexpected intellectual property infringement liability.

The last reading in this chapter describes how systematic management attention to intellectual property infringement risks and claims can aid companies in avoiding infringement liability and in preventing personal liability for corporate officers and directors where corporate actions they have authorized produce unexpected infringement liability for their companies.

READINGS

A. RESPONDING TO PARTIALLY UNDERSTOOD INTELLECTUAL PROPERTY THREATS: THE EXAMPLE OF RISKS ASSOCIATED WITH OPEN SOURCE PRODUCTS

Open source software is increasingly relied upon in corporate environments, but its use raises some unusual intellectual property infringement risks. As noted by one observer:

> "'Open source' software is not new, but it has recently attracted much more attention from in-house counsel and private practitioners. As more companies incorporate open source software into their internal systems and commercial products, lawyers need to ensure that underlying licenses are not violated and that proprietary improvements are not compromised. Not all open source licenses are equally "open," and such software has already prompted multi-billion-dollar litigation. The advantages of open source products far outweigh the risks, so long as users are adequately informed of pertinent issues."

Lori E. Lesser, *Open Source Software: Risks, Benefits, and Practical Realities in the Corporate Environment,* in Practising Law Institute, Open Source Software: Risks, Benefits, and Practical Realities in the Corporate Environment, 808 PLI/Pat. 29, 29 (2004).

The following reading describes the licensing terms under which most open source software is distributed and some of the risks that can arise when open source software is incorporated in broader commercial products.

Lori E. Lesser, Simpson Thacher & Bartlett, LLP, A Hard Look at the Tough Issues in Open Source Licenses
Practising Law Institute Open Source Software 2005: Critical Issues in Today's Corporate Environment (2005)[*]

Introduction

An examination of the predominant "open source" software licenses prompts a multitude of legal questions, many of which the courts have not yet answered. These licenses are designed to be binding contracts just like any other privately-negotiated agreement. Yet, the courts have not yet provided guidance on critical issues, such as the meaning of license terms, their validity and enforceability, the proper parties in any related litigation, and the reasonable penalties for breach. Until such specific guidance is obtained, in-house counsel and private practitioners are examining long-standing general principles of licensing law to advise clients accordingly.

I.   Background on Open Source Software

A.   Creation of Open Source

1. In the early 1980s, Richard Stallman of MIT began creating his own operating system, named GNU (for "GNU's Not Unix"). Stallman and his colleagues had been writing software for the mainframe computer of MIT's Artificial Intelligence Laboratory, but a newly installed mainframe — with proprietary source code — rendered their work moot and obsolete. Stallman founded the Free Software Foundation, and in 1985, Stallman published the "GNU Manifesto," stating his mission to develop a Unix-compatible software system that was and would remain free for users. GNU had many higher-level functions.

2. In 1987, Professor Andrew Tanenbaum developed an open source Unix clone named Minix.

3. In 1991, Linus Torvalds of Finland began creating his own operating system "kernel," which contained "lower level" functionality governing basic interactions with the computer's hardware. The system used inexpensive PC hardware, but had the functionality of a more expensive Unix system. Torvalds posted his source code on the Internet and incorporated many programmers' suggestions and improvements into his system.

4. The combination of Stallman and Torvalds' work became GNU/Linux, and is now known as Linux. The Linux kernel is still licensed under the [General Public License (GPL) discussed below].

B.   Open Source Principles

1. The open source movement believes that software users should have the right to access and modify source code (the part of the code that is readable by human software programmers), which requires legal permission from the copyright owner and physical possession of the code. . . . Source code access is critical to allow the necessary "tinkering" that produces innovation — just like a student annotates a textbook or a mechanic "soups up" an exhaust system. The theory is that, if thousands of programmers have access to source code and exchange their improvements, and innovation will occur more quickly and efficiently.

2. Open source licenses are not uniform in their provisions as to how programmers must share derivative works created from the open source base. Indeed, several popular open source licenses differ in this regard. The GPL license (discussed below) requires users who distribute integrated derivative works to do so without charge.

3. The Open Source Initiative (www.opensource.org) lists 10 principles to qualify a software license as an "open source" license. Dozens of licenses currently comply.

> a. Free distribution
>
> b. Availability of source code
>
> c. Permission to make derivative works
>
> d. Integrity of the author's source code
>
> e. No discrimination against users/groups
>
> f. No discrimination against fields of use
>
> g. Distribution of original license with product
>
> h. License is not product specific
>
> i. No restriction of accompanying software
>
> j. License is technology neutral

C.   Open Source Myths

1. *Open source software is new.* As noted above, the first open source software has its origins in the early 1980s.

2. *Open source software is "free."* The word "free" is frequently used in connection with "open source" software, but it does not mean that the software is dedicated to the public, *Planetary Motion, Inc. v. Techsplosion, Inc.,* 261 F.3d 1188, 1198 (11th Cir. 2001) (noting that software distributed pursuant to GPL license "is not necessarily ceded to the public domain" and the licensor purports to retain ownership rights). Nor does it mean that open source software will always be available without monetary cost. Open source developers may charge for their specific products; however, users can copy and modify the open source code incorporated therein without paying further royalties.

Further, certain open source licenses allow derivative works to remain proprietary, and those owners may extract fees for copying and redistribution of such works. Open source users may need to pay for top-line user support, bug fixing, patches or proprietary applications running on an open source operating system. Stallman has said, "Think free speech, not free beer." Similarly, think "free puppy," due to later accompanying costs.

3. *A prudent company would not give away open source products for free.* Such a strategy may be profitable in the long run, if a vendor sells accompanying hardware, support or training services or compatible applications. Certain Internet companies have profited by offering free content or services, and thereby attracting users and driving them to for-profit services or supporting an advertising base.

4. *There is a standard open source license.* The Open Source Initiative website (www.opensource.org/licenses) lists dozens of open source licenses, including samples from Apache, Apple, BSD, Eclipse, Entessa, GNU, IBM, Intel, Lucent, MIT, Mozilla, Nokia, Python, RealNetworks, Sun, Sybase and Vovida. The GPL and BSD licenses are the more commonly-used and discussed agreements.

5. *Open source products are not mainstream.* Open source products are found at many large U.S. companies and institutions and include: Red Hat Linux (operating system), Apache (webpage server), Tomcat (Java servlet engine), Sendmail (mail server), MySQL (relational database system), Emacs (development tool), Snort (intrusion detection tool), Sun Microsystems' StarOffice (office suite), and Solaris 10 (operating system), BIND (Internet domain name service) and OpenSSL (security protocols).

6. *Open source products are niche products and do not support most user needs.* Personal computers are now being sold with complete open source "office suite programs" (word processor, spreadsheet program, presentation builder, image editor). For home users or corporate staff needing minimal computer access for Internet browsing and e-mail (*e.g.*, complaint departments or sales support), open source products may be sufficient for all daily needs.

I.   Types of Open Source Software Licenses (www.opensource.org)

A.   GNU Model (Free Software Foundation)

1. [The] GNU General Public License, GNU Lesser General Public License, [and] GNU Free Documentation License [cover software and documentation related to the] initial kernel of Linux. *See* www.gnu.org/licenses.

2. These licenses are the most protective, in license terms of preserving the "openness" of open source. The GPL license requires that all modified software be redistributed under the same license. The licenses are several pages long.

3. Provisions of GPL — Summary:

a. Users may copy and distribute verbatim copies of the program's source code, if they publish copyright notice and warranty disclaimers on every copy, and provide the GPL license to every recipient of the program. Users may charge a fee for the physical transfer of a copy of the program or may offer warranty protection for a fee.

b. If users distribute any modifications to the program (which is at the users' discretion), it must be under the above terms, and users must: (i) have the modified files prominently note such modifications and the dates thereof; (ii) distribute or publish any derivative works under the terms of this license and not charge for a license to such works as a whole; and (iii) cause the modified program to print a copyright notice and warranty disclaimer when starting to run.

c. The forced re-licensing of a derivative work does not apply to "identifiable sections of that work that are not derived from the Program, and can be reasonably considered independent and separate works in themselves" that are distributed as "separate works." If such sections are distributed as part of a whole that is a derivative work of the program, such distribution is subject to the GPL.

. . .

B.   BSD (Berkeley Software Distribution) Model

1. OpenBSD, FreeBSD, Apache, [and MIT Licenses are based on this model].

2. The University of California at Berkeley developed the BSD model in the 1970s. To distribute an open source program or derivative work under BSD, in either source code or object code form, one must affix a copyright notice, the license's brief conditions, a disclaimer of warranties and limitation of liability, and a prohibition against using contributors' names to promote products created with the program. BSD users are not, however, required to distribute any derivative work free of charge. These licenses are the least protective of the "openness" of open source works.

3. These licenses are generally short. The license template requires publication of standard copyright notice (e.g., © name and year), publication of a damages and warranty disclaimer and little else. The license provides that redistribution and use of the program are permitted, in source or object code form, with or without modification.

C.   Corporate Authors/Miscellaneous

1. Dozens of open source licenses are offered by corporations and private organizations, including Mozilla, Sun, Nokia, Apple and IBM.

2. The Mozilla public license is a basis for many future ones. In 1998, Netscape released its browser software under an open source license through Mozilla.

3. The licenses written by corporations are drafted by attorneys and have more substance than the BSD models. In style and structure (but not substantive terms), many resemble mass-market object code licenses.

III. Risks of Open Source Software

A. Mandatory Licensing

1. In theory, if an in-house programmer incorporates a small portion of GPL-licensed code into an integrated proprietary product and the integrated product is distributed, the source code to the entire derivative work becomes subject to the GPL license. This specific issue has never been litigated. It is unclear how the "derivative work" subject to the GPL license would be defined — a single module or an entire program. It is also unclear when GPL-protected code is deemed integrated into the derivative work, or when it is sufficiently "independent or separate" so as not to trigger the mandatory licensing obligation.

2. In *Progress Software Corp. v. MySQL AB*, 195 F. Supp.2d 328 (D.Mass. 2002), MySQL moved for a preliminary injunction regarding Progress' distribution of its Gemini program based upon MySQL, pursuant to an end-user license that was not GPL compliant. The court denied the injunction. It noted that a factual dispute remained whether Progress' program was a derivative work governed by the GPL or a separate and independent work not subject to the GPL, but noted that Progress had released Gemini's source code, thereby arguably curing any breach of the GPL. The court further noted that MySQL had not demonstrated irreparable harm, given that the Gemini source code had been released and that Progress planned to withdraw its end use license for commercial users. Meanwhile, given that Progress' product line using MySQL was significant to one of its subsidiaries, Progress had demonstrated that the balance of harm tipped in its favor, regarding its use of MySQL pursuant to the GPL license.

3. [In 2005, a] Munich court . . . enjoined a British software company from selling or distributing software incorporating GPL-licensed code that did not comply with the GPL's terms. *Welte v. Fortinet UK Ltd.*, Landgericht Muenchen 1, No. 21 0 7240105. The firm settled quickly and modified its end-user licenses to comply with the GPL. *See* BNA ELECTRONIC COMEMERCE AND LAW REPORT, Vol. 10, No. 18, May 4, 2005.

4. Recent commentators have noted that the GPL "derivative works" issue is still unresolved, citing *Progress Software v. MySQL. See* Lerner, J., *The Scope of Open Source Licensing*, JOURNAL OF LAW, ECONOMICS AND ORGANIZATION (April 2005); Carver, B., *Share and Share Alike: Understanding and Enforcing Open Source and Free Software Licenses*, 20 BERKTLJ 443, 460 (2005) (referring to *MySQL* case; "Ultimately, the issue of what constitutes a derivative software work must be addressed by statute or the courts. There was some hope that the issue would be decided in a case from 2002, but the court did not reach this issue.").

B. Validity and Enforcement

1. Open source licenses are not signed. Therefore, it is unclear if all open source users or contributors have "accepted" the terms of their open source licenses and formed a valid contract, particularly if the license's terms are embedded in the

program code. Absent a signature (or clicking "I agree"), such licenses arguably function as "browsewrap" agreements that are accepted when the user avails him/herself of the program governed by the license. Browsewrap agreements have had mixed results in the courts in terms of their validity and enforceability.

. . .

2. It is unlikely that a user who has modified open source software will claim he/she did not have a valid license that was properly accepted, because absent such a license, such modifications would amount to copyright infringement.

3. Given that an open source program may have multiple authors worldwide who create overlapping or duplicate improvements of varying sizes and importance, it is unclear who will have standing (or the desire) to bring litigation against a particular user. As with proprietary licenses, an unrelated third party may claim a certain version of open source software infringes its copyrights or patents. Unlike proprietary software, however, there are no warranties (or generally, indemnities) supporting the end user's right to use an open source product against any third-party claims.

4. If software that was previously proprietary and licensed to end users is released as open source, such release may affect the rights and obligations of previous licensees.

C. Litigation

1. Stallman worked vigorously to acquire ownership of the intellectual property rights to GNU, so the license's forced re-licensing of derivative works could not be challenged by third parties claiming to own the copyright in some portion of the program and not to be bound by the GPL license.

2. Torvalds did not engage in similar activities, and the authorship of various portions of Linux is disputed.

3. SCO v. IBM

a. *The SCO Group, Inc. v. International Business Machines Corp.*, Case No. 03-CV-0294 OAK (D. Utah). SCO initially sued IBM in March 2003, alleging that IBM improperly used SCO's "trade secrets" in the Linux operating system, despite the fact that the source code of Linux is publicly available. SCO later amended its complaint to allege that SCO's copyrightable Unix code, and not trade secrets, are improperly incorporated into Linux. IBM has counterclaimed for patent and copyright infringement.

b. In 2001, SCO bought Unix, the AT&T operating system for mainframe and minicomputers, which had been licensed to thousands of users. SCO alleges that fragments of Unix are incorporated into the foundation "kernel" of Linux.

c. In late May 2003, Novell claimed that it owned the Unix rights that SCO claimed as its own. *See SCO Group Inc. v. Novell Inc.*, 377 F. Supp. 2d 1145 (D. Utah June 27, 2005) (denying Novell's motion to dismiss SCO's slander of title claim).

d. SCO has also sued end-user Linux customers — AutoZone and DaimlerChrysler — and sent 1,500 letters to other Linux end-user customers.

e. Red Hat claims in the suit below that SCO has never identified a specific piece of Unix code that was unlawfully copied into Linux.

f. In February 2005, the court denied IBM's motion for summary judgment, but chided SCO for not providing "any competent evidence" that would raise a genuine issue of material fact as to whether IBM committed copyright infringement. Judge Kimball noted that the discovery process was not yet complete and that IBM had yet to hand over certain documents, but invited IBM to re-file the motion for summary judgment at the end of discovery. *See The SCO Group, Inc. v. International Business Machines Corp.*, 2005 WL 318784, 2005 Copr. L. Dec. ¶ 28,957 (D. Utah, Feb. 9, 2005).

g. Trial is expected to begin in early 2007.

4. *Red Hat, Inc. v. The SCO Group, Inc.*, No. Civ. 03-772-SLR, 2004 WL 883400 (D. Del. Apr. 6, 2004). Red Hat sued for a declaratory judgment regarding the potential copyright and patent infringement by Linux of SCO's Unix OS software, citing SCO's public statements that it intended to sue Red Hat after IBM. The court stayed the action pending the resolution of the SCO/IBM litigation in Utah. Red Hat's complaint alleges that SCO's statements "are solely designed to create an atmosphere of fear, uncertainty and doubt about Linux." Comp., ¶ 2.

5. Other cases make passing reference to "open source" software. *See Computer Associates Int'l v. Quest Software, Inc.*, 333 F. Supp.2d 688, 698 (N.D.Ill. 2004) (noting that GPL license restricts modification and subsequent distributions of freeware programs, but finding that program output at issue was not subject to GPL license); *Massachusetts v. Microsoft Corp.*, 373 F.3d 1199, 1228-32 (D.C. Cir. 2004) (addressing open source provision of remedial antitrust consent decree).

D. Remedies

1. Non-compliance with an open source license may amount to a material breach of its terms. As with other intellectual property licenses, every material breach may not rise to the level of copyright infringement. Exceeding the scope of a license (e.g., publishing in an unauthorized country, medium or distribution channel) generally constitutes copyright infringement, while breach of a covenant separate from the license grant (e.g., failure to make timely royalty payments) is only breach of contract. *See Allman v. Capricorn Records*, 2002 WL 1579899 at *1, 2002 Copr. L. Dec. ¶ 28,467 (9th Cir. July 16, 2002); *Sun Microsystems, Inc. v. Microsoft Corp.*, 188 F.3d 1115, 1121 (9th Cir. 1999) (licensor can sue for copyright infringement if licensee acts outside scope of limited license; otherwise, claim is only for breach of contract); *Graham v. James*, 144 F.3d 229, 237 (2d Cir. 1998) (if licensee's breach of license is failure to satisfy condition on license, conduct may rise to infringement).

2. From a plaintiff's point of view, alleging copyright infringement is better, because it allows the plaintiff to seek an injunction, statutory damages and attorney's fees. Further, the plaintiff can bring its case in Federal court. Breach of contract claims, which are litigated in state court absent diversity jurisdiction, generally do not allow such enhanced remedies.

E. Copyright Misuse

1. The issue of copyright misuse is mentioned in connection with open source software. Copyright misuse is use of a copyright in a manner contrary to public policy, such as requiring a copyright licensee to refrain from competitive activities that are <u>not</u> related to the license. It is an affirmative defense to a copyright infringement claim, and to the extent the defense succeeds, the plaintiff's copyright is unenforceable in such instance. *See Video Pipeline, Inc. v. Buena Vista Home Entm't, Inc.*, 342 F.3d 191, 204 (3rd Cir. 2003); *Practice Mgmt. Info. Corp. v. American Medical Assoc.*, 121 F.3d 516, 520-21 (9th Cir. 1997); *Lasercomb America, Inc. v. Reynolds*, 911 F.2d 970, 973 (4th Cir. 1990).

2. A defendant in a copyright infringement case could raise a copyright misuse defense concerning the GPL or similar open source licenses. Yet, this argument seems unlikely to prevail, because the restrictions in the GPL license relate to use of the licensed code itself (or modifications thereto), which the code's creators are under no obligation to license at all. The GPL license also specifically provides that it does not attempt to regulate sections of the user's derivative works that are <u>not</u> derived from the licensed code.

3. A party demanding a license fee for use of patent or copyright dedicated to the public may be liable for patent or copyright misuse, rendering such license unenforceable. *See Assessment Technologies of WI, LLC v. Wiredata, Inc.*, 361 F.3d 434, 437 (7th Cir. 2004) (noting that claim of copyright in public domain data "came close" to copyright misuse). Yet open source software is not public domain, but is licensed with written conditions.

F. Support

1. There is no free lunch. While open source software is initially available for free, not all programs have high-quality vendors offering support, bug fixes and training. User groups, websites and listserves abound of uneven quality.

2. Open source licenses disclaim all warranties and most disclaim indemnification, as well.

NOTES & QUESTIONS

1. What are the sources of operational and infringement risks to product users in adopting an open source software product (such as Linux or the Linux-based product described in the Problem above) versus the risks of adopting an equivalent software product (such as Microsoft Windows) produced and sold by a single software developer?

2. Should a commercial party be able to profit by building a broader, copyrighted product around a core of open source software or is this type of commercial reuse and extension of open source components inconsistent with either the spirit of open source software development or the legally authorized scope of open source software use? What would be the implications for the subsequent use of open source software of simply precluding its incorporation in any commercial product?

3. Some companies marketing products developed through open source processes have sought to reassure their customers that they can acquire and use the products with minimal risks of copyright and patent infringement claims. Agreements governing sales of open source products may include indemnification provisions in which software sellers agree to indemnify buyers for losses stemming from copyright or patent infringement claims, thereby shifting the financial risks of such claims from the buyers to the sellers. In addition, some software sellers have pledged to use their own intellectual property portfolios to respond to infringement claims pressed against their customers based on the customers' use of the sellers' products. For example, Novell, Inc., a major vendor of open source Linux products, has released a policy statement which provides, in part, that:

> "We believe that customers want and need freedom of choice in making decisions about technology solutions. Those considering Novell offerings, whether proprietary or open source, should be able to make their purchasing decisions based on technical merits, security, quality of service and value, not the threat of litigation. Novell intends to continue to compete based on such criteria.
>
> . . .
>
> • As appropriate, Novell is prepared to use our patents, which are highly relevant in today's marketplace, to defend against those who might assert patents against open source products marketed, sold or supported by Novell. Some software vendors will attempt to counter the competitive threat of Linux by making arguments about the risk of violating patents. Vendors that assert patents against customers and competitors such as Novell do so at their own peril and with the certainty of provoking a response. We urge customers to remind vendors that all are best served by using innovation and competition to drive purchasing decisions, rather than the threat of litigation.
>
> • Novell has previously used its ownership of UNIX copyrights and patents to protect customers against similar threats to open source software made by others."

Novell Statement on Patents and Open Source Software, http://www.novell.com/company/ policies/patent/ (last visited on 10/12/2005).

B. INFRINGEMENT INSURANCE

Steven E. Tiller & Briggs Bedigian, Intellectual Property and Technological Insurance Coverage
Maryland Bar Journal, Nov./Dec. 2001, p. 35*

. . .

In light of the emphasis on [intellectual property (IP)] and technical know-how in today's marketplace, insurance coverage for possible infringement and other related claims can be critical to the continued success of any company.

Insurance coverage can provide the funds to defend a claim; pay a judgment in the event of an adverse ruling; and even, in the appropriate situation, provide an IP owner with the resources to bring suit against an infringer. Such coverage is often the difference between life and death for a company facing an infringement claim as such claims are quite expensive to defend. For example, the average patent infringement suit costs between $775,000 and $2.5 million. [*See*] *Finding Intellectual Property Liability Coverage In The New Business Era – Part I*, THE METROPOLITAN CORPORATE COUNSEL, July 2000.

Traditionally, the only potential coverage available for such claims could be found under the advertising injury provision of a business' commercial general liability (CGL) policy. These policies, however, were drafted long before the garage doors began opening in the new technical revolution, and were not designed to cover most of these emerging forms of litigation. The absence of coverage for most infringement claims has led to the development of new types of policies that provide coverage, at a cost, for many types of infringement claims.

1.   IP Coverage Under Traditional CGL Policies

An insurer's duty to defend and/or indemnify generally depends on the allegations comprising the claim against its insured, and the language of the policy. Traditionally, coverage for IP claims has only been found in the advertising injury provisions of CGL policies. These provisions typically provide coverage for damages arising from:

1)   Publication of material that slanders or libels a person or organization, or disparages a person's or organization's goods, products or services;

2)   Publication of material that violates a person's right to privacy;

3)   Misappropriation of advertising ideas or style of doing business; or

4)   Infringement of copyright, title or slogan.

Two criteria must be met before coverage for advertising injuries will be extended. First, the alleged conduct must fall within the scope of one of the enumerated offenses described as an advertising injury. The alleged conduct must also not otherwise fall within the scope of one of the policy's exclusions. Second, the offense must have been committed in the course of advertising the insured's goods, products or services — commonly referred to as the "nexus requirement." If one of these two elements is absent, no coverage will extend.

The majority of courts find a nexus if the following requirements are met:

1)   the complaint filed against the injured alleges an offense covered by the advertising injury provision;

2)   the alleged offense occurred during the term of the policy;

3)   the claim arose out of the insured's advertising activities; and

4)   the offense occurred in the course of the insured's advertising activities.

So where does coverage stand today? The answer to that question can differ depending on what type of intellectual property dispute is in question.

A. Advertising Injury Coverage For Patent Infringement

. . .

Computer technology coupled with the patentability of biotechnology has led to a sharp increase in the number of patent disputes. Attempts to obtain coverage under CGL policies, however, are difficult because it is hard to show that the infringement occurred during the course of the insured's advertising. If the insured is unable to establish a nexus between the allegedly infringing conduct and its advertising efforts, the nexus requirement is not met, and coverage will not extend. Moreover, many CGL policies contain specific exclusions for patent infringement, thereby negating any argument that coverage should apply.

B. Advertising Injury Coverage For Trademark Infringement

It is typically argued that coverage for trademark infringement claims is provided under the provisions for "misappropriation of advertising ideas or style of doing business" and "infringement of title or slogan." Although courts are split on the issue, a majority have found that the language of those two clauses generally grants coverage for trademark infringement claims. *See, e.g., Bay Elec. Supply, Inc.*, 61 F. Supp.2d at 617 (holding that misappropriation of advertising ideas or style of doing business encompasses claims for trademark and trade dress infringement); *Lebas Fashion Imports of USA, Inc. v. ITT Harford Insurance Group*, 50 Cal. App. 4th 548, 565-66 (Cal.App. 1996) (finding the enumeration of "misappropriation of advertising ideas or style" ambiguous and, therefore, holding in favor of the insured).

Other courts, however, have found that there is no duty to cover trademark or trade dress infringement claims. *See, e.g., Callas Enters. Inc. v. Travelers Indem. Co. of America*, 193 F.3d 952, 956 (8th Cir. 1999), following *Advance Watch Co. v. Kemper Nat'l. Ins. Co.*, 99 F.3d 795, 801-802 (6th Cir. 1996) (holding that the "misappropriation of advertising ideas or style of doing business" provisions could not be so broadly construed as to include trademark or trade dress infringement). The Sixth Circuit in *Advance Watch* reasoned that "if the insurer had intended to provide coverage for such liability, they would have referred to it by name in the policy, as they did in the case of infringement of copyright, title or slogan." *Advance Watch*, 99 F.3d at 803.

C. Advertising Injury Coverage For Copyright Infringement

With the advent of the Internet, copyright infringement is as easy as downloading a copyrighted document or computer program onto a hard drive, or forwarding protected material via e-mail. As copyright infringement is specifically mentioned in typical CGL policies, most assume that coverage is a given. However, this may not always be the case. Not every case of copyright infringement is related to the insured's advertising efforts, and therefore coverage may not be provided.

With the uncertainty of coverage for most IP claims, including a complete lack of coverage for any claim not arising out of one's advertising efforts, companies have desperately been looking for alternatives. Insurance companies are finally obliging.

2. Intellectual Property Insurance

Separate IP insurance may benefit both large and small companies. IP can be a business' primary asset and at the very least a valued commodity. In fact, it was estimated in 1999, that of Microsoft's $300 billion market capitalization, $284 billion of that was made up of IP. Kevin M. Quinley, DEFENDING AND HANDLING INTELLECTUAL PROPERTY CLAIMS, Insurance Information Institute, Inc., 1999.

A. Who and What Are Typically Covered By Intellectual Property Insurance?

Prior to the 1980's, IP was generally not considered insurable. IP assets were considered difficult to quantify, and infringement claims were even harder to underwrite. New IP insurance policies, however, have transformed the intangible into the tangible. IP insurance keeps a business' bottom line intact by controlling unexpected costs of litigation, and reducing the pressure a business may feel to settle because of the mountain of legal fees that can accumulate during the course of IP litigation. There are currently two prominent forms of IP coverage: 1) enforcement policies, also known as pursuit, abatement or offensive coverage; and 2) defense (liability) policies.

B. Enforcement Policies

The most common type of IP enforcement policy available today is for patent infringement. This type of policy applies to situations where an insured's patent is allegedly infringed by another, and the insured wishes to bring an infringement claim. These policies typically cover: 1) the cost of bringing suit against an alleged infringer; 2) the cost to defend against counterclaims alleging invalidity of the insured's patent; 3) the cost of reexamination of the insured's patent in the Patent and Trademark Office; and 4) the cost to reissue the patent. Betterley, INTELLECTGUAL PROPERTY INSURANCE MARKET SURVEY 2000, Betterley Risk Consultants, Inc. at p. 8.

These policies come at a cost. Premiums can be expensive, and many companies require validity opinions to be prepared by qualified patent counsel at the cost of the insured.[1]

C. Defense Policies

Defense coverage is more traditional, and generally protects an insured against allegations that it has infringed upon the IP of another. A company's

---

[1] Intellectual property enforcement policies and their use to protect intellectual property owners are described more fully in Chapter 11.

IP needs are often very specialized, and policies designed to cover the unique needs of each area of IP are now available. Moreover, insurers' premiums and coverages are as varying as the products they insure.

The types of policies offered vary with the type of protection sought. Policies are not limited to patent, trademark and copyright infringement policies, or strictly third party liability coverage. In fact, many insurance companies are now offering both first and third party coverage for emerging liabilities.

. . .

The following is a general synopsis . . . of the various types of coverage that are available in today's market:

1) <u>Intellectual property liability insurance</u>: These policies are being offered by a number of carriers who offer blanket coverage for all forms of IP infringement litigation. Such policies generally provide coverage for most IP claims or suits brought against the insured.

2) <u>Patent infringement liability insurance</u>: This type of coverage generally provides coverage for any patent infringement related to the manufacture, use, distribution, or sale of an allegedly infringing product.

3) <u>Warranty and representation insurance</u>: This type of policy generally covers costs associated with the breach of IP warranties and/or representations made in IP transactions, and also provides first party coverage for damages and losses.

4) <u>Technology liability insurance:</u> These policies generally cover damages that the insured is obligated to pay resulting from its wrongful acts in connection with the provision of technological services or products. Technological services include such things as systems analysis, programming, data processing, repair and maintenance of computer products, and design of networks and systems.

5) <u>Intellectual property agreement insurance</u>: These policies generally provide coverage for disputes arising from agreements including licenses, confidentiality, non-disclosure, and other technology or IP related agreements.

6) <u>Media liability insurance</u>: These policies are specially tailored for technology and Internet companies. They generally cover liabilities including Internet advertising and webcasting, as well as material published, transmitted, disseminated, distributed, created, originated, exhibited or displayed on the Internet in the course of business. These policies often cover allegations of defamation, product disparagement, trade libel, infringement of copyright, title or slogan, trademark, trade name, trade dress or service name, plagiarism, piracy, misappropriation of ideas under implied contracts, invasion or infringement of privacy and public disclosure of private facts.

7) <u>Internet professional liability insurance</u>: This type of coverage is also geared to the technology sector, and combines media liability coverage with professional services liabilities, such as Internet technology services (consulting, systems analysis, systems programming, data processing, system integration, development, repair or maintenance of computer products) and

Internet professional services (design, construction or maintenance of internet site, providing electronic mail services, maintaining chat rooms, etc.).

8) <u>Internet and computer network security insurance</u>: This type of policy combines media liability coverage with security liability coverage which covers the failure of hardware, software, or firmware whose function or purpose is to protect a computer from attack, unauthorized access, unauthorized use, disclosure of confidential or private information or transmission of malicious code. Some of these policies also add cyber-extortion coverage, a criminal reward fund and crisis management coverage. Another similar policy provides for asset and income protection coverage that will cover losses attributed to a company's information assets, as well as any lost profits that may occur if such information is lost.

9) <u>Errors and omission insurance:</u> These policies are relatively new and are generally designed to cover damages arising from the insured's negligence arising out of the provision of technology services.

MEZ INDUSTRIES, INC. v. PACIFIC NATIONAL INSURANCE COMPANY
California Court of Appeals
90 Cal.Rptr.2d 721 (Cal.App. 1999)

CROSKEY, J.

This case presents the question of whether a liability insurer providing coverage for "advertising injury" is required to defend its insured in an action charging the insured with *inducement* of patent infringement. When the respondent, Pacific National Insurance Company ("Pacific") refused to provide such a defense to the appellant, Mez Industries, Inc. ("Mez"), Mez filed this action for declaratory relief and breach of contract. The trial court sustained Pacific's demurrer without leave to amend and thereafter entered a judgment of dismissal.

Because we conclude that the advertising injury provisions of Pacific's policy did not provide coverage to Mez for inducement of patent infringement and, in any event, such coverage would have been precluded by Insurance Code section 533, we conclude that no potential for coverage existed as a matter of law and thus no duty to defend ever arose. The trial court ruled correctly and we therefore affirm.

FACTUAL AND PROCEDURAL BACKGROUND

Mez is engaged in the business of manufacturing, distributing and selling components used for the connection of joints in airflow conduction systems (such as central heating and air conditioning systems). It manufactures these components and advertises them for sale through wholesalers to mechanical and sheet metal construction contractors who use the components to create duct systems in various building projects throughout the United States.

On April 10, 1995, Ductmate Industries, Inc. ("Ductmate") filed a complaint against Mez in the United States District Court for the Northern District of Ohio in an action styled as "Ductmate Industries, Inc. v. Mez Industries, Inc.," U.S.D.C. N.D. Ohio Case No. 4:95CV00815 (hereinafter, the "Ductmate action"). Stripped to its relevant essentials, the complaint in that action alleged that Mez had induced its customers to infringe at least four of Ductmate's patents for certain "flange-type duct joint assembl[ies] and seal arrangement[s] [therefor]."[2]

Ductmate's alleged claims of inducement of patent infringement pursuant to 35 U.S.C. § 271(b) were not based upon Mez's manufacture of the individual component parts for a duct system joint assembly, but rather upon those activities of Mez that caused or encouraged *others* to take those component parts and put them together in a way which infringed Ductmate's patents. Those activities by Mez necessarily involved its *advertising* activities, which encouraged and solicited others to buy Mez's products and assemble them in a particular manner. For example, Ductmate featured in its own advertising its "Slide-On Connectors" for use in putting together a conduction system and provided step-by-step instructions for assembly and installation. Mez has distributed a variety of advertising brochures, mailers, and promotional booklets depicting HVAC duct joint assemblies which graphically illustrated how Mez's corners, flanges and seals could work as substitutes for Ductmate's Slide-On-Connectors corner units and related products. In addition, Mez's assembly and installation instructions produced the same HVAC ducts as depicted in Ductmate's advertising materials.

At least for our purposes, there is no contention that Mez's products themselves infringed upon any of Ductmate's patents. Rather, the relevant essence of the Ductmate action is that Mez's advertising, marketing and sales promotion activities solicited, encouraged and induced engineers, contractors, distributors and builders to purchase Mez's products and to combine and assemble them in a manner which did infringe Ductmate's patents.

Mez tendered defense of the Ductmate action to Pacific on or about July 6, 1995. Mez asserted that it was entitled to coverage and a defense of the action under the "Advertising Injury" section of Pacific's liability policy. As relevant to the issues before us, that policy promised both indemnity and a defense for an injury caused by one or both of the following two "offenses" committed *in the course of advertising* goods, products or services in the coverage territory during the policy period:

---

[2] [FN4] Ductmate also alleged other misconduct by Mez including active direct infringement of Ductmate's patents. However, on appeal, the only alleged conduct which Mez claims justifies a defense of the Ductmate action by Pacific are the allegations that Mez induced others to infringe Ductmate's patents. Mez made this clear in the initial paragraph of its Opening Brief: "Mez seeks a determination that Pacific owes it a duty of defense for claims of *inducing patent infringement* under its 'advertising injury' coverage for [1] 'misappropriation of advertising ideas or style of doing business' or [2] 'infringement of title.' " (Italics added.) As will become apparent, such a limitation on its scope of coverage argument was necessary to satisfy the requirement that the alleged misconduct for which a defense was sought had an *advertising* nexus.

(1) "Misappropriation of advertising ideas or style of doing business," and

(2) "Infringement of copyright, title or slogan."[3]

On or about November 22, 1995, after a review of the matter, Pacific denied coverage and refused to provide a defense. On June 4, 1997, Mez filed this action alleging essentially the forgoing facts and asserting that Pacific had wrongfully denied coverage. Mez alleged that it was entitled to a defense and sought a declaratory judgment for Pacific's breach of its contractual obligations under the policy.

Pacific attacked this complaint by demurrer, asserting that, as a matter of law, there could be no potential for coverage and thus no duty to defend. Pacific argued that the claim of inducing patent infringement is simply not a covered offense under the advertising provisions of the policy and, in any event, coverage for such an act would be precluded under section 533. The trial court agreed and, on January 9, 1998, sustained Pacific's demurrer without leave to amend. A judgment of dismissal was thereafter entered on January 27, 1998. Mez has filed this timely appeal.

CONTENTIONS OF THE PARTIES

Mez contends that there is at least a potential for coverage under the Pacific policy. It argues that the offenses of (1) "misappropriation of advertising ideas or style of doing business" and (2) "infringement of copyright, title or slogan" are both ambiguous and each could reasonably include the alleged inducement of patent infringement. Therefore, Mez concludes, Pacific had a duty to provide Mez with a defense to the Ductmate action and the trial court erred when it sustained Pacific's demurrer and entered a judgment of dismissal.

Pacific rejects these contentions and reasserts the same basic arguments which the trial court accepted and upon which it based its ruling.

---

[3] [FN5] The specific provisions of Pacific's policy here at issue are as follows:

"Coverage B—Personal and Advertising Injury Liability

1. Insuring Agreement

a. We will pay those sums that the insured becomes legally obligated to pay as damages because of . . . 'advertising injury' to which this coverage part applies. We will have the right and duty to defend any 'suit' seeking those damages.

b. This insurance applies to:

(1) . . .

(2) 'Advertising injury' caused by an offense *committed in the course of advertising* your goods, products, or services; but only if the offense was committed in the 'coverage territory' during the policy period."

Section 5 of the Primary Policy provides in pertinent part:

"1. 'Advertising Injury' means injury arising out of one or more of the following offenses:

(a) Oral or written publication of material that slanders or libels the person or organization or disparages a person's or organization's goods, products or services;

(b) Oral or written publication of material that violates a person's right of privacy;

(c) Misappropriation of advertising ideas or style of doing business; or

(d) *Infringement* of copyright, *title* or slogan." (Italics added.)

DISCUSSION

. . .

2.   Advertising Injury Coverage Cannot Be Established In This Case

Advertising injury liability has become part of the coverage offered in Commercial General Liability ("CGL") policies only recently. Prior to 1986, this coverage was offered by a separate broad form endorsement for which an additional premium was charged. It is important to understand that this coverage is entirely distinct from the bodily injury and property damage coverage which has long been the standard fare of CGL policies.

Bodily injury and property damage coverage is dependent upon an "accident" or "occurrence" and coverage is not triggered until an injury or damage results. Advertising injury, on the other hand, applies to injury resulting from the commission of certain specified offenses. It does *not* depend upon an accident, but may be based (and often is) on the *intentional* acts of the insured. Thus, even certain intentional torts may be covered (subject, of course, to the statutory exclusion under section 533, which we discuss below). The event triggering coverage is the commission of the specified offense during the policy period, provided that it is committed in the course of advertising goods, products or services.

a.   There Is No Coverage For a Patent Infringement Claim

The specified "offenses" with which we are concerned here are the (1) "misappropriation of an advertising idea or style of doing business" and (2) "infringement of copyright, title or slogan." If Mez's alleged inducement of the infringement of Ductmate's patents fits either of these two offenses, and was committed in the course of Mez's advertisement of its own products, then coverage would be available. It is doubtless because of this latter requirement that Mez does not argue on appeal that coverage is provided for the direct patent infringement which is also alleged in the Ductmate action. Under *relevant* applicable federal law (i.e., prior to the 1996 effective date of the 1994 amendment), patent infringement occurs when a party makes, uses or sells a product incorporating a patented invention. (35 U.S.C. ¶ 271(a).)[4] Where the claim in the underlying action is that an insured directly infringed the patents of another by the *sale* of its products, rather than by

---

[4] [FN8] We note that in 1994, Congress amended the Patent Act to include "offers to sell" (e.g., advertising) as conduct which could constitute patent infringement, and this amendment became effective in 1996. (35 U.S.C. § 271(a); see also Historical and Statutory Notes re 1994 Amendments and Effective Date of 1994 Amendments.) At least one court has concluded that this amendment "indicates that the insured could have an objectively reasonable expectation that it could be prosecuted for advertising injury in a claim for patent infringement." (See *Everett Associates, Inc. v. Transcontinental Ins. Co.* (N.D.Cal.1999) 57 F.Supp.2d 874, 882.) Assuming arguendo that the *Everett* court reached a proper result, a matter on which we express no opinion, this statutory change would appear to have nullified the argument that direct patent infringement could not arise out of an insured's advertising activities. However, the amendment has no impact on the issue before us because the alleged misconduct of Mez occurred prior to 1996 and Mez makes no claim for coverage based upon Ductmate's allegations of patent infringement. Moreover, even though a direct patent infringement might now be committed during the course of an advertising activity, such circumstance does not help us to resolve the question as to whether patent infringement itself will fall within one of the covered "offenses."

the form of the insured's advertisements, then the patent infringing act did not occur in the course of the insured's advertising activities within the meaning of the relevant policy language. (*Bank of the West v. Superior Court* (1992) 2 Cal. 4th 1254, 1275, 10 Cal.Rptr.2d 538, 833 P.2d 545.) An advertising injury must have a causal connection with the insured's advertising activities before there can be coverage. (*Id.* at p. 1277, 10 Cal.Rptr.2d 538, 833 P.2d 545.) As there is no contention here that Mez directly violated any of Ductmate's patents by its advertising activities, Mez cannot claim coverage for the allegations of direct patent infringement. Thus, Mez has limited its coverage argument to the allegations that *inducement* of infringement is alleged by Ductmate and that such allegation is enough to justify coverage.

b. There Is No Coverage For an Inducement of Patent Infringement Claim

Federal law also proscribes *inducing* patent infringement. (35 U.S.C. 271(b).) This section provides that "[w]hoever actively induces infringement of a patent shall be liable as an infringer." However, the alleged infringer must be shown to have *knowingly* induced infringement. "It must be established that the defendant possessed specific intent to encourage another's infringement and not merely that the defendant had knowledge of the acts alleged to constitute inducement. The plaintiff has the burden of showing that the alleged infringer's actions induced infringing acts and that he knew or should have known his actions would induce actual infringements."

Unlike direct infringement, it is possible for inducement to infringe to occur during the course of advertising activities; indeed, advertising has been found to be a sufficient basis for a claim of inducement.[5] (*U.S. Fidelity & Guar. Co. v. Star Technologies* (1996) 935 F.Supp. 1110, 1116; *New Hampshire Ins. v. R.L. Chaides Const.* (N.D.Cal.1994) 847 F.Supp. 1452, 1458.) However, liability can only be found if the inducement is "active"; that is, a party must "purposefully cause, urge or encourage another to infringe." Something *more* is required than simply the advertising of a product for sale. "In addition, the advertisement must instruct or explain to the purchaser exactly how to recreate or reassemble the product into one that infringes a patent." (*U.S. Fidelity & Guar. Co. v. Star Technologies, supra,* 935 F.Supp. at p. 1116; see also *Fromberg, Inc. v. Thornhill* (5th Cir.1963) 315 F.2d 407, 412[defendant advertised and personally demonstrated to purchasers how his device could be inserted into another object to recreate a patented product].)

Having in mind these general principles, we address the two questions which are raised by the parties' briefs as to whether coverage was provided for such conduct under Pacific's policy: (1) is the inducement of patent infringement an advertising offense within the meaning of the policy and, in any event, (2) is coverage under the policy for such an act barred by section 533?

(1) Inducing Patent Infringement Does Not Constitute An Advertising Injury Offense

---

[5] [FN9] As it seems clear, at least from Mez's complaint, that the alleged acts of inducement were committed in the course of Mez's advertising and marketing of its products, we assume, *for purposes of our decision,* that Mez has satisfied the "in the course of advertising" element required under Pacific's policy.

Pacific argues that neither direct patent infringement nor the inducement thereof is included within either the (1) "misappropriation of an advertising idea or style of doing business" or (2) "infringement of copyright, title or slogan." Mez responds that those terms are ambiguous, as they are subject to at least one reasonable interpretation which would include patent infringement or at least its inducement.

It is now settled that the interpretation of an insurance policy is no different than the interpretation of contracts generally. The mutual intention of the parties at the time the contract is formed governs interpretation. Such intent is to be inferred, if possible, solely from the written provisions of the contract. The "clear and explicit" meaning of these provisions, interpreted in their "ordinary and popular sense," unless "used by the parties in a technical sense" or "a special meaning is given to them by usage," will control judicial interpretation.

On the other hand, "'[i]f the terms of a promise are in any respect ambiguous or uncertain, it must be interpreted in the sense in which the promisor believed, at the time of making it, that the promisee understood it.' This rule, as applied to a promise of coverage in an insurance policy, protects not the subjective beliefs of the insurer but, rather, 'the objectively reasonable expectations of the insured.' Only if this rule does not resolve the ambiguity do we then resolve it against the insurer. [¶] In summary, a court that is faced with an argument for coverage based on assertedly ambiguous policy language must first attempt to determine whether coverage is consistent with the insured's objectively reasonable expectations. In so doing, the court must interpret the language in context, with regard to its intended function in the policy. This is because '*language in a contract* must be construed in the context of that instrument as a whole, and in the circumstances of that case, and *cannot be found to be ambiguous in the abstract.*'" (*Bank of the West v. Superior Court, supra,* 2 Cal.4th at pp. 1264-1265, 10 Cal.Rptr.2d 538, 833 P.2d 545; italics in original, citations omitted.)

The *Bank of the West* court made it clear that it was no longer enough to find an abstract ambiguity or a meaning for a disputed word or phrase which was simply "semantically permissible." In order to conclude that an ambiguity exists which will be construed against an insurer, it is necessary first to determine whether the coverage under the policy, which would result from such a construction, is consistent with the insured's *objectively reasonable expectations.* In order to do this, the disputed policy language must be examined *in context* with regard to its intended function in the policy. This requires a consideration of the policy as a whole, the circumstances of the case in which the claim arises, and "common sense." Such an evaluation of an insured's *objectively* reasonable expectations under that criteria may result in a restriction of coverage rather than an expansion. An insured will not be able successfully to claim coverage where a reasonable person would not expect it.

We recently had occasion to apply these principles in the context of a *trademark* infringement dispute. In *Lebas Fashion Imports of USA, Inc. v. ITT Hartford Ins. Group* (1996) 50 Cal.App.4th 548, 59 Cal.Rptr.2d 36 (*Lebas*), we concluded that the advertising offense "misappropriation of an advertising idea or style of doing business" was indeed ambiguous and, *in the context of the facts of that case,* the insured could have objectively reasonable expectations of coverage. However, the scope of our conclusion was necessarily confined by the specific circumstances in which it was reached. In *Lebas,* we were dealing with an insured that allegedly had appropriated the proprietary mark and name of an international distributor of high fashion perfume and cosmetics, and that was utilizing such mark and name in the labeling, marketing and advertising of its own line of clothing. We noted that, contrary to the fundamental purposes of a *patent,* one of the three fundamental purposes of a *trademark* was to advertise the products of the trademark holder and that an infringement of the trademark frequently occurred in the course of advertising. Moreover, a trademark often represented the manner and means of such advertising, or at the least was an integral part thereof, and as such could easily and reasonably be considered to fall within the definition of an "advertising idea" and be considered a part of the trademark holder's "style of doing business." Thus, an insurer's promise to provide coverage for the insured's misappropriation of either an "advertising idea" or a "style of doing business" could reasonably be construed by a layperson insured to include a trademark infringement. This was particularly true in light of the fact that, in *Lebas,* the record reflected that these new policy definitions of advertising injury offenses (which had replaced prior offenses described as "piracy" and "unfair competition") were accompanied by the *deletion* of an exclusion for trademark infringement that had been a part of the prior policy.

Understandably, Mez asks us to apply the same reasoning in this case and to find the policy's misappropriation offense ambiguous. However, we cannot go that far. In *Lebas,* we did not find that clause to be ambiguous in the abstract. We only reached the conclusion we did in the *context* of (1) the language of the policy, (2) the general circumstances of that particular case and (3) "common sense." We examined the policy language in that context with regard to its intended function in the policy and attempted to evaluate the insured's *objectively* reasonable expectations under that criteria. We have examined this same language in Pacific's policy and use the same criteria as we did in *Lebas,* but in the context of the facts in this case, we reach an entirely different result. We do not see how Mez's inducement of the infringement of Ductmate's particular patents reasonably could be considered to be the misappropriation of an "advertising idea" or "style of doing business." Similarly, as we discuss below, we see no reasonable basis for characterizing such inducement as constituting the infringement of a "copyright, title or slogan." As the federal cases we discuss below have said, such a construction would be offensive to both commonly understood meaning as well as common sense.

While we are aware of at least two cases which have concluded that the language in pre-1986 policies which described the offense of "piracy" was ambiguous enough to embrace patent infringement (see *New Hampshire Ins. v. R.L. Chaides Const., supra,* 847 F.Supp. at p. 1456; *National Union Fire Ins. Co. v. Siliconix, Inc.* (N.D.Cal.1989) 729 F.Supp. 77, 79),[6] we are aware of no

---

    [6] [FN14] Mez also cites us to the decision of the Nebraska Supreme Court (*Union Insurance Co. v. Land and Sky, Inc.* (Neb.1995) 247 Neb. 696, 529 N.W.2d 773) which held that an insured, under a policy defining one of the advertising injury offenses as "piracy," was entitled to a defense in a patent infringement action. Not only did that case involve a pre-1986 policy, and is thus not very helpful to us, but also the same insurer had issued the insured an excess policy which had expressly excluded coverage for patent infringement. The *Land and Sky* court found the term "piracy" to be ambiguous primarily because of this inconsistency between these two policies.

California or federal case which has reached a similar result with respect to the *post*-1986 policy language before us.

On the other hand, there are a number of cases which have concluded that the new language is not ambiguous, *at least in the context of a coverage claim for patent infringement,* and that no coverage is provided. Obviously, if patent infringement cannot properly be characterized as an advertising injury offense, then neither could its inducement. In *Owens-Brockway Glass v. International Ins. Co.* (E.D.Cal.1995) 884 F.Supp. 363, the court rejected the coverage claim of an insured who had suffered a judgment for non-willful patent infringement in the sum of $36,485,400.

When the insured sued its insurer to recover the judgment, the court concluded that patent infringement simply was not covered. The *Owens-Brockway* court applied the same principles of policy construction discussed above and then stated:

> "Plaintiff argues that patent infringement is included within the policy language insuring advertising injury as 'infringement of title' or 'misappropriation of style of doing business.' Plaintiff consults the dictionary to find that the word 'title' can refer to ownership of property such as a patent. Under this argument, the phrase 'infringement of . . . title' could refer to infringement of a patent. Similarly, plaintiff argues that 'misappropriation of style of doing business' could refer to patent infringement. Neither claim is reasonable, however, when the words 'title' and 'style of doing business' are examined in the context of their use and in the light of common sense. [¶] First, and perhaps most significantly, there is the glaring absence of the word 'patent' anywhere in the policy language defining advertising injury. The language defining 'advertising injury' includes 'slander[,]' 'libel,' 'right of privacy,' 'advertising ideas,' 'style of doing business,' and 'copyright.' These are specific terms connected to well known legal categories, just as a claim of patent infringement is a distinct legal claim. But there is not a mention of 'patent' anywhere in the definition or elsewhere in the policy. Surely if coverage for patent infringement were anticipated there would be some mention of the term itself just as 'copyright' is explicitly listed. Several courts have commented vigorously on the significance of the omission of any reference to patent in the definition of advertising injury: [¶] [I]t is nonsense to suppose that if the parties had intended the insurance policy in question to cover patent infringement claims, the policy would explicitly cover infringements of 'copyright, title or slogan,' but then include patent infringement, sub silentio, in a different provision, by reference to 'unauthorized taking of . . . [the] style of doing business.' [Citation.] . . . It is even more absurd to suggest that the phrase "infringement of . . . title," as used in the clause "infringement of copyright, title or slogan", encompasses patent infringement or inducement to infringe. Basic common sense dictates that if these policies covered any form of patent infringement, the word "patent" would appear in the quoted "infringement" clauses.' [Citation.] Moreover, as noted above, the policy language at issue here does not include the terms 'piracy' or 'unfair competition'; it lists well recognized and

narrow categories of legal claims among which patent infringement is notably absent. [¶] Second, neither the term 'infringement of title' nor 'misappropriation of style of doing business' suggests coverage of patent claims when these terms are viewed in the context of their use. One of the most significant parts of that context is that both terms are part of the definition of 'advertising injury.' There is nothing about the term 'advertising injury' itself that remotely suggests coverage of patent infringement." (884 F.Supp. at p. 367, fns. omitted.)

In *Gencor Industries v. Wausau Underwriters Ins. Co.* (M.D.Fla.1994) 857 F.Supp. 1560, the court concluded that neither patent infringement nor inducement of infringement were covered offenses under this same policy language. Its reasoning was identical to that expressed by the *Owens-Brockway* court. (857 F.Supp. at p. 1564.) Finally, in *St. Paul Fire & Marine v. Advanced Interventional* (E.D.Va.1993) 824 F.Supp. 583, 584-587, the court, applying California law, reached that same conclusion.

We think the analysis of these federal decisions is persuasive and we adopt their reasoning here. *In the context of the facts and circumstances of this case,* the policy terms "misappropriation of an advertising idea or style of doing business" and "infringement of copyright, title or slogan" simply could not be reasonably read by a layperson to include either patent infringement or the inducement thereof. This conclusion is consistent with the principles of contextual reasonableness which we have already summarized. Clearly, the Ductmate patents did not involve any process or invention which could reasonably be considered an "advertising idea" or a "style of doing business."

With respect to Mez's argument that there is coverage under the "infringement of . . . title . . ." provision in the policy, we reach the same conclusion. Our construction of that phrase is informed by the doctrine of *ejusdem generis* under which a term is interpreted by reference to the surrounding language. (See, e.g., *American Motorists Ins. Co. v. Allied-Sysco Food Services, Inc.* (1993) 19 Cal.App.4th 1342, 1349, 24 Cal.Rptr.2d 106, disapproved of on another ground in *Buss v. Superior Court* (1997) 16 Cal.4th 35, 50, fn. 12, 65 Cal.Rptr.2d 366, 939 P.2d 766 [policy covering "humiliation" was "limited to those cases in which humiliation damages arise out of the types of torts in which it is grouped — i.e., libel, slander, defamation of character, and invasion of the right to privacy"]; *Waranch v. Gulf Insurance Co.* (1990) 218 Cal.App.3d 356, 360-361, 266 Cal.Rptr. 827 ["private occupancy," when grouped with "wrongful entry" and "wrongful eviction," could only mean occupancy of *real property,* not a motor vehicle]; *Martin Marietta Corp. v. Insurance Co. of North America* (1995) 40 Cal.App.4th 1113, 1133, 47 Cal.Rptr.2d 670 [the policy term "other invasion of the right of private occupancy" must be read as similar to terms "eviction" and "trespass" appearing in same coverage phrase]; *Truck Ins. Exchange v. Bennett* (1997) 53 Cal.App.4th 75, 86, 61 Cal.Rptr.2d 497 [coverage for "disparagement" tort "cannot reasonably be read to include any more than those causes of action customarily grouped together into the legal category of defamation"]. Applying this principle here, Mez's contention that a claim of patent infringement falls within the "infringement of . . . title . . . " must be rejected. The advertising offense, "infringement of copyright, title or slogan" must be read as a whole and interpreted by reference to all of the words used, and in full recognition that the words "patent infringement" are *not* included. In our view, reading the phrase as a whole compels the reasonable conclusion that coverage is *at most* provided for claims involving (1) those matters which are protected by copyright statutes and decisions, and (2) those literary, musical, artistic or commercial titles, marks or slogans which are protected by common law principles of unfair competition.[7] The phrase simply cannot reasonably be interpreted to encompass claims involving patent infringement.

A number of courts agree with this conclusion. (*Owens-Brockway Glass v. International Ins. Co., supra,* 884 F.Supp. at p. 368 ["The term 'infringement of title' is part of a list that includes copyright and slogan. In company with these terms, 'title' apparently refers to a name, such as a name of a literary or artistic work, rather than to ownership of an invention or other thing"]; *ShoLodge, Inc. v. Travelers Indem. Co. of Illinois* (6th Cir.1999) 168 F.3d 256, 259-260 [in a service mark infringement case, the court held the term "title" was *unambiguous* and was defined as the "non-copyrightable title of a book, film, or other literary or artistic work"]; *Atlantic Mut. Ins. Co. v. Brotech Corp.* (E.D.Pa.1994) 857 F.Supp. 423, 429 [the court declined to hold infringement of title encompassed patent infringement on the ground that the term "title" referred to a distinctive name or designation, rather than to the legal concept of ownership of property].)

Recently, another court had occasion to construe this same policy language in a case where coverage was sought for a claim of patent infringement asserted in the underlying lawsuit. That court, as do we, placed emphasis on the absence of any reference to "patent infringement" in the policy language. The court then stated, "The drafters of this policy placed 'title' between 'copyright' and 'slogan.' A slogan is a brief, attention-getting phrase used in advertising or promotion. A copyright is the exclusive right, granted by statute to an author or original creator to reproduce, publish and sell the matter and form of a literary, musical or artistic work or production. Neither of these terms has any apparent connection to the concept of ownership interests in property, let alone the legal right to make use, sell or offer to sell a patented invention. Hence, while dictionaries attribute several meanings to the word *title*, including the legal ownership of property (Black's Law Dict. (5th ed. 1979) p. 1331, col. 1), when read in the context of the CGL policy, 'title' can only mean a distinctive name, designation or other appellation." (*Maxconn Inc. v. Truck Ins. Exchange* (1999) 74 Cal.App.4th 1267, 1276-1277, 88 Cal.Rptr.2d 750, fn. omitted.)

---

[7] [FN17] This conclusion is consistent with our Supreme Court's recent decision in *Palmer v. Truck Insurance Exchange* (1999) 21 Cal.4th 1109, 90 Cal.Rptr.2d 647, 988 P.2d 568, where the court considered the scope of the coverage provided under this same clause (1) in the context of a claim for infringement of a registered business mark, (2) where the insured's policy contained an exclusion for claims based on "infringement of registered trade mark service mark or trade name," except for those relating to "titles or slogans." In the presence of such policy language, the work "title" could not subsume "trade mark," "service mark" or "trade name." Therefore, the court concluded, "[o]nly one definition fits: the name of a literary or artistic work. Because these names can be trademarked, adopting this definition of 'title' carves out a limited exception and gives effect to every part of the policy's trademark exclusion clause." (Id. at p. 1117, 90 Cal.Rptr.2d 647, 988 P.2d 568.)

Thus, when read in the context of the entire policy, the general circumstances of this case and simple common sense, the advertising injury provisions simply do not extend to patent infringement. Moreover, even if the policy language is not totally free from some ambiguity, Mez could not, in light of such contextual considerations, have had an *objectively reasonable* expectation of coverage for a claim of *inducing* willful patent infringement. Therefore, such a claim would not be covered as an advertising injury offense.

2.   Coverage For Inducement of Patent Infringement Is Barred By Section 533

As our brief initial discussion of inducing patent infringement demonstrated, in order to be found liable, a party must have the specific intent to induce another to infringe the patent holder's prior right. (*Manville Sales Corp. v. Paramount Systems, Inc., supra,* 917 F.2d at p. 553.) Accordingly it must be shown that "the defendant possessed *specific intent* to encourage another's infringement and *not merely that the defendant had knowledge* of the acts alleged to constitute inducement." (*Id.* at p. 553; italics added; see also *National Presto Industries, Inc. v. West Bend Co.* (Fed.Cir.1996) 76 F.3d 1185, 1194, italics added [the "statutory liability for inducement of [patent] infringement derives from the common law, wherein acts that *the actor* knows will lead to the commission of a wrong by another, place shared liability for the wrong on the actor"].)

In *Dynamis, Inc. v. Leepoxy Plastics, Inc.* (N.D.Ind.1993) 831 F.Supp. 651, the court stated: "'[A] person infringes by actively and *knowingly* aiding and abetting another's direct infringement. Although section 271(b) does not use the word "knowing," the case law and legislative history uniformly assert such a requirement.'" (*Id.* at p. 656, italics in the original, citing *Water Technologies Corp. v. Calco, Ltd., supra,* 850 F.2d at p. 668.) Thus, "it is clear that under ¶ 271(b) an accused infringer must be shown to have actual knowledge of the patent and the infringement *and have the actual intent to induce the infringement.*" (*Id.* at p. 657; italics added.) Absent proof that the defendant "had an actual intent to induce infringement," there is no liability and summary judgment in favor of the judgment must be granted. (*Id.* at p. 657; see also *Hewlett-Packard Co. v. Bausch & Lomb, Inc.* (Fed.Cir.1990) 909 F.2d 1464, 1469, fn. omitted ["we are of the opinion that proof of actual intent to cause the acts which constitute the infringement is a necessary prerequisite to finding active inducement. And it is proof of that intent which is missing in the present case"]; *R2 Medical Systems, Inc. v. Katecho, Inc.* (E.D.Ill.1996) 931 F.Supp. 1397, 1440-1441 [liability for inducing infringement under section 271(b) requires proof that defendant knew that the combination for which its component was especially designed was both patented and infringed and that the defendant "specifically intended that its sale or other challenged acts induce its customers to engage in the conduct that allegedly directly infringes"].)

A "willful act" under section 533 will include either "an act deliberately done for the *express purpose* of causing damage or intentionally performed *with knowledge* that damage is highly probable or *substantially certain* to result."

(*Shell Oil Co. v. Winterthur Swiss Ins. Co.* (1993) 12 Cal.App.4th 715, 742, 15 Cal.Rptr.2d 815; italics added.) It also appears that a willful act includes an intentional and wrongful act in which "the harm is inherent in the act itself." (*J.C. Penney Casualty Ins. Co. v. M.K.* (1991) 52 Cal.3d 1009, 1025, 278 Cal.Rptr. 64, 804 P.2d 689.) In an earlier case, the Supreme Court had said that "even an act which is 'intentional' or 'willful' within the meaning of traditional tort principles will not exonerate the insurer from liability . . . unless it is done with a 'preconceived design to inflict injury.' [Citations.]" (*Clemmer v. Hartford Insurance Co.* (1978) 22 Cal.3d 865, 887, 151 Cal.Rptr. 285, 587 P.2d 1098.) However, the issue to which the *Clemmer* court spoke involved a question of the insured's mental capacity. Subsequent decisions have made clear that the "preconceived design to injure" standard is relevant only when the insured's "mental capacity is an issue or the insured's intent or motive might justify an otherwise wrongful act." (*Shell Oil Co. v. Winterthur Swiss Ins. Co., supra,* 12 Cal.App.4th at p. 740, 15 Cal.Rptr.2d 815; *J.C. Penney Casualty Ins. Co. v. M. K., supra,* 52 Cal.3d at p. 1023, 278 Cal.Rptr. 64, 804 P.2d 689.) Citing *J.C. Penney,* the *Shell Oil* court emphasized that "section 533 precludes *indemnification, whether or not the insured subjectively intended harm,* if the insured seeks coverage for an intentional, wrongful act that is inherently and necessarily harmful." (*Shell Oil Co. v. Winterthur Swiss Ins. Co., supra,* 12 Cal.App.4th at pp. 740-741, 15 Cal.Rptr.2d 815; italics added.)

Although it was speaking in the context of an environmental pollution case, the *Shell Oil* court properly summarized the rule which governs the scope and application of section 533: "We conclude that section 533 prohibits indemnification of more than just intentional acts that are subjectively desired to cause harm and acts that are intentional, wrongful, and necessarily harmful regardless of subjective intent. *A 'willful act' under section 533 must also include a deliberate, liability-producing act that the individual, before acting, expected to cause harm. Conduct for which the law imposes liability, and which is expected or intended to result in damage, must be considered wrongful and willful. Therefore, section 533 precludes indemnification for liability arising from deliberate conduct that the insured expected or intended to cause damage.*" (*Id.* at pp. 742-743, 15 Cal.Rptr.2d 815, italics added.)

We believe that the circumstances presented here clearly come within this analysis of the proper application of section 533. An inducement to patent infringement under 35 U.S.C. § 271(b), as alleged in the underlying *Ductmate* action, could not be committed except as a knowing, intentional and purposeful act that is clearly wrongful and necessarily harmful. A defendant would have to intend the act, that is, to intend that the induced party infringe the patent. Such an impermissible motivation is necessary to liability for the act of inducement and it thus involves willful and intentional misconduct. Obviously, damage would flow in the form of a loss to Ductmate and a gain to Mez through the sale of *its* products. Plainly, such a result would necessarily have to be within Mez's knowledge. Indeed, it would be Mez's presumed purpose. This is enough to satisfy the requirements of section 533.

Thus, even if the post-1986 policy language embraced patent infringement, its inducement would be excluded under section 533. Two recent cases which have directly considered this question have expressly so held. (*Aetna Casualty & Surety Co. v. Superior Court (Watercloud Bed Co.)* (1993) 19 Cal.App.4th 320, 330-333, 23 Cal.Rptr.2d 442; *Intex Plastics Sales Co. v. United Nat. Ins.* (9th Cir.1994) 23 F.3d 254, 256-257.) Mez argues that we should reject those cases as wrongly decided. We decline to do so. Our discussion and analysis, which is based in part on prior decisions of this court examining the scope and breadth of section 533 (see *Downey Venture v. LMI Ins. Co.* (1998) 66 Cal.App.4th 478, 500-502, 78 Cal.Rptr.2d 142 and *B & E Convalescent Center v. State Compensation Ins. Fund* (1992) 8 Cal.App.4th 78, 94, 97-99, 9 Cal.Rptr.2d 894), has caused us to reach the same conclusion as did the *Aetna* and *Intex* courts. We believe they were correctly decided. There is no potential coverage for Mez under the Pacific policy.

3.   Pacific Had No Duty To Defend Mez in the Ductmate Action

What Mez seeks to accomplish in this action is the vindication of its contention that Pacific owed it a duty to defend it in the Ductmate action. It is well settled that where there is no potential for coverage under a liability policy, the insurer owes no duty to defend. It is the potential for coverage under a particular policy, and in light of the specific pleadings and known facts of the third party claim, which establishes the insurer's obligation to defend.

However, where a denial of indemnification is based on the application of section 533, it does not necessarily follow that no duty to defend exists. As we stated in *B & E Convalescent Center,* . . . "'[S]ection 533 precludes only *indemnification* of willful conduct and not the *defense* of an action in which such conduct is alleged. [Citation.] . . . [¶] . . . [E]ven though public policy or section 533 precludes an insurer from indemnifying an insured in an underlying action the duty to defend still exists so long as the "insured reasonably expect[s] the policy to cover the types of acts involved in the underlying suit[.]" [Citation.]' [Citation]. Put another way, 'if the reasonable expectations of an insured are that a defense will be provided for a claim, then the insurer cannot escape that obligation merely because public policy precludes it from indemnifying that claim.' [Citation.]" (*B&E Convalescent Center v. State Compensation Insurance Fund, supra,* 8 Cal.App.4th at p. 93, 9 Cal.Rptr.2d 894, italics in original.)

As we have explained, however, no potential for coverage exists in this case and Mez could not have had *any* objectively reasonable expectation of such coverage. Similarly, to the extent that section 533 alone is relied upon to preclude coverage, we see nothing in this record or in the arguments of Mez which would prompt us to conclude that Mez had any reasonable expectation of a defense even though indemnification was excluded. Therefore, for the reasons discussed above, Pacific owed no duty to defend Mez in the Ductmate action and the trial court correctly sustained Pacific's demurrer to Mez's complaint.

DISPOSITION

The judgment is affirmed. Pacific shall recover its costs on appeal.

NOTES & QUESTIONS

1. Assuming that infringement claims would otherwise be covered by a policy, what types of intellectual property infringement would be excluded from insurance coverage under a provision like that of California Insurance Code ¶ 533 barring insurance for "a loss caused by the willful act of the insured"? What aspect of an infringer's conduct must be willful before insurance is precluded? Why should the limits of coverage be restricted by statute if an insurance company is willing to provide insurance protection against a wider range of infringement-related losses?

2. Should insurance policies covering losses from "misappropriation of style of doing business" be construed broadly to provide recoveries for patent infringement losses incurred by businesses that inadvertently adopt patented business methods for internet transactions or other business activities?

ZURICH INSURANCE CO. v. KILLER MUSIC, INC
United States Court of Appeals for the Ninth Circuit
998 F.2d 674 (1993)

Beezer, Circuit Judge:

Killer Music, Inc., doing business as HLC Partnership; TTBB, Inc., doing business as Killer Tracks; and Ron Hicklin (collectively, "Killer Music") appeal the district court's grant of Zurich Insurance Co.'s ("Zurich") motion for summary judgment on Zurich's declaratory judgment action and the dismissal of Killer Music's counterclaims on a motion for summary judgment. The issues are whether Zurich had a duty to defend and indemnify Killer Music in a suit brought by a third party (Pfeifer) and whether Zurich's denial of coverage was in bad faith. We reverse and remand because we hold that Zurich wrongfully refused to defend Killer Music. We affirm the summary judgment on the bad faith issue.

I

Killer Music contracted with Pfeifer to sell jingles which Pfeifer produced to radio and television stations and movie studios. Killer Music agreed to pay Pfeifer for each jingle sold. The contract also provided that Pfeifer would perform on certain songs, and that he would be paid for these performances when the songs were sold. That contract expired in 1988.

After that date, Killer Music compiled and sold a music library which included Pfeifer songs which had not been sold during the contract period. The songs were not attributed to Pfeifer and no compensation was paid. In April 1990, Pfeifer filed a complaint in which he alleged copyright infringement, false designation of origin, unfair competition, palming off, conversion, and unjust enrichment. He sought punitive and compensatory damages, an accounting, the establishment of a constructive trust, and attorneys' fees.

Killer Music was insured under a Comprehensive General Liability Policy written by Zurich. The policy was sold by DeWitt Stern, an insurance broker. The policy covers "advertising injury," which includes "those sums that the insured becomes legally obligated to pay as damages because of 'personal injury' or 'advertising injury' to which this insurance applies." "Advertising injury" is defined to include injury from infringement of copyright. The policy excludes coverage, however, for advertising injury "arising out of breach of contract."

Killer Music first learned of the Pfeifer litigation when they were notified that Pfeifer had obtained a temporary injunction against them. At this point, Killer Music contacted DeWitt Stern, advised a clerk there that the Pfeifer suit was going to be filed against them, and asked her to check into the matter. Killer Music did not ask that the insurer defend them. The clerk may or may not have contacted persons at Zurich to confer about the policy coverage; at any rate, she advised Killer Music that they were not covered. Another telephone call was made to another clerk that same week, who also reported that there was no coverage. Killer Music never followed up with any written notice of claim either to Zurich or DeWitt, nor did Killer Music transmit any of the court documents to either company.[8]

Killer Music settled with Pfeifer soon after the suit was filed. Under the settlement agreement, Pfeifer transferred his rights to the songs which had been used in the music library, and agreed to drop his suit, in exchange for a $175,000 settlement.

At this point, Killer Music, through counsel, began corresponding with Zurich over the issue of coverage, seeking recovery of defense costs in the suit and indemnification. Zurich responded by filing an action for a declaratory judgment that it had no duty to defend or indemnify. Killer Music counterclaimed and asserted that Zurich breached its duty of good faith. The district court granted Zurich's motions for summary judgment on both its claim and the counterclaim.

. . .

III

Under the contract with Killer Music, Zurich had "the right and duty to defend any 'suit' seeking [damages for 'advertising injury']." "Advertising injury" was defined to include infringement of copyright. Pfeifer alleged copyright infringement, among other causes of action, in his complaint against Killer Music. The policy excludes coverage, however, for advertising injury "arising out of breach of contract." Zurich, based on a reasonable reading of

---

[8] [FN1] The policy provides in relevant part:

> b. If a claim is made or 'suit' is brought against any insured, you [the insured] must see to it that we receive prompt written notice of the claim or 'suit.'
> c. You and any other involved insured must . . . [i]mmediately send us copies of any demands, notices, summonses or legal papers received in connection with the claim or 'suit.'

case law, including *Home Indem. Co. v. Avol*, 706 F.Supp. 728 (C.D.Cal.1989) (applying California law), *aff'd without opinion*, 912 F.2d 469 (9th Cir.1990), and *Allstate Ins. Co. v. Hansten*, 765 F.Supp. 614 (N.D.Cal.1991) (applying California law), determined that Pfeifer's copyright infringement claim arose out of a breach of contract and was therefore not covered. Other cases suggest, however, that the Pfeifer action should be characterized as sounding in tort. *See Fragomeno v. Insurance Co. of the West*, 207 Cal.App.3d 822, 255 Cal.Rptr. 111 (1989); *Fireman's Fund Ins. Co. v. City of Turlock*, 170 Cal.App.3d 988, 216 Cal.Rptr. 796 (1985). Under California law, "the duty to defend is so broad that as long as the complaint contains language creating the potential of liability under an insurance policy, the insurer must defend an action against its insured." *CNA Casualty of California v. Seaboard Sur. Co.*, 176 Cal.App.3d 598, 606, 222 Cal.Rptr. 276 (1986); *Republic Indem. Co. v. Superior Court*, 224 Cal.App.3d 492, 500, 273 Cal.Rptr. 331 (1990). Based on our reading of the California cases, we conclude that there was at least a "potential of liability" so Zurich had a duty to defend Killer Music in that action.

IV

Zurich contends that the claim was not potentially covered because coverage was excluded by operation of California Insurance Code § 533. Section 533 provides that "[a]n insurer is not liable for a loss caused by the willful act of the insured. . . ." According to Zurich, Pfeifer's suit against Killer Music was based on intentional misconduct, a "willful act" by Killer Music. Killer Music argues that the use of Pfeifer's music in the music library was inadvertent and certainly not "willful" as defined in the statute.

A "clear line of authority" in California directs that "even an act which is 'intentional' or 'willful' within the meaning of traditional tort principles will not exonerate the insurer from liability under [§] 533 unless it is done with a 'preconceived design to inflict injury.'" The term "willful" is used to describe "an act done with malevolence." A "'willful act' within the meaning of section 533 means 'something more than the mere intentional doing of an act constituting [ordinary] negligence', and appears to be something more than the intentional violation of a statute."

Killer Music's actions were not proven to be "willful" as a matter of law. While Zurich characterizes Killer Music's infringement as "knowing," Killer Music's president Hicklin, by sworn affidavit, indicated that he did not know that any of Pfeifer's work was being used in the music library and that he "never intended to engage in any unauthorized use of any work owned in whole or in part by Pfeifer." He also disavowed any intent to injure or harm Pfeifer.

Zurich points out that California courts have been willing to find some activities "willful" as a matter of law "if the harm is inherent in the act itself." *B & E Convalescent Center*, 8 Cal.App. 4th at 97, 9 Cal.Rptr.2d 894 (citation omitted). It is true that a subjective desire to injure or harm need not always be proven and can be assumed by the nature of the act. However, copyright infringement is not one of those activities that is "willful" per se. Zurich admits in its brief that "[c]opyright infringement can be innocent or intentional. . . . Innocent infringement may be covered."

The possibility that § 533 might operate to exclude coverage does not excuse Zurich's initial decision to deny coverage. "[I]n order to rely upon Section 533 to justify its refusal to defend, [Zurich] must show that information available to it at that time demonstrated that [Pfeifer] was required to establish that [Killer Music] intended him harm, not merely that it intended to act." Zurich did not demonstrate that Pfeifer was required to prove Killer Music's intent to harm him to succeed on his claim for copyright infringement; indeed, Zurich itself noted that "[c]opyright infringement can be innocent or intentional." We hold that the district court erred in granting Zurich's motion for summary judgment on the basis of § 533.

V

Zurich argues that it had no duty to cover Killer Music's claim since no written notice was given, as required by the policy, and Zurich had no actual or constructive notice of the claim. Although the parties dispute whether Zurich ever received actual notice of the claim from an employee of DeWitt Stern, this question is immaterial since under California Civil Code § 2332 notice to an agent is equivalent to notice to the principal. It is clear that DeWitt Stern must be considered Zurich's agent. The only address on the policy for the insured to contact was DeWitt Stern's. *See* California Civil Code §§ 2300, 2317 (1992). The lack of written notice alone does not excuse Zurich's refusal to defend. Here Zurich's agent had actual notice and, without requesting a copy of the complaint, the agent decided not to defend on the basis of lack of coverage, not inadequate notice. *See, e.g., Clemmer v. Hartford Ins. Co.,* 22 Cal.3d 865, 151 Cal.Rptr. 285, 587 P.2d 1098 (1978) (insurer made no showing that it would have defended if it had had timely tender of defense).

VI

We now address the consequences of Zurich's breach. As to the settlement, the mere fact that Zurich failed to defend does not mean that Zurich is liable for the amount of the settlement. Zurich is liable only for the amount of a "reasonable settlement of the claim in good faith." "A reasonable settlement made by the insured to terminate the underlying claim against him may be used as presumptive evidence of the insured's liability on the underlying claim, and the amount of such liability." This presumption "may be overcome by proof" that the settlement agreement is unreasonable in amount.

We recognize that the settlement agreement represents, in part, an exchange of cash consideration for the rights to Pfeifer's songs, not simply compensation for damages from copyright infringement. We also note that Zurich had no control over the terms of the settlement agreement, which was structured so that Killer Music received the rights to the songs. When the issue of the amount of a reasonable settlement in good faith is addressed on remand, Zurich will have the opportunity to demonstrate that some portion, if not all, of the settlement amount is allocable to the value of the songs which Killer received in the settlement agreement.

By breaching its duty to defend, Zurich is also liable for attorneys' fees as provided in the policy or as "incurred in good faith, and in the exercise of a reasonable discretion" in defending the action. California Civil Code § 2778. Zurich's liability extends to fees arguably allocable to defense of non-covered claims. Zurich is not liable for fees incurred by Killer Music in bringing this action in the district court, since Killer Music "is not entitled to an award of attorney's fees incurred in a separate action in which [it] seeks to enforce [its] right to be defended or to be reimbursed for attorney's fees previously incurred in an action which should have been defended by the insurer."

VII

As to Killer Music's counterclaim alleging bad faith on Zurich's part, there is no evidence of bad faith in this record. Although Zurich breached its duty to defend, "breach of the implied covenant of good faith and fair dealing involves something beyond breach of the contractual duty itself." Zurich did not reasonably investigate the claim to determine coverage, but "without actual presentation of a claim by the insured in compliance with claims procedures contained in the policy, there is no duty imposed on the insurer to investigate the claim." Here it is undisputed that Killer Music failed to follow explicit policy conditions requiring written notice, conditions that were incorporated into the contract to avoid just the sort of out-of-channel coverage decision that took place in this case. The fact that Zurich brought a declaratory judgment action to determine its liability for coverage is not bad faith. The district court did not err in granting Zurich's motion for summary judgment on the bad faith counterclaim.

VIII

We reverse the summary judgment on Zurich's claim and remand for a determination of the damages attributable to a reasonable settlement in good faith and for a determination of attorneys' fees incurred in the defense of the Pfeifer suit. We affirm the grant of Zurich's motion for summary judgment on the bad faith counterclaim. Neither party shall recover costs on appeal.

NOTES & QUESTIONS

1. Why is the duty to defend an insured under a General Liability Policy applicable in a wider range of circumstances than the obligation to compensate the insured's losses? What type of evidence of potentially covered intellectual property infringement liability should be present before the duty to defend is triggered?

2. Why was the type of copyright infringement at issue in the *Killer Music* case sufficiently related to advertising activities to at least arguably involve an "advertising injury" within the coverage of the General Liability Policy present in that case? Did the company infringe any copyrights in its advertising? At what point and in what way were the company's advertising activities related to its infringement liability?

3. Why should General Liability Policies exclude coverage of losses related to breaches of contracts like the copyright royalty agreement present in *Killer*

Music? How might claims under such a contract differ from claims of copyright infringement brought for unauthorized use of the same intellectual property if no licensing and royalty agreement were present?

STATE FARM FIRE AND CASUALTY INSURANCE COMPANY v. WHITE
United States District Court for the Northern District of Georgia
777 F. Supp. 952 (1991)

HAROLD L. MURPHY, District Judge.

This case is before the Court on seven motions for summary judgment filed by the Plaintiff in this action for declaratory judgment. The motions, however, rely on substantially similar legal positions and will therefore be consolidated for the purpose of this Court's discussion.

This action arises out of a companion case pending in this Court and styled *Greg Simms and North Georgia Partnership v. Edward White, et al.,* Civil Action File No. 4:89-cv-306-HLM. In the underlying action Greg Simms and North Georgia Partnership allege that Edward White, Howard Rozell, and Neal Davis, and their various development associations built apartment complexes relying on plans that were written and owned by themselves. Plaintiffs in the underlying action allege that "Defendants are guilty of predicate acts of theft, conversion and/or unjust enrichment from theft and conversion and/or conspiracy to convert to their own use certain architectural and business plans and other intellectual property of the Plaintiff's in that said Defendants jointly and severally have taken and used certain architectural plans, designs, trade dress, and specifications which were and are the property of the Plaintiff and for which the Defendants are liable to the Plaintiffs in conversion, quantum meruit, assumpsit, violation of common law copyright, copyright infringement, and unfair business practices all in violation of State and Federal Law. . . ." Plaintiff in the instant action, through its Motions for summary judgment, seeks a judicial determination that its insurance policies do not provide coverage to the Defendants in the above referenced action.

Plaintiff's argument, presented in basically the same format given that certain of the insurance policies vary in detail, is that the underlying action against the insured sounds in copyright. The insurance policies involved, however, insure only the loss of use of "tangible" property.[9] Plaintiff argues that

---

[9] [FN1] The potentially relevant third party liability coverage, common to all of the subject insurance policies, is as follows:

   "*Coverage L—Business Liability,* the company will pay on behalf of the insured all sums which the insured shall become legally obligated to pay as damages because of bodily injury, property damage or personal injury caused by an occurrence to which this insurance policy applies."

   "*Property damage* means (a) physical injury to or destruction of tangible property which occurs during the policy period including the loss of use thereof at any time resulting therefrom; or (b) loss of use of tangible property which has not been physically injured or destroyed provided such loss of use is caused by an occurrence during the policy period."

the architectural plans allegedly converted by the Defendants can only be considered intangible intellectual property and, therefore, the potential loss of use of these plans is not insured.

Plaintiff thus emphasizes the term "tangible" as it modifies the property loss coverage of the relevant insurance policies to conclude that theft or conversion of intellectual property is not within the coverage definitions. By the same token, claims for copyright violations, and unfair business practices are similarly not covered by the relevant insurance policies. Plaintiff contends that it is entitled to a Court order ratifying this position.

Defendants, generally, disagree. None of these Defendants contend that the policy coverage should extend to claims for copyright infringement; however, all oppose the grant of summary judgment as to other claims. Defendants argue that the claims for copyright violation are only a portion of the underlying Plaintiff's complaint. Laying aside the issue of copyright violation, Defendants argue that the claims for conversion, assumpsit, and quantum meruit, punitive damages, attorney's fees, and costs are covered by the relevant insurance policies.

Defendants argue that the architectural plans are "tangible" property. Once the "idea" which is validly considered intangible intellectual property has been reduced to physical plans and drawings, Defendants contend, they have assumed a tangible form. Consequently the "loss of use" of these plans is a loss of use of tangible property and, therefore, within the policy definition of "property loss."

The resolution of this dispute revolves around the legal definition of "tangible property," the Georgia common law rules of contract construction, and, ultimately, the role of this Court on summary judgment. According to O.C.G.A. 48-8-2(11), tangible property is "property which may be weighed, measured, felt or touched, or is in any manner perceptible to the senses." Likewise, Blacks Law Dictionary defines tangible property as "that which may be felt or touched, and is necessarily corporeal, although it may either be real or personal." Under these definitions an architectural plan, in its physical form, is obviously tangible, its finite mass lending weight and sensory perception.

Plaintiff argues, nonetheless, that the aspects of the architectural plan which lends its tangible qualities are simply the paper and ink. The value of such a plan, Plaintiff contends, is in the intellectual property which is represented on the paper. Plaintiff points out that under Georgia law, "where the language of a contract is clear and unambiguous, and capable of only one *reasonable* interpretation, no construction is necessary or even permissible." *Stern's Gallery, Inc. v. Corporate Property Investors, Inc.,* 176 Ga.App. 586, 337 S.E.2d 29 (1985) (emphasis supplied). According to the Plaintiff, the term "tangible property," applied to the facts of this case, can only reasonably be interpreted as excluding coverage for the loss of use of architectural plans.[10]

In the policies which define the term "occurrence" it is defined as:

> "*Occurrence* means an accident, including continuous or repeated exposure to conditions, which result in bodily injury, or property damage, neither expected nor intended from the standpoint of the insured. . . ."

[10] [FN3] Plaintiff points out that no recovery is sought for the loss of the paper on which the plans were printed, rather it is the loss of the "idea" contained on that paper which the Defendants would be seeking under the policies.

Another relevant principle of contract construction, however, is that "a contract of insurance is construed most strongly against the insurer, particularly where the insurer denies coverage based upon a policy exclusion." Nonetheless in the view of this Court, the conclusive consideration is this Court's role in deciding the instant motions for summary judgment. Plaintiff's motion for summary judgment seeks to absolve itself of any liability for the loss of use the architectural plans in question on the ground that they are not "tangible" property. Both parties agree, however, that the architectural plans, in the sense of their being printed on paper, meet the legal definition of tangible property. Therefore while the parties may argue about the value of the paper printed plan vis-à-vis the concept reproduced on the paper, it seems that at least whatever value is assigned to the paper would fall within insurance policy definition of property loss. Accordingly, what remains is a question of fact regarding the relative valuation of the components of a printed architectural plan. Given that this Court is precluded, on a motion for summary judgment, from resolving genuine issues of material fact, Plaintiff's argument on this point must fail.

Perhaps anticipating this result, Plaintiff in its reply brief has requested an entry at least of partial summary judgment as to the issues which have been admitted or not contested. As this Court reads the pleadings, Defendants Greg Simms and North Georgia Partnership have not challenged Plaintiff's position with respect to policy numbers 81-34-7572-0, 91-23-7016-7, and 1-18-0921-1. Moreover, as to the issue of copyright infringement, none of the Defendants have controverted the Plaintiff's position. In light of the absence of disagreement on these points this Court has no difficulty in granting partial summary judgment.

. . .

NOTES & QUESTIONS

1. Under what circumstances should a physical item containing intellectual property (such as a book, movie, or computer software diskette) be deemed tangible property for purposes of an insurance policy covering losses to tangible property? Where an item of this sort is stolen or destroyed, when will its status as a covered item of tangible property be sufficiently possible to trigger the duty to defend the insured under a policy covering tangible property losses?

AMERICAN CENTURY SERVICES CORP. v. AMERICAN INTERNATIONAL SPECIALTY LINES INSURANCE CO.

United States District Court for the Southern District of New York
2002 U.S. Dist. LEXIS 15016 (Aug. 14, 2002)

LYNCH, J.

On December 20, 1998, defendant American International Specialty Lines Insurance Company ("AISLIC") issued a two-year investment management insurance policy (the "Policy") to plaintiff American Century Services Corporation ("American Century"). For a premium of $414,800, AISLIC offered up to $10,000,000 liability coverage, less a $350,000 retention, for various enumerated risks. In this action, American Century seeks a declaratory judgment, pursuant to 28 U.S.C. § 2201, that the Policy requires AISLIC to pay the costs and settlement amounts of certain patent infringement claims raised by third parties against American Century during the policy period. The plaintiff now moves for summary judgment. After full briefing, and oral argument before this Court on February 8, 2002, the motion will be denied, for the reasons that follow.

BACKGROUND

This dispute concerns coverage for patent infringement claims raised by non-party patent owners Leon Stambler ("Stambler"), whose patents relate to internet security technology, and Ronald A. Katz ("Katz"), whose patents relate to automated telephone technology. American Century, a Missouri corporation with its principal place of business in Kansas City, Missouri, used allegedly infringing internet and telephone technology in providing investment management and related services to a group of mutual funds (the "Funds"). These internet and telephone systems allow American Century customers to obtain account and market information, make transfers between the Funds, and contact American Century representatives. American Century has since settled with Katz. Stambler is not actively pursuing his claim. Plaintiff seeks a declaratory judgment as to coverage for both alleged infringements under its Policy with AISLIC, an Alaskan corporation with its principal place of business in New York.

The first patent infringement claim arrived on March 27, 2000, when Stambler notified American Century that its use of certain secure internet services software infringed his patents. Plaintiff relayed this information to AISLIC on July 3, 2000. (*Id.* Ex. 5.) In a letter dated September 1, 2000, AISLIC responded that "It appears that coverage, *if any,* would fall under Coverage B as the allegation is based upon the insured's use of secure internet services software in the operation of their mutual fund business," Coverage B reaches "all sums which the Insured shall become legally obligated to pay as damages resulting from any claim or claims first made against the Insured . . . for any Wrongful Act of the Insured . . . but only if the Wrongful Act occurs prior to the end of the Policy Period and solely in the course of the management and/or operations of the Fund(s)." AISLIC also concluded that, "[i]f, in fact, [Stambler] has a patent . . . which the insured has used in the management of their mutual fund business without payment of royalties due, then this would be a gaining of profit or advantage to which they are not legally entitled." Defendant concluded that such "royalties owed" fall under Exclusion 4(I)(2), which denies coverage for "any actual or alleged gaining of any profit or advantage to which the Insured is not legally entitled." AISLIC later agreed to advance reasonable defense costs once the $350,000 retention had been exhausted. No settlement has been reached with Stambler, who apparently has not pursued his claim since a letter to plaintiff dated September 29, 2000.

On September 26, 2000, American Century received notice of the second patent infringement claim. This claim came from Katz, who informed American Century that he believed its interactive automated telephone system infringed one or more of his patents. American Century notified

AISLIC of Katz's claim on October 17, 2000. AISLIC again denied coverage. This time, however, AISLIC concluded that on the facts presented neither Coverage A, B, C, D, nor the Policy's amendment for Employment Practices Liability Insurance applied to Katz's claim, and accordingly, did not consider the applicability of any of the Policy's exclusions. American Century settled with Katz for $3,403,321 on February 28, 2001.

In addition to seeking a declaration that the Policy covers Stambler's and Katz's claims, plaintiff demands damages for breach of contract and wrongful denials of coverage, including the costs of bringing this action, compensatory damages for $3,053,321 (the settlement with Katz less the retention), and pre- and post-judgment interest.

DISCUSSION

. . .

III. *Interpretation of the Policy*

Whether an investment management insurance policy of the type issued by AISLIC to American Century covers patent infringement claims is a novel question. Neither plaintiff nor defendant has produced cases on this issue, and the Court's own research suggests that none exist.

Insurance coverage for patent infringement claims, however, is not a new issue and has been frequently debated. The majority of the cases, as well as the academic scholarship on the topic, focus on whether insurers have a duty to defend insureds against infringement claims under the advertising injury provisions of commercial general liability insurance policies. Such policies generally include provisions providing coverage for injuries such as libel, infringement of copyright, or unfair competition, caused in the course of the insured's advertising activities. The New Jersey courts have refused coverage of patent infringement under such policies, concluding that the claims are not within the commonly understood meanings of the covered terms and that to extend the policies to include patent claims, when they are silent on such coverage, would be "nonsense." Such denials of coverage accord with the general trend in other courts throughout the United States, which have usually ruled against insureds seeking to recover from their insurers for patent infringement. *See, e.g.,* Gauntless, *Patents and Insurance,* 4 B.U. J. SCI. & TECH. L. at 6.

Moreover, separate insurance for patent infringement claims is available in the market. "[I]nsisting that the comprehensive policies weren't designed for patent disputes," insurers like American International Group Inc. ("AIG"), which processes claims for AISLIC, and AISLIC itself, have introduced patent-specific plans with higher deductibles and premiums to reflect the greater risks in assessing possible liability. Introduction of such policies "reflects the growing importance of patent protection." Without coverage, insureds face potentially large judgments on their own. On the other hand, "some patent specialists worry that the availability of insurance" will generate more litigation and make insured companies potential targets.

But while this context may highlight the issues at stake in this case, its resolution depends not upon broad issues of patent policy or trends in the insurance business, but upon the meaning of the particular Policy at issue here (specifically, the scope of Coverage B and of the Policy's exclusion for illegally obtained gains). In interpreting the Policy under New Jersey law, we "'are bound to protect the insured to the full extent that any fair interpretation will allow.'" If the language supports two meanings, the one resulting in coverage must be applied.

A. Waiver and Estoppel

American Century argues that AISLIC's defenses should be limited to those cited in its denial letters. In advocating such a limitation, the plaintiff seems to rely on theories of waiver and/or estoppel. Neither prevents the defendant from asserting the defenses raised in its brief.

. . .

Accordingly, AISLIC can argue as to both claims that Coverage B does not include patent infringement and, even if it did, liability is excluded under Exclusion 4(I)(2).

B. Coverage B

Under Coverage B, the defendant must pay on behalf of the plaintiff "all sums which the Insured shall become legally obligated to pay as damages resulting from any claim" for a "Wrongful Act" occurring during the Policy period and "solely in the course of the *management and/or operation* of the Fund(s)." As amended, " 'Wrongful Act' means any breach of duty, neglect, error, misstatement, misleading statement, omission or other act wrongfully done or attempted by the Insured or *so alleged* by any claimant."

Katz and Stambler charged that American Century infringed their patents. Since allegations of wrongdoing are sufficient to trigger coverage under the Policy, it is clear that American Century's use of the allegedly infringing telephone and internet systems was a Wrongful Act for the purpose of coverage. The parties, however, disagree about whether the patented technologies were used in the "management and/or operation" of the Funds. "Under New Jersey law, the words of an insurance contract should be given their everyday and common meaning." The defendant argues that the common meanings of "management" and "operation" do not cover the plaintiff's use of the disputed systems. Specifically, AISLIC claims that "management" and "operation" requires the "application of judgment, skill or education . . . as opposed to a mere technical operation," and that the systems were used merely in the "process of managing the funds."

AISLIC's argument is unpersuasive. Defendant attempts to limit "management" and "operation" to a class of activities far narrower than those understood by those terms. Under New Jersey law, we must "construe words granting coverage liberally." But even without this encouragement to liberal construction, it is difficult to conceive of language broader, in relation to the activities of a business, than the "management and/or operation" of the business. The first listed definition of "management" in WEBSER'S NEW COLLEGIATE DICTIONARY (9th ed.

1985) ("Webster's") is "the act or art of managing: the conducting or supervising of something (as a business)." The more elaborate definition in the current online Oxford English Dictionary ("OED") begins with "the action or manner of managing, in senses of the v[er]b," and the leading definitions of "manage" thus incorporated (following a specialized meaning in the equestrian world) are at least as general: "2. . . . To handle, wield, make use of; . . . 3. a. To conduct or carry on (a war, a business, an undertaking, an operation." "Operation" is equally general in meaning: Webster's first definition is "performance of a practical work or of something involving the practical application of principles or processes." The OED's first non-obsolete meaning is "Working; exertion of force, energy, or influence; actions, activity, agency; manner of working, the way in which anything works."

BLACK'S LAW DICTIONARY (6th ed. 1990) ("BLACK'S") the only source relied on by AISLIC, is not to the contrary. Far from limiting the definition of "management" to exclude technical processes or apply only to the application of investment skills, BLACK'S defines "management" as "[g]overnment, control, superintendence, physical or manual handling or guidance; act of managing by direction or regulation, or administration, as management of family, or of household . . . or of great enterprises." AISLIC attempts to import the concept of "skill and judgment" into this definition from BLACK'sdefinition of "manage" as "[t]o control and direct, to administer, to take charge of. To conduct; to carry on the concerns of a business or establishment. Generally applied to affairs that are somewhat complicated and that involve skill and judgment." Even if this highly selective reading is accepted, it does not disqualify plaintiff's claim. Selecting and installing high technology equipment is surely a part of the "somewhat complicated" business of "conduct[ing]" or "carry[ing] on the concerns of" any modern "business or establishment," and is surely one that involves "skill and judgment."[11]

These definitions would certainly cover anything done in connection with carrying on a business. Surely, the installation of telephone or internet technology by an investment fund to enable its customers to contact the fund, review accounts, and engage in transactions with the fund is an act undertaken in the "conduct" of the fund's business — indeed, in the modern world, the use of such systems in a normal and nearly indispensable aspect of the operation of such a business. It is difficult to imagine what the installation and use of such technology could be called other than a part of the "management and/or operation" of the fund.

Moreover, AISLIC has not offered a reasonable alternative reading of the contract raising a question of fact whose meaning can only be resolved at trial. Whether a contract is ambiguous is a question of law. In determining whether a contract is ambiguous, we look to "'words of the agreement,

---

[11] [FN6] BLACK'S definition of "operation" as "[e]xertion of power; the process of operating or mode of action; an effect brought about in accordance with a definite plan; action; activity," is at least as broad as WEBSTER'S or the OED's. Even if we allow AISLIC's arbitrary decision to ignore the breadth of the definition and to focus solely on the phrase "in accordance with a definite plan," there is no reason to adopt its peculiar conclusion that the adoption of modern communications technology was not part of American Century's "plan . . . to achieve gains for its customers through application of the skill of its employees."

alternative meanings suggested by counsel, and extrinsic evidence offered in support of those meanings." The contract language is not ambiguous. As noted by the plaintiff in oral argument, the Policy was designed "to cover the broad range of risks that mutual fund companies are subject to" and "involves very hefty premiums and also involves a high deductible . . . [T]his is big problem insurance." Coverage B sweeps exceedingly broadly, to cover any allegedly wrongful act undertaken in connection with the conduct of the Funds managed by American Century. Patent infringement is a wrongful act, and the infringements alleged by Katz and Stambler were committed (if they occurred at all) in the ordinary course of conducting — that is, managing and operating — American Century's investment funds.

C. Exclusion 4(I)(2)

Finding that the claims fall into Coverage B, however, does not end the inquiry. The Policy includes an exclusion for illegal profit and advantage, which AISLIC claims applies to patent infringement damages. This exclusion, in keeping with favoring the insured in construction of policies, must be strictly interpreted.

The Policy does not cover "any actual or alleged gaining of profit or advantage to which any Insured is not legally entitled." In a patent infringement action, the patent owner can recover damages for reasonable royalties, lost profits, and other compensatory damages. AISLIC argues that the exclusion precludes coverage of the patent infringement claims here, since those claims seek damages not for actual harms done to Katz and Stambler by American Century, but rather for royalties and profits that they would have received had American Century properly negotiated for licensing the use of their allegedly patented technology. In other words, the infringer must compensate the patentee for the gains and advantages it had while using the patented inventions illegally.

Citing cases from jurisdictions other than New Jersey, American Century argues that the illegal profit or advantage exclusion applies only to claims seeking the disgorgement of gains, and not to the type of claims advanced here. Even interpreting the exclusion strictly, nothing in its language suggests such a limitation. Katz and Stambler alleged that American Century enjoyed the use of their telephone and internet systems without payment. If American Century had identified Katz as the holder of a valid patent before using the telephone system and had agreed to purchase a license to use it, American Century would have paid Katz for the privilege of using the phone system. It would not have been entitled to coverage under the Policy for that license fee, as the Policy only covers Wrongful Acts and not the ordinary costs of doing business, such as payments for the use of desired technologies. If an employee of American Century had stolen tangible goods to be used in the course of its business, and the company then settled a lawsuit by agreeing to pay for the stolen materials, AISLIC would not be required to fund that settlement, because the settlement would simply require American Century to pay for an "actual or alleged gaining of profit or advantage to which the Insured is not legally entitled." To the extent that American Century has agreed with Katz to pay license fees for past and future use of Katz's intellectual property in connection with its business, the same rule applies. Such license fees are simply normal expenses of doing business, against which AISLIC has not contracted to insure the plaintiff, whether they are agreed to and paid with or without a threatened lawsuit.

For these reasons, American Century has not established that it is entitled to a judgment of coverage. AISLIC, on the other hand, has not moved for summary judgment, and may not be entitled to it. Material issues of fact may still exist as to the precise nature of the settlement with Katz or of the claims that Stambler has asserted against American Century.

To the extent that the settlement reflects expenses that plaintiff was required to pay for the past or future use of a valuable technology in the course of its business, such royalties or fees are within the exclusion and are not covered by the Policy. American Century cannot shift to its insurer the cost of patented technology it would like to use by failing to license the technology and waiting to be sued for damages for infringement by the patent holder. American Century has argued, however, that some portion of the settlement extends beyond simple royalties or fees, and represents some additional component of damages beyond what is necessary for Katz to recoup the royalties he would have received if plaintiff had simply negotiated up front for the use of his technology. The Court expresses no opinion, based on the limited record before it, as to whether any portion of the Katz settlement, or any aspect of potential further claims by Stambler, might go beyond recovery of the fair market value of intellectual property American Century used without payment in the course of its business, which it should have to disgorge as an illegal benefit or advantage it gained by appropriation. To the extent, however, that at least some portions of those claims sought restitution for precisely such misappropriation, the claims are to that degree within the exclusion from coverage cited by AISLIC.

Accordingly, plaintiff's motion for summary judgment must be denied.

CONCLUSION

For the reasons stated above, plaintiff's motion for summary judgment is denied.

SO ORDERED.

NOTES & QUESTIONS

If an insurance policy is interpreted like that in *American Century* to exclude recoveries for royalties that the insured should have paid for infringing conduct, what types of patent infringement on the part of an insured will ever produce recoverable losses? Should it matter that the royalties, if paid, would have supported a broader, profit making activity of the insured? Would the same insurance policy exclusion properly apply if payment of the royalties would have added sufficient costs to the insured's related business activities to have produced a net loss for the insured?

C. LIABILITY OF CORPORATE OFFICERS AND DIRECTORS FOR INFRINGEMENT OF INTELLECTUAL PROPERTY INTERESTS

Steven E. Bochner & Susan P. Krause,[12]
Intellectual Property Management and Board Liability
Practising Law Institute, Advanced Securities Law Institute
1065 PLI/Corp 453 (1998)[*]

A Case for Increased Board Scrutiny of Intellectual Property Management

The need for a well thought out strategy, both offensive and defensive, for the management of intellectual property rights, is becomingly increasingly crucial as the pace of patent filings and issuances, infringement claims, and licensing royalties continues to escalate. Moreover, intellectual property is increasingly recognized as a business asset that should produce not only strategic advantages, but a suitable return on research and development investments as well. The cumulative effect of these developments is likely to be that intellectual property will play an increasingly important role in the enterprise value and, as a result, in corporate transactions such as acquisitions, corporate partnering arrangements and public offerings. As further discussed below, these trends create potentially greater liability implications for Boards of Directors under corporate . . . laws in connection with allegations of mismanagement, inattention and/or inadequate disclosure with respect to intellectual property issues. These factors are also likely to lead to increasing Board of Director scrutiny of the management of intellectual property assets.

. . .

Board of Directors' Fiduciary Duties and Intellectual Property

[D]irectors may find themselves subject to potential liability for alleged [breaches of fiduciary duties] arising out of inadequate intellectual property management. A director's fiduciary duty is a creation of state corporate law. A director's fiduciary duties typically fall into two categories, a duty of care and a duty of loyalty.

The duty of care has two facets. First, directors have a duty to carefully consider the implications of corporate actions before permitting the corporation to take them. Second, the Board may be liable for a loss which arises from an unconsidered failure of the Board to act in circumstances in which due attention would, arguably, have prevented the loss. In *In re Caremark*,[13]

---

[12] Mr. Bochner practices corporate and securities law at Wilson Sonsini Goodrich & Rosati, Palo Alto, California. Ms. Krause is the former Vice President, General Counsel, and Secretary of Sirenza Microdevices, Inc. The views expressed are those of the authors only, and do not necessarily represent those of their firm or former corporate employer.

[13] [FN6] In re Caremark International Inc. Derivative Litigation, 698 A.2d 959, 1996 Del. Ch. LEXIS 125 (1996).

the Delaware Chancery Court . . . addressed the legal standard governing a Board's obligation to supervise or monitor corporate performance. In *Caremark*, the corporation had been indicted for breaking a federal law governing payments to participants in drug studies. The plaintiffs in *Caremark* alleged that the Caremark Board breached its duty of care by failing adequately to supervise the conduct of Caremark employees, or institute corrective measures, thereby exposing Caremark to legal liability. In evaluating the plaintiffs' claims, the court in *Caremark* reasoned that a director's obligation includes a duty to "attempt in good faith to assure" the implementation of information and reporting systems in the corporation reasonably designed, in the view of the Board, to provide senior management and the Board with timely, accurate information sufficient to allow each to reach informed judgments concerning compliance with law and business performance. However, the standard set by the *Caremark* court to establish lack of good faith requires a "sustained or systematic failure of the Board to exercise oversight."

Accordingly, as intellectual property management becomes more critical from a strategic, financial and competitive point of view, directors may face similar potential liability based on claims of a breach of fiduciary duty in situations where a company faces a material loss in value due to insufficient attention given to the management of intellectual property assets.

Under most formulations of the duty of care, directors are entitled to the protection of the business judgment rule. The business judgment rule under both Delaware and California law essentially provides that a director shall not be held liable, even for bad business decisions, provided the director acts in good faith and in a manner the director believes to be in the best interests of the corporation and the shareholders, and with such care, including reasonable inquiry, as an ordinarily prudent person in a like position would use under similar circumstances. The purpose of the business judgment rule is to encourage qualified individuals to serve on corporate Boards with the assurance that they will not be second-guessed, and held liable, if they act in good faith following a reasonable investigation. Fiduciary duty cases often turn on whether a reasonable investigation has been performed. In the case of the management of intellectual property assets, the question becomes what amount of oversight and investigation with respect to such assets is sufficient to avoid claims of director inattention or failure to perform a reasonable investigation. While the outcome of such claims is highly fact-specific, prudent Boards will ensure that they are sufficiently briefed on a company's intellectual property management strategy, as well as any attendant risks and uncertainties.

"Red Flags" in Corporate Transactions

Corporate and securities lawyers conducting due diligence in financings and acquisition transactions, as well as management and intellectual property counsel performing similar due diligence investigations, need to be sensitive to potential red flags signaling inadequate attention to intellectual property management. For example, the inability of senior management to articulate the Company's IP strategy may be a sign of trouble. Can senior management describe the Company's intellectual property assets (patents, copyrights, trade secrets, trademarks and domain names), and tie these to core products and features? Also, is there a process for determining when key patents expire and evaluating the potential impact on the company? Another problem area would be a lack of knowledge regarding competition and industry patents, particularly those in the field engaged in aggressive patent licensing activities. Finally, senior management should help implement, and be aware of, a company policy to ensure that newly hired employees, especially those hired from competitors, do not inadvertently or otherwise bring with them or use proprietary information belonging to their employers.

A thorough understanding should be obtained in how intellectual property is used, including use as a competitive barrier to entry, defensively in licensing negotiations and/or to achieve a financial return on research and development investments.

Insufficient involvement of intellectual property counsel is also a potential sign of trouble, as is the absence of a trade secrets policy or appropriate inventions assignment clauses in agreements with employees and consultants.

<u>Recommendations</u>

For many companies, strategic intellectual property management is a new concept. A company's first step in developing a strategy for the management of intellectual property issues is understanding what assets are in its portfolio and how the intellectual property is connected with the company's products and key product features, as well as those of its competitors. A good intellectual property strategy should be able to address the company's needs from an offensive viewpoint (what intellectual property protection is needed for the company's own work) and from a defensive viewpoint (what risks exist for the portion of the company's business which is dependent on intellectual property). A coherent offensive intellectual property strategy should seek to fully utilize the assets owned by the company and extract the maximum value from such assets. Such strategy should determine which patents, copyrights and trade secrets cover which products, establish criteria for which inventions should be patented based on the company's business goals, establish criteria for seeking foreign patents based on the company's business goals and on a realistic assessment of the value of foreign patents, and provide a mechanism to periodically prune out U.S. and foreign patents (as well as pending applications) that no longer provide meaningful coverage. A defensive strategy includes routine monitoring of competitors' issued patents and published patent applications and a system of product clearances (patent and trademark) on all new products.[14]

To minimize the potential liability of corporate officers and directors, management should routinely make presentations to the Board of Directors regarding the company's intellectual property management strategy, including key patents, copyrights and trade secrets, potential infringement issues and other developments which could impact shareholder value. The goal of these sessions is to make sure the Board is performing reasonable oversight

---

[14] [FN8] These points are taken from a list of questions that an attorney can pose to his client listed in Gregory A. Stobbs' article *Evolution or Extinction-Your Intellectual Property Strategy*, published in IPWW OUTLOOK..

regarding key intellectual property issues, and has the protection of the business judgment rule with respect to decisions made. For public companies, particularly during financing activities, part of a Board's due diligence procedures should include an inquiry into material intellectual property matters. Consideration should also be given as to the level of risk disclosure required in public filings and offering documents concerning intellectual property issues. In particular, a public company's obligations in its quarterly and annual reports concerning disclosure of known events, trends, and uncertainties which could likely result in a material impact on the company should be assessed in the context of any intellectual property developments in the company or in the industry generally.

<u>Summary</u>

Intellectual property management, or the lack thereof, is likely to play an increasing role in securities and fiduciary duty litigation as the need to manage intellectual property assets becomes more critical. The rapidly increasing number of patents applied for and issued, patent litigation and licensing activities will have the effect of accelerating these trends. Corporate and intellectual property counsel need to work more closely together in advising Boards of Directors concerning the increasing role of intellectual property on the enterprise value, and the resulting potential for these issues to arise in lawsuits directed against corporations and their directors and officers.

NOTES & QUESTIONS

1. What types of monitoring of intellectual property risks or developments will help to protect corporate directors and officers from personal liability once they have notice of a possible infringement problem associated with their company's practices — for example, if they learn about infringement claims against other companies undertaking similar practices?

2. What are a company's options regarding changes in business practices once company officials learn that the company's present or contemplated actions involve some probability of intellectual property infringement claims?

CHAPTER 13

THE ANTITRUST PERILS OF A DOMINANT INTELLECTUAL PROPERTY POSITION

PROBLEM

Digital Ignition, in order to allay concerns about the service and repair of the company's ignition systems, requires all replacement parts for the systems to be purchased by automobile manufacturers from Digital Ignition. This requirement is imposed under the contracts for the sale of the ignition systems to automobile manufacturers who are incorporating the systems in newly manufactured cars. The provision imposing the requirement is written to apply to manufacturer-owned car dealers that engage in automobile service and repair. The sale of replacement parts is further conditioned on the purchase and use of a special lubrication fluid that Digital Ignition manufactures. While Digital Ignition does not monitor the actual use of the fluid, purchasers of the replacement parts must buy the fluid. Over time, specialized companies have started to repair and maintain the ignition systems of automobiles. These companies work on all brands of ignition systems, including those manufactured by Digital Ignition. Some of these companies have designed their own replacement parts for different brands of ignition systems. Digital Ignition has aggressively pursued patent infringement suits against these companies regarding replacement parts that are asserted to have incorporated Digital Ignition's patented designs. Some of the suits have forced the companies out of the marketplace; others have resulted in licensing arrangements with Digital Ignition for the making of the replacement parts.

Dr. See, the chief executive officer of Digital Ignition, has been very active in the Automobile Manufacturers Association of America (AMAA), an industry organization which engages in a variety of activities, including the setting of manufacturing and performance standards for automobiles. The Electric Automobile Standards Organization (EASO) is a body within the AMAA which proposes standards to the federal government concerning the design and performance of hybrid and electric cars. One standard that EASO has been working on is for the fuel systems of the next generation of hybrid cars that include both gas engines and electric motors in order to optimize fuel efficiency and engine performance. The proposed standard for the fuel systems of hybrid cars incorporates some of Digital Ignition's proprietary technology. Under the policies and procedures of EASO, any member of the AMAA who has proprietary technology which is incorporated in an EASO-proposed standard that is adopted by a federal or state agency must disclose the technology and forebear from enforcing the associated rights in the technology against other members of the AMAA and the government.

FOCUS OF CHAPTER

Intellectual property laws give an owner the right to exclude others, including competitors, from the use of proprietary technology. At the same time, antitrust laws disfavor business conduct that excludes parties from markets or other competitive situations. Ever since the enactment of statutory antitrust laws in the United States in 1890, jurists and practitioners have attempted to reconcile the right to exclude under intellectual property laws with the prohibitions of exclusionary conduct under antitrust laws. In the early twentieth century, the view that the two were irreconcilable prevailed with antitrust trumping intellectual property rights. After World War II, an increased recognition of the importance of intellectual property for stimulating innovation led to a waning of the hostility to intellectual property rights under antitrust law. But it is not necessarily the case that clarity has resulted. Instead, as the material below shows, there is still much disagreement on when the right to exclude needs to be limited by the prohibition on exclusionary conduct.

As a practitioner, you will come across these issues in many ways. First, as an antitrust practitioner, it is very likely that you will have to deal with intellectual property issues, whether in a challenge by the government or in private litigation. Furthermore, to the extent that you represent an intellectual property owner engaged in licensing and contracting, you will need to consider the antitrust implications of your client's business plan. Finally, in negotiating licensing terms for a licensee, you should keep in mind the possible antitrust limitations on what a licensor proposes to include in a licensing arrangement.

The readings in this section are divided into five parts. Section A presents the principal statutes that constitute antitrust law: the Sherman Act, the Clayton Act, and the Federal Trade Commission Act. Together, these three statutes define the powers of the US Department of Justice and the Federal Trade Commission to police anticompetitive behavior. In addition, the National Cooperative Research Act of 1984 and federal antitrust enforcement agencies' 1995 Guidelines on the Licensing of Intellectual Property are discussed. These last two standards respond directly to the problem of applying antitrust principles to limit the right to exclude under intellectual property law. Section B presents a speech given by former Assistant Attorney General for Antitrust Hewett Pate in 2005 on the reconciliation of antitrust concerns and intellectual property rights. The speech discusses general trends in the law and specific cases and provides background for the case studies presented in the remainder of the chapter. Section C presents excerpts from the Court of Appeals opinion reviewing the federal government's antitrust case against the Microsoft Corporation brought in the United States. Section D presents an antitrust consent decree reached by the Federal Trade Commission with the Dell Computer Corporation, which illustrates the contemporary problems raised by intellectual property in standard setting processes. Finally, Section E presents an excerpt from the European Union Competition Commission's ruling against Microsoft to illustrate the international issues raised by the interplay between intellectual property and antitrust laws.

READINGS

A. STATUTORY OVERVIEW

SHERMAN ACT

15 USC §§ 1, 2 (2003)

Section 1. Trusts, etc., in restraint of trade illegal; penalty

Every contract, combination in the form of trust or otherwise, or conspiracy, in restraint of trade or commerce among the several States, or with foreign nations, is declared to be illegal. Every person who shall make any contract or engage in any combination or conspiracy hereby declared to be illegal shall be deemed guilty of a felony, and, on conviction thereof, shall be punished by fine not exceeding $10,000,000 if a corporation, or, if any other person, $350,000, or by imprisonment not exceeding three years, or by both said punishments, in the discretion of the court.

Section 2. Monopolizing trade a felony; penalty

Every person who shall monopolize, or attempt to monopolize, or combine or conspire with any other person or persons, to monopolize any part of the trade or commerce among the several States, or with foreign nations, shall be deemed guilty of a felony, and, on conviction thereof, shall be punished by fine not exceeding $10,000,000 if a corporation, or, if any other person, $350,000, or by imprisonment not exceeding three years, or by both said punishments, in the discretion of the court.

CLAYTON ACT

15 USC §§ 14, 18 (2003)

Section 14. Sale, etc., on agreement not to use goods of competitor

It shall be unlawful for any person engaged in commerce, in the course of such commerce, to lease or make a sale or contract for sale of goods, wares, merchandise, machinery, supplies, or other commodities, whether patented or unpatented, for use, consumption, or resale within the United States or any Territory thereof or the District of Columbia or any insular possession or other place under the jurisdiction of the United States, or fix a price charged therefor, or discount from, or rebate upon, such price, on the condition, agreement, or understanding that the lessee or purchaser thereof shall not use or deal in the goods, wares, merchandise, machinery, supplies, or other commodities of a competitor or competitors of the lessor or seller, where the effect of such lease, sale, or contract for sale or such condition, agreement, or understanding may be to substantially lessen competition or tend to create a monopoly in any line of commerce.

Section 18. Acquisition by one corporation of stock of another

No person engaged in commerce or in any activity affecting commerce shall acquire, directly or indirectly, the whole or any part of the stock or other share capital and no person subject to the jurisdiction of the Federal Trade Commission shall acquire the whole or any part of the assets of another person engaged also in commerce or in any activity affecting commerce, where in any line of commerce or in any activity affecting commerce in any section of the country, the effect of such acquisition may be substantially to lessen competition, or to tend to create a monopoly.

No person shall acquire, directly or indirectly, the whole or any part of the stock or other share capital and no person subject to the jurisdiction of the Federal Trade Commission shall acquire the whole or any part of the assets of one or more persons engaged in commerce or in any activity affecting commerce, where in any line of commerce or in any activity affecting commerce in any section of the country, the effect of such acquisition, of such stocks or assets, or of the use of such stock by the voting or granting of proxies or otherwise, may be substantially to lessen competition, or to tend to create a monopoly.

FEDERAL TRADE COMMISSION ACT

15 USC § 45 (2003)

Section 45. Unfair methods of competition unlawful; prevention by Commission

(a) Declaration of unlawfulness; power to prohibit unfair practices

(1) Unfair methods of competition in or affecting commerce, and unfair or deceptive acts or practices in or affecting commerce, are hereby declared unlawful.

NATIONAL COOPERATIVE RESEARCH ACT

15 USC §§ 4301, 4302 (2003)

Section 4301. Definitions

. . .

(6) The term "joint venture" means any group of activities, including attempting to make, making, or performing a contract, by two or more persons for the purpose of —

(A) theoretical analysis, experimentation, or systematic study of phenomena or observable facts,

(B) the development or testing of basic engineering techniques,

(C) the extension of investigative findings or theory of a scientific or technical nature into practical application for experimental and demonstration purposes, including the experimental production and testing of models, prototypes, equipment, materials, and processes,

(D) the production of a product, process, or service,

(E) the testing in connection with the production of a product, process, or service by such venture,

(F) the collection, exchange, and analysis of research or production information, or

(G) any combination of the purposes specified in subparagraphs (A), (B), (C), (D), (E), and (F), and may include the establishment and operation of facilities for the conducting of such venture, the conducting of such venture on a protected and proprietary basis, and the prosecuting of applications for patents and the granting of licenses for the results of such venture, but does not include any activity specified in subsection (b) of this section.

(b) The term "joint venture" excludes the following activities involving two or more persons:

(1) exchanging information among competitors relating to costs, sales, profitability, prices, marketing, or distribution of any product, process, or service if such information is not reasonably required to carry out the purpose of such venture,

(2) entering into any agreement or engaging in any other conduct restricting, requiring, or otherwise involving the marketing, distribution, or provision by any person who is a party to such venture of any product, process, or service, other than —

(A) the distribution among the parties to such venture, in accordance with such venture, of a product, process, or service produced by such venture,

(B) the marketing of proprietary information, such as patents and trade secrets, developed through such venture formed under a written agreement entered into before June 10, 1993, or

(C) the licensing, conveying, or transferring of intellectual property, such as patents and trade secrets, developed through such venture formed under a written agreement entered into on or after June 10, 1993,

(3) entering into any agreement or engaging in any other conduct —

(A) to restrict or require the sale, licensing, or sharing of inventions, developments, products, processes, or services not developed through, or produced by, such venture, or

(B) to restrict or require participation by any person who is a party to such venture in other research and development activities, that is not reasonably required to prevent misappropriation of proprietary information contributed by any person who is a party to such venture or of the results of such venture,

(4) entering into any agreement or engaging in any other conduct allocating a market with a competitor,

(5) exchanging information among competitors relating to production (other than production by such venture) of a product, process, or

service if such information is not reasonably required to carry out the purpose of such venture,

(6) entering into any agreement or engaging in any other conduct restricting, requiring, or otherwise involving the production (other than the production by such venture) of a product, process, or service,

(7) using existing facilities for the production of a product, process, or service by such venture unless such use involves the production of a new product or technology, and

(8) except as provided in paragraphs (2), (3), and (6), entering into any agreement or engaging in any other conduct to restrict or require participation by any person who is a party to such venture, in any unilateral or joint activity that is not reasonably required to carry out the purpose of such venture.

Section 4302. Rule of reason standard

In any action under the antitrust laws, or under any State law similar to the antitrust laws, the conduct of any person in making or performing a contract to carry out a joint venture shall not be deemed illegal per se; such conduct shall be judged on the basis of its reasonableness, taking into account all relevant factors affecting competition, including, but not limited to, effects on competition in properly defined, relevant research, development, product, process, and service markets. For the purpose of determining a properly defined, relevant market, worldwide capacity shall be considered to the extent that it may be appropriate in the circumstances.

Antitrust Guidelines for the Licensing of Intellectual Property
Issued by the U.S. Department of Justice and
the Federal Trade Commission
April 6, 1995

1. Intellectual property protection and the antitrust laws

1.0 These Guidelines state the antitrust enforcement policy of the U.S. Department of Justice and the Federal Trade Commission (individually, "the Agency," and collectively, "the Agencies") with respect to the licensing of intellectual property protected by patent, copyright, and trade secret law, and of know-how. By stating their general policy, the Agencies hope to assist those who need to predict whether the Agencies will challenge a practice as anticompetitive. However, these Guidelines cannot remove judgment and discretion in antitrust law enforcement. Moreover, the standards set forth in these Guidelines must be applied in unforeseeable circumstances. Each case will be evaluated in light of its own facts, and these Guidelines will be applied reasonably and flexibly.

In the United States, patents confer rights to exclude others from making, using, or selling in the United States the invention claimed by the patent for a period of seventeen years from the date of issue. To gain patent protection, an invention (which may be a product, process, machine, or composition of matter) must be novel, non-obvious, and useful. Copyright protection applies to original works of authorship embodied in a tangible medium of expression. A copyright protects only the expression, not the underlying ideas. Unlike a patent, which protects an invention not only from copying but also from independent creation, a copyright does not preclude others from independently creating similar expression. Trade secret protection applies to information whose economic value depends on its not being generally known. Trade secret protection is conditioned upon efforts to maintain secrecy and has no fixed term. As with copyright protection, trade secret protection does not preclude independent creation by others.

The intellectual property laws and the antitrust laws share the common purpose of promoting innovation and enhancing consumer welfare. The intellectual property laws provide incentives for innovation and its dissemination and commercialization by establishing enforceable property rights for the creators of new and useful products, more efficient processes, and original works of expression. In the absence of intellectual property rights, imitators could more rapidly exploit the efforts of innovators and investors without compensation. Rapid imitation would reduce the commercial value of innovation and erode incentives to invest, ultimately to the detriment of consumers. The antitrust laws promote innovation and consumer welfare by prohibiting certain actions that may harm competition with respect to either existing or new ways of serving consumers.

2. General principles

2.0 These Guidelines embody three general principles: (a) for the purpose of antitrust analysis, the Agencies regard intellectual property as being essentially comparable to any other form of property; (b) the Agencies do not presume that intellectual property creates market power in the antitrust context; and (c) the Agencies recognize that intellectual property licensing allows firms to combine complementary factors of production and is generally procompetitive.

2.1 Standard antitrust analysis applies to intellectual property

The Agencies apply the same general antitrust principles to conduct involving intellectual property that they apply to conduct involving any other form of tangible or intangible property. That is not to say that intellectual property is in all respects the same as any other form of property. Intellectual property has important characteristics, such as ease of misappropriation, that distinguish it from many other forms of property. These characteristics can be taken into account by standard antitrust analysis, however, and do not require the application of fundamentally different principles.

Although there are clear and important differences in the purpose, extent, and duration of protection provided under the intellectual property regimes of patent, copyright, and trade secret, the governing antitrust principles are the same. Antitrust analysis takes differences among these forms of intellectual property into account in evaluating the specific market circumstances in which transactions occur, just as it does with other particular market circumstances.

Intellectual property law bestows on the owners of intellectual property certain rights to exclude others. These rights help the owners to profit from the use of their property. An intellectual property owner's rights to exclude are similar to the rights enjoyed by owners of other forms of private property. As with other forms of private property, certain types of conduct with respect to intellectual property may have anticompetitive effects against which the antitrust laws can and do protect. Intellectual property is thus neither particularly free from scrutiny under the antitrust laws, nor particularly suspect under them.

The Agencies recognize that the licensing of intellectual property is often international. The principles of antitrust analysis described in these Guidelines apply equally to domestic and international licensing arrangements. However, as described in the 1995 Department of Justice and Federal Trade Commission Antitrust Enforcement Guidelines for International Operations, considerations particular to international operations, such as jurisdiction and comity, may affect enforcement decisions when the arrangement is in an international context.

2.2 Intellectual property and market power

Market power is the ability profitably to maintain prices above, or output below, competitive levels for a significant period of time. The Agencies will not presume that a patent, copyright, or trade secret necessarily confers market power upon its owner. Although the intellectual property right confers the power to exclude with respect to the specific product, process, or work in question, there will often be sufficient actual or potential close substitutes for such product, process, or work to prevent the exercise of market power. If a patent or other form of intellectual property does confer market power, that market power does not by itself offend the antitrust laws. As with any other tangible or intangible asset that enables its owner to obtain significant supra-competitive profits, market power (or even a monopoly) that is solely "a consequence of a superior product, business acumen, or historic accident" does not violate the antitrust laws. Nor does such market power impose on the intellectual property owner an obligation to license the use of that property to others. As in other antitrust contexts, however, market power could be illegally acquired or maintained, or, even if lawfully acquired and maintained, would be relevant to the ability of an intellectual property owner to harm competition through unreasonable conduct in connection with such property.

2.3 Pro-competitive benefits of licensing

Intellectual property typically is one component among many in a production process and derives value from its combination with complementary factors. Complementary factors of production include manufacturing and distribution facilities, workforces, and other items of intellectual property. The owner of intellectual property has to arrange for its combination with other necessary factors to realize its commercial value. Often, the owner finds it most efficient to contract with others for these factors, to sell rights to the intellectual property, or to enter into a joint venture arrangement for its development, rather than supplying these complementary factors itself.

Licensing, cross-licensing, or otherwise transferring intellectual property (hereinafter "licensing") can facilitate integration of the licensed property with complementary factors of production. This integration can lead to more efficient exploitation of the intellectual property, benefiting consumers through the reduction of costs and the introduction of new products. Such arrangements increase the value of intellectual property to consumers and to the developers of the technology. By potentially increasing the expected returns from intellectual property, licensing also can increase the incentive for its creation and thus promote greater investment in research and development.

Sometimes the use of one item of intellectual property requires access to another. An item of intellectual property "blocks" another when the second cannot be practiced without using the first. For example, an improvement on a patented machine can be blocked by the patent on the machine. Licensing may promote the coordinated development of technologies that are in a blocking relationship.

Field-of-use, territorial, and other limitations on intellectual property licenses may serve pro-competitive ends by allowing the licensor to exploit its property as efficiently and effectively as possible. These various forms of exclusivity can be used to give a licensee an incentive to invest in the commercialization and distribution of products embodying the licensed intellectual property and to develop additional applications for the licensed property. The restrictions may do so, for example, by protecting the licensee against free-riding on the licensee's investments by other licensees or by the licensor. They may also increase the licensor's incentive to license, for example, by protecting the licensor from competition in the licensor's own technology in a market niche that it prefers to keep to itself. These benefits of licensing restrictions apply to patent, copyright, and trade secret licenses, and to know-how agreements.

. . .

5. Application of general principles

5.0 This section illustrates the application of the general principles discussed above to particular licensing restraints and to arrangements that involve the cross-licensing, pooling, or acquisition of intellectual property. The restraints and arrangements identified are typical of those that are likely to receive antitrust scrutiny; however, they are not intended as an exhaustive list of practices that could raise competitive concerns.

5.1 Horizontal restraints

The existence of a restraint in a licensing arrangement that affects parties in a horizontal relationship (a "horizontal restraint") does not necessarily cause the arrangement to be anticompetitive. As in the case of joint ventures among horizontal competitors, licensing arrangements among such competitors may promote rather than hinder competition if they result in integrative efficiencies. Such efficiencies may arise, for example, from the realization of economies of scale and the integration of complementary research and development, production, and marketing capabilities.

Following the general principles outlined in section 3.4, horizontal restraints often will be evaluated under the rule of reason. In some circumstances, however, that analysis may be truncated; additionally, some restraints may merit per se treatment, including price fixing, allocation of markets or customers, agreements to reduce output, and certain group boycotts.

Example 9

Situation: Two of the leading manufacturers of a consumer electronic product hold patents that cover alternative circuit designs for the product. The manufacturers assign their patents to a separate corporation wholly owned by the two firms. That corporation licenses the right to use the circuit designs to other consumer product manufacturers and establishes the license royalties. None of the patents is blocking; that is, each of the patents can be used without infringing a patent owned by the other firm. The different circuit designs are substitutable in that each permits the manufacture at comparable cost to consumers of products that consumers consider to be interchangeable. One of the Agencies is analyzing the licensing arrangement.

Discussion: In this example, the manufacturers are horizontal competitors in the goods market for the consumer product and in the related technology markets. The competitive issue with regard to a joint assignment of patent rights is whether the assignment has an adverse impact on competition in technology and goods markets that is not outweighed by pro-competitive efficiencies, such as benefits in the use or dissemination of the technology. Each of the patent owners has a right to exclude others from using its patent. That right does not extend, however, to the agreement to assign rights jointly. To the extent that the patent rights cover technologies that are close substitutes, the joint determination of royalties likely would result in higher royalties and higher goods prices than would result if the owners licensed or used their technologies independently. In the absence of evidence establishing efficiency-enhancing integration from the joint assignment of patent rights, the Agency may conclude that the joint marketing of competing patent rights constitutes horizontal price fixing and could be challenged as a per se unlawful horizontal restraint of trade. If the joint marketing arrangement results in an efficiency-enhancing integration, the Agency would evaluate the arrangement under the rule of reason. However, the Agency may conclude that the anticompetitive effects are sufficiently apparent, and the claimed integrative efficiencies are sufficiently weak or not reasonably related to the restraints, to warrant challenge of the arrangement without an elaborate analysis of particular industry circumstances.

5.2 Resale price maintenance

Resale price maintenance is illegal when "commodities have passed into the channels of trade and are owned by dealers." *Dr. Miles Medical Co. v. John D. Park & Sons Co.,* 220 U.S. 373, 408 (1911). It has been held per se illegal for a licensor of an intellectual property right in a product to fix a licensee's resale price of that product. *United States v. Univis Lens Co.,* 316 U.S. 241 (1942); *Ethyl Gasoline Corp. v. United States,* 309 U.S. 436 (1940). [T]he Agencies will enforce the per se rule against resale price maintenance in the intellectual property context.

5.3 Tying arrangements

A "tying" or "tie-in" or "tied sale" arrangement has been defined as "an agreement by a party to sell one product . . . on the condition that the buyer also purchases a different (or tied) product, or at least agrees that he will not purchase that [tied] product from any other supplier." *Eastman Kodak Co. v. Image Technical Services, Inc.,* 112 S. Ct. 2072, 2079 (1992). Conditioning the ability of a licensee to license one or more items of intellectual property on the licensee's purchase of another item of intellectual property or a good or a service has been held in some cases to constitute illegal tying. Although tying arrangements may result in anticompetitive effects, such arrangements can also result in significant efficiencies and pro-competitive benefits. In the exercise of their prosecutorial discretion, the Agencies will consider both the anticompetitive effects and the efficiencies attributable to a tie-in. The Agencies would be likely to challenge a tying arrangement if: (1) the seller has market power in the tying product, (2) the arrangement has an adverse effect on competition in the relevant market for the tied product, and (3) efficiency justifications for the arrangement do not outweigh the anticompetitive effects. The Agencies will not presume that a patent, copyright, or trade secret necessarily confers market power upon its owner.

Package licensing — the licensing of multiple items of intellectual property in a single license or in a group of related licenses — may be a form of tying arrangement if the licensing of one product is conditioned upon the acceptance of a license of another, separate product. Package licensing can be efficiency enhancing under some circumstances. When multiple licenses are needed to use any single item of intellectual property, for example, a package license may promote such efficiencies. If a package license constitutes a tying arrangement, the Agencies will evaluate its competitive effects under the same principles they apply to other tying arrangements.

5.4 Exclusive dealing

In the intellectual property context, exclusive dealing occurs when a license prevents the licensee from licensing, selling, distributing, or using competing technologies. Exclusive dealing arrangements are evaluated under the rule of reason. See *Tampa Electric Co. v. Nashville Coal Co.,* 365 U.S. 320 (1961) (evaluating legality of exclusive dealing under section 1 of the Sherman Act and section 3 of the Clayton Act); *Beltone Electronics Corp.,* 100 F.T.C. 68 (1982) (evaluating legality of exclusive dealing under section 5 of the Federal Trade Commission Act). In determining whether an exclusive dealing arrangement is likely to reduce competition in a relevant market, the Agencies will take into account the extent to which the arrangement (1) promotes the exploitation and development of the licensor's technology and (2) anti-competitively forecloses the exploitation and development of, or otherwise constrains competition among, competing technologies.

The likelihood that exclusive dealing may have anticompetitive effects is related, inter alia, to the degree of foreclosure in the relevant market, the duration of the exclusive dealing arrangement, and other characteristics of the input and output markets, such as concentration, difficulty of entry, and the responsiveness of supply and demand to changes in price in the relevant markets. If the Agencies determine that a particular exclusive dealing arrangement may have an anticompetitive effect, they will evaluate the extent to which the restraint encourages licensees to develop and market the licensed technology (or specialized applications of that technology), increases licensors' incentives to develop or refine the licensed technology, or otherwise increases competition and enhances output in a relevant market.

5.5 Cross-licensing and pooling arrangements

Cross-licensing and pooling arrangements are agreements of two or more owners of different items of intellectual property to license one another or third parties. These arrangements may provide pro-competitive benefits by integrating complementary technologies, reducing transaction costs, clearing blocking positions, and avoiding costly infringement litigation. By promoting the dissemination of technology, cross-licensing and pooling arrangements are often pro-competitive.

Cross-licensing and pooling arrangements can have anticompetitive effects in certain circumstances. For example, collective price or output restraints in pooling arrangements, such as the joint marketing of pooled intellectual property rights with collective price setting or coordinated output restrictions, may be deemed unlawful if they do not contribute to an efficiency-enhancing integration of economic activity among the participants. Compare *NCAA* 468 U.S. at 114 (output restriction on college football broadcasting held unlawful because it was not reasonably related to any purported justification) with *Broadcast Music*, 441 U.S. at 23 (blanket license for music copyrights found not per se illegal because the cooperative price was necessary to the creation of a new product). When cross-licensing or pooling arrangements are mechanisms to accomplish naked price fixing or market division, they are subject to challenge under the per se rule. See *United States v. New Wrinkle, Inc.,* 342 U.S. 371 (1952) (price fixing).

Settlements involving the cross-licensing of intellectual property rights can be an efficient means to avoid litigation and, in general, courts favor such settlements. When such cross-licensing involves horizontal competitors, however, the Agencies will consider whether the effect of the settlement is to diminish competition among entities that would have been actual or likely potential competitors in a relevant market in the absence of the cross-license. In the absence of offsetting efficiencies, such settlements may be challenged as unlawful restraints of trade. Cf. *United States v. Singer Manufacturing Co.,* 374 U.S. 174 (1963) (cross-license agreement was part of broader combination to exclude competitors).

Pooling arrangements generally need not be open to all who would like to join. However, exclusion from cross-licensing and pooling arrangements among parties that collectively possess market power may, under some circumstances, harm competition. Cf. *Northwest Wholesale Stationers, Inc. v. Pacific Stationery & Printing Co.,* 472 U.S. 284 (1985) (exclusion of a competitor from a purchasing cooperative not per se unlawful absent a showing of market power). In general, exclusion from a pooling or cross-licensing arrangement among competing technologies is unlikely to have anticompetitive effects unless (1) excluded firms cannot effectively compete in the relevant market for the good incorporating the licensed technologies and (2) the pool participants collectively possess market power in the relevant market. If these circumstances exist, the Agencies will evaluate whether the arrangement's limitations on participation are reasonably related to the efficient development and exploitation of the pooled technologies and will assess the net effect of those limitations in the relevant market.

Another possible anticompetitive effect of pooling arrangements may occur if the arrangement deters or discourages participants from engaging in research and development, thus retarding innovation. For example, a pooling arrangement that requires members to grant licenses to each other for current and future technology at minimal cost may reduce the incentives of its members to engage in research and development because members of the pool have to share their successful research and development and each of the members can free ride on the accomplishments of other pool members. However, such an arrangement can have pro-competitive benefits, for example, by exploiting economies of scale and integrating complementary capabilities of the pool members, (including the clearing of blocking positions), and is likely to cause competitive problems only when the arrangement includes a large fraction of the potential research and development in an innovation market.

Example 10

Situation: As in Example 9, two of the leading manufacturers of a consumer electronic product hold patents that cover alternative circuit designs for the product. The manufacturers assign several of their patents to a separate corporation wholly owned by the two firms. That corporation licenses the right to use the circuit designs to other consumer product manufacturers and establishes the license royalties. In this example, however, the manufacturers assign to the separate corporation only patents that are blocking. None of the patents assigned to the corporation can be used without infringing a patent owned by the other firm.

Discussion: Unlike the previous example, the joint assignment of patent rights to the wholly owned corporation in this example does not adversely affect competition in the licensed technology among entities that would have been actual or likely potential competitors in the absence of the licensing arrangement. Moreover, the licensing arrangement is likely to have pro-competitive benefits in the use of the technology. Because the manufacturers' patents are blocking, the manufacturers are not in a horizontal relationship with respect to those patents. None of the patents can be used without the right to a patent owned by the other firm, so the patents are not substitutable. As in Example 9, the firms are horizontal competitors in the relevant goods market. In the absence of collateral restraints that would likely raise price or reduce output in the relevant goods market or in any other relevant antitrust market and that are not reasonably related to an efficiency-enhancing integration of economic activity, the evaluating Agency would be unlikely to challenge this arrangement.

5.6 Grantbacks

A grantback is an arrangement under which a licensee agrees to extend to the licensor of intellectual property the right to use the licensee's improvements to the licensed technology. Grantbacks can have pro-competitive effects, especially if they are nonexclusive. Such arrangements provide a means for the licensee and the licensor to share risks and reward the licensor for making possible further innovation based on or informed by the licensed technology, and both promote innovation in the first place and promote the subsequent licensing of the results of the innovation. Grantbacks may adversely affect competition, however, if they substantially reduce the licensee's incentives to engage in research and development and thereby limit rivalry in innovation markets.

A non-exclusive grantback allows the licensee to practice its technology and license it to others. Such a grantback provision may be necessary to ensure that the licensor is not prevented from effectively competing because it is denied access to improvements developed with the aid of its own technology. Compared with an exclusive grantback, a non-exclusive grantback, which leaves the licensee free to license improvements technology to others, is less likely to have anticompetitive effects.

The Agencies will evaluate a grantback provision under the rule of reason, see generally *Transparent-Wrap Machine Corp. v. Stokes & Smith Co.*, 329 U.S. 637, 645-48 (1947) (grantback provision in technology license is not per se unlawful), considering its likely effects in light of the overall structure of the licensing arrangement and conditions in the relevant markets. An important factor in the Agencies' analysis of a grantback will be whether the licensor has market power in a relevant technology or innovation market. If the Agencies determine that a particular grantback provision is likely to reduce significantly licensees' incentives to invest in improving the licensed technology, the Agencies will consider the extent to which the grantback provision has offsetting pro-competitive effects, such as (1) promoting dissemination of licensees' improvements to the licensed technology, (2) increasing the licensors' incentives to disseminate the licensed technology, or (3) otherwise increasing competition and output in a relevant technology or innovation market. See section 4.2. In addition, the Agencies will consider the extent to which grantback provisions in the relevant markets generally increase licensors' incentives to innovate in the first place.

5.7 Acquisition of intellectual property rights

Certain transfers of intellectual property rights are most appropriately analyzed by applying the principles and standards used to analyze mergers, particularly those in the 1992 Horizontal Merger Guidelines. The Agencies will apply a merger analysis to an outright sale by an intellectual property owner of all of its rights to that intellectual property and to a transaction in which a person obtains through grant, sale, or other transfer an exclusive license for intellectual property (i.e., a license that precludes all other persons, including the licensor, from using the licensed intellectual property). Such transactions may be assessed under section 7 of the Clayton Act, sections 1 and 2 of the Sherman Act, and section 5 of the Federal Trade Commission Act.

Example 11

Situation: Omega develops a new, patented pharmaceutical for the treatment of a particular disease. The only drug on the market approved for the treatment of this disease is sold by Delta. Omega's patented drug has almost completed regulatory approval by the Food and Drug Administration. Omega has invested considerable sums in product development and market testing, and initial results show that Omega's drug would be a significant competitor to Delta's. However, rather than enter the market as a direct competitor of Delta, Omega licenses to Delta the right to manufacture and sell Omega's patented drug. The license agreement with Delta is nominally nonexclusive. However, Omega has rejected all requests by other firms to obtain a license to manufacture and sell Omega's patented drug, despite offers by those firms of terms that are reasonable in relation to those in Delta's license.

Discussion: Although Omega's license to Delta is nominally nonexclusive, the circumstances indicate that it is exclusive in fact because Omega has rejected all reasonable offers by other firms for licenses to manufacture and sell Omega's patented drug. The facts of this example indicate that Omega would be a likely potential competitor of Delta in the absence of the licensing arrangement, and thus they are in a horizontal relationship in the relevant goods market that includes drugs for the treatment of this particular disease. The evaluating Agency would apply a merger analysis to this transaction, since it involves an acquisition of a likely potential competitor.

6. Enforcement of invalid intellectual property rights

The Agencies may challenge the enforcement of invalid intellectual property rights as antitrust violations. Enforcement or attempted enforcement of a patent obtained by fraud on the Patent and Trademark Office or the Copyright Office may violate section 2 of the Sherman Act, if all the elements otherwise necessary to establish a section 2 charge are proved, or section 5 of the Federal Trade Commission Act. . . . Inequitable conduct before the Patent and Trademark Office will not be the basis of a section 2 claim unless the conduct also involves knowing and willful fraud and the other elements of a section 2 claim are present. . . . Actual or attempted enforcement of patents obtained by inequitable conduct that falls short of fraud under some circumstances may violate section 5 of the Federal Trade Commission Act. Objectively baseless litigation to enforce invalid intellectual property rights may also constitute an element of a violation of the Sherman Act.

NOTES & QUESTIONS

1. Although common law antitrust law can be dated back to England and continued in the United in the eighteenth and nineteenth century as the restraint of trade doctrine, antitrust law had its statutory origins with the enactment of the Sherman Act in 1890. Judicial glosses on the Sherman Act that in many ways weakened its application were addressed through the enactment of the Clayton Act and the Federal Trade Commission Act in 1914. Prior to 1914, antitrust enforcement entailed private causes of actions and cases brought by the Department of Justice. In 1914, the Federal Trade Commission was created to deal with the policing of harms to competition,

particularly those arising from deceptive and unfair trade practices. These three statutes are the foundation of antitrust law in the United States. Occasionally, Congress has enacted new statutes to address cutting edge issues in antitrust law. One example of such intervention is the National Cooperative Research Act, passed in 1984, to exempt certain joint research ventures from the antitrust laws. For more complex areas of the law, the Department of Justice and the Federal Trade Commission sometimes jointly release guidelines to aid in the application of antitrust law. An example of such guidelines is the 1995 Joint Guidelines on the Licensing of Intellectual Property. The legal documents presented here provide the backbone for understanding the relationship between intellectual property and antitrust, the subject of this chapter. For an excellent history of the origins of U.S. antitrust law, see Hans B. Thorelli, THE FEDERAL ANTITRUST POLICY: ORIGINATION OF AN AMERICAN TRADITION 9-53 (1954).

2. The first two sections of the Sherman Act are the substance of antitrust law. Together they cover the range of anticompetitive activities that antitrust law regulates. Section One of the Sherman Act criminalizes and establishes civil liability for restraints of trade. Incorporating common law doctrine, Section One addresses agreements among two or more firms in an industry to control the competitive process. The underlying principle is that firms in an industry should be competing with each other in order to ensure the best products at the lowest prices to consumers. Cooperation among firms, according to this principle, is a basis for suspicion since such cooperation may serve as a way to raise prices or restrain the quality and quantity of products in the marketplace.

Section Two of the Sherman Act criminalizes and establishes civil liability for anticompetitive conduct by one firm in an industry. Section Two does not make it illegal to be a monopolist, but it is illegal to monopolize or attempt to monopolize. Monopolization occurs when a firm that has a dominant presence in a market engages in conduct that hurts the competitive process. As with Section One, the underlying principle is that competition is the source of strength in an economy. Monopolistic acts that limit the entry of new firms or new products or new ideas into a marketplace are contrary to the principle of competition. Notice an important tension in Section Two: simply being a monopolist is not enough to violate the antitrust laws. Being a monopolist, in other words, is not inconsistent with the principle of competition since one would expect that competition would lead to strong and sometimes large firms surviving through skill and superior ability.

3. The Sherman Act was a controversial piece of legislation when enacted, and some courts attempted to narrow its scope through interpretation. One distinction that arose in the law of Section One was that between per se violations of the Sherman Act and violations under the rule of reason. Per se violations were just that: violations establishing strict liability for certain acts deemed to be anticompetitive independent of any showing of harm. Rule of reason violations, on the other hand, rested on a consideration of competitive harms and benefits that might result from a particular business arrangement. The distinction between per se and rule of reason violations continues today. Two categories of behavior that are considered per se violations are agreements among competitions to set prices (price fixing agreements) and

agreements among competitors to divide up markets geographical (horizontal territorial agreements). In general, agreements that do not fall into one of these categories are analyzed under the rule of reason, which requires a court to consider the economic benefits and harms of an agreement to determine a Section One violation.

4. Congress remedied the confusion created by judicial interpretations of the Sherman Act with the passage of the Clayton Act in 1914. The Clayton Act was more detailed than the Sherman Act with specific provisions designed to limit judicial discretion in applying the law. Two provisions of the Clayton Act are excerpted here. Section 14 deals with restraints placed on purchasers by sellers of products or services; section 18 deals with mergers and acquisitions. The key thing to notice about these provisions is the legal standard for liability that Congress adopted. Under both provisions, liability is imposed if a business activity "substantially lessens competition" or tends to "create a monopoly." These standards were meant to move away from the confusion over per se versus rule of reason violations under Section One of the Sherman Act and confusion about business justifications under Section Two of the Sherman Act to impose antitrust liability upon a finding of harm to competition.

The Clayton Act did not overrule the Sherman Act. Antitrust claims can be based on the Clayton Act, the Sherman Act, or both. For example, a merger or acquisition is actionable under the Clayton Act Section 18 and under Sherman Act, as either a restraint on trade or monopolization. Over time, the standards for analysis of mergers and acquisitions under the two Acts have converged. For a discussion of the application of antitrust law to a merger that involved the acquisition of patent rights, see *SCM Corporation v. Xerox Corporation,* 645 F.2d 1195 (2nd Cir. 1981) ("analyzing the lawfulness of the acquisition of a patent necessitates that we primarily focus upon the circumstances of the acquiring party and the status of the relevant product and geographic markets at the time of acquisition").

Notice also that Clayton Act is more specific than the Sherman Act, meaning that some business conduct may not be actionable under the Clayton Act, but would be actionable under the Sherman Act. For example, if a purchaser places a restraint on the seller of a product (for example, a retailer tells a manufacturer not to sell to any other retailer), the conduct would be actionable under the Sherman Act, but not the Clayton Act (which covers only restraints placed on purchasers by sellers). These idiosyncrasies reflect legislative compromises regarding particular types of antitrust abuses that were viewed with concern at the time each of the Acts was passed. For example, the asymmetry between restraints on purchasers and restraints on sellers under the Clayton Act reflects Congress' belief in 1914 that the practices of manufacturers, which tended to be large entities, were potentially more harmful to competition than the practices of retailers, which were relatively small at the time. Of course, nowadays with the growth of retailers throughout the Twentieth Century, some retailers are larger than many manufacturers. The Sherman Act with its broad provisions, however, reaches the full gamut of business conduct while the Clayton Act remains more narrowly focused.

5. The Federal Trade Commission Act was another innovation in 1914. The Act created the Federal Trade Commission (FTC) as a government agency for policing markets regarding unfair and deceptive trade practices. While the Sherman and Clayton Acts were enacted to prevent harms to the marketplace as a whole, the Federal Trade Commission Act was aimed at preventing harms to consumers resulting from such activities as false advertising or deceptive contract terms. The Federal Trade Commission, however, also deals with mergers and activities and has concurrent jurisdiction with the Department of Justice in reviewing and challenging mergers under the Clayton Act.

6. The National Cooperative Research Act of 1984 was enacted to allow some amount of cooperation among competitors for the purposes of technological innovation and research and development. Prior to the enactment of the NCRA, cooperative ventures would run the risk of being found to be a restraint of trade under the Sherman Act or the Clayton Act. The NCRA exempts "joint ventures" from per se treatment and imposes liability based on the reasonableness of the joint ventures' activities. In addition, if a joint venture files a notification with the Department of Justice, any antitrust damages would be limited to actual damages without the possibility of treble damages. Notice the definition of a joint venture, particularly the exclusions. The exclusions were meant to ensure that anticompetitive agreements among competitors, such as agreements to fix prices, divide territories, or share manufacturing information, were not protected from antitrust scrutiny by being implemented through a joint venture.

7. The 1995 Antitrust Guidelines on the Licensing of Intellectual Property reflect a more flexible treatment of intellectual property licensing under the antitrust laws. The case law in the early to mid-twentieth century demonstrated a hostility to intellectual property under the antitrust laws. Courts would often find that the exclusivity provided by intellectual property, particularly patents, translated into potentially illegal market power under the antitrust laws. In the 1970's, the Department of Justice (DOJ) identified nine specific licensing activities that were clearly forbidden by the antitrust laws:

- Mandatory package licensing, also known as patent pools;

- Tying of unpatented supplies;

- Compulsory payments of royalties in amounts not reasonably related to sales of patented products;

- Mandatory grantbacks;

- Licensee veto power over the licensor's grant of further licenses;

- Restrictions on sales of unpatented products made by patented processes;

- Post-sale restrictions on resale by purchasers of patented products;

- Specifying price licensee can charge on resale of licensed products;

- Tie-outs, which are restrictions on a licensee's ability to sell products that compete with licensor's patented products.

These nine prohibited practices reflected a hostility to the exclusivity of intellectual property law. The 1995 Guidelines clearly show a mellowing by both the DOJ and the FTC, particularly in identifying the pro-competitive benefits of intellectual property licensing. Pay particular attention to the discussion of specific licensing practices in section five of the Guidelines. The discussion of tying is important and should be kept in mind when reading the Microsoft case below. The one area where scrutiny of business practices by federal antitrust officials remains close is the enforcement of invalid patents as discussed in section six of the Guidelines. Keep the Guidelines in mind when reading the consent decree involving Dell below as well as the speech by then Assistant Attorney General Pate in the next section.

B.   THE ANTITRUST-INTELLECTUAL PROPERTY INTERFACE

R. Hewitt Pate, Competition and Intellectual Property in the U.S.: Licensing Freedom and the Limits of Antitrust

Assistant Attorney General, Antitrust Division, U.S. Department of Justice, 2005 EU Competition Workshop, Florence, Italy, June 3, 2005

I.   Introduction

Defining the relationship of intellectual property rights and competition law is an important economic issue in Europe and the United States. This paper attempts to outline some bedrock principles of intellectual property and antitrust policy in the United States, then discuss how they explain, and in some cases require, the current U.S. approach to a series of specific licensing practices. The basic U.S. approach, reflected in the 1995 DOJ/FTC Guidelines for the Licensing of Intellectual Property, calls for flexible application of economic analysis to licensing practices. And the recent trend has been one of increasing convergence in U.S. and European approaches to IP licensing questions, as seen in the new revisions to the Technology Transfer Block Exemption and accompanying guidelines.

The opening question for this workshop asks whether intellectual property is like other property. This question has been discussed to death many times over in recent years, without much improvement on the answer given ten years ago in the 1995 Guidelines. In short, for competition law purposes, intellectual property should be treated in essentially the same way as other forms of property, though this does not mean that it is in all respects the same as other forms of property. "Intellectual property is thus neither particularly free from scrutiny under the antitrust laws, nor particularly suspect under them."

This answer means rejection of the hostility toward intellectual property that held sway in the U.S. during the 1970's. During this era, the Antitrust Division had a section devoted to attacking IP licensing practices that we routinely applaud today. This was the era of the "Nine No Nos," during which we applied per se rules of illegality to many licensing practices. The contention that IP should be treated essentially like other forms of property at that time was meant as a call to curtail hostility toward IP rights, a call for the end of disfavored status for IP.

Today, in contrast, our policy is animated by the recognition that IP licensing is generally pro-competitive. But the modern answer to the question whether IP is like other forms of property also requires rejection of extreme claims of privilege on the part of IP owners. Today, the statement that IP is essentially like other forms of property is often heard in arguments against claims for complete exemption from antitrust scrutiny. The mere presence of an IP right that somehow figures in a course of otherwise anticompetitive conduct does not act as a talisman that wards off all antitrust enforcement. The classic statement on this point is contained in *United States v. Microsoft Corp.*, 253 F.3d 34 (D.C. Cir. 2001) ("Microsoft's primary copyright argument borders upon the frivolous. The company claims an absolute and unfettered right to use its intellectual property as it wishes. . . . That is no more correct than the proposition that use of one's personal property, such as a baseball bat, cannot give rise to tort liability.")

II.   First Principles of U.S. Intellectual Property Law and Antitrust

Sound antitrust enforcement condemns anticompetitive conduct. It does not attempt to regulate the amount of competition in a general sense or address vague questions of fairness. It does not attempt to create an affirmative incentive for pro-competitive conduct, by promising any specific reward or legal recognition for competitors who play by the rules. It focuses on specific anticompetitive actions, as judged by their effects on markets and consumer welfare. Although this narrow focus is a limitation, at the same time it is a great strength — it makes possible objectivity, predictability, and transparency.

Intellectual property laws, by contrast, provide a complex system of affirmative rewards for an important type of pro-competitive behavior — innovation. They take consumer welfare into account, but in different ways than does antitrust. First, they reward innovators with exclusive rights that serve as an incentive to bring new and improved goods and services to market. The hope is that such innovations will lead to increased competition and increased consumer welfare in the long term. Second, they strike a balance between these rights and certain types of public access, such as fair use under copyright law or the disclosure requirement and the limited term of patents. They also include a fail-safe procedure under which a rival or a customer can sue to declare an intellectual property right non-infringed or unenforceable for a number of reasons. So the legislature, via the IP laws, has struck a balance between the rights of IP owners, the rights of consumers, and concerns for a competitive marketplace. This may or may not be the correct balance; nevertheless, it is the one the legislature has chosen.

It is important to understand precisely what reward is offered by the IP laws. Each type of IP right provides "exclusivity" for its owner. What does this exclusivity mean? It does not mean a right to commercialize any invention or creation. The owner of an improvement patent, for example, may find itself blocked from practicing its own patent if it cannot secure permission from the original patentee. Instead, what IP rights provide is the right to exclude others. The right to exclude is not simply one of the rights provided by intellectual property, it is the fundamental right, the foundation upon which the entire IP system is built.

III.   Specific Practices and the Freedom to License

These bedrock principles of antitrust and intellectual property law inform the proper approach to specific licensing and IP-related practices. A decade's experience with the Guidelines, together with subsequent judicial precedent, provides reliable guidance on several issues in the U.S. On many, but not all, of these issues, it is also possible to rely on continued transatlantic convergence.

Unilateral Refusals to License Technology

The subject of unilateral refusals to license intellectual property is one in which the premise that IP is essentially like other forms of property has sometimes been stretched beyond sensible limits. Because, outside the area of IP, antitrust law holds out the possibility of rare exceptions to the principle that parties are free unilaterally to refuse to deal with others, the argument is that there must therefore be some circumstance in which the unilateral, unconditional refusal to license a patent must constitute an antitrust violation. With a single much-criticized exception, this is an argument that has never found support in any U.S. legal decision. At this point in the development of U.S. law, it is safe to say that this argument is without merit.

A unilateral, unconditional refusal to license a valid patent cannot, by itself, result in antitrust liability under U.S. law. It is instructive that the very notion of such liability was not even discussed in the 1995 Guidelines. Instead, the Guidelines unequivocally state that, even in the case of IP that conveys market or monopoly power, that power does not "impose on the intellectual property owner an obligation to license the use of that property to others." This is hardly surprising, as the right to choose whether the license has long been recognized by the U.S. Supreme Court as the core of the patent right. Although the Supreme Court decisions are not directly on point, lower courts have correctly held that the unilateral, unconditional refusal to license a valid patent does not give rise to liability as an improper refusal to deal under Section 2 of the Sherman Act. But of course, while an intellectual property owner has the right to decide not to license its technology, the owner does not have the right to impose conditions on licensees that would effectively extend an intellectual property right beyond the limits of the Patent Act.

The clarity of U.S. law on unilateral refusals was enhanced by last year's Supreme Court decision in *Verizon Communications Inc. v. Law Offices of Curtis V. Trinko, LLP*. In *Trinko*, the Supreme Court found that private plaintiffs did not state an antitrust claim when they alleged a failure by a communications provider, Verizon, to provide adequate assistance to its rivals. The Court showed great skepticism about expanding liability for the refusal to deal because such liability "may lessen the incentive for the monopolist, the rival, or both to invest in . . . economically beneficial facilities" and "also requires antitrust courts to act as central planners . . . a role for which they are ill-suited." The Court posed the question as being whether the narrow list of exceptions to the general rule against liability should be expanded. Although *Trinko* was not an intellectual property case — the rights in that case were governed by the Telecommunications Act — the Supreme Court would apply similar logic under the Patent Act. Given the many cases indicating that the right to exclude is a fundamental right embodied in the patent grant, it is safe to say that liability for the unilateral, unconditional refusal to license a valid patent is not going to be added to the narrow list of exceptions the Court mentioned.

When analyzing the effects of a unilateral refusal to deal, one cannot merely consider the effect on a rival that is refused a license; one must also consider the alternative world in which the IP owner would have had less of an incentive to innovate because he could not be assured of the right to refuse to license. Would that IP owner have chosen to innovate less? If so, would competition or consumer welfare have been better off with the present state of affairs, including the right to refuse? In the short term, it will always be more efficient to disregard the IP right and allow duplication. The IP system rests on the idea of long-term innovation incentives, so we must think about the long-term effects of a rule imposing liability in this context. That is entirely consistent with antitrust policy related to exclusionary conduct, which also focuses on dynamic competition and long-term effects. Where we cannot reliably predict the effects of enforcement decisions, false positives are likely, and the increased uncertainty itself will raise costs to businesses and enforcers.

It is useful to remember that the creation of intellectual property tends to add to consumer choices, rather than to reduce them. The development of intellectual property for new technological solutions usually does not cause older solutions to be withdrawn from a marketplace; instead, it increases competition, which tends to erode the prices of the old solutions over time, increasing choice and consumer welfare. Of course, a patent sometimes issues for an obvious or previously-known solution to a problem, but such a patent should be invalidated, and the proper remedy is to seek invalidation under the patent laws.

Does this mean that the policy on unilateral refusals conflicts with EU law as stated in *IMS Health?* At this time, that it is difficult to tell. The European Court of Justice decision, issued a year ago, began by stating that a refusal to license a copyright "cannot in itself" constitute an abuse of a dominant position. That seems to match the U.S. view on unilateral refusals to license. But the court added that liability might occur if: (1) the refusal prevents the emergence of a new product for which consumer demand exists; (2) the refusal is not justified by any objective considerations; and (3) the refusal excludes competition in a "secondary market." It is not clear how these three factors will be interpreted, or whether the same reasoning would apply to other contexts such as a refusal to license a patent. (Some have observed that the IP right asserted in IMS was relatively weak, and that the lack of a unified European system of IP rights may explain differing attitudes toward antitrust liability in this context.) It will be interesting to see how the *IMS Health* decision is applied, for example in the *Microsoft* appeal. While the Justice Department required Microsoft to make certain IP available to its competitors as part of the agreed remedy for antitrust violations, the European Commission imposed liability for the failure to make IP available. It will be up to the Court of First Instance to determine whether this was permissible under EU law.

"Excessive" Royalties in Standard Setting and Beyond

The Antitrust Division sometimes hears complaints about demands for large royalties. Most frequently, although not always, the complaints arise in the context of a technical standard. According to the complainants, one or more patent holders can "hold up" licensees by waiting until participants are locked into the standard, then charging an allegedly "excessive" royalty for patents that cover the standard. The U.S. Federal Trade Commission has brought antitrust enforcement actions related to this issue in two recent cases, *Rambus* and *Unocal*. Both cases are ongoing.

Bringing a complaint to the Antitrust Division about "excessive" royalties, without more, is a losing strategy. Antitrust enforcers are not in the business of price control. We protect a competitive process, not a particular result, and particularly not a specific price. In fact, if a monopoly is lawfully obtained, whether derived from IP rights or otherwise, we do not even object to setting a monopoly price. A high patent royalty rate, after all, might just reflect that the Patent Act is functioning correctly and the market is rewarding an inventor for a pioneering invention. When a complainant begins a presentation by telling the Antitrust Division that a royalty rate is "excessive," the staff responds that the complainant is putting the cart before the horse. A complaining party must first identify some anticompetitive conduct beyond a mere unilateral refusal to license and beyond the mere attempt to charge, where a lawful monopoly exists, a monopoly price.

Many situations of standard setting "hold up" can be mitigated by disclosure in the ex ante phase, before the standard is set. For example, if all participants are required to disclose their financial interest in any version of the standard — including any patents they own or are seeking on the technology — other participants can adjust their behavior accordingly. If a participant agrees to disclose but then fails to do so, it can be liable for breach of contract or fraud. Such liability would hinge on a pattern of breaches, frauds, or other unlawful conduct. If antitrust liability is also contemplated, it would require, in addition, proof of market effects.

Increasingly, standards development organizations are requiring "reasonable and non-discriminatory" (RAND) licensing, which is a partial solution. A difficulty of RAND, however, is that the parties tend to disagree later about what level of royalty rate is "reasonable." It would be useful to clarify the legal status of ex ante negotiations over price. Some standards development organizations have reported to the Department of Justice that they currently avoid any discussion of actual royalty rates, due in part to fear of antitrust liability. It would be a strange result if antitrust policy is being used to prevent price competition. There is a possibility of anticompetitive effects from ex ante license fee negotiations, but it seems only reasonable to balance that concern against the inefficiencies of ex post negotiations and licensing hold up. It is interesting to note that the EU licensing guidelines already address this point: in their Paragraph 225, the guidelines state that firms normally should be allowed to negotiate royalty rates before a standard setting effort, as well as after a standard is set.

Barriers to discussing licensing rates may not be entirely law-related. Some standard setting participants do not want the distraction of considering licensing terms. Engineers and other technical contributors may prefer to leave the lawyers at home and limit discussions to technical issues alone. So there may be powerful incentives to keep the status quo. If that is the case, this may be yet another area where the outcomes can be imperfect but antitrust does not provide a solution.

Compulsory Licensing

Compulsory licensing is another place where enforcers need to be fully aware of antitrust's limitations. Licensing can be an effective remedy in some contexts; for example, for merger cases, it can serve as a less drastic alternative to a divestiture. But in the first instance, there must be conduct that warrants a remedy — licensing is only a remedy, not a liability theory. And there are practical reasons to tread carefully when considering compulsory licensing: designing and enforcing such licenses is complex and can be an invitation to endless ancillary compliance litigation. As explained in the Trinko case, an enforcement agency should not impose a duty to deal that it cannot reasonably supervise, since this risks assuming the day-to-day controls characteristic of a regulatory agency. For these and other reasons, compulsory licensing of intellectual property as an antitrust remedy should be a rare beast.

"Excessive Patenting" and Patent Enforceability

There has been much talk in recent years, and perhaps worldwide, about whether there is a problem of "excessive patenting," meaning patents being granted too easily or in too great a number. Of course, it is the job of the U.S. Patent and Trademark Office in the Department of Commerce — not the Department of Justice — to make and regulate awards of patent rights. The PTO has mechanisms for reconsidering specific patents and hearing complaints about the patent system as a whole, and it employs untold hundreds of patent experts. The Federal Trade Commission, an independent agency, has issued a useful report on possible improvements to the patent system. The National Academies have also issued a report.

It is open to question whether antitrust analysis, which is specific and effects-based, can be applied to a question as broad as "excessive patenting." To know whether patenting is excessive, we would first have to make a conclusion about the "but-for" world. If fewer patents were granted, would innovation have decreased? Would firms have reduced their research and development in areas that currently are covered by patents, and would the result have been fewer benefits for consumers? Antitrust enforcement is not well suited to answering such questions. These questions should be directed, instead, to the patent authorities or to legislators.

Of course, this point must not be overstated. Part of the patent system is court review of patent enforceability. In the appropriate case the Antitrust Division will examine enforceability and, if necessary, challenge the validity or scope of a patent as part of an antitrust claim. This is not necessary where a patent-related practice will be lawful (or at least, does not violate the antitrust laws) or unlawful regardless of the patent's enforceability. But if the conduct would have violated the antitrust laws in the absence of patent rights, is difficult to address fundamental questions about the but-for world — here, meaning the world that would have existed without the allegedly anti-competitive patent-related practice — unless one knows whether the patent owner could have won an infringement claim. If the patent is valid, all entry before its expiration is a competitive "gift," but if it is invalid, any delay in entry due to threatened patent enforcement is a competitive harm. Just three months ago, an appellate court asserted this need to examine the but-for world in a case involving the antitrust analysis of a patent settlement. According to the court, it is impossible to measure a patent settlement's effect on competition unless one first makes a conclusion about the validity and enforceability of the patent. A petition for rehearing in that case is pending.

IP Rights and Market Power

Last on my list of specific issues is the concept of market power. Intellectual property cannot be presumed to establish market power. While intellectual property grants exclusive rights, these rights are not monopolies in the economic sense: they do not necessarily provide a large share of any commercial market and they do not necessarily lead to the ability to raise prices in a market. A single patent, for example, may have dozens of close substitutes. The mere presence of an intellectual property right does not permit an antitrust enforcer to skip the crucial steps of market definition and determining market effects.

In the view of the Department of Justice and the Federal Trade Commission, the idea that IP rights cannot be presumed to create market power is a settled question. Interestingly, however, there is still some debate in courts that decide private party antitrust claims. In the January 2005 case *Independent Ink*, the Federal Circuit — which handles all direct patent appeals in the United States — held that Supreme Court precedent compelled it to conclude that a patent does raise a presumption of market power in an IP tying case. But even the Federal Circuit disagreed with the presumption; in fact, the Federal Circuit's opinion invited the Supreme Court to reverse. The patentees in this case filed a petition for Supreme Court review. If the Supreme Court agrees to take the case, it would provide a good opportunity to settle the question once and for all.

Many other IP issues arise at the competition law interface. With respect to patent pools, the Antitrust Division has issued several "Business Review Letters" analyzing proposed licensing arrangements. Package licensing, bundling, and tying all receive some coverage in our Guidelines. Our general approach is to avoid rigid tests and instead rely on a review of the likely economic effects to the marketplace as a whole, both in the short term and over the long term, factoring in incentives for pro-competitive innovation. Both IP law and competition law seek to maintain dynamic, robustly innovative markets far into the future, and to that end they properly are willing to tolerate — or rather, offer the inducement of — a degree of private reward and market power in the present day.

IV. Conclusion

We have made great strides in the United States in bringing sound economics to the antitrust analysis of intellectual property. Europe is doing the same with the newly revised Technology Transfer Block Exemption and its accompanying licensing guidelines, both of which embrace an effects-based analysis for licensing transactions. We have experienced significant international convergence in this area and we have every reason to expect more of the same. While some differences remain between the U.S., the EU, and our other important trading partners, the general trend toward convergence is continuing.

NOTES & QUESTIONS

1. The speech by then Assistant Attorney General Pate provides a nice overview of the legal issues presented in this chapter as well as the government's ongoing concerns regarding the intellectual property-antitrust interface. Is the approach described in this speech consistent with the 1995 Guidelines? Mr. Pate certainly takes the Guidelines as his starting point. However, his analysis suggests views on antitrust enforcement that are both more strict and more lenient than those underlying the Guidelines. For example, his emphasis on exclusivity as the foundational right of intellectual property would allow wide room for antitrust enforcement that would curtail business activities involving intellectual property. If an intellectual property owner has only a right to exclude parties from infringing conduct, then the right to commercialize protected intellectual property can still be broadly limited under antitrust laws. At the same time, Mr. Pate suggests that an owner might have wide latitude to license intellectual property, free from the restrictions of antitrust law. Notice Mr. Pate's discussion of the *Trinko* decision, a telecommunications case in which Justice Scalia stated that the Sherman Act "does not give judges carte blanche to insist that a monopolist alter its way of doing business whenever some other approach might yield greater competition." 540 US at 416. What this statement means is not completely clear, but the *Trinko* decision suggests that there may be broad limits to antitrust law when Congress has created exclusive property rights in a particular area to further a regulatory purpose, as Congress did with rights created as part of schemes for telecommunications regulation. Mr. Pate is suggesting that antitrust laws might have similar limitations in the connection with intellectual property rights. The 1995 Guidelines do not go so far as to say that Congress has wide latitude in defining intellectual property rights, in contravention of antitrust laws.

2. The speech makes reference to several cases, some of which (like *Rambus* and *Unocal*) will be discussed below. Mr. Pate expressly discussed a European Union case called *IMS*, which can be found at *IMS Health GmbH & Co. OHG*, Case C-418/01 (April 29, 2004). The case had to do with allegedly anticompetitive uses of a database of pharmaceutical suppliers. As Mr. Pate, the European Union's decision has been a source of ongoing confusion and controversy as the court attempted to balance intellectual property and competition concerns. The treatment of intellectual property under competition law in the European Union is the focus of discussions in Section E, below, particularly with reference to the *Microsoft* case.

3. Standard setting raises very important issues regarding the management of intellectual property and the relationship of the implementations of standards with antitrust law. As Mr. Pate stated in an omitted footnote: "Standards development organizations have identified Sony *Electronics, Inc. v. Soundview Technologies, Inc.*, 157 F. Supp. 2d 180 (D. Conn. 2001), as a case that raises the possibility of antitrust liability for ex ante negotiations. In that decision, a district court refused to dismiss an antitrust claim based on an allegation that standards setters made a group decision, after a standard had been adopted, to refuse to license a patent and to sue to have the patent invalidated. Although the court refused to dismiss the antitrust claim in an initial pretrial ruling, it later dismissed the claim when the patent was found to be invalid." We will discuss standard setting in greater detail below in the context of the Dell consent decree.

4. In 2003 and 2004, the patent system was under intense scrutiny by the FTC and the National Academy of Sciences, each of which released detailed reports identifying potentially anticompetitive effects of the patent system. *See* Fed. Trade Comm'n, To Promote Innovation: The Proper Balance of Competition and Patent Law and Policy (2003); National Academy of Sciences, A Patent System for the 21st Century (2004).

5. Two cases in 2005 illustrate the continuing controversy over the proper balance between intellectual property and antitrust law. In *Schering-Plough Corp. v. FTC*, 402 F3d 1056 (11th Cir. 2005), the appellate court overruled a finding by the district court that a settlement agreement requiring a generic drug manufacturer to stay out of a market was anticompetitive. In *Independent Ink, Inc. v. Illinois Tool Works, Inc.*, 396 F.3d 1342 (Fed. Cir. 2005), the Federal Circuit held that ownership of a patent created the presumption of market power for a tying claim. The Supreme Court will be reviewing the *Independent Ink* decision in its 2005-2006 term to clarify the relationship between patents and market power.

6. Mr. Pate concludes his speech by emphasizing a convergence in United States and European Union competition law towards the use of an effects test in analyzing the uses of intellectual property. The effects test is often advocated as a means to inject economic and business reality into antitrust law. On the other hand, the effects test may also introduce a lack of clarity and predictability into antitrust analyses. Keep this tension in mind when reading the materials below.

C. IMPROPER CONDUCT

1. Restricting Competitors

UNITED STATES v. MICROSOFT
United States Court of Appeals for the District of Columbia
253 F.3d 34 (D.C. Cir. 2001) (Per Curiam)

I. Introduction

A. Background

In July 1994, officials at the Department of Justice ("DOJ"), on behalf of the United States, filed suit against Microsoft, charging the company with, among other things, unlawfully maintaining a monopoly in the operating system market through anticompetitive terms in its licensing and software developer agreements. The parties subsequently entered into a consent decree, thus avoiding a trial on the merits. *See United States v. Microsoft Corp.,* 56 F.3d 1448 (D.C. Cir. 1995) ("Microsoft I"). Three years later, the Justice Department filed a civil contempt action against Microsoft for allegedly violating one of the decree's provisions. On appeal from a grant of a preliminary injunction, this court held that Microsoft's technological bundling of IE 3.0 and 4.0 with Windows 95 did not violate the relevant provision of the consent decree. *United States v. Microsoft Corp.,* 147 F.3d 935 (D.C. Cir. 1998) ("Microsoft II"). We expressly reserved the question whether such bundling might independently violate §§ 1 or 2 of the Sherman Act.

On May 18, 1998, shortly before issuance of the Microsoft II decision, the United States and a group of State plaintiffs filed separate (and soon thereafter consolidated) complaints, asserting antitrust violations by Microsoft and seeking preliminary and permanent injunctions against the company's allegedly unlawful conduct. The complaints also sought any "other preliminary and permanent relief as is necessary and appropriate to restore competitive conditions in the markets affected by Microsoft's unlawful conduct." Relying almost exclusively on Microsoft's varied efforts to unseat Netscape Navigator as the preeminent internet browser, plaintiffs charged four distinct violations of the Sherman Act: (1) unlawful exclusive dealing arrangements in violation of § 1; (2) unlawful tying of IE to Windows 95 and Windows 98 in violation of § 1; (3) unlawful maintenance of a monopoly in the PC operating system market in violation of § 2; and (4) unlawful attempted monopolization of the internet browser market in violation of § 2. The States also brought pendent claims charging Microsoft with violations of various State antitrust laws.

The District Court scheduled the case on a "fast track." The hearing on the preliminary injunction and the trial on the merits were consolidated pursuant to Fed. R. Civ. P. 65(a)(2). The trial was then scheduled to commence on September 8, 1998, less than four months after the complaints had been filed. In a series of pretrial orders, the District Court limited each side to a maximum of 12 trial witnesses plus two rebuttal witnesses. It required that all trial witnesses' direct testimony be submitted to the court in the form of written declarations. The District Court also made allowances for the use of deposition testimony at trial to prove subordinate or predicate issues. Following the grant of three brief continuances, the trial started on October 19, 1998.

After a 76-day bench trial, the District Court issued its Findings of Fact. *United States v. Microsoft Corp.*, 84 F. Supp. 2d 9 (D.D.C. 1999) ("Findings of Fact"). This triggered two independent courses of action. First, the District Court established a schedule for briefing on possible legal conclusions, inviting Professor Lawrence Lessig to participate as amicus curiae. Second, the District Court referred the case to mediation to afford the parties an opportunity to settle their differences. The Honorable Richard A. Posner, Chief Judge of the United States Court of Appeals for the Seventh Circuit, was appointed to serve as mediator. The parties concurred in the referral to mediation and in the choice of mediator.

Mediation failed after nearly four months of settlement talks between the parties. On April 3, 2000, with the parties' briefs having been submitted and considered, the District Court issued its conclusions of law. The District Court found Microsoft liable on the § 1 tying and § 2 monopoly maintenance and attempted monopolization claims, Conclusions of Law, at 35-51, while ruling that there was insufficient evidence to support a § 1 exclusive dealing violation. As to the pendent State actions, the District Court found the State antitrust laws conterminous with §§ 1 and 2 of the Sherman Act, thereby obviating the need for further State- specific analysis. In those few cases where a State's law required an additional showing of intrastate impact on competition, the District Court found the requirement easily satisfied on the evidence at hand.

Having found Microsoft liable on all but one count, the District Court then asked plaintiffs to submit a proposed remedy. Plaintiffs' proposal for a remedial order was subsequently filed within four weeks, along with six supplemental declarations and over 50 new exhibits. In their proposal, plaintiffs sought specific conduct remedies, plus structural relief that would split Microsoft into an applications company and an operating systems company. The District Court rejected Microsoft's request for further evidentiary proceedings and, following a single hearing on the merits of the remedy question, issued its Final Judgment on June 7, 2000. The District Court adopted plaintiffs' proposed remedy without substantive change.

Microsoft filed a notice of appeal within a week after the District Court issued its Final Judgment. This court then ordered that any proceedings before it be heard by the court sitting en banc. Before any substantive matters were addressed by this court, however, the District Court certified appeal of the case brought by the United States directly to the Supreme Court pursuant to 15 U.S.C. § 29(b), while staying the final judgment order in the federal and state cases pending appeal. The States thereafter petitioned the Supreme Court for a writ of certiorari in their case. The Supreme Court declined to hear the appeal of the Government's case and remanded the matter to this court; the Court likewise denied the States' petition for writ of certiorari. *Microsoft Corp. v. United States*, 530 U.S. 1301 (2000). This consolidated appeal followed.

B.   Overview

Before turning to the merits of Microsoft's various arguments, we pause to reflect briefly on two matters of note, one practical and one theoretical.

The practical matter relates to the temporal dimension of this case. The litigation timeline in this case is hardly problematic. Indeed, it is noteworthy that a case of this magnitude and complexity has proceeded from the filing of complaints through trial to appellate decision in a mere three years. See, e.g., *Data Gen. Corp. v. Grumman Sys. Support Corp.*, 36 F.3d 1147, 1155 (1st Cir. 1994) (six years from filing of complaint to appellate decision); *Transamerica Computer Co., Inc. v. IBM*, 698 F.2d 1377, 1381 (9th Cir. 1983) (over four years from start of trial to appellate decision); *United States v. United Shoe Mach. Corp.*, 110 F. Supp. 295, 298 (D. Mass. 1953) (over five years from filing of complaint to trial court decision).

What is somewhat problematic, however, is that just over six years have passed since Microsoft engaged in the first conduct plaintiffs allege to be anticompetitive. As the record in this case indicates, six years seems like an eternity in the computer industry. By the time a court can assess liability, firms, products, and the marketplace are likely to have changed dramatically. This, in turn, threatens enormous practical difficulties for courts considering the appropriate measure of relief in equitable enforcement actions, both in crafting injunctive remedies in the first instance and reviewing those remedies in the second. Conduct remedies may be unavailing in such cases, because innovation to a large degree has already rendered the anticompetitive conduct obsolete (although by no means harmless). And broader structural remedies present their own set of problems, including how a court goes about restoring competition to a dramatically changed, and constantly changing, marketplace. That is just one reason why we find the District Court's refusal in the present case to hold an evidentiary hearing on remedies — to update and flesh out the available information before seriously entertaining the possibility of dramatic structural relief — so problematic.

We do not mean to say that enforcement actions will no longer play an important role in curbing infringements of the antitrust laws in technologically dynamic markets, nor do we assume this in assessing the merits of this case. Even in those cases where forward-looking remedies appear limited, the Government will continue to have an interest in defining the contours of the antitrust laws so that law-abiding firms will have a clear sense of what is permissible and what is not. And the threat of private damage actions will remain to deter those firms inclined to test the limits of the law.

The second matter of note is more theoretical in nature. We decide this case against a backdrop of significant debate amongst academics and practitioners over the extent to which "old economy" § 2 monopolization doctrines should apply to firms competing in dynamic technological markets characterized by network effects. In markets characterized by network effects, one product or standard tends towards dominance, because "the utility that a user derives from consumption of the good increases with the number of other agents consuming the good." Michael L. Katz & Carl Shapiro, *Network Externalities, Competition, and Compatibility,* 75 Am. Econ. Rev. 424, 424

(1985). For example, "[a]n individual consumer's demand to use (and hence her benefit from) the telephone network . . . increases with the number of other users on the network whom she can call or from whom she can receive calls." Howard A. Shelanski & J. Gregory Sidak, *Antitrust Divestiture in Network Industries*, 68 U. Chi. L. Rev. 1, 8 (2001). Once a product or standard achieves wide acceptance, it becomes more or less en- trenched. Competition in such industries is "for the field" rather than "within the field." See Harold Demsetz, *Why Regulate Utilities?*, 11 J.L. & Econ. 55, 57 & n.7 (1968) (emphasis omitted).

In technologically dynamic markets, however, such entrenchment may be temporary, because innovation may alter the field altogether. See Joseph A. Schumpeter, CAPITALISM, SOCIALISM AND DEMOCRACY 81-90 (Harper Perennial 1976) (1942). Rapid technological change leads to markets in which "firms compete through innovation for temporary market dominance, from which they may be displaced by the next wave of product advancements." Shelanski & Sidak, at 11-12 (discussing Schumpeterian competition, which proceeds "sequentially over time rather than simultaneously across a market"). Microsoft argues that the operating system market is just such a market.

Whether or not Microsoft's characterization of the operating system market is correct does not appreciably alter our mission in assessing the alleged antitrust violations in the present case. As an initial matter, we note that there is no consensus among commentators on the question of whether, and to what extent, current monopolization doctrine should be amended to account for competition in technologically dynamic markets characterized by network effects. Compare Steven C. Salop & R. Craig Romaine, *Preserving Monopoly: Economic Analysis, Legal Standards, and Microsoft*, 7 Geo. Mason L. Rev. 617, 654-55, 663-64 (1999) (arguing that exclusionary conduct in high-tech networked industries de- serves heightened antitrust scrutiny in part because it may threaten to deter innovation), with Ronald A. Cass & Keith N. Hylton, Preserving *Competition: Economic Analysis, Legal Standards and Microsoft*, 8 Geo. Mason L. Rev. 1, 36-39 (1999) (equivocating on the antitrust implications of network effects and noting that the presence of network exter-nalities may actually encourage innovation by guaranteeing more durable monopolies to innovating winners). Indeed, there is some suggestion that the economic consequences of network effects and technological dynamism act to offset one another, thereby making it difficult to formulate categorical antitrust rules absent a particularized analysis of a given market. See Shelanski & Sidak, at 6-7 ("High profit margins might appear to be the benign and necessary recovery of legitimate investment returns in a Schumpeterian framework, but they might represent exploitation of customer lock-in and monopoly power when viewed through the lens of network eco-nomics. . . . The issue is particularly complex because, in network industries characterized by rapid innovation, both forces may be operating and can be difficult to isolate.").

Moreover, it should be clear that Microsoft makes no claim that anticom-petitive conduct should be assessed differently in technologically dynamic markets. It claims only that the measure of monopoly power should be differ-ent. [W]e reject Microsoft's monopoly power argument.

II. Monopolization

. . .

B. Anticompetitive Conduct

A firm violates § 2 only when it acquires or maintains, or attempts to acquire or maintain, a monopoly by engaging in exclusionary conduct "as distinguished from growth or development as a consequence of a superior product, business acumen, or historic accident."

In this case, after concluding that Microsoft had monopoly power, the District Court held that Microsoft had violated § 2 by engaging in a variety of exclusionary acts (not including predatory pricing), to maintain its monopoly by preventing the effective distribution and use of products that might threaten that monopoly. Specifically, the District Court held Microsoft liable for: (1) the way in which it integrated IE into Windows; (2) its various dealings with Original Equipment Manufacturers ("OEMs"), Internet Access Providers ("IAPs"), Internet Content Providers ("ICPs"), Independent Software Vendors ("ISVs"), and Apple Computer; (3) its efforts to contain and to subvert Java technologies; and (4) its course of conduct as a whole. Upon appeal, Microsoft argues that it did not engage in any exclusionary conduct.

Whether any particular act of a monopolist is exclusionary, rather than merely a form of vigorous competition, can be difficult to discern: the means of illicit exclusion, like the means of legitimate competition, are myriad. The challenge for an antitrust court lies in stating a general rule for distinguishing between exclusionary acts, which reduce social welfare, and competitive acts, which increase it.

From a century of case law on monopolization under § 2, however, several principles do emerge. First, to be condemned as exclusionary, a monopolist's act must have an "anticompetitive effect." That is, it must harm the competitive process and thereby harm consumers. In contrast, harm to one or more competitors will not suffice. "The [Sherman Act] directs itself not against conduct which is competitive, even severely so, but against conduct which unfairly tends to destroy competition itself."

Second, the plaintiff, on whom the burden of proof of course rests, must demonstrate that the monopolist's conduct indeed has the requisite anticompetitive effect. In a case brought by a private plaintiff, the plaintiff must show that its injury is "of 'the type that the statute was intended to forestall,'"; no less in a case brought by the Government, it must demonstrate that the monopolist's conduct harmed competition, not just a competitor.

Third, if a plaintiff successfully establishes a prima facie case under § 2 by demonstrating anticompetitive effect, then the monopolist may proffer a "pro-competitive justification" for its conduct. If the monopolist asserts a pro-competitive justification — a non-pretextual claim that its conduct is indeed a form of competition on the merits because it involves, for example, greater efficiency or enhanced consumer appeal — then the burden shifts back to the plaintiff to rebut that claim.

Fourth, if the monopolist's pro-competitive justification stands unrebutted, then the plaintiff must demonstrate that the anticompetitive harm of the conduct outweighs the pro-competitive benefit. In cases arising under § 1 of the Sherman Act, the courts routinely apply a similar balancing approach under the rubric of the "rule of reason." The source of the rule of reason is *Standard Oil Co. v. United States,* 221 U.S. 1, 31 S.Ct. 502, 55 L.Ed. 619 (1911), in which the Supreme Court used that term to describe the proper inquiry under both sections of the Act. As the Fifth Circuit more recently explained, "[i]t is clear . . . that the analysis under section 2 is similar to that under section 1 regardless whether the rule of reason label is applied. . . ."

Finally, in considering whether the monopolist's conduct on balance harms competition and is therefore condemned as exclusionary for purposes of § 2, our focus is upon the effect of that conduct, not upon the intent behind it. Evidence of the intent behind the conduct of a monopolist is relevant only to the extent it helps us understand the likely effect of the monopolist's conduct.

With these principles in mind, we now consider Microsoft's objections to the District Court's holding that Microsoft violated § 2 of the Sherman Act in a variety of ways.

1. Licenses Issued to Original Equipment Manufacturers

The District Court condemned a number of provisions in Microsoft's agreements licensing Windows to OEMs, because it found that Microsoft's imposition of those provisions (like many of Microsoft's other actions at issue in this case) serves to reduce usage share of Netscape's browser and, hence, protect Microsoft's operating system monopoly. The reason market share in the browser market affects market power in the operating system market is complex, and warrants some explanation.

Browser usage share is important because. . . a browser (or any middleware product, for that matter) must have a critical mass of users in order to attract software developers to write applications relying upon the APIs it exposes, and away from the APIs exposed by Windows. Applications written to a particular browser's APIs, however, would run on any computer with that browser, regardless of the underlying operating system. "The overwhelming majority of consumers will only use a PC operating system for which there already exists a large and varied set of . . . applications, and for which it seems relatively certain that new types of applications and new versions of existing applications will continue to be marketed. . . ." If a consumer could have access to the applications he desired — regardless of the operating system he uses — simply by installing a particular browser on his computer, then he would no longer feel compelled to select Windows in order to have access to those applications; he could select an operating system other than Windows based solely upon its quality and price. In other words, the market for operating systems would be competitive.

Therefore, Microsoft's efforts to gain market share in one market (browsers) served to meet the threat to Microsoft's monopoly in another market (operating systems) by keeping rival browsers from gaining the critical mass of users necessary to attract developer attention away from Windows as the platform for software development. Plaintiffs also argue that Microsoft's actions injured competition in the browser market — an argument we will examine below in relation to their specific claims that Microsoft attempted to monopolize the browser market and unlawfully tied its browser to its operating system so as to foreclose competition in the browser market. In evaluating the § 2 monopoly maintenance claim, however, our immediate concern is with the anticompetitive effect of Microsoft's conduct in preserving its monopoly in the operating system market.

In evaluating the restrictions in Microsoft's agreements licensing Windows to OEMs, we first consider whether plaintiffs have made out a prima facie case by demonstrating that the restrictions have an anticompetitive effect. In the next subsection, we conclude that plaintiffs have met this burden as to all the restrictions. We then consider Microsoft's proffered justifications for the restrictions and, for the most part, hold those justifications insufficient.

a.   Anticompetitive effect of the license restrictions

The restrictions Microsoft places upon Original Equipment Manufacturers are of particular importance in determining browser usage share because having an OEM pre-install a browser on a computer is one of the two most cost-effective methods by far of distributing browsing software. (The other is bundling the browser with internet access software distributed by an IAP.) The District Court found that the restrictions Microsoft imposed in licensing Windows to OEMs prevented many OEMs from distributing browsers other than IE. In particular, the District Court condemned the license provisions prohibiting the OEMs from: (1) removing any desktop icons, folders, or "Start" menu entries; (2) altering the initial boot sequence; and (3) otherwise altering the appearance of the Windows desktop.

The District Court concluded that the first license restriction — the prohibition upon the removal of desktop icons, folders, and Start menu entries — thwarts the distribution of a rival browser by preventing OEMs from removing visible means of user access to IE. The OEMs cannot practically install a second browser in addition to IE, the court found, in part because "[p]re-installing more than one product in a given category . . . can significantly increase an OEM's support costs, for the redundancy can lead to confusion among novice users." That is, a certain number of novice computer users, seeing two browser icons, will wonder which to use when and will call the OEM's support line. Support calls are extremely expensive and, in the highly competitive original equipment market, firms have a strong incentive to minimize costs.

Microsoft denies the "consumer confusion" story; it observes that some OEMs do install multiple browsers and that executives from two OEMs that do so denied any knowledge of consumers being confused by multiple icons.

Other testimony, however, supports the District Court's finding that fear of such confusion deters many OEMs from pre-installing multiple browsers. Most telling, in presentations to OEMs, Microsoft itself represented that having only one icon in a particular category would be "less confusing for end users." Accordingly, we reject Microsoft's argument that we should vacate the District Court's Finding of Fact 159 as it relates to consumer confusion.

As noted above, the OEM channel is one of the two primary channels for distribution of browsers. By preventing OEMs from removing visible means of user access to IE, the license restriction prevents many OEMs from pre-installing a rival browser and, therefore, protects Microsoft's monopoly from the competition that middleware might otherwise present. Therefore, we conclude that the license restriction at issue is anticompetitive. We defer for the moment the question whether that anticompetitive effect is outweighed by Microsoft's proffered justifications.

The second license provision at issue prohibits OEMs from modifying the initial boot sequence — the process that occurs the first time a consumer turns on the computer. Prior to the imposition of that restriction, "among the programs that many OEMs inserted into the boot sequence were Internet sign-up procedures that encouraged users to choose from a list of IAPs assembled by the OEM." Microsoft's prohibition on any alteration of the boot sequence thus prevents OEMs from using that process to promote the services of IAPs, many of which — at least at the time Microsoft imposed the restriction — used Navigator rather than IE in their internet access software. (Upon learning of OEM practices including boot sequence modification, Microsoft's Chairman, Bill Gates, wrote: "Apparently a lot of OEMs are bundling non-Microsoft browsers and coming up with offerings together with [IAPs] that get displayed on their machines in a FAR more prominent way than MSN or our Internet browser."). Microsoft does not deny that the prohibition on modifying the boot sequence has the effect of decreasing competition against IE by preventing OEMs from promoting rivals' browsers. Because this prohibition has a substantial effect in protecting Microsoft's market power, and does so through a means other than competition on the merits, it is anticompetitive. Again the question whether the provision is nonetheless justified awaits later treatment.

Finally, Microsoft imposes several additional provisions that, like the prohibition on removal of icons, prevent OEMs from making various alterations to the desktop: Microsoft prohibits OEMs from causing any user interface other than the Windows desktop to launch automatically, from adding icons or folders different in size or shape from those supplied by Microsoft, and from using the "Active Desktop" feature to promote third-party brands. These restrictions impose significant costs upon the OEMs; prior to Microsoft's prohibiting the practice, many OEMs would change the appearance of the desktop in ways they found beneficial. (March 1997 letter from Hewlett-Packard to Microsoft: "We are responsible for the cost of technical support of our customers, including the 33% of calls we get related to the lack of quality or confusion generated by your product.... We must have more ability to decide how our system is presented to our end users. If we had a choice of another supplier, based on your actions in this area, I assure you [that you] would not be our supplier of choice.").

The dissatisfaction of the OEM customers does not, of course, mean the restrictions are anticompetitive. The anticompetitive effect of the license restrictions is, as Microsoft itself recognizes, that OEMs are not able to promote rival browsers, which keeps developers focused upon the APIs in

Windows. This kind of promotion is not a zero-sum game; but for the restrictions in their licenses to use Windows, OEMs could promote multiple IAPs and browsers. By preventing the OEMs from doing so, this type of license restriction, like the first two restrictions, is anticompetitive: Microsoft reduced rival browsers' usage share not by improving its own product but, rather, by preventing OEMs from taking actions that could increase rivals' share of usage.

b.   Microsoft's justifications for the license restrictions

Microsoft argues that the license restrictions are legally justified because, in imposing them, Microsoft is simply "exercising its rights as the holder of valid copyrights." Microsoft also argues that the licenses "do not unduly restrict the opportunities of Netscape to distribute Navigator in any event."

Microsoft's primary copyright argument borders upon the frivolous. The company claims an absolute and unfettered right to use its intellectual property as it wishes: "[I]f intellectual property rights have been lawfully acquired," it says, then "their subsequent exercise cannot give rise to antitrust liability. That is no more correct than the proposition that use of one's personal property, such as a baseball bat, cannot give rise to tort liability. As the Federal Circuit succinctly stated: "Intellectual property rights do not confer a privilege to violate the antitrust laws." *In re Indep. Serv. Orgs. Antitrust Litig.,* 203 F.3d 1322, 1325 (Fed.Cir.2000).

Although Microsoft never overtly retreats from its bold and incorrect position on the law, it also makes two arguments to the effect that it is not exercising its copyright in an unreasonable manner, despite the anticompetitive consequences of the license restrictions discussed above. In the first variation upon its unqualified copyright defense, Microsoft cites two cases indicating that a copyright holder may limit a licensee's ability to engage in significant and deleterious alterations of a copyrighted work. The relevance of those two cases for the present one is limited, however, both because those cases involved substantial alterations of a copyrighted work, and because in neither case was there any claim that the copyright holder was, in asserting its rights, violating the antitrust laws.

The only license restriction Microsoft seriously defends as necessary to prevent a "substantial alteration" of its copyrighted work is the prohibition on OEMs automatically launching a substitute user interface upon completion of the boot process.   We agree that a shell that automatically prevents the Windows desktop from ever being seen by the user is a drastic alteration of Microsoft's copyrighted work, and outweighs the marginal anticompetitive effect of prohibiting the OEMs from substituting a different interface automatically upon completion of the initial boot process. We therefore hold that this particular restriction is not an exclusionary practice that violates § 2 of the Sherman Act.

In a second variation upon its copyright defense, Microsoft argues that the license restrictions merely prevent OEMs from taking actions that would reduce substantially the value of Microsoft's copyrighted work: that is, Microsoft claims each license restriction in question is necessary to prevent

OEMs from so altering Windows as to undermine "the principal value of Windows as a stable and consistent platform that supports a broad range of applications and that is familiar to users." Microsoft, however, never substantiates this claim, and, because an OEM's altering the appearance of the desktop or promoting programs in the boot sequence does not affect the code already in the product, the practice does not self-evidently affect either the "stability" or the "consistency" of the platform. Microsoft cites only one item of evidence in support of its claim that the OEMs' alterations were decreasing the value of Windows. That document, prepared by Microsoft itself, states: "there are quality issues created by OEMs who are too liberal with the preinstall process," referring to the OEMs' installation of Windows and additional software on their PCs, which the document says may result in "user concerns and confusion." To the extent the OEMs' modifications cause consumer confusion, of course, the OEMs bear the additional support costs. Therefore, we conclude Microsoft has not shown that the OEMs' liberality reduces the value of Windows except in the sense that their promotion of rival browsers undermines Microsoft's monopoly — and that is not a permissible justification for the license restrictions.

Apart from copyright, Microsoft raises one other defense of the OEM license agreements: It argues that, despite the restrictions in the OEM license, Netscape is not completely blocked from distributing its product. That claim is insufficient to shield Microsoft from liability for those restrictions because, although Microsoft did not bar its rivals from all means of distribution, it did bar them from the cost-efficient ones.

In sum, we hold that with the exception of the one restriction prohibiting automatically launched alternative interfaces, all the OEM license restrictions at issue represent uses of Microsoft's market power to protect its monopoly, unredeemed by any legitimate justification. The restrictions therefore violate § 2 of the Sherman Act.

2. Integration of IE and Windows

Although Microsoft's license restrictions have a significant effect in closing rival browsers out of one of the two primary channels of distribution, the District Court found that "Microsoft's executives believed . . . its contractual restrictions placed on OEMs would not be sufficient in themselves to reverse the direction of Navigator's usage share. Consequently, in late 1995 or early 1996, Microsoft set out to bind [IE] more tightly to Windows 95 as a technical matter."

Technologically binding IE to Windows, the District Court found, both prevented OEMs from pre-installing other browsers and deterred consumers from using them. In particular, having the IE software code as an irremovable part of Windows meant that pre-installing a second browser would "increase an OEM's product testing costs," because an OEM must test and train its support staff to answer calls related to every software product preinstalled on the machine; moreover, pre-installing a browser in addition to IE would to many OEMs be "a questionable use of the scarce and valuable space on a PC's hard drive."

Although the District Court, in its Conclusions of Law, broadly condemned Microsoft's decision to bind "Internet Explorer to Windows with . . . technological shackles," its findings of fact in support of that conclusion center upon three specific actions Microsoft took to weld IE to Windows: excluding IE from the "Add/Remove Programs" utility; designing Windows so as in certain circumstances to override the user's choice of a default browser other than IE; and commingling code related to browsing and other code in the same files, so that any attempt to delete the files containing IE would, at the same time, cripple the operating system. As with the license restrictions, we consider first whether the suspect actions had an anticompetitive effect, and then whether Microsoft has provided a pro-competitive justification for them.

a. Anticompetitive effect of integration

As a general rule, courts are properly very skeptical about claims that competition has been harmed by a dominant firm's product design changes. In a competitive market, firms routinely innovate in the hope of appealing to consumers, sometimes in the process making their products incompatible with those of rivals; the imposition of liability when a monopolist does the same thing will inevitably deter a certain amount of innovation. This is all the more true in a market, such as this one, in which the product itself is rapidly changing. Judicial deference to product innovation, however, does not mean that a monopolist's product design decisions are per se lawful.

The District Court first condemned as anticompetitive Microsoft's decision to exclude IE from the "Add/Remove Programs" utility in Windows 98. Microsoft had included IE in the Add/Remove Programs utility in Windows 95, but when it modified Windows 95 to produce Windows 98, it took IE out of the Add/Remove Programs utility. This change reduces the usage share of rival browsers not by making Microsoft's own browser more attractive to consumers but, rather, by discouraging OEMs from distributing rival products. Because Microsoft's conduct, through something other than competition on the merits, has the effect of significantly reducing usage of rivals' products and hence protecting its own operating system monopoly, it is anticompetitive; we defer for the moment the question whether it is nonetheless justified.

Second, the District Court found that Microsoft designed Windows 98 "so that using Navigator on Windows 98 would have unpleasant consequences for users" by, in some circumstances, overriding the user's choice of a browser other than IE as his or her default browser. Plaintiffs argue that this override harms the competitive process by deterring consumers from using a browser other than IE even though they might prefer to do so, thereby reducing rival browsers' usage share and, hence, the ability of rival browsers to draw developer attention away from the APIs exposed by Windows. Microsoft does not deny, of course, that overriding the user's preference prevents some people from using other browsers. Because the override reduces rivals' usage share and protects Microsoft's monopoly, it too is anticompetitive.

Finally, the District Court condemned Microsoft's decision to bind IE to Windows 98 "by placing code specific to Web browsing in the same files as code that provided operating system functions." Putting code supplying browsing functionality into a file with code supplying operating system functionality "ensure[s] that the deletion of any file containing browsing-specific routines would also delete vital operating system routines and thus cripple Windows. . . ." As noted above, preventing an OEM from removing IE deters it from installing a second browser because doing so increases the OEM's product testing and support costs; by contrast, had OEMs been able to remove IE, they might have chosen to pre-install Navigator alone.

Microsoft denies, as a factual matter, that it commingled browsing and non-browsing code, and it maintains the District Court's findings to the contrary are clearly erroneous. According to Microsoft, its expert "testified without contradiction that '[t]he very same code in Windows 98 that provides Web browsing functionality' also performs essential operating system functions — not code in the same files, but the very same software code."

Microsoft's expert did not testify to that effect "without contradiction," however. A Government expert, Glenn Weadock, testified that Microsoft "design [ed] [IE] so that some of the code that it uses co-resides in the same library files as other code needed for Windows." Another Government expert likewise testified that one library file, SHDOCVW.DLL, "is really a bundle of separate functions. It contains some functions that have to do specifically with Web browsing, and it contains some general user interface functions as well." One of Microsoft's own documents suggests as much. (Microsoft document indicating some functions in SHDOCVW.DLL can be described as "IE only," others can be described as "shell only" and still others can be described as providing both "IE" and "shell" functions)).

In view of the contradictory testimony in the record, some of which supports the District Court's finding that Microsoft commingled browsing and non-browsing code, we cannot conclude that the finding was clearly erroneous. Accordingly, . . . we conclude that such commingling has an anticompetitive effect; as noted above, the commingling deters OEMs from pre-installing rival browsers, thereby reducing the rivals' usage share and, hence, developers' interest in rivals' APIs as an alternative to the API set exposed by Microsoft's operating system.

b.   Microsoft's justifications for integration

Microsoft proffers no justification for two of the three challenged actions that it took in integrating IE into Windows — excluding IE from the Add/Remove Programs utility and commingling browser and operating system code. Although Microsoft does make some general claims regarding the benefits of integrating the browser and the operating system, it neither specifies nor substantiates those claims. Nor does it argue that either excluding IE from the Add/Remove Programs utility or commingling code achieves any integrative benefit. Plaintiffs plainly made out a prima facie case of harm to competition in the operating system market by demonstrating that Microsoft's actions increased its browser usage share and thus protected its operating system monopoly from a middleware threat and, for its part, Microsoft failed to meet its burden of showing that its conduct serves a purpose other than protecting its operating system monopoly. Accordingly, we hold that Microsoft's exclusion of IE from the Add/Remove Programs utility and its commingling of browser and operating system code constitute exclusionary conduct, in violation of § 2.

As for the other challenged act that Microsoft took in integrating IE into Windows — causing Windows to override the user's choice of a default browser in certain circumstances — Microsoft argues that it has "valid technical reasons." Specifically, Microsoft claims that it was necessary to design Windows to override the user's preferences when he or she invokes one of "a few" out "of the nearly 30 means of accessing the Internet." According to Microsoft:

> The Windows 98 Help system and Windows Update feature depend on ActiveX controls not supported by Navigator, and the now-discontinued Channel Bar utilized Microsoft's Channel Definition Format, which Navigator also did not support. Lastly, Windows 98 does not invoke Navigator if a user accesses the Internet through "My Computer" or "Windows Explorer" because doing so would defeat one of the purposes of those features — enabling users to move seamlessly from local storage devices to the Web in the same browsing window.

The plaintiff bears the burden not only of rebutting a proffered justification but also of demonstrating that the anticompetitive effect of the challenged action outweighs it. In the District Court, plaintiffs appear to have done neither, let alone both; in any event, upon appeal, plaintiffs offer no rebuttal whatsoever. Accordingly, Microsoft may not be held liable for this aspect of its product design.

[The court affirmed the district court's findings that Microsoft's exclusive contracts with Internet Access Providers and its dealings with Apple and Intel concerning the development of Java were in violation of Section 2 of the Sherman Act.]

NOTES & QUESTIONS

1. The Department of Justice's case against Microsoft dominated the 1990's and as of this writing, many of the issues continue to be litigated not only in ongoing state claims against Microsoft but also in the European Union. To give you a sense of the baroque drama of the case, here is a timeline of the major developments in the dispute:

1990:   The FTC begins investigation of Microsoft's pricing and exclusionary practices

1993:   An evenly divided FTC board splits on bringing a suit against Microsoft. The Department of Justice takes over the investigation.

1994:   Microsoft and the Department of Justice enter into a settlement under which Microsoft agrees to alter its business practices. One of the terms of the settlement is that Microsoft will not distribute bundled versions of its software, but can distributed integrated products.

1995:   Judge Sporkin rejects the proposal settlement. The D.C. Court of Appeals overturns Judge Sporkin and orders a new judge be assigned to review the settlement. Judge Penfield Jackson is assigned to the case and approves the settlement. Microsoft launches Windows 95 in the Fall.

1996:   The Department of Justice initiates an investigation of Microsoft's practices with respect to Windows 95.

1997:   The Department of Justice brings a lawsuit claiming that Microsoft violated the terms of its settlement agreement in distributing Windows 95 by bundling the Internet Explorer browser with the operating system. Judge Jackson orders a preliminary injunction to keep Microsoft from requiring computer manufacturers to install Internet Explorer. Microsoft appeals the order.

1998:   The D.C. Court of Appeals reverses Judge Jackson's preliminary injunction order, finding that Internet Explorer and Windows were integrated, rather than bundled products. Since the products were integrated, Microsoft was not in violation of the settlement. The Department of Justice, along with several states attorney general, file a suit claiming that Microsoft's conduct was exclusionary and monopolizing.

1999:   Judge Jackson issues his findings of fact against Microsoft, concluding that Microsoft had market power and had acted illegally. Judge Jackson orders Microsoft and the Department of Justice to mediate and appoints Judge Richard Posner as the mediator.

2000:   After the mediation fails, Judge Jackson issues his findings of law and orders Microsoft to be split into two companies.

2001:   The D.C. Court of Appeals overrules Judge Jackson's order to split the company, but does find violations of the law. The appeals court remands to a new judge for determinations of liability. [Note: The D.C. Court of Appeals' opinion is the one excerpted here and in the next section.] Microsoft and the Department of Justice enter into a settlement agreement.

2002:   Judge Colleen Kollar-Kotelly approves the settlement agreement which requires Microsoft to disclose features of the Windows source code to make it easier for companies to create middleware and to allow computer manufacturers to decide which Microsoft features to include on equipment. The states opt out of the settlement.

Microsoft entered into settlement agreements with various states in 2003 and 2004. Many states and private companies continue to pursue the litigation.

2. The *Microsoft* case illustrates the perils that may await a successful high technology company. Some critics of the case claim that Microsoft's only offense was being successful. Certainly, Microsoft's success and size put it on the radar screen of antitrust enforcers. Judge Jackson's decision to split the company into two (an operating system company and an applications company) is one possible response to concerns with company size. This approach, however, ignores some of the synergies that arise between operating systems and applications. Of course, these synergies could still be realized through joint ventures between the two companies. Since joint ventures receive relaxed

treatment under antitrust law, the decision to split the company could potentially lead to even more problems in antitrust enforcement. For this, and other reasons, the rejection of the divestiture remedy by the D.C. Court of Appeals was probably correct. What are the arguments in support of a split? What other remedies are responsive to the problems that the D.C. Court of Appeals identified?

3. While the Court of Appeals rejected the remedy imposed by Judge Jackson, the court did find that Microsoft monopolized the market for computer operating systems. Did the court define the market in a meaningful way? Microsoft made the argument that, given the dynamics of the software industry, its market size was continually threatened by competing systems. The Court of Appeals found this argument unpersuasive, partly because Microsoft's activities were found to shield the company from competitive threats. What were the bad acts that the court found? What are potential business justifications for these acts?

4. It might be helpful to think about the lessons that can be derived from the *Microsoft* case. The company's problems in that case stemmed from licensing and marketing practices that Microsoft engaged in during the 1990's. Do the 1995 Licensing Guidelines offer guidance on the legality or illegality of Microsoft's business practices? Is the Court of Appeals' analysis consistent with the 1995 Guidelines?

2. Tying Arrangement

UNITED STATES v. MICROSOFT
United States Court of Appeals for the District of Columbia
253 F.3d 34 (2001)

[The court's analysis of Microsoft's practices continued:]

IV. Tying

Microsoft also contests the District Court's determination of liability under § 1 of the Sherman Act. The District Court concluded that Microsoft's contractual and technological bundling of the IE web browser (the "tied" product) with its Windows operating system ("OS") (the "tying" product) resulted in a tying arrangement that was per se unlawful. We hold that the rule of reason, rather than per se analysis, should govern the legality of tying arrangements involving platform software products. The Supreme Court has warned that "'[i]t is only after considerable experience with certain business relationships that courts classify them as per se violations. . . .'" While every "business relationship" will in some sense have unique features, some represent entire, novel categories of dealings. As we shall explain, the arrangement before us is an example of the latter, offering the first up-close look at the technological integration of added functionality into software that serves as a platform for third-party applications. There being no close parallel in prior antitrust cases, simplistic application of per se tying rules carries a serious risk of harm. Accordingly, we vacate the District Court's finding of a per se tying violation and remand the case. Plaintiffs may on remand pursue their tying claim under the rule of reason.

The facts underlying the tying allegation substantially overlap with those set forth in Section II.B in connection with the § 2 monopoly maintenance claim. The key District Court findings are that (1) Microsoft required licensees of Windows 95 and 98 also to license IE as a bundle at a single price; (2) Microsoft refused to allow OEMs to uninstall or remove IE from the Windows desktop; (3) Microsoft designed Windows 98 in a way that withheld from consumers the ability to remove IE by use of the Add/Remove Programs utility; and (4) Microsoft designed Windows 98 to override the user's choice of default web browser in certain circumstances. The court found that these acts constituted a per se tying violation. Although the District Court also found that Microsoft commingled operating system-only and browser-only routines in the same library files, it did not include this as a basis for tying liability despite plaintiffs' request that it do so.

There are four elements to a per se tying violation: (1) the tying and tied goods are two separate products; (2) the defendant has market power in the tying product market; (3) the defendant affords consumers no choice but to purchase the tied product from it; and (4) the tying arrangement forecloses a substantial volume of commerce.

Microsoft does not dispute that it bound Windows and IE in the four ways the District Court cited. Instead it argues that Windows (the tying good) and IE browsers (the tied good) are not "separate products," and that it did not substantially foreclose competing browsers from the tied product market.

We first address the separate-products inquiry, a source of much argument between the parties and of confusion in the cases. Our purpose is to highlight the poor fit between the separate-products test and the facts of this case. We then offer further reasons for carving an exception to the per se rule when the tying product is platform software. In the final section we discuss the District Court's inquiry if plaintiffs pursue a rule of reason claim on remand.

A. Separate-Products Inquiry Under the Per Se Test

The requirement that a practice involve two separate products before being condemned as an illegal tie started as a purely linguistic requirement: unless products are separate, one cannot be "tied" to the other. Indeed, the nature of the products involved in early tying cases — intuitively distinct items such as a movie projector and a film. It was not until *Times-Picayune Publishing Co. v. United States,* 345 U.S. 594, 73 S.Ct. 872, 97 L.Ed. 1277 (1953), that the separate-products issue became a distinct element of the test for an illegal tie. Even that case engaged in a rather cursory inquiry into whether ads sold in the morning edition of a paper were a separate product from ads sold in the evening edition.

The first case to give content to the separate-products test was *Jefferson Parish,* 466 U.S. 2, 104 S.Ct. 1551, 80 L.Ed.2d 2. That case addressed a tying arrangement in which a hospital conditioned surgical care at its facility on the purchase of anesthesiological services from an affiliated medical group. The facts were a challenge for casual separate-products analysis because the tied service — anesthesia — was neither intuitively distinct from nor intuitively contained within the tying service — surgical care. A further complication was that, soon after the Court enunciated the per se rule for tying liability, new economic research began to cast doubt on the assumption, voiced by the Court when it established the rule, that " 'tying agreements serve hardly any purpose beyond the suppression of competition.' "

The Jefferson Parish Court resolved the matter in two steps. First, it clarified that "the answer to the question whether one or two products are involved" does not turn "on the functional relation between them. . . ." In other words, the mere fact that two items are complements, that "one . . . is useless without the other," id., does not make them a single "product" for purposes of tying law. Second, reasoning that the "definitional question [whether two distinguishable products are involved] depends on whether the arrangement may have the type of competitive consequences addressed by the rule [against tying]," the Court decreed that "no tying arrangement can exist unless there is a sufficient demand for the purchase of anesthesiological services separate from hospital services to identify a distinct product market in which it is efficient to offer anesthesiological services separately from hospital service."

The Court proceeded to examine direct and indirect evidence of consumer demand for the tied product separate from the tying product. Direct evidence addresses the question whether, when given a choice, consumers purchase the tied good from the tying good maker, or from other firms. The Court took note, for example, of testimony that patients and surgeons often requested specific anesthesiologists not associated with a hospital. Indirect evidence includes the behavior of firms without market power in the tying good market, presumably on the notion that (competitive) supply follows demand. If competitive firms always bundle the tying and tied goods, then they are a single product. Here the Court noted that only 27% of anesthesiologists in markets other than the defendant's had financial relationships with hospitals, and that, unlike radiologists and pathologists, anesthesiologists were not usually employed by hospitals, i.e., bundled with hospital services. With both direct and indirect evidence concurring, the Court determined that hospital surgery and anesthesiological services were distinct goods.

To understand the logic behind the Court's consumer demand test, consider first the postulated harms from tying. The core concern is that tying prevents goods from competing directly for consumer choice on their merits, i.e., being selected as a result of "buyers' independent judgment." With a tie, a buyer's "freedom to select the best bargain in the second market [could be] impaired by his need to purchase the tying product, and perhaps by an inability to evaluate the true cost of either product. . . ." Direct competition on the merits of the tied product is foreclosed when the tying product either is sold only in a bundle with the tied product or, though offered separately, is sold at a bundled price, so that the buyer pays the same price whether he takes the tied product or not. In both cases, a consumer buying the tying product becomes entitled to the tied product; he will therefore likely be unwilling to buy a competitor's version of the tied product even if, making his own price/quality assessment, that is what he would prefer.

But not all ties are bad. Bundling obviously saves distribution and consumer transaction costs. This is likely to be true, to take some examples from the computer industry, with the integration of math co-processors and memory into microprocessor chips and the inclusion of spell checkers in word processors. Bundling can also capitalize on certain economies of scope. A possible example is the "shared" library files that perform OS and browser functions with the very same lines of code and thus may save drive space from the clutter of redundant routines and memory when consumers use both the OS and browser simultaneously. Indeed, if there were no efficiencies from a tie (including economizing on consumer transaction costs such as the time and effort involved in choice), we would expect distinct consumer demand for each individual component of every good. In a competitive market with zero transaction costs, the computers on which this opinion was written would only be sold piecemeal — keyboard, monitor, mouse, central processing unit, disk drive, and memory all sold in separate transactions and likely by different manufacturers.

Recognizing the potential benefits from tying, the Court in Jefferson Parish forged a separate-products test that, like those of market power and substantial foreclosure, attempts to screen out false positives under per se analysis. The consumer demand test is a rough proxy for whether a tying arrangement may, on balance, be welfare-enhancing, and unsuited to per se condemnation. In the abstract, of course, there is always direct separate demand for products: assuming choice is available at zero cost, consumers will prefer it to no choice. Only when the efficiencies from bundling are dominated by the benefits to choice for enough consumers, however, will we actually observe consumers making independent purchases. In other words, perceptible separate demand is inversely proportional to net efficiencies. On the supply side, firms without market power will bundle two goods only when the cost savings from joint sale outweigh the value consumers place on separate choice. So bundling by all competitive firms implies strong net efficiencies. If a court finds either that there is no noticeable separate demand for the tied product or, there being no convincing direct evidence of separate demand, that the entire "competitive fringe" engages in the same behavior as the defendant, then the tying and tied products should be declared one product and per se liability should be rejected.

Before concluding our exegesis of *Jefferson Parish's* separate-products test, we should clarify two things. First, *Jefferson Parish* does not endorse a direct inquiry into the efficiencies of a bundle. Rather, it proposes easy-to-administer proxies for net efficiency. In describing the separate-products test we discuss efficiencies only to explain the rationale behind the consumer demand inquiry. To allow the separate-products test to become a detailed inquiry into possible welfare consequences would turn a screening test into the very process it is expected to render unnecessary.

Second, the separate-products test is not a one-sided inquiry into the cost savings from a bundle. Although *Jefferson Parish* acknowledged that prior lower court cases looked at cost-savings to decide separate products, the Court conspicuously did not adopt that approach in its disposition of tying arrangement before it. Instead it chose proxies that balance costs savings against reduction in consumer choice.

With this background, we now turn to the separate products inquiry before us. The District Court found that many consumers, if given the option, would choose their browser separately from the OS. Turning to industry custom, the court found that, although all major OS vendors bundled browsers with their OS's, these companies either sold versions without a browser, or allowed OEMs or end-users either not to install the bundled browser or in any event to "uninstall" it. The court did not discuss the record evidence as to whether OS vendors other than Microsoft sold at a bundled price, with no discount for a browserless OS, perhaps because the record evidence on the issue was in conflict.

Microsoft does not dispute that many consumers demand alternative browsers. But on industry custom Microsoft contends that no other firm requires non-removal because no other firm has invested the resources to integrate web browsing as deeply into its OS as Microsoft has. (We here use the term "integrate" in the rather simple sense of converting individual goods into components of a single physical object (e.g., a computer as it leaves the OEM, or a disk or sets of disks), without any normative implication that such integration is desirable or achieves special advantages.) Microsoft contends not only that its integration of IE into Windows is innovative and beneficial but also that it requires non-removal of IE. In our discussion of monopoly maintenance we find that these claims fail the efficiency balancing applicable in that context. But the separate-products analysis is supposed to perform its function as a proxy without embarking on any direct analysis of efficiency. Accordingly, Microsoft's implicit argument — that in this case looking to a competitive fringe is inadequate to evaluate fully its potentially innovative technological integration, that such a comparison is between apples and oranges — poses a legitimate objection to the operation of Jefferson Parish's separate-products test for the per se rule.

In fact there is merit to Microsoft's broader argument that Jefferson Parish's consumer demand test would "chill innovation to the detriment of consumers by preventing firms from integrating into their products new functionality previously provided by standalone products — and hence, by definition, subject to separate consumer demand." The per se rule's direct consumer demand and indirect industry custom inquiries are, as a general matter, backward-looking and therefore systematically poor proxies for overall efficiency in the presence of new and innovative integration. The direct consumer demand test focuses on historic consumer behavior, likely before integration, and the indirect industry custom test looks at firms that, unlike the defendant, may not have integrated the tying and tied goods. Both tests compare incomparables — the defendant's decision to bundle in the presence of integration, on the one hand, and consumer and competitor calculations in its absence, on the other. If integration has efficiency benefits, these may be ignored by the *Jefferson* Parish proxies. Because one cannot be sure beneficial integration will be protected by the other elements of the per se rule, simple application of that rule's separate-products test may make consumers worse off.

In light of the monopoly maintenance section, obviously, we do not find that Microsoft's integration is welfare-enhancing or that it should be absolved of tying liability. Rather, we heed Microsoft's warning that the separate-products element of the per se rule may not give newly integrated products a fair shake.

B.   Per Se Analysis Inappropriate for this Case.

We now address directly the larger question as we see it: whether standard per se analysis should be applied "off the shelf" to evaluate the defendant's tying arrangement, one which involves software that serves as a platform for third-party applications. There is no doubt that "[i]t is far too late in the history of our antitrust jurisprudence to question the proposition that certain tying arrangements pose an unacceptable risk of stifling competition and therefore are unreasonable 'per se.'" But there are strong reasons to doubt that the integration of additional software functionality into an OS falls among these arrangements. Applying per se analysis to such an amalgamation creates undue risks of error and of deterring welfare-enhancing innovation.

The Supreme Court has warned that " '[i]t is only after considerable experience with certain business relationships that courts classify them as per se violations. . . .' " Yet the sort of tying arrangement attacked here is unlike any the Supreme Court has considered. The early Supreme Court cases on tying dealt with arrangements whereby the sale or lease of a patented product was conditioned on the purchase of certain unpatented products from the patentee. Later Supreme Court tying cases did not involve market power derived from patents, but continued to involve contractual ties.

In none of these cases was the tied good physically and technologically integrated with the tying good. Nor did the defendants ever argue that their tie improved the value of the tying product to users and to makers of complementary goods. In those cases where the defendant claimed that use of the tied good made the tying good more valuable to users, the Court ruled that the same result could be achieved via quality standards for substitutes of the tied good. Here Microsoft argues that IE and Windows are an integrated physical product and that the bundling of IE APIs with Windows makes the latter a better applications platform for third-party software. It is unclear how the benefits from IE APIs could be achieved by quality standards for different browser manufacturers. We do not pass judgment on Microsoft's claims regarding the benefits from integration of its APIs. We merely note that these and other novel, purported efficiencies suggest that judicial "experience" provides little basis for believing that, "because of their pernicious effect on competition and lack of any redeeming virtue," a software firm's decisions to sell multiple functionalities as a package should be "conclusively presumed to be unreasonable and therefore illegal without elaborate inquiry as to the precise harm they have caused or the business excuse for their use."

Nor have we found much insight into software integration among the decisions of lower federal courts. Most tying cases in the computer industry involve bundling with hardware. Just as Microsoft integrated web browsing into its OS, IBM in the 1970s integrated memory into its CPUs, a hardware platform. A peripheral manufacturer alleged a tying violation, but the District Court dismissed the claim because it thought it inappropriate to enmesh the courts in product design decisions. The court's discussion of the tying claim was brief and did not dwell on the effects of the integration on competition or efficiencies. Nor did the court consider whether per se analysis of the alleged tie was wise. . . .

. . . [T]he nature of the platform software market affirmatively suggests that per se rules might stunt valuable innovation. We have in mind two reasons.

First, as we explained in the previous section, the separate-products test is a poor proxy for net efficiency from newly integrated products. Under per se analysis the first firm to merge previously distinct functionalities (e.g., the inclusion of starter motors in automobiles) or to eliminate entirely the need for a second function (e.g., the invention of the stain-resistant carpet) risks being condemned as having tied two separate products because at the moment of integration there will appear to be a robust "distinct" market for the tied product.

The failure of the separate-products test to screen out certain cases of productive integration is particularly troubling in platform software markets such as that in which the defendant competes. Not only is integration common in such markets, but it is common among firms without market power. We have already reviewed evidence that nearly all competitive OS vendors also bundle browsers. Moreover, plaintiffs do not dispute that OS vendors can and do incorporate basic internet plumbing and other useful functionality into their OS's. Firms without market power have no incentive to package different pieces of software together unless there are efficiency gains from doing so. The ubiquity of bundling in competitive platform software markets should give courts reason to pause before condemning such behavior in less competitive markets.

Second, because of the pervasively innovative character of platform software markets, tying in such markets may produce efficiencies that courts have not previously encountered and thus the Supreme Court had not factored into the per se rule as originally conceived. For example, the bundling of a browser with OS's enables an independent software developer to count on the presence of the browser's APIs, if any, on consumers' machines and thus to omit them from its own package. It is true that software developers can bundle the browser APIs they need with their own products, but that may force consumers to pay twice for the same API if it is bundled with two different software programs. It is also true that OEMs can include APIs with the computers they sell, id., but diffusion of uniform APIs by that route may be inferior. First, many OEMs serve special subsets of Windows consumers, such as home or corporate or academic users. If just one of these OEMs decides not to bundle an API because it does not benefit enough of its clients, ISVs that use that API might have to bundle it with every copy of their program. Second, there may be a substantial lag before all OEMs bundle the same set of APIs — a lag inevitably aggravated by the first phenomenon. In a field where programs change very rapidly, delays in the spread of a necessary element (here, the APIs) may be very costly. Of course, these arguments may not justify Microsoft's decision to bundle APIs in this case, particularly because Microsoft did not merely bundle with Windows the APIs from IE, but an entire browser application (sometimes even without APIs, see id.). A justification for bundling a component of software may not be one for bundling the entire software package, especially given the malleability of software code. Furthermore, the interest in efficient API diffusion obviously supplies a far stronger justification for simple price-bundling than for Microsoft's contractual or technological bars to subsequent removal of functionality. But our qualms about redefining the boundaries of a defendant's product and the possibility of consumer gains from simplifying the work of applications developers makes us question any hard and fast approach to tying in OS software markets.

There may also be a number of efficiencies that, although very real, have been ignored in the calculations underlying the adoption of a per se rule for tying. We fear that these efficiencies are common in technologically dynamic markets where product development is especially unlikely to follow an easily foreseen linear pattern. When IBM first introduced [computer disk] drives in 1956, it sold an integrated product that contained magnetic disks and disk heads that read and wrote data onto disks. Consumers of the drives demanded two functions — to store data and to access it all at once. In the first few years consumers' demand for storage increased rapidly, outpacing the evolution of magnetic disk technology. To satisfy that demand IBM made it possible for consumers to remove the magnetic disks from drives, even though that meant consumers would not have access to data on disks removed from the drive. This componentization enabled makers of computer peripherals to sell consumers removable disks. Over time, however, the technology of magnetic disks caught up with demand for capacity, so that consumers needed few removable disks to store all their data. At this point IBM reintegrated disks into their drives, enabling consumers to once again have immediate access to all their data without a sacrifice in capacity. A manufacturer of removable disks sued. But the District Court found the tie justified because it satisfied consumer demand for immediate access to all data, and ruled that disks and disk heads were one product. . . .

These arguments all point to one conclusion: we cannot comfortably say that bundling in platform software markets has so little "redeeming virtue," and that there would be so "very little loss to society" from its ban, that "an inquiry into its costs in the individual case [can be] considered [ ] unnecessary." We do not have enough empirical evidence regarding the effect of Microsoft's practice on the amount of consumer surplus created or consumer choice foreclosed by the integration of added functionality into platform software to exercise sensible judgment regarding that entire class of behavior. (For some issues we have no data.) "We need to know more than we do about the actual impact of these arrangements on competition to decide whether they . . . should be classified as per se violations of the Sherman Act." Until then, we will heed the wisdom that "easy labels do not always supply ready answers," and vacate the District Court's finding of per se tying liability under Sherman Act § 1. We remand the case for evaluation of Microsoft's tying arrangements under the rule of reason.

Our judgment regarding the comparative merits of the per se rule and the rule of reason is confined to the tying arrangement before us, where the tying product is software whose major purpose is to serve as a platform for third-party applications and the tied product is complementary software functionality. While our reasoning may at times appear to have broader force, we do not have the confidence to speak to facts outside the record, which contains scant discussion of software integration generally. Microsoft's primary justification for bundling IE APIs is that their inclusion with Windows increases the value of third-party software (and Windows) to consumers. Because this claim applies with distinct force when the tying product is platform software, we have no present basis for finding the per se rule inapplicable to software markets generally. Nor should we be interpreted as setting a precedent for switching to the rule of reason every time a court identifies an efficiency justification for a tying arrangement. Our reading of the record suggests merely that integration of new functionality into platform software is a common practice and that wooden application of per se rules in this litigation may cast a cloud over platform innovation in the market for PCs, network computers and information appliances.

NOTES & QUESTIONS

1. The issue facing the Court of Appeals in this part of the *Microsoft* opinion is whether Internet Explorer and Windows constitute one product or two products. If the web browser and operating system constitute one product, then Microsoft could not logically be tying the sale of one product to another. For example, an automobile is a product that consists of many elements. It would be absurd to say that the sale of an automobile constituted a tying sale of tires to the chassis of the car. To determine if a sale involves one product or two, a court must conduct an efficiency analysis to determine if there are identifiable benefits stemming from the combination of different elements into one product. It should be easy to see how an automobile would pass this efficiency test and be considered one product. The problem can become more complicated when services are involved. In *Jefferson Parish*, a case cited by the Court of Appeals, patients challenged a hospital's practice of requiring the use of certain designated anesthesiologists in surgical procedures. Patients reasoned that this practice restricted the supply of anesthesiologists and raised prices. The Supreme Court applied a market analysis in *Jefferson Parish* to conclude that anesthesiological services were a separate product from surgical services. Note, however, that the separate product analysis resolves only the first part of the overall analysis of liability for tying arrangements. If a court finds that there are separate products, the court will then need to consider whether tying the sale of the two products is anticompetitive.

2. How does the Court of Appeals apply the separate products inquiry to software? Keep in mind that, with appropriate reprogramming, software is often divisible into parts. Software with two functions can be divided in some situations into two pieces of software each performing the separate functions. A previous Court of Appeals panel considered whether Internet Explorer and Windows were one product or two under the terms of the 1994 settlement agreement between Microsoft and the Department of Justice. The court was analyzing the term of the agreement that permitted Microsoft to distribute integrated products, but not tied products. The Court of Appeals ruled that the combination of Internet Explorer and Windows constituted an integrated product, as defined in the agreement. In finding an integrated product, the court emphasized the functional interactions between Internet Explorer and Windows. How does the Court of Appeal analyze the separate products issue in the excerpted opinion? The court seems to be particularly sensitive to the unique features of software and the dynamics of high technology markets. Is

there a meaningful way to determine whether individual pieces of software constitute one product or two?

3. The court concludes that per se treatment is not appropriate for analyzing tying claims in the software industry. What is the basis for this conclusion? Is the court basing its conclusion on the nature of software or the structure of software markets? Does the court provide a sense of how to apply the rule of reason to alleged tying agreements in the software industry? Is the analysis a technical one or an economic one? Notice that in *Jefferson Parish*, the analysis rested largely on the demand for the individual services at issue. In the Court of Appeals' review of the 1994 settlement agreement involving Microsoft, the court applied a technical analysis of how software functions. What approach is appropriate for the *Microsoft* case described in the opinion excerpted above?

4. The 1995 Licensing Guidelines state that a tying arrangement will be challenged if (a) the seller has market power in the tying product, (b) the arrangement has an adverse effect on competition in the relevant market for the tied product, and (c) efficiency justifications do not outweigh the anticompetitive effects of the arrangement. Is this approach consistent with the Court of Appeals' analysis in the *Microsoft* opinion excerpted above? Would Microsoft's practices be challenged under the 1995 Licensing Guidelines as an illegal tying arrangement?

D. COOPERATIVE VENTURES

In the Matter of Dell Computer Corporation Consent Order, etc., In Regard to Alleged Violation of Sec. 5 of the Federal Trade Commission Act

Docket No. C-3658
Decision, May 20, 1996

COMPLAINT

Pursuant to the provisions of the Federal Trade Commission Act, and by virtue of the authority vested in it by said Act, the Federal Trade Commission, having reason to believe that the respondent, Dell Computer Corporation, a corporation, has violated the provisions of said Act, and it appearing to the Commission that a proceeding by it in respect thereof would be in the public interest, hereby issues its complaint, stating its charges as follows:

1. Respondent Dell Computer Corporation ("Dell") is a corporation organized, existing and doing business under and by virtue of the laws of the State of Delaware, with its principal office and place of business at 2214 West Braker Lane, Texas.

2. Respondent is a publicly traded for-profit corporation engaged in the innovation, development, manufacture, and sale of personal computer systems throughout the United States. By virtue of its purposes and activities,

respondent is a corporation within the meaning of Section 4 of the Federal Trade Commission Act, 15 U.S.C. 44.

3. Dell's acts and practices, including the acts and practices alleged in this complaint, are in or affect commerce as defined in the Federal Trade Commission Act.

4. In February 1992 Dell became a member of the Video Electronics Standards Association ("VESA"), a non-profit standards-setting association composed of virtually all major U.S. computer hardware and software manufacturers.

5. At or about the same time, VESA began the process of setting a design standard for a computer bus design, later to be known as the VESA Local Bus or "VL-bus." Like all computer buses, the VL-bus carries information or instructions between the computer's central processing unit and the computer's peripheral devices such as a hard disk drive, a video display terminal, or a modem.

6. By June 1992 VESA's Local Bus Committee, with Dell representatives sitting as members, approved the VL-bus design standard, which improved upon then-existing technology by more quickly and efficiently meeting the transmission needs of new, video-intensive software. One year earlier, in July 1991, Dell had received United States patent number 5,036,481 (the "'481 patent"), which, according to Dell, gives it "exclusive rights to the mechanical slot configuration used on the motherboard to receive the VL-bus card." Nonetheless, at no time prior to or after June 1992 did Dell disclose to VESA's Local Bus Committee the existence of the '481 patent.

7. After committee approval of the VL-bus design standard, VESA sought the approval of the VL-bus design standard by all of its voting members. On July 20, 1992, Dell voted to approve the preliminary proposal for the VL-bus standard. As part of this approval, a Dell representative certified in writing that, to the best of his knowledge, "this proposal does not infringe on any trademarks, copyrights, or patents" that Dell possessed. On August 6, 1992, Dell gave final approval to the VL-bus design standard. As part of this final approval, the Dell representative again certified in writing that, to the best of his knowledge, "this proposal does not infringe on any trademarks, copyrights, or patents" that Dell possessed.

8. After VESA's VL-bus design standard became very successful, having been included in over 1.4 million computers sold in the eight months immediately following its adoption, Dell informed certain VESA members who were manufacturing computers using the new design standard that their "implementation of the VL-bus is a violation of Dell's exclusive rights." Dell demanded that these companies meet with its representatives to "determine . . . the manner in which Dell's exclusive rights will be recognized . . . ." Dell followed up its initial demands by meeting with several companies, and it has never renounced the claimed infringement.

9. By engaging in the acts or practices described in paragraphs four through eight of this complaint, respondent Dell has unreasonably restrained competition in the following ways, among others:

(a) Industry acceptance of the VL-bus design standard was hindered because some computer manufacturers delayed their use of the design standard until the patent issue was clarified.

(b) Systems utilizing the VL-bus design standard were avoided due to concerns that patent issues would affect the VL-bus' success as an industry design standard.

(c) The uncertainty concerning the acceptance of the VL-bus design standard raised the costs of implementing the VL-bus design as well as the costs of developing competing bus designs.

(d) Willingness to participate in industry standard-setting efforts has been chilled.

10. The acts or practices of respondent alleged herein were and are to the prejudice and injury of the public. The acts or practices constitute unfair methods of competition in or affecting commerce in violation of Section 5 of the Federal Trade Commission Act. These acts or practices are continuing and will continue, or may recur, in the absence of the relief requested.

DECISION AND ORDER

The Federal Trade Commission ("Commission") having initiated an investigation of certain acts and practices of the respondent named in the caption hereof, and the respondent having been furnished thereafter with a copy of the draft of complaint which the Bureau of Competition proposed to present to the Commission for its consideration and which, if issued by the Commission, would charge respondent with violation of the Federal Trade Commission Act; and

The respondent, its attorneys, and counsel for the Commission having thereafter executed an agreement containing consent order, an admission by the respondent of all jurisdictional facts set forth in the aforesaid draft of complaint, a statement that the signing of said agreement is for settlement purposes only and does not constitute an admission by respondent that the law has been violated as alleged in the complaint, and waivers and other provisions as required by the Commission Rules; and

The Commission having thereafter considered the matter and having determined that it had reason to believe that the respondent has violated the said Act, and that complaint should issue stating its charges in that respect, and having thereupon accepted the executed consent agreement and placed such agreement on the public record for a period of sixty (60) days, and having duly considered the comments received, now in further conformity with the procedure prescribed in Section 2.34 of its Rules, the Commission hereby issues its complaint, makes the following jurisdictional findings and enters the following order:

1. Respondent Dell Computer Corporation is a corporation organized, existing and doing business under and by virtue of the laws of the State of

Delaware, with its offices and principal place of business located at 2214 West Braker Lane, Austin, Texas.

2. The Federal Trade Commission has jurisdiction of this proceeding and of the respondent, and the proceeding is in the public interest.

ORDER

I.

It is ordered, that, as used in this order, the following definitions shall apply:

A. "Respondent" or "Dell" means Dell Computer Corporation, its predecessors, subsidiaries, divisions, groups, and affiliates controlled by Dell Computer Corporation, their successors and assigns, and their directors, officers, employees, agents and representatives.

B. "Designated representative" means the person appointed by Dell to the standard-setting organization who communicates respondent's position regarding respondent's patent rights related to any standard under consideration by the standard-setting organization.

C. "VESA" means the Video Electronics Standards Association, located at 2150 North First Street, Suite 440, San Jose, California.

D. "VL-bus" means the computer local bus design standard VESA established in August 1992 for the transmission of computer information between a computer's central processing unit and certain computer peripheral devices.

E. "'481 patent" means United States patent number 5,036,481.

F. "Commission" means the Federal Trade Commission.

II.

It is further ordered, that, within thirty (30) days after the date this order becomes final, and until the expiration of the '481 patent, respondent shall cease and desist all efforts it has undertaken by any means, including without limitation the threat, prosecution or defense of any suits or other actions, whether legal, equitable, or administrative, as well as any arbitrations, mediations, or any other form of private dispute resolution, through or in which respondent has asserted that any person or entity, by using or applying VL-bus in its manufacture of computer equipment, has infringed the '481 patent.

III.

It is further ordered, that, until the expiration of the '481 patent, respondent shall not undertake any new efforts to enforce the '481 patent by threatening, prosecuting or defending any suit or other action, whether legal, equitable, or administrative, as well as any arbitration, mediation, or other form of private dispute resolution, through or in which respondent claims that any person or entity, by using or applying VL-bus in its manufacture, use or sale of computer equipment, has infringed the '481 patent.

IV.

It is further ordered, that, for a period of ten (10) years after the date this order becomes final, respondent shall cease and desist from enforcing or threatening to enforce any patent rights by asserting or alleging that any person's or entity's use or implementation of an industry design standard, or sale of any equipment using an industry design standard, infringes such patent rights, if, in response to a written inquiry from the standard-setting organization to respondent's designated representative, respondent intentionally failed to disclose such patent rights while such industry standard was under consideration. . . .

DISSENTING STATEMENT OF COMMISSIONER MARY L. AZCUENAGA

Today the Commission issues its complaint and final consent order against Dell Computer Corporation ("Dell"), accompanied by an unusual explanatory statement on behalf of the majority. The case, which was touted in the Commission's press release soliciting public comment as "precedent-setting," has aroused a high degree of interest. Several thoughtful comments have been received.

The complaint against Dell does not articulate a violation of Section 5 of the FTC Act under any established theory of law. Under any novel theory, the competitive implications of the conduct alleged remain unclear. As confirmed by the comments we have received, a host of questions needs to be resolved before the Commission creates a new antitrust-based duty of care for participants in the voluntary standards-setting process.

The statement of the majority appears intended to respond to the concerns raised in the comments. Unfortunately, it does not resolve those concerns. Instead, by failing to take a clear stand on what legal standard it intends to apply, the majority creates more confusion. In its explanatory statement, the majority tries to have it both ways: it manages at once to suggest that this case is based on a traditional theory, which requires a showing of intent, and at the same time to say that this case is based on a novel theory, apparently to explain the absence of any showing or allegation of intent. The complaint and order combined with the explanatory statement of the majority give rise to troubling implications about the duty of care in the standards-setting process.

I. FACTUAL BACKGROUND

This is a case about alleged abuse of the standards-setting process by a patent holder. The facts alleged in the complaint are not complex. The Video Electronics Standards Association ("VESA") is a private standards-setting organization, including as members both computer hardware and software manufacturers. In 1991 and 1992, VESA developed a standard for a computer bus design, called the VESA Local Bus ("VL-bus"). The bus carries information and instructions between the computer's central processing unit and peripheral devices. In August 1992, VESA conducted a vote to approve its VL-bus standard. The VESA ballot required each member's authorized voting representative to sign a statement that "to the best of my knowledge," the proposal did not infringe the member company's intellectual property rights.

According to the Commission's complaint, after adoption of the standard, the VL-bus design was incorporated in many computers. The complaint alleges that Dell subsequently asserted that the "implementation of the VL-bus [by other computer manufacturers] is a violation of Dell's exclusive [patent] rights." For purposes of antitrust analysis, it is important to note that the complaint does not allege that Dell's representative to VESA had any knowledge of the coverage of Dell's relevant patent (known as the "'481" patent) or of the potential infringement by the VL-bus at the time he cast the ballot.

Nothing in the limited information available to the Commission suggests that Dell had any greater role in the development and promulgation of the VESA VL-bus standard than that described in the minimal factual allegations in the complaint. For example, the complaint does not allege that Dell proposed or sponsored the standard, that Dell urged others to vote for the standard, that Dell employees participated in drafting the standard, that Dell employees were present, in person or online, during the committee drafting sessions, that Dell steered the VESA committee toward adopting a standard that incorporated Dell technology, or that Dell had any hand whatsoever in shaping the standard.

The sole act for which Dell is charged with a violation of law is that Dell's voting representative, in voting to adopt the standard, signed a certification that to the best of his knowledge, the proposed standard did not infringe on any relevant intellectual property.

II.   INTENTIONAL FRAUD OR ABUSE OF THE STANDARDS PROCESS

This might have been a routine antitrust case. A traditional antitrust analysis of Dell's conduct would have centered on two questions: whether Dell intentionally misled VESA into adopting a VL-bus standard that was covered by Dell's '481 patent and whether, as a result of the adoption of such a standard, Dell obtained market power beyond that lawfully conferred by the patent. If Dell had obtained market power by knowingly or intentionally misleading a standards-setting organization, it would require no stretch of established monopolization theory to condemn that conduct. Indeed, Section IV of the order against Dell seems to address precisely such a traditional antitrust violation. It prohibits Dell's enforcement of intellectual property rights only if in response to a written inquiry "respondent intentionally failed to disclose such patent rights" during the standards-setting process. (Emphasis added). The public comments, the majority, and I all seem to agree that Section 5 of the Federal Trade Commission Act ("FTC Act") prohibits knowing deception of standards makers to acquire market power and other intentional abuses of the standards process. If the case had gone only this far, it likely would not have elicited comment or controversy.

The novelty of the case against Dell, the reason it has been characterized as precedent-setting, is that the order prohibits Dell from enforcing the '481 patent without any allegation in the complaint that Dell intentionally and knowingly misled VESA and without any allegation that Dell obtained market power as a result of the misstatement at issue. The complaint does not allege that Dell's voting representative was aware either of the patent or of the potential infringement at the time the vote was taken.

The way in which the Commission handles the factual questions of intent and knowledge is critical to the policy issue at the core of this case, which is the nature and extent of the duty under Section 5 of the FTC Act of a member of a standards-setting organization in the standards-setting process. It is one thing to prohibit a knowing misrepresentation or an intentional manipulation; under that standard, it is clear how to avoid liability. It is quite another matter to base liability on constructive knowledge or unsubstantiated inferences. It is possible to assert that Dell "must have" known of the patent, because obviously some people at Dell did know about the patent. That sort of logic leads to a strict liability standard, under which a company would place its intellectual property at risk simply by participating in the standards-setting process. No matter how much money, time and talent a company might devote to avoiding mistakes in the certification process, a mistake still would be possible and potentially very costly.

By finding a violation of Section 5 in the absence of any allegation of a knowing or intentional misrepresentation, the Commission effectively imposes a duty of disclosure on Dell beyond what VESA required. The Commission may have the authority to do this but the question is whether it is advisable. VESA might have required, but did not, that each voting representative certify, on behalf of the entire company, that nothing in its entire patent portfolio overlapped with the standard and have made the certification binding regardless of any mistakes or subsequent, good faith discoveries. Had that been the standard, the process of collecting votes likely would have been quite prolonged and, perhaps, even impossible. Nevertheless, VESA could have structured its process in this more exacting way. Perhaps there is a good reason why it did not.

The theory of antitrust liability for intentional abuse of the standards process is similar to the monopolization theory applied in cases of fraud on the Patent and Trademark Office ("PTO"). In addition, although the decisions of the Court of Appeals for the Federal Circuit in patent cases are not controlling in cases under Section 5 of the FTC Act, it may be useful to consider the principles in those cases.

Two standards have been applied by the courts, respectively, in determining fraud on or inequitable conduct before the PTO. First, to prove fraud on the PTO necessary to make an unlawful monopolization claim, based on the Supreme Court's decision in Walker Process, a party must make out a common law fraud claim, including proof of a material misrepresentation, intentionally made to deceive, and reasonably relied on by the PTO. Second, although the showing of inequitable conduct as a defense to a patent infringement claim is less rigorous than that necessary to establish common law fraud, the Court of Appeals for the Federal Circuit nonetheless requires clear and convincing evidence that the patent applicant failed to disclose material information known to the applicant, or that the applicant submitted false information with the intent to act inequitably. Patent law is not within the institutional expertise of the Commission, but it would seem useful to study the history and policy underlying these strict requirements for establishing liability before setting forth in a different direction and creating new theories under Section 5 of the FTC Act.

III.   ANTICOMPETITIVE EFFECTS

A second notable omission from the Dell complaint is any allegation that the company acquired or extended market power. Instead, paragraph nine of the complaint alleges that Dell unreasonably restrained competition in four ways: (1) industry acceptance of the VL-bus "was hindered"; (2) systems using the VL-bus "were avoided"; (3) uncertainty concerning the acceptance of the VL-bus design standard "raised the costs of implementing the VL-bus design" and "of developing competing bus designs"; and (4) "willingness to participate in industry standards-setting efforts have [sic] been chilled." Assuming the allegations are true, none of them suggests that Dell acquired the power to control price and output in a relevant antitrust market. Indeed, if, as appears from the allegations to be the case, computer producers readily could switch to bus designs that do not incorporate Dell's technology, no monopoly seems possible. The first three allegations regarding delay in acceptance of the standard, avoidance of systems using the VL-bus, and uncertainty about the bus standard, all relate to the speed and breadth of industry acceptance of the standard. Assuming that industry acceptance of the bus was slower or less extensive than it otherwise would have been, those effects do not necessarily translate into higher prices of computers for consumers, restricted output of computers in any relevant geographic market, or any other harm to consumers or competition.

Although the complaint does not allege that Dell acquired market power, the majority asserts in its explanatory statement that "once VESA's VL-bus standard had become widely accepted, the standard effectively conferred market power upon Dell as the patent holder." It is worth noting that even here the majority does not allege that Dell did anything to acquire market power. In addition, the majority fails to identify the relevant market in which market power assertedly was "conferred." Dell is a producer of computers, and the press release announcing that the order had been accepted for public comment stated that Dell restricted competition "in the personal computer industry." Perhaps the majority actually does mean to find that Dell has market power in the personal computer industry; if so, some explanation is needed to make the finding more plausible, and an allegation to that effect in the complaint would seem to be in order.

The fourth allegation in the complaint, that Dell "chilled" willingness to participate in standards-setting, is particularly odd. Under the Dell order, a participant in a VESA-like standards process would be well advised not only to review its patent portfolio carefully before permitting its voting representative to sign a ballot, but if it has valuable intellectual property to protect, it might well consider not voting at all. The danger that voting on a standard might result in the loss of a company's intellectual property rights may dissuade some firms from participating in the standards-setting process in the first place. That would be a curious result indeed for an order resting on a complaint that alleges, as an anticompetitive effect, that "[w]illingness to participate in industry standard-setting efforts ha[s] been chilled."

IV. REMEDY

The relief imposed by the majority seems unnecessarily harsh. The order prohibits Dell from enforcing its '481 patent against any firm using the patented technology to implement the VL-bus design for the life of the patent. In effect, the order requires Dell to provide a global royalty-free license to any firm that may have used the technology in the past, or may use it in the future, to implement the standard. The explanatory statement of the majority indicates that the relief is "carefully limited to the facts of the case," because VESA's disclosure requirement "creates an expectation by its members" that intellectual property rights will be disclosed. This emphasis on an "expectation" sounds like a private patent estoppel case, not a competition case brought in the interest of the public. In any event, the complaint did not allege an "expectation" by VESA members as an element of the offense or of the competitive effects.

The private remedy of patent estoppel should suffice to remedy expectations based on Dell's conduct by barring inappropriate enforcement of a patent claim. The three elements of patent estoppel are: (1) a misleading communication by way of words, conduct or silence by a knowledgeable patentee; (2) reliance by another party on the communication; and (3) material prejudice to the other party if the patent holder is allowed to proceed. If Dell's vote with its accompanying certification was misleading, and if another VESA member relied on the certification to its material prejudice, then the other firm may assert estoppel as a bar to any claims under the patent. The Commission order, however, bars Dell from enforcing its patent without regard to whether the infringer relied on the miscommunication or whether the infringer would be materially prejudiced. If, as the majority suggests in its explanatory statement, an "expectation" is a critical underpinning of the remedy, it seems curious to bar enforcement of the patent without some better proof of expectation.

The anticompetitive effects alleged in the complaint were all highly ephemeral; they involved a delay in industry acceptance of the VL-bus design standard, avoidance of systems using the standard, and increased costs due to uncertainty about acceptance of the VL-bus and development of competing bus designs. As a practical matter, a Commission order, entered in 1996, can do little to correct any uncertainty and delay that might have occurred in early 1993, when Dell asserted the claim. Presumably, companies have long since decided what bus design to select. In a "precedent-setting" matter such as this one, the Commission should attempt to identify the relevant competitive interests and strike a fair balance among them. An order limiting enforcement of an undisclosed patent for an ample period of time to permit modification of the standard to eliminate the patent conflict would be less draconian than the majority's permanent ban on enforcement and seems more proportional to the alleged harm.

V. PUBLIC COMMENTS

Eleven thoughtful comments reflecting diverse viewpoints in the business community have been received. The comments contain a wealth of information and analysis, and I commend them in their entirety to anyone with an interest in this area. The comments reflect an unusual degree of concern and apprehension about the implications of the order. Several of the nation's most significant standards-setting organizations have written to state their opposition to the broad implications of the order and its possible chilling effect on the participation of firms with broad patent portfolios in the standards-setting process. VESA and a few other groups, however, support this or an even stronger order.

Seven commenters strongly opposed the imposition on participants in the standards-setting process of any duty to identify and disclose patents. The American National Standards Institute ("ANSI"), an umbrella organization that accredits standards development organizations, supported liability for failure to disclose relevant patents only insofar as a firm "intentionally and deliberately fails to disclose . . . in an attempt to gain an unfair advantage." ANSI opposed the imposition of any affirmative duty to identify and disclose patents, because it would chill participation in standards development. ANSI also expressed concern that the Dell remedy, which could be characterized as forfeiture of patent rights or mandatory licensing, might harm the United States' position in international negotiations. Five standards development organizations and an intellectual property law bar association filed comments that supported all or parts of ANSI's comment.

The American Intellectual Property Law Association ("AIPLA"), a national bar association of intellectual property attorneys, supported the reconciliation of the rights of standards users and owners of intellectual property as set forth in ANSI's patent policy. AIPLA agreed with ANSI that unless limited to egregious facts, the Dell order will discourage industry cooperation in standards-setting. Because patent disputes in the standards as in other contexts are highly fact specific, AIPLA said that private patent estoppel litigation is a better forum than a Section 5 proceeding to resolve such disputes. AIPLA noted that the Dell remedy constitutes a forfeiture of patent rights or compulsory licensing and said that the remedy is too drastic and inappropriate for many situations.

Several other commenters also endorsed a standard that requires a showing of intent, including the Electronic Industries Association ("EIA"), the Telecommunications Industry Association ("TIA"), the Standards Board of the Institute of Electrical and Electronic Engineers ("IEEE"), and the Alliance for Telecommunications Industry Solutions, Inc. (ATIS).

ANSI addressed the dangers of imposing liability on the basis of an unintentional failure to disclose a patent or of imposing an affirmative obligation to search patent portfolios. For firms with hundreds of employees involved in standards-setting and with tens of thousands of patents, an affirmative obligation to search for patents would present the choice of either avoiding standards-setting or placing their intellectual property at risk. Several other commenters expressed the same concern. The EIA and TIA warned of a "profound chilling effect" on standards-making if Dell is extended to situations of negligent failure to disclose. The Standards Board of the IEEE similarly commented that if "a 'disclose it or lose it' approach becomes the test, the very robust standards-setting activities in industry today will be quickly truncated to a minimal level." Others expressed similar concerns.

The ANSI patent policy reconciles the interests of patent owners with the users of standards. The policy provides that the patent holder must supply ANSI with either:

1. A general disclaimer to the effect that the patent holder does not hold and does not anticipate holding any invention the use of which would be required for, compliance with the proposed standard, or

2. A written assurance that either:

a) A license will be made available to applicants desiring to utilize the license for the purpose of implementing the standard without compensation to the patent holder, or

b) A license will be made available to applicants under reasonable terms and conditions that are demonstrably free of unfair discrimination.

ANSI specifically anticipates and addresses the situation in which intellectual property that bears on a standard is discovered after the standard is adopted. "Under ANSI's patent policy, the patent holder is then required to provide the same assurances to ANSI that are required in situations where patents are known to exist prior to the standard's approval. If those assurances are not forthcoming or if potential users can show that the policy is not being followed, the standard may be withdrawn through the appeals process." Several other commenters follow this ANSI policy. Indeed, the patent policy attached to the VESA comment appears for all practical purposes to be like the ANSI policy.

Two commenters took issue with the statement quoted in the press release announcing the consent order for public comment that "[o]pen, industry-wide standards also benefit consumers because they can be used by everyone without cost." The ITI and the Standards Board of the IEEE disagreed with the view that open standards are standards without cost, observing that the common meaning of an open standard includes standards that incorporate patented technology licensed by the patent owner. It appears from the explanations in the comments that the statement in the Commission's press release was simply a mistake based on a lack of knowledge, rather than an attempt to effect a major change in the way business is done, with the attendant costs and dangers of such a change. The primary significance of this issue is that it illustrates that the Commission does not have a great deal of experience in this area and should tread carefully.

Four comments, including one anonymous comment, supported the imposition of a duty to search for and disclose patents during the standards-setting process. The American Committee for Interoperable Systems ("ACIS") argued that it is appropriate to place the burden to search for patent/standard conflicts on the patent holder because the patent holder is in the better position to determine if its patent reads on the standard. ACIS downplayed the concern about chilling participation in the development of standards and noted that participation in standards-setting is motivated by commercial self-interest and "is not a form of charitable or community service." Bay Networks, Inc., also appears to support a strict liability standard. It would require firms participating in standards-setting to identify and disclose intellectual property rights or waive any such rights needed to practice the standard. Bay Networks argued that a requirement to license on reasonable and nondiscriminatory terms may not be sufficient, because firms may disagree about the meaning of these terms.

VESA favored imposition of a "general duty of members of standards associations to disclose the existence of intellectual property rights (or potential rights) that the member is aware of. . ." In VESA's view, the disclosure duty should not be limited to the engineers involved in the standards-setting process. Instead, VESA favors "implying a duty to disclose on the organization that is participating in the standard-setting activities, as opposed to simply limiting that duty to the engineers involved." VESA would put the burden of showing good faith on the party "belatedly" asserting a patent or other intellectual property rights. The VESA Board Policy for dealing with proprietary standards is very like ANSI's patent policy, which is quoted at pages 6-7 of the ANSI comment. It is not clear why the VESA patent policy was not sufficient to deal with the facts of this case.

Several comments applauded Commission action to halt intentional misrepresentations or intentional abuse of the standards process. These comments appear to be based on the erroneous assumption that the Commission's complaint against Dell alleges knowing, intentional deception of VESA, and they do not address the specific question of conduct that is not based on an allegation of intent or knowing misrepresentation.

NOTES & QUESTIONS

1. The dissent by Commissioner Azcuenaga provides a broader perspective on the case than the majority opinion. The legal issue is the meaning of "unfair or deceptive trade practice" under the Federal Trade Commission Act. What is the basis for concluding that Dell's conduct was deceptive? Unfair? Look at Commissioner Azcuenaga's discussion of Dell's intent and the anticompetitive effects of Dell's conduct. What legal guidance is she providing for companies that participate in standard setting organizations? For a discussion of the impact of antitrust laws on intellectual property issues faced by standard setting organizations, see Mark A. Lemley, *Intellectual Property Rights and Standard Setting Organizations,* 90 CAL. L. REV. 1889, 1937-1948 (2002) (reviewing antitrust limitations on enforcement of intellectual property rights against standard setting organizations).

2. Review the provisions of the National Cooperative Research Act (NCRA) excerpted in Section A. How would that Act deal with Dell's actions with respect to VESA? How would the NCRA deal with VESA itself? Note that the NCRA establishes rule of reason treatment for antitrust claims against joint ventures. Would VESA be considered a joint venture under the NCRA?

3. Standard setting organizations have been the focus of several legal controversies in addition to the dispute leading to the Dell consent decree. In March, 2003, the FTC brought a complaint against Union Oil of California (Unocal) for its activities in persuading the State of California to adopt environmental standards for reformulated gasoline when the company had proprietary rights in emissions data and the gasoline. Unocal did not disclose its proprietary interests and subsequently enforced its patent rights against rival oil companies

attempting to comply with the standard. In November, 2003, an administrative law judge made an initial ruling that Unocal's actions were protected by the Noerr-Pennington doctrine, which immunizes lobbying and political activities from antitrust scrutiny. The matter remains open at the FTC as of this writing.

The computer chip manufacturer Rambus also faced scrutiny for enforcing its patent rights in the design of a computer memory chip against rival company Infineon, which designed its memory board to conform to a standard established by the Joint Electronic Devices Engineering Council (JEDEC). Rambus had been involved with the standard setting process by JEDEC, and Infineon claimed that Rambus had failed to disclose its proprietary interest in the technology that was central to the standard, as required by the rules of JEDEC. After an initial victory at the district court level, Infineon saw its $3.5 million verdict overturned by the Federal Circuit, which held 2-1 that JEDEC's disclosure rules were too amorphous and vague to support a finding of fraud by Rambus. See *Rambus, Inc. v. Infineon Technologies,* 318 F.3d 1081 (C.A.F.C. 2003). In 2002, the FTC initiated a complaint against Rambus for deceiving JEDEC, a complaint that was reminiscent of the complaint in the Dell dispute. In 2004, an administrative law judge dismissed the complaint on the grounds that Rambus had not acted deceptively, that Rambus had not acquired monopoly power as a result of the standard adopted by JEDEC, and that Rambus' conduct did not have anticompetitive effects. The investigation is still active at the FTC, with the agency recently looking into possible perjury and document tampering by the company.

4. How would you counsel a standard setting organization in light of the materials presented? What other issues, in addition to the ones here, would you want to pursue? Would disclosure of a proprietary interest to a standard setting body under a confidentiality agreement be a wise and effective strategy?

E. INTERNATIONAL PERSPECTIVE FROM THE EUROPEAN UNION

European Union Competition Commission Decision of March 24, 2004, relating to a proceeding under Article 82 of the EC Treaty
Case COMP/C-3/37.792 Microsoft

1. PARTIES TO THE PROCEEDINGS

1.1 Microsoft Corporation

(1) Microsoft Corporation ("Microsoft"), a company based in Redmond, state of Washington, USA, manufactures, licenses and supports a wide variety of software products for many computing devices. Its turnover for the fiscal year July 2002 to June 2003 was USD 32,187 million (EUR 30,701 million) on which it earned net profits of USD 13,217 million (EUR 12,607 million). Microsoft employs 55,000 people around the world. Microsoft Europe Middle

East & Africa controls its activities in the European Economic Area ("EEA") from Paris La DÈfense. Microsoft is present in all countries within the EEA.

1.2   The complainant: Sun Microsystems, Inc.

(2) Sun Microsystems Inc. ("Sun"), a company based in Palo Alto, California, USA, provides network computing infrastructure solutions that comprise computer systems (hardware and software), network storage systems (hardware and software), support services and professional and educational services. Its turnover for the fiscal year July 2002 to June 2003 was USD 11,434 million (EUR 10,906 million) on which it suffered a net loss of USD 2,378 million (EUR 2,268 million). Sun employs some 36,100 people around the world. Sun is present in all countries within the EEA.

2.   CHRONOLOGY OF THE PROCEDURE AND BACKGROUND

2.1   The procedure

(3) On 10 December 1998, Sun made an application to the Commission pursuant to Article 3 of Regulation No 17 for the initiation of proceedings against Microsoft ("Sun's Complaint"). Sun alleged that Microsoft enjoyed a dominant position as a supplier of a certain type of software product called operating systems for personal computers ("PC operating systems"). Sun further contended that Microsoft infringed Article 82 of the Treaty by reserving to itself information that certain software products for network computing, called work group server operating systems, need to interoperate fully with Microsoft's PC operating systems. According to Sun, the withheld interoperability information is necessary to viably compete as a work group server operating system supplier.

(4) The case opened pursuant to Sun's complaint was registered as Case IV/C-3/37.345. After a first investigation of the complaint, the Commission, on 1 August 2000, sent a Statement of Objections to Microsoft to give Microsoft opportunity to comment on its preliminary findings of facts and law. The Statement of Objections focused on the interoperability issues that formed the basis of Sun's complaint. Microsoft responded to the Statement of Objections on 17 November 2000.

(5) In the interim (February 2000), the Commission had launched an investigation into Microsoft's conduct on its own initiative, under Regulation No 17, which was registered as Case COMP/C-3/37.792. The investigation carried out under that case concerned more specifically Microsoft's "Windows 2000" generation of PC and work group server operating systems and Microsoft's incorporation of a software product called "Windows Media Player" into its PC operating system products. On 30 August 2001, that investigation resulted in the sending of a second Statement of Objections to Microsoft. The second Statement of Objections concerned issues of interoperability as well as the incorporation of Windows Media Player in Windows. The Commission, by virtue of the second Statement of Objections, joined the relevant findings set

out in the first Statement of Objections to the procedure followed under Case COMP/C-3/37.792. On 16 November 2001, Microsoft responded to the second Statement of Objections.

(6) In its responses to both the first and second Statements of Objections, Microsoft submitted several statements from customers (enterprises and administrations) and system integrators, purportedly supporting its responses to the Commission's objections concerning interoperability. Altogether, 46 such Microsoft customer statements were submitted.

(7) In February and March 2002, the Commission sent a round of requests for information to those 46 customers, with a view to obtaining quantitative data on those customers' use of products relevant to the Commission's investigation.

(8) From April to June 2003, the Commission engaged in a wider market enquiry. For interoperability, on the basis of an independent sample of organisations that use PC and work group server operating systems, a first set of requests for information was sent on 16 April 2003 to 75 companies, all based in the EEA. Those companies, which were selected at random, are from a number of different activity sectors and of different sizes. Some of the 71 companies which responded provided answers for their sub-entities/subsidiaries or for sister-companies in the same group, so the total number of responses was in fact over 100, covering more than 1.2 million client PCs (desktops and laptops). The replies to the questionnaire generated additional queries, and a follow-up questionnaire was therefore sent on 28 May 2003 and on 4 June 2003 to the 62 organizations that at those points in time had already responded to the requests for information of 16 April 2003.

(9) In parallel, 46 requests for information were sent on 16 April 2003 to companies active in areas relevant to the issues raised by the incorporation of Windows Media Player into Windows (content owners, content providers, software developers and associations of such companies). 33 responses were received.

. . .

(11) Throughout the procedure, a significant number of companies, comprising major Microsoft competitors, as well as industrial associations, have been admitted as interested third parties. These are inter alia the Association for Competitive Technology, Time Warner Inc., the Computer & Communications Industry Association, the Computing Technology Industry Association, the Free Software Foundation Europe, Lotus Corporation, Novell Inc, RealNetworks, Inc., and the Software & Information Industry Association. Microsoft has been asked to comment on certain submissions by these interested third parties and by the complainant Sun, and in particular on the comments that these third parties and the complainant made on Microsoft's reply to the second Statement of Objections and on certain submissions that they made following the supplementary Statement of Objections.

. . .

5.   ECONOMIC AND LEGAL ASSESSMENT

. . .

(316) Under Article 82 of the Treaty, any abuse by one or more undertakings having a dominant position within the common market or in a substantial part of it is prohibited as incompatible with the common market in so far as it may affect trade between Member States.

(317) Under Article 54 of the EEA Agreement, any abuse by one or more undertakings of a dominant position within the territory covered by the Agreement or in a substantial part of it is prohibited in so far as it may affect trade between the contracting parties to the Agreement.

(318) Microsoft is an undertaking within the meaning of Article 82 of the Treaty and Article 54 of the EEA Agreement. Its relevant conduct affects the whole of the EEA.

(319) Insofar as Microsoft's conduct affects trade between Member States, Article 82 of the Treaty applies. As regards the effects on competition in Norway, Iceland and Liechtenstein, and the effects on trade between the Community and those countries, as well as between those three countries, Article 54 of the EEA Agreement applies.

(320) Microsoft does not earn more than 33% of its EEA turnover in the EFTA Member States. Therefore, pursuant to Article 56 (1) (c) and Article 56 (3) of the EEA agreement, the Commission is competent in this case to apply both Article 82 of the Treaty and Article 54 of the EEA Agreement.

5.2   Dominant position

(428) A dominant position under Article 82 of the Treaty has been defined by the Court of Justice of the European Communities as a position of economic strength enjoyed by an undertaking which enables it to prevent effective competition being maintained on the relevant market by affording it the power to behave to an appreciable extent independently of its competitors, its customers and ultimately of the consumers.

5.3   Abuses

(542) The fact that an undertaking holds a dominant position is not in itself contrary to the competition rules. However, an undertaking enjoying a dominant position is under a special responsibility not to engage in conduct that may distort competition.

(543) The Court of Justice defined the concept of abuse under Article 82 of the Treaty in the following terms:

> The concept of abuse is an objective concept relating to the behaviour of an undertaking in a dominant position which is such as to influence the structure of a market where, as a result of the very presence of the undertaking in question, the degree of competition is weakened and

which, through recourse to methods different from those which condition normal competition in products or services on the basis of the transactions of commercial operators, has the effect of hindering the maintenance of the degree of competition still existing in the market or the growth of that competition. . . .

(545) In the following, Microsoft's behavior will be assessed pursuant to Article 82 of the Treaty. The behavior assessed can be grouped in the following two categories: Microsoft's refusal to supply interoperability information (Section 5.3.1) and Microsoft's tying of WMP with Windows (Section 5.3.2).

5.3.1 Refusal to supply

(546) In the following recitals (recitals (547) to (791)), it will be established that Microsoft is abusing its dominant position by refusing to supply Sun and other undertakings with the specifications for the protocols used by Windows work group servers in order to provide file, print and group and user administration services to Windows work group networks, and allow these undertakings to implement such specifications for the purpose of developing and distributing interoperable work group server operating system products. As outlined above, it cannot be excluded that ordering Microsoft to disclose such specifications and allow such use of them by third parties restricts the exercise of Microsoft's intellectual property rights.

(547) Although undertakings are, as a rule, free to choose their business partners, under certain circumstances a refusal to supply by a dominant undertaking may constitute an abuse of dominance pursuant to Article 82 of the Treaty, unless it is objectively justified. This may also be the case for a refusal to license intellectual property rights.

. . .

(550) [The] *Magill* [case] concerned the refusal of TV broadcasters to license intellectual property in the form of (copyright-protected) programme listings. The Court of Justice stated that — the refusal by the owner of an exclusive right [copyright] to grant a license, even if it is the act of an undertaking holding a dominant position, cannot in itself constitute abuse of a dominant position. It pointed out, however, that the exercise of an exclusive right by the proprietor may, in exceptional circumstances, involve abusive conduct thereby clarifying that intellectual property rights are not in a different category to property rights as such. On this basis, the Court of Justice upheld the Commission's Decision (and the Court of First Instance's judgment) which mandated compulsory licensing of the right to reproduce the copyrighted programme listings.

(551) There were three sets of exceptional circumstances identified in *Magill*. First, the Court of Justice underlined that the dominant undertakings' refusal prevented the appearance of a new product which the dominant undertakings did not offer and for which there was a potential consumer demand. As such, the refusal was inconsistent in particular with Article 82 (b) of the Treaty, which provides that abuse as prohibited by Article 82 of the Treaty may consist

in limiting production, markets or technical development to the prejudice of consumers. Second, along the lines of Commercial Solvents, the Court of Justice pointed out that the conduct in question enabled the dominant undertakings to reserve to themselves the secondary market of weekly television guides by excluding all competition on that market. Third, the refusal was not objectively justified.

. . .

(555) On a general note, there is no persuasiveness to an approach that would advocate the existence of an exhaustive checklist of exceptional circumstances and would have the Commission disregard a limine other circumstances of exceptional character that may deserve to be taken into account when assessing a refusal to supply.

(558) The case law of the European Courts therefore suggests that the Commission must analyze the entirety of the circumstances surrounding a specific instance of a refusal to supply and must take its decision based on the results of such a comprehensive examination.

(559) It is against this backdrop that in the following sections, the relevant circumstances are examined under which Microsoft's refusal to supply occurs. 5.3.1.1 Refusal to supply

5.3.1.1.1   Refusal to supply Sun

(560) Sun's request and Microsoft's behaviour in response to it have been described above. Sun asked Microsoft to supply, inter alia, the specifications for the protocols used by Windows work group servers in order to provide file, print and group and user administration services to Windows work group networks and allow the use of such specifications for the purpose of developing and distributing interoperable work group server operating system products. Microsoft refuses to provide that information to Sun.

(561) Microsoft denies that there is a proper request and a refusal to supply interoperability information in this case.

(562) First, Microsoft argues that the market definition proposed by the Commission "has the effect of excluding Sun from the product market, so whatever complaints Sun may have had about disclosures of information [. . .] have no relevance to the case ." This is incorrect: Sun is present in the market for work group server operating systems (although its market share is very low). Sun's investment in PC NetLink shows Sun's interest in selling servers that deliver work group server functionality to Windows client PCs. In any case, considering inter alia Sun's strong presence as a server vendor, even if it were absent from the work group server operating system market, quod non, it still would have an interest in entering that market. There is no reason why a refusal to supply an undertaking that has an interest in entering the market should be treated differently to a refusal to supply a company that is already present in the market. In *Magill.* for instance, the company to which supply was refused was not competing in the market that was being monopolized — precisely because such supply had been refused.

(563) Second, Microsoft argues that it "has consistently disclosed large amounts of interface information about its operating systems, a practice that continues with Windows 2000" and that "there is therefore no refusal to supply interface information in this case." This argument is incorrect. The fact that Microsoft discloses certain pieces of interface information does not mean that it does not refuse other pieces of interface information, or that it discloses enough interface information. As outlined above, most elements of the large amount of interface information that Microsoft referred to are obsolete, or unrelated to the request at issue.

(564) Third, Microsoft argues that its refusal to provide Sun with the information that it has requested is not a refusal to supply interface information, because Sun's request was not directed at interface information. It has been established that it is factually incorrect to say that Microsoft does not refuse interface information to its competitors in the work group server operating system market. In this respect, it is also noteworthy that, in its application for initiation of proceedings by the Commission, Sun requested that the Commission order Microsoft to disclose and make available for use sufficient interface information to provide equality of attachment from the server environment to the Microsoft desktop (irrespective of whether the desktop is already part of a network which includes Microsoft server products). After having received a copy of Sun's complaint (and indeed after having received three statements of objections), Microsoft has persisted in its refusal.

(565) Fourth, to the extent that Microsoft's argument is that Sun's request was too broad because it was not limited to the interface information that was essential to market commercially viable work group server operating systems, this argument cannot be accepted either. It is quite an unrealistic proposition to argue that Sun should have explained in detail what minimum level of disclosure of interoperability information relating to Active Directory and COM was sufficient for Microsoft to dispense with its obligations under Community competition law. This would have been all the more difficult since the technologies at stake are complex, and were not fully known by Sun - this lack of information being precisely the reason underpinning Sun's request.

(566) For the sake of clarity, since only the core work group server tasks of file, print and group and user administration are essential to compete in the work group server operating systems, the only refusal at stake in this Decision is a refusal to provide a full specification of the protocols underlying the Windows domain architecture, which organizes the way through which Windows work group servers deliver work group server services to Windows client PCs. The fact that Microsoft has also turned down Sun's request for information that would facilitate cross-platform portability of COM objects does not form part of the conduct treated in this Decision as a refusal to supply.

(567) Finally, Microsoft's argument that the features about which Sun complains are on Windows 2000 Server, not Windows 2000 Professional is worth mentioning. As such, its refusal to Sun would be unrelated to its client PC operating system dominance. However, the features about which Sun complains rely on code present in Microsoft's client PC operating system prod-

ucts. Whilst it is true that Sun's request involves both client-to-server and server-to-server interoperability, in the present case the latter interconnections and interactions are functionally related to the client PC. This link back to the client PC operating system market implies that the competitive value of the information refused derives from Microsoft's market strength in the client PC operating system market. Insofar as Microsoft's refusal is considered abusive, the abuse derives from Microsoft's dominance on the client PC operating system market.

5.3.1.1.2   The refusal at issue is not a refusal to license source code

(568) Microsoft interprets the letter by Mr. Green as "a demand by Sun that Microsoft create a version of [. . .] Active Directory [. . .] that Sun could use on Solaris." Microsoft thus apparently argues that what Sun requested was a disclosure of source code written by Microsoft, and the right to copy or adapt that source code in order to integrate the copied or adapted code in its Solaris product. This interpretation seems to derive from Mr. Green's statement that Sun believes that Microsoft should provide a reference implementation for some or all of the relevant technologies.

(569) It bears reiteration, however, that the conduct that is relevant to this Decision is limited to Microsoft's refusal to supply a full specification of the protocols used by Windows work group servers to deliver work group server services to Windows work group networks, and to allow the use of that specification to build interoperable products.

(570) The distinction between interface specifications and implementation is important in this context. As outlined above, an interface specification describes what an implementation must achieve, not how it achieves it. In a report submitted by Sun, Professor Wirsing, a computer science professor, states that since it does not have to be executable [that is to say to run on a machine], a specification does not have to be concerned with details that are relevant to the implementation (e.g., memory allocation or details of most algorithms used in an actual realisation of the specification). Professor Wirsing illustrates this point by the following example: "[It] is easy to specify when a sequence of numbers is ordered: every number in the sequence is smaller or equal to its successor in the sequence. It is a lot harder to describe an algorithm for sorting a sequence of numbers and to make sure that it is correct."

(571) Not only is it therefore possible to provide interface specifications without giving access to all implementation details, but it has been outlined above that it is common practice in the industry to do so, in particular when open interoperability standards are set. In this respect, it is also noteworthy that, under the US Communications Protocols Licensing Program, licensees are not granted access to Microsoft's source code, but to specifications of the relevant protocols.

(572) In conclusion, Microsoft's refusal to supply as at issue in this Decision is a refusal to disclose specifications and allow their use for the development of compatible products. The present Decision does not contemplate ordering Microsoft to allow copying of Windows by third parties.

5.3.1.1.3   Additional circumstances to consider

5.3.1.1.3.1   Microsoft's refusal to Sun is part of a general pattern of conduct

(573) As outlined above, Microsoft has acknowledged that it does not intend to disclose the information requested by Sun to Sun or to any other work group server operating system vendor. Moreover, many competitors to Microsoft in the work group server operating system market have confirmed that they do not obtain sufficient interoperability information from Microsoft and feel that this puts them at a strong competitive disadvantage vis-à-vis Microsoft. Some of them (Novell, Samba) have argued that Microsoft refused to provide information that they had requested or failed to answer their requests.

(574) Some of Sun's competitors have received more of the relevant information than Sun has. This is for instance the case for SGI, Digital (now HP) and Compaq (now HP). But the licences granted to SGI and Digital only relate to Windows NT technology and not to Windows 2000 technology, whilst the licence granted to Compaq is, in Microsoft's own admission, of much more limited scope than the information requested by Sun, and is aimed at providing a migration path towards Windows.

. . .

(576) Microsoft's policy in licensing certain technologies necessary for interoperability with the Windows domain architecture is further evidence of Microsoft's strategy. At the Oral Hearing, Sun pointed to the following excerpts from testimony given to the US Courts by Mr. Dan Neault, who was Windows Source Licensing Program Manager in Microsoft in 1997:

> [Question to Mr. Neault]: You, in fact, proposed the following; that AT&T would have to agree that it would not enter into any ASU license arrangement with certain specified Microsoft competitors, correct?
>
> [Answer]: Yes.
>
> Q: And those competitors included, among others, Sun Microsystems, Netscape, IBM, Apple, Oracle, Novell, correct?
>
> A: That's correct.

(577) In conclusion, Microsoft's refusal to supply Sun is part of a broader conduct of not disclosing interoperability information to work group server operating system vendors.

5.3.1.1.3.2   Microsoft's conduct involves a disruption of previous levels of supply

(578) It has been highlighted that the European Courts have given weight to circumstances where a refusal to supply constituted a disruption of previous levels of supply.

(579) In this case, many of the already limited disclosures that had been undertaken by Microsoft with respect to Windows NT have been discontinued with the development of Windows 2000.

(580) Because of Microsoft's license of information to AT&T and the development of AS/U, it had been possible for Sun to adapt its work group server operating system products so that servers running them could be domain controllers in a Windows NT 4.0 domain.

(581) Due to the lower level of disclosures for Windows 2000, many protocols that enable Windows 2000 domain controllers to provide enhanced group and user administration to the Windows 2000 domain are not available to Sun. The upshot of this is that a server running Solaris cannot act as a domain controller in a Windows 2000 domain, notwithstanding the fact that Solaris, as Windows 2000 Server or Windows 2003 Server, Standard Edition, includes a state of the art directory service.

(582) Microsoft explains that its products provide a certain degree of backward-compatibility, which means that new versions of its operating system products such as Windows 2000 continue to exhibit certain interfaces that were present in previous versions of its operating system products such as Windows NT 4.0. According to Microsoft, the previous disclosures would still be relevant, and there would therefore be no discontinuation of previous levels of supply.

(583) However, Windows NT 4.0 technology is already outdated technology. It is being replaced by the Windows 2000 technology, which is based on different protocols. Backward compatibility enables the migration to be smoother, but is not intended to offer a durable solution. The intended "end state" of a Windows 2000 domain is the "native-mode," where all Windows NT domain controllers have been upgraded to Windows 2000 and cannot be downgraded back to Windows NT.

(584) In conclusion, by not disclosing the new interface specifications that organize the Windows 2000 domain while it previously disclosed part of the corresponding interface specifications for the Windows NT domain, Microsoft disrupts previous levels of supply.

5.3.1.2   Risk of elimination of competition

(585) In *Magill*, . . . one of the constituent elements of the abuse finding was that the dominant undertakings' behaviour risked eliminating competition. [T]he Court of Justice has clarified that, for the judgment in *Magill* to be relied upon, it was necessary to show that supply is indispensable to carry on business in the market, which means that there is no realistic actual or potential substitute to it.

(586) In this case, Microsoft's behaviour as regards disclosures of interface information must be analysed against the backdrop of two key elements, which have been outlined above. First, Microsoft enjoys a position of extraordinary market strength on the client PC operating system market. Second, interoperability with the client PC operating system is of significant competitive importance in the market for work group server operating systems.

(587) A historic look at the work group server operating system market shows that Microsoft entered this market relatively recently. UNIX vendors

and Novell were the first developers with significant activity and success in this area. Customers had started to build work group networks that contained non-Microsoft work group servers and Microsoft's competitors had a distinct technological lead. The value that their products brought to the network also augmented the client PC operating systems' value in the customers' eyes and therefore Microsoft — as long as it did not have a credible work group server operating system alternative — had incentives to have its client PC operating system interoperate with non-Microsoft work group server operating systems. While entering the work group server operating system market, pledging support for already established technologies was important in gaining a foothold and the confidence of the customers.

(588) Once Microsoft's work group server operating system gained acceptance in the market, however, Microsoft's incentives changed and holding back access to information relating to interoperability with the Windows environment started to make sense. With Windows 2000, Microsoft then engaged in a strategy of diminishing previous levels of supply of interoperability information. This disruption of previous levels of supply concerns elements that pertain to the core tasks that are expected from work group server operating systems, and in particular to the provision of group and user administration services.

(589) . . . Microsoft's refusal puts Microsoft's competitors at a strong competitive disadvantage in the work group server operating system market, to an extent where there is a risk of elimination of competition.

. . .

5.3.2   Tying of Windows Media Player with Windows

(792) In the following recitals, it will be established that Microsoft infringes Article 82 of the Treaty, in particular paragraph (d) thereof, by tying Windows Media Player with the Windows PC operating system. Article 82 (d) provides that abuse as prohibited by that Article may consist in making the conclusion of contracts subject to acceptance by the other parties of supplementary obligations which, by their nature or according to commercial usage, have no connection with the subject of such contracts.

(793) The Commission considers that Microsoft started to tie its streaming media player with Windows 98 Second Edition in May 1999. Whatever bundling Microsoft may have engaged in previously, with Windows 98 Second Edition, Microsoft tied for the first time the product that it offered in the relevant market for streaming media players. It will further be shown that since May 1999, Microsoft has persisted in the abusive behavior by tying WMP with subsequent versions of Windows.

5.3.2.1   Microsoft's conduct fulfills the constituent elements of a tying abuse under Article 82 of the Treaty

(794) Tying prohibited under Article 82 of the Treaty requires the presence of the following elements: (i) the tying and tied goods are two separate products; (ii) the undertaking concerned is dominant in the tying product market;

(iii) the undertaking concerned does not give customers a choice to obtain the tying product without the tied product; and (iv) tying forecloses competition.

(795) It will be established at recitals (799) to (954) that Microsoft's conduct fulfils the constituent elements of tying. Furthermore, it will be shown at recitals (956) to (970) that Microsoft's arguments to justify the tying of WMP do not prevail over the anticompetitive effects of tying.

(796) In discussing the individual elements of tying, the impact of the US Judgment and Microsoft's implementation of it will be examined. This is all the more important as Microsoft argues that the US Settlement (and the US Judgment) has had the practical effect of unbundling WMP and Windows. Microsoft states that it started implementing the US Settlement on 16 December 2001. Accordingly, OEMs would be free to install and promote other non-Microsoft media players. They could ship client PCs free from visible means of access to WMP and hence with RealPlayer or another media player pre-installed as the default player. Microsoft argues that any additional antitrust remedy on the Commission's part would therefore be unnecessary.

(797) As outlined above, the US proceedings focused on Microsoft's anticompetitive conduct of protecting its dominant client PC operating system from competitive threats posed by Netscape's Navigator and Sun's Java. Furthermore, the plaintiffs dropped their tying charge after the Court of Appeals ruled that tying in the case at issue should have been considered under a rule of reason approach and not under the per se approach proposed by the plaintiffs and adopted by the District Court in its Conclusions of Law. As a consequence, after the Court of Appeals' ruling, the District Court had no opportunity to consider whether Microsoft's conduct violated the prohibition of tying under § 1 of the Sherman Act.

(798) Consequently, the US Judgment does not purport to include a remedy for tying. In particular, the US Judgment does not provide for removal of WMP code from the PC operating system (and neither does Microsoft's altered business conduct). Under the US Judgment, Microsoft need only provide a means enabling OEMs and end-users to hide the icon and entries representing the WMP application on the computer screen. The WMP code is still present on top of each Windows operating system Microsoft ships. In her memorandum opinion on the US Judgment, Judge Kollar-Kotelly stated that any order to provide for the removal of software code from Windows would likely be reflected in the imposition of liability for illegal tying, rather than liability for illegal . . . monopoly maintenance.

. . .

5.3.2.3   Conclusion

(978) The Commission does not purport to pass judgment as to the desirability of one unique media player or set of media technologies (for example DRM, formats) coming to dominate the market. However, the manner in which competition unfolds in the media player market, which may or may not bring about such a result, is of competitive concern. Article 82 must be read in the light of its underlying objective which is to ensure that competition in the internal market is not distorted (see Article 3 (g) of the Treaty). To maintain

competitive markets so that innovations succeed or fail on the merits is an important objective of Community competition policy.

(979) Through tying WMP with Windows, Microsoft uses Windows as a distribution channel to anti-competitively ensure for itself a significant competition advantage in the media player market. Competitors, due to Microsoft's tying, are a priori at a disadvantage irrespective of whether their products are potentially more attractive on the merits.

(980) Microsoft thus interferes with the normal competitive process which would benefit users in terms of quicker cycles of innovation due to unfettered competition on the merits. Tying of WMP increases the content and applications barrier to entry which protects Windows and it will facilitate the erection of such a barrier for WMP. A position of market strength achieved in a market characterized by network effects - such as the media player market - is sustainable, as once the network effects work in favor of a company which has gained a decisive momentum, they will amount to entry barriers for potential competitors.

(981) This shields Microsoft from effective competition from potentially more efficient media player vendors which could challenge its position. Microsoft thus reduces the talent and capital invested in innovation of media players, not least its own and anti-competitively raises barriers to market entry. Microsoft's conduct affects a market which could be a hotbed for new and exciting products springing forth in a climate of undistorted competition.

(982) Moreover, tying of WMP allows Microsoft to anti-competitively expand its position in adjacent media-related software markets and weaken effective competition to the eventual detriment of consumers.

(983) Microsoft's tying of WMP also sends signals which deter innovation in any technologies which Microsoft could conceivably take interest in and tie with Windows in the future. Microsoft's tying instills actors in the relevant software markets with a sense of precariousness thereby weakening both software developers' incentives to innovate in similar areas and venture capitalists' proclivity to invest in independent software application companies. A start-up intending to enter or raise venture capital in such a market will be forced to test the resilience of its business model against the eventuality of Microsoft deciding to bundle its own version of the product with Windows.

(984) There is therefore a reasonable likelihood that tying WMP with Windows will lead to a lessening of competition so that the maintenance of an effective competition structure will not be ensured in the foreseeable future. For these reasons, tying WMP with Windows violates the prohibition to abuse a dominant position enshrined in Article 82 of the Treaty and in particular point (d) of the second paragraph thereof.

NOTES & QUESTIONS

1. The European Union Competition Commission initiated an investigation of Microsoft's practices in the early 1990's and joined in the 1994 settlement agreement between Microsoft and the Department of Justice. The timeline leading up to excerpted opinion from 2004 is as follows:

1998:   EU begins probe of Microsoft after a complaint is brought by Sun Microsystems stating anticompetitive conduct in the licensing of its operating system code

2000:   EU launches investigation of Windows 2000.

2001:   EU issues a charge sheet to Microsoft, alleging that the company abused its dominant position in violation of Article 82 of the European Committee Competition Treaty. The charge sheet orders Microsoft to unbundle Media Player from its operating system.

2002:   Microsoft proposes concessions to the EU, such as including software of rival companies on a CD with sales of Windows. The EU rejects the proposals.

2003:   EU submits another charge sheet to Microsoft, ordering changes to Windows 2000.

2004:   EU Competition Chief Mario Monti issues the opinion, excerpted above, fining Microsoft 497 million Euros (613 million US dollars) and ordering the company to unbundle its Media Player from its operating system and to release portions of its source code to rival software companies in facilitate interoperability.

As of this writing, Microsoft is still in negotiations with the EU over compliance with Monti's order. Private suits against Microsoft are also proceeding in the EU.

2. Article 82 of the EC Treaty reads as follows:

Any abuse by one or more undertakings of a dominant position within the common market or in a substantial part of it shall be prohibited as incompatible with the common market insofar as it may affect trade between Member States.

Such abuse may, in particular, consist in:

(a) directly or indirectly imposing unfair purchase or selling prices or other unfair trading conditions;

(b) limiting production, markets or technical development to the prejudice of consumers;

(c) applying dissimilar conditions to equivalent transactions with other trading parties, thereby placing them at a competitive disadvantage;

(d) making the conclusion of contracts subject to acceptance by the other parties of supplementary obligations which, by their nature or according to commercial usage, have no connection with the subject of such contracts.

This provision is the counterpart in the EU to Section 2 of the Sherman Act. Compare the two provisions. Which seems to have more teeth?

3. Read the Commissioner's findings closely. How do they compare with the Court of Appeals' decision? Does the EU approach seem more sensitive to the

special problems posed by software? The argument could be made that the EU approach focuses more closely on business conduct while the US approach adopts a holistic approach to the marketplace. Is this argument borne out by a comparison of the two opinions?

4. The excerpt from the EU opinion, which goes on for several hundred pages in its full form, is presented to illustrate the global pitfalls that might await a high technology company. An understanding of United States law is not sufficient in planning for the global marketplace. Recall that Assistant Attorney General Pate, in the speech reprinted above, stated the need for harmonization of international competition law, especially with respect to the treatment of intellectual property. He also concludes that harmonization is occurring. After reading about the treatment of Microsoft in the United States and the European Union, do you have a sense that the law is harmonizing?

CHAPTER 14

MANAGING THE INTELLECTUAL PROPERTY PORTFOLIO

PROBLEM

Digital Ignition is undertaking an inventory of its intellectual property assets. Dr. See, the company's chief executive officer, would like to determine the best way to develop Digital Ignition's intellectual property portfolio in the company's present areas of technological excellence and to identify areas for further research and innovation leading to additional types of valuable intellectual property interests. He would like your thoughts, as an experienced intellectual property lawyer, on the types of intellectual property management issues that Digital Ignition should consider in this assessment of the company's present intellectual property portfolio and means to alter that portfolio in the future. In assisting him in thinking about this assessment, be sure to give careful consideration to both legal and business strategies regarding Digital Ignition's intellectual property and to the integration of the various areas of law that have been the focus of our studies.

FOCUS OF CHAPTER

Once a company has developed some critical technologies from which it has derived intellectual property assets, the company's executives will often wish to consider how to best maximize the value of these technologies and assets. The legal and business techniques for accomplishing are sometimes called "intellectual property management." You can imagine a company's technologies and intellectual property assets as a portfolio, similar to its financial assets. While managing a financial portfolio most often entails understanding market trends and following fluctuations in returns, managing an intellectual property portfolio entails combining business activity strategies with complementary acquisitions of legal rights and choices about how to enforce those rights. The readings in this chapter describe some of the most important business and legal issues that arise as companies pursue intellectual property portfolio management.

The excerpt from the article by Polk and Parchomovsky in Section A introduces the concept of the patent portfolio and illustrates several methods of patent portfolio management with several case studies. Polk and Parchomovsky argue that companies seek to maximize the value of a set of critical technologies rather than focusing on rights to one key invention or a series of unrelated patents. According to their interpretation, patenting strategies should be seen as attempts by companies to create optimal patent portfolio designs. This excerpt raises provocative questions of how to determine what constitutes an optimal patent portfolio and how to design a patenting strategy to obtain the optimal portfolio.

The readings in Sections B complement the interpretations of Polk and Parchomovsky by discussing how a company can best maximize the value of its intellectual property through joint ventures.

Finally, section C addresses special problems raised by the employment of intellectual property in "experimental uses" aimed at expanding the scope and value of existing knowledge. This type of problem has arisen, in part, through the unlicensed use of patented research tools in order to carry out valuable business or university activities, resulting, in some cases, in additionally valuable discoveries. However, considerable confusion has arisen as to whether this type of use of patented research tools is specially protected from patent infringement liability under either the common law experimental use doctrine long recognized by federal courts or under the more recent statutory experimental use provisions applicable to the pharmaceutical industry. The Supreme Court's 2005 decision in *Merck v. Integra*, excerpted below, assessed some of the issues surrounding the experimental use of research tools. Portions of two amici briefs submitted in the *Merck* case and excerpted below illustrate perspectives on the proper scope of infringement-free experimental use of patented tools that are very different from the tack adopted by the Supreme Court in its *Merck* decision. The impact of threatened infringement liability on the use of research tools provides an illuminating example of how patents affect research and development and product marketing choices.

Together, this set of readings provides an introduction to the theoretical and practical issues of intellectual property management. A consideration of how projected business opportunities and related legal standards affect management decisions provides a flavor of the type of decision making necessary to effectively market and disseminate new technologies in contemporary marketplaces.

READINGS

A. IDENTIFYING THE PATENT PORTFOLIO

R. Polk Wagner & Gideon Parchomovsky, Patent Portfolios
154 U. Penn. L. Rev. 1 (2005)*

[W]e will present three case studies that illustrate how companies employ the portfolio theory to gain and preserve a dominant position in their respective industries. It bears emphasis that the examples we use here are highly representative. There is ample evidence that the desire to achieve a strong patent portfolio shapes the patenting activities of virtually all innovating firms.

A.   Dominating a Technology via a Patent Portfolio: The Case of Qualcomm

Qualcomm rose to prominence in the mid-90s as part of the wave of technology firms that capitalized on the value of their patent portfolios by aggressively pursuing licensing agreements. The leap to superstardom, however, didn't occur until 1999, when the company began spinning off divisions in order to focus squarely on its intellectual property portfolio, and saw its stock soar over 2,000% (noteworthy even amidst the flurry of speculation driving the dot-com bubble). Despite suffering through the subsequent market downturn, the company has experienced significant growth over the past three years, including a $200 million increase in revenue from its licensing division.

This meteoric success can be traced back to 1989, when the four-year-old start-up introduced "code division multiple access" (CDMA) wireless technology as a better alternative to the "time division multiple access" (TDMA) digital system which had just been endorsed by the Cellular Telecommunications Industry Association (CTIA) after a two-year dispute over the industry standards. Despite the network externalities which created a substantial barrier to entry into the wireless market at that time, CDMA eventually supplanted TDMA, largely by virtue of being a superior technology.

Qualcomm's insight was not simply in championing CDMA, but in anticipating future developments and aggressively pursuing an array of patents covering diverse applications of the standard. The benefits to Qualcomm of this approach are two-fold: the company generates a dual revenue stream and prevents competitors from entering any aspect of the CDMA market.

Qualcomm's official statements (in annual reports, press releases, and presentations to both investors and the media) make it clear that the company views the portfolio, rather than the individual patent, as the relevant level of abstraction for managing intellectual property assets. Filings with the SEC further reflect a recognition of the portfolio as a distinct commodity. Finally, the company consistently emphasizes the growing number of patents which it applies for and receives each year, as well as the broad applicability of the portfolio as a whole to a wide range of wireless technologies.

B.   Building Scale and Diversity: The Case of IBM

When it comes to numbers, nobody beats Big Blue. Since 1994, IBM has amassed a total of 24,665 US patents, far more than any other company, each year ranking first on the USPTO's list of top patent earners. Its closest competitor in that regard, Canon Kabushiki Kaisha, received only 16,570 patents during the same period. Moreover, the number of ideas being patented each year is on the rise — several times in the past decade, IBM set new records for the most US patents received by an organization in a single year.

In the 1980s, IBM struggled as the national consciousness came to associate excellence in technology with foreign-produced goods. Moreover, the once-progressive company grew stagnant, falling from its perch as the leader in innovation. But even then, IBM recognized the bargaining value of a robust portfolio, as well as the leverage such a portfolio could provide when seeking to compel licensing agreements from potential infringers (perhaps unscrupulously). Still, after a decade of very public management snafus, analysts and economists were writing the company's obituary.

The turn-around began with the arrival of Lou Gerstner as CEO in 1993, appointed to replace John Akers after the company suffered its worst year ever. Among the changes instituted under Gerstner's watch: substantially increasing efforts to exploit the company's intellectual property assets, mandating a narrower focus on less theoretical and more product-oriented research, and slashing the R&D budget while simultaneously initiating a campaign to increase the number of patents the company received. This led to the remarkable growth of the company's patent portfolio, but also to the significantly reduced ratio of research dollars spent to patents earned. Even taking into account the approximately 28-months required for the average patent prosecution, patent intensity — patents obtained per R&D dollar — at IBM has exploded.

By some measures, IBM's portfolio-building success has come at the price of its patent quality: although the undisputed leader based on sheer numbers, the company lags behind peers such as Microsoft, Cisco and Sun Microsystems on indexes which measure how often a company's patents are cited as prior art and how close its portfolio is to the cutting edge of research. Nevertheless, IBM's dramatic overhaul paid off: the portfolio provides the company's engineers with the freedom to experiment unhindered by concerns of infringing on other's patents, and IBM has turned intellectual property licensing into a "fine art" which division has become so profitable and efficient that IBM now provides the service of counseling other firms on how to maximize income from their own patent portfolios.

C. Assembling a Patent Portfolio from Alternative Sources: The Case of Gemstar

Henry Yuen launched Gemstar in 1989 with a simple dream: to help the nation program its VCRs. He (along with partner David Kwoh) developed an algorithm for converting information about a TV show into a short string of numbers, convinced newspapers and TV Guide to carry the codes in their listings, and designed a set-top box to convert those codes back into instructions telling the device the date, time, and channel of the program the end-user wanted to record. The VCR Plus+ was an immediate success, and Yuen raked in millions.

As the company grew, it sought to apply its patented technology to related emerging fields. Yuen's vision was for Gemstar to assemble a portfolio of patents which could be used to claim coverage over all aspects of on-screen guides and interactive program listings. Although the company conducted some research in-house, Gemstar's primary method of expansion was to acquire smaller companies with potentially valuable patents, and to use the threat of expensive infringement litigation to force competitors either into licensing deals or out of the field.

Gemstar soared through the 1990s with a string of high-profile successes, most notably the acquisition of TV Guide (which resolved a long-standing patent dispute). But Yuen's aggressive strategy prompted an industry backlash, and a series of courtroom defeats led competitors and licensees to question the strength of Gemstar's patent portfolio. Yuen was finally ousted in 2002 following revelations that the company was overstating revenue.

Today, Gemstar still maintains a portfolio of over 260 patents on listing and interactive technologies, and numerous analysts believe the size of this portfolio, combined with a less-combative attitude towards licensees, leaves the company poised for a long-term dominant role in the industry.

NOTES & QUESTIONS

1. What lessons can be learned from these three case studies regarding patent strategy? Does the pursuit of a patent portfolio resolve some of the antitrust issues raised by patent pooling? To what extent are the benefits of lowered antitrust scrutiny offset by the loss in specialization by focusing on a few core patents?

2. The Wagner and Parchomovsky reading discusses Lou Gerstner, chief executive officer of IBM, who cut the company's research and development budget while expanding the company's patent portfolio. How are these strategies consistent? Is there a trade-off between basic research and commercial research? Between improving existing products and developing breakthrough innovations?

3. Clayton M. Christensen, a professor at Harvard Business School, has pointed out that disruptive technologies can cause even well managed companies to fail because of the inability to recognize changes in the marketplace that result from the technologies. He calls this problem "the innovator's dilemma." Does the focus on patent portfolios exacerbate or ameliorate the innovator's dilemma? How would a company design a patent portfolio in order to avoid the dilemma: create a seminal product and then work on improvements or strive to develop a series of breakthrough products?

4. The phenomenon of patent portfolios might also be relevant to copyright and trademark interests. Under copyright law, a copyright owner has the ability to control derivative works and the range of rights in derivative works developed either in-house or through licensing can be understood as defining a copyright portfolio. A copyright portfolio can allow a company to segment a market and serve a wider customer base at a higher return through price discrimination. A copyright strategy emphasizing a portfolio approach should not focus solely on the creation of a single copyrighted work, but rather on the creation of an initial work and a series of derivative works that allow the company involved to pursue a more expansive business strategy. Similarly with trademarks, a company might attempt to use a familiar mark to branch out into different marks. The use of a family of marks, such as the different uses of Coca-Cola (Coca-Cola light, Cherry Coke, etc.) or of McDonald's (Big Mac, McGriddle), allows a company to expand the reach of consumer recognition developed for the company's primary mark. For an excellent discussion of trademark management practices and branding, see Nancy F. Koehn, BRAND NEW: HOW ENTREPRENEURS EARNED CUSTOMER'S TRUST FROM WEDGEWOOD TO DELL (2001).

5. Josh Lerner, a professor at Harvard University and a frequently-cited scholar in the area of patent policy found the following patterns of patenting in a study of 419 biotechnology firms:

> First, firms with high litigation costs are less likely to patent in subclasses with many previous awards by rival biotechnology firms. Firms with the highest litigation costs are twice as likely as others to patent in subclasses with no rival awards. When high-litigation-cost firms do patent in subclasses in which rival biotechnology firms have already patented, they tend to choose less crowded subclasses. In the case of firms with high litigation costs, the preceding award to a rival was 303 days earlier. In the case of other firms' patents, an interval of 208 days separated the last prior rival award.
>
> Second, firms with high litigation costs are less likely to patent in subclasses where firms with low litigation costs have previously patented. A patent awarded to a firm with low litigation costs is followed by an award to a firm with high litigation costs 11 percent of the time; awards to other firms are followed by a patent to a firm with high litigation costs 21 percent of the time. The results are robust to controls for a variety of sample selection biases, such as the changing mixture of firms over time and the different technological focuses of various vintages of firms.

Josh Lerner, *Patenting in the Shadow of Competitors*, 38 J. L. & ECON. 463, 463 (1995). Professor Lerner concludes that his findings are relevant for the criticism that "the 1982 reform of the patent system [with the creation of the Federal Circuit] has led to aggressive efforts by large firms to extract favorable settlements from smaller concerns and consequent distortions in the innovative activity of smaller concerns." *Id.* at 464.

6. Michael Melton, former general counsel for Pitney-Bowes, makes an important distinction between "intellectual capital" (IC) and "intellectual property" (IP). Intellectual capital is defined by the knowledge base of a company, embodied in its technologies and human know-how. Mr. Melton reasons:

> The first element of any IP strategy must be to protect technology important to the corporation. A corporation must develop the appropriate IP infrastructure as a first step in securing protection for all strategically significant technology with particular emphasis on its implementation in the products and services the corporation delivers. The transformation of IC into IP through contracts, patents, copyrights and other IP protection must have a special focus in this plan. Tools must be woven into this fabric to enhance the creation of the most effective barriers to product or service substitution or emulation by our competitors, to safeguard a corporations global market positions and to provide freedom of action for the introduction of new products. This protection should include a focus on technology that if known by competitors would be immediately embraced. In order to identify a competitor's interest, a corporation must deploy appropriate tools for understanding and exploiting the strengths and weaknesses of their competitors. These tools are commonly referred to as corporate intelligence tools.

See Michael Melton, *Transforming Intellectual Capital Into Strategic Corporate Assets*, Practising Law Iinstitute Patents, Copyrights, Trademarks, and Literary Property Course Handbook Series PLI Order No. G0-00JN (February 2001).

7. Are Professor Lerner's findings consistent with Mr. Melton's discussion of the importance of "intellectual capital"? To what extent should the ability to restrain competition shape intellectual property strategies? Needless to say, a company cannot be open about any anti-competitive purpose. At the same time, the exclusivity provided by intellectual property will have some effect on the competitive process. Review the materials in Chapter 13 on antitrust concerns to think about how companies can best pursue an aggressive intellectual property position without crossing the limits imposed by antitrust law.

B. THE CHALLENGES OF JOINT VENTURES

Kurt M. Saunders, The Role of Intellectual Property Rights in Negotiating and Planning a Research Joint Venture
7 Marq. Intell. Prop. L. Rev. 75 (2003)*

. . .

Research has been the wellspring for all of the advanced technological innovations that have appeared in the last twenty years. Indeed, many of the most successful and globally competitive industries in the United States, including computers, semiconductors, pharmaceuticals, aeronautics, and biotechnologies, are the products of basic and applied research. Basic and applied research is usually considered to be the point of departure for dynamic models of technology transfer, leading eventually to product development and diffusion. However, a single firm may not have sufficient resources to undertake a project of research and development alone. In such instances, the firm may consider entering into a research and development collaboration with another firm as a means of pursuing innovation. These types of cooperative efforts have become increasingly prevalent in many industries, benefiting not only the firms involved, but also enhancing overall U.S. economic competitiveness.

As a business endeavor, a joint venture "represents a collaborative effort between [two] companies — [which] may or may not be competitors — to achieve a particular end. . . ." This form of business association combines certain attributes of one firm with complementary features of another firm to engage in a specific project. The enterprise involves special contributions by each partner, rather than the mere pooling of funds by investors to fund a project that is too costly for either to fund alone. Two or more firms form a joint venture to pursue a program of research activities. The partners jointly engage in these activities for the benefit of the joint venture and each of the partners. The partners share risks and investment costs and pool technologies and know-how, to expand the capabilities of each partner. Likewise, the partners may conduct research to develop a product that will be marketed later by the joint venture, or the research joint venture may subsequently license or assign the intellectual property rights to each of the partners for further exploitation. Thus, the primary motives for forming a research joint venture are likely to be the desire to establish a vertical relationship in the market, to achieve an expansion of a geographic market for a product, or to achieve an expansion into related product areas.

The role of intellectual property rights in forming and conducting the research and development effort may be significant; however, intellectual property rights may also be of central concern to the partners and to antitrust regulators even after the project is completed and the research joint venture is dissolved. This Article explores the importance of intellectual property rights in the formation of a research joint venture between two firms. The Article first considers the structural advantages afforded by the joint venture arrangement as to basic and applied research. Next, it identifies the intellectual property rights that the joint venture partners may bring into or develop during the term of their collaboration. This Article then considers the relevant antitrust implications of shared development of intellectual property rights. Finally, it assesses the intellectual property rights concerns that may arise at each stage of the research joint venture life cycle and offers strategies for addressing these concerns during the negotiation and planning stages of the collaboration.

. . .

V.   Intellectual Property Rights and their Part in Planning the Research Joint Venture

Intellectual property rights may be the strategic objective of an inter-firm research collaboration. At the same time, they are a source of risk and uncertainty that impact the planning and organization of the joint venture. There are a multitude of contingencies and considerations that the parties to a research joint venture should address in negotiating and constructing the endeavor. We have already considered a number of such issues so far in this discussion. The threshold issues in all joint ventures concern the compatibility of each firm's expectations and objectives, as well as ongoing administrative matters. For instance: what are the reasons of each partner for forming the joint venture? Will one or more partners be limited in its future actions because of the venture? How will disputes as to purposes of venture be settled? Will such disputes be decided jointly, or does one partner have a controlling vote? Who will manage and direct the venture? How will they be chosen and what is their authority? On the other hand, intellectual property rights raise unique concerns at each stage of the joint venture life cycle. Here, we examine these concerns as they may arise in each phase of this process.

A.   Conveying Pre-Existing Intellectual Property Rights

Intellectual property rights may be conveyed to the research joint venture in the joint venture agreement, a separate license agreement, a separate assignment, or all three. Conveyance of intellectual property rights should be discussed in a joint venture agreement or separate agreement, which references back and between both agreements, and which describes the intellectual property rights and subject matter with specificity, specifying the consideration and defining any license or assignment as exclusive or nonexclusive. As mentioned above, the decision as to whether to assign or license intellectual property rights depends on many factors, including the specifics of the transaction and the nature of the assets.

Other considerations include: the contributing partners' plans as to continued use and exploitation of the intellectual property rights in geographic and product markets, other than those acquired by the joint venture; tax and accounting issues; allocation of rights and responsibilities with respect to prosecution, enforcement, and defense of intellectual property rights infringement claims; the types of intellectual property rights to be granted; and any other legal constraints, such as antitrust, filing, registration requirements, or limitations. The partners should also determine ownership and licensing rights in improvements to, and derivative works of, pre-existing intellectual property rights; intellectual property rights developed by one of the partners after the joint venture is created that would be used by the research joint venture; and intellectual property rights developed by the joint venture. Finally, the partners should decide whether the joint-venture entity will have the right to assign or sublicense rights licensed or granted to it by the partners. If sublicensing rights are granted, the joint venture must ensure that the sublicenses adequately protect the intellectual property rights, including all confidential information and trade secrets, and provide adequate contract defenses, including intended third-party beneficiary status for partners.

B.   Rights and Duties During the Research Joint Venture

The joint venture agreement must also address the respective rights and obligations of the joint venture and the partners with respect to protecting, prosecuting, and obtaining intellectual property rights; pursuing claims of infringement and misappropriation against third parties; and defending such actions brought by third parties. When the joint venture is permitted to use technologies of one partner that are protected by patent or trademark, the partner will want assurances that the joint venture and other partner's use will not damage partner's reputation or decrease the value of its brand name.

Additionally, the joint venture agreement should address responsibility and control issues with respect to litigation against third parties based on the intellectual property. It should also set forth which parties will bear the costs associated with such litigation and how they will share in any recovery. Research partners must agree to maintain records in sufficient detail and in a good scientific manner so as to: permit partners to pursue patent protection for any new invention that results; maintain confidentiality to prevent disclosure of trade secrets or proprietary information; cooperate in perfecting and maintaining intellectual property rights; and implement procedures to protect trade secrets and other confidential information developed during the course of the research joint venture.

C.   Termination of the Research Joint Venture

Negotiation of termination provisions, especially those that govern the disposition of intellectual property acquired during the collaboration, are crucial.

Termination provisions related to intellectual property rights should provide for an orderly disposition of the intellectual property rights both contributed by the partners and created by the research joint venture. Termination provisions should state: which of any original technologies and pre-existing intellectual property rights should be assigned back to the original owner; which of any original technologies and intellectual property rights should be cross-licensed between the partners or sublicensed to the research joint venture (if it is to continue); which jointly developed technologies and intellectual property rights should be licensed or sublicensed to each partner by the research joint venture; which partner is entitled to improvements made to the technology by the research joint venture; and what types of ancillary agreements, such as non-competition or nondisclosure covenants, are reasonably necessary to protect the respective legitimate business interests of the partners.

VI. Conclusion

Individual firms may lack the resources and incentives to invest at a socially optimal level in uncertain research and innovation. Research collaboration among firms can correct such market failures and increase the rate of technology creation and diffusion in an industry. As Congress has recognized, "technological innovation and its profitable commercialization are critical components of the ability of the United States to raise the living standards of Americans and to compete in world markets. . . . [C]ooperative arrangements among nonaffiliated businesses . . . are often essential for successful technological innovation. . . ."

The research joint venture arrangement offers numerous advantages for collaborative basic and applied research and innovation. Intellectual property rights, whether brought into the venture by one or more of the partners or generated during the term of the venture, raise critical concerns about disclosure, ownership, use, and management that should be addressed in the negotiation and planning phase of the collaboration. Antitrust considerations that relate to the cooperative disclosure, ownership, use, and management of intellectual property rights are also relevant. If the partners to a research joint venture are pro-active in addressing these issues, they can anticipate and mange many of the legal risks involved and maximize the many benefits and efficiencies that result from collaboration.

David J. Teece, Profiting from Technological Innovation: Implications for Integration, Collaboration, Licensing and Public Policy
Practising Law Institute
Patents, Copyrights, Trademarks, and Literary Property Course No. G0-007N (October 7-8, 1999)*

EMI's failure to reap significant returns from the CAT scanner can be explained in large measure by [failures in appropriate intellectual property management]. The scanner which EMI developed was of a technical sophistication much higher than would normally be found in a hospital, requiring a high level of training, support, and servicing. EMI had none of these capabilities, could not easily contract for them, and was slow to realize their importance. It most probably could have formed a partnership with a company like Siemens to access the requisite capabilities. Its failure to do so was a strategic error compounded by the very limited intellectual property protection which the law afforded the scanner. Although subsequent court decisions have upheld some of EMI's patent claims, once the product was in the market it could be reverse engineered and its essential features copied. Two competitors, GE and Technicare, already possessed the complementary capabilities that the scanner required, and they were also technologically capable. In addition, both were experienced marketers of medical equipment, and had reputations for quality, reliability and service. GE and Technicare were thus able to commit their R&D resources to developing a competitive scanner, borrowing ideas from EMI's scanner, which they undoubtedly had access to through cooperative hospitals, and improving on it where they could while they rushed to market. GE began taking orders in 1976 and soon after made inroads on EMI. In 1977 concern for rising health care costs caused the Carter Administration to introduce "certificate of need" regulation, which required HEW's approval on expenditures on big ticket items like CAT scanners. This severely cut the size of the available market.

By 1978 EMI had lost market share leadership to Technicare, which was in turn quickly overtaken by GE. In October 1979, Godfrey Houndsfield of EMI shared the Nobel prize for invention of the CT scanner. Despite this honor, and the public recognition of its role in bringing this medical breakthrough to the world, the collapse of its scanner business forced EMI in the same year into the arms of a rescuer, Thorn Electrical Industries, Ltd. GE subsequently acquired what was EMI's scanner business from Thorn for what amounted to a pittance. Though royalties continued to flow to EMI, the company had failed to capture the lion's share of the profits generated by the innovation it had pioneered and successfully commercialized.

If EMI illustrates how a company with outstanding technology and an excellent product can fail to profit from innovation while the imitators succeeded, the story of the IBM PC indicates how a new product representing a very modest technological advance can yield remarkable returns to the developer.

The IBM PC, introduced in 1981, was a success despite the fact that the architecture was ordinary and the components standard. Philip Estridge's design team in Boca Raton, Florida, decided to use existing technology to produce a solid, reliable micro rather than state of the art. With a one-year mandate to develop a PC, Estridge's team could do little else.

However, the IBM PC did use what at the time was a new 16-bit microprocessor (the Intel 8088) and a new disk operating system (DOS) adapted for IBM by Microsoft. Other than the microprocessor and the operating system, the IBM PC incorporated existing micro "standards" and used off-the-shelf parts from outside vendors. IBM did write its own BIOS (Basic Input/Output System) which is embedded in ROM, but this was a relatively straightforward programming exercise.

The key to the PC's success was not the technology. It was the set of complementary assets which IBM either had or quickly assembled around the PC. In order to expand the market for PCs, there was a clear need for an expandable, flexible microcomputer system with extensive applications software. IBM could have based its PC system on its own patented hardware and copyrighted software. Such an approach would cause complementary products to be co-specialized, forcing IBM to develop peripherals and a comprehensive library of software in a very short time. Instead, IBM adopted what might be called an "induced contractual" approach. By adopting an open system architecture, as Apple had done, and by making the operating system information publicly available, a spectacular output of third part software was induced. IBM estimated that by mid-1983, at least 3000 hardware and software products were available for the PC. Put differently, IBM pulled together the complementary assets, particularly software, which success required, without even using contracts, let alone integration. This was despite the fact that the software developers were creating assets that were in part co-specialized with the IBM PC, at least in the first instance.

A number of special factors made this seem a reasonable risk to the software writers. A critical one was IBM's name and commitment to the project. The reputation behind the letters I.B.M. is perhaps the greatest co-specialized asset the company possesses. The name implied that the product would be marketed and serviced in the IBM tradition. It guaranteed that PC-DOS would become an industry standard, so that the software business would not be solely dependent on IBM, because emulators were sure to enter. It guaranteed access to retail distribution outlets on competitive terms. The consequence was that IBM was able to take a product which represented at best a modest technological accomplishment, and turn it into a fabulous commercial success. The case demonstrates the role that complementary assets play in determining outcomes.

The spectacular success and profitability of G.D. Searle's NutraSweet is an uncommon story which is also consistent with the above framework. In 1982, Searle reported combined sales of $74 million for NutraSweet and its table top version, Equal. In 1983, this surged to $336 million. In 1985, NutraSweet sales exceeded $700 million and Equal had captured 50 percent of the U.S. sugar substitute market and was number one in five other countries.

NutraSweet, which is Searle's tradename for aspartame, has achieved rapid acceptance in each of its FDA approved categories because of its good taste and ability to substitute directly for sugar in many applications. However, Searle's earnings from NutraSweet and the absence of a strategic challenge can be traced in part to Searle's clever strategy.

It appears that Searle has managed to establish an exceptionally tight appropriability regime around NutraSweet — one that may well continue for some time after the patent has expired. No competitor appears to have successfully "invented around" the Searle patent and commercialized an alternative, no doubt in part because the FDA approval process would have to begin anew for an imitator who was not violating Searle's patents. A competitor who tried to replicate the aspartame molecule with minor modification to circumvent the patent would probably be forced to replicate the hundreds of tests and experiments which proved aspartame's safety. Without patent protection, FDA approval would provide no shield against imitators coming to market with an identical chemical and who could establish to the FDA that it is the same compound that had already been approved. Without FDA approval on the other hand, the patent protection would be worthless for the product would not be sold for human consumption.

Searle has aggressively pushed to strengthen its patent protection. The company was granted U.S. patent protection in 1970. It has also obtained patent protection in Japan, Canada, Australia, U.K., France, Germany, and a number of other countries. However, most of these patents carry a 17-year life. Since the product was only approved for human consumption in 1982, the 17-year patent life was effectively reduced to five. Recognizing the obvious importance of its patent, Searle pressed for and obtained special legislation in November 1984 extending the patent protection on aspartame for another 5 years. The U.K. provided a similar extension. In almost every other nation, however, 1987 will mark the expiration of the patent.

When the patent expires, however, Searle will still have several valuable assets to help keep imitators at bay. Searle has gone to great lengths to create and promulgate the use of its NutraSweet name and a distinctive "Swirl" logo on all goods licensed to use the ingredient. The company has also developed the "Equal" tradename for a table top version of the sweetener. Trademark law in the U.S. provides protection against "unfair" competition in branded products for as long as the owner of the mark continues to use it. Both the NutraSweet and Equal trademarks will become essential assets when the patents on aspartame expire. Searle may well have convinced consumers that the only real form of sweetener is NutraSweet/Equal. Consumers know most other artificial sweeteners by their generic names — saccharin and cyclamates.

Clearly, Searle is trying to build a position in complementary assets to prepare for the competition which will surely arise. Searle's joint venture with Ajinomoto ensures them access to that company's many years of experience in the production of biochemical agents. Much of this knowledge is associated with techniques for distillation and synthesis of the delicate hydrocarbon compounds that are the ingredients of NutraSweet, and is therefore more tacit than codified. Searle has begun to put these techniques to use in its own $160 million Georgia production facility. It can be expected that Searle will use trade secrets to the maximum to keep this know-how proprietary.

By the time its patent expires, Searle's extensive research into production techniques for L-phenylalanine, and its 8 years of experience in the Georgia plant, should give it a significant cost advantage over potential aspartame competitors. Trade secret protection, unlike patents, has no fixed lifetime and may well sustain Searle's position for years to come.

Moreover, Searle has wisely avoided renewing contracts with suppliers when they have expired. Had Searle subcontracted manufacturing for NutraSweet, it would have created a manufacturer who would then be in a position to enter the aspartame market itself, or to team up with a marketer of artificial sweeteners. But keeping manufacturing in-house, and by developing a valuable tradename, Searle has a good chance of protecting its market position from dramatic inroads once patents expire. Clearly, Searle seems to be astutely aware of the importance of maintaining a "tight appropriability regime" and using co-specialized assets strategically.

NOTES & QUESTIONS

1. The Saunders reading raises many of the issues discussed elsewhere in this text in the chapters on start-up companies, mergers and acquisitions, and antitrust concerns. His discussion is worth comparing with the Michael Melton's views on internal corporate development of intellectual property. When should a company decide to enter into a joint venture rather than develop a new technology in-house? Consider the reading on patent portfolios above. How is the decision to enter into a joint venture affected by a company's patent portfolio strategy? The presence of blocking patents held by the company and another party and the corresponding need for cross-licensing are certainly important concerns that may motivate a company to pursue a joint venture rather than just relying on developing a technology within the protections of the company's own patent portfolio. A company should consider the implications of joint research and development regarding the joint ownership of resulting patents. Finally, many of the intellectual property transfer issues described in the materials on employment law and mergers and acquisitions may also arise in connection with the types of joint venture activities described in the Saunders reading.

2. The Teece reading provides several useful case studies regarding joint venturing and associated intellectual property strategies. Compare the EMI case study with the IBM case study. What explains one company's failure and the other's success? Does the difference stem from different laws, different business strategies, or different technologies and market structure? What could EMI have done differently? Could EMI, for example, have emulated some of IBM's choices?

3. The Teece reading provides an interesting comparison with the earlier discussions of patent portfolios in this chapter. Consider the Searle case study discussed in the Teece article. It could be argued that Searle's success rested not on determining the best mix of patents, but on leveraging its patents to create a market position that was sustainable even after the patents expired. Does this interpretation contradict points made in the patent portfolio article? Teece describes the strategy as one of creating complementary assets that support and sustain new technology. What role does intellectual property play in creating these complementary assets and using them to generate economic and business value? In thinking about this question, keep in mind that some of the value may be appropriated through service contracts and commercialization of specialized know-how that may not always be protected as property.

4. After reading these materials, you should have a sense of the business and legal decisions that are involved in the management of intellectual property. These decisions relate to not only the determination of patenting strategies, but also the coordination of intellectual property acquisition with technological and market realities. In reviewing these materials, try to identify as many different legal and business strategies as possible and see how

each strategy or set of strategies takes advantage of the law, the underlying technology, and the related markets.

C. PATENT PROTECTION FOR RESEARCH TOOLS AND EXPERIMENTAL USE

MERCK KGAA v. INTEGRA LIFESCIENCES I, LTD.
United States Supreme Court
125 S. Ct. 2372 (2005)

Justice SCALIA delivered the opinion of the Court.

This case presents the question whether uses of patented inventions in preclinical research, the results of which are not ultimately included in a submission to the Food and Drug Administration (FDA), are exempted from infringement by 35 U.S.C. § 271(e)(1).

I

It is generally an act of patent infringement to "mak[e], us[e], offe[r] to sell, or sel[l] any patented invention . . . during the term of the patent therefor." § 271(a). In 1984, Congress enacted an exemption to this general rule, see 35 U.S.C. § 271(e)(1), which provides:

> It shall not be an act of infringement to make, use, offer to sell, or sell within the United States or import into the United States a patented invention (other than a new animal drug or veterinary biological product (as those terms are used in the Federal Food, Drug, and Cosmetic Act and the Act of March 4, 1913) . . .) solely for uses reasonably related to the development and submission of information under a Federal law which regulates the manufacture, use, or sale of drugs. . . .

The Federal Food, Drug, and Cosmetic Act (FDCA). . . . is "a Federal law which regulates the manufacture, use, or sale of drugs." Under the FDCA, a drugmaker must submit research data to the FDA at two general stages of new-drug development. First, a drugmaker must gain authorization to conduct clinical trials (tests on humans) by submitting an investigational new drug application (IND). The IND must describe "preclinical tests (including tests on animals) of [the] drug adequate to justify the proposed clinical testing." Second, to obtain authorization to market a new drug, a drugmaker must submit a new drug application (NDA), containing "full reports of investigations which have been made to show whether or not [the] drug is safe for use and whether [the] drug is effective in use." Pursuant to FDA regulations, the NDA must include all clinical studies, as well as preclinical studies related to a drug's efficacy, toxicity, and pharmacological properties.

II

A

Respondents Integra Lifesciences I, Ltd., and the Burnham Institute, own five patents related to the tripeptide sequence Arg-Gly-Asp, known in single-letter notation as the "RGD peptide." U.S. Patent Nos. 4,988,621, 4,792,525, 5,695,997, 4,879,237, and 4,789,734, Supp.App. SA11-SA19. The RGD peptide promotes cell adhesion by attaching to [the] receptors commonly located on the outer surface of certain endothelial cells.

Beginning in 1988, petitioner Merck KGaA provided funding for angiogenesis research conducted by Dr. David Cheresh at the Scripps Research Institute (Scripps). Angiogenesis is the process by which new blood vessels sprout from existing vessels; it plays a critical role in many diseases, including solid tumor cancers, diabetic retinopathy, and rheumatoid arthritis. In the course of his research, Dr. Cheresh discovered that it was possible to inhibit angiogenesis by blocking the [receptors] on proliferating endothelial cells. In 1994, Dr. Cheresh succeeded in reversing tumor growth in chicken embryos, first using a monoclonal antibody (LM609) he developed himself and later using a cyclic RGD peptide (EMD 66203) provided by petitioner. Dr. Cheresh's discoveries were announced in leading medical journals and received attention in the general media.

With petitioner's agreement to fund research at Scripps due to expire in July 1995, Dr. Cheresh submitted a detailed proposal for expanded collaboration between Scripps and petitioner on February 1, 1995. The proposal set forth a 3-year timetable in which to develop "integrin antagonists as angiogenesis inhibitors," beginning with *in vitro* and *in vivo* testing of RGD peptides at Scripps in year one and culminating with the submission of an IND to the FDA in year three. Petitioner agreed to the material terms of the proposal on February 20, 1995 and on April 13, 1995, pledged $6 million over three years to fund research at Scripps. Petitioner's April 13 letter specified that Scripps would be responsible for testing RGD peptides produced by petitioner as potential drug candidates but that, once a primary candidate for clinical testing was in "the pipeline," petitioner would perform the toxicology tests necessary for FDA approval to proceed to clinical trials. Scripps and petitioner concluded an agreement of continued collaboration in September 1995.

Pursuant to the agreement, Dr. Cheresh directed *in vitro* and *in vivo* experiments on RGD peptides provided by petitioner from 1995 to 1998. These experiments focused on EMD 66203 and two closely related derivatives, EMD 85189 and EMD 121974, and were designed to evaluate the suitability of each of the peptides as potential drug candidates. Accordingly, the tests measured the efficacy, specificity, and toxicity of the particular peptides as angiogenesis inhibitors, and evaluated their mechanism of action and pharmacokinetics in animals. Based on the test results, Scripps decided in 1997 that EMD 121974 was the most promising candidate for testing in humans. Over the same period, Scripps performed similar tests on LM609, a monoclonal antibody developed by Dr. Cheresh. Scripps also conducted more basic research on organic mimetics designed to block [the receptors] in a manner similar to the RGD peptides; it appears that Scripps used the RGD peptides in these tests as "positive controls" against which to measure the efficacy of the mimetics.

In November 1996, petitioner initiated a formal project to guide one of its RGD peptides through the regulatory approval process in the United States and Europe. Id., at 129a. Petitioner originally directed its efforts at EMD 85189, but switched focus in April 1997 to EMD 121974. Petitioner discussed

EMD 121974 with officials at the FDA. In October 1998, petitioner shared its research on RGD peptides with the National Cancer Institute (NCI), which agreed to sponsor clinical trials. Although the fact was excluded from evidence at trial, the lower court's opinion reflects that NCI filed an IND for EMD 121974 in 1998.

B

On July 18, 1996, respondents filed a patent-infringement suit against petitioner, Scripps, and Dr. Cheresh in the District Court for the Southern District of California. Respondents' complaint alleged that petitioner willfully infringed and induced others to infringe respondents' patents by supplying the RGD peptide to Scripps, and that Dr. Cheresh and Scripps infringed the same patents by using the RGD peptide in experiments related to angiogenesis. Respondents sought damages from petitioner and a declaratory judgment against Dr. Cheresh and Scripps. Petitioner answered that its actions involving the RGD peptides did not infringe respondents' patents, and that in any event they were protected by the common-law research exemption and 35 U.S.C. § 271(e)(1).

At the conclusion of trial, the District Court held that, with one exception, petitioner's pre-1995 actions related to the RGD peptides were protected by the common-law research exemption, but that a question of fact remained as to whether petitioner's use of the RGD peptides after 1995 fell within the § 271(e)(1) safe harbor. With the consent of the parties, the District Court gave the following instruction regarding the § 271(e)(1) exemption:

> To prevail on this defense, [petitioner] must prove by a preponderance of the evidence that it would be objectively reasonable for a party in [petitioner's] and Scripps' situation to believe that there was a decent prospect that the accused activities would contribute, relatively directly, to the generation of the kinds of information that are likely to be relevant in the processes by which the FDA would decide whether to approve the product in question.
>
> Each of the accused activities must be evaluated separately to determine whether the exemption applies.
>
> [Petitioner] does not need to show that the information gathered from a particular activity was actually submitted to the FDA.

The jury found that petitioner, Dr. Cheresh, and Scripps infringed respondents' patents and that petitioner had failed to show that its activities were protected by § 271(e)(1). It awarded damages of $15 million.

In response to post-trial motions, the District Court dismissed respondents' suit against Dr. Cheresh and Scripps, but affirmed the jury's damage award as supported by substantial evidence, and denied petitioner's motion for judgment as a matter of law. With respect to the last, the District Court explained that the evidence was sufficient to show that "any connection between the infringing Scripps experiments and FDA review was insufficiently direct to qualify for the [§ 271(e)(1) exemption]."

A divided panel of the Court of Appeals for the Federal Circuit affirmed in part, and reversed in part. The panel majority affirmed the denial of judgment as a matter of law to petitioner, on the ground that § 271(e)(1)'s safe harbor did not apply because "the Scripps work sponsored by [petitioner] was not clinical testing to supply information to the FDA, but only general biomedical research to identify new pharmaceutical compounds." It reversed the District Court's refusal to modify the damages award, and remanded for further proceedings. Judge Newman dissented on both points. The panel unanimously affirmed the District Court's ruling that respondents' patents covered the cyclic RGD peptides developed by petitioner. We granted certiorari to review the Court of Appeals' construction of § 271(e)(1).

III

As described earlier, 35 U.S.C. § 271(e)(1) provides that "[i]t shall not be an act of infringement to . . . use . . . or import into the United States a patented invention . . . solely for uses reasonably related to the development and submission of information under a Federal law which regulates the . . . use . . . of drugs." Though the contours of this provision are not exact in every respect, the statutory text makes clear that it provides a wide berth for the use of patented drugs in activities related to the federal regulatory process.

As an initial matter, we think it apparent from the statutory text that § 271(e)(1)'s exemption from infringement extends to all uses of patented inventions that are reasonably related to the development and submission of any information under the FDCA. This necessarily includes preclinical studies of patented compounds that are appropriate for submission to the FDA in the regulatory process. There is simply no room in the statute for excluding certain information from the exemption on the basis of the phase of research in which it is developed or the particular submission in which it could be included.

Respondents concede the breadth of § 271(e)(1) in this regard, but argue that the only preclinical data of interest to the FDA is that which pertains to the safety of the drug in humans. In respondents' view, preclinical studies related to a drug's efficacy, mechanism of action, pharmacokinetics, and pharmacology are not reasonably included in an IND or an NDA, and are therefore outside the scope of the exemption. We do not understand the FDA's interest in information gathered in preclinical studies to be so constrained. To be sure, its regulations provide that the agency's "primary objectives in reviewing an IND are . . . to assure the safety and rights of subjects," but it does not follow that the FDA is not interested in reviewing information related to other characteristics of a drug. To the contrary, the FDA requires that applicants include in an IND summaries of the pharmacological, toxicological, pharmacokinetic, and biological qualities of the drug in animals. The primary (and, in some cases, only) way in which a drugmaker may obtain such information is through preclinical *in vitro* and *in vivo* studies.

Moreover, the FDA does not evaluate the safety of proposed clinical experiments in a vacuum; rather, as the statute and regulations reflect, it asks whether the proposed clinical trial poses an "unreasonable risk." This assessment involves a comparison of the risks and the benefits associated with the proposed clinical trials. As the Government's brief, filed on behalf of the FDA, explains, the "FDA might allow clinical testing of a drug that posed significant safety concerns if the drug had a sufficiently positive potential to address a serious disease, although the agency would not accept similar risks for a drug that was less likely to succeed or that would treat a less serious medical condition." Accordingly, the FDA directs that an IND must provide sufficient information for the investigator to "make his/her own unbiased risk-benefit assessment of the appropriateness of the proposed trial." Such information necessarily includes preclinical studies of a drug's efficacy in achieving particular results.

Respondents contend that, even accepting that the FDA is interested in preclinical research concerning drug characteristics other than safety, the experiments in question here are necessarily disqualified because they were not conducted in conformity with the FDA's good laboratory practices regulations. This argument fails for at least two reasons. First, the FDA's requirement that preclinical studies be conducted under "good laboratory practices" applies only to experiments on drugs "to determine their safety". The good laboratory practice regulations do not apply to preclinical studies of a drug's efficacy, mechanism of action, pharmacology, or pharmacokinetics. Second, FDA regulations do not provide that even safety-related experiments not conducted in compliance with good laboratory practices regulations are not suitable for submission in an IND. Rather, such studies must include "a brief statement of the reason for the noncompliance."

The Court of Appeals' conclusion that § 271(e)(1) did not protect petitioner's provision of the patented RGD peptides for research at Scripps appeared to rest on two somewhat related propositions. First, the court credited the fact that the "Scripps-Merck experiments did not supply information for submission to the [FDA], but instead identified the best drug candidate to subject to future clinical testing under the FDA processes." The court explained:

> The FDA has no interest in the hunt for drugs that may or may not later undergo clinical testing for FDA approval. For instance, the FDA does not require information about drugs other than the compound featured in an [IND] application. Thus, the Scripps work sponsored by [petitioner] was not 'solely for uses reasonably related to' clinical testing for FDA.

Second, the court concluded that the exemption "does not globally embrace all experimental activity that at some point, however attenuated, may lead to an FDA approval process."

We do not quibble with the latter statement. Basic scientific research on a particular compound, performed without the intent to develop a particular drug or a reasonable belief that the compound will cause the sort of physiological effect the researcher intends to induce, is surely not "reasonably related to the development and submission of information" to the FDA. It does not follow from this, however, that § 271(e)(1)'s exemption from infringement categorically excludes either (1) experimentation on drugs that are not ultimately the subject of an FDA submission or (2) use of patented compounds in experiments that are not ultimately submitted to the FDA. Under certain conditions, we think the exemption is sufficiently broad to protect the use of patented compounds in both situations.

As to the first proposition, it disregards the reality that, even at late stages in the development of a new drug, scientific testing is a process of trial and error. In the vast majority of cases, neither the drugmaker nor its scientists have any way of knowing whether an initially promising candidate will prove successful over a battery of experiments. That is the reason they conduct the experiments. Thus, to construe § 271(e)(1), as the Court of Appeals did, not to protect research conducted on patented compounds for which an IND is not ultimately filed is effectively to limit assurance of exemption to the activities necessary to seek approval of a generic drug: One can know at the outset that a particular compound will be the subject of an eventual application to the FDA only if the active ingredient in the drug being tested is identical to that in a drug that has already been approved.

The statutory text does not require such a result. Congress did not limit § 271(e)(1)'s safe harbor to the development of information for inclusion in a submission to the FDA; nor did it create an exemption applicable only to the research relevant to filing an ANDA for approval of a generic drug. Rather, it exempted from infringement all uses of patented compounds "reasonably related" to the process of developing information for submission under any federal law regulating the manufacture, use, or distribution of drugs. We decline to read the "reasonable relation" requirement so narrowly as to render § 271(e)(1)'s stated protection of activities leading to FDA approval for all drugs illusory. Properly construed, § 271(e)(1) leaves adequate space for experimentation and failure on the road to regulatory approval: At least where a drugmaker has a reasonable basis for believing that a patented compound may work, through a particular biological process, to produce a particular physiological effect, and uses the compound in research that, if successful, would be appropriate to include in a submission to the FDA, that use is "reasonably related" to the "development and submission of information under . . . Federal law."

For similar reasons, the use of a patented compound in experiments that are not themselves included in a "submission of information" to the FDA does not, standing alone, render the use infringing. The relationship of the use of a patented compound in a particular experiment to the "development and submission of information" to the FDA does not become more attenuated (or less reasonable) simply because the data from that experiment are left out of the submission that is ultimately passed along to the FDA. Moreover, many of the uncertainties that exist with respect to the selection of a specific drug exist as well with respect to the decision of what research to include in an IND or NDA. As a District Court has observed, "[I]t will not always be clear to parties setting out to seek FDA approval for their new product exactly which kinds of information, and in what quantities, it will take to win that agency's approval." This is especially true at the preclinical stage of drug approval. FDA regulations provide only that "[t]he amount of information on a particular drug that must be submitted in an IND . . . depends upon such factors as the novelty of the drug, the extent to which it has been studied previously, the known or suspected risks, and the developmental phase of the drug." We thus agree with the Government that the use of patented compounds in preclinical studies is protected under § 271(e)(1) as long as there is a reasonable basis for believing that the experiments will produce "the types of information that are relevant to an IND or NDA."

MERCK KGAA v. INTEGRA LIFESCIENCES I, LTD.

Brief of Amici Curiae Applera Corporation and
Isis Pharmaceuticals, Inc. in Support of Respondents

. . .

Amici are companies whose technological contributions epitomize the innovation that the Constitutional mandate for a patent system is intended to promote. Amici's . . . inventions are primarily "platform technologies" in the biotech and pharmaceutical area, the proverbial "shoulders of giants" on which other innovators stand. Indeed, Amici's efforts have led to fundamental enabling technologies such as the polymerase chain reaction ("PCR"), and groundbreaking drug discovery tools such as anti-sense technology. Amici depend on a vibrant patent system that allows them to fund future innovation by licensing these enabling technologies to others.

Applera Corporation is a world-renowned innovator whose inventions routinely establish benchmarks in the global economy and provide springboards for innovation. Through its Applied Biosystems division, Applera has developed and commercialized fundamental instruments and tools that form the foundation for the modern biotech and pharmaceutical industries. These include instruments and basic techniques for automatically synthesizing DNA with any genetic code desired, finding and replicating DNA, and sequencing DNA and proteins. Through its Celera Genomics division, Applera has created tools for gene discovery and sequencing that have accelerated the comprehension of the human genome by decades. Applera's technologies are core to the biotech and pharmaceutical industries and are disseminated through a robust program of licensing that allows all researchers to be lifted by this rising tide of innovation.

Isis Pharmaceuticals is a leading drug discovery and development company focused exclusively on the therapeutic target, RNA. Isis is a pioneer in the field of anti-sense technology, which aims to control protein expression by intervening at the RNA level. Anti-sense technology is one component in a suite of valuable tools that Isis has created to facilitate drug discovery at every stage of the process. Other Isis inventions include technologies for rapid validation of targets, medicinal chemistries and formulations useful in basic research and for optimizing delivery of drug candidates, and improved manufacturing and analytical tests and standards for evaluating therapeutic agents. Isis holds more than 1400 patents worldwide and depends on its ability to license its patent portfolio for its continued success.

Amici generate the tools that constitute the lifeblood of the pharmaceutical industry. Amici's tools are diverse and run the gamut from bench instruments to medicinal chemistries. All of these inventions enable the drug discovery process to proceed while remaining ancillary to the ultimate drug products. Thus, unlike many of the other amici from the pharmaceutical industry, Applera and Isis do not often reap the benefit of the patent term extension granted to certain therapeutics by 35 U.S.C. § 156. However, Amici's businesses are threatened by overaggressive attempts to expand the exemption of 35 U.S.C. § 271(e) in ways that would destroy the value in foundational tool patents. While others espouse unduly one-sided views of the cost of patent law, Amici have witnessed first hand the profound growth that can be achieved when the intellectual property of the entire industry is protected, consistent with the patent laws and the will of Congress.

In sum, Amici are well-positioned to address the balanced trade-off inherent in the patent system that tolerates short term costs of patent licenses to achieve the long term benefits that accrue in a system that rewards all innovation. Amici eschew the short-sighted attempts to shift the costs of invention almost entirely from one set of innovators to another.

II.

INTRODUCTION

Petitioner and its allies ignore the critical word "solely," which sits squarely in the middle of Section 271(e)(1). Indeed, the United States does not address this statutory language until page 20 of its brief — and then the subject is reduced to a footnote. As one would expect, the statutory term "solely" should be given meaning because it is not mere hollow text needlessly cluttering the statute.

The plain text of the statute should not be ignored. Specifically, Section 271(e)(1) provides that the FDA exemption applies "solely for uses reasonably related to the development and submission of information under a Federal Law." Whether viewed from the perspective of a lay person, or a legal scholar trained in statutory construction, these words unmistakably mean that the exemption applies to infringing activities undertaken solely for purposes of regulatory approvals. This is particularly true because the structure of the statute shows that the word "uses" in the phrase "solely for uses" refers to the purposes of the infringing act (e.g., clinical testing, marketing), not to the infringing act itself. Thus, "solely for uses" necessarily means "solely for purposes" reasonably related to the development and submission of information under a federal drug law.

As the statute states in straightforward terms, to qualify for the exemption, the purpose of any infringement must be solely for regulatory reasons — a subjective inquiry. That an infringement could theoretically result in information of a kind that someone might submit to the FDA is insufficient to gain immunity if the information was never even supposed to be used for regulatory purposes at all. Even if it were intended solely to obtain regulatory approvals, such an intent must also be reasonable because the statute provides that the purpose must be "reasonably related" to the regulatory approval process — an objective inquiry. That an infringer commits acts of infringement for the purpose of FDA approval is insufficient to gain immunity if the information generated is not reasonably related to the approval process. Thus, the language and logic of the statute dictate that the exemption has both a subjective and objective requirement. The fatal error in Petitioner's position is that it ignores the statutory term "solely for uses" and consequently ignores the subjective requirement of the statute. Indeed, neither Petitioners, nor its allies, explain what real meaning "solely" would have under their reading of the statute. . . .

Giving "solely" its natural meaning is supported by the legislative history. The legislative history makes clear that the exemption was designed to address improper patent term extensions, not to repeal the patent law broadly in the area of drug and medical device research and development. Section 271(e)(1) was merely intended to avoid the situation where the regulatory approval process resulted in an undeserved de facto extension of a patent's life. It thus makes sense that only activities used for regulatory approvals are exempt under the statute. Although the terms of the statute are not limited to immunizing infringement in the generic drug approval process, the exemption fits that circumstance like a glove. Because a generic drug is a copy of an existing product, there is no drug discovery necessary. What is necessary is to have a generic drug approved by the FDA by the time the patent on the proprietary version of the drug expires. This simply requires immunity from infringement for the development and submission of information to the FDA for regulatory approval to establish the generic copy is what it is supposed to be.

The presence of the phrase "solely for uses" is not a mistake or surplusage because it ensures that the exemption remains balanced as Congress intended. This is not a case where clear statutory language appears to be the unfortunate result of a stumble by the drafter. If that were so, a tough statutory construction question might exist. But it is not so. Respecting the phrase "solely for uses" right-sizes the exemption and honors the sensible policy balance struck by Congress and blessed by the President. A statute that authorizes the uncompensated infringement of a whole class of patents was not undertaken lightly - or without balance. Yet, petitioner and its allies mistreat the exemption as though it were a sweeping suspension of the patent law for the drug discovery and development process generally. To interpret the statute in this way would be manifestly unfair to those who innovate and invest in the technology protected by such patents.

The potential cost of ignoring the term "solely" is staggering. The engine for modern drug discovery is the biotech industry. The biotech industry has provided an increasingly rich set of tools that are used for basic research, drug discovery, and drug development. Yet, if Section 271(e) is construed as the drug companies would like, the patents on such tools could be infringed cost-free. The patents protecting those innovations would lose their value and the incentive to create new tools would diminish dramatically. This is particularly true because the patent rights preventing copying are frequently the main source of value for the large investments made by tool creators.

In sum, limiting the exemption to immunity for infringement "solely for" efforts to obtain regulatory approval avoids major policy problems, properly gives effect to all terms of the statute, and respects the balance memorialized in the plain terms of the statute.

III.

PETITIONER'S REQUEST FOR A BROAD "DRUG RESEARCH AND DEVELOPMENT" EXEMPTION IGNORES THE PLAIN MEANING OF THE STATUTE

A.   The Statutory Term "Solely" Must Be Given Real Meaning

As this Court has explained repeatedly, "it is a cardinal principle of statutory construction" that the Court has a "duty 'to give effect, if possible, to every clause and word of a statute.'" Further, the Court is "reluctant to treat statutory terms as surplusage in any setting" The Court is "especially unwilling" to treat a term as surplusage when it occupies a pivotal place in the statute.

Here, the phrase "solely for uses" occupies a central place in Section 271(e) and cannot be ignored. Not surprisingly, this Court has recognized that "solely" has an established meaning that should be given effect. [Editor's Note: The Amici then extensively cite cases in which the Supreme Court and lower courts adopted a strict construction of the word "solely."]

B.   The Attempts By Petitioner And Its Allies To Address The Meaning Of "Solely" Treat That Term As Surplusage

Petitioner and some of its allies have attempted to respond to the Federal Circuit's reliance on the word "solely" in the statute. However, these attempts are unsatisfying, at best. Petitioner expends only three conclusory sentences on this subject. The gist of Petitioner's argument is that solely "means only that a drug innovator's freedom to use a patented invention under the FDA exemption is not a license to infringe in other ways, such as commercial exploitation." If this were correct, "solely" would merely represent the truism that infringement outside of the exemption is not protected by the exemption. This treatment of "solely" would necessarily render it surplusage in violation of this Court's precedents identified above.

In a different part of its brief, Petitioner makes perfectly clear that it is giving no meaning to the word "solely." Petitioner broadly argues that any experiment that could yield information theoretically relevant to the FDA is protected without regard to whether the purpose of the infringement is for the regulatory approval process at all:

Congress insulated any experiment that would yield the 'information' from any experiment, so long as it would be reasonable for the researcher to believe the experiment could generate information of a sort the FDA considers at some point in its role as a regulator of drugs.

Petitioner's argument expressly would include as exempt an experiment merely if it "could generate information of a sort the FDA considers at some point" even if that is not the purpose of the infringement at all. Petitioner's argument would also include as exempt the identification of drug candidates in the first instance from among thousands of compounds. Yet, this too involves commercial purposes well beyond mere regulatory approvals.

The United States' brief also reads the term "solely" right out of the statute. In its 30-page brief, the United States' argument on this key statutory language is reduced to a footnote. In that footnote, the brief struggles unsuccessfully to justify how the exemption could immunize infringements pursued for commercial purposes, such as marketing and product development, notwithstanding the presence of the word "solely":

> The statute authorizes making, using, selling, or offering to sell a patented invention 'solely for uses reasonably related to the development and submission of information' to the FDA. 35 U.S.C. 271(e)(1). Because "solely" modifies 'uses,' it makes clear that a researcher is not protected by the exemption insofar as he or she engages in uses that are not, in their entirety, reasonably related to the development and submission of information to FDA. 'Solely' does not, however, modify "reasonably related." Thus, as long as the full extent of a particular use is reasonably related to the development and submission of information, that use is protected even if it also advances other objectives, such as product development or marketing. But the exemption is inapplicable to the extent that a portion of the particular use at issue does not satisfy the reasonable relationship test.

Because "solely" modifies "use," if the infringing acts are used, for example, for marketing (marketing obviously is not required for FDA approval), it is simply illogical for the United States to argue that such a "use" is solely for regulatory approval and thus within the statutory scope of the exemption. That the United States could not identify in clear terms a meaning for "solely" under its reading of the statute, illustrates vividly that a broad exemption of the kind now desired by the government is incompatible with the statutory language selected by Congress.

C.   Petitioner And Its Allies Misinterpret The Word "Uses," As Used In Section 271(e)(1), By Conflating It Improperly With "Act Of Infringement"

It is important to appreciate that the second instance of "uses" in the statute — which is in the phrase "solely for uses" — is not referring to "use" as an act of infringement under Section 271(a), but rather refers to the purpose of the otherwise infringing acts.

There are three reasons why this must be true. First, the statute would have used the phrase "acts of infringement" instead of "uses" if that had been the intent. After all, the phrase "act of infringement" was used earlier in the statute when that was what was intended. Second, "acts of infringement" and "uses" mean two very different things and cannot be treated as interchangeable. Section 271(a), the basic direct infringement statute, defines an act of infringement as including the following types of acts: making, using, offering to sell, selling or importing. Indeed, this same list of acts of infringement is recited in Section 271(e)(1). "Use" is only one sub-class of acts of infringement as defined in both Section 271(a) and Section 271(e). Thus, if solely for "uses" in Section 271(e) were to refer to "use" as an act of infringement, instead of "use" as a purpose, it would exclude from the exemption whole classes of acts (selling, making, importing, and offering to sell) that are undisputedly within the exemption. That makes no sense. Third, the phrase "solely for" immediately before "uses" connotes purpose and thus confirms that the overall phrase "solely for uses" refers to the intended purpose of the act and is not merely a reference to an act itself.

Petitioner's and the United States' arguments muddy the waters around "solely" by conflating "act of infringement" and "use" to shift the inquiry to whether a particular infringing act can be reasonably related to the regulatory approval process. This is not the proper question. Because infringing acts have multiple potential purposes, the question is whether the particular purpose of the infringing act is reasonably related to the regulatory approval process. If they are not, as in the dual use situation in which an act both generates regulatory information but is also used for marketing, the act is not "solely for uses reasonably related" to regulatory approval.

Petitioner and the United States short circuit the analysis by asking whether an "experiment," for example, could generate regulatory information. Such a test focuses only on the objective half of the inquiry and improperly suggests that "reasonably related" should modify "act of infringement" instead of the purpose of the infringing act. However, it is necessary, but not sufficient, that a particular class of infringing acts, such as pre-clinical experiments, can be put to regulatory uses. The presence of "solely" in the statute demonstrates that Congress did not intend to immunize all acts that might reasonably be related to FDA approval. Only those acts that are solely used for regulatory approvals are exempt.

Once "act" and "use" are properly distinguished from each other in the context of Section 271(e)(1), it also becomes clear that the "solely for uses" requirement addresses the problem of hindsight in applying the exemption. Indeed, the temptation, to which others fall prey, is to view the drug discovery process teleologically by looking back from the perspective of successful drug screens and consummated IND applications. Such a focus is understandable — the select therapeutics that make it through are the valuable ones. However, by focusing only on the successes (and near misses) the reality of the research process is warped. Every assay and experiment appears directed toward (and reasonably related to) the FDA approval process. The presence of the subjective requirement that acts of infringement must be "solely for" the regulatory approval process returns the focus to the purpose of an "act" at its inception by evaluating what the act is "for" before its fate appears preordained.

In reality, the drug development process is highly uncertain. Some estimate that as many as one thousand different medicines must be tested in order to yield one that enters clinical trials. The pre-IND sieve that screens drug candidates is basic research. Until an IND is filed for a particular therapeutic, a significant if not predominant "use" of the acts of infringement is research and optimization apart from the generation of information that is required or desired by the FDA. When the research landscape is viewed from the perspective of the actor before an IND has been filed, it is clear that acts of infringement cannot be "solely for" the FDA approval process.

IV.

RESPECTING THE WORDS OF SECTION 271(e)(1) RIGHT-SIZES THE EXEMPTION AND ALIGNS IT WITH ITS ORIGINAL PURPOSE

As demonstrated above, for otherwise infringing activity to qualify for the Section 271(e)(1) exemption, it must be used "solely" for purposes of developing and submitting information for regulatory approvals. As Judge Schwarzer explained in Scripps, the legislative history confirms that this interpretation of the statute aligns with the purpose behind the exemption.

When the rhetoric is stripped away, there is not serious dispute about the central purpose behind the enactment of Section 271(e)(1). As documented below, the statute was a carefully circumscribed exemption. It authorized only de minimis uncompensated patent infringement solely for the regulatory approval process. It was intended to permit generic drug makers to perform FDA required bioequivalency testing, which necessarily involves the infringement of the proprietary drug maker's patent rights. The purpose of such testing is to allow the generic drug maker to prove that the proposed generic drug is effectively the same as the proprietary drug before the patents on the proprietary drug expire. This enables the fulfillment of the ultimate goal of having approved generic drugs ready for the market promptly upon the expiration of the patents covering the proprietary drug so there is no de facto patent extension. Because the generic drug makers are not defining a new drug, and a market for the drug has already been established, the exemption is needed for the basic bioequivalency testing. Of course, the purpose of this limited testing is for FDA approval.

The Federal Circuit explained that a central purpose of Section 271(e)(1) was to "ensure that a patentee's rights did not de facto extend past the expiration of the patent term because a generic competitor also could not enter the market without regulatory approval." Petitioner does not contest this analysis of the legislative history. Likewise, Petitioner does not meaningfully deny that the legislative history reflects that Congress foresaw only "a limited amount of testing so that generic manufacturers can establish the bioequivalency of a generic substitute."

On the other hand, Petitioner and its allies do not cite any legislative history that suggests the purpose of the legislation was to exempt broadly drug development from the patent laws.

Where Amici and Petitioner really part company is on the legal consequence of the legislative history. Petitioner reasons that, because the above-quoted legislative history did not trump the statutory language and structure in *Eli Lilly & Co. v. Medtronic, Inc.*, 496 U.S. 661 (1990), it should not do so here. Indeed, Petitioner's central argument is that the legislative history cannot narrow a broad statute.

The statutory interpretation issue here is far different than that presented in Lilly, and Petitioner and its allies uniformly ignore that important difference. Here, the narrow scope of the exemption suggested by the legislative history is mandated by the statutory language "solely for uses," as demonstrated above. It is not in conflict with the statute's structure as it was found to be in Lilly.

In sum, here, both the statutory language and the legislative history support the conclusion that the Section 271(e)(1) exemption is confined to infringing acts "solely" used for the regulatory approvals such as bioequivalency testing. If activities other than bioequivalency testing for generic substitutes fall within some of the broader language of the statute, they must be protected pursuant to standard statutory interpretation principles. However, by its plain terms, activities not used solely for regulatory approvals fall outside the exemption because the statute says so. The legislative history reinforces, rather than undermines, this conclusion.

V.

THE EXEMPTION SOUGHT BY PETITIONER WILL SET BACK, NOT ADVANCE, PUBLIC HEALTH

The broad infringement exemption sought by Petitioner and its allies will harm public health in the long run, not help it. The far-reaching exemption they seek essentially suspends the patent laws as it relates to the drug research and development process. Indeed, Petitioner goes so far as to suggest that if drug research and development relates to the "safety, efficacy, mechanism of action, pharmacology, or pharmacokinetics" any infringement is cost-free because the FDA is interested in those broad topics. One of the more candid drug company briefs expressly pleads that "the FDA exemption should be generously interpreted" because to do otherwise would "complicate" the drug development process.

While there may be some superficial appeal to the emotional argument that patent rights complicate product development and increase prices, the Constitution and experience teach otherwise. While those with a short-term view see the cost of patent enforcement, those with a longer perspective appreciate the incentives created by patent rights in this field, at least as much as in other fields.

These truths are especially relevant in the area of drug discovery tools. Modern drug discovery is buoyed by the rising and swelling tide of innovation in the area of research tools. Some tools make the discovery of new drugs and therapies possible. Examples of such tools are technologies that replicate DNA, decode genes, screen candidate drugs, validate targets and provide manufacturing and analytical standards and tests. Other tools enhance the performance of candidate therapeutics or diagnostic products. Examples of these tools include medicinal chemistries and formulations that make whole classes of drugs work better.

Tools are the common denominator across all possible therapeutic agents — tools are necessary to isolate, analyze, qualify, and optimize every potential drug, and are employed at every stage of the development process. In some cases, a tool is employed to work a permanent improvement to a class of therapeutics. Concerns about preserving the value of tool patents in the face of free-riding by pharmaceutical companies during the term of development are no less implicated where the "tool" is an optimization that is incorporated into a final product that is sold, potentially, years after patents on the tool have expired.

If new drugs are the "fish," the research tools are the fishing poles. If the patent-free development of this year's drugs is perceived by some as in their short-term interest, the patent-incentivized development of future research tools is in the interest of our descendants for generations to come.

One group of commentators explained in stark terms the risk to tool patents posed by an overbroad reading of Section 271(e)(1):

> Since there is generally no use for research tools other than in the research and development process and a third party's interest is to use the technology rather than resell it, extension of the § 271(e)(1) exemption far upstream in the research-and-development process renders research tool patents essentially unenforceable. Consequently, such staple technologies of biotechnology industry patents as recombinant cells, transgenic animals, or high-throughput screening methods and their uses will be essentially unprotectable, thus erasing the value of much of the biotechnology industry and undercutting incentive for further research in this essential area. Because a biotech company would have no proprietary rights to any FDA-approved commercial product discovered or developed by a third party using its patented research tool, the value of these companies is severely and perhaps fatally undercut.

Kevin E. Noonan, *Paradise Lost: The Uncertain Future Of Research Tool Patents*, 15 No.3 J. PROPRIETARY RTS. 1, 8.

Petitioner does not deny that research tools are vitally important or even that patent protection is important for such tools. Instead, it focuses its energy attempting to persuade this Court that "research tools" are not (strictly speaking) at issue in this case. Petitioner's fallback position is that even if the rules created by this case impact tool patents, the Court should not let that get in the way of creating the broad exemption they seek.

In fact, an overbroad interpretation of Section 271(e)(1) unquestionably creates grave risk for the biotech industry generally and tool patents specifically. Even the champions of a broad exemption raise the possibility of restrictions that this Court could invoke to protect tool patents. For example, Petitioner explains that, under certain circumstances, "a court might conclude that the use of a patented research tool is not 'reasonably related' to the development of information for the FDA." Petitioner also notes that the "patented invention" covered by Section 271(e) may not be interpreted to include tool patent inventions. Likewise, the United States observes that "Congress may not have intended to include research tools within the scope of the affected inventions."

Others explain persuasively why these protections should in fact be invoked by this Court to minimize any damage to the biotech community and tool makers; Amici will not belabor those points. In any event, giving "solely" its undeniable meaning goes a long way towards ensuring that the balance struck by Congress is honored and that the exemption does not threaten innovation broadly. As explained above, respecting the word "solely" is also mandated by the straightforward application of standard statutory interpretation principles. Acknowledging the entirety of the text of the statute is not only common sense, but it points to the right result.

IV.

CONCLUSION

For the reasons addressed above, the judgment of the court of appeals should be affirmed.

MERCK KGAA v. INTEGRA LIFESCIENCES I, LTD.

Brief of Amici Curiae Wisconsin Alumni Research Foundation, The American Council on Education, Boston University, The Regents of the University of California, Research Corporation Technologies, The Salk Institute for Biological Studies, University of Alberta and University of Oklahoma in Support of Respondents

INTEREST OF THE AMICI

The Amici include the Wisconsin Alumni Research Foundation ("WARF"), the Regents of the University of California, the American Counsel on Education, Research Corporation Technologies, The Salk Institute for Biological Studies, Boston University, the University of Oklahoma, and the University of Alberta.

The Amici are generally interested in the management, development, licensing, and enforcement of university-related intellectual property that forms a substantial part of the new drug discovery pipeline. As has been recently observed, these institutions, along with biotechnology companies, "perform the risky experiments that lead who knows where. They also develop the cutting-edge tools that permit this research - such as screening methods for new chemicals that might be transformed into medical cures and computer programs to better design those chemicals." As explained herein the university sector's ability to patent technology arising from its research efforts is the basis for transferring such technology to the public for its use and benefit.

To expand the safe harbor of 35 U.S.C. § 271(e)(1) beyond the limits set forth in the statute's plain meaning and identified by the court of appeals below would have an adverse effect on the research community as a whole, and the university research community in particular. Given the normal expectation that innovation follows invention, the corresponding erosion of patent rights that would necessarily accompany an undue expansion of the safe harbor would also bring with it a lag in innovation. Without the protection afforded by viable patents, there would be a lessened interest within the private sector to support university-related research functions.

The performance of the university sector in transferring technology under the seminal University and Small Business Patent Procedures Act, Pub. L. No. 96- 517, sec. 6(a), 94 Stat. 3019 (1980), codified as amended at 35 U.S.C. § 201, et seq. (2000) (commonly known as "the Bayh-Dole Act") has been exemplary. The success of the Act can be traced to two fundamental features embraced in the Patent Act: (1) the certainty and security of title that is essential for academic and non-profit institutions to transfer their patented technologies to the private sector; and (2) the right to exclude others from practicing the patented technology afforded to such institutions under the patent laws. Contravening these features would be anathema to the ability of universities to transfer the technology derived from the conduct of their research functions.

The President's Council of Advisors on Science and Technology (PCAST) reported to the President in 2003 that judicial decisions on "research exemptions," especially as concerns research tool patents, "could be an important factor in future technology transfer practices." PCAST also concluded, and recommended generally, that "[e]xisting technology-transfer legislation works and should not be altered."

Moreover, and without question, the university sector is a key in the discovery of new drugs, as well as other breakthrough technologies, which have served to make the United States the world's technology leader. As an example, the biotechnology industry as we know it today began on university campuses in the United States. With the continued "downsizing" of corporations in this country, the private sector is heavily dependent upon the academic community to perform the basic research function that advances technologies and yields new products and processes that benefit mankind the world over.

As holders of many of the patents directed to inventions which are or may be utilized directed to experimental pursuits, the Amici have a substantial interest in the principal question to be resolved by the Court, namely the appropriate scope of the infringement safe harbor of section 271(e)(1) of the Patent Act.

SUMMARY OF ARGUMENT

The statutory safe harbor provided in section 271(e)(1) was designed by Congress to solve a very specific problem — the de facto extension of a patentee's exclusivity resulting from a competitor's inability to conduct experimentation to obtain regulatory approval necessary to bring otherwise infringing products to market upon the expiration of a patent. The express language of section 271(e)(1), which exempts only those acts "solely for uses reasonably related to the development and submission of information under a Federal law which regulates the manufacture, use, or sale of drugs or veterinary biological products," is purposefully narrow to accomplish that goal. The Petitioner argues for the expansion of section 271(e)(1) that may, in turn, result in an exemption of more than was ever intended by Congress — i.e., general pharmaceutical research.

In addition to being well beyond the intended scope of section 271(e)(1), such an expansion would nullify the commercial value of an entire class of patents — drug research patents, which are paramount tools in the drug discovery process. Not only would such a result be clearly contrary to statutory language, the legislative purposes and objectives of the Bayh-Dole Act, but it would be contrary to treaty obligations entered into by the United States. In the final analysis, it would result in a serious detriment to the drug discovery process, which would benefit neither institutions, such as the Amici, nor pharmaceutical companies such as the Petitioner.

ARGUMENT

I. Introduction

It is a policy conflict that originated well before this case began — the desire to provide the widest range of affordable, lifesaving drug products to the U.S. population versus the recognition that, in order to ensure that such products are developed, the need to provide for patent exclusivity for such products, and the various economic results arising from such exclusivity.

Ironically, large pharmaceutical companies, such as the Petitioner, generally find themselves among the group favoring patent exclusivity, especially in the face of low-priced competition from generic drug manufacturers. Here, of course, the Petitioner argues for drug availability to the detriment of broader patent protection.

In making their stand for narrower patent protection, the Petitioner, and the Amici that have thus far weighed in on behalf of the Petitioner, mischaracterize the issue below as a distinction somehow drawn between generic and pioneer drug products. In fact, the Federal Circuit's decision was not based on any such distinction. Rather, the Federal Circuit ruled, as it should have, in light of the plain language of section 271(e)(1), that, in the safe harbor of that statutory provision exempts from an infringement charge acts "solely for uses reasonably related to the development and submission of information under a Federal law which regulates the manufacture, use, or sale of drugs."

In light of the afore-quoted language, the Federal Circuit correctly ruled that "general biomedical experimentation" was not embraced by the narrow safe harbor to infringement charges provided under section 271(e)(1).

The Amici do not contest the view that the words "reasonably related" in the statute give courts limited leeway to engage in a fact-specific inquiry about whether making, using, or selling a patented invention in the United States are "solely for uses reasonably related" to the statutory safe harbor.

II. Section 271(e)(1) is a Limited Exemption to an Infringement Charge by Design

A. The Original Purpose of Section 271(e)(1)

Section 271 (e)(1), under which the Petitioner originally sought safe harbor below, provides as follows:

> It shall not be an act of infringement to make, use, or sell within the United States . . . a patented invention . . . solely for uses reasonably related to the development and submission of information under a Federal law which regulates the manufacture, use, or sale of drugs or veterinary biological products.

This section was originally part of the Drug Price Competition and Patent Term Restoration Act of 1984 Pub. L. 98-417 (1984), sec. 201, 98 Stat. 1598-1602, codified as amended at 35 U.S.C. § 156 (2002) ("the Act"), which was designed to respond to an unintended extension of the statutory patent term in certain circumstances resulting from the requirement that certain products, such as pharmaceuticals, receive pre-market regulatory approval. Prior to the enactment of the Act, a patentee's potential competitors were often delayed from entering the market once a patent expired because such competitors could not seek their own regulatory approval prior to the expiration of the patent.

This patent term distortion was exacerbated by the Federal Circuit's decision in *Roche Products, Inc. v. Bolar Pharmaceutical Co., Inc.* 733 F.2d 858 (Fed. Cir. 1984), *cert. denied*, 469 U.S. 856 (1984), which "decided that the manufacture, use, or sale of a patented invention during the term of the patent constituted an act of infringement . . . even if it was for the sole purpose of conducting tests and developing information necessary to apply for regulatory approval."

Congress responded to this distortion by providing a narrowly-tailored safe harbor exemption for otherwise infringing activity where such activity is "solely for uses reasonably related to the development and submission of information" to the FDA. In enacting this provision, Congress had in mind the particular plight of competitor drug manufacturers, who would thenceforth be permitted "a limited amount of testing so that generic manufacturers can establish the bioequivalency of a generic substitute." The Federal Circuit recognized, and relied upon, this objective in rendering its decision below.

There is nothing in either section 271(e) itself or in the legislative history therefor that suggests an intent on the part of Congress to exempt from an infringement charge general research. To expand the scope of section 271(e)(1) in a manner so as to include such research "would not confine the scope of § 271(e)(1) to de minimis encroachment on the rights of the patentee."

On the other hand, the Petitioner, and Amici the United States, AARP, and Wyeth, attempt to focus attention on the distinction between pioneer drugs, which require preclinical trials, and generic drugs, which do not, as somehow being the lynchpin of the Federal Circuit's opinion below. The Federal Circuit, of course, made no such bright line distinction in determining the proper scope of the safe harbor of section 271(e)(1). Rather, the Federal Circuit looked at whether the type of research at issue below was "solely . . . reasonably related to the development and submission of information' to the FDA," and whether exempting such research from an infringement charge would have more than a de minimis effect on the patentee's rights.

Nowhere did the Federal Circuit rule that pioneer drug testing is always excluded. In fact, as Amicus the United States notes, "the court of appeals issued an 'errata' sheet indicating that 'the scope of the safe harbor is not limited to generic drug approval'." Rather, the Federal Circuit's inquiry, as it should have been, is whether the research in question, irrespective of whether such research pertains to pioneer or generic drugs is solely reasonably related to the development and submission of information to the FDA.

Indeed, as Amicus the United States acknowledges:

> To be sure, not all research that occurs before the commencement of the clinical phase will necessarily fall within the FDA exemption . . .

the initial stages of basic exploratory research may not be covered by section 271(e)(1).

Further, as Amicus Wyeth notes, "the FDA requires certain preclinical tests to be conducted in accordance with the FDA's Good Laboratory Practice regulations, which are designed to ensure the quality of the studies that form the basis for the application." These Good Laboratory Practices require, inter alia: an FDA inspection (21 C.F.R. § 58.15(a)); particular training and experience levels for laboratory personnel (21 C.F.R. § 58.29); a quality assurance unit (21 C.F.R. § 58.35); animal care and supply facilities (21 C.F.R. §§ 58.43 & 58.45); and many more specific requirements regarding equipment, facilities, and procedures (see generally 21 C.F.R. Part 58).

The record below shows that the 1995 agreement between the Petitioner and Scripps imposed the requirement of assuring Good Laboratory Practices on Scripps. However, the Petitioner is seeking a safe harbor under section 271(e)(1) for experiments conducted before the 1995 agreement, as well as after. In any event, and at the very least, an accused infringer seeking safe harbor for preclinical testing under section 271(e)(1) should be required to make at least a showing that all of the experiments for which safe harbor is sought were conducted according to Good Laboratory Practices, as required by the FDA.

On a related issue, the Petitioner submits that the court below correctly observed that " 'all the research conducted under the Scripps-Merck [1995] agreement' was 'pre-clinical research'." However, it is not clear that the Federal Circuit was using the term "pre-clinical" in the same fashion as the Petitioner, insofar as the Federal Circuit referred to a "pre-clinical" stage antibody that was the subject of a 1990 agreement, well before any "pre-clinical" (as the Petitioner uses that term) research was being conducted.

In sum, the proper question in this matter ultimately becomes whether the research in question relates solely and reasonably to the submission of information to the FDA — not whether such information pertains to pioneer versus generic drug testing. The Federal Circuit answered the proper question below in reaching its decision regarding the scope of section 271(e)(1). . . .

[Editor's Note: The remainder of this section focused on the interpretation of the word "solely" in the statute.]

III.   Research Patents

A.   Reading "Solely" Out of the Statute Would Commercially Neuter Research Patents

Congress certainly could have passed a provision including a safe harbor for any use of a patented invention that related in any way to developing information for submission to the FDA. Doing so, however, would have left all pharmaceutical research patents bereft of value. No research activity that would have otherwise been an infringement of such a patent would have been actionable, as any research activity relates, at least in some remote fashion, to the submission of information to the FDA for approval. Congress, of course, opted not to adopt such a provision, electing rather to adopt the narrower language of section 271(e)(1) containing the word "solely" therein.

Although not an issue with regard to the patents in suit below, a statutory construction that reads the word "solely" out of section 271(e)(1) would effectively neuter all research patents issued in the United States in the aforedescribed way. Such a construction would be inconsistent with the plain language of section 271(e)(1), as well as the Constitutional authority behind the enactment of the Patent Statute, and would violate the intent of Congress that any effect on the rights of patentees resulting from the enactment of section 271(e)(1) be de minimis.

The Federal Circuit put it most persuasively in its opinion below:

> Because the downstream clinical testing for FDA approval falls within the safe harbor, these patented tools would only supply some commercial benefit to the inventor when applied to general research. Thus, exaggerating § 271(e)(1) out of context would swallow the whole benefit of the Patent Act for some categories of biotechnological inventions. Needless to say, the 1984 Act was meant to reverse the effects of Roche under limited circumstances, not to deprive entire categories of inventions of patent protection.

The risk to pharmaceutical research patents in the event the scope of section 271(e)(1) is judicially expanded is empirically shown in *Bristol-Myers Squibb Co. v. Rhone-Poulenc Rorer, Inc.* In that case, the defendant used patented intermediate products to run "hundreds of experiments for purposes of identifying a drug candidate." The types of experiments in which the patented intermediates were used took place very early in the drug discovery and development process. Nonetheless, the court in Bristol- Myers held that the subject research was entitled to the infringement exemption under section 271(e)(1).

In ruling the way it did, the court in Bristol-Myers focused upon "the likelihood of the information generated being relevant to information sought by the FDA, not the likelihood of submission of the new product to the FDA." In other words, according to this reasoning, otherwise infringing preliminary research in which thousands of compounds are screened would be entirely immune under section 271(e)(1) if the type of information generated from such research would be submitted to the FDA if a promising drug product is ultimately identified. This exemption would apply, according to the court in Bristol-Myers, whether such a drug product is identified or not.

In the event that the safe harbor of section 271(e)(1) is unduly expanded, decisions such as that in Bristol-Myers will become commonplace, whittling away at the value of pharmaceutical research patents until nothing is left. The Federal Circuit recognized the value that such patents bring in terms of the discovery of new drugs, an issue in which the Petitioner purports to be deeply concerned — "[a]fter all, patented tools often facilitate general research to identify candidate drugs, as well as downstream safety-related experiments on those new drugs." Expanding section 271(e)(1) to exempt general pharmaceutical research would completely vitiate this value.

The Petitioner, in attempting to deflect the issue regarding pharmaceutical research tool patents, argues that the inventions of such patents could be used "in any context, not just drug research," thereby preserving at least a portion of the value of such patents. One of the very examples cited by the Petitioner — patents directed to a "special assay for screening compounds on the basis of certain properties" — belies this statement, however. In other words, there would be no use other than drug research for such patents. Should the safe harbor of section 271(e)(1) be expanded to include general pharmaceutical research, it is inconceivable that such research patents will have any value left.

Finally, the Petitioner hypothesizes that, notwithstanding any expansion here of the section 271(e)(1) safe harbor, lower courts in the future may very well create judicial exceptions to the safe harbor for drug research patents. This, of course, is pure conjecture. The more likely outcome is that any expansion of the safe harbor by this Court will be read by the courts below as pertaining to all categories of patents, including drug research patents. At the very least, it will be difficult, if not impossible, to draw the bright line that the Petitioner suggests. The end result is that there will be little, if any, value left to such patents.

B.   Neutering Research Patents Would Have the Effect of Thwarting the Purposes of the Bayh-Dole Act and the Attendant Research that the Act Promotes

The ability of universities to obtain intellectual property protection for, inter alia, the research that they perform was a primary aim of the Bayh-Dole Act. The following is the National Institutes of Heath's description of the Act, and the rights and obligations that the Act confers:

> The Bayh-Dole Act . . . provides the statutory basis and framework for federal technology transfer activities, including the patenting and licensing of federally funded inventions by recipient organizations. The Act permits recipients of federal grants and contracts to elect title to patentable 'subject inventions' that arise with the use of federal funds. If recipients elect title, the Act requires them to file patent applications, seek commercialization opportunities, and report back to the funding agency on efforts to obtain utilization of their inventions.

This characterization of the Bayh-Dole Act was echoed by the Council on Governmental Relations:

> [U]nder the Bayh-Dole Act, universities have a mandate to ensure, to the extent possible, that inventions arising from federally funded research are commercialized. It is an obligation they have increasingly embraced since 1980 when the law was enacted.

One of the co-sponsors of the Bayh-Dole Act, Senator Birch Bayh, described the Act as being "a step in the direction of encouraging innovation and productivity in the United States." Further, university investigators "understand that the act provides them the possibility of their advancing mankind, as Pasteur did, which explains their growing enthusiasm to participate."

Diminishing or eliminating the value of research patents owned by universities and university-related research institutions via the section 271(e)(1) safe harbor would thwart the afore-described aims of the Bayh-Dole Act, leaving universities without an effective means of protecting technology generated from their research efforts through the patent laws, and substantially hindering their ability to commercialize the results of such research.

In pursuing patent protection, universities also ensure dissemination of the technology resulting from their basic research activities. Universities, such as the Amici, "develop the cutting-edge tools that permit this research." Patent protection for such research tools ensures the benefits derived by the developers of such tools.

On the other hand, dissemination of technology is not a given for the private sector, which may very well opt for trade secret protection, thereby curtailing knowledge of scientific advances, as well as the opportunity to build upon information developed and disclosed via the patent system. An overextended safe harbor as applied to research patents may encourage more universities to protect technology as trade secrets, licensing the technology as such, thereby resulting in a similar, corresponding reduction in the dissemination of scientific information.

Also of importance to the university sector is the protection of researchers' rights to publish the results of their research, as advancement in academics is generally dependent upon such publication. Effective patent protection ensures the continued ability to publish, and share with the public, such results, while ensuring that a goal of the Bayh-Dole Act, i.e., the commercial viability of such research, is met.

The proposed expansion of the safe harbor risks contravening express Congressional language and intent that section 271(e)(1) interfere only nominally with the rights of the patent holder. Should the afore-described devaluation of drug research patents result from the urged expansion of the section 271(e)(1) safe harbor, the result would be the impairment of the drug discovery process, as well as the frustration of the purpose of another section of the Patent Act, the Bayh-Dole Act.

C. Neutering the Value of Pharmaceutical Research Patents Would Violate the Obligations Imposed on the United States Under TRIPS

The United States is a party to the Agreement on Trade-Related Aspects of Intellectual Property Rights, 1869 U.N.T.S. 299, 33 I.L.M. 1197 (1994) ("TRIPS Agreement"). Pursuant to the TRIPS Agreement:

> Subject to the provisions of paragraphs 2 and 3, patents shall be available for any inventions, whether products or processes, in all fields of technology, provided that they are new, involve an inventive step and are capable of industrial application.

It is true that, pursuant to Article 27(3)(a) of TRIPS, a member state can exclude from patentability "diagnostic, therapeutic and surgical methods for the treatment of humans or animals." However, once a member nation has determined to provide patent protection for a particular class of inventions, a patent owner is to have the exclusive right to prevent others from making, using, offering for sale, selling, or importing the patent subject matter.

A member state may provide for:

[L]imited exceptions to the exclusive rights conferred by a patent, provided that such exceptions do not unreasonably conflict with a normal exploitation of the patent and do not unreasonably prejudice the legitimate interests of the patent owner, taking account of the legitimate interests of third parties.

No less an authority than the United States Constitution provides that treaties made under the authority of the United States, such as TRIPS, "shall be the supreme Law of the Land; and the Judges in every State shall be bound thereby, any Thing in the Constitution or Laws of any State to the Contrary notwithstanding." Any judicial expansion of the section 271(e)(1) safe harbor that would, in essence, strip pharmaceutical research patents of their value, would violate the United States' obligations under TRIPS, and should, therefore, be resisted.

CONCLUSION

For the foregoing reasons, this Court should affirm the decision of the Federal Circuit that general research is not exempt from an infringement charge under section 271(e)(1).

NOTES & QUESTIONS

1. The *Merck* opinion was an eagerly anticipated source of guidance from the Supreme Court. One reason for the attention devoted to this case was the hope that the court would clarify the scope of legitimate, non-infringing experimental use of patented inventions. The Court, in a nine to zero decision, addressed solely the issue of experimental use as permitted under the patent statute. Patent practitioners and scholars were anticipating some discussion of the status of common law experimental use. An amici brief submitted by a number of intellectual property law professors, written on the side of neither party, urged the Court not to narrow or otherwise alter the scope of the common law experimental use doctrine. The Federal Circuit had addressed common law experimental use in its 2002 *Madey* decision (excerpted and discussed in Chapter One). In *Merck*, a majority of the Federal Circuit also sidestepped the common law experimental use issue, much to the chagrin of Judge Newman, who, in a stinging dissent, urged the court to consider to what extent Merck would have been protected by the common law doctrine. The current state of the law appears to be a narrow common law experimental use doctrine as articulated by the Federal Circuit in *Madey* and a broader statutory experimental use doctrine for pharmaceuticals as articulated by the Supreme Court in *Merck*. How would you read the Supreme Court's *Merck* decision as it pertains to the common law experimental use doctrine? Does the opinion's silence reflect deference to the Federal Circuit or does the expansive view of statutory

experimental use adopted in *Merck* signal a need for a broadening of the common law doctrine as well?

2. Under the current state of the law, non-infringing experimental use is quite broad in the pharmaceutical industry and narrow in all other industries (which are covered solely by the common law experimental use doctrine). Does this distinction among industries make sense? Should patent law be industry specific? For the case in favor of industry specific patent law, see Dan L. Burk & Mark A. Lemley, *Is Patent Law Technology-Specific?*, 17 BEKELEY TECH. L. J. 1155 (2002). For contrary arguments, see R. Polk Wagner, *Of Patents and Path Dependency: A Comment on Burk & Lemley*, 18 BEKELEY TECH. L. J. 1341 (2003). Does the *Merck* opinion provide a justification for this different treatment of pharmaceuticals?

3. Review the amici brief submitted by Applera Corporation and other members of the research tool industry on behalf of the respondents. This brief urged the Court to interpret the statutory experimental use doctrine quite narrowly. The position should not be surprising. Members of the research tool industry are concerned that a broad experimental use exception to infringement liability will give researchers a license to use patented research tools without the permission of the patent owner. One strawman argument sometimes raised against the Court's holding in *Merck* is that a broad experiment use exception would allow a company to use a patented microscope if such use was "reasonably related" to clinical trials for new drugs. Is there some kernel of truth to this argument? Could "reasonably related" be read so broadly? Does the *Merck* opinion prevent this seemingly absurd outcome? If so, how?

4. Despite the crucial business and economic interests implicated by the *Merck* case, the Applera amici does not address many of the policy concerns head-on. Instead, the authors of the amici brief present a textual argument that hinges on how to read the word "solely." Is the argument convincing? Justice Scalia is often thought of as a strict constructionist, meaning that he prefers close textual readings of statutes and other legal sources. Does he stray from his strict constructionist leanings in the *Merck* opinion?

5. The second amici brief excerpted was submitted by several universities and research foundations. Like the Applera brief, this brief argued in favor of the position advocated by Integra and recommends a narrow reading of the statutory experimental use exception. Are the interests of the universities submitting this brief the same as those of research tool manufacturers? Why would universities not want a broad experimental use exception to infringement liability? In this regard, reconsider the *Madey* case discussed in Note 1 and excerpted in Chapter One. In that case, Duke University attempted to raise the common law experimental use defense and lost. In the *Merck* case, the universities that submitted the amici brief emphasized the potential negative implications of a broad experimental use exception for university-based research and development and related patenting activity. The brief also claims that a broad experimental use exception would be inconsistent with the goals of the Bayh-Dole Act to foster university-industry collaboration. It should not be surprising that universities take this position. What is perhaps surprising is that no universities submitted a brief in support of Merck and a liberal experimental use exception. Does the silence say something about how universities view

the commercialization of research in general or about the scope of the statutory experimental use exception in particular? Remember that law professors did submit a brief in support of neither party urging the Court not to alter the scope of the common law experimental use exception. Perhaps the silence has less to do with the need for the exception than with the special role of the statutory exception in the pharmaceutical industry.

APPENDIX

INTRODUCTION TO INTELLECTUAL PROPERTY FOR THE NON-SPECIALIST

Contents

I. Types of Intellectual Property Interests

    A.   Patents

    B.   Copyrights

    C.   Trademarks and Servicemarks

    D.   Trade Secrets

II. Patent Laws

    A. What Can Be Patented

        1. Utility Patents

        2. Design Patents

        3. Plant Patents

    B. Conditions for Obtaining a Patent: Novelty and Non-Obviousness

    C. The Role of the Patent Office

    D. Who May Apply For a Patent

    E. Contents of a Patent Application

        1. Regular Patent Application

        2. Provisional Patent Application

    F. Patent Attorneys and Agents

    G. Publication of Patent Applications

    H. Examination of Patent Applications

    I. Nature of Patent Rights

    J. Maintenance Fees

    K. Patent Expiration

    L. Relief for Patent Infringement

    M. Patent Marking and Notices of "Patent Pending"

    N. Patent Assignments and Licenses

        1. Forms of Assignments

        2. Recording of Assignments

        3. Patent Licenses

O. International Considerations
    1. Foreign Patents and Patent Rights
    2. The Paris Convention
    3. The Patent Cooperation Treaty (PCT)
    4. Foreign Filing License
    5. Foreign Applicants for United States Patents

III. Copyright Laws

    A. Copyrightable Works
    B. Copyright Registration
    C. Initial Copyright Ownership
    D. Rights of Copyright Holders
    E. Fair Use Limitations on Copyright Enforcement
    F. Compulsory Licenses as Limitations on
        Copyright Enforcement
    G. Remedies for Copyright Infringement
    H. Duration of Copyright Protections
        1. Works Originally Created on or after January 1, 1978
        2. Works Originally Created before January 1, 1978,
            But Not Published or Registered by That Date
        3. Works Originally Created and Published or
            Registered before January 1, 1978
    I. Transfers of Copyright Interests

IV. Trademark Laws

    A. Characteristics of a Trademark or Service Mark
    B. Items That May Serve as Trademarks
        1. Textual Marks
        2. Graphical Marks
    C. Registering a Trademark
        1. Application Based on Use in Commerce
        2. Application Based on Intent to Use
    D. Role of the USPTO
    E. Bases for Rejection of a Trademark Registration Application
        1. Likelihood of Confusion With an Existing Mark
        2. Other Grounds for Rejection
    F. Impacts of Trademark Registration
    G. Use of Trademark Symbols TM, SM and ®
    H. Duration of Trademark Protections
    I. Trademark Infringement and Remedies
    J. Further Remedies for False Designations of
        Origin or False Descriptions

K. Transfers of Trademark Interests

L. International Considerations

V. Trade Secret Laws

    A. Characteristics of a Trade Secret

    B. Secrecy

    C. Other Significant Factors Indicating That Information
is a Trade Secret

    D. Relationships Between Trade Secret and Patent Protections

        1. Broader Subject Matter Covered by Trade Secrets

        2. Reliance on Trade Secret Protections When
Obtaining Patents

        3. Strategic Choice of Trade Secret Protections
Over Patent Protections

    E. Misappropriation of Trade Secrets

    F. Remedies for Trade Secret Misappropriation

VI. Additional Intellectual Property Protections

    A. Internet Domain Names

    B. Rights of Publicity

    C. Protections Under the Semiconductor Chip Protection Act (SCPA)

I. TYPES OF INTELLECTUAL PROPERTY INTERESTS[1]

A. Patents

A patent for an invention gives the inventor the ability to control the use and commercialization of the invention for a limited period. A United States patent is granted based on an application to and review for legal sufficiency by the United States Patent and Trademark Office (USPTO). Generally, the term of a new patent is 20 years from the date on which the application for the patent was filed in the United States. United States patents are effective only within the United States, U.S. territories, and U.S. possessions. Under certain circumstances, patent term extensions or adjustments may be available.

The right conferred by the patent grant is, in the language of the Patent Act, "the right to exclude others from making, using, offering for sale, or selling" the invention in the United States or "importing" the invention into the United States. What is granted is not the right to make, use, offer for sale, sell or import the invention, but rather the right to exclude others from making, using, offering for sale, selling, or importing the invention. Once a patent is issued, the patentee must enforce the patent without aid of the USPTO.

---

[1] The material in this section is based on United States Patent and Trademark Office, "General Information Concerning Patents," http://www.uspto.gov/web/offices/pac/doc/general/ index. html#faqs.

There are three types of patents:

1) Utility patents covering new and useful processes, machines, articles of manufacture, or compositions of matter, or any new and useful improvements thereof;

2) Design patents covering new, original, and ornamental designs for articles of manufacture; and

3) Plant patents covering distinct and new varieties of asexually reproducing plants.

B. Copyrights

Copyright is a form of protection provided to the authors of "original works of authorship" including literary, dramatic, musical, artistic, and certain other intellectual works, both published and unpublished. The 1976 Copyright Act generally gives the owner of copyright the exclusive right to reproduce the copyrighted work, to prepare derivative works, to distribute copies or phonorecords of the copyrighted work, to perform the copyrighted work publicly, or to display the copyrighted work publicly.

A copyright protects an author's particular form of expression rather than the subject matter of a protected writing. For example, a description of a machine could be copyrighted, but this would only prevent others from copying the description. It would not prevent others from writing a description of their own or from making and using the machine. Copyrights are registered by the Copyright Office of the Library of Congress.

C. Trademarks and Servicemarks

A trademark is a word, name, symbol, or device that is used in trade with goods to indicate the source of the goods and to distinguish them from the goods of others. A servicemark is the same as a trademark except that it identifies and distinguishes the source of a service rather than a product. The terms "trademark" and "mark" are commonly used to refer to both trademarks and servicemarks.   This convention is also used in this Appendix.

Trademark rights may be used to prevent others from using a confusingly similar mark, but not to prevent others from making the same goods as the trademark holder or from selling the same goods or services under a clearly different mark. Trademarks which are used in interstate or foreign commerce may be registered with the USPTO.

D. Trade Secrets

A trade secret may consist of any formula, pattern, device or compilation of information which is used in secret in a person's business, and which gives him an opportunity to obtain an advantage over competitors who do not know or use it. The subject matter of a trade secret must be information that is not widely known or easily ascertainable. Matters of public knowledge or of general knowledge in an industry cannot be appropriated by a person as his trade secret. Matters which are completely disclosed by the goods which a party markets cannot be his trade secret.

Persons who have access to trade secrets in their work can be prevented by legal injunctions from disclosing these secrets to others and from using the trade secrets for purposes other than furthering the interests of the trade secret owner. Persons who acquire trade secrets through wrongful means — for example, by trespass or knowingly causing others to breach their obligations to keep trade secrets confidential — can also be precluded from using or disclosing the trade secrets. Persons who use or disclose trade secrets without the permission of the trade secret owners can be forced to compensate the trade secret holder for resulting damages.

II. PATENT LAWS[2]

The Constitution of the United States gives Congress the power to enact laws relating to patents, in Article I, section 8, which reads: "The Congress shall have the power . . . To promote the Progress of Science and useful Arts, by securing for limited Times to Authors and Inventors the exclusive Right to their respective Writings and Discoveries." Under this grant of power, Congress has from time to time enacted various laws relating to patents. The first patent law was enacted in 1790. The patent laws most recently underwent a general revision in 1952, resulting in the present Patent Act which came into effect January 1, 1953. The Patent Act is codified in Title 35, United States Code. Additionally, on November 29, 1999, Congress enacted the American Inventors Protection Act of 1999 (AIPA), which further revised the patent laws.

The Patent Act specifies the subject matters that can be patented and the conditions for patentability. Federal law authorizes the United States Patent and Trademark Office to administer the law relating to the granting of patents and contains various other provisions relating to patents.

A. <u>What Can Be Patented</u>

Three types of patents are authorized under the Patent Act: utility patents, design patents, and plant patents.

1. Utility Patents

Utility patents are granted for new inventions that are useful. These inventions can be in several forms, including new devices, new compounds or chemicals, and new procedures for undertaking a useful task. Utility patents are by far the most frequently issued type of patent and the form of patent the public is most familiar with. Indeed, when persons refer to a patent, they typically mean a utility patent. This convention will be used here in that, where the text refers to a patent, the interest involved should be presumed to involve a utility patent unless otherwise indicated.

---

[2] The material on United States patent laws in this section is based on United States Patent and Trademark Office, "General Information Concerning Patents," http://www.uspto.gov/web/offices/pac/doc/general/index.html#faqs.

In the language of the Patent Act, any person who "invents or discovers any new and useful process, machine, manufacture, or composition of matter, or any new and useful improvement thereof, may obtain a patent," subject to the conditions and requirements of the law. The word "process" is defined by law as a process, act or method, and primarily includes industrial or technical processes. The term "machine" used in the statute includes artificially created assemblages that operate on some other subject matter, often transforming that additional matter. The term "manufacture" refers to articles that are made, and includes all manufactured articles. The term "composition of matter" relates to chemical compositions and may include mixtures of ingredients as well as new chemical compounds. These classes of subject matter taken together include practically everything that is made by man and the processes for making the products.

The Atomic Energy Act of 1954 restricts patentable subject matter in the atomic energy field, excluding the patenting of inventions useful solely in the utilization of special nuclear material or atomic energy in an atomic weapon.

The Patent Act specifies that patentable inventions must be "useful." The term "useful" in this connection refers to the condition that an invention has a useful purpose and operates to achieve its intended purpose. That is, a machine such as a perpetual motion device which will not operate to achieve its intended purpose would not be deemed useful, and therefore would not qualify for a utility patent.

Judicial interpretations of the Patent Act have defined the limits of the field of subject matter that can be covered by a utility patent. For example, it has been held that the laws of nature, physical phenomena, and abstract ideas are not patentable subject matter.

A patent cannot be obtained upon a mere idea or suggestion. A patent is only available for a new machine, manufacture, chemical or process with specific, implementable details and not for the idea or suggestion of the new invention. A complete description of the actual machine or other subject matter for which a patent is sought is required in a patent application and in the resulting patent if one issues.

2. Design Patents

The Patent Act provides for design patents granted to any person who has invented any new and nonobvious ornamental design for an article of manufacture. A design patent protects only the exterior ornamentation and appearance of an article, and not the article's structural or functional features. If the structural or functional features of an ornamented article are also new, the creator of the article can sometimes obtain a utility patent for these utilitarian aspects of the article in addition to gaining a design patent covering the ornamental features. A design patent has a term of 14 years from its grant, and no fees are necessary to maintain a design patent in force. A design patent is infringed by a party that makes, uses, sells, or imports, without the patent holder's permission, the type of article covered by the design patent augmented by ornamentation that is the same or similar to the design covered by the patent.

3. Plant Patents

The Patent Act also provides for the granting of a patent to anyone who has invented or discovered and asexually reproduced any distinct and new variety of plant, including cultivated sports, mutants, hybrids, and newly found seedlings, other than a tuber-propagated plant or a plant found in an uncultivated state.

Asexually propagated plants are those that are reproduced by means other than from seeds, such as by the rooting of cuttings, by layering, budding, or grafting. Tuber-propagated plants, for which a plant patent cannot be obtained, include plants that are reproduced through a short, thickened portion of an underground branch such as an Irish potato or a Jerusalem artichoke. The term of a plant patent is generally 20 years from the date on which the application for the patent was filed in the United States. A plant patent is infringed by a party that reproduces, uses, sells, or imports the type of plant covered by the plant patent without the patent holder's permission.

Although not covered by the Patent Act, a second sort of intellectual property interest in new plant varieties is recognized under federal law. The Plant Variety Protection Act (PVPA) is a statute administered by the Department of Agriculture that provides intellectual property protection for sexually reproduced plants. Breeders of novel varieties of plants may apply for and obtain a plant variety protection certificate that allows the holder "to exclude others from selling the variety, or offering it for sale, or reproducing it, or importing it, or exporting it, or using it in producing (as distinguished from developing) a hybrid or different variety therefrom," 7 U.S.C. § 2483(a)(1), for a term of 20 years from the date of issuance (or 25 years for vines and trees).

To secure a plant variety protection certificate, an applicant must show that the plant variety is:

(1) new, in the sense that, on the date of filing of the application for plant variety protection, propagating or harvested material of the variety has not been sold or otherwise disposed of to other persons . . . ;

(2) distinct, in the sense that the variety is clearly distinguishable from any other variety the existence of which is publicly known or a matter of common knowledge at the time of the filing of the application;

(3) uniform, in the sense that any variations are describable, predictable, and commercially acceptable; and

(4) stable, in the sense that the variety, when reproduced, will remain unchanged with regard to the essential and distinctive characteristics of the variety with a reasonable degree of reliability commensurate with that of varieties of the same category in which the same breeding method is employed.

7 U.S.C. § 2402(a). Protection certificates issued under the PVPA are distinct from plant patents, which are issued by the Patent and Trademark Office, in that the plants eligible for PVPA protection must be sexually reproducing, while plant patents protect asexually reproducing plants.

In addition to qualifying for protection under a plant patent or a plant variety protection certificate issued under the PVPA, a variety of plant that is new and useful may qualify for protection by a utility patent as an innovative composition of matter.

B. Conditions for Obtaining a Patent: Novelty and Non-Obviousness

The remainder of the discussion here will address utility patents (although design patents and plant patents are subject to parallel rules in many respects). In order for an invention to be patentable it must be "new" as this term is defined in the Patent Act. The Act provides that an invention cannot be patented if: "(a) the invention was known or used by others in this country, or patented or described in a printed publication in this or a foreign country, before the invention thereof by the applicant for patent," or "(b) the invention was patented or described in a printed publication in this or a foreign country or in public use or on sale in this country more than one year prior to the application for patent in the United States. . . ."

If the invention has been described in a printed publication anywhere in the world, or if it was known or used by others in this country before the date that the applicant made his/her invention, a patent cannot be obtained. If the invention has been described in a printed publication anywhere, or has been in public use or on sale in this country more than one year before the date on which an application for patent is filed in this country, a patent cannot be obtained. In this connection it is immaterial when the invention was made, or whether the printed publication or public use was by the inventor himself/herself or by someone else. If the inventor describes the invention in a printed publication or uses the invention publicly, or places it on sale, he/she must apply for a patent before one year has gone by, otherwise any right to a patent will be lost. The inventor must file before the date of public use or disclosure, however, in order to preserve patent rights in many foreign countries.

Even if the subject matter sought to be patented is not exactly shown by the prior art, and involves one or more differences from the most nearly similar thing already known, a patent may still be refused if the differences would be obvious. The subject matter sought to be patented must be sufficiently different from what has been used or described before that it may be said to be nonobvious to a person having ordinary skill in the area of technology related to the invention. For example, the substitution in a device design of one color for another, or a change in size of an object, are frequently changes that are obvious and not patentable.

C. The Role of the Patent Office

Congress established the United States Patent and Trademark Office (USPTO or Patent Office) to issue patents on behalf of the government. The Patent Office as a distinct bureau dates from the year 1802 when a separate official in the Department of State who became known as the "Superintendent of Patents" was placed in charge of patents. The revision of the patent laws enacted in 1836 reorganized the Patent Office and designated the official in charge as Commissioner of Patents. The Patent Office remained in the Department of State until 1849 when it was transferred to the Department of Interior. In 1925 it was transferred to the Department of Commerce where it is today. The name of the Patent Office was changed to the Patent and Trademark Office in 1975 and changed to the United States Patent and Trademark Office in 2000.

The USPTO administers the patent laws as they relate to the granting of patents for inventions, and performs other duties relating to patents. Patent examiners within the USPTO review applications for patents to determine if the applicants are entitled to patents under the law and the USPTO grants the patents when the applicants are so entitled. The USPTO publishes issued patents and most patent applications filed on or after November 29, 2000, at 18 months from the earliest filing date of the applications. The USPTO also issues various publications concerning patents, records assignments of patents, maintains a search room for the use of the public to examine issued patents and records, and supplies copies of records and other papers concerning patents. The USPTO also performs similar functions with respect to the registration of trademarks. The USPTO has no jurisdiction over questions concerning the infringement and enforcement of patents.

The work of examining applications for patents is divided among a number of examining technology centers (TC), each TC having jurisdiction over certain assigned fields of technology. Each TC is headed by group directors and staffed by examiners and support staff. The examiners review applications for patents and determine whether patents can be granted. An appeal can be taken to the Board of Patent Appeals and Interferences from their decisions refusing to grant a patent, and a review by the Director of the USPTO may be had on other matters by petition. The examiners also identify applications that claim the same invention and may initiate proceedings, known as interferences, to determine who was the first inventor.

D. <u>Who May Apply For a Patent</u>

Under United States patent law, only the inventor of a new item or process may apply for a patent, with certain exceptions. If a person who is not the inventor should apply for a patent, the patent, if it were obtained, would be invalid. The person applying for a patent who intentionally misstated that he was the inventor would also be subject to criminal penalties. If the inventor is dead, the application may be made by legal representatives, that is, the administrator or executor of the estate. If the inventor is insane, the application for patent may be made by a guardian. If an inventor refuses to apply for a patent or cannot be found, a joint inventor or, if there is no joint inventor available, a person having a proprietary interest in the invention may apply on behalf of the non-signing inventor.

If two or more persons make an invention jointly, they apply for a patent as joint inventors. A person who makes only a financial contribution is not a joint inventor and cannot be joined in the application as an inventor. It is generally possible to correct an innocent mistake in erroneously omitting an inventor or in erroneously naming a person as an inventor.

Officers and employees of the United States Patent and Trademark Office
are prohibited by law from applying for a patent or acquiring, directly or indirectly, except by inheritance or bequest, any patent or any right or interest in
any patent.

E.   Contents of a Patent Application

1.   Regular Patent Application

An application for a patent is made to the Director of the USPTO and must
include:

> (1)   A written specification of the applicant's invention (a written descrip-
> tion of the invention involved and further information on its use) and
> proposed claims delineating the legally operative scope of the patent
> rights being sought (a textual description of the critical elements
> making up the invention for which a patent is claimed);

> (2)   One or more drawings illustrating the elements of the claimed inven-
> tion where these are required to understand the invention; and

> (3)   Filing fees (which are reduced if the party who will own the patent
> upon issuance is a "small entity" such as an independent inventor, a
> small business concern, or a non-profit organization).

2.   Provisional Patent Application

Since June 8, 1995, the USPTO has offered inventors the option of filing a
provisional application for a patent. This type of simplified application is
designed to provide a lower cost first patent filing in the United States and to
give U.S. applicants parity with foreign applicants. Patent claims are not
required in a provisional application, but the invention for which a patent will
be sought must be described in some clear way. A provisional application
establishes a tentative filing date for the inventor's ultimate regular patent
application. If a regular patent application covering the same invention is
filed within 12 months of the filing of a provisional patent application, the filing date for the provisional application becomes the filing date for the regular
application. However, if a regular application is not filed within 12 months,
the provisional filing has no effect. Provisional applications may not be filed
for new ornamental designs of the sort covered by design patents nor for new
varieties of asexually reproduced plants of the sort covered by plant patents.

F.   Patent Attorneys and Agents

The preparation of a proper patent application and the successful completion of proceedings in the USPTO to obtain a patent are undertakings requiring substantial knowledge of patent law and the rules and procedures of the
USPTO. Inventors may prepare and file their own applications in the USPTO
and conduct related proceedings themselves, but unless they are familiar with
patent laws and USPTO procedures in detail, they may get into considerable
difficulty. While a patent may be obtained in many cases by persons not
skilled in this work, there would be no assurance that the patent obtained

would have commercial value and adequately protect the particular invention involved. Most inventors employ the services of registered patent attorneys or patent agents to aid the inventors in drafting patent applications, in properly filing those applications and related materials, and in responding to rulings regarding the applications by USPTO officials.

Federal patent laws give the USPTO the power to make rules and regulations governing the conduct and registration of patent attorneys and agents. Persons who are not registered by the USPTO for this type of practice are not permitted by law to represent inventors before the USPTO. The USPTO maintains a list or "register" of authorized patent attorneys and agents. To be admitted to this register, a person must comply with the regulations prescribed by the Office, which require a showing that the person is of good moral character and of good repute and that she has the legal and scientific or technical qualifications necessary to render applicants for patents a valuable service. In addition, persons seeking to become patent attorneys or agents must pass a patent bar examination administered by the USPTO, which tests the individual's knowledge of patent laws and USPTO procedures.

The USPTO registers both attorneys at law who have already passed a state bar examination and persons who are not attorneys at law but who have gained specialized knowledge in the narrow area of patent law and USPTO procedure. The former persons are referred to as "patent attorneys" and the latter are referred to as "patent agents." Both patent attorneys and patent agents are equally entitled to prepare patent applications and represent clients before the USPTO. Patent agents, however, cannot conduct patent litigation in the courts or render other legal services since to do so would constitute the unauthorized practice of law. For example, a patent agent can not draw up a contract relating to a patent, such as an assignment or a license agreement, if the state in which he works considers drafting contracts for other individuals to constitute practicing law.

G. **Publication of Patent Applications**

Publication of patent applications is required by the American Inventors Protection Act of 1999 for most plant and utility patent applications filed on or after November 29, 2000. On filing of a plant or utility patent application, an applicant may request that the application not be published, but only if the invention has not been and will not be the subject of an application filed in a foreign country that requires publication 18 months after filing. Publication occurs after the expiration of an 18-month period following the earliest effective filing date or priority date claimed by an application. Following publication, the application for patent is no longer held in confidence by the USPTO and any member of the public may request access to the entire file history of the application. For the rare patent application which is not published under these provisions, the USPTO will only disclose the patent application and its related file history upon the issuance and publication of a patent based on the application.

As a result of publication of a patent application, the applicant may assert provisional rights. These rights provide a patentee with the opportunity to obtain a reasonable royalty from a third party that infringes a published application claim provided actual notice is given to the third party by the applicant and a patent issues from the application with a substantially identical claim. Thus, damages for pre-patent grant infringement by another are now available.

H.   Examination of Patent Applications

Applications, other than provisional applications, are generally reviewed or "examined" by patent examiners within the USPTO. The examination of an application consists of a study of the application for compliance with legal form requirements and a search through U.S. patents, publications of patent applications, foreign patent documents, and available literature, to see if the claimed invention is new, useful and nonobvious. If a patent examiner's decision on patentability is favorable, a patent is granted.

On the average, patents are granted based on about two out of every three applications for patents that are filed. However, in the course of examination, a patent applicant may have voluntarily limited his or her claims to avoid a disfavorable decision by a patent examiner. Hence, while some form of patent issues based on most patent applications, some of the resulting patents are relatively narrow in scope and not what the applicant sought in his or her initial filing.

I.   Nature of Patent Rights

The owner of an issued patent — that is, the patent applicant or an assignee of the applicant's interest in the patent — has the right to exclude others from making, using, offering for sale, or selling the patented invention throughout the United States or importing the invention into the United States and its territories and possessions. Provided that relevant maintenance fees are paid as described below, these patent rights will generally extend for 20 years from the date on which the application for the patent was filed in the United States.

A patent right is essentially negative — that is, it allows the patent holder to bar others from certain actions — making, using, selling, or importing the patented invention — but does not give the patent holder the positive right to undertake these same activities. This is because the making, using, selling, or importing of the invention may be limited by government regulations or restricted by other parties' patent rights concerning components of the invention.

For example, an inventor of a new automobile who has obtained a patent thereon would not be entitled to use the patented automobile in violation of the laws of a state requiring a license, nor could the patentee sell an automobile adhering to the new design if the automobile failed to meet minimum safety standards imposed by law. Similarly, a party may not, by virtue of having a patent on an item, violate federal antitrust laws by selling the patented item through illegal means such as prohibited resale price agreements or entry into combinations in restraint of trade.

Even if the making, sale, use, or importation of a patented item by the patentee would otherwise be lawful, these actions may be restricted because they would infringe the rights of another patent holder having an interest in the same item. For example, if person A gains a patent on a particular design for a sewing machine and person B designs and patents an improvement adding computer controls to the same type of sewing machine, person B can only make, use, sell, or import sewing machines based on the new design upon obtaining the permission of person A so long as the new design still incorporates the patent features of A's original design. However, B will be able to prevent all other parties (including A) from making, using, selling, or importing sewing machines based on the new, improved design covered by B's patent.

J. Maintenance Fees

While the duration of rights stemming from a patent will generally be 20 years from the date on which the application for the patent was filed in the United States, in order for these rights to remain in force for this entire term, the patent holder must periodically pay maintenance fees. A maintenance fee is due 3 1/2, 7 1/2 and 11 1/2 years after the original grant for all patents issuing from applications filed on and after December 12, 1980.

K. Patent Expiration

After a patent has expired anyone may make, use, offer for sale, sell, or import the formerly patented invention without permission of the patentee, provided that matter covered by other unexpired patents is not used. Free public access to a formerly patented invention is part of the public policy bargain under which a patent applicant discloses a patented invention (in a published patent application or issued patent) and ultimately dedicates the invention to the public in exchange for a temporary period of control over the invention during the life of a patent. Any attempt of a patent holder to extend the force or impact of a patent beyond the 20-year term of the patent will generally be seen as patent abuse or a violation of antitrust laws.

L. Relief for Patent Infringement

Patent infringement consists of the unauthorized making, using, offering for sale, or selling any patented invention within the United States or United States Territories, or importing into the United States of any patented invention during the term of the patent. The USPTO has no jurisdiction over questions relating to infringement of patents. In examining applications for patent, no determination is made as to whether the invention sought to be patented infringes any prior patent. An improvement invention may be patentable, but it might also infringe a prior unexpired patent for the invention improved upon.

If a patent is infringed, the patentee may sue for relief in the appropriate federal court — usually the federal district court where the infringement occurred or where the defendant resides. The patentee can typically obtain an injunction to prevent the continuation of the infringement and an award of damages stemming from infringement which has already transpired.

In such an infringement suit, the defendant may contest the validity of the patent in question. While patents are presumed valid once issued and the burden is on a defendant in an infringement suit to establish patent invalidity, patents are invalidated in litigation with substantial frequency. This sometimes results because a defendant threatened with extensive infringement liability uncovers evidence bearing on patentability that was not considered by the USPTO. For example, a defendant might find new evidence of prior knowledge in the field which indicates that the patented invention at issue was not new when created by the patent applicant or that the invention was merely an unpatentable, obvious extension of prior designs.

In addition to challenging the patent at issue, a defendant in a patent infringement action may claim that, even if the patent is valid, the defendant's conduct does not infringe the patent. The patent holder bears the burden of establishing patent infringement. This can be established by proof that the item or process made, used, sold, or imported by the defendant included all of the elements of the patented invention or, if one or more elements are missing, that the defendant's item or process included an equivalent of the missing element or elements. Infringement is determined primarily by the language of the claims of the patent and, if the defendant's item or process does not involve the elements of the patented invention as defined in the patent claims (or equivalents of these elements) there is no patent infringement.

Suits for infringement of patents follow the rules of procedure of the federal courts. The decision of a federal district court regarding patent infringement can be appealed to the Court of Appeals for the Federal Circuit. This court is highly experienced and knowledgeable concerning patent matters, hearing patent appeals from across the country. The rulings of the Court of Appeals for the Federal Circuit often constitute the final word on important patent issues, subject only to being overruled occasionally based on a rare successful appeal of a patent case to the Supreme Court. In addition to cases involving patent infringement which are heard by federal courts, suits turning on contracts for patent assignments and licenses can be decided in state courts, as can cases which are based primarily on state law claims, but which involve patent issues in counterclaims.

If the United States Government infringes a patent, a patentee has a remedy for damages in the United States Court of Federal Claims, but the patentee cannot stop the Government from using the patented invention at issue. The Government may use any patented invention without permission of the patentee, but the patentee is entitled to obtain compensation for the use by or for the Government.

M. Patent Marking and Notices of "Patent Pending"

A patentee who makes or sells patented articles or a person who does so for or under the authorization of the patentee will typically mark the articles with the word "Patent" followed by the number of the patent. If the patent holder does not mark articles in this way, the patentee may not recover damages from an infringer unless the infringer had actual notice of the applicable patent and continued to infringe after gaining such notice. There is no equivalent rule regarding the desirability of giving notice of an applicable patent when a patented process is undertaken.

The marking of an article as patented when it is not in fact patented is against the law and subjects the offender to a substantial penalty.

Some persons mark articles sold with the terms "Patent Applied For" or "Patent Pending." These phrases have no formal legal effect, but do, if used honestly, give purchasers and users of the articles information that an application for a patent has been filed in the USPTO and that patent rights concerning the article may arise in the future. The protection afforded by a patent does not start until the actual grant of the patent (or, in the case of a published patent application, upon the date of publication). False use of these phrases or their equivalents may constitute fraud or an unfair marketing practice providing a basis for recoveries by parties who are injured by the false message conveyed.

N. **Patent Assignments and Licenses**

1. **Forms of Assignments**

A patent is personal property and may be sold to others or mortgaged, bequeathed by a will, and passed to the heirs of a deceased patentee. The Patent Act provides for the transfer or sale of a patent, or of an application for patent, by an instrument in writing. Such an instrument is referred to as an assignment and may transfer the entire interest in the patent. The assignee, when the patent is assigned to him or her, becomes the owner of the patent and has the same rights that the original patentee had.

The Patent Act also provides for the assignment of a part interest, that is, a half interest, a fourth interest, etc., in a patent. A mortgage of a patent passes ownership of the patent to the mortgagee or lender until the mortgage has been satisfied. This will occur when the mortgagor — the borrower — pays the full amount of the loan secured by the mortgage. A conditional assignment also passes ownership of a patent and is regarded as absolute until canceled by the parties or by the decree of a competent court.

An assignment, grant, or conveyance of any patent or application for patent should be acknowledged before a notary public or officer authorized to administer oaths or perform notarial acts. The certificate of such acknowledgment constitutes prima facie evidence of the execution of the assignment, grant, or conveyance.

Sometimes a patent assignment is made before a patent has even issued. For example, it is common for employees of large companies who develop inventions as part of their jobs to be obligated by the terms of their employment to assign their rights in patent applications to their employers. An assignment agreement relating to an application should identify the application by its application number and date of filing, the name of the inventor, and the title of the invention as stated in the application. If an application for a patent has been assigned and the assignment is recorded on or before the date the issue fee for the patent is paid, the patent will be issued to the assignee as owner. If the assignment is of a part interest only, the patent will be issued to the inventor and assignee as joint owners.

2. Recording of Assignments

The USPTO records assignments, grants, and similar instruments in an official registry. The recording of these instruments serves as constructive (that is, legally presumed) notice to other parties of the assignment or other transfer. If an assignment, grant, or conveyance of a patent or an interest in a patent (or an application for patent) is not recorded in the Office within three months from its date and is still unrecorded when a second attempt to transfer the same interest is made, the first transfer is void against a subsequent purchaser of the same interest who takes the interest in exchange for valuable consideration and without notice of the first transfer. This means that if party A holds a patent and transfers it via an assignment to another party B, but B does not record the assignment, A's second assignment of the same patent to C in exchange for valuable consideration will be effective and C will hold the patent unless C had actual notice of the prior assignment to B. This type of impact of the recording statute is aimed at encouraging the recording of patent transfers and at protecting the interests of innocent purchasers such as C who have dealt with parties who appear, from the official records of issued patents and patent assignments, to be the owners of particular patents.

3. Patent Licenses

A patent license does not entail a transfer of patent ownership, but rather involves a grant of rights from a patent holder to another. Patent licenses are either exclusive or nonexclusive. An exclusive license grants the licensee the right to make, use, sell, or import a patented invention (or some portion of these rights) without fear of an infringement action by the patent holder and with the further guarantee that the patent holder will not grant equivalent rights to any other party. A nonexclusive license grants the licensee the right to undertake what would otherwise be infringing actions, but does not provide the licensee with any assurance that the patent holder will not grant equivalent rights to additional parties. In essence, an exclusive license conveys a unique opportunity to the licensee, while a nonexclusive license merely signifies a patent holder's permission for the licensee to proceed with a specified activity concerning a patented invention free from the risk of an infringement suit.

O. International Considerations

1. Foreign Patents and Patent Rights

Since the rights granted by a United States patent extend only throughout the territory of the United States and have no effect in a foreign country, an inventor who wishes patent protection in other countries must apply for a patent in each of the other countries or in regional patent offices (such as the European Patent Office) which can grant patents covering entire regions encompassing several countries.

The laws of many countries differ in various respects from the patent laws of the United States. In most foreign countries, for example, publication of a description of an invention before the date of a patent application will bar the inventor from obtaining a patent. Most foreign countries require that a patented invention must be manufactured in that country after a certain period, usually three years. If there is no manufacturing within this period, the patent involved will be void in some countries, although in most countries the patent will be subject to the grant of compulsory licenses to any persons who apply for licenses.

2. The Paris Convention

Several international treaties specify aspects of patent systems which the signatory countries have agreed to implement in order to create greater uniformity in the patent laws of various countries. One key treaty of this sort, adhered to by 168 countries including the United States, is the Paris Convention for the Protection of Industrial Property. It provides that each country guarantees to the citizens of the other countries the same rights in patent and trademark matters that it gives to its own citizens. This means that, for example, a German inventor applying for a United States patent will have the same opportunity to gain a patent and have the same rights if a patent is issued as would a United States citizen. Similarly, a United States inventor seeking a German patent must be afforded the same opportunities and rights as a German citizen.

The Paris Convention also establishes important rules regarding the right of priority in the case of utility patents and industrial designs (design patents). This right means that, once an applicant files a regular patent application on an invention or design in one of the signatory countries governed by the treaty, the applicant may, within a certain period of time, apply for utility or design patent protection in all the other member countries. The later applications will then be regarded as if they had been filed on the same day as the first application. This right is referred to as one involving "priority" because the applicant's second and subsequent applications, having an effective filing date of the first application, will have priority over patent applications of other parties for the same invention that may have been filed during the gap in time between the first and subsequent applications. Moreover, the later applications, having the benefit of the filing date of the first application, will not be invalidated by any acts accomplished in the intervals between the first and subsequent applications, such as, for example, publication or exploitation of an invention or the sale of copies of items bearing an industrial design. The period in which subsequent applications may be filed in the other countries and still gain the filing date of a first application is 12 months in the case of applications for a utility patent and six months in the case of applications for industrial design or design patent protection.

3. The Patent Cooperation Treaty (PCT)

The Patent Cooperation Treaty (PCT) was created in 1970 to streamline the process of securing patents in multiple countries. An application submitted in accordance with the PCT (sometimes called a "PCT application") reduces the cost and duplication of effort that would otherwise be involved in filing individual patent applications in multiple countries. The treaty, which came into force in 1978, is open to any country that has joined the Paris Convention and is administered by the United Nation's World Intellectual Property Organization (WIPO). Over one hundred countries, including the United States, adhere to the PCT.

Under the PCT, an inventor who wishes to obtain patents in multiple countries has twelve months to file an initial application in one of the countries adhering to the PCT. Typically inventors choose to file in the inventor's home country. The filing date for this initial application establishes the priority date for subsequent filings and designates the other countries adhering to the PCT in which protection will be sought. The patent office in the country of the initial filing conducts a prior art search and publishes the application after eighteen months. The applicant then has thirty months from the priority date to convert the PCT application into parallel foreign patent applications or risk forfeiting patent applications in those countries.

4. Foreign Filing License

Under United States law it is necessary, in the case of inventions made in the United States, to obtain a license from the Director of the USPTO before applying for a patent in a foreign country. Such a license is required if the foreign application is to be filed before an application is filed in the United States or before the expiration of six months from the filing of an application in the United States. The filing of an application for a patent constitutes the request for a foreign filing license and the granting or denial of such request is indicated in the filing receipt mailed to each applicant. After six months from the filing of a United States patent application, a license is not required unless the invention involved has been ordered to be kept secret. If the invention has been ordered to be kept secret, consent to a foreign patent filing must be obtained from the Director of the USPTO during the period when the order of secrecy is in effect.

5. Foreign Applicants for United States Patents

Under the patent laws of the United States, any inventor, regardless of citizenship, may apply for a patent on the same basis as a United States citizen. There are, however, a number of particular points of special interest to applicants located in foreign countries.

The application for a patent in the United States must be made by an inventor and the inventor must sign an oath or declaration confirming that he or she is the inventor of the claimed invention. This differs from the law in many countries where the signature of the inventor and an oath of inventorship are not necessary. If an inventor is dead, an application for a United States patent may be made by his/her executor or administrator, or equivalent, and in the case of mental disability it may be made by his/her legal representative (guardian).

A United States utility patent can not be obtained if an invention was patented abroad before applying in the United States by the inventor or his or her legal representatives if the foreign application was filed more than 12 months before filing in the United States.

An application for a patent filed in the United States by any person who has previously filed an application for a patent for the same invention in a foreign country (provided the country affords similar privileges to citizens of the United States) shall have the same force and effect for the purpose of overcoming intervening acts of others as if filed in the United States on the date on which the application for a patent for the same invention was first filed in the foreign country. This is the case, provided the application for a United States utility patent is filed within 12 months (six months in the case of a design patent) from the earliest date on which any corresponding foreign application was filed.

III. COPYRIGHT LAWS[3]

A. Copyrightable Works

Copyright is a form of protection provided by the laws of the United States to the authors of "original works of authorship," including literary, dramatic, musical, artistic, and certain other intellectual works. This protection is available to both published and unpublished works. In general, a copyright permits the holder to control how a protected work is copied, reused and modified as the basis for further works, and distributed or otherwise communicated to the public.

Copyright protections arise automatically at the moment a work is created and fixed in a tangible form that is perceptible either directly or with the aid of a machine or device. Thus, for example, a person keeping a private diary gains copyright protection in this work as entries are made. A copyright notice is an identifier placed on copies of the work to inform the world of copyright ownership. This notice generally consists of the symbol "©" or word "copyright (or copr.)," the name of the copyright owner, and the year of first publication, e.g., "©2003 John Doe." While use of a copyright notice was once required as a condition of copyright protection, it is now optional. However, even though optional, the use of a copyright notice on a work is often desirable as a means to undercut assertions by persons reading and reproducing the work (or engaging in other infringing acts) that their conduct constituted unknowing or "innocent" infringement not warranting an award of statutory damages.

Copyrights do not protect ideas, concepts, systems, or methods of doing something. A person may express ideas in writing or drawings and claim copyright in the resulting description of the ideas, but copyright will not protect the ideas themselves as revealed in a written or artistic work.

In contrast to works protected by copyrights, many works are in the "public domain." A work of authorship is in the "public domain" if it was once copyrighted but is no longer under copyright protection or if it failed to ever meet the

---

[3]The material on United States copyright laws in this section is based on United States Copyright Office, Copyright Basics, http://www.copyright.gov/circs/circ1.html, and United States Copyright Office, Frequently Asked Questions About Copyright, http://www.copyright.gov/help/faq/.

requirements for copyright protection. Works in the public domain may be used freely without the permission of the former copyright owner or any other party.

B. Copyright Registration

Registration of a copyright with the United States Copyright Office (an agency within the Library of Congress) is not needed to establish copyright protections. However, registration is often desirable for several reasons. The advantages of registration include the following:

- Registration establishes a public record of a copyright interest.

- Before an infringement suit may be filed in court, registration is necessary for works of United States origin.

- If made before or within 5 years of publication, registration will establish prima facie evidence in court of the validity of a copyright and of the facts stated in the certificate of registration received from the Copyright Office.

- If registration is made prior to an infringement of a work, statutory damages and attorney's fees will be available to the copyright owner in court actions. For published works, if the copyright owner registers within three months of publication, statutory damages and attorney's fees are available for any infringement that occurs after publication and before registration.

- Registration allows the owner of the copyright to record the registration with the United States Customs Service for protection against the importation of infringing copies.

To register a copyrighted work, a copyright holder must submit to the Copyright Office a completed application form, a nonrefundable filing fee of $30, and a nonreturnable copy or copies of the work to be registered. A person may register an initial work and then also register an altered version of the work provided that the changes are substantial and creative, something more than just editorial changes or minor alterations. For instance, simply making spelling corrections throughout a work does not warrant a new registration, but adding an additional chapter would.

C. Initial Copyright Ownership

Where a work is created by an independent author, the associated copyright in the work immediately becomes the property of the author. Only the author or those deriving their rights through the author can rightfully claim the copyright.

Different rules regarding initial copyright ownership apply to works produced by an author for another party — referred to as "works made for hire" in the federal copyright statute. One common type of work made for hire is a work created by an employee while working for a large corporation or other employer. In the case of such a work made for hire, the employer and not the employee is considered to be the author of the work and is recognized as the initial copyright holder.

Federal copyright laws define a "work made for hire" as:

"(1) a work prepared by an employee within the scope of his or her employment; or

(2) a work specially ordered or commissioned for use as a contribution to a collective work, as a part of a motion picture or other audiovisual work, as a translation, as a supplementary work, as a compilation, as an instructional text, as a test, as answer material for a test, or as an atlas, if the parties expressly agree in a written instrument signed by them that the work shall be considered a work made for hire. . . ."

In some instances, multiple authors will contribute to the creation of a single work — referred to as a "joint work." The authors of a joint work are co-owners of the copyright in the work, unless there is an agreement to the contrary. Co-owners of a copyright in a work will each be able to authorize copies of the work to be made and to authorize other normally infringing activities unless there is a contrary agreement among the co-owners.

The copyright covering each separate contribution to a periodical or other collective work — such as the copyright covering an individual article included in a magazine where the authors are not employees of the magazine — is distinct from the copyright in the collective work as a whole and vests initially with the author of the contribution.

D. **Rights of Copyright Holders**

The federal Copyright Act generally gives the owner of a copyright the exclusive right to do and to authorize others to do the following:

- *To reproduce* the work in copies or phonorecords;

- To prepare *derivative works* based upon the work;

- *To distribute copies or phonorecords* of the work to the public by sale or other transfer of ownership, or by rental, lease, or lending;

- To *perform the work publicly*, in the case of literary, musical, dramatic, and choreographic works, pantomimes, and motion pictures and other audiovisual works;

- *To display the copyrighted work publicly*, in the case of literary, musical, dramatic, and choreographic works, pantomimes, and pictorial, graphic, or sculptural works, including the individual images of a motion picture or other audiovisual work; and

- In the case of sound recordings, *to perform the work publicly* by means of a *digital audio transmission*.

Certain authors of works of visual art also have rights of attribution and rights to control the integrity of these sorts of works.

In addition to their control over copying of a protected work, copyright holders' exclusive right to authorize the making of derivative works from a protected original work gives these parties considerable control over how elements of a protected work are reused in subsequent works. A derivative work is one that is based or "derived from" a prior work protected by a copyright and that incorporates unchanged or modified versions of protected expression from the original work. Examples of derivative works include translations, musical arrangements, dramatizations, fictionalizations, art reproductions, and condensations.

The opportunity to create derivative works can be a highly valuable offshoot of an initial copyright. For example, the holder of the copyright in a movie such as "Star Wars" can control and license for considerable profit the opportunities to make action figures and other derivative works based on characters from the movie.

Any work in which the editorial revisions, annotations, elaborations, or other modifications represent, as a whole, an original work of authorship may qualify for a copyright as a new derivative work. This copyright interest concerning the derivative work is recognized in addition to the copyright covering the original work on which the derivative work was based. Where these separate copyright interests are held by different parties, all of these parties will need to approve the reproduction of the derivative work, but only the holder of the copyright on the original work needs to approve copying of that work.

Because copyright protections extend only to creative expression and not to the ideas conveyed by the expression, persons are free to reuse the ideas or information that are described in a publicly available copyrighted work so long as the persons do not reuse the particular words or other means of expression used to describe the ideas or information in the copyrighted work. Similarly, copyright protections do not extend to a procedure, process, system, method of operation, concept, principle, or discovery described or otherwise communicated in a copyrighted work.

For example, if an author writes a book explaining a new system for food processing, the copyright in the book, which comes into effect at the moment the work is fixed in a tangible form, will prevent others from publishing the text and illustrations describing the author's ideas for machinery, processes, and merchandising methods. But this copyright will not give the author any rights to prevent others from adopting the ideas for commercial purposes or from developing or using the machinery, processes, or methods described in the book.

A copyright holder generally does not have control over a particular copy of a copyrighted work (such as a single copy of a copyrighted book) once the copy has been sold in a manner authorized by the copyright holder. A buyer's legitimately obtained ownership of a single copy of a work generally gives the owner the right to make full private use of that copy (other than to make an additional copy or other reproduction of the work) and to sell the single copy to another owner. However, mere ownership of a book, manuscript, painting, or any other copy or phonorecord does not give the possessor an interest in the copyright concerning the contents. The law provides that transfer of ownership of any material object that embodies a protected work does not of itself convey any rights in the copyright.

E. Fair Use Limitations on Copyright Enforcement

The rights of copyright holders are limited by several important doctrines. For example, actions that would otherwise constitute copyright infringement are not a basis for liability where they involve "fair use" of copyrighted materials. The nature of a fair use of copyrighted materials is not defined in the Copyright Act. However, in general, uses that are commercially insignificant or that support socially valuable activities (such as political criticism or news reporting) are considered fair use and not infringing. In contrast, uses of materials in ways that are likely to have a negative impact upon the potential market for or value of a copyrighted work are not likely to be viewed as fair uses.

The Copyright Act indicates that the following factors should be considered in determining if a particular use of a copyrighted work is a fair use free from infringement liability:

1. the purpose and character of the use, including whether such use is of commercial nature or is for nonprofit educational purposes;

2. the nature of the copyrighted work;

3. the amount and substantiality of the portion used in relation to the copyrighted work as a whole; and

4. the effect of the use upon the potential market for or value of the copyrighted work.

There is no specific number of words, lines, or notes from a copyrighted work that may safely be reused without permission. Acknowledging the source of copyrighted material when the material is reused does not substitute for obtaining permission and does not automatically constitute fair use.

Examples of activities that courts have regarded as fair use include: quotation of excerpts in a review or criticism for purposes of illustration or comment; quotation of short passages in a scholarly or technical work, for illustration or clarification of the author's observations; use in a parody of some of the content of the work parodied; summary of an address or article, with brief quotations, in a news report; reproduction by a library of a portion of a work to replace part of a damaged copy; reproduction by a teacher or student of a small part of a work to illustrate a lesson; reproduction of a work in legislative or judicial proceedings or reports; incidental and fortuitous reproduction, in a newsreel or broadcast, of a work located in the scene of an event being reported.

F. Compulsory Licenses as Limitations on Copyright Enforcement

Holders of copyrights in certain types of works are also limited in their enforcement rights by "compulsory license" provisions of federal copyright laws. These provisions compel copyright holders to permit the use of certain works in exchange for a defined compensation. However, compulsory licenses apply only to specialized types of copyrightable works.

For example, a compulsory license is available to anyone wishing to record a musical work as soon as phonorecords of a nondramatic musical work have been distributed to the public in the United States under the authority of the copyright owner. This means that, once the holder of a copyright in a musical work authorizes one artist to initially record the work and the resulting recordings are distributed to the pubic, additional artists can rerecord their versions of the work without the permission of the holder of the copyright on the underlying musical work. However, to make these additional recordings, the second and subsequent recording artists must pay the copyright holder a licensing fee. Such provisions establish a "compulsory license" because the licensor has no choice but to allow the use covered by the compulsory license in exchange for the required royalty payment.

Thus, provided that a prior recording of the work by a singer such as Bing Crosby had been authorized and distributed to the public, a singer such as Elvis Presley would be entitled to record a song such as "White Christmas" regardless of whether Irving Berlin, the composer, agreed so long as the second recording artist paid the statutorily-defined royalty for use of the song. Such compulsory license provisions are included in United States copyright laws to encourage rerecording of musical works without allowing the original creators of the works to narrowly constrain how the works may be reused.

G.   Remedies for Copyright Infringement

As a general matter, copyright infringement occurs when a copyrighted work is reproduced, distributed, performed, publicly displayed, or made into a derivative work without the permission of the copyright owner. A copyright holder, through a legal action brought in a federal court, can obtain several types of remedies for past and future copyright infringement.

A federal judge can grant such an injunction as the judge deems reasonable to prevent or restrain infringement of a copyright. A judge can also order the destruction or other reasonable disposition of all copies or phonorecords found to have been made or used in violation of a copyright owner's exclusive rights, and of all plates, molds, matrices, masters, tapes, film negatives, or other items by means of which such copies or phonorecords may be reproduced.

For infringement already completed at the time of a suit, a copyright holder can recover either (1) the copyright owner's actual damages and any additional profits of the infringer or (2) statutory damages.

If a copyright holder elects to seek actual damages, she is entitled to recover the monetary damages suffered as a result of the infringement and any profits of the infringer that are attributable to the infringement and that are not taken into account in computing the actual damages. In establishing the infringer's profits, the copyright owner is required to present proof only of the infringer's gross revenues, and the infringer is required to prove his deductible expenses and the elements of profit attributable to factors other than the copyrighted work.

A copyright holder who establishes copyright infringement can obtain, instead of actual damages and profits, an award of statutory damages.

Statutory damages for all non-willful infringements involved in a lawsuit with respect to any one work shall generally be not less than $750 or more than $30,000 as the judge in the case considers just. For willful infringement — that is, conduct known to infringe an outstanding copyright — statutory damages are authorized up to a limit of $150,000. However, in a case where the infringer sustains the burden of proving, and the judge involved in the case finds, that the infringer was not aware and had no reason to believe that his or her acts constituted an infringement of a copyright, the judge in her discretion may reduce the award of statutory damages to a sum of not less than $200.

H.   Duration of Copyright Protections

1.   Works Originally Created on or after January 1, 1978

A work that is created (fixed in tangible form for the first time) on or after January 1, 1978, is automatically protected from the moment of its creation and is ordinarily given a term of copyright protection enduring for the author's life plus an additional 70 years after the author's death. In the case of "a joint work prepared by two or more authors who did not work for hire," the term lasts for 70 years after the last surviving author's death. For works made for hire, and for anonymous and pseudonymous works (unless the author's identity is revealed in Copyright Office records), the duration of copyright protections will be 95 years from publication or 120 years from creation, whichever period is shorter.

2.   Works Originally Created before January 1, 1978, But Not Published or Registered by That Date

The duration of copyright in these works will generally be computed in the same way as for works created on or after January 1, 1978 — that is, the life-plus-70 or 95/120-year terms will apply to them as well. The law provides that in no case will the term of copyright for works in this category expire before December 31, 2002, and for works published on or before December 31, 2002, the term of copyright will not expire before December 31, 2047.

3.   Works Originally Created and Published or Registered before January 1, 1978

Under the law in effect before 1978, copyright was secured either on the date a work was published with a copyright notice or on the date of registration if the work was registered in unpublished form. In either case, the copyright endured for a first term of 28 years from the date it was secured. During the last (28th) year of the first term, the copyright was eligible for renewal. The Copyright Act of 1976 extended the renewal term from 28 to 47 years for copyrights that were subsisting on January 1, 1978, making these works eligible for a total term of protection of 75 years.

Public Law 105-298, enacted on October 27, 1998, further extended the renewal term of copyrights still subsisting on that date by an additional 20 years, providing for a renewal term of 67 years and a total term of protection of 95 years.

Public Law 102-307, enacted on June 26, 1992, amended the 1976 Copyright Act to provide for automatic renewal of the term of copyrights secured between January 1, 1964, and December 31, 1977. Although the renewal term is automatically provided, the Copyright Office does not issue a renewal certificate for these works unless a renewal application and fee are received and registered in the Copyright Office.

Public Law 102-307 makes renewal registration optional. Thus, filing for renewal registration is no longer required in order to extend the original 28-year copyright term to the full 95 years. However, some benefits accrue from making a renewal registration during the 28th year of the original term.

I. Transfers of Copyright Interests

Transfers of copyright interests are normally made by contract. A contract providing for the transfer of ownership of a copyright interest is referred to as a copyright assignment. Any or all of a copyright owner's exclusive rights or any subdivision of those rights may be transferred, but the transfer of exclusive rights is not valid unless that transfer is in writing and signed by the owner of the rights conveyed or such owner's duly authorized agent. Transfer of a right on a nonexclusive basis does not require a written agreement.

A copyright may also be conveyed by operation of law and may be bequeathed by will or pass as personal property by the applicable laws of intestate succession. A copyright is a personal property right and is subject to the various state laws and regulations that govern the ownership, inheritance, or transfer of personal property.

Federal law includes provisions for the recording in the Copyright Office of transfers of copyright ownership. Although recordation is not required to make a valid transfer between the parties to an assignment agreement, it does provide certain legal advantages and may be required to validate the transfer as against third parties.

Advantages of recording contracts providing for transfers of copyright ownership include:

- Under certain conditions, recordation establishes priorities between conflicting transfers, or between a conflicting transfer and a nonexclusive license.

- Recordation establishes a public record of the contents of the transfer or document.

- Recordation of a document in the Copyright Office provides the advantage of "constructive notice," a legal concept meaning that members of the public are deemed to have knowledge of the facts stated in the document and cannot claim otherwise. The Copyright Act specifies that recordation of a document in the Copyright Office gives all persons constructive notice of the facts stated in the recorded document, but only if:

  1) The document or material attached to it specifically identifies the work to which it pertains so that, after the document is indexed by the Register of Copyrights, it would be revealed by a reasonable search under the title (or registration number) of the work; and

2) The copyright in the work has been registered.

- Recordation may be required to perfect a security interest in a copyright although case law on this point is mixed.

IV. TRADEMARK LAWS[4]

A. <u>Characteristics of a Trademark or Service Mark</u>

A trademark is a word, phrase, symbol or design, or a combination of these, that identifies and distinguishes the source of the goods of one party from those of others. A service mark is the same as a trademark, except that it identifies and distinguishes the source of a service rather than a product. For purposes of the following summary of trademark laws, the terms "trademark" and "mark" should be assumed to refer to both trademarks and service marks.

A broad range of items may serve as trademarks so long as they are capable of being associated with particular sources of goods or services. While most trademarks are comprised of words, phrases, graphic images, or some combination of these, more exotic items such as distinctive smells, colors, or sounds are capable of identifying the source of products and can qualify for trademark protections. Even the shape of a product package — referred to as the product's "trade dress" — can qualify for the equivalent of trademark protections if the shape is distinctive and associated with a particular product source.

Federal trademark laws provide for the registration of trademarks and nationwide protection against the use of confusingly similar marks by persons other than the registered trademark holder. Federal law also protects against trademark dilution — that is, the use of a famous trademark in a manner that weakens or "dilutes" the public's association of the mark with its owner or which entails a scandalous or otherwise distasteful use of the trademark that tarnishes the mark in the eyes of the public. State laws also provide for registration of trademarks within particular states and for the protection of unregistered trademarks within the areas of their actual use.

The summary which follows focuses on federal trademark laws and protections.

B. <u>Items That May Serve as Trademarks</u>

While other types of symbols or designs may also serve as trademarks, most marks are comprised of a distinctive word, phrase, or graphic work. The following are examples of each of these common types of marks along with typical information on the matters that need to be disclosed in the registration of these marks.

1. Textual Marks

If a mark is comprised of a word or phrase, does not depend on the use of a particular font to present the word or phrase, and does not incorporate any further graphical element, a registration may be sought for the word or phrase

---

[4] The material on United States trademark laws in this section is based on United States Patent and Trademark Office, Basic Facts About Trademarks, http://www.uspto.gov/web/offices/tac/doc/basic/ and United States Trademark Office, Frequently Asked Questions About Trademarks, http://www.uspto.gov/web/offices/tac/tmfaq.htm.

itself. If granted, the registration would apply to all forms of presentation as a trademark of the registered word or phrase. Since a merely descriptive term will be refused registration, a word or phrase granted registration will usually be made up or distinctively modified to be different from mere descriptive contents. The following registration material covers a typical textual trademark involving a single coined word.

Applicant's Name: A-OK Software Development Group
Correspondence Address: 100 Main Street, Any Town, MO 12345
Goods and Services: Computer services, namely on-line magazine in the field of business management
Date of First Use: January 15, 1995
Date of First Use in Commerce: May 15, 1995
Standard Character Claim: The mark is presented in standard character format without claim to any particular font style, size or color.

The Mark:

THEORYTEC

---

2.   Graphical Marks

Where the appearance of a mark is one of its distinctive features — either because the mark includes a graphical element or because the mark involves letters or text presented in a particular font or with a particular appearance — protection should be sought for the mark's specific visual form. The following is an example of registration material for a mark which includes both a graphic work and a textual element:

Applicant's Name: Pinstripes, Inc.
Applicantís Address: 100 Main Street, Any Town, MO 12345
Goods and Services: Clothing, namely baseball caps and t-shirts
Date of First Use: Intent-to-Use Application
Date of First Use in Commerce: Intent-to-Use Application

The Mark:

PINSTRIPES

C. **Registering a Trademark**

An application to the USPTO for registration of a trademark must include the following elements:

- the name of the applicant;
- a name and address for correspondence;
- a clear drawing of the mark;
- a listing of the goods or services for which registration is sought; and
- the filing fee for at least one class of goods or services.

The application must be filed in the name of the owner of the mark. The owner of the mark is the person or entity who controls the nature and quality of the goods identified by the mark or the services rendered in connection with the mark. The owner may be an individual, corporation, partnership, or other type of legal entity.

An applicant must list the specific goods or services for which registration is sought, regardless of the basis for the application. Most U.S. applicants base their application on their current use of a mark in commerce, or their intent to use their mark in commerce in the future. In addition, a party may base an application for registration of a trademark in the United States based on an application for trademark registration in another country.

1. **Application Based on Use in Commerce**

If a party has already started using a mark in commerce, the party may file an application for registration of the mark based on that use. For purposes of trademark registration application requirements, "commerce" means all commerce that the United States government may lawfully regulate, including interstate commerce and commerce between the United States and another country. A "use in commerce" is a bona fide use of the mark in the ordinary course of trade, and not a use simply made to reserve rights in the mark. Generally, acceptable uses include the following:

> **For goods:** the mark must appear on the goods, the container for the goods, or displays associated with the goods, and the goods must be sold or transported in commerce.

> **For services:** the mark must be used or displayed in the sale or advertising of the services, and the services must be rendered in commerce.

A "use" based application must include a sworn statement (usually in the form of a declaration) that the mark involved is in use in commerce, listing the date of first use of the mark anywhere and the date of first use of the mark in commerce. The applicant or a person authorized to sign on behalf of the applicant must sign the statement. The application should include a specimen showing use of the mark in commerce.

2. Application Based on Intent to Use

If a party has not yet used a mark when registration is sought, but plans to do so in the future, the party may file based on a good faith or bona fide intention to use the mark in commerce. An "intent to use" application must include a sworn statement (usually in the form of a declaration) that the applicant has a bona fide intention to use the mark in commerce. The applicant or a person authorized to sign on behalf of the applicant must sign the statement.

If a party files for a trademark registration based on an intent to use a mark, the applicant must begin actual use of the mark in commerce before the USPTO will register the mark. After filing an application based on an intent to use, the applicant must later file another form to establish that use of the mark has begun.

D. <u>Role of the USPTO</u>

The United States Patent and Trademark Office (USPTO) reviews trademark applications for federal registration and determines whether an applicant meets the requirements for federal registration. USPTO officials do not decide whether an applicant has the right to use a mark (which differs from the right to register).

After the USPTO determines that a party has met the minimum filing requirements for a registration application, the application is forwarded to an examining attorney. The evaluation of the trademark application by this attorney may take a number of months. The examining attorney reviews the application to determine whether it complies with all applicable rules and statutes and includes all required fees. A complete examination also includes a search for conflicting marks, and a review of the sufficiency of the written application, the drawing, and any specimen.

If the examining attorney decides that a mark should not be registered, the attorney will issue a letter describing the negative "office action" being taken based on the attorney's review and explaining any substantive or procedural deficiencies in the application. If only minor corrections are required, the examining attorney may contact the applicant by telephone or e-mail. If the examining attorney sends a notice of an office action, the applicant's response to the office action must be received in the USPTO within six months of the mailing date of the notice of the office action or the application will be declared abandoned.

If an applicant's response to a negative office action does not overcome all the examiner's objections to the registration of a proposed mark, the examining attorney will issue a final refusal to register the mark. To attempt to overcome a final refusal, the applicant may, for an additional fee, appeal to the Trademark Trial and Appeal Board, an administrative tribunal within the USPTO.

E. Bases for Rejection of a Trademark Registration Application

1. Likelihood of Confusion With an Existing Mark

As part of her review of a trademark application, an examining attorney will search the USPTO records to determine if a conflict — i.e., a likelihood of confusion — exists between the mark in the application and another mark that is registered or for which a registration application is pending in the USPTO. The principal factors considered by the examining attorney in determining whether there would be a likelihood of confusion are:

- the similarity of the marks; and

- the commercial relationship between the goods or services listed in the application and those associated with the potentially conflicting mark.

To create a conflict, marks do not have to be identical, and the goods or services associated with the marks do not have to be the same. It may be enough that the marks are similar and the goods or services are related.

If a conflict exists between a mark in a registration application and a registered mark, the examining attorney will refuse registration on the ground of a likelihood of confusion. If a conflict exists between a mark in a new registration application and a mark in a pending application that was filed before the new application, the examining attorney will notify the second applicant of the potential conflict. If the earlier-filed application results in the registration of the mark involved, the examining attorney will refuse registration of the mark covered by the second application on the ground of a likelihood of confusion.

2. Other Grounds for Rejection

In addition to refusing to register a proposed mark based on a likelihood of confusion with an existing mark, an examining attorney will refuse registration if the new mark is:

- primarily descriptive or deceptively misdescriptive of the goods or services associated with the mark;

- primarily geographically descriptive or deceptively misdescriptive of the goods or services associated with the mark;

- primarily used as a surname; or

- ornamental.

A mark also will be rejected for registration if the mark involves immoral or scandalous matter, deceptive matter, or matter that may disparage, or bring into contempt or disrepute, persons, institutions, beliefs or national symbols.

F.   Impacts of Trademark Registration

Registration of a trademark is not necessary to establish rights in a trademark. However, registering a trademark generally provides the mark owner with several advantages, including establishing:

- constructive notice to the public of the registrant's claim of ownership of the mark;

- a legal presumption of the registrant's ownership of the mark and the registrant's exclusive right to use the mark nationwide on or in connection with the goods and/or services listed in the registration;

- the ability to bring an action concerning the mark in federal court;

- the use of the U.S registration as a basis to obtain registration in foreign countries; and

- the ability to file the U.S. registration with the U.S. Customs Service to prevent importation of infringing foreign goods.

G.   Use of Trademark Symbols TM, SM and ®

Any time a party claims rights in a mark, the party may use the "TM" (trademark) or "SM" (service mark) designation to alert the public to this claim, regardless of whether the party has filed an application for registration of the mark with the USPTO. However, a party can only use the federal registration symbol "®" after the USPTO actually registers a mark and not while an application is pending. Also, a party may use the registration symbol with the mark only on or in connection with the goods or services listed in the federal trademark registration.

H.   Duration of Trademark Protections

Rights in a federally-registered trademark can last indefinitely if the owner continues to use the mark on or in connection with the goods or services specified in connection with registration of the mark and the owner files all necessary documentation in the USPTO at the appropriate times. In general, to keep federal trademark rights in force and avoid the cancellation of the registration of a mark, the owner of a registered mark must periodically file:

- Affidavits of Continued Use or Excusable Nonuse of a Mark; and

- Applications for Renewal of the Registration.

An affidavit of continued use or excusable nonuse of a mark must be filed on a date that falls on or between the fifth and sixth anniversaries of the registration of the mark (or, for an extra fee of $100.00 per trademark class, a trademark holder may file this affidavit within the six-month grace period following the sixth anniversary of registration of the mark). The failure of a trademark owner to file this affidavit in a timely manner will result in cancellation of the registration of the mark.

Between the ninth and tenth anniversaries of the registration of a trademark, and at the end of each successive ten-year period thereafter, a trademark owner must file both an affidavit of continued use or excusable nonuse of the mark and a registration renewal application (or, for an extra fee of $200.00 per class, the owner may file these two documents within the six-month grace period following the normal filing period). The failure to file either of these documents in a timely fashion will result in the cancellation of the registration of the mark.

I. **Trademark Infringement and Remedies**

Federal trademark laws provide that a person who, without the consent of the registrant:

> (a) uses in commerce any reproduction, counterfeit, copy, or colorable imitation of a registered mark in connection with the sale, offering for sale, distribution, or advertising of any goods or services on or in connection with which such use is likely to cause confusion, or to cause mistake, or to deceive; or

> (b) reproduces, counterfeits, copies or colorably imitates a registered mark and applies such reproduction, counterfeit, copy or colorable imitation to labels, signs, prints, packages, wrappers, receptacles, or advertisements intended to be used in commerce upon or in connection with the sale, offering for sale, distribution, or advertising of goods or services on or in connection with which such use is likely to cause confusion, or to cause mistake, or to deceive,

is liable to the registrant for trademark infringement. Remedies available to the registrant in these circumstances include the recovery of damages and the issuance of injunctions barring further infringement.

Damage recoveries for past trademark infringement generally extend to (1) the infringer's profits, (2) any further damages sustained by the trademark registrant, and (3) the costs of the legal action enforcing the registrant's rights. However, where liability is premised on a party's application of an imitation of a registered mark to items in commerce, the owner of the registered trademark will not be entitled to recover profits or damages unless the acts have been committed with knowledge that such imitation is intended to be used to cause confusion, or to cause mistake, or to deceive.

Once trademark infringement is established in a legal action, the court involved may also order that all labels, signs, prints, packages, wrappers, receptacles, and advertisements in the possession of the defendant, bearing the registered mark and all plates, molds, matrices, and other means of making the same, shall be delivered up and destroyed.

A trademark owner establishing trademark infringement is generally also entitled to an injunction barring the defendant from undertaking further infringing activities. The scope of this type of injunction will be determined in accordance with principles of equity and upon such terms as the court in the case deems reasonable.

A trademark owner may also obtain further relief against the attempted importation of goods bearing an unauthorized copy or simulation of a registered trademark. Such relief includes the barring of such goods from entry into the United States and is administered by United States customs officials.

J. Further Remedies for False Designations of Origin or False Descriptions

Section 43(a) of the Lanham Act codifies federal common law protection for trademarks and trade dress. Section 43(a) provides a federal civil cause of action against the "false designation of origin or false description" of a product or service as follows:

(a) Civil action.

(1) Any person who, on or in connection with any goods or services, or any container for goods, uses in commerce any word, term, name, symbol, or device, or any combination thereof, or any false designation of origin, false or misleading description of fact, or false or misleading representation of fact, which —

(A) is likely to cause confusion, or to cause mistake, or to deceive as to the affiliation, connection, or association of such person with another person, or as to the origin, sponsorship, or approval of his or her goods, services, or commercial activities by another person, or

(B) in commercial advertising or promotion, misrepresents the nature, characteristics, qualities, or geographic origin of his or her or another person's goods, services, or commercial activities,

shall be liable in a civil action by any person who believes that he or she is or is likely to be damaged by such act.

Lanham Act § 43(a), 15 U.S.C. § 1125(a) (2005). Note that registration of a mark is not a prerequisite for protection under § 43(a) of the Lanham Act. Most trade dress and product configurations are not registered and therefore depend on § 43(a) for protection.

K. Transfers of Trademark Interests

Federal trademark statutes specify that a registered mark or a mark for which an application to register has been filed shall be assignable with the good will of the business in which the mark is used, or with that part of the good will of the business which is connected with the use of and symbolized by the mark. An assignment agreement transferring a trademark interest must be in writing.

An assignment of a trademark interest can be recorded in the USPTO. While an assignment can be valid without such recording, a transferee gains several advantages from recording a trademark assignment. The recording of an agreement assigning a trademark interest provides prima facie evidence of proper execution of the agreement. In addition, the recording of an assignment provides the initial assignee with protections against an attempt by the assignor to transfer the same trademark interest to a second assignee. In general, a prior assignment shall be void against any subsequent assignee who is a purchaser for valuable consideration without notice of the first assignment, unless the first assignment is recorded in the USPTO within 3 months after the date of the first assignment or prior to the second assignment.

L. **International Considerations**

International trademark applications — meaning both applications by United States parties seeking protection for marks in other countries and applications by foreign parties seeking protection for their marks in the United States — are aided under the provisions of a key treaty called "The Protocol Relating to the Madrid Agreement Concerning the International Registration of Marks" ("Madrid Protocol"). This treaty allows a trademark owner to seek registration for a mark in any of the countries or intergovernmental organizations that have joined the Madrid Protocol by submitting a single registration application, called an international application. The International Bureau ("IB") of the World Intellectual Property Organization ("WIPO") in Geneva, Switzerland administers the international registration system. The Madrid Protocol became effective in the United States on November 2, 2003.

Under the Madrid Protocol, a party seeking international protection for a trademark starts by submitting an international application through the trademark office of the signatory country (the "Contracting Party") in which a basic application or registration is already filed (the "Office of Origin"). The Office of Origin must certify that the information in the international application corresponds with the information in the basic application or registration and forward the international application to the IB. If the IB receives the international application within two months of the date of receipt in the Office of Origin, the date of the international registration is the date of receipt in the Office of Origin. If the IB does not receive the international application within two months of the date it was received by the Office of Origin, the date of the international registration is the date the international application was received by the IB.

The international registration is dependent on the basic application or registration for five years from the international registration date. If the basic application or registration is abandoned, cancelled or expired during this five-year period, the IB will cancel the international registration.

The holder of an international registration may obtain protection in additional Contracting Parties by submitting a subsequent designation. A subsequent designation is a request by the holder of an international registration for an extension of protection of the registration to additional Contracting Parties.

Each Contracting Party designated in an international application or subsequent designation will examine the request for extension of protection as a national trademark application under its domestic laws. There are strict time limits (a maximum of 18 months) for the trademark office of a Contracting Party to enter a refusal of an extension of protection. If the Contracting Party does not notify the IB of a refusal within this time period, the mark is automatically protected. However, the extension of protection may be invalidated in accordance with the same procedures for invalidating a national registration, *e.g.*, by cancellation.

The USPTO may be involved in an international application in any of three capacities:

- **Office of Origin.** The USPTO is the Office of Origin if an international application or registration is based on an application pending in or a registration issued by the USPTO.

- **Office of a Designated Contracting Party.** The USPTO is the Office of a Designated Contracting Party if the holder of an international registration requests an extension of protection under that registration to the United States.

- **Office of the Contracting Party of the Holder.** If the holder of an international registration is a national of, is domiciled in, or has a real and effective industrial or commercial establishment in the United States, the holder can file certain requests with the IB through the USPTO, such as requests to record changes of ownership and restrictions on the holder's right to dispose of an international registration.

V. TRADE SECRET LAWS[5]

A. <u>Characteristics of a Trade Secret</u>

A trade secret is a design, practice, device, or compilation of information which is used in one's business and which gives the trade secret holder an advantage over competitors who do not know or use the trade secret. Common types of trade secrets include a commercially advantageous formula for a chemical compound, a process of manufacturing, a means of treating or preserving materials, a pattern for a machine or other device, or a list of customers.

A trade secret differs from other secret information in a business in that it is not simply information about a single action or ephemeral event in the conduct of a business, as, for example, the amount or other terms of a secret bid for a contract or the salary of certain employees. A trade secret is information about a process or device for ongoing use in the operation of a business. Generally it relates to the production of goods, as, for example, a machine or formula for the production of an article. It may, however, relate to practices used in the sale of goods or to other operations in a business, such as a code for determining discounts, rebates or other concessions in a price list or catalogue, or a list of specialized customers, or a method of bookkeeping or for undertaking other office management practices.

B. <u>Secrecy</u>

The subject matter of a trade secret must be secret. Matters of public knowledge or of general knowledge in an industry cannot be appropriated by one party as a trade secret. Matters which are completely disclosed by (or easily ascertained from) the goods which a party markets cannot be a trade secret.

---

[5] The material on state trade secret laws in this section is based on 29 C.F.R. § 1910.1200 (App. D).

Likewise, information that can easily be obtained from customers or from other publicly available sources can not be a trade secret.

The scope of proper knowledge of a trade secret within a business depends on the way the knowledge involved is used in business activities. It is not requisite that only the proprietors of a business or the senior managers know a trade secret. A trade secret may, without losing protection, be shared with those employees who can advantageously use the information. However, reasonable measures should be taken by a trade secret holder to release the trade secret to as few other parties as possible.

A trade secret holder may also communicate the information involved to others who are pledged to maintain the secrecy of the information. This type of transfer of trade secret information commonly occurs under trade secret licensing agreements in which a trade secret owner allows another party to use a trade secret and the second party agrees to maintain the secrecy of the information and, generally, to pay a royalty to the licensor for use of the trade secret.

Physical security measures should normally be maintained such that, absent improper means of access such as a trespass or theft, parties other than the authorized users of a trade secret will not gain access. Even if such security measures are in place, if a party can rediscover trade secret information through a modest amount of independent research, the information will probably be seen as available to the public and therefore not a proper subject for trade secret protections.

C. Other Significant Factors Indicating That Information is a Trade Secret

Because of the many variations in ways that information may be kept secret and have business significance, an exact standard for determining whether information is a trade secret has not yet been developed. However, courts have indicated that certain factors should be considered in determining whether a trade secret is present in a particular situation. Factors which should be considered in determining whether particular information is a trade secret include: (1) the extent to which the information is known outside of the business seeking trade secret protection; (2) the extent to which the information is known by employees and others involved in the business; (3) the extent of measures taken by the holder of the information to guard its secrecy; (4) the value of the information to the business and its competitors; (5) the amount of effort or money expended by the business in developing the information; and (6) the ease or difficulty with which the information could be properly acquired or duplicated by others.

D. Relationships Between Trade Secret and Patent Protections

1. Broader Subject Matter Covered by Trade Secrets

Trade secret protections are often available for secret designs of useful devices, materials, or processes, the same sorts of designs that can sometimes qualify for patent protections. However, trade secrets can cover many designs for useful devices, materials, and processes which are not patentable subject matter. For example, a trade secret may involve the implementation details of a device design which is unpatentable because it is not new but rather clearly anticipated in the prior design knowledge or "prior art" of the field. Alternatively, a trade secret may involve a design for a device which is new, but that is unpatentable because the design is merely a minor, obvious improvement over prior designs for similar devices and an average practitioner in the field could implement the improvement with modest effort. The fact that a business is relying on particular devices, materials, or processes and the advantages their use may gain for a business can qualify as trade secrets even though the same devices, materials, or processes would not be proper subject matters for patent protections.

Novelty and nonobviousness of useful designs are not requisites for trade secret protection as they are for patentability because the goals of these types of protection differ in fundamental ways. Trade secret protections are primarily aimed at maintaining confidential relationships while patent protections are primarily aimed at encouraging inventive efforts. Novelty and nonobviousness of inventions are essential to patentability because patent rewards and controls are reserved for inventions that are new to the public and not likely to be rediscovered through normal engineering processes. By contrast, trade secret protections are not primarily aimed at rewarding or otherwise encouraging the development of secret processes or devices. Trade secret protections are aimed at discouraging breaches of faith by persons entrusted with trade secrets and deterring reprehensible means of learning another's secret. In order for trade secret protections to act in this manner as a backstop to confidential relationships, it is not appropriate to limit those protections to only circumstances involving the kinds of novelty and nonobvious inventions needed for patentability.

2. Reliance on Trade Secret Protections When Obtaining Patents

Where patentable subject matter is present in a new design for a useful device, material, or process, the inventor of the new design may rely on trade secret protections as a preliminary step in seeking patent protections. A developer of a patentable invention will typically rely on trade secret protections to prevent others from using the new design while a patent application is being prepared and while that application is pending in secret in the USPTO. Once a patent application is published (typically 18 months after filing) or a patent issues, the public disclosure of the design involved will preclude further trade secret protections. However, barring the failure to obtain a patent, the trade secret owner will typically be able to rely on patent protections as a substitute for the trade secret protections that are lost through these disclosures.

In most instances, the patent protections gained in this situation will be superior to the trade secret protections given up. In part, this stems from the fact that a patent holder need not be concerned about maintaining the secrecy of a useful design in order to keep control over use of the design. The holder of a patent can publicize the new availability of the patented invention without concern over maintaining the secrecy of the new invention and without the commercialization limitations such secrecy would otherwise entail. Furthermore, the holder of a patent on a given invention will be able to compel those who independently rediscover the same invention to stop making, using, or selling the invention during the life of the patent, whereas a holder of a trade secret can gain no relief against a party who independently rediscovers the design or information covered by the trade secret.

For many new designs of useful devices, patent protection is the only effective means of maintaining long-term control over the commercial value of the designs because the marketing of devices based on the new designs will disclose the design features and preclude subsequent assertion of trade secret protections. While trade secret laws will give the developer of a new design temporary control over the use of the design until disclosures through product marketing efforts or other public revelations disclose an initially secret design, this sort of brief opportunity to be the sole marketer of a new invention may not achieve enough benefit for the first offeror to offset the costs of developing the new invention. Once it is publicly disclosed, other businesses will be free to use an unpatented design in creating and marketing their own products, but will not be required to pay any of the development costs associated with producing the new design. In such settings, it may pay to be a copier rather than an innovator in manufacturing and marketing new products.

3. Strategic Choice of Trade Secret Protections Over Patent Protections

In some circumstances, businesses may choose to rely on trade secret protections for secret designs even though patent protections would probably be available if sought. This type of business strategy will typically only be advantageous if the commercial value of a trade secret can be realized without publicly revealing the trade secret. For example, a company that develops a new process for manufacturing an item might keep this process a trade secret rather than seeking a patent for the process. Provided that secrecy concerning the means of manufacturing can be maintained — for example, by only using the process in a secure work environment — the commercial value of the cost savings achieved by the new process or the marketing value of the superior product quality resulting from the process can be realized by the firm involved without disclosing and losing the trade secret.

This type of business strategy has one important potential advantage over obtaining a patent for the secret process involved — trade secret protections can be maintained indefinitely, while patent protections will expire with the patent involved, currently at a point 20 years from the date of the patent application leading to the patent. If the secrecy of a process or other trade secret can be maintained over time and the burden of securing such secrecy does not outweigh the advantages of the secret process to the business involved, a business strategy of relying on trade secret protections rather than seeking a patent may be an advantageous means to extend the business value of a new invention beyond the period that patent protections would cover.

Some trade secrets have been maintained over many years and have assertedly achieved significant value over such periods for the firms involved. The most famous example of this type of reliance on trade secret protection is the formula for "Coca-Cola," which was first developed in the 1800's and which is still limited to a few company employees today. The company is able to use this formula to create syrup for drinks in secret and the syrup is then distributed to bottlers for use in preparing Coca-Cola soda without revealing the formula.

E.   Misappropriation of Trade Secrets

Misappropriation of a trade secret — the equivalent of infringement of a patent, copyright, or trademark — involves use of the trade secret in a manner that is not authorized by the trade secret owner. A trade secret can be misappropriated in either of two ways. First, a person who gains access to a trade secret through improper means may misappropriate the trade secret through use. Any use of the trade secret by such a party will be misappropriation since the trade secret owner has not authorized the party's access to the trade secret, much less the use. Second, a person who is given access to a trade secret for a specified use will misappropriate the trade secret if a different use is made. For example, an employee of a business who is given a secret list of store customers to contact them on behalf of the store to see if they would like to purchase additional items would not misappropriate the trade secret in making such calls but would misappropriate the trade secret if he took the information home and used the list to contact parties in conducting a personal business run by the employee.

Where a second business acquires the trade secrets of another concern, whether the use of the information by the second business constitutes trade secret misappropriation may depend on whether the managers of the second business had reason to know that the information was a trade secret of another business. Thus if an individual A works for business B, takes a secret formula from B's files, and then goes to work for business C and uses the same formula for C's benefit claiming that A had developed the formula since coming to work for C, A's use of the trade secret would certainly constitute misappropriation by A since he made use of the formula beyond the scope of any use authorized by B. However, whether the use also constitutes misappropriation by C would depend on whether C had reason to doubt A's claim of having developed the formula and had grounds to believe that A must have brought the formula with him from his former employer. As this example suggests, potential trade secret misappropriation and liability can place significant limits on employee mobility in high-tech industries and constrain the ability to reuse information or techniques learned in one employer's secret work environment after an employee has transferred to a second employer.

F.   Remedies for Trade Secret Misappropriation

If a trade secret is misappropriated (or will be misappropriated through reasonably anticipated future conduct), the proper relief will depend on whether the trade secret has been released to the public through the misappropriation or is still secret. If the information formerly constituting a trade secret has been fully disclosed, it is no longer a trade secret and the owner's loss is the full value of the trade secret. This value, if it can be proven, can generally be recovered from the party whose misappropriation led to the public release of the information.

If misappropriation of a trade secret has not produced a public disclosure, the owner of the trade secret can generally obtain an injunction barring further use of the trade secret by the misappropriator and a damage award compensating the trade secret owner for injury suffered due to the misappropriator's past use of the trade secret.

The nature of a trade secret is an important factor in determining the kind of relief that is appropriate against one who is subject to liability for improper use of the trade secret. Thus, if a trade secret consists of a device or process which is a novel invention, a party that acquires the secret wrongfully would ordinarily be enjoined from further use of the trade secret and required to account for the profits derived from the party's past use. If, on the other hand, the secret consists of modest improvements that a good mechanic could make without resort to the secret, the wrongdoer's liability may be limited to damages over the period in which independent research would have been needed to acquire similar information and an injunction against future use of the improvements made with the aid of the secret may be inappropriate.

VI. ADDITIONAL INTELLECTUAL PROPERTY PROTECTIONS

A. Internet Domain Names

Domain names are the words that are used as part of an Internet address, such as www.intellectualproperty.com. The "com" portion is referred to as the top-level domain name (TLD). Rights in a particular domain name are obtained by being the first to register the domain name with a registry sponsored by the Internet Corporation for Assigned Names and Numbers (ICANN), a private entity that regulates the registration of domain names. The rights obtained through registration are limited by trademark law. For example, if a company registers a domain name that is also a trademark owned by another company (such as www.mcdonalds.com), the domain name registrant very likely will be liable for trademark infringement if the domain name is used in commerce in a way that is likely to confuse consumers. In addition, a company that registers a trademark as a domain name may be liable for cybersquatting under the Anti-Cybersquatting Consumer Protection Act (ACCPA) if the registration was done with a bad faith intent to profit from a trademark owned by someone else and the registrant has no bona fide rights in the domain name. Claims of trademark infringement or violations of the ACCPA are adjudicated in court. Alternatively, claims for cybersquatting can be settled through the Uniform Domain Name Dispute Resolution Process (UDRP) implemented by ICANN. The UDRP is a system of arbitration and is governed at the international and domestic levels by guidelines promulgated by the World Intellectual Property Organization (WIPO).

B. Rights of Publicity

Rights of publicity protect a person's marketable image or persona. State laws specifying these rights create a form of intellectual property by granting an individual the exclusive ability to control the commercial use of his or her identity. Since state laws govern publicity rights, protection varies from state to state. Some states recognize common law rights of publicity while others have codified the rights in statutes. California recognizes both common law and statutory forms of protection for publicity rights.

Generally, rights of publicity protect elements that serve to identify a person, including one's name, voice, signature, likeness, and performance style. Celebrities are commonly the plaintiffs in suits alleging the infringement of rights of publicity. Infringement of publicity rights involves unauthorized commercial use of an element of an individual's identity in a way that identifies the individual. The typical remedy for infringement is an injunction against further unauthorized use of elements of the plaintiff's identity.

C. Protections Under the Semiconductor Chip Protection Act (SCPA)

In 1984, Congress passed the Semiconductor Chip Protection Act (SCPA), 17 U.S.C. §§ 901-914, which establishes a distinct form of intellectual property protection for "mask works" used to create electronic circuitry on semiconductor chips. A mask work is a graphic work used to preserve or "mask" certain elements of semiconductor material from chemical processes in the production of highly sophisticated semiconductor chips. The details of a mask work define the physical layout of elements of a semiconductor chip and, in turn, the electronic characteristics of the chip. Hence, the ability to recreate and reuse a mask work in the production of semiconductor chips is an effective way to replicate the design of a chip. A new semiconductor chip typically costs $100 million to develop, but free riders can copy the chip by replicating and reusing a corresponding mask work for a fraction of the development cost. The SCPA was aimed at discouraging this type of free rider copying by granting the owner of a mask work the exclusive rights "to reproduce the mask work by optical, electronic, or any other means" as part of semiconductor production processes or otherwise and "to import or distribute a semiconductor chip product in which the mask work is embodied." 17 U.S.C. § 905.

The SCPA was enacted in response to concerns that existing patent and copyright laws did not adequately protect semiconductor chips. Designs for semiconductor chips often could not meet the novelty and non-obviousness requirements for patent protection. Copyright protections for images capturing patterns of electronic elements in semiconductor chips were also seen as inadequate because "it was uncertain whether the copyright law could protect against copying of the pattern on the chip itself, if the pattern was deemed inseparable from the utilitarian function of the chip." *Brooktree Corp. v. Advanced Micro Devices,* 977 F.2d 1555, 1561-62 (Fed. Cir. 1992). The Court of Appeals for the Federal Circuit has called the SCPA "an innovative solution to [the] problem of technology-based industry." *Id.* at 1563. The law drew from both copyright and patent law principles, but was "uniquely adapted to semi-conductor mask works, in order to achieve appropriate protection for original designs while meeting the competitive needs of the industry and serving the public interest." *Id.*

TABLE OF CASES

[References are to page numbers; principal cases appear in italics.]

A

Abba Rubber Co. v. Seaquist 278
Abbott Laboratories v. Diamedix Corporation
. . . . 404; *405-409;* 410
Access Beyond Technologies, Inc., In re . . .
561
Adobe Systems, Inc. v. One Stop Micro, Inc.
. . . . 624
Advance Technology Consultants 365
Advance Watch Co. v. Kemper Nat'l. Ins. Co.
. . . . 874
Aetna Casualty & Surety Co. v. Superior
Court (Watercloud Bed Co.) 889
Affiliated Ute Citizens of Utah v. United
States 208; 210; 211; 225; 226
Aldon Accessories Ltd. v. Spiegel, Inc. . . . .
331
Alfus v. Pyramid Technology Corp. . . . 202
*Alliance Pharmaceutical Corp. Securities Liti-
gation, In re* 733; *772-778*
Allis-Chalmers Manufacturing Co. v. Conti-
nental Aviation & Engineering Corp. . . .
381
Allman v. Capricorn Records 870
Allstate Ins. Co. v. Hansten 892
Alna Capital Associates v. Wagner . . . 193;
220-228; 229
Aluminum Co. of America, United States v.
. . . . 436
AMCA Int'l Finance Corp. v. Interstate De-
troit Diesel Allison, Inc. 535
American Can Co. v. Mansukhani . . . 370
*American Century Services Corp. v. American
International Specialty Lines Insurance
Co.* *897-903*
American Cotton Tie Co. v. Simmons . . . .
436
American Motorists Ins. Co. v. Allied-Sysco
Food Services, Inc. 885
American Potato Dryers v. Peters . . . 388
AMP, Inc. v. Fleischhacker 351; 370;
371
Amplicillin Antitrust Litigation, In re . . . .
717
Anderson, United States v. 147n4
Anderson v. Century Prods. Co. 334
Anderson v. Clow 752
Apple Computer Sec. Litig., In re . . . 196;
197; 198; 209; 210; 215; 216
Applied Innovations, Inc. v. Regents of the
University of Minnesota 534

Arachnid, Inc. v. Merit Indus., Inc. . . 337
Arnold v. Society for Sav. Bancorp. (Arnold I)
. . . . 242; 243; 243n5; 245; 249
Arnold v. Society for Sav. Bancorp. (Arnold II)
. . . . 249; 250
Aro Manufacturing Co. v. Convertible Top
Replacement Co. 436; 437; 438
Aronson v. Quick Point Pencil Co. . . . 404;
427-432
Ar-Tik Systems, Inc. v. Dairy Queen, Inc.
. . . . 427
A.S.C.A.P., United States v. 723
Aslakson v. Home Sav. Ass'n 398
Assessment Technologies of WI, LLC v. Wire-
data, Inc. 871
Atlantic Mut. Ins. Co. v. Brotech Corp. . . . .
886
Automatic Radio Mfg. v. Hazeltine Research,
Inc. 480

B

Backman v. Polaroid Corp. 770
Baker v. Allen 183
Baker v. Texas & Pacific R. Co. 331
Ballan v. Upjohn 210; 212
Baltimore & Ohio R.R. Co. v. United States
. . . . 439
Bank Brussels Lambert v. Credit Lyonnais
(Suisse) S.A. 725
Bank of the West v. Superior Court . . 881;
882
Bartsch v. Metro-Goldwyn-Mayer, Inc. . . . .
512; 513; 515
Basic, Inc. v. Levinson 208; 217
Bastian v. Petren Resources Corp. . . . 211
Bates Mach. Co. v. Bates 336
Baxter Int'l, Inc. v. McGaw, Inc. 88
Bay Elec. Supply, Inc. 874
Bayer Corp. 383
Baystate Technologies, Inc. v. Bentley Sys-
tems, Inc. 17
B & E Convalescent Center v. State Compen-
sation Insurance Fund 889; 892
Beltone Electronics Corp. 919
Berliner v. Lotus Development Corp. . . . . .
207
B.F. Goodrich Co. v. Wohlgemuth . . . 381
Bharucha v. Reuters Holdings PLC . . 198
BIEC Int'l, Inc. v. Global Steel Services, Ltd.
. . . . 13
Bildisco, In re 560

[References are to page numbers; principal cases appear in italics.]

Biltmore Pub. Co. v. Grayson Pub. Corp. . . . 326

Biolife Solutions, Inc. v. Endocare, Inc. . . . *654-661*

Bloggild v. Kenner Prods. 516

Blonder-Tongue Laboratories, Inc. v. University of Illinois Foundation . . . 404; *410-416*

Blum 64

BMI v. CBS 515

Bobbs-Merrill Co. v. Straus 442

Boeing Co. v. Sierracin Corp. 287

Bonito Boats v. Thunder Craft Boats 305

Boosey & Hawkes Music Publishers, Ltd. v. The Walt Disney Company . . . 404; *511-516*

Bouchat v. Baltimore Ravens, Inc. 49

Boulez 67

Bouten v. Richard Miller Homes, Inc. 398

Brenner v. Berkowitz 183

Bristol-Myers Squibb Co. v. Rhone-Poulenc Rorer, Inc. 1021

Broadcast Music, Inc. v. Columbia Broadcasting System, Inc. 467; 835; 920

Broadcast Music, Inc. v. Moor Law, Inc. . . . 464

Brown v. Ivie 214

Brulotte v. Thys Co. . . . 404; *425-427*; 430; 432; 489

Brunswick Beacon, Inc. v. Schock-Hopchas Publishing Co. 331

Buffets, Inc. v. Klinke . . 254; *274-277*; 279; 280

Burlington Indus. v. Exxon Corp. . . . 717; 719n14

Burstein v. Applied Extrusion Technologies, Inc. 733; *778-785*

Buss v. Superior Court 885

Buxbom v. Smith 393; 394

C

Cadence Design Systems, Inc. v. Avant! Corp. 273

Callas Enters. Inc. v. Travelers Indem. Co. of America 874

Campbell v. Acuff-Rose Music, Inc. . . . 835

Camp Creek Hospitality Inns, Inc. v. Sheraton Franchise Corporation, ITT . . . 280

Carborundum v. Molten Metal . . 440; 441

Caremark, In re 904; 905

Caremark International, Inc. Derivative Litigation, In re 713

Casey v. Hochman 529

Catapult Entertainment, Inc., In re *572-578*; 579

Cellnet Data Systems, Inc., In re *554-562*; 566; 567

CFLC, Inc., In re 571; 578

Checkers Drive-In Restaurants, Inc. v. Commissioner of Patents and Trademarks . . *538-544*; 549

Chemical Foundation, Inc. v. E.I. du Pont De Nemours & Co. 557

Cherne Indus., Inc. v. Grounds & Assoc., Inc. 399

Chilton 65

Cinnabar 2000 Haircutters, Inc., In re . . . 549

City Bank & Trust Co. v. Otto Fabric, Inc. 155; 156; 156n10

City of Philadelphia v. Fleming Co. . . . 231

Clemmer v. Hartford Insurance Co. . . . 888; 893

CNA Casualty of California v. Seaboard Sur. Co. 892

Coggins 182

Cohen v. Paramount Pictures Corp. . . . 513; 623; 624

Colgate-Palmolive Co. v. Carter Products . . *384-388*

College Savings Bank v. Florida Prepaid Postsecondary Education Expense Board 93; 94

Commerce One, Inc. / Commerce One Operations, Inc. *841-843*

Commerce One Inc., In re 839-841

Commonwealth v. Engleman 306

Community for Creative Non-Violence v. James Earl Reid *328-335*

Compco Corp. v. Day-Brite Lighting, Inc. . . 419

Complete Auto Transit, Inc. v. Brady 160

Comptroller of the Treasury v. Crown Cork & Seal Company (Delaware), Inc. . . . 159; 160; 161

Comptroller of the Treasury v. Syl, Inc. 159; 160; 161

Computer Associates International v. American Fundware, Inc. 16

Computer Associates Int'l v. Quest Software, Inc. 870

Conmar Prods. Corp. v. Universal Slide Fastener Co. 388

Connecticut National Bank v. Fluor Corp. 232

Consumer Product Safety Comm'n v. GTE Sylvania, Inc. 331

[References are to page numbers; principal cases appear in italics.]

Convergent Technologies Sec. Litig., In re
. 754
Convergent Technologies Securities Litigation, In re 199; 202
Crom v. Cement Gun Co. 557
Crowley v. McCoy 343
C Tek Software, Inc., In re 153; 530
C Tek Software, Inc. v. New York State Business Venture Partnership *530-536*
Curtis 1000, Inc. v. Pierce 402
Cybernetic Services, Inc., In re . . 154; 155

D

Dad's Root Beer Co. v. Doc's Beverages . . .
326
Dana Corp. v. American Precision Co. . . . .
436; 437; 438
Danning v. Pacific Propeller 150
Dart Industries, Inc. v. E.I. du Pont De Nemours & Co. 46
Data Gen. Corp. v. Grumman Sys. Support
Corp. 938
Dawn Donut Company v. Hart's Food Stores, Inc. *493-497*
Dawn Donut Co. v. Hart's Food Stores, Inc.
. 404
Dearborn Process Service, Inc., In re . . . .
186; 188
DeGiorgio v. Megabyte International, Inc. . .
254; *273-274*
Della Penna v. Toyota Motor Sales, U.S.A.,
Inc. 395
Del Madera Properties v. Rhodes & Gardner,
Inc. 149n6
Demoulas v. Demoulas Super Markets, Inc.
. . . . 181; 182; 184
DeVries v. Taylor 209
Diamond Scientific Co. v. Ambico . . . 423;
425
Diodes, Inc. v. Franzen 394; 395
Directory Sales Mgmt. Corp. v. Ohio Bell Tel.
Co. 470
Dole 94
Donahue v. Rodd Electrotype Co. of New England, Inc. 181; 184; 187
Downey Venture v. LMI Ins. Co. 889
Dr. Miles Medical Co. v. John D. Park & Sons
Co. 918
DSC Communications Corp. v. Pulse Communications, Inc. 623; 624
Duane Jones Co. v. Burke 13; 326
Dubey v. Abam Building Corp. . . . 187n19
Dubilier Condenser Corporation, United
States v. 312; 314; 317

Ductmate Industries, Inc. v. Mez Industries,
Inc. 878; 888
Dunlap Corp. v. Deering Milliken, Inc. . . . .
450
DuPont 66
Durfee v. Durfee & Canning, Inc. . . . 181;
184
Dynamis, Inc. v. Leepoxy Plastics, Inc. . . . .
887

E

EarthWeb 383
Easter Seal Society for Crippled Children & Adults of Louisiana, Inc. v. Playboy Enterprises 331
Eastman Kodak Co. v. Image Technical Services, Inc. 919
Ed Peters Jewelry Co., Inc. v. C & J Jewelry Co., Inc. *645-650*; 653
Eggiman v. Mid-Century Ins. Co. 341
E.I. duPont de Nemours & Company v. Christopher 254; *281-284*
E.I. du Pont de Nemours & Co. v. Celanese
Corporation of America 495; 498
E.I. duPont de Nemours v. American Potash
& Chemical Corp 374; 381
Eldridge v. Johnston 349
Electrolux Corp. v. Val-Worth, Inc. . . . 326
Eli Lilly & Co. v. Medtronic, Inc. . . . 1013
Elizabeth v. American Nicholson Pavement
Co. 47
Embrex, Inc. v. Service Engineering Corp.
. . . . . 74; 75; *88-90;* 96
Ernst & Ernst v. Hochfelder . . . 205; 227
Escott v. BarChris Construction Corp. . . . .
702; 703; 704; 705; 707; 708
Ethyl Gasoline Corp. v. United States . . . .
918
Eutectic Corp. v Metco, Inc. 716n10
Evans Newton, Inc. v. Chicago Systems Software 331
Everett Associates, Inc. v. Transcontinental
Ins. Co. 880n4
Everett v. Judson 524
Everex Sys., Inc. v. Cadtrak Corp. (In re
CFLC, Inc.) 623; 624

F

Farwell v. Pyle-National Electric Headlight Co. *164-167*
Feit v. Leasco Data Processing Equipment
Corporation 700-710
Fenix Cattle Co. v. Silver (In re Select-A-Seat
Corp.) 563

[References are to page numbers; principal cases appear in italics.]

Fenn v. Yale University 76-84; 96
Fireman's Fund Ins. Co. v. City of Turlock
. . . . 892
First National Trust and Savings Bank of San
Diego 70
Flamm v. Eberstadt 217
Fleming v. International Pizza Supply Corp.
. . . . 185n14
Florida Prepaid Postsecondary Education Ex-
pense Board v. College Savings Bank . .
93; 94; 95; 96
Flynn v. Bass Brothers Enters., Inc. . . . . .
247n7
FMC v. Taiwan Tainan Giant Indus. Co. . . .
19
Fortner Enterprises, Inc. v. United States
Steel Corp. 501
Fortune Sys. Sec. Litig., In re 212
Fox, In re 552
Fragomeno v. Insurance Co. of the West . .
892
Fralich v. Despar 320
*Freedom Wireless, Inc. v. Boston Communica-
tions Group, Inc.* 335-337
Fromberg, Inc. v. Thornhill 881
Fujisawa Pharmaceutical Co. Ltd. v. Kapoor
. . . . 212

G

GAB Business Services, Inc. v. Lindsey &
Newsom Claim Services, Inc. 393
Gaffin v. Teledyne, Inc. 248
Galler v. Galler 184n13
Gardner v. Nike 578
G.A. Thompson and Co., Inc. v. Partridge
. . . . 227; 228
Gencor Industries v. Wausau Underwriters
Ins. Co. 885
Gencor, In re 552
General Electric Co. v. United States . . . .
436; 437; 438
Geoffrey, Inc. v. South Carolina Tax Commis-
sion 161
Georgia-Pacific Corp. v. U.S. Plywood-
Champion Papers, Inc. 43
Gilbert v. El Paso Co. 242
Gill v. Poe & Brown of Georgia, Inc. . . 364
Gill v. United States 315
Gilman, Clinton & Springfield Railroad
Co. v. Kelly 166
Glamorene Products Corp. v. Proctor & Gam-
ble Co. 493
Golden Books Family Entertainment, Inc., In
re 578
Goldstein v. California 429

Gompper v. VISX, Inc. 194; *229-231*
Goodman v. Epstein 219
Graham v. James 870
Graham v. John Deere Co. 410; 412
Greenstone v. Cambex Corporation . . 781;
784; 785
Gregory v. Helvering 62; 160
Greg Simms and North Georgia Partnership v.
Edward White, et al. 895
Guth v. Minn. Min. & Mfg. Co. 336

H

Hagshenas v. Gaylord . . 184n13; 186; 187;
188
Hanover Ins. Co. v. Sutton 182
Hapgood v. Hewitt *579-583;* 606
Harris v. Emus Records Corp. 624
Harris v. Ivax 765
Harry R. Defler Corporation v. Kleeman . .
323-326
Hartford-Empire Co. v. Demuth Glass Works,
Inc. 629
Hartford-Empire Co. v. United States . . . .
476
Health Care Affiliated Services, Inc. v. Lip-
pany 12
Henderson v. Axiam, Incorporated . . . . . .
175-184
Hercules, Inc. v. Exxon Corp. 716n9
Hercules, Inc. v. United States 439
Herman & MacLean 762
Hermes Int'l v. Lederer de Paris Fifth Ave-
nue, Inc. 18
Hernandez, In re 578
Herold v. Herold China & Pottery Co. . . . .
387
Hewlett-Packard Co. v. Bausch & Lomb Inc.
. . . . . 439; 722; 725; 726; 887
Heyden Chemical Corp. v. Burrell & Neidig,
Inc. 278; 279
H.F. Walliser & Co. v. F.W. Maurer & Sons
Co. 314
Hill 67
Hillsborough County v. Automated Medical
Laboratories, Inc. 149
Hilton Int'l Co. v. NLRB 333
H.J. Baker & Bro. v. Organics, Inc. . . 645;
649; 650
Hollinger v. Titan Capital Corp. 206
Holt v. Winpisinger 333
Home Indem. Co. v. Avol 892
H & R Block Eastern Tax Servs. Inc. v. En-
chura 383
Hsu, United States v. 288; 292; 297;
298; 299; 304

[References are to page numbers; principal cases appear in italics.]

Huddleston v. Herman and MacLean . . . .
228
Hughes Tool Co. v. Dresser Industries, Inc.
. . . . 40-43; 44
Husen v. Husen 343; 344
Hutchinson Tel. Co. v. Fronteer Directory Co.
of Minnesota, Inc. 533
Hyde Corporation v. Huffines 282

I

ILG Industries v. Scott 351
IMS Health GmbH & Co. OHG . . 930; 935
Independent Ink, Inc. v. Illinois Tool Works,
Inc. 933; 935
Independent Wireless Tel. Co. v. Radio Corp.
of Am. 407
Indep. Serv. Orgs. Antitrust Litig., In re . .
944
Infinity Prods. Inc. v. Quandt . . . 390; 391
Ingersoll-Rand Co. v. Armand Ciavatta . . .
336; *352-361*
Innovative Constr. Sys., Inc., In re . . . 271
In re . . . *see name of party*
Institute Pasteur v. Cambridge Biotech Cor-
poration 568-572; 579
Intel Corp. v. VIA Techs., Inc. 451
International Business Mach. Corp. v. Sea-
gate Technology, Inc. 383
International Cosmetics Exchange, Inc. v. Ga-
pardis Health & Beauty, Inc. . . *489-492*
International Paper Company v. Ernest
Broadhead 624
International Salt Co. v. United States . . .
452
International Trade Management, Inc. v.
United States 150n7
Intex Plastics Sales Co. v. United Nat. Ins.
. . . . 889
Int'l Cosmetics Exch. Inc. v. Gapardis Health
& Beauty, Inc. 404
Int'l Mgf. Co. v. Landon 473; 474

J

Jabend, Inc. v. Four-Phase Systems, Inc. . . .
214; 215
Jack Winter, Inc. v. Koratron, Inc. . . 717;
718; 719
Jazz Photo Corp. v. International Trade Com-
mission 404; *433-440*
J Bar H, Inc. v. Johnson 188
J.C. Penney Casualty Ins. Co. v. M.K. . . .
888
Jefferson Parish . . 474; 951; 953; 954; 958;
959

Johnson Electric North America Inc. v. Mabuchi North American Corp. 723
Jordan v. Duff and Phelps, Inc. 217
JumpSport, Inc. v. Jumpking, Inc. . . . 789;
818-828

K

Kallok v. Medtronic, Inc. 399; 400
Katz and MCI v. AT&T Corp. 726
Kelley v. Southern Pacific Co. 331
Kennedy v. Wright 184
Kerrigan v. Unity Savings Association . . .
172
Kewanee Oil Co. v. Bicron Corp. 286;
305; 429; 431
Knogo Corporation v. United States . . 682;
715-720
Knorr-Bremse v. Dana Corp. 675
Koppers Coal & Transportation Co. v. United
States 625; 631
Korea Supply 395; 396

L

Labriola v. Pollard Group, Inc. 352
Lamdin v. Broadway Surface Adv. Corp. . . .
326
Landorf v. Glottstein 187n18
Lange, United States v. . . . 254; 256; 257;
290-293; 299
Lasercomb America, Inc. v. Reynolds . . . .
871
L. Batlin & Sons, Inc. v. Snyder 535
Lear, Inc. v. Adkins . . 404; 414; 415; *416-*
422; 423; 430
Learning Curve Toys, Incorporated v. Play-
wood Toys Incorporated . . 254; *258-266;*
273; 279; 280
Learning Publications, Inc., In re . . . 552
Lebas Fashion Imports of USA, Inc. v. ITT
Harford Insurance Group . . . 874; 882;
883
Levitt v. Bouvier 241
LHLC 219
Libbey Glass, Inc. v. Oneida, Ltd. . . . 725
Lightner v. Boston & A. R. Co. 629
Li'l' Red Barn, Inc. v. Red Barn System, Inc.
. . . . 157n11
Linney v. Cellular Alaska Partnership . . .
623
Loew's, Inc., United States v. 468
Lubrizol Enterprises, Inc. v. Richmond Metal
Finishers, Inc. 553; *562-566;* 567
Lucent Information Management, Inc v. Lu-
cent Technologies, Inc. 14

[References are to page numbers; principal cases appear in italics.]

Lueder Constr. Co. v. Lincoln Elec. Co. . . . 343

Lynch v. Vickers Energy Corp. . . 243; 244; 244n6; 245

M

Machen Inc. v. Aircraft Design, Inc. . . 279

Madey v. Duke University 72-75; 96; 1024; 1025

Magill 975; 976; 980

Mai Systems Corp. v. Peak Computer, Inc. 623; 624

Mallinckrodt, Inc. v. Medipart, Inc. . . 439; 442; 466

Mangren Research and Development Corporation v. National Chemical Company, Incorporated . . 266-272; 273; 279

Manville Sales Corp. v. Paramount Systems, Inc. 887

Marion Merrell Dow, Inc. Securities Litigation, In re 199

Maritime Fish Products, Inc. v. World-Wide Fish Products, Inc. 13

Martin Marietta Corp. v. Insurance Co. of North America 885

Martin, United States v. . . . 254; *293-299;* 304

Masonite Corp., United States v. 437

Massachusetts v. Microsoft Corp. 870

Matsushita Electrical Industrial Co., Ltd. v. Cinram International, Inc. . . . 404; *459-465*

Matusalem, In re 553

Max C. McElmurry and White River Tech., Inc. v. Arkansas Power & Light Co., Entergy Corp. and Middle South Utilities . . *310-314*

Maxconn Inc. v. Truck Ins. Exchange 886

Mazer v. Stein 533

McAleer v. United States 315

McClain 65

McCombs v. McClelland 341; 342

McCullough Tool Co. v. Well Surveys, Inc. 478; 479

Mentor Graphics Corp. v. Quickturn Design Systems 425

Merck KGaA v. Integra Lifesciences I, Ltd. 988; *1001-1006; 1007-1016; 1016-1024;* 1025

Metro Traffic Control, Inc. v. Shadow Traffic Network 394

Mez Industries, Inc. v. Pacific National Insurance Company *877-890*

Michoud v. Girod 166

Microsoft Corp., United States v. (Microsoft I) 936

Microsoft Corp., United States v. (Microsoft II) 936

Microsoft Corp. v. DAK Industries, Inc. . . . 552

Microsoft Corp. v. United States 937

Microsoft, United States v. 928; 930; 935; *936-948;* 949; *950-958;* 958; 959

Miller v. Miller 399

Mills Music, Inc. v. Snyder 510

Mills v. The Electric Auto-Lite Co. . . . 225

Mitchell v. Hawley 435

Money Store v. Harriscorp Finance Inc. . . . 493

Monsanto Co. v. McFarling 441; 442; 466

Morris v. Business Concepts Inc. 49

Morton Salt Co. v. G.S. Suppiger Co. 452

Motor City Bagels, LLC v. American Bagel Co. *20-24;* 25; 106

Motorola, Inc. v. Amkor Techonology, Inc. *639-644*

N

Nancey Silvers v. Sony Pictures Entertainment, Inc. *504-509*

Nathenson v. Zonagen, Inc. . . 194; *233-238*

National Bellas Hess, Inc. v. Department of Revenue of Ill. 160

National Development Co. v. Gray . . . 356

National Presto Industries, Inc. v. West Bend Co. 887

National Union Fire Ins. Co. v. Siliconix, Inc. 883

Nat'l Development Co. v. Gray 184

Natta v. Hogan 717

NCAA 920

Network Solutions, Inc. v. Umbro Int'l, Inc. 538

Newbridge Network Securities Litigation, In re 208

New Hampshire Ins. v. R.L. Chaides Const. 881; 883

New Wrinkle, Inc., United States v. . . 920

New York Times Company, Inc. v. Tasini . . 789; *829-835;* 836; 837

Nicolas M. Salgo Assocs. v. Continental Ill. Properties 651; 652

Nike, Inc. v. Eugene McCarthy . . . *345-351*

N.J. Super. 353; 355

NLRB v. Bildisco 561

NLRB v. Hearst Publications, Inc. . . . 331

[References are to page numbers; principal cases appear in italics.]

Nordling v. N. State Power Co. 401
North Chicago Rolling Mill Co. v. St. Louis
    Ore & Steel Co. 589
North Pac. Lumber Co. v. Moore 349
Northwest Wholesale Stationers, Inc. v. Pa-
    cific Stationery & Printing Co. 920
Nowak v. National Car Coupler Co. . . 165
N. Pac. Ry. Co. v. United States 473

O

Oil Resources, Inc., U.S. v. 625
199Z, Inc., In re 158
Online Partners.Com Inc. v. AtlanticNet Me-
    dia Corp. 537
Owens-Brockway Glass v. International Ins.
    Co. 884; 885; 886
Owings v. Rose 341

P

Packard 631
Palmer & Cay of Georgia, Inc. v. Lockton
    Companies, Inc. 363-365
Palmer v. Truck Insurance Exchange . . . .
    886n7
Panavision Int'l, L.P. v. Toeppen 15
Pandol Bros., Inc. v. Indemnity Marine Assur.
    Co. 336
Paragon Trade Brands, Inc. v. Weyerhaeuser
    Company . . 653; 654; 662-674; 675; 676
Paramount Pictures, Inc., United States v.
    468
Parden v. Terminal Railway of the Alabama
    State Docks Department 94
Parsons v. Hornblower & Weeks-Hemphill
   785
Pasteurized Eggs Corp., In re 155
Patrick A. Casey, P.A. v. Joel S. Hochman,
    M.D. 522-525
Pav-Savr Corp. v. Vasso Corp. . . 584-591;
    606
Penick Pharmaceutical, Inc. and Unofficial
    Committee of Equity Holders of Penick
    Pharmaceutical, Inc. v. McManigle . . . .
    525-529
Pennock v. Dialogue 47; 48
People v. Pribich 254; 300-304
Pepsico, Inc. v. William E. Redmond, Jr., and
    the Quaker Oats Company . . . 365-374;
    381
Pepsico v. Grapette Co. 492
Peregrine Entertainment, Ltd., In re . . . . .
    146-153; 154; 155; 158
Peregrine Entertainment, Ltd. v. Capitol Fed-
    eral Savings & Loan of Denver . . . 157

Perrin v. United States 331
Petty 94
Pfaff v. Wells Electronics, Inc. . . 45-49; 49
Pfizer, Inc. Securities Litigation, In re . . .
    201
Phillips v. Frey 284
Pioneer Hi-Bred Int'l, Inc. v. Ottawa Plant
    Food, Inc. 442
Pitcairn v. United States 75
Pitney Bowes, Inc. v. Mestre 516
Pittsburgh Cut Wire Co. v. Sufrin . . . 320
Planetary Motion, Inc. v. Techsplosion, Inc.
   865
Pommer v. Medtest Corporation 193;
    204; 216-220
Potthoff v. Jefferson Lines, Inc. 399
PPG Industries, Inc. v. Guardian Industries
    Corp. 625-633; 644; 651; 652; 654
Practice Mgmt. Info. Corp. v. American Medi-
    cal Assoc. 871
Precisions Industries, Inc. v. Qualitech Steel
    SBQ 567
Principe v. McDonald's Corporation . . 404;
    500-503
ProCD, Inc. v. Zeidenberg 482
Progress Software Corp. v. MySQL AB . . .
    868
Public Citizen Health Research Group v. Na-
    tional Institutes of Health 85
Pure Oil Co. v. Hyman 314

Q

Quill Corp. v. North Dakota 160

R

R2 Medical Systems, Inc. v. Katecho, Inc.
   887
Rambus, Inc. v. Infineon Technologies . . . .
    931; 935; 971
Raquel v. Education Management Corp. . . .
    49
RasterOps Corp. Securities Litigation, In re
    206
Red Hat, Inc. v. The SCO Group, Inc. . . . . .
    870
Reeves v. Hanlon 391-397
Regents of the University of California, In re
    724
Rem Metals Corp. v. Logan 349
Republic Indem. Co. v. Superior Court . . .
    892
Rexford Rand Corp. v. Ancel 184-189
Roberts 219

[References are to page numbers; principal cases appear in italics.]

Robinson v. Baltimore & Ohio R. Co. 331

Rocform Corp. v. Acitelli-Standard Concrete Wall, Inc. 479

Roche Products, Inc. v. Bolar Pharmaceutical Co., Inc. 74; 75; 1019

Roeder v. Alpha Industries, Inc. 770; 772; 783; 784

Roman Cleanser Co., In re 156n11

Roman Cleanser Co. v. National Acceptance Co. 156n11

Romani v. Shearson Lehman Hutton 781; 782

Ronconi v. Larkin 230; 231

Rosenblatt v. Getty Oil Co. 242; 244

Ross v. A.H. Robins Co., Inc. 201

Royal Business Group Inc. v. Realist, Inc. 781

Rubinstein v. Collins 738

Ruth v. Stearns-Roger Mfg. Co. 75

S

Saballus v. Timke 186n17

Saltzberg v. TM Sterling/Austin Assocs., Ltd. 766n2

Santarus, Inc. *742-750*

Santa's Workshop v. Sterling 326

Schatz v. Abbott Laboratories, Inc. . . . 173

Schering-Plough Corp. v. FTC 935

Scherr v. Universal Match Corp. 67

Schmidt v. Central Foundry Co. 314

SCM Corporation v. Xerox Corporation . . . 925

SCO Group, Inc. v. International Business Machines Corp., The 869; 870

SCO Group, Inc. v. Novell Inc., The . . 869

Scott Paper Co. v. Marcalus Mfg. Co. 423; 426

Seachange International, Inc., In re . . 733; *766-772*

Seagate Technology II Securities Litigation, In re 210

Sears, Roebuck & Co. v. Stiffel Co. . . . 419; 429

SEC v. Cherif 370

SEC v. Texas Gulf Sulphur Co. . . . 225; 777

Seiko Epson Corp. v. Nu-Kote Int'l, Inc. . . 549

Seminole Tribe of Florida v. Florida . . . 94

Service Eng'g Corp. v. United States . . 89

Shell Oil Co. v. Winterthur Swiss Ins. Co. 888

Shell Petroleum, Inc. v. Smith 242

Sherleigh Associates, LLC v. Windmere-Durable Holdings, Inc. . . . 732; *755-766*

Sherwin-Williams Co. v. Commissioner of Revenue 71; 162

Sherwin-Williams Co. v. Tax Appeals Tribunal of the Department of Taxation and Finance of the State of New York . . 71

ShoLodge, Inc. v. Travelers Indem. Co. of Illinois 886

Silicon Graphics, Inc. Sec. Litig., In re . . . 230; 231; 232

Silvers v. Sony Pictures Entm't, Inc. . . . 404

Simon v. Merrill, Lynch, Pierce, Fenner and Smith, Inc. 226

Simplified Information Systems, Inc. v. Cannon *529-530*

Singer Company, The, In re 544-548; 549

Singer Manufacturing Co., United States v. 920

Smith v. Atlantic Properties, Inc. 187n20

Snap-On Tools Corp., In re 91

Solari Indus., Inc. v. Malady . . . 358; 359; 361

Solomons v. United States 315

Somerset House, Inc. v. Turnock 370

Sony Electronics, Inc. v. Soundview Technologies, Inc. 935

S.O.S., Inc. v. Payday, Inc. 623; 624

Southwest Whey Inc. v. Nutrition 101, Inc. *591-598;* 606

Spectrum Sports, Inc. v. McQuillan . . 292

Speedry Chem. Products, Inc. v. Carter's Ink Co. 287

Speed Shore Corp. v. Woudenberg Enterprises 454

Spiegel v. Beacon Participations, Inc. 181

SQL Solutions, Inc. v. Oracle Corp. . . . 623; 624; 625

Stac Electronics Securities Litigation, In re 732; *750-755;* 766n2

Standard Oil Co. v. United States . . . 941

Standard Parts Co. v. Peck . . *314-316;* 317

Star Cellular Telephone Company, Inc. v. Baton Rouge CGSA, Inc. 623; 625

State Farm Fire and Casualty Insurance Company v. White *895-897*

State Street Bank v. Signature Financial Services 97

Steinberg v. PRT Group, Inc. 17

Stephenson v. Capano Dev., Inc. 248

Step-Saver Data Systems, Inc. v. Wyse Technology 442; 443; 482

Steranko v. Inforex, Inc. 183n12

Stern's Gallery, Inc. v. Corporate Property Investors, Inc. 896

[References are to page numbers; principal cases appear in italics.]

Stewart v. Abend 532

Storage Technology Corp. Securities Litigation, In re 198

Storage Technology Corp. v. Cisco Systems, Inc. *397-401*

St. Paul Fire & Marine v. Advanced Interventional 885

Stroud v. Grace 242

Studiengesellschaft Kohle m.b.H. v. Shell Oil 422; 423

Summit Inv. & Dev. Corp. v. Leroux (In re Leroux) 570

Sun Microsystems, Inc. v. Microsoft Corp. 623; 870

Superintendent of Insurance of the State of New York v. Bankers Life and Casualty Co. 213

Swaney v. Crawley 399

Syms Corp. v. Commissioner of Revenue . . *60-64;* 71; 72; 162

Syntek Semiconductor Co. Ltd. v. Microchip Technology Inc. 49

T

Tackett v. State Farm Fire & Casualty Ins. Co. 243n5

Taco Cabana v. Two Pesos 498; 499

Tampa Electric Co. v. Nashville Coal Co. . . . 919

Tap Publ'n, Inc. v. Chinese Yellow Pages (New York), Inc. 578

Taylor 69

Telephone Cases 46; 48

Tenneco Packaging Specialty and Consumer Products, Inc. v. S.C. Johnson & Son, Inc. 724

Teradyne, Inc. v. Clear Communications Corp. 370; 371

Texaco Ref. & Mktg., Inc. v. Delaware River Basin Comm'n 624

Texas Instruments v. Hyundai Electronics Industries 404; *444-449; 452-459*

Thompson 314

Timely Products Corp. v. Arron 46

Times-Picayune Publishing Co. v. United States 951

Together Dev. Corp., In re 157

Tonry, In re 552

Topco Associates, Inc., United States v. 503; 504

Toro Co. v. R & R Products Co., The . . 533

Town & Country Serv. v. Newbery . . 325; 326

TR-3 Indus., In re 156n11; 157

TR-3 Indus. v. Capital Bank 156n11

Transamerica Computer Co., Inc. v. IBM . . 938

Transparent-Wrap Machine Corp. v. Stokes & Smith Co. 922

Transportation Design & Technology Inc., In re 155; 156

Treadaway v. Camellia Convalescent Hospitals, Inc. 624

Triangle Film Corp. v. Artcraft Pictures Corp. 394

Trinity Industries, Inc. v. Road Systems, Inc. *85-88*

Triplett v. Lowell 411; 413; 414; 415; 416

Troy Iron & Nail v. Corning 629

Trubowitch 625

Truck Ins. Exchange v. Bennett 885

T.S.C. Industries, Inc. v. Northway, Inc. . . 225; 226; 242; 244

Tulumello v. W.J. Taylor Intl. Construction Co., Inc. 188

Turkish v. Kasenetz 232

TXO Production Co. and Marathon Oil Co. v. M.D. Mark, Inc. 624; *650-653;* 654

Tyson Foods, Inc. v. Conagra, Inc. 327

U

Underhill v. Schenck 326

Union Insurance Co. v. Land and Sky, Inc. 883n6

Union Pacific Railroad Company v. Brent Mower *339-344*

United Mine Workers v. Gibbs 220

United Shoe Machinery Corp., United States v. 715; 716; 720; 938

United States Gypsum Co., United States v. 479

United States v. . . . *see name of defendant party*

University of Colorado Foundation, Inc. v. American Cyanamid Co. 90-92; 96; 481

University of Rochester v. G.D. Searle, Inc. *84*

Univis Lens Co., United States v. . . . 918

Unocal 931; 935

U.S. Bioscience Securities Litigation, In re 205

U.S. Fidelity & Guar. Co. v. Star Technologies 881

U.S. Philips Corporation v. International Trade Commission *465-476*

V

Vantage Point, Inc. v. Parker Bros. . . . 389

[References are to page numbers; principal cases appear in italics.]

Vaupel Textilmaschinen KG v. Meccanica Euro Italia S.P.A. 408

Vendo Company v. Stoner *167-174*

Verizon Communications Inc. v. Law Offices of Curtis V. Trinko, LLP 929; 930; 934

Verson Corporation v. Verson International Group, PLC *633-639;* 644

Verson Wilkins Ltd. v. Allied Products Corp. 633

Video Pipeline, Inc. v. Buena Vista Home Entm't, Inc. 871

Virginia Bankshares, Inc. v. Sandberg . . . 217

Virginia Panel Corp. v. MAC Panel Co. . . . 466

Volt Servs. Group v. Adecco Employment Servs., Inc. 350

Vosgerichian v. Commodore Int'l 205

W

Wall 66

Waranch v. Gulf Insurance Co. 885

Ward 333

Warner-Lambert Pharmaceutical Company v. John J. Reynolds, Inc. . . . 404; *483-488*

Warshaw v. Xoma Corp. 754

Waterman v. Mackenzie . . . 406; 407; 408

Water Technologies Corp. v. Calco, Ltd. . . . 887

Weinberger v. Rio Grande Indus., Inc. . . . 247; 247n7

Well-Made Toy Mfg. Corp. v. Goffa Intern Corp. 49

Well Surveys, Inc. v. Perfo-Log, Inc. . . 404; *477-480*

Welte v. Fortinet UK Ltd. 868

Westcott Chuck Co. v. Oneida Nat. Chuck Co. 326

West Publishing Co. v. Mead Data Central, Inc. 534

Wexler v. Greenberg *318-321;* 322

White's Elecs., Inc. v. Teknetics, Inc. 342

Whitmyer Bros., Inc. v. Doyle . . 358; 359; 361

Whyte v. Schlage Lock Co. 382

Wilbur-Ellis Co. v. Kuther 436; 437

William LeJeune v. Coin Acceptors, Inc. . . . *375-384*

Wilson v. Simpson 435

Windsurfing Int'l. 466

Winegard 410

Wireless Specialty Apparatus Co. v. Mica Condenser Co. 184

Witkop & Holmes Co. v. Boyce 325

World Auxiliary Power Co., In re 154

Worlds of Wonder Securities Litigation, In re 739; 755

W. R. Grace & Co. v. Mouyal . . . 364; 365

X

Xechem Intern., Inc. v. Univ. of Tex. M.D. Anderson Cancer Center *92-96*

Y

Yang, United States v. 299

Z

Zenith Radio Corp. v. Hazeltine Research Inc. 480

Zirn v. VLI Corporation . . . 194; *239-250;* 243n5; 250

Zurich Insurance Co. v. Killer Music, Inc. *890-894;* 895

TABLE OF STATUTES

[References are to page and footnote numbers.]

AMERICAN JOBS CREATION ACT OF 2004
Generally 845; 849
Sec. 882 845

BANKRUPTCY CODE
Generally . . . 153; 539; 541; 543; 549; 559;
561; 562
Ch. 7 . . . . 520; 522; 523; 524; 552
Ch. 11 . . 521; 522; 523; 524; 525; 527; 540;
552; 568; 569; 571; 572; 573; 574;
672
Sec. 35A 551
Sec. 35B 551
Sec. 35C 551
Sec. 35D 551
Sec. 35E 551
Sec. 35F 551
Sec. 101 551
Sec. 362 . . . . 521; 546; 547
Sec. 362(a) 547; 548
Sec. 362(a)(1) 546
Sec. 362(a)(3) 547
Sec. 362(b) 549
Sec. 363(c)(1) 528
Sec. 365 . . . . 521; 549; 557; 563; 564; 566;
573; 574; 575; 644
Sec. 365(a) . . 549; 551; 553; 555; 556; 557;
559; 560; 561; 563; 564; 565; 566;
567; 568; 573; 578
Sec. 365(c) 569; 570; 573; 574; 575
Sec. 365(c)(1) 553; 569; 572; 573; 574;
575; 576; 577; 578
Sec. 365(c)(1)(A) 570; 573; 574; 576
Sec. 365(c)(1)(B) 570; 573; 574
Sec. 365(c)(2) 576; 577
Sec. 365(e) 570
Sec. 365(f) 567; 575
Sec. 365(f)(1) 553; 575; 576
Sec. 365(g) 566
Sec. 365(h) 561; 562
Sec. 365(n) . . 521; 552; 553; 556; 557; 559;
560; 561; 566; 567; 579
Sec. 365(n)(1) 550
Sec. 365(n)(1)(A) 550
Sec. 365(n)(1)(B) 550; 555
Sec. 365(n)(2) 550; 560; 561
Sec. 365(n)(2)(A) 550
Sec. 365(n)(2)(B) 550; 556; 560; 561
Sec. 365(n)(2)(C) 550
Sec. 365(n)(2)(C)(i) 550
Sec. 365(n)(2)(C)(ii) 550

Sec. 365(n)(3) 550
Sec. 365(n)(3)(A) 550
Sec. 365(n)(3)(B) 551
Sec. 365(n)(4) 551
Sec. 365(n)(4)(A) 551
Sec. 365(n)(4)(A)(i) 551
Sec. 365(n)(4)(A)(ii) 551
Sec. 365(n)(4)(B) 551
Sec. 506(c) 538
Sec. 507 538
Sec. 541(a) 545
Sec. 541(a)(1) 527; 528
Sec. 541(a)(6) 527
Sec. 541(a)(7) 527; 528
Sec. 1108 528

BAYH-DOLE ACT
Generally 84; 85; 86; 88; 89; 96; 481;
1016; 1017; 1022; 1023; 1025

BUSINESS REVIEW LETTER, U.S. DEPARTMENT OF JUSTICE, ANTITRUST DIVISION (DEC. 16, 1998) . . . .
473

CLAYTON ACT
Generally 910; 911; 925; 926
Sec. 3 919
Sec. 7 . . . . 482; 922
Sec. 14 . . . . 911; 925
Sec. 18 . . . . 911; 925

CLEAN AIR ACT OF 1970
Generally 443

CODE OF FEDERAL REGULATIONS
17 C.F.R. part 229 739
17 C.F.R. 229.101 739
17 C.F.R. 229.101(a) 739
17 C.F.R. 229.101(c) 739; 740
17 C.F.R. 229.101(c)(1) 739
17 C.F.R. 229.101(c)(1)(i) 739
17 C.F.R. 229.101(c)(1)(ii) 740
17 C.F.R. 229.101(c)(1)(iv) 740
17 C.F.R. 229.101(c)(1)(i)-(x) 739
17 C.F.R. 229.101(c)(1)(x) 740
17 C.F.R. 229.101(c)(1)(xi)-(xiii) 739
17 C.F.R. 229.103 . . . . 741; 772
17 C.F.R. 229.103(2) 741
17 C.F.R. 229.503 741

17 C.F.R. 229.503(c) 741
17 C.F.R. 229.601 741
17 C.F.R. 229.601(b) 741
17 C.F.R. 229.601(b)(10) 741
17 C.F.R. 229.601(b)(10)(i) 741
17 C.F.R. 229.601(b)(10)(ii) 742
17 C.F.R. 229.601(b)(10)(ii)(B) 742
17 C.F.R. 240.10b-5 . . . . 216; 235n2; 753
21 C.F.R. part 58 1020
21 C.F.R. 58.15(a) 1020
21 C.F.R. 58.29 1020
21 C.F.R. 58.35 1020
21 C.F.R. 58.43 1020
21 C.F.R. 58.45 1020
26 C.F.R. 1.170-1 849
37 C.F.R. 1.56 . . . . 717n11
37 C.F.R. 1.56(a) 719n13
37 C.F.R. 1.56(b) 87; 719
37 C.F.R. 201.4(a)(2) 149
37 C.F.R. 201.4(c)(1) 152n9

COPYRIGHT ACT OF 1909

Generally 504; 508

COPYRIGHT ACT OF 1976

Generally 148; 149; 149n6; 150; 151;
                152; 152n9; 153; 155; 157n11;
                327; 328; 330; 331; 504; 507; 508;
                509; 530; 832; 836; 837
Sec. 101 . . . .   328; 329; 330; 331; 332; 333
Sec. 101(1) 328; 329; 330; 331; 332
Sec. 101(2) 330; 331; 332; 333
Sec. 102 330
Sec. 102(a) 529
Sec. 102(a)(1) 529
Sec. 106 . . . . 149n6; 506; 507; 508
Sec. 106-122 506
Sec. 201 508
Sec. 201(a) 330; 333; 529
Sec. 201(b) 330
Sec. 201(c) . . 829; 831; 832; 834; 835; 836
Sec. 201(d) 506
Sec. 203(a) 330
Sec. 205(a) 149; 152
Sec. 205(d) 151
Sec. 302(c) 330
Sec. 304 510
Sec. 304(a) 330
Sec. 411 505
Sec. 501(a) 506
Sec. 501(b) 505; 506; 507
Sec. 601(b)(1) 330

DRUG PRICE COMPETITION AND PATENT TERM RESTORATION ACT OF 1984

Generally 1018

ECONOMIC ESPIONAGE ACT (EEA)

Generally . . .   19; 254; 255; 256; 288; 289;
                290; 296; 299; 306

EC TREATY

Art. 3(g) 982
Art. 82 . . . . . 971; 974; 975; 981; 983; 984
Art. 82(b) 975
Art. 82(d) 981

EUROPEAN UNION COMPETITION COMMISSION DECISION OF MARCH 24, 2004

Generally 971

FEDERAL DECLARATORY JUDGMENT ACT

Generally 483

FEDERAL FOOD, DRUG, AND COSMETIC ACT (FDCA)

Generally 1001

FEDERAL RULES OF CIVIL PROCEDURE

Rule 8(c) 415
Rule 9(b) . . .   752; 753; 762; 779; 781; 782;
                785
Rule 12(b)(6) 95; 230; 233; 236; 752;
                766; 772; 779
Rule 12(c) 415
Rule 19 . . . . 408; 409
Rule 19(a) 408
Rule 19(b) 406
Rule 24(a)(2) 406
Rule 24(b) 406
Rule 26(b)(3) 818; 825; 827; 828
Rule 56 . . . . 415; 773
Rule 56(c) 480
Rule 56(e) 397
Rule 65(a)(2) 936

FEDERAL TRADE COMMISSION ACT

Generally . . .   910; 912; 923; 926; 959; 961;
                970
Sec. 4 960
Sec. 5 . .   499; 919; 922; 923; 959; 961; 963;
                964; 965; 966

[References are to page and footnote numbers.]

Sec. 45 912
Sec. 45(a) 912
Sec. 45(a)(1) 912

FREEDOM OF INFORMATION ACT

Generally 85

GENERAL LAWS

c. 62C, Sec. 33(f) 63
c. 63, Sec. 1 63
c. 93A, Sec. 11 175
c. 231, Sec. 1 183

HELIUM ACT

Generally 443

HOUSE REPORTS

H.R. Rep. No. 96-1307, pt. 1, at 3 (1980) . . 84
H.R. Rep. No. 122 832
H.R. Rep. No. 6840, 97th Cong., 2d Sess. . . . 443
H.R. Rep. No. 9276, 94th Cong., 1st Sess. 443

INTELLECTUAL PROPERTY BANKRUPTCY PROTECTION ACT

Generally 553

INTERNAL REVENUE CODE

Sec.
5 95
102 106
103 106
119 105
120 105
156(g) 105
162 63
170 . . . . . . 845; 845n1; 849; 850; 852
170(a) 849; 850; 851; 852
170(b)(1)(E) 846; 849
170(c) 849; 850
170(f)(2) 850
170(f)(3) 846n3; 850; 851
170(f)(3)(A) 850; 851
170(f)(3)(B)(ii) 850
170(f)(8) 846n5
172 58
174(a) 853
197 845
256 90
271 105
271(b) 887

285 106
365 105
382 59
671 850
1011(b) 846n4
1221(a)(3) 846n2; 852
1231(b)(1)(C) 846n2
1235 . . . . 64; 68; 70
2055 . . . . 845n1
2522 . . . . 845n1
6050L 845

LANHAM TRADEMARK ACT

Generally . . . 157; 157n11; 494; 495; 496; 497; 544
Sec. 5 499
Sec. 8 . . 539; 540; 541; 542; 543; 544; 549
Sec. 45 . . . . 496; 499

NATIONAL COOPERATIVE RESEARCH ACT (NCRA)

Generally 450; 910; 912; 926
Sec. 4301 912
Sec. 4301(6) 912
Sec. 4301(6)(A) 912; 913
Sec. 4301(6)(B) 912; 913
Sec. 4301(6)(C) 912; 913
Sec. 4301(6)(D) 912; 913
Sec. 4301(6)(E) 913
Sec. 4301(6)(F) 913
Sec. 4301(6)(G) 913
Sec. 4301(6)(G)(b) 913
Sec. 4301(6)(G)(b)(1) 913
Sec. 4301(6)(G)(b)(2) 913; 914
Sec. 4301(6)(G)(b)(2)(A) 913
Sec. 4301(6)(G)(b)(2)(B) 913
Sec. 4301(6)(G)(b)(2)(C) 913
Sec. 4301(6)(G)(b)(3) 913; 914
Sec. 4301(6)(G)(b)(3)(A) 913
Sec. 4301(6)(G)(b)(3)(B) 913
Sec. 4301(6)(G)(b)(4) 913
Sec. 4301(6)(G)(b)(5) 913
Sec. 4301(6)(G)(b)(6) 914
Sec. 4301(6)(G)(b)(7) 914
Sec. 4301(6)(G)(b)(8) 914
Sec. 4302 914

NATIONAL LABOR RELATIONS ACT

Generally 331

NATIONAL STOLEN PROPERTY ACT

Generally 288

[References are to page and footnote numbers.]

PATENT ACT(S)
Generally . . 880n4; 930; 1016; 1021; 1023
1836 Act 48
1952 Act . . 46; 91; 154; 155; 406; 508; 509
Sec. 100 46
Sec. 101 46
Sec. 102 47
Sec. 102(b) 45; 46; 47; 48
Sec. 102(g) 46
Sec. 271(e) 1007; 1009; 1010; 1011;
                      1012; 1015; 1019
Sec. 271(e)(1) 1001; 1003; 1004; 1005;
                      1006; 1008; 1009; 1011; 1012;
                      1013; 1014; 1015; 1016; 1017;
                      1018; 1019; 1020; 1021; 1022;
                      1023; 1024

PATENT CODE
Sec. 282 413

PATENT MISUSE REFORM ACT (1988)
Generally 452; 453; 454; 458

PLANT VARIETY PROTECTION ACT
Generally 443

PRESCRIPTION DRUG PATENT LICENSING ACT
Generally 443

PRIVATE SECURITIES LITIGATION REFORM ACT OF 1995 (PSLRA)
Generally . . . 229; 230; 231; 232; 765; 766;
                                          769

PUBLIC LAWS
No. 96-517, Sec. 6(a) 1016
No. 98-417, Sec. 201 1018
No. 108-357 845
No. 194-67 765

RESTATEMENT (SECOND) OF AGENCY
Sec. 220(2) 332
Sec. 228 331
Sec. 312 . . . . 391; 402

RESTATEMENT (SECOND) OF CONTRACTS
Sec. 241 658
Sec. 356 587

RESTATEMENT OF TORTS
Generally 254

RESTATEMENT OF TORTS (1939)
Sec. 757 . . . . . . 257; 262; 273; 285; 387
Sec. 757(a) 286
Sec. 757 cmt. b . . . 273; 285; 359; 388; 431
Sec. 757 cmt. f at 10 283
Sec. 758 cmt. b 389
Sec. 759 285

RESTATEMENT (SECOND) OF TORTS (1978)
Generally 257; 258
Sec. 766 402
Sec. 766 cmt. g 401
Sec. 767 397
Sec. 774A 399
Secs. 766-767 391

RESTATEMENT (THIRD) OF UNFAIR COMPETITION
Generally 257; 265n1
Sec. 39 cmt. e 265n1
Sec. 41 cmt. d 488
Sec. 43 384
Secs. 38-49 285

REVENUE PROCEDURES
69-19 66

REVENUE RULINGS
2003-28 849

SECURITIES ACT OF 1933
Generally 755
Sec. 11 . . . 684n2; 701; 703; 707; 708; 710;
              751; 753; 761; 762; 766; 769; 771;
                                  772; 776; 778
Sec. 11(a) 701; 702
Sec. 11(b) 702
Sec. 11(b)(3) 702; 703
Sec. 11(b)(3)(A) 702
Sec. 11(c) 703
Sec. 12 . . . . 684n2; 769; 771
Sec. 12(2) 778
Sec. 12(a)(2) . . 761; 762; 766; 772; 776; 778
Sec. 15 . . . . 751; 766; 772; 778

SECURITIES EXCHANGE ACT OF 1934
Generally 755
Sec. 10(b) . . . 195; 198; 200; 201; 203; 205;
              208; 209; 210; 213; 214; 215; 216;
              220; 223; 228; 229; 233; 235;
                          235n1; 751; 753; 778

[References are to page and footnote numbers.]

Sec. 20 751
Sec. 20A 229
Sec. 20(a) . . 229; 233; 236; 236n3; 238; 779
Sec. 28(a) 215

SECURITIES EXCHANGE COMMISSION

Generally 235n1
Form S-1 742
Rule 10b-5 . . 195; 196; 198; 201; 203; 205;
            208; 209; 210; 213; 214; 215; 216;
            220; 223; 224; 225; 226; 227; 228;
            233; 235; 235n2; 753; 778 779
Rule 13d-5(b)(1) 712
Rule 131 . . . . 718n12
Rule S-K 735
Rule S-K, Item 103 . . . . 770; 771

SHERMAN ACT

Generally . . . 461; 910; 911; 923; 924; 925;
                            926; 957
Sec. 1 . . 459; 461; 462; 500; 911; 919; 922;
            924; 925; 936; 937; 941; 957; 982
Sec. 2 . . 459; 461; 462; 482; 911; 922; 923;
            924; 925; 929; 936; 937; 938; 940;
            941; 942; 944; 945; 948; 951; 984

TARIFF ACT OF 1930

Sec. 337(a)(1)(B) 466

TECHNICAL ADVICE MEMORANDUM

200249002 . . . . 65; 66

TRADEMARK ACT OF 1946 (See LANHAM TRADEMARK ACT)

TRADE-RELATED ASPECTS OF INTELLECTUAL PROPERTY RIGHTS (TRIPS)

Generally 444; 1023; 1024
Art. 27(2) 444
Art. 27(3)(a) 1023
Art. 31 444
Art. 31(f) 444

TREASURY REGULATIONS

1.170A-1(e) 851
1.170A-7(a)(1) 851
1.170A-7(a)(2)(i) 850
1.170A-7(a)(3) 851
1.170A-7(b)(1) 850
1.170A-7(b)(1)(i) 851
1.170A-13(c)(3) 847n7

1.1011-2 . . . . 846n4
1.1235 68
1.1235-1(b) 70
1.1235-2(a) 64
1.1235-2(f) 68

UNIFORM COMMERCIAL CODE (UCC)

Generally . . 147; 147nn3, 4; 149; 151; 152;
            152n9; 153; 153n9; 154; 155; 157;
                                        692
Art. 9 . . 146; 151; 152; 152n8; 156; 156n10
Sec. 9-504 646
Sec. 9101 151
Sec. 9103(3)(b) 148n5
Sec. 9104 . . . . 152; 156
Sec. 9104(a) 156; 156n10
Sec. 9106 . . . . 147n4
Sec. 9204 . . . . 153n9
Sec. 9302 . . . . 152n8; 153
Sec. 9302(1) 152
Sec. 9302(3) 152n8; 153; 156n10
Sec. 9302(3)(a) 152; 153
Sec. 9302(4) 152; 152n8; 153; 156
Sec. 9312(5) 151
Sec. 9401(1)(c) 152

UNIFORM TRADE SECRETS ACT (UTSA)

Generally 254; 255; 257; 258; 265n1;
            273; 280; 285; 287; 288; 289; 401
Sec. 1 384
Sec. 1(2) 286
Sec. 1(4) 255
Sec. 1 cmt. 265n1

UNITED STATES CODE

7 U.S.C. 2402 443
11 U.S.C. 108(c) 541
11 U.S.C. 301 524
11 U.S.C. 302 524
11 U.S.C. 303 524
11 U.S.C. 348(a) 523
11 U.S.C. 362 . . . . 546; 547
11 U.S.C. 362(a) 538; 541; 542; 543
11 U.S.C. 362(a)(1) 542; 544; 546
11 U.S.C. 362(a)(3) . . . 542; 543; 544; 547
11 U.S.C. 362(b) 549
11 U.S.C. 363 561
11 U.S.C. 365 . . . 557; 563; 564; 566; 574;
                                        575
11 U.S.C. 365(a) . . 551; 553; 554; 555; 556;
            557; 559; 560; 562; 563; 564; 565;
                        566; 567; 568; 573; 578
11 U.S.C. 365(c) 569; 570; 574; 575

[References are to page and footnote numbers.]

11 U.S.C. 365(c)(1) . . . 553; 570; 573; 574; 575; 576; 577; 578
11 U.S.C. 365(c)(1)(A) 574; 576
11 U.S.C. 365(c)(1)(B) 574
11 U.S.C. 365(c)(2) 576; 577
11 U.S.C. 365(e) 570
11 U.S.C. 365(f) 567; 573; 575
11 U.S.C. 365(f)(1) 553; 575; 576
11 U.S.C. 365(g) 566
11 U.S.C. 365(h) 561; 562
11 U.S.C. 365(n) . . 552; 553; 554; 556; 557; 559; 560; 561; 566; 567; 579
11 U.S.C. 365(n)(2) 561
11 U.S.C. 365(n)(2)(B) 561
11 U.S.C. 541(a) 523; 524; 529
11 U.S.C. 541(a)(1) . . . 524; 525; 527; 528
11 U.S.C. 541(a)(5) 525
11 U.S.C. 541(a)(6) . . . 524; 525; 527; 528
11 U.S.C. 541(a)(7) . . . 524; 525; 527; 528
11 U.S.C. 727 522
11 U.S.C. 1107(a) 556
15 U.S.C. 1 . . . . 459; 461; 500; 911
15 U.S.C. 2 . . . . 459; 461; 911
15 U.S.C. 14 911
15 U.S.C. 18 911
15 U.S.C. 29(b) 937
15 U.S.C. 44 960
15 U.S.C. 45 912
15 U.S.C. 45(a) 912
15 U.S.C. 45(a)(1) 912
15 U.S.C. 77k 710; 751; 772; 778
15 U.S.C. 77k(a) 701; 753; 762
15 U.S.C. 77k(b)(3)(A) 702
15 U.S.C. 77k(c) 703
15 U.S.C. 77k(f) 710
15 U.S.C. 77l(a)(2) 762
15 U.S.C. 77o 751; 773; 778
15 U.S.C. 77z-2(c)(1)(A)(i) 233
15 U.S.C. 77z-2(c)(1)(B) 233
15 U.S.C. 77z2(i)(1) 233
15 U.S.C. 78j 223
15 U.S.C. 78j(b) . . . 216; 223; 229; 235n1; 751; 753; 779
15 U.S.C. 78t 751
15 U.S.C. 78t-1 229
15 U.S.C. 78t(a) 229; 236n3; 779
15 U.S.C. 78u-4(b)(1) 229; 230; 232
15 U.S.C. 78u-4(b)(2) 229; 230; 232
15 U.S.C. 78u-5(c)(1)(A)(i) 233
15 U.S.C. 78u-5(c)(1)(B) 233
15 U.S.C. 78u-5(i)(1) 233
15 U.S.C. 77l 772
15 U.S.C. 77l(2) 778
15 U.S.C. 1051-1127 157
15 U.S.C. 1051(a)(1) 497

15 U.S.C. 1051(b) 14
15 U.S.C. 1055 495
15 U.S.C. 1058 539
15 U.S.C. 1060 492
15 U.S.C. 1064 . . . . 494; 540
15 U.S.C. 1072 494
15 U.S.C. 1119 497
15 U.S.C. 1127 . . . . 494; 495
15 U.S.C. 4301 912
15 U.S.C. 4301(6) 912
15 U.S.C. 4301(6)(A) 912; 913
15 U.S.C. 4301(6)(B) 912; 913
15 U.S.C. 4301(6)(b)(1) 913
15 U.S.C. 4301(6)(b)(2) 913; 914
15 U.S.C. 4301(6)(b)(2)(A) 913
15 U.S.C. 4301(6)(b)(2)(B) 913
15 U.S.C. 4301(6)(b)(2)(C) 913
15 U.S.C. 4301(6)(b)(3) 913; 914
15 U.S.C. 4301(6)(b)(3)(A) 913
15 U.S.C. 4301(6)(b)(3)(B) 913
15 U.S.C. 4301(6)(b)(4) 913
15 U.S.C. 4301(6)(b)(5) 913
15 U.S.C. 4301(6)(b)(6) 914
15 U.S.C. 4301(6)(b)(7) 914
15 U.S.C. 4301(6)(b)(8) 914
15 U.S.C. 4301(6)(C) 912; 913
15 U.S.C. 4301(6)(D) 912; 913
15 U.S.C. 4301(6)(E) 913
15 U.S.C. 4301(6)(F) 913
15 U.S.C. 4301(6)(G) 913
15 U.S.C. 4301(6)(G)(b) 913
15 U.S.C. 4302 . . . . 912; 914
17 U.S.C. 567
17 U.S.C. 35E 551
17 U.S.C. 101 . . 148; 149n6; 327; 328; 330; 331; 332; 333; 530
17 U.S.C. 101(1) 328; 330; 331; 332
17 U.S.C. 101(2) 330; 331; 332; 333
17 U.S.C. 102 330
17 U.S.C. 102(a) 833
17 U.S.C. 106 . . 149; 149n6; 506; 507; 508
17 U.S.C. 106(1) 832; 834
17 U.S.C. 106(3) 832; 834
17 U.S.C. 106-122 506
17 U.S.C. 118(b) 835
17 U.S.C. 201 508
17 U.S.C. 201(a) 327; 330; 333
17 U.S.C. 201(b) 328; 330
17 U.S.C. 201(c) . . 829; 831; 832; 834; 835; 836
17 U.S.C. 201(d) 149n6; 506
17 U.S.C. 201(d)(1) 148
17 U.S.C. 201(d)(2) 504
17 U.S.C. 203 510
17 U.S.C. 203(a) 330

[References are to page and footnote numbers.]

17 U.S.C. 203(a)(4)(A) 510
17 U.S.C. 203(b) 510
17 U.S.C. 204(a) 624
17 U.S.C. 205 . . . . 149n6; 149n7
17 U.S.C. 205(a) 148; 152n9
17 U.S.C. 205(c) 149; 152n9
17 U.S.C. 205(c)(2) 149n7
17 U.S.C. 205(d) 151; 506
17 U.S.C. 301 . . . . 149n6
17 U.S.C. 301(a) 149n6
17 U.S.C. 302(c) 330
17 U.S.C. 304 510
17 U.S.C. 304(a) 330
17 U.S.C. 304(c)(6)(A) 510
17 U.S.C. 408 . . . . 149n7
17 U.S.C. 409 . . . . 149n7
17 U.S.C. 410 . . . . 149n7
17 U.S.C. 411 . . . . 44; 150n7
17 U.S.C. 411(a) 44
17 U.S.C. 501(a) 506
17 U.S.C. 501(b) 505; 506; 507; 509
17 U.S.C. 502(a) 835
17 U.S.C. 504(b) 91
17 U.S.C. 601(b)(1) 330
17 U.S.C. 702 . . . . 153n9
17 U.S.C. 9103(3)(d) 148n5
17 U.S.C. ch. 9 551
18 U.S.C. 1341 288
18 U.S.C. 1343 288
18 U.S.C. 1831 . . . . 288; 289
18 U.S.C. 1831-1839 . . . . 19; 288
18 U.S.C. 1831(a) 288
18 U.S.C. 1831(a)(1) 289
18 U.S.C. 1831(a)(2) 289
18 U.S.C. 1831(a)(3) 289
18 U.S.C. 1831(a)(4) 289
18 U.S.C. 1831(a)(5) 289
18 U.S.C. 1831(b) 289
18 U.S.C. 1832 289
18 U.S.C. 1832(a) 297; 298
18 U.S.C. 1832(a)(4) 292; 299
18 U.S.C. 1832(a)(5) 296
18 U.S.C. 1833 289
18 U.S.C. 1834 289
18 U.S.C. 1835 289
18 U.S.C. 1836 289
18 U.S.C. 1837 289
18 U.S.C. 1838 289
18 U.S.C. 1839 . . . . . . 289; 298; 298n4
18 U.S.C. 1839(3) 255; 256; 292; 297
18 U.S.C. 1839(3)(B) 256
18 U.S.C. 1905 288
18 U.S.C. 2314 288
19 U.S.C. 1337(a)(1)(B) 466
26 U.S.C. 170(e)(1)(B)(iii) 845

26 U.S.C. 170(m) 845
28 U.S.C. 291(b) 146n1
28 U.S.C. 636(c) 216
28 U.S.C. 1291 751
28 U.S.C. 1331 220
28 U.S.C. 1498 443
28 U.S.C. 2201 . . . . 428; 483; 898
28 U.S.C. 2202 483
Title 35 68
35 U.S.C. 35B 551
35 U.S.C. 100 46
35 U.S.C. 100(d) 406
35 U.S.C. 101 46
35 U.S.C. 101-103 91
35 U.S.C. 102 . . . . 44; 47; 106
35 U.S.C. 102(b) 45; 46; 47; 48
35 U.S.C. 102(g) 46
35 U.S.C. 103 106
35 U.S.C. 111 . . . . 309; 717
35 U.S.C. 112 717
35 U.S.C. 116-120 91
35 U.S.C. 118 309
35 U.S.C. 119 105
35 U.S.C. 120 105
35 U.S.C. 154 . . . . 314; 426; 432
35 U.S.C. 156 . . . . 1007; 1018
35 U.S.C. 156(g) 105
35 U.S.C. 200 . . . . 84; 85
35 U.S.C. 201(b) 86; 87
35 U.S.C. 201(c) 86
35 U.S.C. 201(e) 86
35 U.S.C. 201 et seq. 1016
35 U.S.C. 202(c)(4) 86; 87
35 U.S.C. 202(c)(6) 86; 87
35 U.S.C. 254-256 91
35 U.S.C. 258 769
35 U.S.C. 261 . . . . 154; 155; 156
35 U.S.C. 261-262 91
35 U.S.C. 271 . . . . 105; 314; 408
35 U.S.C. 271(a) . . 880; 880n4; 1001; 1011
35 U.S.C. 271(b) 878; 881; 887; 888
35 U.S.C. 271(d) 467
35 U.S.C. 271(d)(5) . . . 453; 454; 467; 468
35 U.S.C. 271(e) . . 1007; 1009; 1010; 1011;
                              1012; 1015; 1019
35 U.S.C. 271(e)(1) 1001; 1003; 1004;
                    1005; 1006; 1008; 1009; 1011;
                    1012; 1013; 1014; 1015; 1016;
                    1017; 1018; 1019; 1020; 1021;
                              1022; 1023; 1024
35 U.S.C. 273 104
35 U.S.C. 281 . . . . 406; 508
35 U.S.C. 285 . . . . 106; 415
35 U.S.C. 288 415
35 U.S.C. 365 105

[References are to page and footnote numbers.]

42 U.S.C. 1857h-6 443
49 U.S.C. App. 1403(a) 150
50 U.S.C. 1678 443

UNITED STATES CONSTITUTION

Art. I 91
Art. I, Sec. 8 426
Art. I, Sec. 8, Clause 8 . . . . 505; 529
Fourteenth Amendment 95

UNIVERSITY AND SMALL BUSINESS PATENT PROCEDURES ACT

Generally 1016

U.S. DEPARTMENT OF JUSTICE AND FEDERAL TRADE COMMISSION, ANTITRUST GUIDELINES FOR THE LICENSING OF INTELLECTUAL PROPERTY

Sec. 5.5 472

VISUAL ARTISTS RIGHTS ACT

Generally 804
Sec. 102 807
Sec. 103 807

STATE LAWS

CALIFORNIA BUSINESS AND PROFESSIONAL CODE
Sec. 16600 . . . . 362n4
CALIFORNIA CIVIL CODE
Sec. 2300 893
Sec. 2317 893
Sec. 2332 893
Sec. 2778 894
CALIFORNIA CORPORATIONS CODE
Sec. 1107 . . . . 624; 625
CALIFORNIA INSURANCE CODE
Sec. 533 . . 880; 881; 887; 888; 889; 890;
                           892; 893
CALIFORNIA LABOR CODE
Sec. 2870 . . . . 336; 338
Sec. 2870(a) 338
Sec. 2870(a)(1) 338
Sec. 2870(a)(2) 338
Sec. 2870(b) 338
CALIFORNIA PENAL CODE
Generally 306
Sec. 499c 304
Sec. 499c(a)(9) 303
Sec. 499c(b) 300

Sec. 499c(b)(1) 300
Sec. 499c(b)(2) 300; 303
Sec. 499c(b)(3) 300
Sec. 499c(b)(4) 300
Sec. 499c(c) 300
Sec. 502(c)(4) 303
CALIFORNIA UNIFORM TRADE SECRETS ACT
Generally 273
DELAWARE CODE
8 Del.C. 102(b)(7) . . . 239; 248; 249; 250
8 Del.C. 253 . . . . 241; 246
8 Del.C. 259 630
8 Del.C. 259(a) 631
8 Del.C. 262 . . . . 241; 246
Generally 652
DELAWARE CORPORATIONS CODE
Generally 609; 612
Sec. 251 . . . . 610; 653
Sec. 251(a) 610
Sec. 251(b) 610
Sec. 251(c) 611
Sec. 251(c)(1) 611
Sec. 251(c)(2) 611
Sec. 251(c)(3) 612
Sec. 251(c)(4) 612
Sec. 251(c)(5) 612
Sec. 251(c)(6) 612
Sec. 251(c)(7) 612
Sec. 259 624
Sec. 271 612
Sec. 271(a) 612
Sec. 271(b) 612
FLORIDA BLUE SKY LAW
Generally 226; 228
FLORIDA STATUTES
Sec. 517.301 . . . . . 220; 223; 224; 227
GEORGIA CONSTITUTION (1983)
Art. III, Sec. VI, Par. V (c) 364
GEORGIA STATUTES
OCGA Sec. 13-8-2 364
OCGA Sec. 48-8-2(11) 896
ILLINOIS TRADE SECRETS ACT (ITSA)
765 ILCS 1065/1 258
765 ILCS 1065/1 et seq. 261
765 ILCS 1065/2(d) 261; 265
765 ILCS 1065/3(a) 370
Generally . . 266; 269; 271; 370; 597; 598
ILLINOIS UNIFORM PARTNERSHIP ACT
Generally 585; 586; 590; 591
Sec. 2 586
Sec. 2(a) 586
Sec. 2(a)(II) 586
Sec. 2(b) 586

[References are to page and footnote numbers.]

Sec. 2(c) 586
Sec. 38(2) 589
Sec. 38(2)(b) 586

INDIANA CODE ANNOTATED
Sec. 24-2-3-1(b) 390
Sec. 24-2-3-1(c) 390
Sec. 24-2-3-2 390
Sec. 24-2-3-3 391
Sec. 24-2-3-5 391

**MARYLAND COMMERCIAL LAW II CODE
ANNOTATED**
Secs. 11-1201-11-1209 22
Sec. 11-1208 22

**MARYLAND UNIFORM TRADE SECRETS
ACT (MUTSA)**
Generally 22; 23; 24; 377; 378; 379;
          380; 382; 383
Sec. 11-1201(b) 379
Sec. 11-1201(c) 378
Sec. 11-1202(a) 378; 379

MASSACHUSETTS GENERAL LAWS
Ch. 93A 779

MASSACHUSETTS STATUTES
266 M.G.L.A. 30 306

OHIO REVISED CODE
Generally 652
Sec. 1701.81 630
Sec. 1701.81(A)(4) 631
Sec. 1701.83 630

OREGON REVISED STATUTES
Sec. 653.295 . . . . 347; 349
Sec. 653.295(1) 347; 348
Sec. 653.295(1)(b) 345; 347

RHODE ISLAND GENERAL LAWS
Sec. 6A-9-504 646
Sec. 6A-9-504(4) 646

**TEXAS BUSINESS CORPORATIONS
ACT**
Generally 652; 653

INDEX

[References are to pages.]

A

ACCOUNTING
Generally . . . 57
Reporting distributions from licensing . . 64

ACQUISITIONS (See MERGERS AND AC-
QUISITIONS)

ANTITRUST
Clayton Act . . . 911
Cooperative ventures . . . 959
Cross-licensing . . . 452
European Union perspective . . . 971
Federal Trade Commission Act . . . 912
Licensing
    Antitrust guidelines . . . 914
    Cross-licensing . . . 452
    Limits of antitrust . . . 927
    Trademark licensing . . . 500
National Cooperative Research Act . . . 912
Restricting competition . . . 936
Sherman Act . . . 911
Trademark licensing . . . 500
Tying arrangements . . . 950

ATTORNEYS
Attorney-client privilege (See DUE DILI-
GENCE REVIEWS)
Due diligence reviews (See DUE DILIGENCE
REVIEWS)
Guide to representing startup companies
. . . 109

B

BANKRUPTCY
Generally . . . 519
Automatic stay . . . 538
Bankruptcy estate . . . 522
Licenses
    Generally . . . 549
    Licensee as debtor . . . 568
    Licensor as debtor . . . 554

BUSINESS MODELS
Generally . . . 7
Accounting . . . 57
Forfeitures of intellectual property interests
. . . 44
Licensing (See LICENSING)
Patents (See PATENTS)
Startup companies (See STARTUP COMPA-
NIES)
Taxation (See TAXATION)
Valuation of intellectual property . . . 25

C

CHARITABLE ORGANIZATIONS
Donations of intellectual property . . . 844
Taxation
    Generally . . . 845
    Patents . . . 849

**CONSPIRACY TO STEAL TRADE SE-
CRETS**
Generally . . . 293

COPYRIGHT
Employment issues relating to ownership
. . . 327
Licensing (See LICENSING)

**CORPORATE OFFICERS AND DIREC-
TORS**
Fiduciary duties . . . 163
Liability for infringement . . . 904

D

DEVELOPMENT AND USE (See TECH-
NOLOGY DEVELOPMENT AND USE)

DISCLOSURES
Nonuse and nondisclosure agreements . . . .
339
Securities regulation (See SECURITIES, subhead: Disclosures regarding intellectual
property)

**DISPOSITIONS OF INTELLECTUAL
PROPERTY**
Auctions . . . 838
Charitable organizations, donations to
    Generally . . . 844
    Taxation
        Generally . . . 845
        Patents . . . 849
Open source, releasing to . . . 854
Taxation of charitable donations
    Generally . . . 845
    Patents . . . 849

DUE DILIGENCE REVIEWS
Generally . . . 677
Attorney-client privilege protections
    Generally . . . 714
    Maintaining protections . . . 721
    Scope of protections . . . 715
    Waiving protections . . . 714
Features of review . . . 682
Legal tests for reasonableness . . . 700

[References are to pages.]

E

ECONOMIC ESPIONAGE ACT OF 1996
Generally . . . 288

EMPLOYMENT ISSUES
Generally . . . 307
Contract adjustments
    Generally . . . 333
    Invention assignments . . . 334
Copyright ownership . . . 327
Covenant not to compete
    Generally . . . 345
    Holdover/trailer clauses . . . 352
    Nonsolicitation agreements . . . 362
Hiring experienced high tech employees, risks of
    Intentional interference with contractual or fiduciary relationship . . . 391
    Misappropriation . . . 383
    Third party liability . . . 383
    Wrongful use or disclosure . . . 383
Inevitable disclosures doctrine
    Generally . . . 365
    Risks of applying doctrine . . . 375
Invention assignments . . . 334
Nonsolicitation agreements . . . 362
Nonuse and nondisclosure agreements 339
Patent ownership
    Generally . . . 309
    Hired to invent . . . 314
    Shop rights . . . 310
Preemptive employment restrictions (See subhead: Inevitable disclosures doctrine)
Subsequent employment, restrictions on
    Covenant not to compete
        Generally . . . 345
        Holdover/trailer clauses . . . 352
        Nonsolicitation agreements . . 362
    Nonuse and nondisclosure agreements . . . 339
Trade secrets
    Generally . . . 317
    Implied duties of employees . . . 323
    Subsequent employment (See subhead: Subsequent employment, restrictions on)

EUROPEAN UNION
Antitrust perspective . . . 971

F

FEDERAL GOVERNMENT
Special context for intellectual property . . . 88

FEDERALLY FUNDED RESEARCH
Special context for intellectual property . . . 84

FIDUCIARY DUTIES
Corporate officers . . . 163

FINANCING
Bonds, royalty payments as security for . . . 812
Multidivisional corporations as internal capital markets . . . 790
Patents . . . 130
Security interests in intellectual property
    Generally . . . 145
    Royalty payments as security for bonds . . . 812
Startup companies
    Initial financing . . . 107
    Secured loans . . . 145
    Venture capital . . . 123
Venture capital . . . 123

FORFEITURES
Avoiding forfeitures of intellectual property interests . . . 44

FRAUD
Examples of fraudulent representations . . . 216
Standards for stock sales . . . 195

I

INFRINGEMENT
Insurance
    Enforcement insurance . . . 817
    Infringement insurance . . . 872
Liability of corporate officers and directors . . . 904
Open source, risks associated with . . . 863

INSURANCE
Enforcement insurance . . . 817
Infringement insurance . . . 872

J

JOINT VENTURES
Antitrust considerations . . . 959
Negotiating and planning . . . 993

L

LICENSING
Generally . . . 403
Antitrust
    Generally . . . 927
    Cross-licensing . . . 452

[References are to pages.]

LICENSING—Cont.

Antitrust—Cont.

Guidelines . . . 914

Trademarks . . . 500

Bankruptcy of licensor or licensee (See BANKRUPTCY)

Copyright

Generally . . . 504

Performance rights organizations 515

Unforseen uses . . . 511

Cross-licensing

Generally . . . 444

Antitrust considerations . . . 452

Distributions, taxation and reporting of . . . 64

Establishing and policing . . . 50

Hybrid licensing . . . 516

Negotiation

Generally . . . 50

Royalties . . . 30

Patents (See PATENTS)

Royalties (See ROYALTIES)

Taxation and reporting of distributions . . . 64

Trademarks

Generally . . . 489

Antitrust concerns . . . 500

Control over the mark . . . 493

Patent, hybrid licensing with . . . 516

Trade secrets

Generally . . . 481

Duration of royalties . . . 483

Patent, hybrid licensing with . . . 516

M

MANAGING INTELLECTUAL PROPERTY

Joint ventures, negotiating and managing . . . 993

Patent portfolios, identifying . . . 988

Research tools and experimental use 1001

MERGERS AND ACQUISITIONS

Generally . . . 607

Definitions . . . 609

Liability issues . . . 645

Ownership issues . . . 613

Transfer issues

Generally . . . 654

Inadequate diligence . . . 662

Ineffective transfers . . . 662

P

PATENTS

Business methods . . . 97

PATENTS—Cont.

Charitable donations of patents . . . 849

Employment issues related to patent ownership

Generally . . . 309

Hired to invent . . . 314

Shop rights . . . 310

Estoppel regarding validity of patent . . 416

Financing . . . 130

Identifying and managing a patent portfolio . . . 988

Licensing

Generally . . . 405

Compulsory licenses . . . 443

Cross-licensing

Generally . . . 444

Antitrust considerations . . . 452

First sale doctrine . . . 433

Hybrid licensing . . . 516

Implied transfers . . . 433

Patent packages . . . 477

Patent pools . . . 459

Right to sue for infringement . . . 405

Royalties (See ROYALTIES)

University licensing . . . 480

Validity of patents, challenges to

Estoppel . . . 416

Res judicata . . . 410

Patent packages . . . 477

Patent pools . . . 459

Research tools and experimental use, protection for . . . 1001

Res judicata regarding patent validity 410

Royalties (See ROYALTIES)

Trademark, hybrid licensing with . . . 516

Trade secret, hybrid licensing with . . . 516

University licensing . . . 480

PROSPECTUS

Disclosures (See SECURITIES, subhead: Disclosures regarding intellectual property)

R

ROYALTIES

Bonds, royalty payments as security for . . . 812

Duration of obligation to pay . . . 425

Negotiation . . . 30

Post patent expiration . . . 425

Trade secrets . . . 483

Unpatented, publicly disclosed products . . . 427

[References are to pages.]

S

SECURITIES
Disclosures regarding intellectual property
    Generally . . . 729
    Examples . . . 742
    Misstatements in prospectus . . . 750
    Regulation S-K . . . 739
    SEC Form S-1 . . . 742
Fraud standards . . . 195
Fraudulent representations, examples of . . 216
Misstatements
    In prospectus . . . 750
    In stock sales . . . 191
"Vaporware" . . . 195

SPECIAL CONTEXTS
Federal government . . . 88
Federally funded research . . . 84
State government . . . 90
Universities . . . 72

STARTUP COMPANIES
Attorney's guide to representing . . . 109
Corporate officers, fiduciary duties of 163
Fiduciary duties of corporate officers . . 163
Financing
    Initial financing . . . 107
    Secured loans . . . 145
    Venture capital . . . 123
Initial financing . . . 107
Risk, putting intellectual property at . . 12
Secured loans as basis for financing . . 145
Strategic alliances . . . 113
Tax considerations . . . 158
Venture capital financing . . . 123

STATE GOVERNMENT
Special context for intellectual property . . . 90

T

TAXATION
Generally . . . 57
Allocation among business entities . . . 158
Charitable donations of intellectual property
    Generally . . . 845
    Patents . . . 849
Distributions from licensing . . . 64
Holding companies . . . 158
Startup companies . . . 158

TECHNOLOGY DEVELOPMENT AND USE
Corporations as long-term users . . . 828
Insurance, enforcement . . . 817
Multidivisional corporations as internal capital markets . . . 790

TECHNOLOGY DEVELOPMENT AND USE—Cont.
Open source product development . . . 808; 854
Securitization of intellectual property 812

TERMINATION OF BUSINESS
Generally . . . 579
Bankruptcy (See BANKRUPTCY)

THEFT OF TRADE SECRETS
Generally . . . 288
Actual theft . . . 290
Conspiracy to steal . . . 293
Economic Espionage Act of 1996 . . . 288
Federal laws . . . 288
State laws . . . 299

TRADEMARK LICENSING
Generally . . . 489
Antitrust concerns . . . 500
Control over the mark . . . 493
Patent, hybrid licensing with . . . 516

TRADE SECRETS
Generally . . . 253
Civil protection . . . 257
Criminal protection
    Generally . . . 288
    Actual theft . . . 290
    Conspiracy to steal . . . 293
    Economic Espionage Act of 1996 288
    Federal laws . . . 288
    State laws . . . 299
Elements of trade secrets under UTSA
    Generally . . . 273
    Information . . . 273
    Protection, reasonable efforts of . . 279
    Value through secrecy . . . 274
Employment issues
    Generally . . . 317
    Implied duties of employees . . . 323
    Subsequent employment, restrictions on (See EMPLOYMENT ISSUES, subhead: Subsequent employment, restrictions on)
"Honest discoverer" . . . 286
Inevitable disclosures doctrine
    Generally . . . 365
    Risks of applying doctrine . . . 375
Innocent wrongful user . . . 287
Licensing
    Generally . . . 481
    Duration of royalties . . . 483
    Patent, hybrid licensing with . . . 516
Uniform Trade Secrets Act (UTSA)
    Generally . . . 258

[References are to pages.]

TRADE SECRETS—Cont.
Uniform Trade Secrets Act (UTSA)—Cont.
    Application of act . . . 258
    Elements of trade secrets (See subhead:
      Elements of trade secrets under UTSA)

U

UNIVERSITIES
Licensing of patents . . . 480
Special context for intellectual property . . .
  72

V

**VALUATION OF INTELLECTUAL PROP-
  ERTY**
Generally . . . 25

VENTURE CAPITAL
Startup companies, financing for . . . 123